applying
international
financial
reporting
standards

enhanced edition

applying
international
financial
reporting
standards

enhanced edition

keith
ALFREDSON
Consultant

ken
LEO
Curtin University
of Technology

ruth
PICKER
Senior Partner
Technical Consulting
Group, Global IFRS
Ernst & Young

paul
PACTER
Director,
Global IFRS
Office of Deloitte,
Hong Kong

jennie
RADFORD
Consultant

victoria
WISE
University of
Tasmania

BICENTENNIAL
BICENTENNIAL
1807
WILEY
2007
BICENTENNIAL
BICENTENNIAL

John Wiley & Sons Australia, Ltd

First published 2007 by
John Wiley & Sons Australia, Ltd
42 McDougall Street, Milton, Qld 4064

Offices also in Sydney and Melbourne

Typeset in 10/12 Agfa Rotis Serif

National Library of Australia
Cataloguing-in-Publication data

Applying International Financial Reporting Standards.

Enhanced ed.
Bibliography.
Includes index.
For tertiary students.
ISBN   978 0 470 80823 8.

1. Accounting — Standards. 2. Financial statements
— Standards. I. Alfredson, Keith. II. Title.

657.0218

Cover and internal design images: © Digital Vision,
© Ernst & Young, © PhotoDisc
Anniversary logo design: Richard Pacifico

Edited by Miriana Dasovic

Printed in Singapore by
Kyodo Printing Co (S'pore) Pte Ltd

10 9 8 7 6 5 4 3 2 1

from the profession

Ernst & Young is delighted to support *Applying International Financial Reporting Standards Enhanced Edition* – a definitive guide to International Financial Reporting Standards (IFRSs). The year 2005 was a significant milestone in the accounting profession's history as almost 100 countries adopted one set of international standards for the first time. The challenge for these countries is to achieve global consistency in applying these standards. For example, a French company must account for a business combination in the same way as an Australian or New Zealand company. By contrast, each of these countries in the past had its own national accounting standards, and interpretations were determined at the country level.

This text is an important contribution to the goal of global consistency. It is an invaluable guide to applying IFRSs, written by a distinctive combination of authoritative academics and experienced accounting practitioners. The text is abundant with practical examples, and is groundbreaking in providing those examples in many areas such as business combinations and financial instruments. I am sure that the book will be instructive, not only to those learning about accounting standards for the first time, but also to qualified accountants grappling with the new world of applying IFRSs.

In recent years the role of relevant and reliable financial reporting has been elevated, unfortunately as a result of corporate collapses or misdeeds. Never in my experience has financial reporting been in the media headlines as much as in the past few years. The opportunity for the accounting profession now is to ensure that our financial reporting standards are appropriate, well understood and consistently applied. The International Accounting Standards Board (IASB) has played its part in completing the stable platform of IFRSs. The rest is up to us.

I commend this book to you, as you play your part in understanding and applying IFRSs.

James M Millar
Chief Executive Officer
Ernst & Young Australia
Sydney
August 2006

brief contents

contents

*pre*face

With the completion of the stable platform of International Financial Reporting Standards (IFRSs) in 2004, the International Accounting Standards Board (IASB) established itself as a world leader in the preparation of financial reporting standards. As many countries agreed to adopt these standards, or equivalents to them, many influential national standard-setters such as the United Kingdom, Australia and New Zealand acknowledged that the time had come for an international approach to standard setting. This process is ongoing.

The existence of the new set of IFRSs has had major implications for the way in which financial reporting is undertaken in practice as well as the way in which accounting is taught in tertiary institutions. As with business, a global perspective is required. For universities, educating students to become part of a global business environment requires placing more emphasis on understanding accounting principles rather than applying specific local jurisdictional regulations.

Applying International Financial Reporting Standards Enhanced Edition has been written to meet the needs of accounting students and practitioners in understanding the complexities of IFRSs and applying the stable platform of standards. It concentrates on those financial reporting standards that are not related to specific industries and that therefore have wide application. The book is divided into four sections:

- *Part 1: Framework.* The first chapter in this section provides an overview of the IASB as an organisation. To understand the workings of the IASB, it is helpful to view its history as well as its current structures and decision-making processes. The second chapter contains an analysis of the Framework in relation to the financial reporting standards. An intimate knowledge of the Framework used by the IASB in its development of financial reporting standards enables an understanding of the interrelationships between the standards themselves.

- *Part 2: Elements.* The three elements of accounting are assets, liabilities and equity. This book primarily uses companies as the organisational structure under review, so equity is analysed in relation to the component parts of share capital, retained earnings and other reserves. For assets, the key classes analysed are: inventories; intangibles; leases; and property, plant and equipment. Provisions and contingencies constitute the liability focus, while other standards that cover both assets and liabilities (such as income tax and financial instruments) add to the coverage of the elements. Because of their effects on the recognition and measurement process, the standards on share-based payment, business combinations and impairment are included in this part. The standard on revenue recognition is also analysed.

- *Part 3: Disclosure.* An introduction to the process of selecting and changing accounting policies, as well as the concept of materiality, is provided in the first chapter of this section. The next two chapters provide details about what must be disclosed in the balance sheet, income statement, statement of changes in equity, and the cash flow statement. To complete this section, the preparation of information about the segments of entities is discussed.

- *Part 4: Economic Entities.* This section focuses on organisational structures where an entity has investments in other entities. Much detail is provided on the rationale for and preparation of consolidated financial statements, including the translation of the financial statements of foreign subsidiaries. Accounting for investments in associates and joint ventures is also analysed.

This book has been written by a team of six authors with a range of backgrounds and employment situations. Between us, we have had a long and close association with national accounting standard-setting bodies, and involvement in the practical application of financial reporting standards. Specifically, in relation to IFRSs, members of our author team have been part of the process of developing the stable platform of standards, primarily by working through national standard-setting bodies and providing commentary to the IASB, as well as developing internationally equivalent standards for the local jurisdiction. In addition, we have been employed in helping entities understand the changes in financial reporting standards and have also actively participated in the implementation process.

When writing the chapters, we have endeavoured to ensure that the following common themes flow throughout the book:

- *Financial reporting standards are underpinned by a conceptual framework.* Financial reporting standards are not simply a rulebook to be learned by rote. An understanding of the conceptual basis of accounting, and the rationale behind the principles espoused in particular standards, is crucial to their consistent application in a variety of practical situations.
- *International Financial Reporting Standards are principles based.* Although a specific standard is a stand-alone document, the principles in any standard relate to and are interpreted in conjunction with other standards. This reinforces the conceptual basis of financial reporting standards. To appreciate the application of a specific standard, an understanding of the reasoning within other standards is needed. We have endeavoured where applicable to refer to other financial reporting standards that are connected in principle and application. In particular, extensive references are made to the Basis for Conclusions documents accompanying each standard. This material, although not integral to the standards, explains the reasoning process used by the IASB as well as providing indicators of changes in direction being proposed by the board.
- *Financial reporting standards have a practical application.* The end product of the standard-setting process is applied by accounting practitioners in a variety of organisational structures and practical settings. While a theoretical understanding of a standard is important, practitioners must be able to apply the relevant standard. The author of each chapter has demonstrated the practical application of the financial reporting standards by providing case studies, examples and journal entries (where relevant). The references to practical situations require the reader to pay close attention to the detailed information provided, but such a detailed examination is essential to an understanding of the standards. Having only a broad overview of the basic principles is insufficient.

Many people have been directly and indirectly involved in the writing of this book. Our task was made possible because of the discussions and debates we have had with many colleagues, and by the assistance of staff associated with the standard-setting bodies, particularly at the Australian Accounting Standards Board. We thank them all for their patience and tolerance, as well as the impartation of their knowledge. Writing a book takes time, and this has left less time for family and friends. We thank them also for their support.

Finally, at a time when the world seems to produce situations and pronouncements of ever-increasing complexity, we hope that this book assists in the lifelong learning process in which practitioners and students alike must continuously engage.

Keith Alfredson
Ken Leo
Ruth Picker
Paul Pacter
Jennie Radford
Victoria Wise

September 2006

about the authors

keith ALFREDSON

Keith Alfredson, BCom (Hons), AAUQ, FAICD, FCA, FCPA, is a graduate of the University of Queensland. On graduation in 1963, he joined Arthur Andersen, becoming a partner in 1974 and retiring in 1997. He specialised in the audit of large publicly listed and privately owned entities in addition to acting as an expert on technical accounting issues. Keith was Arthur Andersen's representative on the Australian Urgent Issues Group (UIG). In 1998, he became a senior fellow in the Department of Accounting and Business Information Systems of the University of Melbourne. In May 2000, he was appointed the first full-time chairman of the Australian Accounting Standards Board, a position he held until May 2003. During that period, he also acted as chairman of the UIG.

ken LEO

Ken Leo, BCom (Hons), MBA (Qld), AAUQ, ACA, FCPA, is professor of accounting at Curtin University of Technology, Western Australia. During his 37 years as an academic, he has taught company accounting to both undergraduate and postgraduate students. Since 1981, Ken has been involved in writing books published by John Wiley, and has also written books and monographs for other organisations including CPA Australia, the Group of 100 and the Australian Accounting Research Foundation. As a founding member of the Urgent Issues Group in 1995, Ken served on this body until 2001, and has served on the Australian Accounting Standards Board since 2002.

ruth PICKER

Ruth Picker, BA, FCA, FSIA, FCPA, partner — Technical Consulting Group, Global IFRS.

Ruth has had 24 years' experience with Ernst & Young. Her current position is senior partner in the Technical Consulting Group, Global IFRS. Prior to this she was the firm's professional practice director (PPD) for four years. As professional practice director, Ruth was responsible for directing the firm's accounting and auditing policies, with the ultimate authority on accounting and auditing issues. She is a member of Ernst & Young's global International Financial Reporting Standards (IFRS) Policy Committee. The global IFRS Policy Committee meets three times a week by teleconference and quarterly in London to determine Ernst & Young's global positions on IFRS interpretations. She has recently been appointed to the International Financial Reporting Interpretations Committee (IFRIC). IFRIC is the official interpretative arm of the International Accounting Standards Board. Ruth is the only Australian on IFRIC.

In relation to accounting standards, Ruth is responsible for advising clients on the application of accounting standards to complex transactions.

Ruth was responsible for the preparation of Ernst & Young's Corporate Governance Series (which includes guidance for directors and the results of numerous corporate governance surveys) and subsequent advice to a number of entities in both the private and public sectors on the application of corporate governance.

Ruth has conducted numerous 'Directors' Schools' for listed company boards. These schools were designed by Ruth and are aimed at enhancing the financial literacy of listed company board members.

She is a frequent speaker and author on accounting issues and is actively involved in the Australian accounting standard-setting process. She is an immediate past member and past deputy chair of the Australian Accounting Standards Board (AASB), and served on the Urgent Issues Group (UIG) for three years prior to taking up her position on the AASB.

Ruth has been a long-standing lecturer and taskforce member for the Securities Institute of Australia, serving that organisation for 17 years.

Her written articles have been published in a number of publications, and she is frequently quoted in the media on accounting and governance issues.

Ruth is a member of Ernst & Young's board of partners, and has served as a board member for four years. She is a member of the editorial board of the *Australian Accounting Review*, and a member of the Industry Advisory Committee for the Melbourne Centre for Financial Studies.

In November 2000, Ruth was awarded the inaugural Lynne Sutherland Award — an Ernst & Young award created to recognise those people at Ernst & Young who contribute to the development and retention of women, and who support and enhance the ability of Ernst & Young to attract and retain talented people.

paul PACTER

Paul Pacter holds two concurrent positions as the director of standards for small and medium-sized entities (SMEs) at the International Accounting Standards Board in London, and director in the global IFRS office of Deloitte Touche Tohmatsu in Hong Kong. Previously, Paul worked for the US Financial Accounting Standards Board for 16 years, and was commissioner of finance of the City of Stamford, Connecticut, for seven years. He received his PhD from Michigan State University and is a CPA. He has taught in several MBA programs for working business managers.

jennie RADFORD

Jennie Radford, BCom, DipEd (Melb), MCom (Curtin), ACA, recently retired after 17 years as a lecturer at Curtin University of Technology, Western Australia. She has co-authored two research monographs published by the Group of 100 and the ASCPA. She has also contributed to and co-edited a textbook, *Financial Accounting Issues*, and is a co-author on *Company Accounting*. Jennie was for many years employed as an auditor with the 'Big 4' chartered accounting firms, and has taught both undergraduate and postgraduate courses in her career as an academic.

victoria WISE

Victoria Wise, BCom, MEcon, PhD, FCPA, is a professor in the School of Accounting and Corporate Governance at the University of Tasmania, Hobart. During her 20 years as an academic, she has taught financial accounting and auditing to undergraduate, honours and postgraduate students. Victoria has contributed to more than 120 publications, including books and book chapters, professional journal articles and conference proceedings. Her journal articles focus on International Financial Reporting Standards, regulatory issues, public sector accounting, and consolidated and small business financial reporting. Victoria's current research interests include business regulation and financial literacy.

*ac*knowledgements

The authors and publisher would like to thank the following copyright holders, organisations and individuals for their permission to reproduce copyright material in this book.

Images
• **pp. 171, 554:** Ernst & Young • **pp. 443, 444:** The Brookings Institution • **p. 469:** Skandia Insurance Company Ltd • **p. 470:** 'Management Challenges' from Systematic, *Intellectual Capital Report*, 2004, p. 11. www.systematic.dk • **p. 763:** © 2006 International Accounting Standards Committee Foundation. All rights reserved. No permission granted to reproduce or distribute • **p. 947:** Peter Gerhardy, School of Commerce, Flinders University.

Text
• **pp. 7, 64–5, 76, 95, 109, 134, 138, 140, 142, 167–87, 198–200, 203, 206, 209, 211, 219–21, 231–3, 277–9, 293–4, 299, 304–7, 316, 319, 342–4, 356, 362, 382–3, 384, 385–8, 389–90, 391, 392–3, 397, 399–402, 405, 414, 437–8, 440, 445, 448–9, 453–5, 462, 463–4, 484–5, 487, 488–95, 497–8, 500–3, 505–6, 508, 510, 523–5, 532, 550, 553–5, 557–8, 560–2, 567, 568, 570–3, 574, 575–7, 580, 582–4, 596–8, 600–2, 606, 608, 609, 617, 626–7, 630, 632, 633, 651–2, 654, 656–7, 659–60, 662, 663–4, 676–7, 679–80, 682–3, 684–5, 687, 689, 710–11, 713–14, 724–5, 757–9, 761–2, 767–8, 770–2, 773, 796, 799–802, 808, 811, 813–14, 817–8, 823–5, 827, 834, 867, 888, 940–1, 946, 1054, 1060–1, 1066, 1082, 1103, 1105, 1106, 1109, 1112–13, 1121, 1126, 1128, 1154–5, 1159, 1167, 1186, 1187, 1191, 1192, 1211–19:** © 2006 International Accounting Standards Committee Foundation. All rights reserved. No permission granted to reproduce or distribute • **pp. 24–9:** Extracts from 'Use of IFRSs for reporting by domestic listed companies, by country and region' March 2006 © Deloitte Touche Tohmatsu. All rights reserved • **pp. 29–32:** Extracts from 'IFRSs in your pocket 2006' © Deloitte Touche Tohmatsu. All rights reserved • **pp. 34–7:** Extracts from 'First time adoption of international financial reporting standards' ww.iasplus.com/standard/ifrs01.htm © Deloitte Touche Tohmatsu. All rights reserved • **pp. 63–4:** 'Study pursuant to section 108(d) of the Sarbanes–Oxley Act of 2002 on the adoption by the United States financial reporting system of a principles-based accounting system' © U.S Securities and Exchange Commission • **p. 67:** Standard 'ISA 700' of the IAASB, published by the International Federation of Accountants (IFAC) in October 1992 (with revisions in November 1993 and June 2001) is used with the permission of IFAC. • **pp. 78–9:** Portions of various documents, copyright by the Financial Accounting Standards Board, 401 Merritt 7, PO Box 5116, Norwalk, CT 06856-5116, U.S.A., are reproduced with permission. Complete copies of these documents are available from the FASB. © 2006 International Accounting Standards Committee Foundation. All rights reserved. No permission granted to reproduce or distribute • **pp. 88, 94, 101, 107, 112, 117–18, 322–3, 343, 504, 553, 561, 563, 673, 675, 677, 678, 686, 690–2, 693–4, 735–6, 1083:** Extracts from *Nokia in 2005* © Nokia Corporation • **pp. 89–90:** ICRC — International Committee of the Red Cross • **p. 91:** *Comparative International Accounting Seventh Edition* by Nobes & Parker © Pearson Education Limited 2002 • **p. 92:** © Pearson — data sourced from London Stock Exchange, *Fact File* 2000, p. 19 © London Stock Exchange • **p. 99:** Scott Rochfort/*The Age* • **p. 100:** © Australian Stock Exchange Limited ABN 98 008 624 691 (ASX) 2002. All rights reserved. This material is reproduced with the permission of ASX. This material should not be reproduced, stored in a retrieval system or transmitted in any form whether

in whole or part without the prior written permission of ASX. • **pp. 102–3:** Extracted from ANZ *Renounceable Rights Issue Prospectus*, November 2003 ∑ **pp. 108, 450–2, 464:** Christian Dior • **pp. 119, 776–9:** Extracts from ANZ *Financial Report 2005* © ANZ Bank • **pp. 150, 1083, 1194:** © Bayer • **pp. 152, 558:** Swatch Group • **p. 153:** © Lufthansa • **p. 154:** 'SEC charges McAfee, Inc. with accounting fraud; McAfee agrees to settle and pay a $50 million penalty' 2006 © U.S Securities and Exchange Commission • **p. 155:** 'SEC charges Qwest Communications International Inc. with multi-faceted accounting and financial reporting fraud' 2004 © U.S Securities and Exchange Commission • **p. 156:** 'SEC charges Time Warner with fraud, aiding and abetting frauds by others, and violating a prior cease-and-desist order; CFO, Controller, and Deputy Controller Charged with causing reporting violations' 2005 © U.S Securities and Exchange Commission • **pp. 169, 246–53, 1136:** Ernst & Young • **pp. 257, 262, 279, 280:** Information supplied courtesy of BlueScope Steel Limited • **pp. 260, 270, 273, 274:** e-GAAP update No. 3/2005 (April 2005) 'Share based payments — new and complex IFRS equivalent standard' by Colin Parker FCA (www.gaap.com.au) • **pp. 263, 264, 265, 266, 267–8, 270–1, 272–3, 275, 276–7:** © Commonwealth of Australia 2006. All legislation herein is reproduced by permission but does not purport to be the official or authorised version. It is subject to Commonwealth of Australia copyright. The *Copyright Act 1968* permits certain reproduction and publication of Commonwealth legislation. In particular, s.182A of the Act enables a complete copy to be made by or on behalf of a particular person. For reproduction or publication beyond that permitted by the Act, permission should be sought in writing from the Commonwealth, available from the Australian Accounting Standards Board. Requests in the first instance should be addressed to the Administration Director, Australian Accounting Standards Board, PO Box 204, Collins Street West, Melbourne, Victoria, 8007. © 2006 International Accounting Standards Committee Foundation. All rights reserved. No permission granted to reproduce or distribute • **pp. 383, 522–3, 570, 737–9:** Danisco • **pp. 394, 487, 505, 805, 1157–8, 1160, 1188:** All ASB material is reproduced by kind permission of the Accounting Standards Board UK. For further information please visit www.frc.org.uk/asb or call +44 20 7492 2300. • **pp. 400–1:** © Commonwealth of Australia 2006. All legislation herein is reproduced by permission but does not purport to be the official or authorised version. It is subject to Commonwealth of Australia copyright. The *Copyright Act 1968* permits certain reproduction and publication of Commonwealth legislation. In particular, s.182A of the Act enables a complete copy to be made by or on behalf of a particular person. For reproduction or publication beyond that permitted by the Act, permission should be sought in writing from the Commonwealth, available from the Australian Accounting Standards Board. Requests in the first instance should be addressed to the Administration Director, Australian Accounting Standards Board, PO Box 204, Collins Street West, Melbourne, Victoria, 8007. • **p. 410:** Ruth Picker and Anne-Marie Young, Accounting Brief, April 1999 © Ernst & Young • **pp. 436, 505, 809:** © CPA Australia. Reproduced with the permission of CPA Australia. CPA Australia has used reasonable care and skill in compiling the content of these works. However, CPA Australia makes no warranty as to the accuracy or completeness of any information in these works. No part of these works are intended to be advice, whether legal or professional. As laws change frequently, all readers are advised to undertake their own research or to seek professional advice to keep abreast of any reforms or developments in the law. • **pp. 437, 441–2, 444, 455, 459:** The Brookings Institution • **pp. 438, 439, 446–8, 455, 459-60, 475, 800–2, 805–6, 826–7, 1073–4, 1156–7:** Portions of various documents, copyright by the Financial Accounting Standards Board, 401 Merritt 7, PO Box 5116, Norwalk, CT 06856-5116, U.S.A., are reproduced with permission. Complete copies of these documents are available from the FASB. • **pp. 441, 443, 472:** 'Hail the "age of access"' by David James, *BRW*, 27/4/01, by permission of Journalists Copyright • **p. 456:** Table extracts from 'Publishing industry: the future of intangibles under IAS' by Samantha Harrison © Deloitte Touche Tohmatsu. All rights reserved • **p. 473:** 'Assets: standard deviation, part two' by Nick Tabakoff, *BRW*, 21/05/99, by permission of Journalists Copyright • **p. 474:** Reproduced courtesy *The West Australian* • **pp. 532, 586:** EFRAG — European Financial Reporting Advisory Group • **pp. 586–7:** © Deloitte Touche Tohmatsu. All rights reserved • **pp. 613–15:** Telstra Corporation Limited. Reproduced with permission • **p. 674:** Dresdner Bank • **pp. 680–1:** AngloGold Ashanti • **pp. 773–5:** © Queensland Cotton Holdings Limited • **pp. 779–80:** © Colorado Group Limited • **pp. 780–4:** Wesfarmers Limited • **pp. 827–8:** Examples from pp. 536–38 *Company Accounting in Australia 6th Edition* by Leo & Hoggett © John Wiley & Sons Australia 2005 • **pp. 828–30:** Palamedia Limited • **p. 1055:** Lawrence Revsine © The American Accounting Association • **p. 1058:** *Advanced Accounting Second Edition* by Jeter & Chaney © 2004 John Wiley & Sons Inc. Reprinted with permission of John Wiley & Sons, Inc. • **pp. 1187–91:** © 1978 by AICPA, reproduced with permission. Opinions of the authors are their own and do not necessarily reflect the policies of the AICPA.

Every effort has been made to trace the ownership of copyright material. Information that will enable the publisher to rectify any error or omission in subsequent editions will be welcome. In such cases, please contact the Permissions Section of John Wiley & Sons Australia, Ltd who will arrange for the payment of the usual fee.

PART 1
Framework

PART 1 sets the scene for the study of International Financial Reporting Standards (IFRSs) in two ways – historically and conceptually. Chapter 1 provides a history of the development of IFRSs over the past 40 years, and examines why they are increasingly important as the world's economy globalises. Chapter 1 also outlines how IFRSs are established, which topics have already been addressed, which ones are now on the agenda of the International Accounting Standards Board (IASB), and where in the world IFRSs are being used.

Chapter 2 examines the conceptual framework that the IASB uses in developing IFRSs, including the objective of financial statements, the qualities that make accounting information useful, the basic elements of financial statements (assets, liabilities, equity, income and expenses), and the concepts by which these elements are recognised and measured.

CHAPTER 1
The IASB: history, current structure and processes

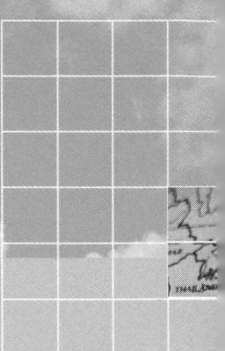

CONCEPTS FOR REVIEW

• This chapter presumes a basic understanding of financial accounting and reporting (such as that gained after a one-year university level introductory accounting course) but does not presume any particular background regarding International Financial Reporting Standards and the International Accounting Standards Board.

LEARNING OBJECTIVES

When you have studied this chapter, you should be able to:
1. understand why accounting information is needed by capital providers
2. explain why there is now a need for global accounting standards when accounting standards have historically been established country by country
3. describe the thinking behind the creation of the International Accounting Standards Committee (IASC) in 1973
4. describe the important achievements of the IASC 1973–2000
5. know what the International Accounting Standards Board (IASB) Framework is
6. recognise the shortcomings of the old IASC that led to its reorganisation into the IASB in 2001
7. explain the structure of the IASB and its related organisations
8. understand the objectives of the IASB, as well as its authority and limitations
9. explain the processes followed by the IASB in establishing International Financial Reporting Standards (IFRSs)
10. know what interpretations of IFRSs are and how they are developed

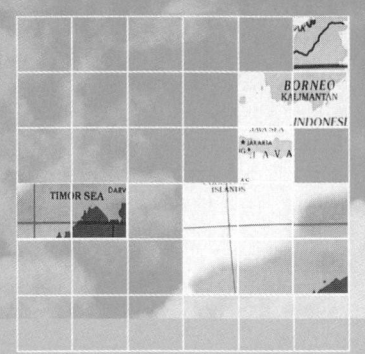

11. know who uses IFRSs today and what the prospects are for expanded use of IFRSs in the next five to ten years
12. understand the steps being taken towards the convergence of IFRSs and US GAAP
13. have a general familiarity with the projects that are currently on the IASB's agenda
14. understand what a company needs to do when it adopts IFRSs for the first time
15. know how International Auditing Standards and International Public Sector (government unit) Accounting Standards are set.

See appendix B to this chapter for a list of common acronyms and abbreviations used in this chapter.

1.1 National accounting standards

A business enterprise that receives capital from investors and creditors or one that is seeking new capital has an obligation to keep its capital providers informed about the entity's performance, condition and prospects. In other words, the business is *accountable* to its investors and creditors. It is also accountable to others who provide resources or an environment in which to operate, such as employees, governments and the community at large. Making this information available in an accurate and understandable format is the role of financial accounting and reporting.

Historically, the rules for what information should be provided and the format that information should take have evolved country by country. By the last quarter of the 20th century, a mechanism for developing and adopting accounting standards had been established in most countries.

In some cases, standard setting has been the responsibility of the public accounting profession, with enforcement of the standards often achieved by law or government regulation. For example, accounting standards are set by the private-sector professional accountancy organisation in Austria, Brazil, Canada, Denmark, Hong Kong, Indonesia, Italy, the Netherlands, New Zealand, the Philippines, South Africa, Sweden, Switzerland and Taiwan. In New Zealand, standards issued by the Financial Reporting Standards Board of the New Zealand Institute of Chartered Accountants must be reviewed and approved by the Accounting Standards Review Board, a government entity.

In other cases, standard setting has been the responsibility of the government. For example, there are government-sponsored accounting standards boards in Argentina, China, Finland, France, Greece, Malaysia, Poland and Saudi Arabia. The Australian Accounting Standards Board (AASB) is a government agency, with a government-appointed oversight body, the Financial Reporting Council, whose members comprise representatives from a range of government and private sector users and preparers of financial statements, including the accounting profession. The chairman of the board is appointed by the government, with other members being appointed by the Financial Reporting Council. In a few countries — among them Germany, Japan, the United Kingdom and the United States — a private-sector standard setter has been established that is independent of the public accounting profession and of government. (Appendix A lists several of the major national accounting standard setters, with links to their websites.)

National accounting standards made sense when companies raised money, and investors and lenders looked for investment opportunities, in their home country. The world's capital markets began to globalise over 30 years ago, and the investment community and the accounting profession quickly recognised the need for a cooperative international effort in the development of accounting standards — and the benefits of a common global accounting language.

1.2 Globalisation of capital markets

Nowadays, investors seek investment opportunities all over the world. Similarly, companies seek capital at the lowest price anywhere. Almost every day you can open a business newspaper and read about a sizable cross-border merger or investment transaction. The problem that this creates for investors, of course, is that accounting differences can completely obscure the comparisons and other analyses that they must make in order to assess various investment opportunities.

In a statement before the Capital Markets, Insurance and Government Sponsored Enterprises Subcommittee of the US House of Representatives in Washington on 7 June 2001,

Paul Volcker, former chairman of the US Federal Reserve Board and former chairman of the International Accounting Standards Committee (IASC) Foundation Board of Trustees, said:

> If markets are to function properly and capital is to be allocated efficiently, investors require transparency and must have confidence that financial information accurately reflects economic performance. Investors should be able to make comparisons among companies in order to make rational investment decisions. In a rapidly globalising world, it only makes sense that the same economic transactions are accounted for in the same manner across various jurisdictions (Volcker 2001).

That the world's financial markets are globalised is undeniable. On many stock exchanges, foreign listings form a large percentage of the total listings. Table 1.1 sets out some representative statistics from early 2006.

TABLE 1.1	Globalisation of the world's securities markets, 2006
Market	Listed companies that are foreign
Australia	4%
Euronext	24%
Germany	17%
London Stock Exchange	16% (by number) 66% (by market capitalisation)
Luxembourg	84%
NASDAQ (US)	10%
New Zealand	18%
New York Stock Exchange	20%
SEC (US): total registered	8% (approximately 1240 foreign registrants out of 13 000 total registered companies)
Singapore	17%
Switzerland	30%

Source: Compiled from information from exchange websites and the website of the World Federation of Exchanges at <www.world-exchanges.org>.

In the United States, the 1240 foreign registrants come from about 55 different countries. The figure of 1240 (correct as of 2006) compares with 491 foreign companies listed in the United States in 1991 and only 173 in 1981. Foreign securities issuers in the United States are permitted to submit financial statements in their national Generally Accepted Accounting Principles (GAAP) provided that they disclose a reconciliation of income and net assets to US GAAP. However, the reconciliation amounts to only a few selected financial figures on two or three pages. All of the monetary amounts in the financial statements and footnotes themselves, and all of the other financial data in the annual and quarterly reports and in filings with the US Securities and Exchange Commission (SEC), which often runs to 100 pages or more, are prepared using the company's national GAAP. This means in many cases different recognition and measurement principles for assets, liabilities and income from the principles used by US companies, as well as different presentation formats and disclosures. Clearly, comparability of most financial figures with similar US companies is often not possible for these foreign companies. American investors cannot be expected to understand 55 different GAAP, so confusion is almost inevitable. Nor is it reasonable to expect the SEC staff, whose job it is to monitor and review the public filings of all 13 000 companies whose securities are publicly traded, to have a thorough understanding of all 55 GAAP. As a result, investor protection can be compromised.

As table 1.1 shows, the situation is similar in Europe and Asia. In fact, users of financial statements in these regions are at an even greater disadvantage than those in the United States, because most European and Asian countries allow foreign companies to provide investors with financial statements prepared using their home-country GAAP without any reconciliation to the GAAP in the investor's country.

1.2.1 Cross-border securities markets

Securities markets themselves are now crossing national boundaries. Euronext, for example, is a recent combination of the former Amsterdam, Brussels, Lisbon and Paris stock exchanges. NASDAQ and London shares can be bought on the stock exchange of Hong Kong. Australian and Malaysian stock exchange shares can be purchased on the Singapore exchange. Merger talks continue among some of the world's largest stock exchanges.

1.2.2 Investing via the Internet

The Internet now enables any investor anywhere to gather corporate financial data posted by companies all over the world, and to enter into securities purchase and sale transactions online in markets and through brokers across the globe. In such an environment, a single set of global accounting and financial reporting standards makes eminent sense.

1.2.3 Benefits of global accounting standards

Among the benefits often cited for a single set of global accounting standards are these:
- easier access to foreign capital markets
- increased credibility of domestic capital markets to foreign capital providers and potential foreign merger partners
- increased credibility to potential lenders of financial statements from companies in less-developed countries
- lower cost of capital to companies
- comparability of financial data across borders
- greater transparency
- greater understandability – a common financial language
- the need for companies to keep only one set of books
- reduced national standard-setting costs
- ease of regulation of securities markets – regulatory acceptability of financial information provided by market participants
- continuation of local implementation guidance for local circumstances
- lower susceptibility to political pressures than national standards
- portability of knowledge and education across national boundaries
- consistency with the concept of a single global professional credential.

In his testimony before the US Senate Committee on Banking, Housing and Urban Affairs on 14 February 2002 in Washington, Sir David Tweedie, chairman of the International Accounting Standards Board (IASB), stated that a single international standard setter was needed for the following four reasons.

1. There is a recognised and growing need for international accounting standards.
2. No individual standard setter has a monopoly on the best solutions to accounting problems.
3. No national standard setter is in a position to set accounting standards that can gain acceptance around the world.
4. There are many areas of financial reporting in which a national standard setter finds it difficult to act alone (Tweedie 2002).

In his remarks to the Economic and Monetary Affairs Committee of the European Parliament on 31 January 2006, Sir David Tweedie commented on the benefits of global accounting standards:

> A common financial language, applied consistently, will enable investors to compare the financial results of companies operating in different jurisdictions more easily and provide more opportunity for investment and diversification. The removal of a major investment risk — the concern that the nuances of different national accounting regimes have not been fully understood — should reduce the cost of capital and open new opportunities for diversification and improved investment returns. This point is particularly relevant at a time when companies, countries and individuals are increasingly dependent upon capital markets to provide a secure retirement for their employees.
>
> For auditors, a single set of accounting standards should enable international audit firms to standardise training and better assure the quality of their work on a global basis. An international approach for accounting should also permit international capital to flow more freely, enabling audit firms and their clients to develop consistent global practice to accounting problems and thus further enhancing consistency. Finally, for regulators, the confusion associated with needing to understand various reporting regimes would be reduced.
>
> The logic behind the case for international standards is clear. I am heartened by the fact that our consultations reveal that there still remains broad support in Europe and elsewhere for the objective of international standards (Tweedie 2006).

LO 3

1.3 Calls for the harmonisation of accounting standards

As the national boundaries of capital markets began to blur, starting in the 1960s and increasing in the 1970s and 1980s, investors, lenders and others who use the financial information that companies report began to complain about the lack of comparability of financial information from one country to the next. They also voiced concerns about the lack of transparency in company reports. By this they meant that the accounting policies used by companies were often hard to understand, and the financial disclosures that companies made were often less than complete. Those concerns led to calls for the harmonisation of accounting standards (making national accounting standards consistent between countries), particularly among countries with developed capital markets. By the 1990s, calls for harmonisation were replaced by calls for a single global set of financial reporting standards that could replace national accounting standards, at least for companies with publicly traded securities.

During this period, many business entities began to expand their operations across national borders; they globalised. National governments regulate and tax businesses that operate within their countries, and regulation and taxation create a need for financial information. As a result, governments and tax authorities also became strong advocates for global accounting standards. For similar reasons, many international bodies — including the World Bank, the International Monetary Fund (IMF), the G7 Finance Ministers, the International Organization of Securities Commissions (IOSCO), the Basel (a.k.a. Basle) Committee on Banking Supervision, the United Nations and the Organisation for Economic Cooperation and Development (OECD) — have publicly urged the adoption of a single set of global accounting standards.

Accountants and others have for many years been aware of the problems caused by having different sets of accounting standards. As early as 1966, professional accountancy bodies in Canada, the United Kingdom and the United States created the Accountants International Study Group (AISG) to develop comparative studies of accounting and auditing practices in the three countries, in the hope that their respective local accounting standards boards would work towards the harmonisation of any differences. The AISG published a total of 20 studies until 1977, when it was disbanded.

1.4 Formation and achievements of the IASC (1973–2000)

In 1972, at the 10th World Congress of Accountants in Sydney, Sir Henry Benson of the United Kingdom put forward a proposal for an International Accounting Standards Committee (IASC). Representatives of the three AISG countries (Canada, the United Kingdom and the United States) discussed the proposal at the congress. Shortly thereafter, the proposal was raised with representatives of several other countries, including Australia, France, Germany, Japan, the Netherlands and Mexico. Together, the nine countries agreed to form the IASC and, in 1973, the IASC opened its doors in London. Each of the countries had a voting seat on the IASC board.

The IASC board was empowered to establish International Accounting Standards (IASs). Each of the signatories to the agreement creating the IASC made a commitment to use their best efforts to bring about the adoption of IASs as their national GAAP.

1.4.1 Structure of the IASC

LO 4

By 2000, the IASC's original nine sponsoring bodies had grown through expansion to encompass 152 professional accounting bodies in 112 countries — all of the members of the International Federation of Accountants (IFAC), which is the global association of national accounting professional bodies. The IASC board that established the IASs eventually grew to have 16 seats, each normally represented by two individuals plus a technical adviser. This meant that at least 48 people normally sat at the IASC board table, deliberating technical issues at meetings held three or four times a year. Thirteen of the 16 seats were held by individual countries or, in a few cases, by pairs of countries. The other three seats were held by a global financial analysts organisation, a global financial executives organisation and a Swiss industry federation.

In addition to the 16 board seats (48 people in all), a number of groups were represented around the board table as observers with the right of the floor. They were the European Commission (EC, generally two people), the US Financial Accounting Standards Board (FASB, one person), the Ministry of Finance of the People's Republic of China (two people), the Basel Committee (one or two people) and IOSCO (up to five people). Including the IASC staff, it was not uncommon for upwards of 70 people to be seated at the IASC board table.

A super-majority vote was required to publish an exposure draft (11 of the 16 IASC board members) and final standard (12 of the 16 members).

1.4.2 Core standards and the IOSCO agreement

As a private sector non-government body, the IASC had no power to force national standard setters to adopt its standards or to require any company to use them. Since it was a global organisation, it could not rely on one national government agency to bring about the widespread adoption and enforcement of its standards. In this regard, the IASC differed from the FASB in the United States, whose standards are imposed on listed companies by the SEC, and also differed from the Accounting Standards Board in the United Kingdom and the Australian Accounting Standards Board in Australia, whose standards are imposed on companies via legislation.

IOSCO is the representative body of the world's securities markets regulators, including the SEC in the US, the Australian Securities and Investments Commission and about 100 similar organisations. High-quality financial information is vital to the operation of an efficient capital market, and differences in the quality of the accounting policies and their enforcement between countries lead to inefficiencies between markets. As regulators of capital markets, IOSCO members have a strong interest in financial reporting that is relevant, reliable, complete and transparent.

From the early 1990s, IOSCO took an active role in encouraging and promoting the improvement and quality of IASs. In 1995, IOSCO and the IASC formally agreed to work on a program of core standards that could be used by publicly listed enterprises when offering securities in foreign jurisdictions. The program identified 40 topics that IOSCO felt had to be addressed in the core standards before IOSCO could recommend International Accounting Standards to its member agencies.

In December 1998, the IASC completed the core set of standards, and IOSCO immediately began a review of these standards. The IOSCO review culminated in May 2000 in a public recommendation from IOSCO that its members allow foreign securities issuers to use International Accounting Standards (IASs), rather than requiring the member's national GAAP, supplemented by reconciliations, disclosure and interpretation where necessary to address outstanding substantive issues at a national or regional level.

WEBLINK   The full text of the IOSCO endorsement can be found on IOSCO's website at <www.iosco.org>.

At about the same time, both the Basel Committee on Banking Supervision and the G7 Finance Ministers similarly endorsed the International Accounting Standards. In its April 2000 report, the Basel Committee on Banking Supervision (2000) said:

> The Committee expresses its support for the standards developed by the IASC. It will continue a close dialogue with the IASC and the banking industry to monitor future developments with care.

The G7 Finance Ministers (1998) themselves issued a public statement saying:

> We call upon ... the IASC to finalise by early 1999 a proposal for a full range of internationally agreed accounting standards. IOSCO, the International Association of Insurance Supervisors and the Basle Committee should complete a timely review of these standards.

1.4.3 Growing pressure for global standards in the late 1990s

The economic crisis that began in 1998 in certain Asian countries and spread to other regions of the world demonstrated the need for reliable and transparent accounting to support sound decision-making by investors, lenders and regulatory authorities. Regulators and economic authorities around the world recognised this need.

The World Bank pushed countries to adopt IASs or develop national standards based on IASs. In some cases, they required IAS reporting as a condition for granting a loan. The US Senate passed a resolution calling on the SEC to study the use of IASs in the United States. The European Commission began to see a common set of accounting standards as a critical pillar in building a single unified capital market in Europe and, after studying whether to develop its own set of standards, it concluded that it would be better to require European companies to use IASs.

The G7 Finance Ministers and the Central Bank Governors also committed themselves to trying to ensure that private sector institutions in their countries comply with internationally agreed principles, standards and codes of best practice. They called on all countries participating in global capital markets to similarly make a commitment to comply with these internationally agreed codes and standards.

1.4.4 Adoption of IASs around the world

The goal of a single set of International Accounting Standards replacing national standards was lofty, and the creators of the IASC in 1973 had recognised it as such. By the beginning of the 21st century, in only one of the nine original IASC countries (Germany) did even a relatively small number of listed companies use IASs as their primary basis of reporting to domestic investors. In four of the nine (France, Germany, the Netherlands and the United Kingdom), nearly all listed companies were required to do so by 2005, and even in these countries national GAAP are likely to remain for unlisted companies. In Australia, the government and the standard setter have replaced national standards with Australian equivalents to International Financial Reporting Standards, effective in 2005. (Starting in 2002, the term 'International Financial Reporting Standards' (IFRSs) replaced the term 'International Accounting Standards' (IASs) as the name used for global accounting standards — see section 1.5.1 of this chapter.) In Canada, the Accounting Standards Board (AcSB) announced in January 2006 that, for publicly traded companies, IFRSs will replace Canadian GAAP over a five-year transition period. In the other three (Japan, Mexico and the United States), the prospects that IASs will replace national GAAP for at least some domestic companies are still uncertain but, it seems fair to say, those prospects are growing.

Because Europe has required IASs for all listed companies starting in 2005 (see section 1.6.1 of this chapter), US companies that are subsidiaries of companies in Europe, or in any other country where international standards replace national GAAP, must prepare financial information using international standards. Similarly, subsidiaries and other investees in Europe and other IAS countries have to comply with international standards.

An increasing number of countries that continue to develop their own GAAP are adopting International Accounting Standards (IASs) almost verbatim (among them Australia, New Zealand, South Africa, Singapore, Hong Kong and the Philippines). Many smaller countries have stopped developing national standards altogether, relying instead on IASs as their national GAAP. Examples include Bahrain, Croatia, Cyprus, the Dominican Republic, Ecuador, Egypt (listed companies only), Haiti, Kenya, Malta, Nepal, Oman, Panama, Tajikistan, the United Arab Emirates (banks only) and Venezuela. Even before Europe moved to international standards for public companies in 2005, foreign issuers and at least some domestic issuers in most European countries were permitted to prepare IAS consolidated financial statements instead of national GAAP statements. Some countries outside Europe also allow or require at least some domestic companies to follow IASs rather than their national GAAP; for example, Hong Kong, Russia and Switzerland. In China, some listed companies whose securities trade in US dollars and can be purchased by non-Chinese investors (known as 'B-shares') must prepare IAS financial statements for investors while still preparing Chinese GAAP statements for government purposes. (A chronology of the history of the IASC and its recent replacement, the IASB, is set out in appendix C to this chapter.)

1.4.5 International Financial Reporting Standards

From its inception in 1973 until it was reorganised into the International Accounting Standards Board (IASB) in early 2001, the IASC developed 41 standards, known as International Accounting Standards. Many of those were revised one or more times over the years. Several were superseded or merged in with other standards. Since 2001, the IASB has revised a number of the IASs and has begun a second series of standards known as International Financial Reporting Standards (IFRSs), starting again with number 1. Figure 1.1 sets out a complete list of the IASs and IFRSs at 30 June 2006. Those not identified as superseded or withdrawn continue in force.

FIGURE 1.1   Complete list of International Accounting Standards, 1973 – June 2006

IAS 1   *Presentation of Financial Statements*

IAS 2   *Inventories*

IAS 3   *Consolidated Financial Statements.* Originally issued in 1976, effective 1977. No longer effective. Superseded in 1989 by IAS 27 and IAS 28.

IAS 4   *Depreciation Accounting.* Withdrawn in 1999, replaced by IAS 16, IAS 22 and IAS 38, all of which were issued or revised in 1998.

IAS 5   *Information to Be Disclosed in Financial Statements.* Originally issued in 1976, effective 1997. No longer effective. Superseded by IAS 1 in 1997.

IAS 6   *Accounting Responses to Changing Prices.* Superseded by IAS 15, which has been withdrawn.

IAS 7   *Cash Flow Statements*

IAS 8   *Accounting Policies, Changes in Accounting Estimates and Errors*

IAS 9   *Accounting for Research and Development Activities.* Superseded by IAS 38, effective 1999.

IAS 10   *Events After the Balance Sheet Date*

IAS 11   *Construction Contracts*

IAS 12   *Income Taxes*

IAS 13   *Presentation of Current Assets and Current Liabilities.* Superseded by IAS 1.

IAS 14   *Segment Reporting*

IAS 15   *Information Reflecting the Effects of Changing Prices.* Withdrawn by the IASB in 2003.

IAS 16   *Property, Plant and Equipment*

IAS 17   *Leases*

IAS 18   *Revenue*

IAS 19   *Employee Benefits*

IAS 20   *Accounting for Government Grants and Disclosure of Government Assistance*

IAS 21   *The Effects of Changes in Foreign Exchange Rates*

IAS 22   *Business Combinations.* Superseded by IFRS 3, effective in 2005.

IAS 23   *Borrowing Costs*

IAS 24   *Related Party Disclosures*

IAS 25   *Accounting for Investments.* Superseded by IAS 39 and IAS 40, effective in 2001.

IAS 26   *Accounting and Reporting by Retirement Benefit Plans*

IAS 27   *Consolidated and Separate Financial Statements*

IAS 28   *Investments in Associates*

IAS 29   *Financial Reporting in Hyperinflationary Economies*

IAS 30   *Disclosures in the Financial Statements of Banks and Similar Financial Institutions.* Superseded by IFRS 7, effective in 2007.

IAS 31   *Interests in Joint Ventures*

IAS 32   *Financial Instruments: Disclosure and Presentation.* Major portions superseded by IFRS 7, effective in 2007. IAS 32 is renamed *Financial Instruments: Presentation.*

IAS 33   *Earnings Per Share*

IAS 34   *Interim Financial Reporting*

(continued)

IAS 35 *Discontinuing Operations.* Superseded by IFRS 5, effective in 2005.
IAS 36 *Impairment of Assets*
IAS 37 *Provisions, Contingent Liabilities and Contingent Assets*
IAS 38 *Intangible Assets*
IAS 39 *Financial Instruments: Recognition and Measurement*
IAS 40 *Investment Property*
IAS 41 *Agriculture*
IFRS 1 *First-time Adoption of International Financial Reporting Standards*
IFRS 2 *Share-based Payment*
IFRS 3 *Business Combinations*
IFRS 4 *Insurance Contracts*
IFRS 5 *Non-current Assets Held for Sale and Discontinued Operations*
IFRS 6 *Exploration for and Evaluation of Mineral Resources*
IFRS 7 *Financial Instruments: Disclosures*

1.4.6   IFRSs: a principles-based approach

International Accounting Standards are more principles based rather than rules based. Principles-based standards focus on establishing general principles derived from an underlying conceptual framework, reflecting the recognition, measurement and reporting requirements for the transactions covered by the standards. By following a principles-based approach, IFRSs tend to include only a limited amount of guidance for applying the general principles to typical transactions, encouraging professional judgement in applying the general principles to other transactions specific to an entity or industry. IFRSs also tend to include qualitative principles (a lease is a finance lease if its term is for the 'major part of the economic life of the asset') rather than quantitative guidelines (a lease is a finance lease if its term is '75% or more of the estimated economic life of the leased property').

By taking a principles-based approach, the international standards tend to have far fewer application examples and numerical thresholds than their US counterparts. Also, the number of published interpretations of IFRSs is minuscule compared to the number of consensuses of the FASB's Emerging Issues Task Force. In addition, very few IFRSs address industry accounting issues whereas many FASB statements deal with individual industries, and these are supplemented by specialised industry accounting guides developed by industry committees of the American Institute of CPAs. Australian and New Zealand accounting standards tend to be more similar to the IFRSs than to US GAAP, and starting in 2005 they reproduce the IFRSs nearly word for word.

LO 5

1.4.7   The IASB Framework

In 1989, the IASC adopted the Framework for the Preparation and Presentation of Financial Statements. The Framework describes the basic concepts by which financial statements are prepared. It defines the objectives of financial reporting and the basic elements of financial statements (assets, liabilities, equity, income, expenses). It sets out concepts of recognition and measurement of the elements. The Framework was developed to serve as a guide to the IASC board in developing accounting standards and as a guide to resolving accounting issues that are not addressed directly in an International Accounting Standard.

The IASB has reaffirmed the Framework, which is now called the IASB Framework. The Framework is not itself a standard, although it must be considered in the absence of an international standard addressing a specific issue. Therefore, it does not define standards for any particular accounting recognition, measurement or disclosure matter. Nor does the Framework override any specific standard if there appears to be a conflict. The International Accounting Standards Board and the US Financial Accounting Standards Board have jointly begun a long-term project to revise and converge their conceptual Frameworks. Chapter 2 of this book discusses the IASB's Framework and outlines the IASB–FASB work program for their joint review of their conceptual Frameworks.

1.4.8 The IASC process for developing standards

The procedures followed by the IASC in issuing final standards always included publishing an exposure draft (ED) for public comment. The ED was an IASC board document and required 11 affirmative votes of the board for issuance. For most agenda projects, the IASC appointed a steering committee of experts on the subject. Most often, the exposure draft was preceded by two documents prepared and issued by the steering committee – a discussion paper (sometimes called an issues paper) setting out the issues, and a draft statement of principles (DSOP) setting out the steering committee's tentative views.

Recognising the need for guidance on implementation questions that might arise as IASs moved into complex accounting areas, the IASC board in 1997 established the Standing Interpretations Committee (SIC). The SIC's role was to consider, on a timely basis, accounting issues that were likely to receive divergent or unacceptable treatment in the absence of authoritative guidance. The SIC considered accounting issues within the context of existing International Accounting Standards and the IASC Framework. That is, it could interpret the meaning of existing requirements but it could not plough new ground.

The SIC followed a due process that included soliciting public input before reaching a final consensus. Once a final interpretation was approved by the SIC, it was submitted to the IASC board, which had to approve the interpretation by a vote of at least 12 of the 16 IASC members before the interpretation took effect. In a few cases, the IASC remanded an interpretation back to the SIC to be reworked. In a few other cases, the IASC did not adopt the final SIC interpretation.

As part of the restructuring of the IASC into the IASB in 2001, the SIC was replaced by the International Financial Reporting Interpretations Committee (IFRIC). IFRIC's interpretations are in a new numbered series taking the form IFRIC 1, IFRIC 2 and so on, the first of which was issued in May 2004. In 2003 and 2004, the IASB made major revisions to many of the IASs that had been issued by the IASC. In making those revisions, the IASB incorporated the provisions of many of the SIC interpretations directly into the revised IASs. Also, starting in 2003, the IASB began issuing IFRSs and, in some cases, incorporated the provisions of several SIC interpretations directly into the new IFRS. As a consequence, many of the original SIC interpretations have now been superseded. Figure 1.2 sets out a list of all of the interpretations issued by the SIC – 31 in all, and the nine interpretations issued so far by IFRIC, with an indication of which ones have been superseded. Note that SIC Draft Interpretations 4, 26, and 34 were issued for public comment but were never finalised.

1.4.9 Implementation guidance

The IASC did not have a practice of publishing staff views or other detailed implementation guidance for its standards and interpretations. The single exception it made was with respect to IAS 39 *Financial Instruments: Recognition and Measurement*. When that standard was issued in December 1998, the IASC recognised the need for practical guidance and formed an IAS 39 Implementation Guidance Committee (IGC). In its two years of existence, the IGC published approximately 250 questions and answers (Q&As) on various issues that had arisen in applying IAS 39. When the IASB revised IAS 39 in

December 2003, the issues addressed in many of the Q&As were incorporated directly into IAS 39. The remaining Q&As are included in the annual bound volume of International Accounting Standards as non-mandatory guidance.

FIGURE 1.2   Complete list of final interpretations, 1997–June 2006

Final interpretations issued by IFRIC

IFRIC 1 *Changes in Existing Decommissioning, Restoration and Similar Liabilities*

IFRIC 2 *Members' Shares in Co-operative Entities and Similar Instruments*

IFRIC 3 *Emission Rights* **Withdrawn**

IFRIC 4 *Determining Whether an Arrangement Contains a Lease*

IFRIC 5 *Rights to Interests Arising from Decommissioning, Restoration and Environmental Rehabilitation Funds*

IFRIC 6 *Liabilities Arising from Participating in a Specific Market – Waste Electrical and Electronic Equipment*

IFRIC 7 *Applying the Restatement Approach under IAS 29 Financial Reporting in Hyperinflationary Economies*

IFRIC 8 *Scope of IFRS 2*

IFRIC 9 *Reassessment of Embedded Derivatives*

Final interpretations issued by the SIC

SIC 1   *Consistency – Different Cost Formulas for Inventories* **Superseded**

SIC 2   *Consistency – Capitalisation of Borrowing Costs* **Superseded**

SIC 3   *Elimination of Unrealised Profits and Losses on Transactions with Associates* **Superseded**

SIC 5   *Classification of Financial Instruments – Contingent Settlement Provisions* **Superseded**

SIC 6   *Costs of Modifying Existing Software* **Superseded**

SIC 7   *Introduction of the Euro*

SIC 8   *First-time Application of IASs as the Primary Basis of Accounting* **Superseded**

SIC 9   *Business Combinations – Classification either as Acquisitions or Unitings of Interests* **Superseded**

SIC 10 *Government Assistance – No Specific Relation to Operating Activities*

SIC 11 *Foreign Exchange – Capitalisation of Losses Resulting from Severe Currency Devaluations* **Superseded**

SIC 12 *Consolidation – Special Purpose Entities*

SIC 13 *Jointly Controlled Entities – Non-Monetary Contributions by Venturers*

SIC 14 *Property, Plant and Equipment – Compensation for the Impairment or Loss of Items* **Superseded**

SIC 15 *Operating Leases – Incentives*

SIC 16 *Share Capital – Reacquired Own Equity Instruments (Treasury Shares)* **Superseded**

SIC 17 *Equity – Costs of an Equity Transaction* **Superseded**

SIC 18 *Consistency – Alternative Methods* **Superseded**

SIC 19 *Reporting Currency – Measurement and Presentation of Financial Statements under IAS 21 and IAS 29* **Superseded**

SIC 20 *Equity Accounting Method – Recognition of Losses* **Superseded**

SIC 21 *Income Taxes – Recovery of Revalued Non-Depreciable Assets*

SIC 22 *Business Combinations – Subsequent Adjustment of Fair Values and Goodwill Initially Reported* **Superseded**

SIC 23 *Property, Plant and Equipment – Major Inspection or Overhaul Costs* **Superseded**

SIC 24 *Earnings Per Share – Financial Instruments that May Be Settled in Shares* **Superseded**

SIC 25 *Income Taxes – Changes in the Tax Status of an Enterprise or its Shareholders*
SIC 27 *Evaluating the Substance of Transactions in the Legal Form of a Lease*
SIC 28 *Business Combinations – 'Date of Exchange' and Fair Value of Equity Instruments* **Superseded**
SIC 29 *Disclosure – Service Concession Arrangements*
SIC 30 *Reporting Currency – Translation from Measurement Currency to Presentation Currency* **Superseded**
SIC 31 *Revenue – Barter Transactions Involving Advertising Services*
SIC 32 *Intangible Assets – Website Costs*
SIC 33 *Consolidation and Equity Method – Potential Voting Rights and Allocation of Ownership Interests* **Superseded**

LO 6 & 7

1.5 Restructuring of the IASC into the IASB

Productive as it was, the IASC suffered from a number of shortcomings, including the following:

- weak relationships with national standard setters
- lack of convergence of IASs and major national GAAP after 25 years of trying
- a full-time workload having to be shouldered by a part-time board
- need for broader sponsorship than is provided by the accounting profession
- lack of widespread recognition of its standards by regulators
- shortage of resources.

Recognising these problems, in 1998 the committee that was entrusted with overseeing the IASC began a comprehensive review of the IASC's structure and operations. That review was completed in 2000. The principal recommendations of the structure review are shown below.

- The large, part-time IASC should be replaced by a smaller and essentially full-time International Accounting Standards Board.
- The new IASB should operate under a broad-based IASC Foundation (IASCF) with trustees representing all regions of the world and all groups interested in financial accounting.
- The new IASB should have a Standards Advisory Council (SAC) to provide counsel to the board.
- The SIC should continue in a slightly modified form as the International Financial Reporting Interpretations Committee (IFRIC).

After some tweaking, the proposals received rapid and widespread support. In November 1999, the IASC board itself approved the constitutional changes necessary for its own restructuring. In May 2000, the IFAC unanimously approved the restructuring. The constitution of the old IASC was revised to reflect the new structure. A new IASC Foundation was incorporated (under the laws of the US state of Delaware), and its trustees were appointed. By early 2001, the members of the IASB and the SAC were appointed, and the new structure became operational. Later that year, the IASB moved into new quarters in London. The technical staff of the IASB comprises over 20 accounting professionals – roughly quadruple the former IASC's professional staff.

The IASB's budget of around US$21 million per year is five times that of the old IASC. The board meets monthly (except for August), usually for four days. Three or four times a year the board meets with the chairpersons of certain major national standard setters, to share information and identify the steps needed for the convergence of accounting standards. Seven of the IASB members have specific liaison responsibilities with these national standard setters. The liaison countries are Australia, Canada, France, Germany, Japan, New Zealand, the United Kingdom and the United States. Liaison involves aligning the board's agenda and joint projects, and seeking mutual agreement on specific accounting questions. The board also meets three times a year with its Standards Advisory Council. (The SAC's role is discussed in section 1.5.5.) Annually, the board hosts a meeting of many national accounting standard setters, with 50 or more countries represented. Figure 1.3 contains a diagram of the new IASB structure.

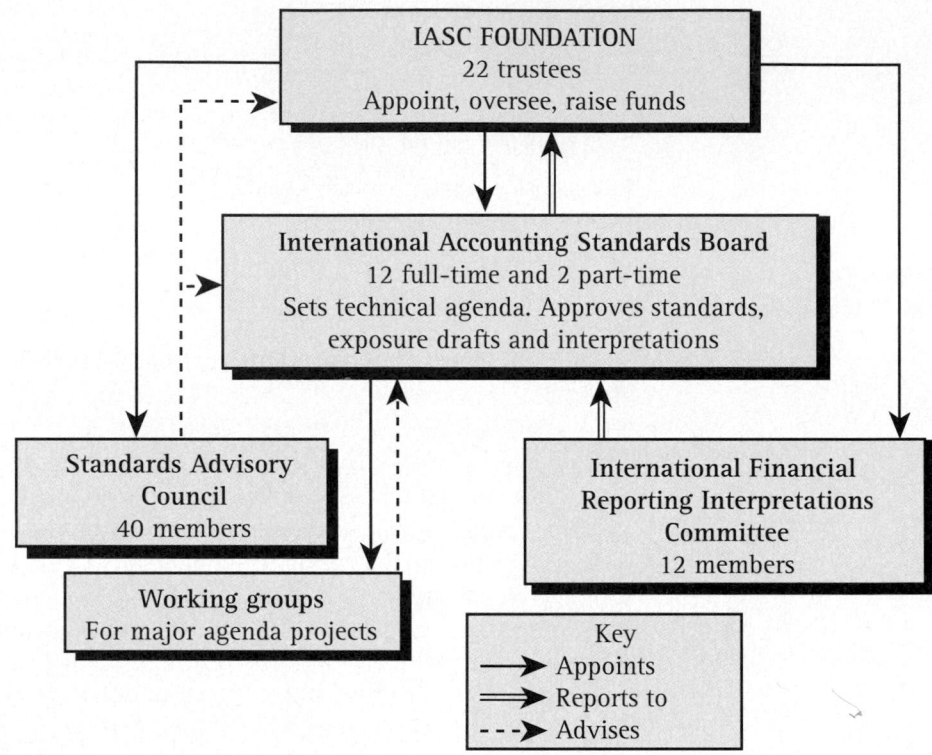

FIGURE 1.3   The structure of the IASB

1.5.1   Naming the standards

The old IASC called its standards International Accounting Standards. The new name for standards issued by the IASB is International Financial Reporting Standards (IFRSs). In one of its earliest actions, the IASB voted to make clear that the IASs issued by the former IASC continue with full force and effect unless and until the IASB amends or replaces them. The IASB announced that the term 'IFRS' should be understood to include IAS. Consistent with that announcement, the term IFRS will be used to refer to the entire body of IASB standards, including the old IASs and interpretations. However, the old IASs have not been renumbered. They remain outstanding until replaced by an IFRS. The IASB has amended some of the old IASs without replacing them, in which case they keep their old IAS number. The IASB has begun to issue a new series of pronouncements known as IFRSs, beginning with IFRS 1 *First-time Adoption of International Financial Reporting Standards*. While some of these will replace the old IASs, others will deal with issues not addressed by the old standards.

1.5.2   Key responsibilities and specific objectives of the IASB

LO 8

The IASB has 14 members, of whom 12 serve full-time and two part-time. The board's principal responsibilities are to:
• develop and issue IFRSs and exposure drafts
• approve interpretations developed by IFRIC.

As set out in the IASB's constitution, the board's objectives are:

(a) to develop, in the public interest, a single set of high quality, understandable and enforceable global accounting standards that require high quality, transparent and comparable information in financial statements and other financial reporting to help participants in the world's capital markets and other users make economic decisions;

(b) to promote the use and rigorous application of those standards; and

(c) in fulfilling the objectives associated with (a) and (b), to take account of, as appropriate, the special needs of small and medium-sized entities and emerging economies; and

(d) to bring about convergence of national accounting standards and International Accounting Standards and International Financial Reporting Standards to high quality solutions (IASC Foundation 2005, p. 3).

In accomplishing its objectives, the IASB has complete responsibility for all technical matters including preparing and issuing International Financial Reporting Standards and exposure drafts, and approving interpretations developed by IFRIC. The IASC Foundation trustees have no involvement in developing IFRSs.

LO 9

1.5.3 IASB due process

Before issuing a final standard, the IASB must publish an exposure draft (ED) for public comment. Sometimes it will also publish a discussion document for public comment on major projects before it issues the ED. It must also consider whether to hold a public hearing or conduct field tests, although there is no requirement to take either one of those steps.

The IASB has full discretion over its technical agenda. It may outsource detailed research or other work to national standard setters or other organisations. The board is responsible for establishing the operating procedures for reviewing comments on EDs and other documents. The IASB will generally form specialist working groups to give advice on major projects, although it is not required to do so. The IASB is required to consult the Standards Advisory Council on major projects, agenda decisions and work priorities. The IASB will normally issue bases for conclusions with both final standards and exposure drafts. All meetings of the IASB are open to public observation. They tend to attract from 20 to 50 observers.

The IASB's use of the term 'advisory groups' rather than the old IASC term 'steering committees' reflects the purely advisory role of these groups: they no longer steer technical projects in a direction supported by the steering committee. Instead, they serve as resources of expertise for the board and its staff.

Standards and exposure drafts must be approved by a vote of 9 of the 14 IASB members. Dissenting opinions are included. Interpretations developed by IFRIC must also be approved by a vote of 9 of the 14 IASB members.

1.5.4 Qualifications of IASB members

The key qualification for IASB membership is professional competence and practical experience. The trustees of the IASC Foundation, who appoint the IASB members, must ensure that the board is not dominated by any particular constituency or regional interest. While there is no specific required number of board members from any particular background, the appointing trustees must ensure that there is 'an appropriate mix of recent practical experience among auditors, preparers, users and academics' (IASC Foundation 2005, para. 21). Appendix D to this chapter identifies the members of the IASB as of August 2006.

1.5.5 Standards Advisory Council (SAC)

The International Accounting Standards Advisory Council (SAC) has approximately 40 members from around 25 countries and seven international organisations. The SAC provides a forum for organisations and individuals with an interest in international financial reporting to participate in the standard-setting process. Members are appointed for a renewable term of three years and have diverse geographic and functional backgrounds.

The SAC normally convenes three times each year at meetings open to the public in order to:

- advise the IASB on priorities in the board's work
- inform the board of the views on major standard-setting projects held by the organisations and individuals on the SAC
- give other advice to the board or to the trustees.

The SAC has an independent chairman, and meets with the board generally three times a year.

LO 10

1.5.6 International Financial Reporting Interpretations Committee (IFRIC)

The International Financial Reporting Interpretations Committee (which in 2002 replaced the Standing Interpretations Committee) has 12 members appointed by the IASC Foundation trustees for three-year terms. IFRIC members are not salaried but their expenses are reimbursed. IFRIC meetings are open to public observation. Approval of draft or final interpretations requires that not more than three voting members vote against the draft or final interpretation. IFRIC is chaired by a non-voting chair, who can be one of the IASB members, the director of technical activities, or a member of the IASB's senior technical staff. In fact, one of the IASB members is the chair of IFRIC.

IFRIC's responsibilities are to:

(a) interpret the application of International Accounting Standards (IASs) and International Financial Reporting Standards (IFRSs) and provide timely guidance on financial reporting issues not specifically addressed in IASs and IFRSs, in the context of the IASB Framework, and undertake other tasks at the request of the IASB;

(b) in carrying out its work under (a) above, have regard to the IASB's objective of working actively with national standard-setters to bring about convergence of national accounting standards and IASs and IFRSs to high quality solutions;

(c) publish after clearance by the IASB Draft Interpretations for public comment and consider comments made within a reasonable period before finalising an Interpretation; and

(d) report to the IASB and obtain its approval for final Interpretations (IASC Foundation 2005, para. 36).

By allowing IFRIC to develop interpretations on financial reporting issues not specifically addressed in an IFRS or IAS, the new IASB constitution has broadened IFRIC's mandate beyond that of the former SIC.

LO 11

1.6 Who uses IFRSs?

As explained in the next section, virtually all listed companies in Europe (about 8000 in total) were required to use IFRSs, starting in 2005. Figure 1.4 identifies some representative companies from among the thousands that had been preparing their financial statements using IFRSs before 2005.

AdidasSolomon	European Investment Bank	Nordic Investment Bank
Air Malta	Eutelsat	Novartis
Alianz	Gazprom	Petroleos de Venezuela
Amadeus Global	Great Nordic	Puma
AngloGold Ltd	Gucci	Roche
Ashanti Goldfields	Gulf Bank	Rostelecom
Austrian Airlines	Henkel	RWE
Bank of Cyprus	Holderbank	Scandinavian Air System
Banka Slovenjie	Hong Kong Land	Schindler
Barbados Shipping	IOSCO	Shanghai Petrochem
Bayer	Jardine Matheson	Statoil (Norway)
Brierley Investments	Lufthansa	StoraEnso
China Petrochemical	Mandarin Oriental	Swatch
Commerzbank	Matav Hungary Telecom	Swiss Air
Consolidated Water	Mexican Maritime Transport	UBS
Czech Telecom	Movenpick	United Saudi Bank
Dairy Farm	Munich Re	Volkswagen
Danisco	National Bank of Kuwait	Wella AG
Dresdner Bank	Nestlé	World Bank
Emirates Bank	Nokia	Zurich Financial Services

FIGURE 1.4   Some companies that prepared IFRS financial statements before 2005

1.6.1 IFRSs in Europe

In June 2000, the European Commission adopted a Financial Reporting Strategy for the 25 European Union (EU) member states that would require 'all listed EU companies to prepare their consolidated accounts in accordance with one single set of accounting standards, namely International Financial Reporting Standards (IFRSs).'

To implement this strategy, the Parliament and Council of the European Union have approved an accounting regulation requiring all European companies listed on a stock exchange in the EU to follow IASB standards in their consolidated financial statements, starting no later than 2005. EU member states are authorised to extend the IFRS requirement to the consolidated financial statements of non-listed companies and also to the separate statements of parent companies. Nineteen of the EU countries, in fact, have permitted (but not required) the non-listed companies to use IFRSs, three EU countries require IFRSs for all or most non-listed companies, and the remaining three require their national GAAP for all non-listed companies. Member states were also authorised to exempt certain companies temporarily from the IFRS requirement – but only until 2007 – in two limited cases: (1) companies that are listed both in the EU and on a non-EU exchange and that currently use US GAAP as their primary accounting standards; and (2) companies that have only publicly traded debt securities. Several EU countries did, in fact, allow the deferral to 2007 for one or both of those small groups of companies. The IFRS requirement applies not only in the 25 EU countries but also in the three additional European Economic Area (EEA) countries that are not in the EU. There are an estimated 8000 listed companies in these 28 countries (all of which must use IFRSs), and upwards of 5 million non-listed companies (most of which are permitted, and some even required, to use IFRSs). Also, many large companies in Switzerland (which is not an EU or EEA member) have long used IFRSs.

In response to a request from the European Commission, the private-sector European Financial Reporting Advisory Group (EFRAG) reviewed International Accounting Standards 1–41 and related SICs and, in June 2002, concluded that: (1) they are not contrary to the fourth and seventh directives; and (2) they meet the required criteria of understandability, relevance, reliability and comparability. Accordingly, EFRAG recommended EU endorsement of the current standards en bloc. Subsequently, EFRAG has continued to make similar recommendations for the revised IASs and new IFRSs that were adopted by the IASB. EFRAG was divided on IAS 39 *Financial Instruments: Recognition and Measurement* and so, in July 2004, chose not to make any recommendation on that standard. EFRAG also recommended that the EU not endorse one of the IFRIC Interpretations (IFRIC 3 *Emission Rights*). The IASB subsequently withdrew IFRIC 3 and is currently reconsidering the question of how to account for tradable emission rights.

Before IASs/IFRSs become officially required under European law, they must be endorsed by an Accounting Regulatory Committee (ARC) of the EC. By February 2006, the ARC had endorsed all of the IASB standards in effect at that time, including both the old IASs (as revised by the IASB), as well as IFRSs 1 to 7, and all the interpretations to IFRIC 6. The ARC has the ongoing responsibility to review and 'endorse for use in Europe' each new IFRS or revised IAS and interpretation.

Because there is not yet a pan-European regulator for all of Europe's securities markets, enforcement of accounting standards is more complicated than when one single regulator regulates the markets, as is the case in Australia and in the United States. To overcome this problem, Europe's securities regulators have joined together to form the Committee of European Securities Regulators (CESR). In mid 2003, CESR published its Standard No. 1 *Enforcement of Standards on Financial Information in Europe*, aimed at developing and implementing a common approach to the enforcement of IFRSs throughout the EU. The document sets out 21 high-level principles that define enforcement, and describes principles that EU member states should adopt in enforcing IFRSs, including the structure of their enforcement authority. It also addresses the selection of financial information to be reviewed for enforcement purposes, the actions available to enforcers (including, in particular, asking for public correction), cross-border coordination, and reporting by enforcement agencies. Furthermore, in July 2003 the EU adopted a 'single prospectus' law under which a prospectus that meets the requirements of the law and that is approved by the securities regulator in one European country is valid in all EU member states. (A prospectus is a disclosure document, including financial statements, that is issued to prospective investors by companies seeking capital.)

Among other recent developments in Europe are the following:

- The European Parliament is considering a proposed new directive (law) on the statutory audit of annual accounts and consolidated accounts. Among other things, it would adopt international standards on auditing throughout the EU and require member states to form auditor oversight bodies.
- The EU directives have been amended to establish the collective responsibility of board members for a company's financial statements.

- In late 2005, the European Commission formed a new European Group of Auditors' Oversight Bodies (EGAOB) to coordinate auditor oversight throughout Europe.
- In late 2005, the European groups of bank regulators, insurance regulators and securities regulators agreed to a plan for cooperation on overlapping enforcement issues, including financial reporting.
- The Committee of European Securities Regulators is developing a plan to make the published financial reports of listed companies available electronically throughout Europe.

1.6.2 IFRSs in the Asia–Pacific region

The Asia–Pacific jurisdictions are taking a variety of approaches towards the convergence of GAAP for domestic companies with IFRSs.

Bangladesh is the only Asian country that now requires IFRSs in place of national GAAP for all domestic listed companies, just as required in Europe. Both Australia and New Zealand have decided to adopt national GAAP that are word-for-word equivalents of IFRSs, but some changes have been made. In both countries:

- Wording has been amended to accommodate the national legislative environment.
- Additional or amended accounting recognition and measurement requirements have been introduced for non-profit and governmental entities that must follow the standards.
- In some cases where the IFRSs allow two accounting policy options, Australia or New Zealand permits only one of the options.
- Additional disclosures have been added.
- There are different effective dates.
- There are different transitional requirements.

Australia's IFRS equivalents took effect in 2005, and New Zealand's will take place in 2007 although adoption from 2005 was permitted. The auditor's report will refer to conformity with national GAAP. The notes to the financial statements of companies in both of those countries will state that the financial statements also conform to IFRSs, as well as to Australian or New Zealand standards. Both of those countries have, in the past, tried to develop a single set of accounting standards that applies not only to business entities but also to government and not-for-profit entities. This broader scope is one of the reasons for the decisions not to replace national GAAP with IFRSs in Australia and New Zealand.

Hong Kong, the Philippines and Singapore have also decided to adopt new national standards that are virtually word-for-word equivalents of IFRSs, but there is sometimes a time lag and, in the case of Singapore, some changes have been made to IFRSs. In these three jurisdictions, the auditor's report refers to the national GAAP, not IFRSs. Certain Chinese companies listed on the stock exchanges in China are required to prepare IFRS financial statements – namely those companies whose shares trade in US dollars and can be purchased by foreign investors. IFRSs are looked to in developing national GAAP to varying degrees in most of the rest of the Asia–Pacific region. Virtually all countries will assert that they base their national GAAP on IFRSs but – as the expression goes – the devil is in the details. The major economies of China, Japan and Korea have adopted only a few national accounting standards that can be described as being the same as the IFRSs. In February 2006, the Ministry of Finance of China announced that it had adopted a new basic standard and 38 new Chinese accounting standards that are substantially in line with the principles in international standards, although a few exceptions are noted. The basic standard is akin to a conceptual framework, and the 38 standards address nearly all of the issues covered in the IFRSs. The new standards will become effective for listed enterprises from 1 January 2007. Other entities are encouraged to adopt them.

Many of the recent accounting standards in India and Thailand are nearly identical to the IFRSs, although significant differences remain in some of the older standards, and not all IFRSs have been adopted. In Laos and Myanmar, some domestic companies may use IFRSs; and in Australia, Hong Kong, New Zealand, Pakistan, Singapore and Thailand, foreign listed companies may use IFRSs. Japan has also permitted foreign companies to use IFRSs in several cases.

1.6.3 IFRSs in Russia

In Russia, banks have been required to use IFRSs since 2004. A bill has been introduced in the legislature to extend IFRSs to additional classes of companies in stages through 2007, although not to small companies.

1.6.4 IFRSs in the United States

In the United States, a foreign Securities and Exchange Commission (SEC) registrant may submit IFRS financial statements, but a reconciliation of earnings and net assets to US GAAP figures is required. In effect, this requires companies to keep two sets of books. Alternatively, foreign registrants can submit to the SEC financial statements prepared using their national GAAP, with a reconciliation to US GAAP, resulting once again in keeping two sets of books. In February 2000 in the US, the SEC issued a concept release, *International Accounting Standards*, inviting views on whether and how IASs might be permitted for foreign registrants, and possibly for domestic registrants as well. The matter continues to be under study by the SEC.

WEBLINK   ↗   The full text of the SEC's concept release can be found on the SEC's website at <www.sec.gov/rules/concept/34-42430.htm>.

In 2002, the United States Congress enacted the *Public Company Accounting Reform and Investor Protection Act* of 2002, also known as the Sarbanes-Oxley Act. The act requires the SEC to conduct a study on the 'adoption by the United States financial reporting system of a principles-based accounting system', including in s. 108(d)(1)(B):

- the extent to which principles-based accounting and financial reporting exists in the United States
- the length of time required for change from a rules-based to a principles-based financial reporting system
- the feasibility of and proposed methods by which a principles-based system may be implemented
- a thorough economic analysis of the implementation of a principles-based system.

As a result of the act, the FASB has invited comment on a proposal for a principles-based approach to US accounting standard setting. The proposal addresses concerns about the increase in the level of detail and complexity in accounting standards.

The Sarbanes-Oxley Act in the US permits the SEC to look to a private-sector accounting standard setter, such as the FASB, provided that the standard setter:

> considers, in adopting accounting principles . . . the extent to which international convergence on high quality accounting standards is necessary or appropriate in the public interest and for the protection of investors (s. 108(b)(1)(A)(v) of the act).

The Sarbanes-Oxley Act created a new Public Company Accounting Oversight Board (PCAOB). Its mission is to protect investors in US securities markets and to further the public interest by ensuring that public company financial statements are audited according to the highest standards of quality, independence and ethics. In April 2003, the PCAOB decided by unanimous vote not to delegate responsibility for setting auditing standards to the accounting profession but, instead, to set the standards itself. Previously, the American Institute of CPAs had promulgated auditing standards in the United States. The PCAOB's auditing standards will include matters of quality control, professional ethics, and independence of auditors from companies whose financial statements they audit. The FASB will continue to set accounting standards in the United States. Nothing in the Sarbanes-Oxley Act or PCAOB regulations would prevent the greater use of IFRSs in the United States.

LO 12

In October 2002, the International Accounting Standards Board and the US Financial Accounting Standards Board jointly issued a memorandum of understanding, marking a significant step towards formalising their commitment to the convergence of US and International Accounting Standards. Both boards added to their agendas a short-term International Convergence project. The FASB also voted to authorise its staff to expand its research project on international convergence. The FASB has already made a number of changes to its standards in the interests of convergence, and it has proposed others.

In April 2005, the US Securities and Exchange Commission (SEC) announced a 'roadmap' that it intends to follow in deciding whether to eliminate the requirement that companies that are registered with the SEC and that publish IFRS financial statements must include a reconciliation of earning and shareholders' equity from IFRS figures to US GAAP figures. The roadmap contemplates (a) the SEC reviewing the 2005 and 2006 filings of IFRS companies, and (b) further steps by the IASB and the FASB to eliminate differences between their two bodies of standards.

In February 2006, the FASB and the IASB published an updated memorandum of understanding (MOU) that reaffirms the boards' shared objective of developing high-quality, common accounting standards for use in the world's capital markets. The MOU is a further elaboration of the objectives and principles first described in the MOU published in October 2002. While the new document does not represent a change in the boards' convergence work program, it does reflect the context of the US SEC's roadmap for removing the reconciliation requirement for non-US companies that use IFRSs and are registered in the United States. It also reflects the work undertaken by the Committee of European Securities Regulators (CESR) to identify areas where accounting standards can be improved. Both the FASB and the IASB note that removing the current reconciliation requirements will require continued progress on the boards' convergence program. Accordingly, the MOU sets out milestones that the FASB and the IASB believe are achievable.

The boards agreed that trying to eliminate differences between standards that are both in need of significant improvement is not the best use of resources. Instead, new common standards should be developed. Consistent with that principle, convergence work will continue to proceed on the following two tracks:
1. The boards will reach a conclusion about whether major differences in focused areas should be eliminated through one or more short-term standard-setting projects and, if so, the goal is to complete or substantially complete work in those areas by 2008.
2. The FASB and the IASB will seek to make continued progress in other areas identified by both boards where accounting practices under US GAAP and IFRSs are regarded as candidates for improvement.

WEBLINK

Deloitte Touche Tohmatsu has published a detailed comparison of IFRSs and US GAAP that is available without charge from its IAS Plus website at
<www.iasplus.com/dttpubs/pubs.htm>.

1.6.5   Canada

In Canada, the Accounting Standards Board (AcSB) announced in January 2006 that, for publicly traded companies, IFRSs will replace Canadian GAAP over a five-year transition period. Canadian public companies whose securities are registered with the US Securities and Exchange Commission will be permitted to use US GAAP instead of Canadian GAAP. For private (non-listed) businesses, the AcSB has begun a comprehensive examination of their financial reporting needs and will determine the most appropriate model for meeting those needs. For not-for-profit organisations, the AcSB will continue to apply those elements of GAAP for profit-oriented enterprises that are applicable to the circumstances, and develop other standards dealing with the special circumstances of the not-for-profit sector. Foreign securities issuers in Canada were permitted, starting in 2004, to use IFRSs without reconciliation to Canadian GAAP.

1.6.6   Use of IFRSs: a global summary

Table 1.2 summarises where and how IFRSs are already used for domestic reporting purposes by listed companies around the world at February 2006.

TABLE 1.2	Use of IFRSs for domestic reporting by listed companies as of February 2006			
Location	IFRSs not permitted	IFRSs permitted	Required for some domestic listed companies	Required for all domestic listed companies
Albania	No stock exchange. Companies use Albanian GAAP			
Argentina	✓			
Armenia				✓
Aruba		✓		
Austria				✓ (a)
Australia				✓ (b)
Bahamas				✓
Bahrain			Banks	
Barbados				✓
Bangladesh				✓
Belgium				✓ (a)
Belize	No stock exchange. Companies may use IFRSs.			
Benin	✓			
Bermuda		✓		
Bolivia		✓		
Botswana		✓		

Location	IFRSs not permitted	IFRSs permitted	Required for some domestic listed companies	Required for all domestic listed companies
Brazil	✓			
Brunei Darussalam		✓		
Bulgaria				✓
Burkina Faso	✓			
Cambodia	No stock exchange. Companies may use IFRSs.			
Cayman Is.		✓		
Canada	✓			
Chile	✓			
China			✓	
Cote D'Ivoire	✓			
Colombia	✓			
Costa Rica				✓
Croatia				✓
Cyprus				✓ (a)
Czech Republic				✓ (a)
Denmark				✓ (a)
Dominica		✓		
Dominican Republic				✓
Ecuador				✓
Egypt				✓
El Salvador		✓		
Estonia				✓ (a)
Finland				✓ (a)
Fiji	✓			
France				✓ (a)
Germany				✓ (a)
Georgia				✓

(continued)

Location	IFRSs not permitted	IFRSs permitted	Required for some domestic listed companies	Required for all domestic listed companies
Ghana	✓			
Gibraltar		✓		
Greece				✓ (a)
Guam	No stock exchange. Companies use US GAAP.			
Guatemala				✓
Guyana				✓
Haiti				✓
Honduras				✓
Hong Kong				✓ (c)
Hungary				✓ (a)
Iceland				✓ (a)
India	✓			
Indonesia	✓			
Ireland				✓ (a)
Israel	✓			
Italy				✓ (a)
Jamaica				✓
Japan	✓			
Jordan				✓
Kazakhstan			Banks	
Kenya				✓
Korea (South)	✓			
Kuwait				✓
Kyrgyzstan				✓
Laos		✓		
Latvia				✓ (a)
Lebanon				✓

Location	IFRSs not permitted	IFRSs permitted	Required for some domestic listed companies	Required for all domestic listed companies
Liechtenstein				✓ (a)
Lesotho		✓		
Lithuania				✓ (a)
Luxembourg				✓ (a)
Macedonia				✓
Malawi				✓
Mali	✓			
Malta				✓ (a)
Malaysia	✓			
Mauritius				✓
Mexico	✓			
Moldova	✓			
Myanmar		✓		
Namibia		✓		
Netherlands				✓ (a)
NL Antilles		✓		
Nepal				✓
New Zealand				2007 (b)
Niger	✓			
Norway				✓ (a)
Oman				✓
Pakistan	✓			
Panama				✓
Papua New Guinea				✓
Peru				✓
Philippines				✓ (c)

(*continued*)

Location	IFRSs not permitted	IFRSs permitted	Required for some domestic listed companies	Required for all domestic listed companies
Poland				✓ (a)
Portugal				✓ (a)
Romania			All large companies	
Russian Federation			✓	Proposed phase-in starting 2006
Saudi Arabia	✓			
Singapore				✓ (c)
Slovenia				✓ (a)
Slovak Republic				✓ (a)
South Africa				✓
Spain				✓
Sri Lanka		✓		
Sweden				✓ (a)
Syria	✓			
Swaziland		✓		
Switzerland		✓		
Taiwan	✓			
Tajikistan				✓
Tanzania				✓
Thailand	✓			
Togo	✓			
Trinidad and Tobago				✓
Tunisia	✓			
Turkey		✓		
Uganda		✓		
Ukraine				✓

Location	IFRSs not permitted	IFRSs permitted	Required for some domestic listed companies	Required for all domestic listed companies
United Arab Emirates			Banks and some others	
United Kingdom				✓ (a)
United States	✓			
Uruguay				✓ (d)
Uzbekistan	✓			
Venezuela				✓
Vietnam	✓			
Yugoslavia				✓
Zambia		✓		
Zimbabwe		✓		

Notes:
(a) Audit report refers to IFRSs as adopted by the EU.
(b) Compliance with IFRSs is stated in a note.
(c) IFRSs adopted virtually in full as national GAAP.
(d) Follows IFRSs as at 29 May 2004.
This table is kept up to date on <www.iasplus.com>.

LO 13

1.7 IASB activities to date

When it started operations in 2001, the IASB was able to hit the ground running because there were a number of projects left in the pipeline from its predecessor. Since then, the IASB has finished most of its initial agenda projects and has added others to its agenda. Figure 1.5 summarises the IASB technical agenda projects as of February 2006.

FIGURE 1.5   Summary of the IASB's agenda projects as of February 2006

Accounting standards for small and medium-sized entities (SMEs)

Status: A discussion paper and recognition and measurement questionnaire were issued. Public round-tables were held. The IASB is developing an exposure draft:
- Standards are intended to be suitable for entities that do not have public accountability (not listed, not a financial institution).
- Will be a single-volume IFRS for SMEs, organised topically.
- There is general agreement that disclosure reductions are needed. The main area of debate is about simplification of recognition and measurement principles in IFRSs for SMEs.

What's next? An exposure draft of an IFRS for SMEs is planned for 2006.

(*continued*)

Business combinations — phase II

Status: In June 2005, the IASB issued exposure drafts dealing with:
- application of the purchase method (joint with FASB; this exposure draft would amend IFRS 3)
- non-controlling (minority) interests (this exposure draft would amend IAS 27).
- non-financial liabilities (this exposure draft would amend the principles for measuring provisions under IAS 37).

What's next? A final standard is expected in mid 2007.

Conceptual Framework

Status: This is a joint project with the FASB designed to align the two boards' conceptual Frameworks. The project is being addressed in eight phases:
- objectives and qualitative characteristics
- elements: recognition and measurement attributes
- initial and subsequent measurement
- reporting entity
- presentation and disclosure
- status of Framework in GAAP hierarchy
- applicability to not-for-profit organisations
- reconsideration of entire Framework.

What's next? Each of the eight phases will be examined in a discussion paper. Papers on objectives and qualitative characteristics are planned for late 2006. Papers on elements and reporting entity are planned for 2007. This project is of more than just academic interest because IAS 8 now requires an entity to look to the Framework if it cannot find guidance on accounting for a particular kind of transaction in the standards or interpretations.

Consolidation, including special purpose entities

Status: The objective of this project is to clarify and provide more rigorous guidance on the concept of 'control' as the basis for preparing consolidated financial statements, including applying that concept to special purpose entities. The board's most recent thinking on the definition of control is as follows:
- ability to direct the strategic financing and operating policies
- ability to access benefits
- ability to use power to maintain, increase or protect benefits.

What's next? An exposure draft is expected in late 2006 or, more likely, 2007.

Financial instruments puttable at fair value

Status: Currently, IAS 32 classifies an instrument as a liability if the issuer cannot avoid paying cash, such as through a holder's put option or a mandatory redemption feature. For many entities — including many SMEs that have buy/sell agreements with owners, as well as most partnerships and cooperatives — IAS 32 classifies as debt what these entities have traditionally regarded as equity capital. Often it is their only investor capital. This project seeks to identify criteria by which financial instruments puttable at a pro rata share of the fair value of the residual interest in the issuer would appropriately be classified as equity. The IASB issued an exposure draft in June 2006.

What's next? Comments are requested by 23 October 2006. A final standard is expected in the first half of 2007.

Government grants and emissions trading schemes

Status: IAS 20 provides many options in accounting for government grants. This project is addressing ways to improve IAS 20, including possibly replacing it with a new standard.

Additionally, in December 2004, IFRIC issued Interpretation 3 *Emission Rights*, which are a form of government grant. The IASB subsequently withdrew that interpretation. The matter of accounting for emission rights is now included in the IAS 20 project.

What's next? The board has noted that certain issues related to recognising and measuring obligations under grants with conditions attached are similar to issues related to recognising and measuring provisions under IAS 37. Because the board is currently reconsidering IAS 37 as part of the Business Combinations Phase II project, in February 2006 the board decided to defer work on the IAS 20 project pending final decisions on the revision of IAS 37, which are expected in mid 2007.

Insurance contracts — phase II

Status: The insurance contracts project was carried forward from the former IASC. It is a comprehensive project addressing all issues on accounting for insurance contracts. However, in May 2002, the IASB agreed to split the project into two phases, so that some components could be put in place by 2005 without delaying the rest of the project.

Phase I: This phase involved issuing an interim standard (IFRS 4) to provide guidance on how existing IFRSs should be applied to insurance contracts. Phase I is now completed.

Phase II: This phase is taking a fresh look at accounting for insurance contracts. In January 2003, the board suspended work on phase II pending completion of phase I. Work on phase II resumed in September 2004 with the appointment of a new working group on insurance. In announcing the working group, the board noted that its predecessor had published an issues paper and a draft statement of principles, and the IASB itself has discussed the project at many board meetings. The board said that it will 'regard the past work as a useful resource, but will not feel bound by it. The only restrictions on a fresh look are the IASB's Framework and the general principles established in the IASB's existing standards.'

What's next? The IASB is expected to publish a discussion paper in 2006 or 2007.

Performance reporting (reporting comprehensive income)

Status: A joint project with FASB. The project is divided into two segments:
- Segment A addresses the following:
  - Which financial statements? Tentatively decided to require an opening (as well as closing) balance sheet, and a statement of all recognised income and expenses.
  - Comparative information.
- Segment B addresses the following:
  - Presentation of information on the face of the required financial statements: What information? What format (line items, columns and so on)?
  - Recycling.
  - Disaggregation (such as segment information).
  - Totals and subtotals.

What's next? The IASB issued an exposure draft on segment A in January 2006. The FASB will not publish an exposure draft on segment A. Instead, it will address the topics in segments A and B together. The timetable for segment B has not been established.

(continued)

Revenue recognition

Status: This is a joint project with the FASB. Tentative decisions include the following:

- Revenue should be recognised on the basis of changes in assets and liabilities arising from contracts with customers – without considering additional criteria, such as the realisation and completion of an earnings process.
- Revenue arises as a result of (a) an unconditional right to receive consideration because a contract deliverable has been delivered, and (b) the extinguishment of the reporting entity's performance obligations to its customers.
- The boards are exploring a revenue recognition approach under which performance obligations would be measured by allocating the customer consideration rather than at the fair value of the obligation (that is, the amount the reporting entity would be required to pay to transfer the performance obligation to a willing third party of comparable credit standing).

What's next? A discussion paper is due in the third quarter of 2006.

Short-term convergence of IFRSs and US GAAP

Status: The objective of this project is to eliminate a variety of differences between IFRSs and US GAAP. The project, which is being done jointly by FASB and IASB, grew out of an agreement reached by the two boards in September 2002. From the IASB side, some aspects of this project have been completed, including many of the changes to IASs in December 2003 as a result of the IASB's Improvements project; IFRS 3 on business combinations and the related revisions to IAS 36 and IAS 38; and IFRS 5 on asset disposals and discontinued operations. Likewise, FASB has converged on a number of points.

What's next? Current convergence projects are underway in the following areas:

- IAS 12 *Income Taxes*. An exposure draft is expected in the second half of 2006.
- IAS 14 *Segment Reporting*. An exposure draft was issued in January 2006. It proposes to adopt the US FAS 131 'management approach' for both defining segments and determining what information is disclosed.
- IAS 23 *Borrowing Costs*. Currently, IAS 23 allows both capitalisation and immediate expensing. The IASB has agreed to require capitalisation and to prohibit immediate expensing, thereby converging with the FASB approach. An exposure draft was issued in the first half of 2006.

 WEBLINK The best places to look for up-to-date information about IASB projects are the IASB's own website at <www.iasb.org> and an IASB-related website maintained by Deloitte Touche Tohmatsu at <www.iasplus.com>.

1.8 Recent trends in International Financial Reporting Standards

The standards issued by the IASC in its last few years, and by the IASB, allow the following observations to be made about trends in IFRSs:

- The recent IFRSs reflect greater use of fair value in measuring transactions and a movement away from the traditional historical-cost basis of measurement. While fair values are somewhat more subjective than a price paid in a past transaction, current values are usually more relevant for economic decision making than past costs. Examples of the use of fair values for measuring profits in recent IFRSs include:
  - financial instruments (required for trading investments and an option to measure most other financial assets and financial liabilities at fair value)
  - assets held for disposal

- impairment recognition (write-down to fair values)
- prohibition of pooling of interests (the required purchase method recognises the fair values of assets and liabilities acquired in a business combination)
- exchanges of similar items of property, plant and equipment
- changes in fair values of investments in real estate
- changes in fair values of agricultural crops, orchards, forests, and livestock prior to harvesting.
- More assets are being reported at fair value, rather than at cost, on the balance sheet. In particular:
  - financial instruments (available-for-sale investments)
  - investment property, including leases of land
  - commodity inventories
  - biological assets and agricultural produce.
- Traditionally, IFRSs had not recognised income until an actual sale was made and the buyer had a legal obligation to pay the seller. This has been called the 'realisation principle' for recognising income. More recently, however, as fair values have been recognised in the balance sheet, the accounting standards have considered most, but not all, value changes to be components of income. As a result, performance reporting becomes key. That is, the income statement should separately report the 'realised' components of income and those components of income that result from changes in the fair values of assets and liabilities even before they have been disposed of.
- Until the last few years, some IFRSs were designed to smooth out the volatility of earnings from period to period by means of cost and revenue deferrals and accruals of future costs. As a result, the balance sheet included deferred costs that did not meet the definition of an asset because they would not result in future cash inflows to the company, as well as deferred revenues and provisions that did not meet the definition of a liability because they did not obligate the company to make a future cash payment. Recent accounting standards have rejected income smoothing as an accounting objective by:
  - taking a weakened corridor approach to pensions
  - taking a balance sheet approach to deferred taxes
  - not allowing accruals for future losses and restructurings
  - using rigorous hedge accounting rules.
- In the past, companies were able to keep certain obligations and expenses off their books because no IFRS required the company to recognise those obligations and expenses. Sometimes, investors found out about the obligations only when a problem developed. Recent accounting standards have moved off-balance-sheet items onto the balance sheet. In particular:
  - special purpose entities
  - derivatives
  - share-based payment.
- Recent IFRSs have substantially expanded financial statement disclosures, especially about judgements, plans and assumptions:
  - greater disclosure about accounting policy choices made by the company
  - judgements made in applying accounting policies
  - disclosure of key sources of estimation uncertainties in financial statement amounts
  - risk-management policies
  - sensitivity analyses.
- Historically, many accounting standards allowed companies to choose between two or more acceptable methods of accounting for the same transaction. Little by little, the IASC and the IASB have eliminated these accounting choices, and the IASB's current projects will eliminate many more.
- Convergence with US GAAP.

1.9 First-time adoption of IFRSs

A company is regarded as a first-time adopter of IFRSs if, for the first time, it makes an explicit and unreserved statement that its general purpose financial statements comply with IFRSs. IFRS 1 *First-time Adoption of International Financial Reporting Standards* prescribes the accounting and disclosure required for first-time adopters.

A first-time adopter will prepare its first IFRS financial statements using the IFRSs that are in effect at the time it first adopts IFRSs. It will use those standards to prepare IFRS financial statements for that year and (at least) the preceding year, and will restate the opening balance sheet of the earliest period presented in conformity with IFRSs.

To illustrate: an entity that adopted IFRSs for the first time in its annual financial statements for the year ended 31 December 2005 was required to do as follows:

1. *Select accounting policies.* The entity selected its accounting policies based on the IFRSs in force at 31 December 2005.
2. *Choose its IFRS reporting periods.* The entity prepared financial statements for at least 2005 and 2004, and restated retrospectively the opening balance sheet (beginning of the first period for which full comparative financial statements are presented) by applying the IFRSs in force at 31 December 2005.
   (a) Since IAS 1 requires that at least one year of comparative prior-period financial information be presented, the opening balance sheet is 1 January 2004 if not earlier.
   (b) If a 31 December 2005 adopter reports selected financial data (but not full financial statements) on an IFRS basis for periods prior to 2004, in addition to full financial statements for 2004 and 2005, that does not change the fact that its opening IFRS balance sheet is as of 1 January 2004.

Certain adjustments are required to move from the entity's previous GAAP to IFRSs. These may include the following:

1. The entity should eliminate previous GAAP assets and liabilities from the opening balance sheet if they do not qualify for recognition under IFRSs. For example:
   (a) IAS 38 does not permit recognising expenditure on any of the following as an intangible asset: research; start-up, pre-operating and pre-opening costs; training; advertising and promotion; and moving and relocation. If previous GAAP recognised these as assets, they are eliminated in the opening IFRS balance sheet.
   (b) If previous GAAP had allowed accrual of liabilities for 'general reserves', restructurings, future operating losses, or major overhauls that do not meet the conditions for recognition as a provision under IAS 37, these are eliminated in the opening IFRS balance sheet.
   (c) If previous GAAP had allowed recognition of reimbursements or contingent assets that are not virtually certain, these are eliminated in the opening IFRS balance sheet.
2. Conversely, the entity should recognise all assets and liabilities required to be recognised by IFRSs even if they were never recognised under previous GAAP. For example:
   (a) IAS 39 requires recognition of all derivative financial assets and liabilities, including embedded derivatives. Derivatives include options, forward and futures contracts, and swaps. These were not recognised under many local GAAP.
   (b) IAS 19 requires an employer to recognise its liabilities under defined benefit plans. These are not just pension liabilities but also obligations for medical and life insurance, vacations, termination benefits, and deferred compensation. In the case of overfunded plans, this would be a defined benefit asset.

(c) IAS 37 requires recognition of provisions as liabilities. Examples include obligations for onerous contracts, decommissioning, site restoration, warranties, guarantees and litigation.

(d) Deferred tax assets and liabilities would be recognised in conformity with IAS 12.

3. The entity should reclassify previous GAAP opening balance sheet items into the appropriate IFRS classification. For example:

(a) IAS 10 does not permit classifying dividends declared or proposed after the balance sheet date as a liability at the balance sheet date. These would be reclassified as retained earnings in the opening IFRS balance sheet.

(b) If previous GAAP had allowed treasury shares (an entity's own shares that it had purchased) to be reported as an asset, the shares would be reclassified as a component of equity under IFRSs.

(c) Items classified as identifiable intangible assets in a business combination accounted for under the previous GAAP may be required to be classified as goodwill under IAS 22 because they do not meet the definition of an intangible asset under IAS 38. The converse may also be true in some cases, and these must be reclassified.

(d) IAS 32 has principles for classifying items as financial liabilities or equity. Thus mandatorily redeemable preferred shares and puttable shares that may have been classified as equity under previous GAAP would be reclassified as liabilities in the opening IFRS balance sheet.

(e) The reclassification principle would apply for the purpose of defining reportable segments under IAS 14 as compared to the entity's former GAAP.

(f) The scope of consolidation might change, depending on the consistency of the previous GAAP requirements with those in IAS 27. In some cases, IFRSs will require consolidated financial statements where they were not required before.

4. The general measurement principle (several significant exceptions are noted below) is to apply IFRSs in measuring all recognised assets and liabilities. Therefore, if an entity adopted IFRSs for the first time in its annual financial statements for the year ended 31 December 2005, in general it would have used the measurement principles in IFRSs in force at 31 December 2005.

5. Adjustments required to move from previous GAAP to IFRSs at the time of first-time adoption should be recognised directly in retained earnings or in another appropriate category of equity at the date of transition to IFRSs.

There are some important exceptions to the general restatement and measurement principles set out above. The following exceptions are individually optional, not mandatory:

1. **Business combinations that occurred before opening balance sheet date**

(a) An entity may keep the original previous GAAP accounting; that is, not restate:
   - previous mergers or goodwill written off from reserves
   - the carrying amounts of assets and liabilities recognised at the date of acquisition or merger
   - how goodwill was initially determined (do not adjust the original purchase price allocation on acquisition).

(b) However, should it wish to do so, an entity can elect to restate all business combinations starting from a date it selects prior to the opening balance sheet date.

(c) In all cases, the entity must make an initial IAS 36 impairment test of any remaining goodwill in the opening IFRS balance sheet, after reclassifying (as appropriate) previous GAAP intangibles to goodwill.

2. **Property, plant and equipment; intangible assets; and investment property carried under the cost model**

(a) These assets may be measured at their fair value at the opening IFRS balance sheet date. (This option applies to intangible assets only if an active market exists.) Fair value becomes the 'deemed cost' going forward under the IFRS cost model. 'Deemed cost' is a surrogate for an actual cost measurement.

(b) If, before the date of its first IFRS balance sheet, the entity had revalued any of these assets under its previous GAAP either to fair value or to a price-index-adjusted cost, that previous GAAP revalued amount at the date of the revaluation can become the deemed cost of the asset under IFRSs.

(c) If, before the date of its first IFRS balance sheet, the entity had made a one-time revaluation of assets or liabilities to fair value because of a privatisation or initial public offering, and the revalued amount became deemed cost under the previous GAAP, that amount (adjusted for any subsequent depreciation, amortisation and impairment) would continue to be deemed cost after the initial adoption of IFRSs. The revaluation would not have to be reversed.

3. IAS 19 — Employee benefits: actuarial gains and losses

An entity may elect to recognise all cumulative actuarial gains and losses for all defined benefit plans at the opening IFRS balance sheet date (that is, reset any corridor recognised under previous GAAP to zero), even if it elects to use the IAS 19 corridor approach for actuarial gains and losses that arise after first-time adoption of IFRSs. If an entity does not elect to apply this exemption, it must restate all defined benefit plans under IAS 19 since the inception of those plans (which may differ from the effective date of IAS 19).

4. IAS 21 — Accumulated translation reserves

An entity may elect to recognise all translation adjustments arising on the translation of the financial statements of foreign entities in accumulated profits or losses at the opening IFRS balance sheet date (that is, reset the translation reserve included in equity under previous GAAP to zero). If the entity elects this exemption, the gain or loss on subsequent disposal of the foreign entity will be adjusted only by those accumulated translation adjustments arising after the opening IFRS balance sheet date. If the entity does not elect to apply this exemption, it must restate the translation reserve for all foreign entities since they were acquired or created.

There are also a number of exceptions to the general restatement and measurement principles set out above that are mandatory. The three most significant are:

1. IAS 39 — Derecognition of financial instruments

A first-time adopter is not permitted to recognise financial assets or financial liabilities that had been derecognised under its previous GAAP in a financial year beginning before 1 January 2001 (the effective date of IAS 39). This is consistent with the transition provision in IAS 39. However, if a special purpose entity was used to effect the derecognition of financial instruments and that entity is controlled at the opening IFRS balance sheet date, the entity must be consolidated.

2. IAS 39 — Hedge accounting

The conditions in IAS 39.72–102 for a hedging relationship that qualifies for hedge accounting are applied as of the opening IFRS balance sheet date. The hedge accounting practices, if any, that were used in periods prior to the opening IFRS balance sheet may not be retrospectively changed. This is consistent with the transition provision in IAS 39. Some adjustments may be needed to take account of the existing hedging relationships under previous GAAP at the opening balance sheet date.

3. Information to be used in preparing IFRS estimates retrospectively

In preparing IFRS estimates retrospectively, the entity must use the inputs and assumptions that had been used to determine previous GAAP estimates in prior periods, provided that those inputs and assumptions are consistent with IFRSs. The entity is not permitted to use information that became available only after the previous GAAP estimates were made, except to correct an error.

Paragraph 36A of IFRS 1 provides an optional exemption from the requirement to restate comparative information to comply with IAS 32, IAS 39 and IFRS 4 to an entity that adopted IFRSs for the first time before 1 January 2006.

IFRS 1 requires disclosures that explain how the transition from previous GAAP to IFRSs affected the entity's reported financial position, financial performance and cash flows. This includes the following:

1. Reconciliations of equity reported under previous GAAP to equity under IFRSs both (a) at the date of the opening IFRS balance sheet and (b) the end of the last annual period reported under the previous GAAP must be disclosed. For an entity that adopted IFRSs for the first time in its 31 December 2005 financial statements, the reconciliations would be as of 1 January 2004 and 31 December 2004.
2. Reconciliations of profit or loss for the last annual period reported under the previous GAAP to profit or loss under IFRSs for the same period must be disclosed.
3. Material adjustments (including error corrections and impairment losses) that were made, in adopting IFRSs for the first time, to the balance sheet, income statement and cash flow statement must be disclosed.
4. Appropriate explanations must be made if the entity has availed itself of any of the specific recognition and measurement exemptions permitted under IFRS 1; for instance, if it used fair values as deemed cost.

LO 15

1.10 International Accounting Standards for the public sector

The IASB's preface to the International Financial Reporting Standards notes that IFRSs are designed to apply to the financial reports of all profit-oriented entities. Although IFRSs are not designed to apply to not-for-profit or government activities, non-profit and government entities 'may find them appropriate'. The International Public Sector Accounting Standards Board (IPSASB) of the International Federation of Accountants (IFAC) develops International Public Sector Accounting Standards (IPSASs) for financial reporting by governments and other public sector entities. In general, the IPSASB uses IFRSs as the starting point in developing its standards. Also, the IPSASB has issued a guideline stating that IFRSs are fully applicable to government business enterprises.

WEBLINK

More information on IPSASs is available at
<www.ifac.org/PublicSector>.

1.11 International Auditing Standards

The International Auditing and Assurance Standards Board (IAASB) is a committee of IFAC that works to improve the uniformity of auditing practices and related services throughout the world by issuing pronouncements on a variety of audit and assurance functions and by promoting their acceptance worldwide. Until 2002, the IAASB was known as the International Auditing Practices Committee (IAPC).

IAASB pronouncements are of four types:
- International Standards on Quality Control and the International Framework for Assurance Engagements, which apply to all types of assurance engagements
- International Standards on Auditing (ISAs) and International Auditing Practice Statements (IAPSs), which apply to audits

- International Standards on Review Engagements, which apply to reviews
- International Standards on Assurance Engagements and International Standards on Related Services, which apply to assurance engagements other than audits and reviews.
  The ISA on the auditor's report on financial statements requires that the auditor's opinion must clearly indicate the financial reporting framework used to prepare the financial statements (including the country of origin of the financial reporting framework when the IFRS Framework is not used). The auditor's opinion must also state whether the financial statements give a true and fair view (or are presented fairly, in all material respects) in accordance with that financial reporting framework and, where appropriate, whether the financial statements comply with statutory requirements.

More information can be found on the IAASB website at <www.ifac.org/iaasb>.

WEBLINK

1.12 Summary

As the world's capital markets globalised in the last quarter of the 20th century, investors and creditors became increasingly frustrated when trying to compare the financial statements of companies in different countries. They urged that accounting standards around the world be harmonised. The International Accounting Standards Committee was formed in 1973, and it developed a body of accounting standards suitable for use around the world. By and large, however, the major developed countries continued to develop and use their own national accounting principles. In 2001, the IASC was reorganised into the International Accounting Standards Board. In 2002, the European Union adopted an accounting regulation requiring all publicly traded EU companies to use International Financial Reporting Standards developed by the IASB, rather than their home-country standards, starting in 2005. Some non-European countries have also replaced their national standards with IFRSs, while other countries have adopted programs that retain their national standards but converge them as closely as possible with IFRSs.

DISCUSSION QUESTIONS

1. You are the financial officer of a successful medium-sized Swiss company. The company has grown to the point where its owners can no longer supply all of the capital the company needs for expansion. The owners have asked you to set out some options for raising capital either within Switzerland or in European Union capital markets. With that in mind, you have begun some discussions with bankers in London, Paris, Frankfurt and Zurich. You have also spoken with several investment bankers about the possibility of an initial public offering on the London Stock Exchange, the Swiss Exchange or Euronext. Currently, your company prepares financial statements in conformity with Swiss GAAP. Swiss law allows you to use IFRSs instead of Swiss GAAP. The owners of the company are hesitant to change to IFRSs because of the cost involved and also their concern that IFRSs would require too much disclosure.

   Required

   List some of the key reasons in favour of switching to IFRSs.

2. Each country has its own laws for everything, from crimes to taxes to health and safety. Is it in a country's best interest to develop its own accounting standards as well?

3. There is less use of IFRSs in North America than elsewhere. Why do you suppose that is?

4. Do you think governments should use International Financial Reporting Standards for the purpose of measuring taxable income in their country, so that income reported to investors and income reported to the tax authorities is identical?

5. Under the approaches to accounting standard setting that have been adopted in Australia and New Zealand, will companies in these countries be following International Financial Reporting Standards?

6. What might be some of the reasons why the European Union decided to require all listed companies to prepare their consolidated financial statements in conformity with IFRSs?

7. What is the difference between International Accounting Standards and International Financial Reporting Standards?

8. The IASB's objective is to develop global accounting standards in the public interest. What does 'in the public interest' mean?

9. Is the IASB's objective of developing a single set of global accounting standards consistent with its objective of bringing about the convergence of national accounting standards and International Accounting Standards?

10. As part of its national economic development program, an Asian country is working vigorously to promote the growth of small high-tech companies. Because these companies tend to have limited cash resources, they compensate their employees partly in shares of their own stock. If the employees work hard and the company prospers, the employees prosper. The accounting standard setter in that country is a board within the national professional accountancy organisation. The standard setter has proposed that the fair value of the shares of stock given to employees should be recognised as a compensation expense in measuring net profit or loss. The high-tech companies do not want to recognise the expense since it will reduce their reported profits or add to their reported losses, thereby discouraging investors from putting capital into the company. Because they think the accounting standard setter is not listening to their concerns, the companies urge their national legislature to intervene by passing a law to prohibit expense recognition for the shares of stock given to employees. They tell the legislators that the accounting standard setter is acting contrary to the country's national economic growth policy.

    Required

    List a few key points that might be made about the proposed legislation from the following points of view:

    (a) an investor in the high-tech companies

    (b) the head of the stock exchange on which many of the high-tech companies are listed

    (c) a legislator.

REFERENCES

Basel Committee on Banking Supervision 2000, *Report to G7 Finance Ministers and Central Bank Governors on International Accounting Standards*, Bank for International Settlements, Basle, Switzerland, April. Available from <www.bis.org>. Quoted material sourced from this publication.

G7 Finance Ministers 1998, *Declaration of G7 Finance Ministers and Central Bank Governors*, 30 October. Available from <www.fsforum.org>. Quoted material sourced from this publication.

IASC Foundation 2005, *IASC Foundation Constitution*, 1 July.

Public Company Accounting Reform and Investor Protection Act (Sarbanes-Oxley Act), (Public Law 107–204).

Tweedie, D 2002, chairman of the International Accounting Standards Board, statement before the Committee on Banking, Housing and Urban Affairs of the United States Senate Washington, DC, 14 February.

—2006, remarks to the Economic and Monetary Affairs Committee of the European Parliament, Brussels, 31 January.

Volcker, PA 2001, chairman of the trustees of the IASC Foundation, statement before the Capital Markets, Insurance and Government Sponsored Enterprises Subcommittee of the United States House of Representatives, Washington, DC, 7 June. Quoted material sourced from this publication.

APPENDICES

APPENDIX A

Websites of organisations mentioned in this chapter

Australian Accounting Standards Board   www.aasb.com.au
Australian Securities and Investments Commission   www.asic.gov.au
Basel Committee on Banking Supervision   www.bis.org/bcbs
Canadian Accounting Standards Board   www.acsbcanada.org
China Accounting Standards Committee   www.casc.gov.cn/internet/internet/en.html
France Conseil National de la Comptabilité   www.minefi.gouv.fr/directions_services/CNCompta
German Accounting Standards Committee   www.drsc.de
International Accounting Standards Board   www.iasb.org
International Association of Insurance Supervisors   www.iaisweb.org
International Auditing and Assurance Standards Board   www.ifac.org/iaasb
International Federation of Accountants   www.ifac.org
International Organization of Securities Commissions   www.iosco.org
Japan Accounting Standards Board   www.asb.or.jp/index_e.html
New Zealand Financial Reporting Standards Board   www.nzica.com
United Kingdom Accounting Standards Board   www.frc.org.uk
US Financial Accounting Standards Board   www.fasb.org
US Public Company Accounting Oversight Board   www.pcaobus.org
US Securities and Exchange Commission   www.sec.gov

APPENDIX B

Common acronyms and abbreviations used in this chapter

AISG	Accountants International Study Group
CICA	Canadian Institute of Chartered Accountants
DSOP	Draft Statement of Principles
EC	European Commission
ED	Exposure draft
EEA	European Economic Area
EFRAG	European Financial Reporting Advisory Group
EU	European Union
FASB	Financial Accounting Standards Board (US)
FEE	Fédération des Experts Comptables Européens (European Federation of Accountants)
GAAP	Generally Accepted Accounting Principles
IAASB	International Auditing and Assurance Standards Board
IAPC	International Auditing Practices Committee (former name of IAASB)
IAPS	International Auditing Practice Statement

IAS	International Accounting Standard (issued by the former IASC)
IASB	International Accounting Standards Board
IASC	International Accounting Standards Committee (replaced by IASB in 2001)
IASCF	International Accounting Standards Committee Foundation
IFAC	International Federation of Accountants
IFAD	International Forum on Accountancy Development
IFRIC	International Financial Reporting Interpretations Committee
IFRS	International Financial Reporting Standard (issued by the IASB)
IGC	IAS 39 Implementation Guidance Committee
IOSCO	International Organization of Securities Commissions
IPSAS	International Public Sector Accounting Standards
IPSASB	International Public Sector Accounting Standards Board
ISA	International Standard on Auditing
OECD	Organisation for Economic Cooperation and Development
PCAOB	Public Company Accounting Oversight Board (US)
PSC	Public Sector Committee of IFAC (former name of IPSASB)
SAC	Standards Advisory Council (of the IASB)
SEC	Securities and Exchange Commission (US)
SIC	Standing Interpretations Committee (of the former IASC)

APPENDIX C

Chronology of the IASC and the IASB

Pre-1973 events leading to the formation of the IASC

1966

- A proposal to create an Accountants International Study Group is agreed to by professional accountancy bodies in Canada, the United Kingdom and the United States in order to develop comparative studies of accounting and auditing practices in the three nations.

1967

- The Accountants International Study Group is created, precursor to the IASC.

1968

- The first AISG study on comparative accounting practices for inventories in Canada, the United Kingdom and the United States is released. The AISG published a total of 20 studies until 1977, when it was disbanded. Some were used by the IASC in its early standards.

1972

- A proposal for the IASC is put forward by Sir Henry Benson at the 10th World Congress of Accountants in Sydney and discussed with the three AISG countries (Canada, the United Kingdom and the United States).
- Further discussions of the Benson proposal take place, and include representatives of Australia, France, Germany, Japan, the Netherlands and Mexico.

The IASC, 1973-2000

1973

- An agreement to establish the IASC is signed by representatives of the professional accountancy bodies in Australia, Canada, France, Germany, Japan, Mexico, the Netherlands, the United Kingdom/Ireland and the United States.
- The IASC opens an office at 3 St Helen's Place, London.
- Paul Rosenfield (from the United States, on secondment from the AICPA) is appointed first secretary of the IASC.
- The IASC holds its inaugural meeting in London on 29 June.

- Sir Henry Benson is elected first chairman of the IASC.
- The IASC adopts its initial agenda of three technical projects: accounting policies, inventories, and consolidated financial statements.
- Steering committees are appointed for the above three projects (these are the first IASC steering committees).
- The first meeting of an IASC steering committee (IAS 1 *Disclosure of Accounting Policies*) is held.
- The IASC holds board meetings in London (2).

Exposure drafts published

- None

Final standards published

- None

1974

- The first associate members of the IASC are admitted: Belgium, India, Israel, New Zealand, Pakistan and Zimbabwe.
- The IASC holds board meetings in London (3) and Paris.

Exposure drafts published

- E1 *Disclosure of Accounting Policies*
- E2 *Valuation and Presentation of Inventories in the Context of the Historical Cost System*
- E3 *Consolidated Financial Statements and the Equity Method of Accounting*

Final standards published

- None

1975

- A proposal is made to create an International Federation of Accountants to replace the International Coordinating Committee for the Accounting Profession.
- The IASC holds board meetings in London (3) and Montreal.

Exposure drafts published

- E4 *Depreciation Accounting*
- E5 *Information to be Disclosed in Financial Statements*

Final standards published

- IAS 1 (1975) *Disclosure of Accounting Policies*
- IAS 2 (1975) *Valuation and Presentation of Inventories in the Context of the Historical Cost System*

1976

- Joseph P Cummings of the United States becomes chairman of the IASC.
- The Central Bank Governors of the Group of Ten fund an IASC project on bank financial statements.
- The IASC holds board meetings in London (2) and Washington.

Exposure drafts published

- E6 *Accounting Treatment of Changing Prices*
- E7 *Statement of Source and Application of Funds*
- E8 *The Treatment in the Income Statement of Unusual Items and Changes in Accounting Estimates and Accounting Policies*

Final standards published

- IAS 3 (1976) *Consolidated Financial Statements*
- IAS 4 (1976) *Depreciation Accounting*
- IAS 5 (1976) *Information to be Disclosed in Financial Statements*

1977

- The IASC constitution is revised to add two seats to the IASC board (in addition to the nine founding countries), bringing the total to 11. Nine votes are required to adopt a standard, giving the nine founding members substantial control. The revised constitution identifies the standard-setting body as the 'Board' of the IASC and not a 'committee'.

- IFAC is formed.
- The AISG is disbanded.
- The IASC holds board meetings in London, Amsterdam and Edinburgh.

Exposure drafts published

- E9   *Accounting for Research and Development Costs*
- E10 *Contingencies and Events Occurring After the Balance Sheet Date*
- E11 *Accounting for Foreign Transactions and Translation of Foreign Financial Statements*
- E12 *Accounting for Construction Contracts*

Final standards published

- IAS 6 (1977) *Accounting Responses to Changing Prices*
- IAS 7 (1977) *Statement of Changes in Financial Position*

1978

- John A Hepworth of Australia becomes chairman of the IASC.
- South Africa and Nigeria join the board, increasing the size of the board to 11.
- The IASC holds board meetings in London (2) and Perth (Australia).
- For the first time, the IASC rejects a proposed standard (based on E11 *Accounting for Foreign Transactions and Translation of Foreign Financial Statements*), and a new steering committee is appointed for a fresh start.
- The IASC begins discussions with the International Federation of Accountants on 'mutual commitments' regarding the relationship between the two bodies.

Exposure drafts published

- E13 *Accounting for Taxes on Income*
- E14 *Current Assets and Current Liabilities*

Final standards published

IAS 8 (1978) *Unusual and Prior Period Items and Changes in Accounting Policies*

IAS 9 (1978) *Accounting for Research and Development Activities*

IAS 10 (1978) *Contingencies and Events Occurring After the Balance Sheet Date*

1979

- Allan VC Cook becomes secretary of the IASC.
- The IASC meets the OECD working group on accounting standards.
- The IASC holds board meetings in London (2) and Mexico City.

Exposure drafts published

- None

Final standards published

- IAS 11 (1979) *Accounting for Construction Contracts*
- IAS 12 (1979) *Accounting for Taxes on Income*
- IAS 13 (1979) *Presentation of Current Assets and Current Liabilities*

1980

- JA (Hans) Burggraaff of the Netherlands becomes chairman of the IASC.
- The IASC publishes a discussion paper on bank disclosures (a project funded by the Central Bank Governors of the Group of Ten).
- The IASC holds board meetings in London, Berlin and Dublin.
- The United Nations Intergovernment Working Group on Accounting and Reporting meets for the first time. The IASC proposes a cooperative working arrangement with the UN group.

Exposure drafts published

- E15 *Reporting Financial Information by Segment*
- E16 *Accounting for Retirement Benefits in the Financial Statements of Employers*
- E17 *Information Reflecting the Effects of Changing Prices*

- E18 *Accounting for Property, Plant and Equipment in the Context of the Historical Cost System*
- E19 *Accounting for Leases*

Final standards published

- None

1981

- Geoffrey B Mitchell becomes secretary of the IASC. The title is changed to 'Secretary-General' during his tenure.
- The IASC Consultative Group is formed to advise the IASC on agenda projects and priorities. Consultative Group members represent both accounting and non-accounting organisations with an interest in financial reporting (stock exchanges, bankers, lawyers, business, unions, government, the UN, World Bank, OECD, etc.). The first meeting is held in October 1981.
- The IASC begins a joint project on accounting for income taxes with standard setters from the Netherlands, the United Kingdom and the United States.
- The IASC holds board meetings in London (2) and Tokyo.

Exposure drafts published

- E20 *Revenue Recognition*
- E21 *Accounting for Government Grants and Disclosure of Government Assistance*
- E22 *Accounting for Business Combinations*

Final standards published

- IAS 14 (1981) *Reporting Financial Information by Segment*
- IAS 15 (1981) *Information Reflecting the Effects of Changing Prices*

1982

- Stephen Elliott of Canada becomes chairman of the IASC.
- The IASC and IFAC make mutual commitments. The IASC board is expanded to up to 17 members, including 13 country members appointed by the Council of IFAC and up to four representatives of organisations with an interest in financial reporting. All members of IFAC are members of the IASC. IFAC recognises and will look to the IASC as the global accounting standard setter. The special constitutional status of the nine founding members of the IASC is eliminated.
- The IASC holds board meetings in London (2) and Amsterdam.

Exposure drafts published

- E23 *Accounting for the Effects of Changes in Foreign Exchange Rates*
- E24 *Capitalisation of Borrowing Costs*

Final standards published

- IAS 16 (1982) *Accounting for Property, Plant and Equipment*
- IAS 17 (1982) *Accounting for Leases*
- IAS 18 (1982) *Revenue Recognition*

1983

- Italy joins the IASC board.
- The expanded IASC board under the revised constitution takes effect.
- The IASC holds board meetings in London, Edinburgh and Paris.
- The title of the senior staff executive is changed from 'Secretary' to 'Secretary-General'.

Exposure drafts published

- E25 *Disclosure of Related Party Transactions*

Final standards published

- IAS 19 (1983) *Accounting for Retirement Benefits in the Financial Statements of Employers*
- IAS 20 (1983) *Accounting for Government Grants and Disclosure of Government Assistance*
- IAS 21 (1983) *Accounting for the Effects of Changes in Foreign Exchange Rates*
- IAS 22 (1983) *Accounting for Business Combinations*

1984
- Taiwan joins the IASC board.
- The IASC holds a formal meeting with the US Securities and Exchange Commission.
- The IASC holds board meetings in London, Toronto and Dusseldorf.

Exposure drafts published
- E26 *Accounting for Investments*

Final standards published
- IAS 23 (1984) *Capitalisation of Borrowing Costs*
- IAS 24 (1984) *Related Party Disclosures*

1985
- John L Kirkpatrick of the United Kingdom becomes chairman of the IASC.
- David Cairns becomes secretary-general of the IASC.
- The IASC participates in an OECD forum on global accounting harmonisation.
- The IASC responds to SEC proposals for a multinational prospectus.
- The IASC holds board meetings in London, Rome and New York.

Exposure drafts published
- E27 *Accounting and Reporting by Retirement Benefit Plans*

Final standards published
- None

1986
- Financial analysts (International Coordinating Committee of Financial Analysts Associations) get a seat on the IASC board.
- The IASC co-sponsors a conference with the New York Stock Exchange and International Bar Association on the globalisation of financial markets.
- The IASC holds board meetings in London, Dublin and Amsterdam.

Exposure drafts published
- E28 *Accounting for Investments in Associates and Joint Ventures*

Final standards published
- IAS 25 (1986) *Accounting for Investments*

1987
- Georges Barthes de Ruyter of France becomes chairman of the IASC.
- The IASC begins its Comparability and Improvements project. Its objective is to reduce or eliminate alternatives, and make standards more detailed and prescriptive rather than flexible and descriptive of current practice.
- The International Organization of Securities Commissions joins the Consultative Group and supports the Comparability project.
- The IASC publishes its first bound volume of International Accounting Standards.
- The IASC holds board meetings in Sydney and Edinburgh.

Exposure drafts published
- E29 *Disclosures in the Financial Statements of Banks*
- E30 *Consolidated Financial Statements and Accounting for Investments in Subsidiaries*
- E31 *Financial Reporting in Hyperinflationary Economies*

Final standards published
- IAS 26 (1987) *Accounting and Reporting by Retirement Benefit Plans*

1988
- Jordan, Korea and the Nordic Federation (representing accounting bodies in Norway, Denmark, Sweden, Finland and Iceland) join the IASC board. They replace Mexico, Nigeria and Taiwan.
- The Financial Instruments project is started in conjunction with the Canadian Accounting Standards Board.

- The IASC publishes a survey on the use of IASs.
- The FASB joins the Consultative Group and becomes an observer at the IASC board table.
- The IASC holds board meetings in Dusseldorf, Toronto and Copenhagen.

Exposure drafts published
- Exposure Draft: *Framework for the Preparation and Presentation of Financial Statements*

Final standards published
- None

1989
- The European Accounting Federation supports international harmonisation and greater European involvement in the IASC.
- IFAC adopts a public sector guideline to require government business enterprises to follow IASs.
- The IASC holds board meetings in Brussels and New York.
- The IASC publishes its Framework for the Preparation and Presentation of Financial Statements.

Exposure drafts published
- E32 *Comparability of Financial Statements*
- E33 *Accounting for Taxes on Income*
- E34 *Disclosures in the Financial Statements of Banks and Similar Financial Institutions*
- E35 *Financial Reporting of Interests in Joint Ventures*

Final standards published
- IAS 27 (1989) *Consolidated Financial Statements and Accounting for Investments in Subsidiaries*
- IAS 28 (1989) *Accounting for Investments in Associates*
- IAS 29 (1989) *Financial Reporting in Hyperinflationary Economies*

1990
- *Statement of Intent — Comparability of Financial Statements* is released.
- Arthur R Wyatt of the United States becomes chairman of the IASC.
- The European Commission joins the Consultative Group and takes a seat at the IASC board table as an observer. Bank regulators and asset valuers also join the Consultative Group.
- A program to seek external funding is launched.
- The IASC holds board meetings in Amsterdam, Paris and Singapore.

Exposure drafts published
- None

Final standards published
- IAS 30 (1990) *Disclosures in the Financial Statements of Banks and Similar Financial Institutions*
- IAS 31 (1990) *Financial Reporting of Interests in Joint Ventures*

1991
- The IASC organises a conference of national standard setters in conjunction with the FEE and the FASB.
- The US FASB indicates its support for International Accounting Standards.
- The IASC holds board meetings in London, Milan and Seoul.

Exposure drafts published
- E36 *Cash Flow Statements*
- E37 *Research and Development Activities*
- E38 *Inventories*
- E39 *Capitalisation of Borrowing Costs*
- E40 *Financial Instruments*

Final standards published
- None

1992

- The IASC constitution is revised.
- The IASC holds board meetings in Madrid, Amman and Chicago.

Exposure drafts published

- E41 *Revenue Recognition*
- E42 *Construction Contracts*
- E43 *Property, Plant and Equipment*
- E44 *The Effects of Changes in Foreign Exchange Rates*
- E45 *Business Combinations*
- E46 *Extraordinary Items, Fundamental Errors and Changes in Accounting Policies*
- E47 *Retirement Benefit Costs*

Final standards published

Revision:

- IAS 7 (revised 1992) *Cash Flow Statements*

1993

- Eiichi Shiratori of Japan becomes chairman of the IASC.
- India replaces Korea on the board.
- The IASC and IOSCO agree on a list of core standards.
- The Comparability and Improvements project is completed with the approval of 10 revised IASs. However, IOSCO does not endorse IASs at this time for use in cross-border securities offerings.
- The South African Institute of Chartered Accountants decides that South African accounting standards should be based on IASs, and the existing South African GAAP are to be revised.
- The IASC holds board meetings in Tokyo, London and Oslo.

Exposure drafts published

- None

Final standards published

Revisions:

- IAS 2 (revised 1993) *Inventories*
- IAS 8 (revised 1993) *Net Profit or Loss for the Period, Fundamental Errors and Changes in Accounting Policies*
- IAS 9 (revised 1993) *Research and Development Costs*
- IAS 11 (revised 1993) *Construction Contracts*
- IAS 16 (revised 1993) *Property, Plant and Equipment*
- IAS 18 (revised 1993) *Revenue*
- IAS 19 (revised 1993) *Retirement Benefit Costs*
- IAS 21 (revised 1993) *The Effects of Changes in Foreign Exchange Rates*
- IAS 22 (revised 1993) *Business Combinations*
- IAS 23 (revised 1993) *Borrowing Costs*

1994

- The IASC board meets with standard setters to discuss E48 *Financial Instruments*.
- Accounting educators join the Consultative Group.
- The World Bank agrees to fund the Agriculture project.
- The establishment of the IASC Advisory Council is approved, with responsibilities for oversight and finances.
- IOSCO accepts 14 IASs and identifies some specific issues to be addressed in the remaining core standards (the 'Shiratori letters').
- The FASB agrees to work with the IASC on a joint Earnings Per Share project.

- The G4+1 group, which includes the IASC as the '+1', publishes its first *Study on Future Events*.
- The IASC holds board meetings in Edinburgh and Budapest.

Exposure drafts published

- E48 *Financial Instruments*
- E49 *Income Taxes*

Final standards published

- None

1995

- Michael Sharpe of Australia becomes chairman of the IASC.
- Sir Bryan Carsberg becomes secretary-general of the IASC.
- The IASC agrees with IOSCO to complete the core standards by 1999. IOSCO states that if the core standards are successfully completed, IOSCO will review them with the objective of endorsing IASs for cross-border offerings.
- The first German companies report under IASs.
- The Federation of Swiss Holding Companies takes a seat on the IASC board.
- Malaysia and Mexico replace Italy and Jordan on the board. India and South Africa agree to share board seats with Sri Lanka and Zimbabwe respectively.
- The World Bank's accounting handbook states that 'in the absence of any superior national standards, the Bank requires the use of IASs in the preparation of financial statements'.
- The European Commission supports the IASC/IOSCO agreement and concludes that IASs should be followed by EU multinationals.
- The IASC holds board meetings in Dusseldorf, Amsterdam and Sydney.

Exposure drafts published

- E50 *Intangible Assets*
- E51 *Reporting Financial Information by Segment*

Final standards published

New:

- IAS 32 (1995) *Financial Instruments: Disclosure and Presentation*

1996

- The IASB accelerates its core standards program by one year, with completion planned by the end of 1998.
- The International Association of Financial Executives Institutes joins the IASC board. IOSCO takes a seat at the IASC board table as an observer.
- The IASC starts a joint project on Provisions with the UK Accounting Standards Board.
- A study by the EU Contact Committee finds IASs compatible with EU directives, with minor exceptions.
- The US SEC announces its support of the IASC's objective to develop, as expeditiously as possible, accounting standards that could be used for preparing financial statements used in cross-border offerings.
- The US Congress calls for 'a high-quality comprehensive set of generally accepted international accounting standards'.
- The Australian Stock Exchange supports a program to harmonise Australian standards with IASs.
- The World Trade Organization encourages the successful completion of International Accounting Standards.
- The IASC holds board meetings in Brussels, Stockholm and Barcelona.

Exposure drafts published

- E52 *Earnings Per Share*
- E53 *Presentation of Financial Statements*
- E54 *Employee Benefits*

Final standards published
Revision:
- IAS 12 (revised 1996) *Income Taxes*

1997
- The Standing Interpretations Committee is formed with 12 voting members.
- The IASC and FASB issue similar earnings per share standards. The IASC, FASB and CICA issue new segments standards with relatively minor differences.
- An IASC discussion paper proposes fair value for all financial assets and financial liabilities. The IASC holds 45 consultation meetings in 16 countries.
- Actuaries join the Consultative Group.
- The Arab Society of Certified Accountants calls for all of its 22 member countries to adopt IASs as their national GAAP (the 'Dubai Declaration').
- APEC (Asia–Pacific Economic Cooperation) expresses its support of the efforts of the IASC to develop International Accounting Standards.
- A joint working group on financial instruments is formed with national standard setters.
- The People's Republic of China becomes a member of IFAC and joins the IASC board as an observer.
- The IASC sponsors a conference in Hong Kong of accounting standard setters from 20 countries.
- The FEE calls on Europe to use the IASC Framework.
- The US SEC reports to Congress on the outlook for a successful completion of a set of International Accounting Standards that would be acceptable in the United States.
- A strategy working party is formed to make recommendations regarding the future structure and operation of the IASC following completion of the core standards. Its first meeting is held in April.
- The IASC sets up its Internet website.
- The IASC holds board meetings in London, Johannesburg, Beijing and Paris.

Exposure drafts published
- E55 *Impairment of Assets*
- E56 *Leases*
- E57 *Interim Financial Reporting*
- E58 *Discontinuing Operations*
- E59 *Provisions, Contingent Liabilities and Contingent Assets*
- E60 *Intangible Assets*
- E61 *Business Combinations*

Final standards published
New:
- IAS 33 (1997) *Earnings Per Share*

Revisions:
- IAS 1 (revised 1997) *Presentation of Financial Statements*
- IAS 14 (revised 1997) *Segment Reporting*
- IAS 17 (revised 1997) *Leases*

Final interpretations published
- SIC 1 *Consistency – Different Cost Formulas for Inventories*
- SIC 2 *Consistency – Capitalisation of Borrowing Costs*
- SIC 3 *Elimination of Unrealised Profits and Losses on Transactions with Associates*

1998
- Stig Enevoldsen of Denmark becomes chairman of the IASC.
- New laws in Belgium, France, Germany and Italy allow large companies to use IASs domestically in their consolidated financial statements.
- The first official translation of IASs (into German) occurs.

- IFAC/IASC membership expands to Latin America (with new member bodies in Bolivia, Costa Rica, El Salvador, Guatemala, Honduras and Nicaragua) as well as Haiti, Iran and Vietnam. This brings membership to 140 bodies in 101 countries.
- The IFAC Public Sector Committee begins a program to develop International Public Sector Accounting Standards based on IASs.
- A strategy working party proposes structural changes (including a bicameral standard-setting structure) and closer ties to national standard setters.
- In response to the Asian financial crisis, the G8 Summit, the G7 Finance Ministers, the Central Bank Governors, the World Bank and the IMF all call for rapid completion and global adoption of high-quality International Accounting Standards.
- The International Federation of Stock Exchanges expresses support for IASs.
- IASs are published on CD-ROM.
- The IASC completes the core standards with the approval of IAS 39 in December.
- The IASC holds board meetings in London, Kuala Lumpur, Niagara-on-the-Lake, Zurich and Frankfurt.

Exposure drafts published
- E62 *Financial Instruments: Recognition and Measurement*
- E63 *Events After the Balance Sheet Date*

Final standards published
New:
- IAS 34 (1998) *Interim Financial Reporting*
- IAS 35 (1998) *Discontinuing Operations*
- IAS 36 (1998) *Impairment of Assets*
- IAS 37 (1998) *Provisions, Contingent Liabilities and Contingent Assets*
- IAS 38 (1998) *Intangible Assets*
- IAS 39 (1998) *Financial Instruments: Recognition and Measurement*

Revisions:
- IAS 16 (revised 1998) *Property, Plant and Equipment*
- IAS 19 (revised 1998) *Employee Benefits*
- IAS 22 (revised 1998) *Business Combinations*
- IAS 32 (revised 1998) *Financial Instruments: Disclosure and Presentation*

Final interpretations published
- SIC 5 *Classification of Financial Instruments – Contingent Settlement Provisions*
- SIC 6 *Costs of Modifying Existing Software*
- SIC 7 *Introduction of the Euro*
- SIC 8 *First-time Application of IASs as the Primary Basis of Accounting*
- SIC 9 *Business Combinations – Classification either as Acquisitions or Unitings of Interests*
- SIC 10 *Government Assistance – No Specific Relation to Operating Activities*
- SIC 11 *Foreign Exchange – Capitalisation of Losses Resulting from Severe Currency Devaluations*
- SIC 12 *Consolidation – Special Purpose Entities*
- SIC 13 *Jointly Controlled Entities – Non-Monetary Contributions by Venturers*
- SIC 14 *Property, Plant and Equipment – Compensation for the Impairment or Loss of Items*

1999
- IOSCO begins its review of the IASC core standards.
- The IASC board meetings are opened to public observation, and the first public meeting is held in Washington in March.
- G7 Finance Ministers and the IMF urge support for IASs to 'strengthen the international financial architecture'.

- The new IFAC International Forum on Accountancy Development commits to support the 'use of International Accounting Standards as the minimum benchmark for raising national accounting standards' worldwide.
- An EC study finds no significant conflicts between IASs and the European directives. The EC adopts a financial services action plan that includes the use of IASs as 'European GAAP'.
- The FEE 'reporting strategy for Europe' strongly supports the use of IASs in Europe without requiring compliance with EC accounting directives, as well as the phasing out of US GAAP.
- The Eurasian Federation of Accountants and Auditors plans to adopt IASs in Commonwealth of Independent States (CIS) countries.
- Various meetings of the strategy working party are held to discuss the comments on its initial proposal and to develop final recommendations. The working party publishes a revised proposal.
- The IASC board unanimously approves restructuring into a 14-member board (12 full-time) under an independent board of trustees.
- The IASC board appoints a nominating committee, chaired by the US SEC chairman, Arthur Levitt, to select its first trustees under the new IASC structure.
- Looking beyond financial statements, the IASC publishes a study of business reporting on the Internet.
- The IASC holds board meetings in Washington, Warsaw, Venice and Amsterdam.

Exposure drafts published
- E64 *Investment Property*
- E65 *Agriculture*

Final standards published
Revision:
- IAS 10 (revised 1999) *Events After the Balance Sheet Date*

Final interpretations published
- SIC 15 *Operating Leases – Incentives*
- SIC 16 *Share Capital – Reacquired Own Equity Instruments (Treasury Shares)*

2000
- Thomas E Jones (a UK citizen, with his career primarily in the United States) becomes chairman of the IASC.
- SIC meetings are opened to public observation.
- The Basel Committee expresses support for IASs and for efforts to harmonise accounting internationally.
- The SEC issues a concept release inviting comments on the use of International Accounting Standards in the United States.
- As part of its restructuring program, the IASC board approves a new constitution.
- IOSCO recommends that its members allow multinational issuers to use IASC standards in cross-border offerings and listings, supplemented by reconciliations, disclosure and interpretation where deemed locally necessary.
- The nominating committee announces the initial trustees of the restructured IASC. Paul Volcker, former US Federal Reserve Board chairman, will chair the board of trustees.
- The IASC member bodies approve the IASC's restructuring and a new IASC constitution.
- The European Commission announces a plan to require all EU-listed companies to use IASs starting no later than 2005.
- The IASC trustees name Sir David Tweedie (chairman of the UK Accounting Standards Board) as the first chairman of the restructured IASC board.

- The trustees announce a search for new board members. Over 200 applications are received.
- The IASC board approves limited revisions to IAS 12, IAS 19 and IAS 39.
- The IASC publishes the first batch of *Implementation Guidance Q&As* on IAS 39.
- IAS 41 *Agriculture* is approved at the last meeting of the IASC board, and is published in 2001.
- The IASC holds board meetings in Sao Paulo, Copenhagen, Tokyo and London.
- As one of its last official acts, the IASC board approves a statement to the new IASC board commenting on projects to be carried forward and possible additional projects to be undertaken.

Exposure drafts published
- E66 *Financial Instruments: Recognition and Measurement – Limited Revisions to IAS 39*
- E67 *Pension Plan Assets*
- E68 *Income Tax Consequences of Dividends*

Final standards published
New:
- IAS 40 (2000) *Investment Property*
Revisions:
- IAS 12 (revised 2000) *Income Taxes*
- IAS 19 (revised 2000) *Employee Benefits*
- IAS 28 (revised 2000) *Accounting for Investments in Associates*
- IAS 31 (revised 2000) *Financial Reporting of Interests in Joint Ventures*

Final interpretations published
- SIC 17 *Equity – Costs of an Equity Transaction*
- SIC 18 *Consistency – Alternative Methods*
- SIC 19 *Reporting Currency – Measurement and Presentation of Financial Statements under IAS 21 and IAS 29*
- SIC 20 *Equity Accounting Method – Recognition of Losses*
- SIC 21 *Income Taxes – Recovery of Revalued Non-Depreciable Assets*
- SIC 22 *Business Combinations – Subsequent Adjustment of Fair Values and Goodwill Initially Reported*
- SIC 23 *Property, Plant and Equipment – Major Inspection or Overhaul Costs*
- SIC 24 *Earnings Per Share – Financial Instruments that May Be Settled in Shares*
- SIC 25 *Income Taxes – Changes in the Tax Status of an Enterprise or its Shareholders*

2001
- The trustees appoint the initial 14 members of the International Accounting Standards Board.
- In March 2001, the IASC trustees activate part B of the IASC's new constitution and establish a non-profit Delaware corporation, named the International Accounting Standards Committee Foundation, to oversee the IASB.
- On 1 April 2001, the new IASB takes over from the IASC the responsibility for setting International Accounting Standards. The new board holds its first meeting, adopts existing IASs and SICs, and deliberates its agenda and other issues.
- The trustees appoint 49 charter members to the IASB Standards Advisory Council. The first SAC meeting is held in July.
- The European Commission presents legislation requiring the use of IASC standards for all listed companies no later than 2005.
- The European Financial Reporting Advisory Group is created by the accounting profession, preparers, users and national standard setters in EU countries to advise the European Commission on the acceptability of individual IASs for Europe, as well as to respond to IASB comment documents.
- European directives are amended to allow compliance with IAS 39.

- The IASB moves into new offices at 30 Cannon Street, London.
- The IASB meets with chairs of those national accounting standard-setting bodies that have a formal liaison relationship with the IASB – Australia/New Zealand, Canada, France, Germany, Japan, the United Kingdom and the United States – to begin coordinating agendas and setting out convergence goals.
- The IASB adopts its initial agenda of nine technical projects and agrees to have an advisory or monitoring role on 16 additional projects being worked on by partner national standard setters.
- Debate over the IASB's stock options project reaches US Congress.
- The seven largest accounting firms strongly endorse IASs for Europe.
- The new SEC chief accountant urges global convergence of accounting standards.
- The trustees appoint the members of the restructured Standing Interpretations Committee.
- IFAD publishes GAAP 2000 – a comparison of IASs and GAAP in 53 countries – as part of its effort to bring national GAAP up to an IAS benchmark.
- The IASB holds board meetings in London (6), Washington and Paris.

Exposure drafts published
- Exposure Draft: *Preface to International Financial Reporting Standards*

Final standards published
New:
- IAS 41 (2001) *Agriculture* (approved by the old IASC board in December 2000)

Final interpretations published
- SIC 27 *Evaluating the Substance of Transactions in the Legal Form of a Lease*
- SIC 28 *Business Combinations – 'Date of Exchange' and Fair Value of Equity Instruments*
- SIC 29 *Disclosure – Service Concession Arrangements*
- SIC 30 *Reporting Currency – Translation from Measurement Currency to Presentation Currency*
- SIC 31 *Revenue – Barter Transactions Involving Advertising Services*
- SIC 33 *Consolidation and Equity Method – Potential Voting Rights and Allocation of Ownership Interests*

2002
- IASB chairman Sir David Tweedie and IASC foundation chairman Paul Volcker testify at a US Senate hearing on accounting and investor protection issues raised by Enron and other public companies.
- The IASB issues its first exposure draft and final standard on an accounting issue (IAS 19 *Employee Benefits: The Asset Ceiling*).
- The SIC is renamed the International Financial Reporting Interpretations Committee, with a mandate to both interpret existing IASs and IFRSs and provide timely guidance on matters not addressed in an IAS or IFRS.
- Europe adopts regulations requiring all listed companies, including banks and insurance companies, to prepare their consolidated accounts in accordance with IASs from 2005.
- IASB board member Robert Herz is appointed chairman of the US Financial Accounting Standards Board. John T Smith, partner at Deloitte Touche Tohmatsu, replaces Mr Herz on the IASB.
- The IASB issues its first exposure draft of a standard that will be in its new series of International Financial Reporting Standards: ED1 *First-time Application of International Financial Reporting Standards.*

Exposure drafts published
- Exposure Draft: *Amendment to IAS 19, Employee Benefits: The Asset Ceiling*
- Exposure Draft: *Improvements to International Accounting Standards*
- Exposure Draft ED1: *First-Time Application of International Financial Reporting Standards*
- Exposure Draft: *Amendments to IAS 32, Financial Instruments: Disclosure and Presentation, and IAS 39, Financial Instruments: Recognition and Measurement*

Final standards published

Revisions:

- *Preface to International Financial Reporting Standards* (2002), replaced *Preface to Statements of International Accounting Standards* (1982)

IAS 19 (Revised 2002) *Employee Benefits*

Final interpretations published

- SIC 32 *Intangible Assets – Website Costs*

2003

- The IASB holds public round-table discussions on financial instruments. Representatives of 108 organisations participate.
- The IASB adopts the first standard in its new series of International Financial Reporting Standards.
- IFRIC publishes its first draft interpretation.
- The EC Accounting Regulatory Committee endorses existing IASs (except IAS 32 and IAS 39).

Exposure drafts published

- ED 4 *Disposal of Non-current Assets and Presentation of Discontinued Operations*
- ED 5 *Insurance Contracts*
- *Fair Value Hedge Accounting for a Portfolio Hedge of Interest Rate Risk*

Final standards published

New:

- IFRS 1 (2003) *First-time Adoption of International Financial Reporting Standards*

Revisions:

- IAS 1 *Presentation of Financial Statements*
- IAS 2 *Inventories*
- IAS 8 *Accounting Policies, Changes in Accounting Estimates and Errors*
- IAS 10 *Events After the Balance Sheet Date*
- IAS 16 *Property, Plant and Equipment*
- IAS 17 *Leases*
- IAS 21 *The Effects of Changes in Foreign Exchange Rates*
- IAS 24 *Related Party Disclosures*
- IAS 27 *Consolidated and Separate Financial Statements*
- IAS 28 *Investments in Associates*
- IAS 31 *Interests in Joint Ventures*
- IAS 32 *Financial Instruments: Presentation and Disclosure*
- IAS 33 *Earnings per Share*
- IAS 39 *Financial Instruments: Recognition and Measurement*
- IAS 40 *Investment Property*

Final interpretations published

- SIC 32 *Intangible Assets – Website Costs*

2004

- The IASB and various European groups engage in extensive discussions about IAS 32 and IAS 39.
- The European Commission endorses all IASs and IFRSs for use in Europe except for two sections of IAS 39 that are 'carved out'.
- Australia, Hong Kong, New Zealand and the Philippines adopt improved IASs and IFRSs virtually word-for-word as national GAAP.
- The IASB and the Accounting Standards Board of Japan begin the Convergence project.
- The IASB initiates an internal review of its deliberative processes.

- The IASC Foundation trustees propose constitutional changes, including super-majority vote.
- The first webcasts are made of an IASB board meeting.
- The first IFRIC interpretation is published.
- The first IASB discussion paper is published: *Preliminary Views on Accounting Standards for Small and Medium-sized Entities.*

Exposure drafts published

- ED 6 *Exploration for and Evaluation of Mineral Resources*
- ED 7 *Financial Instruments: Disclosures*
- *Amendments to IFRS 3 Business Combinations: Combinations by Contract Alone or Involving Mutual Entities*
- *Amendments to IAS 19 Employee Benefits: Actuarial Gains and Losses, Group Plans and Disclosures*
- *Amendments to IAS 39 Financial Instruments: Recognition and Measurement – The Fair Value Option*
- *Amendments to IAS 39 Financial Instruments: Recognition and Measurement – Financial Guarantee Contracts and Credit Insurance*
- *Amendments to IAS 39 Financial Instruments: Recognition and Measurement – Cash Flow Hedge Accounting of Forecast Intragroup Transactions*
- *Amendments to IAS 39 Financial Instruments: Recognition and Measurement – Transition and Initial Recognition of Financial Assets and Financial Liabilities*

Final standards published

New:

- IFRS 2 *Share-based Payment*
- IFRS 3 *Business Combinations*
- IFRS 4 *Insurance Contracts*
- IFRS 5 *Non-current Assets Held for Sale and Discontinued Operations*
- IFRS 6 *Exploration for and Evaluation of Mineral Assets*

Revisions:

- IAS 19 *Employee Benefits (Actuarial Gains and Losses, Group Plans and Disclosures)*
- IAS 36 *Impairment of Assets*
- IAS 38 *Intangible Assets*
- IAS 39 *Financial Instruments: Recognition and Measurement (Macro Hedging, Transition)*

Final interpretations published

New:

- IFRIC 1 *Changes in Existing Decommissioning, Restoration and Similar Liabilities*
- IFRIC 2 *Members' Shares in Co-operative Entities and Similar Instruments*
- IFRIC 3 *Emission Rights*
- IFRIC 4 *Determining Whether an Arrangement Contains a Lease*
- IFRIC 5 *Rights to Interests Arising from Decommissioning, Restoration and Environmental Rehabilitation Funds*

Revisions:

- SIC 12 *Consolidation – Special Purpose Entities (Scope amendment)*

2005

- Meetings of the IASB working groups are opened to public observation.
- Constitutional changes are adopted, including expanding the IASCF trustees from 19 to 22, raising the IASB vote from simple majority to 9 out of 14, and appointing an independent chair of SAC.
- An IASB board member is appointed as chair of IFRIC.
- The SEC publishes a 'roadmap' to eliminating reconciliation from IFRSs to US GAAP.
- The first independent chairman of SAC is appointed.

- A new IASB publication series is proposed but abandoned after public comments.
- The IASCF trustees form the Trustee Appointments Advisory Group.

Exposure drafts published

- *Amendments to IFRS 1 First-time Adoption of International Financial Reporting Standards and IFRS 6 Exploration for and Evaluation of Mineral Resources*
- *Amendments to IAS 19 Employee Benefits*
- *Amendments to IAS 27 Consolidated and Separate Financial Statements*
- *Amendments to IAS 37 Provisions, Contingent Liabilities and Contingent Assets*
- *Replacement of IFRS 3 Business Combinations*

Final standards published

New:

- IFRS 7 *Financial Instruments: Disclosures*

Revisions:

- *IAS 39 Financial Instruments: Recognition and Measurement – Cash Flow Hedge Accounting of Forecast Intragroup Transactions*
- *IAS 39 Financial Instruments: Recognition and Measurement – Fair Value Option*
- *Amendments to IFRS 1 First-time Adoption of International Financial Reporting Standards and IFRS 6 Exploration for and Evaluation of Mineral Resources*
- *Amendments to IAS 39 Financial Instruments: Recognition and Measurement and IFRS 4 Insurance Contracts with respect to financial guarantee contracts*
- *Amendments to IAS 1 Presentation of Financial Statements with respect to capital disclosures*
- *Amendment to IAS 21 The Effects of Changes in Foreign Exchange Rates with respect to net investment in a foreign operation*

Final interpretations published

New:

- *IFRIC 6 Liabilities Arising from Participating in a Specific Market – Waste Electrical and Electronic Equipment*
- *IFRIC 7 Applying the Restatement Approach under IAS 29 Financial Reporting in Hyperinflationary Economies*

Revisions:

- *IFRIC 3 Emission Rights – Withdrawn*

APPENDIX D

Members of the IASB as at August 2006

Sir David Tweedie, chairman. Sir David became the first IASB chairman on 1 January 2001, having served from 1990 to 2000 as the first full-time chairman of the UK Accounting Standards Board. Before that, he was national technical partner for KPMG and was a professor of accounting in his native Scotland. He worked on international standard-setting issues as a member of the IASC. His term expires on 30 June 2011.

Thomas E Jones, vice chairman. As the former principal financial officer of Citicorp and chairman of the IASC board, Tom Jones brings extensive experience in standard setting and the preparation of financial accounts for financial institutions. A British citizen, Mr Jones has worked in Europe and the United States. His term expires on 30 June 2009.

Mary E Barth. As a part-time board member, Mary Barth, a US citizen, retains her position as senior associate dean of the Graduate School of Business at Stanford University. Professor Barth was previously a partner at Arthur Andersen. Her term expires on 30 June 2009.

Hans-Georg Bruns. Mr Bruns has served as the chief accounting officer for Daimler-Chrysler and has been head of a principal working group of his home country's German

Accounting Standards Committee. He was responsible for addressing the accounting issues related to the DaimlerChrysler merger. His term expires on 30 June 2011.

Anthony T Cope. Mr Cope, a British citizen, joined the US FASB in 1993. Before this, he worked as a financial analyst in the United States for 30 years. As a member of the IASC Strategy Working Party, he was closely involved with the IASC's restructuring, and served as FASB's observer at IASC board meetings for the IASC's last five years. His term expires on 30 June 2007.

Jan Engstrom. Jan Engstrom, a Swedish citizen, held senior financial and operating positions with the Volvo Group, including serving on the management board and as chief financial officer. He also was the chief executive officer of the Volvo Bus Corporation. His term expires on 30 June 2009.

Robert P Garnett. Mr Garnett was the executive vice president of finance for Anglo American plc, a South African company listed on the London Stock Exchange. He has worked as a preparer and analyst of financial statements in his native South Africa. He serves as chairman of IFRIC. His term expires on 30 June 2010.

Gilbert Gelard. Having been a partner at KPMG in his native France, Gilbert Gelard has extensive experience with French industry. Mr Gelard speaks eight languages and has been a member of the French standard-setting body, CNC. He was also a member of the former IASC board. His term expires on 30 June 2010.

James J Leisenring. Jim Leisenring has worked on issues related to accounting standard setting over the last three decades, as the vice chairman and more recently as director of international activities of the FASB in his home country. While at the FASB, Mr Leisenring served for several years as the FASB's observer at meetings of the former IASC board. His term expires on 30 June 2010.

Warren McGregor. Mr McGregor developed an intimate knowledge of standard-setting issues with his work over 20 years at the Australian Accounting Research Foundation, where he ultimately became the chief executive officer. His term expires on 30 June 2011.

Patricia O'Malley. Ms O'Malley was the first full-time chair of the Accounting Standards Board of Canada. She has worked on issues related to global standard setting since 1983 and brings with her a broad experience on work with financial instruments. Before joining the Canadian board, Ms O'Malley was a technical partner at KPMG in Canada. Her term expires on 30 June 2007.

John T Smith. As a part-time member of the board, Mr Smith continues to be a partner at Deloitte & Touche (US). He was a member of the FASB's Emerging Issues Task Force, Derivatives Implementation Group, and Financial Instruments Task Force. He served on the IASC Task Force on Financial Instruments and chaired the IASC's IAS 39 Implementation Guidance Committee. He was a member of the IASC, SIC and IFRIC. His term expires on 30 June 2007.

Philippe Danjou. Mr Danjou was director of the accounting division of Autorité des Marchés Financiers (AMF), the French securities regulator. He graduated from l'École des Hautes Études Commerciales (HEC), then qualified as a chartered accountant and registered statutory auditor, and rose to be an audit partner with Arthur Andersen & Co (Paris). He was also the executive director of the French Ordre des Experts Comptables (OEC) from 1982 until 1986. His term expires on 30 June 2011.

Tatsumi Yamada. Tatsumi Yamada was a partner at ChuoAoyama Audit Corporation (a member firm of PricewaterhouseCoopers) in Tokyo. He brings extensive experience with international standard setting as a Japanese member of the former IASC board between 1996 and 2000. His term expires on 30 June 2011.

IASB contact information

General inquiries:
30 Cannon Street
London EC4M 6XH
United Kingdom
Telephone: +44-20-7246-6410
Fax: +44-20-7246-6411
General email: <iasb@iasb.org>
Office hours: Monday–Friday, 08:30–18:00 London time
Website: <www.iasb.org>

IASC Foundation Publications Office
30 Cannon Street
London EC4M 6XH
United Kingdom
Publications orders phone: +44-20-7332-2730
Publications orders email: <publications@iasb.org>
Publications fax: +44-20-7332-2749
Office hours: Monday–Friday, 09:30–17:30 London time

CHAPTER 2
The conceptual Framework of the IASB

CONCEPTS FOR REVIEW

Before studying this chapter, you should understand or, if necessary, revise:

- basic financial accounting and reporting concepts, particularly the general format and content of a set of financial statements (such as that gained after a one-year university level introductory accounting course)
- the material in chapter 1 of this book.

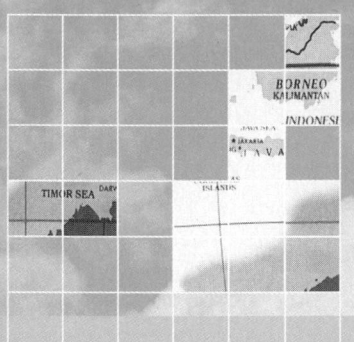

LEARNING OBJECTIVES

When you have studied this chapter, you should be able to:

1. understand the purpose of the IASB Framework – who uses it and why
2. explain the difference between general purpose financial statements and special purpose financial statements
3. describe the primary groups of users at which general purpose financial statements are aimed
4. understand the IASB's objective for general purpose financial statements
5. explain how financial statements meet users' needs for information about financial position, performance and changes in financial position
6. understand the accrual basis and going concern assumptions
7. identify the qualities that make financial statements useful, in particular, understand the concept of materiality and the trade-off between relevance and reliability
8. define the basic elements of financial statements – assets, liabilities, equity, income and expenses
9. understand the principles for recognising the elements of financial statements
10. be aware of the various bases for measuring the elements of financial statements
11. be aware of the joint IASB and FASB project to update and converge their conceptual Frameworks.

2.1 Introduction

In 1989, the International Accounting Standards Committee (IASC), predecessor to the International Accounting Standards Board (IASB), adopted the Framework for the Preparation and Presentation of Financial Statements. In 2001, the IASB 're-adopted' the Framework.

LO 1

2.2 Purpose and status of the Framework

The Framework describes the basic concepts that underlie financial statements prepared in conformity with International Financial Reporting Standards (IFRSs). The Framework serves as a guide to the IASB in developing accounting standards and as a guide to resolving accounting issues that are not addressed directly in an International Financial Reporting Standard.

However, the Framework is not itself an IASB standard. Therefore, it does not define principles for any particular accounting recognition, measurement or disclosure matter. Nor does the Framework override any specific IASB standard if there appears to be a conflict. The Framework:

- defines the objective of financial statements
- identifies the qualitative characteristics that make information in financial statements useful
- defines the basic elements of financial statements and the concepts for recognising and measuring them in financial statements.

When IAS 8 *Accounting Policies, Changes in Accounting Estimates and Errors* was revised in 2003, the IASB added a hierarchy of sources by which an entity would choose its accounting policies. In the absence of a specific standard addressing an issue, an entity is required to look to the IASB Framework. This means that entities preparing IFRS financial statements must become familiar with the Framework, because it is unlikely that IFRSs will provide clear accounting guidance for every single transaction that an entity encounters.

2.2.1 How is the Framework used?

Since the Framework is not a standard, you might wonder who uses it and how they use it. The Framework has a variety of uses.

1. Most importantly, the Framework guides the IASB and International Financial Reporting Interpretations Committee (IFRIC) members in deliberating and establishing International Financial Reporting Standards and interpretations of these standards. In the absence of a framework, each board member inevitably would debate accounting standards questions premised on his or her own professional experience – their personal frameworks. Unfortunately, as in any debate, different premises can lead to different equally logical conclusions. For example, a board member who felt that accounting should smooth earnings volatility to help financial analysts assess long-term trends might favour a deferral-and-amortisation approach for certain kinds of costs. Another board member, however, who felt that assets must have clear future benefits in terms of expected cash flows to the entity might reject a deferral-and-amortisation approach. Both board members would have logic on their side. The difference, of course, is in the premises to their reasoning. The Framework provides a set of 'givens' in the debate over accounting standards. The members of the IASB (currently 14 in number) change from time to time. New board members have an obligation to accept the Framework as a given or, if they disagree with some aspects of the Framework, to work to change these aspects.

2. Basing a set of accounting standards on the underlying IASB Framework helps ensure that the body of standards is internally consistent, at least to the maximum extent possible. For instance, one of the things the Framework does is define the basic elements of financial statements – assets, liabilities, equity, income and expenses. When an accounting issue that comes before the IASB involves whether to accrue a provision (liability and related expense) for a contingency of uncertain amount or timing – such as a pending lawsuit – the Framework definition of a liability becomes a 'given', and the debate should centre on whether the particular contingency in question meets the agreed definition of a liability.

3. Preparers and auditors of financial statements use the Framework as a point of reference to resolve an accounting question in the absence of a standard or interpretation that specifically deals with the question. It is not possible for any set of accounting standards to provide clear answers to all accounting questions – and certainly not a principles-based body of accounting standards such as that promulgated by the IASB. Judgement is required in answering specific questions that the standards do not address. The Framework establishes boundaries for the exercise of judgement in preparing financial statements.

4. The IASB Framework establishes precise terminology by which people can discuss accounting questions. To illustrate, agreement on the definition of 'liability' helps in deciding whether things known variously as obligations, commitments, contingencies, provisions, accruals and the like qualify for recognition as liabilities in the balance sheet. Consider a company that has chosen to self-insure for fire losses. (Self-insure means the company has decided to retain all or some portion of its risk of loss from fire damage to its property rather than to pay an insurance premium for the insurance company to take on the risk.) Assume that an uninsured fire loss is expected to occur once every three years, and the first year goes by without a loss. An accounting question arises as to whether it is appropriate for the company to accrue one-third of the estimated loss as an expense of the first year and as a liability at the end of the first year. Without a conceptual Framework, the company might well analyse the question in terms of earnings volatility. If the once-in-every-three-years fire loss is recognised in its entirety in measuring net profit in the year it occurs, with no loss recognised in the other two years, earnings will appear volatile. Wishing to avoid reporting earnings volatility, the company might conclude that accrual of one-third of the expected fire loss as an expense and a year-end obligation for the loss is appropriate in the first year. By defining the elements of financial statements rigorously, the Framework focuses the debate on whether the obligation meets the definition of a liability. (Incidentally, accruals for self-insured losses that have not yet happened would fail the test for liability under the existing IASB Framework because the Framework defines a liability in terms of a present obligation arising from a past event. In the case of our self-insured company, the loss event would be an actual fire. A loss event has not yet occurred by the end of the first year, so there is no liability under the Framework at that date. Simply put, the entity does not owe anything to anyone.)

5. The Framework reduces the volume of standards. Without the Framework, each accounting question would have to be answered ad hoc, and there would be pressure from the preparers, auditors and users of financial statements for more detailed standards. The Framework provides direction for resolving questions without the need for increasingly specific standards.

6. The Framework makes it more likely that the standards will be 'principles based' rather than detailed rules that try to cover every conceivable potential situation. As the US Securities and Exchange Commission (2003, p. 5) said in its report, principles-based standards should:

   - Be based on an improved and consistently applied conceptual framework;
   - Clearly state the accounting objective of the standard;

- Provide sufficient detail and structure so that the standard can be operationalized and applied on a consistent basis;
- Minimize exceptions from the standard;
- Avoid use of percentage tests ("bright-lines") that allow financial engineers to achieve technical compliance with the standard while evading the intent of the standard.

7. By providing parameters for the exercise of judgement, the Framework reduces the need for interpretations and other detailed implementation guidance.

8. By adding rigour and discipline, the Framework enhances public confidence in financial reports. Users of financial statements make comparisons, and comparability is diminished if financial statement preparers use their own judgement on an ad hoc, company-by-company basis. No matter how well intentioned that judgement may be, financial statements can lose credibility if they lack a conceptual underpinning.

2.2.2   Authority of the Framework

The IASB addressed the role of the Framework in its *Preface to International Financial Reporting Standards*, adopted by the board in May 2002:

> IFRSs are based on the Framework, which addresses the concepts underlying the information presented in general purpose financial statements. The objective of the Framework is to facilitate the consistent and logical formulation of IFRSs. The Framework also provides a basis for the use of judgement in resolving accounting issues (para. 8).

Further, the preface described the due process steps that the IASB follows in developing an International Financial Reporting Standard. Step one noted in the preface is:

> The staff are asked to identify and review all of the issues associated with the topic and to consider the application of the Framework to the issues (para. 18(a)).

An identical step one is set out in the due process followed by the International Financial Reporting Interpretations Committee in developing Interpretations.

Despite these benefits, you might still be wondering whether the Framework has any real effect, or whether preparers and auditors of financial statements can choose to ignore it since it is not a standard. Until recently, the Framework might appropriately have been called 'non-binding'. According to IAS 1 *Presentation of Financial Statements*:

> An entity whose financial statements comply with IFRSs shall make an explicit and unreserved statement of such compliance in the notes. Financial statements shall not be described as complying with IFRSs unless they comply with all the requirements of IFRSs (para. 14).

Because the Framework is not mentioned in that requirement of IAS 1, some people concluded that it lacked authority. Whether that view was ever accurate, it is certainly no longer the case. As a result of the addition in 2003 of the following two paragraphs to IAS 8 *Accounting Policies, Changes in Accounting Estimates and Errors*, the IASB clarified that the Framework cannot be ignored. IAS 8 is an authoritative, binding standard, and it states that the Framework is the first place to which a preparer or auditor must look in the absence of a specific standard or interpretation:

> 10. In the absence of a Standard or an Interpretation that specifically applies to a transaction, other event or condition, management shall use its judgement in developing and applying an accounting policy that results in information that is:
>   (a) relevant to the economic decision-making needs of users; and
>   (b) reliable, in that the financial statements:
>   (i) represent faithfully the financial position, financial performance and cash flows of the entity;
>   (ii) reflect the economic substance of transactions, other events and conditions, and not merely the legal form;

(iii) are neutral, i.e. free from bias;

(iv) are prudent; and

(v) are complete in all material respects.

11. In making the judgement described in paragraph 10, management shall refer to, and consider the applicability of, the following sources in descending order:

(a) the requirements and guidance in Standards and Interpretations dealing with similar and related issues; and

(b) the definitions, recognition criteria and measurement concepts for assets, liabilities, income and expenses in the Framework.

2.3 General purpose financial statements

LO 2

The Framework addresses general purpose financial statements, which are the financial statements that an entity prepares and presents at least annually to meet the common information needs of a wide range of users external to the entity. Therefore, the Framework does not necessarily apply to special purpose financial reports such as reports to tax authorities, reports to government regulatory authorities, prospectuses prepared in connection with securities offerings, and reports prepared in connection with proposed business combinations.

The Framework focuses on the financial statements of business entities, which would include both privately owned and state-owned business entities. The Framework does not necessarily apply to the financial statements of governments, government non-business units or other not-for-profit entities, although most of the concepts in the Framework would seem to be equally relevant to those types of entities.

The Framework acknowledges that some parties who use the general purpose financial statements of an entity may have the power to obtain information in addition to that contained in the financial statements. For example, a major lender often can negotiate to obtain whatever special information it deems necessary to make its lending decision. Nonetheless, that major lender still has a use for the general purpose financial statements. After all, lenders are bankers, not accountants, and even a lender with clout is likely to look to the accounting standard setters to define the accounting principles and presentation formats on which borrowers' financial statements should be based. Furthermore, many present and potential investors, creditors, vendors, and others who seek financial information about the entity do not have the same power as the major lender to get special information. They must rely on the general purpose financial statements to meet their information needs.

2.4 Users and their information needs

LO 3

The Framework identifies the principal classes of users of general purpose financial statements as:

- present and potential investors
- lenders
- suppliers and other trade creditors
- employees
- customers
- governments and their agencies
- the general public.

All of these categories of users rely on financial statements to help them in making various kinds of economic and public policy decisions.

The Framework also concludes that, because investors are providers of risk capital to the entity, financial statements that meet their needs will also meet most of the general financial information needs of the other classes of financial statement users. Common to all of these user groups is their interest in the ability of an entity to generate cash and cash equivalents, and the timing and certainty of those future cash flows. Therefore, the Framework regards investors as the primary, overriding user group.

The Framework notes that financial statements cannot provide all the information that users may need to make economic decisions. For one thing, financial statements show the financial effects of past events and transactions, whereas the decisions that most users of financial statements have to make relate to the future. The information in financial statements helps users to make their own forecasts. Further, financial statements provide only a limited amount of the non-financial information needed by users of financial statements. Financial statements cannot meet all of the diverse information needs of these user groups. However, there are information needs that are common to all users, and general purpose financial statements focus on meeting those needs.

While the concepts in the Framework are likely to lead to information that is useful to the management of an entity in running the business, the Framework does not purport to address their information needs. The same can be said for the IFRSs and interpretations themselves.

2.5 Responsibility for financial statements

The management of an entity has the primary responsibility for preparing and presenting the entity's financial statements. This responsibility is noted in the auditor's report in most countries. Some countries require that company management include, as part of the financial statements, an explicit statement of management's responsibility for the financial statements. The auditor's responsibility is to form and express an opinion as to whether the financial statements are prepared, in all material respects, in accordance with International Financial Reporting Standards or some other identified financial-reporting framework. The fact that financial statements are audited does not relieve management of its fundamental responsibility for preparing and presenting the financial statements.

In a very real sense, there is a conflict of interest if the auditor is responsible for preparing the financial statements and also responsible for forming and expressing an independent opinion on whether those statements have been properly prepared.

International Standard on Auditing (ISA) 700, *The Auditor's Report on Financial Statements*, requires that the auditor's report include a statement that the financial statements are the responsibility of the entity's management. The auditor's report must also explain that the auditor's responsibility is to express an opinion on the financial statements based on the audit. The standard wording of an unqualified auditor's report set out in ISA 700 is shown in figure 2.1.

INDEPENDENT AUDITOR'S REPORT

[Appropriate addressee]

We have audited the accompanying financial statements of ABC Company, which comprise the balance sheet as at December 31, 20X1, and the income statement, statement of changes in equity and cash flow statement for the year then ended, and a summary of significant accounting policies and other explanatory notes.

Management's responsibility for the financial statements

Management is responsible for the preparation and fair presentation of these financial statements in accordance with International Financial Reporting Standards. This responsibility includes: designing, implementing and maintaining internal control relevant to the preparation and fair presentation of financial statements that are free from material misstatement, whether due to fraud or error; selecting and applying appropriate accounting policies; and making accounting estimates that are reasonable in the circumstances.

Auditor's responsibility

Our responsibility is to express an opinion on these financial statements based on our audit. We conducted our audit in accordance with International Standards on Auditing. Those standards require that we comply with ethical requirements and plan and perform the audit to obtain reasonable assurance whether the financial statements are free from material misstatement.

An audit involves performing procedures to obtain audit evidence about the amounts and disclosures in the financial statements. The procedures selected depend on the auditor's judgment, including the assessment of the risks of material misstatement of the financial statements, whether due to fraud or error. In making those risk assessments, the auditor considers internal control relevant to the entity's preparation and fair presentation of the financial statements in order to design audit procedures that are appropriate in the circumstances, but not for the purpose of expressing an opinion on the effectiveness of the entity's internal control. An audit also includes evaluating the appropriateness of accounting policies used and the reasonableness of accounting estimates made by management, as well as evaluating the overall presentation of the financial statements.

We believe that the audit evidence we have obtained is sufficient and appropriate to provide a basis for our audit opinion.

Opinion

In our opinion, the financial statements give a true and fair view of (*or 'present fairly, in all material respects,'*) the financial position of ABC Company as of December 31, 20X1, and of its financial performance and its cash flows for the year then ended in accordance with International Financial Reporting Standards.

[Auditor's signature]

[Date of the auditor's report]

[Auditor's address]

FIGURE 2.1   Wording of an unqualified auditor's report
Source: ISA 700 (effective for auditors' reports dated on or after 31 December 2006).

LO 4

2.6 The objective of financial statements

The Framework states that the objective of financial statements is to provide information about the financial position, performance and changes in financial position of an entity that is useful to a wide range of users in making economic decisions. This may not seem very profound, but decision usefulness as an objective of financial statements has been the subject of heated debate. By their nature, economic decisions are forward looking: Should I invest in this company? Should I sell my investment? Should I vote to keep the current management or replace them? Should I lend to this company and, if so, what rate is appropriate to compensate me for my risks? If I sell goods or services to this company on credit, will the company have enough cash in the short term to pay my invoice? Is this company financially secure enough for me to quit my current job and go to work for the company instead?

All of those decisions are future-oriented, and the objective of financial statements as set out in the IASB Framework is to help people make these sorts of decisions. Some accountants disagree with that objective. They argue that the objective of financial statements is strictly to be a scorecard of the past; namely, how well did the management of the company do with the resources that were entrusted to it? This is sometimes called the 'stewardship objective' of financial statements. The IASB Framework does not reject the stewardship objective. But it says that people want to know about the past (stewardship), not merely out of curiosity, but because they want to use the information about the past to help them in making future-oriented economic decisions. Thus, financial statements prepared in conformity with IFRSs serve both a stewardship objective and an economic decision-making objective, but the decision-making objective is overriding.

LO 5

2.6.1 Financial position

One of the objectives of financial statements is to provide information about an entity's financial position:
- What assets does the entity own?
- What does it owe?
- What are the residual equity interests in the entity's net assets?

The financial position of an entity is affected by the economic resources it controls, its financial structure, its liquidity and solvency, and its capacity to adapt to changes in the environment in which it operates. The balance sheet (sometimes called the statement of financial position or statement of financial condition) presents this kind of information.

2.6.2 Performance

Performance is the ability of an entity to earn a profit on the resources that have been invested in it. Information about the amount and variability of profits helps in forecasting future cash flows from the entity's existing resources and in forecasting potential additional cash flows from additional resources that might be invested in the entity.

The Framework states that information about performance is primarily provided in an income statement (sometimes called the statement of profit and loss or the statement of financial performance), but that explanation is somewhat out of date. IAS 1 (revised after the Framework was written) added a fourth basic financial statement, the statement showing changes in equity. It is important to look to both the income statement and the equity statement in assessing performance because several International Financial Reporting Standards provide that certain items of income and expense should be reported directly in equity, thereby bypassing the income statement, sometimes permanently and sometimes only temporarily. In the latter case, the amounts reported directly in equity are removed from equity at some future date and, at that time, recycled through the income statement. Examples of income and expense items required by International Financial Reporting Standards to be reported initially directly in equity are shown below.
- Changes in fair value of available-for-sale financial assets (investments in equity and debt securities) are reported directly in equity until the financial asset is sold, at which

time the cumulative fair value change is removed from equity and flowed through the income statement (IAS 39 *Financial Instruments: Recognition and Measurement*).

- Major classes of property, plant and equipment (such as land, buildings and equipment) are remeasured to fair value at each balance sheet date, with the change in fair value reported in a 'revaluation reserve' directly in equity. When the asset is ultimately sold or otherwise disposed of, the cumulative fair value change remains in equity and is not recycled through the income statement (IAS 16 *Property, Plant and Equipment*). Revaluation of land, buildings and equipment is an option under IAS 16. The other alternative is to measure these assets at historical cost, and recognise depreciation and impairment losses while the asset is held.

- Foreign currency translation adjustments arising when the financial statements of a foreign operation are translated from the foreign currency into the reporting company's currency are reported directly in equity. The amount of the exchange differences previously deferred in equity is recognised as income or expense (recycled) in the period in which any gain or loss on disposal of the foreign entity is recognised (IAS 21 *The Effects of Changes in Foreign Exchange Rates*).

- Companies have an option of reporting actuarial gains and losses on their pension funds directly in equity when they arise. Actuarial gains and losses are differences between actual experience and the assumptions made by the company about such things as employee turnover, mortality, and earnings on pension-plan assets in making its prior estimates of pension obligations.

These value changes are part of an entity's performance, but under existing IFRSs they are not reported in the income statement. Rather, they show up in the equity statement. Therefore, in assessing performance, both of those financial statements must be considered. The International Accounting Standards Board is working on a project on how best to report performance. A key tentative conclusion is that performance should be reported in a single financial statement instead of being scattered among several. Further, every item of income and expense should be reported once — and only once (no recycling) — in the combined performance statement.

An entity's performance is of particular interest to equity investors (shareholders) and providers of long-term debt capital. For them, the income and equity statements are paramount, because the company's ability to provide a return on their capital investment depends on the company's operating performance, not on its current bank account and near-term collections of receivables. On the other hand, short-term creditors (vendors, suppliers, employees and so on) are generally more interested in current financial condition and liquidity, so they are more likely to focus on the balance sheet and cash flow statement.

2.6.3   Changes in financial position

Users of financial statements seek information about the sources and uses of an entity's cash and cash equivalents such as bank deposits during the reporting period. Cash comes into and goes out of an entity from three broad categories of activity: its operations (producing and selling its goods and services), its investing activities (buying and selling long-lived assets and financial investments), and its financing activities (raising and repaying debt and equity capital). The cash flow statement provides this kind of information. In a sense, the income statement analyses changes in one line in the balance sheet — retained earnings — and the cash flow statement provides insight into changes in all of the other line items in the balance sheet.

Ultimately, all investors, creditors, and other capital providers to an entity want to get cash out of their investment. They can do that in various ways. They receive cash when they receive dividend or interest payments. They receive cash when the principal on their debt investments is paid when due. They receive cash when their receivables are paid off. They receive cash when they sell their investment securities. The cash flow statement helps them assess the prospects of receiving cash from the entity.

Investors can even receive cash without selling their investments by using their securities as collateral on borrowings. In that case, the one who lends to the investor is interested in the entity's prospects of generating cash because that affects the liquidity of the collateral.

2.6.4 Notes and supplementary schedules

The financial statements also contain notes and supplementary schedules and other information that (a) explain items in the balance sheet and income statement, (b) disclose the risks and uncertainties affecting the entity, and (c) explain any resources and obligations not recognised in the balance sheet. The notes also sometimes contain information that meets disclosure requirements arising under national laws or regulations.

The IASB Framework does not spell out a list of specific topics that should be covered in the notes to an entity's financial statements. No single IASB standard does that, although many individual standards require specific items of disclosure.

LO 6

2.7 Underlying assumptions

The Framework sets out the underlying assumptions of financial statements. These are known as the accrual basis of accounting and the going concern assumption.

2.7.1 Accrual basis

Accounting recognises the effects of transactions and other events when they occur rather than only when cash or its equivalent is received or paid, and accounting reports these effects in the financial statements of the periods to which they relate. This is known as the accrual basis of accounting. The accrual basis recognises that a company's financial position and performance can change without any cash changing hands, although it usually occurs with a right to receive cash or an obligation to pay cash in the future. Accrual accounting recognises these changes when they occur.

An alternative to the accrual basis of accounting is the cash basis of accounting, which recognises changes in financial position and performance only when cash is received or paid. The cash basis is not consistent with the IASB Framework.

2.7.2 Going concern

The financial statements presume that an entity will continue in operation indefinitely or, if that presumption is not valid, disclosure and a different basis of reporting are required.

An entity that is not a going concern is likely to be liquidated (assets sold and liabilities paid off) in the near term. If it is not being completely liquidated, its operations will be materially scaled back through partial liquidation. The users of the financial statements of such an entity will have a great interest in the net amount of cash that can be generated from the entity's assets in the very short term. IASB standards are not necessarily designed to provide this kind of information. Rather, as the Framework indicates, IASB standards presume that the entity will continue to operate for the foreseeable future and therefore will generate its cash flows from operations rather than from liquidation sales.

LO 7

2.8 Qualitative characteristics of financial statements

These characteristics are the attributes that make the information in financial statements useful to investors, creditors and others. The Framework identifies four principal qualitative characteristics.

1. understandability
2. relevance
3. reliability
4. comparability.

2.8.1 Understandability

Information should be presented in a way that is readily understandable by users who have a reasonable knowledge of business and economic activities and accounting, and who are willing to study the information diligently.

2.8.2 Relevance

Information in financial statements is relevant when it influences the economic decisions of users. It can do that by (a) helping them evaluate past, present or future events relating to an entity; and (b) confirming or correcting past evaluations they have made.

Materiality

Materiality is a component of relevance. Information is material if its omission or misstatement could influence the economic decisions of users. Conversely, if information does not have a bearing on the economic decisions of users, it is immaterial and therefore lacks relevance. Neither the IASB Framework nor individual International Financial Reporting Standards provide quantified measures of materiality that can be applied in preparing financial statements generally. Several IFRSs contain quantified guidance on materiality for a very narrow use; for example, to determine whether a business or geographical segment is large enough to be reported separately (IAS 14 *Segment Reporting*) or to determine whether actuarial gains and losses on pension funds are large enough to warrant immediate accounting recognition (IAS 19 *Employee Benefits*). But there is no overall quantified measure.

Timeliness

Timeliness is another component of relevance. To be useful, information must be provided to users within the time period in which it is most likely to bear on their decisions. Stale information does not bear on users' decisions and is therefore not relevant.

2.8.3 Reliability

Information in financial statements is reliable if it is free from material error and bias and can be depended on by users to represent events and transactions faithfully. Measurement difficulties can sometimes cause information not to be reliable. Information is also not reliable when it is purposely designed to influence users' decisions in a particular direction (the information lacks neutrality). The IASB Framework identifies several attributes that make information reliable.

Representational faithfulness

To be reliable, information must represent accurately the transaction or other circumstance that the information purports to present. Consider a bank that includes a portfolio of loans receivable among its assets. If the economy of the country in which the bank operates is in a significant recession so that a substantial portion of these loans are non-performing (interest or principal payments are not being made on schedule), representational faithfulness requires measurement of those loans in the balance sheet at not more than the present value of amounts reasonably expected to be collected. Accounting cannot ignore the reality of the recession just because it might make a big dent in the bank's reported equity or might force it to report losses to the government and its investors and depositors. Nor would it be representationally faithful to ignore today's reality of the problem loans because the bank management is confident that the economy will turn around next year or the year after. After all, the balance sheet is trying to present the true current financial condition of the bank.

Substance over form

Financial statements should reflect the substance of transactions and not necessarily their legal form. For example, if an entity leases a machine under a non-cancellable lease that covers the entire economic life of the asset, and the lease payments approximate the payments that the entity would have made if it had signed a purchase agreement to buy the asset and pay for it over the life of the asset, the substance of the lease transaction is no different from the purchase transaction. Substance over form would require the same accounting no matter whether the legal document is labelled a lease or a purchase agreement.

Neutrality

The Framework is clear that accounting information must be decision-neutral. This means that the information is not designed in a way that intentionally leads the users of that information to make an economic decision that the preparer of the information would like them to make. Some examples are shown below.

- Accounting standards should not allow debt to be kept off the balance sheet, if the debt meets the definition of a liability (this is sometimes called 'off-balance-sheet financing'), simply to enhance the entity's capacity to borrow additional funds or to reduce its future borrowing cost. A potential lender might make the wrong decision about whether to extend a loan to the entity and what price to charge for it.
- Principles of revenue and expense measurement should not be designed in such a way as to smooth out volatility of income and expenses from period to period simply because investors prefer to invest in stable rather than volatile entities. This holds true even if the entity will have a higher cost of capital as a consequence. If its performance is volatile, its financial statements should show that volatility.
- Accounting should not avoid appropriate loan loss recognition simply because recognising the bad debts would cause the financial statements of some banks to report a precarious financial condition. This holds true even if the government fears that reporting serious financial problems in the banking sector is politically or socially unwise.
- The balance sheet of a company that makes a commitment to provide medical insurance coverage to employees after they retire should reflect the liability resulting from that commitment. This holds true even if the company threatens to stop providing the coverage if it has to accrue the obligation.

Saying that accounting information should be decision-neutral is entirely consistent with saying that accounting information should be relevant. Relevance requires that the information bear on the economic decisions that users want to make. Neutrality requires that the information be free from bias toward any particular economic decision; that is, it should be purely factual.

Prudence

Prudence is the inclusion of a degree of caution in the exercise of the judgements needed in making the estimates required under conditions of uncertainty, such that assets or income are not overstated and liabilities or expenses are not understated. While there is nothing wrong with healthy scepticism — accounting recognition and measurement decisions usually involve some judgement — prudence has sometimes been used to justify the deliberate overstatement of liabilities or expenses, or the deliberate understatement of assets or income. When this happens, the financial statement measurements lose their reliability. Consequently, prudence is not a qualitative characteristic in the IASB Framework. The Framework concludes that prudence can be exercised only within the context of the other qualitative characteristics in the Framework, particularly relevance and the faithful representation of transactions in financial statements.

Completeness

Reliability requires that the financial statements must report what they purport to report completely, subject to constraints of cost and materiality. Omissions make financial statements just as wrong as unreliable or irrelevant information.

Balance between benefit and cost

The IASB Framework states that the benefits that users of financial statements derive from information should exceed the cost of providing that information. While this seems an eminently sensible principle, it is one that is difficult to implement because the evaluation of benefits and costs is a judgemental process. The benefits accrue not only to the users of financial statements (ability to make better economic decisions) but also to the preparers of financial statements (potentially lower cost of capital) and to society (better allocation and pricing of resources). The costs of providing information include not only the obvious costs of preparing the information (accounting and computer systems, audits and so on) but also indirect costs such as the benefits the information provides to a company's competitors. The IASB and other accounting standard setters must nonetheless assess costs and benefits as part of their standard-setting processes.

2.8.4   Trade-off between relevance and reliability

There is sometimes a trade-off between relevance and reliability – and judgement is required to provide the appropriate balance. For the most part, that judgement is made by the accounting standard setter (the IASB). In some cases, the standard setter asks the preparer of financial statements to make the judgement about balancing relevance and reliability in applying individual standards. Two examples are shown below.

- In adopting IAS 41 *Agriculture*, the IASB determined that the fair values of biological assets (livestock, crops, orchards, timberlands and the like) and agricultural produce (harvested commodities) are more relevant to users of financial statements than the historical costs of those items. Therefore, IAS 41 requires accounting for those items at fair value. The board recognised, however, that sometimes it is simply not possible to get a reliable measure of the fair value of certain biological assets. Therefore, IAS 41 includes a 'reliability exception' to the fundamental fair value measurement principle. This 'reliability exception' places the burden of judgement on the preparer and auditor of the financial statements and is an illustration of the trade-off between relevance and reliability.
- In IAS 39 *Financial Instruments: Recognition and Measurement*, the IASB concluded that measurement of investments in debt and equity securities classified as available for sale or held for trading at fair value is more relevant to users of financial statements than measurement at cost.

2.8.5   Comparability

Users must be able to compare the financial statements of an entity over time so that they can identify trends in its financial position and performance. Users must also be able to compare the financial statements of different entities to make decisions about where to invest their capital and at what price. Disclosure of accounting policies is essential for comparability.

2.8.6   Supremacy of relevance and reliability

Section 2.2.2 of this chapter explained that in 2003 the IASB clarified the authority of the Framework by amending IAS 8 *Accounting Policies, Changes in Accounting Estimates and Errors* to require that the Framework be the first place to which a preparer or auditor must look in the absence of a specific standard or interpretation. This change to IAS 8 also restructured the Framework's hierarchy of the qualitative characteristics to place relevance and reliability as the twin overriding qualities of financial statements, and to place representational faithfulness, substance over form, neutrality, prudence and completeness as subqualities under reliability.

2.9   The elements of financial statements

Financial statements portray the financial effects of transactions and other events by grouping them into broad classes according to their economic characteristics. These broad classes are known as the elements of financial statements. The elements directly related to financial position (balance sheet) are:

- assets
- liabilities
- equity.

The elements directly related to performance (income statement) are:

- income
- expenses.

The cash flow statement reflects both income statement elements and changes in balance sheet elements. The cash flow statement does not present any additional elements of financial statements.

2.9.1   Definitions of the elements relating to financial position

- Asset — a resource controlled by the entity as a result of past events and from which future economic benefits are expected to flow to the entity.
- Liability — a present obligation of the entity arising from past events, the settlement of which is expected to result in an outflow from the entity of resources embodying economic benefits.
- Equity — the residual interest in the assets of the entity after deducting all its liabilities.

In the definitions of asset and liability, the term 'economic benefits' is used. In these contexts, economic benefits means future flows of cash or other assets. Thus, an asset is expected to help generate cash or other assets coming into the entity, and a liability is expected to result in cash or other assets flowing out of the entity.

Both the asset and liability definitions refer to 'past events'. These are key parts of the definitions because they have led, in various IASB standards, to prohibitions of cost deferrals and liability accruals whose sole purpose is to smooth out earnings volatility. If a loss event has not yet happened, the past event criterion would prohibit liability recognition. If the entity does not already have a right to future benefits as a result of some past event, it cannot defer costs as assets.

2.9.2   Definitions of the elements relating to performance

- Income — increases in economic benefits during the accounting period in the form of inflows or enhancements of assets or decreases of liabilities that result in increases in equity, other than those relating to contributions from equity participants.
- Expense — decreases in economic benefits during the accounting period in the form of outflows or depletions of assets, or the incurrence of liabilities that result in decreases in equity other than those relating to distributions to equity participants.

The definition of income encompasses both revenue and gains. Revenue arises in the course of the normal operating activities of the entity, such as the sales of goods and services produced by the entity. Revenue is referred to by a variety of different names including sales, turnover, fees, interest, dividends, royalties and rent. Gains represent other items that meet the definition of income but that do not result from the normal sales of goods and services produced by the entities. To illustrate, an entity sells one of the factories in which it manufactures its products. The selling price is higher than the depreciated carrying amount of the factory, so the net profit on the sale of the factory is a gain. Sales of the products produced in the entity's factories are revenue. Gains represent increases in economic benefits and so are not really different in nature from revenue. Hence, the IASB Framework does not treat them as a separate financial statement element. However, they are usually reported in separate lines in the performance statement (income statement) because they may have different probabilities of recurring in the future. Also, gains are usually reported on a net basis (net of the related expenses), whereas revenues are reported gross.

The definition of expenses encompasses losses as well as those expenses that arise in the course of the ordinary activities of an entity. Expenses that arise in the course of the ordinary activities of an entity may include cost of sales, wages, marketing costs, administrative costs and depreciation. They usually take the form of an outflow or depletion of assets such as cash and cash equivalents, inventory, property, plant and equipment. Losses represent other items that meet the definition of expenses and may or may not arise in the course of the ordinary activities of the entity. To illustrate: a company has excess cash and invests the cash in certain marketable securities. When it needs the cash, it sells the securities at a time when their fair value has declined below cost. A loss is recognised. The entity is not in the securities investment business, so the loss may be thought of as non-operating, but it is really not much different from losing money on sales of goods that the entity has manufactured. Because losses, like expenses, represent decreases in economic benefits, the IASB Framework does not treat them as a separate financial statement element, although they are often presented or disclosed separately.

LO 9

2.10 Recognition of the elements of financial statements

Recognition is the process of incorporating in the balance sheet or income statement an item that meets the definition of an element and satisfies both the following criteria for recognition:
- Probable economic benefits – it is probable that any future economic benefit associated with the item will flow to or from the entity.
- Measurement reliability – the item's cost or value can be measured reliably.

All items that satisfy these recognition criteria should be recognised in the balance sheet or income statement. Disclosure in the notes is not a substitute for such recognition.

Based on those general criteria, the recognition criteria for the elements of financial statements under the IASB Framework are as follows:
- An asset is recognised in the balance sheet when it is probable that the future economic benefits will flow to the entity and the asset has a cost or value that can be measured reliably.
- A liability is recognised in the balance sheet when it is probable that an outflow of resources embodying economic benefits will result from the settlement of a present obligation and the amount at which the settlement will take place can be measured reliably.
- Income is recognised in the income statement when an increase in future economic benefits related to an increase in an asset or a decrease in a liability has arisen that can be measured reliably. This means, in effect, that recognition of income occurs simultaneously with the recognition of increases in assets or decreases in liabilities (for example, the net increase in assets arising from a sale of goods or services, or the decrease in liabilities arising from the waiver of a debt payable).

• Expenses are recognised when a decrease in future economic benefits related to a decrease in an asset or an increase in a liability has arisen that can be measured reliably. This means, in effect, that recognition of expenses occurs simultaneously with the recognition of an increase in liabilities or a decrease in assets (for example, the accrual of employee wage and benefit entitlements or the depreciation of equipment).

Because equity is the arithmetic difference between assets and liabilities, a separate recognition criterion for equity is not needed in the IASB Framework.

Many of the individual IFRSs specify principles for recognising specific types of assets, liabilities, income or expenses. One of the standards (IAS 18 *Revenue*) is somewhat like an extension of the IASB Framework in that it sets out concepts for recognising revenue. Those concepts are shown in the next section.

2.10.1 Recognition of revenue from the sale of goods

Revenue arising from the sale of goods should be recognised when all of the following criteria have been satisfied (IAS 18, paragraph 14):
• The seller has transferred to the buyer the significant risks and rewards of ownership.
• The seller retains neither continuing managerial involvement to the degree usually associated with ownership nor effective control over the goods sold.
• The amount of revenue can be measured reliably.
• It is probable that the economic benefits associated with the transaction will flow to the seller.
• The costs incurred or to be incurred in respect of the transaction can be measured reliably.

2.10.2 Recognition of revenue from the rendering of services

For revenue arising from the rendering of services, revenue should be recognised by reference to the stage of completion of the transaction at the balance sheet date (the percentage-of-completion method), provided that all of the following criteria are met (IAS 18, paragraph 20):
• The amount of revenue can be measured reliably.
• It is probable that the economic benefits will flow to the seller.
• The stage of completion at the balance sheet date can be measured reliably.
• The costs incurred, or to be incurred, in respect of the transaction can be measured reliably.

When the above criteria are not met, revenue arising from the rendering of services should be recognised only to the extent of the expenses recognised that are recoverable (IAS 18, paragraph 26). This is known as a 'cost-recovery approach'.

2.10.3 Recognition of revenue from interest, royalties and dividends

For interest, royalties and dividends, so long as it is probable that the economic benefits will flow to the entity and the amount of revenue can be measured reliably, revenue should be recognised as follows (IAS 18, paras 29–30):
• Interest should be recognised using the effective interest method set out in IAS 39, paragraphs 9 and AG5–AG8.
• Royalties should be recognised on an accruals basis in accordance with the substance of the relevant agreement.
• Dividends should be recognised when the shareholder's right to receive payment is established.

LO 10

2.11 Measurement of the elements of financial statements

Measurement involves assigning monetary amounts at which the elements of the financial statements are to be recognised and reported. The Framework acknowledges that a variety of measurement bases are used today to different degrees and in varying combinations in financial statements, including:

- historical cost
- current replacement cost
- net realisable value
- present value (discounted expected future cash flows).

Historical cost is the measurement basis most commonly used today, but it is usually combined with other measurement bases. Historical costs are often adjusted for depreciation, amortisation and other write-downs, so the financial statement measurement basis is really unamortised historical cost.

Net realisable value is an asset's selling price or a liability's settlement amount. In some cases, an asset's selling price is reduced by estimated selling costs and a liability's settlement amount includes estimated costs of settling.

The IASB Framework does not include concepts or principles for selecting which measurement basis should be used for particular elements of financial statements or in particular circumstances. The qualitative characteristics do provide some guidance, however, particularly the characteristics of relevance and reliability. Nonetheless, after covering the objectives of financial statements, qualitative characteristics, and elements definitions quite thoroughly in 98 paragraphs, the Framework addresses measurement in only three paragraphs. It is fair to say that this is a significant deficiency in the Framework because, first and foremost, accounting boils everything down to monetary amounts. The balance sheet does not just list descriptions of the entity's assets, it assigns monetary amounts to them (measurements). The same applies to the other elements of financial statements.

Because the Framework does not include concepts for choosing the proper measurement attribute for various elements, the IASB standards today result in what is called a 'mixed attribute accounting model', with different measurement bases for different types of assets, liabilities, income and expenses. Some members of the IASB have a tendency to favour fair value measurements if at all possible (reliable). Other members lean towards cost-based measures. Since the Framework does not provide concepts for choosing between these two often-divergent bases for measurement, the measurement bases prescribed in individual IASB standards are rather ad hoc in nature. The IASB has recognised this deficiency and has begun working on a conceptual measurement project that will ultimately expand the IASB Framework in this critical area.

LO 11

2.12 The IASB's current Conceptual Framework project

The IASB and the US Financial Accounting Standards Board are currently working on a joint project designed to update and align the two boards' conceptual Frameworks. The project is being addressed in eight phases:

- objectives and qualitative characteristics
- elements: recognition and measurement attributes
- initial and subsequent measurement

- reporting entity
- presentation and disclosure
- status of Framework in GAAP hierarchy
- applicability to not-for-profit entities
- reconsideration of the entire Framework.

The two boards have already reached some tentative decisions on objectives and qualitative characteristics, which are discussed below.

2.12.1 Objectives

The boards have tentatively concluded that financial reports should aim to provide information to a wide range of users rather than focus on the information needs of existing common shareholders only. The Framework should identify the primary users as present and potential investors and creditors and their advisers. Later in the project, the boards will consider whether financial reporting should also provide information to meet the information needs of particular types of users, such as different kinds of equity participants.

The objective is to provide information about the entity to the external users who lack the power to prescribe the information they require and therefore must rely on the information provided by an entity's management. The entity's management will also be interested in that information. However, because management has the power to obtain the information it requires, any additional information needs of management are beyond the scope of the Framework.

2.12.2 Qualitative characteristics

The two boards have tentatively concluded to identify the following five primary qualitative characteristics of accounting information (US FASB & IASB 2006):

1. *Relevance* is an essential qualitative characteristic. To be relevant, information must be capable of making a difference in the economic decisions of users by helping them evaluate the effect of past and present events on future net cash inflows (predictive value) or confirm or correct previous evaluations (confirmatory value), even if it is not now being used. Being "capable of making a difference," rather than "now being used", is a change from the present IASB *Framework*.
   a. *Predictive value* is a characteristic of financial reporting information that is used, or could be used, to make predictions. Financial reporting information is not intended, in itself, as a prediction or as synonymous with statistical predictability or persistence.
   b. *Confirmatory value* rather than feedback value is a change in terminology from the present FASB framework.
   c. *Timeliness* is a third aspect of relevance; information must be available when the users need it.

2. *Faithful representation* of real-world economic phenomena is an essential qualitative characteristic. Representations are faithful (there is correspondence or agreement between the accounting measures or descriptions in the financial reports and the economic phenomena they purport to represent) when the measures and descriptions are verifiable and neutral. Therefore, faithful representation requires verifiability and neutrality, and not subordinating substance to form. The common conceptual framework will discuss thoroughly what faithful representation means and what it does not mean. The common framework will change the current IASB and FASB frameworks by replacing the widely misinterpreted term *reliability* with *faithful representation*.
   a. *Verifiability* of financial reporting information provides assurance to users that such information faithfully represents what it purports to represent and that the information is free from material error, complete, and neutral. Descriptions and measures that can be directly verified through consensus among observers are preferable to descriptions or measures that can only be indirectly verified.

b. *Neutrality* means that financial reporting information must be free from bias intended to influence a decision or outcome. To that end, the common conceptual framework should not include conservatism or prudence among the desirable qualitative characteristics of financial reporting information. However, the framework should note the continuing need to be careful in the face of uncertainty.

c. Although empirical research may provide evidence useful in standard-setting decisions, for example, in assessing trade-offs between desirable qualities, the conceptual framework project should not seek to develop empirical measures of faithful representation or its component qualities.

3. *Comparability* is an important characteristic of financial reporting information and should be included in the converged conceptual framework. Comparability, which enables users to identify similarities in and differences between economic phenomena, should be distinguished from consistency (the consistent use of accounting methods). Concerns about comparability or consistency should not preclude financial reporting information that is of greater relevance or that more faithfully represents the economic phenomena that information purports to represent. If such concerns arise, disclosures can help to compensate for lessened comparability or consistency.

4. *Understandability* also is an essential characteristic of financial reporting information and should be included in the converged conceptual framework. Information is made more understandable by aggregating, classifying, characterizing, and presenting it clearly and concisely. Whether reported information is sufficiently understandable depends on who is using it. The information in general purpose external financial reports should be understandable to financial statement users who have a reasonable knowledge of business and economic activities and accounting and a willingness to study the information with reasonable diligence. Relevant information should not be excluded because it is too complex or difficult for some users to understand.

5. *Materiality* relates not only to relevance, but also to faithful representation. Materiality should be included in the converged framework as a screen or filter to determine whether information is sufficiently significant to influence the decisions of users in the context of the entity, rather than as a qualitative characteristic of financial reporting information.

2.12.3 Next steps

Each of the eight phases will be examined in a discussion paper. The two boards published identical discussion papers on objectives and qualitative characteristics in July 2006. Papers on elements and reporting entity are planned for 2007.

2.13 Summary

The IASB Framework describes the basic concepts that underlie financial statements prepared in conformity with International Financial Reporting Standards. The Framework serves as a guide to the board in developing accounting standards and in resolving accounting issues that are not addressed directly in an International Financial Reporting Standard.

The Framework identifies the principal classes of users of an entity's general purpose financial statements and states that the objective of financial statements is to provide information – about the financial position, performance and changes in financial position of an entity – that is useful in making economic decisions. It specifies the qualities that make financial information useful; namely, understandability, relevance, reliability and comparability. The Framework also defines the basic elements of financial statements (assets, liabilities, equity, income and expenses) and discusses the criteria for recognising and measuring them.

The IASB and the FASB are jointly working on a project to revise and conform their conceptual Frameworks.

1. Why is a conceptual Framework needed if we have a comprehensive body of accounting standards such as the IFRSs?
2. Who are the main users of the conceptual Framework? For what purposes do these use the Framework?
3. What are general purpose financial statements? What might be an example of 'special purpose financial statements' as distinct from 'general purpose financial statements'?
4. Who does the IASB see as the primary users of general purpose financial statements?
5. What is the problem if the auditor is engaged both to prepare the company's financial statements and to audit them?
6. What is financial position? Which financial statement presents financial position?
7. What is performance? Which financial statements present performance?
8. Does performance include only (a) the results when an entity sells its goods and services or, in addition, (b) changes in the values of its assets while it holds them even in the absence of a sale transaction?
9. What are some examples of information that you can learn from the cash flow statement that is not apparent from the balance sheet and income statement?
10. Relevance is one of the key qualities of the information in financial statements. What does relevance mean? For what is the information relevant?
11. Explain by means of an example what is meant by the 'trade-off of relevance and reliability' in accounting information.
12. Under the IASB Framework, an asset is recognised 'when it is probable that the future economic benefits will flow to the entity'. What future economic benefits does that principle refer to? Is it always cash flows to the entity? If not, what are other examples of future economic benefits?
13. What is the difference between consistency of accounting information and comparability of accounting information?
14. The IASB and the FASB in their current joint project to converge their conceptual Frameworks have decided to replace the qualitative characteristic of 'reliability' (described in section 2.8.3) with 'faithful representation of real-world economic phenomena' (described in section 2.12.2). What do you see as the benefits (or shortcomings) of that proposed change?

EXERCISES

EXERCISE 2.1 ★

What is income?

A government gives a piece of land to a company. The company builds a factory on the land and agrees to employ a certain number of people at the factory for a certain period of time. Considering the definition of income in the IASB Framework, do you think the fair value of the land is income to the company or is it a direct credit to equity?

EXERCISE 2.2 ★

Meaning of faithful representation and reliability

A company buys a costly item of electronic equipment that it expects will have a useful life of six years, and it depreciates the asset over that period. By the end of year 3, the item of equipment is obsolete and the company is no longer using it. It is still in the company's balance sheet at the remaining undepreciated one-half of original cost, which the company says (a) is a faithful representation of its circumstances since the company still owns the asset, and (b) is a reliable measure of the asset. Comment on the company's view.

EXERCISE 2.3	★

General purpose financial statements

In some countries, the income tax authority requires companies to prepare a balance sheet and income statement that conform to national laws for measuring taxable income. Would those financial statements be 'general purpose financial statements'? Why?

EXERCISE 2.4	★

Company managers as users of financial statements

The IASB does not include the management of a company as one of the primary users of general purpose financial statements. Why do you suppose that is?

EXERCISE 2.5	★

What is income?

An oil and gas exploration company reports that its engineers and geologists have discovered what they believe to be a sizable quantity of new petroleum reserves on a property in which the company has a one-half interest. The company's share price rises significantly on this announcement. Under the IASB Framework, would income be recognised?

EXERCISE 2.6	★

Authority of the Framework

A company's senior financial officer says 'I always follow IFRSs in preparing my company's financial statements. But the IASB's Framework is a lot of conceptual theory that doesn't affect me directly. It's not an accounting standard, so I have never read it.' Is the IASB Framework a standard? Is it relevant to preparing IFRS financial statements? If so, how?

PROBLEMS	

PROBLEM 2.1	★

Relevant information for an investment company

A year ago you bought shares of stock in an investment company. The investment company in turn buys, holds and sells shares of business entities. You want to use the financial statements of the investment company to assess its performance over the past year.

(a) What financial information about the investment company's holdings would be most relevant to you?

(b) Compare the reliability of the financial statements if the investment company buys only shares in listed companies with their reliability if the company invests in shares of private high-tech companies.

(c) The investment company earns profits from appreciation of its investment securities and from dividends received. How would the concepts of recognition in the IASB Framework apply here?

PROBLEM 2.2	★

Meaning of 'probable future benefits'

The IASB Framework includes 'probable future economic benefits' as a condition for recognising an element of financial statements. How would you interpret 'probable' in this context?

PROBLEM 2.3	★

Measuring inventories of gold and silver

IAS 2 *Inventories* allows producers of gold and silver to measure inventories of these commodities at selling price even before they have sold them, which means a profit is recognised at production. In nearly all other industries, however, profit is recognised only when the inventories are sold to outside customers. What concept/s in the Framework might the IASB have considered with regard to accounting for gold and silver production?

PROBLEM 2.4 ★

Recognising a loss from a lawsuit

The law in your community requires store owners to shovel snow and ice from the pavement in front of their shops. You failed to do that, and a pedestrian slipped and fell, resulting in serious and costly injury. The pedestrian has sued you. Your lawyers say that while they will vigorously defend you in the lawsuit, you should expect to lose $25 000 to cover the injured party's costs. A court decision, however, is not expected for at least a year. What aspects of the IASB Framework might help you in deciding the appropriate accounting for this situation?

PROBLEM 2.5 ★

Financial statements of a real estate investor

An entity purchases a rental property for $10 million as an investment. The building is fully rented, and is in a prosperous area. At the end of the current year, the entity hires an appraiser who reports that the fair value of the building is $15 million plus or minus 10%. Depreciating the building over 50 years would reduce the carrying amount to $9.8 million.

(a) What are the relevance and reliability accounting considerations in deciding how to measure the building in the entity's financial statements?

(b) Does the IASB Framework lead to measuring the building at $15 million? Or at $9.8 million? Or at some other amount?

PROBLEM 2.6 ★

Need for the Framework v. interpretations

Applying the Framework is subjective and requires judgement. Would the IASB be better off to abandon the Framework entirely and instead rely on a very active interpretations committee that develops detailed guidance in response to requests from constituents?

PROBLEM 2.7 ★

Conservatism

'When I studied accounting, we were taught always to be conservative in recognition or measurement. When in doubt, don't put the asset on the balance sheet or, if it's there, write it down at the first sign of trouble. Never recognise profit until a sale takes place.' How do this person's comments relate to the IASB Framework?

PROBLEM 2.8 ★

Authoritativeness of the Framework

Was the IASB wise in amending IAS 8 to make the Framework the mandatory source of guidance on an accounting question in the absence of a special standard dealing with the subject? What are the pluses and minuses of doing this?

PROBLEM 2.9 ★

Meaning of 'decision useful'

What is meant by saying that accounting information should be 'decision useful'?

PROBLEM 2.10 ★★

Performance of a business entity

A financial analyst says: 'I advise my clients to invest for the long term. Buy good stocks and hang onto them. Therefore I am interested in a company's long-term earning power. Accounting standards that result in earnings volatility obscure long term earning power. Accounting should report earning power by deferring and amortising costs and revenues.' How does the IASB Framework relate to this analyst's view of financial statements?

PROBLEM 2.11 ★★

Going concern

What measurement principles might be most appropriate for a company that has ceased to be a going concern (for example, it is in bankruptcy and the receiver is seeking buyers for its assets)?

PROBLEM 2.12 ★★

Economic consequences of accounting standards

After the OPEC oil embargo of 1973, the US government passed a law aimed at encouraging domestic exploration for oil and gas in order to make the US less dependent on foreign suppliers. At about the same time, the FASB proposed an accounting standard that would have required oil and gas exploration companies to charge to expense, immediately, all unsuccessful exploration costs (no oil or gas discovered). Some exploration companies had been capitalising and amortising such unsuccessful costs. They said the FASB's proposed new standard would cause them to report losses, their sources of venture capital would disappear, and they would stop their exploration activities, which is contrary to government economic policy. How does the IASB Framework relate to the accounting question? Focus on the issue of neutrality.

PROBLEM 2.13 ★★

Assessing probabilities in accounting recognition

The IASB Framework defines an asset as a resource from which future economic benefits are expected to flow. 'Expected' means it is not certain, and involves some degree of probability. At the same time the Framework establishes, as a criterion for recognising an asset, that 'it is probable that any future economic benefit associated with the item will flow to or from the entity.' Again, an assessment of probability is required. Is there a redundancy, or possibly some type of inconsistency, in including the notion of probability in both the asset definition and recognition criteria?

PROBLEM 2.14 ★★

Purchase orders

An airline places a non-cancellable order for a new airplane with one of the major commercial aircraft manufacturers at a fixed price, with delivery in 30 months and payment in full to be made at delivery.
(a) Under the IASB Framework, do you think the airline should recognise any asset or liability at the time it places the order?
(b) One year later, the price of this airplane model has risen by 5%, but the airline had locked in a fixed, lower price. Under the Framework, do you think the airline should recognise any asset (and gain) at the time when the price of the airplane rises? If the price fell by 5% instead of rising, do you think the airline should recognise a liability (and loss) under the Framework?

PROBLEM 2.15 ★★

Defining an asset

The Framework definition of an asset is: 'An asset is a resource controlled by the entity as a result of past events and from which future economic benefits are expected to flow to the entity.' When one company (the parent) owns 100% of another company (the subsidiary), the parent prepares consolidated financial statements in which the subsidiary's assets (as well as its liabilities, revenues and expenses) are added line by line to those of the parent. Is this consistent with the Framework definition of an asset? What definition of 'entity' is being used when consolidated financial statements are prepared?

WEBLINK

Visit these websites for additional information:

www.iasb.org   www.iasplus.com
www.asic.gov.au   www.ifac.org
www.aasb.com.au   www.nzica.com
www.accaglobal.com   www.capa.com.my

REFERENCES

US Financial Accounting Standards Board & International Accounting Standards Board 2006, *Conceptual Framework – Joint Project of the IASB and FASB*, viewed 28 April 2006, <www.fasb.org/project/conceptual_framework.shtml>

US Securities and Exchange Commission 2003, *Study Pursuant to Section 108(d) of the Sarbanes-Oxley Act of 2002 on the Adoption by the United States Financial Reporting System of a Principles-Based Accounting System*, 26 July, viewed 2 May 2006, <www.sec.gov/news/studies/principlesbasedstand.htm>.

PART 2
Elements

PART 2 examines accounting issues and international standards relating to the elements of financial statements – assets, liabilities, revenues and equity. Chapter 3 deals with the recognition of movements in equity. Revenue and its recognition are discussed in chapter 4. Accounting standards on financial instruments and tax-effect accounting are covered in chapters 6 and 8 respectively. Chapter 5 focuses on liabilities in the form of provisions and contingent liabilities. Accounting for equity and financial instruments is covered in chapter 7. Chapters 9–11 and 14 are concerned with the recognition, measurement and disclosure of inventories; property, plant and equipment; intangibles; and leased assets. Differences in accounting for assets and liabilities acquired via business combinations are addressed in chapter 12. Chapter 13 is concerned with the judgements used in accounting for assets, with the application of an impairment test.

CHAPTER 3
Shareholders' equity: share capital and reserves

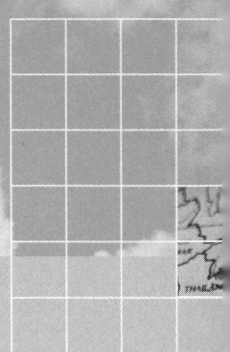

Before studying this chapter, you should understand or, if necessary, revise:
- the IASB Framework.

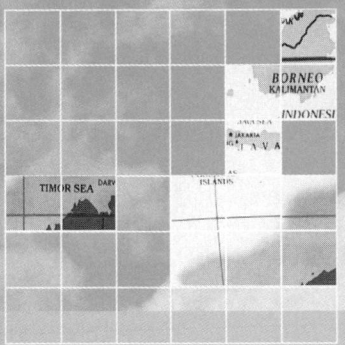

When you have studied this chapter, you should be able to:
1. distinguish between different forms of corporate entities
2. understand the key features of the corporate structure
3. account for the issue of both par value and no-par shares
4. account for share placements
5. account for rights issues
6. account for options
7. account for bonus issues
8. understand the rationale behind share buy-backs and the accounting treatment thereof
9. account for movements in retained earnings, including dividends
10. understand the nature of reserves other than retained earnings
11. prepare note disclosures in relation to equity, as well as a statement of changes in equity.

3.1 Shareholders' equity

The purpose of this chapter is to introduce the various components of the equity section of the balance sheet, namely contributed capital and reserves. The element of capital will differ depending on the nature of the organisation, whether a sole proprietorship, partnership or company. Reserves comprise equity attributable to the owners of the entity other than amounts directly contributed by the owners. An example of the equity section of the balance sheet of a for-profit entity is shown in figure 3.1. It contains an extract from the consolidated balance sheet of Nokia Corporation as at 31 December 2005. The accounts were prepared in accordance with International Financial Reporting Standards (IFRSs), and the extract relating to the shareholders' equity of the group is shown in figure 3.1. Note that the two key components are share capital and reserves.

| | Notes | December 31 | |
		2005 EURm	2004 As revised EURm
SHAREHOLDERS' EQUITY AND LIABILITIES			
Capital and reserves attributable to equity holders of the parent			
Share capital	23	266	280
Share issue premium		2 458	2 366
Treasury shares, at cost		(3 616)	(2 022)
Translation differences		69	(126)
Fair value and other reserves	22	(176)	13
Retained earnings	25	13 154	13 720
		12 155	14 231
Minority interests		205	168
Total equity		12 360	14 399

FIGURE 3.1 Shareholders' equity
Source: Nokia (2005, p. 7).

With a sole proprietor, having a single owner means there is little reason for distinguishing between capital (potentially the initial investment in the business) and profits retained in the business for investment purposes.

Traditionally with partnerships, the rights and responsibilities of the partners are specified in a partnership agreement. This document details how the profits and losses of the partnership are to be divided between the partners, including rules relating to distributions on dissolution of the partnership. In accounting for partnerships, a distinction is generally made for each partner between a capital account, to which amounts invested by a partner are credited, and a current account or retained earnings account, to which a partner's share of profits are credited and from which any drawings are debited. As with a sole proprietorship, there generally is no real distinction between capital contributed and profits retained (unless there is some other specification in the partnership agreement, which is unlikely). Both amounts represent the ongoing investment by the partners. On dissolution of the partnership, the distribution to partners is unaffected by whether an equity balance is capital or retained earnings.

With companies, the situation is different because their formation is generally governed by legislation, and there is normally a clear distinction made between contributed capital and profits retained in the entity. However, it must be understood that, although the laws governing companies in a particular country may require a distinction between capital and other forms of owners' equity, from an accounting point of view there is no real difference between the various classifications of owners' equity. In other words, apart from any legal restrictions such as applying to the distribution of dividends, whether an entity has $200 000 of capital and $100 000 of retained earnings, or $100 000 of capital and $200 000 of retained earnings, is of no real importance. In essence, the entity has $300 000 of equity.

This chapter concentrates on the company as the organisational form of interest, with the major account reflecting contributed equity being share capital. However, as noted above, there is no reason, apart from legal reasons specific to a particular jurisdiction, for the organisational form to require major differences in accounting for the equity of an entity.

LO 1

3.2 Types of companies

Generally, companies can be distinguished by the nature of the ownership, and the rights and responsibilities of the shareholders. Two types of companies are examined in the next section: not-for-profit companies and for-profit companies.

3.2.1 Not-for-profit companies

'Not-for-profit' is not defined in International Financial Reporting Standards. In Australia, whose accounting standards are equivalent to international standards, a not-for-profit entity is defined as an 'entity whose principal objective is not the generation of profit'.

Not-for-profit companies can be divided into government or public sector companies and private not-for-profit sector entities:

- Entities may be established by the government to undertake various activities of the government, such as the supply of water or electricity, the provision of communications and the running of an airline. The government may own all the issued shares of the company, or a controlling interest in the entity. For the government enterprise to be classified as not-for-profit, the primary objective of the entity must be something other than the earning of profit.
- Organisations such as charities may form companies as their preferred organisational structure to limit their liability. The companies may be limited by guarantee, whereby members undertake to contribute a guaranteed amount in the event the company goes into liquidation, but have no rights to dividends or distributions on liquidation. Alternatively, the company may be a non-public company, sometimes called a proprietary company or a closed corporation, where the shares are held by a limited number of shareholders and the shares are not available for purchase by the public.

An example of the equity section of the balance sheet of a not-for-profit entity is shown in figure 3.2, which contains an extract from the 2005 balance sheet of the International Committee of the Red Cross (ICRC) whose financial statements are prepared in accordance with IFRSs. As noted in section 5.2.1 of the significant accounting policies section of the ICRC's 2005 annual report: 'Currently, IFRS do not contain specific guidelines for non-profit organizations and non-governmental organizations concerning the accounting treatment and the presentation of the consolidated financial statements.'

Restricted Reserves	Notes	2005	2004
Total Funds & Foundations	5.3.12	14 462	11 987
Funding of Field Operations	5.3.13		
Field operations with temporary deficit financing		−38 945	−9 487
Donor-restricted contributions		61 943	8 064
Total Funding of Field Operations		22 998	−1 423
Total Restricted Reserves		**37 460**	**10 564**
Unrestricted Reserves			
Reserves designated by the Assembly	5.3.14		
Future operations		147 691	127 605
Operational risks		26 166	25 000
Assets replacement		116 969	99 351
Financial risks		14 933	12 176
Human resources		10 694	8 294
Specific projects		4 516	2 580
Total Designated Reserves		320 969	275 006
Other Unrestricted Reserves			
General reserve		12 500	12 500
Retained surplus at beginning of the year		1 900	1 900
Total Other Unrestricted Reserves		14 400	14 400
Total Unrestricted Reserves		**335 369**	**289 406**
Total RESERVES		**372 829**	**299 970**

FIGURE 3.2   Extract from the balance sheet at 31 December 2005 (in Swiss franc '000) of the International Committee of the Red Cross
Source: International Committee of the Red Cross (2005).

3.2.2   For-profit companies

For-profit companies may take a number of forms:

- Proprietary or closed corporations may be established with limited membership and restrictions on obtaining funds from the public. In some countries, a distinction is made between large and small proprietary companies, with the size being measured in relation to accounting numbers such as gross revenue and gross assets as well as other variables such as the number of employees. Where a proprietary company is classified as large, there is an increased responsibility in relation to the disclosure of information.
- Public companies or open corporations generally have a large number of issued shares, with the ownership being widespread. These companies rely on the public for subscription to share offers as well as the provision of debt funding via secured loans such as debentures or through unsecured loans.

For-profit companies may be:

- listed − their shares are traded on a stock exchange
- unlisted − the shares are traded through brokers and financial institutions
- limited by guarantee − the members undertake to contribute a guaranteed amount in the event of the company going into liquidation
- unlimited − members are liable for all the debts of the company
- no-liability − members are not required to pay any calls on their shares if they do not wish to continue being shareholders in the company.

The exact rights and responsibilities of shareholders in relation to the different forms of companies will differ according to the relevant companies legislation and other laws specific to the country or countries in which the company operates.

As noted by Nobes & Parker (2002, pp. 21–3) the types of organisations and ownership differ substantially across countries:

> In Germany, France and Italy, capital provided by banks is very significant, as are small family-owned businesses. By contrast, in the United States and the United Kingdom there are large numbers of companies that rely on millions of private shareholders for finance ...
>
> A proposed grouping of countries into types by financial system has been formalized by Zysman (1983) as follows:
>
> 1. capital market systems (e.g. United Kingdom, United States)
> 2. credit-based government systems (e.g. France, Japan)
> 3. credit-based financial institution systems (e.g. Germany).
>
> A further point of comparison between 'equity' and 'credit' countries is that, in the latter countries, even the relatively few listed companies may be dominated by shareholders who are bankers, governments or founding families. For example, in Germany, the banks in particular are important owners of companies as well as providers of debt finance ... In such countries as Germany, France or Italy, the banks or the state will, in many cases, nominate directors and thus be able to obtain information and affect decisions.

Table 3.1 shows the distribution of the world's largest 500 companies by country, measured by revenue. The United States of America and Japan contain the largest number of top companies. Table 3.2 shows the major stock exchanges of the world and the market capitalisation of the companies on those exchanges. Many companies list on a number of stock exchanges; Nokia, for example, is quoted on the following stock exchanges:

- HEX, Helsinki (quoted since 1915)
- Frankfurter Wertpapierborse (quoted since 1988)
- Stockholmsborsen (quoted since 1983)
- New York Stock Exchange (quoted since 1994).

Countries with larger capital markets tend to dominate the overall world market, as movements in these markets have immediate effects on other economies. Note, however, that the size of a country's market does not necessarily correlate with the sophistication of the accounting and regulatory regimes of that country.

TABLE 3.1	Share of the world's top 500 companies (distribution by revenue)		
Australia	9	Luxembourg	1
Belgium	3	Malaysia	1
Belgium/Netherlands	1	Mexico	2
Brazil	3	Netherlands	14
Britain	35	Norway	2
Britain/Netherlands	2	Russia	3
Canada	13	Saudi Arabia	1
China	16	Singapore	1
Denmark	2	South Korea	11
Finland	3	Spain	8
France	39	Sweden	7
Germany	37	Switzerland	11
India	5	Taiwan	2
Ireland	1	Thailand	1
Italy	8	Turkey	1
Japan	81	United States of America	176
			500

Source: Fortune magazine (2005).

TABLE 3.2	Major stock exchanges at 1 January 2000			
Country	Exchange	Domestic listed companies	Market capitalisation of domestic listed companies	Market capitalisation as % of United Kingdom
Europe				
France	Paris	980	918	50
Germany	Federation of Exchanges	933	888	48
Italy	Italian	264	451	25
Netherlands	Amsterdam	424	504	27
Spain	Madrid	718	267	15
Switzerland	–	239	420	23
United Kingdom	London	2 292	1 834	100
North America				
Canada	Toronto	1 409	488	27
United States	NASDAQ	4 400	3 218	176
	New York	2 619	7 135	389
Asia				
China	Hong Kong	688	376	21
Japan	Tokyo	1 894	2 764	151
Australasia				
Australia	Australian	1 217	263	14

Source: Based on London Stock Exchange, *Fact File*, 2000, p. 19 and cited in Nobes & Parker (2002, p. 12).

LO 2

3.3 Key features of the corporate structure

The choice of the company as the preferred form of organisational structure brings with it certain advantages, such as limited liability to shareholders. It also comes with certain disadvantages, such as making the entity subject to increasing government regulation including the forced and detailed disclosure of information about the company. Some features of the company structure that affect the subsequent accounting for a company are described below.

The use of share capital

The ownership rights in a company are generally represented by shares; that is, the share capital of a company comprises a number of units or shares. Each share represents a proportional right to the net assets of the company and, within a class of shares, all shares have the same equal rights. These shares are generally transferable between parties. As a result, markets have been established to provide investors with an ability to trade in shares. Where active markets exist, such as with organised stock exchanges, the fair value of a company's shares at a point in time may be reliably determined. A further advantage of transferability is that a change in ownership by one shareholder selling shares to a new investor does not have an effect on the continued existence and operation of the company.

Besides the right to share equally in the net assets, and hence the profits and losses of a company, each share has other rights, including:

• *the right to vote for directors of the company.* This establishes the right of shareholders to have a say as owners in the strategic direction of the company. Where there are a large number of owners in a company, there is generally a separation between ownership and management. The shareholders thus employ professional managers (the directors) to manage the organisation, these managers then providing periodic reports to the shareholders on the financial performance and position of the company. Some directors are executive directors, being employed as executives in the company, while others have non-executive roles. The directors are elected at the annual general meeting of the company, and shareholders exercise their voting rights to elect the directors. The shareholders may vote in person, or by proxy. In relation to the latter, a shareholder may authorise another party to vote on his or her behalf at the meeting; the other party could be the chairman of the company's board.

- *the right to share in assets on the winding-up or liquidation of the company.* The rights and responsibilities of shareholders in the event of liquidation are generally covered in legislation specific to each country, as are the rights of creditors to receive payment in preference to shareholders.
- *the right to share proportionately in any new issues of shares of the same class.* This right is sometimes referred to as the pre-emptive right. It ensures that a shareholder is able to retain the same proportionate ownership in a company, and that this ownership percentage cannot be diluted by the company issuing new shares to other investors, possibly at prices lower than the current fair value. However, the directors may be allowed to make limited placements of shares under certain conditions.

Limited liability

When shares are issued, the maximum amount payable by each shareholder is set. Even if a company incurs losses or goes into liquidation, the company cannot require a shareholder to provide additional capital. In some countries, shares are issued with a specific amount stated on the share certificate, this amount being called the par value of the share. For example, a company may issue one million shares each with a par value of $1, the company then receiving share capital of $1 million.

Par value shares may also be issued at a premium. For example, where a company requires share capital of $2 million, one million $1 shares may be issued at a premium of $1 per share; in this case, each shareholder is required to pay $2 per share. Similarly, par value shares may be issued at a discount. For example, where a company issues $1 shares at a discount of 20c, the company requires each shareholder to pay 80c per share. The only real purpose of the par value is to establish the maximum liability of the shareholder in relation to the company. Legislation in some countries restricts the issue of shares at a discount, and also establishes the subsequent uses of any share premium received on a share.

Note that the par value does not represent a fair or market value of the share. At the issue date, it would be expected that the par value, plus the premium or minus the discount, would represent the market value of the share. In some countries, such as Australia, the use of par value shares has been replaced by the issue of shares at a specified price with no par value. For example, a company may issue 1000 shares in 2004 at $3 per share, and in 2007 it may issue another 1000 shares at $5 per share. In 2007, the company then has 2000 shares and a share capital of $8000. The issue price becomes irrelevant subsequent to the issue, the key variables being the number of shares issued and the amount of share capital in total. The liability of each shareholder is limited to the issue price of the shares at the time of issue.

The feature of limited liability protects shareholders by limiting the contribution required of shareholders. This then places limitations on the ability of creditors to access funds for the repayment of company debts. To protect creditors, many countries have enacted legislation that prohibits companies from distributing capital to shareholders in the form of dividends. Dividends are then payable only from profits, not out of capital.

Different forms of capital

Shares are issued with specific rights attached. Shares are then given different names to signify differences in rights.

The most common form of share capital is the ordinary share or common stock. These shares have no specific rights to any distributions of profit by the company, and ordinary shareholders are often referred to as 'residual' equity holders in that these shareholders obtain what is left after all other parties' claims have been met. An example of a company that has only one class of share is Nokia. Information on its shares as at 31 December 2005 was provided in its 2005 annual report in note 15 to the financial statements of the parent company. Part of this information is shown in figure 3.3.

Share capital and shares Dec. 31, 2005	2005	2004	2003	2002	2001
Share capital, EURm	266	280	288	287	284
Shares (1000, par value EUR 0.06)	4 433 887	4 663 761	4 796 292	4 787 907	4 737 530
Number of registered shareholders[1]	126 352	142 095	133 991	129 508	116 352

(1) Each account operator is included in the figure as only one registered shareholder.

FIGURE 3.3 Share capital, Nokia
Source: Nokia (2005, p. 44).

Another form of share capital is the preference share. As the name implies, holders of preference shares generally have a preferential right to dividends over the ordinary shareholders. Note firstly that the name of the instrument does not necessarily indicate the rights associated with that instrument. As is discussed in chapter 6, some preference shares are in reality not equity but liabilities, or they may be compound instruments being partially debt and partially equity. Secondly, the rights of preference shareholders may be very diverse. Some preference shares have a fixed dividend; for example, a company may issue preference shares at $10 each with a 4% dividend per annum, thus entitling the shareholder to a 40c dividend per annum. Other common features of preference shares are:

- *cumulative versus non-cumulative shares.* Where a preference share is cumulative, if a dividend is not declared in a particular year, the right to the dividend is not lost but carries over to a subsequent year. The dividends are said to be in arrears. With non-cumulative shares, if a dividend is not paid in a particular year, the right to that dividend is lost.
- *participating versus non-participating shares.* A participating share gives the holder the right to share in extra dividends. For example, if a company has issued 8% participating preference shares and it pays a 10% dividend to the ordinary shareholders, the preference shareholders may be entitled to a further 2% dividend.
- *convertible versus non-convertible shares.* Convertible preference shares may give the holder the right to convert the preference shares into ordinary shares. The right to convert may be at the option of the holder of the shares or at the option of the company itself. As explained in chapter 6, convertible preference shares may need to be classified into debt and equity components.
- *converting preference shares.* With convertible preference shares, whether a conversion into ordinary shares ever occurs depends upon the exercise of an option, but with converting preference shares the terms of issue are such that the shares must convert into ordinary shares at a specified point of time. As explained in chapter 6, converting preference shares may need to be classified as debt.
- *redeemable versus non-redeemable shares.* Subsequent to their issue, redeemable preference shares may be bought back from the shareholders by the company at a price generally established in the terms of issue of the shares. The option to redeem is normally held by the company.

Returns to shareholders

As already noted, the shareholders of ordinary shares have no specific rights to dividends, being residual equity holders. Whether a dividend is paid depends on the decisions made by the directors. Regulations in some countries may specify from which equity accounts the dividends can be paid, or whether the company has to meet solvency tests before paying dividends. In some cases, the directors may be allowed to propose a dividend at year-end, but this proposal may have to be approved by the shareholders in the annual general meeting.

LO 3

3.4 Contributed equity: issue of share capital

Once a business has decided to form a public company, it will commence the procedures necessary to issue shares to the public. The initial offering of shares to the public to invest in the new company is called an initial public offering (IPO). To arrange the sale of the shares, the business that wishes to float the company usually employs a promoter, such as a stockbroker or a financial institution, with expert knowledge of the legal requirements and experience in this area. Once the promoter and the managers of the business agree on the structure of the new company, a prospectus is drawn up and lodged with the regulating authority. The prospectus contains information about the current status of the business and its future prospects.

In order to ensure that the statements in the prospectus are accurate, a process of due diligence is undertaken by an accounting firm and a report attached. To ensure that the sale of shares is successful, an underwriter may be employed. The role of the underwriter is to advise on such matters as the pricing of the issue, the timing of the issue and how the issue will be marketed. One of the principal reasons for using an underwriter is to ensure that all the shares are sold, as the underwriter agrees to acquire all shares that are not taken up by the public.

The costs of issuing the shares can then be quite substantial and could amount to 10% of the amount raised. The costs include costs associated with preparing and printing the relevant documentation and marketing the share issue, as well as the fees charged by the various experts consulted which could include accountants, lawyers and taxation specialists. Accounting for these costs is covered in paragraph 31 of IFRS 3 *Business Combinations*:

> Similarly, the costs of issuing equity instruments are an integral part of the equity issue transaction, even when the equity instruments are issued to effect a business combination, rather than costs directly attributable to the combination. Therefore, entities shall not include such costs in the cost of a business combination. In accordance with IAS 32 *Financial Instruments: Disclosure and Presentation*, such costs reduce the proceeds from the equity issue.

The costs are then treated as a reduction in share capital such that the amount shown in share capital immediately after the share issue is the net amount available to the company for operations. The accounting for share issue costs is demonstrated in the next section.

Any costs associated with the formation of the company that cannot be directly related to the issue of the shares, such as registration of the company name, are expensed as the cost is incurred. These outlays do not meet the definition of an asset as there are no expected future economic benefits associated with these outlays that can be controlled by the company.

3.4.1 Issue of no-par shares

ILLUSTRATIVE EXAMPLE 3.1

Issue of no-par shares

Malaga Ltd issues 500 no-par shares for cash at $10 each, incurring share issue costs of $450. Malaga Ltd records on its share register the number of shares issued, and makes the following journal entry:

Cash	Dr	5 000	
Share capital	Cr		5 000
(Issue of 500 $10 shares)			
Share capital	Dr	450	
Cash	Cr		450
(Share issue costs)			

If cash is collected from applicants for shares before the shares are issued, the company records the cash received in a cash trust account, and raises an application account to record the balance prior to the issue of the shares. For example, if application monies of $5000 were collected during the month of January and the shares were issued at the end of January, the journal entries would be:

January 1–30	Cash trust	Dr	5 000	
	Application	Cr		5 000
	(Monies received from applicants for shares)			
31	Application	Dr	5 000	
	Share capital	Cr		5 000
	(Issue of shares applied for)			
	Cash	Dr	5 000	
	Cash trust	Cr		5 000
	(Transfer from cash trust on issue of shares)			

The reason for raising the cash trust account is that there may be a minimum number of applications that have to be received in order for the share issue to proceed. When the minimum subscription is not received or applicants are allotted fewer shares than they applied for, application monies collected are paid back to the applicants via the cash trust account.

Shares in limited liability companies are generally issued on a fully paid basis, but, in some cases, shares may be issued so that part of the issue price is payable immediately and part is required to be paid later. In this case, at the appropriate date the company has to make a call on the shareholders for the subsequent payment.

ILLUSTRATIVE EXAMPLE 3.2

Calls on no-par shares

Mataro Ltd issues 500 no-par shares at $10, the terms of issue requiring the shareholders to pay $6 immediately and $4 in one year's time. The initial journal entry is:

Cash	Dr	3 000	
Share capital	Cr		3 000
(Issue of shares)			

The following journal entry is made in one year's time:

Call	Dr	2 000	
Share capital	Cr		2 000
(Call of $4 on 500 shares)			

When the call money is received from shareholders, the following journal entry is made:

Cash	Dr	2 000	
Call	Cr		2 000
(Receipt of call money)			

Directors may be given the power under the regulations governing the company's operations to forfeit shares where the call is not paid. For example, assume that in illustrative example 3.2 the holders of 10 shares declined to pay the $4 call. The company then forfeits the shares, and the following journal entry is made:

Share capital	Dr	100	
Call	Cr		40
Forfeited shares account	Cr		60
(Forfeiture of 10 shares called to $10 and paid to $6 per share)			

Depending on the regulations in the country in which the company is incorporated, the balance in the forfeited shares account may be refunded to the shareholders and the shares cancelled; in this case the account is classified as a liability. If the balance in the forfeited shares account is retained by the company, the account could be called 'Forfeited shares reserve' and be included in equity. Alternatively, the company could decide to reissue the shares. For example, the shares could be reissued as fully paid to $10 per share on payment of $8 per share, with the forfeited shares account being used to fund the difference as well as any costs of reissue. Assuming all the shares were reissued, incurring costs of $5, and any balance of the reserve being returned to the former shareholders, the journal entries are shown on the next page.

Cash	Dr	80	
Forfeited shares account	Dr	20	
Share capital	Cr		100
(Reissue of shares)			
Forfeited shares account	Dr	40	
Share issue costs payable	Cr		5
Payable to shareholders	Cr		35
(Share issue costs and monies refundable to shareholders)			
Share issue costs payable	Dr	5	
Payable to shareholders	Dr	35	
Cash	Cr		40
(Payment of amounts owing)			

3.4.2   Issue of par value shares

Shares issued at a premium

Where shares are issued at a premium, the excess over the par value is credited to an equity account which may be called share premium, additional paid-in capital or share capital in excess of par. The share premium is then a component of contributed equity.

ILLUSTRATIVE EXAMPLE 3.3

Issue of par value shares at a premium

Bilbao Ltd issues 5000 shares of $1 par value at a premium of $2 per share. The journal entry is:

Cash	Dr	15 000	
Share capital	Cr		5 000
Share premium	Cr		10 000
(Issue of shares at a premium)			

Shares issued at a discount

Where shares are issued at a discount, the account used in relation to the discount can be the same as that used for a premium, or it can be a separate discount account. The accounting treatment will vary depending on the regulations governing discounts in particular jurisdictions.

ILLUSTRATIVE EXAMPLE 3.4

Issue of par value shares at a discount

Pampiona Ltd issued 5000 shares of $2 par value at a 50c discount. The journal entry is:

Cash	Dr	7 500	
Discount on shares	Dr	2 500	
Share capital	Cr		10 000
(Issue of shares at a discount)			

3.4.3 Oversubscriptions

An issue of shares by a company may be so popular that it is oversubscribed; that is, there are more applications for shares than shares to be issued. Some investors may then receive an allotment of fewer shares than they applied for, or may not be allotted any shares at all.

An example of shares being oversubscribed was reported in the Melbourne newspaper *The Age* in relation to the share offer made by the airline Virgin Blue in 2003 (see figure 3.4).

$5 billion: Virgin float offer swamped

Virgin Blue's public share offer has tapped into growing interest in the sharemarket, with applications of more than $5 billion for only $558 million of stock.

Investors apparently shrugged off any concerns about a threat to Virgin's growth plans and sharemarket float from Qantas's fledgling discount offshoot, JetStar.

Virgin claims its public offer closed more than 10 times oversubscribed and at the top of its price range.

With Virgin Blue set to start trading on the Australian Stock Exchange with $2.3 billion market capitalisation, the two questions lingering yesterday were whether Sir Richard Branson would reduce his 29.1 per cent stake, and what publicity stunt the Virgin founder had in store for Monday's listing ceremony.

Sir Richard hinted that he might well increase the shares available through the float to 29 per cent of Virgin Blue, which would cut his interest to 25.1 per cent, when he paid credit to the '250 institutions worldwide and many thousands of our customers' who applied for shares.

'Although we have been told by our advisers that demand was over 10 times subscribed at the $2.25 price, we have decided not to price the offering any higher to hopefully allow for a decent aftermarket for the many staff and supporters of Virgin Blue,' Sir Richard said in a statement.

With the float costing Virgin Blue about $20 million, advisers Goldman Sachs, JBWere and Credit Suisse First Boston will get 2.5 per cent of the funds raised plus a 0.5 per cent bonus, worth an estimated $16.7 million.

FIGURE 3.4 Oversubscription of shares
Source: Rochfort, S (2003).

In most cases, excess application monies are simply refunded to the applicants. When this happens, the appropriate journal entries are:

Application	Dr	XXX	
Share capital	Cr		XXX
(Issue of shares applied for)			
Application	Dr	XXX	
Cash	Dr	XXX	
Cash trust	Cr		XXX
(Transfer from cash trust and refund of excess application money)			

Depending on the company's constitution or the terms of the prospectus, an entity may retain the excess application money as an advance on future calls. In this case the journal entry is:

Application	Dr	XXX	
Calls in advance	Cr		XXX
Share capital	Cr		XXX
(Issue of shares)			

ILLUSTRATIVE EXAMPLE 3.5

Oversubscription of shares

Ibiza Ltd was incorporated on 1 July 2005. The directors offered to the general public 100 000 ordinary shares for subscription at an issue price of $2. The company received applications for 200 000 shares. The directors then decided to issue 150 000 shares, returning the balance of application money to the unsuccessful applicants.

The appropriate journal entries are:

Cash trust	Dr	400 000	
Application	Cr		400 000
(Money received on application)			
Application	Dr	300 000	
Share capital	Cr		300 000
(Issue of shares)			
Cash	Dr	300 000	
Application	Dr	100 000	
Cash trust	Cr		400 000
(Transfer of cash on issue of shares and refund of excess application money)			

LO 4

3.5 Contributed equity: subsequent movements in share capital

Having floated the company, the directors may at a later stage decide to make changes to the share capital. These changes may result in both increases and decreases in the share capital of the company. For example, in Australia the Australian Stock Exchange (ASX) reported the information shown in figure 3.2 in relation to equity capital issues on the ASX. Note that the popularity of the various types changes over time as the economy changes.

Type	1990	1995	2000
	A$m	A$m	A$m
New floats	463	4 112	10 250
Rights issues	2 347	2 867	2 147
Placements	1 060	2 104	[a]12 358
Options, calls, staff plans	1 043	1 633	3 068
Dividend reinvestment	2 514	3 264	3 719
Total	7 427	13 980	31 542

[a] Includes the $6.4 billion second instalment on second Telstra issue

FIGURE 3.5 Equity capital issues on the Australian Stock Exchange
Source: Australian Stock Exchange (2001, p. 34).

In its 2005 annual report, Nokia reported the authorisation given by shareholders at the annual general meeting to the board of directors to increase the entity's share capital. This authorisation is shown in figure 3.6.

Authorization to increase the share capital

The Board of Directors had been authorized by Nokia shareholders at the Annual General Meeting held on March 25, 2004 to decide on an increase of the share capital by a maximum of EUR 55 500 000 offering a maximum of 925 000 000 new shares. In 2005, the Board of Directors did not increase the share capital on the basis of this authorization. The authorization expired on March 25, 2005.

At the Annual General Meeting held on April 7, 2005 Nokia shareholders authorized the Board of Directors to decide on an increase of the share capital by a maximum of EUR 53 160 000 within one year from the resolution of the Annual General Meeting. The increase of the share capital may consist of one or more issues offering a maximum of 886 000 000 new shares with a par value of EUR 0.06 each. The share capital may be increased in deviation from the shareholders' pre-emptive rights for share subscription provided that from the company's perspective important financial grounds exist such as financing or carrying out of an acquisition or another arrangement or granting incentives to selected members of the personnel. In 2005, the Board of Directors did not increase the share capital on the basis of this authorization. The authorization is effective until April 7, 2006.

At the end of 2005, the Board of Directors had no other authorizations to issue shares, convertible bonds, warrants or stock options.

The Board of Directors proposes to the Annual General Meeting convening on March 30, 2006 that the Board of Directors be authorized to resolve to increase the share capital of the company by issuing new shares, stock options or convertible bonds in one or more issues. The increase of the share capital through issuance of new shares, subscription of shares pursuant to stock options and conversion of convertible bonds into shares, may amount to a maximum of EUR 48 540 000 in total.

As a result of share issuance, subscription of shares pursuant to stock options and conversion of convertible bonds into shares an aggregate maximum of 809 000 000 new shares with a par value of EUR 0.06 may be issued. The authorization is proposed to be effective until March 30, 2007, or in the event that the new Companies Act has been approved by the time of the Annual General Meeting, and enters into force latest on March 30, 2007, this authorization is proposed to be effective until June 30, 2007.

FIGURE 3.6 An authorisation to increase share capital
Source: Nokia (2005, p. 45).

3.5.1 Placements of shares

Rather than issue new shares through an issue to the public or current shareholders, the company may decide to place the shares with specific investors such as life insurance companies and superannuation funds. The advantages to the company of a placement of shares are:

- *speed* – a placement can be effected in a short period of time
- *price* – because a placement is made to other than existing shareholders, and to a market that is potentially more informed and better funded, the issue price of the new shares may be closer to the market price at the date of issue
- *direction* – the shares may be placed with investors who approve of the directions of the company, or who will not interfere in the formation of company policies
- *prospectus* – in some cases, a placement can occur without the need for a detailed prospectus to be prepared.

There are potential disadvantages to the existing shareholders from private placements in that the current shareholders will have their interest in the company diluted as a result of the placement. In some countries, the securities regulations place limits on the amounts of placements of shares without the approval of existing shareholders. Further disadvantages to current shareholders can occur if the company places the shares at a large discount. Again, securities laws are generally enacted to ensure that management cannot abuse the placement process and that current shareholders are protected.

ILLUSTRATIVE EXAMPLE 3.6

Placement of shares

Palma Ltd placed 5000 no-par ordinary shares at $5 each with Majorca Ltd.
The entry in the journals of Palma Ltd is:

Cash	Dr	25 000	
Share capital	Cr -		25 000
(Placement of shares)			

LO 5

3.5.2   Rights issues

A rights issue is an issue of new shares with the terms of issue giving existing shareholders the right to an additional number of shares in proportion to their current shareholding; that is, the shares are offered pro rata. For example, an offer could be made to each shareholder to buy two new shares on the basis of every 10 shares currently held. If all the existing shareholders exercise their rights and take up the shares, there is no change in each shareholder's percentage ownership interest in the company.

Rights issues may be renounceable or non-renounceable. If renounceable, existing shareholders may sell their rights to the new shares to another party during the offer period. As shown on its website in November 2003, the ANZ Bank in Australia issued a prospectus for a 2-for-11 fully underwritten renounceable rights issue to existing shareholders of ANZ of approximately 276.7 million new ordinary shares at an issue price of A$13 per new ordinary share to raise approximately A$3597 million as a part of the purchase price for the acquisition of the National Bank of New Zealand Group. On page 14 of the prospectus, the ANZ Bank (2003) listed the choices available to the eligible shareholders:

- take up the rights in full: the shareholders would thereby apply for the new shares on the appropriate application form, attaching a cheque or money order for $13 per share applied for. The bank noted (page 8) that until the new ordinary shares were allotted, ANZ would hold the application monies in a bank account.
- sell the rights in full on the Australian or New Zealand Stock Exchanges (ASX or NZSX). The shareholders would then instruct their stockbrokers to sell the rights. The prospectus specified the dates on which rights trading would conclude, and shareholders with unsold rights would have to make a final decision on whether to acquire the new shares themselves or forgo the opportunity to take up the new shares. In the event of the rights being unsold, and the existing shareholders not taking up the new shares, the underwriters would deal with the rights.
- sell part of the rights on ASX or NZSX and take up the balance
- transfer all or part of the rights to another person other than via ASX or NZSX. The existing shareholder would then forward to the ANZ a completed renunciation form, the transferee's application form and cheque or money order.

- do nothing. In this case, the underwriters would endeavour to sell the rights to institutional investors at a minimum of $13 per share, with the proceeds less brokerage and other expenses being paid to the existing shareholders.

If the rights issue is non-renounceable, a shareholder is not allowed to sell his or her rights to the new shares and must either accept or reject the offer to acquire new shares in the company.

A major difference between an issue of shares to the public and a rights issue is that with the former, the offer comes from the applicant (the prospective shareholder) and it is for the company to accept or reject the offer. With a rights issue, the prospectus constitutes an offer, which may be accepted or rejected by the existing shareholder.

ILLUSTRATIVE EXAMPLE 3.7

Rights issue

Tarragona Ltd planned to raise $3.6 million from shareholders through a renounceable one-for-six rights issue. The terms of the issue were 6 million no-par shares to be issued at 60c each, applications to be received by 15 April 2006. The rights issue was fully underwritten. By the due date, the company had received applications for 5 million shares from existing shareholders or parties to whom they had sold their rights. The underwriter acquired the other 1 million shares, and the shares were issued on 20 April 2006.

The journal entries in the company's records are:

15 April	Cash	Dr	3 000 000	
	Application	Cr		3 000 000
	(Application monies)			
	Receivable from underwriter	Dr	600 000	
	Application	Cr		600 000
	(Amount due from underwriter)			
20 April	Cash	Dr	600 000	
	Receivable from			
	underwriter	Cr		600 000
	(Receipt from underwriter)			
	Application	Dr	3 600 000	
	Share capital	Cr		3 600 000
	(Issue of shares)			

LO 6

3.5.3 Options

A company-issued share option is an instrument that gives the holder the right but not the obligation to buy a certain number of shares in the company by a specified date at a stated price. For example, a company could issue options that gave an investor the right to acquire shares in the company at $2 each, with the options having to be exercised before 31 December 2007. The option holder is taking a risk in that the share price may not reach $2 (the option is 'out of the money') or the share price may exceed $2 (the option is 'in the money').

Where the option holder exercises the option, the company increases its share capital as it issues the shares to the option holder. The company could issue these options to its employees as a part of their remuneration package; or in conjunction with another share issue, rights issue or placement as an incentive to take up the shares offered. The option may be issued free. In the case of options issued to employees, for example, the employees may receive the options as payment for past service. Alternatively, the options may only vest; that is, be exercisable if certain conditions are met, such as the employee remaining with the company for a specified period of time. Accounting for such options is covered in IFRS 2 *Share-based Payment*, the details of which are beyond the scope of this chapter. One of the key features of IFRS 2 is the establishment of the measurement principles in relation to such options. In particular, at the date the options are granted, the fair value of the options is determined and this is used in accounting for the options.

To illustrate: assume a company at 30 June 2004 issues 100 options valued at $1 each to a key executive as a payment for past services. Each option entitles the executive to acquire a share in the company at a price of $3, the current market price of the company shares being $2.90. Assume that on 30 November the share price reaches $3.10 and the executive exercises the option. The journal entries required are shown below.

30 June	Wages expense	Dr	100	
	Options	Cr		100
	(Options granted to executive)			
30 November	Cash	Dr	300	
	Options	Dr	100	
	Share capital	Cr		400
	(Exercise of options issued)			

If the share price did not reach $3 within the specified life of the option, then the options would lapse. According to IFRS 2, paragraph 16, the company is then allowed to transfer the balance of the options account to other equity accounts.

Where the options are sold to investors, the company will record an increase in equity. For example, assume A Ltd issued 20 000 options at 50c each to acquire shares in A Ltd at $4 per share. The initial entry recorded by A Ltd is:

	Cash	Dr	10 000	
	Options*	Cr		10 000
	(Issue of options)			

* This account may be called 'Options reserve' or simply 'Other equity'

Options generally have to be exercised by a specific date. Assume that in the case of A Ltd the options had to be exercised by 30 June 2004, and the holders of 18 000 options exercised their rights to acquire A Ltd shares. The journal entries required are:

	Cash	Dr	72 000	
	Share capital	Cr		72 000
	(Issue of shares on exercise of options)			
	Options	Dr	9 000	
	Share capital	Cr		9 000
	(Exercise of options)			

Note that the issue price of those options exercised is treated as part of share capital; in essence, these shareholders are paying $4.50 for their shares in A Ltd. However, the journal entries shown may not always be the appropriate ones. The journal entries that need to be made when options are issued may be affected in particular jurisdictions by legal and taxation implications. For example, in Australia it is possible to 'taint' share capital by transferred amounts to that account from retained earnings or other reserves. This affects the subsequent taxation of dividends and returns of capital. The choice of equity accounts used and accounting for movements between these accounts must always be taken after gaining an understanding of legal and taxation effects.

For the options not exercised, the entity could transfer the options balance of $1000 to share capital or a reserve account including retained earnings. Again, legal and taxation implications should be considered in choosing the appropriate accounts to be used. For the example above where the holders of 2000 options did not exercise those options, the journal entry required when the options lapse is:

Options	Dr	1 000	
Options reserve	Cr		1 000
(Transfer of lapsed options)			

3.5.4 Share warrants

Another form of option is the company-issued warrant. The difference between a warrant and an option is that the warrant is generally attached to another form of financing. For example, the warrant may be attached to an issue of debt, or be given as an incentive to acquire a large parcel of shares in a share issue as an incentive to be involved in the capital raising. The warrants may be detachable or non-detachable. If the latter, then they cannot be traded separately from the shares or debt package to which they were attached. In either case, the warrant has a value and accounting for the issue of warrants is the same as that shown in the previous section for options.

LO 7

3.5.5 Bonus issues

A bonus issue is an issue of shares to existing shareholders in proportion to their current shareholdings at no cost to the shareholders. The company uses its reserves balances or retained earnings to make the issue. The bonus issue is a transfer from one equity account to another, so it does not increase or decrease the equity of the company. Instead, it increases the share capital and decreases another equity account of the company.

To illustrate: assume a company has a share capital consisting of 500 000 shares. If it makes a 1-for-20 bonus issue from its $100 000 general reserve, it will issue 25 000 shares pro rata to its current shareholders. The journal entry required is:

General reserve	Dr	100 000	
Share capital	Cr		100 000
(Bonus issue of 25 000 shares			
from general reserve)			

Although the bonus issue does not have any effect on the equity of the company, empirical evidence from research into the stockmarket effects of bonus issues shows that share prices tend to increase as a result of bonus issues. The explanation for this effect is that the bonus issue is generally an indicator of future dividend increases. Other reasons for a company making a bonus issue include defending against a takeover bid, particularly following the revaluation of the entity's assets; providing a return to the shareholders; or lowering the current price of the company's shares in the expectation that a lower price per share may make them more tradeable.

3.5.6 Share-based transactions

A company may acquire assets, including other entities, with the consideration for the acquisition being shares in the company itself. Accounting for this form of transaction is covered in chapter 12. Accounting for share-based payments is covered in chapter 7.

LO 8

3.6 Share capital: subsequent decreases in share capital

A company may decrease the number of shares issued by buying back some of its own shares. The extent to which a company may buy back its own shares and the frequency with which it may do so are generally governed by specific laws within a jurisdiction. A key feature of such regulations is the protection of creditors, as the company is reducing equity by using cash that would have been available to repay debt. Companies may undertake a share buy-back to:
- increase the worth per share of the remaining shares
- manage the capital structure by reducing equity
- most efficiently manage surplus funds held by the company, rather than pay a dividend or reinvest in other ventures.

IFRSs do not prescribe any accounting treatment for share buy-backs. Consider the situation where an entity has issued the following no-par shares over a period of years:

200 000 shares at $1.00	$200 000
100 000 shares at $1.50	150 000
200 000 shares at $2.00	400 000
500 000 shares	$750 000

Assume the total equity of the entity consists of:

Share capital	$ 750 000
Asset revaluation surplus	20 000
Retained earnings	230 000
	$1 000 000

If the company now buys back 50 000 shares for $2.20 per share, a total of $110 000, what accounts should be affected by the buy-back? Is it necessary to determine which shares from past issues have been repurchased?

In essence, the composition of the $1 million equity of the entity is relatively unimportant — it is all equity. The composition is only important if there are tax or dividend distribution issues associated with particular accounts. In the absence of such considerations, whether the equity is share capital or retained earnings is irrelevant. This is demonstrated below:

	Equity composition A	or	Equity composition B
Share capital (500 000 shares)	$ 750 000		$ 550 000
Asset revaluation surplus	20 000		150 000
Retained earnings	230 000		300 000
	$1 000 000		$1 000 000

The composition of equity here is *per se* irrelevant. Hence, in accounting for the share buy-back, it is immaterial what accounts are affected. The $110 000 write-off could conceivably be taken totally against share capital or retained earnings, or proportionally against all three components of equity. One possible entry is:

Share capital	Dr	100 000	
Retained earnings	Dr	10 000	
Cash	Cr		110 000
(Buy-back of 50 000 shares for $110 000)			

If the shares had been issued at a specific par value, then it would be necessary to identify which particular parcel of shares had been repurchased. The share capital would be reduced by the relevant number of shares repurchased times the par value, and the share premium reduced by the appropriate amount relating to that raised on the original issue of shares not identified as being repurchased. However, any remaining balance could be adjusted against any equity account other than share capital and share premium account.

An example of a repurchase of shares is that undertaken by Nokia and reported in note 15 of its 2005 annual report. This is shown in figure 3.7.

At the Annual General Meeting held on March 25, 2004, Nokia shareholders authorized the Board of Directors to repurchase a maximum of 230 million Nokia shares. In 2005, Nokia repurchased 54 million Nokia shares on the basis of this authorization.

At the Annual General Meeting held on April 7, 2005, Nokia shareholders authorized the Board of Directors to repurchase a maximum of 443 200 000 Nokia shares, representing less than 10% of the share capital and the total voting rights, and to resolve on the disposal of a maximum of 443 200 000 Nokia shares. In 2005, a total of 261 010 000 Nokia shares were repurchased under this buy-back authorization, as a result of which the unused authorization amounted to 182 190 000 shares on December 31, 2005. No shares were disposed of in 2005 under the respective authorization. The shares may be repurchased under the buy-back authorization in order to carry out the company's stock repurchase plan. In addition, the shares may be repurchased in order to develop the capital structure of the company, to finance or carry out acquisitions or other arrangements, to settle the company's equity-based incentive plans, to be transferred for other purposes, or to be cancelled. The authorization to dispose of the shares may be carried out pursuant to terms determined by the Board in connection with acquisitions or in other arrangements or for incentive purposes to selected members of the personnel. The Board may resolve to dispose the shares in another proportion than that of the shareholders' pre-emptive rights to the company's shares, provided that from the company's perspective important financial grounds exist for such disposal. These authorizations are effective until April 7, 2006.

The Board of Directors proposes to the Annual General Meeting convening on March 30, 2006 that the Board of Directors be authorized to repurchase a maximum of 405 million Nokia shares by using unrestricted shareholders' equity. Further, the Board of Directors proposes that the Annual General Meeting authorize the Board of Directors to resolve to dispose a maximum of 405 million Nokia shares. These authorizations are proposed to be effective until March 30, 2007, or in the event that the new Companies Act has been approved by the time of the Annual General Meeting, and enters into force latest on March 30, 2007, these authorizations are proposed to be effective until June 30, 2007.

FIGURE 3.7 Repurchase of shares
Source: Nokia (2005, p. 45).

In some countries, when shares are reacquired, they are held in treasury for reissue instead of being cancelled. Such shares are then referred to as 'treasury shares', and are essentially the same as unissued share capital. For example, if an entity acquires 10 000 of its own shares at $12 per share, it would pass the following entry to record this repurchase:

Treasury shares	Dr	12 000	
Cash	Cr		12 000
(Repurchase of shares)			

In Nokia's 2005 balance sheet (see figure 3.1), the treasury shares are shown as a reduction in total equity because the share capital of the entity has effectively been reduced by the repurchase of the shares. In Christian Dior's 2005 annual report, the fashion house reports treasury shares as part of its current assets. This accounting treatment is explained in note 2.9 to Dior's annual report, shown in figure 3.8.

2.9 – Treasury shares
Treasury shares are recorded at acquisition cost.

Shares held under French market regulations governing stock price adjustments, shares held for employee stock option plans and shares held by subsidiaries on a short-term basis are recorded as assets in the balance sheet.

Shares held under stock option plans are attributed to these plans, for their duration; these shares are recorded as 'less than a year' in the balance sheet when the corresponding options can be exercised immediately or in a period less than a year, and stay classified as 'more than a year' until this date.

When the market value of the treasury shares … becomes less than the acquisition price, a provision for depreciation equal to the amount of the difference is recorded.

For treasury shares allocated to option plans, the calculation of depreciation is made on a per-plan basis when the market value of the share is greater than the option exercise price and in relation to the average cost price for all plans in question when the market value of the share is less than the option exercise price. Moreover, when the value of the shares allocated to option plans, net of depreciation, is greater than the exercise price stipulated by each of the plans, a provision for risks and charges is recorded for the amount of the difference.

In case of disposal of treasury shares, the cost price of the disposed parcel is established according to the first-in first-out (FIFO) method.

Treasury Shares held for a long-term basis or for the purpose of future cancellation or exchange are deducted from shareholders' equity, including the realized capital gains and losses.

FIGURE 3.8 Treasury shares
Source: Dior (2005, p. 77).

3.7 Reserves

'Reserves' is the generic term for all equity accounts other than contributed equity. A major component is the retained earnings account. This account accumulates the annual profit or loss earned by an entity, and is the primary account from which appropriations are made in the form of dividends. As noted in paragraph 99 of IAS 1 *Presentation of Financial Statements*, this standard requires all items of income and expense recognised in a period to be included in profit or loss unless another standard requires otherwise. Hence, in general, the retained earnings account will accumulate the profit or loss earned over the life of the entity. However, as paragraph 99 also notes, other standards require some gains and losses to be reported directly as changes in equity. Some examples are:

- revaluation of property, plant and equipment (see chapter 10)
- particular foreign exchange differences (see chapter 24)
- remeasurements of available-for-sale financial assets (see chapter 8).

These gains and losses are then recognised as part of reserves. As noted in section 3.8.2, entities are required to disclose movements in these accounts in the statement of changes in equity.

LO 9

3.7.1 Retained earnings

'Retained earnings' has the same meaning as 'retained profits' and 'accumulated profit or loss'. The key change in this account is the addition of the profit or loss for the current period. The main other movements in the retained earnings account are:

- dividends paid or declared
- transfers to and from reserves
- changes in accounting policy and errors (see IAS 8 *Accounting Policies, Changes in Accounting Estimates and Errors,* discussed in detail in chapter 15).

Dividends are a distribution from the company to its owners. It is generally the case, under companies legislation, that dividends can be paid only from profits, and not from capital. In some jurisdictions, companies must comply with a solvency test before paying dividends. The purpose in both situations is to protect the creditors, as any money paid to shareholders is money unavailable for paying creditors.

Dividends are sometimes divided into interim and final dividends. Interim dividends are paid during the financial year, while final dividends are declared by the directors at year-end for payment sometime after balance date. In some companies, the eventual payment of the final dividends is subject to approval of the dividend by the annual general meeting. With the final dividend, there is some debate as to when the company should raise a liability for the dividend, particularly where payment of the dividend is subject to shareholder approval. Some would argue that until approval is received there is only a contingent liability, the entity not having a present obligation to pay the dividend until approval is received. Others argue that there is a constructive obligation existing at balance date and, given customary business practice, the entity has a liability at balance date.

In this regard, paragraphs 12 and 13 of IAS 10 *Events after the Balance Sheet Date* state:

12. If an entity declares dividends to holders of equity instruments (as defined in IAS 32 *Financial Instruments: Disclosure and Presentation*) after the balance sheet date, the entity shall not recognise those dividends as a liability at the balance sheet date.

13. If dividends are declared (i.e. the dividends are appropriately authorised and no longer at the discretion of the entity) after the balance sheet date but before the financial statements are authorised for issue, the dividends are not recognised as a liability at the balance sheet date because they do not meet the criteria of a present obligation in IAS 37. Such dividends are disclosed in the notes in accordance with IAS 1 *Presentation of Financial Statements.*

If the dividends are not declared at balance sheet date, no liability is recognised at balance date. When shareholder approval is required for dividends declared prior to balance date, a liability should be recognised only once the annual general meeting approves the dividends, because before that date the entity does not have a present obligation. Until that occurs, the declared dividend is only a contingent liability. (See chapter 5 for further discussion on provisions and contingencies.) It is expected that companies that prefer to raise a liability at year-end will change their regulations or constitution so that dividends can be declared without the need for shareholder approval.

ILLUSTRATIVE EXAMPLE 3.8

Dividends

During the period ending 30 June 2005, the following events occurred in relation to Alicante Ltd:

2004	
25 Sept.	Annual general meeting approves the final dividend of $10 000.
30 Sept.	Alicante Ltd pays the final dividend to shareholders.

2005	
10 Jan.	Alicante Ltd pays an interim dividend of $8 000.
30 June	Alicante Ltd declares a final divided of $12 000, this dividend requiring shareholder approval at the next AGM.

Required

Prepare the journal entries to record the dividend transactions of Alicante Ltd.

Solution

2004				
25 Sept.	Dividends declared	Dr	10 000	
	Dividends payable	Cr		10 000
	(Dividend of $10 000 authorised by annual meeting)			
30 Sept.	Dividends payable	Dr	10 000	
	Cash	Cr		10 000
	(Payment of dividend)			
2005				
10 Jan.	Interim dividend paid	Dr	8 000	
	Cash	Cr		8 000
	(Payment of interim dividend)			

Notes:
1. No entry is required in relation to the final dividend of $12 000. A contingent liability would be recorded in the notes to the 2005 financial statements.
2. The journal entries contain temporary accounts such as 'Dividends declared' and 'Interim dividend paid'. These accounts are useful in preparing the statement of changes in equity (see section 3.8.2) as well as in the worksheet used in the preparation of consolidated financial statements (see chapter 20). At the end of the reporting period, these temporary accounts are transferred to retained earnings:

	Retained earnings	Dr	18 000	
	Dividends declared	Cr		10 000
	Interim dividend paid	Cr		8 000
	(Closing entry)			

LO 10

3.7.2   Other components of equity

Some examples of reserves other than retained earnings are shown below.

Asset revaluation surplus

IAS 16 *Property, Plant and Equipment* allows entities a choice in the measurement of these assets. In particular, entities may choose between measuring the assets at cost (the cost model) or at fair value (the revaluation model). If the fair value basis is chosen, revaluation increments are recognised directly in equity via an asset revaluation surplus. (Details of the accounting under a fair value basis for property, plant and equipment is covered in chapter 10.)

The requirement to use the asset revaluation surplus is effectively a measure adopted by the IASB to stop the increase in the fair value of the assets being recognised immediately in the income statement. It may be argued that this is an application of the prudence concept in that the fair values of the assets may decline in a later period, and to allow the recognition in income of movements in the fair values of assets would introduce volatility into the income statement numbers. However, it may equally be argued that this accounting treatment results in the income statement not showing the total performance of the entity over the period.

Having created an asset revaluation surplus, an entity is not restricted in its subsequent disposition. It may be used for payment of dividends or be transferred to other reserve accounts including retained earnings. Amounts recognised directly in the asset revaluation surplus cannot subsequently be recognised in the income statement even when the revalued asset is disposed of.

Foreign currency translation differences

These differences arise when foreign operations are translated from one currency into another currency for presentation purposes. (Details of the establishment of this account are found in chapter 24.) The changes in wealth as a result of the translation process are thereby not taken through the income statement, and are recognised in income only if and when the investor disposes of its interest in the foreign operation.

Fair value differences

Under IAS 39 *Financial Instruments: Recognition and Measurement*, paragraph 55, gains and losses on available-for-sale financial assets are recognised directly in equity until the financial asset is derecognised. At this time, the cumulative gain or loss previously recognised in equity is recognised in profit or loss. This is a situation where the IASB allows the recycling of reserves to income, an accounting treatment unavailable with other reserves.

ILLUSTRATIVE EXAMPLE 3.9

Reserves

As an example of the disclosure of reserves, the consolidated balance sheet of Nokia at 31 December 2005 contained the information shown in figure 3.9. The translation differences are the result of translating the financial statements of foreign subsidiaries.

		December 31	
	Notes	2005 EURm	2004 As revised EURm
Capital and reserves attributable to equity holders of the parent			
Share capital	23	266	280
Share issue premium		2 458	2 366
Treasury shares, at cost		(3 616)	(2 022)
Translation differences		69	(126)
Fair value and other reserves	22	(176)	13
Retained earnings	25	13 154	13 720
		12 155	14 231
Minority interests		205	168
Total equity		12 360	14 399

FIGURE 3.9 Example of equity accounts including reserves
Source: Nokia (2005, p. 7).

Entities may make transfers between these reserve accounts, or between reserve accounts and other equity accounts such as retained earnings. Where there is a bonus share dividend, a transfer may be made between reserve accounts and share capital. When accounting for retained earnings, as when accounting for dividends, temporary accounts (namely 'Transfer to/from reserve') are used, these being closed at the end of the period to retained earnings. Chapter 10 discusses in detail the application of the revaluation model to property, plant and equipment and the use of that model. IAS 16 *Property, Plant and Equipment* requires the use of an asset revaluation surplus account in accounting for a revaluation increment. Although not specifically stated in IAS 16, increases in an asset revaluation surplus cannot be made via transfers from other reserves or retained earnings because the surplus arises as a result of applying the revaluation model. Paragraph 41 of IAS 16 covers the accounting for an asset revaluation surplus subsequent to its creation. There is no requirement that an asset revaluation surplus must be transferred to retained earnings on derecognition of a revalued asset. IAS 16, however, allows transfers from the surplus account when a revalued asset is derecognised or progressively as the asset is used by the entity.

ILLUSTRATIVE EXAMPLE 3.10

Reserve transfers

During the period ending 30 June 2006, the following events occurred in relation to Espanola Ltd:

10 Jan.	$10 000 transferred from retained earnings to general reserve
18 Feb.	$4000 transferred from asset revaluation surplus to retained earnings
15 June	Bonus share dividend of $50 000, half from general reserve and half from retained earnings

Required

Prepare the journal entries to record these transactions.

Solution

2006				
10 Jan.	Transfer from retained earnings General reserve (Transfer to general reserve)	Dr Cr	10 000	 10 000
18 Feb.	Asset revaluation surplus Transfer to retained earnings (Transfer from asset revaluation surplus)	Dr Cr	4 000	 4 000
15 June	General reserve Bonus dividend paid Share capital (Bonus issue of shares)	Dr Dr Cr	25 000 25 000	 50 000

30 June	Retained earnings
	Transfer to retained earnings
	    Transfer from retained earnings
	    Bonus dividend paid
	(Closing entry)
		Dr
		Dr
		Cr
		Cr
			31 000
			4 000
				
				10 000
				25 000

LO 11

3.8 Disclosure

Disclosures in relation to equity are detailed in IAS 1 *Presentation of Financial Statements*. The disclosures relate to specific items of equity as well as the preparation of a statement of changes in equity.

3.8.1 Specific disclosures

The specific disclosures illustrated in figure 3.10 are required by paragraphs 76, 125 and 126 of IAS 1.

FIGURE 3.10 Specific disclosures on equity required by IAS 1

	IAS 1 para.
Note 21: Company information Mallorca Ltd is a public company registered in Barcelona, Spain. The company's principal activities are the manufacture of woollen goods, ranging from clothing to furnishings for homes and offices. The company is a subsidiary of Montoro Ltd.	*126(a),* *(b), (c)*
Note 22: Share capital and reserves The company has only one class of share capital, namely ordinary shares. Details in relation to these shares are: • 2 million shares have been authorised for issue by the company	*76(a)* *(i)*
	(continued)

• 500 000 shares have been issued fully paid to €3, and 250 000 shares have been issued at €4, but are paid only to €3 per share	*(ii)*
• the shares issued are no-par shares.	*(iii)*

Number of shares issued at 1 January 2006	500 000	*(iv)*
Issued during 2006	250 000	
Number of shares issued at 31 December 2006	750 000	

There are no restrictions on dividends payable to the shareholders.	*(v)*
There are no shares held by subsidiaries or associates of Mallorca Ltd, and the company has not repurchased any shares issued.	*(vi)*
The company has issued 50 000 options to current shareholders, each option entitling the holder to buy an ordinary share in Mallorca Ltd at €2.70, the options having to be exercised by 30 June 2007.	*(vii)*

Reserves	*76(b)*
The plant maintenance reserve of €140 000 was established to inform those with a financial interest in the company that it had a major claim on future funds in relation to the need to maintain the plant in accordance with Spanish government regulations. The asset revaluation surplus of €95 000 has arisen as the company uses the revaluation model to measure its landholdings. Retained earnings accumulates the annual profit or loss of the entity, other than gains or losses taken directly to equity, and the balance at reporting date represents the undistributed profits of the entity.	

Note 23: Dividends	*125(a)*
The directors of Mallorca Ltd in January 2007 proposed dividends of €1 per share for fully paid shares and €0.75 for the partly paid shares, giving a total proposed dividend of €687 500. These dividends have not been recognised in the accounts because their payment is subject to approval by the shareholders at the annual general meeting.	

3.8.2   Statement of changes in equity

Paragraph 96 of IAS 1 requires the preparation of a statement of changes in equity. This paragraph requires the statement to show the following:

(a) profit or loss for the period
(b) each item of income and expense that, as required by other standards, is recognised directly in equity (for example, increases in asset revaluation surplus), and the total of these items
(c) total income and expense for the period, calculated as the sum of (a) and (b)
(d) the cumulative effect of changes in accounting policy and the correction of errors recognised under IAS 8 *Accounting Policies, Changes in Accounting Estimates and Errors*. (See chapter 15 for a detailed analysis of IAS 8.)

Paragraph 97 of IAS 1 contains details of information that may also be included on the face of the statement of changes in equity. If the only information provided on the face of the statement is that required by paragraph 96, the statement must be titled a 'statement of recognised income and expenses'.

Paragraph 97 of IAS 1 also requires the disclosure (either on the face of the statement of changes in equity or in the notes) of:

(a) the amounts of capital transactions with owners — such as new issues of shares or repurchases of shares — and distributions to owners (dividends)
(b) the balance of retained earnings at the beginning of the period and at the balance sheet date, and the movements for the period — this will include dividends and transfers to and from reserves

(c) a reconciliation between the carrying amount of each class of contributed equity capital and each reserve at the beginning and end of the period, separately disclosing each change.

As noted in paragraph 101 of IAS 1, these requirements can be met in a number of ways, including using a columnar format. The statement of changes in equity must contain the information in paragraph 96 of IAS 1. The information required by paragraph 97 may be included in the statement of changes in equity or disclosed in the notes.

Figure 3.11 is a pro-forma report showing the information required on the face of the statement of changes in equity as per paragraph 96 of IAS 1, and figure 3.12 is a pro-forma statement showing the information required by paragraph 97 as a note to the accounts. Figure 3.13 illustrates a statement of changes in equity combining the disclosures required by paragraphs 96 and 97 in a columnar fashion. Figure 3.14 contains the statement of changes in shareholders' equity for the year ended 30 September 2005 as prepared by the ANZ Bank in Australia. This illustrates the pro-forma note disclosures in figure 3.12.

XYZ Group
Statement of recognised income and expense
for the year ended 30 June 2005

	Note	Consolidated		The company	
		2005	2004	2005	2004
		$ million	$ million	$ million	$ million
Gain/loss on revaluation of properties					
Available for sale investments: Valuation gains/(losses) taken to equity ... Transferred to profit or loss on sale					
Exchange differences on translation of foreign operations					
Gain/loss on business combination					
Net income recognised directly in equity					
Profit for the period					
Total recognised income and expense for the period					
	Note	Consolidated		The company	
		2005	2004	2005	2004
Attributable to: Equity holders of the parent Minority interest					
Effect of changes in accounting policy: Equity holders of the parent Minority interest					

FIGURE 3.11 Pro-forma statement of changes in equity in accordance with IAS 1, para. 96

NOTE
Statement of changes in equity for the year ended 30 June 2005
In $millions

	Note	Consolidated		Attributable to shareholders of the parent		The company	
		2005	2004	2005	2004	2005	2004
Share capital							
Balance at start of year							
Dividend reinvestment plan							
Group employee share acquisition scheme							
Group share option scheme							
New issues							
Share buy-back							
Balance at end of year							
Reserves							
Asset revaluation surplus							
Balance at start of year							
Revaluation increment							
Transfers							
Balance at end of year							
Foreign currency translation differences							
Balance at start of year							
Currency translation adjustments							
Balance at end of year							
Business combination valuation reserve							
Balance at start of year							
Increments – new business combinations							
Transfers to other reserves							
Balance at end of year							
Retained earnings							
Total income and expense for the period							
Balance of retained earnings at start of year							
Total available for appropriation							
Dividends paid or declared							
Balance of retained earnings at end of year							
Total equity at end of year							

FIGURE 3.12 Pro-forma note disclosures relating to the statement of changes in equity in accordance with IAS 1, para. 97

FIGURE 3.13   Statement of changes in equity

Consolidated financial statements according to IFRS

Consolidated statements of changes in shareholders' equity, IFRS

Group, EURm	Number of shares (000s)	Share capital	Share issue premium	Treasury shares	Translation differences	Fair value and other reserves	Retained earnings	Before minority interests	Minority interests	Total
Balance at January 1, 2003	4 786 762	287	2 225	(20)	135	(7)	11 661	14 281	173	14 454
Impact of implementing IAS 39(R)						(21)	21			
Revised balance at January 1, 2003	4 786 762	287	2 225	(20)	135	(28)	11 682	14 281	173	14 454
Tax benefit on stock options exercised			13					13		13
Translation differences					(375)			(375)	(33)	(408)
Net investment hedge gains					155			155		155
Cash flow hedges, net of tax[1]						10		10		10
Available-for-sale investments, net of tax						98		98		98
Other increase, net							40	40	8	48
Profit[1]							3 543	3 543	54	3 597
Total recognized income and expense				—	(220)	108	3 583	3 484	29	3 513
Share issue related to acquisitions	1 225	—	18					18		18
Stock options exercised	7 160	1	22					23		23
Stock options exercised related to acquisitions			(6)					(6)		(6)
Share-based compensation[1][2]			41					41		41
Acquisition of treasury shares	(95 339)			(1 363)				(1 363)		(1 363)
Reissuance of treasury shares	460			10				10		10
Dividend							(1 340)	(1 340)	(38)	(1 378)
Total of other equity movements		1	75	(1 353)	—	—	(1 340)	(2 617)	(38)	(2 655)
Revised balance at December 31, 2003	4 700 268	288	2 313	(1 373)	(85)	80	13 925	15 148	164	15 312
Translation differences					(119)			(119)	(16)	(135)
Net investment hedge gains					78			78		78
Cash flow hedges, net of tax[1]						(1)		(1)		(1)
Available-for-sale investments, net of tax						(66)		(66)		(66)
Other decrease, net							(1)	(1)	(5)	(6)
Profit[1]							3 192	3 192	67	3 259

(continued)

Consolidated financial statements according to IFRS
Consolidated statements of changes in shareholders' equity, IFRS

	Number of shares (000s)	Share capital	Share issue premium	Treasury shares	Translation differences	Fair value and other reserves	Retained earnings	Before minority interests	Minority interests	Total
Total recognized income and expense				–	(41)	(67)	3 191	3 083	46	3 129
Stock options exercised	5	–	–							–
Stock options exercised related to acquisitions			(8)					(8)		(8)
Share-based compensation[1][2]			53					53		53
Acquisition of treasury shares	(214 120)			(2 661)				(2 661)		(2 661)
Reissuance of treasury shares	788			14				14		14
Cancellation of treasury shares		(8)	8	1 998			(1 998)	–		–
Dividend					–	–	(1 398)	(1 398)	(42)	(1 440)
Total of other equity movements		(8)	53	(649)	–	–	(3 396)	(4 000)	(42)	(4 042)
Revised balance at December 31, 2004	4 486 941	280	2 366	(2 022)	(126)	13	13 720	14 231	168	14 399

Source: Nokia (2005, p. 10).

Statement of changes in shareholders' equity for the year ended 30 September 2005

	Note	Consolidated 2005 $m	Consolidated 2004 $m	Consolidated 2003 $m	The company 2005 $m	The company 2004 $m
Share capital						
Ordinary shares						
Balance at start of year		8 005	4 175	3 939	8 005	4 175
Dividend reinvestment plan		153	135	115	153	135
Group employee share acquisition scheme		16	47	48	16	47
Group share option scheme		104	86	73	104	86
Group share buyback		(204)	–	–	(204)	–
Rights issues		–	3 562	–	–	3 562
Balance at end of year		8 074	8 005	4 175	8 074	8 005
Preference shares						
Balance at start of year		987	2 212	1 375	987	2 212
New issues[1]		871	–	987	871	–
Buyback of preference shares		–	(1 225)	–	–	(1 225)
Retranslation of preference shares		–	–	(150)	–	–
Balance at end of year		1 858	987	2 212	1 858	987
Total share capital		9 932	8 992	6 387	9 932	8 992
Asset revaluation reserve[2]						
Balance at start and end of year		31	31	31	415	401
Revaluation of investment in controlled entities		–	–	–	–	14
Total asset revaluation reserve		31	31	31	415	415
Foreign currency translation reserve[3]						
Balance at start of year		218	(239)	117	233	228
Currency translation adjustments, net of hedges after tax		(443)	233	(356)	(213)	5
Transfer from general reserve		–	224	–	–	–
Total foreign currency translation reserve (FCTR)		(225)	218	(239)	20	233
General reserve[4]						
Balance at start of year		181	239	237	11	55
TrUEPrS preference share gain on buy back		–	180	–	–	180
Transfers (to) from retained profits/FCTR		–	(238)	2	–	(224)
Total general reserve		181	181	239	11	11
Capital reserve[4]		149	149	149	–	–
Total reserves		136	579	180	446	659
Retained profits						
Balance at start of year		8 336	7 203	5 600	6 996	6 398
Net profit attributable to shareholders of the Company		3 018	2 815	2 348	2 227	1 972
Total available for appropriation		11 354	10 018	7 948	9 223	8 370
Transfers from (to) reserves		–	14	(2)	–	224
Ordinary share dividends provided for or paid	7	(1 877)	(1 598)	(641)	(1 877)	(1 598)
Preference share dividends paid	7	(84)	(98)	(102)	–	–
Retained profits at end of year		9 393	8 336	7 203	7 346	6 996
Total shareholders' equity attributable to shareholders of the Company		19 461	17 907	13 770	17 724	16 647

The notes appearing on pages 6 to 107 form an integral part of these financial statements

1 2005 relates to the issue of 500 000 Euro Trust securities raising $875m net of issue costs of $4m. 2003 relates to the issue of 10 million ANZ Stapled Exchangeable Preferred Securities (ANZ StEPS), raising $1 billion less issue costs of $13 million. Refer note 30

Nature and purpose of reserves

2 Asset revaluation reserve
Prior to 1 October 2000, the asset revaluation reserve was used to record certain increments and decrements on the revaluation of non-current assets. As the Group has elected to adopt deemed cost in accordance with AASB 1041, the balance of the reserve is not available for future non-current asset write downs while the Group remains on the deemed cost basis

3 Foreign currency translation reserve
Exchange differences arising on translation of foreign self-sustaining operations are taken to the foreign currency translation reserve, as described in accounting policy note 1(v)

4 General reserve and Capital reserve
The balance of these reserves have resulted from prior period allocations of retained profits and may be released to retained profits

FIGURE 3.14 Disclosures relating to the statement of changes in equity

Source: ANZ Bank (2005).

3.9 Summary

The corporate form of organisational structure is a popular one in many countries, particularly because of the limited liability protection that it affords to shareholders. These companies' operations are financed by a mixture of equity and debt. In this chapter the focus is on the equity of a corporate entity. The components of equity recognised generally by companies are share capital, other reserves and retained earnings. Share capital in particular is affected by a variety of financial instruments developed in the financial markets, offering investors instruments with an array of risk-return alternatives. Each of these equity alternatives has its own accounting implications. The existence of reserves is driven by traditional accounting as well as the current restrictions in some accounting standards for some wealth increases to be recognised directly in equity rather than in current income. Even though definite distinctions are made between the various components of equity, it needs to be recognised that they are all equity and differences relate to jurisdictional differences in terms of restrictions on dividend distribution, taxation effects and differences in rights of owners. IAS 1 requires detailed disclosures in relation to each of the components of equity.

1. Discuss the nature of a reserve. How do reserves differ from the other main components of equity?
2. A company announces a final dividend at the end of the financial year. Discuss whether a dividend payable should be recognised.
3. The telecommunications industry in a particular country has been a part of the public sector. As a part of its privatisation agenda, the government decided to establish a limited liability company called Telecom Plus, with the issue of 10 million $3 shares. These shares were to be offered to the citizens of the country. The terms of issue were such that investors had to pay $2 on application and the other $1 per share would be called at a later time. Discuss:
   (a) the nature of the limited liability company, and in particular the financial obligations of acquirers of shares in the company
   (b) the journal entries that would be required if applications were received for 11 million shares.
4. Why would a company wish to buy back its own shares? Discuss.
5. A company has a share capital consisting of 100 000 shares issued at $2 per share, and 50 000 shares issued at $3 per share. Discuss the effects on the accounts if:
   (a) the company buys back 20 000 shares at $4 per share
   (b) the company buys back 20 000 shares at $2.50 per share.
6. A company has a share capital consisting of 100 000 shares having a par value of $1 per share and issued at a premium of $1 per share, and 50 000 shares issued at $2 par and $1 premium. Discuss the effects on the accounts if:
   (a) the company buys back 20 000 shares at $4 per share
   (b) the company buys back 20 000 shares at $2.50 per share.
7. Discuss the nature of a rights issue, distinguishing between a renounceable and a non-renounceable issue.
8. What is a private placement of shares? What are the advantages and disadvantages of such a placement?
9. Discuss whether it is necessary to distinguish between the different components of equity rather than just having a single number for shareholders' equity.
10. For what reasons may a company make an appropriation of its retained earnings?

EXERCISE 3.1 ★   Reserves and dividends

Prepare journal entries to record the following unrelated transactions of a public company:
(a) payment of interim dividend of $30 000
(b) transfer of $52 000 from the asset revaluation surplus to the general reserve
(c) transfer of $34 000 from the general reserve to retained earnings
(d) payment of 240 000 bonus shares, fully paid, at $2 per share from the general reserve.

EXERCISE 3.2 ★   Dividends

Spain Ltd's share capital currently consists of 40 000 ordinary shares issued with a par value of $5 per share, and 20 000 10% preference shares issued at $10 each. In relation to the preference shares, dividends have not been paid for the two years prior to the current year. The company plans to pay out $100 000 in dividends in the current period, meeting all past obligations (where applicable) to shareholders.

Determine how much each class of shares should receive under the following situations:
(a) the preference shares are non-cumulative and non-participating
(b) the preference shares are cumulative and non-participating
(c) the preference shares are cumulative and participating. Assume that the participation agreement requires that the ordinary shareholders receive the same percentage of dividend as the preference shareholders, and that any balance of dividends to be paid is shared in proportion to the issued share capital of each class.

EXERCISE 3.3   ★

Rights issue

Pamplona Ltd had share capital of one million $1 shares, fully paid. As it needed finance for certain construction projects, the company's management decided to make a non-renounceable rights issue to existing shareholders of 200 000 new shares at an issue price of $5 per share. The rights issue was to be fully underwritten by Finance Brokers Ltd. The prospectus was issued on 15 February 2005 and applications closed on 15 March 2005. Costs associated with the rights issue and the eventual issue of the shares were $10 000.

(a) If 80% of the rights were exercised by the due date, provide journal entries made by Pamplona Ltd in relation to the rights issue and the eventual share issue.

(b) If the rights issue was not underwritten and any unexercised rights lapsed, what would be the required journal entries?

EXERCISE 3.4   ★

Share issue, options

Madrid Ltd has the following shareholders' equity at 1 January 2006:

Share capital – 500 000 shares	$1 240 000
Asset revaluation surplus	350 000
Retained earnings	110 000

On 1 March the company decided to make a public share issue to raise $600 000 for new capital development. The company issued a prospectus inviting applications for 200 000 $3 shares, payable in full on application. Shareholders who acquired more than 10 000 shares were allowed to buy options at 50 cents each. These options enabled the owner to buy shares in Madrid Ltd at $3.50 each, the acquisition having to occur before 31 December 2006.

By 25 March the company had received applications for 250 000 shares and for 20 000 options. The shares and options were allotted on 2 April, and money returned to unsuccessful applicants on the same day. All applicants who acquired options also received shares.

By 31 December 2006, the company's share price had reached $3.75. Holders of 18 000 exercised their options in December. The remaining options lapsed.

Required

Prepare the journal entries in the records of Madrid Ltd in relation to the equity transactions in 2006.

EXERCISE 3.5   ★★

Issue of ordinary and preference shares

Prepare journal entries and ledger accounts to record the following transactions for Castile Ltd:

2005	
01 April	A prospectus was issued inviting applications for 100 000 ordinary shares at an issue price of $1.50, fully payable on application. The prospectus also offered 100 000 10% preference shares at an issue price of $2, fully payable on application. The issue was underwritten at a commission of $4500, being $500 relating to the issue of ordinary shares and the balance for preference shares. All unsuccessful application monies were to be returned to the applicants.
10 April	Applications closed with the ordinary issue oversubscribed by 40 000 shares and the preference shares undersubscribed by 15 000 shares.
15 April	100 000 ordinary shares were allotted and applications for 40 000 shares were rejected and money refunded. 100 000 preference shares were also allotted.
20 April	The underwriter paid for the shares allocated to her, less the commission due.

EXERCISE 3.6   ★★

Rights issue, placement of shares

The shareholders' equity of Cadiz Ltd on 1 January 2006 was:

Share capital – 200 000 shares fully paid	$400 000
General reserve	200 000
Retained earnings	100 000

The following transactions occurred during the year ended 31 December 2006:

1. On 1 February 2006, a renounceable one-for-two rights issue was made to existing shareholders. The issue price was $2 per share, payable in full on application. The issue was underwritten for a commission of $5000. The issue closed fully subscribed on 31 March, the holders of 40 000 shares having transferred their rights. The underwriting commission was paid on 5 March.
2. On 30 June 2006, 10 000 shares were privately placed with Spanish Investments Ltd at $2 per share.

Required

Prepare the general journal entries to record the above transactions.

PROBLEMS

PROBLEM 3.1   ★

Dividends, calls on shares and bonus issue

The equity of Barcelona Ltd at 1 January 2006 was as follows:

Share capital		
600 000 shares fully paid	$600 000	
400 000 shares issued for $1 and paid to 50c	200 000	$ 800 000
General reserve		200 000
Plant maintenance reserve		50 000
Retained earnings		80 000
Total equity		**$1 130 000**

The following events occurred during the year:

25 June	Interim dividend of 10c per share paid, with partly paid shares receiving a proportionate dividend.
10 July	Call of 50c per share on the partly paid shares.
31 July	Collection of call money.
15 Sept.	Bonus share issue of one share for each 10 shares held, at $1 per share, allocated from general reserve.
31 Dec.	Directors announce that a dividend of 20c per share will be paid in September, subject to approval at the February annual general meeting. Transfer of plant maintenance reserve to general reserve. The company earned a profit of $60 000

Required

(a) Prepare the journal entries to give effect to the above events.
(b) Prepare the equity section of the balance sheet at 31 December 2006.

PROBLEM 3.2   ★★   Share issue, options

On 30 June 2004, the equity accounts of Valencia Ltd consisted of:

175 000 'A' ordinary shares, issued at $2.50 each, fully paid	$437 500
50 000 6% cumulative preference shares, issued at $3 and paid to $2	100 000
Options (20 000 at 56c each)	11 200
Accumulated losses	(6 250)

As the company had incurred a loss for the year ended 30 June 2004, no dividends were declared for that year. The options were exercisable between 1 March 2005 and 30 April 2005. Each option allowed the holder to buy one 'A' ordinary share for $4.50.

The following transactions and events occurred during the year ended 30 June 2005:

2004 25 July	The directors made the final call of $1 on the preference shares.
31 August	All call monies were received except those owing on 7500 preference shares.
7 September	The directors resolved to forfeit 7500 preference shares for non-payment of the call. The constitution of the company directs that forfeited amounts are not to be refunded to shareholders. The shares will not be reissued.
1 November	The company issued a prospectus offering 30 000 'B' ordinary shares payable in two instalments: $3 on application and $2 on 30 November 2006. The offer closed on 30 November.
30 November	Applications for 40 000 'B' ordinary shares were received.
1 December	The directors resolved to allot the 'B' ordinary shares pro rata with all applicants receiving 75% of the shares applied for. Excess application monies were allowed to be held. The shares were duly allotted.
5 December	Share issue costs of $5200 were paid.
2005 30 April	The holders of 15 000 options applied to purchase shares. All monies were sent with the applications. All remaining options lapsed. The shares were duly issued.

Required

(a) Prepare general journal entries to record the above transactions.
(b) If Valencia Ltd buys back 25 000 preference shares for $3.50 per share, what factors would its accountant have to consider in determining how best to record the transaction in the accounts?

PROBLEM 3.3   ★★   Issue of option and shares, forfeiture of shares

Prepare ledger accounts to record the following transactions for Andalusia Ltd:

2006 01 July	A prospectus was issued inviting applications for 100 000 ordinary shares at an issue price of $3, with $2 payable on application and the balance payable on 10 June 2007. The prospectus also offered 50 000 10% preference shares at $2, fully payable on application. The issue was underwritten at a commission of $6500, allocated equally between the classes of shares.

21 July	Applications closed with the ordinary share issue oversubscribed by 20 000 and the preference shares undersubscribed by 15 000.
31 July	All shares were allotted, and application money refunded to unsuccessful applicants for ordinary shares.
14 Aug.	The underwriter paid amounts less commission.
01 Dec.	The directors resolved to give each ordinary shareholder, free of charge, one option for every two shares held. The options are exercisable prior to 1 June 2007 and allow each holder to acquire one ordinary share at an exercise price of $2.70. Options not exercised prior to that date lapse.
2007 01 June	The holders of 40 000 options elected to exercise those options and 40 000 shares were issued.
10 June	The balance payable on the ordinary shares was received from holders of 95 000 ordinary shares.
15 June	The shares on which call money was not received were forfeited.
25 June	The forfeited shares were placed with a financial institution, paid to $3 on payment of $2.80. The cash was received from the financial institution, and any balance in the forfeited shares account returned to the former shareholders. Reissue costs amounted to $550.

PROBLEM 3.4 ★★   Buy-back of shares

Seville Ltd decided to repurchase 10% of its ordinary shares under a buy-back scheme for $5.60 per share. At the date of the buy-back, the equity of Seville Ltd consisted of:

Share capital – 4 million shares fully paid	$4 000 000
General reserve	600 000
Retained earnings	1 100 000

The costs of the buy-back scheme amounted to $3500.

Required
(a) Prepare the journal entries to account for the buy-back. Explain the reasons for the entries made.
(b) Assume that the buy-back price per share was equal to 70c per share. Prepare journal entries to record the buy-back, and explain your answer.
(c) Assume that, instead of the share capital shown above, Seville Ltd had issued 1 million shares at a par value of $1 and a share premium of $3 per share. Rework your answers to (a) and (b) under this new scenario.

PROBLEM 3.5 ★★   Rights issue, call on shares, issue of options

The share capital of Cordoba Ltd on 30 June 2006 was:

120 000 'A' ordinary shares issued at $1.50, paid to 75c	$ 90 000
50 000 'B' ordinary shares issued at $2.00, fully paid	100 000
100 000 9% preference shares issued at $1, paid to 80c	80 000
	$ 270 000

The following transactions occurred during 2006 and 2007:

2006	
01 Nov.	The company makes a one-for-five rights offer to its 'B' ordinary shareholders. The rights are renounceable, and allow holders to obtain 'B' ordinary shares for $2.25 per share, payable in full on application.
30 Nov.	The holders of 40 000 'B' ordinary shares accept the rights offer by the expiry date. The shares are duly allotted.
2007 16 Jan.	A call of 75c per share is made on all 'A' ordinary shares. All call money except that owed by the holder of 10 000 shares is received by 31 January.
05 Feb.	Shares on which calls are unpaid are forfeited and cancelled.
17 Mar.	To assist with cash flow difficulties, the company issued a prospectus inviting offers for 50 000 options to acquire 'A' ordinary shares at an issue price of 60c per option, payable in full on application. Each option, exercisable prior to 31 December 2007, allows the holder to acquire one 'A' ordinary share for $1.78.
31 Mar.	Offers had been received for 35 000 options and these were duly allotted.
31 Dec.	The holders of 25 000 options had exercised their options, with money paid on exercise, and 25 000 'A' ordinary shares were issued. The remaining options lapsed. Costs of issuing the shares amounted to $2000.

Required
Prepare journal entries to record the above transactions in the records of Cordoba Ltd.

PROBLEM 3.6 ★★★   Share issue, options, statement of changes in equity

On 30 June 2004, the equity accounts of Cadiz Ltd consisted of:

120 000 ordinary shares, issued at $2.50 each, fully paid	$300 000
Options (80 000 at 50c each)*	40 000
General reserve	30 000
Forfeited shares reserve	2 000
Retained earnings	75 000

* The options were exercisable between 1 May 2005 and 31 May 2005. Each option allowed the holder to buy one ordinary share for $3 each.

Additional information
The following transactions and events occurred during the year ended 30 June 2005:
• The final 6c per share dividend for the year ended 30 June 2004 was paid on 27 September 2004. Shareholder approval to pay the dividend had been obtained at the annual general meeting on 20 September.
• On 1 October, the directors issued a prospectus offering 40 000 ordinary shares at an issue price of $2.80, payable $2 on application and 80c as a future call. The closing date for application was 31 October 2004. The share issue was underwritten by Support Stockbrokers for a fee of $2500, payable on 15 November 2005.
• By 31 October 2004, applications for 50 000 shares had been received.
• On 5 November 2004, the directors allotted the shares pro rata, with applicants receiving 80% of their requested shares. The company's constitution allows excess application monies to be retained and used to offset future calls payable.

- On 15 November 2004, the underwriting fee was paid.
- On 31 December 2004, the directors announced an interim dividend of 3c per share payable in cash on 1 February.
- To raise funds for expansion, the directors sold a parcel of 80 000 ordinary shares to Espana Superannuation Fund on 28 April 2005 at an issue price of $2.90 per share.
- By 31 May 2005, the holders of 65 000 options had indicated that they wished to purchase shares. On 2 June 2005, 65 000 ordinary shares were issued with monies being payable by 21 June. Options not exercised duly lapsed.
- All outstanding monies were received with respect to shares issued to option holders.
- Profit for the year was $69 420. On 30 June 2005, the directors decided to:
  - transfer $30 000 to the general reserve
  - declare a final 5c per share dividend. Shareholder approval for this dividend will be sought at the annual general meeting in September 2005.

Required

(a) Prepare general journal entries, including any closing entries required, to record the above transactions. (Narrations are not required, but show all workings.)
(b) Prepare a statement of changes in equity for the year ended 30 June 2005.
(c) Cadiz Ltd has recognised a 'Forfeited shares reserve' as part of equity. Explain how and why such a reserve would be created.

PROBLEM 3.7 ★★★ Shares, options, dividends and reserve transfers

The equity of Toledo Ltd at 30 June 2007 consisted of:

400 000 ordinary 'A' shares issued at $2.00, fully paid	$800 000
300 000 ordinary 'B' shares issued at $2.00, called to $1.20	360 000
50 000 6% preference shares issued at $1.50, fully paid	75 000
Share options issued at 60c, fully paid	24 000
Retained earnings	318 000

The options were exercisable before 28 February 2008. Each option entitled the holder to acquire two ordinary 'C' shares at $1.80 per share, the amount payable on notification to exercise the option.

The following transactions occurred during the year ended 30 June 2008:

2007 15 Sept.	The preference dividend and the final ordinary dividend of 16c per fully paid share, both declared on 30 June 2007, were paid. The directors do not need any other party to authorise the payment of dividends.
01 Nov.	A one-for-five renounceable rights offer was made to ordinary 'A' shareholders at an issue price of $1.90 per share. The expiry date on the offer was 30 November 2007. The issue was underwritten at a commission of $3000.
30 Nov.	Holders of 320 000 shares accepted the rights offer, paying the required price per share, with the renounced rights being taken up by the underwriter. Ordinary 'A' shares were duly issued.
10 Dec.	Money due from the underwriter was received.
2008 10 Jan.	The directors transferred $35 000 from retained earnings to a general reserve.

(continued)

28 Feb.	As a result of options being exercised, 70 000 ordinary 'C' shares were issued. Unexercised options lapsed.
30 Apr.	The directors made a call on the ordinary 'B' shares for 80c per share. Call money was payable by 31 May.
31 May	All call money was received except for that due on 15 000 shares.
18 June	Shares on which the final call was unpaid were forfeited.
26 June	Forfeited shares were reissued, credited as paid to $2, for $1.80 per share, the balance of the forfeited shares account being refundable to the former shareholders.
27 June	Refund paid to former holders of forfeited shares.
30 June	The directors declared a 20c per share final dividend to be paid on 15 September 2008.

Required
(a) Prepare general journal entries to record the above transactions.
(b) Prepare the equity section of the balance sheet as at 30 June 2008.

PROBLEM 3.8   ★★★   Dividends, share issues, share buy-backs, options and movements in reserves

Granada Ltd, a company whose principal interests were in the manufacture of fine leather shoes and handbags, was formed on 1 January 2005. Prior to the 2008 period, Granada Ltd had issued 110 000 ordinary shares:
- 95 000 $30 shares were issued for cash on 1 January 2005
- 5000 shares were exchanged on 1 February 2006 for a patent that had a fair value at date of exchange of $240 000
- 10 000 shares were issued on 13 November 2007 for $50 per share.

At 1 January 2008, Granada Ltd had a balance in its retained earnings account of $750 000, while the general reserve and the asset revaluation surplus had balances of $240 000 and $180 000 respectively. The purpose of the general reserve is to reflect the need for the company to regularly replace certain of the shoe-making machinery to reflect technological changes.

During the 2008 financial year, the following transactions occurred:

15 Feb.	Granada Ltd paid a $25 000 dividend that had been declared in December 2007. Liabilities for dividends are recognised when they are declared by the company.
10 May	10 000 shares at $55 per share were offered to the general public. These were fully subscribed and issued on 20 June 2008. On the same date, another 15 000 shares were placed with major investors at $55 per share.
25 June	The company paid a $20 000 interim dividend.
30 June	The company revalued land by $30 000, increasing the asset revaluation surplus by $21 000 and the deferred tax liability by $9000.
01 July	The company early adopted IAS X in relation to insurance. The transitional liability on initial adoption was $55 000 more than the liability recognised under the previous accounting standard. This amount was recognised directly in retained earnings.

22 July	Granada Ltd repurchased 5000 shares on the open market for $56 per share. The repurchase was accounted for by writing down share capital and retained earnings by an equal amount.
16 Nov.	Granada Ltd declared a 1-for-10 bonus issue to shareholders on record at 1 October 2008. The whole of the general reserve was used to create this bonus issue.
01 Dec.	The company issued 100 000 options at 20 cents each, each option entitling the holder to acquire an ordinary share in Granada Ltd at a price of $60 per share, the options to be exercised by 31 December 2009. No options had been exercised by 31 December 2008.
31 Dec.	Granada Ltd calculated that its profit for the 2008 year was $150 000. It declared a $30 000 final dividend, transferred $40 000 to the general reserve, and transferred $30 000 from the asset revaluation surplus to retained earnings.

Share issue costs amount to 10% of the worth of any share issue.

Required

(a) Determine the balances of each of the equity accounts of Granada Ltd at 31 December 2008.

(b) Prepare the statement of changes in equity for Granada Ltd for the year ended 31 December 2008.

PROBLEM 3.9 ★★★   Share issues, options, rights issues, dividends, reserve transfers

The equity of Santiago Ltd on 30 June 2004 (balance date) consisted of:

280 000 ordinary shares, issued at $2.40 each and called to $2.40	$672 000
Calls in arrears (24 000 shares × 80c)	(19 200)
General reserve	290 000
Retained earnings	53 780

Additional information

The following transactions and events relating to share issues and options occurred during the year ended 30 June 2005:

• On 15 July 2004, the directors forfeited the shares on which the call was outstanding. Forfeited shares are not to be reissued and the company's constitution requires that any forfeited amounts be refunded to the former shareholders. Refund cheques were sent on 26 July 2004. Any outstanding dividends were still payable to former shareholders.

• On 1 August 2004, a rights offer (offering 5% preference shares at an issue price of $2.80 per share) was made to existing shareholders on the basis of one preference share for every two ordinary shares held. Shares were payable in full on allotment and rights were renounceable. The issue was underwritten for a fee of $5000.

• The rights offer closed undersubscribed on 31 August 2004, and rights in respect of 40 000 shares were transferred to the underwriter. On 1 September 2004, the shares were allotted. The underwriter paid for its allotment of shares, net of its fee, on 10 September 2004. All other monies were received by 21 September 2004.

• On 1 March 2005, the directors offered for sale 100 000 options at 10c each. Each option gave the holder the right to purchase one ordinary share for $2.80 each. Options were exercisable between 1 April 2006 and 30 June 2006. The option offer closed with 80 000 applications being received. Options were duly allotted on 2 April 2005.

The following transactions and events relating to dividends and reserve transfers occurred during the year ended 30 June 2005:

- On 29 September 2004, the final dividend of 10c per share for the year ended 30 June 2004 was paid. The dividend had been declared on 28 June 2004. Shareholder approval is not required for a declaration of dividends.
- On 2 January 2005, the directors declared and paid an ordinary interim share dividend of one ordinary share, valued at $3, for every four ordinary shares held. The dividend was funded from the general reserve.
- On 30 June 2005, the directors transferred $30 000 from the general reserve to retained earnings, declaring the 5% preference dividend as well as a final ordinary dividend of 8c per share. The loss for the year ended 30 June 2005 was $36 000.

Required

(a) Prepare general journal entries to record the transactions relating to share issues and options for the year ending 30 June 2005.

(b) Prepare general journal entries, including any closing entries required, to record the transactions relating to dividends and reserve transfers for the year ended 30 June 2005.

(c) If the company's constitution required all dividends to be approved by the share-holders at the annual general meeting before they could be paid, explain how and why your recording of the dividend payment on 29 September 2004 would change. Assume shareholder approval was granted on 20 September 2004.

Visit these websites for additional information:

www.iasb.org   www.iasplus.com
www.asic.gov.au   www.ifac.org
www.aasb.com.au   www.nzica.com
www.accaglobal.com   www.capa.com.my

REFERENCES

ANZ Bank 2003, *Prospectus*, Australia and New Zealand Banking Group Limited, viewed 24 November 2003, <www.anz.com.au>.

−2005, *2005 ANZ Financial Report*, Australia and New Zealand Banking Group Limited, viewed 2 March 2005, <www.anz.com.au>.

Australian Stock Exchange 2001, *Fact book: statistics to 31 December 2000*, available for down-loading from the Australian Stock Exchange website at <www.asx.com.au>.

Dior 2005, *Full annual report 2004*, Christian Dior, Paris, viewed 29 August 2006, <www.dior-finance.com/en>.

Fortune magazine 2005, 'Fortune global 500', 25 July, available from <http://money.cnn.com/magazines/fortune/global500/2005>.

International Committee of the Red Cross 2005, *ICRC Annual report 2005*, Switzerland, viewed 29 August 2006, <www.icrc.org>.

Nobes, C & Parker, R 2002, *Comparative international accounting* 7th edn, Pearson Education Limited, England.

Nokia 2005, *Nokia in 2005*, Nokia Corporation, Finland, viewed 29 August 2006, <www.nokia.com>.

Rochfort, S 2003, '$5 billion: Virgin float offer swamped', *The Age*, 6 December, page 1.

CHAPTER 4
Revenue recognition

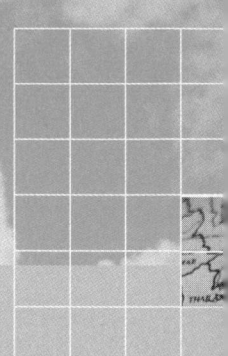

ACCOUNTING STANDARDS

International: IAS 18 *Revenue*
Australia: AASB 118 *Revenue*
New Zealand: NZ IAS 18 *Revenue*

CONCEPTS FOR REVIEW

Before studying this chapter, you should understand or, if necessary, revise:
- the IASB Framework, in particular the criteria for recognition of income
- IAS 18 *Revenue*, focusing on the principles for measuring revenue and recognising revenue from interest, royalties and dividends, and from the sale of goods and the rendering of services
- the appendix to IAS 18, which sets out 20 revenue recognition examples.

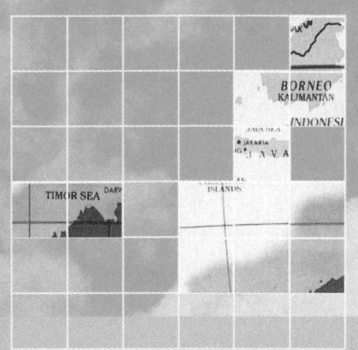

LEARNING OBJECTIVES

When you have studied this chapter, you should be able to:
1. understand what revenue is and how it relates to the element of financial statements known as income
2. describe how revenue recognition and measurement are fundamental to measuring the profit or loss of an entity during a reporting period
3. determine when revenue from the sale of goods is normally recognised
4. determine when revenue from the rendering of services is normally recognised
5. determine when revenue from interest, royalties, and dividends is normally recognised
6. understand how to measure revenue
7. be aware of a number of exceptions to these normal revenue-recognition principles.

LO 1

4.1 Revenue

The IASB Framework for the Preparation and Presentation of Financial Statements (examined in chapter 2) points out that investors, lenders, creditors and other users of the financial statements of a business entity are interested in information about the entity's performance over a period of time. Performance is the ability of an entity to earn a profit on the resources that have been invested in it. Information about the amounts and variability of profits helps in forecasting future cash flows from the entity's existing resources and in forecasting potential additional cash flows from additional resources that might be invested in the entity.

How does an entity earn a profit? It sells goods and services or takes in other kinds of income in amounts that exceed its expenses. So, to assess performance, we need information about income and expenses. The Framework (para. 70) recognises this and defines two basic elements of financial statements relating to performance, income and expenses:

(a) Income is increases in economic benefits during the accounting period in the form of inflows or enhancements of assets or decreases of liabilities that result in increases in equity, other than those relating to contributions from equity participants.

(b) Expenses are decreases in economic benefits during the accounting period in the form of outflows or depletions of assets or incurrences of liabilities that result in decreases in equity, other than those relating to distributions to equity participants.

The definition of income encompasses both revenue and other items of income that are not revenue. The distinction depends on whether the item of income is part of the ordinary or main activities of the entity (in which case it is revenue) or other activities (in which case it is income but not revenue). IAS 18 (para. 7) defines revenue as follows:

> *Revenue* is the gross inflow of economic benefits during the period arising in the course of the ordinary activities of an entity when those inflows result in increases in equity, other than increases relating to contributions from equity participants.

Profit is the residual amount that remains after expenses have been deducted from income. Profit is not a separate element of financial statements; it is simply the arithmetical difference between income minus expenses.[1]

LO 2

4.1.1 IAS 18 *Revenue*

Paragraph 1 of IAS 18 establishes the principles for recognising revenue from:

(a) the sale of goods [whether manufactured by the seller or purchased by the seller for resale];

(b) the rendering of services; and

(c) the use by others of entity assets yielding interest, royalties and dividends.

Other International Financial Reporting Standards (IFRSs) address aspects of revenue recognition in specific industries, and these matters are expressly excluded from the scope of IAS 18. For example:

- IAS 11 *Construction Contracts* covers revenue derived from the rendering of services pursuant to a construction contract (for example, revenue earned by builders, project managers and architects).

---

1. It is actually simplistic to think about profit as a single amount — an arithmetical difference between two other numbers. There are different types of 'profit', for example, profit that arises from selling goods and services to outside customers and profit that arises from holding assets whose fair values increase during the holding period. Some items of profit relate to an entity's ongoing operations, while other items of profit may relate to activities that have been sold or terminated and will not continue. Some items of profit may be one-off (non-recurring) gains. The IASB is addressing how to report the various components of 'profit' in its Performance Reporting project.

- IAS 17 *Leases* applies to recognition of income from leases by a lessor.
- IAS 28 *Investments in Associates* and IAS 31 *Interests in Joint Ventures* spell out how an investor recognises income from investments in which it has significant influence or joint control.
- IFRS 4 *Insurance Contracts* specifies how an insurance company should recognise revenue.
- IAS 39 *Financial Instruments: Recognition and Measurement* prescribes revenue recognition principles for most classes of financial assets (such as investments).
- IAS 41 *Agriculture* provides revenue recognition principles for an entity engaged in agricultural activity (farming, livestock raising, forestry, cultivating orchards, plantations, floriculture, fish farming and so on).

Another exclusion from the scope of IAS 18 is how an oil and gas company or a mining company should recognise revenue from the extraction of minerals from the ground. This is a complex area for which, at the moment, an IASB standard does not exist.

4.1.2 The importance of revenue in reporting performance

Revenue usually is the largest single item in financial statements. Users of financial statements assess the trends, growth and components of an entity's revenues as an indicator of the entity's past performance and future prospects.

Revenue is the most fundamental determinant of an entity's profit. Almost invariably, the higher an entity's revenue, the greater will be its profits. It may seem quite straightforward to say that revenue is an inflow of economic benefits, but great accounting debates arise over when those inflows occur and how to measure them.

To illustrate an issue about the timing of revenue recognition, consider a sale of goods by a manufacturer to a distributor, who will resell those same goods to the ultimate customer. When should the manufacturer recognise revenue? When it delivers the goods to the distributor, or when the distributor resells the goods to the final customer? What if the distributor has the right to return any unsold goods to the manufacturer, and the distributor only pays the manufacturer when the goods are sold to the final customer? Does it make a difference if title to the goods (legal ownership) passes to the distributor when the goods are initially delivered to the distributor, versus title passing directly from the manufacturer to the final customer when the final customer takes possession? Does it make a difference whether it is the distributor or the manufacturer who is responsible for theft and fire loss while the goods are in the possession of the distributor?

ILLUSTRATIVE EXAMPLE 4.1

How to measure revenue

To illustrate a 'how to measure revenue' issue, consider a sale of goods for $100 by a manufacturer to an ultimate customer in each of the following cases:

A. The customer pays cash of $100 when goods are delivered.
B. Goods are delivered to the customer, who agrees to pay $100 on normal 30-day payment terms (the manufacturer sends an invoice for $100).
C. Goods are delivered to the customer, who agrees to pay $50 one year after delivery and another $50 two years after delivery. Thirty days before each payment is due, the manufacturer sends invoices for $50.

→

While most accountants would agree that the manufacturer should recognise revenue of $100 at the time of delivery in cases A and B (the delay of payment in B is negligible), many would question whether it is appropriate to measure revenue of $100 at the time of delivery in case C.[2] In case C, the manufacturer is wearing two hats — that of a manufacturer and that of a financing institution. Surely the manufacturer in case C would have been willing to accept something less than $100 if cash were paid up-front, if for no other reason than it could take that cash, invest it and have the full $100 after two years. For simplicity, assume that the customer would have had to borrow at a 10% rate of interest to obtain the cash to pay up-front in case C, and if the manufacturer had been paid cash up-front it could have invested that cash at 10%. The present value of $50 for one year at 10% is about $45, and the present value of $50 for two years at 10% is about $41. Most accountants would measure the manufacturer's revenue at $86 ($45 + $41) at the time of delivery and, thereafter, the manufacturer would recognise interest income of about $9 (10% × 45 plus 10% × 41) in year one and about $5 in year two.

---

2. Technically, slightly more revenue should be recognised in case A than in case B, because the seller in case A has the use of the $100 thirty days earlier than in case B. However, because of the short period of time, this difference is generally regarded as immaterial.

Studies show that revenue recognition is the single largest category of financial statement restatements (corrections of errors in previously-issued financial statements). For instance, in October 2002 the US General Accounting Office (GAO, since renamed the Government Accountability Office) published a 272-page report to the US Senate on financial statement restatements. The GAO said that from January 1997 to June 2002, issues involving revenue recognition (misreported or non-reported revenue) accounted for 38% of the 919 announced restatements of earnings by US companies whose securities are publicly traded. Revenue recognition was also the primary reason for restatements each individual year. The GAO found that restatements for improper revenue recognition resulted in larger drops in market capitalisation (the total value of a company's outstanding shares) than any other type of restatement (GAO, p. 24):

> In the 3 trading days surrounding the initial announcement of a restatement, the stock prices of most of the restating publicly traded companies that we analyzed decreased by almost 10 percent and, in total, these companies lost more than $100 billion in market capitalization ... We found that restatements involving revenue recognition accounted for more than half of these losses.

The GAO report cited a range of ways in which revenues were improperly recognised, including: recognising revenue although significant contingencies were unresolved; recognising revenue before delivery took place; recognising software revenue before services were performed; and reporting revenue at gross rather than net amounts. There are some real-world examples in section 4.9 of this chapter.

4.1.3   Distinction between revenue and income

Revenue arises in the course of the normal ('ordinary') operating activities of an entity — sales of the goods that it produces and the services that it renders to customers. In other words, revenue is a subset of income. To illustrate, a manufacturing company earns its revenue from selling the products made in its factories. A wholesaling or retailing company earns its revenue from reselling merchandise that it has purchased. Of course, the manufacturer, wholesaler or retailer may earn extra income in other ways that are incidental to its main revenue-generating activities. For instance, it may have a certain amount of extra cash on which it earns interest through bank deposits or the purchase of investment securities. Because the manufacturer, wholesaler or retailer is not in the investment business, the interest that it earned is generally regarded as income but not revenue. On the other hand, a financial institution (such as a bank, insurance company or stockbroker) is likely to regard interest as revenue because investing is part of its ordinary operating activities.

As businesses diversify, the distinction between ordinary operating activities and other operating activities becomes less clear. For example, department stores that have their own credit card programs often make a sizable portion of their income from the interest paid by customers on their credit card accounts. Should the interest income be classified as part of normal operating activities – in which case it is revenue – or not? Or what if a retailer whose IT department has developed particularly good inventory-tracking computer software sells that software to another retailer in a one-off transaction? Is that revenue? Neither the IASB Framework nor IAS 18 is entirely clear on the distinction between revenue and other income.

4.1.4 Distinction between revenue and profit

Revenue is the gross amount of economic benefits (inflows of cash or other assets) that an entity receives from selling its goods or services in the ordinary course of business. Profit is the net amount of benefits received from selling those goods and services after deducting all related costs and expenses. As an extremely simple illustration, a retail store sells for $10 inventory that cost $4. Additional expenses during the period are $3. In this case, revenue for the period is $10 and profit is $3. If that retail store happened to earn interest of $1 during that period because it had put idle cash in an interest-earning bank account, its revenue would still be $10 for the period but its income would be $11 (the $10 of revenue plus the $1 of interest income) and its profit would be $4.

4.1.5 Terminology

Revenue is reported in the income statement.[3] That is a requirement of IAS 1 *Presentation of Financial Statements*. It is almost always the top line in the income statement but it is not always labelled 'revenue'.

Revenue is referred to by a variety of different names including sales, sales revenue, gross income, gross receipts (though receipts suggests cash whereas revenue is normally measured on an accrual basis) and turnover. Specialised kinds of revenue are often referred to by their nature, for example, fees, interest, dividends, royalties and rent.

4.1.6 Revenue versus gains

Gains are another subset of income, just as revenue is. Gains represent other items that meet the definition of income but that do not result from normal sales of the goods and services produced by the entity. Rather, they arise from transactions that are incidental to the entity's main revenue-generating activities. Gains represent increases in economic benefits and as such are not really different in nature from revenue. Hence, the IASB Framework does not treat them as a separate financial statement element.

---

3. In March 2006, the International Accounting Standards Board published an exposure draft proposing to change the name of the income statement to the 'statement of recognised income and expense'.

Generally, gains are reported net of related expenses. To illustrate, a manufacturer sells one of its factories. The selling price is more than the depreciated carrying amount of the factory. The net profit on the sale of the factory is a gain. Gross amounts received or receivable on sales of the products produced in the entity's factories are revenue.

4.1.7 Amounts collected as an agent

Revenue includes only the gross inflows of economic benefits that an entity receives for its own benefit. Sometimes an entity is required by law or contract, as part of a sale transaction, to collect on behalf of third parties amounts such as sales tax and value added tax (VAT). These collections are not economic benefits that flow to the entity. They must be remitted to the government or other party promptly, and they do not result in increases in the equity of the collecting entity. Therefore, they are excluded from revenue.

A similar situation arises when a business entity acts as an agent for another business entity. Consider, for instance, a travel agent. The travel agent books a flight for a customer on behalf of the airline. The airline's price for the ticket is $100. The customer pays the travel agent $100. The travel agent remits $95 to the airline and keeps the remaining $5 as its commission for selling the flight ticket. How much revenue did the travel agency earn — $100 (with related expense of $95) or $5? Under IAS 18, amounts collected on behalf of the principal in a transaction (in this case the airline) are not revenue. Therefore, revenue in this case is the amount of commission.

Judgement is needed to determine whether an agency relationship exists. A travel agency would not be an agent if it chartered an airplane for a specific trip and then sold seats on the charter flight, taking the risk of being left with unsold seats. In that case, the travel agency is operating as a principal, and the full amount of the ticket sales would be included in its revenue and the cost of the charter would be included in its expenses.

4.1.8 Internal transactions and revenue generation

When one component of a reporting entity makes a sale to another component of the same reporting entity, revenue is not recognised. This is because there is no inflow of economic benefits to the reporting entity as a whole. For that reason, revenues and related expenses on transactions between two subsidiaries are eliminated in the consolidated financial statements. The same goes for 'sales' from one department to another at various steps in an entity's manufacturing process.

4.2 Principles for recognising revenue

Under the IASB Framework (para. 92), income is recognised in the income statement when 'an increase in future economic benefits related to an increase in an asset or a decrease of a liability has arisen that can be measured reliably'. This means, in effect, that recognition of income occurs simultaneously with the recognition of increases in assets or decreases in liabilities — for example, the increase in cash or receivables arising on a sale of goods or services.

Why does the income recognition criterion in Framework paragraph 92 refer to an increase in benefits 'related to an increase in an asset or a decrease of a liability'? Because some events that will probably add to an entity's future economic benefits do not meet the asset recognition criteria and therefore are not recognised as income to the entity. An entity is likely to benefit when the primary economy in which it operates strengthens. But that alone is not income to the entity because no asset is recognised. (Of course, the strengthening of the economy may affect existing assets — the fair values of the entity's investments in shares traded on the local stock exchange may rise, for instance — and income would be recognised.) Likewise, an entity may well benefit from research and technological discoveries but, because the criteria in IAS 38 *Intangible Assets* for recognising self-created intangible assets are very strict, those discoveries alone do not result in the recognition of assets and therefore of income.

4.2.1 Accrual basis

The principle of accrual accounting (discussed in chapter 2) applies to the recognition of revenue. Under the accrual basis of accounting, the effects of transactions and other events are recognised when they occur rather than when cash or its equivalent is received or paid, and accounting principles recognise those effects in the financial statements of the periods to which they relate.

Thus, on a normal sale of goods or services on credit, the seller recognises revenue when the customer takes delivery and assumes a legal obligation to pay the seller in the future. However, there are certain constraints on applying the accrual basis. These will be discussed later in this chapter.

4.2.2 Matching of revenue and related expenses

Revenues and expenses that relate to the same transaction are recognised simultaneously. This is commonly referred to as the matching of revenues and expenses. Therefore, when revenue from the sale of goods is recognised, the cost of the goods sold is recognised as an expense. If revenue is recognised, other related expenses (such as warranty expense) must also be accrued. Normally, the other related expense can be measured reliably. However, if the related future expenses cannot be measured reliably, accrual of the revenue is not appropriate under IAS 18. In such a circumstance, any amount that the seller has received before revenue is recognised is reported as a liability.

4.2.3 Identifying the transaction

The criteria for recognising revenue in IAS 18 are usually applied separately to each sale transaction or service transaction. However, IAS 18 acknowledges that a single transaction may sometimes involve two or more separate revenue-producing components (sometimes called 'multiple deliverables'), and it may be necessary to apply the recognition criteria to the separately identifiable components to reflect the substance of the transaction. Applying the criteria to separate components may result in deferring a portion of revenue received up-front because it relates to a component of the transaction for which the revenue recognition criteria have not yet been met. Here are several examples:

- *Sale of products that include free servicing for a fixed period of time.* IAS 18 provides that an amount of revenue relating to the subsequent servicing would be deferred and recognised as revenue of the period during which the servicing is performed.
- *Sale of software with after-sale support, bug fixes and/or product enhancements.* IAS 18 provides that when the selling price of a product includes an identifiable amount for subsequent servicing (for example, after-sales support and product upgrades without additional charge), that amount is deferred and recognised as revenue over the period during which the service is performed. The amount deferred is that which will cover the expected costs of the services under the agreement, together with a reasonable profit on those services.
- *Subscriptions to publications and similar items.* The revenue recognition principles in IAS 18 would be applied separately to each individual subscription item. Therefore,

revenue is recognised when the items are shipped, in proportion to the sales value of each individual item relative to the total estimated sales value of all of the items.

- *Franchise fees that cover both initial supplies and services and continuing services.* IAS 18 requires that the franchisor defer the portion of the fee relating to continuing services and recognise it as revenue over the service period.

Sometimes the converse may be appropriate. That is, it might be necessary to combine two or more revenue-generating transactions when they are linked in such a way that the commercial effect cannot be understood separately. For example, an entity may sell goods and at the same time enter into a separate agreement to repurchase the goods at a later date. While the initial 'sale' transaction may on its own seem to meet the criteria for revenue recognition, the repurchase obligation negates the substantive effect of the sale transaction. IAS 18 would require that the two transactions be dealt with together.

Another less clear example under IAS 18 might be a non-cancellable two-year contract for connection to a broadband Internet service. Under the contract, the customer pays a set-up charge of $50 and then pays $20 per month for 24 months for the broadband connection. The broadband company incurs costs of $30 for the set-up. Should the broadband company treat this as two separate transactions — one for the set-up (recognising revenue of $50 and expenses of $30) and the other for the $20 monthly connection? Or should the broadband company treat it as one single transaction — in which case both the $50 and the $30 would be recognised proportionally over the 24 months? Surely the customer paid the $50 set-up charge solely to get 24 months of broadband connection service. That is, the set-up and the monthly connection are a single integrated transaction. While IAS 18 is not crystal clear in this regard, accountants are likely to treat the set-up and monthly access as one integrated revenue-producing transaction.

LO 3

4.3 Recognising revenue from the sale of goods

Under IAS 18, revenue from the sale of goods is recognised only when all the following conditions have been satisfied (IAS 18, para. 14):

(a) all of the significant risks and rewards of ownership are transferred to the buyer
(b) the seller has no continuing managerial involvement or effective control over the goods
(c) the amount of revenue can be measured reliably
(d) it is probable that economic benefits will flow to the seller
(e) the costs of the transaction (including future costs) can be measured reliably.

Condition (a) is probably the most difficult to assess. In most transactions, the significant risks and rewards of ownership are transferred to the buyer when the goods are delivered. At that point, the buyer has assumed the risks of loss, damage, obsolescence and declines in fair value. At the same time, the buyer has obtained the right to use the asset, and it is the buyer who will benefit from an increase in its fair value. At that point, the seller obtains a right to consideration (that is, a receivable) in exchange for the goods that have been delivered. Typically, delivery of the goods triggers revenue recognition — but not always.

IAS 18 identifies several examples of situations in which the entity may retain the significant risks and rewards of ownership even after delivery has taken place (IAS 18, para. 16):

- the entity retains an obligation for unsatisfactory performance not covered by normal warranty provisions
- the receipt of the revenue from a particular sale is contingent on the buyer reselling the goods
- the goods are shipped subject to installation, and the installation is a significant part of the contract that has not yet been completed by the entity

- the buyer has the right to rescind the purchase for a reason specified in the sales contract, and the entity is uncertain about the probability of return.

It is not necessary for every conceivable risk to be transferred before revenue is recognised. Insignificant risks may be retained and revenue can still be recognised. On the other hand, revenue recognition is deferred if significant risks are retained. Judgement is needed. The next few sections illustrate this.

4.3.1 Passing of title to the buyer

To protect the collectability of the amount due, the seller may retain legal title to the goods until payment has been made in full. For example, an automobile dealer may retain title to the car until the buyer has made the final payment. This may make it easier for the dealer to legally repossess the car if the buyer defaults on payment.

Normally, retaining legal title does not prevent revenue recognition under IAS 18. However, if the retention of title indicates that collectability is uncertain, then revenue recognition is not appropriate.

4.3.2 Right of return

The seller offers customers a right of return or a right of exchange if the customer is not satisfied with the purchase. Revenue is recognised under IAS 18 in this case, provided the seller can reliably estimate future returns and recognises a liability for returns based on experience and other factors.

4.3.3 Laws requiring the seller to retain certain risks

In some jurisdictions, the law imposes certain obligations on the seller, and if the seller fails to meet those obligations the sale can be rescinded. For example, in some jurisdictions a sale may be rescinded if the product is not merchantable (fit for sale), if it is not fit for its advertised purpose, if it has certain inherent manufacturing flaws, or if the seller does not have the legal right to sell. Such legal obligations do not prevent revenue recognition if they are insignificant or, if significant, are reliably measurable and an appropriate liability is recognised.

4.3.4 Seller holds the goods at buyer's request

The buyer can request the seller to hold onto the goods until the buyer asks for delivery. Sometimes this is purely a convenience for the buyer – for example, if it is probable that delivery will be made, the seller has the goods ready for delivery, title has already passed to the buyer and the buyer has been invoiced. In this case, revenue is normally recognised. On the other hand, if the seller does not have the goods ready for delivery (planning, instead, to acquire or manufacture them when the buyer requests delivery), then revenue is not recognised. In this case, the seller has received a binding order but has not yet made a sale because it still has significant obligations to fulfil.

4.3.5 Buyer's right to inspect and reject

Sometimes the buyer has a right to inspect the goods after it takes delivery to assess the quality, and the buyer can return any goods it deems to be of inferior quality. In such cases, revenue is recognised only after the buyer has notified the seller of a satisfactory inspection or after the time period for rejection has elapsed.

4.3.6 Consignment sales

A consignment sale is one in which the owner transfers possession of goods, but not title to the goods, to a third party. The third party is responsible for selling the goods and remitting the proceeds to the owner, usually less a commission. If the goods do not sell after a specified period of time, the goods are returned to the owner.

In a consignment sale, the owner has retained most of the significant risks and rewards of ownership (lack of demand, price declines, obsolescence and so on). The owner will recognise revenue only when the third party sells the goods to the ultimate customer. In effect, the third party is acting as an agent for the seller and not as a customer.

4.3.7 Channel stuffing

Sometimes a seller will take actions to inflate its revenue (and therefore its profit) by deliberately sending retailers along its distribution channel more products than the distributor would normally keep in its inventory to meet demand. An example of such an action would be price reductions or other incentives to induce extra sales near the end of a reporting period. This is known as 'channel stuffing'. By channel stuffing, the seller beefs up its revenue in one period, but either (a) the distributor will send the excess items back to the seller in the subsequent period, or (b) the distributor will simply purchase far less than normal in the subsequent period. Essentially, channel stuffing will catch up with the seller because it cannot maintain sales at that rate.

IAS 18 does not address channel stuffing directly. While all of the five conditions for recognising revenue from the sale of goods (discussed at the start of section 4.3) might appear to have been met, the substance of a channel stuffing transaction is that it is a device for manipulating revenue and profits rather than an income-producing transaction.

4.3.8 Estimating future costs

Condition (e) in IAS 18 paragraph 14 requires that the seller be able to estimate future costs such as warranty and repair costs. If those future costs cannot be estimated reliably, revenue recognition is deferred.

To illustrate, an entity builds and installs a chemical processing facility for a customer. The facility uses new technology that has been tested only in a small prototype, not a full-sized plant. The entity has guaranteed that the facility will process X litres per hour, and the entity is contractually committed to do whatever re-engineering and reconstruction is necessary after start-up to achieve the guaranteed throughput. If the entity cannot estimate reliably the future costs involved, under IAS 18 it must defer recognition of revenue.

LO 4

4.4 Recognising revenue from rendering services

Under IAS 18, revenue from rendering services is recognised by reference to the stage of completion of the service project so long as the following conditions are satisfied (IAS 18, para. 20):
- the amount of revenue can be measured reliably
- it is probable that economic benefits will flow to the service provider
- the stage of completion of the transaction can be measured reliably
- the costs of the transaction (including future costs) can be measured reliably.

This method is sometimes called the 'percentage of completion method'. If these conditions are met, revenue (and related costs) are recognised as the service activity progresses, with profit recognised as the difference between the recognised revenue and related costs. If there is an excess of revenue recognised over payments received, the excess is reported as a receivable. If a service contract is expected to result in a loss (past and estimated future costs are less than the contractual revenue), the loss is recognised in full.

If the outcome of a service contract cannot be measured reliably, revenue is recognised only to the extent of the expenses recognised that are recoverable. This is known as the 'cost-recovery method'. Profit is recognised only after all costs have been recovered.

LO 5

4.5 Recognising revenue from use of the entity's assets by others

4.5.1 Interest

Interest revenue is earned when a lender allows another party to use the lender's funds in exchange for payment of interest and repayment of the borrowed funds at a future date. Under IAS 18, interest revenue is recognised on a time-proportion basis using the effective interest method.

ILLUSTRATIVE EXAMPLE 4.2

Calculating interest revenue

To illustrate the effective interest method, an investor purchases a five-year, $1000 5% bond for $957.88. The maturity amount is $1000. The bond pays $50 cash interest per year (5% × $1000). The investor was able to purchase the bond for the 'discounted' amount of $957.88 because the current market rate of interest for a bond of this risk and maturity is 6%, but this bond only pays cash interest of 5%. The discount is the compensating factor. The investor would recognise interest revenue as shown in column (b) of the following table:

Year	(a) Cash interest received	(b) Interest income (d) × 6%	(c) Amortisation of discount (b) − (a)	(d) Investment on balance sheet
				$957.88
1	$50.00	$57.47	$7.47	$965.35
2	$50.00	$57.92	$7.92	$973.27
3	$50.00	$58.40	$8.40	$981.67
4	$50.00	$58.90	$8.90	$990.57
5	$50.00	$59.43	$9.43	$1000.00

Column (b) reflects interest revenue recognised by the effective interest method. The alternative would be to amortise the $42.12 total discount ($1000.00 − $957.88) on a straight-line basis over the five years, resulting in interest income of $58.424 ($50 + ($42.12/5)) each year for the five years. IAS 18 does not permit straight-line amortisation unless the difference between the effective interest method and the straight-line method is immaterial.

Incidentally, the total interest revenue recognised under both methods is identical. The sum of amounts in column (b) above and five times $58.424 are the same. The only difference is in the timing of the interest revenue recognition.

4.5.2 Royalties

Royalties are fees earned for allowing another party to use an entity's intangible assets such as copyrights, trademarks, brand names, patents, technology, computer software, music copyrights, record masters, motion picture films and digital images. Revenue from royalties is recognised on an accrual basis in accordance with the substance of the relevant agreement. Normally, this means that revenue is recognised by the straight-line method (equal amounts per period over the duration of the agreement).

If a royalty becomes receivable only when a specific event occurs (such as the showing or broadcasting of a motion picture), revenue is recognised when the event occurs. On the other hand, if a licence to exhibit or broadcast a motion picture provides for the payment of a licence fee regardless of whether or when the licensee actually exhibits or broadcasts the film, revenue is recognised at the time of sale.

4.5.3 Dividends

Dividend revenue is recognised when the shareholder's right to receive the dividend is established. Under most legal systems, that right is established only when the board of directors or other governing body legally declares a dividend by formal vote. If a dividend-paying entity normally declares its dividends on 1 April and 1 October each year, the dividend recipient preparing financial statements as of 31 December would not recognise dividend revenue for the three-month period October to December because its legal right to a dividend has not yet been established.

LO 6

4.6 Measurement of revenue

Under IAS 18, revenue is measured at the 'fair value of the consideration received or receivable'. In this context, 'consideration' is a legal term meaning the bargained exchange of items of value between buyer and seller. Fair value under this standard is the amount for which an asset could be exchanged, or a liability settled, between knowledgeable, willing parties in an arm's-length transaction. (The IASB uses this same definition of fair value throughout its standards.)

4.6.1 Cash transactions

Measurement of the consideration is generally an easy task in a transaction involving cash or cash equivalents (such as a cheque). It is the amount of cash paid. If the cash payment is in a foreign currency rather than the entity's main currency, the foreign currency is translated into the main currency at the exchange rate on the date the cash is received.

4.6.2 Normal credit transactions

If payment of the cash is deferred (that is, the sale is a credit transaction rather than a cash transaction), then the nature and perhaps the measurement of the consideration change. In this case, the consideration that the seller gets is a legal claim against the buyer.

Under IAS 18 (para. 9), the seller must determine whether the payment is due in normal payment terms customary in that industry. In some industries, this is 30 days; in others, 60 or even 90 days. If the payment is due under customary payment terms, the amount of revenue is measured based on the amount of cash receivable without discounting.

4.6.3 ## Deferred payment terms equivalent to a financing transaction

If the terms call for deferred payment such that the arrangement effectively constitutes a financing transaction, IAS 18 requires that the seller recognise both sales revenue and interest income. Sales revenue is measured at the discounted present value of the future payments. Sometimes this is known as 'imputing interest'.

ILLUSTRATIVE EXAMPLE 4.3

Imputing interest

The seller sells an item of machinery on the following terms:
• Down payment of $100 000
• Annual payments of $100 000 for 10 years (total $1 million).
The published cash price for the machine is $800 000 but recent cash sales have been for about $775 000. If the buyer were to borrow money to purchase the machine today, it would pay 8% interest.

Under IAS 18, it is not appropriate for the seller to recognise revenue of $1 100 000 ($100 000 down payment plus 10 future payments of $100 000 each) in full, up-front, at the time of the sale. The substance of this transaction is that the seller is not only selling the machine but is also financing the buyer's purchase. The seller is earning income from selling the machine and from interest.

To measure how much revenue the seller should recognise up-front, we need to calculate the discounted present value of the consideration the seller will receive. It is easy to do with an electronic spreadsheet such as Microsoft Excel. (If you do not have an electronic spreadsheet, you can use the present value tables in appendix A of chapter 14.) Excel has a built-in function for the present value of an annuity (equal payments for a defined number of periods at a given interest rate). The function is:

PV(interestrate,numberofpayments,amountperpayment)

So in our example, in an Excel cell, we put:

=PV(.08,10,100000)

The result is $671 008. We can prepare an amortisation schedule as follows (also easily done with an electronic spreadsheet):

(a) Payment number	(b) Payment ($)	(c) (e) × 8% Interest at 8% ($)	(d) (b) − (c) Repayment of principal ($)	(e) (e) − (d) Principal balance ($)
				671 008
1	100 000	53 681	46 319	624 689
2	100 000	49 975	50 025	574 664
3	100 000	45 973	54 027	520 637
4	100 000	41 651	58 349	462 288
5	100 000	36 983	63 017	399 271
6	100 000	31 942	68 058	331 213
7	100 000	26 497	73 503	257 710
8	100 000	20 617	79 383	178 327
9	100 000	14 266	85 734	92 593
10	100 000	7 407	92 593	0

→

Under IAS 18, the seller would recognise revenue of $771 008 at the time of sale ($100 000 down payment plus the present value of the 10 future annual payments of $100 000 each). This $771 008 is the fair value of the consideration that the seller has received. The seller's cost of the machine would be recognised as an expense at the time of sale. In each of the 10 subsequent years, the seller will recognise interest income as shown in column (c) above.

IAS 18 allows a second method of measuring the revenue. Since the normal cash sale price for the machine is $775 000, we could have used an electronic spreadsheet to calculate the implicit rate of interest in the transaction (that is, the rate of interest that would exactly equate 10 payments of $100 000 with the net $675 000 cash sales price minus the down payment). The result would have been a rate a tiny fraction higher than 8%. An amortisation schedule would be prepared as shown above, using that rate of interest. It would appear negligibly different from the schedule shown above.

LO 7

4.7 Other revenue recognition issues

4.7.1 Trade discounts

Some goods have a published 'list price' or 'regular retail price'. The seller of such goods generally offers substantial discounts to resellers of such goods — discounts of 30%, 40% and the like. These are known as trade discounts. Recognising revenue for the full 'list price' and an offsetting expense for the amount of the trade discount is not permitted under IAS 18. The seller must recognise revenue net of the trade discount.

4.7.2 Volume rebates

Some sellers offer customers a 'volume rebate' based on the amount of goods purchased in a time period such as one year. Once the required volume is reached, the prices of past transactions during the period are, in effect, reduced by means of a rebate of a portion of the revenue to the buyer.

IAS 18 is clear that revenue does not include volume rebates. If the volume rebate period coincides with the financial reporting period, this does not pose any special measurement problem. A measurement problem may arise, however, if those periods are different.

ILLUSTRATIVE EXAMPLE 4.4

Volume rebates

A seller's policy is that if a customer's total purchases during the year exceed $1 million, the customer will be entitled to an extra 2% reduction in the purchase prices including amounts paid during the portion of the year before the $1 million level was achieved.

Assume the seller prepares quarterly financial statements and that, during the first quarter, a particular customer has made $300 000 in purchases. Assume, further, that the seller expects this customer to make total purchases in excess of $1 million for the year. In the first quarter, the seller would recognise revenue not of $300 000 but of $294 000 (net of the 2% expected rebate). If the seller has collected the entire $300 000 during the first quarter, it would report a liability of $6000 at the end of the first quarter. This represents the volume rebate expected to be paid to the customer or netted against that customer's future purchases during the remainder of the year.

4.7.3 VAT and sales taxes

In many jurisdictions, a seller is required by law to collect sales tax and value added tax (VAT) relating to the goods or services that the entity sells. Sometimes the quoted sales price includes the tax; at other times, the tax is added separately to the invoice. In all of these cases, the seller is merely acting as a tax collector for the government. The tax collections must be remitted promptly to the government, and they do not provide any benefit to the seller. One of the conditions for recognising revenue is that economic benefits will flow to the seller. Since this is not true with respect to monies that the seller is merely collecting on behalf of a government, IAS 18 requires that the taxes be excluded from revenue. It is inappropriate to include them in revenue and then to report an offsetting 'tax expense'.

4.7.4 Exchanges of goods or services

Sometimes two sellers of goods will exchange (swap) goods or services that are of a similar nature and value for reasons of convenience, industry practice or cost savings. For example, to meet customer demands, two car dealers may swap cars that are similar but perhaps of a different colour. Or crude oil suppliers might exchange inventories in various locations to fulfil demand on a timely basis in a particular location. Sometimes a small amount of cash is also exchanged to adjust for slight differences in the fair values of the two sides of the transaction.

Under IAS 18, exchanges of goods or services of a similar nature and value do not result in revenue. Instead, the acquired asset is recognised at the carrying amount of the asset given up, and revenue is recognised only when the acquired asset is sold to an outside customer.

On the other hand, when goods are sold or services are rendered in exchange for dissimilar goods or services, the exchange is regarded as a transaction that generates revenue — unless it is clear that the transaction lacks commercial substance (IAS 18, para. 12). The revenue is measured at the fair value of the goods or services received, adjusted by the amount of any cash or cash equivalents transferred. When the fair value of the goods or services received cannot be measured reliably, the revenue is measured at the fair value of the goods or services given up, adjusted by the amount of any cash or cash equivalents transferred.

IAS 18 does not elaborate on 'dissimilar'. Here is an example that most accountants would agree generates revenue under IAS 18: a law firm provides legal services to a computer company and, instead of being paid in cash, the computer company provides computer equipment, software, installation and training to the law firm. Both the law firm and the computer company would recognise revenue. Each would measure revenue based on the fair value of what it received.

4.7.5 Barter transactions involving advertising services

The exchanges of goods or services for dissimilar goods or services described in the preceding section are sometimes referred to as barter transactions. Barter transactions may be entered into because the parties do not have cash, want to avoid payment of taxes or for other reasons. In some developing or transitional economies, barter transactions comprise a substantial portion of gross domestic product.

As a result of some abuses in applying the general principle for recognising revenue from exchanges of dissimilar goods and services in the area of bartered advertising services, the IASB's interpretations committee published an interpretation of IAS 18 restricting the recognition of revenue in these cases. Bartered advertising can involve swaps of advertisements on the Internet, in broadcast media or in published media. For most barter transactions, IAS 18 permits the 'seller' to recognise revenue if either the fair value of the goods or services received, or the fair value of the goods and services given up, can be measured reliably.

In the case of a barter transaction involving advertising, however, the interpretation says that the fair value of advertising services received cannot be measured with sufficient reliability to warrant revenue recognition. Nonetheless, a seller may be able to measure reliably the fair value of the advertising services it provides in a barter transaction, but only by reference to its non-barter income-producing advertising transactions that:

- involve advertising similar to the advertising in the barter transaction
- occur frequently
- represent a predominant number of transactions and amount when compared to all transactions to provide advertising that is similar to the advertising in the barter transaction
- involve cash and/or another form of consideration (such as marketable securities, non-monetary assets, and other services) that has a reliably measurable fair value
- do not involve the same counterparty as in the barter transaction.

Only if the seller has sufficient non-barter (that is, cash) advertising revenue to meet these conditions is it permitted to recognise revenue from bartered advertising transactions.

4.7.6 Subscriptions to publications

Often, the items involved in a subscription are of similar value in each time period. Magazine and newspaper subscriptions are typical examples. Subscription revenue is recognised on a straight-line basis over the subscription period. If the customer pays before the subscription has been delivered, the revenue received in advance is recognised as a liability (obligation to deliver future subscription items).

Sometimes the items involved in a subscription may have significantly different values. For example, the IASB sells annual subscriptions to its publications, including an annual 2400-page bound volume of its standards plus monthly newsletters. Clearly, the bound volume is of significantly greater value than the individual monthly newsletters, and revenue would be recognised accordingly.

4.8 Illustrative real-world revenue examples

The following examples extracted from the annual financial statements of various companies illustrate many of the principles applied in recognising revenue.

4.8.1 Revenue from services provided by a bank

Banks earn revenue from fees for providing various kinds of services. Some of these fees relate to services provided over a period of time, and other fees relate to individual transactions. In figure 4.1, a major Swiss bank using IFRSs describes how it recognises revenue from various kinds of fees.

UBS AG
Annual financial statements
Year ended 31 December 2004
Notes to the financial statements
Note 1 Summary of significant accounting policies
Note k — Fee income
UBS earns fee income from a diverse range of services it provides to its customers. Fee income can be divided into two broad categories: income earned from services that are provided over a certain period of time, for which customers are generally billed on an annual or semi-annual basis, and income earned from providing transaction-type services. Fees earned from services that are provided over a certain period of time are recognized ratably over the service period. Fees earned from providing transaction-type services are recognized when the service has been completed. Fees or components of fees that are performance linked are recognized when the performance criteria are fulfilled.

The following fee income is predominantly earned from services that are provided over a period of time: investment fund fees, fiduciary fees, custodian fees, portfolio and other management and advisory fees, insurance-related fees, credit-related fees and commission income. Fees predominantly earned from providing transaction-type services include underwriting fees, corporate finance fees and brokerage fees.

FIGURE 4.1   Recognising revenues from fees
Source: UBS AG (2004, p. 82).

4.8.2 VAT, rebates, returns, discounts, uncertainties

The accounting policy note about revenue recognition in the annual financial statements of AstraZeneca (a British pharmaceutical company) for the year ended 31 December 2005 illustrates a number of points discussed in this chapter, including:

- revenue does not include value added taxes collected on behalf of a government
- revenue does not include sales between components that are part of a single reporting entity
- estimated sales returns are deducted from revenue
- settlement allowances are not include in revenue
- revenue is not recognised when there is significant uncertainty about the amount or collectability of consideration to be received
- revenue is not recognised when future after-sale costs cannot be estimated reliably.

An extract from AstraZeneca's 2005 statements is provided in figure 4.2.

AstraZeneca
Annual financial statements for the year ended 31 December 2005
Accounting policies
Revenue
Sales exclude inter-company sales and value-added taxes and represent net invoice value less estimated rebates, returns and settlement discounts. Sales are recognised when the significant risks and rewards of ownership have been transferred to a third party. No revenue is recognised when there are significant uncertainties regarding the consideration to be received or the costs associated with the transaction.

FIGURE 4.2   Items included in recognising revenue
Source: AstraZeneca (2005, p. 87).

4.8.3   Sales taxes, rebates, customer acceptance, royalties, VAT, returns, discounts, uncertainties

The accounting policy note about revenue recognition in the annual IFRS financial statements of Bayer AG (a German pharmaceutical company) for the year ended 31 December 2005 is shown in figure 4.3. It illustrates a number of points discussed in this chapter, including:

- revenue does not include sales taxes collected on behalf of a government
- revenue is measured net of estimated provisions for rebates
- when there are customer acceptance provisions, revenue is deferred until acceptance
- multiple deliverables
- royalties from the licensing of technology
- up-front payments, before the goods or services have been delivered, are not revenue.

Bayer AG
Annual report for the year ended 31 December 2005
Notes to the consolidated financial statements
Note 4.3 Basic recognition and valuation principles
Net sales and other operating income
Sales are recognized upon transfer of risk or rendering of services to third parties and are reported net of sales taxes and rebates. Revenues from contracts that contain customer acceptance provisions are deferred until customer acceptance occurs.

Where sales of products or services involve the provision of multiple elements which may contain different remuneration arrangements such as prepayments, milestone payments, etc. — for example research and development alliances and co-promotion agreements — they are assessed to determine whether separate delivery of the individual elements of such arrangements comprises more than one unit of accounting. The delivered elements are separated if (1) they have value to the customer on a stand-alone basis, (2) there is objective and reliable evidence of the fair value of the undelivered element(s) and (3) if the arrangement includes a general right of return relative to the delivered element(s), delivery or performance of the undelivered element(s) is considered probable and substantially in the control of the company. If all three criteria are fulfilled, the appropriate revenue recognition convention is then applied to each separate accounting unit.

Allocations to provisions for rebates to customers are recognized in the period in which the related sales are recorded. These amounts are deducted from net sales. Payments relating to the sale or outlicensing of technologies or technological expertise — once the respective agreements have become effective — are immediately recognized in income if all rights to the technologies and all obligations resulting from them have been relinquished under the contract terms and Bayer has no continuing obligation to perform under the agreement. However, if rights to the technologies continue to exist or obligations resulting from them have yet to be fulfilled, the payments received are recorded in line with the actual circumstances.

Upfront payments and similar non-refundable payments received under these agreements are recorded as deferred revenue and recognized in income over the estimated performance period stipulated in the agreement. Non-refundable milestone payments linked to the achievement of a significant and substantive technical/regulatory hurdle in the research and development process, pursuant to collaborative agreements, are recognized as revenue upon the achievement of the specified milestone. Revenues such as license fees, rentals, interest income or dividends are recognized according to the same principles.

FIGURE 4.3   Multiple revenue-recognition issues including sales taxes, rebates, customer acceptance, multiple deliverables, royalties and up-front payments
Source: Bayer AG (2005, p. 94).

4.8.4 Revenue does not include equity method associates and joint ventures

Under IFRSs, an investment in an associate — a company in which the investor has significant influence but not control — is accounted for by the equity method. Under the equity method, the investor includes on its income statement one line representing its proportionate share in the net profit or loss of the investee. So, if company X's 25% ownership of company Y gives X significant influence but not control, and if Y's profit for the year is $100, X's income statement shows one line 'equity in income of Y $25'. Because Y's profit of $100 is a net number (its revenues minus its expenses), X's 25% share of the $100 is also a net amount. It is not included in X's revenue but, rather, is reported separately on X's income statement. Figure 4.4 contains an example from a Hong Kong-listed food manufacturing and distributing company that uses IFRSs.

> **Dairy Farm International Holdings Limited**
> **Annual report 2004**
> **Principal accounting policies**
> **M. SALES**
> Sales consist of the gross value of goods sold to customers, excluding sales taxes. This does not include sales generated by associates and joint ventures.

FIGURE 4.4   Separate recognition of profits of associates and joint ventures that are equity accounted
Source: Dairy Farm International Holdings Limited (2004, p. 20).

4.8.5 Delivery, passing of title, licensing, effective interest method

The 2005 IFRS financial statements of Esprit Holdings Limited (a clothing and cosmetics retailer and wholesaler) illustrate:
- revenue recognition at delivery and passing of title
- royalty revenue from licensing
- effective interest method for recognising interest revenue.

An extract from the statements is shown in figure 4.5.

FIGURE 4.5   Recognising revenue arising from the sale of goods, licensing and interest

> **Esprit Holdings Limited**
> **Notes to the financial statements**
> **Year ended 30 June 2005**
>
> **Note 2 Summary of significant accounting policies**
>
> **(n) Revenue recognition**
>
> Revenue comprises the fair value for the sale of goods and services, net of value-added tax, rebates and discounts and after eliminating sales within the Group. Revenue is recognized as follows:
>
> *(i) Sales of goods — wholesale*
> Sales of goods are recognized on the transfer of risks and rewards of ownership, which generally coincides with the time when the goods are delivered to the customer and title has been passed.
>
> *(continued)*

(ii) Sales of goods — retail
Sales of goods are recognized on sale of a product to the customer. Retail sales are usually in cash or by credit card.

(iii) Licensing income
Licensing income is recognized on an accruals basis in accordance with the substance of the relevant agreements.

(iv) Interest income
Interest income is recognized on a time proportion basis using the effective interest method

Source: Esprit Holdings Limited (2005, p. 78).

4.8.6 Revenue from barter transactions, core versus incidental revenue

The Swatch Group Ltd (manufacturer of watches) will exchange (barter) timekeeping services and display equipment that it manufactures in return for advertising and identification rights. This is an exchange of dissimilar items and, under IAS 18, is recognised at the fair value of consideration received (advertising and identification rights) or (if more reliably measurable) the fair value of the consideration given up (timing services and display equipment). An extract from the 2004 financial statements is shown in figure 4.6.

The Swatch Group Ltd
Annual financial statements for 2004
Changes in accounting policies
Changes in accounting treatment of Olympic Games activities
The Swatch Group has given a provisional commitment to supply the timekeeping and sports results displays for the Olympic Games up to the year 2010 in return for advertising and identification rights. All in all, this results in a net expense for the Group. Since timekeeping is not a core activity of the Group, these transactions will in future be presented in the financial statements as gross amounts under the items 'Other operating income' and 'Other operating expenses', and will not be included in Group sales.

FIGURE 4.6 Incidental revenue arising from barter transactions
Source: The Swatch Group Ltd (2004, p. 118).

4.8.7 Distinction between revenue and income

Under IAS 18, items of income that are incidental to the entity's main revenue-generating activities are not included in revenues but instead are reported separately as other income. The 2004 IFRS financial statements of Lufthansa AG (a German airline) shown in figure 4.7 provide an illustration.

Lufthansa AG
Annual report for 2004
Financial statements
Note 9 Other operating income
Items excluded from revenue and reported as other operating income:

	2004	2003
Income from disposal of fixed assets	€446	€258
Income from reversal of impairment losses	6	12
Foreign currency translation gains	374	527
Reversal of provisions	195	179
Income from rebilling of accounts payable	32	110
Commissions earned	80	68
Rebilling of charges for EDP distribution systems	33	31
Release of allowances for receivables/elimination of accounts payable	38	40
Hiring out of staff	29	34
Compensation received for damages	29	23
Rental income	28	28
Income from the subleasing of aircraft	3	10
Income from disposal of current financial assets	34	8
Other operating income	426	400
	1 753	1 728

FIGURE 4.7 The distinction between items disclosed as revenue and those as other operating income
Source: Lufthansa AG (2004, p. 146).

4.8.8 Consignment sales made through agents

Under IAS 18, when an owner transfers goods to a third party in a consignment sale, the third party is acting as the owner's selling agent, not as a buyer of the goods. Accordingly, the owner will not recognise revenue until the third party sells the goods to the ultimate customer. The 2004 IFRS financial statements shown in figure 4.8 of Gazprom, a Russian natural gas company, provide an illustration.

Gazprom
Financial report 2004
Explanatory notes to the 2004 accounting reports
Revenue recognition
Sales made under the terms of an agent agreement are recognized by the Company, acting as a consignor (principal), upon receipt of a corresponding notice from the commissioner (agent) that gas or refined products have been delivered to the customer.

FIGURE 4.8 Recognising revenue from consignment sales
Source: Gazprom (2004, p. 25).

4.9   A few real-world revenue recognition problems

With revenue being the most fundamental determinant of an entity's profit, company mangers may sometimes attempt to find ways to increase the revenue reported in the financial statements. The following examples illustrate ways in which a few companies have tried to inflate their reported revenue.

4.9.1   Channel stuffing

In the United States, the Securities and Exchange Commission (SEC) charged McAfee, Inc. (a computer security-software manufacturer) with accounting fraud, and early in 2006 McAfee agreed to settle and pay a $50 million penalty. The fraud related to channel stuffing, a revenue recognition issue discussed in section 4.3.7. Figure 4.9 contains an excerpt from the SEC's 4 January 2006 announcement of the complaint and settlement.

The Commission alleges in its complaint that McAfee used a variety of undisclosed ploys during the period to aggressively oversell its products to distributors in amounts that far exceeded the public's demand for the products. While engaging in this channel-stuffing, McAfee improperly recorded the sales to distributors as revenue. McAfee offered its distributors lucrative sales incentives that included deep price discounts and rebates in an effort to persuade the distributors to continue to buy and stockpile McAfee products. McAfee also secretly paid distributors millions of dollars to hold the excess inventory, rather than return it to McAfee for a refund and consequent reduction in McAfee's revenues. In other instances, McAfee used an undisclosed, wholly-owned subsidiary, Net Tools, Inc., to repurchase inventory that McAfee had oversold to its distributors. The complaint further alleges that McAfee took action to conceal the fraud from investors by, among other things, wrongly recording in its books the payments and discounts that it offered to distributors, and improperly manipulating reserve accounts to increase inadequate sales reserves and cover the costs of the distributor payments. The complaint alleges that McAfee defrauded investors by reporting false and materially misleading financial and other information in periodic reports, financial statements, and securities registration statements that McAfee filed with the Commission, and in press releases and other public statements.

FIGURE 4.9   An allegation of channel stuffing
Source: Securities and Exchange Commission (2006).

4.9.2   US$3.8 billion multifaceted revenue recognition fraud

The US SEC charged Qwest Communications International Inc., one of the largest telecommunications companies in the United States, with securities fraud and other violations of the federal securities laws. The Commission's complaint alleged that, between 1999 and 2002, Qwest fraudulently recognised over $3.8 billion in revenue and excluded $231 million in expenses as part of a 'multi-faceted fraudulent scheme to meet optimistic and unsupportable revenue and earnings projections'. Without admitting or denying the allegations in the complaint, Qwest consented to entry of a judgement enjoining it from violating the antifraud, reporting, books and records, internal control, proxy, and securities registration provisions of the federal securities laws.

The fundamental issues included:

- reporting as revenue (rather than as a gain or other income) the sale of its principal income-producing asset
- sham exchanges of similar fibre optical cable capacity with other companies, with revenue recognised

- front-ending of revenue that should have been recognised ratably over a contract period.

Figure 4.10 contains an excerpt from the SEC's 21 October 2004 settlement announcement.

Fraudulent use of non-recurring revenue

After its initial public offering in 1997, Qwest touted itself as a progressive, new-generation technology company with enormous growth potential. Beginning in 1999, in fact, Qwest's CEO consistently predicted publicly that Qwest would achieve double-digit revenue and earnings growth. By mid-1999, it became clear to Qwest senior management that the market for telecommunications services was declining and that revenue from those services would not sustain Qwest's projected revenue and earnings growth.

To 'fill the gap' between its actual and projected revenue, Qwest, at the direction of its senior management, began selling indefeasible rights of use (IRUs). An IRU is an irrevocable right to use a specific fiber strand or specific amount of fiber capacity for a specified time period. Thus, to meet revenue expectations that it created, Qwest sold what the company had previously identified in Commission filings and press releases as its 'principal asset.' When the demand for IRUs declined, Qwest engaged in IRU 'swaps' whereby Qwest bought IRUs from other companies in exchange for agreements from those companies to buy IRUs from Qwest. As another 'gap filler,' Qwest sold capital equipment.

Both IRU and equipment sales were referred to internally as 'one hit wonders.' Indeed, the investment community generally discounted such non-recurring revenue sources when valuing telecommunications companies because non-recurring revenue sources were not sustainable. Qwest's use of one-time transactions to fill the gap between actual and projected revenue became so common that many Qwest employees likened the practice to an 'addiction' and the non-recurring IRU and equipment sale transactions as Qwest's 'heroin.'

In Commission filings and other public statements, Qwest fraudulently characterized non-recurring revenue from IRU and equipment transactions as recurring 'data and Internet service revenues,' thereby masking its declining financial condition and artificially inflating its stock price.

Fraudulent accounting for IRU and equipment sale transactions

In addition to fraudulently characterizing non-recurring revenue as recurring revenue, Qwest ignored generally accepted accounting principles ('GAAP') by recognizing upfront revenue from IRU transactions and equipment sales. Qwest, in fact, employed fraudulent devices such as backdated contracts and secret side agreements to conceal the fact that its IRU and equipment transactions did not meet GAAP's requirements for upfront revenue recognition. Under GAAP, Qwest should either have not recognized any revenue on these transactions or recognized revenue ratably over the lives of the contracts.

FIGURE 4.10   Fraudulent use of non-recurring revenue
Source: Securities and Exchange Commission (2004).

4.9.3   Internet advertising revenue fraud

The US SEC charged Time Warner Inc. (formerly known as AOL Time Warner) in March 2005 with materially overstating online advertising revenue and the number of its Internet subscribers, and with aiding and abetting three other securities frauds. Figure 4.11 contains an excerpt from the SEC's 4 January 2006 announcement of the complaint and settlement.

Fraudulent round-trip transactions to inflate online advertising revenue
Beginning in mid-2000, stock prices of Internet-related businesses declined precipitously as, among other things, sales of online advertising declined and the rate of growth of new online subscriptions started to flatten. Beginning at this time, and extending through 2002, the company employed fraudulent round-trip transactions that boosted its online advertising revenue to mask the fact that it also experienced a business slow-down. The round-trip transactions ranged in complexity and sophistication, but in each instance the company effectively funded its own online advertising revenue by giving the counterparties the means to pay for advertising that they would not otherwise have purchased. To conceal the true nature of the transactions, the company typically structured and documented round-trips as if they were two or more separate, bona fide transactions, conducted at arm's length and reflecting each party's independent business purpose. The company delivered mostly untargeted, less desirable, remnant online advertising to the round-trip advertisers, and the round-trip advertisers often had little or no ability to control the quantity, quality, and sometimes even the content of the online advertising they received. Because the round-trip customers effectively were paying for the online advertising with the company's funds, the customers seldom, if ever, complained.

FIGURE 4.11   Internet advertising revenue fraud
Source: Securities and Exchange Commission (2005).

4.10   Presentation of revenue

IAS 1 *Presentation of Financial Statements* requires that revenue be presented separately on the face of the income statement. IAS 18 requires that the amount of each significant category of revenue recognised during the period be presented separately, including (at a minimum) each of the following:
- revenue from the sale of goods
- revenue from the rendering of services
- interest
- royalties
- dividends.

Moreover, if any of the above categories includes revenue arising from exchanges of goods and services (rather than transactions that will ultimately be settled in cash), those amounts of revenue must be disclosed separately.

4.11   Summary

Revenue is the gross inflow of economic benefits to an entity during the period arising in the course of its ordinary operating activities. IAS 18 *Revenue* establishes the principles for recognising revenue from the sale of goods, the rendering of services, and the use by others of entity assets yielding interest, royalties and dividends.
Recognition
- *Sale of goods.* Revenue is recognised only when all the following conditions have been satisfied:
  - all of the significant risks and rewards of ownership are transferred to the buyer
  - the seller has no continuing managerial involvement or effective control over the goods

- the amount of revenue can be measured reliably
- it is probable that economic benefits will flow to the seller
- the costs of the transaction (including future costs) can be measured reliably.

The cost of the goods sold is recognised as an expense in the same period as the related revenue is recognised (sometimes called 'matching').

- *Rendering of services*. Revenue is recognised by reference to the project's stage of completion, known as the 'percentage of completion method'. If the stage of completion or future costs cannot be measured reliably, revenue is recognised on a cost-recovery basis.
- *Interest*. Revenue is recognised using the effective interest method as set out in IAS 39.
- *Royalties*. Revenue is recognised on an accrual basis in accordance with the substance of the agreement.
- *Dividends*. Revenue is recognised when the shareholder's right to receive payment is established.

Measurement

- Revenue is measured at the fair value of the consideration received or receivable.

1. What is the difference between income and revenue?
2. What is the difference between revenue and gains?
3. What do accountants mean when they say they match revenues and expenses to measure profit?
4. Which of the following is not a synonym for revenue?
   (a) Sales
   (b) Gross income
   (c) Profit
   (d) Turnover
5. What is the principle for recognising revenue under the IASB Framework?
6. What is the accrual basis of accounting, and how does it apply to revenue recognition?
7. What criteria does IAS 18 require for recognising revenue from the sale of goods?
8. A company sells certain goods, and the buyer takes delivery. Give three examples of future costs that the selling company might have to accrue concurrent with revenue recognition.

9. What is the basic principle for measuring revenue under IAS 18?
10. What is 'channel stuffing' and how might it affect revenue recognition?
11. IAS 18 requires the percentage-of-completion method for what type of revenue?
12. To induce a buyer to make a major purchase, the seller allows the buyer to defer payment for one year, with no interest. IAS 18 requires that the seller 'impute' interest in recognising revenue. What does that mean?
13. A municipality imposes a 10% occupancy tax on hotel rooms. The hotel adds the tax to the guest's bill at checkout. The hotel is required to remit all taxes collected to the municipality at the end of each month. The hotel bookkeeper tells you that the 'matching principle' requires the hotel to include the 10% occupancy tax collections in its revenue, and to recognise, at the same time, a related and equal tax expense. Do you agree? Why?

EXERCISE 4.1 ★

Revenue — multiple deliverables

A company selling natural gas for heating and cooking extends its gas pipeline network to a neighbourhood with single-family homes that currently use electricity for heating and cooking. To secure new customers, the company offers to install a connecting gas pipe into the customer's home without charge if the customer signs a three-year non-cancellable contract to purchase natural gas. If the customer does not wish to sign a three-year contract, the installation charge is $600. It costs the company $420 to do the installation. Customer X signs the three-year contract and the gas company installs the pipeline to that home.

Required
(a) Argue the case that the gas company should recognise the entire $600 as revenue at the time of installation.
(b) Argue the case that the gas company should spread the $600 as revenue over the three-year contract period.
(c) What would be the difference, if any, if in all cases there is free installation and the customer is not required to sign a contract?

EXERCISE 4.2 ★

Revenue — layaway sales

Company R is a retailer that offers 'layaway' sales to its customers. Company R retains the merchandise, sets it aside in its inventory, and collects a cash deposit from the customer. Company R does not require the customer to enter into an instalment note or other fixed payment commitment or agreement when the initial deposit is received. The merchandise is not released to the customer until the customer pays the full purchase price. If the customer fails to pay the remaining purchase price within two years, the customer forfeits its cash deposit. If the merchandise is lost, damaged or destroyed, company R either must refund the cash deposit to the customer or provide replacement merchandise.

Required

When do you think company R should recognise revenue from a layaway sale? State your reasons.

EXERCISE 4.3 ★

Revenue — payment in full, non-cancellable sale

Company M manufactures goods to its customers' specifications. Orders are not cancellable. Because the goods would be of no use to other customers, and to avoid bad debt losses, company M requires each customer to pay in full at the time the order is placed. Company M can estimate its manufacturing costs reliably. On 10 January, Company M receives an order for $100 000 of goods specially designed to meet the needs of customer X, with payment in full. Delivery will be 28 February.

Required

When should company M recognise the revenue? State your reasons.

EXERCISE 4.4 ★★

Revenue — licensing

Company F is a film production company. A film that it released six months ago met with both critical and box office success. Company F grants a licence to television network N to broadcast the film once (N will choose the date and time) during the next 12 months for a licence fee of $1 million. The fee is paid and the film is delivered to N up-front. The contract prohibits company F from granting a broadcast licence to any other television station or network that broadcasts within N's broadcast area during the 12-month period.

Required

(a) How should company F recognise the $1 million revenue?
   (i) Up-front
   (ii) When the network actually broadcasts the film
   (iii) Spread evenly over the 12-month period
   (iv) In some other way
   Why?
(b) Some people might say that the network paid not only for its right to broadcast the film one time but also for the inability of any of its competitors to broadcast the film during the 12-month period. How might this bear on revenue recognition?

EXERCISE 4.5 ★★

Revenue — membership fees

Company F operates a fitness centre. It generates revenue from annual membership fees of $960 per person. The membership contract requires the customer to pay the entire annual membership fee ($960) at the outset of the contract. However, the customer has the unilateral right to cancel at any time during its term and receive a time-proportional refund of the fee. (A customer cancelling halfway through the year gets a $480 refund, for example.)

Based on historical data collected over time for a large number of homogeneous transactions, Company F estimates that approximately 4% of the customers will request a refund each month before the end of the membership contract term. Company F's data for the past five years indicate that significant variations between actual and estimated cancellations have not occurred, and Company F does not expect significant variations to occur in the foreseeable future. Company F can reliably estimate its costs of providing membership services for the year.

Required

Do you think that Company F should recognise in earnings the revenue for the membership fees (adjusted to reflect the expected refunds) and accrue the costs to provide membership services at the outset of the arrangement? State your reasons.

PROBLEMS	

PROBLEM 4.1 ★

Revenue recognition — goods

A manufacturer sells goods to customer A, who has an unlimited right of return. If customer A cannot sell those goods to a third party, customer A may return the goods to the manufacturer for a credit against future purchases from the manufacturer (but not for a cash refund).

Required

Under the IASB Framework, what should the manufacturer do?
(a) Recognise revenue when the goods are delivered to Customer A, with an appropriate allowance for estimated returns
(b) Recognise revenue when Customer A resells the goods to a third party

PROBLEM 4.2 ★

Revenue recognition — promotion costs

Company E sells food products to end consumers. To promote a certain product, company E's suppliers will give cash to company E in return for prime placement of its product in Company E's stores. These are sometimes called 'slotting fees'.

Required

Under IAS 18, how should company E account for the slotting fees received?
(a) As revenue
(b) As a reduction of the cost of food products purchased from suppliers
State your reasons.

PROBLEM 4.3 ★

Revenue recognition — transfer of title

When goods are shipped free on board (FOB) shipping point, title passes to the buyer when the goods are shipped, and the buyer is responsible for any loss in transit. On the other hand, when goods are shipped free on board (FOB) destination, title does not pass to the buyer until delivery, and the seller is responsible for any loss in transit. How do those factors affect revenue recognition under IAS 18?

PROBLEM 4.4 ★

Revenue from sale of gift certificates

Company G sells gift certificates that can be used to buy its merchandise. Under the IASB Framework, should sales revenue for gift certificates:
(a) be recognised at the time that the gift certificate is purchased?
(b) not be recognised until the gift certificate is redeemed for merchandise?

PROBLEM 4.5 ★★

Revenue recognition — services

A travel agency makes an airplane reservation for a customer, collects $1000 from the customer, delivers the ticket to the customer, remits $930 to the airline and retains $70 as commission. The travel agency acts purely as agent for the airline, assuming no responsibility for the flight.

Required

Based on the definition and recognition criteria for income in the IASB Framework and in IAS 18, do you think the travel agency had:
(a) $1000 of revenue and $930 of expenses, leaving a $70 gross profit?
(b) $70 of commission revenue, with the $1000 and the $930 not reflected in its income statement?

PROBLEM 4.6 ★★   Revenue recognition — value added tax

Company B operates in a country with a 17% VAT. The VAT is billed to the customer and remitted monthly to the government. Company B sells goods for $100 and bills the customer $117. Calculate the amount of revenue that company B should recognise under IAS 18.

PROBLEM 4.7 ★★   Revenue recognition — gross or net?

Company C operates an Internet site from which it sells the products of various manufacturers. Customers select products from the website and provide credit card and shipping information. The manufacturers establish the selling price. Company C receives the order and authorisation from the credit card company and passes the order on directly to the relevant manufacturer, who ships the product directly to the customer. Company C does not take delivery of or title to the goods, and has no risk of loss or other responsibility for the product. The manufacturer is responsible for all product returns, defects and disputed credit card charges. Company C's fee is 20% of the sales price. It remits the remaining 80% to the manufacturer.

Required

Explain how, under IAS 18, Company C should recognise revenue for a $100 transaction.
(a) As revenue of $100, with $80 expense also recognised for the amount remitted to the manufacturer
(b) As revenue of $20

PROBLEM 4.8 ★★   Revenue recognition — retailer

Company D owns and operates a department store. However, it leases out a portion of its floor space to a brand-name perfume company. Decisions regarding staffing, shop design, furnishing, products to be sold, and other operating matters relating to the leased department are made by the perfume company.

Required

Under the IASB Framework, do you think that it is appropriate for company D to include in its revenue (and in its cost of goods sold) the amount of sales (and cost of goods sold) of a leased or licensed department in the store? What is Company D selling — perfume or floor space?

PROBLEM 4.9 ★★   Revenue recognition — up-front fees

Company F provides mobile phone services. Customers must pay a non-refundable up-front activation fee plus a monthly usage fee. The monthly usage fee more than covers company F's operating costs. The costs incurred by Company F to activate the phone service are nominal.

Required

Under IAS 18, do you think the activation fee should be:
(a) recognised as revenue at the time the service is activated?
(b) spread as revenue over the estimated period over which the customer will use company F's mobile phone services (the 'customer relationship period')? State your reasons. (*Hint:* You need to determine exactly what company F is selling to its customers.)

PROBLEM 4.10 ★★★   Deferred revenue payments

On 2 January 2008, seller S sells and delivers an item of equipment to buyer B for $100 000. The sale contract requires B to pay $20 000 each year for five years from the date of purchase, without interest. Based on B's credit rating, it could borrow money at 10% to finance this purchase.

Required

Calculate:

(a) The amount of revenue from the sale of goods (if any) that S should recognise on 2 January 2008 (date of sale) and each year 2008 to 2012.

(b) The amount of interest income (if any) that S should recognise each year 2008 to 2012.

WEBLINK

Visit these websites for additional information:

www.iasb.org   www.iasplus.com
www.asic.gov.au   www.ifac.org
www.aasb.com.au   www.nzica.com
www.accaglobal.com   www.capa.com.my

REFERENCES

AstraZeneca 2005, *Annual report and form 20-F information 2005*, <www.astrazeneca.com>.

Bayer AG 2005, *Bayer annual report 2005*, <www.bayer.com>.

Dairy Farm International Holdings Limited 2004, *Annual report 2004*, <www.dairyfarmgroup.com>.

Esprit Holdings Limited 2005, *Annual report 04–05*, <www.esprit.com>.

Gazprom 2004, *Financial report 2004*, <www.gazprom.ru>.

General Accounting Office (US) 2002, GAO report number GAO-03-138, *Financial statement restatements: trends, market impacts, regulatory responses, and remaining challenges*, 23 October, <www.gao.gov>.

Lufthansa AG 2004, *Annual report for 2004*, <www.lufthansa.com>.

Securities and Exchange Commission (US) 2004, *SEC charges Qwest Communications International Inc. with multi-faceted accounting and financial reporting fraud*, viewed 11 April 2006, <www.sec.gov/news/press/2004-148.htm>.

—2005, *SEC charges Time Warner with fraud, aiding and abetting frauds by others, and violating a prior cease-and-desist order; CFO, controller, and deputy controller charged with causing reporting violations*, viewed 11 April 2006, <www.sec.gov/news/press/2005-38.htm>.

—2006, *SEC charges McAfee, Inc. with accounting fraud; McAfee agrees to settle and pay a $50 million penalty*, viewed 11 April 2006, <www.sec.gov/news/press/2006-3.htm>.

The Swatch Group Ltd 2004, *Annual report 2004*, <www.swatchgroup.com>.

UBS AG 2004, *Financial report 2004*, <www.ubs.com>.

CHAPTER 5
Provisions, contingent liabilities and contingent assets

ACCOUNTING STANDARDS

International: IAS 37 *Provisions, Contingent Liabilities and Contingent Assets*

Australia: AASB 137 *Provisions, Contingent Liabilities and Contingent Assets*

New Zealand: NZ IAS 37 *Provisions, Contingent Liabilities and Contingent Assets*

CONCEPTS FOR REVIEW

Before studying this chapter, you should understand or, if necessary, revise:
- the IASB Framework, in particular the definitions of and recognition criteria for liabilities and assets
- the concept of the time value of money and discounted cash flows.

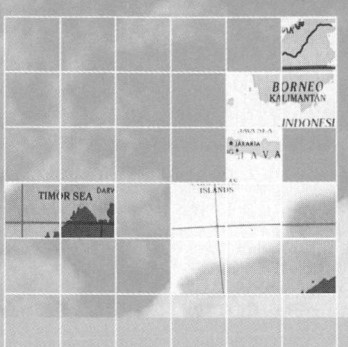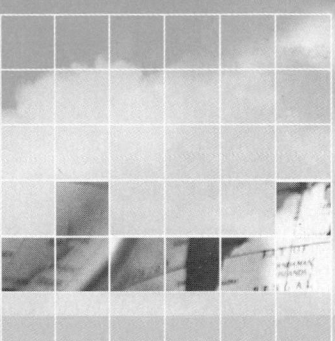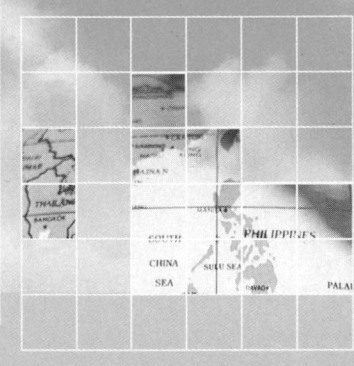

LEARNING OBJECTIVES

When you have studied this chapter, you should be able to:
1. understand the concept of a provision
2. understand how to distinguish provisions from other liabilities
3. understand the concept of a contingent liability
4. describe how to distinguish a provision from a contingent liability
5. explain when a provision should be recognised
6. explain how a provision, once recognised, should be measured
7. apply the definitions, recognition and measurement criteria for provisions and contingent liabilities to practical situations
8. understand the concept of a contingent asset
9. describe the disclosure requirements for provisions and contingent liabilities
10. describe the disclosure requirements for contingent assets.

5.1   Introduction to IAS 37

IAS 37 deals with the recognition, measurement and presentation of provisions and contingent assets and contingent liabilities. The standard contains specific requirements regarding the recognition of restructuring provisions and onerous contracts.

The standard:

- defines provisions and specifies recognition criteria and measurement requirements for the recognition of provisions in financial statements
- defines contingent liabilities and contingent assets and prohibits their recognition in the financial statements but requires their disclosure when certain conditions are met
- requires that where provisions are measured using estimated cash flows the cash flows be discounted to their present value at the reporting date and specifies the discount rate to be used for this purpose
- prohibits providing for future operating losses
- defines onerous contracts and requires the estimated net loss under onerous contracts to be provided for
- specifies recognition criteria for restructuring provisions and identifies the types of costs that may be included in restructuring provisions
- requires extensive disclosures relating to provisions, recoveries, contingent liabilities and contingent assets.

5.1.1   Scope

IAS 37 prescribes the accounting and disclosure for all provisions, contingent liabilities and contingent assets except:

(a) those resulting from financial instruments (see chapter 6) and those arising in insurance entities from contracts with policyholders

(b) those resulting from executory contracts, except where the contract is onerous (Executory contracts are contracts under which neither party has performed any of its obligations or both parties have partially performed their obligations to an equal extent.)

(c) those covered by another IAS. For example, certain types of provisions are also addressed in standards on:
- construction contracts (see IAS 11 *Construction Contracts*)
- income taxes (see IAS 12 *Income Taxes*, covered in chapter 8)
- leases (see IAS 17 *Leases*, covered in chapter 14). However, as IAS 17 contains no specific requirements to deal with operating leases that have become onerous, IAS 37 applies to such cases
- employee benefits (see IAS 19 *Employee Benefits*)
- insurance contracts (see IFRS 4 *Insurance Contracts*).

Some amounts sometimes described as provisions may relate to the recognition of revenue; for example, where an entity gives guarantees in exchange for a fee. This may also be described as 'deferred revenue'. IAS 37 does not address the recognition of revenue. IAS 18 *Revenue* identifies the circumstances in which revenue is recognised and provides practical guidance on the application of the recognition criteria.

Sometimes the term 'provision' is also used in the context of items such as depreciation, impairment of assets and doubtful debts. These are adjustments to the carrying amounts of assets and are not addressed in IAS 37. Refer to IAS 36 *Impairment of Assets*, which is covered in chapter 13.

Other IASs specify whether expenditures are treated as assets or as expenses. These issues are not addressed in IAS 37. Accordingly, IAS 37 neither prohibits nor requires capitalisation of the costs recognised when a provision is made. Refer to IAS 38 *Intangible Assets*, which deals partly with this issue, and is covered in chapter 11.

IAS 37 applies to provisions for restructuring (including discontinued operations). Where a restructure meets the definition of a discontinued operation, additional disclosures may be required by IFRS 5 *Non-current Assets Held for Sale and Discontinued Operations*. IFRS 3 *Business Combinations* deals with accounting for restructuring provisions arising in business combinations. This chapter covers the relevant requirements of IFRS 3.

LO 1

5.2 Definition of a provision

Paragraph 49 of the IASB Framework defines a liability as:

> a present obligation of the entity arising from past events, the settlement of which is expected to result in an outflow from the entity of resources embodying economic benefits.

A provision is a subset of liabilities (i.e. it is a type of liability). Paragraph 10 of IAS 37 defines a provision as:

> a liability of uncertain timing or amount.

It is this *uncertainty* that distinguishes provisions from other liabilities.

The IASB Framework states that an essential characteristic of a liability is that the entity has a present obligation. An obligation is a duty or responsibility to act or perform in a certain way. Obligations may be legally enforceable as a consequence of a binding contract, for example. This is normally the case with amounts payable for goods or services received, which are described as 'payables' or 'trade creditors'. However, legal enforceability is not a necessary requirement to demonstrate the existence of a liability. An entity may have an equitable or constructive obligation, arising from normal business practice or custom, to act in an equitable manner. Alternatively, the obligation is construed from the circumstances. Determining whether an equitable or constructive obligation exists is often more difficult than identifying a legal obligation. IAS 37 does not specifically acknowledge the concept of an equitable obligation; however, it does define a constructive obligation, in paragraph 10, as:

> an obligation that derives from an entity's actions where:
> (a) by an established pattern of past practice, published policies or a sufficiently specific current statement, the entity has indicated to other parties that it will accept certain responsibilities; and
> (b) as a result, the entity has created a valid expectation on the part of those other parties that it will discharge those responsibilities.

A present obligation exists only where the entity has no realistic alternative but to make the sacrifice of economic benefits to settle the obligation.

For example, assume that an entity makes a public announcement that it will match the financial assistance provided by other entities to victims of a natural disaster and, because of custom and moral considerations, has no realistic alternative but to provide the assistance. (In this case the events have already taken place – the natural disaster – and the public announcement is the obligating event).

Importantly, a decision by the entity's management or governing body does not, by itself, create a constructive obligation. This is because the management or governing body would retain the ability to reverse that decision. A present obligation would come into existence when the decision was communicated publicly to those affected by it. This would result in the valid expectation that the entity would fulfil the obligation, thus leaving the entity with little or no discretion to avoid the sacrifice of economic benefits.

LO 2

5.3 Distinguishing provisions from other liabilities

A provision may arise from either a legal or constructive obligation. As stated previously, the key distinguishing factor is the uncertainty relating to either the timing of settlement or the amount to be settled.

Paragraph 11 of IAS 37 gives an example of the distinction between liabilities and provisions as follows. It states that trade payables and accruals are liabilities because:

(a) trade payables are liabilities to pay for goods or services that have been received or supplied and have been invoiced or formally agreed with the supplier; and

(b) accruals are liabilities to pay for goods or services that have been received or supplied but have not been paid, invoiced or formally agreed with the supplier, including amounts due to employees (for example, amounts relating to accrued vacation pay). Although it is sometimes necessary to estimate the amount or timing of accruals, the uncertainty is generally much less than for provisions.

Accruals are often reported as part of trade and other payables, whereas provisions are reported separately.

Note, however, that employee benefits are addressed specifically by IAS 19 *Employee Benefits*, and are not included in the scope of IAS 37.

Some examples of typical provisions include provisions for warranty, restructuring provisions and provisions for onerous contracts. These are discussed in more detail later in this chapter.

LO 3

5.4 Definition of a contingent liability

Paragraph 10 of IAS 37 defines a contingent liability as:

(a) a possible obligation that arises from past events and whose existence will be confirmed only by the occurrence or non-occurrence of one or more uncertain future events not wholly within the control of the entity; or

(b) a present obligation that arises from past events but is not recognised because:

 (i) it is not probable that an outflow of resources embodying economic benefits will be required to settle the obligation; or

 (ii) the amount of the obligation cannot be measured with sufficient reliability.

The definition of a contingent liability is interesting because it encompasses two distinctly different concepts. The first, part (a) of the definition, is the concept of a *possible* obligation. This fails one of the essential characteristics of a liability — the requirement for the existence of a present obligation. If there is no present obligation, only a possible one, there is no liability. Hence, part (a) of the definition does not meet the definition of a liability such that one could argue that the term 'contingent *liability*' is misleading, because items falling into category (a) are not liabilities by definition.

Part (b) of the definition, on the other hand, deals with liabilities that fail the recognition criteria. They are present obligations, so they meet the essential requirements of the definition of liabilities, but they do not meet the recognition criteria (probability of outflow of economic benefits and reliability of measurement).

LO 4

5.5 Distinguishing a contingent liability from a provision

Contingent liabilities are not recognised in the financial statements but must be disclosed in the financial statements unless the possibility of an outflow in settlement is remote.

Paragraph 12 of IAS 37 states that:

> In a general sense, all provisions are contingent because they are uncertain in timing or amount. However, within this Standard the term 'contingent' is used for liabilities and assets that are not recognised because their existence will be confirmed only by the occurrence or non-occurrence of one or more uncertain future events not wholly within the control of the entity. In addition, the term 'contingent liability' is used for liabilities that do not meet the recognition criteria.

The following example (figure 5.1) illustrates the difference between a contingent liability and a provision. Note, however, that financial guarantees are specifically covered by IAS 39 and must be accounted for in accordance with that standard or IFRS 4 (see chapter 6).

When *Endeavour Limited* provides a guarantee to a bank in relation to a bank loan provided to *Tower Limited*:
- If *Tower Limited* is solvent and able to repay the loan without breaching any debt covenants, a contingent liability exists and disclosure thereof is required in the notes to the financial statements of *Endeavour Limited*;
- If *Tower Limited* has breached the debt covenants and it is probable that *Endeavour Limited* will be called upon as guarantor of the loan by the Bank, a provision should be recognised by *Endeavour Limited* for the amount likely to be paid to the Bank. This assumes that there is still uncertain 'timing or amount', otherwise the amount would be a liability.

FIGURE 5.1   Example of the difference between a provision and a contingent liability
Source: Ernst & Young (2002a).

LO 5   5.6   The recognition criteria for provisions

The recognition criteria for provisions are the same as those for liabilities as set out in the IASB Framework. Curiously, IAS 37 also includes part of the definition of a liability in its recognition criteria for provisions (part (a) of the recognition criteria below). The reason for this is most likely the desire of the standard setters to distinguish between provisions and contingent liabilities, but it is arguable whether this needs to be done via the recognition criteria, since the definitions are sufficiently clear.

Paragraph 14 of IAS 37 states that a provision should be recognised when:

(a) an entity has a present obligation (legal or constructive) as a result of a past event;
(b) it is probable that an outflow of resources embodying economic benefits will be required to settle the obligation; and
(c) a reliable estimate can be made of the amount of the obligation.
If these conditions are not met, no provision shall be recognised.

The concept of probability is discussed in the IASB Framework and deals essentially with the likelihood of something eventuating. If it is more likely rather than less likely to eventuate, IAS 37 regards the outflow as probable. Probability is assessed for each obligation separately, unless the obligations form a group of similar obligations (such as product warranties) in which case the probability that an outflow will be required in settlement is determined by assessing the class of obligations as a whole.

Paragraphs 15 and 16 of IAS 37 discuss the concepts of a present obligation and probability, giving some useful examples:

> 15. In rare cases it is not clear whether there is a present obligation. In these cases, a past event is deemed to give rise to a present obligation if, taking account of all available evidence, it is more likely than not that a present obligation exists at the balance sheet date.

16. In almost all cases it will be clear whether a past event has given rise to a present obligation. In rare cases, for example in a law suit, it may be disputed either whether certain events have occurred or whether those events result in a present obligation. In such a case, an entity determines whether a present obligation exists at the balance sheet date by taking account of all available evidence, including, for example, the opinion of experts. The evidence considered includes any additional evidence provided by events after the balance sheet date. On the basis of such evidence:

(a) where it is more likely than not that a present obligation exists at the balance sheet date, the entity recognises a provision (if the recognition criteria are met); and

(b) where it is more likely that no present obligation exists at the balance sheet date, the entity discloses a contingent liability, unless the possibility of an outflow of resources embodying economic benefits is remote [in which case no disclosure is made].

A past event that leads to a present obligation is called an obligating event. As discussed in the section on constructive obligations, for an event to be an obligating event the entity must have no realistic alternative to settling the obligation created by the event. In the case of a legal obligation this is because the settlement of the obligation can be enforced by law. In the case of a constructive obligation the event needs to create a valid expectation in other parties that the entity will discharge the obligation.

Reliable estimation is the final criterion for recognition of a provision. Although the use of estimates is a necessary part of the preparation of financial statements, in the case of provisions the uncertainty associated with reliable measurement is greater than for other liabilities. Accordingly, IAS 37 goes on to give more detailed guidance on measurement of provisions, which we will discuss later in the chapter. However, it is expected that except in very rare cases an entity will be able to determine a reliable estimate of the obligation.

Note the use of the concept of 'probability' in the recognition criteria for liabilities, including provisions, contrasted with the use of the concept of 'possibility' in determining whether or not a contingent liability should be disclosed. Paragraph 86 of IAS 37 requires contingent liabilities to be disclosed in the financial statements 'unless the possibility of an outflow in settlement is remote'. IAS 37 interprets 'probable' as meaning more likely rather than less likely. IAS 37 does not, however, provide any further guidance on what it means by 'possibility'. In plain English terms 'probability' addresses the likelihood of whether or not something will happen, whereas 'possibility' has a broader meaning – virtually anything is possible, but how probable is it? Given this distinction, we should assume that the intention of IAS 37 is that most contingent liabilities should be disclosed and that only in very rare circumstances is no disclosure appropriate.

Contingent liabilities need to be continually assessed to determine whether or not they have become actual liabilities. This is done by considering whether the recognition criteria for liabilities have been met. If it becomes probable that an outflow of economic benefits will be required for an item previously dealt with as a contingent liability, a provision is recognised in the financial statements in the period in which the change in probability occurs.

5.7 Putting it all together — a useful decision tree

In sections 5.2 through 5.6 we discussed the definitions of provisions and contingent liabilities, the recognition criteria for provisions and when a contingent liability must be disclosed. The decision tree (figure 5.2) on the opposite page summarises this discussion. The decision tree is based on appendix B of IAS 37 but has been modified to aid understanding.

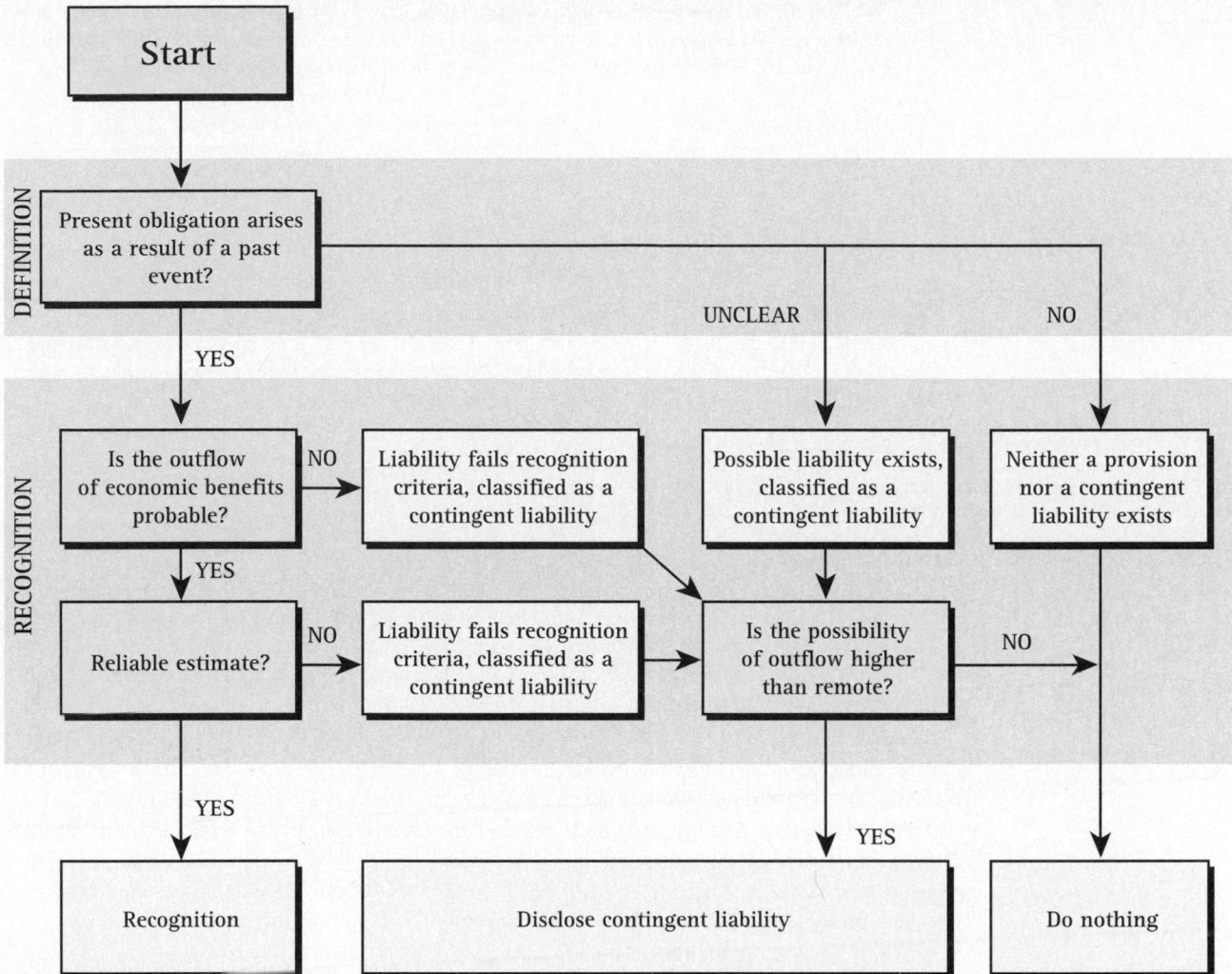

FIGURE 5.2 Decision tree
Source: Ernst & Young (2002b).

LO 6

5.8 Measurement of provisions

5.8.1 Best estimate

When measuring a provision, the amount recognised should be the *best estimate* of the consideration required to settle the present obligation at the balance sheet date. This amount is often expressed as the amount which represents, as closely as possible, what the entity would rationally pay to settle the present obligation immediately or to provide consideration to a third party to assume it. The fact that it is difficult to measure the provision and that estimates have to be used does not mean that the provision is not reliably measurable.

Paragraphs 39 and 40 of IAS 37 address the issue of how to deal with the uncertainties surrounding the amount to be recognised as a provision:

39. Uncertainties surrounding the amount to be recognised as a provision are dealt with by various means according to the circumstances. Where the provision being measured involves a large population of items, the obligation is estimated by weighting all possible outcomes by their associated probabilities. The name for this statistical method of estimation is 'expected value'. The provision will therefore be different depending on

whether the probability of a loss of a given amount is, for example, 60 per cent or 90 per cent. Where there is a continuous range of possible outcomes, and each point in that range is as likely as any other, the mid-point of the range is used.

> **Example**
>
> An entity sells goods with a warranty under which customers are covered for the cost of repairs of any manufacturing defects that become apparent within the first six months after purchase. If minor defects were detected in all products sold, repair costs of 1 million would result. If major defects were detected in all products sold, repair costs of 4 million would result. The entity's past experience and future expectations indicate that, for the coming year, 75% of the goods sold will have no defects, 20% of the goods sold will have minor defects and 5% of the goods sold will have major defects. In accordance with paragraph 24, an entity assesses the probability of an outflow for the warranty obligations as a whole.
>
> The expected value of the cost of repairs is:
>
> $$(75\% \text{ of nil}) + (20\% \text{ of 1 m}) + (5\% \text{ of 4 m}) = 400\,000$$

40. Where a single obligation is being measured, the individual most likely outcome may be the best estimate of the liability. However, even in such a case, the entity considers other possible outcomes. Where other possible outcomes are either mostly higher or mostly lower than the most likely outcome, the best estimate will be a higher or lower amount. For example, if an entity has to rectify a serious fault in a major plant that it has constructed for a customer, the individual most likely outcome may be for the repair to succeed at the first attempt at a cost of 1000, but a provision for a larger amount is made if there is a significant chance that further attempts will be necessary.

The provision is measured before tax. Any tax consequences are accounted for in accordance with IAS 12 *Income Taxes*.

The need to use judgement in determining the best estimate is clearly evident. Judgement is used in assessing, inter alia:

- what the likely consideration required to settle the obligation will be
- when the consideration is likely to be settled
- whether there are various scenarios that are likely to arise
- what the probability of those various scenarios arising will be.

The distinguishing characteristic of provisions — the uncertainty relating to either the timing of settlement or the amount to be settled — is clearly illustrated in the above discussion. Because of the extent of judgement required in measuring provisions, auditors focus more on auditing provisions than on other normal liabilities such as trade creditors and accruals. This is particularly the case if a change in one of the assumptions, such as the probability of a particular scenario eventuating or the likely consideration required to settle the obligation, would have a material impact on the amount recognised as a provision and thus on the financial statements.

5.8.2 Risks and uncertainties

IAS 37 requires that the risks and uncertainties surrounding the events and circumstances should be taken into account in reaching the best estimate of a provision. Paragraph 43 states:

> Risk describes variability of outcome. A risk adjustment may increase the amount at which a liability is measured. Caution is needed in making judgements under conditions of uncertainty, so that income or assets are not overstated and expenses or liabilities are not understated. However, uncertainty does not justify the creation of excessive provisions or a deliberate overstatement of liabilities. For example, if the projected costs of a particularly adverse outcome are estimated on a prudent basis, that outcome is not then deliberately treated as more probable than is realistically the case. Care is needed to avoid duplicating adjustments for risk and uncertainty with consequent overstatement of a provision.

5.8.3 Present value

Provisions are required to be *discounted to present value* where the effect of discounting is material. IAS 37 requires that the discount rate used must be a pre-tax rate that reflects current market assessments of the time value of money and the *risks specific to the liability*. Where future cash flow estimates have been adjusted for risk, the discount rate should not reflect this risk.

In practical terms it is often difficult to determine reliably a liability-specific discount rate. Also, the higher the discount rate the lower the amount that will be recognised as a liability. This seems counter-intuitive — the higher the risk attached to the liability the lower the amount at which it is recognised. A more appropriate way to factor in risk would be to use it in assessing the probability of outcomes (as discussed in 5.8.1) and then use a risk-free rate in discounting the cash flows. Paragraph 78 of IAS 19 *Employee Benefits* states that the discount rate for long-term employee benefit obligations should be determined by reference to market yields at balance date on high-quality corporate bonds or, where there is no deep market in such bonds, the market yield on government bonds. The currency and term of the corporate bonds or government bonds should be consistent with the currency and estimated term of the employee benefit obligations. Although there may be some debate about how to determine the risk-free rate, market yields on high-quality corporate bonds or government bonds are reasonable approximations. It is unclear why IAS 37 and IAS 19 are inconsistent, but given that IAS 19 is a more recent standard than IAS 37, we expect that IAS 37 will be modified to be consistent with IAS 19.

The following illustrative example shows the way a provision should be measured, taking into account risks and the time value of money.

ILLUSTRATIVE EXAMPLE 5.1

Measuring a provision

An entity estimates that the expected cash outflows to settle its warranty obligations at balance date are as follows. (Note that probability of cash outflows has already been assessed similarly to the example in 5.8.1 and, accordingly, no further adjustment for risk is made.) The entity has used a discount rate based on government bonds with the same term and currency as the expected cash outflows.

Expected cash outflow	Timing	Discount rate	Present value of cash outflow
400 000	In 1 year	6.0%	377 358
100 000	In 2 years	6.5%	88 166
20 000	In 3 years	6.9%	16 371
Present value			481 895

5.8.4 Future events

Anticipated future events expected to affect the amount required to settle the entity's present obligation must be reflected in the amount provided, when there is reliable evidence that they will occur.

As an example, paragraph 49 of IAS 37 states:

> Expected future events may be particularly important in measuring provisions. For example, an entity may believe that the cost of cleaning up a site at the end of its life will be reduced by future changes in technology. The amount recognised reflects a reasonable expectation of technically qualified, objective observers, taking account of all available evidence as to the technology that will be available at the time of the clean-up. Thus it is appropriate to include, for example, expected cost reductions associated with increased experience in applying existing technology or the expected cost of applying existing technology to a larger or more complex clean-up operation than has previously been carried out. However, an entity does not anticipate the development of a completely new technology for cleaning up unless it is supported by sufficient objective evidence.

5.8.5 Expected disposal of assets

Gains from the expected disposal of assets must not be taken into account when measuring the amount of a provision, even if the expected disposal is closely linked to the event giving rise to the provision. Rather, when the gain on disposal is made it should be recognised at that time in accordance with the relevant international accounting standard. Therefore, it is clear that only expected cash *outflows* must be taken into account in measuring the provision. Any cash inflows are treated separately from the measurement of the provision.

5.8.6 Reimbursements

When some of the amount required to settle a provision is expected to be recovered from a third party IAS 37 requires that the recovery be recognised as an asset, but only when it is *virtually certain* that the reimbursement will be received if the entity settles the obligation. This differs from the normal asset recognition criteria, which require that the inflow of future economic benefits be *probable*. Presumably, the standard setters were concerned about an uncertain asset related to an uncertain liability, and therefore decided to make the recognition criteria stricter for these types of assets. When such an asset is recognised the amount should not exceed the amount of the provision. IAS 37 allows the income from the asset to be set off against the expense relating to the provision in the income statement. However, it does not mention set off in the balance sheet of the asset and the provision. One of the disclosures required, in paragraph 85(c), is the amount of any asset that has been recognised for expected reimbursements; therefore, it is reasonable to assume that IAS 37 did not intend for the provision and asset to be set off in the balance sheet.

5.8.7 Changes in provisions and use of provisions

IAS 37 requires provisions to be reviewed at each balance sheet date and adjusted to reflect the current best estimate. If it is no longer probable that an outflow of resources embodying economic benefits will be required to settle the obligation, the provision should be reversed.

Where discounting is used, the carrying amount of a provision increases in each period to reflect the passage of time. This increase is recognised as borrowing cost. This is similar to the way finance lease liabilities are accounted for under IAS 17 *Leases*, as shown in chapter 14.

A provision should be used only for expenditures for which the provision was originally recognised. Illustrative example 5.2 shows how a provision is accounted for where discounting is applied and where the provision is adjusted to reflect the current best climate.

ILLUSTRATIVE EXAMPLE 5.2

Accounting for a provision

Company A estimates that it will be required to pay $100 000 in three years time to settle a warranty obligation. The discount rate applied is 5.5%. The probability of cash outflows has been assessed in determining the $100 000.

The following table shows how the provision is accreted over the three years:

A. Year	B. Present value at the beginning of the year	C. Interest expense at 5.5% (B × 5.5%)	D. Cash flows	E. Present value at the end of the year (B + C − D)
1	85 161	4 683	–	89 844
2	89 844	4 942	–	94 786
3	94 786	5 214	(100 000)	–

Journal entries are as follows:

On initial recognition in year 1			
Warranty expense	Dr	85 161	
Warranty provision	Cr		85 161
On recognition of interest in year 1			
Interest expense	Dr	4 683	
Warranty provision	Cr		4 683
On recognition of interest in year 2			
Interest expense	Dr	4 942	
Warranty provision	Cr		4 942
On recognition of interest in year 3			
Interest expense	Dr	5 214	
Warranty provision	Cr		5 214
On settlement of provision, end of year 3			
Warranty provision	Dr	100 000	
Cash	Cr		100 000

Now assume the same facts as above except that, at the end of year 2, company A re-estimates the amount to be paid to settle the obligation at the end of year 3 to be $90 000. The appropriate discount rate remains at 5.5%.

The present value of $90 000 at the end of year 2 is $85 306. Company A thus adjusts the provision by $9480 ($94 786–85 306) to reflect the revised estimated cash flows.

Journal entries are as follows:

Revision of estimate at end of year 2			
Warranty provision	Dr	9 480	
Warranty expense (income statement)	Cr		9 480
On recognition of interest in year 3			
Interest expense	Dr	4 694	
Warranty provision ($85 306 × 5.5% rounded)	Cr		4 694
On settlement of provision, end of year 3			
Warranty provision	Dr	90 000	
Cash	Cr		90 000

The re-estimated cash flows are adjusted against the warranty expense recorded in the income statement, while the unwinding of the discount continues to be recorded as interest expense. Any change in the discount rate used would also be adjusted against interest expense.

5.9 Application of the definitions, recognition and measurement rules

5.9.1 Future operating losses

IAS 37 states that provisions must not be recognised for future operating losses. Even if a sacrifice of future economic benefits is expected, a provision for future operating losses is not recognised because a past event creating a present obligation has not occurred. This is because the entity's management will generally have the ability to avoid incurring future operating losses by either disposing of or restructuring the operation in question. An expectation of future operating losses may, however, be an indicator that an asset is impaired and the requirements of IAS 36 *Impairment of Assets* should be applied.

5.9.2 Onerous contracts

An onerous contract is defined in paragraph 10 of IAS 37 as:

> a contract in which the unavoidable costs of meeting the obligations under the contract exceed the economic benefits expected to be received under it.

If an entity is a party to an onerous contract, a provision for the present obligation under the contract must be recognised. The reason these losses should be provided for is that the entity is contracted to fulfil the contract. Therefore, entry into an onerous contract gives rise to a present obligation.

Examples of onerous contracts include:

- where an electricity supplier has entered into a contract to supply electricity at a price lower than the price that it is contracted to receive it at
- where a manufacturer has entered into a supply contract at a price below the costs of production.

IAS 37 does not go into a lot of detail regarding onerous contracts and the requirements of the standard are quite vague in this area. Therefore, judgement has to be applied on a case-by-case basis to assess whether or not individual contracts qualify as onerous contracts under the standard.

For the purpose of raising a provision in respect of an onerous contract, the amount to be recognised is the least net cost of exiting the contract; that is, the lesser of:

- the cost of fulfilling the contract, and
- any compensation or penalties arising from failure to fulfil the contract.

5.9.3 Restructuring provisions

Perhaps the most controversial aspect of IAS 37 is the recognition criteria for restructuring provisions. IFRS 3 *Business Combinations* addresses restructuring provisions arising as part of a business combination, whereas IAS 37 addresses restructuring provisions arising other than as part of a business combination. Although the fundamental criteria are consistent, IFRS 3 has more prescriptive requirements than IAS 37. For ease of discussion, both types of restructuring provision are discussed here.

During the 1990s, standard setters in various jurisdictions set tougher rules on when a restructuring provision could be recognised, particularly when the provision related to the acquisition of a business. The reason for the crackdown was the tendency for companies to create restructuring provisions deliberately to avoid the recognition of an expense in future periods. The following example illustrates this point.

ILLUSTRATIVE EXAMPLE 5.3

Restructuring provisions

Assume company A acquires company B on 1 February 2005. The identifiable net assets of company B are $400 million and company A pays $500 million cash as purchase consideration. The goodwill arising on acquisition is thus $100 million. Company A then decides to create a restructuring provision of $60 million for future possible restructuring activities related to company B. Company A records the following additional entry as part of its acquisition accounting entries:

Goodwill	Dr	60m	
Restructuring provision	Cr		60m

Why does company A have an incentive to record this entry? The entry increases the amount recorded as goodwill, and in the 1990s goodwill was required to be amortised in most jurisdictions. Why would company A want to expose itself to future goodwill amortisation? The answer is that because the restructuring provision was recorded directly against goodwill, an expense for the restructuring will *never* be recorded. When company A incurs the expenditure in the future, the outflows will be recorded against the provision. Company A would likely have been able to highlight goodwill amortisation as a separate item either in its income statement or the attached notes, and thus would have been satisfied that the amortisation expense was effectively quarantined from the rest of its reported profit. The benefit for company A was that the restructuring expense never affected its profit, and thus the creation of the restructuring provision as part of the acquisition entries protected company A's future profits.

Rules to make it more difficult to record restructuring provisions were introduced in the United States and the United Kingdom. In the United States, the requirements for the recognition of restructuring provisions are contained primarily in Emerging Issues Task Force (EITF) Consensus EITF 94-3 and EITF 95-3. In addition, the Securities and Exchange Commission (SEC) issued a staff accounting bulletin (SAB) 100, which clarified how the SEC interprets certain aspects of the EITFs previously mentioned.

In the United Kingdom, FRS 7 *Fair Values in Acquisition Accounting* addresses the required accounting for restructuring provisions.

IAS 37 and IAS 22 (superseded by IFRS 3) were the least prescriptive of these requirements but, when IFRS 3 *Business Combinations* superseded IAS 22, it came more into line with UK requirements.

Paragraph 70 of IAS 37 provides the following examples of events that may be considered as restructurings:

(a) sale or termination of a line of business;
(b) the closure of business locations in a country or region or the relocation of business activities from one country or region to another;
(c) changes in management structure, for example, eliminating a layer of management; and
(d) fundamental reorganisations that have a material effect on the nature and focus of the entity's operations.

In broad terms, to be able to raise a restructuring provision, three conditions need to be met. First, the entity must have a *present obligation (either legal or constructive)* to restructure such that it cannot realistically avoid going ahead with the restructuring and thus incurring the costs involved. Second, only costs that are *directly and necessarily* caused by the restructuring and *not associated with the ongoing activities* of the entity may be included in a restructuring provision. Third, if the restructuring involves the sale of an operation, no obligation is deemed to arise for the sale of an operation until the entity is committed to the sale by a *binding sale agreement*.

Each of these requirements is considered in more detail below.

Present obligation

Usually a restructuring is initiated by management and thus it is rare that a legal obligation will exist for a restructuring. IAS 37 therefore focuses on the conditions that need to be met for a constructive obligation to exist. As we saw earlier, a constructive obligation is defined in paragraph 10 as:

> an obligation that derives from an entity's actions where:
> (a) by an established pattern of past practice, published policies or a sufficiently specific current statement, the entity has indicated to other parties that it will accept certain responsibilities; and
> (b) as a result, the entity has created a valid expectation on the part of those other parties that it will discharge those responsibilities.

In respect of restructuring provisions, paragraph 72 of IAS 37 states that a constructive obligation to restructure arises only when an entity:

> (a) has a detailed formal plan for the restructuring identifying at least:
> (i) the business or part of a business concerned;
> (ii) the principal locations affected;
> (iii) the location, function, and approximate number of employees who will be compensated for terminating their services;
> (iv) the expenditures that will be undertaken; and
> (v) when the plan will be implemented; and
> (b) has raised a valid expectation in those affected that it will carry out the restructuring by starting to implement that plan or announcing its main features to those affected by it.

Therefore, we see that the entity needs to have a *detailed formal plan* and must have raised a *valid expectation* in those affected. In respect of restructuring provisions arising as part of an acquisition, IAS 22 (now superseded by IFRS 3) went even further, with the following three additional requirements:

First, *at or before the date of acquisition*, the acquirer must have developed the *main features of a plan* that involves terminating or reducing the activities of the acquiree. The main features include items such as compensating employees for termination, closing facilities of the acquiree, eliminating product lines of the acquiree and terminating contracts of the acquiree that have become onerous because of the acquisition. Second, the main features of the plan must be *announced at or before the date of acquisition*, in order to meet the 'valid expectation' test in IAS 37. Third, the *detailed formal plan* required by IAS 37 must be developed by the *earlier of three months* after the date of acquisition and the date when the financial statements are authorised for issue.

IAS 22 allowed the restructuring provision to be recorded in the books of the *acquirer* (i.e. as part of the acquirer's acquisition entries), provided the criteria for recognition were met. This is in contrast to FRS 7. According to FRS 7, the identifiable assets and liabilities to be recognised should be only those of the *acquired entity* that existed at the acquisition date. FRS 7 is explicit in saying that provisions for restructuring would be recognised as identifiable liabilities only if the commitments had been made before the date of acquisition. It even goes so far as to say that only if the acquired entity was demonstrably committed to the expenditure whether or not the acquisition was completed, would it have a liability.

In October 1998 the Australian companies' regulator, the Australian Securities and Investments Commission (ASIC), issued a media release announcing that it had required St George Bank to adjust its financial statements for 1998 for a $120 million restructuring liability that had been recorded against goodwill in its 1997 financial statements. ASIC's view was that the restructuring provision could not be recognised because it did not relate to restructuring costs of the acquired entity. This was ASIC's interpretation of Urgent Issues Group (UIG) Abstract 8 *Accounting for Acquisitions – Recognition of Restructuring Costs as Liabilities* (ASIC 1998).

When the Australian Accounting Standards Board (AASB) issued its equivalent of IAS 37 (AASB 1044) in 2001, it amended the requirements of IAS 37 to reflect ASIC's view and required that the restructuring provision be a liability of the acquired entity. AASB 1044 was not very clear on this issue and it continued to be a controversial area for a number of years. Finally, in 2004, the IASB issued IFRS 3, which amended IAS 22 to require that the liability be a liability of the acquiree, recognised in accordance with IAS 37. As a result, no additional criteria are required by IFRS 3, and the three additional requirements of IAS 22 were removed.

Recording restructuring provisions

Where a provision for restructuring costs arises on the acquisition of an entity, it must be recognised as a liability in the balance sheet of the acquiree and not in the books of the acquirer or as a consolidation entry. The provision for the restructuring costs must be taken into account by the acquirer when measuring the fair value of the net assets acquired. Illustrative example 5.4 demonstrates this principle further.

ILLUSTRATIVE EXAMPLE 5.4

Recording restructuring provisions

Assume company X acquires company Y, a manufacturing company that has a head office in the city centre and a manufacturing plant in an industrial area. As part of the acquisition plans, company X decides to close company Y's head office premises and move company Y's staff to company X's own city premises. Company Y will be paying for the office closure costs.

Assume that the cost of closing company Y's office premises is $120 000. Company Y will record the following journal entry at the date of acquisition:

Restructuring costs (P+L)	Dr	120 000	
Restructuring provision (B/S)	Cr		120 000

In determining the fair value of the net assets acquired in company Y (in accordance with IFRS 3), company X will include the restructuring provision.

We saw above that in order to satisfy the 'valid expectation' test in IAS 37, the entity needs to have started to implement the detailed formal plan or announced the main features to those affected by it. An entity can do this in the following ways:

- By the entity having already entered into firm contracts to carry out parts of the restructuring. These contracts would be of such a nature that they effectively force the entity to carry out the restructuring. This would be the case if they contained severe penalty provisions or the costs of not fulfilling the contract were so high that it would effectively leave the entity with no alternative but to proceed.
- By starting to implement the detailed restructuring. This could include, for example, selling assets, notifying customers that supplies will be discontinued, notifying suppliers that orders will be ceasing, dismantling plant and equipment, and terminating employees' service.

- By announcing the main features of the plan to those affected by it (or their representatives). There may be a number of ways in which such an announcement could be made. It could be through written communication, meetings or discussions with the affected parties.

It is important that the communication is made in such a way that it raises a valid expectation in the affected parties such that they can be expected to act as a result of the communication, and by them doing so the entity would be left with no realistic alternative but to go ahead with the restructuring. For example, affected employees would start looking for other employment and customers would seek alternative sources of supply.

Figure 5.3 provides examples of where a present obligation does and does not arise on a restructuring as a result of an acquisition.

Example 1

The acquired entity has developed a detailed plan for the restructuring. Details of the plan have not been made public but, as at the date of acquisition, agreement about key features of the plan has been reached with, or information about the plan has been disclosed to, relevant third parties. These parties include employee representatives, lessors and regulatory bodies. As at the acquisition date, no elements of the plan had begun to be implemented.

A present obligation exists because the key features of the plan have been communicated to those affected and a detailed plan has been developed. The fact that parts of the plan have not begun to be implemented at the acquisition date does not negate the constructive obligation. Importantly, the *acquired entity* has the obligation.

Example 2

The acquiring entity has developed a detailed plan for the restructuring as at the date of acquisition. That plan involves the closure of a number of operating sites if the acquisition is successful and the retrenchment of all employees at those sites. As at the date of acquisition, key features of the plan have not been made public; however, employee representatives have been informed. Lessors of premises that will no longer be required have been informed of the entity's intentions, and negotiations on potential lease-termination penalty costs have commenced. Expressions of interest have been sought regarding the sale of plant and equipment that will be surplus should the acquisition proceed. Preliminary commitments have been made, and, conditional on the acquisition proceeding, agreements have been reached with third parties regarding the relocation or alternative supply of certain goods and services currently provided from the sites to be closed. The planned restructuring is such that on closure of the sites the continued employment of affected employees is not possible.

A present obligation does not exist for the *acquired entity*, so no provision is required.

FIGURE 5.3 Examples of the existence of a present obligation under IFRS 3 and IAS 37

Qualifying restructuring costs

The second requirement for recognition of a restructuring provision is that the provision can include only costs that are directly and necessarily caused by the restructuring and not associated with the ongoing activities of the entity (IAS 37, para. 80).

Examples of the types of costs that would be included in a restructuring provision include the costs of terminating leases and other contracts as a direct result of the restructuring; costs of operations conducted in effecting the restructuring, such as employee remuneration while they are engaged in such tasks as dismantling plant, disposing of surplus stocks and fulfilling contractual obligations; and costs of making employees redundant.

Paragraph 81 of IAS 37 specifically indicates that the types of costs excluded from provisions for restructuring would be the costs of retraining or relocating the continuing staff, marketing costs and costs related to investment in new systems and distribution networks. These types of costs relate to the future conduct of the entity and do not relate to present obligations.

These requirements relating to the types of costs that qualify as restructuring costs apply equally to internal restructurings as well as to restructurings occurring as part of an acquisition. Figure 5.4 provides examples of costs that qualify as restructuring costs and figure 5.5 provides examples of costs that *do not* qualify as restructuring costs.

Example 1

A restructuring plan includes discontinuing operations currently performed in a facility that is leased under an operating lease. A lease-cancellation penalty fee payable on terminating the lease is a restructuring cost.

Example 2

A restructuring plan includes relocating operations currently performed in a facility leased by the acquired entity to a site that is owned by the acquirer. The lessor will not release the acquired entity from the lease agreement and will not permit the acquirer or acquiree to sublease the facility. The acquirer does not intend to re-open the facility prior to the lease's expiration. The leased space provides no future benefit to the enterprise. The lease payments for the remaining non-cancellable term of the operating lease after operations cease are a restructuring cost.

FIGURE 5.4   Examples of costs that qualify as restructuring costs

Example 1

The acquired entity used to share computer resources with its previous parent company. Therefore, the restructuring plan includes activities to separate the acquired entity from its previous parent and establish independent computer resources. The costs include costs of installing a LAN, moving head office PCs, moving a call centre, moving dedicated systems and acquisitions of new software. Such costs are not restructuring costs because they are associated with the ongoing activities of the entity.

Example 2

The restructuring plan includes costs to hire outside consultants to identify future corporate goals and strategies for organisational structure. The consultants' costs are not restructuring costs because they are associated with the ongoing activities of the entity.

FIGURE 5.5   Examples of costs that do not qualify as restructuring costs

It is important to note that, although certain costs have occurred only because of restructuring (i.e. they would not have had to be incurred had the restructuring not taken place), this fact alone does not qualify them for recognition as restructuring costs. They also have to be costs that are not associated with the ongoing activities of the entity.

Binding sale agreement

The final requirement for recognition of a restructuring provision is that if the restructuring involves the sale of an operation, no obligation is deemed to arise for the sale until the entity is committed to the sale by a binding sale agreement (IAS 37, para. 78). Paragraph 79 explains:

> Even when an entity has taken a decision to sell an operation and announced that decision publicly, it cannot be committed to the sale until a purchaser has been identified and there is a binding sale agreement. Until there is a binding sale agreement, the entity will be able to change its mind and indeed will have to take another course of action if a purchaser cannot be found on acceptable terms. When the sale of an operation is envisaged as part of a restructuring, the assets of the operation are reviewed for impairment, under IAS 36 *Impairment of Assets*. When a sale is only part of a restructuring, a constructive obligation can arise for the other parts of the restructuring before a binding sale agreement exists.

5.9.4 Other applications

The examples in figures 5.6 to 5.14, sourced from IAS 37 and modified to aid understanding, illustrate other applications of the recognition requirements of IAS 37.

A manufacturer gives warranties at the time of sale to purchasers of its product. Under the terms of the contract for sale the manufacturer undertakes to make good, by repair or replacement, manufacturing defects that become apparent within three years from the date of sale. On past experience, it is probable (i.e. more likely than not) that there will be some claims under the warranties.

Present obligation as a result of a past obligating event – The obligating event is the sale of the product with a warranty, which gives rise to a legal obligation.

An outflow of resources embodying economic benefits in settlement – Probable for the warranties as a whole.

Conclusion – A provision is recognised for the best estimate of the costs of making good under the warranty products sold before the balance sheet date.

FIGURE 5.6 Warranties
Source: IAS 37, Appendix C, Example 1.

An entity in the oil industry causes contamination but cleans up only when required to do so under the laws of the particular country in which it operates. One country in which it operates has had no legislation requiring cleaning up, and the entity has been contaminating land in that country for several years. At 31 December 2000, it is virtually certain that a draft law requiring a clean up of land already contaminated will be enacted shortly after the year end.

Present obligation as a result of a past obligating event – The obligating event is the contamination of the land (past event) which gives rise to a present obligation because of the virtual certainty of legislation requiring cleaning up.

An outflow of resources embodying economic benefits in settlement – Probable.

Conclusion – A provision is recognised for the best estimate of the costs of the clean-up.

FIGURE 5.7 Contaminated land — legislation virtually certain to be enacted
Source: IAS 37, Appendix C, Example 2A.

An entity in the oil industry causes contamination and operates in a country where there is no environmental legislation. However, the entity has a widely published environmental policy in which it undertakes to clean up all contamination that it causes. The entity has a record of honouring this policy.

Present obligation as a result of a past obligating event – The obligating event is the contamination of the land, which gives rise to a constructive obligation because the conduct of the entity has created a valid expectation on the part of those affected by it that the entity will clean up contamination.

An outflow of resources embodying economic benefits in settlement – Probable.

Conclusion – A provision is recognised for the best estimate of the costs of clean-up [the entity has a constructive obligation].

FIGURE 5.8 Contaminated land and constructive obligation
Source: IAS 37, Appendix C, Example 2B.

An entity operates an offshore oilfield where its licensing agreement requires it to remove the oil rig at the end of production and restore the seabed. Ninety per cent of the eventual costs relate to the removal of the oil rig and restoration of damage caused by building it, and 10 per cent arise through the extraction of oil. At the balance sheet date, the rig has been constructed but no oil has been extracted.

Present obligation as a result of a past obligating event – The construction of the oil rig creates a legal obligation under the terms of the licence to remove the rig and restore the seabed and is thus an obligating event. At the balance sheet date, however, there is no obligation to rectify the damage that will be caused by extraction of the oil.

An outflow of resources embodying economic benefits in settlement – Probable.

Conclusion – A provision is recognised for the best estimate of 90 per cent of the eventual costs that relate to the removal of the oil rig and restoration of damage caused by building it. These costs are included as part of the cost of the oil rig. The 10 per cent of costs that arise through the extraction of oil are recognised as a liability when the oil is extracted.

FIGURE 5.9 Offshore oilfield
Source: IAS 37, Appendix C, Example 3.

A retail store has a policy of refunding purchases by dissatisfied customers, even though it is under no legal obligation to do so. Its policy of making refunds is generally known.

Present obligation as a result of a past obligating event – The obligating event is the sale of the product, which gives rise to a constructive obligation because the conduct of the store has created a valid expectation on the part of its customers that it will refund purchases.

An outflow of resources embodying economic benefits in settlement – Probable. A proportion of goods are returned for refund.

Conclusion – A provision is recognised for the best estimate of the costs of refunds.

FIGURE 5.10 Refunds Policy
Source: IAS 37, Appendix C, Example 4.

Under new legislation, an entity is required to fit smoke filters to its factories by 30 June 2000. The entity has not fitted the smoke filters.

(a) At the balance sheet date of 31 December 1999:
Present obligation as a result of a past obligating event – There is no obligation because there is no obligating event either for the costs of fitting smoke filters or for fines under the legislation.

Conclusion – No provision is recognised for the cost of fitting the smoke filters.

(b) At the balance sheet date of 31 December 2000:
Present obligation as a result of a past obligating event – There is still no obligation for the costs of fitting smoke filters because no obligating event has occurred (the fitting of the filters). However, an obligation might arise to pay fines or penalties under the legislation because the obligating event has occurred (the non-compliant operation of the factory).

An outflow of resources embodying economic benefits in settlement – Assessment of the probability of incurring fines and penalties by non-compliant operation depends on the details of the legislation and the stringency of the enforcement regime.

Conclusion – No provision is recognised for the costs of fitting smoke filters. However, a provision is recognised for the best estimate of any fines and penalties that are more likely than not to be imposed.

FIGURE 5.11 Legal requirement to fit smoke filters
Source: IAS 37, Appendix C, Example 6.

An entity operates profitably from a factory that it has leased under an operating lease. During December 2000 the entity relocates its operations to a new factory. The lease on the old factory continues for the next four years. It cannot be cancelled and the factory cannot be re-let to another user.

Present obligation as a result of a past obligating event – The obligating event is the signing of the lease contract, which gives rise to a legal obligation.

An outflow of resources embodying economic benefits in settlement – When the lease becomes onerous, an outflow of resources embodying economic benefits is probable. (Until the lease becomes onerous, the entity accounts for the lease under IAS 17 *Leases.*)

Conclusion – A provision is recognised for the best estimate of the unavoidable lease payments.

FIGURE 5.12 An onerous contract
Source: IAS 37, Appendix C, Example 8.

Some assets require, in addition to routine maintenance, substantial expenditure every few years for major refits or refurbishment and the replacement of major components. IAS 16 *Property, Plant and Equipment* gives guidance on allocating expenditure on an asset to its component parts where these components have different useful lives or provide benefits in a different pattern.

A furnace has a lining that needs to be replaced every five years for technical reasons. At the balance sheet date, the lining has been in use for three years.

Present obligation as a result of a past obligating event – There is no present obligation.

Conclusion – No provision is recognised.

The cost of replacing the lining is not recognised because, at the balance sheet date, no obligation to replace the lining exists independently of the company's future actions — even the intention to incur the expenditure depends on the company deciding to continue operating the furnace or replace the lining. Instead of a provision being recognised, the depreciation of the lining takes account of its consumption (i.e. it is depreciated over five years). The re-lining costs incurred are capitalised with the consumption of each new lining shown by depreciation over the subsequent five years.

FIGURE 5.13 Repairs and maintenance: refurbishment costs — no legislative requirement
Source: IAS 37, Appendix C, Examples 11 and 11A.

An airline is required by law to overhaul its aircraft once every three years.

Present obligation as a result of a past obligating event — There is no present obligation.

Conclusion — No provision is recognised.

The costs of overhauling aircraft are not recognised as a provision for the same reasons as the cost of replacing the lining is not recognised as a provision in Example 11A. Even a legal requirement to overhaul does not make the costs of overhaul a liability because no obligation exists to overhaul the aircraft independently of the entity's future actions — the entity could avoid the future expenditure by its future actions, for example by selling the aircraft. Instead of a provision being recognised, the depreciation of the aircraft takes account of the future incidence of maintenance costs (i.e. an amount equivalent to the expected maintenance costs is depreciated over three years).

FIGURE 5.14 Repair and maintenance: refurbishment costs — legislative requirement
Source: IAS 37, Appendix C, Example 11B.

It is interesting to contrast figures 5.13 and 5.14 with figures 5.7 and 5.8. In figures 5.7 and 5.8, the entity had a present obligation for the costs of clean-up or removal, which were independent of the cost and useful life of the asset in question. In addition, in those examples the entity was unable to avoid the clean-up or removal, although it could be argued that it could avoid those actions and incur any resultant fines (as in figure 5.11). In that case, provision would be made for the best estimate of the costs of non-compliance with the relevant legislation.

5.10 Contingent assets

LO 8

Paragraph 10 of IAS 37 defines a contingent asset as:

> a possible asset that arises from past events and whose existence will be confirmed only by the occurrence or non-occurrence of one or more uncertain future events not wholly within the control of the entity.

Paragraph 31 states that an entity should *not recognise* a contingent asset. Paragraph 89 requires that a contingent asset be *disclosed* where an inflow of benefits is probable.

Note the lack of symmetry between the definition of a contingent asset and a contingent liability. The definition of a contingent liability includes both possible liabilities and liabilities that fail the recognition criteria. A contingent asset includes only possible assets. The standard setters were presumably concerned with overstatement of assets and therefore wanted to apply a more stringent test to the definition, although arguably an asset that fails the recognition criteria is more of an asset than a possible asset! Further, IAS 37 permits a contingent asset to be reclassified and recognised as an actual asset only when it has become virtually certain that an inflow of economic benefits will arise. Contrast this with the test of probability which is applied to asset recognition generally. It could be argued that IAS 37 is biased towards ensuring that contingent liabilities are disclosed in almost all circumstances and reclassified and recognised as actual liabilities as soon as they meet the liability recognition criteria. Contingent assets, however, can be disclosed only in rare circumstances and reclassified to actual assets only when they meet strict recognition criteria. This bias could be criticised as being against the IASB's own Framework which, although it recognises the qualitative characteristic of prudence, states that:

> ... the exercise of prudence does not allow, for example, ... the deliberate understatement of assets or income, or the deliberate overstatement of liabilities or expenses, because the financial statements would not be neutral and, therefore, not have the quality of reliability (IASB Framework, para. 37).

An example of a contingent asset would be the possible receipt of damages arising from a court case which, as at the balance date, has been decided in favour of the entity. The hearing to determine damages, however, will be held after the balance date. The outcome of the hearing is outside the control of the entity, but the receipt of damages is probable because the case has been decided in the entity's favour. The asset meets the definition of a contingent asset because it is possible that the entity will receive the damages and the hearing is outside its control. In addition, the contingent asset is disclosed because it is probable that the damages (the inflow of economic benefits) will flow to the entity.

LO 9 & 10

5.11 Disclosure

The disclosure requirements of IAS 37 are self-explanatory and are reproduced below:

84. For each class of provision, an entity shall disclose:
    (a) the carrying amount at the beginning and end of the period;
    (b) additional provisions made in the period, including increases to existing provisions;
    (c) amounts used (i.e. incurred and charged against the provision) during the period;
    (d) unused amounts reversed during the period; and
    (e) the increase during the period in the discounted amount arising from the passage of time and the effect of any change in the discount rate.
    Comparative information is not required.
85. An entity shall disclose the following for each class of provision:
    (a) a brief description of the nature of the obligation and the expected timing of any resulting outflows of economic benefits;
    (b) an indication of the uncertainties about the amount or timing of those outflows. Where necessary to provide adequate information, an entity shall disclose the major assumptions made concerning future events, as addressed in paragraph 48; and
    (c) the amount of any expected reimbursement, stating the amount of any asset that has been recognised for that expected reimbursement.
86. Unless the possibility of any outflow in settlement is remote, an entity shall disclose for each class of contingent liability at the balance sheet date a brief description of the nature of the contingent liability and, where practicable:
    (a) an estimate of its financial effect, measured under paragraphs 36–52;
    (b) an indication of the uncertainties relating to the amount or timing of any outflow; and
    (c) the possibility of any reimbursement.
89. Where an inflow of economic benefits is probable, an entity shall disclose a brief description of the nature of the contingent assets at the balance sheet date, and, where practicable, an estimate of their financial effect, measured using the principles set out for provisions in paragraphs 36–52.
91. Where any of the information required by paragraphs 86 and 89 is not disclosed because it is not practicable to do so, that fact shall be stated.

92. In extremely rare cases, disclosure of some or all of the information required by paragraphs 84–89 can be expected to prejudice seriously the position of the entity in a dispute with other parties on the subject matter of the provision, contingent liability or contingent asset. In such cases, an entity need not disclose the information, but shall disclose the general nature of the dispute, together with the fact that, and reason why, the information has not been disclosed.

The disclosures required for contingent liabilities and assets necessarily involve judgement and estimation. Many analysts consider the contingent liabilities note to be one of the most important notes provided by a company because it helps the analyst to make his or her own decision about the likely consequences for the company and is useful in providing an overall view of the company's exposures. Thus, the use of the exemption permitted in paragraph 92 should be treated with caution because it could be interpreted as a deliberate concealing of the company's exposures.

An example of the disclosures required by paragraph 85 is included in appendix D of IAS 37, shown in figure 5.15.

A manufacturer gives warranties at the time of sale to purchasers of its three product lines. Under the terms of the warranty, the manufacturer undertakes to repair or replace items that fail to perform satisfactorily for two years from the date of sale. At the balance sheet date, a provision of 60 000 has been recognised. The provision has not been discounted as the effect of discounting is not material. The following information is disclosed:

A provision of 60 000 has been recognised for expected warranty claims on products sold during the last three financial years. It is expected that the majority of this expenditure will be incurred in the next financial year, and all will be incurred within two years of the balance sheet date.

FIGURE 5.15 Warranties
Source: IAS 37, Appendix D, Example 1.

5.12 Expected future developments

In June 2005, the IASB issued an exposure draft proposing significant changes to IAS 37 as part of its program to amend IFRS 3 (see chapter 12). The exposure draft proposed amendments to the title of IAS 37 (to 'Non-financial Liabilities'), new definitions of contingencies, and new recognition and measurement criteria. The proposed changes are so far-reaching that they have attracted widespread concern by respondents to the exposure draft. At the date of updating this textbook, there is doubt as to whether the proposed changes will eventuate in their current form, and to attempt to discuss them in more detail would only confuse readers.

5.13 Summary

IAS 37 deals with the recognition, measurement and presentation of provisions and contingent assets and contingent liabilities. The standard contains specific requirements regarding the recognition of restructuring provisions and onerous contracts.

The standard:
- defines provisions and specifies recognition criteria and measurement requirements for the recognition of provisions in financial statements
- defines contingent liabilities and contingent assets and prohibits their recognition in the financial statements but requires their disclosure when certain conditions are met

- requires that where provisions are measured using estimated cash flows, that the cash flows be discounted to their present value at the reporting date and specifies the discount rate to be used for this purpose
- prohibits providing for future operating losses
- defines onerous contracts and requires the estimated net loss under onerous contracts to be provided for
- specifies recognition criteria for restructuring provisions and identifies the types of costs that may be included in restructuring provisions
- requires extensive disclosures relating to provisions, recoveries, contingent liabilities and contingent assets.

DISCUSSION QUESTIONS

1. How is present value related to the concept of a liability?
2. Define (a) a contingency and (b) a contingent liability.
3. What are the characteristics of a provision?
4. Define a constructive obligation.
5. What is the key characteristic of a present obligation?
6. What are the recognition criteria for provisions?
7. At what point would a contingent liability become a provision?

EXERCISES

EXERCISE 5.1

Recognising a provision

Qantas awards members of its Frequent Flyer program one free round-the-world ticket for every 200 000 kilometres flown. How would the free ticket award be accounted for?

EXERCISE 5.2

Recognising a provision

When should liabilities for each of the following items be recorded in the accounts of the business entity?
(a) Acquisition of goods by purchase on credit
(b) Salaries
(c) Annual bonus paid to management
(d) Dividends

EXERCISE 5.3

Recognising a provision

The government introduces a number of changes to the value added tax system. As a result of these changes, company A, a manufacturing company, will need to retrain a large proportion of its administrative and sales workforce in order to ensure continued compliance with the new taxation regulations. At the balance sheet date, no retraining of staff has taken place.

Required
Should Company A provide for the costs of the staff training at the balance sheet date?

EXERCISE 5.4 ★★

Recognising a provision

Company B, a listed company, provides food to function centres that host events such as weddings and engagement parties. After an engagement party held by one of company B's customers in June 2005, 100 people became seriously ill, possibly as a result of food poisoning from products sold by company B. Legal proceedings were commenced seeking damages from company B, which disputed liability by claiming that the function centre was at fault for handling the food incorrectly. Up to the date of authorisation for issue of the financial statements for the year to 30 June 2005, company B's lawyers advised that it was probable that company B would not be found liable. However, two weeks after the financial statements were published, company B's lawyers advised that, owing to developments in the case, it was probable that company B would be found liable and the estimated damages would be material to the company's reported profits.

Required

Should company B recognise a liability for damages in its financial statements at 30 June 2005? How should it deal with the information it receives two weeks after the financial statements are published?

EXERCISE 5.5

Restructuring costs

A division of an acquired entity will be closed and activities discontinued. The division will operate for one year after the date of acquisition, after which all divisional employees will be retrenched except for the retention of some employees retained to finalise closure of the division.

Required

Which of the following costs, if any, are restructuring costs?
(a) The costs of employees (salaries and benefits) to be incurred after operations cease and that are associated with the closing of the division
(b) The costs of leasing the factory space occupied by the division for the year after the date of acquisition
(c) The costs of modifying the division's purchasing system to make it consistent with that of the acquirer's

EXERCISE 5.6

Restructuring costs

Company Z acquires company Y. The restructuring plan, which satisfies the criteria for the existence of a present obligation under IAS 37 and IFRS 3, includes an advertising program to promote the new company image. The restructuring plan also includes costs to retrain and relocate existing employees of the acquired entity.

Required

Are these costs restructuring costs?

EXERCISE 5.7 ★★

Distinguishing between liabilities, provisions and contingent liabilities

Identify whether each of the following would be a liability, a provision or a contingent liability, or none of the above, in the financial statements of company A as at its balance date of 30 June 2005. Assume that company A's financial statements are authorised for issue on 24 August 2005.
(a) An amount of $35 000 owing to company Z for services rendered during May 2005
(b) Long-service leave, estimated to be $500 000, owing to employees in respect of past services
(c) Costs of $26 000 estimated to be incurred for relocating employee D from company A's head office location to another city. The staff member will physically relocate during July 2005.
(d) Provision of $50 000 for the overhaul of a machine. The overhaul is needed every five years and the machine was five years old as at 30 June 2005.
(e) Damages awarded against Company A resulting from a court case decided on 26 June 2005. The judge has announced that the amount of damages will be set at a future date, expected to be in September 2005. Company A has received advice from its lawyers that the amount of the damages could be anything between $20 000 and $7 million.

EXERCISE 5.8 ★★

Contingent liabilities — disclosure

A customer filed a lawsuit against company A in June 2005, for costs and damages allegedly incurred as a result of the failure of one of company A's electrical products. The amount claimed was $3 million. Company A's lawyers have advised that the amount claimed is extortionate and that company A has a good chance of winning the case. However, the lawyers have also advised that, if company A loses the case, its expected costs and damages would be about $500 000.

Required

How should company A disclose this event in its financial statements as at 30 June 2005?

EXERCISE 5.9 Recognising a provision

In each of the following scenarios, explain whether or not company G would be required to recognise a provision.

(a) As a result of its plastics operations, company G has contaminated the land on which it operates. There is no legal requirement to clean up the land, and company G has no record of cleaning up land that it has contaminated.

(b) As a result of its plastics operations, company G has contaminated the land on which it operates. There is a legal requirement to clean up the land.

(c) As a result of its plastics operations, company G has contaminated the land on which it operates. There is no legal requirement to clean up the land, but company G has a long record of cleaning up land that it has contaminated.

EXERCISE 5.10 Risk and present value of cash flows

Using examples, explain how a liability-specific discount rate could cause the amount calculated for a provision to be lower when the risk associated with that provision is high. How could this problem be averted in practice?

PROBLEMS

PROBLEM 5.1 Measuring a restructuring provision

Company T's directors decided on 3 May 2005 to restructure the company's operations as follows:

• Factory Z would be closed down and put on the market for sale.

• 100 employees working in factory Z would be retrenched on 31 May 2005, and would be paid their accumulated entitlements plus three months wages.

• The remaining 20 employees working in factory Z would be transferred to factory X, which would continue operating.

• Five head-office staff would be retrenched on 30 June 2005, and would be paid their accumulated entitlements plus three months wages.

As at company T's balance sheet date of 30 June 2005, the following transactions and events had occurred:

• Factory Z was shut down on 31 May 2005. An offer of $4 million has been received for factory Z but there is no binding sales agreement.

• The 100 retrenched employees have left and their accumulated entitlements have been paid. However, an amount of $76 000, representing a portion of the three months wages for the retrenched employees, has still not been paid.

• Costs of $23 000 were expected to be incurred in transferring the 20 employees to their new work in factory X. The transfer is planned for 14 July 2005.

• Four of the five head-office staff who have been retrenched have had their accumulated entitlements paid, including the three months wages. However, one employee, Jerry Perry, remains in order to complete administrative tasks relating to the closure of factory Z and the transfer of staff to factory X. Jerry is expected to stay until 31 July 2005. His salary for July will be $4000 and his retrenchment package will be $13 000, all of which will be paid on the day he leaves. He estimates that he would spend 60% of his time administering the closure of factory Z, 30% on administering the transfer of staff to factory X, and the remaining 10% on general administration.

Required

Calculate the amount of the restructuring provision recognised in company T's financial statements as at 30 June 2005, in accordance with IAS 37.

PROBLEM 5.2   Calculation of a provision

In May 2005, company A relocated employee R from company A's head office to an office in another city. As at 30 June 2005, company A's balance sheet date, the costs were estimated to be $40 000. Analysis of the costs is as follows:

Costs for shipping goods	$ 3 000
Airfare	6 000
Temporary accommodation costs (May and June)	8 000
Temporary accommodation costs (July and August)	9 000
Reimbursement for lease break costs (paid in July; lease was terminated in May)	2 000
Reimbursement for cost-of-living increases (for the period 15 May 2005–15 May 2006)	12 000

Required

Calculate the provision for relocation costs for company A's financial statements as at 30 June 2005. Assume that IAS 37 applies to this provision and that the effect of discounting is immaterial.

PROBLEM 5.3   Restructuring provisions on acquisition

Company A acquires company B, effective 1 March 2005. At the date of acquisition, company A intends to close a division of company B. As at the date of acquisition, management has developed and the board has approved the main features of the restructuring plan and, based on available information, best estimates of the costs have been made. As at the date of acquisition, a public announcement of company A's intentions has been made and relevant parties have been informed of the planned closure. Within a week of the acquisition being effected, management commences the process of informing unions, lessors, institutional investors and other key shareholders of the broad characteristics of its restructuring program. A detailed plan for the restructuring is developed within three months and implemented soon thereafter.

Required

Should company A create a provision for restructuring as part of its acquisition accounting entries? Explain your answer. How would your answer change if all the circumstances are the same as those above except that company A decided that, instead of closing a division of company B, it would close down one of its own facilities?

PROBLEM 5.4   ★★★   Comprehensive problem

ChubbyChocs Ltd, a listed company, is a manufacturer of confectionery and biscuits. Its balance date is 30 June. Relevant extracts from its financial statements at 30 June 2005 are shown opposite.

Current liabilities		
Provisions		$
Provision for warranties		270 000
Non-current liabilities		
Provisions		
Provision for warranties		160 715
Non-current assets		
Plant and equipment	$	
At cost	2 000 000	
Accumulated depreciation	600 000	
Carrying amount	1 400 000	

Plant and equipment has a useful life of 10 years and is depreciated on a straight-line basis.

Note 36 — Contingent liabilities

ChubbyChocs is engaged in litigation with various parties in relation to allergic reactions to traces of peanuts alleged to have been found in packets of fruit gums. ChubbyChocs strenuously denies the allegations and, as at the date of authorising the financial statements for issue, is unable to estimate the financial effect, if any, of any costs or damages that may be payable to the plaintiffs.

The provision for warranties at 30 June 2005 was calculated using the following assumptions (there was no balance carried forward from the prior year):

Estimated cost of repairs – products with minor defects	$1 000 000
Estimated cost of repairs – products with major defects	$6 000 000
Expected % of products sold during FY 2005 having no defects in FY 2006	80%
Expected % of products sold during FY 2005 having minor defects in FY 2006	15%
Expected % of products sold during FY 2005 having major defects in FY 2006	5%
Expected timing of settlement of warranty payments – those with minor defects	All in FY 2006
Expected timing of settlement of warranty payments – those with major defects	40% in FY 2006, 60% in FY 2007
Discount rate	6%. The effect of discounting for FY 2006 is considered to be immaterial.

During the year ended 30 June 2006, the following occurred:
1. In relation to the warranty provision of $430 715 at 30 June 2005, $200 000 was paid out of the provision. Of the amount paid, $150 000 was for products with minor

defects and $50 000 was for products with major defects, all of which related to amounts that had been expected to be paid in the 2006 financial year.

2. In calculating its warranty provision for 30 June 2006, ChubbyChocs made the following adjustments to the assumptions used for the prior year:

Estimated cost of repairs – products with minor defects	No change
Estimated cost of repairs – products with major defects	$5 000 000
Expected % of products sold during FY 2006 having no defects in FY 2007	85%
Expected % of products sold during FY 2006 having minor defects in FY 2007	12%
Expected % of products sold during FY 2006 having major defects in FY 2007	3%
Expected timing of settlement of warranty payments – those with minor defects	All in FY 2007
Expected timing of settlement of warranty payments – those with major defects	20% in FY 2007, 80% in FY 2008
Discount rate	No change. The effect of discounting for FY 2007 is considered to be immaterial.

3. ChubbyChocs determined that part of its plant and equipment needed an overhaul – the conveyer belt on one of its machines would need to be replaced in about May 2007 at an estimated cost of $250 000. The carrying amount of the conveyer belt at 30 June 2005 was $140 000. Its original cost was $200 000.

4. ChubbyChocs was unsuccessful in its defence of the peanut allergy case and was ordered to pay $1 500 000 to the plaintiffs. As at 30 June 2006, ChubbyChocs had paid $800 000.

5. ChubbyChocs commenced litigation against one of its advisers for negligent advice given on the original installation of the conveyer belt referred to in (4) above. In April 2006 the court found in favour of ChubbyChocs. The hearing for damages had not been scheduled as at the date the financial statements for 2006 were authorised for issue. ChubbyChocs estimated that it would receive about $425 000.

6. ChubbyChocs signed an agreement with BankSweet to the effect that ChubbyChocs would guarantee a loan made by BankSweet to ChubbyChocs' subsidiary, CCC Ltd. CCC's loan with BankSweet was $3 200 000 as at 30 June 2006. CCC was in a strong financial position at 30 June 2006.

Required

Prepare the relevant extracts from the financial statements (including the notes) of ChubbyChocs at at 30 June 2006, in compliance with IAS 37 and related International Accounting Standards. Include comparative figures where required. Show all workings separately. Perform your workings in the following order:

(a) Calculate the warranty provision as at 30 June 2005. This should agree with the financial statements provided in the question.

(b) Calculate the warranty provision as at 30 June 2006.

(c) Calculate the movement in the warranty provision for the year.

(d) Calculate the prospective change in depreciation required as a result of the shortened useful life of the conveyer belt.

(e) Determine whether the unpaid amount owing as a result of the peanut allergy case is a liability or a provision.

(f) Determine whether the receipt of damages for the negligent advice meets the definition of an asset or a contingent asset.

(g) Determine whether the bank guarantee meets the definition of a provision or a contingent liability. (Ignore recent amendments to IAS 39 in this regard.)

(h) Prepare the financial statement disclosures.

WEBLINK

Visit these websites for additional information:

www.iasb.org   www.iasplus.com
www.asic.gov.au   www.ifac.org
www.aasb.com.au   www.nzica.com
www.accaglobal.com   www.capa.com.my

REFERENCES

ASIC 1998, *Media release 98/314*, Australian Securities and Investments Commission, October.

Ernst & Young 2002a, 'Provisions, contingent liabilities and contingent assets', *Accounting Brief*, January, Australia.

—2002b, AH 217 'Accounting for provisions', *Accounting handbook*, Australia.

CHAPTER 6
Financial instruments

ACCOUNTING STANDARDS

International: IAS 32 *Financial Instruments: Disclosure and Presentation*

IAS 39 *Financial Instruments: Recognition and Measurement*

Australia: AASB 132 *Financial Instruments: Disclosure and Presentation*

AASB 139 *Financial Instruments: Recognition and Measurement*

New Zealand: NZ IAS 32 *Financial Instruments: Disclosure and Presentation*

NZ IAS 39 *Financial Instruments: Recognition and Measurement*

CONCEPTS FOR REVIEW

Before studying this chapter, you should understand or, if necessary, revise:

- the IASB Framework, in particular the definitions of and recognition criteria for assets and liabilities
- basic financial statement ratios indicating solvency and liquidity
- the use of a financial calculator to calculate the effective interest rate
- IAS 21 *The Effects of Changes in Foreign Exchange Rates*.

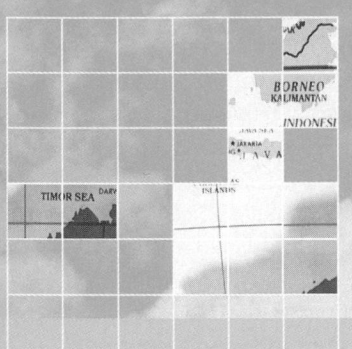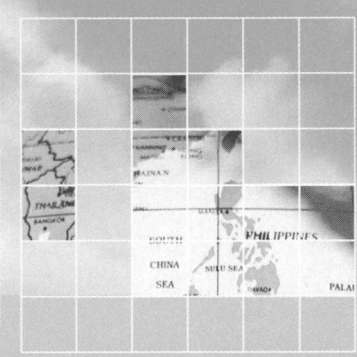

LEARNING OBJECTIVES

When you have studied this chapter, you should be able to:

1. understand the concept of financial instruments
2. understand and apply the definitions of financial assets and financial liabilities
3. understand the concept of a derivative
4. distinguish between equity instruments and financial liabilities
5. understand the concept of a compound financial instrument
6. determine the classification of revenues and expenses arising from financial instruments
7. determine when financial assets and financial liabilities may be offset
8. describe the main disclosure requirements of IAS 32
9. understand the scope of IAS 39
10. understand the concepts of a derivative and embedded derivative
11. distinguish between the four categories of financial instruments specified in IAS 39
12. understand and apply the recognition criteria for financial instruments
13. understand and apply the measurement criteria for each category of financial instrument
14. have an overall understanding of the rules of hedge accounting set out in IAS 39 and be able to apply the rules to simple common cash flow and fair value hedges.

6.1 Introduction to IAS 32 and IAS 39

Accounting for financial instruments has been the most controversial area in the development of the IASB's 'stable platform' of standards adopted in 2005. Indeed, the controversy surrounding IAS 39 in particular almost derailed the IASB's plans for adopting IFRSs in Europe for financial years beginning on or after 1 January 2005. As late as 30 June 2004, IAS 39 had still not been completed because changes continued to be proposed or made in response to lobbying from various European interested parties, notably the banks. The controversial aspects of the standards were largely those relating to hedge accounting.

Because IAS 32 and IAS 39 are complex standards, this chapter aims to provide an overall explanation of the requirements. It emphasises those areas most commonly affecting the majority of reporting entities, and places less emphasis on specialised areas.

IAS 32 was developed before IAS 39. It sets out the definitions of financial instruments, financial assets and financial liabilities, distinguishes between financial liabilities and equity instruments, and prescribes detailed disclosures. The standard was developed separately from IAS 39 because consensus on the recognition, derecognition, measurement and hedging rules for financial instruments was difficult to achieve. Therefore the standard setters first established classification and disclosure rules, anticipating that increased disclosure by reporting entities would provide more information, not only for users, but also for the standard setters. Increased disclosure helps to provide standard setters with information that assists in developing further standards.

IAS 39 was originally based largely on the similar FASB standard in the United States, Statement of Financial Accounting Standards No. 133 (SFAS 133) *Accounting for Derivative Instruments and Hedging Activities*. FASB standards have historically been rule-based rather than principle-based, and this explains why IAS 39 is considerably more rule-based than other IASB standards. As IAS 39 was amended repeatedly during 2003 and 2004, it moved further away from SFAS 133 but still reflects many of the same rules.

Each standard is addressed separately in this chapter. IAS 32 and IAS 39 each contain Application Guidance, which is abbreviated in this chapter as AG. IAS 39 also contains Implementation Guidance.

IFRS 7 *Financial Instruments: Disclosures* was issued in late 2005 and is applicable to annual reporting periods beginning on or after 1 January 2007, with early adoption permitted. The standard supercedes the disclosure requirements of IAS 32. In order to avoid confusion, this chapter does not address IFRS 7 as most reporting entities are not expected to adopt that standard until 2007/2008.

WEBLINK For an analysis of the differences between IAS 32 and IFRS 7, refer to <www.ey.com/ifrs> for the publication *IFRS 7: Financial Instruments: Disclosures*, published in February 2006.

6.2 IAS 32 *Financial Instruments: Disclosure and Presentation*

LO 1

6.2.1 What is a financial instrument?

IAS 32, paragraph 11, defines a financial instrument as:

> any contract that gives rise to a financial asset of one entity and a financial liability or equity instrument of another entity.

Financial assets and financial liabilities are terms defined in IAS 32 (see section 6.2.2 of this chapter). Financial assets are defined from the perspective of the *holder* of the instrument, whereas financial liabilities and equity instruments are defined from the perspective of the *issuer* of the instrument.

An equity instrument is defined in paragraph 11 as:

> any contract that evidences a residual interest in the assets of an entity after deducting all of its liabilities.

The most common type of equity instrument is an ordinary share of a company. The holder of the shares is not entitled to any fixed return on or of its investment; instead, the holder receives the residual after all liabilities have been settled. This applies both to periodic returns (where dividends are paid after interest on liabilities has been paid) and capital returns (when a company is wound up, all liabilities are settled before shareholders are entitled to any return of their investment).

Note that the definition of a financial instrument is two-sided: the contract must always give rise to a financial asset of one party, with a corresponding financial liability or equity instrument of another party. So, for example, a contract that gives the seller of a product the right to receive cash from the purchaser creates a receivable for the seller (a financial asset) and a payable for the purchaser (a financial liability).

Financial instruments include primary instruments such as cash, receivables, investments and payables, as well as derivative financial instruments such as financial options and forward exchange contracts. Derivative financial instruments, or derivatives, are instruments that *derive* their value from another underlying item such as a share price or an interest rate. (The definition of a derivative is discussed in section 6.3.2 of this chapter.)

Financial instruments do *not* include non-financial assets such as property, plant and equipment, or non-financial liabilities such as provisions for restoration. Contracts to buy or sell non-financial items are also usually not financial instruments. Many commodity contracts fall into this category (contracts to buy or sell oil, cotton, wheat and so on). These commodity contracts are thus outside the scope of IAS 32, but the standard encourages reporting entities with commodity contracts to follow the disclosure requirements (IAS 32, AG 24). Certain commodity contracts are, however, included within the scope of IAS 32. These include contracts to buy or sell non-financial items that can be settled net (in cash) or by exchanging financial instruments, or in which the non-financial item is readily convertible into cash. Contracts to buy or sell gold might fall into the latter category and hence might be caught by IAS 32 (IAS 32, para. 8).

Note also that the definition of a financial instrument requires there to be a contractual right or obligation. Therefore liabilities or assets that are not contractual – such as income taxes that are created as a result of statutory requirements imposed by governments, or constructive obligations as defined in IAS 37 *Provisions, Contingent Liabilities and Contingent Assets* (see chapter 5) – are not financial instruments.

In addition, certain financial assets and liabilities lie outside the scope of the standard (IAS 32, para. 4). These include employee benefits accounted for under IAS 19, and investments in subsidiaries, associates and joint ventures that are accounted for under IAS 27 *Consolidated and Separate Financial Statements*, IAS 28 *Investments in Associates* and IAS 31 *Interests in Joint Ventures*.

LO 2

6.2.2   Financial assets and financial liabilities

A financial asset is defined in paragraph 11 of IAS 32 as follows:

> any asset that is:
> (a) cash
> (b) an equity instrument of another entity
> (c) a contractual right:
> > (i) to receive cash or another financial asset from another entity; or

(ii) to exchange financial assets or financial liabilities with another entity under conditions that are potentially favourable to the entity; or

(d) a contract that will or may be settled in the entity's own equity instruments and is:

  (i) a non-derivative for which the entity is or may be obliged to receive a variable number of the entity's own equity instruments; or

  (ii) a derivative that will or may be settled other than by the exchange of a fixed amount of cash or another financial asset for a fixed number of the entity's own equity instruments. For this purpose the entity's own equity instruments do not include instruments that are themselves contracts for the future receipt or delivery of the entity's own equity instruments.

Examples of common financial assets in each of the categories of the definition include:

(a) Cash – either cash on hand or the right of the depositor to obtain cash from the financial institution with whom it has deposited the cash

(b) An equity instrument of another entity – ordinary shares held in another entity, commonly known as share investments

(c) A contractual right

  (i) to receive cash or another financial asset – trade accounts receivable, notes receivable, loans receivable

  (ii) to exchange under potentially favourable conditions – an option held by the holder to purchase shares in a specified company at less than the market price.

Part (d) of the definition was added in amendments made to IAS 39 in 2003 and 2004. The amendments were made in response to issues arising from the classification of certain complex financial instruments as liabilities or equity. (Liability/equity classification is discussed in section 6.2.4 of this chapter.)

A financial liability is defined in paragraph 11 of IAS 32 as follows:

any liability that is:

(a) a contractual obligation:

  (i) to deliver cash or another financial asset to another entity; or

  (ii) to exchange financial assets or financial liabilities with another entity under conditions that are potentially unfavourable to the entity; or

(b) a contract that will or may be settled in the entity's own equity instruments and is:

  (i) a non-derivative for which the entity is or may be obliged to deliver a variable number of the entity's own equity instruments; or

  (ii) a derivative that will or may be settled other than by the exchange of a fixed amount of cash or another financial asset for a fixed number of the entity's own equity instruments. For this purpose the entity's own equity instruments do not include instruments that are themselves contracts for the future receipt or delivery of the entity's own equity instruments.

Examples of common financial liabilities in each of the categories of the definition include:

(a) A contractual obligation

  (i) to deliver cash or another financial asset – trade accounts payable, notes payable, loans payable

  (ii) to exchange under potentially unfavourable conditions – an option written (i.e. issued) by the issuer to sell shares in a specified company at less than the market price.

Part (b) of the definition was added in amendments made to IAS 39 in 2003 and 2004. The amendments were made in response to issues arising from the classification of certain complex financial instruments as liabilities or equity. (Liability/equity classification is discussed in section 6.2.4 of this chapter.)

Table 6.1 contains a summary of common financial instruments.

TABLE 6.1	Summary of common financial instruments		
Financial assets	Financial liabilities	Equity instruments
Cash	Bank overdraft	Ordinary shares
Accounts receivable	Accounts payable	Certain preference shares
Notes receivable	Notes payable	
Loans receivable	Loans payable	
Derivatives with potentially favourable exchange conditions	Derivatives with potentially unfavourable exchange conditions	
	Certain preference shares	

LO 3

6.2.3 Demystifying derivatives

The concept of a derivative may appear daunting because there are numerous derivative financial instruments in the market that seem complex and difficult to understand. However, as already noted, fundamentally all derivatives simply *derive* their value from another underlying item such as a share price or an interest rate. Derivative financial instruments create rights and obligations that have the effect of transferring between the parties to the instrument one or more of the financial risks inherent in an underlying primary financial instrument. On inception, derivative financial instruments give one party a contractual right to exchange financial assets or financial liabilities with another party under conditions that are potentially favourable, while the other party has a contractual obligation to exchange under potentially unfavourable conditions.

Figure 6.1 provides an option contract as an example of a derivative.

FIGURE 6.1   How an option contract works

An option contract

Party A buys an option that entitles it to purchase 1000 shares in company Z at $3 a share, at any time in the next six months. The shares in company Z are the *underlying* financial instruments from which the option derives its value. The option is thus the derivative financial instrument. The amount of $3 a share is called the *exercise price* of the option.

Party B sells the option to party A. Party A is called the *holder* of the option, and party B is called the *writer* of the option. Party A will usually pay an amount called a *premium* to purchase the option. The amount of the premium is less than what party A would have to pay for the shares in company Z.

Assume that at the date of the option contract the market price of shares in company Z is $2.60.

The financial instrument created by this transaction is a contractual right of party A to purchase the 1000 shares in company Z at $3 a share (a financial asset of party A), and a contractual obligation of party B to sell the shares in company Z to party A at $3 a share (a financial liability of party B). Party A's right is a financial asset because it has the right to exchange under potentially favourable conditions to itself. Thus, if the share price of company Z rises above $3, party A will exercise its option and require party B to deliver the shares at $3 a share. Party A will have benefited from this transaction by acquiring the shares in company Z at less than the market price. Conversely, party B's obligation is a financial liability because it has the obligation to exchange under potentially unfavourable conditions to itself. Thus, if the shares in Company Z rise to $3.20, party A will purchase the shares from party B for $3000. If party A had had to purchase the shares on the market, it would have paid $3200.

(continued)

Party B may have made a loss from this transaction, depending on whether it already held the shares in company Z, or had to go out and buy them for $3200 and then sell them to party A for $3000, or had entered into other derivative contracts with other parties enabling it to purchase the shares at less than $3000.

What if the share price in company Z never exceeds $2.60 over the six-month term of the option? In this case, party A will not exercise the option and the option will lapse. The option is termed 'out-of-the money' from party A's perspective — it has no value to party A because the exercise price is higher than the market price. Once the share price rises above $3, the option is termed 'in-the money'. Party A is not compelled to exercise its option, even if it is in-the-money. From party A's perspective, it has a right to exercise the option should it so choose. However, if party A exercises its option, party B is then compelled to deliver the shares under its contractual obligation.

IAS 32, AG 17, notes that the nature of the holder's right and of the writer's obligation is not affected by the likelihood that the option will be exercised.

In simple terms, parties to derivative financial instruments are taking bets on what will happen to the underlying financial instrument in the future. In the example in figure 6.1, party A was taking a bet that the share price in company Z would rise above $3 within six months, and party B was taking a bet that it wouldn't. Party B would most likely hedge its bet by doing something to protect itself should the market price rise above $3. It could do this by entering into another derivative with another party, enabling party B to purchase shares from that other party at $3. Often a chain of derivative financial instruments will be created in this way. Party A will probably not know anything about the chain created. (Hedging is discussed in section 6.3.6 of this chapter.)

IAS 32 does not prescribe recognition and measurement rules for derivatives; these are addressed in IAS 39. Instead, IAS 32 includes derivatives in the definition of financial instruments. Other types of derivatives include interest rate swaps, forward exchange contracts, and futures contracts.

LO 4

6.2.4

Distinguishing financial liabilities from equity instruments

IAS 32 is very prescriptive in the area of distinguishing between financial liabilities and equity instruments. This area, commonly known as the debt versus equity distinction, is of great concern to many reporting entities because instruments classified as liabilities rather than equity affect:

- a company's gearing and solvency ratios
- debt covenants with financial institutions (usually a requirement that specified financial ratios of the borrower do not exceed predetermined thresholds; if they do exceed the thresholds, the financial institution has a right to require repayment of the loan)
- whether periodic payments on these instruments are treated as interest or dividends
- regulatory requirements for capital adequacy (banks and other financial institutions are required by their regulators to maintain a certain level of capital, which is calculated by reference to assets and equity).

Accordingly, reporting entities are often motivated, when raising funds, to issue instruments that are classified as equity for accounting purposes. In the years since IAS 32 was first issued, many complex instruments were devised by market participants specifically to achieve equity classification under IAS 32. Some of these instruments were liabilities in substance but were able to be classified technically as equity, notwithstanding a 'substance over form' test in IAS 32. As a result, the standard setters amended IAS 32 in 2003–04 to create specific rules designed to address these complex instruments. Unfortunately, the rules are now more complicated than the instruments themselves, so this section will address the key principles of liability versus equity classification only.

IAS 32, paragraph 15, states:

> The issuer of a financial instrument shall classify the instrument, or its component parts, on initial recognition as a financial liability, a financial asset or an equity instrument in accordance with the substance of the contractual arrangement and the definitions of a financial liability, a financial asset and an equity instrument.

To avoid any doubt, paragraph 16 goes on to repeat and clarify the definition of a financial liability. It states that an instrument shall be classified as an equity instrument if, and only if, *both* conditions (a) and (b) below are met:

(a) The instrument includes no contractual obligation:
    (i) to deliver cash or another financial asset to another entity; or
    (ii) to exchange financial assets or financial liabilities with another entity under conditions that are potentially unfavourable to the issuer.
(b) If the instrument will or may be settled in the issuer's own equity instruments, it is:
    (i) a non-derivative that includes no contractual obligation for the issuer to deliver a variable number of its own equity instruments; or
    (ii) a derivative that will be settled only by the issuer exchanging a fixed amount of cash or another financial asset for a fixed number of its own equity instruments.

Part (a) is clearly referring to the definition of a financial liability. Part (b) helps to clarify the amendments to the definitions of a financial asset and a financial liability (discussed in section 6.2.2 of this chapter). In essence, the rules in part (b) are trying to establish who bears 'equity risk' in complex transactions where an entity issues a financial instrument that will or may be settled in its own shares.

The concept of equity risk is useful for both part (b) of the test and generally in determining whether an instrument is equity or a liability. Note, however, that part (a) of the test turns only on whether or not the issuer has a contractual obligation.

Part (a) of the equity/liability test: contractual obligation

The examples in figure 6.2 apply part (a) of the equity/liability test, together with the equity risk concept.

FIGURE 6.2   Applying part (a) of the equity/liability test

Example 1: Ordinary shares

Company A wants to raise funds of $1 million. It does so by issuing ordinary shares to the public. The holders of those shares are exposed to equity risk (they are not entitled to any fixed return on or of their investment, and receive the residual left over after all liabilities have been settled) in respect of both periodic payments and capital returns. If there is no profit after interest on liabilities and other contractual obligations have been paid, then there are no dividends. If, on winding up, there are no assets after all liabilities have been settled, there is nothing returned to the shareholders. This is the fundamental nature of equity risk. The ordinary shares issued by company A are equity instruments of company A. Under part (a) of the test, company A has no contractual obligation to its ordinary shareholders.

Company A would record the following journal entry on initial recognition:

| Cash (financial asset) | Dr | 1 000 000 | |
| Ordinary share capital (equity) | Cr | | 1 000 000 |

Example 2: Non-cumulative, non-redeemable preference shares

Company A decides to issue preference shares instead of ordinary shares. It issues one million preference shares for $1 each. Each preference shareholder is entitled to

(continued)

a non-cumulative dividend of 5% annually. (A non-cumulative dividend means that, if in any year a dividend is not paid, the shareholder forfeits it.) The preference shareholders rank ahead of ordinary shareholders on the winding-up of the company. The preference shares are non-redeemable (the holders of the shares cannot get their money back).

Under part (a) of the test, company A has no contractual obligation to the preference shareholders, either to pay dividends or to return the cash. Therefore the preference shares are equity instruments of company A. In addition, applying the concept of equity risk reveals that the preference shareholders are exposed to equity risk, although it is lower than for the ordinary shareholders.

Company A would record the following journal entry on initial recognition:

Cash (financial asset)	Dr	1 000 000	
Preference share capital (equity)	Cr		1 000 000

Example 3: Cumulative, redeemable preference shares

Company A issues one million preference shares for $1 each, and each preference shareholder is entitled to a *cumulative* dividend of 5% annually. The preference shareholders rank ahead of ordinary shareholders on the winding-up of the company. The preference shares are redeemable for cash *at the option of the holder*.

Under part (a) of the test, company A now has a contractual obligation to the preference shareholders – both in respect of dividends and to return the cash. Company A must pay the dividends and, if in any period it cannot pay, it must make up the payment with the next dividend. Furthermore, company A must repay the money whenever the holder demands repayment. Therefore, the preference shares are financial liabilities of company A. In addition, applying the concept of equity risk reveals that the preference shareholders are not exposed to equity risk – they are guaranteed a periodic return of 5% and they can require that their cash be returned. They bear the same risk as would a lender to the company. A lender's risk is generally credit risk (the risk that company A will fail to discharge its obligations) and liquidity risk (the risk that company A will fail to raise funds to enable it to redeem the liability on demand).

Company A would record the following journal entry on initial recognition:

Cash (financial asset)	Dr	1 000 000	
Preference share liability (financial liability)	Cr		1 000 000

Example 4: Cumulative, redeemable preference shares

Company A issues one million preference shares for $1 each, and each preference shareholder is entitled to a *cumulative* dividend of 5% annually. The preference shareholders rank ahead of ordinary shareholders on the winding-up of the company. The preference shares are redeemable for cash *at the option of company A*.

Under part (a) of the test, company A now has a contractual obligation to the preference shareholders, but only in respect of dividends. It cannot be required to return the cash, since redemption is at its own option. In addition, applying the concept of equity risk reveals that the preference shareholders are partially exposed to equity risk – they are guaranteed a periodic return of 5% but they cannot require that their cash be returned. IAS 32, AG 25, confirms that preference shares redeemable at the option of the issuer are not financial liabilities. IAS 32, AG 26, clarifies that, when preference shares are non-redeemable, the other rights that attach to them determine the appropriate classification. It states that when distributions, whether cumulative or non-cumulative, are at the discretion of the issuer, the shares are equity instruments.

However, neither AG 25 nor AG 26 is particularly useful in helping decide what to do if the distributions are not discretionary. Is it possible for the preference share to be part liability and part equity? The answer, in theory, is yes. IAS 32 contains a section on **compound financial instruments** (discussed in section 6.2.5 of this chapter). In practice, though, such splitting of the instrument would be difficult to achieve. This is further complicated by having to split the 'dividend' into an interest component and a dividend component (see section 6.2.7). The discussion in AG 26 implies that cumulative dividends, on their own, would not be sufficient to cause a preference share to be classified as a liability, and that the overall substance of the arrangement must be considered. Unfortunately, it then goes on to give examples of where the distribution payments create a financial liability in substance, but says that even then the cumulative dividends do not create a liability. Therefore, in this example, the preference shares are equity instruments of company A.

Company A would record the following journal entry on initial recognition:

Cash (financial asset)	Dr	1 000 000	
Preference share capital (equity)	Cr		1 000 000

Paragraph 17 of IAS 32 reiterates that a critical feature in differentiating a financial liability from an equity instrument is the existence of a contractual obligation of the issuer. Paragraph 18 then goes on to state that the substance of a financial instrument, rather than its legal form, governs its classification on the entity's balance sheet. Some financial instruments, such as the preference shares in example 3 of figure 6.2, take the legal form of equity but are liabilities in substance. Other financial instruments, such as the preference shares in example 4 of figure 6.2, may combine features associated with equity instruments and those associated with financial liabilities. Sometimes the combined features result in the financial instrument being split into its component parts (see section 6.2.5 of this chapter).

Another example (added to IAS 32 in the 2003–04 revisions) of a financial instrument whose legal form may be equity but whose accounting classification is a financial liability is a puttable instrument. A puttable instrument gives the holder the right to put the instrument back to the issuer for cash or another financial asset. This is so even when the amount of cash/other financial asset is determined on the basis of an index or another amount that may increase or decrease. For example, certain mutual funds, unit trusts and partnerships provide their unit holders or members with a right to redeem their interests in the issuer at any time for cash equal to their proportionate share of the net asset value of the issuer. Traditionally, unit holder funds have been classified as equity because the legal form of their interest was equity. However, under paragraph 18 of the revised IAS 32, it is clear that these are financial liabilities. This will be a significant change to the presentation of financial statements for unit trusts.

Paragraphs 19 and 20 of IAS 32 go on to explain that an entity has a contractual obligation to deliver cash/other financial assets notwithstanding:

- any restrictions on the entity's ability to meet its obligation (such as access to foreign currency)
- that the obligation may be conditional on the counterparty exercising its redemption right (as in example 3 of figure 6.2 − redemption is at the option of the holder and therefore could be considered to be conditional on the holder exercising its right to

redeem. However, this does not negate the fact that the issuer has a contractual obligation to redeem the shares, because it cannot avoid its obligation should it be required to redeem by the holder)

- that the financial instrument does not explicitly establish a contractual obligation to deliver cash/other financial assets. A contractual obligation may be implied in the terms and conditions of the instrument. Unfortunately, the guidance in paragraph 20 contradicts the guidance on preference shares in AG 26. AG 26 states that non-redeemable preference shares are equity instruments, notwithstanding a term that prevents ordinary share dividends from being paid if the preference share dividend is not paid, or from being paid on the issuer's expectation of profit or loss for a period. A fairly common term in certain non-redeemable preference shares is that the dividend is 'discretionary' but, if the preference dividend is not paid, then ordinary dividends cannot be paid. If these terms exist in the preference shares of highly profitable companies, one could argue under paragraph 20 of IAS 32 that the implicit terms and conditions of the preference shares require the dividend to be paid. However, AG 26 states that such conditions do not create a financial liability of the issuer.

Part (b) of the equity/liability test: settlement in the entity's own equity instruments

Paragraph 21 of IAS 32 states that a contract is not an equity instrument solely because it may result in the receipt or delivery of the entity's own equity instruments. As noted earlier in this section, such an instrument can be classified as an equity instrument under paragraph 16(b) of IAS 32 only if it is:

(i) a non-derivative that includes no contractual obligation for the issuer to deliver a variable number of its own equity instruments; or

(ii) a derivative that will be settled only by the issuer exchanging a fixed amount of cash or another financial asset for a fixed number of its own equity instruments.

Part (i) will be examined first. Assume listed company A has an obligation to deliver to party B as many of company A's own ordinary shares as will equal $100 000. The number of shares that company A will have to issue will vary depending on the market price of its own shares. If company A's shares are each worth $1 at the date of settlement of the contract, it will have to deliver 100 000 shares. If company A's shares are each worth 50c at the date of settlement of the contract, it will have to deliver 200 000 shares. Company A has a contractual obligation at all times to deliver $100 000 to party B; that is, the value is fixed, and so the number of shares to be delivered will vary. Therefore, company A's financial instrument fails the test in part (i) and the instrument is a financial liability. Applying the concept of equity risk, the *holder* of the financial instrument (party B) is not exposed to equity risk because it will always receive $100 000 regardless of the market price of company A's shares. A true equity risk-taker will be exposed to share price fluctuations — this reflects the residual nature of an equity risk-taker's investment.

Now examine part (ii). Assume listed company A issues a share option to party B that entitles party B to buy 100 000 shares in company A at $1 each in three months time. This financial instrument meets the conditions for equity classification under part (ii) because it is a derivative that will be settled by issuing a fixed number of shares for a fixed amount. Assume that, at the date of the grant of the option, company A's share price is $1. If in three months time company A's share price exceeds $1, party B will exercise its option and company A must issue its shares to party B for $100 000. If, however, in three months time company A's share price falls below $1, party B will not exercise its option and company A will not issue any shares. Applying the concept of equity risk reveals that the *holder* of the financial instrument (party B) is exposed to equity risk because it is not guaranteed to receive $100 000 in value. Whether or not it receives

$100 000 is entirely dependent on the market price of company A's shares. As a true equity risk-taker, it is exposed to share price fluctuations; this reflects the residual nature of an equity risk-taker's investment. Party B will have paid a premium to company A for the option. Paragraph 22 of IAS 32 states that this premium is added directly to company A's equity, consistent with the classification of the instrument as an equity instrument.

Contingent settlement provisions and settlement options

Sometimes, when a financial instrument requires an entity to deliver cash/other financial assets, the terms of settlement are dependent on the occurrence or non-occurrence of uncertain future events that are beyond the control of both the issuer and the holder. Examples of such events include changes in a share market index, the consumer price index or the issuer's future revenues. The issuer of such an instrument does not have the unconditional right to avoid delivering the cash/other financial assets, so paragraph 25 of IAS 32 requires such instruments to be classified as financial liabilities unless they meet certain rare exceptions. For example, assume that company A issues preference shares to party B, the terms of which entitle party B to redeem the preference shares for cash if company A's revenues fall below a specified level. Because neither company A nor party B can control the level of company A's revenues, the settlement provision is considered to be contingent. However, because company A cannot avoid repaying party B should company A's revenues fall below the specified level, company A does not have an unconditional right to avoid repayment. Thus the preference shares are a financial liability of company A.

It is common for financial instruments to contain a choice of settlement. For example, preference shares may be redeemed for cash or for the issuer's ordinary shares. Sometimes the choice is the issuer's; sometimes it is the holder's. Paragraph 26 of IAS 32 requires that, when a *derivative* financial instrument gives one party a choice over how it is settled, it is a financial asset or a financial liability unless all of the settlement alternatives would result in it being an equity instrument. An example is a share option that the issuer can decide to settle net in cash or by exchanging its own shares for cash. Because not all of the settlement options would result in an equity instrument being issued, the option must be classified as a financial asset or liability. Note that the likely outcome is not taken into account; the fact that cash settlement may be required is sufficient to create a financial asset or liability.

Paragraph 26 does not address non-derivative financial instruments. Therefore, where a non-derivative financial instrument such as a preference share may be redeemed for cash or for the issuer's own ordinary shares, paragraph 26 does not apply. Instead, paragraph 16 would be applied to determine whether or not there is (a) a contractual obligation to deliver cash/other financial assets, or (b) a contractual obligation to deliver a variable number of the issuer's ordinary shares. Note that both (a) and (b) must be answered in the negative for equity classification to apply. So, for example, if the *issuer* of the preference share has the option to redeem for cash or for a variable number of its ordinary shares, the first question to ask is: does the issuer have a contractual obligation to deliver cash? If redemption is at the issuer's option, the issuer has *no* contractual obligation to redeem *at all* and therefore arguably the second question about the number of ordinary shares is irrelevant. Indeed, paragraph 16(b) asks whether or not the issuer has a contractual obligation to deliver a variable number of its own shares and, since redemption is at the issuer's option, it has no such contractual obligation, even though the number of shares that potentially will be issued is variable. Therefore, all other things being equal, the preference shares will be classified as equity. On the other hand, if redemption is at the *holder's* option, the instrument would be classified as a liability, because the issuer has a contractual obligation to deliver cash/other financial assets or ordinary shares because the holder has the right to call for redemption. This is so even if the number of ordinary shares is fixed, because the holder's right to redeem for cash means that paragraph 16(a) is met.

LO 5

6.2.5   ## Compound financial instruments

Paragraph 28 of IAS 32 requires an issuer of a non-derivative financial instrument to determine whether it contains both a liability and an equity component. Such components must be classified separately as financial liabilities, financial assets or equity instruments.

Paragraph 29 goes on to explain that this means that an entity recognises separately the components of a financial instrument that (a) creates a financial liability of the entity, and (b) grants an option to the holder of the instrument to convert it into an equity instrument of the entity. A common example of such a financial instrument is a convertible bond or note that entitles the holder to convert the note into a fixed number of ordinary shares of the issuer. From the perspective of the *issuer*, such an instrument comprises two components: (a) a financial liability, being a contractual obligation to deliver cash/other financial assets in the form of interest payments and redemption of the note, and (b) an equity instrument, being an option issued to the holder entitling it to the right, for a specified period of time, to convert the note into a fixed number of ordinary shares of the issuer. Note that the number of shares to be issued must be fixed, otherwise the option would not meet the definition of an equity instrument under paragraph 16(b) as discussed above.

Classification of the liability and equity components is made on initial recognition of the financial instrument and is not revised as a result of a change in the likelihood that the conversion option may be exercised. This is because, until such time as the conversion option is either exercised or lapses, the issuer has a contractual obligation to make future payments.

How does the issuer measure the separate liability and equity components? Paragraphs 31 and 32 of IAS 32 prescribe that the financial liability must be calculated first, with the equity component by definition being the residual. The example in figure 6.3 illustrates how this is done.

Example 5: Compound financial instrument − a convertible note

Company A issues 2000 convertible notes on 1 July 2004. The notes have a three-year term and are issued at par with a face value of $1000 per note, giving total proceeds at the date of issue of $2 million. The notes pay interest at 6% annually in arrears. The holder of each note is entitled to convert the note into 250 ordinary shares of company A at any time up to maturity.

When the notes are issued, the prevailing market interest rate for similar debt (similar term, similar credit status of issuer and similar cash flows) without conversion options is 9%. This rate is higher than the convertible note's rate because the holder of the convertible note is prepared to accept a lower interest rate given the implicit value of its conversion option.

The issuer calculates the contractual cash flows using the market interest rate (9%) to work out the value of the holder's option, as follows:

Present value of the principal: $2 million payable in three years time:	$1 544 367
Present value of the interest: $120 000 ($2 million × 6%) payable annually in arrears for three years	303 755
Total liability component	1 848 122
Equity component (by deduction)	151 878
Proceeds of the note issue	$2 000 000

The journal entries at the date of issue are as follows:

Cash	Dr	2 000 000	
Financial liability	Cr		1 848 122
Equity	Cr		151 878

The equity component is not remeasured (IAS 32, para. 22) and thus remains at $151 878 until the note is either converted or redeemed. If the note is converted, the remaining liability component is transferred to equity. If the note is redeemed, the equity component remains in equity despite redemption.

FIGURE 6.3   A convertible note, allocating the components between liability and equity
Source: Adapted from IAS 32, Illustrative Example 9, paras IE35–IE36.

6.2.6 Putting it all together

The liability/equity distinction rules in IAS 32 can rarely be applied in isolation. Unfortunately, IAS 32 does not contain a clear hierarchy to assist in determining which rules take precedence. Is it the substance over form rule in paragraph 15? Is it the definition rule in paragraph 15? Is it the contractual obligation rule in paragraph 16? Is it the 'settlement in own equity' rules? Is it the settlement options or contingent settlement provisions rules? Is it the components rule in paragraph 28?

Take our redeemable preference shares in example 4 of figure 6.2. Company A issued one million preference shares for $1 each, and each preference shareholder is entitled to a *cumulative* dividend of 5% annually. The preference shareholders rank ahead of ordinary shareholders on the winding-up of the company. The preference shares are redeemable for cash *at the option of company A*. Assume that a few more terms and conditions have been added. Instead of the shares being redeemable only for cash, they are redeemable for cash or *for a fixed number of ordinary shares* at the option of company A, at any time after five years. The shares also contain a conversion option, entitling the holder to convert to a fixed number of ordinary shares of company A at any time up to five years. In addition, although the dividends are cumulative, they can be paid only if company A's profit exceeds $250 000, indexed annually.

Table 6.2 helps to answer the questions, taking each set of five years separately.

TABLE 6.2	Applying the various liability/equity rules as a whole	
Liability/equity rules	First five years	After five years
Contractual obligation to deliver cash?	No	No (issuer's option)
Contractual obligation to exchange under potentially unfavourable conditions?	No	No
Derivative or non-derivative?	Non-derivative	Non-derivative
If a non-derivative, contractual obligation to deliver shares?	Yes (holder's option to convert)	No (issuer's option to redeem)
Are shares to be delivered fixed or variable?	Fixed, therefore equity classification	Fixed

(continued)

Liability/equity rules	First five years	After five years
If a derivative, settled by fixed cash/fixed number of shares?	N/A	N/A
Contingent settlement provisions?	Yes – the dividends are paid only if profit targets are met[1]	Yes – the dividends are paid only if profit targets are met
If a derivative, terms of settlement options?	N/A	N/A
Compound financial instrument?	Yes – holder has the option to convert to a fixed number of ordinary shares	No
Substance over form?	Equity[2]	Equity
Classification	Equity	Equity

Notes:

1. Under paragraph 25 of IAS 32, the dividend conditions meet the contingent settlement definition and would require liability classification, but AG 26 refutes this by stating that the dividends are at the discretion of the issuer.
2. Although the instrument is a compound instrument for the first five years, there is no liability component because the substance of the entire instrument is equity given the other terms and conditions. This assumes that the dividend payments are discretionary. Therefore no splitting into component parts is required.

LO 6

6.2.7 Interest, dividends, gains and losses

Paragraph 35 of IAS 32 requires the income statement classification of items relating to financial instruments to match their balance sheet classification. Thus, income statement items relating to financial liabilities and financial assets are classified as income or expenses, or gains or losses. These are usually interest expense, interest income and dividend income. Distributions to holders of equity instruments are debited directly to equity. Usually these are dividends. These principles also apply to the component parts of a compound financial instrument.

Table 6.3 summarises these principles.

TABLE 6.3	Classification of revenues, expenses and equity distributions	
Balance sheet classification	Income statement classification	Statement of changes in equity
Equity instrument		Dividends distributed
Financial liability	Interest expense	
Financial asset	Interest income, dividend income	

The transaction costs of an equity transaction are deducted from equity, net of tax, but only to the extent to which they are incremental costs directly attributable to the equity transaction that otherwise would have been avoided (IAS 32, para. 37). Examples of such costs include registration and other regulatory fees, legal and accounting fees and stamp duties. These costs are required to be shown separately under IAS 1 *Presentation of Financial Statements*.

LO 7

6.2.8 Offsetting a financial asset and a financial liability

Paragraph 42 of IAS 32 states that a financial asset and a financial liability shall be offset and the net amount presented when, and only when, an entity:

(a) currently has a legally enforceable right to set off the recognised amounts; and

(b) intends either to settle on a net basis, or to realise the asset and settle the liability simultaneously.

The underlying rationale of this requirement is that when an entity has the right to receive or pay a single net amount and intends to do so, it has effectively only a single financial asset or financial liability. Note that the right of set-off must be legally enforceable and therefore usually stems from a written contract between two parties. In rare cases, there may be an agreement between three parties allowing a debtor to apply an amount due from a third party against the amount due to a creditor. Assume, for example, that company A owes company B $1000, and company Z owes company A $1000. Company A has therefore recorded in its books the following:

| Amount receivable from company Z | Dr | 1 000 | |
| Amount owing to company B | Cr | | 1 000 |

Provided there is a legal right of set-off allowing company A to offset the amount owing to company B against the amount owed by company Z, the amounts may be offset in company A's accounts. Both company B and company Z must be parties to this legal right of set-off with company A.

The conditions for offsetting are strict and essentially require written legal contracts resulting in net cash settlement. Many arrangements that create 'synthetic' (manufactured) offsetting are not permitted under IAS 32. Paragraph 49 provides examples of common cases where offsetting is not permitted.

LO 8

6.2.9 Disclosures

IAS 32 contains many pages dealing with disclosures, but only relatively few 'black letter' requirements. This chapter does not address these requirements in detail, and readers are expected to have a general understanding of the requirements only.

The purpose of the disclosure requirements is to provide information to enhance understanding of the significance of financial instruments to an entity's financial position, performance and cash flows; and to assist in assessing the amounts, timing and certainty of future cash flows associated with those instruments.

Transactions in financial instruments may result in an entity assuming or transferring to another party one or more of the financial risks described in table 6.4. The purpose of the required disclosures is to assist users in assessing the extent of such risks related to financial instruments.

TABLE 6.4	Financial risks pertaining to financial instruments
Type of risk	Description
Market risk	• *Currency risk* – the risk that the value of a financial instrument will fluctuate because of changes in foreign exchange rates • *Fair value interest rate risk* – the risk that the value of a financial instrument will fluctuate because of changes in market interest rates. For example, the issuer of a financial liability that carries a fixed rate of interest is exposed to decreases in market interest rates, such that the issuer of the liability is paying a higher rate of interest than the market rate. • *Price risk* – the risk that the value of a financial instrument will fluctuate as a result of changes in market prices Market risk embodies the potential for both loss and gain.

(continued)

Type of risk	Description
Credit risk	The risk that one party to a financial instrument will fail to discharge an obligation and cause the other party to incur a financial loss
Liquidity risk	The risk that an entity will encounter difficulty in raising funds to meet commitments associated with financial instruments. This is also known as funding risk. For example, as a financial liability approaches its redemption date, the issuer may experience liquidity risk if its available financial assets are insufficient to meet its obligations.
Cash flow interest rate risk	The risk that the future cash flows of a financial instrument will fluctuate because of changes in market interest rates

IAS 32 does not prescribe either the format or the location of the required disclosures. (An illustrative disclosure is provided in appendix A to this chapter.)

The main headings of required disclosures and a brief summary of the requirements are set out in table 6.5. For full details, refer to the text of IAS 32.

TABLE 6.5	Summary of the disclosure requirements of IAS 32
Main heading	Summarised requirements
Risk-management policies and hedging activities (paras 56–9)	• Description of financial risk-management objectives and policies • Policy for hedging each main type of forecast transaction for which hedge accounting is used • Specified details of hedge transactions • Specified details of hedge gains or losses recognised in equity/removed from equity
Terms, conditions and accounting policies (paras 60–6)	• Terms and conditions for each class of financial asset and financial liability • Accounting policies and methods adopted for recognition and measurement • Whether 'regular way' purchases and sales of financial assets are accounted for at trade date or settlement date
Interest rate risk (paras 67–75)	• For each class of financial asset and financial liability, information about exposure to interest rate risk including contractual repricing or maturity dates and **effective interest rates** (this information is usually presented in tabular form; see appendix A of this chapter for an illustration)

Credit risk (paras 76–85)	• For each class of financial asset and other credit exposures, information about exposure to credit risk including
	  – maximum credit risk exposure at the balance date in the event of other parties failing to meet their obligations. This excludes the fair value of any security given
	  – significant concentrations of credit risk. Concentrations of credit risk may arise, for example, from exposure to a single debtor or to a group of debtors with similar characteristics, such as an industry concentration

Fair value (paras 86–93)	• For each class of financial asset and financial liability, disclosure of the fair value of that class of assets and liabilities in a way that permits it to be compared with the corresponding carrying amount in the balance sheet • If certain financial assets required to be measured at fair value under IAS 39 are carried at cost because their fair value cannot be measured reliably, reasons why fair value cannot be measured reliably. In this case, the fair value does not have to be disclosed • Methods and significant assumptions applied in determining fair values for each class of financial asset and financial liability, and whether fair values are determined by reference to published price quotations on an active market or are estimated using a valuation technique • Whether the financial statements include financial instruments measured at fair value using a valuation technique not supported by observable market prices • The total amount recognised in the income statement of the change in fair value estimated using such a valuation technique

Main heading	Summarised requirements
Derecognition (para. 94(a))	• Specified details where a financial asset has been transferred, or another arrangement has been entered into, and the transfer or other arrangement does not qualify for derecognition under IAS 39
Collateral (paras 94(b) and (c))	• Carrying amount of financial assets pledged as collateral (security) for liabilities and contingent liabilities • Specified details where an entity has accepted collateral that it is permitted to sell or repledge
Compound financial instruments with multiple embedded derivatives (para. 94(d))	• Specified details
Financial assets and financial liabilities at fair value through profit or loss (see section 6.3.3 of this chapter) (paras 94(e)(i))	• Specified details
Reclassification (para. 94(j))	• If an entity has reclassified a financial asset to one being measured at cost or amortised cost from being measured at fair value, reasons for the reclassification (see section 6.3.5 of this chapter)

Income statement and equity (para. 94(k))	• Material items of income, expense, gains and losses, whether included in profit and loss or in equity. Disclose at least:
	  – total interest income and total interest expense for financial assets and financial liabilities not measured at fair value through profit or loss
	  – any gain or loss recognised directly in equity/removed from equity, for available-for-sale financial assets (see section 6.3.3 of this chapter)
	  – the amount of interest income accrued on impaired financial assets (see section 6.3.5 of this chapter)

Impairment (para. 94(l))	• Nature and amount of any impairment loss recognised in profit or loss, separately for each class of financial asset
Defaults and breaches (para. 94(m))	• Specified details when there have been defaults and breaches during the period

6.3 IAS 39 *Financial Instruments: Recognition and Measurement*

The stated objective of IAS 39 (see paragraph 1) is to establish principles for recognising and measuring financial assets, financial liabilities and some contracts to buy or sell non-financial items. Arguably, IAS 39 establishes rules rather than principles. Because the standard is very complex, particularly in its application to financial institutions, this chapter addresses only the more common applications of IAS 39 and aims to provide a general understanding of its requirements.

LO 9

6.3.1 Scope of IAS 39

IAS 39 applies to all entities and to all types of financial instruments, with nine exceptions set out in paragraph 2. The exceptions in themselves are complicated, so only an overview of them will be provided. The exceptions are:

1. Investments in subsidiaries, associates and joint ventures that are accounted for under IAS 27, IAS 28 and IAS 31. However, certain investments in such entities may be

accounted for under IAS 39 if so permitted by IAS 27, IAS 28 and IAS 31. For example, IAS 27 permits investments in subsidiaries, associates and jointly controlled entities to be carried at cost or, under IAS 39, in the investor's own separate (not consolidated) financial statements. Also, investments in subsidiaries, associates and jointly controlled entities are measured under IFRS 5 *Non-current Assets Held for Sale and Discontinued Operations* if they are held exclusively for disposal.

2. Rights and obligations under leases to which IAS 17 *Leases* applies. However, certain lease receivables and finance lease payables are subject to the derecognition and impairment provisions of IAS 39. Also, embedded derivatives in leases are subject to IAS 39.

3. Employers' rights and obligations under employee benefit plans to which IAS 19 *Employee Benefits* applies.

4. Rights and obligations arising under insurance contracts, with certain exceptions. Insurance contracts are covered by their own standard, but contracts issued by insurers that are *not* insurance contracts (such as investment contracts) are covered by IAS 39.

5. Financial instruments issued by the entity that meet the definition of an equity instrument in IAS 32. This applies only to the *issuer* of the equity instrument. The *holder* of such an instrument will have a financial asset that is covered by IAS 39.

6. Financial guarantee contracts, such as letters of credit, that provide for specified payments to be made to reimburse the holder of the contract for a loss it incurs because a specified debtor fails to make payment when due under a debt instrument if they are measured under IFRS 4 *Insurance Contracts*. Financial guarantee contracts *are* otherwise subject to the provisions of IAS 39. For example, a financial guarantee contract that provides for the issuer to make payments to the holder if the credit rating of a specified debtor falls below a particular level is within the scope of IAS 39 unless the reporting entity explicitly asserts that it regards such a contract as an insurance contract and applies IFRS 4 to such a contract.

7. Contracts for contingent consideration in a business combination. This exemption applies only to the acquirer.

8. Rights to payments to reimburse the entity for expenditure it is required to make to settle a liability that it recognises as a provision in accordance with IAS 37.

9. Loan commitments that cannot be settled net in cash or another financial instrument, unless the loan commitment is measured at fair value through profit or loss (see section 6.3.3 of this chapter) under IAS 39, in which case it is covered by IAS 39. Loan commitments outside the scope of IAS 39 are measured under IAS 37 or IAS 18.

10. Contracts between an acquirer and a vendor in a business combination to buy or sell an acquiree at a future date.

11. Financial instruments to which IFRS 2 *Share-based Payment* applies.

As discussed in section 6.2.1 of this chapter, contracts to buy or sell *non*-financial items are generally not financial instruments. Certain commodity contracts are, however, included within the scope of IAS 32. These include contracts to buy or sell non-financial items that can be settled net (in cash) or by exchanging financial instruments, or in which the non-financial item is readily convertible into cash.

Similarly, IAS 39 includes within its scope contracts to buy or sell non-financial items that can be settled net (in cash) or by another financial instrument, or by exchanging financial instruments. The exception to this is contracts entered into and that continue to be held for the purpose of the receipt or delivery of a non-financial item in accordance with the entity's expected purchase, sale or usage requirements (para. 5).

For example, an entity may enter into a contract to buy a machine in two months time for $50 000. The entity places an order and agrees to pay cash for the machine on standard credit terms after delivery. This contract is a contract for the purchase of a non-financial item and is settled *gross* in cash. The entity would not record any liability to pay for the machine until delivery of the machine because, until that time, it does not have a contractual obligation to pay the supplier since the supplier has not yet supplied the machine. Such a contract is outside the scope of IAS 39. However, if the entity is owed an amount of $45 000 by the supplier, and agrees to settle the purchase of the machine *net* by paying $5000 on delivery, IAS 39 catches the contract. Under IAS 39, the entity has a financial liability at the date of entering into the contract even though the machine has not yet been delivered.

The required journal entry on initial recognition of the amount owing by the supplier would be:

Amount owed by supplier	Dr	45 000	
Revenue (say)	Cr		45 000

At the date of entering into the contract to settle net, the journal entry would be:

Right to receive machine	Dr	5 000	
Financial liability	Cr		5 000

On delivery of the machine, the journal entries would be:

Cost of machine	Dr	45 000	
Amount owed by supplier	Cr		45 000
Financial liability	Dr	5 000	
Cash	Cr		5 000
Cost of machine	Dr	5 000	
Right to receive machine	Cr		5 000

This accounting would be required unless the entity can prove that the contract was entered into and continues to be held for the purpose of the receipt or delivery of a non-financial item in accordance with the entity's expected purchase, sale or usage requirements. Ideally, such terms should be explicitly written into these contracts in order to avoid any doubt.

This example shows how far reaching the scope of IAS 39 is and demonstrates that it applies to contracts equally proportionately unperformed (where both parties to the contract have equal unperformed rights and obligations) unless they are specifically scoped out. Traditionally, contracts equally proportionately unperformed have not been accounted for. Common examples of such contracts are normal purchase and sale agreements, such as the purchase of the machine described above. A purchaser does not usually account for the right to receive a machine and the corresponding obligation to pay for it at the date of making a purchase order. Similarly, the supplier does not usually account for the right to receive payment for the machine, and a corresponding obligation to deliver it, at the date of receiving the purchase order. Both parties commence recognition at the date of delivery, which is the date at which the equally unperformed rights and obligations are performed. IAS 39 clearly requires accounting on a rights and obligations basis unless the contracts giving rise to those rights and obligations are scoped out of the standard – hence the scoping out of normal purchases and sales of non-financial items. However, as soon as the contract becomes something other than normal, with terms that embody financial assets and liabilities (as in the example above), a rights-and-obligations approach is required.

LO 10   6.3.2   Derivatives and embedded derivatives

Paragraph 9 of IAS 39 defines a derivative. As explained in section 6.2.3 of this chapter, derivatives *derive* their value from another underlying item such as a share price or an interest rate. The definition requires *all* of the following three characteristics to be met:

- its value must change in response to a change in an underlying variable such as a specified interest rate, price, or foreign exchange rate
- it must require no initial net investment or an initial net investment that is smaller than would be required for other types of contracts with similar responses to changes in market factors
- it is settled at a future date.

Typical examples of derivatives are futures and forward, swap and option contracts. A typical option contract was discussed in section 6.2.3. A derivative usually has a notional amount, which is an amount of currency, a number of shares or other units specified in a contract. However, a derivative does not require the holder or writer to invest or receive the notional amount at the inception of the contract. In the example in figure 6.1, where party A buys an option that entitles it to purchase 1000 shares in company Z at $3 a share at any time in the next six months, the 1000 shares is the notional amount. However, a notional amount is not an essential feature of a derivative. For example, a contract may require a fixed payment of $2000 if a specified interest rate increases by a specified percentage. Such a contract is a derivative even though there is no notional amount (IAS 39, AG 9).

Many option contracts require a premium to be paid to the writer of the option. The premium is less than what would be required to purchase the underlying shares or other underlying financial instruments and thus option contracts meet the definition of a derivative.

Derivatives may exist on a stand-alone basis, or they may be embedded in other financial instruments. An embedded derivative is a component of a combined (or 'hybrid') instrument that also includes a non-derivative host contract, with the effect that some of the cash flows of the combined instrument vary in a way similar to a stand-alone instrument (IAS 39, para. 10). An embedded derivative cannot be contractually detached from the host contract, nor can it have a different counterparty from that of the host instrument.

For example, section 6.2.5 of this chapter showed that a common example of a compound financial instrument is a convertible bond or note that entitles the holder to convert the note into a fixed number of ordinary shares of the issuer. From the perspective of the *issuer*, such an instrument comprises two components: (a) a financial liability, being a contractual obligation to deliver cash/other financial assets in the form of interest payments and redemption of the note; and (b) an equity instrument, being an option issued to the holder entitling it to the right, for a specified period of time, to convert the note into a fixed number of ordinary shares of the issuer. The equity instrument is an embedded derivative. The issuer of the convertible note records the embedded derivative as an equity instrument under IAS 32 and this is specifically excluded from the scope of IAS 39 (para. 2(d)). The holder of the convertible note records the embedded derivative, being a derivative embedded in its financial asset, under IAS 39.

Paragraph 11 of IAS 39 requires an embedded derivative to be separated from the host contract if, and only if, the following three conditions are met:

- the economic characteristics and risks of the embedded derivative are *not closely related* to the economic characteristics and risks of the host contract
- a separate instrument with the same terms as the embedded derivative would meet the definition of a derivative

- the combined instrument is not measured at fair value through profit or loss. This means that a derivative embedded in a combined financial instrument measured at fair value through profit or loss is not separated, even if it could be separated. This is because the separated embedded derivative would be required to be measured at fair value anyway.

If an embedded derivative is separated, it is generally required to be measured at fair value. If fair value cannot be reliably measured, then the entire contract must be measured at fair value through profit or loss (IAS 39, paras. 12 and 9).

The following are examples of instruments where the economic characteristics and risks of the embedded derivative are *not closely related* to the economic characteristics and risks of the host contract:

- a put option embedded in a debt instrument that allows the holder to require the issuer to reacquire the instrument for an amount of cash that varies on the basis of the change in an equity or commodity price or index. This is because the host is a debt instrument and the variables are not related to the debt instrument
- an equity conversion feature embedded in a host convertible debt instrument (as discussed in section 6.2.5 of this chapter)
- an option to extend the remaining term to maturity of a debt instrument without a concurrent adjustment to the market rate of interest at the time of the extension
- commodity-indexed interest or principal payments embedded in a host debt instrument or insurance contract by which the amount of interest or principal is indexed to the price of the commodity (such as gold).

IAS 39, AG 30, contains other examples of such instruments. It goes on to give examples of instruments where the economic characteristics and risks of the embedded derivative *are* closely related to the economic characteristics and risks of the host contract. These examples are very prescriptive and not clearly principle-based.

LO 11

6.3.3　The four categories of financial instruments

The four categories of financial instruments are set out in paragraph 9 of IAS 39. Table 6.6 summarises the requirements of paragraph 9 and provides common examples of financial instruments likely to fall into each of the four categories.

TABLE 6.6	The four categories of financial instruments		
Category	Characteristics	Other requirements	Examples
A financial asset or financial liability *at fair value through profit or loss*	(a) It is classified as *held for trading*; or (b) Upon initial recognition it *is designated by the entity as at fair value through profit or loss*. Any financial asset or financial liability may be so designated, provided it meets certain conditions and except for investments in equity instruments that do not have a quoted market price and whose fair value cannot be measured reliably.	In order to be classified as held for trading, a financial asset or financial liability must be: (i) acquired or incurred principally for the purpose of selling or repurchasing it in the near term; (ii) part of a portfolio of identified financial instruments that are managed together and for which there is evidence of a recent actual pattern of short-term profit-taking; or (iii) a derivative (except for a derivative that is a hedging instrument).	Share portfolio held for short-term gains; forward exchange contract; interest rate swap; call option

(continued)

Category	Characteristics	Other requirements	Examples
Held-to-maturity investments	(a) Are *non-derivative* financial assets with *fixed or determinable payments* and *fixed maturity*; and (b) The entity has the *positive intention and ability to hold* these investments to maturity.	Excludes investments • designated as at fair value through profit or loss; • designated as available-for-sale; and • that meet the definition of loans and receivables. Note that the ability to designate an investment as held-to-maturity relies heavily on management intent. Accordingly, IAS 39 contains a 'punishment' for managers who do not act according to their intent: if an entity sells or reclassifies more than an insignificant amount of held-to-maturity investments during the current financial year or the two preceding financial years, then the entity shall not classify any financial assets as held-to-maturity.	Commercial bill investments; government bonds; corporate bonds; converting notes (that will convert at a fixed date in future); fixed-term/maturity debentures
Loans and receivables	*Non-derivative* financial assets with *fixed or determinable payments* that are *not quoted* in an active market	Excludes loans and receivables: • designated as at fair value through profit or loss; • intended to be sold in the near term, which must be classified as held-for-trading; • designated as available-for-sale; and • those for which the holder may not recover substantially all of its initial investment, other than because of credit deterioration, which must be classified as available-for-sale.	Accounts receivable; loans to other entities; mortgage loans (financial institutions); credit card receivables
Available-for-sale financial assets	*Non-derivative financial assets that are designated as available-for-sale and do not fall into any of the above three categories*		Ordinary share investments; convertible notes; preference share investments

Note that only the first category in table 6.6 is applicable to financial assets and financial liabilities. All the other categories apply to financial assets only.

LO 12

6.3.4 Recognition criteria

Paragraph 14 of IAS 39 states that an entity shall recognise a financial asset or a financial liability on its balance sheet when, and only when, the entity becomes a party to the contractual provisions of the instrument. (This requirement to recognise rights and obligations arising under contractual agreements was discussed in section 6.3.1 of this chapter.) AG 35 provides other examples of applying the recognition criteria, as follows:

• Unconditional receivables and payables are recognised as assets or liabilities when the entity becomes a party to the contract and, as a consequence, has a legal right to receive or a legal obligation to pay cash. Normal trade debtors and trade creditors would fall into this category.
• Assets to be acquired and liabilities to be incurred under a firm commitment to purchase or sell goods or services are generally not recognised until at least one of the

parties has performed under the agreement. However, this is subject to the rules set out in the scope paragraph of IAS 39 (discussed in section 6.3.1 of this chapter). Thus, if a firm commitment to buy or sell non-financial items is within the scope of IAS 39, its net fair value is recognised as an asset or liability on the commitment date.

- A forward contract within the scope of the standard is also recognised as an asset or liability at the commitment date. When an entity becomes party to a forward contract, the rights and obligations at the commitment date are often equal, so that the net fair value of the forward is zero. The example in figure 6.4 illustrates how a forward foreign exchange contract is accounted for on initial recognition.

Accounting for a forward foreign exchange contract on initial recognition

Company A enters into a forward foreign exchange contract with company B to receive US$10 000 in three months time, at a forward rate of A$1.00 = US$0.70.

At the date of entering into the contract, the exchange rate (the spot rate at that date) was A$1.00 = US$0.68.

At the date of entering into the contract, company A must recognise its rights and obligations under the contract, which are:
- a right to receive US$10 000 at the forward rate in three months time, which equals A$14 285
- an obligation to pay for the US$10 000 in three months time by delivering A$14 285.

Accordingly, company A records the following journal entries on initial recognition:

Forward foreign exchange receivable	Dr	14 285
Forward foreign exchange payable	Cr	14 285

However, because the net fair value of the contract is zero on initial recognition, no asset or liability is recognised.

FIGURE 6.4   Accounting for a forward foreign exchange contract on initial recognition

Note the following:
- Option contracts within the scope of the standard are recognised as assets or liabilities when the holder or writer becomes a party to the contract.
- Planned future transactions, no matter how likely, are not assets and liabilities because the entity has not become a party to a contract.

LO 13

6.3.5   ## Measurement

The measurement rules in IAS 39 address:
1. initial measurement
2. subsequent measurement
3. fair value measurement considerations ('the fair value hierarchy')
4. reclassifications
5. gains and losses
6. impairment and uncollectability of financial assets.

The rules are applied distinctly to each of the four categories of financial instruments discussed in section 6.3.3 of this chapter.

1. Initial measurement

Paragraph 43 of IAS 39 requires that, on initial recognition, financial assets and financial liabilities must be measured at fair value. Fair value is defined in paragraph 9 as:

the amount for which an asset could be exchanged, or a liability settled, between knowledgeable, willing parties in an arm's length transaction.

The concept of fair value will be discussed later in this section.

In addition, paragraph 43 requires that transaction costs directly attributable to the acquisition or issue of the financial asset or liability must be added to the fair value, except for financial assets and liabilities measured at fair value through profit or loss. Transaction costs are defined in paragraph 9 as:

> incremental costs that are directly attributable to the acquisition, issue or disposal of a financial asset or financial liability. An incremental cost is one that would not have been incurred if the entity had not acquired, issued or disposed of the financial instrument.

IAS 39, AG 13, provides further guidance. Examples of transaction costs include fees and commissions paid to agents, advisers, brokers and dealers; levies by regulatory agencies and securities exchanges; and transfer taxes and duties (such as stamp duties). Transaction costs do not include debt premiums or discounts, financing costs or internal administrative or holding costs.

The fair value of a financial instrument on initial recognition is normally the transaction price (the fair value of the consideration given or received). However, if part of the consideration given or received is for something other than the financial instrument, then the fair value must be estimated using valuation techniques. For example, if a company provides an interest-free loan to its employees, part of the consideration is given in the form of recognition of employee services or loyalty rather than for the entire loan itself. The fair value of the loan must be calculated by discounting the future cash flows using a market rate of interest for a similar loan (similar as to currency, term and credit rating). Any additional amount lent is accounted for as an expense unless it qualifies for recognition as some other type of asset. Figure 6.5 provides an example.

Initial measurement of an interest-free loan

Company Z provides interest-free loans to 10 employees for a five-year term, payable at the end of five years. The total loan amount is $200 000. A market rate of interest for a similar five-year loan is 5%. The present value of this receivable, being the future cash flows discounted at 5%, is approximately $157 000. Therefore, $43 000 is an expense to company Z on initial recognition of the loan.

Company Z would record the following journal entries:

Loans receivable	Dr	157 000	
Expenses	Dr	43 000	
Cash	Cr		200 000

FIGURE 6.5   Initial measurement of an interest-free loan

2. Subsequent measurement

Subsequent measurement depends on whether or not the item is a financial asset or financial liability, and on which of the categories applies.

Financial assets are measured as follows (IAS 39, para. 45):

1. 'At fair value through profit or loss' – at fair value. This includes all derivatives, other than those subject to the hedge accounting rules (see section 6.3.6 of this chapter).
2. Held-to-maturity investments – at amortised cost.
3. Loans and receivables – at amortised cost.
4. Available-for-sale financial assets – at fair value.

An exception is given for investments in equity instruments that do not have a quoted market price in an active market and whose fair value cannot be measured reliably. Such equity instruments, and any linked derivatives, must be measured at cost. Furthermore, if any of these financial assets are hedged items, they are subject to the hedge accounting measurement rules (see section 6.3.6 of this chapter).

Amortised cost is defined in paragraph 9 of IAS 39 as follows:

> the amount at which the financial asset or financial liability is measured at initial recognition minus principal repayments, plus or minus the cumulative amortisation using the effective interest method of any difference between that initial amount and the maturity amount, and minus any reduction (directly or through the use of an allowance account) for impairment or uncollectability.

The effective interest method is defined in paragraph 9 as:

> a method of calculating the amortised cost of a financial asset or a financial liability ... and of allocating the interest income or interest expense over the relevant period.

The effective interest rate is defined in paragraph 9 as:

> the rate that exactly discounts estimated future cash payments or receipts through the expected life of the financial instrument or, when appropriate, a shorter period to the net carrying amount of the financial asset or financial liability.

The effective interest rate must be calculated considering all contractual terms of the instrument. It includes all fees, transaction costs, premiums and discounts. (A calculator with a finance function is needed to calculate the effective interest rate.)

Illustrative example 6.1 provides an example of how amortised cost is calculated.

ILLUSTRATIVE EXAMPLE 6.1

Calculation of amortised cost (based on IAS 39, Implementation Guidance B.26)

Company A purchases a debt instrument with a five-year term for its fair value of $1000 (including transaction costs). The instrument has a principal amount of $1250 (the amount payable on redemption) and carries fixed interest of 4.7% annually. The annual cash interest income is thus $59 ($1250 × 0.047). Using a financial calculator, the effective interest rate is calculated as 10%. The debt instrument is classified as a held-to-maturity investment.

The following table sets out the cash flows and interest income for each period, using the effective interest rate of 10%:

A. Year	B. Amortised cost at beginning of year	C. Interest income ($B \times 10\%$)	D. Cash flows	E. Amortised cost at end of year ($B + C - D$)
2005	1 000	100	59	1 041
2006	1 041	104	59	1 086
2007	1 086	109	59	1 136
2008	1 136	113	59	1 190
2009	1 190	119	59 + 1 250	–

→

The journal entries to record this transaction on initial recognition and throughout the life of the instrument are as follows:

On initial recognition in 2005:

| Held-to-maturity investment | Dr | 1 000 | |
| Cash | Cr | | 1 000 |

On recognition of interest in 2005:

Held-to-maturity investment	Dr	41	
Cash	Dr	59	
Interest income	Cr		100

On recognition of interest in 2006:

Held-to-maturity investment	Dr	45	
Cash	Dr	59	
Interest income	Cr		104

On recognition of interest in 2007:

Held-to-maturity investment	Dr	50	
Cash	Dr	59	
Interest income	Cr		109

On recognition of interest in 2008:

Held-to-maturity investment	Dr	54	
Cash	Dr	59	
Interest income	Cr		113

On recognition of interest in 2009:

Held-to-maturity investment	Dr	60	
Cash	Dr	59	
Interest income	Cr		119

On redemption of investment in 2009:

| Cash | Dr | 1 250 | |
| Held-to-maturity investment | Cr | | 1 250 |

Financial liabilities are measured subsequent to initial recognition at amortised cost except for those designated as 'at fair value through profit or loss', which must be measured at fair value (IAS 39, para. 47). There are four exceptions to this rule:

1. Derivative liabilities linked to investments in equity instruments that do not have a quoted market price in an active market and whose fair value cannot be measured reliably. Such linked derivatives must be measured at cost. This mirrors the exemption for derivative assets.
2. Financial liabilities arising in certain circumstances when a financial asset is transferred under the derecognition rules. These are outside the scope of this chapter.
3. Financial guarantee contracts (see section 6.3.1). After initial recognition, an issuer of such a contract shall measure it at the *higher* of
   (i) the amount determined in accordance with IAS 37 and
   (ii) the amount initially recognised less, where appropriate, cumulative amortisation recognised in accordance with IAS 18 *Revenue*.

A common example of a financial guarantee contract is a parent company's guarantee of its subsidiary's loan. Unless the parent company applies IFRS 4 to such a guarantee, it must apply IAS 39. (This applies in the parent company's separate accounts.)

4. Commitments to provide a loan at a below-market interest rate. The measurement rules are the same as for (3) above.

If any of these financial liabilities are hedged items, they are subject to the hedge accounting measurement rules (see section 6.3.6 of this chapter).

Illustrative example 6.2 provides an example of a financial liability measured at amortised cost.

ILLUSTRATIVE EXAMPLE 6.2

A financial liability measured at amortised cost

Company L enters into an agreement with company B to lend it $1 million (plus transaction costs of $25 000) on 1 July 2005. The interest to be paid is 5% for each of the first two years and 7% for each of the next two years, annually in arrears. The loan must be repaid after four years. The annual cash interest expense is thus $50 000 ($1 million × 0.05) for each of the first two years and $70 000 ($1 million × 0.07) for each of the next two years. Using a financial calculator, the effective interest rate is calculated as 6.67%. Company B measures the financial liability at fair value on initial recognition and subsequently at amortised cost in accordance with IAS 39, paragraphs 43 and 47.

The following table sets out the cash flows and interest expense for each period, using the effective interest rate of 6.67%:

A. Year	B. Amortised cost at beginning of year	C. Interest expense (B × 6.67%)	D. Cash flows	E. Amortised cost at end of year (B + C − D)
2005	975 000	65 014	50 000	990 014
2006	990 014	66 015	50 000	1 006 029
2007	1 066 029	67 083	70 000	1 003 112
2008	1 003 112	66 888	70 000 + 1 000 000	–

The journal entries to record this transaction on initial recognition and throughout the life of the instrument in the books of company B are as follows:

On initial recognition in 2005:

Cash	Dr	975 000	
Bond – liability	Cr		1 000 000
Bond – liability	Dr	25 000	

On recognition of interest in 2005:

Interest expense	Dr	65 014	
Bond – liability	Cr		15 014
Cash	Cr		50 000

On recognition of interest in 2006:

Interest expense	Dr	66 015	
Bond – liability	Cr		16 015
Cash	Cr		50 000

On recognition of interest in 2007:

Interest expense	Dr	67 083	
Bond – liability	Cr		2 917
Cash	Cr		70 000

On recognition of interest in 2008:

Interest expense	Dr	66 888	
Bond – liability	Cr		3 112
Cash	Cr		70 000

On repayment of liability in 2008:

Interest expense	Dr	0	
Bond – liability	Dr	1 000 000	
Cash	Cr		1 000 000

3. Fair value measurement considerations

Paragraph 48 of IAS 39 refers readers to paragraphs AG 69 to AG 82 for guidance in determining fair value. These paragraphs set out what has become known as 'the fair value hierarchy', which is the order in which sources of fair value should be determined. This order is as follows:

(a) active market: quoted price
(b) no active market: valuation technique
(c) no active market: equity instruments.

(a) Active market: quoted price

A financial instrument is regarded as quoted in an active market if quoted prices are readily and regularly available from an exchange, dealer, broker, industry group, pricing service or regulatory agency; and if those prices represent actual and regularly occurring market transactions on an arm's-length basis. Examples include the Australian Stock Exchange and the Sydney Futures Exchange. The existence of a quoted price in an active market is the best evidence of fair value. Appropriate market prices are determined as shown in table 6.7.

TABLE 6.7	Determining the appropriate market price
Type of financial asset/liability	Appropriate market price
Financial asset held	Current bid price (what the market is offering to buy that asset for)
Financial liability to be issued	Current bid price
Financial asset to be acquired	Current asking price or offer price (what the market is asking to sell that asset for)
Financial liability held	Current asking price or offer price

When there is an active market but a current bid or asking price is not available, then the price of the most recent transaction provides evidence of the current fair value – so long as there has been no significant change in economic circumstances since the most recent transaction.

(b) No active market: valuation technique

If the market for a financial instrument is not active, an entity establishes fair value by using a valuation technique. Valuation techniques include:

- recent arm's-length transactions
- current fair value of another instrument that is substantially the same
- discounted cash flow analysis
- option pricing models.

The valuation technique should rely as much as possible on market inputs and as little as possible on entity-specific inputs. Inputs to valuation techniques include:

- the time value of money (interest at the basic or risk-free rate); these can be derived from observable government bond rates and are often quoted in financial publications
- credit risk (the premium over the basic interest rate for credit risk)
- foreign currency exchange rates; these are quoted daily in financial publications
- equity prices
- volatility (the expected magnitude of change in the item's price).

In applying discounted cash flow analysis, an entity should use a discount rate equal to the prevailing rate of return for a similar financial instrument. The characteristics that need to be similar are the credit quality of the instrument, the term to maturity and the currency. Short-term receivables and payables with no stated interest rate (such as trade debtors and trade creditors) may be measured at the original invoice price if the effect of discounting is immaterial.

(c) No active market: equity instruments

It was seen earlier in this section that paragraph 45 of IAS 39 provides an exception for investments in equity instruments that do not have a quoted market price in an active market and whose fair value cannot be measured reliably. Such equity instruments, and any linked derivatives, must be measured at cost. AG 80 states that such an instrument *is* regarded as being reliably measurable if (a) the variability in the range of reasonable fair value estimates is not significant, and (b) the probabilities of the various estimates within the range can be reasonably assessed and used in estimating fair value.

In all cases, fair value must be calculated on the presumption that the entity is a going concern. Fair value is not, therefore, the amount that an entity would receive or pay in a forced transaction, involuntary liquidation or distressed sale.

4. Reclassifications

IAS 39 contains various prescriptive rules on the reclassification of financial instruments. The rules are aimed at preventing inconsistent gain or loss recognition and the use of arbitrage between the categories. In summary:

- Paragraph 50 of IAS 39 states that an entity shall not reclassify a financial instrument into or out of the fair value through profit or loss category while it is held or issued.
- Held-to-maturity items can or must be reclassified to the available-for-sale category. This may occur because of a change in management's intention, or because of breaking the rules allowing held-to-maturity classification (see table 6.6, pages 217–18).
- In rare circumstances, a financial instrument may be reclassified from a fair value measurement basis to a cost basis. These are set out in paragraph 54.

5. Gains and losses

A gain or loss arising from the change in fair value of a financial instrument that is *not* part of a hedging relationship (see section 6.3.6 of this chapter) is recognised, in accordance with the four categories, as follows (IAS 39, para. 55):

1. 'At fair value through profit or loss' – in profit or loss.
2. Held-to-maturity investments – in profit or loss. This occurs when the asset is derecognised or impaired, and through the amortisation process.
3. Loans and receivables – in profit or loss. This occurs when the asset is derecognised or impaired, and through the amortisation process.
4. Available-for-sale financial assets – directly in equity, through the statement of changes in equity. When the financial instrument is derecognised, the cumulative amount remaining in equity is removed from equity and 'recycled' back to profit or loss. This rule is subject to four exceptions, all of which must be recognised in profit or loss:
   (a) impairment losses
   (b) foreign exchange gains and losses
   (c) interest calculated using the effective interest rate method
   (d) dividends on available-for-sale equity instruments.

6. Impairment and uncollectability of financial assets

Paragraph 58 of IAS 39 states that an entity shall assess at each balance date whether there is *objective evidence* that a financial asset is impaired. Objective evidence includes observable data about the following loss events (IAS 39, paras 58–61):

(a) significant financial difficulty of the issuer
(b) a breach of contract or default in interest or principal payments
(c) a lender granting concessions to the borrower that the lender would not otherwise consider
(d) it becoming probable that a borrower will enter bankruptcy or other financial reorganisation (such as administration)
(e) the disappearance of an active market for the financial asset because of financial difficulties
(f) observable data indicating that there is a measurable decrease in the estimated future cash flows from a group of financial assets since the original recognition of those assets. This applies mainly to large groups of receivables where companies determine whether a provision for doubtful debts is required for the group. Traditionally, entities such as banks have made a 'general provision' for impairment of a group of receivables because individual customers in that group are relatively small. IAS 39 limits the creation of such general provisions to circumstances where there are observable and directly correlating data. Such data may include, for example, an increased number of delayed payments or customers reaching their maximum credit limit in the group; national or local economic conditions that correlate with defaults on the assets within the group, such as a decrease in property prices for mortgages in the relevant area; a decrease in oil prices for loans to oil producers; or an increase in the unemployment rate in the geographical area of the borrowers
(g) in respect of investments in equity instruments, significant changes with an adverse effect that have taken place in the technological, market, economic or legal environment in which the issuer operates.

Under paragraph 60, the following events are *not*, on their own, objective evidence that a financial asset is impaired:

(a) the disappearance of an active market because an entity's financial instruments are no longer actively traded
(b) a downgrade of an entity's credit rating
(c) a decline in the fair value of a financial asset below its cost/amortised cost. For example, a decline in the fair value of an investment in a fixed-term *debt instrument* that results from an increase in the risk-free interest rate does not necessarily mean

that the investment is impaired, if the investment is being held to maturity. However, a significant or prolonged decline in the fair value of an investment in an *equity instrument* below its cost is objective evidence of impairment.

Impairment losses are recognised, in accordance with the four categories, as follows (IAS 39, paras 63–70):

(a) 'At fair value through profit or loss' – not applicable – the impairment rules do not apply to such instruments.

(b) Held-to-maturity investments – the amount of the loss is measured as the difference between the asset's carrying amount and the present value of expected future cash flows discounted at the asset's original effective interest rate. The carrying amount of the asset is reduced either directly or through use of an allowance account (traditionally termed a 'provision'). The amount of the loss must be recognised in profit or loss. An impairment loss should be reversed only if there is objective evidence of an event after the impairment was recognised, such as an improvement of the debtor's credit rating. The reversal is recognised in profit and loss. The reversal must not result in the carrying amount of the asset exceeding what the amortised cost would have been had the impairment not been recognised at the date the impairment is reversed.

(c) Loans and receivables – as for held-to-maturity investments.

(d) Available-for-sale financial assets – the cumulative loss that has been recognised directly in equity must be removed from equity and recognised in profit or loss. This includes any decline in fair value already recognised in equity plus the impairment loss. Reversals of impairment losses are permitted only for investments in *debt* instruments. The requirement for objective evidence of a reversal is the same as for categories (b) and (c) above, but there is no limit on the upward reversal because the asset is measured at fair value. Reversals of impairment losses for investments in *equity* instruments through profit or loss are not permitted. Effectively, this means that the cost of the equity investment must be reset at the impaired value, and any future upward changes in fair value must be recorded directly in equity.

Once a financial asset has been written down as a result of an impairment loss, interest income is recognised thereafter using the rate of interest used to discount the future cash flows for the purpose of measuring the impairment loss (IAS 39, AG 93).

Illustrative example 6.3 builds on illustrative example 6.1 by demonstrating the calculation of an impairment loss for a held-to-maturity investment.

ILLUSTRATIVE EXAMPLE 6.3

Impairment loss on a held-to-maturity investment

Company A purchases a debt instrument with a five-year term for its fair value of $1000 (including transaction costs). The instrument has a principal amount of $1250 (the amount payable on redemption) and carries fixed interest of 4.7% annually. The annual cash interest income is thus $59 ($1250 × 0.047). Using a financial calculator, the effective interest rate is calculated as 10%. The debt instrument is classified as a held-to-maturity investment. During 2007, the issuer of the instrument is in financial difficulties and it becomes probable that the issuer will be put into administration by a receiver. The fair value of the instrument is estimated to be $636 at the end of 2007, calculated by discounting the expected future cash flows at 10%. No cash flows are received during 2008. At the end of 2008, the issuer is released from administration and company A receives a letter from the receiver stating that the issuer will be able to meet all of its remaining obligations, including interest and repayment of principal.

The following table sets out the cash flows and interest income for each period, using the effective interest rate of 10%:

A. Year	B. Amortised cost at beginning of year	C. Interest income (B × 10%)	D. Cash flows	E. Amortised cost at end of year (B + C − D)
2005	1 000	100	59	1 041
2006	1 041	104	59	1 086
2007	1 086	109	59	1 136
2008	1 136	113	59	1 190
2009	1 190	119	59 + 1 250	–

The journal entries for 2005, 2006 and 2007 are the same as set out in illustrative example 6.1. At the end of 2007, company A records the following journal entry:

Expense (profit and loss)	Dr	500	
Held-to-maturity investment	Cr		500

The asset's carrying value is now $636:

A. Year	B. Amortised cost, less impairment losses, at beginning of year	C. Interest income (B × 10%)	D. Cash flows	E. Amortised cost at end of year (B + C − D)
2008	636	64	–	700

During 2008, company A records interest as 10% of $636 in accordance with IAS 39, paragraph AG 93:

Held-to-maturity investment	Dr	64	
Interest income	Cr		64

At the end of 2008, company A has objective evidence that the impairment loss has been reversed. The limit on the amount of the reversal is what the amortised cost of the asset would have been at the date of reversal had the impairment loss not been recorded. According to the first table above, this amount would have been $1190 at the end of 2008. The asset's carrying value at the end of 2008 was $700, so the reversal of the impairment loss is $490 ($1190 − $700). The journal entry is as follows:

Held-to-maturity investment	Dr	490	
Income (profit and loss)	Cr		490

The journal entries for 2009 are then the same as shown in illustrative example 6.1.

Illustrative example 6.4 shows the calculation of an impairment loss on an available-for-sale investment in a debt instrument and in an equity instrument.

ILLUSTRATIVE EXAMPLE 6.4

Impairment loss on an available-for-sale investment

Part A: In a debt instrument

Company I invests in a debt instrument on 1 July 2005. At this date, the cost and fair value of the instrument is $100 000. The instrument is classified as available-for-sale and so is measured at fair value, and changes in fair value are recorded directly in equity. The following table sets out the changes in the fair value of the debt instrument, and the nature of the change in each year:

Year	Fair value change	Nature of change
2006	($10 000)	No objective evidence of impairment
2007	($20 000)	Objective evidence of impairment
2008	$15 000	Objective evidence of reversal of impairment

The journal entries (ignoring interest income) recorded by company A are shown below.

On initial recognition on 1 July 2005:

Available-for-sale investment	Dr	100 000	
Cash	Cr		100 000

Change in fair value for 2006:

Equity	Dr	10 000	
Available-for-sale investment	Cr		10 000

Impairment loss for 2007:

Expense (profit and loss)	Dr	30 000	
Available-for-sale investment	Cr		20 000
Equity	Cr		10 000

(The above entry is necessary because paragraph 67 of IAS 39 requires the cumulative loss recognised in equity to be transferred to profit and loss.)

Reversal of impairment loss in 2008:

Available-for-sale investment	Dr	15 000	
Income (profit and loss)	Cr		15 000

Part B: In an equity instrument

Assume exactly the same facts as in part A, except that the investment is in an equity instrument. All the journal entries will be the same, except for the entry in 2008, which will be as follows:

Increase in fair value in 2008 (not a reversal of an impairment loss):

Available-for-sale investment	Dr	15 000	
Equity	Cr		15 000

Table 6.8 summarises the measurement rules of IAS 39 discussed earlier in this section of the chapter.

TABLE 6.8	Summary of the measurement rules in IAS 39				
Category of financial asset/ liability	Initial measurement	Subsequent measurement	Reclassifications	Gains and losses	Impairment
A financial asset or financial liability *at fair value through profit or loss*	Fair value	Fair value, unless a hedging instrument[1] or hedged item	Not permitted	Recognised in profit or loss, unless a hedging instrument[1] or hedged item	Not applicable
Held-to-maturity investments	Fair value plus transaction costs	Amortised cost, unless a hedged item	May or must be reclassified to available-for-sale	Recognised in profit or loss, unless a hedged item	Loss, recognised in profit or loss. Reversal of impairment loss permitted subject to conditions. Limit on extent of reversal
Loans and receivables	Fair value plus transaction costs	Amortised cost, unless a hedged item	Not permitted	Recognised in profit or loss, unless a hedged item	Loss, recognised in profit or loss. Reversal of impairment loss permitted subject to conditions. Limit on extent of reversal
Available-for-sale financial assets	Fair value plus transaction costs	Fair value, unless a hedged item	Not permitted	Recognised in equity, unless a hedged item. Four exceptions where gains/losses must be recognised in profit or loss. Amounts in equity are recycled to profit or loss when the asset is derecognised	Loss, recognised in profit or loss. This includes any decline in fair value already recorded in equity. Reversal of impairment loss permitted only for debt investments, subject to conditions. No limit on extent of reversal. Reversal of impairment loss through profit or loss prohibited for equity investments
Other financial liabilities	Fair value plus transaction costs	Amortised cost, unless a hedged item	Not permitted	Recognised in profit or loss, unless a hedged item	Not applicable

Note:

1. This category includes derivatives that may be effective hedging instruments. The financial assets in the other categories may be hedged items (the item being hedged) but cannot be hedging instruments.

LO 14

6.3.6   Hedge accounting

Entities enter into hedge arrangements for economic reasons; namely, to protect themselves from the types of risks discussed in section 6.2.9 – currency risk, fair value interest rate risk, price risk and so on. Hedge accounting generally results in a closer matching of the balance sheet effect with the profit or loss effect, and protects the income statement from volatility caused by changes in fair value from period to period. The hedge accounting rules in IAS 39 are very prescriptive. They are best put into perspective by remembering that the standard is based heavily on SFAS 133, and that the standard's implicit preference is for fair value measurement so that, in order to qualify for hedge accounting, entities need to meet strict specified criteria.

Two important concepts need to be understood:
1. the hedging instrument
2. the hedged item.

The hedging instrument

Paragraph 9 of IAS 39 defines a hedging instrument as:

> a designated derivative or (for a hedge of the risk of changes in foreign currency exchange rates only) a designated non-derivative financial asset or non-derivative financial liability whose fair value or cash flows are expected to offset changes in the fair value or cash flows of a designated hedged item ...

An instrument must meet eight essential criteria for it to be classified as a hedging instrument:
1. It must be *designated* as such. This means that management must document the details of the hedging instrument and the item it is hedging, at the inception of the hedge.
2. It *must* be a *derivative* unless criterion 3 is met.
3. It is hedging *foreign currency* exchange risk, in which case it can be a non-derivative.
4. It must be expected to *offset changes* in the fair value or cash flows of the hedged item.
5. It must be with a party *external* to the reporting entity — external to the consolidated group or individual entity being reported on (para. 73). There is one exception to this rule in respect of intragroup monetary items when certain conditions are met (para. 80).
6. It *cannot be split* into component parts, except for separating the time value and intrinsic value in an option contract, and the interest element and spot price in a forward contract (para. 74).
7. A proportion of the entire hedging instrument, such as 50% of the notional amount, may be designated as the hedging instrument. However, a hedging relationship may *not be designated for only a portion of the time* period during which the hedging instrument remains outstanding (para. 75).
8. A single hedging instrument may be designated as a hedge of more than one type of risk provided that (a) the risks hedged can be identified clearly, (b) the effectiveness of the hedge can be demonstrated, and (c) there is specific designation of the hedging instrument and different risk positions (para. 76).

Examples of hedging instruments are forward foreign currency exchange contracts, interest rate swaps and futures contracts. Written options cannot be hedging instruments of the writer because the potential exposure to loss is greater than the potential gain on the hedged item (IAS 39, AG 94), so they do not meet criterion 4.

The hedged item

IAS 39 provides the following definitions:
• a hedged item (para. 9)

> an asset, liability, firm commitment, highly probable forecast transaction or net investment in a foreign operation that (a) exposes the entity to risk of changes in fair value or future cash flows and (b) is designated as being hedged ...

• a forecast transaction (para. 9)

> an uncommitted but anticipated future transaction.

An example of a forecast transaction is expected future sales or purchases.

- a firm commitment (para. 9)

  a binding agreement for the exchange of a specified quantity of resources at a specified price on a specified future date or dates.

  An example of a firm commitment is a purchase order to buy a machine for $50 000 in three months time.

Paragraph 78 of IAS 39 permits groups of assets, liabilities and so on to be the hedged item, provided they have similar risk characteristics and proportionate fair value changes (para. 83). However, under paragraph 84, a net position cannot be hedged (for example, the net of a group of similar assets and similar liabilities). Certain exceptions to this were introduced in mid 2004 to meet the concerns of financial institutions that routinely hedge net positions as part of their asset/liability management. This was one of the reasons that financial institutions were initially so opposed to the introduction of IAS 39, as it would affect their standard hedging practices.

The hedged item can be a financial item or a non-financial item. If it is a *financial item*, such as an interest-bearing investment, the risk being hedged may be only *part of the total risks* in that item, provided that effectiveness can be measured (para. 81). For example, an interest-bearing investment potentially exposes the holder to interest rate risk, credit risk and price risk. The holder may choose to hedge only the interest rate exposure, or only the credit risk, and so on. The reason for this is that the component risks of financial items can be readily identified.

Note that a held-to-maturity investment cannot be a hedged item with respect to interest rate risk or prepayment risk because, by definition, the investment must be held to maturity and thus these risks should not eventuate (para. 79). However, such an instrument may be a hedged item with respect to foreign currency risk and credit risk.

However, if the hedged item is a *non-financial item*, the risk being hedged must be the *total risks* because of the difficulty in isolating and measuring the component risks in non-financial items. The only exception to this is foreign currency risk, which may be separately hedged (para. 82).

Derivatives cannot be designated as hedged items because they are deemed held for trading and measured at fair value through profit or loss.

The conditions for hedge accounting and the three types of hedge

Hedge accounting recognises the offsetting effects on profit or loss of changes in the fair values of the hedging instrument and the hedged item. Paragraph 88 of IAS 39 sets out the five conditions that must be met in order for hedge accounting to be applied:

1. At the inception of the hedge, there must be formal *designation and documentation* of the hedging relationship and the entity's risk-management objective and strategy for undertaking the hedge. That documentation must include identification of:
   - the hedging instrument
   - the hedged item
   - the nature of the risk being hedged
   - how the entity will assess hedge effectiveness.
2. The hedge must be expected to be *highly effective* in achieving offsetting changes in fair value or cash flows attributable to the hedged risk. 'Highly effective' is elaborated on in AG 105 of IAS 39, which explains that changes must almost fully offset each other and actual results must be within a range of 80%–125%. For example, if actual results are a loss on a hedging instrument of $120 and a corresponding gain on the hedged item of $100, offset can be measured by 100/120 (being 83%) or by 120/100 (being 120%). Effectiveness is assessed, at a minimum, at the time an entity prepares its interim or annual financial statements (AG 106).

3. For cash flow hedges (discussed below), a forecast transaction that is the subject of the hedge must be highly probable and must present an exposure to variations in cash flows that could affect profit or loss. 'Highly probable' is explained further in the Implementation Guidance at F3.7 as meaning a much greater likelihood than 'more likely than not' (the meaning of 'probable').

4. The effectiveness of the hedge can be reliably measured.

5. The hedge is assessed on an ongoing basis and must be determined actually to have been highly effective throughout the financial reporting periods for which the hedge was designated.

Hedge effectiveness is defined in paragraph 9 as:

> the degree to which changes in the fair value or cash flows of the hedged item that are attributable to a hedged risk are offset by changes in the fair value or cash flows of the hedging instrument.

The three types of hedging relationships are:

- fair value hedge
- cash flow hedge
- hedge of a net investment in a foreign operation as defined in IAS 21. This is accounted for in a similar manner to cash flow hedges, but will not be discussed further in this chapter.

Note the following points:

- A fair value hedge is a hedge of the exposure to changes in fair value of an asset, liability or unrecognised firm commitment.
- A cash flow hedge is a hedge of the exposure to variability in cash flows of a recognised asset or liability, or a highly probable forecast transaction.
- Paragraph 87 of IAS 39 states that a hedge of the foreign currency risk of a firm commitment may be accounted for as either a fair value hedge or a cash flow hedge.
- A simple way of remembering the difference between the two types of hedge is that a cash flow hedge locks in future cash flows, whereas a fair value hedge does not.
- The most commonly occurring hedge transactions for average reporting entities are interest rate hedges and foreign currency hedges.

As an example of a simple cash flow hedge, assume that company B has a borrowing with lender bank L that carries a variable rate of interest. Company B is worried about its exposure to future increases in the variable rate of interest and decides to enter into an interest rate swap with bank S. The borrowing is the hedged item, and the risk being hedged is interest rate risk. Under the interest rate swap, bank S pays company B the variable interest rate, and company B pays bank S a specified fixed interest rate. The interest rate swap is the hedging instrument. The net cash flows for company B are its payments of a fixed interest rate, so it has locked in its cash flows. This is therefore a cash flow hedge, assuming all the required criteria of IAS 39 are met. Figure 6.6 illustrates this example of a simple cash flow hedge.

There is no exchange of principal in an interest rate swap — the cash flows are simply calculated using the principal as the basis for the calculation. For the example illustrated in figure 6.6, assume that the hedged item is a borrowing of $100 000 with a variable interest rate, currently 5%. The fixed rate under the interest rate swap is 6%. For the relevant period, company B will pay bank L $100 000 × 5% = $5000. Under the swap, company B will pay a net $1000 (receive $100 000 × 5% and pay $100 000 × 6%). Thus, company B's net cash outflow is $5000 + $1000 = $6000, which is the fixed rate. Note that bank L is not a party to the swap — it continues to receive payments from company B under its borrowing arrangement. Company B has locked in its cash flows at $6000, and has certainty that this is what it will pay over the term of the swap. Currently the cash flows are higher than what it would pay under a variable rate, but company B has entered into the swap in the expectation that the variable rate will rise.

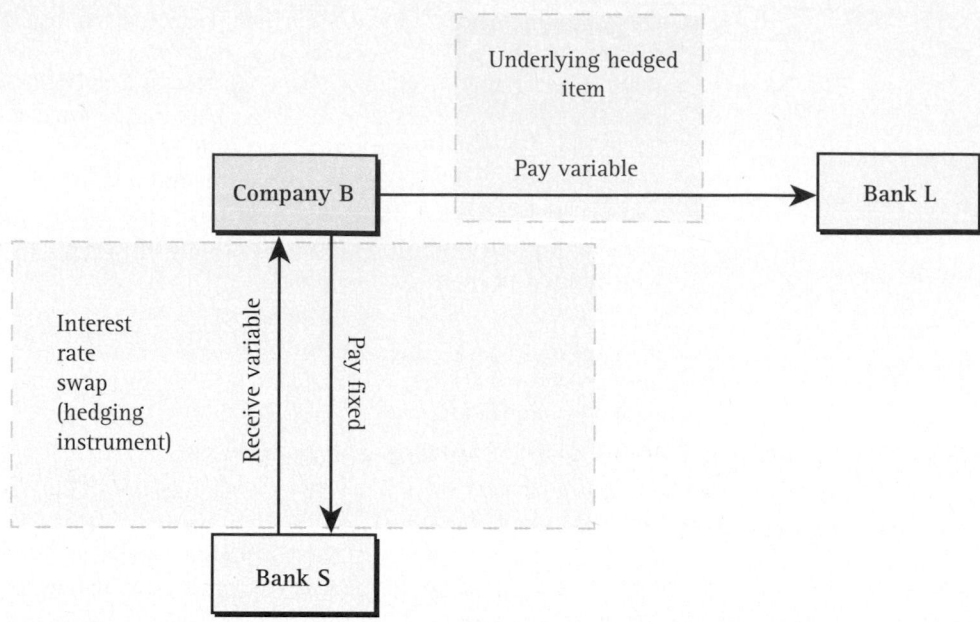

FIGURE 6.6 A simple cash flow hedge

Table 6.9 sets out the main requirements for fair value hedges and cash flow hedges.

TABLE 6.9	Summary of the main requirements of IAS 39 for fair value hedges and cash flow hedges	
	Fair value hedge	Cash flow hedge
Hedged item	Fair value exposures in a recognised asset or liability or unrecognised firm commitment (para. 86)	Cash flow variability exposures in a recognised asset or liability or highly probable forecast transaction (para. 86)
Gain or loss on hedging instrument	Recognised immediately in profit and loss (para. 89)	Fully effective portion recognised directly in equity (para. 95). Ineffective portion recognised immediately in profit and loss (para. 95)
Gain or loss on hedged item	Adjust hedged item and recognise in profit and loss (para. 89). This applies even if the hedged item is otherwise measured at cost.[1] It also applies to available-for-sale investments (see exception to general rule of gain/loss recognition in section 6.3.5 of this chapter).	Not applicable because the exposure being hedged is future cash flows that are not recognised
Hedge ineffectiveness is recorded in profit or loss	Automatically, since the entire gain or loss on both the hedged item and the hedging instrument is recorded in profit and loss	Must be calculated and separated from the amount recorded in equity
Timing of recycling of hedge gains/ losses in equity to profit and loss (paras 97–100)	Not applicable	Hedge of a forecast transaction that subsequently results in the recognition of a *financial* asset or financial liability: during the periods in which said asset/liability affects profit and loss, e.g. when the interest income or expense is recognised (para. 97) Hedge of a forecast transaction that subsequently results in the recognition of a *non-financial* asset or non-financial liability: either (a) during the periods in which said asset/liability affects profit and loss, e.g. when the depreciation expense is recognised; or

Fair value hedge	Cash flow hedge
	(b) include immediately in the initial cost of said asset/liability (para. 98). In this case, the amount is not included in profit and loss
	Entities must choose between (a) or (b) as their adopted accounting policy and must apply consistently to all such transactions (para. 99)

Note:
1. If the hedged item is measured at amortised cost, then the fair value adjustment is amortised to profit or loss, using a recalculated effective interest rate (para. 92).

A simple fair value hedge is demonstrated in illustrative example 6.5.

ILLUSTRATIVE EXAMPLE 6.5

A simple fair value hedge

Company Z has an investment in an equity instrument classified as an available-for-sale investment. The cost of the investment on 1 July 2005 was $250 000. On 1 September 2005, company Z enters into a derivative futures contract to hedge the fair value of the investment. All the conditions for hedge accounting are met, and the hedge qualifies as a fair value hedge because it is a hedge of an exposure to changes in the fair value of a recognised asset. At the next reporting date, 30 September 2005, the fair value of the investment (hedged item) was $230 000, based on quoted market bid prices. The fair value of the derivative (hedging instrument) at that date was $18 000. Company Z would record the journal entries shown below.

On initial recognition of the investment 1 July 2005:

Available-for-sale investment	Dr	250 000	
Cash	Cr		250 000

On entering into the futures contract 1 September 2005:
No entries because the net fair value is zero.

On remeasurement at 30 September 2005:

Expense (profit and loss)	Dr	20 000	
Available-for-sale investment	Cr		20 000
Futures contract	Dr	18 000	
Income (profit and loss)	Cr		18 000

The hedge is within the effectiveness range of 85%–120% (actual range is 90%–111%), so the hedge accounting may continue. The net effect of the hedge is that company Z records a net loss in profit and loss of $2000. The ineffective portion of the hedge ($2000) is recorded automatically in profit and loss. Note that the decline in fair value of the available-for-sale investment is recorded in profit and loss, even though the normal accounting for such investments is to recognise fair value changes directly in equity. This exception is made specifically for hedge accounting, to enable the matching effect of the hedging instrument with the hedged item in profit and loss to occur.

A cash flow hedge of a firm commitment is demonstrated in illustrative example 6.6.

ILLUSTRATIVE EXAMPLE 6.6

Cash flow hedge of a firm commitment (based on IAS 39, Implementation Guidance F.5.6)

On 30 June 2005, Company A enters into a forward exchange contract to receive foreign currency (FC) of 100 000 and deliver local currency (LC) of 109 600 on 30 June 2006. It designates the forward exchange contract as a hedging instrument in a cash flow hedge of a firm commitment to purchase a specified quantity of paper on 31 March 2006, and the resulting payable. Payment for the paper is due on 30 June 2006. All hedge accounting conditions in IAS 39 are met.

Note that a hedge of foreign currency risk in a firm commitment may be either a cash flow hedge or a fair value hedge (IAS 39, para. 87). Company A has elected to account for it as a cash flow hedge. Company A has also elected to apply IAS 39, paragraph 98(b), and adjust the cost of non-financial items acquired as a result of hedged forecast transactions.

The following table sets out the spot rate, forward rate and fair value of the forward contract at relevant dates:

Date	Spot rate	Forward rate to 30 June 2006	Fair value of forward contract
30 June 2005	1.072	1.096	–
31 December 2005	1.080	1.092	(388)[1]
31 March 2006	1.074	1.076	(1 971)
30 June 2006	1.072	–	(2 400)

Journal entries are shown below.

At 30 June 2005:

Forward contract	Dr	LC0	
Cash	Cr		LC0
(Initial recognition of forward contract)			

On initial recognition, the forward contract has a fair value of zero (IAS 39, para. 43).

At 31 December 2005:

Equity	Dr	LC388	
Forward contract (liability)	Cr		LC388
(Recording the change in the fair value of the forward contract)			

At 31 March 2006:

Equity	Dr	LC1 583	
Forward contract (liability)	Cr		LC1 583
(Recording the change in the fair value of the forward contract)			
Paper (purchase price)	Dr	LC107 400	
Paper (hedging loss)	Dr	LC1 971	
Equity	Cr		LC1 971
Payable	Cr		LC107 400

The last entry recognises the purchase of the paper at the spot rate (1.074 × FC100 000), and removes the cumulative loss that has been recognised in equity and includes it in the initial measurement of the purchased paper (IAS 39.98(b)). The paper is thus recognised effectively at the forward rate, and the hedge has been 100% effective.

At 30 June 2006:

Payable	Dr	LC107 400	
Cash	Cr		LC107 200
Profit and loss	Cr		LC200
(Recording settlement of the payable at the spot rate and associated exchange gain)			
Profit and loss	Dr	LC429	
Forward contract	Cr		LC429
(Recording loss on forward contract between 1 Apr. 06 and 30 Jun. 06)			

The forward contract has been effective in hedging the commitment and the payable up to this date. However, the loss on the contract is recognised in profit and loss because the hedge is no longer of a firm commitment but of the fair value of a recognised liability (the payable). The movement must be recorded in profit or loss because the hedge arrangement is now a fair value hedge.

Forward contract	Dr	LC2 400	
Cash	Cr		LC2 400
(Recording net settlement of forward contract)			

If this transaction had been designated as a fair value hedge, then the entries recorded in equity for the cash flow hedge would instead be recorded as an asset or liability (IAS 39, para. 93). Paragraph 94 then requires the initial carrying amount of the asset acquired to be adjusted for the cumulative amount recognised in the balance sheet. The adjusted journal entries would be as follows:

At 31 December 2005:

Asset	Dr	LC388	
Forward contract (liability)	Cr		LC388
(Recording change in fair value of forward contract)			

At 31 March 2006:

Asset	Dr	LC1 583	
Forward contract (liability)	Cr		LC1 583
(Recording change in fair value of forward contract)			
Paper (purchase price)	Dr	LC107 400	
Paper (hedging loss)	Dr	LC1 971	
Asset	Cr		LC1 971
Payable	Cr		LC107 400
(Recording purchase of paper and transferring cumulative amount recognised as an asset to the cost of the paper)			

Note:

1. This can be calculated if the applicable yield curve in the local currency is known. Assuming the rate is 6%, the fair value is calculated as follows: {([1.092 × 100 000]–109 600)/1.06(6/12)}.

Discontinuing hedge accounting

Under paragraph 91 of IAS 39, a fair value hedge must be discontinued prospectively if one of the following occurs:

(a) The hedging instrument expires or is sold, terminated or exercised.

(b) The hedge no longer meets the criteria for hedge accounting.

(c) The entity revokes the designation.

Under paragraph 101 of IAS 39, a cash flow hedge must be discontinued prospectively if one of the following occurs:

(a) The hedging instrument expires or is sold, terminated or exercised. In this case, the cumulative gain or loss that remains recognised in equity from the period when the hedge was effective should remain in equity until the forecast transaction occurs. When the transaction occurs, paragraphs 97, 98 or 100 apply.

(b) The hedge no longer meets the criteria for hedge accounting. In this case, the cumulative gain or loss that remains recognised in equity from the period when the hedge was effective should remain in equity until the forecast transaction occurs. When the transaction occurs, paragraphs 97, 98 or 100 apply.

(c) The forecast transaction is no longer expected to occur. In this case, the cumulative gain or loss that remains recognised in equity from the period when the hedge was effective should be recognised in profit or loss.

(d) The entity revokes the designation. In this case, the cumulative gain or loss that remains recognised in equity from the period when the hedge was effective should remain in equity until the forecast transaction occurs or is no longer expected to occur. When the transaction occurs, paragraphs 97, 98 or 100 apply. If the forecast transaction is no longer expected to occur, the cumulative gain or loss that remains recognised in equity from the period when the hedge was effective should be recognised in profit or loss.

The rationale behind these requirements is that hedge accounting is required for the time that the hedge was effective. If the forecast transaction occurs, then the transaction benefits from the hedge for the time that the hedge was effective. If the forecast transaction does not occur, then there is no transaction to benefit from the hedge.

6.4 Summary

IAS 32 defines financial instruments, financial assets, financial liabilities and derivatives; distinguishes between financial liabilities and equity instruments; and prescribes detailed disclosures. It sets prescriptive rules for distinguishing financial liabilities from equity instruments, and for accounting for compound financial instruments that have elements of both. It requires that interest, dividends, gains and losses be accounted for consistent with the balance sheet classification of the related financial assets and financial liabilities. It also sets prescriptive requirements for offsetting a financial asset and a financial liability. Finally, it contains a lengthy set of disclosure requirements.

IAS 39 requires all financial instruments including derivatives to be initially recorded at fair value. It defines an embedded derivative and establishes rules for separating an embedded derivative from the host contract. It creates four categories of financial instruments. Each category has its own rules for measurement, including initial and subsequent measurement, reclassifications, gains and losses and impairment.

IAS 39 permits hedge accounting provided that strict criteria are met. These include meeting specified conditions before hedge accounting can be applied, meeting the definition of a hedging instrument and a hedged item, and identifying which of the three types of hedge the hedge transaction meets. IAS 39 prescribes when hedge accounting must be discontinued and how the discontinuation must be accounted for. It also contains rules for the derecognition of financial instruments, but these are not addressed in this chapter.

These two standards contain more rules (and consequent exceptions to the rules) than any other IFRSs, making it difficult for preparers and users to apply the standards with confidence. Practical application of the standards, particularly IAS 39, is in its infancy because few companies in the world have yet applied the 2005 versions of the standards.

DISCUSSION QUESTIONS

1. Discuss the concept of 'equity risk' and how it is useful in determining whether a financial instrument is a financial liability or an equity instrument of the issuer.

2. Discuss why the standard setters first set rules on presentation and disclosure of financial instruments before tackling recognition and measurement. Do you think the earlier creation of IAS 32 assisted in the development of IAS 39?

3. Does IAS 32 contain a clear hierarchy to be used in determining whether a financial instrument is a financial liability or an equity instrument of the issuer? Explain your answer.

4. What is the purpose of IAS 32's disclosure requirements?

5. Describe the main risks that pertain to financial instruments.

6. Explain how a concentration of credit risk may arise for trade accounts receivable.

7. IAS 39 applies a 'rights and obligations approach' to the recognition of financial instruments. Discuss.

8. Explain what an economic hedge is. Will hedge accounting always result in the same outcome as an economic hedge?

9. Distinguish, explain and discuss the meaning of 'highly effective' and 'highly probable' in the context of the hedge accounting rules in IAS 39.

EXERCISES

EXERCISE 6.1 ★ Classification of revenues and expenses

Classify the following items as income statement/statement of changes in equity.
(a) Dividends paid on non-redeemable preference shares
(b) Dividends paid on preference shares redeemable at the holder's option
(c) Interest paid on a five-year, fixed interest note
(d) Interest paid on a convertible note classified as a compound instrument

EXERCISE 6.2 ★ Scope of IAS 32

Which of the following is a financial instrument (that is, a financial asset, financial liability, or equity instrument in another entity) within the scope of IAS 32? Give reasons for your answer.
(a) Cash
(b) Investment in a debt instrument
(c) Investment in a subsidiary
(d) Provision for restoration of a mine site
(e) Buildings owned by the reporting entity
(f) Forward contract entered into by a bread manufacturer to buy wheat
(g) Forward contract entered into by a gold producer to hedge the future sales of gold
(h) General sales tax payable

EXERCISE 6.3 ★ Scope of IAS 39

Which of the following is a financial instrument (that is, a financial asset, financial liability, or equity instrument in another entity) within the scope of IAS 39? Give reasons for your answer.
(a) Provision for employee benefits
(b) Deferred revenue
(c) Prepayments
(d) Forward exchange contract
(e) 3% investment in private company
(f) A percentage interest in an unincorporated joint venture
(g) A non-controlling interest in a partnership

(h) A non-controlling interest in a discretionary trust
(i) An investment in an associate
(j) A forward purchase contract for wheat to be used by the entity to make flour
(k) As for part (j), but the entity regularly settles the contracts net in cash or takes delivery of the underlying wheat and sells it shortly after making a dealer's margin
(l) Leases
(m) Trade receivables

| EXERCISE 6.4 | | **Impairment** |

State whether each of the following statements is true or false.
(a) Financial assets measured 'at fair value through profit or loss' must be tested annually for impairment.
(b) A reversal of an impairment loss on a held-to-maturity investment is recognised in profit and loss.
(c) A reversal of an impairment loss on an available-for-sale investment in a debt instrument is not permitted.
(d) A reversal of an impairment loss on an available-for-sale investment in an equity instrument is not permitted.

| EXERCISE 6.5 | | **Hedging** |

State whether each of the following statements is true or false.
(a) In any hedge relationship there needs to be a hedged item and a hedging instrument.
(b) A hedging instrument must always be a derivative.
(c) A cash flow hedge locks in a reporting entity's future cash flows.
(d) A forecast transaction is an uncommitted but anticipated future transaction.
(e) In order to qualify for hedge accounting, there must be formal designation and documentation of the hedging relationship and the entity's risk-management objective and strategy for undertaking the hedge.
(f) The documentation and designation in (e) may occur at any time.

| EXERCISE 6.6 | ★★ | **Categorising common financial instruments under IAS 32** |

Categorise each of the following common financial instruments as financial assets, financial liabilities or equity instruments – of the issuer or the holder, as specified.
(a) Loans receivable (holder)
(b) Loans payable (issuer)
(c) Ordinary shares of the issuer
(d) The holder's investment in the ordinary shares in part (c)
(e) Redeemable preference shares of the issuer, redeemable at any time at the option of the holder
(f) The holder's investment in the preference shares in part (e)

| EXERCISE 6.7 | ★★ | **Categorising common financial instruments under IAS 39** |

Categorise each of the following common financial instruments in one of the four categories specified in IAS 39. Assume that the entity does not elect the 'at fair value through profit or loss category'.
(a) Loans receivable (holder)
(b) Loans payable (issuer)
(c) Ordinary shares of the issuer

    (d) The holder's investment in the ordinary shares in part (c)

    (e) Redeemable preference shares of the issuer, redeemable at any time at the option of the holder

    (f) The holder's investment in the preference shares in part (e)

EXERCISE 6.8 ★★

Offsetting a financial asset and a financial liability

In each of the situations below, state whether the financial asset and financial liability must be offset in the books of company A as at 30 June 2006, and explain why.

(a) Company A owes company B $500 000, due on 30 June 2007. Company B owes company A $300 000, due on 30 June 2007. A legal right of set-off between the two companies is documented in writing, and the parties have indicated their intent to settle the amounts on a net basis.

(b) Company A owes company B $500 000, due on 30 June 2007. Company B owes company A $300 000, due on 31 March 2007. A legal right of set-off between the two companies is documented in writing, and the parties have indicated their intent to settle the amounts on a net basis whenever possible.

(c) Company A owes company B $500 000, due on 30 June 2007. Company C owes company A $300 000, due on 30 June 2007.

(d) Company A owes company B $500 000, due on 30 June 2007. Company C owes company A $500 000, due on 30 June 2007. A legal right of set-off between the three companies is documented in writing, and the parties have indicated their intent to settle the amounts on a net basis.

(e) Company A owes company B $500 000, due on 30 June 2007. Company A has plant and equipment with a fair value of $500 000 that it pledges to company B as collateral for the debt.

EXERCISE 6.9 ★★

Financial instruments categories and measurement

Identify which of the four categories specified in IAS 39 each of the following items belongs to in the books of company H, the holder. Also identify how each item will be measured.

(a) Forward exchange contract

(b) Five-year government bond paying interest of 5%

(c) Trade accounts receivable

(d) Trade accounts payable

(e) Mandatory converting notes paying interest of 6% (the notes must convert to a variable number of ordinary shares at the expiration of their term)

(f) Investment in a portfolio of listed shares held for capital growth

(g) Investment in a portfolio of listed shares held for short-term gains

(h) As in part (e), except that in the previous year company H sold the majority of its held-to-maturity investments to company Z

(i) Borrowings of $1 million, carrying a variable interest rate

---

PROBLEMS

PROBLEM 6.1 ★

Distinguishing financial liabilities from equity instruments (1)

Company A issues 100 000 $1 convertible notes. The notes pay interest at 7%. The market rate for similar debt without the conversion option is 9%. The note is not redeemable, but it converts at the option of the holder into however many shares that will have a value of exactly $100 000.

Required

Determine whether this financial instrument should be classified as a financial liability or equity instrument of company A. Give reasons for your answer.

PROBLEM 6.2   ★★   Distinguishing financial liabilities from equity instruments (2)

Company A issues 100 000 $1 redeemable convertible notes. The notes pay interest at 5%. They convert at any time at the option of the holder into 100 000 ordinary shares. The notes are redeemable at the option of the holder for cash after five years. Market rates for similar notes without the conversion option are 7%.

Required

Determine whether this financial instrument should be classified as a financial liability or equity instrument of company A. Give reasons for your answer.

PROBLEM 6.3   ★★★   Distinguishing financial liabilities from equity instruments (3)

Company A issues 100 000 $1 redeemable convertible notes. The notes pay interest at 5%. They convert at any time at the option of the holder into 100 000 ordinary shares. The notes are redeemable at the option of the issuer for cash after five years. If after five years the notes have not been redeemed or converted, they cease to carry interest. Market rates for similar notes without the conversion option are 7%.

Required

Determine whether this financial instrument should be classified as a financial liability or equity instrument of company A. Give reasons for your answer.

PROBLEM 6.4   ★★★   Distinguishing financial liabilities from equity instruments (4)

Company A issues 100 000 $1 redeemable convertible notes. The notes pay interest at 5%. The notes are redeemable after five years at the option of the issuer for cash or for a variable number of shares (calculated according to a formula). If after five years the notes have not been redeemed or converted, they continue to carry interest at a new market rate to be determined at the expiration of the five years.

Required

Determine whether this financial instrument should be classified as a financial liability or equity instrument of company A. Give reasons for your answer.

PROBLEM 6.5   ★★★   Distinguishing financial liabilities from equity instruments (5)

Company A issues redeemable preference shares with a fixed maturity date. The shares are redeemable only on maturity at the option of the holder. The shares carry a cumulative 6% dividend.

Required

Determine whether this financial instrument should be classified as a financial liability or equity instrument of company A. Give reasons for your answer.

PROBLEM 6.6   ★★★   Distinguishing financial liabilities from equity instruments (6)

Company A issues redeemable preference shares. The shares are redeemable for cash at the option of the issuer. The shares carry a cumulative 6% dividend. In addition, the preference share dividend can be paid only if a dividend on ordinary shares is paid for the relevant period. Company A is highly profitable and has a history of paying ordinary dividends at a yield of about 4% annually without fail for the past 25 years. Company A issued the preference shares after considering various options to raise finance for building a new factory. The market interest rate for long-term debt at the time the preference shares were issued was 7%.

Required

Determine whether this financial instrument should be classified as a financial liability or equity instrument of company A. Give reasons for your answer.

PROBLEM 6.7 ★★★ Accounting for a compound financial instrument

The facts from example 5 of figure 6.3 are repeated below:

Company A issues 2000 convertible notes on 1 July 2004. The notes have a three-year term and are issued at par with a face value of $1000 per note, giving total proceeds at the date of issue of $2 million. The notes pay interest at 6% annually in arrears. The holder of each note is entitled to convert the note into 250 ordinary shares of company A at any time up to maturity.

When the notes are issued, the prevailing market interest rate for similar debt (similar term, similar credit status of issuer and similar cash flows) without conversion options is 9%. This rate is higher than the convertible note's rate because the holder of the convertible note is prepared to accept a lower interest rate given the implicit value of its conversion option.

The issuer calculates the contractual cash flows using the market interest rate (9%) to work out the value of the holder's option, as follows:

Present value of the principal: $2 million payable in three years time:	$1 544 367
Present value of the interest: $120 000 ($2 million × 6%) payable annually in arrears for three years	303 755
Total liability component	1 848 122
Equity component (by deduction)	151 878
Proceeds of the note issue	$2 000 000

Required

Prepare the journal entries to account for this transaction for each year of its term under each of the following circumstances.

(a) The holders exercise their conversion option at the expiration of the note's term.
(b) The holders do not exercise their option and the note is repaid at the end of its term.
(c) The holders exercise their option at the end of year 2.

PROBLEM 6.8 ★★★ Amortised cost, journal entries

Company B issues a bond with a face value of $500 000 on 1 July 2007. Transaction costs incurred amount to $12 000. The bond pays interest at 6% per annum, in arrears. The bond must be repaid after five years.

Required

Prepare the journal entries to record this transaction on initial recognition and throughout the life of the bond in the books of company B.

PROBLEM 6.9 ★★★   Embedded derivatives

Identify which of the following embedded derivatives must be separated from the relevant host contract. In each case, state also how the host contract and the embedded derivative should be measured in the books of the holder. Assume that the host instrument is not measured at fair value through profit or loss.

(a) An equity conversion feature embedded in a convertible debt instrument
(b) An embedded derivative in an interest-bearing host debt instrument, where the embedded derivative derives its value from an underlying interest rate index and can change the amount of interest that would otherwise be paid on the host debt instrument
(c) An embedded cap (upper limit) on the interest rate on a host debt instrument, where the cap is at or above the market rate of interest when the debt instrument is issued
(d) As in part (c), except that the cap is below the market rate of interest

WEBLINK

Visit these websites for additional information:

www.iasb.org   www.iasplus.com
www.asic.gov.au   www.ifac.org
www.aasb.com.au   www.nzica.com
www.accaglobal.com   www.capa.com.my

APPENDIX

APPENDIX A   Illustrative disclosures of financial instruments under IAS 32

The following is an extract from Ernst & Young's illustrative financial statements, notes 23 and 24 from 'Endeavour (International) Limited'. The notes illustrate disclosures required under the Australian-equivalent standard of IAS 32. They incorporate all AASB standards on issue as at 31 December 2005.

NOTES TO THE FINANCIAL STATMENTS (CONTINUED) FOR THE YEAR ENDED 30 JUNE 2006	AASB 101.8(e)
23 FINANCIAL RISK MANAGEMENT OBJECTIVES AND POLICIES (Comment page 168)	
The Group's principal financial instruments, other than derivatives, comprise bank loans, debentures, convertible non-cumulative redeemable preference shares, finance leases and hire purchase contracts, cash and short-term deposits.	AASB 132.56
The main purpose of these financial instruments is to raise finance for the Group's operations.	AASB 132.57
The Group has various other financial instruments such as trade debtors and trade creditors, which arise directly from its operations.	AASB 132.57
The Group also enters into derivative transactions, principally interest rate swaps and forward currency contracts. The purpose is to manage the interest rate and currency risks arising from the Group's operations and its sources of finance.	AASB 132.57
It is, and has been throughout the period under review, the Group's policy that no trading in financial instruments shall be undertaken.	AASB 132.56
The main risks arising from the Group's financial instruments are interest rate risk, liquidity risk, foreign currency risk and credit risk. The board reviews and agrees policies for managing each of these risks and they are summarised below.	AASB 132.56
The Group also monitors the market price risk arising from all financial instruments. The magnitude of this risk that has arisen over the year is discussed in note 24.	AASB 132.57
The Group's accounting policies in relation to derivatives are set out in note 2.	AASB 132.60(b)
Interest rate risk The Group's exposure to market risk for changes in interest rates relates primarily to the Group's long-term debt obligations.	AASB 132.92(c)
The Group's policy is to manage its interest cost using a mix of fixed and variable rate debt.	AASB 132.4(a)
The group's policy is to keep between 25% and 55% of its borrowings at fixed rates of interest.	AASB 132.4(a)
To manage this mix in a cost-efficient manner, the Group enters into interest rate swaps, in which the Group agrees to exchange, at specified intervals, the difference between fixed and variable interest amounts calculated by reference to an agreed-upon notional principal amount.	AASB 132.4(c)
These swaps are designated to hedge underlying debt obligations.	AASB 132.4(c)

NOTES TO THE FINANCIAL STATMENTS (CONTINUED) FOR THE YEAR ENDED 30 JUNE 2006	AASB 101.8(e)

23 FINANCIAL RISK MANAGEMENT OBJECTIVES AND POLICIES (continued)

At 30 June 2006, after taking into account the effect of interest rate swaps, approximately 50% of the Group's borrowings are at a fixed rate of interest.	AASB 132.4(a)
Foreign currency risk As a result of significant investment operations in the United States, the Group's balance sheet can be affected significantly by movements in the US$/A$ exchange rates.	AASB 132.4
Prior to the years presented, the Group did not seek to hedge this exposure, but following the increased focus of the Group on the US market, the Group has changed its policy.	AASB 132.4(a)
The Group now seeks to mitigate the effect of its structural currency exposure by borrowing in US$. Between 20% and 50% of the Group's investment in non-Australian operations will be hedged in this way.	AASB 132.57, 58(a)
The Group also has transactional currency exposures. Such exposure arises from sales or purchases by an operating unit in currencies other than the unit's measurement currency.	AASB 132.4(a)
Approximately 23% of the Group's sales are denominated in currencies other than the reporting currency of the operating unit making the sale, whilst almost 95% of costs are denominated in the unit's reporting currency.	AASB 132.4(a)
The Group requires all its operating units to use forward currency contracts to eliminate the currency exposures on any individual transactions in excess of $100 000 for which payment is anticipated more than one month after the Group has entered into a firm commitment for a sale or purchase.	AASB 132.4(a)
The forward currency contracts must be in the same currency as the hedged item.	AASB 132.1(a)
It is the Group's policy not to enter into forward contracts until a firm commitment is in place.	AASB 132.4(a)
It is the Group's policy to negotiate the terms of the hedge derivatives to match the terms of the hedged item to maximise hedge effectiveness.	AASB 132.4(a)
At 30 June 2006, the Group had hedged 75% of its foreign currency sales for which firm commitments existed at the balance sheet date, extending to September 2006.	AASB 132.4(c)
Commodity price risk The Group's exposure to price risk is minimal.	AASB 132.4(a)
Credit risk The Group trades only with recognised, creditworthy third parties.	AASB 132.4
It is the Group policy that all customers who wish to trade on credit terms are subject to credit verification procedures.	AASB 132.4
In addition, receivable balances are monitored on an ongoing basis with the result that the Group's exposure to bad debts is not significant.	AASB 132.4(a)
	(continued)

NOTES TO THE FINANCIAL STATMENTS (CONTINUED) FOR THE YEAR ENDED 30 JUNE 2006	AASB 101.8(e)

23 FINANCIAL RISK MANAGEMENT OBJECTIVES AND POLICIES (continued)

Credit risk (continued)

For transactions that are not denominated in the measurement currency of the relevant operating unit, the Group does not offer credit terms without the specific approval of the Head of Credit Control.

AASB 132.4(a)

Due to unforeseen circumstances, one exposure has arisen in the year as a result of the liquidation of a significant overseas customer.

AASB 132.94(j)

Although credit terms had not been extended to this customer, in accordance with the policy above, the Group had sought to hedge the foreign currency exposure and had entered into a forward contract for this purpose.

AASB 132.5

At the balance sheet date the loss on this contract was $149 000, and has been charged to the income statement. This is further discussed in note 24.

AASB 132.85

In light of the above exposure, the directors have reassessed the Group's strategies for managing credit and transactional foreign currency exposure, but are of the continued view that they remain appropriate for the Group's circumstances.

AASB 132.4(a)

With respect to credit risk arising from the other financial assets of the Group, which comprise cash and cash equivalents, available-for-sale financial assets and certain derivative instruments, the Group's exposure to credit risk arises from default of the counter party, with a maximum exposure equal to the carrying amount of these instruments.

AASB 139.2

There are no significant concentrations of credit risk within the Group.

AASB 132.94(j)(i)

Liquidity risk

The Group's objective is to maintain a balance between continuity of funding and flexibility through the use of bank overdrafts, bank loans, debentures, preference shares, finance leases and hire purchase contracts.

The Group's policy is that not more than 35% of borrowings should mature in any 12-month period. 9.4% of the Group's debt will mature in less than one year at 30 June 2006 (2005: 16.3%).

AASB 132.4

24 FINANCIAL INSTRUMENTS (Comment page 168)

Fair values

Set out below is a comparison by category of carrying amounts and fair values of all the Group's financial instruments that are carried in the financial statements at other than fair values.

AASB 132.86

The fair value of the liability portion of the convertible non-cumulative redeemable preference shares is estimated using an equivalent market interest rate for a similar convertible bond.

AASB 132.92(a)

24 FINANCIAL INSTRUMENTS (continued)

	Carrying amount		Fair value		
	2006 $'000	2005 $'000	2006 $'000	2005 $'000	AASB 132.86
CONSOLIDATED					
Financial assets					
Cash	16 492	14 916	16 492	14 916	
Trade receivables	17 906	24 290	17 236	24 492	
Forward currency contracts	152	153	152	153	
Available-for-sale financial assets	2 141	1 798	2 141	1 798	
Loan notes	500	–	517	–	
Other financial assets (non-current)	3 053	1 393	3 004	1 261	
Financial liabilities					
Bank overdraft	(966)	(2 650)	(966)	(2 650)	
Trade payables	(20 671)	(22 670)	(20 671)	(22 670)	
Interest-bearing loans and borrowings:					
Obligations under finance leases and hire purchase contracts	(1 070)	(1 146)	(1 063)	(1 216)	
Floating rate borrowings*	(12 128)	(9 575)	(12 912)	(8 723)	
Fixed rate borrowings	(9 183)	(8 963)	(9 250)	(8 731)	
Convertible non-cumulative redeemable preference shares	(2 696)	(2 568)	(2 623)	(2 485)	
Forward currency contracts	(170)	(254)	(170)	(254)	
Interest rate swap	(35)	–	(35)	–	

*   Includes 8.25% secured loan carried at fair value as a result of the fair value hedge discussed below.

	Carrying amount		Fair value		
	2006 $'000	2005 $'000	2006 $'000	2005 $'000	
PARENT					
Financial assets					
Cash	10 076	3 599	10 076	3 599	
Trade receivables	9 919	17 298	9 864	17 432	
Available-for-sale financial assets	989	801	989	801	
Other financial assets (non-current)	198	198	194	182	
Financial liabilities					
Trade payables	(11 080)	(11 570)	(11 080)	(11 570)	
Interest-bearing loans and borrowings:					
Obligations under finance leases and hire purchase contracts	(1 070)	(1 121)	(1 063)	(1 191)	
Floating rate borrowings	(4 919)	(4 868)	(4 919)	(4 868)	
Convertible non-cumulative redeemable preference shares	(2 696)	(2 568)	(2 623)	(2 485)	

Market values have been used to determine the fair value of listed convertible non-cumulative redeemable preference shares and listed available-for-sale financial assets.

AASB 132.92(b)

The fair value of derivative items has been calculated by discounting the expected future cash flows at prevailing interest rates

AASB 132.92(b)

(*continued*)

24 FINANCIAL INSTRUMENTS (continued)

Interest rate risk

The following table sets out the carrying amount, by maturity, of the financial instruments that are exposed to interest rate risk:

AASB 132.67
AASB 132.71

Year ended 30 June 2006	< 1 year $'000	>1–<2 years $'000	>2–<3 years $'000	>3–<4 years $'000	>4–<5 years $'000	> 5 years $'000	Total $'000
CONSOLIDATED							
Fixed rate							
Loan notes	–	–	500	–	–	–	500
Obligations under finance leases and hire purchase contracts	(87)	(492)	(491)	–	–	–	(1 070)
8% debentures	–	(347)	(344)	(339)	(348)	(1 996)	(3 374)
$5 809 000 bank loan	–	–	–	–	(5 809)	–	(5 809)
Convertible non-cumulative redeemable preference shares	–	–	–	–	–	(2 696)	(2 696)
Floating rate							
Cash assets	16 492	–	–	–	–	–	16 492
Bank overdrafts	(966)	–	–	–	–	–	(966)
$1 500 000 bank loan	(1 407)	–	–	–	–	–	(1 407)
$2 500 000 bank loan	–	–	(1 235)	–	(1 251)	–	(2 486)
$2 000 000 bank loan	–	–	–	(2 000)	–	–	(2 000)
Share of joint venture operation loan	–	–	–	–	(510)	–	(510)
Secured bank loan	–	–	–	–	–	(3 479)	(3 479)
8.25% secured loan US$1 500 000*	–	–	–	–	–	(2 246)	(2 246)
Interest rate swap*	–	–	–	–	–	(35)	(35)

AASB 132.74(a)

AASB 132.71(a)

AASB 132.71(b)
AASB 132.74(a)

* effect of interest rate swap is discussed below

	< 1 year $'000	>1–<2 years $'000	>2–<3 years $'000	>3–<4 years $'000	>4–<5 years $'000	> 5 years $'000	Total $'000
PARENT							
Fixed rate							
Obligations under finance leases and hire purchase contracts	(87)	(492)	(491)	–	–	–	(1 070)
Convertible non-cumulative redeemable preference shares	–	–	–	–	–	(2 696)	(2 696)
Floating rate							
Cash assets	10 076	–	–	–	–	–	10 076
$500 000 bank loan	(433)	–	–	–	–	–	(433)
$2 500 000 bank loan	–	–	(1 235)	–	(1 251)	–	(2 486)
$2 000 000 bank loan	–	–	–	(2000)	–	–	(2 000)

AASB 132.71(a)

AASB 132.71(b)
AASB 132.74(a)

Refer to note 20 for disclosure of effective interest rates.

**NOTES TO THE FINANCIAL STATMENTS (CONTINUED)
FOR THE YEAR ENDED 30 JUNE 2006**

AASB 101.8(e)

24 FINANCIAL INSTRUMENTS (continued)

Year ended 30 June 2006	< 1 year $'000	>1–<2 years $'000	>2–<3 years $'000	>3–<4 years $'000	>4–<5 years $'000	> 5 years $'000	Total $'000	
CONSOLIDATED								AASB 132.74(a)
Fixed rate								AASB 132.71(a)
Obligations under finance leases and hire purchase contracts	(51)	(131)	(476)	(488)	–	–	(1 146)	
8% debentures	–	–	(337)	(341)	(334)	(2 142)	(3 154)	
$5 809 000 bank loan	–	–	–	–	–	(5 809)	(5 809)	
Convertible non-cumulative redeemable preference shares	–	–	–	–	–	(2 568)	(2 568)	
Floating rate								AASB 132.71(b)
Cash assets	14 916	–	–	–	–	–	14 916	AASB 132.74(a)
Bank overdrafts	(2 650)	–	–	–	–	–	(2 650)	
$1 400 000 bank loan	(1 357)	–	–	–	–	–	(1 357)	
$2 500 000 bank loan	–	–	–	(1 009)	–	(1 220)	(2 229)	
$2 000 000 bank loan	–	–	–	–	(2 000)	–	(2 000)	
Share of joint venture operation loan	–	–	–	–	–	(500)	(500)	
Secured bank loan	–	–	–	–	–	(3 489)	(3 489)	
PARENT								
Fixed rate								AASB 132.71(a)
Obligations under finance leases and hire purchase contracts	(51)	(131)	(476)	(463)	–	–	(1 121)	
Convertible non-cumulative redeemable preference shares	–	–	–	–	–	(2 568)	(2 568)	
Floating rate								AASB 132.71(b)
Cash assets	3 599	–	–	–	–	–	3 599	AASB 132.74(a)
$700 000 bank loan	(639)	–	–	–	–	–	(639)	
$2 500 000 bank loan	–	–	–	(1 009)	–	(1 220)	(2 229)	
$2 000 000 bank loan	–	–	–	–	(2 000)	–	(2 000)	

Interest on financial instruments classified as floating rate is repriced at intervals of less than one year. Interest on financial instruments classified as fixed rate is fixed until maturity of the instrument.

AASB 132.67

The other financial instruments of the Group and Parent that are not included in the above tables are non-interest bearing and are therefore not subject to interest rate risk.

AASB 132.67

Hedging activities
Cash flow hedges
At 30 June 2006, the Group held two foreign exchange contracts designated as hedges of expected future sales to customers in the United States for which the Group has firm commitments.

AASB 132.58(a),(b)

(continued)

**NOTES TO THE FINANCIAL STATMENTS (CONTINUED)
FOR THE YEAR ENDED 30 JUNE 2006**

AASB 101.8(e)

24 FINANCIAL INSTRUMENTS (continued)

Hedging activities (continued)

The Group also has two foreign exchange contracts outstanding at 30 June 2006 designated as hedges of expected future purchases.

AASB 132.58(a),(b)

The exchange contracts are being used to reduce the exposure to foreign exchange risk. The terms of these contracts are as follows:

AASB 132.58(c)

	Maturity	Exchange rate
Sell		
US$500 000	29 July 2006	A$/US$ 0.74
US$1 200 000	1 August 2006	A$/US$ 0.71
Buy		
A$298 000	13 August 2006	US$/A$ 1.33
A$103 000	25 September 2006	US$/A$ 1.39

AASB 132.58 (b)

The terms of the foreign exchange contracts have been negotiated to match the terms of the commitments.

AASB 132.58(b)

However, the purchaser of the item expected to be settled in August 2006 has recently gone into liquidation, and the hedge is no longer considered effective as the transaction is no longer probable.

AASB 132.58(d)

As a consequence, an unrealised gain of $29 000, with deferred income tax of $17 000 relating to the July 2006 forward exchange contract is included in equity and a loss of $141 000 relating to the August 2006 forward exchange contract is included in the income statement for the year.

AASB 132.59(a),(b)

As at 30 June 2006, a net unrealised gain of $54 000, with deferred income tax of $31 000 is included in equity in respect of these contracts.

AASB 132.59(a)

At 30 June 2005, the Group held two foreign exchange contracts to hedge future sales and two contracts to hedge future purchases that are deferred in the balance sheet. The terms of these contracts are as follows:

AASB 132.58(a),(b)

	Maturity	Exchange rate
Sell		
US$400 000	19 July 2004	A$/US$ 0.68
US$218 000	29 July 2004	A$/US$ 0.69
Buy		
A$128 000	16 August 2004	US$/A$ 1.47
A$197 000	23 September 2004	US$/A$ 1.45

AASB 132.58(b)

Fair value hedge
At 30 June 2006, the Group had an interest rate swap agreement in place with a notional amount of US$1 500 000 whereby it receives a fixed rate of interest of 8.25% and pays a variable rate equal to the BBSW on the notional amount.

AASB 132.58(a),(b)

The swap is being used to hedge the exposure to changes in the fair value of its 8.25% secured loan. The secured loan and interest rate swap have the same critical terms (note 20).

AASB 132.58(c)

NOTES TO THE FINANCIAL STATMENTS (CONTINUED)
FOR THE YEAR ENDED 30 JUNE 2006

AASB 101.8(e)

24 FINANCIAL INSTRUMENTS (continued)

Hedging activities (continued)

Hedge of net investments in foreign entities

Included in other loans at 30 June 2006, is a borrowing of US$1 500 000 (A$2 246 000 including the effect of interest rate swap discussed above), which has been designed as a hedge of the net investments in the US subsidiaries, Wireworks Inc. and Sprinklers Inc. and is being used to reduce the exposure to foreign exchange risk.

AASB 132.58(a),(b),(c)

Gains or losses on the retranslation of this borrowing are transferred to equity to offset any gains or losses on translation of the net investments in the subsidiaries.

AASB 132.58(d)

CHAPTER 7
Share-based payment

ACCOUNTING STANDARDS

International: IFRS 2 *Share-based Payment*
Australia: AASB 2 *Share-based Payment*
New Zealand: NZ IFRS 2 *Share-based Payment*

CONCEPTS FOR REVIEW

Before studying this chapter, you should understand or, if necessary, revise:
- the IASB Framework, in particular, the definitions of and recognition criteria for assets and liabilities
- IAS 32 *Financial Instruments: Disclosure and Presentation* for contracts within the scope of paragraphs 8–10, which are excluded under IFRS 2
- IAS 39 *Financial Instruments: Recognition and Measurement*, particularly the contracts within the scope of paragraphs 5–7, which are excluded under IFRS 2; and the rules for distinguishing financial liabilities from equity instruments.

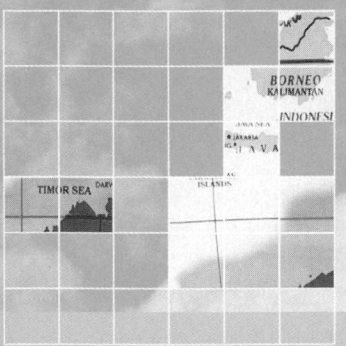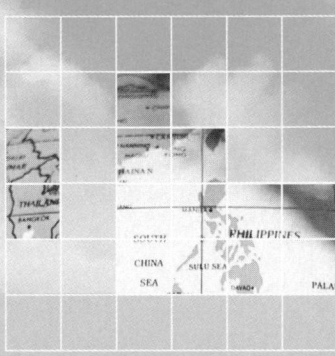

LEARNING OBJECTIVES

When you have studied this chapter, you should be able to:
1. understand the concept of a share-based payment
2. distinguish between cash-settled and equity-settled share-based payment transactions
3. understand and apply the accounting for equity-settled and cash-settled share-based payment transactions
4. apply the requirements of IFRS 2 in respect of measuring transactions at fair value
5. understand the concept of vesting
6. be aware of minimum inputs to option-pricing models
7. understand the concept of a share option reload feature
8. apply the accounting treatment for modifications to granted equity instruments
9. describe and apply the disclosure requirements of IFRS 2.

7.1 Introduction to IFRS 2 *Share-based Payment*

The purpose of this chapter is to examine share-based payments. The international accounting standard covering share-based payments is IFRS 2 *Share-based Payment*. The standard was first issued in 2003 and was amended for financial statements covering periods beginning on or after 1 January 2004.

Share plans and share option plans are becoming an increasingly common feature of remuneration for directors, senior managers and executives, and many other employees as a means of aligning employees' interests with those of the shareholders, and encouraging employee retention. The corporate governance statement provided by Macquarie Bank Limited in its 2005 annual review presents a rationale for engaging in share-based payment transactions with employees. It also provides examples of the types of vesting performance and market conditions that might be incorporated into some employee share plans. The Macquarie Bank approach to remuneration is summarised in figure 7.1.

> The Bank's approach to remuneration is designed to align staff and shareholder interests as well as to optimise shareholder returns over the short and long term ... The Bank ensures that it attracts high quality staff and retains them by offering a competitive performance-driven remuneration package that encourages both long-term commitment and superior performance ... Staff remuneration has three components. They are base salary, variable (at risk) performance pay and a long-term incentive in the form of options ... Executive Directors have performance hurdles on options whereby the Bank's return on ordinary equity is compared to an external reference group.

FIGURE 7.1   Macquarie Bank's remuneration approach
Source: Macquarie Bank Ltd (2005, p. 58).

Some entities may also issue shares or share options to pay for the purchase of property or for professional advice or services. Before the issue of IFRS 2, there was no requirement to identify the expenses associated with this type of transaction or to measure and recognise such transactions in the financial statements of an entity. Standard setters have argued that recognising the cost of share-based payments in the financial statements of entities improves the relevance, reliability and comparability of that financial information, helps users of financial information to understand better the economic transactions affecting an entity and supports resource allocation decisions (FASB 2004).

Under IFRS 2, all such transactions with employees or other parties — whether to be settled in cash (or other assets) or equity instruments of an entity — must now be recognised in the entity's financial statements. The standard adopts the view that all share-based payment transactions ultimately lead to expense recognition, and it requires entities to reflect the effects of such transactions in profit or loss. It is generally expected that the introduction of IFRS 2 will lower the earnings of entities that are significant users of share-based payment transactions as a means of compensating their employees. Whether or not the goods or services received under share-based payment transactions are expensed immediately depends on principles for asset recognition.

BlueScope Steel Ltd, one of Australia's top 200 listed companies (by market capitalisation) applied the Australian version of IFRS 2 (AASB 2 *Share-based Payment*) from 1 January 2005. In its half-year financial statements (note 1(iv) *Share-based payments*), BlueScope Steel Ltd discloses the measurement and accounting approaches it has taken to dealing with share-based payment transactions that vest before this date. The adverse impact of IFRS 2 (and AASB 2) on expenses is clear in the extracts from BlueScope Steel's financial statements presented in figure 7.2.

> **BlueScope Steel Ltd**
> **Notes to the financial statements**
> **Interim financial report — 31 December 2005**
>
> **1   Summary of significant accounting policies**
> *(iv) Share-based payments*
> *... Shares awards and rights granted before 7 November 2002 and/or vested before 1 January 2005*
> No expense is recognised in respect of these share awards and rights.
>
> *Shares awards and rights granted after 7 November 2002 and vested after 1 January 2005*
> The fair value of share awards and rights issued ... is recognised as an employee benefit expense with a corresponding increase in equity ...
>
> **9   Explanation of transition to Australian equivalents to IFRSs**
> *(g) Share-based payments*
> ... Upon transition to [Australian] IFRS, the Group is required to expense the fair value of share rights awarded to senior executives under the 2003 and 2004 Long Term Incentive Plans (LTIP) and any future awards. In addition, the fair value of any shares provided under the General Employee Share Plans (GESP) from 1 January 2005 onwards are required to be expensed. Under [Australian] GAAP, the shares under all these plans would have been issued at nil cost and with no expense recognised.

FIGURE 7.2   BlueScope's measurement and accounting approaches to share-based payment
Source: BlueScope Steel Ltd (2005b, pp. 21, 36).

WEBLINK   The financial reports of BlueScope Steel Limited can be found in the investors section of the company's website at <www.bluescopesteel.com>.

LO 1   7.1.1   Scope of IFRS 2

Measurement principles and specific requirements for three forms of share-based payment transactions are dealt with in IFRS 2. The three forms of share-based payment transactions are:

1. equity-settled share-based payment transactions, in which the entity receives goods or services as consideration for equity instruments of the entity (including shares or share options)
2. cash-settled share-based payment transactions, in which the entity acquires goods or services by incurring liabilities to the supplier for amounts that are based on the value of the shares or other equity instruments of the entity
3. other transactions in which the entity receives or acquires goods or services, and the terms of the arrangement provide either the entity or the supplier (counterparty) of the goods or services with a choice of whether the transaction is settled in cash (or other assets) or by the issue of equity instruments.

The accounting treatment differs depending on the form of settlement. The three forms and the essential features of share-based payment transactions are summarised in table 7.1.

TABLE 7.1	The form and features of share-based payment transactions
Form	Features
Equity-settled share-based payment	Entity receives goods or services as consideration for its own equity instruments
Cash-settled share-based payment	Entity acquires goods or services by incurring liabilities for amounts based on the value of its own equities
Other	Entity receives or acquires goods or services and the entity, or the supplier, has the choice of whether the transaction is settled in cash or equity instruments

IFRS 2 does not apply to share-based payment transactions in which the entity receives or acquires goods or services as part of the net assets acquired in a business combination to which IFRS 3 *Business Combinations* applies. This means that equity instruments issued in a business combination in exchange for control of the acquiree are not within the scope of IFRS 2. However, equity instruments granted to employees of the acquiree in their capacity as employees are within the scope of IFRS 2. Also within the scope of IFRS 2 are the cancellation, replacement or other modification of share-based payment arrangements because of a business combination or other equity restructuring. Excluded under paragraph 6 of IFRS 2 are share-based payment transactions in which the entity receives or acquires goods or services under a contract within the scope of paragraphs 8–10 of IAS 32 *Financial Instruments: Disclosure and Presentation* or paragraphs 5–7 of IAS 39 *Financial Instruments: Recognition and Measurement*.

Any transfers of an entity's equity instruments by its shareholders to parties that have supplied goods or services to the entity are considered, under paragraph 3 of IFRS 2, to be share-based payment transactions (unless the transfer is clearly for a purpose other than payment for goods or services supplied to the entity). This treatment also applies to transfers of equity instruments of the entity's parent, or equity instruments of another entity in the same group as the entity, to parties that have supplied goods or services.

A transaction with an employee in the employee's capacity as a holder of equity instruments of the entity is not regarded as within the scope of the standard (paragraph 4). If, for example, the employee is a member of a class of equity that is granted the right to acquire additional equity at a price that is less than fair value, the granting, or exercise of that right by the employee is excluded from the requirements of IFRS 2.

7.2   Recognition

Paragraph 7 of IFRS 2 requires that goods or services received in a share-based payment transaction be recognised when they are received. A corresponding increase in equity must be recognised if the goods or services were received in an equity-settled share-based payment transaction, or an increase in a liability must be recognised if the goods or services were acquired in a cash-settled share-based payment transaction.

Usually an expense arises from the consumption of goods or services. For example, services are normally consumed immediately, so an expense is recognised as a service is rendered. If goods are consumed over a period of time or, in the case of inventories, sold at a later date, an expense will be recognised when the goods are consumed or sold. Sometimes it may be necessary to recognise an expense before the goods or services are consumed or sold because they do not qualify for recognition as assets. This may occur if an entity acquires goods as part of the research phase of a project. Even though the goods may not have been consumed, they will not qualify for recognition as assets under other International Financial Reporting Standards (IFRSs). When the goods or services received or acquired in a share-based payment transaction do not qualify for recognition as an asset, they must be expensed (IFRS 2, para. 8).

A share-based payment transaction would, depending on the principles for asset or liability recognition, be recognised in journal entries as shown below.

LO 3

Asset or Expense	Dr	XXX	
Equity	Cr		XXX
(Recognition of an equity-settled share-based payment)			
Asset or Expense	Dr	XXX	
Liability	Cr		XXX
(Recognition of a cash-settled share-based payment)			

A significant feature of IFRS 2 is the differential accounting treatment it applies to transactions settled in cash and to transactions that are equity-settled. If a share-based payment transaction is settled in cash, the general principle employed in IFRS 2 is that the goods or services received and the liability incurred are measured at the fair value of the liability. The fair value of the liability is remeasured at each reporting date and at the date of settlement, and any changes in fair value are recognised in profit or loss. For share-based payment transactions that are equity-settled, the general principal is that the goods or services received and the corresponding increase in equity are measured at the grant date at the fair value of the goods or services received. If the fair value cannot be measured reliably, the goods or services are measured indirectly by reference to the fair value of the equity instruments granted.

Under this approach a differential accounting treatment of changes in the fair value of equity instruments occurs, based on whether a transaction is classified as a liability or as equity. The fair value of transactions classified as equity is measured at grant date and subsequent value changes are ignored. In contrast, the fair value of transactions classified as liabilities (debt) are adjusted to fair value at each reporting date and the resulting profit or loss is included in income.

In the view of the AAA Committee (2004) this differential accounting treatment, based on the form of settlement, is a case of 'form over substance'. The committee has expressed a concern that it can bring with it several undesirable consequences ranging from 'transaction structuring to meet reporting goals' to 'estimate manipulation that goes uncorrected due to a lack of *truing up*' (AAA 2004, p. 66). The committee argues that items that are economically identical, such as the outflow of an entity's resources through share-based payment transactions, should be accounted for in the same way.

LO 4

7.3 Equity-settled share-based payment transactions

The goods or services received in equity-settled share-based payment transactions and the corresponding increase in equity must be measured at the fair value of the goods or services unless that fair value cannot be estimated reliably (IFRS 2, para. 10). For transactions with parties other than employees, there is a rebuttable presumption in IFRS 2 (para. 13) that the fair value of goods or services can be estimated reliably. In the rare cases where the entity cannot estimate the fair value reliably, paragraph 10 requires that the goods or services and the corresponding increase in equity be measured indirectly by reference to the fair value of the equity instruments granted at the date the goods are obtained or the counterparty renders the service.

It is normally considered that the fair value of services received in transactions with employees cannot be measured reliably. Thus, the fair value of the services received from employees is measured by reference to the equity instruments granted, at grant date. In summary, under IFRS 2, equity-settled share-based payments are measured and recognised as follows:

| Asset or Expense
    Equity
(Recognition of a share-based payment in which fair value of goods or services can be reliably estimated) | Dr
Cr | Fair value of goods or services received or acquired |
| Asset or Expense
    Equity
(Recognition of a share-based payment where fair value of goods or services cannot be reliably estimated) | Dr
Cr | Fair value of the equity instruments granted |

LO 5

7.3.1 Transactions in which services are received

Certain conditions may need to be satisfied before the counterparty to a share-based payment transaction becomes entitled to receive cash (or other assets) or equity instruments of the entity. When the conditions have been satisfied, the counterparty's entitlement has *vested*.

If the equity instruments vest immediately, the counterparty is not required to serve a specified period of service before becoming unconditionally entitled to those equity instruments (IFRS 2 para. 14). On grant date, the services received would be recognised in full together with the corresponding increase in equity. However, if the equity instruments do not vest until a period of service has been completed, paragraph 15 requires that the services and the corresponding increase in equity be accounted for as the services are rendered across the vesting period. This recognition approach is summarised in table 7.2.

TABLE 7.2	Vesting conditions and the recognition of services
Vesting circumstances	Treatment
Equity instrument vests immediately	Recognise the goods or services and the increase in equity on grant date
Equity instrument does not vest until the counterparty completes a period of service	Recognise the goods or services and the increase in equity as they are received across the vesting period

Source: Adapted from e-GAAP 3/2005.

The granting of equity instruments in the form of share options to employees conditional on completing a two-year period of service accounted for over the two-year vesting period is demonstrated in illustrative example 7.1.

ILLUSTRATIVE EXAMPLE 7.1

Recognition of share options as services are rendered across the vesting period

The Alessandro Company grants 100 share options to each of its 50 employees. Each grant is conditional upon the employee working for the Alessandro Company for the next two years. At grant date, the fair value of each share option is estimated to be $25.

According to IFRS 2, paragraph 15(a), the Alessandro Company will recognise the following amounts during the vesting period for services received from the employees as consideration for the share options granted.

Year	Calculation	Remuneration expense for period $	Cumulative remuneration expense $
1	(100 × 50 options) × $25 × 1/2 years	62 500	62 500
2	(100 × 50 options) × $25 − $62 500	62 500	125 000

7.3.2 Transactions measured by reference to the fair value of the equity instruments granted

Determining the fair value of equity instruments granted

Paragraph 11 of IFRS 2 states that, if share-based payment transactions are with employees, it is not usually possible to measure the fair value of services received. If it is not possible to reliably estimate the value of goods or services received from other counterparties to share-based transactions, the transaction is measured by reference to the fair value of the equity instruments granted. If market prices are not available, or if the equity instruments are subject to terms and conditions that do not apply to traded equity instruments, then a valuation technique must be used to estimate what the price of the equity instruments would have been, in an arm's length transaction, on the measurement date.

While IFRS 2 (appendix B11–41) discusses the inputs to option-pricing models such as the Black–Scholes–Merton formula, the choice of model is left to the entity. The valuation technique chosen must be consistent with generally accepted valuation methodologies for pricing financial instruments. It must also account for the terms and conditions of the equity instruments (for example, whether or not an employee is entitled to receive dividends during the vesting period), and any other factors and assumptions that knowledgeable, willing market participants would consider in setting the price. For instance, many employee share options have long lives, are usually exercisable after the vesting period and before the end of the options' life. If options are exercised early, the binomial option-pricing model might be used because such models are more versatile than the Black–Scholes model in incorporating early exercise (Saly, Jagannathan & Huddart 1999, p. 223). Option-pricing models 'typically price an option by finding a portfolio, comprised of the underlying asset and a risk-free investment, that replicates the payoffs of the option on its expiration date' (Benninga & Sarig 2005, p. 376).

Appendix B of IFRS 2 supplies the following list of factors that all option-pricing models take into account as a minimum:

- exercise price of the option
- life of the option
- current price of the underlying shares
- expected volatility of the share price
- dividends expected on the shares
- risk-free interest rate for the life of the option.

Expected volatility is a measure of the amount by which a price is expected to fluctuate during a period. Volatility is typically expressed in annualised terms, for example,

LO 6

daily, weekly or monthly price observations. Often there is likely to be a range of reasonable expectations about future volatility, dividends and exercise date behaviour. If so, an expected value should be calculated by weighting each amount within the range by its associated probability of occurrence.

Expectations about the future are generally based on experience and modified if the future is reasonably expected to differ from the past. For instance, if an entity with two distinctly different lines of business disposes of the one that was significantly less risky than the other, historical volatility may not be the best information on which to base reasonable expectations for the future. In other circumstances, historical information may not be available. For example, unlisted entities will have no historical data on share prices, and newly listed entities will have little data available.

Whether expected dividends should be taken into account when measuring the fair value of shares or options granted depends on whether the counterparty is entitled to dividends or dividend equivalents. Generally, the assumption about expected dividends is based on publicly available information.

The risk-free interest rate is the implied yield currently available on zero-coupon government issues of the country in whose currency the exercise price is expressed, with a remaining term equal to the expected term of the option being valued (IFRS 2, appendix B37). It may be necessary to use an appropriate substitute if no such government issues exist or if circumstances indicate that the implied yield on zero-coupon government issues is not representative of the risk-free interest rate (for example, in high inflation economies).

BlueScope Steel (discussed earlier in this chapter) discloses its use of a binomial model in the determination of the grant-date fair value of share awards and rights. A relevant extract from BlueScope Steel's half-year report appears in figure 7.3. BlueScope Steel provides further explanation of the inputs to the binomial option-pricing model in the remuneration report contained in its directors report (see figure 7.4).

> **BlueScope Steel Ltd**
> **Notes to the financial statements**
> **Interim financial report — 31 December 2005**
>
> **2   Critical accounting estimates**
> *(iv) Share-based payment transactions*
> ... The fair value is determined by an external valuer using a binomial model. These calculations require assumptions to be made.

FIGURE 7.3   Use of option-pricing models, example 1
Source: BlueScope Steel Ltd (2005b, p. 23).

> **BlueScope Steel Ltd**
> **30 June 2005**
> **Directors' report**
>
> External valuation advice from PricewaterhouseCoopers Securities Limited has been used to determine the value of the Executive Share Rights at grant date for each award. The valuation has been made using the Binomial Option Pricing Model using standard option pricing inputs such as the underlying stock price, exercise price, expected dividends, expected risk free interest rates and expected share price volatility. In addition, specific factors in relation to the likely achievement of performance hurdles and employment tenure have been taken into account.

FIGURE 7.4   Use of option-pricing models, example 2
Source: BlueScope Steel Ltd (2005a, p. 45).

Treatment of vesting conditions

If a grant of equity instruments is conditional on satisfying certain vesting conditions such as remaining in the entity's employment for a specified period of time, the vesting conditions are not taken into account when estimating the fair value of the equity instruments at the measurement date. Instead, vesting conditions are accounted for by adjusting the number of equity instruments included in the measurement of the transaction amount so that the amount recognised for goods or services received as consideration for the equity instrument is based on the number of equity instruments that eventually vest. On a cumulative basis, this means that if a vesting condition is not satisfied then no amount is recognised for goods or services received.

A situation where employees leave during the vesting period, and the number of equity instruments expected to vest varies, is demonstrated in illustrative example 7.2.

ILLUSTRATIVE EXAMPLE 7.2

Grant where the number of equity instruments expected to vest varies

Company A grants 100 share options to each of its 50 employees. Each grant is conditional on the employee working for the company for the next three years. The fair value of each share option is estimated to be $25. On the basis of a weighted average probability, the company estimates that 10% of its employees will leave during the three-year period and therefore forfeit their rights to the share options.

During the year immediately following grant date (year 1) three employees leave, and at the end of year 1 the company revised its estimate of total employee departures over the full three-year period from 10% (five employees) to 16% (eight employees). During year 2 a further two employees leave, and the company revised its estimate of total employee departures across the three-year period down to 12% (six employees). During year 3 a further employee leaves, making a total of six (3 + 2 + 1) employees who have departed. A total of 4400 share options (44 employees × 100 options per employee) vested at the end of year 3.

Year	Calculation	Remuneration expense for period $	Cumulative remuneration expense $
1	(5000 options × 84%) × $25 × 1/3 years	35 000	35 000
2	([5000 options × 88%] × $25 × 2/3 years) − $35 000	38 333	73 333
3	(4400 options × $25) − $73 333	36 667	110 000

Source: Adapted from AASB 2, IG11.

In addition to continuing in employment with the entity, employees may be granted equity instruments that are conditional on the achievement of a performance condition. Where the length of the vesting period varies according to when the performance condition is satisfied, the estimated length of the vesting period at grant date is based on the most likely outcome of the performance condition (IFRS 2, para. 15(b)).

A grant of shares with a performance condition linked to the level of an entity's earnings and in which the length of the vesting period varies is demonstrated in illustrative example 7.3.

ILLUSTRATIVE EXAMPLE 7.3

Grant with a performance condition linked to earnings

At the beginning of year 1 company C grants 100 shares to each of its 50 employees, conditional on the employee remaining in the company's employ during the three-year vesting period. The shares have a fair value of $20 per share at grant date. No dividends are expected to be paid over the three-year period. Additionally, the vesting conditions allow the shares to vest at the end of:

- year 1 if the company's earnings have increased by more than 18%
- year 2 if earnings have increased by more than 13% averaged across the two-year period
- year 3 if earnings have increased by more than 10% averaged across the three-year period.

By the end of year 1, company C's earnings have increased by only 14% and three employees have left. The company expects that earnings will continue to increase at a similar rate in year 2 and the shares will vest at the end of year 2. It also expects that a further three employees will leave during year 2, and therefore that 44 employees will vest in 100 shares each at the end of year 2.

Year	Calculation	Remuneration expense for period $	Cumulative remuneration expense $
1	(44 employees × 100 shares) × $20 × 1/2 years	44 000	44 000

By the end of year 2 the company's earnings have increased by only 10%, resulting in an average of only 12% ([14% + 10%]/2) and so the shares do not vest. Two employees left during the year. The company expects that another two employees will leave during year 3 and that its earnings will increase by at least 6%, thereby achieving the average of 10% per year.

Year	Calculation	Remuneration expense for period $	Cumulative remuneration expense $
2	([43 employees × 100 shares] × $20 × 2/3 years) − $44 000	13 333	57 333

Another three employees leave during year 3 and the company's earnings have increased by 8%, resulting in an average increase of 10.67% over the three-year period. Therefore, the performance condition has been satisfied. The 42 remaining employees (50 − [3 + 2 + 3]) are entitled to receive 100 shares each at the end of year 3.

Year	Calculation	Remuneration expense for period $	Cumulative remuneration expense $
3	([42 employees × 100 shares] × $20) − $57 333	26 667	84 000

Source: Adapted from AASB 2, IG12.

An entity may also grant equity instruments to its employees with a performance condition and where the exercise price varies. This particular situation is demonstrated in illustrative example 7.4.

ILLUSTRATIVE EXAMPLE 7.4

Grant of equity instruments where the exercise price varies

At the beginning of year 1 Excelsior Company granted 5000 share options with an exercise price of $40 to an executive, conditional upon the executive remaining with the company until the end of year 3. The exercise price drops to $30 if Excelsior Company's earnings increase by an average of 10% per year over the three-year period. On grant date the estimated fair value of the share options with an exercise price of $40 is $12 per option and, if the exercise price is $30, the estimated fair value of the options is $16 per option.

During year 1 the company's earnings increased by 12% and they are expected to continue to increase at this rate over the next two years. During year 2 the company's earnings increased by 13% and the company continued to expect that the earnings target would be achieved. During year 3 the company's earnings increased by only 3%. The earnings target was therefore not achieved and so the 5000 vested share options will have an exercise price of $40. The executive completed three years service and so satisfied the service condition.

Year	Calculation	Remuneration expense for period $	Cumulative remuneration expense $
1	5000 options × $16 × 1/3 years	26 667	26 667
2	(5000 options × $16 × 2/3 years) − $26 667	26 666	53 333
3	(5000 options × $12) − $53 333	6 667	60 000

Source: Adapted from AASB 2, IG12.

Because the exercise price varies depending on the outcome of a performance condition that is not a market condition, the effect of that performance condition (the possibility that the exercise price might be either $40 or $30) is not taken into account when estimating the fair value of the share options at grant date. Instead, the entity estimates the fair value of the share options at grant date and ultimately revises the transaction amount to reflect the outcome of the performance condition.

Paragraph 21 of IFRS 2 requires that market conditions (such as a target share price) be taken into account when estimating the fair value of equity instruments. The goods or services received from a counterparty who satisfies all other vesting conditions (such as remaining in service for a specified period of time) are recognised whether or not the market condition is satisfied.

A grant of equity instruments with a market condition is demonstrated in illustrative example 7.5.

ILLUSTRATIVE EXAMPLE 7.5

Grant with a market condition

At the beginning of year 1 Petrovic Company grants 5000 share options to a senior executive, conditional on that executive remaining in the company's employ until the end of year 3. The share options cannot be exercised unless the share price has increased from $15 at the beginning of year 1 to above $25 at the end of year 3. If the share price is above $25 at the end of year 3, the share options can be exercised at any time during the next seven years (that is, by the end of year 10). The company applies an option-pricing model that takes into account the possibility that the share price will exceed $25 at the end of year 3 and the possibility that the share price will not exceed $25 at the end of year 3. It estimates the fair value of the share options with this embedded market condition to be $9 per option. The executive completes three years service with the Petrovic Company.

Year	Calculation	Remuneration expense for period $	Cumulative remuneration expense $
1	5000 options × $9 × 1/3 years	15 000	15 000
2	(5000 options × $9 × 2/3 years) − $15 000	15 000	30 000
3	(5000 options × $9) − $30 000	15 000	45 000

Source: Adapted from AASB 2, IG13.

As noted above, because the executive has satisfied the service condition, the company is required to recognise these amounts irrespective of the outcome of the market condition.

LO 7

Treatment of a reload feature

Employee share options often include features that are not found in exchange-traded options. One such feature, the reload, 'entitles the holder to automatically receive new options when the original option is exercised' (Saly, Jagannathan & Huddart 1999, p. 219). Although a reload feature can add considerably to an option's value, it is not considered feasible to value the reload feature at grant date. Under paragraph 22 of IFRS 2, a reload feature is not taken into account when estimating the fair value of the options granted at measurement date. Instead, a reload feature is accounted for as a new option grant if and when a reload option is subsequently granted.

After vesting date

Having recognised the goods or services received and a corresponding increase in equity, paragraph 23 of IFRS 2 prevents an entity from making a subsequent adjustment to total equity after vesting date. For example, if an amount is recognised for services received from an employee, it may not be reversed if the vested equity instruments are later forfeited or, in the case of share options, if the options are not subsequently exercised. This restriction applies only to total equity; it does not preclude an entity from transferring amounts from one component of equity to another.

If the fair value of the equity instruments cannot be reliably estimated

In the event that the fair value of equity instruments cannot be reliably estimated, they must instead be measured at their intrinsic value (IFRS 2, para. 24(a)). Intrinsic value is measured at the date the goods are obtained or the services rendered, at each subsequent reporting date and at the date of final settlement. Any change in intrinsic value must be recognised in profit or loss. For a grant of share options, the share-based payment arrangement is finally settled when the options are exercised or forfeited, or when they lapse. The amount to be recognised for goods or services is based on the number of equity instruments that ultimately vest or are exercised. The estimate must be revised if subsequent information indicates that the number of share options expected to vest differs from previous estimates. On vesting date, the estimate is then revised to equal the number of equity instruments that ultimately vest.

Illustrative example 7.6 provides an example of the application of the intrinsic value method of accounting for share-based payment transactions.

ILLUSTRATIVE EXAMPLE 7.6

Grant of share options accounted for by applying the intrinsic value method

At the beginning of year 1, Anand Company granted 100 share options each to its 50 employees. The share options will vest at the end of year 3 if the employees remain employed by the company at that date. The share options have a life of five years. The exercise price is $60, which is also Anand Company's share price at the grant date. The company concludes that it cannot reliably estimate the fair value of the share options at the grant date.

Anand Company's share price during years 1–5 and the number of share options exercised during years 4–5 are set out below. Share options may be exercised only at year-end.

Year	Share price at year-end	Number of share options exercised at year-end
1	63	0
2	65	0
3	75	0
4	88	2600
5	100	1700

A   At the end of year 1 three employees have left, and the company estimates that a further seven employees will leave during years 2 and 3. Hence, only 80% of the share options are expected to vest.

Year	Calculation	Remuneration expense for period $	Cumulative remuneration expense $
1	(50 × 100 options × 80%) × ($63 − $60) × 1/3 years	4000	4000

B   Two employees have left during year 2, and the company revises its estimate of the number of share options expected to vest to 86%.
C   Two more employees leave during year 3, so there are 4300 share options vested at the end of year 3 (100 × [50 − (3 + 2 + 2)]).

→

	Year	Calculation	Remuneration expense for period $	Cumulative remuneration expense $
B	2	(50 × 100 options × 86% × [$65 − $60] × 2/3 years) − $4000	10 333	14 333
C	3	(43 × 100 options × [$75 − $60]) − $14 333	50 167	64 500

In accordance with paragraph 24 of IFRS 2, Anand Company will recognise the following amounts in years 4 and 5:

Year	Calculation	Remuneration expense for period $	Cumulative remuneration expense $
4	(1700 outstanding options × [$88 − $75]) + (2600 exercised options × [$88 − $75])	55 900	120 400
5	(1700 exercised options × [$100 − $88])	20 400	140 800*

Source: Adapted from AASB 2, IG16.   *(1700 options × [$100 − $60]) + (2600 options × [$88 − $60])

If share options are forfeited after vesting date or lapse at the end of the share option's life, then paragraph 24(b) of IFRS 2 requires the amount previously recognised for goods or services to be reversed.

Paragraph 25 requires that if a grant of equity instruments is settled during the vesting period, the settlement must be accounted for as an acceleration of vesting, and the amount that would otherwise have been recognised for services received over the remainder of the vesting period is, instead, recognised immediately. Any payment made by the entity on settlement is accounted for as the repurchase of equity instruments (a deduction from equity). Any excess of payment amount over the intrinsic value of the equity instrument measured at repurchase date must be recognised as an expense.

7.3.3 Modifications to the terms and conditions on which equity instruments were granted

An entity might choose to modify the terms and conditions on which it granted equity instruments. For example, it might change (reprice) the exercise price of share options previously granted to employees at prices that were higher than the current price of the entity's shares; it might accelerate the vesting of share options to make the options more favourable to employees; or it might remove or alter a performance condition. If the exercise price of options is modified, the fair value of the options changes. A reduction in the exercise price would increase the fair value of share options. Irrespective of any modifications to the terms and conditions on which equity instruments are granted, paragraph 27 of IFRS 2 requires the services received, measured at the grant-date fair value of the equity instruments granted, to be recognised unless those equity instruments do not vest.

Some companies provide for retesting (repricing) to allow for the potential volatility of earnings and the cyclical nature of the market. The 2005 annual financial statements of

BlueScope Steel Limited (referred to earlier in this chapter) indicate that the group has anticipated that potential volatility in its earnings could adversely affect its share-based payments arrangements. BlueScope Steel discloses the provision it has made if this event occurs.

The incremental effects of modifications that increase the total fair value of the share-based payment arrangement, or that are otherwise beneficial to the employee, must also be recognised. The incremental fair value is the difference between the fair value of the modified equity instrument and that of the original equity instrument, both estimated at the date of modification (IFRS 2, appendix B43(a)). Similarly, if the modification increases the number of equity instruments granted, the fair value of the additional equity instruments granted, measured at the date of modification, must be included in the measurement of the amount recognised for services received.

If the modification occurs during the vesting period, the incremental fair value granted is included in the measurement of the amount recognised for services received over the period from the modification date until the date when the modified equity instruments vest, in addition to the amount based on the grant-date fair value of the original equity instruments that is recognised over the remainder of the original vesting period. If the modification occurs after the vesting date, the incremental fair value granted is recognised immediately, or over the vesting period if the employee is required to complete an additional period of service before becoming unconditionally entitled to those modified equity instruments.

The terms or conditions of the equity instruments granted may be modified in a manner that reduces the total fair value of the share-based payment arrangement or that is not otherwise beneficial to the employee. If this occurs, IFRS 2 (appendix B44) requires the services received as consideration for the equity instruments granted to be accounted for as if that modification had not occurred (that is, the decrease in fair value is not to be taken into account).

Paragraph 28 of IFRS 2 specifies the accounting treatment if equity instruments are cancelled or settled during the vesting period. If a modification reduces the number of equity instruments granted to an employee, the reduction is to be accounted for as a cancellation of that portion of the grant. If a grant of equity instruments is cancelled during the vesting period (other than by forfeiture), the cancellation or settlement must be accounted for as an acceleration of vesting, and the amount that would otherwise have been recognised for services received over the remainder of the vesting period must be recognised immediately. Further, any payment made to the employee on the cancellation or settlement must be accounted for as the repurchase of an equity interest (as a deduction from equity) except to the extent that the payment exceeds the fair value of the equity instruments granted, measured at repurchase date. Any excess must be recognised as an expense.

If new equity instruments are granted to the employee in replacement of the cancelled instruments, the replacement equity instruments must be accounted for in the same way as a modification of the original grant (IFRS 2, para. 28(c)). The incremental fair value will be the difference between the fair value of the replacement equity instruments and the net fair value of the cancelled equity instruments at the date the replacement equity instruments are granted. The net fair value of the cancelled equity instruments is their fair value immediately before the cancellation, less the amount of any payment made to the employee on cancellation of the equity instruments that is accounted for as a deduction from equity. If new equity instruments granted are not identified as replacement equity instruments for the cancelled equity instruments, they must be accounted for as a new grant of equity instruments.

If vested equity instruments are repurchased, IFRS 2 (para. 29) specifies that the payment made to the employee is to be accounted for as a deduction from equity. If the payment exceeds the fair value of the equity instruments repurchased, the excess is recognised as an expense.

The accounting requirements for modifications to the terms and conditions on which equity instruments were granted are summarised in table 7.3.

LO 8

TABLE 7.3	Accounting requirements for modification to granted equity instruments
Modification	Accounting treatment
Modification increases the fair value of the equity instruments granted measured immediately before and after the change	*General* Include the incremental fair value granted in the amount recognised for services received *Change occurs during vesting period* In addition to the amount based on the grant-date fair value of the original equity instruments, which is recognised over the remainder of the original vesting period, include the incremental fair value in the amount recognised for services received over the period from the date of change until the date when the modified equity instruments vest *Change occurs after the vesting period* The incremental fair value granted is recognised immediately, or over the vesting period where the employee is required to complete an additional period of service before becoming unconditionally entitled to those changed equity instruments
Modification increases the number of equity instruments granted	Include the fair value of the additional equity instruments granted, measured at the date of the change, in the amount recognised for services received
Modification changes the vesting conditions in a manner that is beneficial to the employee	Take the changed vesting arrangements into account
Modification reduces the fair value of the equity instruments granted or is not otherwise beneficial to the employee	Continue to account for the services received as if that change had not occurred

Source: Adapted from e-GAAP 3/2005.

Illustrative example 7.7 demonstrates the accounting treatment of a repricing modification to the terms and conditions of share options already granted.

ILLUSTRATIVE EXAMPLE 7.7

Grant of equity instruments that are subsequently repriced

Grace Corporation grants 100 share options to each of its 50 employees, conditional upon the employee remaining in service over the next three years. The corporation estimates that the fair value of each option is $15. On the basis of a weighted average probability, the corporation also estimates that 10 employees will leave during the three-year vesting period and therefore forfeit their rights to the share options.

A   Four employees leave during year 1, and the corporation estimates that a further seven employees will depart during years 2 and 3. By the end of year 1 the corporation's share price has dropped, and it decides to reprice the share options. The repriced share options will vest at the end of year 3. At the date of repricing, Grace Corporation estimates that the fair value of each of the original share options is $5 and the fair value of each repriced share option is $8. The incremental value is $3 per share option, and this amount is recognised over the remaining two years of the vesting period along with the remuneration expense based on the original option value of $15.

Year	Calculation	Remuneration expense for period $	Cumulative remuneration expense $
A 1	(50 − 11) employees × 100 options × $15 × 1/3 years	19 500	19 500

B   During year 2 a further four employees leave, and the corporation estimates that another four employees will leave during year 3 to bring the total expected employee departures over the three-year vesting period to 12 employees.

Year	Calculation	Remuneration expense for period $	Cumulative remuneration expense $
B 2	([50 − 12] employees × 100 options) × ([$15 × 2/3 years] + [$3 × 1/2 years]) − $19 500	24 200	43 700

C   A further three employees leave during year 3. For the remaining 39 employees (50 − [4 + 4 + 3]), the share options vested at the end of year 3.

Year	Calculation	Remuneration expense for period $	Cumulative remuneration expense $
C 3	([50 − 11] employees × 100 options × [$15 + $3]) − $43 700	26 500	70 200

Source: Adapted from AASB 2, IG15.

7.4 Cash-settled share-based payment transactions

Paragraphs 30–33 of IFRS 2 set out the requirements for share-based payment transactions in which an entity incurs a liability for goods or services received, based on the price of its own equity instruments. Such transactions are known as *cash-settled* share-based payment transactions. The fair value of the liability involved is remeasured at each reporting date and at the date of settlement, and any changes in the fair value are recognised in profit or loss for the period. In contrast, the fair value of *equity-settled* share-based payment transactions is determined at grant date, and remeasurement of the granted equity instruments at subsequent reporting dates and settlement date does not occur.

Examples of cash-settled share-based payment transactions included in paragraph 31 of IFRS 2 are share appreciation rights that might be granted to an employee as part of a remuneration package. Share appreciation rights entitle the holder to a future cash payment (rather than an equity instrument) based on increases in the share price. Another example is where an employee is granted rights to shares that are redeemable, providing the employee with a right to receive a future cash payment.

There is a presumption in IFRS 2 that the services rendered by employees in exchange for the share appreciation rights have been received. Where share appreciation rights vest immediately, the services and the associated liability must be recognised immediately. Where the share appreciation rights do not vest until the employees have completed a specified period of service, the services received and the associated liability to pay for those services are recognised as the employees render service. The liability is measured, initially and at each reporting date until settled, at the fair value of the share appreciation rights by applying an option-pricing model that takes into account the terms and conditions on which share appreciation rights were granted, and the extent to which employees have rendered service (para. 33).

Illustrative example 7.8 provides an example of the accounting treatment for cash-settled share appreciation rights.

ILLUSTRATIVE EXAMPLE 7.8

Cash-settled share appreciation rights

Bert Company grants 100 share appreciation rights (SARs) to each of its 50 employees, conditional upon the employee not leaving the company in the next three years. The company estimates the fair value of the SARs at the end of each year in which a liability exists as shown below. The intrinsic values of the SARs at the date of exercise (which equal the cash paid out) at the end of years 3, 4 and 5 are also shown. All SARs held by employees remaining at the end of year 3 will vest.

Year	Fair value	Intrinsic value
1	$14.40	
2	$15.50	
3	$18.20	$15.00
4	$21.40	$20.00
5		$25.00

A   During year 1 three employees leave, and the company estimates that a further six will leave during years 2 and 3.

B   A further four employees leave during year 2, and the company estimates that three more employees will depart during year 3.

	Year	Calculation	Expense $	Liability $
A	1	(50 − 9) employees × 100 SARs × $14.40 × 1/3 years	19 680	19 680
B	2	([50 − 10] employees × 100 SARs × $15.50 × 2/3 years) − $19 680	21 653	41 333

C   Two employees leave during year 3.
D   At the end of year 3, 15 employees have exercised their SARs.
E   Another 14 employees exercise their SARs at the end of year 4.
F   The remaining 12 employees exercise their SARs at the end of year 5.

	Year	Calculation	Expense $	Liability $
C	3	([50 − 9 − 15] employees × 100 SARs × $18.20) − $41 333	5 987	47 320
D		15 employees × 100 SARs × $15	22 500	
E	4	([26 − 14] employees × 100 SARs × $21.40) − $47 320	(21 640)	25 680
		14 employees × 100 SARs × $20	28 000	
F	5	(0 employees × 100 SARs × $25) − $25 680	(25 680)	0
		12 employees × 100 SARs × $25	30 000	
		Total	80 500	

Source: Adapted from AASB 2, IG19.

7.5   Share-based payment transactions with cash alternatives

Some share-based payment transactions may provide either the entity or the counter-party with the choice of having the transaction settled in cash (or other assets) or by the issue of equity instruments. If the entity has incurred a liability to settle in cash or other assets, the transaction is treated as a cash-settled share-based payment transaction. If no such liability has been incurred, paragraph 34 of IFRS 2 requires that the transaction be treated as an equity-settled share-based payment transaction. The accounting treatment is summarised in table 7.4.

TABLE 7.4	Accounting treatment of share-based payment transactions
Arrangement	Accounting treatment
A liability to settle in cash or other assets has been incurred	Cash-settled share-based payment transaction
No liability to settle in cash or other assets has been incurred	Equity-settled share-based payment transaction

Source: Adapted from e-GAAP 3/2005.

7.5.1 Share-based payment transactions where the counterparty has settlement choice

If the counterparty to a share-based payment transaction has the right to choose whether a transaction is settled in cash or equity instruments, a compound financial instrument has been created that includes a debt component and an equity component. The debt component represents the counterparty's right to demand a cash settlement, and the equity component represents the counterparty's right to demand settlement in equity instruments.

IFRS 2 (paras 35, 36) requires that transactions with employees be measured at fair value on measurement date, by taking into account the terms and conditions on which rights to cash and equity were granted. For transactions with others, in which the fair value of goods or services is measured directly, the equity component is to be measured as the difference between the fair value of the goods or services received and the fair value of the debt component at the date the goods or services are received. The fair value of the debt component must be measured before the fair value of the equity component (para. 37), allowing for the fact that the counterparty must forfeit the right to receive cash in order to receive equity instruments. The measurement of compound financial instruments with employees (and with other counterparties) is summarised in table 7.5.

TABLE 7.5	Measurement of compound financial instruments
Counterparty	Measurement approach
Employees	Measure fair value (FV) of the debt component and then FV of the equity component, at measurement date, taking into account the terms and conditions on which rights to cash or equity were granted
Parties other than employees	Equity component is the difference between FV of goods or services received and FV of the debt component, at the date the goods or services are received

The goods or services received in respect of each component of the compound financial instrument must be accounted for separately. For the debt component, the goods or services acquired and a liability to pay for those goods or services is recognised as the counterparty supplies goods or renders service, in the same manner as other cash-settled share-based payment transactions. For the equity component, the goods or services received and the increase in equity are recognised as the counterparty supplies goods or renders services, in the same manner as other equity-settled share-based payment transactions. The accounting treatment is summarised in table 7.6.

TABLE 7.6	Separate recognition of debt and equity components in compound financial instruments
Component	Recognition
Debt	Recognise goods or services acquired and the liability for payment as the counterparty supplies the goods and services
Equity	Recognise goods or services acquired and the increase in equity as the counterparty supplies the goods or services

Source: Adapted from e-GAAP 3/2005.

At settlement date, the liability must be remeasured to fair value (IFRS 2, para. 39). If equity instruments are issued rather than a settlement paid in cash, the liability must be transferred directly to equity as consideration for the equity instruments. If the counterparty elects to take a cash settlement, that payment is to be applied to settle the liability. Any equity component previously recognised must remain within equity although the issuing entity is not precluded from making a transfer within equity.

A grant of shares with a cash alternative subsequently added that provides an employee with a settlement choice is demonstrated in illustrative example 7.9.

ILLUSTRATIVE EXAMPLE 7.9

Grant of shares with a cash alternative subsequently added

At the beginning of year 1 Rosario Corporation granted 10 000 shares with a fair value of $24 per share to a senior manager, conditional on the manager remaining in the corporation's employ for three years. By the end of year 2 the share price had dropped to $15 per share. At that date the corporation added a cash alternative to the grant, giving the manager the right to choose whether to receive the 10 000 shares or cash equal to the value of the shares on vesting date. On vesting date the share price had dropped to $12.

Year	Calculation	Asset/ expense $	Equity $	Liability $
1	10 000 shares × $24 × 1/3 years	80 000	80 000	

The addition of the cash alternative at the end of year 2 created an obligation to settle in cash. The Rosario Corporation must recognise the liability to settle in cash based on the fair value of the shares at the modification date and the extent to which the specified services have been received. The liability must be remeasured at each subsequent reporting date and at the date of settlement.

Year	Calculation	Asset/ expense $	Equity $	Liability $
2	(10 000 shares × $24 × 2/3 years) − $80 000	80 000	80 000	
	10 000 shares × $15 × 2/3 years		(100 000)	100 000*

Year	Calculation	Asset/ expense $	Equity $	Liability $
3	(10 000 shares × $24) − $160 000	80 000	30 000	50 000*
	(10 000 shares × $12) − $150 000	(30 000)		(30 000)
	Total	210 000	90 000	120 000**

* Total liability at date of modification is $150 000 ($15 × 10 000 shares).
** Total liability at date of settlement is $120 000 ($12 × 10 000 shares).

Source: Adapted from AASB 2, IG15.

An example of a share-based payment transaction in which an employee has a right to choose either a cash settlement or an equity settlement is demonstrated in illustrative example 7.10.

Share-based payment transaction where employee has settlement choice

Company A grants to each of its 10 senior executives a choice between receiving a cash payment equivalent to 1000 shares or receiving 1200 shares. The grant is conditional on the completion of three years service with the company. If the share alternative is chosen, the shares must be held for two years after vesting date. At grant date the company's share price is $25 per share. At the end of years 1, 2 and 3 the share price is $27, $28 and $30 respectively. The company does not expect to pay dividends in the next three years. After taking into account the effects of post-vesting transfer restrictions, the company estimates that the grant-date fair value of the share alternative is $24 per share.

The fair value of the cash alternative is $250 000 (10 × 1000 shares × $25), and the fair value of the equity alternative is $288 000 (10 × 1200 shares × $24). Therefore, the fair value of the equity component of the compound instrument is $38 000 ($288 000 − $250 000). Company A will recognise the following amounts:

Year	Calculation	Asset/ expense $	Equity $	Liability $
1	Liability component (10 × 1000 × $27 × 1/3 years) Equity component ($38 000 × 1/3 years)	90 000 12 667	12 667	90 000
2	Liability component (10 × 1000 × $28 × 2/3 years) − $90 000 Equity component ($38 000 × 1/3 years)	96 667 12 667	12 667	96 667
3	Liability component (10 × 1000 × $30) − $186 667 Equity component ($38 000 × 1/3 years)	113 333 12 666	12 666	113 333

At the end of year 3, the employees must choose whether to take the cash or equity. At settlement, the liability must be remeasured to its full value. If all employees choose the cash settlement, the liability is $300 000 (10 × 1000 × $30). If cash is paid on settlement it must be applied to settle the liability in full, with any previously recognised equity instrument remaining within equity.

Year	Calculation	Asset/ expense $	Equity $	Liability $
End year 3	*Choice 1:* *Cash equivalent to 10 × 1000 shares × $30* Cash settlement of $300 000 paid Totals	338 000	38 000	(300 000) 0

If the employees choose the equity issue, the liability is transferred direct to equity (IFRS 2, para. 39) as the consideration for the equity instruments that were issued. If all employees choose the equity alternative, the amount of the liability transferred to equity is $300 000.

Year	Calculation	Asset/ expense $	Equity $	Liability $
End year 3	*Choice 2:* *Equity issue of 10 × 1200 shares* 12 000 shares issued Totals	338 000	300 000 338 000	(300 000) 0

Source: Adapted from AASB 2, IG21.

7.5.2 Share-based payment transactions where the entity has settlement choice

Where an entity has a choice of whether to settle in cash or equity instruments, it must determine whether it has a present obligation to settle in cash. Paragraph 41 of IFRS 2 states that an entity has a present obligation to settle in cash if the choice of settlement in equity instruments has no commercial substance (perhaps the entity is legally prohibited from issuing shares), the entity has a past practice or a stated policy of settling in cash, or if it generally settles in cash whenever the counterparty asks for cash settlement. If a present obligation exists, the transaction must be accounted for as a cash-settled share-based payment transaction. If a present obligation to settle in cash does not exist, the transaction is accounted for as an equity-settled share-based payment transaction.

On settlement, if the entity elects to settle in cash, paragraph 43(a) of IFRS 2 determines that the cash payment is to be accounted for as the repurchase of an equity interest, resulting in a deduction from equity. Where there is an equity settlement, no further accounting adjustments are required. If, on settlement, the entity selects the settlement alternative with the higher fair value, at settlement date an additional expense for the excess value given must be recognised. The excess value is either the difference between the cash paid and the fair value of the equity instruments that would otherwise have been issued, or the difference between the fair value of the equity instruments issued and the amount of cash that would otherwise have been paid, whichever is applicable.

LO 9

7.6 Disclosures

Paragraphs 44–52 of IFRS 2 prescribe various disclosures relating to share-based payments. The objective of these disclosures is to provide significant additional information to assist financial report users to understand the nature and extent of share-based payment arrangements that existed during the reporting period. Three principles underpin the disclosures required by IFRS 2. These are that the disclosures must enable the users of the financial statements to understand:
- the nature and extent of the share-based payment arrangements (para. 44)
- how the fair value of goods or services received, or the fair value of equity instruments granted during the period, was determined (para. 46)

- the effect of share-based payment transactions on the entity's profit or loss for the period and on its financial position (para. 50).

Paragraph 45 of IFRS 2 specifies the disclosures necessary to give effect to the principle in paragraph 44 as including at least the following:

- a description of each type of share-based payment arrangement that existed at any time during the period, including the general terms and conditions of each arrangement, such as vesting requirements, the maximum term of options granted, and the methods of settlement.

An entity with substantially similar types of share-based payment arrangements may aggregate this information unless separate disclosure of each arrangement is necessary to enable users to understand the nature and extent of the arrangements.

Other specific disclosures required by paragraph 45 are the number and weighted average exercise prices of share options for options that:

- are outstanding at the beginning of the period
- are granted during the period
- are forfeited during the period
- are exercised during the period
- have expired during the period
- are outstanding at the end of the period
- are exercisable at the end of the period.

In relation to share options exercised during the period, the weighted average share price at the date of exercise must be disclosed. If the options were exercised on a regular basis throughout the period, the weighted average share price during the period may be disclosed instead. For share options outstanding at the end of the period, the range of exercise prices and weighted average remaining contractual life must be disclosed. If the range of exercise prices is wide, the outstanding options must be divided into ranges that are meaningful for assessing the number and timing of additional shares that may be issued and the cash that may be received upon exercise of those options.

If the fair value of goods or services received as consideration for equity instruments of the entity has been measured indirectly by reference to the fair value of the equity instruments granted, the following information must be disclosed (para. 47):

- the weighted average fair value of share options granted during the period, at the measurement date, and information on how the fair value was measured including:
  - the option-pricing model used and the inputs to that model including the weighted average share price, exercise price, expected volatility, option life, expected dividends, the risk-free interest rate, and any other inputs to the model including the assumptions made to incorporate the effects of expected early exercise
  - how expected volatility was determined, including an explanation of the extent to which expected volatility was based on historical volatility
  - whether, and how many, other features of the option grant (such as a market condition) were incorporated into the measurement of fair value
- for equity instruments other than share options granted during the period, the number and weighted average fair value at the measurement date, and information on how that fair value was measured, including:
  - if not measured on the basis of an observable market price, how fair value was determined
  - whether and how expected dividends were incorporated
  - whether and how any other features of the equity instruments were incorporated
- for share-based payment arrangements that were modified during the period:
  - an explanation of the modifications
  - the incremental fair value granted as a result of the modifications and information on how the incremental fair value granted was measured.

If the entity has measured the fair value of goods or services received during the period directly, it is required to disclose how that fair value was determined (for example, at market price).

If the entity has rebutted the assumption that the fair value of goods or services received can be estimated reliably, it is required to disclose that fact (para. 49) together with an explanation of why the presumption was rebutted.

Paragraph 51 gives effect to the principle that an entity must disclose information that enables financial statement users to understand the effect of share-based payment transactions on the entity's profit or loss for the period and on its financial position. This paragraph requires disclosure of at least the following:

- the total expense recognised for the period arising from share-based payment transactions in which the goods or services received did not qualify for recognition as assets, including separate disclosure of that portion of the total expense that arises from transactions accounted for as equity-settled share-based payment transactions
- for liabilities arising from share-based payment transactions:
  - the total carrying amount at the end of the period
  - the total intrinsic value at the end of the period of liabilities for which the counterparty's right to cash or other assets had vested by the end of the period.

Finally, paragraph 52 requires the disclosure of such other additional information as may be needed to enable the users of the financial statements to understand: the nature and extent of the share-based payment arrangements; how the fair value of goods or services received, or the fair value of equity instruments granted was determined; and the effect of share-based payment transactions on the entity's profit or loss and on its financial position.

An extract relating to share-based payment disclosures for BlueScope Steel Ltd appears in figure 7.5.

BlueScope Steel Limited
Notes to the financial statements
Interim financial report — 31 December 2005

1   Summary of significant accounting policies
(iv) Share-based payments
The Group provides benefits in the form of share-based payment transactions to employees. There are currently two plans in place providing these benefits.
- *The General Employee Share Plan ('GESP')*
  GESP is a share awards program which, at the determination of the Board, issues eligible employees with a grant of ordinary BlueScope Steel shares ...
- *The Long Term Incentive Plan ('LTIP')*
  LTIP is a share rights program which, at the determination of the Board, provides eligible senior managers with the right to acquire ordinary BlueScope Steel shares at a later date subject to the satisfaction of certain performance criteria ...
For further details of share rights and awards granted, refer to the 30 June 2005 Remuneration Report.

FIGURE 7.5 Disclosure of accounting policy for share-based payments
Source: BlueScope Steel Ltd (2005b, p. 23).

Further disclosure details are provided in BlueScope's annual report. A relevant extract from the 30 June 2005 remuneration report (a section of the annual report) is provided in figure 7.6.

BlueScope Steel Ltd
30 June 2005
Remuneration report

(iii) September 2003 Award
Vesting Requirements

TSR Performance Hurdle	% of Share Rights that Vest	
75th – 100th percentile	100%	If the performance hurdles are not met at the end of the first performance period (or are only partially met), four subsequent performance periods will apply. The subsequent performance periods commence on 1 October 2003 and end on 31 March 2007, 30 September 2007, 31 March 2008 and 30 September 2008 respectively. Vesting at a subsequent performance period will only occur if the vesting requirements have been met and any previous percentile rankings are exceeded.
51st – <75th percentile	A minimum of 52% plus a further 2% for each increased percentage ranking. Any unvested share rights will be carried over to be assessed at subsequent performance periods.	
<51st percentile	All share rights will be carried over to be assessed at subsequent performance periods.	

Details of the September 2003 Award

	Nil Priced Share Rights	
Grant Date	24 October 2003 (All executives excluding Managing Director and Chief Executive Officer) 13 November 2003 (Managing Director and Chief Executive Officer)	1 External valuation advice from PricewaterhouseCoopers Securities Limited has been used to determine the value of the Executive Share Rights at grant date. Currently these fair values are not recognised as expenses in the financial statements. However, were these grants to have been expensed they would have been amortised over the vesting period resulting in an estimated increase in employee benefits expense of $3.3 million for the year ended 30 June 2005 (2004: $2.3 million). Note that no adjustment to this amount has been made to reflect actual forfeiture of shares.
Exercise Date (subject to vesting requirements)	From 1 October 2006	
Expiry Date	30 September 2008	
Share Rights Granted	3 183 800	
Number of Participants at Grant Date	144	
Number of current Participants	141	
Exercise Price	Nil	
Fair Value Estimate at Grant date[1]	$9 678 752	
Share Rights Lapsed since Grant Date	109 453	

FIGURE 7.6 Disclosure of accounting policy for share-based payments
Source: BlueScope Steel Ltd (2005a, p. 46).

7.7 Summary

IFRS 2 deals with the recognition and measurement of share-based payment transactions. Share-based payment transactions are arrangements in which an entity receives goods or services as consideration for its own equity instruments, or acquires goods or services for amounts that are based on the price of its equity instruments. The main feature of the standard is that it requires recognition in the financial statements of the goods or services acquired or received under share-based payment arrangements, regardless of whether the form of settlement is cash or equity and regardless of whether the counterparty involved is an employee or other party.

If a share-based payment transaction is settled in cash, the general principle employed in IFRS 2 is that the goods or services received and the liability incurred are measured at the fair value of the liability. Until it is settled, the fair value of the liability is remeasured at each reporting date and at the date of settlement, and any changes in fair value are recognised in profit or loss. For transactions that are equity-settled, the general principle is that the goods or services received and the corresponding increase in equity are measured at the grant date, and at the fair value of the goods or services received. If the fair value cannot be measured reliably, the goods or services are measured indirectly by reference to the fair value of the equity instruments granted.

Another important feature of IFRS 2 is that it allows an entity to choose appropriate option-valuation models to determine fair values and to tailor those models to suit the entity's specific circumstances. Determining the fair value of options where various models may be used, and where various estimates are required, will do little to reduce ambiguity in valuation. Finally, IFRS 2 includes a lengthy set of disclosure requirements aimed at enabling financial statement users to understand the nature, extent and effect of share-based payment arrangements, and how the fair value of goods or services received or equity instruments granted was determined.

DISCUSSION QUESTIONS

1. Why do standard setters formulate rules on the measurement and recognition of share-based payment transactions?
2. What is the hierarchy, contained in IFRS 2, to be used in determining the accounting treatment for a share-based payment transaction?
3. Why are some services received in share-based payment transactions classified initially as assets rather than expenses?
4. What is the difference between equity-settled and cash-settled share-based payment transactions?
5. What is the different accounting treatment for instruments classified as debt and those classified as equity?
6. Why might market prices not be available for some equity instruments such as share options?
7. What are the factors required under IFRS 2 to be taken into account in option-pricing models?
8. When is it appropriate to use another interest rate in place of the 'risk-free' interest rate?
9. What is a 'reload' feature? Explain why it is not taken into account when valuing options.
10. What are the circumstances that cause a share-based payment transaction to be measured by reference to the fair value of equity instruments granted?
11. What is the difference between a debt component and an equity component that is created when a counterparty to a share-based payment transaction has settlement choice?
12. What is the definition of each of the following terms?
    (a) Vest
    (b) Reload feature
    (c) Market condition
13. Are the following statements true or false?
    (a) Goods or services received in a share-based payment transaction must be recognised when they are received.
    (b) Historical volatility provides the best basis for forming reasonable expectations of the future price of share options.
    (c) Share appreciation rights entitle the holder to a future equity instrument based on the profitability of the issuer.

EXERCISES

EXERCISE 7.1   ★   Scope of IFRS 2

Which of the following is a share-based payment transaction within the scope of IFRS 2? Give reasons for your answer.
(a) Goods acquired from a supplier by incurring a liability based on the market price of the goods
(b) An invoiced amount for professional advice provided to an entity, charged at an hourly rate, and to be settled in cash
(c) Services provided by an employee to be settled in equity instruments of the entity
(d) Supply of goods in return for cash or equity instruments at the discretion of the supplier
(e) Dividend payment to employees who are holders of an entity's shares

EXERCISE 7.2   ★   Recognition principles

Company A, a listed company, organises major sporting events. It acquires crowd control equipment in return for a liability for an amount based on the price of 1000 of its own shares.

Required

Is this a share-based payment transaction? Should company A recognise the acquisition cost as an asset or an expense? Explain.

EXERCISE 7.3   ★   Recognition journal entries

Anson Company received the legal title to land in exchange for the issue of 8000 of its own ordinary shares with a fair value of $5 each.

Required

Prepare an appropriate journal entry to recognise this transaction in the accounting records of Anson Company.

EXERCISE 7.4 ★

Categorising

An entity grants 10 000 shares to a senior manager in return for services rendered.

Required

Should the entity recognise the cost of these services as a liability or a component of equity? Explain.

EXERCISE 7.5 ★

Equity-settled share-based payment transactions

On 1 January 2005, Jentec Corporation announces a grant of 250 share options to each of its 20 senior executives. The grant is conditional on the employee continuing to work for Jentec Corporation for the next three years. The fair value of each share option is estimated to be $14. On the basis of a weighted average probability, Jentec Corporation estimates that 10% of its senior executives will leave during the vesting period.

Required

Prepare a schedule setting out the annual and cumulative remuneration expense to be recognised by Jentec Corporation for services rendered as consideration for the share options granted.

EXERCISE 7.6 ★

Determining the value of equity instruments granted

On 30 June 2006, the Jameson Group granted 100 share options to each of its 20 most senior executives. As the share options are subject to certain conditions that do not apply to Jameson's traded shares, an option-pricing model was used to determine the grant-date fair value of the options.

Required

List the factors that option-pricing models take into account.

EXERCISE 7.7 ★★

Cash-settled share-based payment transactions

An entity receives inventory from a supplier in exchange for a liability based on the price of 5000 of the entity's own shares. At the date of receiving the inventory, the entity's shares have a market value of $9.50 each.

Required

Measure the value of this transaction and prepare an appropriate journal entry to recognise it.

EXERCISE 7.8 ★★

Modifications to equity-settled share-based payment transactions

At the beginning of year 1, the Beatty Corporation grants 50 share options to each of its 120 employees, conditional on the employee remaining in the employ of Beatty Corporation over the next two years. The corporation estimates that the fair value of the options on grant date is $12. On the basis of a weighted average probability, the Beatty Corporation estimates that 15% of its employees will leave during the vesting period. At the end of year 1 eight employees have left, and the Beatty Corporation estimates that a further nine will leave during year 2. By the end of year 1 the corporation's share price has dropped, and it decides to reprice the share options. It estimates that the fair value of the original share options is $7 and the fair value of the repriced share options is $10. Nine employees leave during year 2.

Required

Prepare a schedule setting out the remuneration expense to be recognised at the end of years 1 and 2.

EXERCISE 7.9 ★★   Share-based payment transactions in which the entity has the settlement choice

For the following share-based payment arrangements, discuss whether they are 'debt' or 'equity' settled transactions.

(a) Entity A incurs a liability based on the price of its own share options for services received from a director of the entity.

(b) Entity A acquires property from entity B in exchange for 800 of entity A's shares.

(c) Entity A grants share options to each of its 10 senior executives in return for services to be received over the next two years.

EXERCISE 7.10 ★★★   Share-based payment transactions in which the counterparty has the settlement choice

Norah Company grants 5000 shares with a fair value of $30 to one of its directors, conditional on that director remaining as a director for three years from the grant date. By the end of the first year, the share price has dropped to $23 per share. At this date the company added a cash alternative to the grant, giving the director the choice of receiving the shares or receiving cash equal to the value of the shares on vesting date. On vesting date, the share price has dropped to $18.

Required

Prepare a schedule that recognises the extent to which services have been received at the end of each year, and the obligation to settle in cash.

EXERCISE 7.11 ★★★   Disclosure

State whether each of the following items is true or false.

(a) Information about share-based payment arrangements that are substantially the same may be aggregated.

(b) The number and weighted average exercise prices of share options outstanding at the beginning and the end of each period must be disclosed.

(c) Option-pricing models used in valuing share options must be identified.

(d) For equity instruments other than share options, it is not necessary to disclose information on how expected dividends were incorporated into the measure of fair value.

(e) The total expense arising from share-based payment transactions in which the services qualified for recognition as assets must be disclosed.

PROBLEMS

PROBLEM 7.1 ★   Accounting for a grant where the number of equity instruments expected to vest varies

Company A grants 80 share options to each of its 200 employees. Each grant is conditional on the employee working for the company for the three years following the grant date. On grant date, the fair value of each share option is estimated to be $12. On the basis of a weighted average probability, the company estimates that 20% of its employees will leave during the three-year vesting period.

During year 1, 15 employees leave and the company revises its estimate of total employee departures over the full three-year period from 20% to 22%.

Required

Prepare a schedule setting out the annual and cumulative remuneration expense for year 1.

PROBLEM 7.2   ★

Accounting for a grant of share options where the exercise price varies

At the beginning of 2005, Francois Company grants 3000 employee share options with an exercise price of $45 to its newly appointed chief executive officer, conditional on the executive remaining in the company's employ for the next three years. The exercise price drops to $35 if Francois Company's earnings increase by an average of 30% per year over the three-year period. On grant date, the estimated fair value of the employee share options with an exercise price of $35 is $22 per option. If the exercise price is $40, the options have an estimated fair value of $17 each.

During 2005, Francois Company's earnings increased by 8% and are expected to continue to increase at this rate over the next two years.

Required

Prepare a schedule setting out the annual remuneration expense to be recognised by Francois Company and the cumulative remuneration expense for 2005.

PROBLEM 7.3   ★

Accounting for a grant with a market condition

At the beginning of 2005 RoyalPark Corporation grants 10 000 share options to a senior marketing executive, conditional on that executive remaining in the company's employ until the end of 2007. The share options cannot be exercised unless the share price has increased from $20 at the beginning of 2005 to above $30 at the end of 2007. If the share price is above $30 at the end of 2007, the share options can be exercised at any time during the following five years. The RoyalPark Corporation applies a binomial option-pricing model that takes into account the possibility that the share price will exceed $30 at the end of 2007 and the possibility that the share price will not exceed $30 at the end of 2007. The fair value of the share options with this market condition is estimated to be $14 per option.

Required

Calculate the annual and cumulative remuneration expense to be recognised by Royal-Park Corporation for 2005.

PROBLEM 7.4   ★★

Disclosure

X Corporation operates a share option plan for its officers, employees and consultants for up to 10% of its outstanding shares. Under this plan, the exercise price of each option equals the closing market price of the shares on the day before the grant. Each option has a term of five years and vests one-third on each of the three years following grant date. Before this financial period, the X Corporation has accounted for its share option plan on settlement date and no expense has been recognised.

Required

Prepare an appropriate memorandum outlining the disclosures that will need to be made in X Corporation's financial statement following the adoption of IFRS 2.

Application of the intrinsic value method

At the beginning of 2005, DateNews Company grants 2000 share options to each of its 50 most senior executives. The share options have a life of five years and will vest at the end of year 3 if the executives remain in service until then. The exercise price is $50 and DateNews Company's share price is also $50 at the grant date. As the company's share options have characteristics significantly different from those of other traded share options, the use of option-pricing models will not provide a reliable measure of fair value at grant date.

The company's share price during years 1–3 is shown below.

Year	Share price at year-end	Estimated number of executives departing in each year	Number of executives remaining at year-end	Number of share options exercised at year-end
1	53	3	46	0
2	55	2	44	0
3	65	1	43	0

Required
Calculate the annual and cumulative remuneration expense to be recognised by DateNews Company for each of the three years.

Accounting for cash-settled share-based payment transactions

Vincento Corporation grants 1000 share appreciation rights (SARs) to 10 senior managers, to be taken in cash within two years of vesting date on condition that the managers do not leave in the next three years. The SARs vest at the end of year 3. Vincento Corporation estimates the fair value of the SARs at the end of each year in which a liability exists as shown below. The intrinsic value of the SARs at the date of exercise at the end of year 3 is also shown.

Year	Fair value	Intrinsic value	Number of managers who exercised their SARs
1	$4.40		
2	$5.50		
3	$10.20	$9.00	4

During year 1, one employee leaves and Vincento Corporation estimates that a further two will leave before the end of year 3. One employee leaves during year 2 and the corporation estimates that another employee will depart during year 3. One employee leaves during year 3. At the end of year 3, four employees exercise their SARs.

Required
Prepare a schedule setting out the expense and liability that Vincento Corporation must recognise at the end of each of the first three years.

PROBLEM 7.7 ★★★ Accounting for a share-based payment transaction where the counterparty has settlement choice

Tuffin Corporation operates a share plan that grants each of its 100 employees a choice between receiving a cash payment equivalent to 200 shares or receiving 300 shares. The grant is conditional on the employee completing three years service with Tuffin Corporation. If the share alternative is chosen, the shares must be held for four years after vesting date.

At grant date, Tuffin Corporation's share price is $9 per share. At the end of years 1, 2 and 3, the share price is $11, $12 and $15 respectively. Tuffin Corporation has no plan to issue dividends in the next three years. After taking into account the effect of the post-vesting transfer restriction, the Tuffin Corporation estimates that the fair value of the share alternative at grant date is $8 per share. Assume that no employees leave during the vesting period.

Required

Prepare a schedule setting out the liability and equity amounts that Tuffin Corporation must recognise according to IFRS 2. Show also the accounting treatment if (1) all employees choose settlement in cash, and (2) all employees choose the equity alternative.

WEBLINK

Visit these websites for additional information:

www.iasb.org   www.iasplus.com
www.asic.gov.au   www.ifac.org
www.aasb.com.au   www.nzica.com
www.accaglobal.com   www.capa.com.my

REFERENCES

AAA Financial Accounting Standards Committee 2004 (Maines, LA, Bartov, E, Beatty, AL, Botosan, CA, Fairfield, PM, Hirst, DE, Iannoconi, TE, Mallett, R, Venkatachalam, M & Vincent, L), 'Evaluation of the IASB's proposed accounting and disclosure requirements for share-based payment', *Accounting Horizons*, vol. 18, no. 1, pp. 65–76.

Australian Accounting Standards Board 2004, AASB 2 *Share-based Payment*.

Benninga, SZ & Sarig, OH 1997, *Corporate finance: a valuation approach*, international edition, McGraw-Hill.

BlueScope Steel Limited 2005a, 'Directors' report', *Annual report 2004/05*, viewed 19 June 2006, <www.bluescopesteel.com>.

—2005b, *Interim financial report – 31 December 2005*, viewed 19 June 2006, <www.bluescope steel.com>.

FASB 2004, 'FASB issues final statement on accounting for share-based payment', news release 12/16/04, Financial Accounting Standards Board, viewed 21 June 2006, <www.fasb.org/news/nr121604_ebc.shtml>.

IASC Foundation 2005, International Financial Reporting Standard 2 *Share-based Payment*.

Macquarie Bank Limited 2005, *Annual review*, viewed 20 March 2006, <www.macquarie.com.au/au/about_macquarie/acrobat/annualreview2005.pdf>.

Parker, C 2005, 'Share-based payment – new and complex IFRS equivalent standard', GAAP update no. 3/2005, April, Accountnet Pty Ltd.

Saly, PJ, Jagannathan, R & Huddart, SJ 1999, 'Valuing the reload features of executive stock options', *Accounting Horizons*, vol. 13, no. 3, pp. 219–40.

CHAPTER 8
Income taxes

ACCOUNTING STANDARDS

International: IAS 12 *Income Taxes*
Australia: AASB 112 *Income Taxes*
New Zealand: NZ IAS 12 *Income Taxes*

CONCEPTS FOR REVIEW

Before studying this chapter, you should understand or, if necessary, revise:
- the principles of accrual accounting
- the concept of an asset in the IASB Framework
- the concept of a liability in the Framework
- the concept of a revenue in the Framework
- the concept of an expense in the Framework.

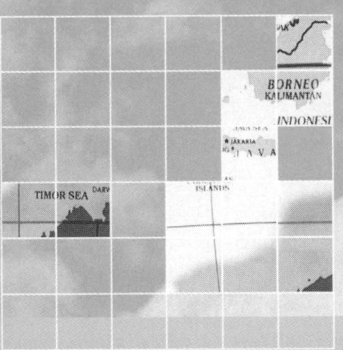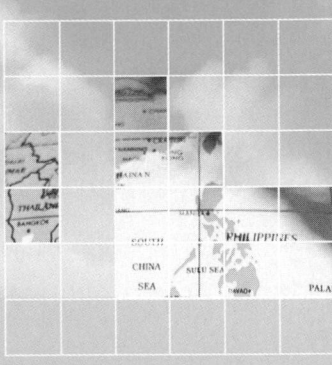

LEARNING OBJECTIVES

When you have studied this chapter, you should be able to:
1. understand the nature of income tax
2. understand differences in accounting treatments and taxation treatments for a range of transactions
3. explain the concept of tax-effect accounting
4. calculate and account for current taxation expense
5. understand the recognition requirements for current tax
6. account for the payment of tax
7. explain the nature of and accounting for tax losses
8. calculate and account for movements in deferred taxation accounts
9. understand and apply the recognition criteria for deferred tax items
10. account for changes in tax rates
11. account for amendments to prior year taxes
12. explain the presentation requirements of IAS 12
13. implement the disclosure requirements of IAS 12.

LO 1

8.1 The nature of income tax

Income taxes are levied by governments on income earned by individuals and entities in order to raise money to fund the provision of government services and infrastructure. The percentage payable and the determination of taxable income are governed by income tax legislation administered by a dedicated government body, such as the Australian Taxation Office. Tax payable is normally determined annually with the lodgement of a taxation document, although some jurisdictions may require payment by instalment, with estimates of tax payable being made on a periodic basis.

This chapter analyses the accounting standard IAS 12 *Income Taxes*. According to paragraph 1 of IAS 12, the standard applies in accounting for income taxes, including all domestic and foreign taxes based on taxable profits. It also applies to withholding taxes that are payable by a subsidiary, associate or joint venture on distributions to a reporting entity. The standard does not deal with methods of accounting for government grants or investment tax credits, but it does deal with accounting for tax effects arising in respect of such transactions.

At first glance, accounting for income tax appears to be a simple matter of calculating the liability owing, recognising the liability and expense, and recording the eventual payment of the amount outstanding. Such a simplistic approach applies only if accounting profit is the same amount as taxable profit and the respective profits have been determined by the same rules. Because this is generally not the case, accounting for income taxes can be a complicated exercise; hence the need for an accounting standard.

LO 2

8.2 Differences between accounting profit and taxable profit

Accounting profit is defined in IAS 12, paragraph 5, as 'profit or loss for a period before deducting tax expense', profit or loss being the excess (or deficiency) of revenues less expenses for that period. Such revenues and expenses would be determined and recognised in accordance with accounting standards and the conceptual Framework. Taxable profit is defined in the same paragraph as 'the profit for a period, determined in accordance with the rules established by the taxation authorities, upon which income taxes are payable'. Taxable profit is the excess of taxable income over taxation deductions allowable against that income. Thus, accounting profit and taxable profit – because they are determined by different principles and rules – are unlikely to be the same figure in any one period. Tax expense cannot be determined by simply multiplying the accounting profit by the applicable taxation rate. Instead, accounting for income taxes involves identifying and accounting for the differences between accounting profit and taxable profit. These differences arise from a number of common transactions and may be either permanent or temporary in nature.

8.2.1 Permanent differences

Permanent differences between accounting profit and taxable profit arise when the treatment of a transaction by taxation legislation and accounting standards is such that amounts recognised as part of accounting profit are never recognised as part of taxable profit, or vice versa. In some jurisdictions, for example, entities are allowed to deduct from their taxable income more than 100% of expenditure incurred on certain research and development activities undertaken during the taxation period. As a result of this extra deduction, taxable profit for the period is lower than accounting profit, and the extra amount is never recognised as an expense for accounting purposes. Other examples of permanent differences include income never subject to taxation, and expenditure incurred by an entity that will never be an allowable deduction. Where such differences exist, taxable profit will never equal accounting profit. No accounting requirements other than disclosure exist for these permanent differences (see section 8.15 of this chapter).

8.2.2 Temporary differences

Temporary differences between accounting profit and taxable profit arise when the period in which revenues and expenses are recognised for accounting purposes is different from the period in which such revenues and expenses are treated as taxable income and allowable deductions for tax purposes. Interest revenue recognised on an accrual basis, for example, may not be taxable income until it is received as cash. Similarly, insurance paid in advance may be tax-deductible when paid but is not recognised in calculating accounting profit as an expense until a later period. The key feature of these differences is that they are temporary, because sooner or later the amount of interest revenue will equal the amount of taxable interest income, and the amount deducted against taxable income for insurance will equal the insurance expense offset against accounting revenue. However, in any one individual accounting/taxation period, these amounts will differ when calculating accounting profit and taxable profit respectively.

Differences that result in the entity paying more tax in the future (for example, when interest is received) are known as taxable temporary differences. Differences that result in the entity recovering tax via additional deductible expenses in the future (for example, when accrued expenses are paid) are known as deductible temporary differences. The existence of such temporary differences means that income tax payable that is calculated on taxable profit will vary in the current period from that based on accounting profit, but tax payments will eventually catch up. This is demonstrated in illustrative example 8.1.

ILLUSTRATIVE EXAMPLE 8.1

Reversal of temporary difference

Assume that the accounting profit of Ludlow Ltd for the year ended 30 June 2007 was $150 000, including $5600 in interest revenue of which only $4000 had been received in cash. The company income tax rate is 30%.

If tax is not payable on interest until it has been received in cash, the company's taxable profit will differ from its accounting profit, and a taxable temporary difference will exist in respect of the $1600 interest receivable. If accounting profit for the next year is also $150 000 and the outstanding interest is received in August 2008, tax payable for the years ending 30 June 2007 and 2008 is calculated as follows:

	2007	2008
Accounting profit	$150 000	$150 000
Interest revenue	(1 600)	1 600
Taxable profit	$148 400	$151 600
Tax payable (30%)	44 520	45 480

Note that tax of $90 000, which is equal to 30% of $300 000 (being 2 × $150 000), is paid over the two years. The temporary difference created in 2007 is reversed in 2008. The same process occurs with all temporary differences although it may take a number of periods for a complete reversal to occur.

Appendix A to IAS 12 gives examples of temporary differences arising from different treatments of transactions for accounting and taxation purposes, some of which are listed below. These examples are not all-inclusive, so the relevant taxation legislation for specific jurisdictions should be consulted to determine if additional differences exist.

Circumstances that give rise to taxable temporary differences

Such circumstances include the following:

1. Interest revenue is received in arrears and is included in accounting profit on a time-apportionment basis but is included in taxable profit on a cash basis.
2. Revenue from the sale of goods is included in accounting profit when goods are delivered but is included in taxable profit only when cash is collected.
3. Depreciation of an asset is accelerated for tax purposes (the taxation depreciation rate is greater than the accounting rate).
4. Development costs are capitalised and amortised to the income statement but are deducted in determining taxable profit in the period in which they are incurred.
5. Prepaid expenses have already been deducted on a cash basis in determining the taxable profit of the current or previous periods.
6. Depreciation of an asset is not deductible for tax purposes and no deduction will be available for tax purposes when the asset is sold or scrapped (see section 8.9 of this chapter).
7. A borrower records a loan at the proceeds received (which equal the amount due at maturity) less transaction costs, and the carrying amount of the loan is subsequently increased by amortising the transaction costs to accounting profit. The transaction costs are deducted for tax purposes in the period when the loan was first recognised.
8. A loan payable is measured on initial recognition at the amount of the net proceeds (net of transaction costs), and the transaction costs are amortised to accounting profit over the life of the loan. These transaction costs are not deductible in determining the taxable profit of future, current or prior periods (see section 8.9).
9. The liability component of a compound financial instrument (such as a convertible bond) is measured at a discount to the amount repayable on maturity, after assigning a portion of the cash proceeds to the equity component (see chapter 6 of this book). The discount is not deductible in determining taxable profit or loss.
10. Financial assets or investment property are carried at fair value, which exceeds cost, but no equivalent adjustment is made for tax purposes.
11. An entity revalues property, plant and equipment, but no equivalent adjustment is made for tax purposes.
12. The carrying amount of an asset is increased to fair value in a business combination that is an acquisition, but no equivalent adjustment is made for tax purposes.
13. Impairment of goodwill is not deductible in determining taxable profit, and the cost of the goodwill would not be deductible on disposal of the business (see section 8.9).

Temporary differences arising in circumstances 7, 8, 9 and 12 are beyond the scope of this chapter. The tax treatment of temporary differences arising from fair-value accounting and revaluation to fair value (items 10 and 11) are discussed and illustrated in section 10.6.1 of this book.

Circumstances that give rise to deductible temporary differences

Such circumstances include the following:

1. Retirement benefit costs are deducted in determining accounting profit because service is provided by the employee, but are not deducted in determining taxable profit until the entity pays either retirement benefits or contributions to a fund. Similar temporary differences arise in relation to other accrued expenses – such as product warranties, leave entitlements and interest – which are deductible on a cash basis in determining taxable profit.

2. Accumulated depreciation of an asset in the financial statements is greater than the cumulative depreciation allowed up to the balance sheet date for tax purposes. That is, the accounting depreciation rate is greater than the allowable taxation depreciation rate.

3. The cost of inventories sold before the balance sheet date is deducted in determining accounting profit when goods or service are delivered, but is deducted in determining taxable profit only when cash is collected.

4. The net realisable value (see chapter 9 of this book) of an item of inventory, or the recoverable amount (see chapter 10) of an item of property, plant and equipment, is less than the previous carrying amount. The entity therefore reduces the carrying amount of the asset, but that reduction is ignored for tax purposes until the asset is sold.

5. Research costs (or organisation or other start-up costs) are recognised as an expense in determining accounting profit, but are not permitted as a deduction in determining taxable profit until a later period.

6. Income is deferred in the balance sheet but has already been included in taxable profit in current or prior periods (for example, subscriptions received in advance).

7. A government grant that is included in the balance sheet as deferred income will not be taxable in a future period (see section 8.9 of this chapter).

8. Financial assets or investment property are carried at fair value, which is less than cost, but no equivalent adjustment is made for tax purposes. (Temporary differences arising in these circumstances are beyond the scope of this chapter.)

In summary, income tax payable in any one period is affected by differences between items used to determine accounting profit and taxable profit. Some revenue items are not taxable, have already been taxed or will not be taxed until some future period/s. Some expense items are not deductible, have already been deducted or may be deducted in some future period/s. Additionally, extra deductions for which no expense will ever be incurred may be allowable under taxation legislation. The illustrative examples, exercises and problems in this chapter assume that the revenue from selling goods and services is taxable irrespective of whether cash has been received for the sale, and that the cost of goods sold is an allowable deduction irrespective of whether cash has been paid to acquire those goods.

LO 3

8.3   Accounting for income taxes

As the objective paragraph of IAS 12 points out:

> The principal issue in accounting for income taxes is how to account for the current and future tax consequences of:
> (a) the future recovery (settlement) of the carrying amount of assets (liabilities) that are recognised in an entity's balance sheet; and
> (b) transactions and other events of the current period that are recognised in an entity's financial statements.

IAS 12 requires the tax consequences of transactions and other events to be accounted for in the same manner and the same period as the transactions themselves. Thus, if a transaction is recognised in profit or loss for the period, so too is the related tax payable or tax benefit. Similarly, if a transaction is adjusted directly to equity, so too is the related tax effect. Differing accounting and taxation rules (as discussed in section 8.2) mean that the actual payment (deduction) of tax relating to revenue (expense) items may take place in both current and/or future accounting periods but IAS 12, paragraph 58, requires that the total income tax expense relating to transactions is recorded in the current year irrespective of when it will be paid or deducted.

To illustrate: an entity recognises interest revenue of $21 000 for the year ended 30 June 2008. Of this amount, $15 000 has been received in cash and a receivable asset has been raised for the remaining $6000. Tax legislation regards interest revenue as taxable only when it has been received. Therefore, the entity will pay tax of $4500 ($15 000 × 30%) in the current year and tax of $1800 ($6000 × 30%) in the following year when the $6000 receivable is paid. If the entity were to record only the current tax payable amount as income tax expense, the profit for the year would be overstated by $1800 given that $6300 of the interest revenue recognised for the year (not $4500) will eventually be paid to the taxation authorities and will not be available for use by the entity. To ensure that the profit after-tax figure for the year is both relevant and reliable, IAS 12 requires the entity to record an income tax expense of $6300 for the current year in respect to the interest revenue. This tax is payable via a current liability amount of $4500 and a deferred (future) liability of $1800.

The need to recognise both current and future tax consequences of current year transactions means that each transaction has two tax effects:

1. tax payable on profit earned for the year may be reduced or increased because the transaction is not taxable or deductible in the current year
2. future tax payable may be reduced or increased when that transaction becomes taxable or deductible.

If only current tax payable is recorded as an expense, then the profit for the current year will be understated or overstated by the amount of tax or benefit to be paid or received in future years. Similarly, in the years that the tax or benefit on these transactions is paid or received, income tax expense will include amounts relating to prior periods and therefore be understated or overstated. As IAS 12 requires income tax expense to reflect all tax effects of transactions entered into during the year regardless of when the effects occur, two calculations are required at balance date:

- the calculation of current tax liability, which determines the amount of tax payable for the period
- the calculation of movements in deferred tax effects relating to assets and liabilities recognised in the balance sheet, which determines the net effect of deferred taxes and deductions arising from transactions during the year.

Acknowledging the current and future tax consequences of all items recognised in the balance sheet (subject to certain exceptions) should make the information about the tax implications of an entity's operations and financial position more relevant and reliable.

LO 4   8.4 Calculation of current tax

Current tax is the recognition of taxes payable to the taxation authorities in respect of a particular period. The current tax calculation involves identifying differences between accounting revenues and taxable income, and between accounting expenses and allowable deductions, for transactions during the year, as well as reversing temporary differences from prior years that occur in the current period. Accounting profit for the period is adjusted by these differences to calculate taxable profit, which is then multiplied by the current tax rate to determine current tax payable.

When selecting the tax rate to apply, the requirements of IAS 12, paragraph 46, must be considered. This paragraph states:

> Current tax liabilities (assets) for the current and prior periods shall be measured at the amount expected to be paid to (recovered from) the taxation authorities, using the tax rates (and tax laws) that have been enacted or substantively enacted by the balance sheet date.

Therefore, if a tax rate has changed — or, in some jurisdictions, if a change has been announced — the rate applicable to the taxable profit for the period must be applied.

Identifying permanent and temporary differences in the current year's profit is a relatively simple exercise. All revenues and expenses are reviewed for amounts that are not taxable or deductible. Identifying reversals of prior year temporary differences may require referring back to prior year worksheets, transactions posted to asset and liability accounts during the current year, or reconstructions of ledger accounts. (The latter method is used in this chapter.) Such reversals include, where applicable, accrued expenses that have been paid and are now deductible, bad debts written off and now deductible, accrued revenue that has been received and is now taxable, and prepaid expenses deducted in a prior period but now included in accounting profit.

Once the differences have been isolated, there are two ways that the current tax could be determined: (1) the net differences could be adjusted against accounting profit to derive taxable profit, or (2) the gross amounts of items with differences could be added back or deducted against accounting profit. (The latter method is adopted in this chapter.) A worksheet is used to perform this reconciliation between accounting profit and taxable profit using the following formula:

> Accounting profit (loss)
>   + (–) accounting expenses not deductible for tax
>   + (–) accounting expenses where the amount differs from deductible amounts
>   + (–) taxable income where the amount differs from accounting revenue
>   – (+) accounting revenues not subject to taxation
>   – (+) accounting revenue where the amount differs from taxable income
>   – (+) deductible amounts where the amount differs from accounting expense
> = taxable profit

The current tax rate is then applied to taxable profit to derive the current tax payable.

ILLUSTRATIVE EXAMPLE 8.2

Determination of current tax worksheet

Bristol Ltd's accounting profit for the year ended 30 June 2007 was $250 450. Included in this profit were the following items of revenue and expense:

Amortisation – development project	$30 000
Impairment of goodwill expense	7 000
Depreciation – equipment (15%)	40 000
Entertainment expense	12 450
Insurance expense	24 000
Doubtful debts expense	14 000
Proceeds on sale of equipment	30 000
Carrying amount of equipment sold	36 667
Rent revenue	25 000
Annual leave expense	54 000

→

At 30 June 2007, the company's draft balance sheet showed the following balances:

	30 June 2007	30 June 2006
Assets		
Cash	$ 55 000	$ 65 000
Accounts receivable	295 000	277 000
Allowance for doubtful debts	(16 000)	(18 000)
Inventories	162 000	185 000
Prepaid insurance	30 000	25 000
Rent receivable	3 500	5 500
Development project	120 000	–
Accumulated amortisation	(30 000)	–
Equipment	200 000	266 667
Accumulated depreciation	(90 000)	(80 000)
Goodwill	35 000	35 000
Accumulated impairment expense	(14 000)	(7 000)
Deferred tax asset	?	24 900
Liabilities		
Accounts payable	310 500	294 000
Provision for annual leave	61 000	65 000
Mortgage loan	100 000	150 000
Deferred tax liability	?	57 150
Current tax liability	?	12 500

Additional information
1. Taxation legislation allows Bristol Ltd to deduct 125% of the $120 000 spent on development during the year.
2. Bristol Ltd has capitalised development expenditure relating to a filter project and amortises the balance over the period of expected benefit (four years).
3. The taxation depreciation rate for equipment is 20%.
4. The equipment sold on 30 June 2007 cost $66 667 when it was purchased three years ago.
5. Neither entertainment expenditure nor goodwill impairment expense is deductible for taxation purposes.
6. The company income tax rate is 30%.

Calculation of current tax payable
Before completing the worksheet, all differences between accounting and taxation figures must be identified:

1. Development project
There are two differences here: a permanent difference arising from the extra 25% deduction allowed by tax legislation, and a temporary difference arising from the treatment of the development costs. For accounting purposes, the $120 000 has been capitalised and will be amortised over four years; for tax purposes, the entire expenditure is deductible in the current year. The tax deduction for development is therefore: $150 000 (being $120 000 + [25% × $120 000]).

→

2. Impairment of goodwill expense

No deduction is allowed for impairment expense, so the taxation deduction is nil. Paragraph 21 of IAS 12 does not permit the recognition of the deferred tax liability arising from the taxable temporary difference created (see section 8.9 of this chapter). Therefore, a permanent difference exists.

3. Depreciation expense – equipment

Because equipment is being depreciated at a faster rate for taxation purposes, a temporary taxable difference will exist. The amount of depreciation deductible is $53 333.40 (being $266 667 × 20%).

4. Entertainment expense

No deduction is allowed for entertainment expenditure, so the taxation deduction is nil and there is a permanent difference between accounting profit and taxable profit.

5. Insurance expense

Insurance expenditure is deductible when incurred. The existence of a prepaid insurance asset account on the balance sheet indicates that the insurance payment and insurance expense figures are different. It is therefore necessary to reconstruct the asset account to identify if any part of the expense has already been deducted for taxation purposes. This is done as follows:

Prepaid insurance			
Opening balance	$25 000	Closing balance	$30 000
Insurance paid	29 000	Insurance expense	24 000
	54 000		54 000

The insurance paid figure of $29 000 represents the deduction allowable in determining taxable profit. The expense figure of $24 000 shows that the payment made includes $5000 for insurance cover for the next accounting period. When this amount is expensed, no deduction will be available against taxable profit.

6. Allowance for doubtful debts

If, under taxation legislation, no deduction is allowed for bad debts until they have been written off, the taxation amount for doubtful debts will be nil. The draft balance sheet shows that an allowance was raised in the previous year, so any debts written off against that allowance are deductible in the current year. To determine the amount (if any) of that write-off, the ledger account is reconstructed as follows:

Allowance for doubtful debts			
Closing balance	$16 000	Opening balance	$18 000
Bad debts written off	16 000	Doubtful debts expense	14 000
	32 000		32 000

The allowable deduction for bad debts written off is therefore $16 000.

7. Proceeds on sale of equipment

All this revenue is taxable, so there is no permanent or temporary difference.

8. Carrying amount of equipment sold

The gain or loss on the sale of equipment is different for accounting and taxation purposes, and is calculated as follows:

	Accounting	Taxation
Cost	$66 667	$66 667
Accumulated depreciation	30 000	40 000
Carrying amount	36 667	26 667
Proceeds	30 000	30 000
Gain (loss)	$ (6 667)	$ 3 333

Because the sales proceeds are recognised for both accounting and taxation purposes, the difference in the loss or gain on sale is caused by the two methods recognising different carrying amounts for the asset sold. This difference is caused by the use of different depreciation rates. When preparing the current tax worksheet, adjusting for the different carrying amounts effectively adjusts for the difference in the gain or loss on sale.

9. Rent revenue

Rent revenue is taxable when received. The presence on the balance sheet of a rent receivable asset indicates that part of the revenue has not yet been received as cash and is not taxable in the current year. A temporary difference therefore exists in respect of rent, as demonstrated by reconstructing the ledger account:

Rent receivable			
Opening balance	$ 5 500	Closing balance	$ 3 500
Rent revenue	25 000	Cash received	27 000
	30 500		30 500

In this instance, the cash received figure represents rent received for two different accounting periods: $5500 outstanding at the end of the prior year, and $21 500 for the current year. Thus, the taxable amount combines the reversal of last year's temporary difference and the tax payable on the current year's income. A temporary difference still exists for the $3500 rent for this year not yet received in cash.

10. Annual leave expense

Annual leave is deductible when paid in cash. The provision for annual leave indicates the existence of unpaid leave and therefore a taxation temporary difference. This is demonstrated by reconstructing the ledger account:

Provision for annual leave			
Closing balance	$ 61 000	Opening balance	$ 65 000
Leave paid	58 000	Leave expense	54 000
	119 000		119 000

The reconstruction reveals a payment of $58 000, which is deductible in the current year and represents a partial reversal of the temporary difference related to the opening balance. As none of the current year expense has been paid, no deduction is available this year and a further temporary difference is created.

This chapter assumes that sales revenue and cost of goods sold are taxable/deductible even when not received/paid in cash, so there are no differences with respect to the accounts receivable or accounts payable balances. If different assumptions applied, then the amounts of cash received for sales and cash paid for inventory would need to be determined in order to calculate the current tax payable.

Figure 8.1 contains the current worksheet used to calculate the current tax liability for Bristol Ltd.

Bristol Ltd Current tax worksheet for the year ended 30 June 2007		
Accounting profit		$250 450
Add:		
Amortisation of development expenditure	$ 30 000	
Impairment of goodwill expense	7 000	
Depreciation expense	40 000	
Entertainment expense	12 450	
Insurance expense	24 000	
Doubtful debts expense	14 000	
Carrying amount of equipment sold (accounting)	36 667	
Annual leave expense	54 000	
Rent received (tax)	27 000	245 117
		495 567
Deduct:		
Rent revenue (accounting)	25 000	
Carrying amount of equipment sold (tax)	26 667	
Bad debts written off	16 000	
Insurance paid	29 000	
Development costs paid	150 000	
Annual leave paid	58 000	
Depreciation of equipment for tax	53 333	(358 000)
Taxable profit		137 567
Current liability @ 30%		$ 41 270

FIGURE 8.1   Completed current tax worksheet for Bristol Ltd

LO 5

8.5 Recognition of current tax

Paragraph 12 of IAS 12 states:

> Current tax for current and prior periods shall, to the extent unpaid, be recognised as a liability. If the amount already paid in respect of current and prior periods exceeds the amount due for those periods, the excess shall be recognised as an asset.

Additionally, paragraph 58 of the standard requires current tax to be recognised as income or an expense and included in the profit or loss for the period, except to the extent that the tax relates to a transaction recognised directly in equity or to a business combination. Therefore, the following journal entry is required to recognise the current tax payable for Bristol Ltd at 30 June 2007:

30 June 2007			
Income tax expense (current)	Dr	41 270	
Current tax liability	Cr		41 270
(Recognition of current tax liability)			

8.6 Payment of tax

Taxation legislation may require taxation debts to be paid annually upon lodgement of a taxation return or at some specified time after lodgement (such as on receipt of an assessment notice, or at a set date or time). Alternatively, the taxation debt may be paid by instalment throughout the taxation year. In some jurisdictions, payments in advance relating to next year's estimated taxable profit may be required. Where one annual payment is required, the entry is:

Current tax liability	Dr	41 270	
Cash	Cr		41 270
(Payment of current liability)			

If payment by instalment is required, the process is a little more complicated. To pay by instalment, an estimate of taxable profit needs to be made; hence the reference in paragraph 12 of IAS 12 to amounts paid in excess of the amount due. To illustrate the process of payment by instalment, assume that Bristol Ltd (from illustrative example 8.2) has to pay tax quarterly and has paid the following amounts for the first three quarters of the 2006–07 taxation year:

28 October 2006	$ 9 420
28 January 2007	10 380
28 April 2007	10 750

The journal entry to record the first payment is:

Income tax expense	Dr	9 420	
Cash	Cr		9 420
(Payment of first quarterly taxation instalment)			

Similar entries are passed at 28 January 2007 and 28 April 2007. At 30 June 2007, because the tax liability has been partially paid, an adjustment is required on the current tax worksheet to determine the balance of tax owing in relation to the 2006–07 year (see next page).

Bristol Ltd Current tax worksheet (extract) for the year ended 30 June 2007	
Taxable profit	$137 567
Tax payable @ 30%	41 270
Less Tax already paid ($9420 + $10 380 + $10 750)	(30 550)
Current tax liability	10 720

The adjusting journal entry becomes:

30 June 2007			
Income tax expense (current)	Dr	10 720	
Current tax liability	Cr		10 720
(Recognitiion of current tax liability)			

LO 7

8.7 Tax losses

Tax losses are created when allowable deductions exceed taxable income. IAS 12 envisages three possible treatments for tax losses: they may be carried forward, carried back, or simply lost. Where taxation legislation allows tax losses to be carried forward and deducted against future taxable profits, the carry-forward may be either indefinite or for a limited number of years. Other restrictions – such as requiring losses to be deducted against non-taxable income on recoupment – may also apply. Carry-forward tax losses create a deductible temporary difference and therefore a deferred tax asset in that the company will pay less tax on future taxable profits. The recognition of a deferred tax asset for tax losses is discussed in detail in section 8.9.2 of this chapter.

ILLUSTRATIVE EXAMPLE 8.3

Creation and recoupment of carry-forward tax losses

The following information relates to Canterbury Ltd for the year ended 30 June 2008:

Accounting loss	$ 7 600
Depreciation expense	14 700
Depreciation deductible for tax	20 300
Entertainment expense (not tax-deductible)	10 000
Income tax rate	30%

→

The calculation of the tax loss appears below:

Canterbury Ltd Current tax worksheet (extract) for the year ended 30 June 2008	
Accounting loss	$ (7 600)
Add:	
Depreciation expense	14 700
Entertainment expense	10 000
	17 100
Deduct:	
Depreciation deduction	(20 300)
Tax loss	(3 200)
Deferred tax asset @ 30%	$ 960

Assuming that recognition criteria are met, the adjusting journal entry is:

30 June 2008			
Deferred tax asset (tax losses)	Dr	960	
Income tax income	Cr		960
(Recognition of deferred tax asset from tax loss)			

If Canterbury Ltd then makes a taxable profit of $23 600 for the year ending 30 June 2009, the loss is recouped as follows:

Canterbury Ltd Current tax worksheet (extract) for the year ended 30 June 2009	
Taxable profit before tax loss	$23 600
Tax loss recouped	(3 200)
Taxable profit	20 400
Current tax liability @ 30%	$ 6 120

The adjusting journal entry is:

30 June 2009			
Income tax expense (current)	Dr	7 080	
Deferred tax asset (tax losses)	Cr		960
Current tax liability	Cr		6 120
(Recognition of current tax liability and reversal of deferred tax asset from tax loss)			

In jurisdictions where taxation legislation allows the current year's tax losses to be carried back, paragraph 13 of IAS 12 requires that: 'The benefit relating to a tax loss that can be carried back to recover current tax of a previous period shall be recognised as an asset'. Paragraph 14 further states that the recognition should take place in the period of the tax loss, because 'it is probable that the benefit will flow to the entity and the benefit can be reliably measured'.

Using the facts from illustrative example 8.3, the adjusting journal entry becomes:

30 June 2008			
Current tax asset	Dr	960	
Income tax expense	Cr		960
(Recognition of tax receivable on offset of tax loss against prior year taxable profit)			

LO 8

8.8 Calculation of deferred tax

As already explained, IAS 12 adopts the philosophy that the tax consequences of transactions that occur during a period should be recognised in income tax expense for that period. Where a transaction has two effects, both have to be recognised. The existence of temporary differences between accounting profit and taxable profit was identified earlier in the chapter. These temporary differences result in the carrying amounts of an entity's assets and liabilities being different from the amounts that would arise if a balance sheet was prepared for the taxation authority. The latter are referred to as the tax base of an entity's assets and liabilities. At balance date, a comparison of an entity's carrying amounts of assets and liabilities and their tax bases will reveal the temporary differences that exist, and adjustments will then be made to deferred assets and liabilities. (The reference to 'deferred' tax adjustments comes from the fact that assets and liabilities reflect future inflows and outflows to an entity. The deferred tax balances are related to these future flows, and hence are deferred to the future rather than affecting current tax.) For assets such as goodwill and entertainment costs payable, differences between their tax bases and carrying amounts may be caused by permanent differences. Such differences will not give rise to deferred tax adjustments.

The following steps are required to calculate deferred tax:

1. Determine the carrying amounts of items recognised on the balance sheet and their tax bases.
2. Determine the assessable and deductible temporary differences relating to the future tax consequences of items recognised at the end of the current period.
3. Calculate and recognise the deferred tax assets and liabilities arising from these temporary differences after taking into account any relevant recognition exceptions (see section 8.8.5 of this chapter) and offset considerations (see section 8.14.1).
4. Recognise the net movement in deferred tax assets and liabilities during the period as deferred tax expense or income in the profit or loss (unless an accounting standard requires recognition directly in equity or as part of a business combination).

The first three steps are carried out on a worksheet. The final step requires an adjusting journal entry.

8.8.1 Determining carrying amounts

Carrying amounts are asset and liability balances net of valuation allowances, accumulated depreciation, amortisation and impairment losses (for example, accounts receivable less allowance for doubtful debts).

8.8.2 ## Determining tax bases

Tax bases need to be calculated for assets and liabilities.

Tax bases of assets

The economic benefits embodied in an asset are normally taxable when recovered by an entity through the use or sale of that asset. The entity may then be able to deduct all or part of the cost or carrying amount of the asset against those taxable amounts when determining taxable profits.

Paragraph 7 of IAS 12 describes the tax base of an asset as:

> the amount that will be deductible for tax purposes against any taxable economic benefits that will flow to an entity when it recovers the carrying amount of the asset. If those economic benefits will not be taxable, the tax base of the asset is equal to its carrying amount.

The following formula can be applied to derive the tax base from the carrying amount of the asset:

Carrying amount – Future taxable amounts + Future deductible amounts = Tax base

Figure 8.2 contains examples of the calculation of tax bases for assets.

	Carrying amount	Future taxable amounts*	Future deductible amounts	Tax base
Prepayments $3000: fully deductible for tax when paid	$ 3 000	$(3 000)	$ 0	$ 0
Trade receivables less $2000 allowance for doubtful debts: sales revenue is already included in taxable profit	50 000	0	2 000	52 000
Plant and equipment costing $10 000 has a carrying value of $5400: accumulated depreciation at tax rates is $6500	5 400	(5 400)	3 500**	3 500
Loan receivable $25 000: loan repayment will have no tax consequences	25 000	0	0	25 000
Interest receivable $1000: recognised as revenue but not taxable until received	1 000	(1 000)	0	0

*Future taxable amounts are equal to carrying amounts unless economic benefits have already been included in taxable profit.
**The deductible amount represents the original cost of the asset less the accumulated depreciation based on taxation depreciation rates (being $10 000 – 6500 = 3500).

FIGURE 8.2 Calculation of the tax base of assets

The formula for calculating the tax base of an asset can be rearranged as follows:

Carrying amount – Tax base = Future taxable amounts – Future deductible amounts

In other words, a temporary difference (the difference between the carrying amount and the tax base) occurs when the future taxable amount is different from the future deductible amount.

Figure 8.2 illustrates the following situations:
- Where the future benefits are taxable, the carrying amount equals the future taxable amount. Hence, the tax base equals the future deductible amount. This can be seen in figure 8.2 for prepayments, plant and equipment, and interest receivable.

- Where there are no future taxable amounts, generally the deductible amount is zero and the tax base equals the carrying amount. In figure 8.2, this applies to the loan receivable. An exception is trade receivables where, although the future taxable amount is zero, the future deductible amount is not zero because of the existence of doubtful debts. In this case, the tax base equals the sum of the carrying amount and the future deductible amount.

Tax bases of liabilities

Liabilities, other than those relating to unearned revenue, do not create taxable amounts. Instead, settlement gives rise to deductible items.

Paragraph 8 of IAS 12 describes the tax base of a liability as:

> its carrying amount, less any amount that will be deductible for tax purposes in respect of that liability in future periods. In the case of revenue received in advance, the tax base of the resulting liability is its carrying amount, less any amount of the revenue that will not be taxable in future periods.

The following formula can be applied to derive the tax base from the carrying amount of the liability:

$$\text{Carrying amount} + \text{Future taxable amounts} - \text{Future deductible amounts} = \text{Tax base}$$

Figure 8.3 contains examples of the calculation of tax base for liabilities.

	Carrying amount	Future taxable amounts	Future deductible amounts	Tax base
Provision for annual leave $3900: not deductible for tax until paid	$ 3 900	$ 0	$(3 900)	$ 0
Trade payables $34 000: expense already deducted from taxable income	34 000	0	0	34 000
Subscription revenue received in advance $500: taxed when received	500	(500)	0	0
Loan payable $20 000: loan repayment will have no tax consequences	20 000	0	0	20 000
Accrued expenses $6700: deductible when paid in cash	6 700	0	(6 700)	0
Accrued penalties $700: not tax-deductible	700	0	0	700

FIGURE 8.3 Calculation of the tax base of liabilities

Figure 8.3 illustrates two situations:
- Where the carrying amount equals the future deductible amount, the tax base is zero. This applies to provisions for annual leave and accrued expenses.
- Where there is no future deductible amount, the carrying amount equals the tax base. This applies to trade payables and the loan payable.

Some items may have a tax base but are not recognised as assets and liabilities in the balance sheet. Paragraph 9 of IAS 12 provides the example of research costs that are recognised as an expense in determining accounting profit in the period in which they are incurred but are not allowed as a deduction in determining taxable profit until a later period. Additionally, under paragraph 52 the manner in which an asset/liability is recovered/settled may affect the tax base of that asset/liability in some jurisdictions.

8.8.3 Calculating temporary differences

When the carrying amount of an asset or liability is different from its tax base, a temporary difference exists. Temporary differences effectively represent the expected net future taxable amounts arising from the recovery of assets and the settlement of liabilities at their carrying amounts. Therefore, a temporary difference cannot exist where there are no future tax consequences from the realisation or settlement of an asset or liability at its carrying value.

Taxable temporary differences

A taxable temporary difference exists when the future taxable amount of an asset or liability exceeds any future deductible amounts. This is demonstrated in illustrative example 8.4.

ILLUSTRATIVE EXAMPLE 8.4

Calculation of a taxable temporary difference

An asset, which cost 150, has an accumulated depreciation of 50.
Accumulated depreciation for tax purposes is 90 and the tax rate is 25%.

Carrying amount	= 100
Future taxable amount	= 100
Future deductible amount	= 60
Tax base	= 100 − 100 + 60
	= 60 (= 150 cost less 90 tax depreciation)

Because the future taxable amount is greater than the future deductible amount, a temporary tax difference exists. In other words, the expectation is that the entity will pay income taxes in the future, when it recovers the carrying amount of the asset, because it expects to earn 100 but receive a tax deduction of 60. The entity has a liability to pay tax on that extra 40. As the payment occurs in the future, the liability is referred to as a 'deferred tax liability'.

Source: Adapted from IAS 12, paragraph 16.

Deductible temporary differences

A deductible temporary difference exists when the future taxable amount of an asset or liability is less than any future deductible amounts. This is demonstrated in illustrative example 8.5.

ILLUSTRATIVE EXAMPLE 8.5

Calculation of a deductible temporary difference

An entity recognises a liability of 100 for accrued product warranty costs. For tax purposes, the product warranty costs will not be deductible until the entity pays claims. The tax rate is 25%.

→

Carrying amount	= 100
Future taxable amount	= 0
Future deductible amount	= 100
Tax base	= 100 + 0 − 100
	= 0

As the future deductible amount is greater than the future taxable amount, a deductible temporary difference exists. In other words, in settling the liability for its carrying amount, the entity will reduce its future tax profits and hence its future tax payments. The entity then has an expected benefit relating to the future tax deduction. As the benefits are to be received in the future, the asset raised is referred to as a 'deferred tax asset'.

Source: Adapted from IAS 12, paragraph 25.

8.8.4   Calculating deferred tax liabilities and deferred tax assets

Paragraphs 15 and 24 of IAS 12 require (with some exceptions) that a deferred tax liability and a deferred tax asset be recognised for all taxable temporary differences and all deductible temporary differences, and that a total be determined for taxable temporary differences and for deductible temporary differences. An appropriate tax rate can then be applied to these totals to derive the balance of deferred tax liability and deferred tax asset at the end of the period. Paragraph 47 of the standard specifies that:

> Deferred tax assets and liabilities shall be measured at the tax rates that are expected to apply to the period when the asset is realised or the liability settled, based on tax rates (and tax laws) that have been enacted or substantively enacted by the balance sheet date.

Thus, if the tax rate is currently 30% but will rise to 32% in the next reporting period, deferred amounts should be measured at 32%. Should a change be enacted (or substantively enacted) between reporting date and the time of completion of the financial statements, no adjustment needs to be made to the tax balances recognised. However, disclosure of any material impacts should be made by note in compliance with IAS 10 *Events after the Balance Sheet Date*.

Different tax rates may be required when temporary differences are expected to reverse in different periods and a change of tax rate is probable, or when temporary differences relate to different taxation jurisdictions. Additionally, consideration should be given to the manner in which an asset/liability is recovered/settled in jurisdictions where the manner of recovery/settlement determines the applicable tax rate (IAS 12, para. 52).

Before determining the amounts of deferred tax liabilities and deferred tax assets, consideration must be given to the recognition criteria mandated by the accounting standard. (See section 8.9 of this chapter.)

8.8.5   Excluded differences

Paragraphs 15 and 24 of IAS 12 mandate the following exceptions to the requirement that a deferred tax liability and a deferred tax asset (subject to probability assessment) be recognised for all taxable and deductible temporary differences:

(a) the initial recognition of goodwill; or
(b) goodwill for which amortisation is not deductible for tax purposes
(c) the initial recognition of an asset or liability in a transaction which:
   (i) is not a business combination; and
   (ii) at the time of the transaction, affects neither accounting profit nor taxable profit (tax loss).

Goodwill

Goodwill is the excess of the cost of the business combination over the acquirer's interest in the net fair value of the identifiable assets, liabilities and contingent liabilities (see chapter 12). In jurisdictions where impairment of goodwill is not deductible, a taxable temporary difference is created because the tax base of goodwill is always nil. IAS 12 does not permit the recognition of the deferred tax liability relating to goodwill, because goodwill is a residual amount and recognising the deferred tax amount would increase the carrying amount of goodwill (IAS 12, para. 21). In jurisdictions where goodwill can be 'depreciated' for tax purposes, a deferred tax liability may be recognised if the carrying amount of the asset remains unimpaired.

Initial recognition of an asset or liability

A temporary difference may arise on the initial recognition of an asset or liability if the carrying amount is not equal to the tax base (for example, if part or all of the cost of an asset is not deductible for tax purposes). The accounting treatment of the temporary difference depends on the nature of the transaction that created the asset or liability.

When deferred tax arises on the acquisition of an entity or business, and it has not been recognised by the acquiring or acquired entity before the acquisition, it must be recognised and taken into account in measuring the amount of goodwill or excess. Deferred tax balances are recognised if they arise from temporary differences related to assets and liabilities that have affected pre-tax accounting profit or taxable profit at or before the time of initial recognition. This most commonly occurs when items are recognised for accounting and tax purposes in different reporting periods. Examples include prepayments, deferred income and accrued expenses.

If the exception provided in paragraph 15 of IAS 12 did not exist, an entity would be allowed to recognise the deferred tax liability or asset, and adjust the carrying amount of the asset or liability by the same amount, for a transaction that was not a business combination and affected neither accounting nor taxable profits. However, the standard setters considered that: 'Such adjustments would make the financial statements less transparent' (IAS 12, para. 22(c)), and so prohibited the recognition of such deferred tax amounts. Fortunately, such items are rare and would occur only where assets have a taxable value deemed by tax laws to be different from the cost of the asset. Such deferred amounts include:

- motor vehicles acquired where the total cost is in excess of a depreciation cost limit set by tax legislation
- the 'roll over' of the tax base of assets to an acquiring entity so that future tax deductions are limited to an amount that is different from the consideration paid
- a non-taxable government grant related to an asset that is deducted from the carrying amount of the asset, but for tax purposes is not deducted from the asset's depreciable amount (its tax base).

In addition to prohibiting the recognition of deferred tax amounts on the initial recognition of the asset or liability, IAS 12 also prohibits recognition of any subsequent changes to the unrecognised deferred tax liability or asset as the asset is depreciated (para. 22(c)).

8.8.6 Deferred tax worksheet

A deferred tax worksheet is shown in illustrative example 8.6. The purpose of the deferred tax worksheet is to calculate the movements in the deferred tax asset and the deferred tax liability accounts during the current period. Determining the temporary differences relating to assets and liabilities allows the closing balances of the deferred tax accounts to be calculated. A consideration of the beginning balances and movements during the year allows the calculation of the adjustments required to achieve those closing balances. All assets and liabilities may be included in the worksheet; alternatively, only those expected to have different accounting and tax bases could be shown.

ILLUSTRATIVE EXAMPLE 8.6

Deferred tax worksheet

Using the information provided in illustrative example 8.2 on pages 295–6, the deferred tax worksheet for Bristol Ltd is shown in figure 8.4.

Bristol Ltd Deferred tax worksheet as at 30 June 2007						
	Carrying amount	Future taxable amount	Future deductible amount	Tax base	Taxable temporary differences	Deductible temporary differences
	$	$	$	$	$	$
Relevant assets						
Receivables[1]	279 000	0	16 000	295 000		16 000
Prepaid insurance[2]	30 000	(30 000)	0	0	30 000	
Rent receivable[3]	3 500	(3 500)	0	0	3 500	
Development project[4]	90 000	(90 000)	0	0	90 000	
Equipment[5]	110 000	(110 000)	80 000	80 000	30 000	
Goodwill[6]	21 000	(21 000)	0	0	21 000	
Relevant liabilities						
Provision for annual leave[7]	61 000	0	(61 000)	0		61 000
Total temporary differences					174 500	77 000
Excluded differences[8]					(21 000)	–
Temporary differences					153 500	77 000
Deferred tax liability[9]					46 050	
Deferred tax asset[9]						23 100
Beginning balances[10]					(17 150)	(24 900)
Movement during year[11]						
Adjustment[10]					28 900 Cr	(1 800) Cr

FIGURE 8.4 Deferred tax worksheet for Bristol Ltd

1. The carrying amount of receivables $279 000 ($295 000 – 16 000) represents the cash that the company expects to receive after allowing for any doubtful debts. Tax on this amount has already been paid via sales revenue recognised in the current year, so the future taxable amount is zero. The allowance for doubtful debts raised as an expense in the current year is not deductible against taxable profit until the

debts actually go 'bad' and are written out of the accounts receivable balance. Thus, there is a future deduction of $5000 available. The tax base for receivables is $283 000, being the total of all debts outstanding at 30 June 2007 (doubtful or otherwise). Because the future deductible amount is greater than the future taxable amount, a deductible temporary difference of $5000 exists in respect of receivables.

2. The prepaid insurance asset represents insurance monies that have been paid for insurance cover in the year ended 30 June 2008. The recovery of these benefits results in the flow of taxable economic benefits to Bristol Ltd, giving a future taxable amount of $30 000. This amount was paid in the year ended 30 June 2007 and was allowed as a deduction against the taxable profit for that year. This means that no deduction is available when the $30 000 is expensed in the year ended 30 June 2008, giving a tax base for the asset of $0. As the future taxable amount exceeds the future deductible amount, a taxable temporary difference of $30 000 exists in respect of prepaid insurance.

3. The rent receivable asset represents monies to be received relating to revenue earned in the year ended 30 June 2007. The recovery of these benefits results in the flow of taxable economic benefits to Bristol Ltd. Hence, a future taxable amount of $3500 exists. As this is a revenue item, no future deduction is available. The tax base is $0 because the cash received affects taxable profit in the year of receipt. As the future taxable amount exceeds the future deductible amount, a taxable temporary difference of $3500 exists in respect of the rent receivable.

4. The development project asset represents the future economic benefits expected to arise from development work undertaken in the current year. When those benefits are received, they are taxable. The total expenditure on development was deducted from taxable profit in the current year, so no future deduction is available. The tax base is $0 as the cash paid has already reduced taxable profit in the current year. As the future taxable amount exceeds the future deductible amount, a taxable temporary difference of $90 000 exists in respect of the development project.

5. The carrying amount of equipment represents the future economic benefits expected to be received from that asset over the remainder of its useful life, $110 000 ($200 000 − $90 000). When those benefits are received, they are taxable. Bristol Ltd will be able to claim a deduction against those taxable benefits, but only to the extent of the carrying amount of the asset for taxation purposes. As the depreciation rate for tax purposes is greater than the accounting rate, the future deduction is only $80 000, being the original cost of $200 000 less $120 000 (that is, three years accumulated depreciation at 20% per annum). As the future taxable amount exceeds the future deductible amount, a taxable temporary difference of $30 000 exists in respect of equipment.

6. The carrying amount of goodwill represents the future economic benefits expected to be received. Those benefits are taxable when received but, unlike equipment, no deduction against the benefits is available. The tax base of goodwill is $0 as taxation law does not allow a deduction for any amounts paid to acquire goodwill. As the future taxable amount exceeds the future deductible amount, a taxable temporary difference of $21 000 exists in respect of goodwill.

→

7. The provision for annual leave represents leave accrued by employees as at balance date. As the leave represents future payments, there is no future taxable amount. When those payments are made, they are fully deductible against taxable profit. The tax base at 30 June 2007 is $0 because leave payments are only deductible in the year of payment. As the future deductible amount exceeds the future taxable amount, a deductible temporary difference of $61 000 exists in respect of the annual leave provision.

8. The adjustment for excluded differences recognises that IAS 12 (paras 15 and 24) has prohibited the recognition of deferred tax amounts relating to certain temporary differences (see section 8.6.5). Paragraph 15 prohibits the recognition of the taxable temporary difference relating to goodwill, so it is removed from the total temporary differences existing at 30 June 2007.

9. The deferred tax liability figure of $46 050 is the future tax payable as a result of the existence of taxable temporary differences of $153 500. The deferred tax asset figure of $23 100 is the future deductions available as a result of the existence of deductible temporary differences of $77 000. These figures represent the closing balances of the deferred tax accounts.

10. Deferred tax amounts may accumulate over time — for example, the taxable temporary difference for equipment represents three years differentials between accounting and taxation depreciation charges. This means that the deferred tax accounts have an opening balance representing prior year differences. If no adjustment is made for the opening balance, the deferred tax amounts are overstated. Accordingly, the opening balances are deducted from the total balances in order to determine the adjustment necessary to account for changes (additions and reversals) to deferred tax items during the current year. These adjustments are shown on the last line of the worksheet and form the basis of the adjusting journal entry for deferred tax. Positive figures are increases and negative figures are decreases in the account balances.

11. Normally, the deferred tax accounts are only adjusted each balance date after the worksheet has been completed. Occasionally, however, adjustments are made to the deferred accounts during the year so the 'movements' line is used to adjust for such changes. Adjustments could be made for:
    - recoupment of prior year tax losses (see section 8.7)
    - a change in tax rates (see section 8.10)
    - an amendment to a prior year tax return (see section 8.11)
    - revaluation of property, plant and equipment items (see section 8.12)
    - business combinations (see section 8.13).

LO 9

8.9 Recognition of deferred tax liabilities and deferred tax assets

The existence of temporary taxable and deductible differences may not result in the recognition of deferred tax assets and liabilities. Paragraphs 15 and 24 of IAS 12 specify recognition criteria that must be met before recognition occurs.

8.9.1   Deferred tax liabilities

Deferred tax liabilities must be recognised for all taxable temporary differences (except as outlined below). A liability is recognised when, and only when, it is probable that an outflow of resources embodying economic benefits will result from the settlement of a present obligation, and the amount at which the settlement will take place can be measured reliably (IASB Framework, para. 91). There is no need to explicitly consider the recognition criteria for a deferred tax liability, because it is always probable that resources will flow from the entity to pay the tax associated with taxable temporary differences. As the carrying amount of the asset or liability giving rise to the taxable temporary difference is recovered or settled, the temporary difference will reverse and give rise to taxable amounts in future periods.

8.9.2   Deferred tax assets

Deferred tax assets must be recognised for all deductible temporary differences (subject to certain exceptions) and from the carry forward of tax losses, but only to the extent that is it *probable* that future taxable profits will be available against which the temporary differences can be utilised.

An asset is recognised when it is probable that the future economic benefits will flow to the entity, and the asset has a cost or value that can be measured reliably (IASB Framework, para. 89). According to paragraph 85 of the Framework, probability refers to the degree of uncertainty about whether the future economic benefits associated with the asset will flow to the entity. This probability must be assessed using the best evidence available based on the conditions at balance date. The reversal of deductible temporary differences results in deductions against the taxable profits of future periods. Economic benefits in the form of reductions in tax payments will flow to the entity only if it earns sufficient taxable profits against which the deductions can be offset. Therefore, an entity recognises deferred tax assets only when it is probable that taxable profits will be available against which the deductible temporary differences can be utilised (IAS 12, para. 27). The realisation of a deferred tax asset would be probable where:

- there are sufficient taxable temporary differences relating to the same taxation authority and the same taxable entity that are expected to reverse in the same period as the deductible temporary differences, or in periods to which a tax loss arising from the deferred tax asset can be carried back or forward (para. 28)
- there would be taxable temporary differences arising if unrecognised increases in the fair values of assets were recognised
- it is probable that there will be other sufficient taxable profits arising in future periods against which to utilise the deductions
- other factors indicate that it is probable that the deductions can be realised.

If there are insufficient taxable temporary differences available against which to offset the deductible temporary differences, an entity can recognise a deferred tax asset only to the extent that sufficient taxable profits will be made in the future or that tax planning opportunities are available to create future taxable profits (IAS 12, para. 29). The following examples of tax planning opportunities that may be available in some jurisdictions are given in paragraph 30 of the standard:

- electing to have interest income taxed on either a received or a receivable basis
- deferring the claim for certain deductions from taxable profit
- selling, and perhaps leasing back, assets that have appreciated but for which the tax base has not been adjusted to reflect such appreciation
- selling an asset that generates non-taxable income in order to purchase another investment that generates taxable income.

A history of accounting losses, or the existence of unused tax losses, provides evidence that future taxable profits are unlikely to be available for the utilisation of deductible temporary differences. In these circumstances, the recognition of deferred tax assets would require either the existence of sufficient taxable temporary differences or convincing evidence that future taxable profits will be earned. In assessing the likelihood that tax losses will be utilised, the entity should consider whether:

- future budgets indicate that there will be sufficient taxable income derived in the foreseeable future
- the losses arise from causes that are unlikely to recur in the foreseeable future
- actions can be taken to create taxable amounts in the future
- there are existing contracts or sales backlogs that will produce taxable amounts
- there are new developments or favourable opportunities likely to give rise to taxable amounts
- there is a strong history of earnings other than those giving rise to the loss, and the loss was an aberration and not a continuing condition.

Where, on the balance of the evidence available, it is not probable that deductible temporary differences will be utilised in the future, no deferred tax asset is recognised. This probability assessment must also be applied to deferred tax assets that have previously been recognised and, if it is no longer probable that the benefits of such assets will flow to the entity, the carrying amount must be derecognised by passing the following entry:

30 June			
Income tax expense	Dr	XXX	
Deferred tax asset	Cr		XXX
(Derecognition of deferred tax assets where recovery is no longer probable)			

At each reporting date, the entity should reassess the probability of recovery of all unrecognised deferred tax assets; it should recognise these assets to the extent that it is now probable that future taxable profit will allow the deduction of the temporary difference on its reversal. Changes in trading conditions, new taxation legislation, or a business combination may all contribute to improving the chance of recovering the deferred tax benefits. Paragraph 60 of IAS 12 requires that any adjustment to deferred tax be recognised in the income statement except to the extent that it relates to items previously charged or credited to equity.

ILLUSTRATIVE EXAMPLE 8.7

Recognition of deferred tax adjustments

Using the figures calculated in illustrative example 8.6 on page 309, and assuming that the recognition criteria for deferred tax assets can be met, the adjusting journal for deferred tax movements is:

30 June 2007			
Income tax expense (deferred)	Dr	30 700	
Deferred tax asset	Cr		1 800
Deferred tax liability	Cr		28 900
(Recognition of movements in deferred tax balances for the year)			

These movements can be checked back to the current worksheet as follows:
- Deferred tax assets arise in respect of doubtful debts and annual leave. In the current year, additional deductions of $2000 (doubtful debts) and $4000 (leave) are received. This indicates that more deductible temporary differences had been reversed than had been created, resulting in a decrease of $6000 in future deductions and a $1800 decrease in the deferred tax asset.
- Deferred tax liabilities arise in respect of development expenditure, equipment, insurance and rent. In the current year, additional deductions of $90 000 (development), $13 333 (depreciation) and $5000 (insurance) are offset by additional taxable amounts of $10 000 (sale of equipment) and $2000 (rent revenue), giving a net extra increase in taxable temporary differences and a $28 900 increase in the deferred tax liability. The posting of this entry results in the deferred tax ledger accounts appearing as follows:

Deferred tax asset					
1/7/06	Balance b/d	24 900	30/6/07	Income tax expense	1 800
			30/6/07	Balance c/d	23 100
		24 900			24 900
1/7/07	Balance b/d	23 100			

Deferred tax liability					
30/6/07	Balance c/d	46 050	1/7/06	Balance b/d	17 150
			30/6/07	Income tax expense	28 900
		46 050			46 050
			1/7/07	Balance b/d	46 050

If the two taxation adjusting journals – current and deferred – are combined, then the total income tax expense recorded for the year ended 2007 by Bristol Ltd is:

Income tax expense (current) (see page 300)	$41 270
Income tax expense (deferred) (see above)	30 700
Total	$71 970

This figure represents the total tax consequences of the transactions recorded in profit and loss for the year. It can be checked in this way: The accounting profit for the year is $250 450. All items of revenue and expense are taxable or deductible with the exception of goodwill impairment and entertainment expense. The development expenditure during the year gave rise to an 'extra' deduction of $30 000 against taxable profit. If the accounting profit adjusted for these permanent differences is multiplied by the tax rate, the result represents the total tax payable above (both now and in the future):

Accounting profit	$250 450
Add Non-deductible amortisation	7 000
Add Non-deductible entertainment expense	12 450
Less Additional deduction for development	(30 000)
Taxable net profit	239 900
Tax @ 30%	$ 71 970

Thus, the income tax expense for the year has been reconciled.

Figure 8.5 below provides a flowchart summarising the accounting for deferred tax items.

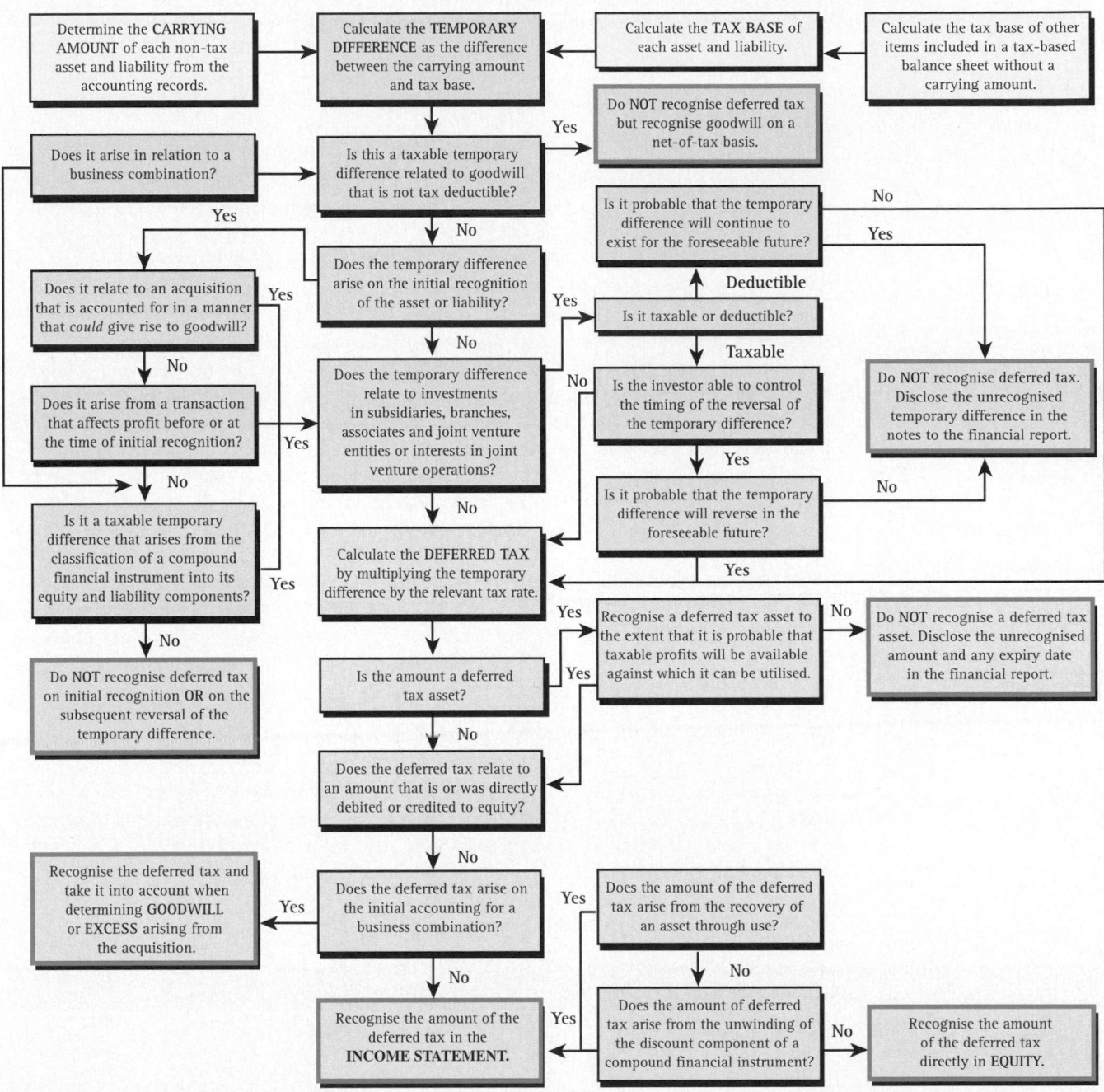

FIGURE 8.5 Accounting for deferred tax items
Source: Adapted from Deloitte Touche Tohmatsu (2001).

8.9.3   Recognition of deferred amounts arising from investments

Where taxable or deductible temporary differences are associated with investments in subsidiaries, branches and associates, and with interests in joint ventures, the deferred tax liabilities and deferred tax assets associated with these temporary differences must be raised in accordance with paragraphs 39 and 44 of IAS 12. Temporary differences arise when the carrying amount of an investment or the interest in a joint venture differs from its tax base. Such differences may be caused by:

- the existence of undistributed profits of subsidiaries, branches, associates and joint ventures
- changes in foreign exchange rates when a parent and its subsidiary are based in different countries
- a reduction in the carrying amount of an investment in an associate to its recoverable amount.

The recognition of a deferred tax liability in relation to investments is required, by paragraph 39 of IAS 12, except where both of the following conditions are satisfied:

(a) the parent, investor or venturer is able to control the timing of the reversal of the temporary difference; and

(b) it is probable that the temporary difference will not reverse in the foreseeable future.

Because there is no definition of or discussion about the meaning of the term 'foreseeable future', managerial judgement is required to determine whether the facts and circumstances associated with a particular investment satisfy the above criteria.

As both branches and subsidiaries are 'controlled' by the parent, the first condition would always be met for such investments. However, where the temporary difference arises with respect to undistributed profits in an associate and the investor cannot control the declaration of dividends from those profits, a deferred tax liability would be recognised.

Deferred tax assets associated with investments would normally arise when the investment has been written down to the recoverable amount, or when the application of fair value or equity accounting has written it down below its tax base. The recognition of such a deferred tax asset is allowed only to the extent that the temporary difference will reverse in the foreseeable future and taxable profit will be available against which the temporary difference can be utilised (IAS 12, para. 44).

| LO 10 |

8.10 Change of tax rates

When a new tax rate is enacted (or substantively enacted), the new rate should be applied in calculating the current tax liability and adjustments to deferred tax accounts during the year. It should also be applied to the deferred amounts recognised in prior years. A journal adjustment must be passed to increase or reduce the carrying amounts of deferred tax assets and liabilities, in order to reflect the new value of future taxable or deductible amounts. Paragraph 60 of IAS 12 requires the net amount arising from the restatement of deferred tax balances to be recognised in the income statement, except to the extent that the deferred tax amounts relate to items previously charged or credited to equity.

ILLUSTRATIVE EXAMPLE 8.8

Change of tax rate

As at 30 June 2007, the balances of deferred tax accounts for Eton Ltd were:

Deferred tax asset	$29 600
Deferred tax liability	(72 800)

In September 2007, the government reduced the company tax rate from 40 cents to 30 cents in the dollar, effective from 1 July 2007. The recorded deferred tax balances

→

represent the tax effect of future taxable amounts and future deductible amounts at 40 cents in the dollar, so they are now overstated and must be adjusted as follows:

	Deferred tax asset	Deferred tax liability
Opening balance	$29 600	$72 800
Adjustment for change in tax rate: ([40 − 30]/40)	(7 400)	(18 200)
Restated balance	$22 200	$54 600

The adjusting journal entry is:

Deferred tax liability	Dr	18 200	
Deferred tax asset	Cr		7 400
Income tax expense	Cr		10 800
(Recognition of the impact of a change of tax rate on deferred tax amounts)			

LO 11

8.11 Amended prior year tax figures

In taxation jurisdictions where entities self-assess their taxable profit, it is possible that the taxation authority will amend that assessment by changing the amount of taxable or deductible items. This amendment could result in the entity being liable to pay extra tax or becoming eligible for a taxation refund. Upon receipt of an amended assessment, the entity should analyse the reason for the adjustment and consider whether both current and deferred tax are affected. For example, if an entity has used an incorrect taxation depreciation rate, then the amendment to the correct rate will change both the prior year taxable profit and future taxable profits across the economic life of the depreciable asset. If only current tax for the previous year has changed, the following journal entry would be passed:

Income tax expense	Dr	XXX	
Current tax liability	Cr		XXX
(Amendment to prior year current tax on receipt of amended assessment)			

If the amendment also changes a deferred item, the new temporary difference will need to be calculated and the carry-forward balance adjusted accordingly. In the depreciation example used above, the adjustment (assuming the accounting depreciation rate is lower than the rate used to calculate taxable income) is:

Income tax expense	Dr	XXX	
Deferred tax liability	Cr		XXX
Current tax liability	Cr		XXX
(Amendment to prior year current tax and deferred tax liability on receipt of amended assessment)			

Any amendment to the deferred tax liability or the deferred tax asset arising from amended assessments would appear on the deferred tax worksheet as a 'movement' adjustment.

8.12 Items credited or charged directly to equity

In general, the amount of current and deferred tax arising in a period must be adjusted directly to equity if it relates to an amount that is or was directly charged or directly credited to equity (IAS 12, para. 61). Examples of such items are:

- revaluation of items of property, plant and equipment to fair value (see chapter 10). At the time of revaluation, an adjustment must be made to the balance of the deferred tax liability account. For example, if an item of plant is revalued upwards from 100 to 200 and the tax rate is 30%, the entity would pass the following journal entry:

Plant	Dr	100	
Deferred tax liability	Cr		30
Asset revaluation surplus	Cr		70
(Revaluation of plant to fair value)			

- an adjustment to the opening balance of retained earnings resulting from either a change in accounting policy that is applied retrospectively or from the correction of a fundamental error
- exchange differences arising on the translation of the financial statements of a foreign entity (see chapter 24)
- amounts arising on the initial recognition of the equity component of a compound financial instrument (see chapter 6).

Where it is difficult to identify the amount of current or deferred tax relating to items charged or credited directly to equity, as may happen when graduated rates of income tax are applicable or a tax rate or rule has changed, a reasonable allocation should be made pro rata (IAS 12, para. 63).

8.13 Deferred tax arising from a business combination

The amount of deferred tax arising in relation to the acquisition of an entity or business is recognised (subject to the recognition criteria) and included as part of net assets acquired when determining the goodwill or excess arising on acquisition. (Further discussion of the determination of goodwill and excess can be found in chapter 12.) When a deferred tax asset of the acquiree not recognised at the date of a business combination is subsequently recognised by the acquirer, the resulting deferred tax income is recognised in the income statement. Additionally, paragraph 68 of IAS 12 requires that the amount of goodwill recognised on acquisition must be adjusted to the amount that would be recorded had the deferred tax asset been recognised on acquisition, and must recognise the reduction in the carrying amount of the goodwill as expense. The same paragraph provides an illustrative example.

LO 12

8.14 Presentation in the financial statements

IAS 12 specifies the way in which tax items (revenues, expenses, assets and liabilities) are to be presented in the financial statements, including the circumstances in which items can be offset.

8.14.1 Tax assets and tax liabilities

Tax assets and tax liabilities must be classified as current and non-current as required by IAS 1 *Presentation of Financial Statements* (para. 51) and presented on the face of the balance sheet in accordance with IAS 1, paragraphs 68(m) and 70. Paragraph 71 of IAS 12 allows current tax assets and current tax liabilities to be offset only when the entity has a legally enforceable right to offset the amount, and intends either to settle on a net basis or to realise the asset and settle the liability simultaneously. A legal right to set off the accounts would normally exist where the accounts relate to income taxes levied by the same taxing authority.

Deferred tax assets and deferred tax liabilities can be offset only if a legally enforceable right to offset current amounts exists; and the deferred items relate to income taxes levied by the same taxing authority on the same taxable entity, or on different taxable entities which intend either to settle on a net basis or to realise the asset and settle the liability simultaneously in each future period in which significant deferred amounts will reverse (IAS 12, para. 74).

Consequently, entities operating in a single country will normally offset both current and deferred tax assets and liabilities, and show only a net current tax liability or asset and a net deferred asset or liability.

8.14.2 Tax expense

The tax expense (or income) related to profit or loss for the period is required to be presented on the face of the income statement (IAS 12, para. 77).

LO 13

8.15 Disclosures

Paragraphs 79–82A of IAS 12 contain the required disclosures relating to income taxes. These disclosures are very detailed, and provide significant additional information about the makeup of income tax expense (or income), and both taxable and deductible temporary differences. Paragraph 79 requires the tax expense figure shown on the income statement to be broken down into its various components (examples of which are listed in paragraph 80), such as current tax expense and deferred tax arising from temporary differences. Paragraph 81 requires a wide range of disclosures including tax relating to equity and discontinued operations, changes in tax rates, and unrecognised deferred tax assets and liabilities.

Paragraph 81 also requires two detailed reconciliations to be prepared:

- Paragraph 81(c) requires entities to disclose 'an explanation of the relationship between tax expense (income) and accounting profit'. This essentially reconciles expected tax — accounting profit multiplied by tax rate — to the actual tax expense recognised. The reconciliation enables financial statement users to understand why the relationship between accounting profit and income tax expense is unusual, the factors causing the variance, and factors that could affect the relationship in the future. Entities are allowed to reconcile in either or both of the following ways:
  - a numerical reconciliation between tax expense and expected tax
  - a numerical reconciliation between the average effective tax rate (tax expense divided by the accounting profit) and the applicable tax rate.

  Irrespective of the reconciliation method used, entities must disclose the basis on which the applicable tax rate is computed.

- Paragraph 81(g) requires disclosure of the following information for deferred tax items recognised on the balance sheet:

  in respect of each type of temporary difference, and in respect of each type of unused tax losses and unused tax credits:
  - (i) the amount of the deferred tax assets and liabilities recognised in the balance sheet for each period presented
  - (ii) the amount of the deferred tax income or expense recognised in the income statement, if this is not apparent from the changes in the amounts recognised in the balance sheet.

Normally, the second part of the paragraph 81(g) disclosure is required only if a change in tax rate or legislation has occurred during the year, or if some other event causes an adjustment to a deferred account during the period.

When an entity has suffered tax losses in either the current or previous period, and recognised a deferred tax asset related to those losses that is dependent on earning future taxable profits in excess of those arising on the reversal of taxable temporary differences, paragraph 82 requires disclosure of the amount of the deferred tax asset and the nature of the evidence supporting its recognition.

Paragraph 82A applies only in those jurisdictions where tax rates vary according to the quantum of profit or retained earnings distributed as dividends. In this situation, paragraph 82A requires the entity to disclose the nature and amounts (to the extent practicable) of the potential income tax consequences that would result from the payment of dividends to its shareholders.

Figure 8.6 (below and opposite) provides an illustration of the disclosures required by IAS 12.

Note 4: Income tax expense	Notes	2006 $	2005 $	IAS 12 para. no.
Major components of income tax expense				*79*
Current tax expense		126 600	117 600	*80(a)*
Deferred tax from origination and reversal of temporary differences		(20 250)	11 320	*80(c)*
Deferred tax relating to tax rate change		250	–	*80(d)*
Benefit from unrecognised tax loss used to reduce current tax expense		(1 500)	–	*80(e)*
Income tax expense		105 100	128 920	*80(f)*
Tax relating to items charged (credited) direct to equity				
Deferred tax relating to revaluation of land		12 500	–	*80(h)*
Reconciliation of tax expense to prima facie tax on accounting profit				*81(b)*
The applicable tax rate is the Australian company income tax rate of 30% (2005: 40%)				*81(c)(i)*
The prima facie tax on accounting profit differs from the tax expense provided in the accounts as follows:				
Accounting profit		402 000	397 000	
Prima facie tax at 30% (2005: 40%)		120 600	158 800	
Tax effect of non-deductible expenses				
Goodwill impairment		3 900	5 200	
Non-taxable revenue		(1 500)	(2 000)	
Entertainment		3 600	2 300	
		126 600	164 300	
Increase in beginning deferred taxes resulting from reduction in tax rate		250	–	
Reduction in current tax from recoupment of tax losses		(1 500)	–	
Tax effect of net movements in items giving rise to:*				
Deferred tax assets		(8 250)	3 200	
Deferred tax liabilities		(12 000)	(38 580)	
Tax expense		105 100	128 920	*81(d)*

Note 4: Income tax expense	Notes	2006 $	2005 $	IAS 12 para. no.
Change in tax rate As of 1 July 2005, the company tax rate changed from 40% to 30%				*81(d)*

*These figures represent the net effect of movements in assets and liabilities during the year which have increased or decreased current tax. The details can be found in disclosures required by paragraph 81(g)(ii).

Unrecognised deferred tax assets Tax losses in respect of which deferred tax has not been recognised as it is not probable that benefits will be received		20 000	40 000	*81(e)*
Unrecognised deferred tax liabilities Aggregate of temporary differences associated with investments in subsidiaries for which deferred tax liabilities have not been recognised		16 000	16 000	*81(f)*
Deferred tax assets and liabilities The following items have given rise to deferred tax assets:				
Accounts receivable		12 000	15 000	
Employee entitlements		24 000	22 000	
Total deferred tax assets		36 000	37 000	
The following items have given rise to deferred tax liabilities:				
Land		12 500	–	
Plant and equipment		15 000	36 000	
Total deferred tax liabilities		27 500	36 000	
Offset of deferred tax asset against liability		36 000	37 000	
Net deferred tax asset (liability)		8 500	(1 000)	*81(g)(i)*
Deferred tax expenses (income) recognised in the income statement for each type of temporary difference* Deferred tax expense in relation to:				
Plant and equipment		(12 000)	(38 580)	
Total deferred tax expense		(12 000)	(38 580)	
Deferred tax income in relation to:				
Accounts receivable		750	1 200	
Employee entitlements		7 500	2 000	
Total deferred tax income		8 250	3 200	*81(g)(ii)*

*This disclosure is required only if the movements in deferred items cannot readily be ascertained from other disclosures made with respect to deferred assets and liabilities. This is the case in this situation because the change in tax rate adjustments has obscured the movements in deferred items.

FIGURE 8.6 Illustrative disclosures required by IAS 12

Figure 8.7 (below and opposite) shows the income tax notes to the financial statements of Nokia Corporation for the year ended 31 December 2005, which were prepared in accordance with International Financial Reporting Standards (IFRSs).

NOTES TO THE NOKIA CORPORATION FINANCIAL STATMENTS (CONTINUED)

13 INCOME TAXES

	2005 EURm	2004 As revised EURm	2003 As revised EURm
Income tax expense			
Current tax	(1 262)	(1 403)	(1 684)
Deferred tax	(19)	(43)	(13)
Total	(1 281)	(1 446)	(1 697)
Finland	(759)	(1 128)	(1 114)
Other countries	(522)	(318)	(583)
Total	(1281)	(1 446)	(1 697)

The differences between income tax expense computed at statutory rates (in Finland 26% in 2005 and 29% in 2004 and 2003) and income taxes recognised in the consolidated income statement is reconciled as follows at December 31:

	2005 EURm	2004 As revised EURm	2003 As revised EURm
Income tax expense at statutory rate	1 295	1 372	1 555
Amortization of goodwill	–	28	46
Impairment of goodwill	–	–	58
Provisions without income tax benefit/expense	11	–	–
Taxes for prior years	1	(34)	56
Taxes on foreign subsidiaries' profits in excess of (lower than) income taxes at statutory rates	(30)	(130)	(77)
Operating losses with no current tax benefit	–	–	8
Net increase in provisions	22	67	14
Change in deferred tax rate	–	26	–
Deferred tax liability on undistributed earnings	8	60	–
Adoption of IAS 39(R) and IFRS 2	–	11	(2)
Other	(26)	46	39
Income tax expense	1 281	1 446	1 697

At December 31, 2005, the Group had loss carry forwards, primarily attributable to foreign subsidiaries of EUR 92 million (EUR 105 million in 2004 and EUR 186 million in 2003), most of which will expire between 2006 and 2023.

In the beginning of 2005, the corporate tax rate in Finland was reduced from 29% to 26%. The impact of the change on the Profit and loss account through change in deferred taxes in 2004 was EUR 26 million. In 2005, there was no impact on the Profit and loss account through a change in deferred tax.

Income taxes include a tax benefit from a tax refund from previous years of EUR 48 million in 2005.

NOTES TO THE NOKIA CORPORATION FINANCIAL STATMENTS (CONTINUED)

13 INCOME TAXES (Continued)

Certain of the Group companies' income tax returns for periods ranging from 1998 through 2004 are under examination by tax authorities. The Group does not believe that any significant additional taxes in excess of those already provided for will arise as a result of the examinations.

During 2004, the Group analyzed its future foreign investments plans with respect to certain foreign investments. As a result of this analysis, the Group concluded that it could no longer represent that all foreign earnings may be permanently reinvested. Accordingly, the Group recorded the recognition of a EUR 60 million deferred tax liability in 2004. In 2005, the deferred tax liability was EUR 68 million.

27 DEFERRED TAXES

	2005 EURm	2004 EURm
Deferred tax assets:		
Intercompany profit in inventory	49	41
Tax losses carried forward	7	12
Warranty provision	107	118
Other provisions	170	174
Fair value gains/losses	43	–
Untaxed reserves	88	88
Other temporary differences	228	190
Total deferred tax assets	692	623
Deferred tax liabilities:		
Untaxed reserves	(24)	(30)
Fair value gains/losses	–	(28)
Undistributed earnings	(68)	(60)
Other	(59)	(61)
Total deferred tax liabilities	(151)	(179)
Net deferred tax asset	541	444
The tax charged to shareholders' equity is as follows:		
Fair value and other reserves, fair value gains/losses	93	(7)

In 2005, the corporate tax rate in Finland reduced from 29% to 26%. The decrease of tax rate had no impact on deferred taxes in 2005 (a reduction of EUR 26 million in net deferred tax assets in 2004).

During 2004, the Group analyzed the majority of its future foreign investment plans with respect to foreign investments. As a result of this analysis, the Group concluded that it could no longer represent that all foreign earnings may be permanently reinvested. Accordingly, the Group recorded the recognition of a EUR 68 million deferred tax liability during 2005 (EUR 60 million in 2004).

At December 31, 2005 the Group had loss carry forwards of EUR 71 million (EUR 67 million in 2004) for which no deferred tax asset was recognized due to uncertainty of utilization of these loss carry forwards. These loss carry forwards will expire in years 2006 through 2011.

FIGURE 8.7 Income tax notes to the consolidated financial statements of Nokia Corporation
Source: Nokia (2005, pp. 21, 29).

8.16 Summary

This chapter analyses the content of IAS 12 *Income Taxes* and provides guidance on its implementation. The principal issue in accounting for taxes is how to account for the current and future tax consequences of transactions and other events of the current period. The accounting standard requires entities to recognise (with limited exceptions) deferred tax liabilities and deferred tax assets when the recovery or settlement of an asset or liability will result in larger or smaller tax payments than would occur if such settlement or recovery had no tax consequence. The tax consequences of transactions are to be accounted for in the same way as the transaction to which they are related. Therefore, for transactions recognised in the income statement, all related tax effects are also recognised in the income statement. Where a transaction requires a direct adjustment to equity, so do any tax effects. Deferred tax assets, particularly those relating to tax losses, are recognised only if it is probable that the entity will have sufficient taxable profit in the future against which the tax benefit can be offset. All deferred tax liabilities must be recognised in full. IAS 12 requires extensive disclosures to be made in relation to both current and deferred tax items.

DISCUSSION QUESTIONS

1. What is the main principle of tax-effect accounting as outlined in IAS 12?
2. Explain the meaning of a temporary difference as it relates to deferred tax calculations and give three examples.
3. Explain how accounting profit and taxable profit differ, and how each is treated when accounting for income taxes.
4. In tax-effect accounting, the creation of temporary differences between the carrying amount and the tax base for assets and liabilities leads to the establishment of deferred tax assets and liabilities in the accounting records. List examples of temporary differences that create:
   (a) deferred tax assets
   (b) deferred tax liabilities.
5. In IAS 12, criteria are established for the recognition of a deferred tax asset and a deferred tax liability.

Identify these criteria, and discuss any differences between the criteria for assets and those for liabilities.
6. What is a 'tax loss' and how is it accounted for?
7. 'Despite the fact that deferred tax liabilities and assets are recognised in respect of certain assets and liabilities, the income tax expense (or benefit) of such items is always recognised in the current year.' Is this statement true? Discuss.
8. What action should be taken when a tax rate or tax rule changes? Why?
9. Are all temporary differences that exist at balance date recognised as deferred tax assets or deferred tax liabilities?
10. In determining whether deferred tax assets relating to tax losses are to be recognised, what factors should be taken into consideration?

EXERCISES

EXERCISE 8.1 ★ Tax effects of a temporary difference

The following information was extracted from the records of Plymouth Ltd for the year ended 30 June 2005:

Plymouth Ltd Deferred tax worksheet (extract) as at 30 June 2005						
	Carrying amount	Future taxable amount	Future deductible amount	Tax base	Taxable temporary differences	Deductible temporary differences
Relevant assets Equipment	$60 000	$(60 000)	$108 000	$108 000		$48 000

Equipment is depreciated at 25% p.a. straight-line for accounting purposes, but the allowable rate for taxation is 20% p.a.

Required
Assuming that no equipment is purchased or sold during the years ended 30 June 2006 and 30 June 2007, calculate:
(a) the accounting expense and tax deduction for each year
(b) the impact of depreciation on the taxable profit for each year
(c) the movement in the temporary difference balance for each year.

EXERCISE 8.2 ★ Calculation of current tax

Salisbury Ltd made an accounting profit before tax of $40 000 for the year ended 30 June 2008. Included in the accounting profit were the following items of revenue and expense.

Donations to political parties (non-deductible)	5 000
Depreciation – machinery (20%)	15 000
Annual leave expense	5 600
Rent revenue	12 000

For tax purposes the following applied:

Depreciation rate for machinery	25%
Annual leave paid	6 500
Rent received	10 000
Income tax rate	30%

Required
1. Calculate the current tax liability for the year ended 30 June 2008, and prepare the adjusting journal entry.
2. Explain your treatment of rent items in your answer to part 1.

EXERCISE 8.3   ★   Calculation of deferred tax

The following information was extracted from the records of Darlington Ltd for the year ended 30 June 2008:

Darlington Ltd Balance sheet (extract) as at 30 June 2008		
Assets		
Accounts receivable	$ 25 000	
Allowance for doubtful debts	(2 000)	$23 000
Machines	100 000	
Accumulated depreciation – machines	(25 000)	75 000
Liabilities		
Interest payable		1 000

Additional information
The accumulated depreciation for tax purposes at 30 June 2008 was $50 000.
The tax rate is 30%.

Required
Prepare a deferred tax worksheet to identify the temporary differences arising in respect of the assets and liabilities in the balance sheet, and to calculate the balance of the deferred tax liability and deferred tax asset accounts at 30 June 2008. Assume the opening balance of the deferred tax accounts was $0.

EXERCISE 8.4   ★   Calculation of current tax

Humber Ltd recorded an accounting profit before tax of $100 000 for the year ended 30 June 2009. Included in the accounting profit were the following items of revenue and expense.

Entertainment expenses (non-deductible)	$ 2 000
Depreciation – vehicles (10%)	17 000
Rent revenue	2 500
For tax purposes the following applied:	
Depreciation rate – vehicles	15%
Rent received	$3 000
Income tax rate	30%

Required

1. Use a current tax worksheet to calculate the current tax liability for the year ended 30 June 2009. Prepare the adjusting journal entry.
2. Explain the future tax effect of the adjustment made in part 1 for interest received/revenue.

EXERCISE 8.5 ★★

Creation and reversal of temporary differences

The following are all independent situations. Prepare the journal entries for deferred tax on the creation or reversal of any temporary differences. Explain in each case the nature of the temporary difference. Assume a tax rate of 30%.

1. The entity has an allowance for doubtful debts of $10 000 at the end of the current year relating to accounts receivable of $125 000. The prior year balances for these accounts were $8500 and $97 500 respectively. During the current year, debts worth $9250 were written off as uncollectible.
2. The entity sold a vehicle at the end of the current year for $15 000. The vehicle cost $100 000 when purchased three years ago, and had a carrying amount of $25 000 when sold. The taxation depreciation rate for equipment of this type is $33\frac{1}{3}\%$.
3. The entity has recognised an interest receivable asset with a beginning balance of $17 000 and an ending balance of $19 500 for the current year. During the year, interest of $127 000 was received in cash.
4. At the end of the current year, the entity has recognised a liability of $4000 in respect of outstanding fines for non-compliance with safety legislation. Such fines are not tax-deductible.

EXERCISE 8.6 ★★

Creation and reversal of a temporary difference

Lincoln Ltd purchased equipment on 1 July 2003 at a cost of $25 000. The equipment had an expected economic life of five years and was to be depreciated on a straight-line basis. The taxation depreciation rate for equipment of this type is 15% p.a. straight-line. On 30 June 2005, Lincoln Ltd reassessed the remaining economic life of the equipment from three years to two years, and the accounting depreciation charge was adjusted accordingly. The equipment was sold on 30 June 2006 for $15 000. The company tax rate is 30%.

Required

For each of the years ended 30 June 2004, 2005 and 2006, calculate the carrying amount and the tax base of the asset and determine the appropriate deferred tax entry. Explain your answer.

EXERCISE 8.7 ★★   Payment of income tax and amended assessment

Dover Ltd calculated its current tax liability at 30 June 2006 to be $57 500. This tax was paid in the following instalments:

28 October 2005	$13 200
28 January 2006	11 600
28 April 2006	15 200
28 July 2006	17 500

On 1 November 2006, an amended assessment notice was received from the taxing authority. It disallowed a donation for $1500 claimed as a deduction, and amended the taxation depreciation rate used for vehicles from 50% to 30%. The accounting depreciation rate is 25%. As a result, further tax of $1950 was paid on 31 December 2006. The company tax rate is 30%.

Required

Prepare all journal entries necessary to record the taxation transactions for the period to 31 December 2006.

EXERCISE 8.8 ★★★   Calculation of deferred tax, and adjustment entry

The following information was extracted from the records of Oxford Ltd as at 30 June 2007:

Asset (liability)	Carrying amount	Tax base
Accounts receivable	$150 000	$175 000
Motor vehicles	165 000	125 000
Provision for warranty	(12 000)	0
Deposits received in advance	(15 000)	0

The depreciation rates for accounting and taxation are 15% and 25% respectively. Deposits are taxable when received, and warranty costs are deductible when paid. An allowance for doubtful debts of $25 000 has been raised against accounts receivable for accounting purposes, but such debts are deductible only when written off as uncollectible.

Required

1. Calculate the temporary differences for Oxford Ltd as at 30 June 2007. Justify your classification of each difference as either a deductible temporary difference or a taxable temporary difference.
2. Prepare the journal entry to record deferred tax for the year ended 30 June 2007 assuming no deferred items had been raised in prior years.

PROBLEMS

PROBLEM 8.1 ★   Current and deferred tax

Liverpool Ltd has determined its accounting profit before tax for the year ended 30 June 2006 to be $256 700. Included in this profit are the items of revenue and expense shown opposite.

Royalty revenue (non-taxable)	$ 8 000
Proceeds on sale of building	75 000
Entertainment expense	1 700
Depreciation expense – buildings	7 600
Depreciation expense – plant	22 500
Carrying amount of building sold	70 000
Doubtful debts expense	4 100
Annual leave expense	46 000
Insurance expense	4 200
Development expense	15 000

The company's draft balance sheet at 30 June 2006 showed the following assets and liabilities:

Assets		
Cash		$ 2 500
Accounts receivable	$ 21 500	
Less Allowance for doubtful debts	(4 100)	17 400
Inventory		31 600
Prepaid insurance		4 500
Land		75 000
Buildings	170 000	
Less Accumulated depreciation	(59 500)	110 500
Plant	150 000	
Less Accumulated depreciation	(67 500)	82 500
Deferred tax asset (opening balance)		9 600
		333 600
Liabilities		
Accounts payable		25 000
Provision for annual leave		10 000
Deferred tax liability (opening balance)		6 000
Loan		140 000
		$181 000

Additional information

(a) Quarterly income tax instalments paid during the year were:

28 October 2005	$18 000
28 January 2006	17 500
28 April 2006	18 000

with the final balance due on 28 July 2006.

(b) The tax depreciation rate for plant (which cost $150 000 three years ago) is 20%. Depreciation on buildings is not deductible for taxation purposes.

(c) The building sold during the year had cost $100 000 when acquired six years ago. The company depreciates buildings at 5% p.a., straight-line. Any gain (loss) on sale of buildings is not taxable (i.e. not deductible).

(d) During the year, the following cash amounts were paid:

Annual leave	$52 000
Insurance	3 700

(e) Bad debts of $3500 were written off against the allowance for doubtful debts during the year.

(f) The $15 000 spent (and expensed) on development during the year is not deductible for tax purposes until 30 June 2007.

(g) Liverpool Ltd has tax losses amounting to $12 500 carried forward from prior years.

(h) The company tax rate is 30%.

Required

1. Determine the balance of any current and deferred tax assets and liabilities for Liverpool Ltd as at 30 June 2006.

2. Prepare any necessary journal entries.

PROBLEM 8.2   ★   Calculation of movements in deferred tax accounts

The balance sheets of Leeds Ltd at 30 June 2009 showed the following net assets:

	2009	2008
Assets		
Cash	80 000	85 000
Inventory	170 000	155 000
Receivables	500 000	480 000
Allowance for doubtful debts	(55 000)	(40 000)
Plant	500 000	500 000
Accumulated depreciation	(260 000)	(210 000)
Deferred tax asset	?	40 500
Liabilities		
Accounts payable	290 000	260 000
Provision for long-service leave	60 000	45 000
Rent received in advance	25 000	20 000
Deferred tax liability	?	38 100

Additional information

• Accumulated depreciation of plant for tax purposes was $315 000 at 30 June 2008, and depreciation for tax purposes for the year ended 30 June 2009 amounted to $75 000.

• The tax rate is 30%.

Required

Prepare a worksheet to calculate the balance-day adjustment to deferred tax asset and liability accounts as at 30 June 2009, and show the necessary journal entry.

PROBLEM 8.3   ★   Calculation of current tax liability and adjusting journal entry

The profit before tax, as reported in the income statement of Stanstead for the year ended 30 June 2008, amounted to $60 000, including the following revenue and expense items:

Rent revenue	$3 000
Government grant received (non-taxable)	1 000
Bad debts expense	6 000
Depreciation of plant	5 000
Annual leave expense	3 000
Entertainment costs (non-deductible)	1 800
Depreciation of buildings (non-deductible)	800

The balance sheet of the company at 30 June 2008 showed the following net assets.

	2008	2007
Assets		
Cash	8 000	8 500
Inventory	17 000	15 500
Receivables	50 000	48 000
Allowance for doubtful debts	(5 500)	(4 000)
Office supplies	2 500	2 200
Plant	50 000	50 000
Accumulated depreciation	(26 000)	(21 000)
Buildings	30 000	30 000
Accumulated depreciation	(14 800)	(14 000)
Goodwill (net)	7 000	7 000
Deferred tax asset	?	4 050
Liabilities		
Accounts payable	29 000	26 000
Provision for long-service leave	6 000	4 500
Provision for annual leave	4 000	3 000
Rent received in advance	2 500	2 000
Deferred tax liability	?	3 150

Additional information
- Accumulated depreciation of plant for tax purposes was $31 500 at 30 June 2007, and depreciation for tax purposes for the year ended 30 June 2008 amounted to $75 000.
- The tax rate is 30%.

Required
Prepare a worksheet to calculate taxable income and the company's current tax liability as at 30 June 2008, and prepare the balance-day adjustment journal.

PROBLEM 8.4   ↓ ★★   Calculation of current tax, and prior year amendment

The accounting profit before tax of Norwich Ltd for the year ended 30 June 2007 was $22 240. It included the following revenue and expense items:

Government grant (non-taxable)	$ 3 600
Proceeds from sale of plant	33 000
Carrying amount of plant sold	30 000
Entertainment expense (non-deductible)	11 100
Doubtful debts expense	8 100
Depreciation expense – plant	24 000
Insurance expense	12 900
Annual leave expense	15 400

The draft balance sheet as at 30 June 2007 included the following assets and liabilities:

	2007	2006
Accounts receivable	$156 000	$147 500
Allowance for doubtful debts	(6 800)	(5 200)
Prepaid insurance	3 400	5 600
Plant	240 000	290 000
Accumulated depreciation – plant	(134 400)	(130 400)
Deferred tax asset	?	9 990
Provision for annual leave	14 100	9 700
Deferred tax liability	?	9 504

Additional information

- In November 2006, the company received an amended assessment for the year ended 30 June 2006 from the taxing authority. The amendment notice indicated that an amount of $4500 claimed as a deduction had been disallowed. Norwich Ltd has not yet adjusted its accounts to reflect the amendment.
- For tax purposes, the carrying amount of plant sold was $26 000. This sale was the only movement in plant for the year.
- The tax deduction for plant depreciation was $28 800. Accumulated depreciation at 30 June 2006 for taxation purposes was $156 480.
- In the previous year, Norwich Ltd had made a tax loss of $18 400. Norwich Ltd recognised a deferred tax asset in respect of this loss.
- The tax rate is 30%.

Required

Show all workings.

1. Prepare the journal entry necessary to record the amendment to the prior year's taxation return.
2. Prepare the current tax worksheet and journal entry/entries to calculate and record the current tax for the year ended 30 June 2007.
3. Justify your treatment of annual leave expense in the current tax worksheet.
4. Calculate the temporary difference as at 30 June 2007 for each of the following assets. Explain how these differences arise and why you have classified them as either deductible temporary differences or taxable temporary differences:
   (a) plant
   (b) accounts receivable.

PROBLEM 8.5 ★★   Current and deferred tax with tax rate change

You have been asked by the accountant of Manchester Ltd to prepare the tax-effect accounting adjustments for the year ended 30 June 2007. Investigations revealed the following information:

(a) In September 2005, the government reduced the company tax rate from 40 cents to 30 cents in the dollar, effective from 1 July 2006.
(b) The profit for the year ended 30 June 2007 was $920 000.
(c) The assets and liabilities at 30 June were:

	2007	2006
Accounts receivable	$235 000	$200 000
Allowance for doubtful debts	(13 000)	(12 000)
Inventory	250 000	220 000
Land	100 000	100 000
Buildings	800 000	800 000
Accumulated depreciation – buildings	(99 000)	(70 000)
Plant	600 000	600 000
Accumulated depreciation – plant (accounting)	(190 000)	(120 000)
Development expenditure		
– costs incurred	320 000	200 000
– accumulated amortisation	(144 000)	(80 000)
Deferred tax asset	?	29 600
Goodwill (net)	–	20 000
Accounts payable	170 000	150 000
Deferred tax liability	?	72 000
Provision for long-service leave	36 000	28 000
Provision for warranty claims	32 000	34 000

(d) The company is entitled to claim a tax deduction of 125% for development expenditure in the year of expenditure. The company has adopted the accounting policy of capitalising and then amortising the expenditure over five years.

(e) Revenue for the year included:

Non-taxable income	$126 000

(f) Expenses brought to account included:

Depreciation – buildings	$29 000
Depreciation – plant	70 000
Impairment – goodwill (non-deductible)	20 000
Amortisation – development expenditure	64 000

(g) Accumulated depreciation on plant for tax purposes was $180 000 on 30 June 2006, and $285 000 on 30 June 2007.

(h) Bad debts of $14 000 were written off during the year, and warranty repairs to the value of $22 000 were carried out. There was no tax deduction for long-service leave in the current year.

(i) Buildings are depreciated in the accounting records but no deduction is allowed for tax purposes.

Required

1. Prepare the journal entry to account for the change in the income tax rate in September 2005.
2. Prepare the worksheets and journal entries to calculate and record the current tax liability, and any movements in deferred tax assets and liabilities in accordance with IAS 12, for the year ended 30 June 2007.

PROBLEM 8.6 ★★ Recognition of deferred tax assets

Sunderland Ltd incurred an accounting loss of $7560 for the year ended 30 June 2005. The current tax calculation determined that the company had incurred a tax loss of $12 500. Taxation legislation allows such losses to be carried forward and offset against future taxable profits. The company had the following temporary differences:

	30 June 2005	30 June 2004	Expected period of reversal
Deductible temporary differences:			
Accounts receivable	$12 000	$10 000	2006
Plant and equipment	5 000	7 500	2006/2007 equally
Taxable temporary differences:			
Interest receivable	1 500	2 500	2006
Prepaid insurance	10 000	20 000	2006

At 30 June 2004, Sunderland Ltd had recognised a deferred tax liability of $6750 and a deferred tax asset of $5250 with respect to temporary differences existing at that date. No adjustment has yet been made for temporary differences existing at 30 June 2005.

Required

1. Discuss the factors that Sunderland Ltd should consider in determining the amount (if any) to be recognised for deferred tax assets at 30 June 2005.
2. Calculate the amount (if any) to be recognised for deferred tax assets at 30 June 2005. Justify your answer.

Current and deferred tax

The accounting profit before tax for the year ended 30 June 2008 for York Ltd amounted to $18 500 and included:

Depreciation – motor vehicle (25%)	$ 4 500
Depreciation – equipment (20%)	20 000
Rent revenue	16 000
Royalty revenue (non-taxable)	5 000
Doubtful debts expense	2 300
Entertainment expense (non-deductible)	1 500
Proceeds on sale of equipment	19 000
Carrying amount of equipment sold	18 000
Annual leave expense	5 000

The draft balance sheet at 30 June 2006 contained the following assets and liabilities:

	2006	2005
Assets		
Cash	$ 11 500	$ 9 500
Receivables	12 000	14 000
Allowance for doubtful debts	(3 000)	(2 500)
Inventory	19 000	21 500
Rent receivable	2 800	2 400
Motor vehicle	18 000	18 000
Accumulated depreciation – motor vehicle	(15 750)	(11 250)
Equipment	100 000	130 000
Accumulated depreciation – equipment	(60 000)	(52 000)
Deferred tax asset	?	6 450
		136 100
Liabilities		
Accounts payable	15 655	21 500
Provision for annual leave	4 500	6 000
Current tax liability	?	7 600
Deferred tax liability	?	2 745
		37 845

Additional information
- The company can claim a deduction of $15 000 (15%) for depreciation on equipment, but the motor vehicle is fully depreciated for tax purposes.
- The equipment sold during the year had been purchased for $30 000 two years before the date of sale.
- The company tax rate is 30%.

Required
1. Determine the balance of any current and deferred tax assets and liabilities for York Ltd as at 30 June 2006, using appropriate worksheets. Show all workings.
2. Prepare any necessary journal entries.

★★   Disclosures

The following taxation worksheets relate to Lyme Regis Ltd's taxation adjustments for the years ending 30 June 2005 and 30 June 2006. Using these worksheets, prepare appropriate notes to the financial statements for 30 June 2006 in accordance with IAS 12 disclosure requirements.

Lyme Regis Ltd Current tax worksheet for the year ended 30 June 2005		
Accounting profit before tax		$2 042 686
Add:		
Depreciation building – non-deductible	$108 000	
Entertainment expense – non-deductible	86 800	
Legal expense – non-deductible	79 200	
Political donations – non-deductible	9 900	
Penalty – non-deductible	20 800	
Doubtful debts expense	123 000	
Depreciation expense – equipment	120 000	
Depreciation expense – furniture and fittings	720 000	
Depreciation expense – motor vehicles	160 000	
Annual leave expense	680 000	
Insurance expense	254 200	
Long-service leave expense	22 000	
Amortisation – patent	100 000	
Rent expense	309 600	
Interest expense	28 000	
Supplies expense	404 800	
Carrying amount of equipment sold	550 000	
Interest received for tax purposes	187 550	3 963 850
		6 006 536
Deduct:		
Interest revenue	186 050	
Political donations deductible	100	
Carrying amount of equipment sold – taxation	400 000	
Debts written off	92 300	
Depreciation – equipment (taxation)	150 000	
Depreciation – furniture and fittings (taxation)	960 000	
Depreciation – motor vehicles (taxation)	200 000	
Annual leave paid	495 000	
Interest paid	28 000	
Insurance paid	256 400	
Development expenditure – additional deduction	25 000	
Amortisation – patent (taxation)	150 000	
Supplies purchased	402 200	
Rent paid	312 500	(3 657 550)
Taxable income		2 348 986
Total tax payable (35%)		822 145
Less Tax already paid		(546 271)
Current tax liability		$ 275 874

	Carrying amount	Future taxable amount	Future deductible amount	Tax base	Taxable temporary differences	Deductible temporary differences
Lyme Regis Ltd **Deferred tax worksheet** **at 30 June 2005**						
Relevant assets						
Accounts receivable (net)	$2 406 000	$ 0	$ 123 000	$2 259 000		$ 123 000
Interest receivable	18 000	(18 000)	0	0	$ 18 000	
Consumable supplies	118 400	(118 400)	0	0	118 400	
Prepaid insurance	59 400	(59 400)	0	0	59 400	
Prepaid rent	12 900	(12 900)	0	0	12 900	
Building	3 492 000	(3 492 000)	0	2 560 000	3 492 000	
Furniture and fittings	3 470 000	(3 470 000)	2 560 000	450 000	910 000	
Motor vehicles	520 000	(520 000)	450 000	150 000	70 000	
Equipment	240 000	(240 000)	150 000	50 000	90 000	
Patent	200 000	(200 000)	50 000		150 000	
Relevant liabilities						
Interest payable	7 000	0	(7 000)	0		7 000
Provision for long-service leave	220 800	0	(220 800)	0		220 800
Provision for annual leave	704 000	0	(704 000)	0		704 000
Temporary differences					4 920 700	1 054 800
Excluded differences					3 492 000	
Net temporary differences					1 428 700	1 054 800
Deferred tax liability (35%)					500 045	
Deferred tax asset (35%)						369 180
Beginning balances					(397 080)	(326 840)
Movement during year (tax rate)					49 635	40 855
Adjustment					$ 152 600	$ 83 195
					Credit	Debit

Lyme Regis Ltd Current tax worksheet for the year ended 30 June 2006		
Accounting profit before tax		$1 900 591
Add:		
Depreciation building – non-deductible	$ 168 000	
Entertainment expense – non-deductible	95 600	
Legal expense – non-deductible	87 000	
Political donations – non-deductible	10 900	
Amortisation – development expenditure	40 000	
Doubtful debts expense	160 600	
Depreciation expense – equipment	135 000	
Depreciation expense – furniture and fittings	963 750	
Depreciation expense – motor vehicles	160 000	
Annual leave expense	652 000	
Insurance expense	276 300	
Long-service leave expense	48 400	
Amortisation – patent	100 000	
Rent expense	356 400	
Supplies expense	458 300	
Carrying amount of equipment sold	90 000	
Interest received for tax purposes	140 650	3 942 900
		5 843 491
Deduct:		
Interest revenue	150 650	
Political donations – deductible	100	
Carrying amount of equipment sold – taxation	37 500	
Debts written off	123 000	
Depreciation – equipment (taxation)	168 750	
Depreciation – Furniture and fittings (taxation)	1 285 000	
Depreciation – Motor vehicles (taxation)	200 000	
Annual leave paid	680 000	
Insurance paid	282 600	
Research and development paid (125%)	150 000	
Amortisation – patent (taxation)	50 000	
Supplies purchased	504 400	
Rent paid	358 350	(3 990 350)
Taxable income		1 853 141
Total tax payable (35%)		648 599
Less Tax already paid		(475 000)
Current tax liability		173 599

Lyme Regis Ltd Deferred tax worksheet at 30 June 2006						
	Carrying amount	Assessable amount	Deductible amount	Tax base	Taxable temporary differences	Deductible temporary differences
Relevant assets						
Accounts receivable (net)	$2 588 400	$ 0	$160 600	$2 749 000		$ 160 600
Interest receivable	8 000	(8 000)	0	0	$ 8 000	
Consumable supplies	164 500	(164 500)	0	0	164 500	
Prepaid insurance	65 700	(65 700)	0	0	65 700	
Prepaid rent	14 850	(14 850)	0	0	14 850	
Building	6 424 000	(6 424 000)	0	0	6 424 000	
Furniture and fittings	3 406 250	(3 406 250)	2 175 000	2 175 000	1 231 250	
Motor vehicles	360 000	(360 000)	250 000	250 000	110 000	
Equipment	465 000	(465 000)	393 750	393 750	71 250	
Patent	100 000	(100 000)	0	0	100 000	
Development expenditure	80 000	(80 000)	0	0	80 000	
Relevant liabilities						
Interest payable	7 000	0	(7 000)	0		7 000
Provision for long-service leave	269 200	0	(269 200)	0		269 200
Provision for annual leave	676 000	0	(676 000)	0		676 000
Temporary differences					8 269 550	1 112 800
Excluded differences					(6 424 000)	
Net temporary differences					1 845 550	1 112 800
Deferred tax liability (35%)					645 943	
Deferred tax asset (35%)						389 480
Beginning balances					(500 045)	(369 180)
Movement during year						
Adjustment					145 898	20 300
					Credit	Debit

PROBLEM 8.9 ★★★ Current and deferred tax with prior year losses

The accounting profit before tax of Cambridge Ltd was $175 900. It included the following revenue and expense items:

Government grant (non-taxable)	$ 3 600
Interest revenue	11 000
Long-service leave expense	7 000
Doubtful debts expense	4 200
Depreciation – plant (15% p.a., straight-line)	33 000
Rent expense	22 800
Entertainment expense (non-deductible)	3 900

The draft balance sheet as at 30 June 2005 included the following assets and liabilities:

	2005	2004
Cash	$ 9 000	$ 7 500
Accounts receivable	83 000	76 800
Allowance for doubtful debts	(5 000)	(3 200)
Inventory	67 100	58 300
Interest receivable	1 000	–
Prepaid rent	2 800	2 400
Plant	220 000	220 000
Accumulated depreciation – plant	(99 000)	(66 000)
Deferred tax asset	?	30 360
Accounts payable	71 200	73 600
Provision for long-service leave	64 000	61 000
Deferred tax liability	?	720

Additional information
- The tax depreciation rate for plant is 10% p.a., straight-line.
- The tax rate is 30%.
- The company has $15 000 in tax losses carried forward from the previous year. A deferred tax asset was recognised for these losses. Taxation legislation allows such losses to be offset against future taxable profit.

Required
1. Prepare the worksheets and journal entries to calculate and record the current tax liability and the movements in deferred tax accounts for the year ended 30 June 2005.
2. Justify your treatment of the interest revenue in the current tax worksheet. Explain how and why this leads to the deferred tax consequence shown in the deferred tax worksheet.

WEBLINK

Visit these websites for additional information:

www.iasb.org   www.iasplus.com
www.asic.gov.au   www.ifac.org
www.aasb.com.au   www.nzica.com
www.accaglobal.com   www.capa.com.my

REFERENCES

Deloitte Touche Tohmatsu 2001, *Accounting for income tax: a guide to revised accounting standards AASB 1020 and AAS 3 'Income Taxes'*, Deloitte Touche Tohmatsu, Australia.
Nokia 2005, *Nokia in 2005*, Nokia Corporation, Finland, viewed 8 May 2006, <www.nokia.com>.

CHAPTER 9
Inventories

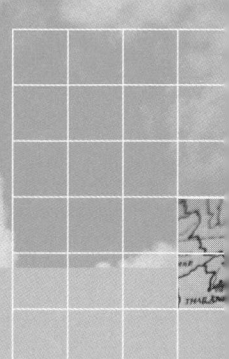

ACCOUNTING STANDARDS

International: IAS 2 *Inventories*
Australia: AASB 102 *Inventories*
New Zealand: NZ IAS 2 *Inventories*

CONCEPTS FOR REVIEW

Before studying this chapter, you should understand or, if necessary, revise:
- the concept of an asset in the IASB Framework
- the concept of an expense in the IASB Framework.

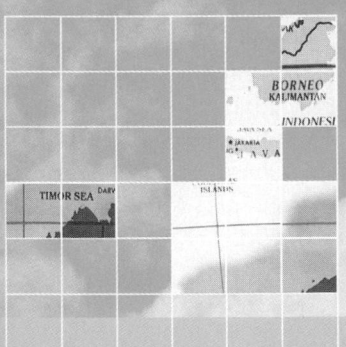

LEARNING OBJECTIVES

When you have studied this chapter, you should be able to:
1. understand the nature of inventories
2. understand how to measure inventories
3. explain what is included in the cost of inventory
4. account for inventory transactions using both the periodic and the perpetual methods
5. explain and apply end-of-period procedures for inventory under both periodic and perpetual methods
6. explain why cost flow assumptions are required
7. apply both FIFO and weighted average cost formulas
8. explain the net realisable value basis of measurement
9. account for adjustments to net realisable value
10. account for inventory expenses
11. implement the disclosure requirements of IAS 2.

9.1 The nature of inventories

For retailing and manufacturing entities inventory is the most active asset, and may make up a significant proportion of current assets. The cost of goods sold during the period is normally the largest expense of such entities.

The main accounting standard analysed in this chapter is IAS 2 *Inventories*. The standard was first issued as IAS 2 in October 1975, revised in 1993, amended in 1999 and 2000, exposed in May 2002 as a part of the *Exposure Draft of Proposed Improvements to International Accounting Standards*, and issued in its present form in 2003.

According to paragraph 2 of IAS 2, the standard applies in accounting for all inventories except work in progress arising under construction contracts (covered by IAS 11 *Construction Contracts*); financial instruments and biological assets related to agricultural activity and agricultural produce at the point of harvest (IAS 41 *Agriculture*).

Paragraph 6 of IAS 2 defines inventories as follows:

Inventories are assets:
(a) held for sale in the ordinary course of business;
(b) in the process of production for such sale; or
(c) in the form of materials or supplies to be consumed in the production process or in the rendering of services.

Note the following points arising from this definition:

1. The assets are held for sale in the ordinary course of business. The accounting standards do not define 'ordinary', but IFRS 5 *Non-current Assets Held for Sale and Discontinued Operations* requires that non-current assets held for sale are to be distinguished from inventories. This indicates that the term 'inventories' should be applied only to those assets that are always intended for sale or use in producing saleable goods or services.

2. Accounting for assets held for use by the entity is covered by other accounting standards according to their nature. IAS 16 *Property, Plant and Equipment* covers tangible assets such as production equipment; IAS 38 *Intangible Assets* covers intangible assets such as patents.

3. Supplies or materials such as stationery would not be treated as inventories unless they are held for sale or are used in producing goods for sale.

4. IAS 16, paragraph 8, states that 'spare parts and servicing equipment are usually carried as inventory' unless those spare parts are expected to be used during more than one period, or can be used only in conjunction with an item of property, plant and equipment. This standard clearly envisages that spare parts as inventory are those items consumed regularly during the production process, such as bobbin winders on commercial sewing machines.

5. In the case of a service provider, inventories include the costs of the service for which the entity has not yet recognised the related revenue (IAS 2, para. 8).

6. The assets are current assets because they satisfy the following criteria for classification as 'current' set out in paragraph 57 of IAS 1 *Presentation of Financial Statements*:
   - it is expected to be realised in, or is intended for sale or consumption in the entity's normal operating cycle
   - it is held primarily for the purpose of being traded.

   The operating cycle of an entity is the time between the acquisition of assets for processing and their realisation in cash or cash equivalents. In some industries, such as retailing, the operating cycle may be very short, but for others, like winemaking, the operating cycle could cover a number of years. When the entity's operating cycle is not clearly identifiable, its duration is assumed to be 12 months (IAS 1, para. 59).

To illustrate: Nokia Corporation, based in Finland, prepares its financial statements in accordance with International Financial Reporting Standards (IFRSs). The extract from

Nokia's notes to the consolidated financial statements at 31 December 2005, as shown in figure 9.1, indicates what is contained in inventories.

NOTES TO THE CONSOLIDATED FINANCIAL STATEMENTS (CONTINUED)		
19 INVENTORIES		
	2005 EURm	2004 EURm
Raw materials, supplies and other	361	326
Work in progress	685	477
Finished goods	622	502
Total	1 668	1 305

FIGURE 9.1 Extract from the consolidated financial statements of Nokia
Source: Nokia (2005, p. 23).

In this chapter, accounting for inventory is considered as follows:
- initial recognition of inventory – determining the cost of inventory acquired or made
- recording of inventory transactions using either the periodic or perpetual inventory methods, including end-of-period procedures and adjustments
- assignment of costs to inventory using the FIFO or weighted average cost flow assumptions
- measurement subsequent to initial recognition – determining the amount at which the asset is reported subsequent to acquisition, including any write-down to net realisable value.

LO 2

9.2 Initial recognition of inventory

According to paragraph 9 of IAS 2: 'Inventories shall be measured at the lower of cost and net realisable value'. As the purpose of acquiring or manufacturing inventory items is to sell them at a profit, inventory will initially be recognised at cost. Two specific industry groups have been exempted from applying the lower of cost and net realisable value rule, namely:
(a) producers of agricultural and forest products, agricultural produce after harvest and minerals and mineral products, to the extent that they are measured at net realisable value in accordance with well-established practices in those industries
(b) commodity broker-traders who measure their inventories at fair value less costs to sell.

In these cases, movements in net realisable value or fair value less any selling costs incurred during the period are recognised in the income statement. Where inventories in these industries are measured by reference to historical cost, the lower of cost and net realisable value rule mandated by paragraph 9 would still apply.

LO 3

9.3 Determination of cost

The first step in accounting for inventory is its initial recognition at cost. IAS 2, paragraph 10, specifies three components of cost:
- costs of purchase
- costs of conversion
- other costs incurred in bringing the inventories to their present location and condition.

Costs of conversion apply only to manufacturing entities where raw materials and other supplies are purchased and then converted to other products.

9.3.1 Costs of purchase

Paragraph 11 of IAS 2 states that the costs of purchase comprise the purchase price, import duties and other taxes (other than those subsequently recoverable by the entity from the taxing authorities), transport, handling and other costs directly attributable to the acquisition of finished goods, materials and services. Trade discounts, rebates and other similar items are deducted in determining the costs of purchase.

Terms of sale

In identifying the costs of purchase, consideration must be given to the terms of sale relating to inventory items because such terms determine the treatment of transport costs associated with purchase. If goods are sold FOB (free on board) shipping point, freight costs incurred from the point of shipment are paid by the buyer, and are included in the costs of purchase. If goods are sold FOB destination, the seller pays all freight costs.

Transaction taxes

Many countries levy taxes on transactions involving the exchange of goods and services, and require entities engaging in such activities to collect and remit the tax to the government. If such a 'goods and services tax' or 'value added tax' exists, care must be taken to exclude these amounts from the costs of purchase if they are recoverable by the entity from the taxing authorities.

Trade and cash discounts

Trade discounts are reductions in selling prices granted to customers. Such discounts may be granted as an incentive to buy, as a means to quit ageing inventory or as a reward for placing large orders for goods. Because the discount reduces the purchase cost, it is deducted when determining the cost of inventory. Cash or settlement discounts are offered as incentives for early payment of amounts owing on credit sales. Credit terms appear on invoices or contracts and often take the form '2/7, n/30', which means that the buyer will receive a 2% discount if the invoice is paid within seven days of the invoice date or will get 30 days to pay without discount. Some entities may also impose an interest penalty for late payment.

Divergent accounting practices have arisen over time in respect of settlement discounts, with some countries treating the discount as a reduction in the cost of inventories and others treating the discount as revenue. This issue was settled when the International Financial Reporting Interpretations Committee (IFRIC) stated in November 2004 that 'settlement discounts should be deducted from the cost of inventories' (IASB 2004). Thus, discounts received are to be treated as a deduction from the cost of inventories rather than as discount revenue. On the other hand, rebates that specifically and genuinely refund selling expenses are not to be deducted from the cost of inventories.

Deferred payment terms

Where an item of inventory is acquired for cash or short-term credit, determination of the purchase price is relatively straightforward. One variation that may arise is that some or all of the cash payment is deferred. In this case, as noted in paragraph 18 of IAS 2, the purchase cost contains a financing element — the difference between the amount paid and a purchase on normal credit terms — which must be recognised as interest expense over the period of deferral.

9.3.2 Costs of conversion

IAS 2, paragraph 12, identifies costs of conversion as being the costs directly related to the units of production, such as direct labour, plus a systematic allocation of fixed and variable production overheads that are incurred in converting materials into finished goods. Variable overheads are indirect costs of production that vary directly with the volume of production and are allocated to each unit of production on the basis of actual use of production facilities. Fixed overheads, such as depreciation of production machinery, remain relatively constant regardless of the volume of production and are allocated to the cost of inventory on the basis of normal production capacity. Where a production process simultaneously produces one or more products, the costs of conversion must be allocated between products on a systematic and rational basis (para. 14). Costing methodologies are a managerial accounting issue and outside the scope of this book.

9.3.3   Other costs

Other costs can be included only if they are 'incurred in bringing the inventories to their present location and condition' (IAS 2, para. 15). Such costs could include specific design expenses incurred in producing goods for individual customers. IAS 23 *Borrowing Costs* allows borrowing costs such as interest to be included in the cost of inventories but only where such inventories are a qualifying asset; that is, one which takes a substantial period of time to get ready for its intended use or sale. Inventory items would rarely meet this criterion.

9.3.4   Excluded costs

The following costs are specifically listed in paragraph 16 of IAS 2 as costs that cannot be included in the cost of inventories and must be recognised as expenses when incurred:

- abnormal amounts of wasted materials, labour or other production costs
- storage costs, unless those costs are necessary in the production process before a further production stage
- administrative overheads that do not contribute to bringing inventories to their present location and condition
- selling costs.

9.3.5   Cost of inventories of a service provider

Service providers, such as cleaners, would normally measure any inventories at the cost of production. Because a service is being provided, such costs would consist primarily of labour and other personnel costs for those employees directly engaged in providing the service. The costs of supervisory personnel and directly attributable overheads may also be included, but paragraph 19 of IAS 2 prohibits the inclusion of labour and other costs relating to sales and general administrative personnel. Profit margins or non-attributable overheads that are built into the prices charged by service providers cannot be factored into the value of inventories. Such inventory assets would be recognised only for services 'in-progress' at reporting date for which the service provider has not as yet recognised any revenue (for example, where a catering firm has provided meals for 10 days as at balance date but bills the client on a fortnightly basis).

9.3.6   Cost of agricultural produce harvested from biological assets

IAS 41 *Agriculture* requires inventories of agricultural produce, such as wheat and oranges, to be measured at their fair value less estimated point-of-sale costs at the point of harvest. IAS 2, paragraph 20, deems this value to be 'cost' for the purposes of applying the requirements of the inventory standard.

9.3.7   Estimating cost

Techniques for determining cost such as the standard cost method or the retail method may be used for convenience so long as the resulting values approximate cost. Manufacturing entities determine a 'standard' value of materials, direct and indirect labour and overheads for each product based on normal levels of efficiency and capacity utilisation. Adjustments are made at the end of the reporting period to account for variances between standard and actual costs. Standard costs must be regularly reviewed and amended as required. The retail method is used to measure inventories of large numbers of rapidly changing items with similar margins for which it is impractical to use other costing methods. Supermarket and department store chains most often employ this method of approximating cost. Cost is determined by reducing the sales value of the inventory by an appropriate percentage gross margin or an average percentage margin. In applying this method, care must be taken to ensure that gross margins are adjusted for goods that have been discounted below their original selling price.

ILLUSTRATIVE EXAMPLE 9.1

Determination of cost

Florence Ltd, an Australian company, received the following invoice from Genoa Garments Ltd, an Italian garment manufacturer.

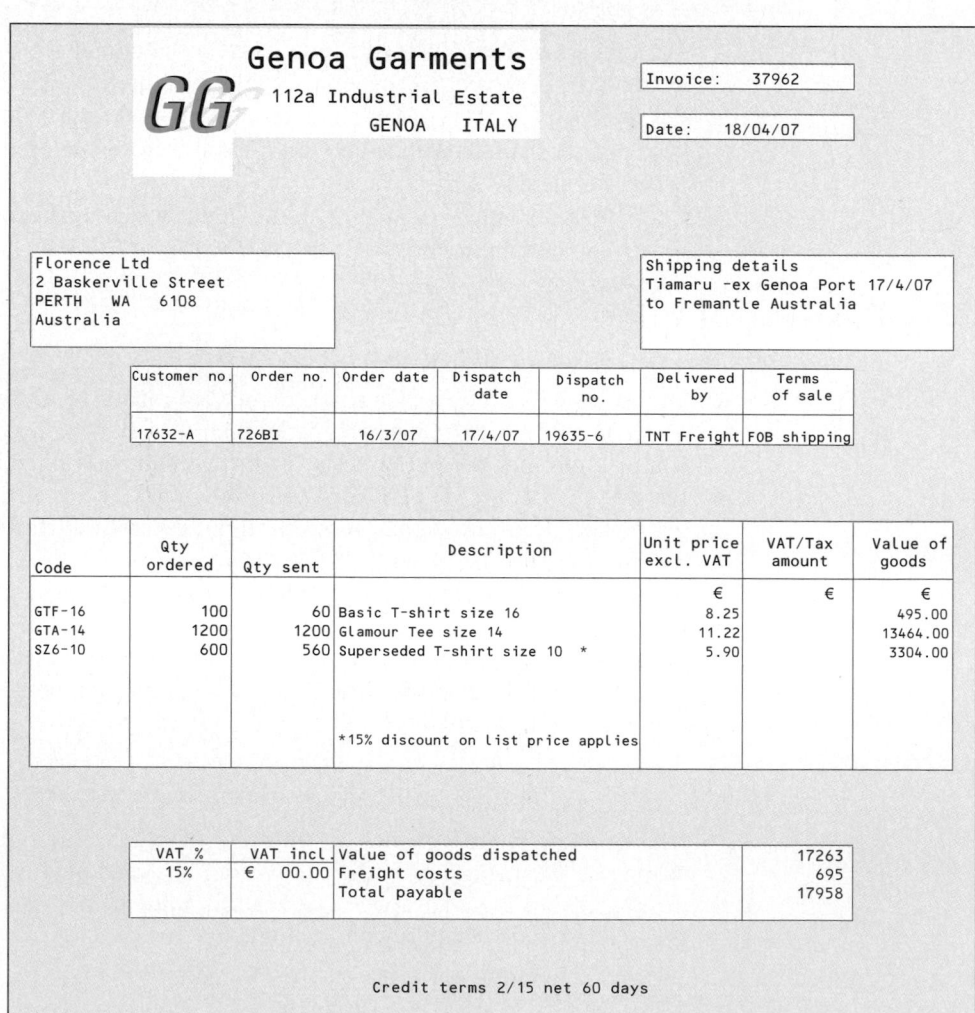

Genoa Garments
GG 112a Industrial Estate
GENOA   ITALY

Invoice: 37962

Date: 18/04/07

Florence Ltd
2 Baskerville Street
PERTH   WA   6108
Australia

Shipping details
Tiamaru -ex Genoa Port 17/4/07
to Fremantle Australia

Customer no.	Order no.	Order date	Dispatch date	Dispatch no.	Delivered by	Terms of sale
17632-A	726BI	16/3/07	17/4/07	19635-6	TNT Freight	FOB shipping

Code	Qty ordered	Qty sent	Description	Unit price excl. VAT	VAT/Tax amount	Value of goods
				€	€	€
GTF-16	100	60	Basic T-shirt size 16	8.25		495.00
GTA-14	1200	1200	Glamour Tee size 14	11.22		13464.00
SZ6-10	600	560	Superseded T-shirt size 10 *	5.90		3304.00
			*15% discount on list price applies			

VAT %	VAT incl.		
15%	€ 00.00	Value of goods dispatched	17263
		Freight costs	695
		Total payable	17958

Credit terms 2/15 net 60 days

The goods arrived at Fremantle port on 29 May 2007 and were held in a bond store pending payment of import duties and taxes. After the payment of storage costs of A$145, import duty at 1.5% of the total value of goods in Australian dollars, goods and services tax (GST) of 10% and local freight charges of A$316, the goods were finally delivered to Florence Ltd's warehouse on 6 June 2007. The invoice was received on 8 June and a liability of $A29 439.34 recorded using the exchange rate of A$1 = €0.61 at that date. The invoice was paid in full on 8 July by the remittance of €28 964.52 (at an exchange rate of A$1 = €0.62). Florence Ltd paid A$167 to acquire the euros. Upon receipt of the goods, Florence Ltd attaches its own logo to the T-shirts and repackages them for sale. The cost of this further processing is A$2.54 per T-shirt.

Problem

What is the cost of this inventory?

Solution

The cost of inventory would include the following amounts:

Purchase price	€17 263.00
Shipping costs	695.00
	€17 958.00
Conversion to Australian dollars:	
€17 958 ÷ 0.61	29 439.34
Storage costs − bond store	145.00
Import duty ($28 300 × 1.5%)	424.50
Freight costs	316.00
Foreign exchange commission	167.00
Logo and repackaging	
(1820 items × $2.54)	4 622.80
Total cost	A$ 35 114.64

Where a cost per unit for each type of T-shirt is required, some method of allocating the 'generic' costs of shipping, storage, freight and foreign exchange commission would need to be employed. In this case, such costs could be allocated on a per garment basis. For example, the cost per unit for the Basic T-shirts would be:

	A$
Purchase price (€8.25 ÷ A$0.61)	13.52
Import duty (1.5% × $13.52)	0.20
Shipping and other costs*	0.97
Logo and repackaging	2.54
Cost per unit	$17.23

*(A$145 + 316 + 167 + [€695 ÷ 0.61] = A$1767.34/1820 garments = A$0.97 per garment)

Note that the exchange gain of $474.82 arising from the change in euro–dollar exchange rates between the recognition of the liability and its payment cannot be incorporated in the calculation of cost as it is not associated with the acquisition transaction. Additionally, the GST of 10% payable is not included as it is a transaction tax receivable by Florence Ltd against GST collected on sale of inventory.

LO 4

9.4 Accounting for inventory

There are two main methods of accounting for inventory: the periodic method and the perpetual method.

9.4.1 Periodic method

Under the periodic method, the amount of inventory is determined periodically (normally annually) by conducting a physical count and multiplying the number of units by a cost per unit to value the inventory on hand. This amount is then recognised as a current asset. This balance remains unchanged until the next count is taken. Purchases and returns of inventory during the reporting period are posted directly to expense accounts. Cost of goods sold during the year is determined as follows:

> Opening inventory + Purchases + Freight inwards − Purchase returns
> − Cash discounts received − Closing inventory = Cost of goods sold

Accounting for inventory using the periodic method is cost effective and easy to apply, but its major disadvantage is that the exact quantity and cost of inventory cannot be determined on a day-to-day basis, and this might result in lost sales or unhappy customers. Additionally, it is not possible to identify stock losses or posting errors, resulting in accounting figures that might be inaccurate or misleading.

9.4.2 Perpetual method

Under the perpetual method, inventory records are updated each time a transaction involving inventory takes place. Thus, up-to-date information about the quantity and cost of inventory on hand will always be available, enabling the entity to provide better customer service and maintain better control over this essential asset. This system is more complicated and expensive than the periodic method but, with the advent of user-friendly computerised accounting packages and point-of-sale machines linked directly to accounting records, most businesses today can afford to and do use the perpetual method.

The perpetual method requires a subsidiary ledger to be maintained, either manually or on computer, with a separate record for each inventory item detailing all movements in both quantity and cost. This subsidiary record is linked to the general ledger account for inventory, and regular reconciliations are carried out to ensure the accuracy and completeness of the accounting records. This reconciliation process is discussed in section 9.5 of this book.

ILLUSTRATIVE EXAMPLE 9.2

Comparing the periodic and the perpetual inventory methods

Palermo Ltd sells garden furniture settings. This example illustrates the journal entries necessary to record the normal inventory transactions that would occur during an accounting period, and the reporting of gross profit from the sale of inventory under both accounting systems.

The inventory account in the general ledger of Palermo Ltd at the beginning of the year under both methods is shown opposite.

→

Inventory			
1 July 2007	Balance b/d (10 units @ $670)	6 700	

The following transactions took place during the year:

(a) Purchased 354 settings (FOB shipping) at $670 each on credit terms of 2/10, n/30 from Taormina Pty Ltd.

(b) Sold, on credit, 352 settings for $975 each.

(c) Returned four settings to the supplier.

(d) Seven settings were returned by customers.

The journal entries necessary to record these transactions under both inventory accounting methods are shown below.

PALERMO LTD
Journal entries

Perpetual inventory method   *Periodic inventory method*

(a) Purchased 354 settings (FOB shipping) at $670 each on credit terms of 2/10, n/30 from Taormina Pty Ltd.

	Dr	Cr		Dr	Cr
Inventory	237 180		Purchases	237 180	
A/cs payable		237 180	A/cs payable		237 180

(b) Sold, on credit, 352 settings for $975 each.

	Dr	Cr		Dr	Cr
A/cs receivable	343 200		A/cs receivable	343 200	
Sales revenue		343 200	Sales revenue		343 200
Cost of goods sold	235 840				
Inventory		235 840			

(c) Returned four settings to the supplier.

	Dr	Cr		Dr	Cr
A/cs payable	2 680		A/cs payable	2 680	
Inventory		2 680	Purchase returns		2 680

(d) Seven settings were returned by customers.

	Dr	Cr		Dr	Cr
Sales returns	6 825		Sales returns	6 825	
A/cs receivable		6 825	A/cs receivable		6 825
Inventory	4 690				
Cost of goods sold		4 690			

Important differences to note between the two methods of accounting for inventory:

- Purchases are posted directly to the asset account under the perpetual method, and are posted to expense accounts under the periodic method.
- When goods are sold, a second entry is necessary under the perpetual method to transfer the cost of those goods from the inventory account to the expense account, cost of goods sold.
- When goods are returned to suppliers, the return is adjusted directly to inventory under the perpetual method, and is posted to a purchase returns account under the periodic method.
- When goods are returned from customers, a second journal entry is necessary under the perpetual method to transfer the cost of these goods out of the cost of goods sold account and back into the inventory account.
- Under the periodic method, freight is normally posted to a separate account. Under the perpetual method, freight is included in the cost of inventory unless the amounts are immaterial, in which case freight costs would be accumulated in a separate expense account.
- If inventory items being returned to the supplier have been paid for, an accounts receivable account would be opened pending a cash refund from the supplier.
- If sales returns have been paid for, an accounts payable entry would be raised to recognise the need to refund cash to the customer.
- Under the periodic method, cash settlement discounts would be posted to a separate ledger account. Under the perpetual method, settlement discounts would be deducted from the cost of inventory.

After posting the journal entries, the general ledger account would appear as shown below.

Perpetual inventory method

Inventory			
1/7/07 Balance b/d	6 700	Cost of goods sold	235 840
A/cs payable	237 180	A/cs payable	2 680
Cost of goods sold	4 690	Balance b/d	10 050
	248 570		248 570
Balance c/d	10 050		

Periodic inventory method

Inventory		
1/7/07 Balance	6 700	

Assuming that the physical count at the end of the reporting period found 15 settings on hand at a cost of $670 each, the gross profit earned on these would be determined as follows:

PALERMO LTD
Determination of gross profit

Perpetual inventory method

Sales revenue	343 200
Less Sales returns and allowances	6 825
Net sales revenue	336 375
Cost of goods sold	231 150
Gross profit	**$ 105 225**

Periodic inventory method

Sales revenue		343 200
Less Sales returns		6 825
Net sales revenue		336 375
Cost of goods sold		
Opening inventory	6 700	
Add Purchases	237 180	
	243 880	
Less Purchase returns	2 680	
Goods available for sale	241 200	
Less Closing inventory	10 050	
Cost of goods sold		231 150
Gross profit		$ 105 225

Note that, in this example, the same gross profit is reported irrespective of the inventory recording method adopted. However, where adjustments are made for damaged or lost inventory, the gross profit will be different under the perpetual method.

LO 5

9.5   End-of-period accounting

To ensure that reported figures for inventory, cost of goods sold and other expenses are accurate and complete, certain procedures must be carried out at the end of each accounting period. It is essential that good internal controls be instituted to ensure that inventory is protected from fraud or loss and that inventory figures are complete and accurate. This section examines the physical count, end-of-year cut-off and essential reconciliation procedures.

9.5.1   Physical count

Under the periodic method, inventory must be counted at the end of each accounting period to determine the value of closing inventory. Periodic counts are made under the perpetual method to verify the accuracy of recorded quantities for each inventory item, although not necessarily at balance date, if inventory differences are historically found to be immaterial.

The way in which the physical count is conducted will depend on the type of inventory and the accounting system of the entity. Stockpiled inventory such as mineral sands may require the use of surveyors to measure quantities on hand and assay tests to determine mineral content.

The following are some steps that are generally taken to ensure the accuracy of a physical count:

- The warehouse, retail store or storage facility should be arranged so as to facilitate counting and clearly segregate non-inventory items.
- Cut-off procedures should be put in place and final numbers of important documents such as dispatch notes and invoices recorded. (Cut-off procedures are discussed in greater detail in section 9.5.2.)
- Prenumbered count sheets, tags or cards should be produced detailing inventory codes and descriptions. A supervisor should record all numbers used and account for spoiled documents to ensure that the count details are complete. Alternatively, where inventory items have bar codes, electronic scanners can be used to record the count.
- Counting should be done in teams of at least two people: one counter and one checker. All team members should sign the count records.

- Any damaged or incomplete items located during the count should be clearly listed on the count records.
- The supervisor should ensure that all goods have been counted before the count sheets are collected.

Perpetual method

Once the physical count is complete, under the perpetual method the quantities on hand are then compared to recorded quantities and all discrepancies investigated. Recording errors cause discrepancies; for example, the wrong code number or quantity might have been entered, or a transaction might not have been processed in the correct period. Alternatively, discrepancies may reveal losses of goods caused by damage or fraud. Recording errors can be corrected but the value of goods that have been lost should be written off using the following entry:

Inventory losses	Dr	5 000	
Inventory	Cr		5 000
(Recognition of inventory losses during the period)			

Unless they are immaterial, inventory losses must be disclosed separately in the notes to the financial statements (see section 9.9 of this chapter).

Periodic method

Once the count is completed, under this method the count quantities are then costed and the value of inventory brought to account. This adjustment can be done in a number of ways, but the simplest is to post the following two journal entries:

Opening inventory (cost of goods sold)	Dr	79 600	
Inventory	Cr		79 600
(Transfer of opening balance to expense)			
Inventory	Dr	87 100	
Closing inventory (cost of goods sold)	Cr		87 100
(Recognition of final inventory balance)			

Under the periodic method, inventory losses and fraud cannot be identified and recorded as a separate expense. The movement in inventory balances plus the cost of purchases is presumed to represent the cost of goods sold during the reporting period.

9.5.2 Cut-off procedures

Under both periodic and perpetual methods there is a need to ensure that, when a physical count is conducted, there is a proper cut-off of the record keeping so that the accounting records reflect the results of the physical count and include all transactions relevant to the accounting period while excluding those that belong to other periods. For all inventory transactions (sales, purchases and returns) it is possible for inventory records to be updated before transaction details are posted to the general ledger accounts. For example, goods are normally entered into inventory records when the goods are received, but accounts payable records will not record the liability until the invoice arrives because shipping documents may not record price details. Under the periodic method, there is a need to ensure a proper cut-off between the general ledger recording of goods received, shipped and returned, and the inventory counted. Under the perpetual method, there is a need to ensure that all inventory movements are properly recorded in the perpetual records, so a valid comparison is made between inventory counted and the perpetual record quantities. Further, if the perpetual method is not integrated with the general ledger, there is also a need to ensure a proper cut-off between the general ledger and the perpetual records. Thus, at balance date it is essential that proper cut-off procedures be implemented.

The following cut-off errors could arise:

- Goods have been received into inventory, but the purchase invoice has not been processed.
- Goods have been returned to a supplier, and deleted from inventory, but the credit note has not been processed.
- Goods have been sold and dispatched to a customer, but the invoice has not been raised.
- Goods have been returned by a customer, but the credit note has not been issued.

If inventory movements have been processed before invoices and credit notes, adjusting entries are needed to bring both sides of the transaction into the same accounting period.

9.5.3 Goods in transit

Accounting for goods in transit at balance date will depend upon the terms of trade. Where goods are purchased on an FOB shipping basis, the goods belong to the purchaser from the time they are shipped, and should be included in inventory/accounts payable at accounting date. All such purchases in transit will need to be identified and the following adjusting journal entry posted:

Goods in transit (inventory)	Dr	1 500	
Accounts payable	Cr		1 500
(Recognition of inventory in transit at accounting date)			

If goods are purchased on FOB destination terms, no adjustment will be required because the goods still legally belong to the supplier.

If goods are sold on FOB destination terms, they belong to the entity until they arrive at the customer's premises. Because the sale will have been recorded in the current year, the following adjusting entries will be required to remove that sale and reinstate the inventory:

Inventory	Dr	3 000	
Cost of goods sold	Cr		3 000
(Reversal of sale for goods in transit at accounting date)			
Sales revenue	Dr	4 500	
Accounts receivable	Cr		4 500
(Reversal of sale for goods in transit at accounting date)			

9.5.4 Consignment inventory

Care must be taken in the treatment of consignment inventory. Under a consignment arrangement, an agent (the consignee) agrees to sell goods on behalf of the consignor on a commission basis. The transfer of goods to the consignee is not a legal sale/purchase transaction. Legal ownership remains with the consignor until the agent sells the goods to a third party. Steps must be taken to ensure that goods held on consignment are not included in the physical count. Equally, goods owned by the entity that are held by consignees must be added to the physical count.

9.5.5 Control account/subsidiary ledger reconciliation

This end-of-period procedure is required only under the perpetual method. The general ledger account balance must be reconciled with the total of the subsidiary ledger (manual or computerised). Recording errors and omissions will cause the reconciliation process to fail. Any material discrepancies should be investigated and corrected. This process will identify only amounts that have not been posted to both records; it cannot identify errors within the subsidiary records, such as posting a purchase to the wrong inventory item code. However, the physical count/recorded figure reconciliation will isolate these errors.

ILLUSTRATIVE EXAMPLE 9.3

End-of-period adjustments

Bill Smith, trading as Rimini Pty Ltd, completed his first year of trading as a toy wholesaler on 30 June 2008. He is worried about his end-of-year physical and cut-off procedures.

The inventory ledger account balance at 30 June 2008, under the perpetual inventory method, was $78 700. His physical count, however, revealed the cost of inventory on hand at 30 June 2008 to be only $73 400. While Bill expected a small inventory shortfall due to breakage and petty theft, he considered this shortfall to be excessive.

Upon investigating reasons for the inventory 'shortfall', Bill discovered the following:

- Goods costing $800 were sold on credit to R Riccione for $1300 on 26 June 2008 on FOB destination terms. The goods were still in transit at 30 June 2008. Rimini Pty Ltd recorded the sale on 26 June 2008 but did not include these goods in the physical count.
- Included in the physical count were $2200 of goods held on consignment.
- Goods costing $910 were purchased on credit from Cattolica Ltd on 25 June 2008 and received on 28 June 2008. The purchase was unrecorded at 30 June 2008 but the goods were included in the physical count.
- Goods costing $400 were purchased on credit from Urbina Supplies on 23 June 2008 on FOB shipping terms. The goods were delivered to the transport company on 27 June 2008. The purchase was recorded on 27 June 2008 but, as the goods had not yet arrived, Rimini Pty Ltd did not include these goods in the physical count.
- At 30 June 2008 Rimini Pty Ltd had unsold goods costing $3700 out on consignment. These goods were not included in the physical count.
- Goods costing $2100 were sold on credit to Montevarchi Ltd for $3200 on 24 June 2008 on FOB shipping terms. The goods were shipped on 28 June 2008. The sale was unrecorded at 30 June 2008 and Rimini Pty Ltd did not include these goods in the physical count.

→

- Goods costing $1500 had been returned to Gubbio Garments on 30 June 2008. A credit note was received from the supplier on 5 July 2008. No payment had been made for the goods prior to their return.

These transactions and events must be analysed to determine if adjustments are required to the ledger accounts (general and subsidiary) and/or the physical count records as follows:

Workings

	Recorded balance $	Physical count $
Balance prior to adjustment	78 700	73 400
Add Goods sold, FOB destination and in transit at 30 June	800	800
Less Goods held on consignment	–	(2 200)
Add Unrecorded purchase	910	–
Add Goods purchased, FOB shipping and in transit at 30 June	–	400
Add Goods out on consignment	–	3 700
Less Unrecorded sale	(2 100)	–
Less Unrecorded purchase returns	(1 500)	–
	$76 810	$76 100

If, after all adjustments are made, the recorded balance cannot be reconciled to the physical count, the remaining discrepancy is presumed to represent inventory losses and a final adjustment is made as follows:

Adjusted balances	76 810	76 100
Inventory shortfall	(710)	–
	$76 100	$76 100

The following journal entries are necessary on 30 June 2008 to correct errors and adjust the inventory ledger accounts:

RIMINI PTY LTD General journal			
2008 30 June			
Sales revenue	Dr	1 300	
Accounts receivable (R Riccione)	Cr		1 300
(Correction of sale recorded in error)			
Inventory (Item X)	Dr	800	
Cost of goods sold	Cr		800
(Correction of sale recorded in error)			
Inventory (Item Y)	Dr	910	
Accounts payable (Cattolica Ltd)	Cr		910
(Correction of unrecorded purchase)			

RIMINI PTY LTD General journal (*continued*)			
Accounts receivable (Montevarchi Ltd)	Dr	3 200	
Sales revenue	Cr		3 200
(Correction of unrecorded sale)			
Cost of goods sold	Dr	2 100	
Inventory (Item Z)	Cr		2 100
(Correction of unrecorded sale)			
Accounts payable (Gubbio Garments)	Dr	1 500	
Inventory (Item W)	Cr		1 500
(Correction of unrecorded purchase return)			
Inventory losses and write-downs	Dr	710	
Inventory	Cr		710
(Unexplained variance (physical/records) written off)			

LO 6

9.6 Assigning costs to inventory on sale

The nature of inventory held by an entity does not affect its initial recognition at cost but has a significant impact when that inventory is sold. As shown in illustrative example 9.2, under the perpetual system the cost of inventory items is transferred to a 'Cost of goods sold' expense account on sale, and under the periodic system a 'Cost of goods sold' figure is calculated on balance date. This is an easy task if the nature of inventory is such that it is possible to clearly identify the exact inventory item that has been sold and its cost, but what if it is not possible to identify exactly the cost of the item sold? How can you measure the cost of a tonne of wheat when it is extracted from a stockpile consisting of millions of tonnes acquired at different prices over the accounting period?

IAS 2 addresses this problem by mandating two different rules for the assigning of cost to inventory items sold. The rules differ depending on the nature of inventory held. Paragraph 23 states that:

> The cost of inventories of items that are not ordinarily interchangeable and goods or services produced and segregated for specific projects shall be assigned by using specific identification of their individual costs.

Thus, if the inventory held consists of items that can be individually identified because of their unique nature or by some other means, or cannot be individually identified but have been acquired for a specific project, then the exact cost of the item sold must be recorded as cost of goods sold expense.

Paragraph 25 states that:

> The cost of inventories, other than those dealt with in paragraph 23, shall be assigned by using the first-in, first-out (FIFO) or weighted average cost formula.

This means that, where a specific cost cannot be identified because of the nature of the item sold, then some method has to be adopted to estimate that cost. This process is known as 'assigning' cost. Most inventory items fall into this category, for example, identical items of food and clothing and bulk items like oil and minerals. There are many methods of assigning a cost to inventory items sold but IAS 2 restricts entities to a choice between two methods — FIFO and weighted average.

9.6.1 First-in, first-out (FIFO) cost formula

LO 7

The FIFO formula assumes that items of inventory that were purchased or produced first are sold first, and the items remaining in inventory at the end of the period are those most recently purchased or produced (IAS 2, para. 27). Thus, more recent purchase costs are assigned to the inventory asset account, and older costs are assigned to the cost of goods sold expense account.

Consider this example: there are 515 DVD players on hand at 30 June 2008, and recent purchase invoices showed the following costs:

- 28 June   180 players at $49.00
- 15 June   325 players at $48.50
- 31 May   200 players at $47.00.

The value of ending inventory is found by starting with the most recent purchase and working backwards until all items on hand have been priced (on the assumption that it is not known when any particular DVD player was sold). The value of ending inventory would be $25 052.50 (being 180 players at $49 + 325 players at $48.50 + 10 players at $47).

Many proponents of the FIFO method argue that this method best reflects the physical movement of inventory, particularly perishable goods or those subject to changes in fashion or rapid obsolescence (as in the case of DVD players). If the oldest goods are normally sold first, then the oldest costs should be assigned to expense.

9.6.2 Weighted average cost formula

Under the weighted average cost formula, the cost of each item sold is determined from the cost of similar items purchased or produced during the period. The average may be calculated on a periodic basis (weighted average), or as each additional shipment is received (moving average).

Using a periodic basis, the cost of inventory on hand at the beginning of the period plus all inventory purchased during the year is divided by the total number of items available for sale during the period (opening quantity plus purchased quantity). This produces the cost per unit. For example: inventory on hand at 1 January 2009 was valued at $3439.78, consisting of 134 units at an average of $25.67 each. During the year the following purchases were made:

- 200 units at $27.50 = $5 500.00
- 175 units at $28.35 = $4 961.25
- 300 units at $29.10 = $8 730.00
- 120 units at $29.00 = $3 480.00.

At the end of the year, the weighted average cost of inventory would be calculated as:

$$\$3439.78 + 5500.00 + 4961.25 + 8730.00 + 3480.00 = \$26\,111.03 \div 929 \text{ units} = \$28.11 \text{ per unit}$$

Using the moving average method, the average unit cost is recalculated each time there is an inventory purchase or purchase return. This is demonstrated in illustrative example 9.4.

ILLUSTRATIVE EXAMPLE 9.4

Application of cost formulas

The following information has been extracted from the records of Positano Parts about one of its products. Positano Parts uses the perpetual inventory method and its reporting date is 31 December.

		No. of units	Unit cost $	Total cost $
2006				
01/01	Beginning balance	800	7.00	5 600
06/01	Purchased	300	7.05	2 115
05/02	Sold @ $12.00 per unit	1 000		
19/03	Purchased	1 100	7.35	8 085
24/03	Purchase returns	80	7.35	588
10/04	Sold @ $12.10 per unit	700		
22/06	Purchased	8 400	7.50	63 000
31/07	Sold @ $13.25 per unit	1 800		
04/08	Sales returns @ $13.25 per unit	20		
04/09	Sold @ $13.50 per unit	3 500		
06/10	Purchased	500	8.00	4 000
27/11	Sold @ $15.00 per unit	3 100		

Required

1. Calculate the cost of inventory on hand at 31 December 2006 and the cost of goods sold for the year ended 31 December 2006, assuming:
   (a) the FIFO cost flow assumption
   (b) the moving average cost flow assumption (round the average unit costs to the nearest cent, and round the total cost amounts to the nearest dollar).
2. Prepare the trading section of the income statement for the year ended 31 December 2006, assuming:
   (a) the FIFO cost flow assumption
   (b) the moving average cost flow assumption.

Part 1. (a) First-in, first-out cost formula

Date	Details	Purchases No. units	Unit cost	Total cost	COGS No. units	Unit cost	Total cost	Balance[1] No. units	Unit cost	Total cost
01/01	Inventory balance							800	7.00	5 600
06/01	Purchases	300	7.05	2 115				800	7.00	5 600
								300	7.05	2 115
05/02	Sales				800	7.00	5 600			
					200	7.05	1 410	100	7.05	705
19/03	Purchases	1 100	7.35	8 085				100	7.05	705
								1 100	7.35	8 085
24/03	Purchase returns	(80)	7.35	(588)				100	7.05	705
								1 020	7.35	7 497
10/04	Sales				100	7.05	705			
					600	7.35	4 410	420	7.35	3 087
22/06	Purchases	8 400	7.50	63 000				420	7.35	3 087
								8 400	7.50	63 000
31/07	Sales				420	7.35	3 087			
					1 380	7.50	10 350	7 020	7.50	52 650
04/08	Sales returns[2]				(20)	7.50	(150)	7 040	7.50	52 800
04/09	Sales				3 500	7.50	26 250	3 540	7.50	26 550
06/10	Purchases	500	8.00	4 000				3 540	7.50	26 550
								500	8.00	4 000
22/11	Sales				3 100	7.50	23 250	440	7.50	3 300
								500	8.00	4 000
				76 612			74 912			

Notes: 1. As it is assumed the earliest purchases are sold first, a separate balance of each purchase at a different price must be maintained.

2. The principle of 'last out–first in' is applied to sales returns.

Part 1. (b) Moving average cost formula

Date	Details	Purchases No. units	Unit cost	Total cost	COGS[2] No. units	Unit cost	Total cost	Balance No. units	Unit cost[1]	Total cost
01/01	Inventory balance							800	7.00	5 600
06/01	Purchases	300	7.05	2 115				1 100	7.01	7 715
05/02	Sales				1 000	7.01	7 010	100	7.01	705
19/03	Purchases	1 100	7.35	8 085				1 200	7.33	8 790
24/03	Purchase returns	(80)	7.35	(588)				1 120	7.32	8 202
10/04	Sales				700	7.32	5 124	420	7.32	3 078
22/06	Purchases	8 400	7.50	63 000				8 820	7.49	66 078
31/07	Sales				1 800	7.49	13 482	7 020	7.49	52 596
04/08	Sales returns				(20)	7.49	(150)	7 040	7.49	52 746
04/09	Sales				3 500	7.49	26 215	3 540	7.49	26 531
06/10	Purchases	500	8.00	4 000				4 040	7.56	30 531
22/11	Sales				3 100	7.56	23 436	940	7.56	7 095
				76 612			75 117			

Notes: 1. The average cost per unit is recalculated each time there is a purchase or a purchase return at a different cost.

2. The 'average' cost on the date of sale is applied to calculate the 'cost of goods sold'.

Part 2.

POSITANO PARTS Income statement (extract) for the year ended 31 December 2006		
	FIFO $	Moving average $
Sales revenue	138 070	138 070
Less Sales returns	(265)	(265)
Net sales	137 805	137 805
Less Cost of goods sold	(74 912)	(75 117)
Gross profit	$ 62 893	$ 62 688

Because the purchase price has been rising throughout the year, using the FIFO formula produces a lower cost of goods sold (higher gross profit) and a higher inventory balance than the moving average formula.

9.6.3 Which cost formula to use?

The choice of method is a matter for management judgement and depends upon the nature of the inventory, the information needs of management and financial statement users, and the cost of applying the formulas. For example, the weighted average method is easy to apply and is particularly suited to inventory where homogeneous products are mixed together, like iron ore or spring water. On the other hand, first-in, first-out may be a better reflection of the actual physical movement of goods, such as those with use-by dates where the first produced must be sold first to avoid loss due to obsolescence, spoilage or legislative restrictions. Entities with diversified operations may use both methods because they carry different types of inventory. Using diverse methods is acceptable under IAS 2, but paragraph 26 cautions that 'a difference in geographical location of inventories (or in the respective tax rules), by itself, is not sufficient to justify the use of different cost formulas'. The nature of the inventory itself should determine the choice of formula.

9.6.4 Consistent application of costing methods

Once a cost formula has been selected, management cannot randomly switch from one formula to another. Because the choice of method can have a significant impact on an entity's reported profit and asset figures, particularly in times of volatile prices, indiscriminate changes in formulas could result in the reporting of financial information that is neither comparable nor reliable. Accordingly, paragraph 13 of IAS 8 *Accounting Policies, Changes in Accounting Estimates and Errors* requires that accounting policies be consistently applied to ensure comparability of financial information. Changes in accounting policies are allowed (IAS 8, para. 14) only when required by an accounting standard or where the change results in reporting more relevant and reliable financial information. Therefore, unless the nature of inventory changes, it is unlikely that the cost formulas will change. A switch from the FIFO to the weighted average method must be disclosed in accordance with the requirements of IAS 8, in particular paragraph 19. This paragraph requires the change to be applied retrospectively, and the information disclosed as if the new accounting policy had always been applied. Hence, a change from the FIFO method to the weighted average method would require adjustments to the financial statements to show the information as if the weighted average method had always been applied. Adjustments can be taken through the opening balance of retained earnings. Comparative information would also need to be restated.

9.7 Net realisable value

LO 8

As the measurement rule mandated by IAS 2 for inventories is the 'lower of cost and net realisable value' (para. 9), an estimate of net realisable value must be made to determine if inventory must be written down. Normally, this estimate is done before preparing the financial reports but, where management become aware during the reporting period that goods or services can no longer be sold at a price above cost, inventory values should be written down to net realisable value. The rationale for this measurement rule, according to paragraph 28 of IAS 2, is that 'assets should not be carried in excess of amounts expected to be realised from their sale or use'.

Net realisable value is the net amount than an entity expects to realise from the sale of inventory in the ordinary course of business. It is defined in paragraph 6 of IAS 2 as 'the estimated selling price in the ordinary course of business less the estimated costs of completion and the estimated costs necessary to make the sale'. Net realisable value is specific to an individual entity and is not necessarily equal to fair value less selling costs. Fair value is defined as 'the amount for which an asset could be exchanged, or a liability settled, between knowledgeable, willing parties in an arm's length transaction' (IAS 2, para. 6).

Net realisable value may fall below cost for a number of reasons including:

- a fall in selling price (e.g. fashion garments)
- physical deterioration of inventories (e.g. fruit and vegetables)
- product obsolescence (e.g. computers and electrical equipment)
- a decision, as part of an entity's marketing strategy, to manufacture and sell products for the time being at a loss (e.g. new products)
- miscalculations or other errors in purchasing or production (e.g. overstocking)
- an increase in the estimated costs of completion or the estimated costs of making the sale (e.g. air-conditioning plants).

9.7.1 Estimating net realisable value

Estimates of net realisable value must be based on the most reliable evidence available at the time the estimate is made (normally balance date) of the amount that the inventories are expected to realise. Thus, estimates must be made of:

- expected selling price
- estimated costs of completion (if any)
- estimated selling costs.

These estimates take into consideration fluctuations of price or cost occurring after balance date to the extent that such events confirm conditions existing at balance date. The purpose for which inventory is held should be taken into account when reviewing net realisable values. For example, the net realisable value of inventory held to satisfy firm sales or service contracts is based on the contract price. If the sales contracts are for less than the inventory quantities held, the net realisable value of the excess is based on general selling prices. Estimated selling costs include all costs likely to be incurred in securing and filling customer orders such as advertising costs, sales personnel salaries and operating costs, and the costs of storing and shipping finished goods.

It is possible to use formulas based on predetermined criteria to initially estimate net realisable value. These formulas normally take into account, as appropriate, the age, past movements, expected future movements and estimated scrap values of the inventories. However, the results must be reviewed in the light of any special circumstances not anticipated in the formulas, such as changes in the current demand for inventories or unexpected obsolescence.

9.7.2 Materials and other supplies

IAS 2, paragraph 32, states that materials and other supplies held for use in the production of inventories are not written down below cost if the finished goods in which they will be incorporated are expected to be sold at or above cost. When the sale of finished goods is not expected to recover the costs, then materials are to be written down to net realisable value. IAS 2 suggests that the replacement cost of the materials or other supplies is probably the best measure of their net realisable value.

LO 9

9.7.3 Write-down to net realisable value

Inventories are usually written down to net realisable value on an item-by-item basis. Paragraph 29 of IAS 2 states that 'it is not appropriate to write inventories down on the basis of a classification of inventory, for example, finished goods, or all the inventories in a particular industry or geographical segment'. Where it is not practical to separately evaluate the net realisable value of each item within a product line, the write-down may be applied on a group basis provided that the products have similar purposes or end uses, and are produced and marketed in the same geographical area. IAS 2 generally requires that service providers apply the measurement rule only on an item-by-item basis, as each service ordinarily has a separate selling price.

The journal entry to process the write-down would be:

Inventory write-down expense	Dr	800	
Inventory	Cr		800
(Write-down to net realisable value)			

9.7.4 Reversal of prior write-down to net realisable value

If the circumstances that previously caused inventories to be written down below cost change, or if a new assessment confirms that net realisable value has increased, the amount of a previous write-down can be reversed (subject to an upper limit of the original write-down). This could occur if an item of inventory written down to net realisable value because of falling sales prices is still on hand at the end of a subsequent period and its selling price has recovered.

The journal entry to process the reversal would be:

Inventory	Dr	800	
Inventory write-down expense	Cr		800
(Write-up to revised net realisable value)			

ILLUSTRATIVE EXAMPLE 9.5

Application of measurement rule

Venice Pty Ltd retails gardening equipment and has four main product lines: mowers, vacuum blowers, edgers and garden tools. At 30 June 2006, cost and net realisable values for each line were as shown below.

Application of lower of cost and net realisable value measurement rule				
Inventory item	Quantity	Cost per unit $	NRV per unit $	Lower of cost and NRV $
Mowers	16	215.80	256.00	3 452.80
Vacuum blowers	113	62.35	**60.00**	6 780.00
Edgers	78	27.40	36.00	2 137.20
Garden tools	129	12.89	**11.00**	1 419.00
Inventory at the lower of cost and net realisable value				$13 789.00

The following journal entry would be required to adjust inventory values to net realisable value:

30 June 2006

Inventory write-down expense	Dr	509.36	
Inventory	Cr		509.36
(Write-down to net realisable value — vacuum blowers $265.55 (113 × $2.35) and garden tools $243.81 (129 × $1.89))			

LO 10

9.8 Recognition as an expense

Paragraph 34 of IAS 2 requires the following items to be recognised as expenses:
- carrying amount of inventories in the period in which the related revenue is recognised, in other words, cost of goods sold
- write-down of inventories to net realisable value and all losses
- reversals of write-downs to net realisable value.

The only exception to this rule relates to inventory items used by an entity as components in self-constructed property, plant or equipment. The cost of these items would be capitalised and recognised as an expense via depreciation.

LO 11

9.9 Disclosure

Paragraph 36 of IAS 2 contains the required disclosures relating to inventories. Before preparing the disclosure note, inventories on hand will need to be classified into categories because paragraph 36(b) requires 'the carrying amount in classifications appropriate to the entity' to be disclosed. Common classifications suggested in paragraph 37 are merchandise, production supplies, materials, work in progress and finished goods. Figure 9.2 provides an illustration of the disclosures required by IAS 2.

	IAS 2 Para. no.
Note 1: Summary of accounting policies (extract)	
Inventories	
Inventories are valued at the lower of cost and net realisable value. Costs incurred in bringing each product to its present location and condition are accounted for as follows: • raw materials – purchase cost on a first-in, first-out basis • finished goods and work in progress – cost of direct material and labour and proportion of manufacturing overheads based on normal operating capacity • production supplies – purchase cost on a weighted average cost basis.	36(a)

Note 6: Inventories

	Notes	2006 $000	2005 $000	
Inventories carried at lower of cost and net realisable value				
At cost:				36(b)
Raw materials		1 257	1 840	
Work in progress		649	721	
Finished goods		3 932	4 278	
Production supplies		385	316	
Total carrying amount		6 223	7 155	
Inventories carried at net realisable value				
Obsolete goods		269	174	36(c)
Less Costs to sell		(31)	(18)	
Total carrying amount		238	156	

In respect to inventory, the following items have been recognised as expenses during the period:			
Cost of sales	11 674	10 543	36(d)
Write-down to net realisable value	26	18	36(e)
Reversal of write-down[a]	(3)	–	36(f)

[a] A prior year write-down was reversed during the current period as a result of an increase in selling price for that inventory item.	36(g)
Inventory with a carrying amount of $570 000 has been pledged as security for loans to the company.	36(h)

FIGURE 9.2   An example of illustrative disclosures required by IAS 2

9.10 Summary

The purpose of this chapter is to analyse the content of IAS 2 *Inventories* and provide guidance on its implementation. The principal issue in accounting for inventories is the determination of cost and its subsequent recognition as an expense, including any write-down to net realisable value (IAS 2, *Objective*). One key decision in recognising inventory is the selection of an appropriate method for allocating costs between individual items of inventory to determine the cost of goods sold and the cost of inventory on hand. Following the initial recognition of the inventory, cost must be compared to net realisable value, and the value of inventory written down where net realisable value falls below cost. IAS 2 requires disclosures to be made in relation to the inventories held by an entity and the accounting policies adopted with respect to these assets.

DISCUSSION QUESTIONS

1. Define 'cost' as applied to the valuation of inventory.
2. What is meant by the term 'net realisable value'? Is this the same as fair value? If not, why not?
3. Explain the concept of lower of cost and net realisable value for inventory.
4. Which is more expensive to maintain: a perpetual inventory system, or a periodic inventory system? Why?
5. In what circumstances must assumptions be made in order to assign a cost to inventory items when they are sold?
6. 'Estimating the value of inventory is not sufficiently accurate to justify using such an approach. Only a full physical count can give full accuracy.' Discuss.
7. What is the difference between the first-in, first-out method and the weighted average method of assigning cost?
8. Compare and contrast the impact on the reported profit and asset value for an accounting period of the first-in, first-out method and the weighted average method.
9. Why is the lower of cost and net realisable value rule used in the accounting standard? Is it permissible to revalue inventory upwards? If so, when?
10. What impact do the terms of trade have on the determination of the quantity and value of inventory on hand where goods are in transit on balance date?

EXERCISES

EXERCISE 9.1 ★ Consignment of inventory

Sestri Levante Ltd reported in a recent financial statement that approximately $12 million of merchandise was received on consignment. Should the company recognise this amount on its balance sheet? Explain.

EXERCISE 9.2 ★ Selection of cost assumption

Under what circumstances would each of the following inventory cost methods be appropriate?
(a) Specific identification
(b) Last-in, first-out
(c) Average cost
(d) First-in, first-out
(e) Retail inventory

EXERCISE 9.3 ★ Balance sheet classification

Where, if at all, should the following items be classified on a balance sheet?
(a) Goods out on approval to customers
(b) Goods in transit that were recently purchased FOB destination
(c) Land held by a real estate firm for sale
(d) Raw materials
(e) Goods received on consignment
(f) Stationery supplies

EXERCISE 9.4 ★ Disclosures relating to inventory

Milan Pty Ltd reported inventory in its balance sheet as follows:
Inventories $11 247 900
What additional disclosures might be necessary to present the inventory fairly?

EXERCISE 9.5 ★ Recording inventory transactions

Sammi Solerno began business on 1 March 2009. Sammi balances the books at month-end and uses the periodic inventory system. Sammi's transactions for March 2009 are detailed on the next page.

01   Sammi invested $16 000 cash and $10 000 office equipment into the business.
02   Purchased merchandise from B Rossano on account for $4800 on terms of 2/15, n/30.
05   Sold merchandise to S Matera on account for $1200 on terms of 2/10, n/30.
08   Purchased merchandise for cash, $860 on cheque no. 003.
12   Purchased merchandise from N Nardo on account for $2000 on terms of 2/10, n/30.
14   Paid B Rossano for 2 March purchase on cheque no. 004.
15   Received $1176 from S Matera in payment of the account.
21   Sold merchandise to Fondi Ltd on account for $1600 on terms of 2/10, n/30.
21   Paid N Nardo for 12 March purchase on cheque no. 005.
22   Purchased merchandise from B Gela on account for $2400 on terms of 2/15, n/30.
23   Sold merchandise for $1300 cash.
25   Returned defective merchandise that cost $600 to B Gela.
28   Paid salaries of $1400 on cheque no. 006.

Required
Prepare journal entries for March 2009, using the pro-forma journals provided.

Cash receipts journal

Date	Account	Ref.	Cash	Disc. all.	Sales	A/c rec.	Other

Cash payments journal

Date	Account	Ch.	Ref.	Other	A/c pay.	Purch.	Cash	Disc. rec.

Purchases journal				
Date	Account	Terms	Ref.	Amount

Sales journal				
Date	Account	Terms	Ref.	Amount

General journal				
Date	Account	Ref.	Dr	Cr

EXERCISE 9.6   ★   Determining inventory cost and cost of goods sold (periodic)

Select the correct answer. Show any workings required and provide reasons to justify your choice.

1. The cost of inventory on hand at 1 January 2010 was $25 000 and at 31 December 2010 was $35 000. Inventory purchases for the year amounted to $160 000, freight outwards expense was $500, and purchase returns were $1400. What was the cost of goods sold for the year ended 31 December 2001?
   (a) $148 100   (c) $149 100
   (b) $148 600   (d) $150 000

2. The following inventory information relates to K Cagliari, who uses a periodic inventory system and rounds the average unit cost to the nearest dollar:
   Beginning inventory   10 units @ average cost of $25 each = $250
   January purchase   10 units @ $24 each
   July purchase   39 units @ $26 each
   October purchase   20 units @ $24 each
   Ending inventory   25 units
   What is the cost of ending inventory using the weighted average costing method?
   (a) $625   (c) $618.75
   (b) $620   (d) $610

EXERCISE 9.7   ★   Assigning cost (perpetual)

Select the correct answer. Show any workings required and provide reasons to justify your choice.

Ancona uses the perpetual inventory method. Ancona's inventory transactions for August 2009 were as follows:

		No.	Unit cost	Total cost
01 Aug.	Beginning inventory	20	$4.00	$80.00
07 Aug.	Purchases	10	$4.20	$42.00
10 Aug.	Purchases	20	$4.30	$86.00
12 Aug.	Sales	15	?	?
16 Aug.	Purchases	20	$4.60	$92.00
20 Aug.	Sales	40	?	?
28 Aug.	Sales returns	3	?	?

1. Using this information, assume that Ancona uses the FIFO cost flow method and that the sales returns relate to the 20 August sales. The sales return should be costed back into inventory at what unit cost?
   (a) $4.00   (c) $4.30
   (b) $4.20   (d) $4.60

2. Assuming that Ancona uses the moving average cost flow method, the 12 August sales should be costed at what unit cost?
   (a) $4.16   (c) $4.06
   (b) $4.07   (d) $4.00

EXERCISE 9.8 ★★ End-of-period adjustments

An extract from Messina Ltd's unadjusted trial balance as at 30 June 2008 appears below. Messina Ltd has a 30 June reporting date and uses the perpetual method to record inventory transactions.

	$	$
Inventory	194 400	
Sales		631 770
Sales returns	6 410	
Cost of goods sold	468 640	
Inventory losses	12 678	

Additional information
- On 24 June 2008, Messina Ltd recorded a $1320 credit sale of goods costing $1200. These goods, which were sold on FOB destination terms and were in transit at 30 June 2008, were included in the physical count.
- Inventory on hand at 30 June 2008 (determined via physical count) had a cost of $195 600 and a net realisable value of $194 740.

Required
1. Prepare any adjusting journal entries required on 30 June 2008.
2. Prepare the trading section of the income statement for the year ended 30 June 2008.

EXERCISE 9.9 ★★ End-of-period adjustments

A physical count of inventory at 31 December 2008 revealed that Verona Pty Ltd had inventory on hand at that date with a cost of $441 000. Verona Pty Ltd uses the periodic method to record inventory transactions. Inventory at 1 January 2008 was $397 000. The annual audit identified that the following items were excluded from this amount:
- Merchandise of $61 000 is held by Verona Pty Ltd on consignment. The consignor is Padua Ltd.
- Merchandise costing $38 000 was shipped by Verona Pty Ltd FOB destination to a customer on 31 December 2008. The customer was expected to receive the goods on 6 January 2009.
- Merchandise costing $46 000 was shipped by Verona Pty Ltd FOB shipping to a customer on 29 December 2008. The customer was scheduled to receive the goods on 2 January 2009.
- Merchandise costing $83 000 shipped by a vendor FOB destination on 31 December 2008 was received by Verona Pty Ltd on 4 January 2009.
- Merchandise costing $51 000 purchased FOB shipping was shipped by the supplier on 31 December 2008 and received by Verona Pty Ltd on 5 January 2009.

Required
1. Based on the above information, calculate the amount that should appear for inventory on Verona Pty Ltd's balance sheet at 31 December 2008.
2. Prepare any journal entries necessary to adjust the inventory general ledger account to the amount calculated in part 1.

EXERCISE 9.10 ★★ Applying the lower of cost and NRV rule

The following information relates to the inventory on hand at 30 June 2009 held by Catania Ltd.

Item No.	Quantity	Cost per unit $	Cost to replace $	Estimated selling price $	Cost of completion and disposal $
A1458	600	2.30	2.41	3.75	0.49
A1965	815	3.40	3.26	3.50	0.55
B6730	749	7.34	7.35	10.00	0.95
D0943	98	1.23	1.14	1.00	0.12
G8123	156	3.56	3.56	5.70	0.67
W2167	1 492	6.12	6.15	7.66	0.36

Required

Calculate the value of inventory on hand at 30 June 2009 in accordance with the requirements of IAS 2.

PROBLEMS

PROBLEM 9.1 ★ Assignment of cost (periodic and perpetual)

Select the correct answer. Show any workings required and provide reasons to justify your choice.

Cremona Ltd's inventory transactions for April 2011 are shown below.

	Purchases			COGS			Balance		
Date	No. units	Unit cost	Total cost	No. units	Unit cost	Total cost	No. units	Unit cost	Total cost
01 April							20	$8.00	$160.00
04	90	$8.40	$756.00						
07	100	$8.60	$860.00						
10				50					
13	(20)	$8.60	($172.00)						
18				70					
21				(5)					
29				40					

1. If Cremona Ltd uses the perpetual inventory system with the moving average cost flow method, the 18 April sale would be costed at what unit cost?
   (a) $8.60   (c) $8.44
   (b) $8.46   (d) $8.42
2. If Cremona Ltd uses the periodic inventory system with the FIFO cost flow method, what would be the cost of goods sold for April?
   (a) $1303.00   (c) $1310.00
   (b) $1508.60   (d) $1324.00

3. If Cremona Ltd uses the perpetual inventory system with the FIFO cost flow method, the 21 April sale return (relating to the 18 April sale) would be costed at what unit cost?

(a) $8.00   (c) $8.40
(b) $8.60   (d) $8.50

4. If Cremona Ltd uses the periodic method with the weighted average cost flow method, what would be the value of closing inventory at 30 April 2011? (Round average cost to the nearest cent.)

(a) $295.40   (c) $253.20
(b) $301.00   (d) $297.50

PROBLEM 9.2   ★★   Balance-date adjustments

Stromboli Outfitters sells outdoor adventure equipment. The entity uses the perpetual inventory method to account for inventory transactions and assigns costs using the moving average method. All purchases and sales are made on FOB destination, 30-day credit terms.

At 30 June 2009, the balance of the inventory control account in the general ledger was $248 265 after the special journal totals were posted but before the balance-date adjusting entries were prepared and posted.

A physical count showed goods worth $256 100 to be on hand. Investigations of the discrepancy between the general ledger account balance and the count total revealed the following:

• Damaged ropes worth $1200 were returned to the supplier on 29 June, but this transaction has not yet been recorded.

• During the stocktake, staff found that a box of leather gloves worth $595 had suffered water damage during a recent storm. The gloves were damaged beyond repair and so were not included in the count, but they are still recorded in the inventory records.

• Equipment worth $1500, which was sold for $2500 on 29 June, was still in transit to the customer on 30 June. The sale was recorded on 29 June and the equipment was not included in the physical count.

• An error occurred when posting the purchase journal totals for May 2009. The correct total of $25 100 was erroneously posted as $21 500.

• The physical count included goods worth $7600 that were being held on consignment for All Weather Gear Pty Ltd.

• An all-terrain kit worth $1570 was returned by a customer on 28 June. The sales return transaction was correctly journalised and posted to the ledgers, but the kit was not returned to the warehouse and therefore was not included in the physical count.

Required

Adjust and reconcile the inventory control ledger account balance to the physical account (adjusted as necessary).

Note: Problems 9.3, 9.4 and 9.5 concern the same entity, Seahorses Emporium, because the three problems have been designed so that they can be combined to form a single comprehensive problem.

PROBLEM 9.3   ★★★   Assignment of cost

Seahorses Emporium is a gift shop situated in a small fishing village. The business carries a range of merchandise that it accounts for under the perpetual inventory method. Cost is assigned using the FIFO cost flow method. All purchases are on FOB shipping terms, with 30 days credit. The reporting date is 30 June.

The following information lists the transactions during October 2007 for one item of inventory (wall plaques):

Date	Detail	Number	Unit cost
Oct. 01	Opening balance	45	6.40
04	Purchase	50	6.50
08	Sale	60	
11	Purchase	70	6.60
14	Purchase return	10	6.60
19	Sale	70	
24	Sale return (on 19 Oct. sale)	5	
28	Purchase	40	6.70

Required

For the inventory item (wall plaques), calculate October's cost of goods sold expense and the cost of inventory on hand at 31 October 2007. Round all figures to the nearest cent.

PROBLEM 9.4 ★★★   Balance-date reconciliation and NRV

Seahorses Emporium is a gift shop situated in a small fishing village. The business carries a range of merchandise that it accounts for under the perpetual inventory method. Cost is assigned using the FIFO cost flow method. All purchases are on FOB shipping terms, with 30 days credit. The reporting date is 30 June.

A physical count of inventory at 30 June 2008 found inventory worth $189 650. The inventory control ledger account at that date had a balance of $193 700. Investigations of the discrepancy between these two figures revealed the following:

- An unopened carton containing posters worth $420 had not been included in the count.
- Seven large conch shells were found to be damaged beyond repair and were not recorded in the count. The shells, worth $220, are still recorded in the inventory records.
- Goods costing $590 were ordered on 27 June 2008 and delivered to the transport company by the supplier on 29 June. As the goods were in transit on 30 June, they were not included in the count. The purchase was recorded when the goods arrived at the shop on 2 July 2008.
- Seahorses Emporium has a number of paintings on display in local restaurants on a consignment basis. The paintings are worth $4200 and were not included in the count.
- A brass telescope had been sold for $1200 on 30 June. As the telescope was still in the shop awaiting collection by the owner, it was included in the count. The telescope cost $950.
- Five missing dolphin statues worth $160 could not be located and are presumed to have been stolen from the shop.

Required

1. Reconcile the inventory control ledger account balance with the physical count figure (adjust both figures as necessary).
2. Prepare any journal entries necessary to achieve the reconciliation.

PROBLEM 9.5 ★★★   Balance-date reconciliation and NRV

Seahorses Emporium is a gift shop situated in a small fishing village. The business carries a range of merchandise that it accounts for under the perpetual inventory method. Cost is assigned using the FIFO cost flow method. All purchases are on FOB shipping terms, with 30 days credit. The reporting date is 30 June.

IAS 2 requires inventory to be recorded at the lower of cost and net realisable value. C Bligh, the owner of Seashells Emporium, assessed the net realisable value of her inventory at 30 June 2008 and concluded that the net realisable value of all items (except barometers) exceeded cost. The six barometers on hand cost $150 each, but C Bligh is of the opinion that they will need to be discounted to $90 in order to sell them.

Required

Explain what is meant by the term 'net realisable value' and detail the action C Bligh must take in respect to the wall barometers.

PROBLEM 9.6 ★★   Allocating cost (weighted average), reporting gross profit and applying the NRV rule

Pisa Ltd wholesales bicycles. It uses the perpetual inventory method and allocates cost to inventory on a moving average basis. The company's reporting date is 31 March. At 1 March 2009, inventory on hand consisted of 350 bicycles at $82 each and 43 bicycles at $85 each. During the month ended 31 March 2009, the following inventory transactions took place (all purchase and sales transactions are on credit):

01 March	Sold 300 bicycles for $120 each.
03	Five bicycles were returned by a customer. They had originally cost $82 each and were sold for $120 each.
09	Purchased 55 bicycles at $91 each.
10	Purchased 76 bicycles at $96 each.
15	Sold 86 bicycles for $135 each.
17	Returned one damaged bicycle to the supplier. This bicycle had been purchased on 9 March.
22	Sold 60 bicycles for $125 each.
26	Purchased 72 bicycles at $98 each.
29	Two bicycles, sold on 22 March, were returned by a customer. The bicycles were badly damaged so it was decided to write them off. They had originally cost $91 each.

Required

1. Calculate the cost of inventory on hand at 31 March 2009 and the cost of goods sold for the month of March. (Round the average unit cost to the nearest cent, and round the total cost amounts to the nearest dollar.)
2. Show the inventory general ledger control account (in T-format) as it would appear at 31 March 2009.
3. Calculate the gross profit on sales for the month of March 2009.

PROBLEM 9.7 ★★   Assigning cost and reporting gross profit using different cost methods

The following information has been extracted from the records of Trieste Trading about one of its products. Trieste Trading uses the perpetual inventory system and its reporting date is 30 September.

		No. of units	Unit cost $	Total cost $
2006				
01/10	Beginning balance	1 600	14.00	22 400
06/10	Purchased	600	14.10	8 460
05/11	Sold @ $24.00 per unit	2 000		
19/12	Purchased	2 200	14.70	32 340
24/12	Purchase returns	160	14.70	2 352
10/01	Sold @ $24.20 per unit	1 400		
22/03	Purchased	16 800	15.00	252 000
30/04	Sold @ $26.50 per unit	3 600		
04/05	Sales returns @ $26.50 per unit	40		
04/06	Sold @ $27.00 per unit	7 000		
06/08	Purchased	1 000	16.00	16 000
27/09	Sold @ $30.00 per unit	6 200		

Required
1. Calculate the cost of inventory on hand at 30 September 2006 and the cost of goods sold for the year ended 30 September 2006, using:
   (a) the FIFO cost method
   (b) the moving average cost method (round the average unit costs to the nearest cent, and round the total cost amounts to the nearest dollar).
2. Prepare the trading section of the income statement for the year ended 30 September 2006, using:
   (a) the FIFO cost method
   (b) the moving average cost method.

PROBLEM 9.8   ★★   End-of-year adjustments

The inventory control account balance of Firenze Fashions at 30 June 2007 was $221 020 using the perpetual inventory method. A physical count conducted on that day found inventory on hand worth $220 200. Net realisable value for each inventory item held for sale exceeded cost. An investigation of the discrepancy revealed the following:
- Goods worth $6600 held on consignment for Portofino Accessories had been included in the physical count.
- Goods costing $1200 were purchased on credit from Roma Ltd on 27 June 2007 on FOB shipping terms. The goods were shipped on 28 June 2007 but, as they had not arrived by 30 June 2007, were not included in the physical count. The purchase invoice was received and processed on 30 June 2007.
- Goods costing $2400 were sold on credit to Arezzo Pty Ltd for $3900 on 28 June 2007 on FOB destination terms. The goods were still in transit on 30 June 2007. The sales invoice was raised and processed on 29 June 2007.
- Goods costing $2730 were purchased on credit (FOB destination) from San Gimignano Handbags on 28 June 2007. The goods were received on 29 June 2007 and included in the physical count. The purchase invoice was received on 2 July 2007.

- On 30 June 2007, Firenze Fashions sold goods costing $6300 on credit (FOB shipping) terms to Pisa's Boutique for $9600. The goods were dispatched from the warehouse on 30 June 2007 but the sales invoice had not been raised at that date.
- Damaged inventory items valued at $2650 were discovered during the physical count. These items were still recorded on 30 June 2007 but were omitted from the physical count records pending their write-off.

Required

Prepare any journal entries necessary on 30 June 2007 to correct any errors and to adjust inventory.

PROBLEM 9.9 ★★★   Allocating cost (FIFO), reporting gross profit and applying the NRV rule

Como Ltd wholesales bicycles. It uses the perpetual inventory method and allocates cost to inventory on a first-in, first-out basis. The company's reporting date is 31 March. At 1 March 2009, inventory on hand consisted of 350 bicycles at $82 each and 43 bicycles at $85 each. During the month ended 31 March 2009, the following inventory transactions took place (all purchase and sales transactions are on credit):

01 March	Sold 300 bicycles for $120 each.
03	Five bicycles were returned by a customer. They had originally cost $82 each and were sold for $120 each.
09	Purchased 55 bicycles at $91 each.
10	Purchased 76 bicycles at $96 each.
15	Sold 86 bicycles for $135 each.
17	Returned one damaged bicycle to the supplier. This bicycle had been purchased on 9 March.
22	Sold 60 bicycles for $125 each.
26	Purchased 72 bicycles at $98 each.
29	Two bicycles, sold on 22 March, were returned by a customer. The bicycles were badly damaged so it was decided to write them off. They had originally cost $91 each.

Required

1. Calculate the cost of inventory on hand at 31 March 2009 and the cost of goods sold for the month of March.
2. Show the inventory general ledger control account (in T-format) as it would appear at 31 March 2009.
3. Calculate the gross profit on sales for the month of March 2009.
4. IAS 2 requires inventories to be measured at the lower of cost and net realisable value. Identify three reasons why the net realisable value of the bicycles on hand at 31 March 2009 may be below their cost.
5. If the net realisable value is below cost, what action should Como Ltd take?

PROBLEM 9.10 ★★★   Assigning costs and end-of-period adjustments

Naples Retailing Ltd is a food wholesaler that supplies independent grocery stores. The company operates a perpetual inventory system, with the first-in, first-out method used to assign costs to inventory items. Freight costs are not included in the calculation of unit costs. Transactions and other related information regarding two of the items (baked beans and plain flour) carried by Naples Ltd are given below for June 2009, the last month of the company's reporting period.

	Baked beans	Plain flour
Unit of packaging	Case containing 25 × 410 g cans	Box containing 12 × 4 kg bags
Inventory @ 1 June 2009	350 cases @ $19.60	625 boxes @ $38.40
Purchases	1. 10 June: 200 cases @ $19.50 plus freight of $135 2. 19 June: 470 cases @ $19.70 per case plus freight of $210	1. 3 June: 150 boxes @ $38.45 2. 15 June: 200 boxes @ $38.45 3. 29 June: 240 boxes @ $39.00
Purchase terms	2/10, n/30, FOB shipping	n/30, FOB destination
June sales	730 cases @ $28.50	950 boxes @ 40.00
Returns and allowances	A customer returned 50 cases that had been shipped in error. The customer's account was credited for $1425.	As the June 15 purchase was unloaded, 10 boxes were discovered damaged. A credit of $384.50 was received by Naples Retailing Ltd.
Physical count at 30 June 2009	326 cases on hand	15 boxes on hand
Explanation of variance	No explanation found — assumed stolen	Boxes purchased on 29 June still in transit on 30 June
Net realisable value at 30 June 2009	$29.00 per case	$38.50 per box

Required

1. Calculate the number of units in inventory and the FIFO unit cost for baked beans and plain flour as at 30 June 2009 (show all workings).
2. Calculate the total dollar amount of the inventory for baked beans and plain flour, applying the lower of cost and net realisable rule on an item-by-item basis. Prepare any necessary journal entries (show all workings).

PROBLEM 9.11   Allocating cost (moving average), end-of-period adjustments and write-downs to NRV

Part A

Mario Alghero uses the perpetual inventory method and special journals, balances the books at month-end and uses control accounts and subsidiary ledgers for all accounts receivable and accounts payable. All sales and purchases are made on 2/10, n/30, FOB destination terms. The moving average method is used to assign cost to inventory items.

The information overleaf has been extracted from Mario's books and records for May and June 2008.

	$
Inventory control ledger account balance at 31 May	20 367.30
Accounts payable control ledger account balance at 31 May	7 973.60
Inventory purchases on credit during June	11 248.90
Cash paid to trade creditors during June	15 123.40
Discount received during June	438.90
Inventory sales on credit during June	15 020.00

Inventory ledger card balances at 1 June:

Pool filters	43 @ $232.50	9 997.50
Pool pumps	21 @ $493.80	10 369.80
		20 367.30

The credit inventory purchases during June comprised the following:

04	5 pool pumps @ $476.10 each	2 380.50
17	3 pool pumps @ $491.30 each	1 473.90
18	12 pool filters @ $236.70 each	2 840.40
24	2 pool pumps @ $491.30	982.60
29	15 pool filters @ $238.10	3 571.50
		11 248.90

The credit inventory sales during June comprised the following:

01	1 pool pump @ $520 and 1 pool filter @ $300	820
05	18 pool filters @ $300	5 400
18	4 pool pumps @ $550	2 200
23	15 pool filters @ $330	4 950
28	5 pool filters @ $330	1 650
		15 020

Other movements in inventory during June were:

09	2 pool filters, sold 5 June (not paid for) were returned by the customer
20	3 pool filters purchased 18 June (not paid for) were returned to the supplier
26	1 pool pump, purchased 4 June (paid for) was returned to the supplier

Required

1. Prepare the perpetual inventory records for June 2008.
2. Prepare the inventory control and accounts payable control general ledger accounts (in T-format) for the month of June 2008.

Part B

At 30 June 2008, Mario conducted a physical stocktake that found 14 pool filters and 26 pool pumps on hand. An investigation of discrepancies between the inventory card balances and the physical count showed that the 15 pool filters purchased on 29 June 2008 were still in transit from the supplier's factory on 30 June 2008, and one pool pump, sold on 18 June, had been returned by a customer on 30 June. No adjustment has been made in the books for the sales return. The customer had not paid for the returned pump.

Required

Prepare any general journal entries necessary to correct the inventory control general ledger account balance as at 30 June 2008. (Narrations are not required, but show all workings). Do not adjust the perpetual inventory records prepared in Part A.

Part C

On 30 June 2008, Mario determined that his inventory items have the following net realisable values:

Pool filters $232 each
Pool pumps $546 each.

Required

1. What does the term 'net realisable value' mean?
2. What sources of evidence could Mario examine to determine net realisable value?
3. What action should Mario take as at 30 June 2008 with respect to these net realisable values? Why?

WEBLINK

Visit these websites for additional information:

www.iasb.org   www.iasplus.com
www.asic.gov.au   www.ifac.org
www.aasb.com.au   www.nzica.com
www.accaglobal.com   www.capa.com.my

REFERENCES

IASB 2004, *IFRIC Update*, November, IASB.

Nokia 2005, *Nokia in 2005*, Nokia Corporation, Finland, viewed on 22 February 2005, <www.nokia.com>.

CHAPTER 10
Property, plant and equipment

ACCOUNTING STANDARDS

International: IAS 16 *Property, Plant and Equipment*
Australia: AASB 116 *Property, Plant and Equipment*
New Zealand: NZ IAS 16 *Property, Plant and Equipment*

CONCEPTS FOR REVIEW

Before studying this chapter, you should understand or, if necessary, revise:
* the concept of an asset in the IASB Framework
* the concept of an expense in the IASB Framework.

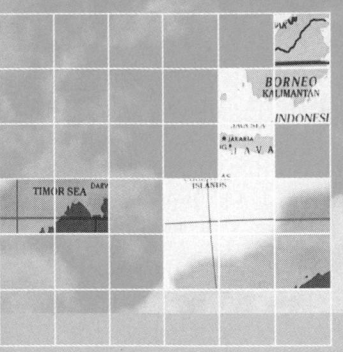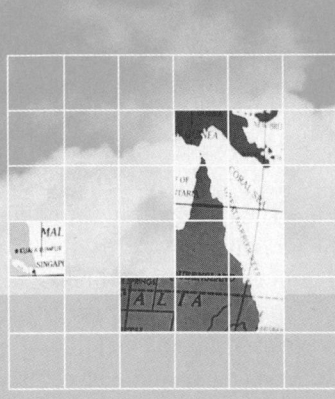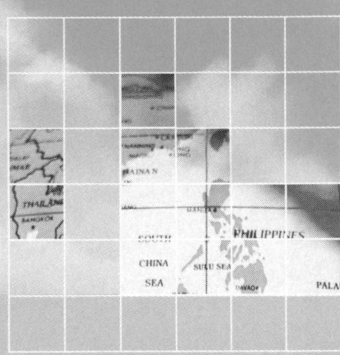

When you have studied this chapter, you should be able to:

1. understand the nature of property, plant and equipment
2. understand the recognition criteria for initial recognition of property, plant and equipment
3. understand how to measure property, plant and equipment on initial recognition
4. explain how to measure purchase price
5. explain what is included in directly attributable costs
6. explain the alternative ways in which property, plant and equipment can be measured subsequent to initial recognition
7. understand the nature and calculation of depreciation
8. explain the revaluation model of measurement
9. apply the revaluation model with revaluation increments
10. apply the revaluation model with revaluation decrements
11. apply the revaluation model after transfers have been made from asset revaluation surplus
12. determine depreciation for assets measured at a revalued amount
13. account for derecognition
14. implement the disclosure requirements of IAS 16.

10.1 The nature of property, plant and equipment

The accounting standard analysed in this chapter is IAS 16 *Property, Plant and Equipment*. The standard was first issued as IAS 16 in March 1982, amended on numerous occasions, exposed in May 2002 as part of the International Accounting Standard Board (IASB) project on improvements to International Accounting Standards (IASs), and issued in its present form in 2004. As a result of this process, the IASB has clarified selected matters and provided additional guidance. It has not reconsidered the fundamental approach to the accounting for property, plant and equipment contained in IAS 16.

According to paragraph 2 of IAS 16, the standard applies in accounting for property, plant and equipment except where another standard requires or permits a different accounting treatment. IAS 16 does not apply to property, plant and equipment classified as held for sale in accordance with IFRS 5 *Non-current Assets Held for Sale and Discontinued Operations*; biological assets related to agricultural activity as these are accounted for under IAS 41 *Agriculture*; or mineral rights and mineral reserves such as oil, gas and similar non-regenerative resources. However, IAS 16 does apply to property, plant and equipment used to develop or maintain biological assets and mineral rights and reserves.

Paragraph 6 of IAS 16 defines property, plant and equipment as follows:

Property, plant and equipment are tangible items that:

(a) are held for use in the production or supply of goods or services, for rental to others, or for administrative purposes; and

(b) are expected to be used during more than one period.

Note the following:

- The assets are 'tangible' assets. The distinction between tangible and intangible assets is discussed in depth in chapter 11. However, a key feature of tangible assets is that they are physical assets, such as land, rather than non-physical, such as patents and trade-marks.
- The assets have specific uses within an entity; namely, for use in production/supply, rental or administration. Assets that are held for sale, including land, or held for investment are not included under property, plant and equipment. Instead, assets held for sale are accounted for in accordance with IFRS 5.
- The assets are non-current assets, the expectation being that they will be used for more than one accounting period.

Property, plant and equipment may be divided into classes for disclosure purposes, a class of assets being a grouping of assets of a similar nature and use in an entity's operations. Examples of classes of property, plant and equipment are land, machinery, motor vehicles and office equipment. To illustrate: the international food preparation company Danisco, based in Denmark, prepares its financial reports in accordance with International Financial Reporting Standards (IFRSs). The notes to the balance sheet of Danisco, at 31 December 2005, as shown in figure 10.1, provide an indication of what is contained in that category as well as the reasons for the movements in this category of assets.

In this chapter, accounting for property, plant and equipment is considered as follows:

- recognition of the asset – the point at which the asset is brought into the accounting records
- initial measurement of the asset – determining the initial amount at which the asset is recorded in the accounts
- measurement subsequent to initial recognition – determining the amount at which the asset is reported subsequent to acquisition, including the recording of any depreciation of the asset
- derecognition of the asset.

13. Property, Plant and Equipment

DKK million	Land and buildings	Plant and machinery	Fixtures, fittings, tools and equipment	Prepayments and assets under construction	Leased plant and equipment	Total
Cost at 1 May 2004	4 236	9 958	891	289	49	15 423
Exchange adjustment of opening value	(41)	(111)	(6)	(9)	(2)	(169)
Additions due to new activities	472	545	74	46	–	1 137
Additions	129	164	92	372	–	757
Disposals	(33)	(79)	(83)	(5)	–	(200)
Transferred from associates	237	261	54	13	–	565
Transferred to (from) other items	19	279	7	(306)	–	(1)
Total	5 019	11 017	1 029	400	47	17 512
Depreciation and writedowns at 1 May 2004	(1 688)	(5 067)	(637)	–	(31)	(7 423)
Exchange adjustment of opening value	13	69	4	–	2	88
Depreciation of disposals during the year	9	68	72	–	–	149
Depreciation and writedowns for the year	(181)	(603)	(96)	–	(3)	(883)
Transferred (to) from other items	(20)	18	3	–	–	1
Total	(1 867)	(5 515)	(654)	–	(32)	(8 068)
Balance at 30 April 2005	3 152	5 502	375	400	15	9 444
Balance at 30 April 2004	2 548	4 891	254	289	18	8 000

FIGURE 10.1 Property, plant and equipment of Danisco
Source: Danisco (2005, p. 49).

10.2 Initial recognition of property, plant and equipment

LO 2

Paragraph 7 of IAS 16 contains the principles for recognition of property, plant and equipment:

> The cost of an item of property, plant and equipment shall be recognised as an asset if, and only if:
> (a) it is probable that future economic benefits associated with the item will flow to the entity; and
> (b) the cost of the item can be measured reliably.

This is a *general* recognition principle for property, plant and equipment. It applies to the initial recognition of an asset, when parts of that asset are replaced, and when costs are incurred in relation to that asset during its useful life. To recognise a cost as an asset, the outlay must give rise to the expectation of future economic benefits.

The criteria for recognition in paragraph 7 differ from the recognition criteria for the elements of financial statements in paragraph 83 of the IASB Framework. Under the Framework, an asset can be recognised when the cost or value can be measured with reliability; under IAS 16, recognition can occur only if the *cost* can be measured reliably. Assets for which the cost cannot be reliably measured but whose initial fair value can be measured reliably cannot be recognised in the entity's records.

10.2.1 Asset versus expense

For most items of property, plant and equipment, the entity will incur some initial expenditure. One of the key problems for the entity is determining whether the outlay should be expensed or capitalised as an asset. As paragraph 7 of IAS 16 states, the elements of that decision relate to whether or not the entity expects there to be future economic benefits, whether the receipt of those benefits is probable, and whether the benefits will flow specifically to the entity. As noted in paragraph 90 of the Framework, the expensing of outlays:

> does not imply either that the intention of management in incurring expenditure was other than to generate future economic benefits for the entity or that management was misguided. The only implication is that the degree of certainty that economic benefits will flow to the entity beyond the current accounting period is insufficient to warrant the recognition of an asset.

As property, plant and equipment consists of physical assets such as land and machinery, such assets are normally traded in a market. One test of the existence of future benefits is then to determine whether or not there exists a market for the item in question. A problem with some assets is that once items have been acquired and installed, there is no normal market for them. However, in many cases, the expected economic benefits arise because of the use of that asset in conjunction with other assets held by the entity. At a minimum, the future benefits would be the scrap value of the item. Where the assets are intangible, such as costs associated with the generation of software, the absence of a physical asset causes more problems in terms of asset recognition. Chapter 11 discusses in detail the problems associated with the recognition of intangible assets.

10.2.2 Separate assets — components

The total property, plant and equipment of an entity can be broken down into separate assets. This is sometimes referred to as a 'components' approach to asset recognition. An entity allocates the amount initially recognised in respect of an asset to its component parts and accounts for each component separately. Paragraph 9 of IAS 16 notes that the identification of a separate item or component of plant and equipment requires the exercise of judgement, the standard not prescribing the unit of measure for recognition (that is, what constitutes an item of property, plant and equipment). The key element in determining whether an asset should be further subdivided into its component parts is an analysis of what is going to happen in the future to that asset. Having identified an asset, the entity wants to recognise the expected benefits as they are consumed by the entity, with the recognition being in the period in which the benefits are received. Hence, if an asset has a number of components that have different useful lives then, in order for there to be an appropriate recognition of benefits consumed, components with different useful lives need to be identified and accounted for separately.

For example, consider an aircraft as an item of property, plant and equipment. Is it sufficient to recognise the aircraft as a single asset? An analysis of the aircraft may reveal that there are various components of the aircraft that have different useful lives. Component parts of the aircraft include the engines, the frame of the aircraft and the fittings (seats, floor coverings and so on). It may be necessary to refit the aircraft every five years, while the engines may last twice as long. Similarly, an entity that deals with the refining of metals may have a blast furnace, the lining of which needs to be changed periodically. The lining of the blast furnace therefore needs to be separated from the external structure in terms of asset recognition and subsequent accounting for the asset. Further, as noted in paragraph 9 of IAS 16, it may be appropriate to aggregate individually insignificant items (such as moulds, tools and dies) and apply the criteria to the aggregate value.

10.2.3 Generation of future benefits

Paragraph 11 of IAS 16 notes that certain assets may not of themselves generate future benefits, but instead it may be necessary for the entity itself to generate future benefits. For example, some items of property, plant and equipment may be acquired for safety or environmental reasons, such as equipment associated with the safe storage of dangerous chemicals. The entity's generation of the benefits from use of the chemicals can occur only if the safety equipment exists. Hence, even if the safety equipment does not of itself generate cash flows, its existence is necessary for the entity to be able to use chemicals within the business.

LO 3

10.3 Initial measurement of property, plant and equipment

Having established that an asset can be recognised, the entity must then assign to it a monetary amount. Paragraph 15 of IAS 16 contains the principles for initial measurement of property, plant and equipment: 'An item of property, plant and equipment that qualifies for recognition as an asset shall be measured at its cost'. Paragraph 16 specifies three components of cost, namely:

- purchase price
- directly attributable costs
- initial estimate of the costs of dismantling and removing the item or restoring the site on which it is located.

These items are considered separately in the following sections.

LO 4

10.3.1 Purchase price

'Purchase price' is not defined in IAS 16, but paragraph 16(a) states that the purchase price includes import duties and non-refundable purchase taxes, and is calculated after deducting any trade discounts and rebates. The essence of what constitutes purchase price is found in the definition of cost in paragraph 6 of the standard, which states: 'Cost is the amount of cash or cash equivalents paid or the fair value of the other consideration given to acquire an asset at the time of its acquisition or construction'.

Where an item of property, plant and equipment is acquired for cash, determination of the purchase price is relatively straightforward. One variation that may arise is that some or all of the cash payment is deferred. In this case, as noted in paragraph 23 of IAS 16, the cost is the cash price equivalent at the recognition date, determined by measuring the cash payments on a present value basis (done by discounting the cash flows). Interest is then recognised as the payments are made.

More difficulties arise where the exchange involves assets other than cash. In a non-cash exchange, the acquiring entity receives a non-cash asset and in return provides a non-cash asset to the seller. In measuring the cost of the asset acquired, the question is whether the measurement should be based on the value of the asset given up by the acquirer, or by reference to the value of the asset acquired from the seller. In relation to the application of the cost principle of measurement, note the following:

1. Cost is determined by reference to the fair value of what is given up by the acquirer rather than by the fair value of the item acquired. The cost represents the sacrifice made by the acquirer. This principle is inherent in the definition of cost in paragraph 6 of IAS 16. Further, paragraph 26 states that where both the fair value of what is given up by the acquirer and the asset received are reliably measurable, then the fair value of the asset given up is used to measure the cost of the asset received, unless the fair value of the asset received is more clearly evident. 'More clearly evident' presumably relates

to the cost and difficulty of determining the fair value as, in the paragraph 26 example, the fair values of both the asset received and the asset given up can be measured reliably.

2. Cost is measured by reference to fair value (paragraph 24). The term 'fair value' is defined in paragraph 6 of the standard: Fair value is the amount for which an asset could be exchanged between knowledgeable, willing parties in an arm's-length transaction.

Fair value is basically market value; in economic terms, it represents the opportunity cost of giving up an asset or assuming a liability. Note that the process of determining fair value necessarily involves judgement and estimation. The acquiring company is not actually trading the items given up in the marketplace for cash, but is trying to estimate what it would get for those items if it did so. Hence, the determination of fair value is only an estimation. A further practical problem in determining fair value is that the nature of the market in which the goods given up are normally traded may make estimation difficult. The market may be highly volatile with prices changing daily, or the market may be relatively inactive. Where no ready market exists for the goods being traded, it may be necessary to obtain a reasonable estimate of fair value by reference to a market for similar goods.

If the acquirer gives up an asset at fair value, and the carrying amount of the asset is different from the fair value, then the entity will recognise a gain or a loss. According to paragraph 34 of IAS 1 *Presentation of Financial Statements*, gains and losses on the disposal of non-current assets are reported by deducting from the proceeds on disposal the carrying amount of the asset and related selling expenses.

Assume then that an entity acquires a piece of machinery and gives in exchange a block of land. The land is carried by the entity at original cost of $100, and has a fair value of $150. The journal entry to record the acquisition of the machinery is:

Machinery	Dr	150	
Proceeds on sale of land	Cr		150
(Sale of land in exchange for machinery)			
Land	Dr	100	
Carrying amount of land sold	Cr		100
(Carrying amount of land sold)			

The entity then reports a gain on sale of land of $50.

If instead of giving land in exchange, the entity issued shares having a fair value of $150, the journal entry is:

Machinery	Dr	150	
Share capital	Cr		150
(Acquisition of machinery by issue of shares)			

Further discussion on the measurement of the fair value of equity instruments issued by the acquirer in exchange for assets is found in chapter 12.

3. Paragraph 24 of IAS 16 requires the use of fair value to measure the cost of an asset received unless the exchange transaction lacks commercial substance. Commercial substance is concerned with whether the transaction has a discernible effect on the economics of an entity. Paragraph 25 states that an exchange transaction has commercial substance if:

(a) *the configuration (risk, timing and amount) of the cash flows of the asset received differs from the configuration of the cash flows of the asset transferred*. This would not occur if similar assets, such as an exchange of commodities like oil or milk were exchanged as would occur where, for example, suppliers exchanged inventories in various locations to fulfil demand on a timely basis in a particular location; or

(b) *the entity-specific value of the portion of the entity's operations affected by the transaction changes as a result of the exchange.* Paragraph 6 defines 'entity-specific value' as 'the present value of the cash flows an entity expects to arise from the continuing use of an asset and from its disposal at the end of its useful life or expects to incur when settling a liability'. If there is no change in the expected cash flows to the entity as a result of the exchange, as in the case of the exchange of similar items, then the transaction lacks commercial substance; and

(c) *the difference in (a) or (b) is significant relative to the fair value of the assets exchanged.* In both (a) and (b), the change in cash flows or configuration must be material, with materiality being measured in relation to the fair value of the assets exchanged.

Where the transaction lacks commercial substance, the asset acquired is measured at the carrying amount of the asset given up.

4. Paragraph 24 of IAS 16 also covers the situation where, in an exchange of assets, neither the fair value of the assets given up nor the fair value of the assets acquired can be measured reliably. Such situations could occur where the assets exchanged are both traded in weak markets where market transactions are infrequent. In this situation, the acquirer measures the cost of the asset acquired at the carrying amount of the asset given up.

Acquisition date

One of the problems in recording the acquisition of an item of property, plant and equipment relates to the determination of the fair values of the assets involved in the exchange. As noted above, accounting for the asset exchange requires that potentially both the fair values of the assets acquired and assets given up must be determined. However, where the markets for these assets are volatile, choosing the appropriate fair value may be difficult. This can be seen where an entity issues shares in exchange for an asset. The fair value of the shares issued may change on a daily basis. At what point in time should the fair values be measured?

Some likely dates that may be considered are:

- the date the contract to exchange the assets is signed
- the date the consideration is paid
- the date on which the assets acquired are received by the acquirer
- the date on which an offer becomes unconditional.

The advantage of these dates is that they relate to a point of time that can be determined objectively, such as the date the item of property, plant and equipment arrives at the acquirer's premises. A problem is that there may be a number of dates involved if, for example, an item of equipment arrives in stages or payment for the equipment is to be made in instalments over time.

The date on which the fair values should be measured is the date on which the acquirer *obtains control of the asset or assets acquired* – hereafter referred to as the 'acquisition date'. The definition of cost in paragraph 6 of IAS 16 refers to the 'time of its [the asset's] acquisition'. There is no specific date defined in the standard. In IFRS 3 *Business Combinations*, acquisition date is defined as 'the date on which the acquirer effectively obtains control of the acquiree'.

The measurement of the fair value relates to the date the assets acquired are recognised in the records of the acquirer. At this date, the acquirer must be able to reliably measure the cost of the asset. Recognition of an asset requires the acquirer to have control of expected future benefits. Hence, when the item acquired becomes the asset of the acquirer (that is, when the expected benefits come under the control of the acquirer), this is the point in time when the measurements of the fair values of assets acquired and given up are made. Paragraph 23 of IAS 16 states that the cost of an item of property, plant and equipment is the cash price equivalent at the 'recognition date'. Recognition date is normally the same as acquisition date.

Acquisition of multiple assets

The above principles as stated in IAS 16 apply to the acquisition of individual items of property, plant and equipment. However, an acquisition may consist of more than one asset, such as a block of land and a number of items of machinery. The acquirer may acquire the assets as a group, paying one total amount for the bundle of assets. The cost of acquiring the bundle of assets is determined as per IAS 16, namely by measuring the fair value of what is given up by the acquirer to determine the purchase price, and adding to this any directly attributable costs. However, even if the total cost of the bundle of assets can be determined, for accounting purposes it is necessary to determine the cost of each of the separate assets as they may be in different classes, or some may be depreciable and others not. No guidance is given in this standard for determining the costs of each of the assets. However, IFRS 3 *Business Combinations*, paragraph 4, states that:

> When an entity acquires a group of assets or net assets that does not constitute a business, it shall allocate the cost of the group between the individual identifiable assets and liabilities in the group based on their relative fair values at the date of acquisition.

In this situation, the cost of each asset to be recorded separately is calculated by allocating the cost of the bundle of assets over the assets acquired in proportion to the fair values of the assets acquired. To illustrate this allocation procedure, assume an entity acquired land, buildings and furniture at a total cost of $300 000 cash. In order to separately record each asset acquired at cost, the entity determines the fair value of each asset, for example:

	Fair value
Land	$ 40 000
Buildings	200 000
Furniture	80 000
	$320 000

The total cost of $300 000 is then allocated to each asset on the basis of these fair values as follows:

Land	40 000/320 000 × $300 000	=	$ 37 500
Buildings	200 000/320 000 × $300 000	=	187 500
Furniture	80 000/320 000 × $300 000	=	75 000
			$300 000

The acquisition of the three assets is recorded by the entity as follows:

Land	Dr	37 500	
Buildings	Dr	187 500	
Furniture	Dr	75 000	
Cash	Cr		300 000
(Acquisition of assets for cash)			

Under IAS 16, the basic principle of recording assets acquired is to record at cost. Where a bundle of assets is acquired, the cost of the separate assets must be estimated, and the fair values of the assets acquired can be used in this process. Where the cost of the assets in total is less than the sum of the fair values of the assets acquired, a bargain purchase has been made. However, as the assets are to be recognised initially at cost, no gain is recognised on acquisition.

LO 5

10.3.2 **Directly attributable costs**

The key feature of those costs included in the cost of acquisition is that they are directly attributable *to bringing the asset to the location and condition necessary for it to be capable of operating in the manner intended by management* (IAS 16, para. 16).

Costs to be included

Paragraph 17 of IAS 16 provides examples of directly attributable costs:
- costs of employee benefits arising directly from the construction or acquisition of the item of property, plant and equipment
- costs of site preparation
- initial delivery and handling costs
- installation and assembly costs – where buildings are acquired, associated costs could be the costs of renovation
- costs of testing whether the asset is functioning properly
- professional fees.

It can be seen that all these costs are incurred prior to the use of the asset, and are necessary in order for the asset to be usable by the entity. Note, however, the use of the word 'necessary'. There may be costs incurred that were not necessary; for example, the entity may have incurred fines, or a concrete platform may have been placed in the wrong position and had to be destroyed and a new one put in the right place. These costs should be written off to an expense rather than being capitalised as part of the cost of the acquired asset.

A further cost that may be capitalised into the cost of an item of property, plant and equipment is that of borrowing costs. Borrowing costs, being interest and other costs associated with the borrowing of funds, are accounted for under IAS 23 *Borrowing Costs*. Borrowing costs are generally recognised as an expense in the period in which they are incurred. However, paragraph 11 of IAS 23 allows for an alternative treatment, where borrowing costs that are directly attributable to the acquisition, construction or production of a qualifying asset may be capitalised as part of the cost of the asset. (A qualifying asset is one that necessarily takes a substantial period of time to get ready for its intended use or sale, such as a building.)

Costs not to be included

Paragraphs 19 and 20 of IAS 16 contain examples of costs that should not be included in directly attributable costs:
- *costs of opening a new facility.* These costs are incurred after the item of property, plant and equipment is capable of being used; the opening ceremony, for example, does not enhance the operating ability of the asset.
- *costs of introducing a new product or service, including costs of advertising and promotional activities.* These costs do not change the location or working condition of the asset.
- *costs of conducting business in a new location or with a new class of customer (including costs of staff training).* Unless the asset is relocated, there is no change in the asset's ability to operate.
- *administration and other general overhead costs.* These costs are not directly attributable to the asset, but are associated generally with the operations of the entity.

- *costs incurred while an item capable of operating in the manner intended by management has yet to be brought into use or is operated at less than full capacity.* These costs are incurred because of management's decisions regarding the timing of operations rather than being attributable to getting the asset in a position for operation.
- *initial operating losses, such as those incurred while demand for the item's output builds up.* These are not incurred prior to the asset being ready for use.
- *costs of relocating or reorganising part or all of the entity's operations.* If a number of currently operating assets are relocated to another site, then the costs of relocation are general, not directly attributable to the item of property, plant and equipment.

Income earned

Paragraph 17(e) of IAS 16 notes that the cost of the asset should be determined after deducting the net proceeds from selling any items produced when bringing the asset to that location and condition, such as proceeds from the sale of samples produced during the testing process. The principle here is that any flows, whether in or out, that occur before the asset is in a position to operate as management intends must be taken into account in determining the cost of the asset. The testing process is a necessary part of readying the asset for its ultimate use. Paragraph 21 provides an example of where income may be earned before the asset is ready for use but should not be included in the calculation of the cost of the asset. The example given is of income earned from the use of the construction site as a car park while there is a delay prior to the construction of a building. These revenues have nothing to do with the creation of the asset. They are incidental to the development activity, and should be separately recognised.

Acquisition for zero or nominal cost

An entity may acquire an asset for zero cost, or be required to pay an amount substantially different from the fair value of the asset. For example, a charitable organisation such as the Red Cross may be given a computer for no charge, or be required to pay only half price for a block of land or a building. Applying IAS 16, where there is zero cost, the entity receiving the asset would not record the asset. In the case of a heavily discounted asset, the asset would be recorded at the cost, namely the purchase price paid plus the directly attributable costs.

It is not appropriate to apply IAS 18 *Revenue* to recognise the asset at fair value and record revenue on receipt of the asset. Paragraph 1 of IAS 18 limits the application of the standard to three types of transactions, not including the acquisition of assets. However, the asset could be recognised subsequent to acquisition at fair value if the revaluation model (as described in section 10.6 of this chapter) is applied to that asset and to other assets in its class.

10.3.3   Costs of dismantling, removal or restoration

At the date the asset is initially recognised, an entity is required to estimate any costs necessary to eventually dismantle and remove an asset and restore its site. For example, when an asset such as an offshore oil platform is constructed, an entity knows that in the future it is required by law to dismantle and remove the platform in such a manner that the environment is cared for. The construction of the platform gives rise to a liability for restoration under IAS 37 *Provisions, Contingent Liabilities and Contingent Assets* (see chapter 5). The expected costs, measured on a present value basis, are capitalised into the cost of the platform as the construction of the platform brings with it the responsibility of disposing of it. Acceptance of the liability for dismantling and removal is an essential part of bringing the asset to a position of intended use. As with directly attributable costs, the dismantling and removal costs are depreciated over the life of the asset. There may be restoration costs associated with the use of land, such as where the land is used for mining or farming. These costs are capitalised into the cost of the land at the acquisition date and, although the land is not depreciated, the restoration costs are depreciated over the period in which the benefits from use of the land are received.

As explained in paragraphs BC14–BC15 of the Basis for Conclusions on IAS 16, due to the limited scope of the revisions undertaken during the Improvements project, the IASB concentrated on the initial estimate of the costs of dismantling, removal and restoration. Issues relating to changes in that estimate, changes in interest rates, and the emergence of obligations subsequent to the asset's acquisition are not covered in IAS 16. However, the IASB did note that, regardless of whether the obligation is incurred when the item is acquired or when it is being used, the obligation's underlying nature and its association with the asset are the same. Hence, where obligations arise because of the use of an asset, these should be included in the cost of the asset.

LO 6

10.4 Measurement subsequent to initial recognition

At the point of initial recognition of an item of property, plant and equipment, the asset is measured at cost, which is the purchase price plus directly attributable costs and removal/restoration costs. After this initial recognition, an entity has a choice on the measurement basis to be adopted. IAS 16, paragraph 29, recognises two possible measurement models:
• the cost model
• the revaluation model.

The choice of model is an accounting policy decision. That policy is not applied to individual assets but to an entire class of property, plant and equipment. Hence, for each class of assets, an entity must decide the measurement model to be used. Having chosen a particular measurement model for a specific class of assets, the entity may later change to the alternative basis. For example, an entity that initially chose the revaluation model may at a later date change to the cost model. In order to change from one basis to another, the principles of IAS 8 *Accounting Policies, Changes in Accounting Estimates and Errors* must be applied. Paragraph 14 of IAS 8 states:

> An entity shall change an accounting policy only if the change:
> (a) is required by a Standard or an Interpretation; or
> (b) results in the financial statements providing reliable and more relevant information about the effects of transactions, other events or conditions on the entity's financial position, financial performance or cash flows.

It is part (b) that establishes the principle for change. The key is whether the change in measurement basis will make the financial statements more useful to users; in particular, will the information be more relevant and/or more reliable? In general, a change from the cost model to the revaluation model would be expected to increase the relevance of information provided because more current information is being made available. However, the change may make the information less reliable, as the determination of fair value requires estimation to occur. The entity would need to assess the overall benefit of the change in order to justify the change. In contrast, changing from the revaluation model would generally lead to a decrease in the relevance of the information. However, it may be that the determination of fair value has become so unreliable that the fair values determined have little meaning. Again, a judgement of the relative trade-offs between relevance and reliability need to be made.

Paragraph 17 of IAS 8 notes that the accounting for a change from the cost model to the revaluation model constitutes a change in accounting policy, but the accounting for such a change is done in accordance with the principles in IAS 16 rather than those in IAS 8, namely by applying the principles of the revaluation model. No such statement is made about a change from fair value back to cost. It would appear that the accounting for this would be based on IAS 8, paragraph 22 in particular. This paragraph requires the change to be applied retrospectively, and the information disclosed as if the new accounting policy had always been applied. Hence, a change from the revaluation model to the cost model would require adjustments to the accounting records to show the information as if the cost model had always been applied. Adjustments can be taken through the opening balance of retained earnings. Comparative information would also need to be restated.

10.5   The cost model

Paragraph 30 of IAS 16 states: 'After recognition as an asset, an item of property, plant and equipment shall be carried at its cost less any accumulated depreciation and any accumulated impairment losses'. The cost is as described in section 10.3 of this chapter, and includes outlays incurred up to the point where the asset is at the location and in the working condition to be capable of operating in the manner intended by management. Note that this entails management determining a level of operations, a capacity of production or a use for the item of property, plant and equipment. In getting a machine to an appropriate working condition, management may need to undertake certain outlays to keep the machine running efficiently at that level. In relation to a vehicle that is needed to take a driver from Point A to Point B, the car needs to run efficiently and at a required safety level, and is not expected to break down. In order for this to occur, the car needs to be regularly serviced, have tune-ups and incur any other routine checks. Costs associated with keeping the item of property, plant and equipment at the required working condition are expensed, and not added to the depreciable cost of the asset. These costs are generally referred to as repairs and maintenance.

Similar examples can be seen with other assets, such as escalators that need to be regularly maintained to ensure they achieve the basic task of moving passengers from one level to another. Most items of plant with moving parts require some form of regular maintenance. Paragraph 12 of IAS 16 notes the existence of these 'repairs and maintenance' costs, stating that these costs should not be capitalised into the cost of the asset. These costs relate to the day-to-day servicing of the asset and consist primarily of labour and consumables, but may also include the cost of small parts. Costs of repairs and maintenance are expensed as incurred.

Subsequent to acquisition, management may also outlay funds refining the ability of the asset to operate. These are not outlays associated with repairs, maintenance or replacement. Examples of such expenditures relate to outlays designed to increase the remaining useful life of the asset, to increase its capacity, to improve the quality of the output, and to adjust the asset to reduce operating costs.

A decision to capitalise these outlays requires the application of the recognition principle in paragraph 7 of IAS 16. Capitalisation requires there to be an increase in probable future economic benefits associated with the asset; that is, it should be probable that the expenditure increases the future economic benefits embodied in the asset in excess of its standard of performance assessed at the time the expenditure is made. Note the timing of the assessment process: at the time the expenditure is made. The comparison is not with the original capacity to operate or the expected future benefits at acquisition, but with the capacity existing at the time the subsequent expenditure is made. Hence, if the capacity of the asset had reduced over time, expenditure to revive the asset to its original capacity would be capitalised. The assessment of capacity requires judgement, and needs to take into account matters such as the level of maintenance performed prior to the incurrence of the subsequent expenditure. The latter could not include the costs of any as yet unperformed maintenance work.

LO 7

10.5.1 ## Depreciation

Under the cost model, after initial recognition, an asset continues to be recorded at its original cost. Adjustments are made only for depreciation and impairment losses. (Impairment losses are discussed in chapter 13.) The main point of the following discussion is to determine the depreciation in relation to an item of property, plant and equipment.

In order to understand the accounting principles for depreciation, it is necessary to consider the definitions of depreciation, depreciable amount, useful life and residual value contained in paragraph 6 of IAS 16:

> *Depreciation* is the systematic allocation of the depreciable amount of an asset over its useful life.

> *Depreciable amount* is the cost of an asset, or other amount substituted for cost, less its residual value.

> *Useful life* is:
> (a) the period over which an asset is expected to be available for use by an entity; or
> (b) the number of production or similar units expected to be obtained from the asset by an entity.

> The *residual value* of an asset is the estimated amount that the entity would currently obtain from disposal of the asset, after deducting the estimated costs of disposal, if the asset were already of the age and in the condition expected at the end of its useful life.

Process of allocation

Depreciation is a process of allocation. Assets by definition are expected future benefits and, as noted in section 10.2, the initial recognition of an item of property, plant and equipment requires that it is probable that the future benefits will flow to the entity. On acquiring these benefits, an entity will have expectations as to the period over which these benefits are to be received and the pattern of these benefits (for example, they could be received evenly over the life of the asset). The purpose of determining the depreciation charge for the period is to measure the consumption of benefits allocable to the current period, ensuring that, over the useful life of the asset, each period will be allocated its fair share of the cost of the asset acquired. This principle is found in paragraphs 50 and 60 of IAS 16:

> 50. The depreciable amount of an asset shall be allocated on a systematic basis over its useful life.
> 60. The depreciation method used shall reflect the pattern in which the asset's future economic benefits are expected to be consumed by the entity.

It could be argued that there are two concepts of depreciation, namely:
- a process of allocation
- a change in the value of an asset.

There are at least three variables that cause a change in value of an asset over the period:
1. a reduction in value due to the use of the asset over the period
2. an increase/decrease in the value due to a change in the general price level
3. a change in the specific price level for this type of asset.

When depreciation is calculated as an allocation of the cost of the asset, what is being measured is variable (1) above. If an asset is measured at a revalued amount such as its fair value, and if depreciation is measured as the change in the fair value over the period, then the amount calculated would be a mixture of all the above variables. If the increase in price levels is so high that the fair value of an asset increases over the period, then there would be no depreciation calculated at all.

By describing depreciation as a process of allocation, the IASB is effectively arguing that an increase in value is not sufficient justification for not depreciating an asset. The IASB wants to consider separately the consumption of benefits and the changes in value over a period. In its 1996 discussion paper, *Measurement of tangible fixed assets,* the Accounting Standards Board in the United Kingdom provided the following example to illustrate the difference between consumption and changes in value:

> Even where there are no general price changes, a change in the value of a tangible asset might still not reflect the consumption of economic benefits of the asset. For example, the drop in value of a new car during its first year would be unlikely to equate to the consumption of economic benefits of the car during the same period resulting from the use of the car. This difference occurs because the price change reflects the market's evaluation of the decline in economic benefits, which may differ from that made by a business. In this example the price change reflects the market's evaluation of the additional economic benefits a new car has over a second-hand car (e.g. the purchaser of a new car can specify exactly what features he wants while the purchaser of a second-hand car cannot, a new car has a known history etc.), but does not reflect the business's evaluation of the remaining economic benefits (para. 5.15).

Under IAS 16, the depreciation charge for the period reflects the consumption of the economic benefits over the period and ignores the fall in the asset's fair value. As paragraph 52 of the standard states, depreciation is recognised even if the fair value of an asset is greater than its carrying amount. However, depreciation is not recognised if the asset's residual value exceeds the carrying amount.

As is noted later in this chapter, where a revalued amount is used rather than cost, the depreciation charge affects current period income, while an increase in the value of the asset affects revaluation surplus. If both amounts affected income, then it would be important to determine whether it is useful to try to measure separately the two components of the change in value of the asset. If depreciation is capitalised into the cost of production, it may be argued that only the amount relating to the consumption of benefits should affect the cost of inventory produced.

Methods of depreciation

The accounting policy that an entity must adopt for depreciation is specified in paragraphs 50 and 60 of IAS 16, namely the systematic allocation of the cost or other revalued amount of an asset over its useful life in a manner that reflects the pattern in which the asset's future economic benefits are expected to be consumed. There are many methods of allocation, depending on the pattern of benefits. Paragraph 62 of the standard notes three methods:

- *Straight-line method.* This is used where the benefits are expected to be received evenly over the useful life of the asset. The depreciation charge for the period is calculated as:

$$\frac{\text{Depreciable amount}}{\text{Useful life}} = \frac{\text{Cost less residual value}}{\text{Useful life}}$$

If an item of plant had an original cost of \$100 000, a residual value of \$10 000, and a useful life of four years, the depreciation charge per annum is:

$$\text{Depreciation expense p.a.} = 1/4(\$100\,000 - \$10\,000)$$
$$= \$22\,500$$

The journal entry is:

Depreciation expense – plant	Dr	22 500	
Accumulated depreciation – plant	Cr		22 500
(Depreciation on plant per annum)			

Note that both the residual value and the useful life may change during the life of the asset as expectations change.

- *Diminishing balance method.* This method is used where the pattern of benefits is such that more benefits are received in the earlier years in the life of the asset. As the asset increases in age, the benefits per annum are expected to reduce.

  It is possible to calculate a rate of depreciation that would result in the depreciable amount being written off over the useful life, with the depreciation charge per annum being calculated by multiplying the rate by the carrying amount at the beginning of the year. The formula is:

$$\text{Depreciation rate} = 1 - \sqrt[n]{\frac{r}{c}}$$

where
n = useful life
r = residual value
c = cost or other revalued amount

Using the same information as in the example for the straight-line method, the depreciation rate under the diminishing balance method is:

$$\text{Depreciation rate} = 1 - \sqrt[4]{\frac{10\,000}{100\,000}}$$
$$= 44\% \text{ approximately}$$

The depreciation expense per annum following acquisition of the item of plant at the beginning of the first year is:

Year 1 depreciation expense = 44% × $100 000	= $44 000
Year 2 depreciation expense = 44% × $56 000	= $24 640
Year 3 depreciation expense = 44% × $31 360	= $13 798
Year 4 depreciation expense = $17 562 – $10 000	= $ 7 562

The depreciation charge then reflects a decreasing pattern of benefits over the asset's useful life.

- *Units of production method.* This method is based on the expected use or output of the asset. Variables used could be production hours or production output.

  Using the above example again, assume that over the four-year life of the asset the expected output of the asset is as follows:

Year 1	17 000 units
Year 2	15 000 units
Year 3	12 000 units
Year 4	6 000 units
	50 000 units

The depreciation expense in each of the four years is:

$$
\begin{aligned}
\text{Year 1 depreciation expense} &= 17/50 \times \$90\,000 = \$30\,600 \\
\text{Year 2 depreciation expense} &= 15/50 \times \$90\,000 = \$27\,000 \\
\text{Year 3 depreciation expense} &= 12/50 \times \$90\,000 = \$21\,600 \\
\text{Year 4 depreciation expense} &= 6/50 \times \$90\,000 = \$10\,800 \\
&\ \underline{\$90\,000}
\end{aligned}
$$

IAS 16 does not specify the use of any specific method of depreciation. The method chosen by an entity should be based on which method most closely reflects the expected pattern of consumption of the future economic benefits embodied in the asset.

Paragraph 61 of IAS 16 requires that an entity review the depreciation method chosen to ensure that it is providing the appropriate systematic allocation of benefits. The review process should occur at least at the end of each financial year. If there has been a change in the pattern of benefits such that the current method is inappropriate, the method should be changed to one that reflects the changed pattern of benefits. This change is not a change in an accounting policy, simply a change in accounting method. As such it is accounted for as a change in an accounting estimate, with the application of IAS 8. Under paragraph 36 of IAS 8, the change is recognised prospectively with adjustments being made to the amounts recognised in the current period and future periods as appropriate.

The depreciation method is applied from the date the asset is available for use; that is, when it is in the location and condition necessary for it to perform as intended by management. As noted in paragraph 55 of IAS 16, depreciation continues even if the asset is temporarily idle, dependent on movements in residual value and expected useful life. However, under methods such as the units of production method, no depreciation is recognised where production ceases.

Useful life

Determination of useful life requires estimation on the part of management, as the way in which an item of property, plant and equipment is used and the potential for changes in the market for that item affect estimates of useful life. Paragraph 56 of IAS 16 provides the following list of factors to consider in determining useful life:

(a) the *expected usage* of the asset by the entity; usage is assessed by reference to the asset's expected capacity or physical output
(b) the expected *physical wear and tear*, which depends on operational factors such as the number of work shifts for which the asset is to be used and the repair and maintenance program of the entity, and the care and the maintenance of the asset while idle
(c) *technical or commercial obsolescence* arising from changes or improvements in production, or from a change in the market demand for the product or service output of the asset. For example, computers may be regarded as having a relatively short useful life. The actual period over which they may be expected to work is probably considerably longer than the period over which they may be considered to be technologically efficient. The useful life for depreciation purposes is related to the period over which the entity intends to use them, which is probably closer to their technological life than the period over which they would be capable of being used
(d) *legal or similar limits* on the use of the asset, such as expiry dates of related leases.

There is no necessary relationship between useful life to the entity and the economic life of the asset. Management may want to hold only relatively new assets, and a policy of replacement after specified periods of time may mean that assets are held for only a proportion of their economic lives. In other words, useful life for the purpose of calculating depreciation is defined in terms of the asset's expected usefulness to the entity. As noted earlier, the useful life of an asset covers the entire time the asset is available for use, including the time the asset is idle but available for use.

As noted in paragraph 58 of IAS 16, land is a special type of asset. Unless the land is being used for a purpose where there is a limited life imposed on the land, such as a quarry, it is assumed to have an unlimited life. Such land is not subject to depreciation. Hence, in accounting for land and buildings, these assets are dealt with separately so that buildings are made subject to depreciation. If, however, the cost of land includes the expected costs of dismantling, removal or restoration, then these costs are depreciated over the period in which the benefits from use of the land are received.

Just as the depreciation method requires a periodic review, so the useful life of an asset is subject to review. According to paragraph 51 of IAS 16, the review should occur at least at each year-end. A change in the assessment of the useful life will result in a change in the depreciation rate used. As this is a change in accounting estimate, changes are made prospectively in accordance with IAS 8, paragraph 36.

ILLUSTRATIVE EXAMPLE 10.1

Assessment of useful life

An entity is in the business of making camera lenses. The machine primarily used in this process is very well made, and could be expected to provide a service in making the lenses currently demanded for another 20 years. As the machine is computer driven, the efficiency of making lenses is affected by the sophistication of the computer program to define what is required in a lens. Technological advances are being made all the time, and it is thought that a new machine with advanced technology will be available within the next five years. The type of lens required is also a function of what cameras are considered to be in demand by consumers. Even if there is a change in technology, it is thought that cameras with the old style lens could still be marketable for another seven years.

Problem
What useful life should management use in calculating depreciation on the machine?

Solution
Three specific time periods are mentioned:
- physical life: 20 years
- technical life: 5 years
- commercial life: 7 years.

A key element in determining the appropriate life is assessing the strategy used by management in marketing its products. If management believe that to retain its market share and reputation it needs to be at the cutting edge of technology, five years would be appropriate. If, however, the marketing strategy is aimed at the general consumer, seven years could be appropriate. In essence, management needs to consider at what point it most likely expects to replace the machine.

Residual value

Note again the definition of residual value in paragraph 6 of IAS 16:

> The *residual value* of an asset is the estimated amount that the entity would currently obtain from disposal of the asset, after deducting the estimated costs of disposal, if the asset were already of the age and in the condition expected at the end of its useful life.

Residual value is an estimate based on what the entity would currently obtain from the asset's disposal; that is, what could be obtained at the time of the estimate – not at the expected date of disposal at the end of the useful life. The estimate is based on what could be obtained from disposal of similar assets that are currently, at the date of the estimate, at the end of their useful lives, and which have been used in a similar fashion to the asset being investigated. Where assets are unique, this estimation process is much more difficult than for assets that are constantly being replaced. For an asset such as a vehicle, which may have a useful life of 10 years, the residual value of a new vehicle is the net amount that could be obtained now for a 10-year-old vehicle of the same type as the one being depreciated. In many cases, the residual value will be negligible or scrap value.

This form of assessment means that the residual value will not be adjusted for expected changes in prices. Basing the residual value calculation on current prices relates to the adoption in IASB 16 of depreciation as a process of allocating economic benefits. If the residual value were adjusted for future prices, then there may be no measure of benefits consumed during the period as the residual value may exceed the carrying amount at the beginning of the period. It is also debatable whether the residual value should take into account possible technological developments. In relation to computers it may reasonably be expected that there will be such changes within a relatively short period of time, whereas with motor vehicles trying to predict cars being powered with other than oil is more difficult. Management is not required to be a predictor of future inventions. Expectations of technological change are already built into current second-hand asset prices. Management should then take into account reasonable changes in technological development and the effect on prices. Where assets are expected to be used for the whole or the majority of their useful lives, the residual values are zero or immaterial in amount.

In paragraphs BC28–BC29 of the Basis for Conclusions on IAS 16, the IASB raises the issue of why an entity deducts an asset's residual value from the cost of the asset for measurement of depreciation. Two reasons are proposed. First, the objective is one of precision; that is, reducing the amount of depreciation so that it reflects the item's net cost. The second is one of economics; that is, stopping depreciation if the entity expects the asset to increase in value by an amount greater than it will diminish. The IASB did not adopt either the net cost or the economic objective completely. Expected increases in value do not override the need to depreciate an asset. An increase in the expected residual value of an asset because of past events affects the depreciable amount; expectations of future changes in residual value other than the effects of expected wear and tear will not.

Where residual values are material, an entity must, under paragraph 51 of IAS 16, review the residual value at each financial year-end. If a change is required, again the change is a change in estimate and is accounted for prospectively as an adjustment to future depreciation.

It is possible that the review of the residual value of an asset may lead to depreciation 'credits'. Consider the following situation:

Asset at cost	$100
Useful life	4 years
Depreciation method	Straight-line
Residual value at acquisition	$60

The entity would then charge depreciation at $10 per annum. If at the start of year 3, the residual value is estimated to be $90, what should the depreciation charge be in years 3 and 4?

At the end of year 2, the carrying amount of the asset is $80, being cost of $100 less two years' depreciation of $10 per annum. At the start of year 3, there is a change in an estimate, namely to the residual value. Under IAS 8, the change in estimate must be adjusted against the current period and any future periods affected by the change. In this case, both years 3 and 4 are equally affected by the change in the estimated residual value. Hence, in both these years the entity should recognise a depreciation credit of $5 (50% of $90 – $80), with a corresponding debit to accumulated depreciation. The depreciation credit reduces the entity's total depreciation expense for the period.

Components depreciation

It has been mentioned previously in this chapter that a components approach requires that an entity allocate the cost of an asset to its component parts and account for each component separately; for example, the cost of an aeroplane is allocated to such parts as the frame, the engines and the fittings. According to paragraph 43 of IAS 16, *each part* of an item of property, plant and equipment with a *cost that is significant* in relation to the total cost of the item shall be depreciated *separately*. In other words, an entity is required to separate each item of property, plant and equipment into its significant parts or components, with each part or component being separately depreciated. Any remainder is also depreciated separately.

Paragraph 13 of the standard discusses the replacement or renewal of the components of an asset:

> Under the recognition principle in paragraph 7, an entity recognises in the carrying amount of an item of property, plant and equipment the cost of replacing part of such an item when the cost is incurred if the recognition criteria are met. The carrying amount of those parts that are replaced is derecognised in accordance with the derecognition provisions of this Standard (see paragraphs 67–72).

As is consistent with accounting for all separate items of property, plant and equipment, once an acquired asset is separated into the relevant components, if one of those components needs regular replacing or renewing, the component is generally accounted for as a separate asset. The replaced asset is depreciated over its useful life, and derecognised on replacement.

To illustrate the accounting for components, consider the case of a building with a roof that periodically needs replacing. If the roof is accounted for as a separate component, then the roof is accounted for as a separate asset and is depreciated separately. On replacement, paragraph 13 of IAS 16 is applied, and the carrying amount (if any) of the old roof is written off. In order for this derecognition to occur, it is necessary to know the original cost of the roof and the depreciation charged to date. The new roof is accounted for as the acquisition of a new asset, assessed under paragraph 7 and, if capitalised as an asset, is subsequently depreciated. If, however, the roof is not treated as a separate component from the acquisition date of the building, then on replacement of the roof, the recognition principle in paragraph 7 and the derecognition principle in paragraph 13 also apply. An entity cannot carry both the replacement and the replaced portion as assets. Calculation of the amount to be derecognised is more difficult where no separate component is recognised because the depreciation of the building has not been separated from the depreciation of the roof.

Another example of dealing with a component of an asset arises where assets are subject to regular major inspections to ensure that they reach the requisite safety and quality requirements. Under paragraph 14 of IAS 16, such major inspections may be capitalised as a replacement component. In order for the cost of the inspection to be capitalised, the recognition criteria in paragraph 7 of the standard must be met. In particular, it must be probable that future economic benefits associated with the outlay will flow to the entity. For example, if there is a five-year inspection of aircraft by a specific party, and this is required every five years in order for the plane not to be grounded, then the cost of the inspection provides benefits to the owner of the aircraft for that period of time by effectively providing a licence to continue flying. The capitalised amount is then depreciated over the relevant useful life, most probably the time until the next inspection.

LO 8   ## 10.6 The revaluation model

Use of the revaluation model of measurement is the alternative treatment to the cost model. Paragraph 31 of IAS 16 states:

> After recognition as an asset, an item of property, plant and equipment whose fair value can be measured reliably shall be carried at a revalued amount, being its fair value at the date of the revaluation less any subsequent accumulated depreciation and subsequent accumulated impairment losses. Revaluations should be made with sufficient regularity to ensure that the carrying amount does not differ materially from that which would be determined using fair value at the balance sheet date.

In relation to this paragraph, note the following points:

1. The measurement basis is fair value, defined in paragraph 6 as 'the amount for which an asset could be exchanged between knowledgeable, willing parties in an arm's length transaction'. The fair value is usually the market value for the asset. However, where there is not an active, liquid market, approximations of fair value may be made using surrogate measures such as depreciated replacement cost. It is also possible to apply market indexes of price changes to estimate fair value.

2. IAS 16 does not specify how often revaluations must take place. The principle established is that the revaluations must be of sufficient regularity such that the carrying amount of the asset does not materially differ from fair value. The frequency of revaluations depends on the nature of the assets themselves. For some assets, frequent revaluations are necessary because of continual change in the fair values due to a volatile market. For other assets, revaluation every three or five years may be appropriate (para. 34). Paragraph 38 notes that assets may be revalued on a rolling basis provided that the total revaluation is completed within a short period of time, and that at no time is the total carrying amount of the class of assets materially different from fair value.

In providing guidance to its constituents on the frequency of revaluations, the Australian Accounting Standards Board provided the following information in its Australian Guidance accompanying its standard AASB 116, a standard equivalent to IAS 16:

> G6 An entity assesses at each reporting date whether there is any indication that a revalued asset's carrying amount may differ materially from that which would be determined if the asset were revalued at the reporting date. If any such indication exists, the entity determines the asset's fair value and revalues the asset to that amount.
>
> G7 In assessing whether there is any indication that a revalued asset's carrying amount may differ materially from that which would be determined if the asset were revalued at the reporting date, an entity considers, as a minimum, the following indications:
>
> External sources of information
>
> (a) significant changes affecting the entity have taken place during the period, or will take place in the near future, in the technological, market, economic or legal environment in which the entity operates or in the market to which an asset is dedicated;
>
> (b) the carrying amount of the net assets of the entity is more than its market capitalisation;
>
> (c) during the period, a price index relevant to the asset has undergone a material change;
>
> Internal sources of information
>
> (d) evidence is available of obsolescence or physical damage of an asset;
>
> (e) significant changes affecting the entity have taken place during the period, or are expected to take place in the near future, in the extent to which, or manner in which, an asset is used or is expected to be used. Adverse changes include the asset becoming idle, or plans to dispose of an asset before the previously expected date, and

reassessing the useful life of an asset as finite rather than indefinite. Favourable changes include capital expenditure incurred during the period to improve or enhance an asset in excess of its standard of performance assessed immediately before the expenditure is made; and

(f) evidence is available from internal reporting that indicates that the economic performance of an asset is, or will be, worse/better than expected.

3. According to paragraph 32 of IAS 16, the fair value of land and buildings 'is usually determined from market-based evidence by appraisal normally undertaken by professionally qualified valuers'. It is then the responsibility of management to determine whether there has been sufficient change in the market for the assets held at fair value to warrant a formal appraisal by professional valuers. With items of plant and equipment, the fair value is usually their market value determined by appraisal.

Paragraph 36 of IAS 16 notes that the revaluation model is not applied to individual items of property, plant and equipment; instead, the accounting policy is applied to a class of assets. Hence, for each class of assets, management must choose whether to apply the cost model or the revaluation model.

A class of property, plant and equipment 'is a grouping of assets of a similar nature and use in an entity's operations' (IAS 16, para. 37). Examples of separate classes are:

- land
- land and buildings
- machinery
- ships
- aircraft
- motor vehicles
- furniture and fixtures
- office equipment (para. 37).

There are two purposes for requiring revaluation to be done on a class rather than on an individual asset basis. First, this limits the ability of management to 'cherry-pick' or selectively choose which assets to revalue. Second, the requirement to have all assets within the class measured on a fair value basis means that there is consistent measurement for the same type of assets in the entity.

According to paragraph 31 of IAS 16, where an asset is carried at a revalued amount, recognition of an asset should occur only when the fair value can be measured reliably. One question arising here is that, if a class of assets is being carried at fair value but there are assets within that class for which the fair value cannot be reliably measured, should those assets be written off because the recognition criteria cannot be met? The problem is that writing off these assets provides less relevant information than including the assets at cost.

The question then is whether, in order to be able to adopt the revaluation model, the fair values need to be capable of being reliably measured for all assets within the class. The problem with allowing some assets within a class to be at fair value and others at cost is that an entity can cherry pick which assets are going to be measured at what amount. This amounts to selective revaluation. The only way to stop selective revaluation is for the IASB to require the use of the fair value method only where *all* assets within the class can be reliably measured at fair value.

LO 9   10.6.1   Applying the revaluation model: revaluation increments

Paragraphs 39 and 40 of IAS 16 contain the principles for applying the fair value method to revaluation increments. These paragraphs apply to individual items of property, plant and equipment. In other words, even though revaluations are done on a class-by-class basis, the accounting is done on an asset-by-asset basis.

The first part of paragraph 39 of IAS 16 states: 'If an asset's carrying amount is increased as a result of a revaluation, the increase shall be credited directly to equity under the heading of revaluation surplus'. Note that the increase is taken directly to equity, rather than through the income statement. In accordance with paragraph 42 of IAS 16, the effects of any taxes on income need to be accounted for in accordance with IAS 12 *Income Taxes*. A revaluation of an asset causes a change between the tax base and the carrying amount of the asset, giving rise to a temporary difference, and a deferred tax liability needs to be raised (see para. 20 of IAS 12). As the increase in equity goes directly to equity, the tax effect is recognised via the revaluation surplus account; that is, this account is shown on an after-tax basis.

ILLUSTRATIVE EXAMPLE 10.2

Revaluation increments and tax effect

On 1 January 2005, an entity carries an item of land at a cost of $100 000, this amount also being the tax base of the asset. The land is revalued to $120 000. The tax rate is 30%.

The tax base of the asset is $100 000 and the new carrying amount is $120 000, giving rise to a taxable temporary difference of $20 000. A deferred tax liability of $6000 must be raised to account for the expected tax to be paid in relation to the increase in expected benefits from the asset. The asset revaluation surplus raised will be the net after-tax increase in the asset ($20 000 − $6000 = $14 000). The appropriate accounting entries on revaluation of the asset are shown in figure 10.2.

Land	Dr	20 000	
Asset revaluation surplus	Cr		20 000
(Revaluation of asset)			
Asset revaluation surplus	Dr	6 000	
Deferred tax liability	Cr		6 000
(Tax effect of revaluation)			

These two entries could be combined as follows:

Land	Dr	20 000	
Deferred tax liability	Cr		6 000
Asset revaluation surplus	Cr		14 000
(Revaluation of asset with associated tax effect)			

FIGURE 10.2 Journal entries for revaluation with associated tax effect

Where the item of property, plant and equipment is depreciable, there are two possible accounting treatments under paragraph 35 of IAS 16:
1. restate proportionately with the change in the gross carrying amount of the asset so that the carrying amount of the asset after revaluation equals its revalued amount; or
2. eliminate the accumulated depreciation balance against the gross carrying amount of the asset and the net amount is then restated to the fair value of the asset. This method is applied in this chapter.

ILLUSTRATIVE EXAMPLE 10.3

Revaluation increments and depreciable assets

On 30 June 2006, an item of plant has a carrying amount of $42 000, being the original cost of $70 000 less accumulated depreciation of $28 000. The fair value of the asset is $50 000. The tax rate is 30%. The entries are shown in figure 10.3.

The revaluation may be done in two steps:
Step 1: Revalue the asset, disregarding the tax effect, and eliminate the accumulated depreciation.

Accumulated depreciation	Dr	28 000	
Plant	Cr		20 000
Asset revaluation surplus	Cr		8 000
(Revaluation of asset)			

Step 2: Adjust for the tax effect of the revaluation.

Asset revaluation surplus	Dr	2 400	
Deferred tax liability	Cr		2 400
(Recognition of deferred tax liability as a direct adjustment against the asset revaluation surplus: 30% × $8000)			

The two entries could be *combined* as follows:

Accumulated depreciation	Dr	28 000	
Plant	Cr		20 000
Deferred tax liability	Cr		2 400
Asset revaluation surplus	Cr		5 600
(Revaluation of asset with associated tax effect)			

FIGURE 10.3 Revaluation increment and depreciable assets

ILLUSTRATIVE EXAMPLE 10.4

Revaluation increment and the tax-effect worksheet

Assume that the depreciable asset in illustrative example 10.3 was acquired for $70 000 on 1 July 2005 to be used in the business. Depreciation rates are on a straight-line basis at 20% p.a. for accounting and 35% for tax. The tax rate is 30%.
On 30 June 2006, the carrying amount and the tax base of the asset are as follows:

	Accounting	Tax
Original cost	$70 000	$70 000
Acumulated depreciation	14 000	24 500
Net amount	56 000	45 500

Hence, the taxable temporary difference at 30 June 2006 is $10 500 ($56 000 − $45 500), with a deferred tax liability of $3150 being recognised.

On 30 June 2007, the asset has a carrying amount and tax base as follows:

	Accounting	Tax
Original cost	$70 000	$70 000
Acumulated depreciation	28 000	49 000
Net amount	42 000	21 000

Assume that on this date the asset is revalued to $50 000. The appropriate entry is:

2007 30 June	Accumulated depreciation	Dr	28 000	
	Plant	Cr		20 000
	Deferred tax liability	Cr		2 400
	Asset revaluation surplus	Cr		5 600
	(Revaluation of asset with associated tax effect)			

For the purpose of determining required entries for tax-effect accounting at the end of the year, the carrying amount of the asset on 30 June 2007 in the accounting records is now $50 000, but its tax base is unchanged at $21 000. This gives a taxable temporary difference of $29 000, and a total deferred tax liability of $8700 at a 30% tax rate. Since $2400 of the deferred tax liability is already recognised in the revaluation entry above, the total credit to the deferred tax liability needs to be only $6300. As the beginning deferred tax liability for the year is $3150, the adjustment required in the current year ending 30 June 2006 is $3150 ($6300 – $3150). In order to recognise the adjustment to the deferred tax liability, the appropriate entry under IAS 12 is as follows:

2007 30 June	Income tax expense	Dr	3 150	
	Deferred tax liability	Cr		3 150
	(Recognition of deferred tax liability)			

The tax-effect worksheet is shown in figure 10.4.

	Carrying amount $	Taxable amount $	Deductible amount $	Tax base $	Taxable temporary differences $	Deductible temporary differences $
Plant	50 000	(50 000)	21 000	21 000	29 000	
Temporary difference					29 000	
Deferred tax liability					8 700	
Beginning balance					3 150	
Movement during the year					2 400	
Adjustment					3 150	

FIGURE 10.4 Tax-effect worksheet on revaluation of assets

Revaluation increment reversing previous revaluation decrement

The full text of paragraph 39 of IAS 16 is as follows:

> If an asset's carrying amount is increased as a result of a revaluation, the increase shall be credited directly to equity under the heading of revaluation surplus. However, the increase shall be recognised in profit or loss to the extent that it reverses a revaluation decrease of the same asset previously recognised in profit or loss.

Hence, a revaluation increment is credited to an asset revaluation surplus unless the increment reverses a revaluation decrement previously recognised as an expense. After the accounting treatment for revaluation decrements is discussed in the next section, illustrative example 10.7 on page 407 demonstrates entries for this situation.

LO 10

10.6.2 Applying the revaluation model: revaluation decrements

Paragraph 40 of IAS 16 states:

> If an asset's carrying amount is decreased as a result of a revaluation, the decrease shall be recognised in profit or loss. However, the decrease shall be debited directly to equity under the heading of revaluation surplus to the extent of any credit balance existing in the revaluation surplus in respect of that asset.

As with revaluation increments, this paragraph covers two situations: a revaluation decrement, and a revaluation decrement following a previous revaluation increment.

The accounting for a revaluation decrement involves an immediate recognition of an expense in the period of the revaluation. As the change in the carrying amount of the asset directly affects income, the tax effect is dealt with in the normal workings of tax-effect accounting. Hence, no extra tax-effect entries outside those generated via the tax-effect worksheet are necessary in accounting for revaluation decrements.

ILLUSTRATIVE EXAMPLE 10.5

Revaluation decrement

Assume an item of plant has a carrying amount of $50 000, being original cost of $60 000 less accumulated depreciation of $10 000. If the asset is revalued downwards to $24 000, the appropriate journal entry is:

Accumulated depreciation	Dr	10 000	
Expense – downward revaluation of asset	Dr	26 000	
Plant	Cr		36 000
(Downward revaluation of plant)			

In relation to the tax-effect worksheet, if the carrying amount and the tax base in this example were the same immediately prior to the revaluation, then there would be a deductible temporary difference of $26 000. A deferred tax asset of $7800 would be raised via the tax-effect worksheet analysis on balance date.

Decrement reversing previous revaluation increment

Where an asset revaluation surplus has been raised via a previous revaluation increment, in accounting for a subsequent revaluation decrement for the same asset, the surplus must be eliminated before any expense is recognised. In adjusting for the prior revaluation increment, both the asset revaluation surplus and the related deferred tax liability must be reversed.

ILLUSTRATIVE EXAMPLE 10.6

Decrement reversing previous increment

Assume an entity has a block of land with a carrying amount of $200 000, this having been previously revalued upwards from $100 000. The following entry was passed:

Land	Dr	100 000	
Deferred tax liability	Cr		30 000
Asset revaluation surplus	Cr		70 000
(Revaluation of plant)			

If the asset is *revalued downwards to $160 000*, the $40 000 write-down is a partial reversal of the previous upward revaluation. The adjustment is then a reduction in the deferred tax liability of $12 000 (i.e. $40 000 × 30%), and a reduction in the asset revaluation surplus of $28 000 ($40 000 [1 − 30%]). The appropriate journal entry is:

Deferred tax liability	Dr	12 000	
Asset revaluation surplus	Dr	28 000	
Land	Cr		40 000
(Downward revaluation of land)			

If the asset is *revalued downwards to $80 000*, which is a reduction of $120 000, the asset is written down to an amount $20 000 less than the original cost of the asset. The downward revaluation then requires the elimination of the deferred tax liability and the asset revaluation surplus, as well as recognition of an expense of $20 000. The appropriate entry is:

Deferred tax liability	Dr	30 000	
Asset revaluation surplus	Dr	70 000	
Expense – downward revaluation of land	Dr	20 000	
Land	Cr		120 000
(Downward revaluation of land)			

The tax-effect worksheet, assuming the original revaluation increment occurred in a previous period, is shown in figure 10.5.

	Carrying amount $	Taxable amount $	Deductible amount $	Tax base $	Taxable temporary differences $	Deductible temporary differences $
Land	80 000	(80 000)	100 000	100 000		20 000
Temporary difference						20 000
Deferred tax liability						6 000
Beginning balance						(30 000)
Movement during the year						30 000
Adjustment						6 000

FIGURE 10.5   Tax-effect worksheet on revaluation of assets

The tax-effect worksheet shows that the entity would recognise a deferred tax asset of $6000, reflecting the fact that the carrying amount of the asset is $20 000 less than the tax base.

Net revaluation increment reversing previous revaluation decrement

Where an asset is revalued upwards, an asset revaluation surplus is credited except where the increment reverses a revaluation decrement previously recognised as an expense. In this case, the revaluation increment must be recognised as income.

ILLUSTRATIVE EXAMPLE 10.7

Revaluation increment reversing previous decrement

Assume an entity has an item of plant whose current carrying amount is $200 000 (accumulated depreciation being $20 000). The asset had cost $300 000. It was revalued downwards from a carrying amount of $270 000 to $220 000, with the following accounting entry being passed:

Expense – downward revaluation of plant	Dr	50 000	
Accumulated depreciation	Dr	30 000	
Plant	Cr		80 000
(Downward revaluation of plant)			

If the asset is now assessed as having *a fair value of $230 000*, the appropriate revaluation entry is:

Accumulated depreciation	Dr	20 000	
Plant	Dr	10 000	
Income on revaluation of plant	Cr		30 000
(Upward revaluation of plant)			

If the asset is assessed as having *a fair value of $280 000*, the accounting entry recognises the increase of $80 000 as consisting partly of revenue, being the reversal of the previous $50 000 write-down, and partly of revaluation surplus. The appropriate entry is:

Accumulated depreciation	Dr	20 000	
Plant	Dr	60 000	
Income on revaluation of plant	Cr		50 000
Deferred tax liability	Cr		9 000
Asset revaluation surplus	Cr		21 000
(Upward revaluation of plant)			

10.6.3 Effects of accounting on an asset-by-asset basis

If the fair value basis of measurement is chosen, IAS 16 requires that it be applied to items of property, plant and equipment on a class-by-class basis. However, in accounting for revaluation increments and decrements, the accounting is done on an individual asset basis within the class. In the April 1999 edition of Ernst & Young's *Accounting Brief* in Australia, written by Ruth Picker and Anne-Marie Johnson, it was argued that a better accounting treatment would be to account for revaluation increments and decrements on a class-by-class basis. The rationale for this is based on the different treatment for increments and decrements, in that revaluation increments are taken to a revaluation surplus and so do not affect current period income, while revaluation decrements are taken as an expense to the income statement. Picker and Johnson (1999) provided the example in figure 10.6 to illustrate their argument.

Class A assets	Carrying value $000	Fair value $000	Increment/(decrement) $000
Asset 1	100	150	50
Asset 2	100	80	(20)
Asset 3	100	75	(25)
Total	300	305	5

FIGURE 10.6   Revaluation by asset or class of asset?
Source: Picker & Johnson (1999).

Applying IAS 16, the revaluation surplus for asset 1 would be increased by $50 000 before tax, while an expense of $45 000 for assets 2 and 3 would be taken as an expense to the current period's income statement. According to the authors, this then 'exacerbates the effect of the existing bias' in IAS 16 towards taking gains to surpluses and losses to the income statement. A further problem is that it could cause 'gaming' in terms of what constitutes an individual asset for revaluation purposes.

LO 11   10.6.4   Applying the revaluation model: transfers from asset revaluation surplus

Paragraph 41 of IAS 16 covers the accounting for the asset revaluation surplus subsequent to its creation. There are two circumstances where the asset revaluation surplus may be transferred to retained earnings. Note that there is no requirement that the asset revaluation surplus must be transferred, only a specification of situations where it may be transferred. The *first* situation is where the asset is derecognised (i.e. removed from the balance sheet, for example, by sale of the asset). In this case, the whole or part of the surplus may be transferred. The *second* situation is where an asset is being used up over its useful life, a proportion of the revaluation surplus may be transferred to retained earnings, the proportion being in relation to the depreciation on the asset. In this case, the amount of the surplus transferred would be equal to the difference between depreciation based on the original cost, and depreciation based on the revalued amount, adjusted for the tax effect relating to the surplus. This second situation is shown in illustrative example 10.8.

ILLUSTRATIVE EXAMPLE 10.8

Transferring revaluation surplus to retained earnings

Assume an item of plant was acquired for $100 000. The asset was immediately revalued to $120 000. The asset has an expected useful life of 10 years, and the tax rate is 30%. The revaluation entry is:

Plant	Dr	20 000	
Deferred tax liability	Cr		6 000
Asset revaluation surplus	Cr		14 000
(Revaluation of plant)			

At the end of the first year, depreciation expense of $12 000 would be recorded. As the asset is being used up at 10% per annum, the entity may transfer 10% of the asset revaluation surplus to retained earnings:

Asset revaluation surplus	Dr	1 400	
Retained earnings	Cr		1 400
(Transfer from asset revaluation surplus to retained earnings)			

Transfers from the asset revaluation surplus may also occur where a bonus issue of share capital is made from the asset revaluation surplus. There is no specific statement in IAS 16 in relation to the reinstatement of transfers from the asset revaluation surplus. However, as the surplus is created only via an upward revaluation of assets, it is expected that the IASB would not allow reinstatement once transfers from the asset revaluation surplus have been made. These transfers may cause a problem if there is a downward revaluation of the asset subsequent to the transfer because, although the balance of the revaluation surplus may have changed, the related deferred tax liability has not been altered.

ILLUSTRATIVE EXAMPLE 10.9

Bonus share issue from asset revaluation surplus

Assume an entity has an item of plant that was revalued in the past from $100 000 to $200 000. The journal entry, based on a tax rate of 30%, is:

Plant	Dr	100 000	
Deferred tax liability	Cr		30 000
Asset revaluation surplus	Cr		70 000
(Revaluation of plant)			

The entity then used $30 000 of the asset revaluation surplus to issue bonus shares, leaving a balance of $40 000 in the asset revaluation surplus. The asset was subsequently written down from a carrying amount of $150 000 to $70 000, a reduction of $80 000. The appropriate journal entry for the downward revaluation is:

Asset revaluation surplus	Dr	40 000	
Deferred tax liability	Dr	24 000	
Expense — downward revaluation of plant	Dr	16 000	
Accumulated depreciation	Dr	50 000	
Plant	Cr		130 000
(Write-down of plant subsequent to upward revaluation and bonus issue)			

In relation to this entry, note the following:
• The balance of $40 000 in the asset revaluation surplus must first be used to write down the asset; the asset revaluation surplus can never be adjusted so as to have a debit balance.

- As a deferred tax liability of $30 000 was raised in relation to the upward revaluation of the asset, this must be reduced by $24 000 (30% × $80 000). The adjustment relates to the revaluation decrement grossed up for any related recognised current tax and deferred tax.
- The balance after adjusting the asset revaluation surplus and the deferred tax liability is debited to current period expense. It arises because of the past transfer of the asset revaluation surplus to share capital.
- The balance of the deferred tax liability is $6000, representing the difference between the tax base of $100 000 and the carrying amount of $120 000.

A further problem arising from transfers from the asset revaluation surplus in situations such as a bonus issue of shares occurs where a number of assets are being revalued. IAS 16 requires the accounting for the asset revaluation surplus to be done on an asset-by-asset basis. Where there is a bonus issue from the asset revaluation surplus, the entity will have to identify which assets are being affected by the use of the asset revaluation surplus for the bonus issue. Any basis of choosing which assets are affected is purely arbitrary. In addressing this issue, Picker and Johnson (1999, p. 4) made the following comments:

For example, where the asset revaluation surplus is reduced through the issue of bonus shares, a number of methods may be adopted to record it:

- Use of the surplus may be allocated to specific asset(s), thereby reducing or eliminating the revaluation surplus attached to those assets only, and has no effect on the revaluation surplus attached to other assets.

- Adopting a FIFO or LIFO basis, such that use of the surplus is allocated to the revaluation surplus of asset(s) which has been there the longest/shortest, and has no effect on the revaluation surplus of other assets.

- Proportionate allocation to reduce the revaluation surplus attached to each and every asset which has been revalued.

Each method is valid, but will have different impacts on the results of an entity in the event that any reversals of revaluations are required, affecting the comparability between entities.

The last method available would appear to result in the ability of the entity to retain both separate debit and credit balances in the surplus, as any allocation would not be made until such time as values change. This method can potentially be used to manipulate the results and performance of the entity.

The potential also arises for entities to change the basis of allocating each issue from the surplus. For example they may elect to pro-rata the use across all assets for one issue, but on the next issue, a different basis may be adopted because of changes in the circumstances, and therefore distort the financial performance.

10.6.5 Applying the revaluation model: depreciation of revalued assets

Section 10.5.1 of this chapter discusses the accounting treatment for depreciation under IAS 16. As noted, the term 'depreciable amount' includes 'other amount substituted for cost'. This includes fair value. Paragraph 50 of IAS 16 notes that depreciation is a process of allocation. Hence, even though an asset is measured at fair value, depreciation is not determined simply as the change in fair value of the asset over a period. As with the cost method, depreciation for a period is calculated after considering the pattern of economic benefits relating to the asset and the residual value of the asset.

ILLUSTRATIVE EXAMPLE 10.10

Depreciation of revalued assets

Assume an entity has an item of plant that was revalued to $1000 at 30 June 2005. The asset is expected to have a remaining useful life of five years, with benefits being received evenly over that period. The residual value is calculated to be $100. Consider two situations.

Situation 1

At 30 June 2006, no formal revaluation occurs and the management of the entity assess that the carrying amount of the plant is not materially different from fair value.

The appropriate journal entry for the 2005–06 period is:

2006	Depreciation expense	Dr	180	
30 June	Accumulated depreciation	Cr		180
	(Depreciation on plant			
	1/5[$1000 – $100])			

The asset is reported in the balance sheet at a carrying amount of $820, equal to a gross amount of $1000 less accumulated depreciation of $180, the carrying amount being equal to fair value.

Situation 2

At 30 June 2006, a formal revaluation occurs and the external valuers assess the fair value of the plant to be $890. Tax rate is 30%.

The appropriate journal entries for the 2005–06 period are:

2006	Depreciation expense	Dr	180	
30 June	Accumulated depreciation	Cr		180
	(Depreciation on plant			
	1/5[$1000 – $100])			
	Accumulated depreciation	Dr	180	
	Plant	Cr		110
	Deferred tax liability	Cr		21
	Asset revaluation surplus	Cr		49
	(Revaluation of plant)			

In other words, there is a two-step process. Depreciation is allocated in accordance with normal depreciation principles. Then, as a formal revaluation occurs, the accumulated depreciation is written off and the asset revalued to fair value. The asset is reported in the balance sheet at fair value of $890 with no associated accumulated depreciation.

It may be argued that the accounting in situation 2 is inappropriate. Whereas the depreciation charge affects the income statement, the revaluation of the asset goes to revaluation surplus, and is never taken to the income statement. The economic benefits in relation to the asset for the period are not only that achieved by consumption of the asset, but also those obtained by changes in the market value of the asset. However, these are accounted for differently under IAS 16. It could then be argued that the appropriate depreciation under situation 2 should be the change in fair value over the period, namely $110 ($1000 – $890), with the journal entry being:

Depreciation expense	Dr	110	
Accumulated depreciation	Cr		110
(Depreciation on plant)			

No revaluation entry is then necessary. Note, however, that this entry is not allowed under IAS 16.

Subsequent to revaluation, the entity should reassess the useful life and residual value of the revalued asset because these may change as a result of economic changes affecting the entity and its use of assets. Using the example in scenario 2, following the revaluation at 30 June 2006, assume the entity determines that the residual value is $110 and the remaining useful life is four years. In the 2006–07 period, the depreciation entry is:

Depreciation expense	Dr	195	
Accumulated depreciation	Cr		195
(Depreciation on plant			
1/4[$890 − $110])			

10.7 Choosing between the cost model and the revaluation model

Given that IAS 16 allows entities a choice between the cost model and the revaluation model, it is of interest to consider what motivates entities to choose between the two measurement models.

Arguments relating to the choice of models generally claim that a current price (a fair value) will provide more relevant information than a past price (the original cost), while the costs associated with continuously determining the present price reduces the incentive, on a cost-benefit basis, to move to current values. Certainly the requirement under IAS 16 to continuously adjust the carrying amounts of assets measured at fair value so that they are not materially different from current fair values provides a cost disincentive to management to adopt the revaluation model. Costs associated with adopting the revaluation model include the cost of employing valuers, annual costs associated with reviewing the carrying amounts to assess whether a revaluation is necessary, extra record-keeping costs associated with the revaluations, including accounting for the associated revaluation increments and decrements, and increased audit costs relating to the review of changing revalued amounts. In January 2002, Ernst & Young in Australia reported on entities changing valuation methods when it became a requirement in that country for entities using the fair value basis to adopt the equivalent of the current IAS 16 accounting procedures. Previously, entities could revalue assets on an irregular basis rather than keeping the fair values continuously current. Ernst & Young (2002) reported that:

- of the entities surveyed, 40% reported a change in measurement basis for one or more classes of non-current assets
- of those entities reporting a change in the measurement basis, all changed from the fair value basis to the cost basis. No entities changed from the cost basis to the fair value basis.

Ernst & Young (p. 8) argued that:

[t]he number of entities changing measurement basis to cost would appear to indicate that the costs associated with keeping the revaluations up to date at each reporting period outweighs the perceived benefits associated with improved relevance and reliability of financial information by recognising fair value adjustments.

A further factor that influences some entities' measurement choice in favour of the cost model is harmonisation with US GAAP, which does not allow the revaluation of non-current assets.

Another factor that entities have to consider when choosing their measurement bases for classes of property, plant and equipment is the effect of the model on the income statement. Where assets are measured on a fair value basis, the depreciation per annum would be expected to be higher as the depreciable amount is higher. In the 2002 Ernst & Young study (p. 3), it was reported that:

> [o]f those entities reverting to original cost as the measurement basis for a class of non-current asset, a reduction in annual depreciation expense (and therefore an increase in profit) ranging from $500 000 to $1.1 million resulted.

Besides the effect of lower depreciation, there will be the effect on the disposal of the asset. Where an asset is measured at fair value, there is expected to be an immaterial amount of profit or loss on sale as, at the time of sale, the recorded amount of the asset should be close to that of the market price. For an asset measured at cost, any gain or loss on sale will be reported in the income statement.

What, apart from increased relevance and reliability arguments, are the incentives for management to use the revaluation model? The effect of adopting the revaluation model is to increase the entity's assets and equities (via the revaluation surplus). Hence, entities that need to report higher amounts in these areas would consider adoption of the revaluation model. The incentives for entities to adopt fair value measures then tend to be entity-specific because the entities face pressures relating to external circumstances. Examples of such pressures are shown below.

- Entities with debt covenants generally have constraints relating to their debt-asset ratios, such as the requirement that the debt-asset ratio must not exceed 50%. Hence, for an entity with increasing debt, adoption of the revaluation model for a class of assets that is increasing in value will ease pressures on the debt-asset ratio by increasing the asset base of the entity. This assumes that the debt covenant allows revaluations to be taken into account in measuring assets.
- An entity's reported profit figure may be under scrutiny from a specific source, such as a trade union seeking reasons to support claims for higher pay, or regulators looking at monopoly control within an industry.

Where there are pressures to report lower profits, adoption of the revaluation model provides scope for higher depreciation charges, with increases in the values of the non-current assets not affecting the income statement. With lower reported profits and higher asset/equity bases, any judgements made by reviewing ratios such as rates of return on assets or equity will result in the entity being seen in a less favourable light.

However, as noted above, the incentives relating to playing with profit and asset numbers tend to rely on users of the information having no knowledge of accounting rules or movements in prices within industries or sectors, or being unable to make comparisons across entities within an industry segment. One of the key elements of analysing entities within an industry is comparability of information. If all entities in the sector are applying the cost model, analysts can make their judgements by comparing the information between the entities and applying information from sources other than accounting reports, such as movements in price indices. The entity then has less reason to incur the costs of adopting the revaluation model of measurement.

LO 13

10.8 Derecognition

As noted in paragraph 3 of IAS 16, the standard does not apply to non-current assets classified as held for sale and accounted for under IFRS 5. (Chapter 12 contains a discussion of the accounting for these assets.) IAS 16 then deals with the disposal of non-current assets that have not previously been classified as held for sale.

Paragraph 67 of IAS 16 identifies two occasions where derecognition of an item of property, plant and equipment should occur:
1. on disposal, such as the sale of the asset
2. when no future economic benefits are expected, either from future use or from disposal.

When items of property, plant and equipment are sold, regardless of whether there are many or few remaining economic benefits, the selling entity will recognise a gain or loss on the asset, this being determined as the difference between the net proceeds from sale and the carrying amount of the asset at the time of sale (IAS 16, para. 71). In calculating the net proceeds from sale, any deferred consideration must be discounted, and the proceeds calculated at the cash price equivalent (IAS 16, para. 72). As the carrying amount is net of depreciation and impairment losses, it is necessary to calculate the depreciation from the beginning of the reporting period to the point of sale. Failing to do this, whether under the cost model or the revaluation model, would be out of step with the key principle established in IAS 16 that depreciation is a process of allocation and each period must bear its fair share of the cost or revalued amount of the asset.

The gain or loss on sale is included in the profit or loss for the period, with the gains not being classified as revenue. IAS 1, paragraph 34, requires only the disclosure of the gain or loss on sale, as opposed to separate disclosure of the income and the carrying amount of the asset sold. In paragraph BC35 of the Basis of Conclusions on IAS 16, the IASB argued that:

> users of financial statements would consider these gains and the proceeds from an entity's sale of goods in the course of its ordinary activities differently in their evaluation of an entity's past results and their projections of future cash flows. This is because revenue from the sale of goods is typically more likely to recur in comparable amounts than are gains from sales of items of property, plant and equipment. Accordingly, the Board concluded that an entity should not classify as revenue gains on disposals of items of property, plant and equipment.

However, in preparing a cash flow statement, as shown in the illustrative example accompanying IAS 7 *Cash Flow Statements*, proceeds from the sale of property, plant and equipment are normally shown as a cash flow from investing activities.

ILLUSTRATIVE EXAMPLE 10.11

Disposals of assets

An entity acquired an item of plant on 1 July 2002 for $100 000. The asset had an expected useful life of 10 years and a residual value of $20 000. On 1 January 2005, the entity sold the asset for $81 000.

Required
Prepare the journal entries relating to this asset in the year of sale.

Solution
At the point of sale, the depreciation on the asset must be calculated for that part of the year for which the asset was held prior to sale. Hence, for the half-year prior to sale, under the straight-line method, depreciation of $4000 ($0.5 \times 1/10[\$100\,000 - \$20\,000]$) must be charged as an expense. The entry is:

$\longrightarrow$

Depreciation expense	Dr	4 000	
Accumulated depreciation	Cr		4 000
(Depreciation charge up to point of sale)			

The gain or loss on sale is the difference between the proceeds on sale of $81 000 and the carrying amount at time of sale of $80 000 ($100 000 − 2.5[1/10 × $80 000]), which is $1000. The required journal entries are:

Cash	Dr	81 000	
Proceeds on disposal of asset	Cr		81 000
(Sale of asset)			
Carrying amount of asset sold	Dr	80 000	
Accumulated depreciation	Dr	20 000	
Plant	Cr		100 000
(Carrying amount of asset sold)			

In the above example, the asset was sold for $81 000. Assume that the asset, now referred to as plant A, was traded in for another asset, plant B. Plant B had a fair value of $280 000, with the entity making a cash payment of $202 000 as well as giving up plant A. The trade-in amount is then $78 000. The journal entries to record this transaction are:

Carrying amount of plant A sold	Dr	80 000	
Accumulated depreciation	Dr	20 000	
Plant A	Cr		100 000
(Disposal of plant A)			
Plant B	Dr	280 000	
Cash	Cr		202 000
Proceeds on sale of plant A	Cr		78 000
(Acquisition of plant B in exchange for cash and trade-in of plant A)			

LO 14

10.9 Disclosure

Paragraphs 73–79 of IAS 16 contain the required disclosures relating to property, plant and equipment. Information in paragraph 73 is required on a class-by-class basis, while paragraph 77 relates only to assets stated at revalued amounts. Paragraph 79 contains information that entities are encouraged to disclose, but are not required to do so. Figure 10.7 provides an illustration of the disclosures required by IAS 16.

FIGURE 10.7   Illustrative disclosures required by IAS 16

Note 1: Summary of accounting policies (extract)	IAS 16 Para.
Property, plant and equipment	
Freehold land and buildings on freehold land are measured on a fair value basis. At each balance date, the value of each asset in these classes is reviewed to ensure that it does not differ materially from the asset's fair value at that date. Where necessary, the asset is revalued to reflect its fair value. In June 2004, revaluations were carried out by an independent valuer; since then valuations have been made internally. The basis for the assessment of fair value has been by reference to observable transactions in the property market, including an analysis of prices paid in recent market transactions for similar properties. No other valuation techniques were used.	*73(a)* *77(a)* *77(b) (c), (d)* *77(a)*
All other classes of property, plant and equipment are measured at cost.	
Depreciation	
Depreciation is provided on a straight-line basis for all property, plant and equipment, other than freehold land.	*73(b)*
The useful lives of the assets are:	*73(c)*

	2006	2005
Freehold buildings	40 years	40 years
Plant and equipment	5 to 15 years	5 to 15 years

Note 10: Property, plant and equipment

	Land and buildings		Plant and equipment		IAS 16 Para.
	2006	2005	2006	2005	
	$000	$000	$000	$000	
Balance at beginning of year	1 861	1 765	2 840	2 640	*73(d)*
Accumulated depreciation	400	364	(732)	520	
Carrying amount	1 461	1 401	2 108	2 120	
Additions	–	123	755	372	*73(e)(i)*
Disposals	(466)	(18)	(181)	(158)	*73(e)(ii)*
Acquisitions via business combinations	739	–	412	–	*73(e)(iii)*
Impairment losses	–	–	(100)	–	*73(e)(v)*
Depreciation	(20)	(36)	(161)	(212)	*73(e)(vii)*
Transfer to assets held for sale	(438)	–	(890)	–	*73(e)(ix)*
Net exchange differences	11	(9)	8	(14)	*73(e)(viii)*
Carrying amount at end of year	1 287	1 461	1 951	2 108	*73(d)*
Property, plant and equipment					
At cost	1 707	1 861	2 944	2 840	
Accumulated depreciation and impairment losses	(420)	(400)	(993)	(732)	
Carrying amount at end of year	1 287	1 461	1 951	2 108	

For the freehold land and buildings measured at fair value, the carrying amount that would have been recognised if they had been carried at cost is:			77(e)
	2006 $000	2005 $000	
Carrying amount at end of year	942	824	
Plant and equipment of $420 000 have been pledged as security for loans to the company.			74(a)
The company has entered into a contract to acquire $640 000 of plant equipment over the next two years.			74(c)
Activity in the revaluation surplus for land and buildings is as follows:			77(f)
	2006 $000	2005 $000	
Balance at beginning of year	309	303	
Revaluation surplus on land and buildings	42	9	
Deferred tax liability	(13)	(3)	
Balance at end of year	338	309	
There are no restrictions on the distribution of the balance of the surplus to shareholders.			

10.10 Summary

The purpose of this chapter is to analyse the content of IAS 16 *Property, Plant and Equipment* and provide guidance on its implementation. The principal issues in accounting for property, plant and equipment are the timing of recognition of the assets, the determination of their carrying amounts and the depreciation charges to be recognised in relation to them (IAS 16, *Objective*). The key issue in recognising the asset is in determining its cost to the acquiring entity, particularly in determining which amounts should be capitalised into the cost. After the initial recognition of the asset, a decision has to be made about which measurement basis to apply, this being made on a class-by-class basis. IAS 16 provides a benchmark treatment of cost and an allowed alternative of fair value. Regardless of which measurement basis is used, the asset is subject to depreciation. The initial method chosen for depreciation and the useful life of an asset must be reviewed periodically and, if necessary, adjusted. Subsequent to use, assets may be replaced or retired. IAS 16 requires extensive disclosures to be made in relation to the property, plant and equipment held by an entity, and the movements in those assets.

1. Explain why accountants determine depreciation in relation to assets such as equipment.

2. In determining the depreciation charge for a period, specify the questions that an accountant needs to answer.

3. The management of an entity has decided to use the fair value basis for the measurement of its equipment. Some of this equipment is very hard to obtain and has in fact increased in value over the current period. Management is arguing that, as there has been no decline in fair value, no depreciation should be charged on these pieces of equipment. Discuss.

4. Surfers Ltd uses tractors as a part of its operating equipment, and it applies the straight-line depreciation method to depreciate these assets. Surfers Ltd has just taken over Paradise Ltd, which uses similar tractors in its operations. However, Paradise Ltd has been using a diminishing balance method of depreciation for these tractors. The accountant in Surfers Ltd is arguing that for both entities the same depreciation method should be used for tractors. Provide arguments for and against this proposal.

5. A company is in the movie rental business. Movies are generally kept for two years and then either sold or destroyed. However, management wants to show increased profits, and believes that the annual depreciation charge can be lowered by keeping the movies for three years. Discuss.

6. A new accountant has been appointed to the firm of Geelong Ltd, which owns a large number of depreciable assets. Upon analysing the firm's depreciation policy, the accountant has implemented a new policy based on the principle that the depreciation rate for particular assets should measure the decline in the value of the assets. Discuss this policy change.

7. A new accountant has been appointed to Darwin Ltd and has implemented major changes in the calculation of depreciation. As a result, some parts of the factory have much larger depreciation charges. This has incensed some operations managers who believe that, as they take particular care with the maintenance of their machines, their machines should not attract large depreciation charges that reduce the profitability of their operations and reflect badly on their management skills. The operations managers plan to meet the accountant and ask for change. How should the new accountant respond?

8. The management of Cairns Ltd has been analysing the financial reports provided by the accountant, who has been with the firm for a number of years. Management has expressed its concern over depreciation charges being made in relation to the company's equipment. In particular, it believes that the depreciation charges are not high enough in relation to the factory machines because new technology applied in that area is rapidly making the machines obsolete. Management's concern is that the machines will have to be replaced in the near future and, with the low depreciation charges, the fund will not be sufficient to pay for the replacement machines. Discuss.

9. Townsville Ltd has acquired a new building. Which of the following items should be included in the cost of the building?
   (a) Stamp duty
   (b) Real estate agent's fees
   (c) Architect's fees for drawings for internal adjustments to the building to be made prior to use
   (d) Interest on the bank loan to acquire the building, and an application fee to the bank to get the loan, which is secured on the building
   (e) Cost of changing the name on the building
   (f) Cost of changing the parking bays
   (g) Cost of refurbishing the lobby to the building to attract customers and make it more user friendly

10. Rockhampton Ltd has acquired a new machine, which it has had installed in its factory. Which of the following items should be capitalised into the cost of the building?
    (a) Labour and travel costs for managers to inspect possible new machines and for negotiating for a new machine
    (b) Freight costs and insurance to get the new machine to the factory
    (c) Costs for renovating a section of the factory, in anticipation of the new machine's arrival, to ensure that all the other parts of the factory will have easy access to the new machine
    (d) Cost of cooling equipment to assist in the efficient operation of the new machine
    (e) Costs of repairing the factory door, which was damaged by the installation of the new machine
    (f) Training costs of workers who will use the machine

11. Maryborough Ltd has acquired a new building for $500 000. It has incurred incidental costs of $10 000 in the acquisition process for legal fees, real estate agent's fees and stamp duties. Management believes that these costs should be expensed because they have not increased the value of the building and, if the building was immediately resold, these amounts would not be recouped. In other words, the fair value of the building is considered to still be $500 000. Discuss how these costs should be accounted for.

12. Discuss the merits of using a 'class of assets' basis for accounting for revaluation increments and decrements rather an 'individual assets' basis.

13. Discuss the role of surpluses in the financial reporting structure. In particular, consider why asset revaluation surpluses are used in accounting for the revaluation of assets and the subsequent disposal of these assets.

EXERCISES

EXERCISE 10.1 ★ Revaluation of assets

In the 30 June 2006 annual report of Sydney Ltd, the equipment was reported as follows:

Equipment (at cost)	$500 000
Accumulated depreciation	150 000
	350 000

The equipment consisted of two machines, machine A and machine B. Machine A had cost $300 000 and had a carrying amount of $180 000 at 30 June 2006, while Machine B had cost $200 000 and was carried at $170 000. Both machines are measured using the cost model, and depreciated on a straight-line basis over a 10-year period.

On 31 December 2006, the directors of Sydney Ltd decided to change the basis of measuring the equipment from the cost model to the revaluation model. Machine A was revalued to $180 000 with an expected useful life of six years, and machine B was revalued to $155 000 with an expected useful life of five years.

At 30 June 2007, machine A was assessed to have a fair value of $163 000 with an expected useful life of five years, while machine B's fair value was $136 500 with an expected useful life of four years.

The tax rate is 30%.

Required
1. Prepare the journal entries during the period 1 July 2006 to 30 June 2007 in relation to the equipment.
2. According to accounting standards, on what basis may management change the method of asset measurement; for example, from cost to fair value?

EXERCISE 10.2 ★ Revaluation of assets

On 30 June 2005, the balance sheet of Melbourne Ltd showed the following non-current assets after charging depreciation:

Building	$300 000	
Accumulated depreciation	(100 000)	$200 000
Motor vehicle	120 000	
Accumulated depreciation	(40 000)	80 000

The company has adopted fair value for the valuation of non-current assets. This has resulted in the recognition in prior periods of an asset revaluation surplus for the building of $14 000. On 30 June 2005, an independent valuer assessed the fair value of the building to be $160 000 and the vehicle to be $90 000. The income tax rate is 30%.

Required
1. Prepare any necessary entries to revalue the building and the vehicle as at 30 June 2005.
2. Assume that the building and vehicle had remaining useful lives of 25 years and four years respectively, with zero residual value. Prepare entries to record depreciation expense for the year ended 30 June 2006 using the straight-line method.

EXERCISE 10.3 ★★

Depreciation

Perth Ltd was formed on 1 July 2005 to provide delivery services for packages to be taken between the city and the airport. On this date, the company acquired a delivery truck from Fremantle Trucks. The company paid cash of $50 000 to Fremantle Trucks, which included government charges of $600 and registration of $400. Insurance costs for the first year amounted to $1200. The truck is expected to have a useful life of five years. At the end of the useful life, the asset is expected to be sold for $24 000, with costs relating to the sale amounting to $400.

The company went extremely well in its first year, and the management of Perth Ltd decided at 1 July 2006 to add another vehicle, a flat-top, to the fleet. This vehicle was acquired from a liquidation auction at a cash price of $30 000. The vehicle needed some repairs for the elimination of rust (cost $2300), major servicing to the engine (cost $480) and the replacement of all tyres (cost $620). The company believed it would use the flat-top for another two years and then sell it. Expected selling price was $15 000, with selling costs estimated to be $400. On 1 July 2006, both vehicles were fitted out with a radio communication system at a cost per vehicle of $300. This was not expected to have any material effect on the future selling price of either vehicle. Insurance costs for the 2006–07 period were $1200 for the first vehicle and $900 for the newly acquired vehicle.

All went well for the company except that, on 1 August 2007, the flat-top that had been acquired at auction broke down. Perth Ltd thought about acquiring a new vehicle to replace this one but, after considering the costs, decided to repair the flat-top instead. The vehicle was given a major overhaul at a cost of $6500. Although this was a major expense, management believed that the company would keep the vehicle for another two years. The estimated selling price in three years' time is $12 000, with selling costs estimated at $300. Insurance costs for the 2007–08 period were the same as for the previous year.

Required
Prepare the journal entries for the recording of the vehicles and the depreciation of the vehicles for each of the three years. The financial year ends on 30 June.

EXERCISE 10.4 ★★

Depreciation

Hobart Ltd constructed a building for use by the administration section of the company. The completion date was 1 July 2000, and the construction cost was $840 000. The company expected to remain in the building for the next 20 years, at which time the building would probably have no real salvage value and have to be demolished. It is expected that demolition costs will amount to $15 000. In December 2006, following some severe weather in the city, the roof of the administration building was considered to be in poor shape so the company decided to replace it. On 1 July 2007, a new roof was installed at a cost of $220 000. The new roof was of a different material to the old roof, which was estimated to have cost only $140 000 in the original construction, although at the time of construction it was thought that the roof would last for the 20 years that the company expected to use the building. Because the company had spent the money replacing the roof, it thought that it would delay construction of a new building, thereby extending the original life of the building from 20 years to 25 years.

Required

Discuss how you would account for the depreciation of the building and how the replacement of the roof would affect the depreciation calculations.

EXERCISE 10.5   ★★★

Depreciation calculation

On 1 July 2004, Brisbane Airlines acquired a new aeroplane for a total cost of $10 million. A breakdown of the costs to build the aeroplane was given by the manufacturers:

Aircraft body	$3 000 000
Engines (2)	4 000 000
Fitting out of aircraft:	
Seats	1 000 000
Carpets	50 000
Electrical equipment – passenger seats	200 000
– cockpit	1 500 000
Food preparation equipment	250 000

All costs include installation and labour costs associated with the relevant part.

It is expected that the aircraft will be kept for 10 years and then sold. The main value of the aircraft at that stage is the body and the engines. The expected selling price is $2.1 million, with the body and engines retaining proportionate value.

Costs in relation to the aircraft over the next 10 years are expected to be as follows:

- *Aircraft body.* This requires an inspection every two years for cracks and wear and tear, at a cost of $10 000.
- *Engines.* Each engine has an expected life of four years before being sold for scrap. It is expected that the engines will be replaced in 2008 for $4.5 million and again in 2012 for $6 million. These engines are expected to incur annual maintenance costs of $300 000. The manufacturer has informed Brisbane Airlines that a new prototype engine with an extra 10% capacity should be on the market in 2010, and that existing engines could be upgraded at a cost of $1 million.
- *Fittings.* Seats are replaced every three years. Expected replacement costs are $1.2 million in 2007 and $1.5 million in 2013. The repair of torn seats and faulty mechanisms is expected to cost $100 000 per annum. Carpets are replaced every five years. They will be replaced in 2009 at an expected cost of $65 000, but will not be replaced before the aircraft is sold in 2014. Cleaning costs per annum amount to $10 000. The electrical equipment (such as the TV) for each seat has an annual repair cost of $15 000. It is expected that, with the improvements in technology, the equipment will be totally replaced in 2010 by substantially better equipment at a cost of $350 000. The electrical equipment in the cockpit is tested frequently at an expected annual cost of $250 000. Major upgrades to the equipment are expected every two years at expected costs of $250 000 (in 2006), $300 000 (in 2008), $345 000 (in 2010) and $410 000 (in 2012). The upgrades will take into effect the expected changes in technology.
- *Food preparation equipment.* This incurs annual costs for repair and maintenance of $20 000. The equipment is expected to be totally replaced in 2010.

Required

1. Discuss how the costs relating to the aircraft should be accounted for.
2. Determine the expenses recognised for the 2004–05 financial year.

EXERCISE 10.6 ★★★   Revaluation of assets and tax-effect accounting

Adelaide Ltd acquired a machine on 1 July 2003 at a cost of $100 000. The machine has an expected useful life of five years, and the company adopts the straight-line basis of depreciation. The tax depreciation rate for this type of machine is 12.5% p.a. The company tax rate is 30%.

Adelaide Ltd measures this asset at fair value. Movements in fair values are as follows:

30 June 2004	$85 000	Remaining useful life: 4 years
30 June 2005	60 000	Remaining useful life: 3 years
30 June 2006	45 000	

Due to a change in economic conditions, Adelaide Ltd sold the machine for $45 000 on 30 June 2006. The asset was revalued to fair value immediately prior to sale.

Required
1. Provide the journal entries used to account for this machine over the period 2003–06.
2. For each of the three years ended 30 June 2004, 2005 and 2006 respectively, calculate the carrying amount and the tax base of the asset, and determine the appropriate tax-effect entry in relation to the machine. Explain your answer.

PROBLEMS

PROBLEM 10.1 ★★   Acquisition and sale of assets, depreciation

Tugan's Turf Farm owned the following items of property, plant and equipment as at 30 June 2004:

Land (at cost)		$120 000
Office building (at cost)	150 000	
Accumulated depreciation	(23 375)	126 625
Turf cutter (at cost)	65 000	
Accumulated depreciation	(42 367)	22 633
Water desalinator (at fair value)		189 000

Additional information (at 30 June 2004)
- The straight-line method of depreciation is used for all depreciable items of property, plant and equipment. Depreciation is charged to the nearest month and all figures are rounded to the nearest dollar.
- The office building was constructed on 1 April 2000. Its estimated useful life is 20 years and it has an estimated residual value of $40 000.
- The turf cutter was purchased on 21 January 2001, at which date it had an estimated useful life of five years and an estimated residual value of $3200.
- The water desalinator was purchased and installed on 2 July 2003 at a cost of $200 000. On 30 June 2004, the plant was revalued upwards by $7000 to its fair value on that day. Additionally, its useful life and residual value were re-estimated to nine years and $18 000 respectively.

The following transactions occurred during the year ended 30 June 2005:
(*Note:* All payments are made in cash.)
- On 10 August 2004, new irrigation equipment was purchased from Pond Supplies for $37 000. On 16 August 2004, the business paid $500 to have the equipment delivered to the turf farm. B Digger was contracted to install and test the new system. In the course

of installation, pipes worth $800 were damaged and subsequently replaced on 3 September. The irrigation system was fully operational by 19 September and B Digger was paid $9600 for his services. The system has an estimated useful life of four years and a residual value of $0.

- On 1 December 2004, the turf cutter was traded in on a new model worth $80 000. A trade-in allowance of $19 000 was received and the balance paid in cash. The new machine's useful life and residual value were estimated at six years and $5000 respectively.
- On 1 January 2005, the turf farm's owner Terry Clifford decided to extend the office building by adding three new offices and a meeting room. The extension commenced on 2 February and was completed by 28 March at a cost of $49 000. The extension is expected to increase the useful life of the building by four years and increase its residual value by $5000.
- On 30 June 2005, depreciation expense for the year was recorded. The fair value of the water desalination plant was $165 000.

Required

(Show all workings and round amounts to the nearest dollar.)

1. Prepare general journal entries to record the transactions and events for the year ended 30 June 2005 (narrations are not required).
2. What does the term 'residual value' mean? Explain how and when it is measured.
3. Justify your journal entry to record the revaluation of the water desalination plant as at 30 June 2005 by reference to the requirements of IAS 16.

PROBLEM 10.2   ★★   Acquisitions, disposals, depreciation

Mandurah Ltd purchased equipment on 1 July 2002 for $39 800 cash. Transport and installation costs of $4200 were paid on 5 July 2002. Useful life and residual value were estimated to be 10 years and $1800 respectively. Mandurah Ltd depreciates equipment using the straight-line method to the nearest month, and reports annually on 30 June. The company tax rate is 30%.

In June 2004, changes in technology caused the company to revise the estimated total life from 10 years to five years, and the residual value from $1800 to $1200. This revised estimate was made before recording the depreciation for the financial year ended 30 June 2004.

On 30 June 2004, the company adopted the revaluation model to account for equipment. An expert valuation was obtained showing that the equipment had a fair value of $30 000 at that date.

On 30 June 2005, depreciation for the year was charged and the equipment's carrying amount was remeasured to its fair value of $16 000.

On 30 September 2005, the equipment was sold for $8400 cash.

Required

(Show all workings and round amounts to the nearest dollar.)

1. Prepare general journal entries to record the transactions and events for the period 1 July 2002 to 30 September 2005. (Narrations are not required.)
2. Given that the company adopted the revaluation model on 30 June 2004, why does it continue to charge depreciation on the equipment? Explain fully by reference to the requirements of IAS 16.

PROBLEM 10.3   ★★   Revaluation of assets

On 1 July 2005, Toowoomba Ltd acquired two assets within the same class of plant and equipment. Information on these assets is shown overleaf.

	Cost	Expected useful life
Machine A	$100 000	5 years
Machine B	60 000	3 years

The machines are expected to generate benefits evenly over their useful lives. The class of plant and equipment is measured using fair value.

At 30 June 2006, information about the assets is as follows:

	Fair value	Expected useful life
Machine A	$84 000	4 years
Machine B	38 000	2 years

On 1 January 2007, machine B was sold for $29 000 cash. On the same day, Toowoomba Ltd acquired machine C for $80 000 cash. Machine C has an expected useful life of four years. Toowoomba Ltd also made a bonus issue of 10 000 shares at $1 per share, using $8000 from the general reserve and $2000 from the asset revaluation surplus created as a result of measuring machine A at fair value.

At 30 June 2007, information on the machines is as follows:

	Fair value	Expected useful life
Machine A	$61 000	3 years
Machine C	68 500	1.5 years

The income tax rate is 30%.

Required

Prepare the journal entries in the records of Toowoomba Ltd to record the described events over the period 1 July 2005 – 30 June 2007, assuming reporting dates are 30 June 2006 and 30 June 2007.

PROBLEM 10.4 ★★   Determining the costs of assets

Newcastle Ltd uses many kinds of machines in its operations. It constructs some of these machines itself and acquires others from the manufacturers. The following information relates to two machines that it has recorded in the 2005–06 period. Machine A was acquired, and machine B was constructed by Newcastle Ltd itself.

Machine A	
Cash paid for equipment, including GST of $8000	$88 000
Costs of transporting machine – insurance and transport	3 000
Labour costs of installation by expert fitter	5 000
Labour costs of testing equipment	4 000
Insurance costs for 2005–06	1 500
Costs of training for personnel who will use the machine	2 500
Costs of safety rails and platforms surrounding machine	6 000
Costs of water devices to keep machine cool	8 000
Costs of adjustments to machine during 2005–06 to make it operate more efficiently	7 500
Machine B	
Cost of material to construct machine, including GST of $7000	$77 000
Labour costs to construct machine	43 000
Allocated overhead costs – electricity, factory space etc.	22 000

Allocated interest costs of financing machine	10 000
Costs of installation	12 000
Insurance for 2005–06	2 000
Profit saved by self-construction	15 000
Safety inspection costs prior to use	4 000

Required
Determine the amount at which each of these machines should be recorded in the records of Newcastle Ltd. For items not included in the cost of the machines, note how they should be accounted for.

PROBLEM 10.5 ★★

Classification of acquisition costs

Armidale Ltd commenced operations on 1 July 2005. During the following year, the company acquired a tract of land, demolished the building on the land and built a new factory. Equipment was acquired for the factory and, in March 2006, the plant was ready to commence operation. A gala opening was held on 18 March, with the local head parliamentarian opening the factory. The first items were ready for sale on 25 March.

During this period, the following inflows and outflows occurred:

- While searching for a suitable block of land, Armidale Ltd placed an option to buy with three real estate agents at a cost of $100 each. One of these blocks of land was later acquired.

• Payment of option fees	$300
• Receipt of loan from bank	400 000
• Payment to settlement agent for title search, stamp duties and settlement fees	10 000
• Payment of arrears in rates on building on land	5 000
• Payment for land	100 000
• Payment for demolition of current building on land	12 000
• Proceeds from sale of material from old building	5 500
• Payment to architect	23 000
• Payment to council for approval of building construction	12 000
• Payment for safety fence around construction site	3 400
• Payment to construction contractor for factory building	240 000
• Payment for external driveways, parking bays and safety lighting	54 000
• Payment of interest on loan	40 000
• Payment for safety inspection on building	3 000
• Payment for equipment	64 000
• Payment of freight and insurance costs on delivery of equipment	5 600
• Payment of installation costs on equipment	12 000
• Payment for safety equipment surrounding equipment	11 000
• Payment for removal of safety fence	2 000
• Payment for new fence surrounding the factory	8 000
• Payment for advertisements in the local paper about the forthcoming factory and its benefits to the local community	500
• Payment for opening ceremony	6 000
• Payments to adjust equipment to more efficient operating levels subsequent to initial operation	3 300

Required
Using the information provided, determine what assets Armidale Ltd should recognise and the amounts at which they would be recorded.

Acquisitions, disposals, trade-ins, overhauls, depreciation

Davy Jones is the owner of Kalbarri Fishing Charters. The business's final trial balance on 30 June 2004 (reporting date) included the following balances:

Processing plant (at cost, purchased 4 April 2002)	$148 650
Accumulated depreciation − processing plant	(81 274)
Charter boats	291 200
Accumulated depreciation − boats	(188 330)

The following boats were owned at 30 June 2004:

Boat	Purchase date	Cost	Estimated useful life	Estimated residual value
1	23 February 2000	$62 000	5 years	$3 000
2	09 September 2000	$66 400	5 years	$3 400
3	06 February 2001	$78 600	4 years	$3 600
4	20 April 2002	$84 200	6 years	$3 800

Additional information

Kalbarri Fishing Charters calculates depreciation to the nearest month using straight-line depreciation for all assets except the processing plant, which is depreciated at 30% on the diminishing value method. Amounts are recorded to the nearest dollar.

Part A

The following transactions and events occurred during the year ended 30 June 2005:

2004	
26 July	Traded in boat 1 for a new boat (boat 5) which cost $84 100. A trade-in allowance of $8900 was received and the balance was paid in cash. Registration and stamp duty costs of $1500 were also paid in cash. Davy Jones estimated boat 5's useful life and residual value at six years and $4120 respectively.
04 Dec.	Overhauled the processing plant at a cash cost of $62 660. As the modernisation significantly expanded the plant's operating capacity and efficiency, Davy Jones decided to revise the depreciation rate to 25%.
2005	
26 Feb.	Boat 3 reached the end of its useful life but no buyer could be found, so the boat was scrapped.
30 June	Recorded depreciation.

Required

Prepare general journal entries (narrations are required) to record the transactions and events for the year ended 30 June 2005.

Part B

On March 26, Davy Jones was offered fish-finding equipment with a fair value of $9500 in exchange for boat 2. The fish-finder originally cost its owner $26 600 and had a carrying value of $9350 at the date of offer. The fair value of boat 2 was $9100.

Required

If Davy Jones accepts the exchange offer, what amount would the business use to record the acquisition of the fish-finding equipment? Why? Justify your answer by reference to the requirements of IAS 16 relating to the initial recognition of a property, plant and equipment item.

Part C

What is meant by the term 'useful life'. What factors should be considered when determining an asset's useful life?

PROBLEM 10.7 ★★★   Acquisitions, revaluations, replacements, depreciation

Albany Trading operates in a very competitive field. To maintain its market position, it purchased two new machines for cash on 1 January 2003. It had previously rented its machines. Machine A cost $40 000 and machine B cost $100 000. Each machine was expected to have a useful life of 10 years, and residual values were estimated at $2000 for machine A and $5000 for machine B.

On 30 June 2004, Albany Trading adopted the revaluation model to account for the class of machinery. The fair values of machine A and machine B were determined to be $32 000 and $90 000 respectively on that date. The useful life and residual value of machine A were reassessed to eight years and $1500. The useful life and residual value of machine B were reassessed to be eight years and $4000.

On 2 January 2005, extensive repairs were carried out on machine B for $66 000 cash. Albany Trading expected these repairs to extend machine B's useful life by 3.5 years, and it revised machine B's estimated residual value to $9450.

Due to technological advances, Albany Trading decided to replace machine A. It traded in machine A on 31 March 2005 for new machine C, which cost $64 000. A $28 000 trade-in was allowed for machine A, and the balance of machine C's cost was paid in cash. Transport and installation costs of $950 were incurred in respect to machine C. Machine C was expected to have a useful life of eight years and a residual value of $8000.

Albany Trading uses the straight-line depreciation method, recording depreciation to the nearest month and the nearest dollar. Its reporting date is 30 June.

On 30 June 2005, fair values were determined to be $140 000 and $65 000 for machines B and C respectively.

Required

1. Prepare general journal entries to record the above transactions and the depreciation journal entries required on each reporting date up to 30 June 2005. (Narrations are not required but show all workings.)
2. Explain why depreciation is still being charged for the machines even though they are now being measured under the revaluation model.
3. What is an asset's 'useful life' and how is it determined?

PROBLEM 10.8 ★★★   Depreciation calculation

Esperence Ltd operates a factory that contains a large number of machines designed to produce knitted garments. These machines are generally depreciated at 10% per annum on a straight-line basis. In general, machines are estimated to have a residual value on disposal of 10% of cost. At 1 July 2005, Esperence Ltd had a total of 64 machines, and the balance sheet showed a total cost of $420 000 and accumulated depreciation of $130 000. During the 2005–06 period, the transactions shown overleaf occurred.

- On 1 September 2005, a new machine was acquired for $15 000. This machine replaced two other machines. One of the two replaced machines was acquired on 1 July 2002 for $8200. It was traded in on the new machine, with Knitting Ltd making a cash payment of $8800 on the new machine. The second replaced machine had cost $9000 on 1 April 2003 and was sold for $7300.
- On 1 January 2006, a machine that had cost $4000 on 1 July 1996 was retired from use and sold for scrap for $500.
- On 1 January 2006, a machine that had been acquired on 1 January 2003 for $7000 was repaired because its motor had been damaged from overheating. The motor was replaced at a cost of $4800. It was expected that this would increase the life of the machine by an extra two years.
- On 1 April 2006, Esperence Ltd fitted a new form of arm to a machine used for putting special designs onto garments. The arm cost $1200. The machine had been acquired on 1 April 2003 for $10 000. The arm can be used on a number of other machines when required and has a 15-year life. It will not be sold when any particular machine is retired, but retained for use on other machines.

Required
1. Record each of the transactions. The reporting date is 30 June.
2. Determine the depreciation expense for Esperence Ltd for the 2005–06 period.

PROBLEM 10.9 ★★★   Revaluation of assets and tax-effect accounting

For Ballarat Ltd, profit before income tax for the year ended 30 June 2005 amounted to $375 000, including the following expenses:

Depreciation of plant	$50 000
Goodwill impairment*	13 000
Long-service leave	40 000
Holiday pay	30 000
Doubtful debts	55 000
Entertainment*	12 000
Depreciation of furniture	5 000
*Non-deductible for taxation	

The balance sheet of Ballarat Ltd at 30 June 2004 and 2005 showed the net assets of the company as follows:

Assets	2004	2005
Cash	$ 73 000	$ 82 000
Inventory	127 000	158 000
Receivables	430 000	585 000
Allowance for doubtful debts	(20 000)	(40 000)
Plant (net)	350 000	320 000
Furniture (net)	75 000	65 000
Goodwill	63 000	50 000
Deferred tax asset	21 000	?
Liabilities		
Payables	247 000	265 000
Provision for long-service leave	30 000	50 000
Provision for holiday pay	20 000	30 000
Deferred tax liability	11 250	?

Additional information
- Plant and furniture are different classes of assets. Both are measured at fair value. The furniture was revalued downward to $65 000 at 30 June 2005. Furniture had not previously been revalued upwards. Tax depreciation for the year ended 30 June 2005 was $7500, giving a carrying amount for tax purposes at 30 June 2005 of $55 000. The plant was revalued upwards at 30 June 2005 to $320 000. Tax depreciation on plant was $75 000, giving a carrying amount for tax purposes at 30 June 2005 of $250 000.
- Total bad debts written off for the 2004–05 year were $35 000.
- The tax rate is 30%.

Required
1. Calculate, by using worksheets, the amounts of income tax expense and current and deferred income tax assets/liabilities for the year ended 30 June 2005.
2. Prepare the deferred tax asset and deferred tax liability accounts.
3. Prepare an income statement for the year ended 30 June 2005.

PROBLEM 10.10 ★★★   Revaluation of assets

On 1 July 2005, Wollongong Ltd acquired a number of assets from Bathurst Ltd. The assets had the following fair values at that date:

Plant A	$300 000
Plant B	180 000
Furniture A	60 000
Furniture B	50 000

In exchange for these assets, Wollongong Ltd issued 200 000 shares with a fair value of $3 per share. The assets constituted a business entity. Any goodwill is subject to annual impairment tests.

The directors of Wollongong Ltd decided to measure plant at fair value and furniture at cost. The plant was considered to have a further 10-year life with benefits being received evenly over that period, whereas furniture is depreciated evenly over a five-year period.

At 31 December 2005, Wollongong Ltd assessed the carrying amounts of its assets as follows:
- Plant A was valued at $296 000, with an expected remaining useful life of eight years.
- Plant B was valued at $168 000, with an expected remaining useful life of eight years.
- Furniture A's carrying amount was considered to be less than its recoverable amount.
- Furniture B's recoverable amount was assessed to be $40 000, with an expected remaining useful life of four years.
- The goodwill was not impaired.

Appropriate entries were made at 31 December 2005 for the half-yearly accounts.

On 15 February 2006, Wollongong Ltd made a bonus issue of shares: 5600 shares fully paid to $1 per share were issued from the plant A asset revaluation surplus.

At 30 June 2006, Wollongong Ltd assessed the carrying amounts of its assets as follows:
- Plant A was valued at $274 000.
- Plant B was valued at $153 500.
- The carrying amounts of furniture were less than their recoverable amounts.

The tax rate is 30%.

Required
1. Prepare the journal entries passed during the 2005–06 period in relation to the non-current assets in accordance with IAS 16.

2. Assume that the asset revaluation surplus for plant was based on a class-by-class calculation rather than on the individual asset method required by IAS 16. Prepare the journal entries for the 2005–06 period in relation to plant.
3. Comment on the effects on the income statement in relation to the revaluation methods for plant adopted in parts 1 and 2 of this problem.

PROBLEM 10.11 ★★★ Cost of acquisition

Broome Ltd started business early in 2004. During its first nine months, Broome Ltd acquired real estate for the construction of a building and other facilities. Operating equipment was purchased and installed, and the company began operating activities in October 2004. The company's accountant, who was not sure how to record some of the transactions, opened a Property ledger account and recorded debits and (credits) to this account as follows.

1. Cost of real estate purchased as a building site.	$ 170 000
2. Paid architect's fee for design of new building.	23 000
3. Paid for the demolition of an old building on the building site purchased in 1.	28 000
4. Paid land tax on the real estate purchased as a building site in 1.	1 700
5. Paid excavation costs for the new building.	15 000
6. Made the first payment to the building contractor.	250 000
7. Paid for equipment to be installed in the new building.	148 000
8. Received from sale of salvaged materials from demolishing the old building.	(6 800)
9. Made final payment to the building contractor.	350 000
10. Paid interest on building loan during construction.	22 000
11. Paid freight on equipment purchased.	1 900
12. Paid installation costs of equipment.	4 200
13. Paid for repair of equipment damaged during installation.	2 700
Property ledger account balance	$1 009 700

Required

1. Prepare a schedule with the following column headings. Analyse each transaction, enter the payment or receipt in the appropriate column, and total each column.

Item No.	Land	Land improvements	Building	Manufacturing equipment	Other

2. Prepare the journal entry to close the $1 009 700 balance of the property ledger account.

PROBLEM 10.12 ★★★ Depreciation

Springs Manufacturing, which started operations on 1 September 2002, is owned by Alice Ltd. Alice Ltd's accounts at 31 December 2005 included the following balances:

Machinery (at cost)	$ 91 000
Accumulated depreciation – machinery	48 200
Vehicles (at cost; purchased 21 November 2004)	46 800
Accumulated depreciation – vehicles	19 656
Land (at cost; purchased 25 October 2002)	81 000
Building (at cost; purchased 25 October 2002)	185 720
Accumulated depreciation – building	28 614

Details of machines owned at 31 December 2005 are as follows:

Machine	Purchase date	Cost	Useful life	Residual value
1	7 October 2002	$43 000	5 years	$2 500
2	4 February 2003	$48 000	6 years	$3 000

Additional information
- Alice Ltd calculates depreciation to the nearest month and balances the records at month-end. Recorded amounts are rounded to the nearest dollar, and the reporting date is 31 December.
- Alice Ltd uses straight-line depreciation for all depreciable assets except vehicles, which are depreciated on the diminishing balance at 40% p.a.
- The vehicles account balance reflects the total paid for two identical delivery vehicles, each of which cost $23 400.
- On acquiring the land and building, Alice Ltd estimated the building's useful life and residual value at 20 years and $5000 respectively.

The following transactions occurred from 1 January 2006:

2006 03 Jan.	Bought a new machine (machine 3) for a cash price of $57 000. Freight charges of $442 and installation costs of $1758 were paid in cash. The useful life and residual value were estimated at five years and $4000 respectively.
22 June	Bought a second-hand vehicle for $15 200 cash. Repainting costs of $655 and four new tyres costing $345 were paid for in cash.
28 Aug.	Exchanged machine 1 for office furniture that had a fair value of $12 500 at the date of exchange. The fair value of machine 1 at the date of exchange was $11 500. The office furniture originally cost $36 000 and, to the date of exchange, had been depreciated by $24 100 in the previous owner's books. Alice Ltd estimated the office furniture's useful life and residual value at eight years and $540 respectively.
31 Dec.	Recorded depreciation.
2007 30 April	Paid for repairs and maintenance on the machinery at a cash cost of $928.
25 May	Sold one of the vehicles bought on 21 November 2004 for $6600 cash.
26 June	Installed a fence around the property at a cash cost of $5500. The fence has an estimated useful life of 10 years and zero residual value. (Debit the cost to a land improvements asset account.)
31 Dec.	Recorded depreciation.
2008 05 Jan.	Overhauled machine 2 at a cash cost of $12 000, after which Alice Ltd estimated its remaining useful life at one additional year and revised its residual value to $5000.

(continued)

20 June	Traded in the remaining vehicle bought on 21 November 2004 for a new vehicle. A trade-in allowance of $3700 was received and $22 000 was paid in cash. Stamp duty of $500 and registration and third-party insurance of $800 were also paid for in cash.
04 Oct.	Scrapped the vehicle bought on 22 June 2006, as it had been so badly damaged in a traffic accident that it was not worthwhile repairing it.
31 Dec.	Recorded depreciation.

Required

Prepare general journal entries to record the above transactions.

PROBLEM 10.13 ★★★   Depreciation

Cairns Ltd started operations on 1 October 2002. Its accounts at 30 June 2005 included the following balances:

Machinery (at cost)	$ 98 000
Accumulated depreciation – machinery	47 886
Vehicles (at cost; purchased 20 February 2003)	160 000
Accumulated depreciation – vehicles	89 440
Land (at cost; purchased 20 March 2005)	75 000
Building (at cost; purchased 20 March 2005)	290 600
Accumulated depreciation – building	3 420
Land improvements (at cost; purchased 20 March 2005)	18 000
Accumulated depreciation – land improvements	300

Details of machines owned at 30 June 2005 were:

Machine	Purchase date	Cost	Useful life	Residual value
1	2 October 2002	$25 000	4 years	$2 500
2	27 December 2002	42 000	5 years	4 000
3	29 July 2003	31 000	4 years	3 000

Additional information
- Cairns Ltd calculates depreciation to the nearest month and balances the records at month-end. Recorded amounts are rounded to the nearest dollar, and the reporting date is 30 June.
- Cairns Ltd uses straight-line depreciation for all depreciable assets except vehicles, which are depreciated on the diminishing balance at 30% p.a.
- The vehicles account balance reflects the total paid for four identical delivery vehicles, which cost $40 000 each.
- On acquiring the land and building, Cairns Ltd estimated the building's useful life and residual value at 20 years and $17 000 respectively.
- The land improvements account balance reflects a payment of $18 000 made on 20 March 2005 for driveways and a car park. On acquiring these land improvements, Cairns Ltd estimated their useful life at 15 years with no residual value.

The following transactions occurred from 1 July 2005:

03/08/05	Purchased a new machine (machine 4) for a cash price of $36 000. Installation costs of $1800 were also paid. Cairns Ltd estimated the useful life and residual value at five years and $3500 respectively.
15/11/05	Paid vehicle repairs of $600.
30/12/05	Exchanged one of the vehicles for items of fixtures that had a fair value of $17 000 at the date of exchange. The fair value of the vehicle at the date of exchange was $16 000. The fixtures originally cost $50 000 and had been depreciated by $31 000 to the date of exchange in the previous owner's books. Cairns Ltd estimated the fixtures' useful life and residual value at five years and $2500 respectively.
10/03/06	Sold machine 1 for $5000 cash.
30/06/05	Recorded depreciation expense.
20/09/06	Traded in machine 3 for a new machine (machine 5). A trade-in allowance of $10 000 was received for machine 3 and $34 000 was paid in cash. Cairns Ltd estimated machine 5's useful life and residual value at six years and $5000 respectively.
30/12/06	Scrapped machine 2, as it was surplus to requirements and no buyer could be found for it.
08/02/07	Paid $8000 to overhaul machine 4, after which machine 4's useful life was estimated at two remaining years and its residual value was revised to $5000.
30/06/07	Recorded depreciation expense.

Required
Prepare general journal entries to record the above transactions.

WEBLINK

Visit these websites for additional information:

www.iasb.org   www.iasplus.com
www.asic.gov.au   www.ifac.org
www.aasb.com.au   www.nzica.com
www.accaglobal.com   www.capa.com.my

REFERENCES

Accounting Standards Board 1996, *Measurement of tangible fixed assets*, discussion paper, Accounting Standards Board UK.

Danisco 2005, *Annual report 2004/05*, viewed March 2006, <www.danisco.com>.

Ernst & Young 2002, *The impact of AASB 1041 'Revaluation of Non-current Assets': a survey of corporate Australia's adoption of the new standard*, Ernst & Young Australia, January.

Picker, R & Johnson, A-M 1999, 'Asset revaluations and impairment', *Accounting Brief*, April.

CHAPTER 11
Intangible assets

ACCOUNTING STANDARDS

International: IAS 38 *Intangible Assets*
Australia: AASB 138 *Intangible Assets*
New Zealand: NZ IAS 38 *Intangible Assets*

CONCEPTS FOR REVIEW

Before studying this chapter, you should understand or, if necessary, revise:

- the Framework issued by the IASB
- accounting for property, plant and equipment, particularly:
  - criteria for recognition
  - concepts of depreciation
  - application of the cost model
  - application of the revaluation model.

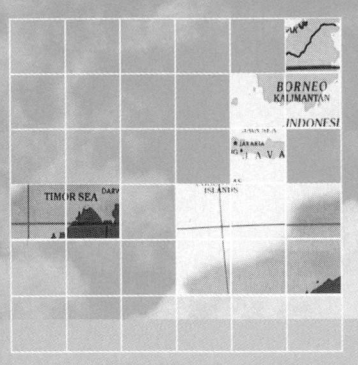
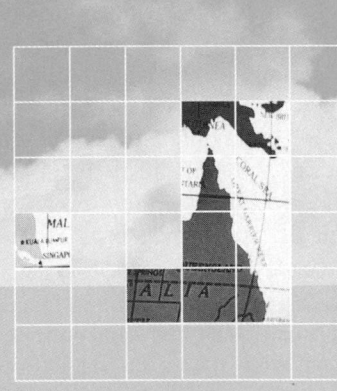

When you have studied this chapter, you should be able to:

1. understand the key characteristics of an intangible asset
2. discuss why intangibles have become progressively more important over time
3. explain whether some intangible items meet the criterion of control, as used in the definition of an asset
4. discuss measurement problems and relevance considerations in accounting for intangibles
5. explain the criteria relating to the initial recognition and measurement of intangible assets
6. discuss the accounting for internally generated assets, particularly research and development
7. discuss potential inconsistencies in the recognition of internally generated and acquired intangibles
8. explain how to account for intangibles subsequent to initial recognition
9. explain the principles relating to the amortisation of intangibles
10. explain the accounting for retirement and disposal of intangible assets
11. apply the disclosure requirements of IAS 38
12. discuss innovative suggestions for improving the reporting of intangible assets.

11.1 Introduction

Chapter 10 addressed the accounting standards for the tangible assets of property, plant and equipment. Chapter 11 now examines the standards for intangible assets. The International Accounting Standards Board (IASB) believes that it is necessary to distinguish between tangible assets (such as property, plant and equipment) and intangible assets (such as patents and brand names). In analysing the accounting for intangible assets, the question that must always be kept at the forefront is whether there should be any difference in the accounting treatment for tangible and intangible assets. What is it that is different about intangible assets that requires a separate accounting standard, and presumably different accounting rules, for intangible and tangible assets?

Historically, it is common for entities to report all their tangible assets on the balance sheet but be less consistent in the reporting of intangible assets. As a result, there are sometimes large differences between the market value of an entity and its recorded net assets. As Jenkins and Upton (2001, p. 4) noted:

> The problem that confronts businesses, users of business and financial reporting, standard-setters and regulators is how best to understand and communicate the difference between the value of a company (usually expressed as the market capitalisation) and the accounting book value of that company.

To assist in understanding the difference between these two numbers, Jenkins and Upton (2001, p. 5) provided the analysis shown in figure 11.1. Item 6 in this figure is not an area that accounting can directly address, although the quality of the accounting may affect the degree to which it exists. How can accounting assist in providing more information about what causes the gap between accounting book value and market capitalisation numbers? How much information should be provided about all the assets and liabilities of an entity? What should be in the financial statements and what should be in the notes to those statements? These are questions for accounting standard setters to solve.

1. Accounting book value	$XXX
2. + Market assessments of differences between accounting measurement and underlying value of recognised assets and liabilities	XXX
3. + Market assessments of the underlying value of items that meet the definition of assets and liabilities but are not recognised in financial statements (for example, patents developed through internal research and development)	XXX
4. + Market assessments of intangible value drivers or value impairers that do not meet the definition of assets and liabilities (for example, employee morale)	XXX
5. + Market assessments of the entity's future plans, opportunities and business risks	XXX
6. + Other factors, including puffery, pessimism and market psychology	XXX
7. Market capitalisation	$XXX

FIGURE 11.1 Differences between market capitalisation and accounting book value
Source: Jenkins & Upton (2001, p. 5).

The standards on accounting for intangibles are contained in IAS 38 *Intangible Assets*. In its 2004 revision, the IASB did not attempt to revisit all areas of accounting for intangibles. Its emphasis in this revision was to reflect changes as a result of decisions made in its Business Combinations project, particularly relating to accounting for intangibles acquired as part of a business combination. Hence, there still may exist areas of inconsistency between accounting for intangibles obtained outside a business combination and those acquired as part of a business combination.

IAS 38 covers the accounting for all intangible assets except, as detailed in paragraphs 2 and 3, those specifically covered by another accounting standard – financial assets; and mineral rights and expenditure on exploration for, or development and extraction of, minerals, oil, natural gas and similar non-regenerative resources. Other standards that include accounting for specific intangible assets are:

- intangible assets held by an entity for sale in the ordinary course of business (IAS 2 *Inventories* and IAS 11 *Construction Contracts*)
- intangible assets arising from insurance contracts with policyholders (IFRS 4 *Insurance Contracts*)
- deferred tax assets (IAS 12 *Income Taxes*)
- leases within the scope of IAS 17 *Leases*
- assets arising from employee benefits (IAS 19 *Employee Benefits*)
- goodwill acquired in a business combination (IFRS 3 *Business Combinations*)
- non-current intangible assets held for sale (IFRS 5 *Non-current Assets Held for Sale and Discontinued Operations*).

LO 1

11.2   The nature of intangible assets

Paragraph 8 of IAS 38 defines an intangible asset as 'an identifiable non-monetary asset without physical substance'. Note that intangible assets are non-monetary assets. Being assets, they are resources controlled by the entity from which future economic benefits are expected to flow to the entity. Monetary assets are defined in paragraph 8 as 'money held and assets to be received in fixed or determinable amounts of money'. Apart from excluding monetary assets, there are two key characteristics of intangible assets, namely:
- they are identifiable
- they lack physical substance.

The concept of intangibles used in IAS 38 is the same as that used in Statement of Financial Accounting Standards No. 142 (SFAS 142) *Goodwill and Other Intangible Assets* issued by the Financial Accounting Standards Board (FASB) in the United States in June 2001. Other writers, such as Baruch Lev, have similar definitions. For example, Lev stated (2001, p. 5) that: 'An intangible asset is a claim to future benefits that does not have a physical or financial (a stock or a bond) embodiment'.

The two key characteristics of an intangible asset are now considered in detail.

11.2.1   Identifiability

The emphasis on the criterion of identifiability arose out of the Business Combinations project and the concern that, in allocating the cost of the combination to the assets and liabilities acquired, the intangible assets acquired were distinguished from goodwill. As paragraph BC8 of the Basis for Conclusions on IAS 38 notes, identifiability is seen as the characteristic that conceptually distinguishes other intangible assets from goodwill. The purpose then is to ensure that an entity identifies and discloses its assets rather than having them subsumed into goodwill.

IAS 38 does not contain a definition of 'identifiable'. However, paragraph 12 of this standard sets down two criteria, one of which must be met for an asset to be classified as identifiable. Paragraph 12 states:

An asset meets the identifiability criterion in the definition of an intangible asset when it:
(a) is separable, i.e. is capable of being separated or divided from the entity and sold, transferred, licensed, rented or exchanged, either individually or together with a related contract, asset or liability; or
(b) arises from contractual or other legal rights, regardless of whether those rights are transferable or separable from the entity or from other rights and obligations.

The criterion of separability tests whether an entity can divide an asset from other assets and deal with it as an individual asset. Not only must the asset be able to be seen as a separate item, it must be capable of being transferred to another party. Assets such as high staff morale and customer relationships may be capable of being named and discussed, and actions may be taken to adjust the levels of them within an entity, but such assets cannot be transferred to another entity. A further reason for requiring an asset to be separable prior to recognition is that it makes the measurability of the asset easier. Exchangeable assets are potentially going to have markets from which prices can be obtained, in contrast to non-exchangeable assets.

In most if not all cases, separable assets are capable of being exchanged by an entity because the entity has a *contractual or legal right* to make the exchange. However, as noted in paragraph BC10 of the Basis for Conclusions on IAS 38:

> some contractual-legal rights establish property interests that are not readily separable from the entity as a whole. For example, under the laws of some jurisdictions some licences granted to an entity are not transferable except by sale of the entity as a whole.

The existence of the legal rights to these assets was seen as being a factor that distinguished some assets from other assets that were to be included in goodwill. Hence, separability was not seen as the only criterion for identifiability.

In his discussion of the interrelationship between tangible and intangible assets, Upton (2001, p. 61) commented: 'With control comes the ability to buy, sell, or withhold from the market — characteristics of the everyday notion of an asset'. Upton then interpreted the meaning of 'control' to require identifiability, implying that expected benefits cannot be controlled if the benefits are not separable, and the entity does not have the ability to transfer them to another entity. He also noted:

> The definition of an asset is derived from sensible economics and everyday use of language. The more complex answer is that monetary measurement is impossible without a notion like control (p. 62).

Non-physical assets cannot be recognised unless they are identifiable. The reason for this restriction is that it makes the subsequent measurement of assets easier.

Figure 11.2 contains a list of assets that could potentially meet the identifiability criteria. The list is included in appendix A to the FASB Statement of Financial Accounting Standards No. 141 (SFAS 141) *Business Combinations*. Note that the assets identified in the first column, those based on contractual/legal rights, may also meet the separability criterion.

In the 1999 exposure draft (ED) to SFAS 141, the FASB provided a different list of identifiable intangible assets that might be acquired in a business combination. The list in SFAS 141, issued in 2001, differs from the list in the 1999 ED in that the SFAS 141 list requires the application of the same identifiability criteria as in IAS 38. As a result, the following assets included in the 1999 list were excluded from the 2001 list, because they were not seen as meeting the identifiability criteria:

- customer base
- customer service capability
- presence in geographic markets or locations
- non-union status or strong labour relations
- ongoing training or recruiting programs
- outstanding credit ratings and access to capital markets
- favourable government relations.

As noted earlier, one of the problems with non-separable assets is the ability to measure them. Some assets, such as an excellent workforce and a high level of customer satisfaction, are interrelated in that very good employees will lead to high customer satisfaction. To recognise these as separate assets would raise difficulties in determining the value of one separately from the other. With the measurement of tangible assets, the emphasis is generally not on measuring the benefits from the asset, but on recording the cost of the asset. Benefits from assets are often measured at the level of a cash-generating unit rather than at the individual asset level, as is the case when determining impairment of assets (see chapter 13 of this book).

	Contractual/ legal rights	Separable
Marketing-related intangible assets		
Trademarks, trade names	✓	
Service marks, collective marks, certification marks	✓	
Trade dress (unique colour, shape or package design)	✓	
Newspaper mastheads	✓	
Internet domain names	✓	
Non-competition agreements	✓	
Customer-related intangible assets		
Customer lists		✓
Order or production backlog	✓	
Customer contracts and related customer relationships	✓	
Non-contractual customer relationships		✓
Artistic-related intangible assets		
Plays, operas, ballets	✓	
Books, magazines, newspapers, other literary works	✓	
Musical works such as compositions, song lyrics, advertising jingles	✓	
Pictures, photographs	✓	
Video and audiovisual material, including motion pictures, music videos, television programs	✓	
Contract-based intangible assets		
Licensing, royalty, stand-still agreements	✓	
Advertising, construction, management, service or supply contracts	✓	
Lease agreements	✓	
Construction permits	✓	
Franchise agreements	✓	
Operating and broadcast rights	✓	
Use rights such as drilling, water, air, mineral, timber cutting and route authorities	✓	
Servicing contracts such as mortgage servicing contracts	✓	
Employment contracts	✓	
Technology-based intangible assets		
Patented technology	✓	
Computer software and mask works	✓	
Unpatented technology		✓
Databases, including title plants		✓
Trade secrets, such as secret formulas, processes, recipes	✓	

FIGURE 11.2 Identifiable intangible assets

Source: Appendix A to the FASB Statement of Financial Accounting Standards No. 141 (SFAS 141) *Business Combinations*.

11.2.2   Lack of physical substance

Lack of physical substance is a key characteristic in the definition of an intangible asset. It is the characteristic that separates assets such as property, plant and equipment from intangible assets, in that property, plant and equipment would generally meet the criterion of identifiability.

It should be noted at the outset that some intangible assets may be associated with a physical item, such as software contained on a computer disk. However, the asset is really the software and not the disk itself. As noted in paragraph 4 of IAS 38, judgement in some cases is required to determine which element, tangible or intangible, is most important to the classification of the asset. Use of the physical substance characteristic is interesting in that paragraph 56 of the IASB Framework states that:

> physical form is not essential to the existence of an asset; hence patents and copyrights, for example, are assets if future economic benefits are expected to flow from them to the entity and if they are controlled by the entity.

If physical substance is not intrinsic to the determination of assets, why then is it necessary to distinguish between physical and non-physical assets?

Many writers in the accounting literature would not agree that separating assets on a physical/non-physical basis is useful in subclassifying assets. For example:

> Indeed, once we agree that assets are future economic benefits, tangibility and even legal ownership are irrelevant for accountants; it is only some confused 'physicalist' prejudice that might persuade them otherwise (Napier & Power 1992, pp. 85–95).

> ... the **lack of physical existence** is not of itself a satisfactory criterion for distinguishing a tangible from an intangible asset. Such assets as bank deposits, accounts receivable, and long-term investments lack physical substance, yet accountants classify them as tangible assets (Kieso & Weygandt 1992, p. 589).

There are a number of problems with defining intangible assets in terms of physical existence. The *first* problem is that it conflicts with the way in which accountants have traditionally classified assets. Non-monetary items such as investments in equity or debt instruments, leases, and deferred costs such as research and development expenditure have not generally been classified as intangible assets. Monetary items such as receivables, prepayments and deferred tax assets are similarly not classified as intangible assets.

The *second* problem relates to why accountants would want to classify assets on the basis of whether they have physical substance. There are an infinite number of ways of classifying items; for example, by colour, size or shape. The choice of classification must have a purpose. Are preparers or users of accounts interested in how many assets can be touched and how many cannot be touched? It is doubtful that this is the case. In determining the appropriate criterion for classifying assets, there must be an explanation for the relevance of the classification. If useful information is the purpose of the classification, accountants' actions in practice, as well as lack of supporting logic in the accounting literature, raise doubts whether physical substance is the appropriate basis for classifying assets.

The *third* problem with using the physical substance criterion is the potential conflict with the IASB Framework as quoted above. Based on the definition of assets as future economic benefits, all assets are intangible in that they represent a collection of perceived economic benefits. Thus, it is not the block of land or item of plant that is the asset; it is the economic benefits embodied in that physical item that constitutes the asset. A key example of this is leased assets. It is not the physical leased motor vehicle that is the asset, but the economic benefits from that physical item that constitutes the asset. In relation to leased items, Stevenson (1989, p. 5) noted that 'we can quickly slip back to physical concepts of assets if we are not careful'.

The *fourth* problem with the criterion of physical substance is that tangibility is not an indication of the worth of an asset. As James (2001a) noted:

> Accounting for new-economy organisations is often problematic, because much of the value lies in intangibles: brands, customer relationships and knowledge. Spotless Services is an example. The company has maintained a relatively stable share price during a period when its tangible assets (NTA) went negative (the NTA is now positive). The reason is that Spotless's assets are mostly intangible; in recognition of this, the company no longer includes the NTA in its public accounts because, according to the company secretary, it is not relevant.

Interestingly, IAS 38 has no discussion on the characteristic of 'physical substance', yet four paragraphs are devoted to the control characteristic of an asset.

Why then distinguish non-physical assets? Lev (2001, p. 5) provides some answers. He defined an intangible asset as 'a claim to future benefits that does not have a physical or financial (a stock or a bond) embodiment.' He then used the terms 'intangibles', 'knowledge assets' and 'intellectual capital' interchangeably, as he saw the term 'intangibles' being used by accountants, 'knowledge assets' by economists, and 'intellectual capital' in the management and legal literature. He summarised (p. 7) intangible assets as being non-physical sources of value (claims to future benefits) generated by innovation (or discovery, relating to innovations, research and development), unique organisational designs (relating to brands, organisational structures and marketing savvy), or human resource practices (relating to unique personnel and compensation policies, recruitment successes and low turnover of employees).

The reason for distinguishing between physical and non-physical assets is that the very nature of a non-physical asset means that the accounting standards for the recognition and measurement of non-physical assets may have to be different from those for tangible assets. What are these unique characteristics and how do they cause a problem? Consider the following characteristics raised by Lev (2001):

- *Intangible assets are non-rival assets* (p. 22). They can be used at the same time for multiple purposes, such as an airline reservation system that can service many customers. There is no opportunity cost of using the asset.
- *The assets are characterised by large fixed (sunk) costs and negligible marginal (incremental) cost* (pp. 22–3). Examples of this are the development of a headache tablet and the creation of a computer software program.
- *Many intangibles are not subject to the diminishing returns characteristic of physical assets* (p. 23). Production of more computer disks does not reduce the worth of the software asset. There may be increasing returns to scale. For example, a university may develop a software program for student enrolment that can be valuable for ongoing use by the university and may also be sold to other universities, thereby increasing the return on the original investment.
- *Intangibles may have network effects* (p. 26); that is, the value of the item increases as the number of people using the item increases. The utility of such items as a computer game (X-Box or PlayStation), a telephone network (Vodaphone or Nokia), or a computer program (Microsoft Word or Excel spreadsheets) increases as more people use the same item.
- *Intangibles may be more difficult to manage and operate than tangible assets* (p. 32). Physical assets such as buildings are harder to steal and copy.
- *Property rights are harder to determine* (p. 33). Investments in employee training and advertising are areas where it is hard to exclude others from securing some of the benefits.
- *The relationship between the investment and the ultimate benefits is hard to track.* Are the extra sales due to the training of the employees, or because the item has become trendy?

- *The relationship between the investment and the return is skewed* (p. 39). Many investments in intangibles result in failure while some are a huge success. The investment is then often high risk. As Lev (p. 39) noted, a key element in intangibles is that success relies on a discovery. Investments in tangible assets tend to occur after the discovery, and alternative uses including the sale of the assets do not depend on discovery.

- *There is in general an absence of organised and competitive markets* (p. 42). Intangibles such as brand names may be sold but, given the unique nature of most intangibles, there is no active market for them. The sale of a brand name in one industry has no bearing on the potential for sale of another brand, even in the same industry. Lev (p. 47) argues that markets in intangibles lack *transparency*, so, 'details of licensing deals and alliances are generally not made public, and acquired intangibles are usually bundled with other assets'.

- *There is a high degree of uncertainty regarding the future benefits of intangible assets.* This is a general statement as there are some physical assets that also exhibit uncertainty in relation to expected benefits. As Egginton (1990, p. 194) stated:

  > For example, there could be more uncertainty over the future benefits of the tangible oil and gas reserves of a section of ocean than over the future benefits of the intangible European rights to the Coca-Cola brand name.

Lev (2001, p. 47) summarised the above discussion as follows:

> Intangibles are inherently difficult to trade. Legal property rights are often hazy, contingent contracts are difficult to draw, and the cost structure of many intangibles (large sunk costs, negligible marginal costs) is not conducive to stable pricing. Accordingly, at present there are no active, organized markets in intangibles. This could soon change with the advent of Internet-based exchanges, but it will require specific enabling mechanisms, such as valuation and insurance schemes. Private trades in intangibles in the form of licensing and alliances proliferate, but they do not provide information essential for the measurement and valuation of intangibles.

Because non-physical assets have the above characteristics, they cause particular problems for accountants. The two key activities for accountants in relation to assets are the recognition and measurement of the assets. With non-physical assets, the determination of when they should be recognised (Should one wait for a point of discovery? Does an asset exist when the investment is made? Is there an asset at the point employee training occurs?), and how they should be measured (Where is the market? Can the specific benefits be isolated? Are the property rights over the expected benefits fuzzy?), is in general more difficult for non-physical assets. Hence, the need for a specific standard on non-physical assets arises from the need for extra guidance on the recognition and measurement of those assets — not because such assets are of any greater or lesser value than physical assets. With physical assets, where there are thin markets or where the assets are of a specialised nature, the guidance in IAS 38 could be considered to be equally applicable to tangible assets.

LO 2

11.2.3 Why have intangibles become important?

For quite some time, writers in the business press have noted a change in the factors that cause a company to be valuable. For example, Gottliebsen (1987, p. 6) noted a change in the composition of valuable assets in modern entities:

> Around the world, Japanese manufacturers established brands such as Sony, Toyota, Nissan, National, Honda and Mazda that have become household names. Their plans to move a vast amount of their productive capacity from Japan to the US reveal that the really fragile asset is the so-called 'tangible asset' — the bricks, mortar and plant that represented the old manufacturing capacity, now to be scrapped. The real tangible asset that endured was the brands — now to be produced for the US market from a different place.

As evidence that intangibles have been increasing in importance over time, Lev (2001, p. 9) reported the average price-to-book ratio of the Standard and Poor 500 companies over the period 1977 to March 2001. Figure 11.3 shows that the mean market-to-book ratio has continuously increased over this period of time, reaching a ratio of 6:1 in March 2001. As Lev noted (p. 8), this means that of every six dollars of market value, only one dollar appears on the balance sheet, while the remaining five dollars represent intangible assets.

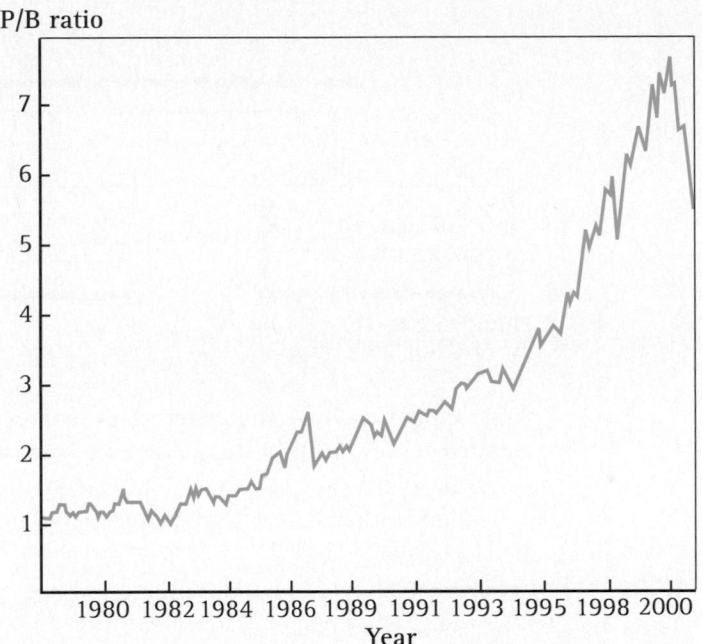

FIGURE 11.3   Average price-to-book ratio of the S&P 500 companies, December 1977 – March 2001
Source: Reproduced in Lev (2001, p. 9).

Lev's arguments are supported by James (2001b), who stated that there was a growing gap between the book values of companies — a measure based mostly on tangible assets — and the market price of companies. He noted that this effect occurred not only in the USA but also in countries like Australia:

> McKinsey estimates that in the US, the market to book value (share price versus the accounting value) for all public companies has risen from below two times in 1990 to 3.5 (it peaked at four in the bull market). This measure, called Tobin's Q, is a rough measure of the increased importance of intangible assets (because book values tend not to have accurate estimates of intangible assets such as knowledge and brands), and the rising differential suggests that intangibles are becoming more important to the value of listed companies. Stukey [the Sydney-based managing partner of consultancy McKinsey & Company] says the trend has not been as extreme in Australia, but there has been a similar increase in the gap between book value and market value. He says the Tobin's Q measure for the Australian stockmarket is now about 2.5.
>
> The Australian Stock Exchange says that, in December 1997, the average share price was 2.1 times net tangible assets. By January this year [2001], the ratio of price to net tangible assets (NTA) was more than three times, a doubling of the gap between NTA and share prices in less than four years.

Lev (2001, pp. 8–9) asked why intangibles are more important now than in the 1960s, 1970s and 1980s. He argued that the surge in intangibles was driven by the 'unique combination of two related economic forces'; namely, intensified business competition and the advent of information technologies. He provided numerous examples to support his case, and the diagram in figure 11.4 illustrates his argument.

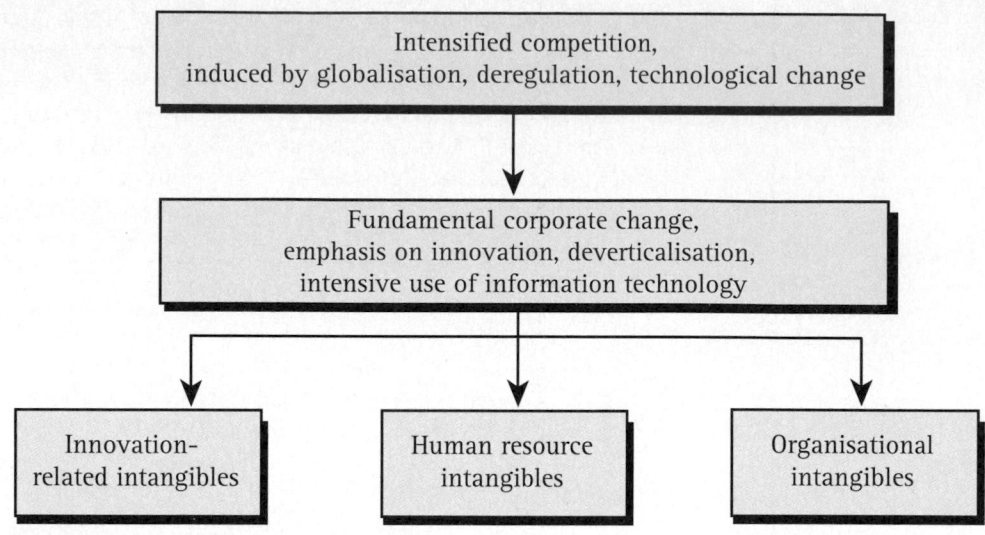

FIGURE 11.4 The ascendancy of intangibles
Source: Lev (2001, p. 18).

In support of his argument that modern entities are more dependent on their employees, Lev (2001, p. 13) quoted research done by Bhide (2000) arguing that:

> The enormous loss from employee turnover is demonstrated by the finding that 71 per cent of the firms in the Inc.500 list (a group of young, fast-growing companies) were established by persons who replicated or modified innovations developed within their former employers.

Baltes (1997, p. 7) was another who viewed a change in the world economy and believed it was more important than ever to consider accounting for 'softer' assets:

> In a decade characterized by exploding global competition, a shift from manufacturing-oriented firms to service-oriented firms and almost perpetual reengineering, more and more companies are paying far greater attention to the measurement of 'soft' or 'intangible' assets — intellectual capital, training, human resources, brand image and, most important, customer satisfaction.

The questions from an accounting perspective are whether financial reporting has experienced a similar degree of change over the same period, and whether financial reports are providing information about the variables that describe the new economy.

LO 3   11.2.4   ## The definition of an asset and identifying intangible assets

Paragraph 49 of the IASB Framework describes an asset as 'a resource controlled by the enterprise'. Paragraphs 13–16 of IAS 38 discuss the application of the characteristic of 'control' and the classification of certain items as intangible assets.

The crux of the debate is whether items (as noted earlier by the FASB) that probably do not meet the identifiability criterion — such as effective advertising programs, trained staff, favourable government relations and fundraising capabilities — qualify as assets. According to paragraphs 13–16 of IAS 38, items such as market and technical knowledge (para. 14), staff skills, specific management or technical talent (para. 15) and a portfolio of customers, market share, customer relationships and customer loyalty (para. 16) do not meet the definition of intangible assets. The key reason for excluding such items as assets is the interpretation of the term 'control' as used in the definition of an asset. According to paragraph 13 of IAS 38, control normally stems from 'legal rights that are enforceable in a court of law'. In the absence of legal rights, it is more difficult to demonstrate control.

An outspoken critic of the definition of an asset has been Walter Schuetze, former chief accountant of the Securities and Exchange Commission (SEC) in the United States and former member of the FASB. He argued (1993, p. 67) that the 'FASB's definition is so complex, so abstract, so open-ended, so all-inclusive, and so vague that we cannot use it to solve problems'. He further stated (2001, p. 12):

> The definition does not discriminate and help us to decide whether something or anything on the margin is an asset. That definition describes an empty box. A large empty box. A large empty box with sideboards.

Because of this, he proposed that assets be defined as 'cash, contractual claims to cash or services, and items that can be sold separately for cash'. This definition incorporates ideas of separability/exchangeability and legal contracts for benefits. He considered the concept of control to be too vague to be operational.

Samuelson (1996, p. 156) agreed with Schuetze that the definition of assets is 'too complex and ambiguous and admits too much to the category of assets'. He noted (p. 156) that, with the advent of the conceptual framework and the dropping of the matching concept, many people have expected that several deferred costs would no longer appear as assets in entities' balance sheets. However, this has not happened. Both writers did not believe that an asset is determinable by considering whether or not the expected benefits are controlled.

Further insights into the definition of an asset can be obtained by analysing the definition of a liability. As Samuelson (1996, p. 147) noted: 'In the conceptual framework of the FASB, assets are the most fundamental accounting elements. Liabilities are defined, in essence, as negative assets'. In the definition of liabilities in the IASB Framework, there is no characteristic similar to control. Yet, for both asset and liability definitions, there are common characteristics of expected future benefits/outflows and existence of a past transaction. However, in determining present obligations, the mere intention to sacrifice economic benefits in the future is not sufficient to give rise to a liability. As paragraph 61 of the Framework states, the existence of a liability depends on the present obligation being such that:

> the economic consequences of failing to honour the obligation, for example, because of the existence of a substantial penalty, leave the entity with little, if any, discretion to avoid the outflow of resources to another party.

Although most obligations are legally enforceable because they arise from contractual or other legal rights, paragraph 60 of the Framework provides examples of liabilities where there are no legal contracts: 'Obligations also arise, however, from normal business practice, custom and a desire to maintain good business relations or act in an equitable manner'. For example, a provision for long-service leave and a deferred tax liability can be recognised as liabilities well before there is any legal enforceability, presumably on the grounds of past experience and/or normal business practice. Both are based on expectations of what might occur. With long-service leave provisions, provisions are based on expected retention rates because employees may change jobs before becoming eligible for payment.

Compare this with an entity that invests in its future staff by outlaying funds on training programs. The entity has invested in its staff, but it has no control over whether staff remain employed by it. Nevertheless, it has an expectation that it will receive most if not all of the benefits from the training programs. If the staff stay, the entity has control over the benefits from the increased sales that arise from the training programs. Access to the future benefits that arise from the well-trained staff who stay with the entity can be denied to other entities. Not all the expected benefits may eventuate but, if they do, they belong to the entity. In fact, if past experience indicates that the entity has a fine record of retaining staff, it can be inferred or construed from the facts in the particular situation that the benefits will flow to the entity. So, if custom and usual business practice are a guide, the benefits will flow to the entity. Although the staff could decide to go to another entity and provide it with the benefits of their training, that entity cannot argue that there are any grounds, such as normal business practice, for suggesting that this will occur. The second entity may form an expectation that the other entity's staff will change employment but there are no legal, equitable or constructive reasons for suggesting that its expectation is any more than a hope.

The debate over the 'real' assets of today's entities is heightened with the existence of Internet or dotcom entities. Some of these entities have high values but very little non-current assets or inventory. As King and Henry (1999) noted, the value of these entities lies in their intellectual capital: 'In fact, a common saying about them is that "the assets walk out the door every night"'. King and Henry did not even question whether these items were assets, being more interested in the question of reliability of measurement. They noted:

> Major banks, such as BT Commercial (part of Bankers Trust, now Deutsche Bank), have lent literally hundreds of millions of dollars to companies like Zenith, Strohs, and Florsheim with the firms' trade names and patents as collateral ... Appraisals are relevant and reliable enough for America's largest banks, so they should also be relevant and reliable for individual investors.

Such difficulties in determining whether certain intangibles meet the definition of an asset caused the IASB to introduce the further test of identifiability. By requiring identifiability for recognition of intangibles, the IASB diffused the debate as to whether an item such as good staff relations is an asset. Regardless of whether it is an asset, it is not an intangible asset because it does not meet the identifiability criterion, and so can only be recognised, if at all, as part of goodwill. However, reducing the number of assets recognised in the financial statements because of measurement problems may also reduce the relevance of the information provided in those financial statements.

11.3 Recognition and initial measurement

IAS 38 establishes standards in relation to the recognition and initial measurement of intangible assets. In order to provide some questions to consider when analysing these standards, it is worthwhile to consider some issues raised by Upton (2001). This is done in the following section.

LO 4

11.3.1 Measurement and relevance issues

In his analysis of intangibles, Upton (2001, p. 53) noted that there are four criteria to consider in determining the information that should be recognised in the financial statements:
- *Definitions* – does the item meet the definition of one of the elements of financial statements?
- *Measurability* – does the item have an attribute that is measurable with sufficient reliability?
- *Relevance* – is the information about the item capable of making a difference in user decisions?
- *Reliability* – is the information representationally faithful, verifiable and neutral?
  He noted further that these criteria were also subject to a cost-benefit constraint.

In this context, Upton (2001, p. 54) observed that FASB Statement No. 2 *Accounting for Research and Development* required that all outlays on research and development be charged to expense. Similarly, in IAS 38, the IASB requires all outlays on research to be expensed, and specific criteria must be met before outlays on development can be capitalised. In FASB No. 2, the following reasons were given for the decision to expense outlays:
- uncertainty of future benefits
- lack of causal relationship between outlay and eventual outcome

- inability to measure future benefits
- lack of usefulness of information about capitalised costs in assessing future performance of an entity.

As Upton noted, these reasons go to the heart of the measurement and relevance issues associated with recognising items in the financial statements. He made a number of insightful comments concerning the issues of measurement and relevance. These are discussed below.

Issues of measurement

Upton (2001) made the following observations:

- *Without a clear boundary, there is a risk that any measurement will double count.* One problem in recognising and measuring intangible assets is the possibility that the same benefits are also included in the measurement of another intangible. For example, if an entity has good staff morale, this will contribute as well to a high level of customer satisfaction. Both lead to the increase in the profitability of an entity. However, measuring these two items separately creates the danger of valuing the same income stream twice. If measurements are based purely on the capitalisation of costs, this is less likely to happen.
- *Retrospective capitalisation may be a useful measure.* If all outlays on areas such as research are initially expensed, it may be useful to allow the retrospective capitalisation of these outlays when a level of success is achieved. Whether the capitalisation of all past outlays is appropriate is, however, questionable.
- *Recognition of in-process assets may be a useful measure.* When an entity outlays funds to either develop some software or find a cure for some disease, the expected results are highly uncertain. One possibility in terms of overcoming the 'expense everything' syndrome is to have a class of in-process assets, and to accumulate costs into in-process accounts. There is no doubt that some in-process information is valuable. In fact, effort expended to date is information for which other entities are willing to pay. An analogy can be made with financial options, for which there may be no value at expiration date.
- *Cross-fertilisation and multigenerational factors.* In some research programs, such as the development of medical cures, it is possible that research will never be totally wasted. The researcher may not find the desired cure for AIDS but, as a result of the research, the information discovered about blood may assist in providing solutions for other medical problems. Expensing purely because no cure for AIDS was found is being too prescriptive in relation to relating outlays to specified outcomes. Similarly, amounts may be spent on developing software that is continuously being updated. However, elements of the software in the first generation device may still be an important foundation in subsequent devices. To expense all previous outlays just because a new version of the asset is developed is again short-sighted.
- *There are two 'gaps' that frustrate attempts to recognise intangible assets.* The first is the 'time gap', which is the gap between the outlay and the determination of the outcome. The longer the gap, the more reluctant standard setters will be to allow capitalisation. The second is the 'correlation gap', which relates the expense to the eventual outcome. For example, were outlays on the AIDS cure related to the information obtained on blood clotting?

Issues of relevance

Upton (2001) also made the following observations:

- *Relevance of capitalised cost information.* An adage popular in the oil industry is 'What you spend doesn't matter. What you found does.' With many intangible assets, the level of expenditure is not proportional to the eventual worth of the outcome. To capitalise costs then does not indicate the potential worth of the outcome or the asset, assuming it has any.

- *Uncertainty does not mean irrelevance.* Accounting does not require certainty for information to be useful. As noted earlier, companies are willing to pay for in-process assets, even though the eventual result is uncertain. It is also true that any entity that does not spend money on developing software or finding medical cures will not produce these products. In terms of causal relationships, entities into drug research will find drug cures even if they are not the ones originally sought. Potentially causal relationships should not be sought on individual research projects but rather on a combination of research projects.
- *Cost information may not be as relevant as fair value but it may be more reliable.* One of the problems of accumulating costs is that the asset may be overstated because the level of costs does not directly relate to the level of benefits. However, the accumulation of costs is at least a reliable measure. If an entity attempts to measure the fair value of an intangible asset, even though the fair value may be more relevant, the measure may be less reliable. To choose between accumulated costs and fair value is to trade off relevance and reliability. However, just because something can be measured reliably, it should not mean that this is what should be disclosed. The measurement attribute must be a relevant one.
- *Volatility of information.* The worth of an entity is affected by events such as a safety recall, a shift in customer tastes, or the success of rival entities and their brands. If information about these events is not disclosed and disclosure is limited to the physical assets, can users obtain a real view of what is happening to the entity? The information on these items may be volatile, but to exclude them may create a financial impression that the entity is in a constantly steady state.

As Upton noted, the determination of relevance and reliable measurement is subject to a cost-benefit test. The costs of any rules on intangibles are borne by the entities preparing the financial statements and by the auditors. The users of the financial statements also incur costs relating to keeping up with accounting rules and adapting their financial analysis models. Unfortunately, while the costs may be quantifiable, the benefits in terms of the incremental information to the users are difficult to measure. Although some research has shown that disclosure of capitalised research and development costs is useful, the benefits relative to the costs have not been empirically demonstrated.

LO 5

11.3.2 ## Criteria for recognition and initial measurement

After determining that an asset exists and that the asset meets the definition of an intangible asset, the asset must meet the two criteria in paragraph 21 of IAS 38 before it can be recognised. The criteria are:

- it is *probable* that the future economic benefits attributable to the asset will flow to the entity
- the *cost* of the asset can be measured *reliably*.

These criteria are the same as those for the recognition of property, plant and equipment in IAS 16 *Property, Plant and Equipment*. If the cost of the asset cannot be reliably measured, but the fair value is determinable, an asset cannot be recognised under either IAS 16 or IAS 38 because both standards require initial measurement at cost. As noted later, this has consequences for the recognition of intangible assets that are internally generated rather than acquired, as well as causing differences in the balance sheets of entities that internally generate assets and those that acquire assets.

In relation to the initial measurement of an intangible asset, paragraph 24 of IAS 38 states that: 'An intangible asset shall be measured initially at cost'. Having required the reliable measurement of cost as one of the recognition criteria, this cost forms the basis for initial measurement.

11.3.3   Separate acquisition

In recognising assets acquired separately, paragraph 25 of IAS 38 notes that 'the probability recognition criterion in paragraph 21(a) is always considered to be satisfied for separately acquired intangible assets'. The IASB argues that the price paid for the asset automatically takes into account the probability of the expected benefits being received; hence, it is unnecessary to apply a further probability test. For example, if an asset had expected cash inflows of $1000, and the probability of these inflows being received was 40%, then an acquirer would pay $400 for the asset. The IASB argues that these benefits are now automatically probable. Further, paragraph 26 notes that the cost of a separately acquired intangible asset can usually be measured reliably. The measurement of cost may be more difficult if the exchange involves the acquirer giving up non-monetary assets rather than cash.

As with property, plant and equipment, the cost of an asset is the sum of the purchase price and the directly attributable costs (IAS 38, para. 27). The purchase price is measured as the fair value of what is given up by the acquirer in order to acquire the asset, and the directly attributable costs are those necessarily incurred to get the asset into the condition where it is capable of operating in the manner intended by management. (These concepts are discussed further in this book in sections 10.3.1 and 10.3.2 of chapter 10 in relation to property, plant and equipment.) The principles of accounting for separately acquired intangibles and property, plant and equipment are the same.

11.3.4   Acquisition as part of a business combination

When assets are acquired as part of a business combination, they are initially recognised at fair value in accordance with IFRS 3 *Business Combinations*. According to paragraph 33 of IAS 38, the cost of such an intangible asset is its fair value at the acquisition date. This is probably a debatable proposition, particularly if there exists an excess on acquisition.

As with separately acquired assets, paragraph 33 of IAS 38 provides that, where intangible assets are acquired as part of a business acquisition, the effect of probability is reflected in the fair value measurement of the asset. Hence, the probability recognition criterion is automatically met. In IFRS 3, paragraph 37(c), the criterion for recognition of an intangible asset acquired in a business combination is simply that 'its fair value can be measured reliably'. As noted in paragraph BC18 of the Basis for Conclusions on IAS 38, the assumption that the probability test is automatically met is in conflict with the recognition criteria for assets in the Framework. However, the IASB expects to revisit this inconsistency in a forthcoming concepts project.

Further, it is argued in paragraph 35 of IAS 38 that the requirement for reliability of measurement is also normally met. In earlier exposure drafts, it was proposed that this criterion would also always be met; in fact, that the reliability of measurement test would be 'subsumed' within the identifiability criterion. However, the reliability test was reinstated because field tests of the standard revealed that there were situations where reliable measurement was not possible (see para. BC21 of the Basis for Conclusions on IAS 38). Due to the undesirability of acquired intangibles being subsumed into goodwill because of arguments that they could not be reliably measured, the IASB placed the following statements in IAS 38:

- the fair value can normally be measured with sufficient reliability (para. 35)
- for an intangible asset with a finite useful life, there is a rebuttable presumption that its fair value can be measured reliably (para. 35)

- a specification that the only circumstances where it might not be possible to measure the fair value reliably are where the asset arises from legal or other contractual rights and is either not separable, or separable but there is no history or evidence of exchange transactions for the same or similar assets (para. 38).

In dissenting from the issue of IAS 38, Professor Whittington argued that the probability test in paragraph 21(a) should be applied in testing the recognition of all intangibles, stating that issues relating to the recognition criteria in the Framework should be resolved before having different recognition criteria for intangible assets acquired in a business combination. The justification for different criteria is presumably that there is an increased relevance of information in reporting the separate intangible assets rather than subsuming them into goodwill.

The application of these recognition requirements means that an acquirer may, in recognising separately the acquiree's intangible assets, recognise intangible assets that the acquiree has not recognised in its records, such as in-process research and development that cannot be recognised under IAS 38 as internally generated assets (discussed later in this section). It can be seen that entities that acquire intangible assets in a business combination will be able to, and in fact are required to, recognise intangible assets that are not separately recognisable when acquired by other means.

Paragraph 24 of IAS 38 requires that intangible assets be initially measured at cost. In a business combination, the costs of the individual assets acquired are measured by reference to the fair values of those assets. Paragraphs 39–41 discuss the measurement of these fair values. Various measures of these fair values are possible:

- *Quoted market prices in an active market.* An active market is defined in paragraph 8 as one which has all the following conditions:
  (a) the items traded within the market are homogeneous
  (b) willing buyers and sellers can normally be found at any time
  (c) prices are available to the public.
  Where there is an active market, the fair value is determined by reference to quoted market prices. It is expected that active markets will be rare for intangible assets.
- *Recent transactions.* Where there is no active market, reference must be made to other sources of information, such as recent transactions in the same or similar items. One of the problems with intangible assets is that their unique nature in many cases precludes the use of information from other transactions.
- *Measurement techniques.* With the increasing importance of intangible assets, there has been a growing establishment of entities who specialise in measuring intangible assets, particularly brand names. These valuation firms measure the worth of intangible assets by using variations of present value techniques, and multiples of variables such as royalty rates. As noted in paragraph 41 of IAS 38, these methods should 'reflect current transactions and practices in the industry'.

Figure 11.5 contains a list of the brands recognised by Christian Dior in its 2004 balance sheet. According to note 2.3 in the 2004 annual report, 'Only the acquired brands that are well known and individually identifiable are recorded as assets, using their value at the time of purchase. This value is not amortized.' The procedures used for those valuations are detailed in figure 11.5. Note that the following valuation methods are used: the royalties method, the margin differential method, the replacement cost method and the comparison method.

FIGURE 11.5 Brands and their valuation

NOTE 3 — BRANDS AND OTHER INTANGIBLE ASSETS

(millions of euros)		2004		2003	2002
	Gross value	Depreciation Amortization	Net value	Net value	Net value
Brands (*)	8 495	(108)	8 387	8 460	8 771
Leasehold acquisition rights	228	(95)	133	139	137
Other	307	(203)	104	106	98
Total	9 030	(406)	8 624	8 705	9 006

(*) Brands break down as follows:

(millions of euros)			2004		2003	2002
	Currency	Gross value	Depreciation Amortization	Net value	Net value	Net value
Louis Vuitton		2 058	–	2 058	2 058	2 058
Henessy		1 067	–	1 067	1 067	1 067
Fendi		807	–	807	807	807
Moët		732	–	732	732	732
Parfums Christian Dior		610	–	610	610	610
Guerlain		441	–	441	441	441
Céline		351	(70)	281	281	281
Veuve Clicquot		244	–	244	244	244
Parfums Givenchy		152	–	152	152	152
Loewe		122	–	122	122	122
Château d'Yquem		108	–	108	108	108
Krug		100	–	100	100	100
Other (<EUR 100m)		315	(29)	286	318	326
Total brands in euros		7 107	(99)	7 008	7 040	7 048
Tag Heuer	CHF	804		804	796	854
Donna Karan New York	USD	380		380	410	494
Ebel	CHF	–		–	–	125
Other (<EUR 100m)		204	(9)	195	214	250
Total brands in foreign currencies		1 388	(9)	1 379	1 420	1 723
TOTAL		8 495	(108)	8 387	8 460	8 771

- The leasehold rights primarily represent the stores under the Louis Vuitton brand and the Sephora banner.
- The acquired brands not detailed in the 'other' item above are primarily:
  - Wines and Spirits: Newton Vineyards, MountAdam;
  - Fashion and Leather Goods: Givenchy, Kenzo, Christian Lacroix, Berluti, Thomas Pink, and Pucci;
  - Perfumes and Cosmetics: Parfums Kenzo, Make Up for Ever, BeneFit Cosmetics and Fresh;
  - Watches and Jewelry: Zenith, Fred, Chaumet and Omas;
  - Other activities: La Tribune and Investir newspapers.

The brands are primarily valued by the cash flow method, i.e. based on the provisional cash flows generated by the brands. Other methods are used as a complement: the royalties method, which gives the brand a value equal to the capitalization of the royalties which must be paid to use it; the margin differential method, which applies only to cases where it is possible to measure the revenue generated by a brand compared to an unbranded product; the replacement cost method for an equivalent brand, especially in terms of advertising expenses; finally, the comparison method, which uses multiples of net sales and income from recent transactions involving similar brands or multiple markets applicable to the activities concerned.

(*continued*)

The provisional data used in the cash flow methods come from the budgets and plans established by the management of the company that uses the brand. The provisional cash flows are discounted and, when several scenarios are used, a probability of the occurrence is allocated to each one of them. The discount rate used integrates the rate of return expected by an investor in the business field in question and the risk premium appropriate to that business.

At the end of 2004, these calculations were made on the basis of the following parameters:
– The growth rate to infinity used in determining provisional cash flows was most often 2%; the brand positioning in its market, its maturity or growth potential in some cases justified a percentage half a point higher or lower.
– The discount rates used, differentiated on the basis of the business and the risk specific to the brand, were as follows:

Wines and Spirits	6.5% to 7.0%
Other luxury brands	8.0% to 8.5%
Selective retailing	7.0%

• The change in the value of the brands on the balance sheet over the year breaks down as follows:

(millions of euros)	Gross value	Depreciation Amortization	Net value
Balance at December 31, 2003	8 681	(221)	8 460
Impact of changes in consolidation	(155)	131	(24)
Changes in depreciation and amortization	–	(19)	(19)
Impact of currency fluctuations	(31)	1	(30)
Balance at December 31, 2004	8 495	(108)	8 387

The impact of changes in consolidation on gross value, and amortization and depreciation, includes 116 million euros from the sale of the Ebel group (see Note 1 – Changes in consolidation).

Source: Dior (2005a, pp. 81–2).

11.3.5   Acquisition by way of a government grant

According to paragraph 44 of IAS 38, some intangible assets, such as licences to operate radio or television stations, are allocated to entities via government grants. These intangibles are accounted for in accordance with IAS 20 *Accounting for Government Grants and Disclosure of Government Assistance*, with an entity initially recognising both the intangible asset and the grant at fair value.

11.3.6   Exchanges of intangible assets

One of the problems with exchanges of intangible assets is the reliable measure of the cost of the acquired asset, particularly where comparable market transactions are infrequent. The following measures will need to be considered in determining that cost:
• the fair value of the asset given up
• the fair value of the asset received, if this is more clearly evident than the fair value of the asset given up
• the carrying amount of the asset given up, when neither of the fair values can be measured reliably.

11.3.7   Internally generated goodwill

Paragraph 48 of IAS 38 states categorically that internally generated goodwill is not recognised as an asset. Hence, goodwill can be recognised only when it is acquired as part of a business combination and measured in accordance with IFRS 3 *Business Combinations.*

The reason given in paragraph 49 of IAS 38 for non-recognition is that goodwill is not identifiable; that is, it is not separable, nor does it arise from contractual or other legal rights. This argument seems strange because identifiability is the test for recognising an intangible asset separately from goodwill, rather than recognising goodwill itself. A second reason given for non-recognition, as stated in paragraph 49, is that the cost of internally generated goodwill cannot be reliably determined. The fair value of goodwill could be determined by comparing the fair value of the entity as a whole and subtracting the sum of the fair values of the identifiable net assets of the entity. However, under IAS 38, the principle for recognition is that identifiable intangible assets as well as goodwill must initially be measured at cost, not at fair value. As is discussed in more detail in the next section, this principle makes the recognition of internally generated intangibles harder than the recognition of acquired intangibles.

LO 6

11.3.8   Internally generated intangible assets

Accounting for internally generated assets requires the application of a number of extra rules, potentially leaving the IASB open to criticism for lack of consistency in the accounting for acquired intangibles versus internally generated intangibles. As Jenkins and Upton (2001, p. 6) noted, genealogy is not an essential characteristic of an asset. Therefore, the accounting should not automatically be different according to whether an asset arises from a business combination or is internally generated.

The problem from an accounting point of view with internally generated intangibles is determining at what point of time an asset should be recognised. An entity may outlay funds in an exploratory project; for example, developing software to overcome a specific problem, or designing a tool for a special purpose. There is no guarantee of success at the commencement of the project. The program may not work or the tool may be unsatisfactory for the purpose. Should the accountant capitalise the costs from the commencement of the project, or wait until there is some indication of success? A further problem with some intangible assets such as brand names is whether the costs outlaid relate solely to increasing the worth of the brand name or simply enhancing the overall reputation of the entity.

The IASB's solution to the problem of when to commence capitalising costs is to classify the generation of the asset into two phases: the research phase, and the development phase. These terms are defined in paragraph 8 of IAS 38 as follows:

> *Research* is original and planned investigation undertaken with the prospect of gaining new scientific or technical knowledge and understanding.

> *Development* is the application of research findings or other knowledge to a plan or design for the production of new or substantially improved materials, devices, products, processes, systems or services before the start of commercial production or use.

It can be seen from these definitions that the earlier stages of a project are defined as research and, at some point in time, the project moves from a research phase to a development phase. Examples of research activities are given in paragraph 56 of IAS 38, such as the search for new knowledge or for alternatives for materials, devices, products, processes, systems or services. Examples of development activities are found in paragraph 59, such as the design, construction and operation of a non-commercial pilot plant, and the design of pre-production prototypes and models. From an accounting perspective, expenditure on research is expensed when incurred (paragraph 54), while expenditure on development is capitalised as an intangible asset. It is obviously important to be able to distinguish one phase from the other.

Paragraph 57 of IAS 38 is the key paragraph in this regard. It contains a list of criteria, all of which must be met in order for a development outlay to be capitalised. In order to capitalise development outlays, an entity must be able to demonstrate all of the following:

(a) the technical feasibility of completing the intangible asset so that it will be available for use or sale.

(b) its intention to complete the intangible asset and use or sell it.

(c) its ability to use or sell the intangible asset.

(d) how the intangible asset will generate probable future economic benefits. Among other things, the entity can demonstrate the existence of a market for the output of the intangible asset or the intangible asset itself or, if it is to be used internally, the usefulness of the intangible asset.

(e) the availability of adequate technical, financial and other resources to complete the development and to use or sell the intangible asset.

(f) its ability to measure reliably the expenditure attributable to the intangible asset during its development.

Given the degree of difficulty in distinguishing research activities from development activities, it would seem simpler for the IASB to disregard any attempt to distinguish between the two activities and simply allow capitalisation when the criteria in paragraph 57 are met. In other words, for an entity to decide whether or not to capitalise an outlay, the decision is not going to be based on an application of the definitions of research and development, but rather on whether the criteria in paragraph 57 are met. If the criteria are met, it will then be decided that the project is in the development stage. The definitions of research and development are then superfluous. The recognition criteria for an internally generated intangible asset are then those contained in paragraphs 18, 21 and 57 of IAS 38.

The criteria in paragraph 57 are designed to assist in determining whether, in relation to a project, it is probable that there will be future benefits flowing to the entity. If there are markets for the output, the project is feasible; and the resources are available to complete the project, then it becomes probable that there will be future cash inflows. The criteria in paragraph 57 are then an elaboration − the provision of more detailed requirements − on the criteria in paragraph 18. This approach in IAS 38 provides more certainty in obtaining comparable accounting across entities than simply relying on an accounting principle that states that, if there are probable expected future benefits, an entity should capitalise the outlay.

If the paragraph 57 criteria are all met, IAS 38 requires the intangible asset to be measured at cost. This cost is not, however, the total cost relating to the project. The amount to be capitalised is the 'sum of expenditure incurred from the date when the intangible asset first meets the recognition criteria in paragraphs 21, 22 and 57' (para. 65). Paragraph 71 explicitly prohibits the reinstatement of amounts previously expensed. Recognition of an asset that is not yet available for use requires an entity to subject that asset to an annual impairment test as per IAS 36 *Impairment of Assets*. Paragraphs 66–7 of IAS 38 note that the cost comprises all directly attributable costs necessary to create, produce and prepare the asset to be capable of operating in a manner intended by management, and provide examples of such costs as well as items that are not components of the cost.

In his discussion of this issue, Lev argued that the immediate expensing of all outlays distorted current and future earnings. He stated (2001, p. 124):

> Given the heightened uncertainty, it makes sense to recognize intangible investments when the uncertainty about benefits is considerably resolved.

His solution to the problem was to have a recognition principle based on the achievement of technological feasibility. He argued (p. 125):

> A major advantage of the proposed asset recognition is its allowance of managers to convey important information about the progress and success of the development program. Indiscriminate capitalization of all expenditures on intangibles does not provide such information.

It can be seen that the criteria in IAS 38 are in line with Lev's views, although the feasibility expressed in the standard require both technological and economic feasibility.

Upton (2001, p. 66) viewed the identification of such a recognition principle as 'interesting', but was still concerned that entities could manipulate the criteria to suit their ends:

> Might some managers conjure assets from thin air in an attempt to pump up the balance sheet? Might others turn a blind eye to discovered assets in an attempt to pump up future operating results (by avoiding amortization)? Both possibilities are real, and either could damage the credibility of financial reporting.

Jenkins and Upton (2001, p. 8) noted, first, that the conceptual framework does not require certainty of future benefits prior to the recognition of an asset and, second, that there is evidence that companies are willing to pay for in-process research and development even though the ultimate result may be uncertain. Upton's suggestion (2001, p. 66) for resolving the problem was to couple the criterion of technological feasibility with a requirement for retrospective capitalisation or value-based measurement. In either case, management would be required to establish the asset, rather than having no asset because all outlays were expensed, and subsequent periods would bear their share of the amortisation of the asset as well as recognition of the benefits.

It may seem that the use of the terms 'research' and 'development', which may be associated with such assets as patents and software development, are not applicable to all internally generated intangibles, such as brand names. However, it needs to be remembered that all intangible assets must meet the identifiability criterion, one part of which is separability, which is the capability of being separated and sold or transferred. In relation to certain assets, paragraph 63 of IAS 38 provides a major exclusion in an entity's ability to capitalise internally generated intangibles: 'Internally generated brands, mastheads, publishing titles, customer lists and items similar in substance shall not be recognised as intangible assets'.

The IASB has concluded that, even though the criteria in paragraph 57 (a) to (f) are met, the listed items in paragraph 63 cannot be recognised. As paragraph 64 states, the IASB does not believe that the costs associated with developing the listed assets can be distinguished from the cost of developing the business as a whole. For example, it may be argued that funds spent on developing a brand name also enhance the overall image of the entity, and therefore the outlays cannot be solely attributable to the brand name.

The non-recognition of internally generated intangibles in the publishing industry may cause major problems. In a 2002 Deloitte & Touche publication, Samantha Harrison provided the data in figure 11.6 to show the importance of intangibles within the publishing industry in the United Kingdom, and examples of the market in publishing assets.

Examples of intangibles as a percentage of net worth

	NBV publishing rights/newspaper titles as a % of net assets
Reed Elsevier	115%
Trinity Mirror plc	133%
Daily Mail and General Trust plc	58%
Johnston Press plc	167%
Emap plc	126%
Highbury House Communications plc	88%

Examples of publishing acquisitions in 2000/2001

Acquirer	Acquiree	Date	Fair value of titles acquired	Total purchase price
Scottish Radio Holdings plc	(i) Kilkenny People Holdings (ii) Ireland on Sunday Ltd	23 June 2000 19 July 2000	£20.4m £6.5m	£24.3m £6.2m
Trinity Mirror plc	Southnews plc	28 November 2000	£345.7m	£293.0m
Reed Elsevier	Harcourt General Inc.	12 July 2001	£1658.0m	£3084.0m

FIGURE 11.6 Intangibles in the publishing industry
Source: Harrison (2002).

The criteria in paragraph 57 of IAS 38 are demonstrated in illustrative example 11.1.

ILLUSTRATIVE EXAMPLE 11.1

Applying the criteria in paragraph 57 of IAS 38

Pretoria Ltd is a highly successful engineering company that manufactures filters for air-conditioning systems. Due to its dissatisfaction with the quality of the filters currently available, on 1 January 2006 it commenced a project to design a more efficient filter. The following notes record the events relating to that project.

2006
January   Spent $145 000 on the salaries of company engineers and consultants who conducted basic tests on available filters with varying modifications.
February   Spent $165 000 on developing a new filter system, including the production of a basic model. It became obvious that the model in its current form was not successful due to the material in the filter not being as effective as required.
March   Acquired the fibres division of Durban Ltd for $330 000. The fair values of the tangible assets of this division were:

Property, plant and equipment	$180 000
Inventories	60 000

This business was acquired because one of the products it produced was a fibrous compound, sold under the brand name Springbok, that Pretoria Ltd considered would be excellent for including in the filtration process.

By buying the fibres division, Pretoria Ltd acquired the patent for this fibrous compound. Pretoria Ltd valued the patent at $50 000 and the brand name at $40 000, using a number of valuation techniques. The patent had a further 10-year life but was renewable on application. Further costs of $54 000 were incurred on the new filter system during March.

April   Spent a further $135 000 on revising the filtration process to incorporate the fibrous compound. By the end of April, Pretoria Ltd was convinced that it now had a viable product because preliminary tests showed that the filtration process was significantly better than any other available on the market.

May   Developed a prototype of the filtration component and proceeded to test it within a variety of models of air-conditioners. The company preferred to sell the filtration process to current manufacturers of air-conditioners if the process worked with currently available models. If this proved not possible, the company would then consider developing its own brand of air-conditioners using the new filtration system. By the end of May, the filtration system had proved successful on all but one of the currently available commercial models. Costs incurred were $65 000.

June   Various air-conditioner manufacturers were invited to demonstrations of the filtration system. Costs incurred were $25 000, including $12 000 for food and beverages for the prospective clients. The feedback from a number of the companies was that they were prepared to enter negotiations for acquiring the filters from Pretoria Ltd. The company now believed it had a successful model and commenced planning the production of the filters. Ongoing costs of $45 000 to refine the filtration system, particularly in the light of comments by the manufacturers, were incurred in the latter part of June.

Required

Explain the accounting for the various outlays incurred by Pretoria Ltd.

Solution

The main problem in accounting for the costs is determining at what point of time costs can be capitalised. This is resolved by applying the criteria in paragraph 57 of IAS 38:

- *Technical feasibility.* At the end of April, the company believed that the filtration process was technically feasible.
- *Intention to complete and sell.* At the end of April, the company was not yet sure that the system was adaptable to currently available models of air-conditioners. If this was not so, it would have to test whether development of its own brand of air-conditioners would be a commercial proposition. Hence, it was not until the end of May that the company was convinced it could complete the project and had a product that it could sell.
- *Ability to use or sell.* By the end of May, the company had a product that it believed it had the ability to sell. Being a filter manufacturer, it knew the current costs of competing products and so could make an informed decision about the potential for the commercial sale of its own filter.
- *Existence of a market.* The market comprised the air-conditioning manufacturers. By selling to the manufacturers, the company had the potential to generate probable future cash flows. This criterion was met by the end of May.

→

- *Availability of resources.* From the beginning of the project, the company was not short of resources, being a highly successful company in its own right.
- *Ability to measure costs reliably.* Costs are readily attributable to the project throughout its development.

On the basis of the above analysis, the criteria in paragraph 57 of IAS 38 were all met at the end of May. Therefore, costs incurred before this point are expensed, and those incurred after this point are capitalised. Hence, the following costs would be written off as incurred:

January	$145 000
February	165 000
March	54 000
April	135 000
May	65 000

In acquiring the fibres division from Durban Ltd, Pretoria Ltd would pass the following entry:

Property, plant and equipment	Dr	180 000	
Inventories	Dr	60 000	
Brand	Dr	40 000	
Patent	Dr	50 000	
Cash	Cr		330 000
(Acquisition of assets)			

The patent would initially be depreciated over a 10-year useful life. However, this would need to be reassessed upon application of the fibrous compound to the air-conditioning filtration system. This alternative use may extend the expected useful life of the product, and hence of the patent. The brand name would be depreciated over the same useful life of the patent, because it is expected that the brand has no real value unless backed by the patent.

The company would then capitalise development costs of $45 000 in June.

The marketing costs incurred in June of $25 000 would be expensed because they are not part of the development process.

LO 7

11.3.9 Explaining the non-recognition of internally generated assets

There are a number of problems associated with the IASB's treatment of internally generated assets versus that required for acquired intangibles. In particular, there are inconsistencies in the accounting for internally generated intangibles and intangibles acquired in a business combination. Note in this regard:

- *The initial recognition of intangible assets.* IAS 38 requires intangible assets to be initially recognised at cost. However, for assets acquired in a business combination, an intangible asset can be recognised at fair value. Internally generated intangibles cannot be recognised, even if the fair value can be reliably measured. For example, outlays on research cannot be recognised as an asset. However, if an entity acquires another entity that has in-process research, an intangible asset can be recognised if the fair value can be measured reliably. Further, the research so recognised can be revalued if this class of asset is measured at fair value.

- *The measurement of fair value.* One of the reasons given in paragraph BCZ38(c) of the Basis for Conclusions on IAS 38 for disallowing the recognition of intangible assets is the impossibility of determining the fair value of an intangible asset reliably if no active market exists for the asset, and active markets are unlikely to exist for internally generated intangible assets. However, for intangible assets recognised in a business combination, it is assumed that fair value can be measured (hopefully reliably) without the existence of active markets. IAS 38 allows the use of other measurement techniques or even what an entity would have paid based on the best information available. Hence, in a business combination, the fair values of intangibles can be measured reliably using measures determined outside an active market, but these same measures cannot be used to measure the fair values of internally generated assets for asset recognition purposes. As a protection, the requirements of IAS 36 *Impairment of Assets* can be applied to both acquired and internally generated intangible assets.
- *Brands, mastheads, publishing titles and customer lists.* Paragraph 63 of IAS 38 prohibits the recognition of internally generated brands and items similar in substance. However, such assets can be recognised when acquired in a business combination (as well as if acquired as a separate asset). As far as the measurement of the fair value of these assets, the argument presented in the point above applies – if the fair value of a brand can be determined in a business combination then it can be determined if internally generated. Further, it has been noted previously that the reason given in paragraph 64 of IAS 38 for non-recognition of internally generated brands is that the cost of these items 'cannot be distinguished from the cost of developing the business as a whole'. If this argument is true for internally generated brands, then surely it is equally true for acquired brands. How is it possible in a business combination to distinguish acquired brands from acquired goodwill? How can the cost of acquiring a brand in a business combination be distinguished from acquiring a business as a whole?

Lev (2001, pp. 85–91) believed that the non-capitalisation of internally generated intangibles is a question of politics, stating:

> The main reason for the intangibles' information failure lies, in my opinion, in the complex web of motives of the major players in the information arena: managers, auditors, and well-connected financial analysts.

He argued that:

- *managers prefer to inflate future profits.* Where major investments in research and development are written off, this is a guarantee that future revenues and earnings derived from these acquisitions will be reported unencumbered by the major expense item, the amortisation of the intangible asset. The effects on ratios such as rates of return on assets and equity are better in the future if write-offs occur now rather than periodic amortisations later.
- *investors generally consider write-offs as one-time items, of no consequence for valuation.* A number of large hits is considered better than periodic amortisation. Investors discount the effect of one-time write-offs and cheer the improved profitability of subsequent years.
- *immediate expensing obviates the need to provide explanations in case of failure.* Writing off assets denotes failure, and managers prefer to avoid questions and lawsuits. Further, failure always attracts more attention than success.

Upton (2001, pp. 80–3) raised further arguments to support the non-recognition of intangible assets:

- *cost and benefit.* Accounting rules involve entities in incurring costs, such as those for running analytical models, measuring fair values, and paying auditors to review the measures.

- *lack of relevance of capitalised numbers.* Is there a sufficient nexus between the capitalised costs and the expected future benefits? For knowledge-based assets, the measurement of the benefits may be impossible.
- *volatility.* Recognising intangible assets in the balance sheet produces a subtle source of volatility in, or at least reduced control over, reported income. If intangible assets are recognised and amortised, the amortisation continues without regard to current activity.

11.3.10   Recognition of an expense

Paragraphs 68–71 of IAS 38 cover the issue of when expenditure on an intangible asset should be expensed. However, if the prior rules in IAS 38 are followed, then the appropriate outlays are expensed when the criteria are not met. These paragraphs add nothing particularly new to the accounting for intangible assets.

Paragraph 71, however, has major import. This paragraph prohibits the recognition at a later date of past expenditure as assets. In other words, if amounts relating to research have been expensed, these amounts cannot then be capitalised, nor can appropriate adjustments to equity be made, when an intangible asset is created at the development stage. As noted earlier, Upton suggested a possible role for the retroactive capitalisation of expenses, because it forced entities to recognise and subsequently amortise their assets. Upton (2001, p. 64) also noted that retroactive capitalisation did not offer a solution to the non-capitalisation of assets such as brands, as these assets lack a series of discrete expenditures. It may be that acceptance of fair value as well as historical cost measures is necessary to solve some of these issues.

LO 8   11.4   Measurement subsequent to initial recognition

11.4.1   Measurement basis

Consistent with IAS 16, after the initial recognition of an intangible asset at cost, an entity must choose for each class of intangible asset whether to measure the assets using the *cost model* or the *revaluation model* – see paragraph 72 of IAS 38. (These models are discussed in greater detail in chapter 10 of this book.)

Cost model

Under the cost model, the asset is recorded at the initial cost of acquisition and is then subject to amortisation (see section 11.4.2 of this chapter) and impairment testing (see chapter 13 of this book).

Revaluation model

Under the revaluation model, the asset is carried at fair value, and is subject to amortisation and impairment charges. As with property, plant and equipment, if this model is chosen, revaluations are made with sufficient regularity so that the carrying amount of the asset does not materially differ from the current fair value at balance date.

One specification that applies to intangible assets but is not required for property, plant and equipment is how the fair value is to be measured. Under paragraph 75 of IAS 38, the fair value must be determined by reference to an active market. An active market is defined in paragraph 8 of IAS 38 as a market where items traded are homogeneous, where willing buyers and sellers can normally be found at any time, and where prices are available to the public. This means that an intangible asset acquired in a business combination, and measured at fair value using some measurement technique, cannot subsequently use that same measurement technique if it adopts the revaluation model. In the absence of an active market, the intangible asset would be kept at the fair value determined at the date of the business combination and accounted for by the cost basis. As paragraph 76 notes, the choice of revaluation model does not allow the recognition of intangible assets that cannot be recognised initially at cost. However, paragraph 77 allows an asset for which only part of the cost was recognised to be fully revalued to fair value.

Paragraph 78 of IAS 38 states that intangibles such as brands, newspaper mastheads, patents and trademarks cannot be measured at fair value, as there is no active market for these assets because they are unique. As with the recognition of these types of intangible assets, the IASB has stated specifically that they can be measured only at cost.

Selection of the revaluation model requires all assets in the one class to be measured at fair value. Because of the insistence on using active markets for the measurement of fair value, the IASB recognises that there will be cases where fair values cannot be determined for all assets within one class. Hence, under paragraph 81 of IAS 38, where there is no active market for an asset, the asset can be measured at cost even if the class is measured using the revaluation model. Further, if the ability to measure the asset at fair value disappears because the market for the asset no longer meets the criteria to be classified as active, the asset is carried at the latest revalued amount and effectively accounted for under the cost model. If the market again becomes active, the revaluation model can be resumed.

Accounting for intangible assets measured using the revaluation model is exactly the same as for property, plant and equipment (see chapter 10 of this book). Where there is a revaluation increment, the asset is increased and the increase is credited directly to a revaluation surplus. However, if the revaluation increment reverses a previous revaluation decrement relating to the same asset, the revaluation increase is recognised as income (IAS 38, para. 85). Any accumulated amortisation would be eliminated at the time of revaluation.

Where there is a revaluation decrement, the decrease is recognised as an expense unless there has been a previous revaluation increment. In the latter case, the adjustment must first be made against any existing revaluation surplus before recognising an expense (IAS 38, para. 86). Any accumulated amortisation would be eliminated at the time of the revaluation.

As with a revaluation surplus on property, plant and equipment, paragraph 87 of IAS 38 states that the revaluation surplus may be transferred to retained earnings when the surplus is realised on the retirement or disposal of the asset. Alternatively, the revaluation surplus may progressively be taken to retained earnings in proportion to the amortisation of the asset.

11.4.2   Subsequent expenditures

Paragraph 20 of IAS 38 discusses subsequent expenditures in general. It is argued in this paragraph that the unique nature of intangibles means that subsequent expenditures should be expensed rather than capitalised. Subsequent expenditures maintain expected benefits rather than increase them. Further, with many subsequent expenditures, it may be difficult to attribute them to specific intangible assets rather than to the entity as a whole. Paragraph 20 notes that with the paragraph 63 intangibles, whether acquired or internally generated, subsequent expenditures are always expensed.

Paragraph 42 provides specific guidance on subsequent expenditures relating to acquired in-process research and development projects. Effectively, the same criteria for initially recognising an asset and expensing are applied to account for subsequent expenditures. The results of this application are to:
• expense research outlays
• expense development outlays not meeting the criteria in paragraph 57
• add to the acquired in-process research or development project if the development expenditure satisfies the paragraph 57 criteria.

11.4.3 ## Amortisation of intangible assets
Useful life

A key determinant in the amortisation process for intangible assets is whether the useful life is finite or indefinite. If finite, then the asset has to be amortised over that life. If the asset has an indefinite life, then there is no annual amortisation charge. Paragraph 88 of IAS 38 states:

> An entity shall assess whether the useful life of an intangible asset is finite or indefinite and, if finite, the length of, or number of production or similar units constituting, that useful life. An intangible asset shall be regarded by the entity as having an indefinite useful life when, based on an analysis of all the relevant factors, there is no foreseeable limit to the period over which the asset is expected to generate net cash inflows for the entity.

The term 'indefinite' does not mean that the asset has an infinite life; that is, that it is going to last forever. As paragraph 91 notes, an indefinite life means that, with the proper maintenance, there is no foreseeable end to the life of the asset. Paragraph 90 provides a list of factors that should be considered in determining the useful life of the asset:

(a) the expected usage of the asset by the entity and whether the asset could be managed efficiently by another management team
(b) typical product life cycles for the asset, and public information on estimates of useful lives of similar assets that are used in a similar way
(c) technical, technological, commercial or other types of obsolescence
(d) the stability of the industry, and changes in market demand
(e) expected actions by competitors
(f) the level of maintenance expenditure required and the entity's ability and intent to reach such a level
(g) the period of control over the asset and legal or similar limits on the use of the asset
(h) whether the useful life of the asset is dependent on the useful lives of other assets of the entity.

Paragraph 94 of IAS 38 notes that, as a general rule, assets whose lives are dependent on contractual or legal lives will be amortised over those lives or shorter periods in some cases. If renewal is possible, then the useful life applied can include the renewal period providing there is evidence to support renewal by the entity without significant cost. Figure 11.7 (below and opposite) contains two examples from those in the illustrative examples accompanying IAS 38 in relation to the assessment of useful lives.

Example 4 An acquired broadcasting licence that expires in five years
The broadcasting licence is renewable every 10 years if the entity provides at least an average level of service to its customers and complies with the relevant legislative requirements. The licence may be renewed indefinitely at little cost and has been renewed twice before the most recent acquisition. The acquiring entity intends to renew the licence indefinitely and evidence supports its ability to do so. Historically, there has been no compelling challenge to the licence renewal. The technology used in broadcasting is not expected to be replaced by another technology at any time in the foreseeable future. Therefore, the licence is expected to contribute to the entity's net cash inflows indefinitely.

The broadcasting licence would be treated as having an indefinite useful life because it is expected to contribute to the entity's net cash inflows indefinitely. Therefore, the licence would not be amortised until its useful life is determined to be finite. The licence would be tested for impairment under IAS 36 annually and whenever there is an indication that it may be impaired.

Example 7 An acquired trademark used to identify and distinguish a leading consumer product that has been a market-share leader for the past eight years
The trademark has a remaining legal life of five years but is renewable every 10 years at little cost. The acquiring entity intends to renew the trademark continuously and evidence supports its ability to do so. An analysis of (1) product life cycles, (2) market, competitive and environmental trends, and (3) brand extension opportunities provides evidence that the trademarked product will generate net cash inflows for the acquiring entity for an indefinite period.

The trademark would be treated as having an indefinite useful life because it is expected to contribute to net cash inflows indefinitely. Therefore, the trademark would not be amortised until its useful life is determined to be finite. It would be tested for impairment under IAS 36 annually and whenever there is an indication that it may be impaired.

FIGURE 11.7 Examples of indefinite lives for intangible assets
Source: Illustrative examples, IAS 38.

Rather than considering the existence of an indefinite life for intangible assets, the IASB could have set a maximum useful life such as 40 years. However, as noted in paragraph BC63 of the Basis for Conclusions on IAS 38, the IASB considers that writing standards in such a fashion would not accord with the principle that the accounting numbers should be representationally faithful. The principles in IAS 38 provide management with more discretion but allow for the provision of more relevant information. In order for an intangible asset (such as a trademark) to have an indefinite life, an entity is required to outlay funds on an annual basis to maintain the trademark. Consider in this regard the annual expenditure by softdrink companies to maintain the value of their trademarks. The annual profit figure is then affected by these outlays. To require amortisation charges to be levied as well, when the asset is being maintained, would be to affect the income statement twice.

Intangible assets with finite useful lives

Paragraph 97 of IAS 38 states the principles relating to the amortisation period and choice of amortisation method. In general, the principles of amortisation are the same as those for depreciating property, plant and equipment under IAS 16. In both cases, the process involves the allocation of the depreciable amount on a systematic basis over the useful life, with the method chosen reflecting the pattern in which the expected benefits are expected to be consumed by the entity. Paragraph 98 notes that an amortisation method will rarely result in an amortisation charge that is lower than that if a straight-line method had been used. Further, in accordance with paragraph 104, the amortisation period and amortisation method should be reviewed at least at the end of each annual reporting period, which is the same for property, plant and equipment.

However, IAS 38 contains a number of rules that are specific to intangible assets, presumably because of the relative uncertainty associated with these assets:

- Where the pattern of benefits cannot be determined reliably, the straight-line method shall be used (para. 97). This is presumably to bring some consistency and comparability into the calculations.
- The residual value shall be assumed to be zero unless:
  - there is a commitment by a third party to purchase the asset at the end of its useful life; or
  - there is an active market for the asset, and
    (a) residual value can be determined by reference to that market; and
    (b) it is probable that such a market will exist at the end of the asset's useful life (para. 100).

Any changes in residual value, amortisation method or useful life are changes in accounting estimates, and accounted for prospectively with an effect on the current and future amortisation charges.

Intangible assets with indefinite useful lives

As noted earlier, where an intangible asset has an indefinite useful life, there is no amortisation charge (IAS 38, para. 107). As with finite useful lives, the useful life of an intangible that is not being amortised must be reviewed each period (para. 109). Any change from indefinite to finite useful life for an asset is treated as a change in estimate, and affects the amortisation charge in current and future periods. Intangible assets with indefinite useful lives are subject to annual impairment tests (see chapter 13 of this book).

An example of an amortisation policy adopted by a company applying IFRSs is shown in figure 11.8. It contains the note disclosure in relation to the amortisation of brands and trade names provided by Christian Dior in its 2004 annual report.

2.2.2 Amortization of brands and trade names

Under French standards, brands are not amortized.

Under IFRS, pursuant to IAS 38, intangible assets with a specified life are amortized over their useful life, according to the straight-line method. Assets of indefinite life are not amortized but are subject to an annual impairment test.

The classification of a brand or trade name as an asset of indefinite life results from the following indicators in particular:
- the global positioning of the brand or trade name on its market in terms of volume of activity, international presence, and reputation;
- prospects for long-term profitability;
- the degree of exposure to circumstantial risks;
- a major event occurring in the activity sector that might affect the future of the brand or trade name;
- the age of the brand or trade name.

The amortization expense and any depreciation expense are included in operating income.

Upon first application of IFRS, amortization is calculated retroactively from the date of acquisition.

Until January 1, 2004, brands and trade names considered as amortizable under IFRS are principally the Fashion and Leather Goods brands (apart from Louis Vuitton), and Perfumes start-ups. As of January 1, 2004, the brands below continue to be amortized. The amortization periods in years are as follows:

Newton	30	Thomas Pink	20
Mountadam	30	Kenzo[1]	40
Fresh	15	Stefano Bi	40
Make Up for Ever	15	Omas	20
L'Eléphant	15	Samaritaine	20

(1) including Perfumes

FIGURE 11.8   Amortisation of intangibles
Source: Dior (2005b, pp. 9–10).

LO 10

11.5 Retirements and disposals

Accounting for the retirements and disposals of intangible assets is identical to that for property, plant and equipment under IAS 16. In particular, under IAS 38:

- intangible assets shall be derecognised on disposal or when there are no expected future benefits from the asset (para. 112)
- gains or losses on disposal are calculated as the difference between the proceeds on disposal and the carrying amount at point of sale, with amortisation calculated up to the point of sale (para. 113)
- amortisation of an intangible with a finite useful life does not cease when the asset becomes temporarily idle or is retired from active use (para. 117).

LO 11

11.6 Disclosure

Paragraph 118 of IAS 38 requires disclosures for each class of intangibles, and for internally generated intangibles to be distinguished from other intangibles. Examples of separate classes are given in paragraph 119:

- brand names
- mastheads and publishing titles
- computer software
- licences and franchises
- copyrights, patents and other industrial property rights, service and operating rights
- recipes, formulas, models, designs and prototypes
- intangible assets under development.

Disclosures required by paragraph 118 (a) and (b) would be contained in note 1 to the financial statements, as illustrated in figure 11.9. Disclosures required by paragraphs 118 and 122 of IAS 38 are illustrated in figure 11.10.

Other disclosures required, where relevant, by paragraph 118 of IAS 38 are:

- the line item in the income statement in which any amortisation of intangible assets is included (118(d))
- increases or decreases during the period resulting from revaluations under paragraphs 75, 85 and 86 and from impairment losses recognised or reversed directly in equity (118(e)(iii))
- impairment losses reversed in profit or loss during the period (118(e)(v)).

FIGURE 11.9 Illustrative disclosures required by paragraph 118(a) and (b) of IAS 38

Note 1: Summary of significant accounting policies (extract)	IAS 38
Intangible assets Intangible assets are initially recognised at cost. Intangible assets that have indefinite useful lives are tested for impairment on an annual basis. Intangible assets that have finite useful lives are amortised over those lives on a straight-line basis.	*Para. 118* *(b)*
Patents and copyrights These have all been acquired by the company. Costs relating to these assets are capitalised and amortised on a straight-line basis over the following periods: Patent – packaging 5 years Patent – tools 10 years Copyright 10 years	 *(b)*

(continued)

Licence The licence relating to television broadcasting rights is determined to be indefinite.	*(a)*
Research and development Research costs are expensed as incurred. Development costs are expensed except for those for which it is probable that they will generate future economic benefits, this being determined by an analysis of factors such as technical feasibility and the existence of markets. Such costs are currently being amortised on a straight-line basis over the following periods: Tool design project 5 years Water cooling project 10 years	*(a)* *(b)*

FIGURE 11.10   Illustrative disclosures required by paragraphs 118 and 122 of IAS 38

Note 11. Intangible assets	IAS 38
Details about the company's intangible assets are provided below. All intangibles are considered to have finite useful lives except for a patent held for a tool used in the manufacture of steel windmills. As this tool is able to substantially lessen the cost of manufacturing windmills, and all entities manufacturing windmills acquire the special tool from the company for use in their production process, the continued use of the tool in the manufacturing process is considered to be infinite. Hence, the patent is considered to have an indefinite life. The tool has a carrying amount of $155 000 [2005: $155 000]. Apart from the above, the main items constituting the intangible assets of the Company are:	*Para. 122* *(a)*

	Carrying amount		Remaining amortisation period		
	2006 $000	2005 $000	2006 years	2005 years	*(b)*
Patents and copyrights					
Patent – packaging	31	45	7	8	
Patent – tools	52	66	5	6	
Copyright – manuals	15	24	3	4	
Deferred development expenditure					
Tool design	322	312	5	6	
Packaging design	95	110	3	4	

	Patents and copyrights		Deferred development expenditure		Para. 118
	2006 $000	2005 $000	2006 $000	2005 $000	
Balance at beginning of year, at cost	576	545	592	362	(c)
Accumulated amortisation	276	234	166	110	
Carrying amount at beginning of year	300	311	426	251	
Additions:					(e)(i)
Acquisition of subsidiary	–	22	–	54	
Internal development	–	–	72	182	
Acquired separately	10	15	–	–	
Disposals	(15)	–	–	–	(e)(ii)
Amortisation	(38)	(32)	(52)	(44)	(e)(vi)
Impairment	–	(10)	–	(12)	(e)(iv)
Exchange differences	5	(6)	5	(5)	(e)(vii)
Carrying amount at end of year	262	300	451	426	
Intangible assets:					
At cost	557	576	669	592	(c)
Accumulated amortisation	295	276	218	166	
Carrying amount at end of year	262	300	451	426	

Paragraph 122 of IAS 38 also requires the following disclosures, if relevant:
- for intangible assets acquired by way of a *government grant* and initially recognised at fair value (122(c)):
  - the fair value initially recognised for these assets
  - their carrying amount
  - whether they are measured after recognition under the cost model or the revaluation model.
- the existence and carrying amounts of intangible assets whose *title is restricted* and the carrying amounts of intangible assets *pledged as security* for liabilities (122(d)).
- the amount of *contractual commitments* for the acquisition of intangible assets (122(e)).

Paragraph 124 details further disclosures where intangible assets are carried at revalued amounts. An example of this disclosure is contained in figure 11.11.

Paragraph 126 requires disclosure of the aggregate amount of research and development expenditure recognised as an expense during the period. Paragraph 128 lists disclosures that are encouraged but not required:
- a description of any fully amortised intangible asset that is still in use
- a brief description of significant intangible assets controlled by the entity but not recognised as assets because they did not meet the recognition criteria in IAS 38.

	IAS 38
Intangibles carried at revalued amounts	*Para.*
The company has recognised its Internet domain name as an intangible asset. The asset was recognised initially at cost in 2004. The	*124*
revaluation model was used to measure this asset from 1 January	*(a)(i)*
2005. At balance date, 31 December 2006, the carrying amount of this	*(a)(ii)*
asset is $52 500. If the cost method had continued to be applied, the	*(a)(iii)*
carrying amount would have been $33 600.	
The revaluation surplus in relation to this asset is as follows:	*(b)*

	2005	2006
Balance at 1 January 2005	$48 000	$45 000
Increment	4 500	3 000
Balance at 31 December 2006	$52 500	$48 000

There are no restrictions on the distribution of this balance to shareholders.	
The method used to value this asset is based on an analysis of sales of similar Internet domain names. There is a ready market in such names, and prices are readily available from brokers. In valuing the domain name, it is assumed that use of the Internet for marketing and communicating information to potential investors will continue to enjoy its current popularity for at least the next 10 years.	*(c)*

FIGURE 11.11   Disclosures required by paragraph 124 of IAS 38

LO 12

11.7 Innovative measures of intangibles

It has already been noted that there is often a large difference between the capitalised value of an entity and the net assets reported by that entity. Even with the adoption of IAS 38, the strictness of the rules relating to the recognition of internally generated intangibles means that there will not be an expansion in the recognition of intangible assets by entities. In some cases, there will be a reduction where, prior to the adoption of IAS 38, internally generated assets such as brand names and mastheads were recognised in the accounts. The purpose of this section is to note the existence of an ever-increasing volume of literature suggesting new ideas in reporting about the value of entities. Many of these innovative ideas are concerned with providing information about the content of the unreported assets of an entity. The aim of this section is to suggest that the accounting profession needs to ensure that it does not get left behind by other information professionals in the provision of information about the value of an entity and the variables that determine that value.

Figure 11.4 (page 444) shows Lev's breakdown of intangibles into innovation-related, human resource and organisational intangibles. This analysis of the composition of intangibles has been undertaken by a number of international companies. Skandia, a company based in Sweden, issued its *Intellectual capital prototype report* in 1998. In this report, Skandia divided the market value of an entity into financial capital and intellectual capital, which was further broken down into customer capital, organisational capital and human capital. This view of the market value of an entity is reproduced in figure 11.12.

WEBLINK ↗

Skandia's report can be found on its website at <www.skandia.com/en/ir/annual reports.shtml>.

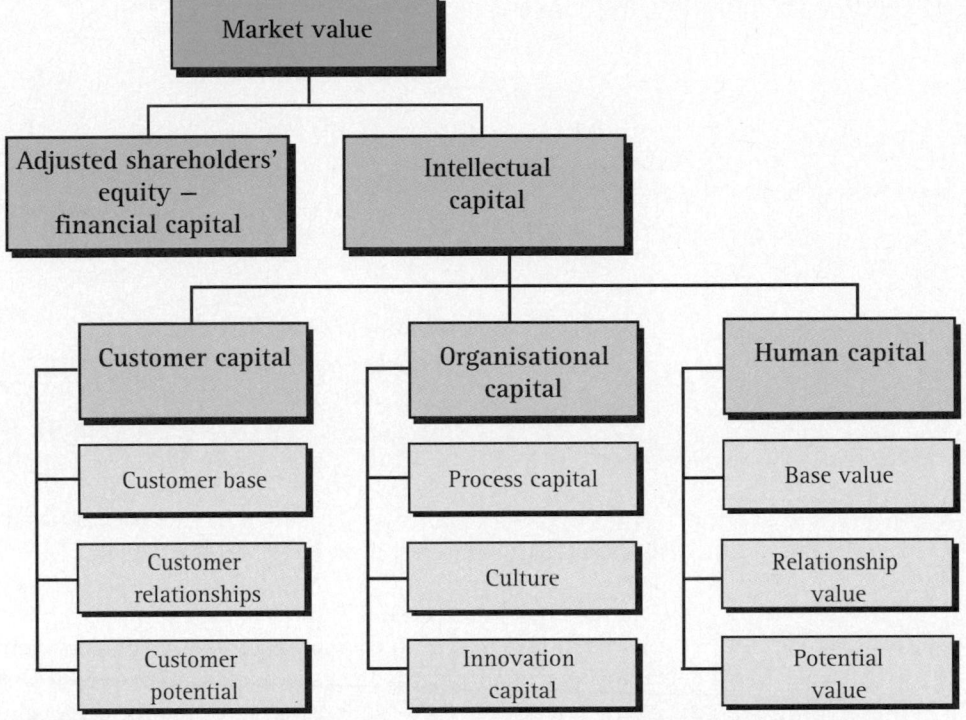

Intellectual capital consists of human capital and structural capital.

Structural capital consists of customer capital and organisational capital; that is, everything that is left once the employee goes home, such as information systems, databases and IT software.

Organisational capital can be broken down into process capital (value-creating and non-value-creating processes), culture, and innovation capital (intangible rights, trademarks, patents, knowledge recipes and business secrets).

Human capital can be broken down into competence, relationships and values.

FIGURE 11.12   Intellectual capital — the Skandia view
Source: Skandia (1998).

The Danish company Systematic, whose strategic business areas are mission critical systems for the defence and health-care sectors and complex software development, published its *Intellectual capital report* in 2004. The primary target groups for this report were customer groups, both present and future, employees and cooperation partners. Systematic identified three managerial challenges within knowledge management:

- partnership with customers
- software process improvement
- employee care and competence development.

This is depicted diagrammatically in figure 11.13.

Systematic's report can be found at <www.systematic.dk>.

WEBLINK ↗

Systematic's
management challenges

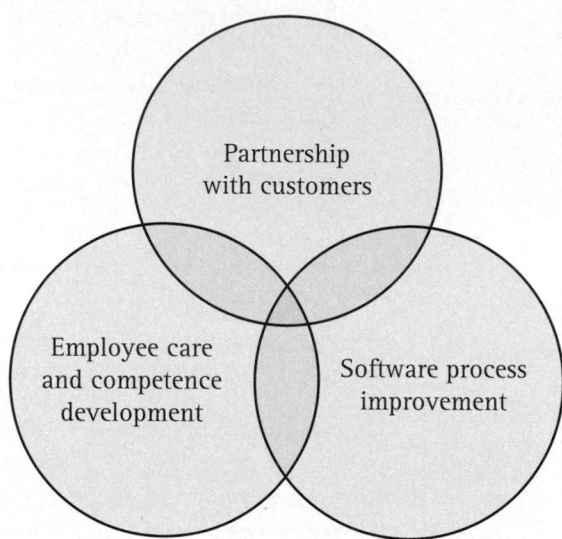

FIGURE 11.13 Management challenges — Systematic
Source: Systematic (2004, p. 11).

When analysing the above reports on the intellectual capital of these organisations, the major point to consider is this: the purpose of the reports is to provide more information about variables in the organisation that management believes add value to the organisation. For example, under IAS 38, an assembled workforce is not allowed to be capitalised as an asset even within a business combination, and funds spent on training employees must be expensed. Hence, the financial reports do not recognise any attempts by management to increase the human capital of the organisation. The question for accountants to consider is whether there are ways in which human capital can be measured, and whether the measures are sufficiently reliable (and relevant) to be included in the financial statements. There have been many attempts to measure human capital. Andrew Mayo (2001) provides an excellent summary of proposed measures in chapter 3 of his book.

Most measures are, however, not directed at including the information in financial reports. A key element in analysing the measures is to determine the variables that various authors see as important and the different ways in which these are measured. For example, Mayo (2001, pp. 58–60) reviewed the Balanced Scorecard approach as developed by Kaplan and Norton in 1992. He noted that, in terms of employee capabilities, three outcome measurements identified were:

• employee satisfaction
• employee retention, and
• employee productivity

with these being driven by the following enablers:

• staff competencies
• technology infrastructure, and
• the climate for action.

Such measures are not suitable for inclusion in financial reports. It is expected that, in the foreseeable future, information on aspects of capital other than financial capital will not be included in the financial statements themselves. However, companies will endeavour to plug the information gap by providing additional reports. Some accounting firms have become involved with these reports; for example, the Systematic 2004 *Intellectual capital report* was audited by Deloitte & Touche in Denmark.

In the Systematic report, the following comment was made: 'Better train people and risk they leave — than do nothing and they stay'. Perhaps this can be adapted for the accounting profession as follows: 'Better become involved in the measurement of intangibles — than risk being left out of the information provision business'.

11.8   Summary

Management in the 21st century is not unfamiliar with the existence of intangible assets and their importance to the success of their companies. However, in many cases, an analysis of the balance sheets of those companies does not provide an indication of the importance of intangible assets. IAS 38 is in many ways a conservative document because it places many restrictions on the recognition of intangible assets. In addition to providing information on the concepts and principles in IAS 38, this chapter has concentrated on explaining the reasons for differences in the accounting for tangible and intangible assets. Standard setters always have the problem of determining the most appropriate mix between relevance and reliability of what is reported in financial statements. Given the unique nature of many intangible assets, although the critics of accounting continue to point to the relevance of information about intangible assets, the problem of determining reliable measurements is one with which both business and the standard setters will continue to grapple.

DISCUSSION QUESTIONS

1. Explain the difference between intangible assets and tangible assets.
2. Discuss whether goodwill is an intangible asset.
3. Explain the difference between 'research' and 'development'.
4. Explain why outlays on research are accounted for differently from outlays on development.
5. Why does IAS 38 not allow the recognition of internally generated goodwill?
6. What is an 'active' market?
7. Explain the term 'identifiable', and identify assets that would be excluded from intangible assets as a result of this criterion being included in the definition of an intangible asset.
8. Explain why intangible assets have become more important to companies in recent years.
9. How might fair value be measured in accounting for intangibles in a business combination?
10. Discuss the use of the revaluation model in accounting for intangible assets.
11. Discuss why brands may be recognised as an intangible asset in a business combination but cannot be recognised when internally generated.
12. Discuss the determination of the useful life of an intangible asset when considering the amortisation of these assets.
13. Discuss the recognition criteria for intangible assets and how it applies to assets acquired separately as well as those acquired in a business combination.
14. What measurement problems arise in accounting for intangible assets?
15. Why might managers of corporations prefer not to expense outlays relating to internally generated intangible assets?

EXERCISES

EXERCISE 11.1 ★   Nature of intangible assets

David James (2001b) in his article stated:

> The Australian company Health Communications Network (HCN), for example, has most of its balance sheet assets in the form of either cash or intangible assets. In its 2000–01 annual report, out of combined assets of $49.7 million, cash assets were $20.4 million and intangible assets were $22.2 million. Plant and equipment were only $1.47 million.
>
> This is characteristic of the shift to intangible assets, but the recent fate of HCN demonstrates some of the difficulties of ownership in the post-industrial environment. The company was the subject of a public furore when it was alleged it had plans to sell prescription information, collected from general practitioners, to undisclosed third parties, possibly pharmaceutical companies. The matter has been referred to the privacy commissioner, but the message is clear: just because a company possesses information, does not mean it can always do with it as it wishes. HCN 'owns' the information, but this does not give it the same rights of ownership as, say, ownership of plant and equipment.

Required

Using the information in the above quotation, discuss the characteristics of intangible assets.

EXERCISE 11.2 ★   Recognition of intangible assets

David James (2001b) in his article stated:

> According to its 1999–2000 annual report, Qantas had total assets of $12 billion. Intangible assets were only $25 million, around 2% of the asset base. Yet Stuckey believes the airline's intangibles are of far greater importance to the company. 'Qantas is interesting because it combines a fantastic brand — an intangible asset — with a heap of capital-intensive tangible assets — the planes they have tried to keep well utilised. They have done very well in an industry that has been a real financial under-performer internationally. They stand out as one of the best performers in that sector.

Required

In relation to a major airline such as Qantas, discuss what intangible assets are probably not on the balance sheet, and possible reasons for their non-recognition.

EXERCISE 11.3   ★

Amortisation of intangibles

Nick Tabakoff (1999) in his article stated:

> ASIC (Australian Securities and Investments Commission) may have plans to change the treatment of television licences in company accounts, as a precursor to the possible introduction of IAS 38. The commission is seeking the views of the main television networks regarding a change to the accounting rules that apply to their licences which, as intangibles, may be amortised. They have not been amortised in the past because of the view held by leading media companies that licences have an ongoing life.
>
> Some ASIC officials beg to differ — because licences need to be reapplied for and renewed every five years, they should be amortised on the grounds that they could be taken away by the Government at any time. The Seven and Nine television networks have been steadily increasing the value placed on their television licences in recent years, a practice that would almost certainly be prevented if IAS 38 was introduced.

Required

Obtain access to the most recent financial reports of your local television stations, and review their policies and accounting for television licences. Critically analyse the arguments for and against the non-amortisation of these assets.

EXERCISE 11.4   ★

Reporting intangibles

Nick Tabakoff (1999) in his article stated:

> News Corporation is far from convinced of the merits of the standard [IAS 38]. At the Australian division, News Limited, finance director and deputy chief executive Peter McCourt, says: 'The reason you get standards like that is that they are prepared by people who are not really responsible to anybody. The business community gains nothing from writing off the value of intangibles over a limited time frame. If the standard comes in, the market will simply add back the amortisation.'
>
> McCourt believes the standard penalises companies that are acquisitive when it comes to intangible assets. He can see no reason for the existence of the standard. 'Who is it aimed at, who is being better informed by taking that charge? I don't think it gets you anywhere.'
>
> He is not alone in getting worked up about preventing accountants from minimising the values placed on intangibles. Even the legendary Berkshire Hathaway chief Warren Buffett has strong views on the issue. He has been quoted as saying: 'Amortisation of intangibles is rubbish. It distorts true cashflows and thus economic reality. For example, the economic earnings of Disney are much greater than reported earnings. Accounting is pushing people to do things that are nuts.'

Required

These comments were made prior to the latest revisions to IAS 38. Comment on whether the current IAS 38 has addressed the issues raised in this article.

EXERCISE 11.5   ★

Nature of intangible assets

In their article, Whiting and Chapman (2003) consider whether the value of rugby players, being a team's most valuable asset, should be placed on the balance sheet. Obtain a copy of the article, critically analyse the arguments made in it and assess whether there should be any changes made to IAS 38 as a result.

EXERCISE 11.6   ★★   Accounting for brands

In the article below, it was reported that the clothing and footwear giant Pacific Brands was set to list on the stockmarket with a $1 billion plus initial public offering (IPO). Patersons Securities analyst, Rob Brierley, was quoted as saying that 'The high brand awareness will certainly be its [Pacific Brand's] marketing strength'.

A history of most popular brands

Pacific Brands can trace its history back to 1893 when it began making Dunlop bicycle tyres.

Along the way, it has collected an astonishing array of brands, many remarkable stories in their own right.

Bonds, one of the company's flagship brands, was founded in 1915 by American immigrant George A. Bond who started out making hosiery and gloves in Sydney. In 1928, Bonds underwear and hosiery secured Charles Kingsford-Smith and Charles Ulm on their historic first flight across the Pacific.

King Gee workwear has been with Australians for more than 75 years, with the first overalls produced in tiny rented premises in Sydney. Its name is derived from a colloquial expression popular during the reign of King George V.

According to PacBrands' website 'King Gee' became Australian slang for a show-off. 'For example, in the 1920s someone who had a high opinion of themselves might have attracted the comment, "he's so good he thinks he's King G",' it said.

Holeproof was first made in Australia in the late 1920s when a hosiery manufacturer started turning out ladieswear under licence from the Holeproof Hosiery Company in the US. The company opened its first Australian mill in Melbourne in 1930, becoming the first manufacturer to make and market Australian-made, self-supporting socks.

Unique Corsets, later better known as bra maker Berlei, was already nearly 20 years old by then.

Founded by Fred R. Burley with a nominal capital of £10 000 in Sydney, the company set out 'to design, manufacture and sell corsets and brassieres of such perfect fit, quality and workmanship as will bring pleasure and profit to all concerned'.

Clarks shoes go back even further, to 1825, and a small sheepskin slipper business founded by Cyrus and James Clark in the small English village of Street. Sixty years later, the company was credited with creating the first shoe to follow the natural shape of the foot — 'a revolutionary concept in its time'.

Source: Peacock, S (2004).

Required
Given the perceived importance of the brands to the success of the IPO, discuss whether the IASB in IAS 38 has adopted too conservative an approach to the accounting for brands.

EXERCISE 11.7   ★   Amortisation of intangibles

X Ltd holds a trademark that is well known within consumer circles and has enabled the company to be a market leader in its area. The trademark has been held by the company for nine years. The legal life of the trademark is five years, but is renewable by the company at little cost to it.

Required
Discuss how the company should determine the useful life of the trademark, noting in particular what form of evidence it should collect to justify its selection of useful life.

EXERCISE 11.8   ★★   Recognition and amortisation of intangibles

A company that sells DVDs by sending emails to prospective customers has acquired a customer list from another company that also markets its products in a similar fashion. The company estimates that it will generate sales from the list for a minimum of two years, and a maximum of three years. The company intends to add names to the list from answers to a questionnaire attached to each of the emails. This should extend the useful life of the list for another year.

Required
Discuss how the company should account for the cost of the customer list. If the cost is capitalised, discuss the determination of the useful life over which the asset is amortised.

EXERCISE 11.9 ★★   Reporting intangibles

In its 2005 annual report, Compusoft Corporation reported €352 million of intangibles and total assets of €80 652 million. Note 8 to the report disclosed details about the entity's intangible assets, including the following breakdown:

June 30 in € millions	Gross carrying amount	Accumulated amortisation
Contract-based	566	(382)
Technology-based	240	(131)
Marketing-based	42	(11)
Customer-related	31	(3)
	879	(527)

Required

Discuss the importance of intangible assets to computing and software companies such as Compusoft, and analyse whether there are aspects of IAS 38 that prevent such companies from disclosing more information about their intangible assets.

EXERCISE 11.10 ★★   Accounting for brands

Simon Evans (2003) in his article reported that a small Victorian wine producer was planning to raise up to $7 million and list on the Australian Stock Exchange. The report stated that Warrenmang Ltd, based in the Pyrenees region in north-west Victoria, has been set up to acquire the Warrenmang, Bazzini and Masoni business and brands. The company hoped to list on the Australian Stock Exchange in February 2004.

Required

Discuss potential problems associated with the recognition of brands by the acquiring entity.

EXERCISE 11.11 ★★   Accounting for brands

Wayne Upton (2001, p. 71) in his discussion of the lives of intangible assets noted that the formula for Coca-Cola has grown more valuable over time, not less; and that Sir David Tweedie, chairman of the IASB, jokes that the brand name of his favourite Scotch whisky is older than the United States of America and, in Sir David's view, the formula for Scotch whisky has contributed more to the sum of human happiness.

Required

Outline the accounting for brands under IAS 38, and discuss the difficulties for standard setters in allowing the recognition of all brands and formulas on balance sheets.

EXERCISE 11.12 ★★   Recognition of intangible assets

Upton (2001, p. 50) notes:

> There is a popular view of financial statements that underlies and motivates many discussions of intangible assets. That popular view often sounds something like this:
>
> If accountants got all the assets and liabilities into financial statements, and they measured all those assets and liabilities at the right amounts, stockholders' equity would equal market capitalization. Right?

Comment on the truth of this 'popular view'.

PROBLEMS

PROBLEM 11.1 ★

Research and development

Because of the low level of rainfall in Simonstown, householders find it difficult to keep their gardens and lawns sufficiently watered. As a result, many householders have installed bores that allow them to access underground water suitable for using on the garden. This is a cheaper option than incurring excess water bills by using the government-provided water system. One of the problems with much of the bore water is that its heavy iron content leaves a brown stain on paths and garden edges. This can make homes look unsightly and lower their value.

Noting this problem, Strand Laboratories believed that it should research the problem with the goal of developing a filter system that could be attached to a bore and remove the effects of the iron content in the water. This process if developed could be patented and filters sold through local reticulation shops.

In 2001, Strand commenced its work on the problem, resulting in August 2005 in a patent for the NoMoreIron filter process. Costs incurred in this process were as follows:

		$000
2001–02	Research conducted to develop filter	125
2002–03	Research conducted to develop filter	132
2003–04	Design and construction of prototype	152
2004–05	Testing of models	51
2005–06	Fees for preparing patent application	12
2006–07	Research to modify design	34
2007–08	Legal fees to protect patent against cheap copies	15

Required
Discuss how the company should account for each of these outlays.

PROBLEM 11.2 ★

Recognition of intangibles

Soweto Ltd is unsure of how to obtain computer software. Four possibilities are:
A. Purchase computer software externally, including packages for payroll and general ledger.
B. Contract to independent programmers to develop specific software for the company's own use.
C. Buy computer software to incorporate into a product that the company will develop.
D. Employ its own programmers to write software that the company will use.

Required
Discuss whether the accounting will differ depending on which method is chosen.

PROBLEM 11.3 ★

Research and development

Stellenbosch Laboratories Ltd manufactures and distributes a wide range of general pharmaceutical products. Selected audited data for the financial year ended 31 December 2005 are as follows:

Gross profit	$ 17 600 000
Profit before income tax	1 700 000
Income tax expense	500 000
Profit for the period	1 200 000
Total assets:	
Current	7 300 000
Non-current	11 500 000

The company uses a standard mark-up on cost.

From your audit files, you ascertain that total research and development expenditure for the year amounted to $4 700 000. This amount is substantially higher than in previous years and has eroded the profitability of the company. Mr Bosch, the company's finance director, has asked for your firm's advice on whether it is acceptable accounting practice for the company to carry foward any of this expenditure to a future accounting period.

Your audit files disclose that the main reason for the significant increase in research and development costs was the introduction of a planned five-year laboratory program to attempt to find an antidote for the common cold. Salaries and identifiable equipment costs associated with this program amounted to $2 350 000 for the current year.

The following additional items were included in research and development costs for the year:

(a) Costs to test a new tamper-proof dispenser pack for the company's major selling line (20% of sales) of antibiotic capsules – $760 000. The new packs are to be introduced in the 2006 financial year.

(b) Experimental costs to convert a line of headache powders to liquid form – $590 000. The company hopes to phase out the powder form if the tests to convert to the stronger and better handling liquid form prove successful.

(c) Quality control required by stringent company policy and by law on all items of production for the year – $750 000.

(d) Costs of a time and motion study aimed at improving production efficiency by redesigning plant layout of existing equipment – $50 000.

(e) Construction and testing of a new prototype machine for producing hypodermic needles – $200 000. Testing has been successful to date and is nearing completion. Hypodermic needles accounted for 1% of the company's sales in the current year, but it is expected that the company's market share will increase following introduction of this new machine.

Required

Respond to Mr Bosch's question for each item above.

PROBLEM 11.4   ★   Recognition of intangibles

Ladysmith Ltd has recently diversified by taking over the operations of Kimberley Ltd at a cost of $10 million. Kimberley Ltd manufactures and sells a cleaning cloth called the 'Supaswipe', which was developed by Kimberley's highly trained and innovative research staff. The unique nature of the coating used on the 'Supaswipe' has resulted in Kimberley Ltd acquiring a significant share of the South African market. A recent expansion into the equatorial African market has proved successful. As a result of the takeover, Ladysmith Ltd acquired the following assets:

	Fair value (at date of acquisition)
Land and buildings	$3 200 000
Production machinery	2 000 000
Inventory	1 800 000
Accounts receivable	700 000
	7 700 000

In addition to the above, Kimberley owned, but had not recognised, the following:

• Trademark – 'Supaswipe'
• Patent   – formula for the special coating.

The research staff of Kimberley Ltd have agreed to join the staff of Ladysmith Ltd and will continue to work on a number of projects aimed at producing specialised versions of the 'Supaswipe'.

The directors have requested your assistance in accounting for the acquisition of Kimberley Ltd. In particular, they are uncertain as to the treatment of the $2.3 million discrepancy between the assets recorded by Kimberley Ltd and the price paid for the company.

Required

Write to the directors outlining the alternative courses of action available in relation to the $2.3 million discrepancy. Your reply should cover the issues of asset recognition, measurement, classification and subsequent accounting treatment.

PROBLEM 11.5   ★   Research and development

Capetown Ltd has been involved in a project to develop an engine that runs on extracts from sugarcane. It commenced the project in February 2004. Between the commencement date and 30 June 2004, the balance date for the company, Capetown Ltd spent $254 000 on the project. At 30 June 2004, there was no indication that the project would be commercially feasible, although the company had made significant progress and was sufficiently sure of future success that it was prepared to outlay more funds on the project.

After spending a further $120 000 during July and August, the company had built a prototype that appeared to be successful. The prototype was demonstrated to a number of engineering companies during September, and a number of these companies expressed interest in the further development of the engine. Convinced that it now had a product that it would be able to sell, Capetown Ltd spent a further $65 000 during October adjusting for the problems that the engineering firms had pointed out. On 1 November, Capetown Ltd applied for a patent on the engine, incurring legal and administrative costs of $35 000. The patent had an expected useful life of five years, but was renewable for a further five years upon application.

Between November and December 2004, Capetown Ltd spent an additional amount of $82 000 on engineering and consulting costs to develop the project such that the engine was at manufacturing stage. These resulted in changes in the overall design of the engine, and costs of $5000 were incurred to add minor changes to the patent authority.

On 1 January 2005, Capetown Ltd invited tenders for the manufacture of the engine for commercial sale.

Required

Discuss how Capetown Ltd should account for these costs. Provide journal entries with an explanation why these are the appropriate entries.

PROBLEM 11.6   ★★★   Recognition of intangibles

Bitterfontein Ltd is a South African mail-order film developer. Although the photo-developing business in South Africa is growing slowly, Bitterfontein Ltd has reported significant increases in sales and net income in recent years. While sales increased from $50 million in 1998 to $120 million in 2004, profit increased from $3 million to $12 million over the same period. The stock market and analysts believe that the company's future is very promising. In early 2005, the company was valued at $350 million, which is three times its 2004 sales and 26 times its estimated 2005 profit.

What is the secret of Bitterfontein Ltd's success? Company management and many investors attribute the company's success to its marketing flair and expertise. Instead of competing on price, Bitterfontein Ltd prefers to focus on service and innovation, including:

- offering customers a CD of their photos and a set of prints from the same roll of film for a set price
- giving customers (at no extra charge) a 'picture index' showing miniphotos of every photo on the roll
- giving every customer a replacement roll (at no extra charge) with every development order.

As a result of such innovations, customers accept prices that are 60% above those of competing discount-film developers, and Bitterfontein Ltd maintains a gross profit margin of around 40%.

Nevertheless, some investors have doubts about the company because they are uneasy about certain accounting policies it has adopted. For example, Bitterfontein Ltd capitalises the costs of its direct mailings to prospective customers ($4.2 million at 30 June 2004) and amortises them on a straight-line basis over three years. This practice is considered to be questionable as there is no guarantee that customers will be obtained and retained from direct mailings.

In addition to the mailing lists developed by in-house marketing staff, Bitterfontein Ltd purchased a customer list from a competitor for $800 000 on 4 July 2005. This list is also recognised as a non-current asset. Bitterfontein Ltd estimates that this list will generate sales for at least another two years, more likely another three years. The company also plans to add names, obtained from a telephone survey conducted in August 2005, to the list. These extra names are expected to extend the list's useful life by another year.

Bitterfontein Ltd's 2004 balance sheet also reported $7.5 million of marketing costs as non-current assets. If the company had expensed marketing costs as incurred, 2004 net income would have been $10 million instead of the reported $12 million. The concerned investors are uneasy about this capitalisation of marketing costs, as they believe that Bitterfontein Ltd's marketing practices are relatively easy to replicate. However, Bitterfontein Ltd argues that its accounting is appropriate. Marketing costs are amortised at an accelerated rate (55% in the 1st year, 29% in the 2nd year, and 16% in the 3rd year), based on 15 years knowledge and experience of customer purchasing behaviour.

Required

Explain how Bitterfontein Ltd's costs should be accounted for under IAS 38 *Intangible Assets*, giving reasons for your answer.

WEBLINK

Visit these websites for additional information:

www.iasb.org   www.iasplus.com
www.asic.gov.au   www.ifac.org
www.aasb.com.au   www.nzica.com
www.accaglobal.com   www.capa.com.my

REFERENCES

Baltes, M 1997, 'Measuring non-financial assets', *Wharton Alumni Magazine*, winter, pp. 7–12. Quoted material sourced from this publication.

Dior 2005a, *Full annual report 2004*, Christian Dior, Paris, viewed 29 August 2006, <www.dior-finance.com/en>.

—2005b, *Full annual report 2004 (part 2): implementation of IFRS*, Christian Dior, Paris, viewed 29 August 2006, <www.dior-finance.com/en>.

Eccles, RG, Herz, RH, Keegan, EM & Phillips, DMH 2001, *The ValueReporting^TM revolution: moving beyond the earnings game*, John Wiley, New York.

Egginton, DA 1990, 'Towards some principles for intangible asset accounting', *Accounting and Business Research*, summer, pp. 193–205.

Evans, S 2003, 'Winery presses ahead with float', *The Australian Financial Review*, 9 December.

Gottliebsen, R 1987, 'Recognising the value of intangible assets', *Business Review Weekly*, 13 February, p. 6. Quoted material sourced from this publication.

Harrison, S 2002, *Publishing industry: the future of intangibles under IAS*, Deloitte & Touche, UK.

James, D 2001a, 'Intangible virtues', *Business Review Weekly*, 4 May.

—2001b, 'Hail the "age of access"', *Business Review Weekly*, 27 April.

Jenkins, E & Upton, W 2001, 'Internally generated intangible assets: framing the discussion', *Australian Accounting Review*, vol. 11, no. 2, pp. 4–11.

Kieso, DE & Weygandt, JJ 1992, *Intermediate accounting*, 7th edn, John Wiley, New York.

King, AM & Henry, JM 1999, 'Valuing intangible assets through appraisals', *Strategic Finance*, vol. 81, no. 5, pp. 32–7. Quoted material sourced from this publication.

Lev, B 2001, *Intangibles: management, measurement, and reporting*, Brookings Institution Press, Washington, DC.

Mayo, A 2001, *The human value of the enterprise*, Nicholas Brealey Publishing, London.

Napier, C & Power, M 1992, 'Professional research, lobbying and intangibles: a review essay', *Accounting and Business Research*, winter, pp. 85–95.

Peacock, S 2004, 'A history of most popular brands', *The West Australian*, 14 February, p. 73.

Samuelson, RA 1996, 'The concept of an asset in accounting theory', *Accounting Horizons*, vol. 10, no. 3, pp. 147–57. Quoted material sourced from this publication.

Schuetze, WP 1993, 'What is an asset?', *Accounting Horizons*, vol. 7, no. 3, pp. 66–70. Quoted material sourced from this publication.

—2001, 'What are assets and liabilities? Where is true north? (Accounting that my sister would understand)', *Abacus*, vol. 37, no. 1, pp. 1–25. Quoted material sourced from this publication.

Skandia 1998, *Intellectual capital prototype report*, viewed June 2006, <www.skandia.com/en/ir/annualreports.html>.

Stevenson, K 1989, 'The precedent in Australian thinking', paper presented at the accounting forum on off-balance-sheet structures, conducted by the Australian Accounting Research Foundation and sponsored by Coopers & Lybrand, Sydney.

Systematic 2004, *Intellectual capital report*, viewed June 2006, <www.systematic.dk>.

Tabakoff, N 1999, 'Assets: standard deviation', *Business Review Weekly*, 21 May.

Upton, WS 2001, *Business and financial reporting, challenges from the new economy*, Financial Accounting Series No. 219-A, Financial Accounting Standards Board, Norwalk, Connecticut, USA.

Whiting, R & Chapman, K 2003, 'Sporting glory – the great intangible', *Australian CPA*, February.

CHAPTER 12
Business combinations

ACCOUNTING STANDARDS

International: IFRS 3 *Business Combinations*
Australia: AASB 3 *Business Combinations*
New Zealand: NZ IFRS 3 *Business Combinations*

CONCEPTS FOR REVIEW

Before studying this chapter, you should understand or, if necessary, revise:
- the IASB Framework
- the accounting for intangibles
- the nature of contingent liabilities.

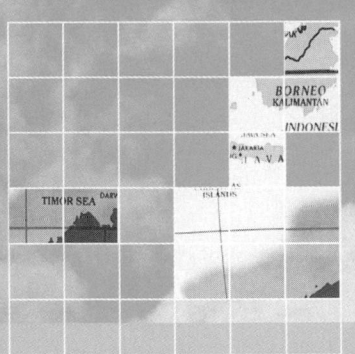

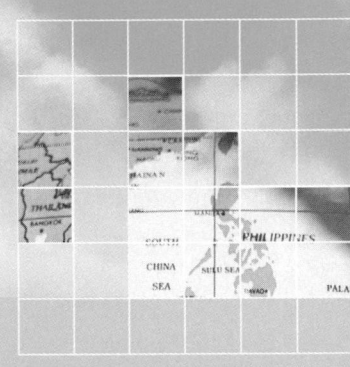

When you have studied this chapter, you should be able to:

1. understand the nature of a business combination and its various forms
2. explain the basic steps in the purchase method of accounting for business combinations
3. understand how to identify an acquirer
4. explain the differences between the various important dates used in accounting for business combinations
5. explain what is meant by fair value, and the fair value hierarchy
6. determine how to measure the cost of the business combination
7. account for directly attributable costs, and costs of issuing debt and equity instruments
8. determine the allocation of the cost of the business combination
9. understand the components of goodwill and how to account for it
10. explain an excess on acquisition and how to account for it
11. explain the difference between pre- and post-acquisition equity
12. account in the records of the acquiree
13. account for subsequent adjustments to the initial accounting for a business combination
14. provide the disclosures required under IFRS 3
15. explain possible changes as a result of Phase II considerations in the 2005 exposure draft.

LO 1

12.1 The nature of a business combination

The accounting standard relevant for accounting for business combinations is IFRS 3 *Business Combinations*. A 'business combination' is defined in appendix A of IFRS 3 as:

> The bringing together of separate entities or businesses into one reporting entity.

The term 'business' is defined in appendix A as:

> An integrated set of activities and assets conducted and managed for the purpose of providing:
>
> (a) a return to investors; or
>
> (b) lower costs or other economic benefits directly and proportionately to policyholders or participants.
>
> A business generally consists of inputs, processes applied to those inputs, and resulting outputs that are, or will be, used to generate revenues. If goodwill is present in a transferred set of activities and assets, the transferred set shall be presumed to be a business.

The purpose of defining a business is to distinguish between the acquisition of a group of assets – such as a number of desks, bookcases and filing cabinets – and the acquisition of an entity that is capable of producing some form of output. Accounting for a group of assets is based on standards such as IAS 16 *Property, Plant and Equipment* (see chapter 10 of this book) rather than IFRS 3. Paragraph 4 of IFRS 3 requires the accounting for a group of assets not constituting a business combination to be at cost, determined by reference to the relative fair values of the individual assets acquired. Note in the definition of a business that goodwill is acquired only as part of a business, and not as part of a group of assets not constituting a business. Hence, if goodwill is acquired, the group of assets acquired must constitute a business, and accounting for the business combination is in accordance with IFRS 3.

Consider the situation in figure 12.1 in which entity A acquires a mining division from entity B by issuing its shares to entity B. In this situation, entity A is considered to be the acquirer, as it obtains control of the mining business from entity B. In analysing the substance of the transaction, entity A is acquiring a business from entity B and selling shares in itself to entity B. Entity B is acquiring shares from entity A and selling a mining division to entity A. However, entity B is not undertaking a business combination. It is acquiring a single asset, shares in A. In contrast, entity A is acquiring a business, namely the mining division from entity B. Both entity A and entity B are acquiring assets and giving up some form of consideration. However, only entity A is undertaking a business combination.

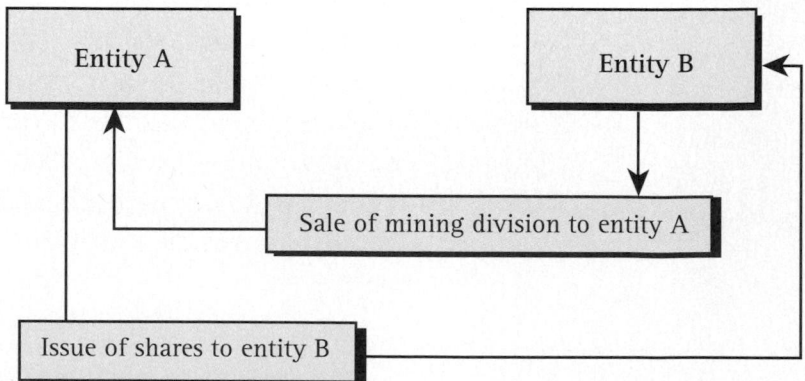

FIGURE 12.1   Identification of a business combination

The definition of a business combination requires the bringing together of businesses into a reporting entity. 'Reporting entity' is defined in appendix A to IFRS 3 as follows:

> An entity for which there are users who rely on the entity's general purpose financial statements for information that will be useful to them for making decisions about the allocation of resources. A reporting entity can be a single entity or a group comprising a parent and all of its subsidiaries.

Chapter 19 of this book discusses the concept of a reporting entity in relation to business combinations that result in the formation of a group comprising a parent and its subsidiaries. However, in the current chapter, it is assumed that the entity resulting from the business combination is a single entity. The combination of separate businesses requires joining the assets and liabilities of the acquirer with those acquired from the acquiree. Assuming the existence of two companies, A Ltd and B Ltd, the following general forms of business combinations are covered in this chapter:

1. A Ltd acquires all the assets and liabilities of B Ltd.

    B Ltd continues as a company, holding shares in A Ltd.

2. A Ltd acquires all the assets and liabilities of B Ltd.

    B Ltd liquidates.

3. C Ltd is formed to acquire all the assets and liabilities of A Ltd and B Ltd.

    A Ltd and B Ltd liquidate.

4. A Ltd acquires a group of net assets of B Ltd, the group of net assets constituting a business for example, a division, branch or segment of B Ltd.

    B Ltd continues to operate as a company.

Obtaining control over the net assets of another entity could be achieved by one entity acquiring the shares of another entity on the open market and, because of the quantity of shares acquired, being able to control the policies of the other entity. Accounting for this form of business combination requires the application of the principles discussed in this chapter, but the application further involves the preparation of consolidated financial statements, as discussed in chapters 19 to 24.

There are many other forms of business combinations that can occur, such as A Ltd acquiring the assets only of B Ltd, and B Ltd paying off the liabilities and then liquidating. Alternatively, A Ltd may acquire all the assets and only some of the liabilities of B Ltd, and B Ltd pays the remaining liabilities before liquidating. The number of possible arrangements is quite large, but most situations are covered by consideration of the three alternatives in figure 12.2.

FIGURE 12.2 General forms of business combinations

1. *A Ltd acquires net assets of B Ltd* A Ltd: • Receipt of assets and liabilities of B Ltd • Outlay of cost of combination, such as shares, cash or other consideration	1. *B Ltd continues, holding shares in A Ltd* B Ltd: • Sale of assets and liabilities to A Ltd • Gain or loss on sale • Receipt of purchase consideration e.g. shares, cash, or other consideration
2. *A Ltd acquires net assets of B Ltd* A Ltd: • As for part 1 above, A Ltd	2. *B Ltd liquidates* B Ltd: • Liquidation account, including gain/loss on liquidation • Receipt of purchase consideration • Distribution of purchase consideration to appropriate parties, including shareholders via the shareholders' distribution account

(continued)

3. *C Ltd formed* C Ltd: • Formation of C Ltd with issue of shares • Acquisition of assets and liabilities of A Ltd and B Ltd • Payment for net assets of A Ltd and B Ltd via cash outlays or issue of shares in C Ltd	3. *A Ltd and B Ltd liquidate* A Ltd and B Ltd: • As for part 2 above, B Ltd

IFRS 3 applies to all the business combinations except those listed in paragraph 3 of the standard, namely:

1. *where the business combination results in the formation of a joint venture.* Such a business combination is accounted for under IAS 31 – *Interests in Joint Ventures* (see chapter 26)
2. *where the business combinations involve entities or businesses under common control.* According to appendix A, such a business combination occurs where all of the combining entities or businesses ultimately are controlled by the same party or parties both before and after the combination and where control is not transitory. This situation could arise where P Ltd owns 100% of the shares of S Ltd. The directors of P Ltd form a new entity, X Ltd, wholly owned by P Ltd, which acquires all the issued shares of S Ltd in an internal reconstruction. All the combining entities are controlled by P Ltd both before and after the reconstruction.
3. *where the business combinations involve two or more mutual entities.* A mutual entity is defined in appendix A as an entity other than an investor-owned entity, such as a mutual insurance company or a mutual cooperative entity that provides lower costs or other economic benefits directly and proportionately to its policy-holders or participants.
4. *business combinations where the reporting entity is formed as a result of a contract without obtaining an ownership interest.* Dual listed corporations are an example of this form of business combination (see chapter 19 for further discussion).

IFRS 3 is the result of the first step, Phase 1, in a two-stage process being undertaken by the International Accounting Standards Board (IASB) in its deliberations on accounting for business combinations. In June 2005, the IASB issued the *Exposure Draft of Proposed Amendments to IFRS 3 Business Combinations* (referred to in this chapter as the Amendments ED), containing the Phase II proposals. This chapter deals with the application of IFRS 3 as issued in 2004. Section 12.7 contains a summary of the proposed changes to the current IFRS 3 under the Phase II exposure draft.

LO 2

12.2 Accounting for a business combination — basic principles

The accepted method of accounting for a business combination under IFRS 3 is the *purchase method*. The key steps in this method are noted in paragraph 16 of the standard:
• Identify an acquirer: the business combination is viewed from the perspective of the combining entity that is the acquirer.
• Measure the cost of the business combination.
• Allocate the cost of the business combination to the assets acquired, both tangible and intangible, and the liabilities and contingent liabilities assumed.

These steps result in determining the existence of any goodwill or excess on combination which must be accounted for.

Paragraph IN7 of IFRS 3 contains a more complete summary of the requirements of IFRS 3. Figure 12.3 contains a summary of these major features of IFRS 3.

IFRS 3 requires:
(a) the use of the purchase method
(b) an acquirer to be identified
(c) the measurement of the cost of a business combination
(d) the allocation of the cost of combination to identifiable assets acquired and liabilities and contingent liabilities assumed
(e) the assets, liabilities and contingent liabilities to be measured initially at fair value at acquisition date
(f) goodwill acquired to be recognised
(g) that goodwill not be amortised but tested for impairment annually
(h) that any excess on combination be accounted for by a reassessment of the assets and liabilities acquired and, where appropriate, by recognising any excess immediately in profit or loss
(i) disclosure of information that enables users to evaluate the nature and effect of business combinations effected in the current period and previous periods, as well as post-balance-sheet date
(j) disclosure of information that enables users to evaluate changes in the carrying amount of goodwill.

FIGURE 12.3   Key requirements of IFRS 3

LO 3

12.2.1   Identifying the acquirer

Paragraph 17 requires that an acquirer be identified in every business combination. It has been argued by some accountants that there are business combinations where it is impossible to identify an acquirer. For example, in its response to the Amendments ED, the Accounting Standards Board in the UK stated that:

> we have reservations about requiring the acquisition [purchase] method for *all* business combinations. In certain circumstances it may not be possible to identify an acquirer and therefore the use of acquisition accounting (which reflects acquisition of one entity by another) may not faithfully represent the business combination. We consider that 'true' mergers do occur ... (Accounting Standards Board UK 2005, p. 8).

Application of the purchase method does, however, require the identification of an acquirer. As explained later (see section 12.3.2 of this chapter), the purchase method requires the assets and liabilities of the acquiree to be measured at fair value. Consider a situation where entity A enters into a business combination with entity B. If entity A were identified as the acquirer, then it would be the assets and liabilities of entity B that would be measured at fair value, whereas if entity B were identified as the acquirer, it would be entity A's assets and liabilities that would be recorded at fair value.

Paragraph 17 of IFRS 3 states that the acquirer is 'the combining entity that obtains control of the other combining entities or businesses'. The key criterion then in identifying an acquirer is that of control. This term is the same as that used in IAS 27 *Consolidated and Separate Financial Statements* for identifying a parent–subsidiary relation (see chapter 19 of this book), and is defined in paragraph 19 of IFRS 3 as 'the power to govern the financial and operating policies of an entity or business so as to obtain benefits from its activities'. In some situations it is very easy to identify an acquirer. For example, if entity A acquires more than half the shares of entity B, then entity A will have control over entity B because its majority shareholding will give entity A more than half of the voting rights of entity B as well as control of entity B's board.

In other situations, identification of an acquirer requires judgement. Consider the situation where entity A combines with entity B. To effect the combination, a new company (entity C) is formed, which issues shares to acquire all the shares of both entities A and B. The subsequent organisational structure is then:

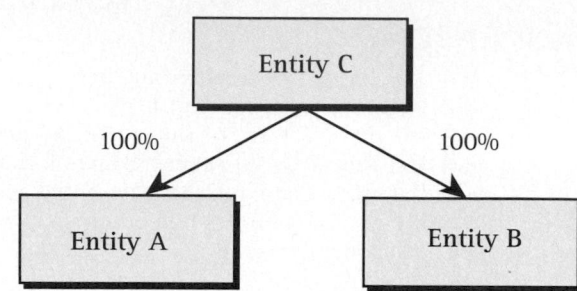

As entity C is created solely to formalise the organisational structure, it is not the acquirer although it may be considered to be the legal parent of both the other entities. As noted in paragraph 22 of IFRS 3, one of the entities that existed prior to the combination must be identified as the acquirer. As noted earlier, if entity A is identified as the acquirer, then the assets and liabilities of entity B (the acquiree) will be measured at fair value. Paragraph 20 of IFRS 3 provides some indicators to assist in assessing which entity is the acquirer:

- *Which entity is the largest?* This could be measured by reference to the fair value of each of the combining entities. In a takeover, it is normally the largest company that takes over the smaller company (that is, the larger company is the acquirer).
- *What has been the consideration passed in the exchange — which entity has issued shares to effect the exchange?* If entity X issues shares to acquire the shares of entity Y, then it is more likely that entity X is the acquirer because its shares are held by shareholders of the combining entities.
- *Has one entity paid cash or other assets for the shares of another entity?* If entity X had paid cash for the shares of entity Y, then entity X is most likely the acquirer because it is acquiring the voting rights in entity Y.
- *Which entity initiated the exchange?* Normally the entity that is the acquirer is the one that undertakes action to take over the acquiree.
- *Which management governs the combined entities subsequent to the combination?* If the management of entity X governs the combined entities X and Y, then it is most likely that entity X has obtained control of entity Y. As noted in paragraph 21, in a reverse acquisition, entity X may issue its shares to acquire the shares of entity Y. However, because of the number of X shares given to the former Y shareholders relative to those held by the shareholders in entity X prior to the combination, the former shareholders in entity Y may have the majority of shares in entity X and be able to determine the operating and financial policies of the combined entities.

Determining the controlling entity is the key to identification of the acquirer. However, doing so may not be straightforward in many business combinations, and the accountant might be required to make a reasoned judgement based on the circumstances.

LO 4

12.2.2 Selecting the right date

Appendix A of IFRS 3 contains definitions of three dates that are relevant to a business combination where one entity acquires an operation from or shares in another entity:

acquisition date	The date on which the acquirer effectively obtains control of the acquiree.
agreement date	The date that a substantive agreement between the combining parties is reached and, in the case of publicly listed entities, announced to the public. In the case of a hostile takeover, the earliest date that a substantive agreement between the combining parties is reached is the date that a sufficient number of the acquiree's owners have accepted the acquirer's offer for the acquirer to obtain control of the acquiree.

date of exchange   When a business combination is achieved in a single exchange transaction, the date of exchange is the acquisition date. When a business combination involves more than one exchange transaction, for example when it is achieved in stages by successive share purchases, the date of exchange is the date that each individual investment is recognised in the financial statements of the acquirer.

Acquisition date is probably the most important definition as it is the date the business combination occurs. A business combination involves the joining together of assets under the control of a specific party or parties. Therefore, the business combination occurs at the date the assets or net assets are under the control of the acquirer. This date is the acquisition date.

An entity may acquire control of another entity via the acquisition of sufficient shares to give it control of the voting power of that entity. The date the shares in the other entity are acquired is the date of exchange. If the controlling parcel of shares is acquired on the one date (for example, if A Ltd acquires 60% of the shares of B Ltd on 1 July 2005), then the date of exchange is also the acquisition date (in this example, 1 July 2005). If, however, A Ltd acquired its 80% holding in a number of steps, such as 10% on 1 July 2002, 20% on 1 January 2004 and 30% on 1 July 2005, then there are three dates of exchange, with the third date of exchange (1 July 2005) being also the acquisition date, because it is on this date that A Ltd has sufficient shares to enable it to control B Ltd. The agreement date is discussed in section 12.3.1 of this chapter in relation to determining the fair value of equity instruments issued by the acquirer.

It should be noted in relation to the acquisition date that the criterion used to determine that date is control, being the date the acquirer controls the net assets acquired from the acquiree. Other dates that are important during the process of the business combination may be:

- the date the contract is signed
- the date the consideration is paid
- a date nominated in the contract
- the date on which assets acquired are delivered to the acquirer
- the date on which an offer becomes unconditional.

These dates may be important, but determination of acquisition date does not depend on when the acquirer receives physical possession of the assets acquired, or actually pays out the consideration to the acquiree. The use of control as the key criterion to determine acquisition date ensures that the substance of the transaction determines the accounting rather than the form of the transaction. For example, assets acquired may be delivered in stages, or payments made for these assets may be made over a period of time with a number of payments being required.

The definition of acquisition date then relates to the point of time when the net assets of the acquiree become the net assets of the acquirer – in essence, the date on which the acquirer can recognise the net assets acquired in its own records. This approach is consistent with the IASB Framework in that an asset is defined in terms of future economic benefits that are controlled by an entity.

There are three main areas where the selection of the date affects the accounting for a business combination:

- The consideration paid by the acquirer is determined as the sum of the fair values of assets given, equity issued and/or liabilities undertaken in exchange for the net assets or shares of another entity. This measurement is made at the *date of exchange*. The choice of date affects the measure of fair value. For example, in the case of shares listed on a stock exchange, the market price of these shares may fluctuate on a daily basis. The choice of the date of exchange affects the choice of which particular market price is used in calculating the fair value of shares issued by the acquirer as consideration.

- The net assets acquired are measured at the fair value of these assets and liabilities. This measurement occurs at the *acquisition date*. Again, the choice of fair value is affected by the choice of the acquisition date.
- Where the acquirer purchases shares in the acquiree, the choice of acquisition date affects the classification of the acquiree's equity into pre-acquisition and post-acquisition equity, and the subsequent accounting for dividends. This issue is considered in detail in section 12.3.6 of this chapter subsequent to an analysis of the appropriate accounting in the records of the acquirer and acquiree.

LO 5

12.2.3 Determination of fair value

Fair value is defined in appendix A to IFRS 3 as follows:

> The amount for which an asset could be exchanged, or a liability settled, between knowledgeable, willing parties in an arm's length transaction.

Fair value is basically market value. However, the process of determining fair value necessarily involves judgement and estimation. The acquiring entity is not actually trading the items in the marketplace for cash, but is trying to estimate what the exchange price would be if it did so. Hence, the determination of fair value involves estimation.

To assist in the determination of fair value, the IASB developed a 'fair value hierarchy'. the purpose of which is to provide a list of ways in which fair value can be measured in a business combination, in order of preference. As noted in the Project Summary for Business Combinations (Phase II) as at January 2004, the IASB believes:

> that the fair value of individual items acquired in a business combination should be determined by focussing on their place and condition on the date of the business combination and assessing the amounts for which they could be exchanged, given those characteristics, between willing buyers and sellers absent a business combination.

Measurement under the IASB fair value hierarchy is as follows:

1. *Level 1* — The estimate of fair value shall be determined by reference to *observable prices of market transactions* for identical assets or liabilities at or near the measurement date whenever that information is available.

2. *Level 2* — If (1) is not available, the estimate of fair value shall be determined by *adjusting observable prices of market transactions for similar assets or liabilities* that occur at or near the measurement date. A similar asset or liability is one that is reasonably comparable; for example, one having similar patterns of cash flows that can be expected to respond similarly to those of the item being measured to changes in economic conditions. Generally, when an asset or liability is sufficiently similar to an asset or liability being measured, adjustments for any difference are objectively determinable. For example, similar assets could be identical in all respects except for location. If the only difference between two assets was their location, the fair value would equal the observable price of an identical item in a different location plus costs to ship the item to the identical location as the asset being measured.

3. *Level 3* — If neither (1) nor (2) is available, the estimate of fair value shall be determined using *other valuation techniques*. Valuation techniques shall be consistent with the objective of estimating fair value and incorporate assumptions that marketplace participants would use whenever market-based information is available without undue cost or effort. If market-based information is not available without undue cost and effort, an entity may use as inputs its own assumptions as a practical expedient. However, for any valuation technique, market inputs shall be maximised and use of internal estimates and assumptions shall be minimised. For example, if an entity is aware of unique advantages or disadvantages that it possesses, such as favourable labour rates or superior processing or manufacturing technologies, it should adjust its entity-specific assumptions so that the inputs into the valuation process or model reflect those that marketplace participants would incorporate in an estimate of fair value.

A similar hierarchy is used in IAS 38 *Intangible Assets*, paragraphs 39–41. Paragraph 21 of this standard requires that intangible assets be initially measured at cost. In a business combination, the costs of the individual assets acquired are measured by reference to the fair values of those assets. Various measures of these fair values are possible:

- *Quoted market prices.* An active market is defined in paragraph 8 as one which has all the following conditions:
  - (a) the items traded within the market are homogeneous
  - (b) willing buyers and sellers can normally be found at any time
  - (c) prices are available to the public.

  Where there is an active market, the fair value is determined by reference to quoted market prices.
- *Recent transactions.* Where there is no active market, reference must be made to other sources of information, such as recent transactions in the same or similar items. One of the problems with intangible assets is that their unique nature in many cases precludes the use of information from other transactions.
- *Measurement techniques.* With the increasing importance of intangible assets, there has been a growing establishment of entities who specialise in measuring intangible assets, particularly brands. These valuation firms measure the worth of intangible assets by using variations of present value techniques, and multiples of variables such as royalty rates. As noted in paragraph 41 of IAS 38, these methods should 'reflect current transactions and practices in the industry to which the asset belongs'.

The hierarchy in IAS 38 is not substantially different from that identified for assets acquired and liabilities assumed in a business combination. However, there are still issues that need to be discussed by the IASB, such as whether the market referred to is wholesale or retail, whether it should take into account geographical markets, and whether it is the exit price or the entry price that should be considered.

Further, in appendix A to IAS 39 *Financial Instruments: Recognition and Measurement*, paragraphs AG69–AG82 consider the measurement of fair value for financial instruments, with a hierarchy of active market with quoted prices, no active market and using recent market transactions, and no active market and valuation techniques.

LO 6

12.3 Accounting in the records of the acquirer

Where the acquirer acquires a business from another entity, it has to measure the fair value of both the consideration paid for the net assets acquired and the assets, liabilities and contingent liabilities acquired. Where the acquirer acquires shares in the acquiree, the acquirer will record the shares acquired and the consideration paid.

12.3.1 Accounting for the cost of a business combination

Paragraph 24 of IFRS 3 states:

> The acquirer shall measure the cost of a business combination as the aggregate of:
>
> (a) the fair values, at the date of exchange, of assets given, liabilities incurred or assumed, and equity instruments issued by the acquirer, in exchange for control of the acquiree; plus
>
> (b) any costs directly attributable to the business combination.

Note the following:

- The objective is to measure the cost of the business combination to the acquirer.
- Cost is determined by measuring what is given up or sacrificed by the acquirer.
- Cost is measured by determining the fair values of the consideration given by the acquirer.
- The fair values of the consideration are measured at the date of exchange.
- The cost is the sum of the fair values of the consideration plus directly attributable costs.

In a specific exchange, the consideration paid to the acquiree could include just one form of consideration, such as cash, but could equally well consist of a number of forms such as cash, shares and non-current assets. These are considered separately in the following pages.

Cash or other monetary assets

The fair value is the amount of cash or cash equivalent dispersed. The amount is usually readily determinable. One problem that may occur arises when the settlement is deferred to a time subsequent to the exchange date. According to paragraph 26 of IFRS 3:

> when settlement of all or any part of the cost of a business combination is deferred, the fair value of that deferred component shall be determined by discounting the amounts payable to their present value at the date of exchange, taking into account any premium or discount likely to be incurred in settlement.

For a deferred payment, the fair value to the acquirer is the amount the entity would have to borrow to settle the debt immediately. Hence, the discount rate used is the entity's incremental borrowing rate.

Use of cash to acquire net assets would result in the acquirer recording the following form of entry at the date of exchange:

Net assets	Dr	XXX	
Cash	Cr		XXX
Payable to acquiree	Cr		XXX
(Acquisition of net assets with partially deferred payment)			

When the deferred payment is made to the acquiree, the interest component needs to be recognised:

Payable to acquiree	Dr	XXX	
Interest expense	Dr	XXX	
Cash	Cr		XXX
(Payment of deferred amount)			

Non-monetary assets

Non-monetary assets consist of assets such as property, plant and equipment, investments, licences and patents. As noted earlier, if active second-hand markets exist, fair values can be obtained by reference to those markets. The items sold in the market may not be exactly the same as those being exchanged in the business combination, and an estimate of fair value for the specific item may have to be made. Where active markets do not exist, other means of valuation, including the use of expert valuers, may be used.

The acquirer is effectively selling the non-monetary asset to the acquiree. Hence, it is earning income equal to the fair value on the sale of the asset. Where the carrying amount of the asset in the records of the acquirer is different from fair value, a gain or loss on sale of the asset is recognised at exchange date.

Use of a non-monetary asset such as plant as part of the consideration to acquire net assets results in the acquirer recording the following entries (assume a cost of plant of $180, a carrying amount of $150 and fair value of $155):

Net assets acquired	Dr	XXX	
Proceeds on sale of plant	Cr		155
Other consideration payable	Cr		XXX
(Acquisition of net assets)			
Accumulated depreciation − plant	Dr	30	
Carrying amount of plant sold	Dr	150	
Plant	Cr		180
(Derecognition of plant sold)			

The acquirer thus recognises a gain on sale of $5. An alternative entry to recognise the gain is:

Net assets acquired	Dr	XXX	
Accumulated depreciation – plant	Dr	30	
Plant	Cr		180
Gain on sale	Cr		5
Other consideration payable	Cr		XXX
(Acquisition of net assets and recognition of gain on sale)			

Equity instruments

If an acquirer issues its own shares as consideration, it will need to determine the fair value of those shares at the date of exchange. For listed entities, reference is made to the quoted prices of the shares. As noted in paragraph 27 of IFRS 3, 'The published price at the date of exchange of a quoted equity instrument provides the best evidence of the instrument's fair value and shall be used, except in rare circumstances'. The only event that the standard recognises as causing the published price to be an unreliable indicator is when the purchase price has been affected by the thinness of the market. Paragraph 27 further notes that in such a case the fair value could be estimated by reference to the fair value of the acquirer, taking a proportional amount as being the value of the shares. Where the equity instruments were the only form of consideration paid, the fair value could be determined by reference to the fair value of the net assets acquired.

It should be noted that the fair value of the equity instruments is measured, according to paragraph 27 of IFRS 3, at the date of exchange. There has been considerable ongoing debate within the accounting community about which date should be used to measure the fair value of equity instruments issued. As reported in the January 2004 Project Summary on Business Combinations (Phase II), page 7, the IASB and the FASB (Financial Accounting Standards Board) have discussed two alternative models: the acquisition date model (equity instruments would be measured on the date the acquirer obtains control over the business acquired), and the agreement date model (equity instruments would be measured on the date a substantive agreement is reached between the acquirer and the target's management).

Some of the arguments raised in favour of the *agreement date model* were:

- The agreement date more effectively identifies the value of the acquired business that is negotiated between the parties to the transaction.
- Fluctuations in the price of the acquirer's equity instruments between the agreement date and the acquisition date could be due to factors unrelated to the business combination. If acquisition date is used, the consideration paid will include the effects of these factors, thus affecting the value of the net assets of the acquiree recorded.
- At the agreement date, the parties are essentially committed to the transaction such that neither party can renege on the agreements without adverse consequences. The value of the transaction should not be revalued after that date.
- The fair value at agreement date reflects the bargained exchange price between the entities involved in the exchange. Movements in the price of the acquirer's equity instruments after the agreement date will be affected by the market's reaction to the agreement. These fluctuations should not be considered in the value of the business combination transaction since they were not specifically negotiated by the acquirer and the management of the acquiree. Further, at agreement date, there is probably some correlation between the fair value of the net assets to be received in the future and the fair value of the equity interests given as consideration. Movements in the value of the net assets and movements in the value of the equity instruments between agreement date and acquisition date are probably unrelated.

The following arguments were presented in favour of the *acquisition date model*:

- There is not a strong conceptual basis for either the acquisition date or agreement date. In this case, the simpler of the two methods should be used.
- The measurement on the acquisition date is a fairly universal concept in accounting.
- The acquisition date model values net assets or equity given up on the same date as the identifiable assets and liabilities. The agreement date model adds confusion, since the purchase consideration is valued on one date and the acquired assets and liabilities are measured on a later date.
- As the share price of the acquirer usually declines after a combination is announced, the acquisition date is less likely to require an immediate write-down of goodwill.

The IASB noted there were valid arguments for both models. It subsequently voted to support acquisition date, being the date that control passes from the acquiree to the acquirer, in the interests of convergence with the FASB. Two key reasons were given:

- the consideration given and the assets acquired and liabilities assumed would be measured on the same date, including the residual goodwill
- all of the consideration would be measured on the same date.

However, for the purposes of IFRS 3, the appropriate date for measurement of the fair value of equity instruments issued is the date of exchange.

Liabilities undertaken

The fair values of liabilities undertaken are best measured by the present values of future cash outflows. As noted in paragraph 28 of IFRS 3, future losses or other costs expected to be incurred as a result of the combination are not liabilities of the acquirer and are therefore not included in the calculation of the fair value of consideration paid.

LO 7

Directly attributable costs

In addition to the consideration paid by the acquirer to the acquiree, a further item to be considered in determining the cost of the business combination is the costs directly attributable to the combination, which includes costs 'such as professional fees paid to accountants, legal advisers, valuers and other consultants to effect the combination' (IFRS 3, para. 29). In IAS 16 *Property, Plant and Equipment* and IAS 38 *Intangible Assets*, directly attributable costs are considered as a part of the cost of acquisition and capitalised into the cost of the asset acquired.

The capitalisation of directly attributable costs is consistent with the adoption by IFRS 3 of the cost model in measuring the cost of the combination.

Costs of issuing debt and equity instruments

In issuing equity instruments such as shares as part of the consideration paid, transaction costs such as stamp duties, professional advisers fees, underwriting costs and brokerage fees may be incurred. According to paragraph 31 of IFRS 3, these costs are an integral part of the equity issue transaction and therefore must be recognised by the acquirer directly in equity. This is in accordance with IAS 32 *Financial Instruments: Disclosure and Presentation*, as such costs reduce the proceeds from the equity issue. Hence, if costs of $1000 are incurred in issuing shares as part of the consideration paid, the journal entry in the records of the acquirer is:

Share capital	Dr	1 000	
Cash	Cr		1 000
(Costs of issuing equity instruments)			

Similarly, as stated in paragraph 30 of IFRS 3, the costs of arranging and issuing financial liabilities are an integral part of the liability issue transaction. These costs are included in the initial measurement of the liability.

Contingencies

Paragraph 32 of IFRS 3 states:

> When a business combination agreement provides for an adjustment to the cost of the combination contingent on future events, the acquirer shall include the amount of that adjustment in the cost of the combination at the acquisition date if the adjustment is *probable* and can be measured reliably.

Paragraph 33 of IFRS 3 provides two examples of contingencies. The first is where, because the future income of the acquirer is regarded as uncertain, the agreement contains a clause that requires the acquirer to provide additional consideration to the acquiree if the income of the acquirer is not equal to or exceeds a specified amount over some specified period. The second situation is where the acquirer issues shares to the acquiree and the acquiree is concerned that the issue of these shares may make the market price of the acquirer's shares decline over time. Therefore, the acquirer may offer additional cash or shares if the market price falls below a specified amount over a specified period of time. The acquirer must measure the fair value of these contingent considerations and include the amounts in the fair value of the consideration paid.

According to paragraph 32 of IFRS 3, in order to include contingencies in the fair value of the consideration paid, the amount must be probable and able to be measured reliably. Paragraph 33 states that:

> It is usually possible to estimate the amount of any such adjustment at the time of initially accounting for the combination without impairing the reliability of the information, even though some uncertainty exists.

If the contingencies are not recognised in the calculation of the fair value of the consideration given, and if the adjustment becomes probable and can be measured reliably, an adjustment is made to the amount of consideration paid, with a subsequent adjustment to goodwill acquired (paragraph 33).

ILLUSTRATIVE EXAMPLE 12.1

Cost of a business combination

The trial balance below represents the financial position of Auckland Ltd at 1 January 2005.

AUCKLAND LTD
Trial balance as at 1 January 2005

	Debit	Credit
Share capital		
Preference — 6000 fully paid shares		$ 6 000
Ordinary — 30 000 fully paid shares		30 000
Retained earnings		21 500
Equipment	$42 000	
Accumulated depreciation — equipment		10 000
Inventory	18 000	
Accounts receivable	16 000	
Patents	3 500	
Debentures		4 000
Accounts payable		8 000
	$79 500	$79 500

→

At this date, the business of Auckland Ltd is acquired by Wellington Ltd, with Auckland Ltd going into liquidation. The terms of acquisition are as follows:

1. Wellington Ltd is to take over all the assets of Auckland Ltd as well as the accounts payable of Auckland Ltd.
2. Costs of liquidation of $350 are to be paid by Auckland Ltd with funds supplied by Wellington Ltd.
3. Preference shareholders of Auckland Ltd are to receive two fully paid shares in Wellington Ltd for every three shares held or, alternatively, $1 per share in cash payable at exchange date.
4. Ordinary shareholders of Auckland Ltd are to receive two fully paid ordinary shares in Wellington Ltd for every share held or, alternatively, $2.50 in cash, payable half at the exchange date and half in one year's time.
5. Debenture holders of Auckland Ltd are to be paid in cash out of funds provided by Wellington Ltd. These debentures have a fair value of $102 per $100 debenture.
6. All shares being issued by Wellington Ltd have a fair value of $1.10 per share. Holders of 3000 preference shares and 5000 ordinary shares elect to receive the cash.
7. Costs of issuing and registering the shares issued by Wellington Ltd amount to $40 for the preference shares and $100 for the ordinary shares.
8. Costs expected to be incurred in delivering and installing the acquired assets amount to $1000.

The calculation of the cost of the business combination to Wellington Ltd is shown in figure 12.4. The incremental borrowing rate for Wellington Ltd is 10% per annum.

COST OF THE BUSINESS COMBINATION

			Fair value
Purchase consideration:			
Cash: Costs of liquidation		$ 350	
Preference shareholders (3000 × $1.00)		3 000	
Ordinary shareholders			
• payable immediately (1/2 × 5000 × $2.50)		6 250	
• payable later (1/2 × 5000 × $2.50 × 0.909 091)*		5 682	
Debentures, including premium ($4000 × 1.02)		4 080	$19 362
Shares: Preference shareholders (2000 × $1.10)		2 200	
Ordinary shareholders (50 000 × $1.10)		55 000	57 200
Cost of consideration paid to Auckland Ltd			76 562
Directly attributable costs:			
Incidental costs			1 000
Cost of the business combination			**$77 562**

*$5682 is the cash payable in one year's time discounted at 10% p.a.

FIGURE 12.4 Cost of the business combination

In acquiring the net assets of Auckland Ltd, Wellington Ltd passes the journal entries shown in figure 12.5.

1 January 2005			
Net assets acquired	Dr	77 562	
Consideration payable	Cr		19 362
Share capital – preference	Cr		2 200
Share capital – ordinary	Cr		55 000
Costs payable	Cr		1 000
(Acquisition of the net assets of Auckland Ltd)			
Consideration payable	Dr	13 680	
Cash	Cr		13 680
(Payment of cash consideration to Auckland Ltd:			
$19 362 less $5682 payable later)			
Costs payable	Dr	1 000	
Cash	Cr		1 000
(Payment of directly attributable costs)			
Share capital – ordinary	Dr	100	
Share capital – preference	Dr	40	
Cash	Cr		140
(Share issue costs)			
1 January 2006			
Consideration payable	Dr	5 682	
Interest expense	Dr	568	
Cash	Cr		6 250
(Balance of consideration paid)			

FIGURE 12.5   Journal entries in the acquirer's records

LO 8

12.3.2 Allocating the cost of the business combination

Paragraph 36 of IFRS 3 includes the following statement:

> The acquirer shall, at the acquisition date, allocate the cost of a business combination by recognising the acquiree's identifiable assets, liabilities and contingent liabilities that satisfy the recognition criteria in paragraph 37 at their fair values at that date ...

Note the following:
- The allocation, including the measurement of fair values, occurs at acquisition date.
- The allocation requires the recognition of:
  - identifiable tangible assets
  - identifiable intangible assets
  - liabilities
  - contingent liabilities.
- The measurement is at fair value.

Each of the items recognised as a result of the allocation and the recognition criteria in paragraph 37 of IFRS 3 are considered separately below.

Identifiable tangible assets

According to the IASB Framework, paragraph 83, there are two tests to be met prior to the recognition of an asset: the expected future benefits flowing to the entity must be probable, and the cost or value of the asset must be able to be reliably measured.

Paragraph 37(a) of IFRS 3 provides similar recognition criteria for tangible assets recognised in a business combination. Tangible assets acquired as part of a business combination are separately recognised by the acquirer if:

> in the case of an asset other than an *intangible* asset, it is probable that any associated future economic benefits will flow to the acquirer, and its fair value can be measured reliably ...

In appendix B to IFRS 3, paragraph B16, the following guidance is given for the measurement of fair value for identifiable tangible assets:

1. *Financial instruments traded in an active market.* The acquirer uses current market values.
2. *Financial instruments not traded in an active market.* The acquirer uses estimated values that take into consideration features such as price-earnings ratios, dividend yields and expected growth rates of comparable securities of entities with similar characteristics.
3. *Receivables, beneficial contracts and other identifiable assets.* The acquirer uses the present values of the amounts to be received, determined at appropriate current interest rates, less allowances for uncollectability and collection costs, if necessary. However, discounting is not required for short-term receivables, beneficial contracts and other identifiable assets when the difference between the nominal and discounted amounts is not material.
4. *Inventories of:*
   - *finished goods and merchandise.* The acquirer uses selling prices less the sum of (1) the costs of disposal and (2) a reasonable profit allowance for the selling effort of the acquirer based on profit for similar finished goods and merchandise
   - *work in progress.* The acquirer uses selling prices of finished goods less the sum of (1) costs to complete, (2) costs of disposal and (3) a reasonable profit allowance for the completing and selling effort based on profit for similar finished goods
   - *raw materials.* The acquirer uses current replacement costs.
5. *Land and buildings.* The acquirer uses market values.
6. *Plant and equipment.* The acquirer uses market values, normally determined by appraisal. When there is no evidence of market value because of the specialised nature of the plant and equipment, or because the items are rarely sold except as part of a continuing business, they are valued at their depreciated replacement cost.
7. *Net employee benefit assets for defined benefit plans.* The acquirer uses the present value of the defined benefit plan obligation less the fair value of any plan assets. However, an asset is recognised only to the extent that it will be available to the acquirer in the form of refunds from the plan or a reduction in future contributions.
8. *Tax assets.* The acquirer uses the amount of the tax benefit arising from tax losses or the taxes payable in respect of the taxable profit, assessed from the perspective of the combined entity. The tax asset is determined after allowing for the tax effect of restating identifiable assets, liabilities and contingent liabilities to their fair values and is not discounted. (Note that the requirement not to discount the tax assets means that the amount used is not equal to fair value.)

Intangible assets

Paragraph 37(c) of IFRS 3 requires the acquirer to recognise separately each intangible asset acquired if it satisfies the following criteria:

> in the case of an intangible asset ..., its fair value can be measured reliably.

Note that, unlike tangible assets, there is no probability test, only a reliability test.

Accounting for intangible assets acquired in a business combination is covered in IFRS 38 (see chapter 11). Paragraph 33 of this standard states that the fair value of an intangible asset reflects market expectations about the probability that the future economic benefits embodied in the asset will flow to the entity. For example, if the expected benefits for an item of plant are $1000 and the probability of receiving these benefits is 90%, then the fair value of the plant is $900. The fair value measurement incorporates the probability of receiving the benefits. Therefore, the probability test established in the IASB Framework is always satisfied.

Paragraph 35 of IAS 38 states that the fair value of an intangible asset acquired in a business combination *can normally be measured with sufficient reliability* to qualify for separate recognition. Paragraph 35 further states that, if an intangible asset acquired in a business combination has a finite useful life, there is a *rebuttable presumption* that its fair value can be measured reliably. Hence, the IASB's expectation is that intangible assets acquired in a business combination will always be separately recognised. Paragraph 38 considers that the only circumstance where separate recognition is not possible is where the asset:

- is not separable; or
- is separable, but there is no history or evidence of exchange transactions for the same or similar assets.

To illustrate the application of the recognition criteria for intangible assets, paragraph 34 of IAS 38 considers the case of an in-process research and development project not recognised by the acquiree at acquisition date. For the acquirer to recognise this asset as a part of the business combination, it must test to see if the project meets the definition of an intangible asset, and if the fair value can be measured reliably.

Paragraphs 39–41 of IFRS 38 provide information on how the fair value of intangible assets acquired in a business combination should be measured. In essence, fair value will be determined:

1. by reference to an active market as defined in IFRS 38; or
2. if no active market exists, on a basis that reflects the amounts the acquirer would have paid for the assets in arm's-length transactions between knowledgeable, willing parties, based on the best information available (this requires the consideration of the outcome of recent transactions for similar assets); or
3. valuation techniques may be used if their objective is to measure fair value and if they reflect current transactions and practices in the industry to which the asset belongs.

Paragraph BC96 of the Basis for Conclusions on IFRS 3 states that the IASB recognises that there is an inconsistency between the recognition criteria for assets in the Framework and those required for intangible assets acquired in a business combination in that, with the latter, there is no probability test. However, the IASB believed that the role of probability in measurement of fair values should be part of an overall project reviewing the Framework. It could also be argued that, if there is no need for a probability test for intangible assets, the test should also be dropped for tangible assets and for liabilities.

As a part of its illustrative examples accompanying IFRS 3, the IASB provided the following examples of items acquired in a business combination that would meet the definition of an intangible asset:

Marketing-related intangible assets

> Trademarks, trade names, service marks, collective marks and certification marks
> Internet domain names
> Trade dress — unique colour, shape or package design
> Newspaper mastheads
> Non-competition agreements

Customer-related intangible assets

> Customer lists
> Order or production backlog
> Customer contracts and the related customer relationships
> Non-contractual customer relationships

(continued)

Artistic-related intangible assets

    Plays, operas and ballets
    Books, magazines, newspapers and other literary works
    Musical works such as compositions, song lyrics and advertising jingles
    Pictures and photographs
    Video and audiovisual material, including films, music videos and television programs

Contract-based intangible assets

    Licensing, royalty and standstill agreements
    Advertising, construction, management, service or supply contracts
    Lease agreements
    Construction permits
    Franchise agreements
    Operating and broadcasting rights
    Use rights such as drilling, water, air, mineral, timber-getting and route authorities
    Servicing contracts such as mortgage servicing contracts
    Employment contracts priced below their market value

Technology-based intangible contracts

    Patented technology
    Computer software and mask works
    Unpatented technology
    Databases
    Trade secrets such as secret formulas, processes or recipes

Liabilities

Paragraph 37(b) of IFRS 3 establishes the recognition criteria for liabilities assumed as part of a business combination. Separate recognition occurs if:

> in the case of a liability other than a contingent liability, it is probable that an outflow of resources embodying economic benefits will be required to settle the obligation, and its fair value can be measured reliably ...

As with identifiable tangible assets, both the probability and the reliability tests must be met in order to separately recognise liabilities assumed in a business combination.

Paragraph B16 of appendix B to IFRS 3 provides the following guidance on the recognition of liabilities:

- *Net employee benefit liabilities for defined benefit plans.* The acquirer uses the present value of the defined benefit plan obligation less the fair value of any plan assets.
- *Tax liabilities.* The acquirer uses the amount of the tax benefit arising from tax losses or the taxes payable in respect of profit or loss, assessed from the perspective of the combined entity. The tax liability is determined after allowing for the tax effect of restating identifiable assets, liabilities and contingent liabilities to their fair values and is not discounted.
- *Accounts and notes payable, long-term debt, liabilities, accruals and other claims payable.* The acquirer uses the present values of amounts to be dispersed in meeting the liabilities determined at appropriate current interest rates. However, discounting is not required for short-term liabilities when the difference between the nominal and discounted amounts is not material.
- *Onerous contracts and other identifiable liabilities of the acquiree.* The acquirer uses the present values of amounts to be disbursed in meeting the obligations determined at appropriate current interest rates.

In paragraph 41 of IFRS 3, it is stated that only the liabilities of the acquiree that existed at the acquisition date are to be recognised separately by the acquirer. One of the areas of concern is whether or not an acquirer should recognise a liability in relation to outlays associated with restructuring the acquiree. Paragraph 41(a) states that the acquirer should recognise a provision for restructuring only when, at the acquisition date, the acquiree has an existing liability for restructuring recognised in accordance with IAS 37 *Provisions, Contingent Liabilities and Contingent Assets*. Paragraph 72 of IAS 37 sets down the conditions for recognition of restructuring provisions (see chapter 5). Note that the requirement is for the acquiree, not the acquirer, to have such a liability at acquisition date.

Paragraphs BC76–BC87 of the Basis for Conclusions on IFRS 3 provide information on why the IASB formed this policy. Those in favour of the acquirer recognising a liability even where the acquiree did not have a liability at acquisition date argue that the acquirer will take the possibility of reconstruction and the associated costs into account in determining the price paid for the acquiree, so the liability should be recognised at acquisition. The IASB rejected this argument on the grounds that the acquirer did not have a liability at the acquisition date for such costs, in the same way as there should be no recognition by the acquirer of any expected future losses of the acquiree.

A further alternative considered by the IASB in paragraph BC86 is for the liability to be raised by the acquirer; that is, as a liability incurred by the acquirer as part of the cost of the business combination. The IASB stated that the acquirer could raise such a liability only if the conditions for recognising a restructuring provision as set down in IAS 37 are met. This means that the acquirer, at or before the acquisition date, must have developed a detailed formal plan for the restructuring or raised valid expectations that it will carry out a restructuring.

Paragraph 42 of IFRS 3 discusses the accounting for payments triggered by a business combination. For example, an entity may have contractual arrangements with certain of its employees that certain payments will be made to them in the event of a business combination. These arrangements are often referred to as 'golden parachutes'. Before the business combination, these are contingent liabilities of the acquiree and are generally unrecognised because the payments would not meet the probability recognition criterion. In the event of a business combination occurring, the payments become probable and, at the time of the acquisition, the acquiree would recognise the expected payments as a liability. In accounting for the business combination, the acquirer would then recognise these expected payments as one of the assumed liabilities.

Contingent assets and liabilities

Contingent assets and liabilities are discussed in greater detail in chapter 5 as part of the discussion of IAS 37 *Provisions, Contingent Liabilities and Contingent Assets*. Appendix A to IFRS 3 contains the following definition of a contingent liability:

Contingent liability has the meaning given to it in IAS 37 *Provisions, Contingent Liabilities and Contingent Assets*, i.e.:
(a) a possible obligation that arises from past events and whose existence will be confirmed only by the occurrence or non-occurrence of one or more uncertain future events not wholly within the control of the entity; or
(b) a present obligation that arises from past events but is not recognised because:
  (i) it is not probable that an outflow of resources embodying economic benefits will be required to settle the obligation; or
  (ii) the amount of the obligation cannot be measured with sufficient reliability.

Note that there are two types of contingent liabilities: real liabilities (present obligations) that are not recognised because of a failure to meet the recognition criteria, and non-liabilities (possible obligations).

Paragraph 37(c) of IFRS 3 provides the criteria for recognition by the acquirer of contingent liabilities of the acquiree:

in the case of ... a contingent liability, its fair value can be measured reliably.

As with intangible assets, the only test for recognition of contingent liabilities is the reliability test. The probability test is assumed to be met because the fair value measurement takes the probability factors into consideration. Hence, contingent liabilities not recognised in the records of the acquiree may be recognised in the records of the acquirer as a result of the business combination.

Paragraph B16(l) of appendix B to IFRS 3 provides the following guidance in relation to measurement of the fair value of a contingent liability:

> for contingent liabilities of the acquiree, the acquirer shall use the amounts that a third party would charge to assume those contingent liabilities. Such an amount shall reflect all expectations about possible cash flows and not the single most likely or the expected maximum or minimum cash flow.

There are three problems associated with the IFRS 3 requirements in relation to contingent liabilities:

1. As discussed in relation to intangible assets, not requiring a probability test as well as a reliability test conflicts with the IASB Framework and the criteria for recognition of liabilities.

2. It was noted earlier that there are two types of contingent liabilities: possible liabilities and real liabilities. Where an acquiree has a real liability that is recognised as a contingent liability due to a failure to meet the probability test, then it is conceivable under point 1 above that an acquirer could recognise such a liability in its records. However, IFRS 3 also requires an acquirer to recognise possible liabilities of the acquiree in its records. This seems to be a major problem with the IASB Framework and the definition of liabilities as present obligations.

3. IFRS 3 requires the recognition of contingent liabilities of the acquiree, but not contingent assets. Paragraph BC117 of the Basis for Conclusions on IFRS 3 recognises this inconsistency and suggests that the IASB decided to leave contingent assets to Phase II of the Business Combinations project.

A further issue relating to contingent liabilities is the accounting for these items *subsequent to* their initial recognition. Paragraph 48 of IFRS 3 states:

> After their initial recognition, the acquirer shall measure contingent liabilities that are recognised separately in accordance with paragraph 36 at the higher of:
>
> (a) the amount that would be recognised under IAS 37, and
>
> (b) the amount initially recognised less, where appropriate, cumulative amortisation recognised in accordance with IAS 18 *Revenue*.

Contingent liabilities are not recognised under IAS 37, but liabilities in general are measured as the best estimate of the expenditure required to settle the obligation at balance date. IAS 18 establishes criteria for the recognition of revenue and hence the non-recognition of revenue if these criteria are not met. A liability may be recognised in such circumstances. Application of the criteria in IAS 18 determines when a liability may be derecognised and revenue recognised.

LO 9

12.3.3 Goodwill

Paragraph 51 of IFRS 3 states:

> The acquirer shall, at the acquisition date:
>
> (a) recognise goodwill acquired in a business combination as an asset; and
>
> (b) initially measure that goodwill at its cost, being the excess of the cost of the business combination over the acquirer's interest in the net fair value of the identifiable assets, liabilities and contingent liabilities recognised in accordance with paragraph 36.

Note the following:

• The cost of the business combination is measured at the date of exchange.

• The allocation process determines the identifiable assets, liabilities and contingent liabilities to be measured at fair value at acquisition date.

• Goodwill is measured at the acquisition date as the difference between the above two amounts.

> Goodwill = Cost of the business combination
> *less*
> Acquirer's interest in the net fair value of the acquiree's identifiable assets, liabilities and contingent liabilities.

- Goodwill is an asset.

Goodwill is defined in appendix A to IFRS 3 as: 'Future economic benefits arising from assets that are not capable of being individually identified and separately recognised'. The criterion of 'being individually identified' relates to the characteristic of 'identifiability' as used in IAS 38 *Intangible Assets* to distinguish intangible assets from goodwill. Note paragraph 11 of IAS 38 in this regard:

> The definition of an intangible asset requires an intangible asset to be identifiable to distinguish it from goodwill. Goodwill acquired in a business combination represents a payment made by the acquirer in anticipation of future economic benefits from assets that are not capable of being individually identified and separately recognised. The future economic benefits may result from synergy between the identifiable assets acquired or from assets that, individually, do not qualify for recognition in the financial statements but for which the acquirer is prepared to make a payment in the business combination.

In order to be identifiable, an asset must be capable of being separated or divided from the entity, or arise from contractual or other legal rights. The notion of being 'separately recognised' is also then a part of the criterion of 'identifiability'. This criterion is discussed further in chapter 11.

Goodwill is then a residual, after the acquirer's interest in the identifiable tangible assets, intangible assets, liabilities and contingent liabilities of the acquiree is recognised.

The components of goodwill

Johnson and Petrone (1998, p. 295) identified six components of goodwill:

1. *Excess of the fair values over the book values of the acquiree's recognised assets*. In a business acquisition, as assets acquired are measured at fair value, these excesses should not exist. Subsequent to the acquisition, the acquiree's goodwill could include such excesses where assets are measured at cost.
2. *Fair values of other net assets not recognised by the acquiree*. The assets of concern here are those tangible assets which are incapable of reliable measurement by the acquirer, and non-physical assets that do not meet the identifiability criteria for intangible assets.
3. *Fair value of the 'going concern' element of the acquiree's existing business*. This represents the ability of the acquiree to earn a higher return on an assembled collection of net assets than would be expected from those net assets operating separately. This reflects synergies of the assets, as well as factors relating to market imperfections such as an ability of an entity to earn a monopoly profit, or where there are barriers to competitors entering a particular market.
4. *Fair value from combining the acquirer's and acquiree's businesses and net assets*. This stems from the synergies that result from the combination, the value of which is unique to each combination.
5. *Overvaluation of the consideration paid by the acquirer*. This relates to errors in valuing the consideration paid by the acquirer, and may arise particularly where shares are issued as consideration, with differences in prices for small parcels of shares as opposed to controlling parcels of shares. There could also be overvaluation of the fair values of the assets acquired. This component could then relate to all errors in measuring the fair values in the business combination.
6. *Overpayment (or underpayment) by the acquirer*. This may occur if the price is driven up in the course of bidding. Conversely, goodwill could be understated if the acquiree's net assets were obtained through a distress or fire sale.

In paragraph BC130 of the Basis for Conclusions on IFRS 3, the IASB recognises components 3–6 in the previous list as being components of goodwill. Johnson and Petrone (1998, p. 295) and the IASB (paragraph BC131) recognised that components 5 and 6 were not conceptually part of goodwill, but rather relate to measurement errors. The two components that are seen as part of goodwill are then components 3 and 4. Component 3 is described by Johnson and Petrone (p. 296) as 'going-concern goodwill' and component 4 as 'combination goodwill', with the combination of the components being referred to as 'core goodwill'. This is represented diagrammatically in figure 12.6.

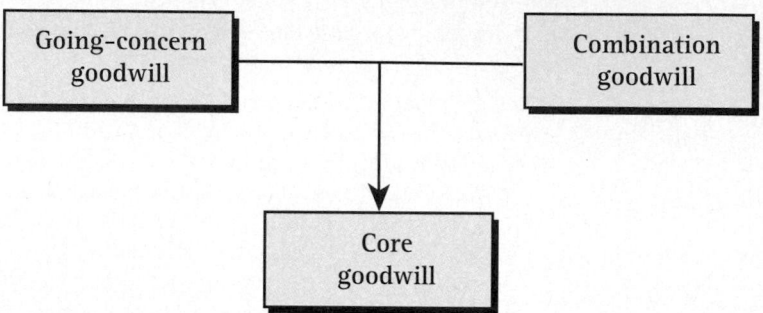

FIGURE 12.6 Two components of core goodwill
Source: Data derived from Johnson & Petrone (1998).

It is this 'core goodwill' that the IASB is concerned with in determining how to account for goodwill. The IASB (paragraphs BC133–BC135) recognises that components such as 5 and 6 are not really assets, but also acknowledges that it is not feasible to measure the separate components of goodwill. Rather than write the whole of goodwill off because it contained components 5 and 6, the IASB argues that it is more representationally faithful to recognise goodwill as an asset.

Figure 12.7 contains an extract from the Nokia 2005 annual report relating to that entity's acquisition of Intellisync. Note the company's description of the items that are expected to generate goodwill.

Acquisition of Intellisync

In February 2006, the Group acquired 100 percent of the outstanding common shares of Intellisync (NASDAQ: SYNC) for cash consideration of approximately EUR 368 million. Intellisync delivers wireless email and other applications over an array of devices and application platforms across carrier networks. The Group believes it is positioned to deliver the industry's most complete offering for the development, deployment and management of mobility in the enterprise and the acquisition will enhance the Group's ability to respond to customer needs in this fast growing market. Intellisync will be integrated into the Enterprise Solutions business upon acquisition and its results of operations from that date will be included in the Group's consolidated financial statements The purchase price allocation is being performed with the assistance of a third party.

Assets acquired are expected to be EUR 51 million and liabilities EUR 17 million with a majority of the excess recognised as goodwill. The principal items that are expected to generate goodwill are the value of the synergies between Intellisync and the Group and the acquired workforce, neither of which qualifies as a separate amortizable intangible asset. None of the goodwill is expected to be deductible for tax purposes. The Group does not expect to write off any in-process R&D or dispose of any one of the acquired operations.

FIGURE 12.7 Components of goodwill
Source: Nokia (2005, p. 34).

Is goodwill an asset?

Whether core goodwill is an asset is considered in detail in Johnson and Petrone (1998, pp. 296–302) and in Miller and Islam (1988). There are many other articles in the accounting literature that discuss this issue, because it has been a source of much debate in the accounting literature. Of the accounting standard-setting bodies that have considered the issue, the Accounting Standards Board in the United Kingdom in 1997, in its Financial Reporting Standard 10 *Goodwill and Intangible Assets*, took the view that goodwill is not an asset (*Summary*, para. b):

> Goodwill arising on acquisition is neither an asset like other assets nor an immediate loss in value. Rather, it forms the bridge between the cost of an investment shown as an asset in the acquirer's own financial statements and the values attributed to the acquired assets and liabilities in the consolidated financial statements. Although purchased goodwill is not in itself an asset, its inclusion amongst the assets of the reporting entity, rather than as a deduction from shareholders' equity, recognises that goodwill is part of a larger asset, the investment, for which management remains accountable.

As defined in the IASB Framework, an asset has essentially three characteristics: expected future economic benefits, control over the benefits, and the benefits have arisen as the result of a past event. There is little debate over whether goodwill is a repository of expected future economic benefits, as this is evidenced by the fact that the acquirer has been prepared to pay extra consideration over and above an amount equal to the fair value of the acquiree's identifiable net assets. Similarly, the existence of the business combination is seen as a past event. The key area of debate is whether the entity has control over the benefits.

The meaning of 'control' in relation to intangibles is discussed in chapter 11 of this book. It is argued there that the IASB, because of the debates over whether items such as well-trained employees or marketing outlays are assets, introduces the identifiability criterion to ensure that the only items recognised as intangible assets are those that are separable or arise from contractual or other legal rights. Paragraph BC132 of the Basis for Conclusions on IFRS 3 recognises that goodwill arises in part because of factors, such as having a well-trained workforce and loyal customers, that are not seen as controllable by the entity and therefore are not assets.

The problem with goodwill is that it is a unique asset. It arises as a residual. As Leo et al. (1995, pp. 44–7) noted, the key difference between identifiable net assets and goodwill is measurement:

> The difference between the measurement method used for goodwill and that for measurement of all other assets of the business is whether the method involves determining the value of the business as a whole or part thereof.

The authors (p. 46) defined unidentifiable assets as those assets that meet the recognition criteria and cannot be measured without measuring the total net assets of a business entity. The existence of goodwill is dependent on the measurement of the entity as a whole. In recognising this, the IASB argued in paragraph BC132 of the Basis for Conclusions on IFRS 3 that:

> in the case of core goodwill, control is provided by means of the acquirer's power to direct the policies and management of the acquiree. Therefore, the Board concluded that core goodwill meets the *Framework's* definition of an asset.

As a residual, goodwill includes any assets, liabilities and contingent liabilities of the acquiree that do not meet the criteria in paragraph 37 of IFRS 3 for separate recognition at acquisition date.

Subsequent accounting for goodwill

Paragraph 54 of IFRS 3 states:

> After initial recognition, the acquirer shall measure goodwill acquired in a business combination at cost less any accumulated impairment losses.

Hence, having recognised the goodwill arising in the business combination, it follows that:

- goodwill is not subject to amortisation but is subject to an annual impairment test as detailed in IAS 36 *Impairment of Assets* (see chapter 13).
- goodwill cannot be revalued because IAS 38 *Intangible Assets* does not allow the recognition of internally generated goodwill.

The IASB did consider the use of amortisation methods in accounting for goodwill subsequent to initial recognition. However, as noted in paragraph BC140 of the Basis for Conclusions on IFRS 3, the IASB:

> agreed that achieving an acceptable level of reliability in the form of representational faith-fulness, while at the same time striking some balance between what is practicable, was the primary challenge ...

Further:

> the useful life of acquired goodwill and the pattern in which it diminishes generally are not possible to predict, yet its amortisation depends on such predictions.

Given then the arbitrary nature of any amortisation method, the IASB preferred to rely on the application of a rigorous impairment test to account for goodwill.

Accounting for goodwill

As noted earlier, goodwill is calculated as the excess of the cost of the business combination over the acquirer's interest in the net fair value of the identifiable assets, liabilities and contingent liabilities of the acquiree. Hence, to calculate goodwill, as a part of the acquisition analysis it is necessary to calculate the cost of the combination, being the sum of the fair value of the consideration paid and any directly attributable costs, and the net fair value of the identifiable assets, liabilities and contingent liabilities acquired. A comparison of these two amounts determines the existence of goodwill. The acquirer then recognises goodwill as an asset in the same way as for all other identifiable assets acquired.

ILLUSTRATIVE EXAMPLE 12.2

Acquisition analysis

Using the figures from illustrative example 12.1 on pages 495–7, assume that Wellington Ltd assesses the fair values of the identifiable assets, liabilities and contingent liabilities of Auckland Ltd to be as follows:

Equipment	$36 000
Inventory	20 000
Accounts receivable	9 000
Patents	4 000
Furniture	6 000
	75 000
Accounts payable	8 000
	$67 000

In determining the entries to be passed by the acquirer, it is useful to prepare an acquisition analysis that consists of a comparison of cost of the business combination and the net fair value of the identifiable assets, liabilities and contingent liabilities acquired. The acquisition analysis for this example is shown in figure 12.8.

Net fair value of identifiable assets, liabilities and contingent liabilities acquired:

Equipment	$36 000
Inventory	20 000
Accounts receivable	9 000
Patents	4 000
Furniture	6 000
	75 000
Accounts payable	8 000
Net fair value acquired	$67 000

Cost of the business combination:
This was calculated in figure 12.4 on page 496 as $77 562.

Goodwill acquired:

Net fair value acquired	= $67 000
Cost of business combination	= $77 562
Goodwill	= $77 562 − $67 000
	= $10 562

FIGURE 12.8   Acquisition analysis by the acquirer

The journal entries in the records of Wellington Ltd at acquisition date are as shown in figure 12.9.

Journal of Wellington Ltd			
Equipment	Dr	36 000	
Inventory	Dr	20 000	
Accounts receivable	Dr	9 000	
Patents	Dr	4 000	
Furniture	Dr	6 000	
Goodwill	Dr	10 562	
Accounts payable	Cr		8 000
Consideration payable	Cr		19 362
Share capital − preference	Cr		2 200
Share capital − ordinary	Cr		55 000
Costs payable	Cr		1 000
(Acquisition of the assets and liabilities of Auckland Ltd)			
Consideration payable	Dr	13 680	
Cash	Cr		13 680
(Payment of cash consideration)			
Costs payable	Dr	1 000	
Cash	Cr		1 000
(Payment of directly attributable costs)			
Share capital − ordinary	Dr	100	
Share capital − preference	Dr	40	
Cash	Cr		140
(Share issue costs)			

FIGURE 12.9   Journal entries in the acquirer, including recognition of goodwill

LO 10   12.3.4   Accounting for an excess

Where the acquirer's interest in the net fair value of the acquiree's identifiable assets, liabilities and contingent liabilities is greater than the cost of the business combination, the difference is called an 'excess'. In equation format, it can be represented as follows:

> Excess = Acquirer's interest in the net fair value of the acquiree's identifiable assets, liabilities and contingent liabilities
> *less*
> Cost of the business combination

The existence of an excess, according to paragraph 57 of IFRS 3, is due to one or more of the following three components:

- errors in measuring the fair value of either the consideration given or the assets, liabilities and contingent liabilities acquired
- a requirement of another accounting standard to measure identifiable assets acquired at an amount that is not fair value but is treated as though it is fair value for the purpose of measurement in a business combination; for example, deferred tax assets and liabilities are not discounted when their fair values are measured
- a bargain purchase; this could occur because the acquirer has excellent negotiation skills, or because the acquiree has made a sale for other than economic reasons or is forced to sell due to specific circumstances such as cash flow problems.

The IASB adopts the view that most business combinations are an exchange of equal amounts, given markets in which the parties to the business combinations are informed and willing participants in the transaction. Therefore, the existence of an excess is expected to be an unusual or rare event.

Paragraph 56 of IFRS 3 details the accounting procedure for an excess:

> If the acquirer's interest in the net fair value of the identifiable assets, liabilities and contingent liabilities recognised in accordance with paragraph 36 exceeds the cost of the business combination, the acquirer shall:
>
> (a) reassess the identification and measurement of the acquiree's identifiable assets, liabilities and contingent liabilities and the measurement of the cost of the combination; and
>
> (b) recognise immediately in profit or loss any excess remaining after that reassessment.

The first step in accounting for an excess is to reassess the measurements used in the acquisition analysis. This is in accord with the expectation that the existence of an excess is a rare occurrence, and that a prime cause is errors in measurement. If errors are not the cause, then the other major cause is the existence of a bargain purchase. The acquirer then recognises the excess as income immediately.

The IASB has considered and rejected other accounting treatments of the excess, such as the following:

- *Allocate the excess across the assets acquired in some fashion.* This method is seen as being consistent with the cost approach adopted in IFRS 3. However, it was rejected by the IASB (see paragraphs BC151–BC153 of the Basis for Conclusions on IFRS 3) because of the arbitrariness of the allocation, Phase II considerations relating to the working principle (see section 12.7 of this chapter), and the measurement problems that could arise subsequent to the allocation because the assets affected by the allocation would not be recognised at fair value.
- *Recognise the excess as a liability.* The problem with this approach is that the credit balance does not meet the definition as a liability. Similarly, to treat the item as a deferred credit and write it back to income over a period of time requires the recognition of an account which has no place within the elements recognised in the IASB Framework. Further, there is no obvious basis for choice of method for writing off the deferred credit.

ILLUSTRATIVE EXAMPLE 12.3

Excess on acquisition

Using the information of the cost of the business combination from illustrative examples 12.1 and 12.2, assume the fair values of the identifiable assets and liabilities of Auckland Ltd are assessed to be:

Equipment	$45 000
Inventory	25 000
Accounts receivable	9 000
Patents	5 000
Furniture	6 000
	90 000
Accounts payable	8 000
	$82 000

The acquisition analysis now shows:

Net fair value of assets and liabilities acquired	= $82 000
Cost of the business combination	= $77 562
Excess on acquisition	= $82 000 − $77 562
	= $4438

Assuming that the reassessment process did not result in any changes to the fair values calculated, the first journal entry in Wellington Ltd to record the acquisition of the net assets of Auckland Ltd is:

Equipment	Dr	45 000	
Inventory	Dr	25 000	
Accounts receivable	Dr	9 000	
Patents	Dr	5 000	
Furniture	Dr	6 000	
Accounts payable	Cr		8 000
Consideration payable	Cr		19 362
Share capital – preference	Cr		2 200
Share capital – ordinary	Cr		55 000
Costs payable	Cr		1 000
Excess (profit and loss)	Cr		4 438
(Acquisition of assets and liabilities acquired from Auckland Ltd, and the excess)			

12.3.5 ## Accounting by the acquirer for shares acquired in an acquiree

Where an entity acquires shares rather than the net assets of another entity, the acquirer records the shares acquired in accordance with paragraph 43 of IAS 39 *Financial Instruments: Recognition and Measurement*, namely at fair value plus transactions costs. It is expected that, in the majority of cases, the fair value of the shares acquired will equal the fair value of the consideration paid. The basic form of the journal entries in the records of the acquirer is shown overleaf.

Shares in acquiree	Dr	XXX	
Share capital	Cr		XXX
Cash	Cr		XXX
(Acquisition of shares in another entity)			

ILLUSTRATIVE EXAMPLE 12.4

Acquisition of shares in an acquiree

Assume that Wellington Ltd acquired all the issued shares in Auckland Ltd for $80 000, giving in exchange $10 000 cash and 20 000 shares in Wellington Ltd, the latter having a fair value of $3.50 per share. Transaction costs of $500 were paid in cash. Share issue costs were $1000. The journal entries in the records of Wellington Ltd at the acquisition date are as shown in figure 12.10.

Journal of Wellington Ltd			
Shares in Auckland Ltd	Dr	80 500	
Cash	Cr		10 500
Share capital	Cr		70 000
(Acquisition of shares in Auckland Ltd)			
Share capital	Dr	1 000	
Cash	Cr		1 000
(Costs of issuing shares to Auckland Ltd)			

FIGURE 12.10 Accounting for the acquisition of shares

LO 11

12.3.6 Pre-acquisition equity and the acquisition date

The effects of choosing the acquisition date are discussed in section 12.2.2 of this chapter. One of these effects relates to the determination of pre-acquisition equity and the effects on accounting for dividends. Accounting for dividends is affected by whether the dividend is paid from pre-acquisition or post-acquisition equity. In this regard, note the definition of the cost method in paragraph 4 of IAS 27 *Consolidated and Separate Financial Statements*:

> The cost method is a method of accounting for an investment whereby the investment is recognised at cost. The investor recognises income from the investment only to the extent that the investor receives distributions from retained earnings of the investee arising after the date of acquisition. Distributions received in excess of such earnings are regarded as a recovery of investment and are recognised as a reduction of the cost of the investment.

This principle is also recognised in paragraph 32 of IAS 18 *Revenue*. Dividends from pre-acquisition equity are treated as a reduction in the investment account because they are a return to the acquirer of equity that was previously paid for. Dividends from post-acquisition equity are revenue to the acquirer because they are appropriated from equity earned subsequent to the acquisition date. The determination of the acquisition date is very important as it affects how dividends are accounted for, and may affect the income reported by an entity that is receiving dividends from its investments in other entities.

To illustrate, consider the situation where A Ltd acquires all the issued shares of B Ltd, shown in figure 12.11. Assume that the retained earnings balance of B Ltd is:

1 July 2006	$10 000
15 July 2005	12 000
31 July 2006	15 000

Assume that B Ltd pays a dividend of $1000 on 1 August 2006. As A Ltd owns all the shares in B Ltd, it will receive all the dividend paid by B Ltd. What is the journal entry in the records of A Ltd to record the receipt of the dividend?

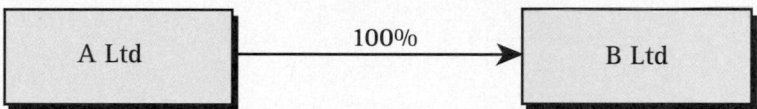

FIGURE 12.11   A Ltd acquires all the issued shares of B Ltd.

The answer depends on first determining the acquisition date in relation to A Ltd's acquisition of shares in B Ltd, and then calculating the profits from which the dividends were paid. Assume the acquisition date is 15 July 2006. *If* the dividend is paid from the $3000 earned between 15 and 31 July, then the dividend is from post-acquisition profits (that is, from profits earned subsequent to the acquisition date). In that case, the dividend received by the acquirer, A Ltd, is considered to be revenue to the acquirer. A Ltd would then pass the following entry:

Cash	Dr	1 000	
Dividend revenue	Cr		1 000
(Post-acquisition dividend from B Ltd)			

If the dividend is paid by B Ltd from profits earned prior to 15 July, the dividend is a pre-acquisition dividend. In that case, the dividend represents a cash return to the acquirer of part of the original equity acquired. Hence, the amount of the consideration paid for the investment is reduced by the amount of any such dividend. The entry in A Ltd is shown below.

Cash	Dr	1 000	
Shares in B Ltd	Cr		1 000
(Pre-acquisition dividend from B Ltd)			

If the dividend paid on 1 August is from the $3000 earned between 15 and 31 July, note the difference that a choice of acquisition date makes. If the acquisition date is 15 July, then the dividend is a post-acquisition dividend and recognised as revenue by A Ltd. If the acquisition date is 31 July, then the dividend is a pre-acquisition dividend and is a return of the investment to A Ltd. The choice of acquisition date affects how the acquirer accounts for dividends. Note then that an entity needs to specify from which profits a dividend is paid.

LO 12

12.4   Accounting in the records of the acquiree

Where the acquirer purchases the acquiree's assets and liabilities, the acquiree may continue in existence or liquidate. The accounts affected in the acquiree by the business combination will differ according to the actions of the acquiree.

12.4.1 Acquiree does not liquidate

In the situation where the acquiree disposes of a business, the journal entries required in the records of the acquiree are shown in figure 12.12. Under IAS 16 *Property, Plant and Equipment*, when an item of property, plant and equipment is sold, gains or losses are recognised in the income statement. Similarly, on the sale of a business, the acquiree recognises a gain or loss.

Journal of acquiree			
Receivable from acquirer	Dr	XXX	
Liability A	Dr	XXX	
Liability B	Dr	XXX	
Liability C	Dr	XXX	
Asset A	Cr		XXX
Asset B	Cr		XXX
Asset C	Cr		XXX
Gain on sale of operation*	Cr		XXX
(Sale of operation)			
*Separate proceeds on sale and carrying amounts of assets sold could be recognised			
Shares in acquirer	Dr	XXX	
Cash	Dr	XXX	
Receivable from acquirer	Cr		XXX
(Receipt of consideration from acquirer)			

FIGURE 12.12   Journal entries in acquiree on sale of business

12.4.2 Acquiree liquidates

The entries required in the records of the acquiree when it sells *all* its net assets to the acquirer are shown in figure 12.13. The accounts of the acquiree are transferred to two accounts: the liquidation account, and the shareholders' distribution account.

To the *liquidation account* are transferred:
- all assets taken over by the acquirer, including cash if relevant, as well as any assets not taken over and which have a zero value, including goodwill
- all liabilities taken over
- expenses of liquidation if paid by the acquiree
- consideration from the acquirer as proceeds on sale of net assets
- all reserves, including retained earnings.

The balance of the liquidation account is then transferred to the shareholders' distribution account.

To the *shareholders' distribution account* are transferred:
- the balance of share capital
- the balance of the liquidation account
- that portion of the consideration received from the acquirer that is distributed to the shareholders. Some of the consideration received by the acquiree may be used to pay for liabilities not assumed by the acquirer, and for liquidation expenses.

Journal of acquiree			
Liquidation	Dr	XXX	
Asset A	Cr		XXX
Asset B	Cr		XXX
Asset C	Cr		XXX
(Transfer of all assets acquired by acquirer, at their carrying amounts)			
Liability A	Dr	XXX	
Liability B	Dr	XXX	
Liability C	Dr	XXX	
Liquidation	Cr		XXX
(Transfer of all liabilities assumed by the acquirer)			
Liquidation	Dr	XXX	
Cash	Cr		XXX
(Liquidation expenses if paid by the acquiree)			
Receivable from acquirer	Dr	XXX	
Liquidation	Cr		XXX
(Consideration for net assets sold)			
Cash	Dr	XXX	
Shares in acquirer	Dr	XXX	
Receivable from acquirer	Cr		XXX
(Receipt of consideration)			
Other reserves	Dr	XXX	
Retained earnings	Dr	XXX	
Liquidation	Cr		XXX
(Transfer of reserves)			
Liquidation	Dr	XXX	
Shareholders' distribution	Cr		XXX
(Transfer of balance of liquidation)			
Share capital	Dr	XXX	
Shareholders' distribution	Cr		XXX
(Transfer of share capital)			
Shareholders' distribution	Dr	XXX	
Cash	Cr		XXX
Shares in acquirer	Cr		XXX
(Distribution of consideration to shareholders)			

FIGURE 12.13 Journal entries in acquiree on liquidation after sale of net assets

ILLUSTRATIVE EXAMPLE 12.5

Entries in the acquiree's records

Using the information from illustrative example 12.1 on pages 495–7, the entries in the records of Auckland Ltd are shown in figure 12.14 (below and opposite).

Journal of Auckland Ltd			
Liquidation	Dr	69 500	
Accumulated depreciation – equipment	Dr	10 000	
Equipment	Cr		42 000
Inventory	Cr		18 000
Accounts receivable	Cr		16 000
Patents	Cr		3 500
(Assets taken over)			
Accounts payable	Dr	8 000	
Liquidation	Cr		8 000
(Liabilities taken over)			
Liquidation	Dr	350	
Liquidation expenses payable	Cr		350
(Liquidation expenses)			
Liquidation	Dr	80	
Debenture holders payable	Cr		80
(Premium on debentures to be paid on redemption)			
Receivable from Wellington Ltd	Dr	76 562	
Liquidation	Cr		76 562
(Consideration receivable)			
Cash	Dr	13 680	
Shares in Wellington Ltd	Dr	57 200	
Receivable from Wellington Ltd	Cr		70 880
(Receipt of consideration from acquirer)			
Retained earnings	Dr	21 500	
Liquidation	Cr		21 500
(Transfer of retained earnings)			
Liquidation	Dr	36 132	
Shareholders' distribution	Cr		36 132
(Balance of liquidation account transferred to shareholders' distribution)			
Share capital – ordinary	Dr	30 000	
Share capital – preference	Dr	6 000	
Shareholders' distribution	Cr		36 000
(Transfer of share capital)			

Debentures	Dr	4 000	
Debenture holders payable	Cr		4 000
(Transfer of debentures to payable account)			
Liquidation expenses payable	Dr	350	
Debenture holders payable	Dr	4 080	
Cash	Cr		4 430
(Payment of liabilities)			
Shareholders' distribution	Dr	72 132	
Cash	Cr		9 250
Shares in Wellington Ltd	Cr		57 200
Receivable from Wellington Ltd	Cr		5 682
(Payment to shareholders)			

FIGURE 12.14 Liquidation of acquiree

12.4.3 Acquirer buys only shares in the acquiree

When the acquirer buys only shares in the acquiree, there are no entries in the records of the acquiree because the transaction is between the acquirer and the shareholders of the acquiree entity. The acquiree itself is not involved.

LO 13

12.5 Subsequent adjustments to the initial accounting for a business combination

The initial accounting for a business combination requires a determination of the fair values to be used in relation to the consideration paid as well as of the assets, liabilities and contingent liabilities acquired. It may be that at the end of the reporting period subsequent to the acquisition date, these amounts can be determined only provisionally. In order to provide a report, the acquirer must use the information available at reporting date, based on provisional fair value information. Paragraph 62 of IFRS 3 allows an acquirer 12 months from the acquisition date to determine the relevant fair values to be used in accounting for the business combination.

Once the initial accounting is complete (that is, up to 12 months after the acquisition date), apart from three exceptions relating to paragraphs 33, 34 and 65 of IFRS 3 (see below), any changes to the accounting for the business combination shall be made only to correct an error, and must be accounted for in accordance with IAS 8 *Accounting Policies, Changes in Accounting Estimates and Errors*. This requires a retrospective adjustment and a restatement of the financial statements as if the error had never occurred.

Paragraph 32 of IFRS 3 requires that, when the business combination agreement includes an adjustment to the cost that is contingent on a future event, the cost of the combination will include that adjustment if it is probable and can be measured reliably. Adjustments may be contingent, for example, on the level of income earned by the acquirer, or the market price of the shares issued by the acquirer being maintained.

Subsequent to the acquisition date, a number of events can occur in relation to that contingency:

- *The future events may not occur or the estimate may need to be revised.* Under paragraph 33 of IFRS 3, an adjustment to the cost of the combination is made, with a subsequent adjustment to goodwill. To illustrate, assume that A Ltd acquires all the net assets of B Ltd in exchange for shares in A Ltd. A Ltd agreed to pay B Ltd $1 for every $10 that the profit of A Ltd falls below $100 000 in the following year. A Ltd estimates that there is a 10% probability that the profit will be only $90 000, and estimates the fair value of the extra consideration to be $100 (10% × 1/10($100 000 − $90 000)). Hence, A Ltd raises a payable of $100 (for simplicity, discounting is disregarded). One year later, A Ltd reports a profit of $95 000 and pays B Ltd $50. A Ltd would pass the following entry:

Consideration payable	Dr	100	
Goodwill	Cr		50
Cash	Cr		50
(Contingent consideration paid)			

The adjustment to the cost of combination affects the goodwill recognised.

In the case of equity instruments, an increase in share capital is recognised at the date of exchange based upon the fair value of shares expected to be issued. These are not remeasured subsequent to initial recognition. This will be illustrated using the same example as above but assuming that A Ltd agrees to issue B Ltd an additional 100 shares if the market price of A Ltd shares drops below the market price of $25 at exchange date. A Ltd estimates the probability of this occurring as 10%. At the date of exchange, A Ltd would recognise share capital of $250 (10% × 100 × $25). Regardless of whether the shares are issued or not, there is no subsequent journal entry. This is based on the principle in IFRS 39 that financial instruments that are classified as equity should not be remeasured subsequent to initial recognition.

- *Where the adjustment was not included in the original calculation of the cost of the combination because the measurement criteria were not met, the adjustment could become probable and be able to be measured reliably.* Under paragraph 34, an adjustment is made to the cost of the combination, with a subsequent adjustment to goodwill or excess.
- *The acquirer could be required to make a subsequent payment to the seller as compensation for a reduction in assets given or equity instruments issued.* Under paragraph 35, where the acquirer is required to issue additional equity instruments or debt instruments, no increase in the cost of the combination is recognised. In the case of the issue of additional shares, the fair value of shares originally issued now simply reflects a lower fair value per share issued.

Paragraph 65 of IFRS 3 relates to the recognition of deferred taxes after the initial accounting is complete. If deferred tax assets acquired were not separately recognised during the initial accounting but are subsequently realised, the accounting for such subsequent recognition requires:

- a recognition of the tax assets and income, under IAS 12 *Income Taxes*
- a reduction in the carrying amount of goodwill to the amount that would have been recognised at acquisition date if the tax assets had been recognised at that date as an expense.

As noted in paragraphs BC167 and BC169 of the Basis for Conclusions on IFRS 3, the IASB carried forward without reconsideration from the replaced standard, IAS 22 *Business Combinations*, the requirements relating to the adjustments after the initial accounting is complete. These accounting requirements for the adjustments are exceptions to the basic principle that the initial accounting for a business combination should be adjusted only to correct errors. This is because IFRS 3 requires the fair value measures to be calculated at the date of exchange and the date of acquisition. Changes in these amounts are either errors or the result of post-acquisition events. Accounting for these adjustments was to be reconsidered in Phase II of the Business Combinations project, as discussed in section 12.7 of this chapter.

ILLUSTRATIVE EXAMPLE 12.6

Comprehensive example

Christchurch Ltd's major business is in the pet food industry. It makes a number of canned pet foods, primarily for cats and dogs, as well as having a very promising line in dry dog food. It has been interested for some time in the operations of Dunedin Ltd, an entity that deals with the processing of grain products for a number of other industries including flour-processing, health foods and, in more recent times, the production of grain products for feeding birds. Given its interest in the pet food industry and its desire to stay as one of the leaders in this area, Christchurch Ltd commenced negotiations with Dunedin Ltd to acquire its birdseed product division.

Negotiations commenced in July 2005. After months of discussion between the relevant parties of both companies, an agreement was reached on 15 February 2006 for Christchurch Ltd to acquire the birdseed division. The agreement document was taken to the board of directors of Dunedin Ltd, who ratified the agreement on 1 March 2006. The net assets were exchanged on this date.

The net assets of the birdseed division at 1 March 2006, showing the carrying amounts at that date and the fair values as estimated by Christchurch Ltd from documentation supplied by Dunedin Ltd, were as follows:

	Carrying amount	Fair value
Plant and equipment	$160 000	$167 000
Land	70 000	75 000
Motor vehicles	30 000	32 000
Inventory	24 000	28 000
Accounts receivable	18 000	16 000
Total assets	302 000	318 000
Accounts payable	35 000	35 000
Bank overdraft	55 000	55 000
Total liabilities	90 000	90 000
Net assets	$202 000	$228 000

Details of the consideration Christchurch Ltd agreed to provide in exchange for the net assets of the division are described below:

- 100 000 shares in Christchurch Ltd — movements in the share price were as follows:

1 July 2005	$1.00
1 October 2005	1.10
1 January 2006	1.15
1 February 2006	1.30
15 February 2006	1.32
16 February 2006	1.45
1 March 2006	1.50

- Because of doubts as to whether it could sustain a share price of at least $1.50, Christchurch Ltd agreed to supply cash to the value of any decrease in the share price below $1.50 for the 100 000 shares issued, this guarantee of the share price lasting until 31 July. Christchurch Ltd believed that there was a 90% chance that the share price would remain at $1.50 and a 10% chance that it would fall to $1.48.

→

- Cash of $40 000, half to be paid on date of exchange and half in one year's time.
- Supply of a patent relating to the manufacture of packing material. This has a fair value of $60 000 but has not been recognised in the records of Christchurch Ltd because it resulted from an internally generated research project.
- Dunedin Ltd was currently being sued for damages relating to a claim by a bird breeder who had bought some seed from the company, and claimed that this resulted in the death of some its prime breeding pigeons. Christchurch Ltd agreed to pay any resulting damages in relation to the court case. The expected damages were $40 000. Lawyers estimated that there was only a 20% chance of losing the case.

Christchurch Ltd supplied the cash on the acquisition date as well as surrendering the patent. The shares were issued on 5 March, the costs of issuing the shares amounting to $1000. The incremental borrowing rate for Christchurch Ltd is 10% per annum. Directly attributable costs paid by Christchurch Ltd in relation to the acquisition amounted to $5000.

On 1 June 2006, Christchurch Ltd, having taken possession of the plant and equipment, reassessed the fair value to be $165 000. Plant and equipment is depreciated on a straight-line basis at 10% per annum.

On 31 July, the share price of Christchurch Ltd's shares was $1.52.

Required

Prepare the journal entries in the records of the acquirer.

Solution

Acquisition analysis

Net fair value of assets and liabilities acquired:

Plant and equipment	$167 000
Land	75 000
Motor vehicles	32 000
Inventory	28 000
Accounts receivable	16 000
	318 000
Accounts payable	35 000
Bank overdraft	55 000
Provision for damages (20% × $40 000)	8 000
	98 000
	$220 000

Cost of the business combination:

Purchase consideration:		
Shares	100 000 × $1.50	$150 000
Guarantee	10% ($1.50 − $1.48) × 100 000	200
Cash	Payable now	20 000
	Deferred ($20 000 × 0.909 091)	18 182
Patent		60 000
		248 382
Directly attributable costs		5 000
		$253 382

→

Goodwill:

($253 382 − $220 000)	$ 33 382

The journal entries in the acquirer, Christchurch Ltd, are shown in figure 12.15.

Journal of Christchurch Ltd			
2006			
1 March			
Plant and equipment	Dr	167 000	
Land	Dr	75 000	
Motor vehicles	Dr	32 000	
Inventory	Dr	28 000	
Accounts receivable	Dr	16 000	
Goodwill	Dr	33 382	
Accounts payable	Cr		35 000
Bank overdraft	Cr		55 000
Provision for damages	Cr		8 000
Share capital	Cr		150 000
Provision for loss in value of shares	Cr		200
Cash	Cr		20 000
Consideration payable	Cr		18 182
Acquisition costs payable	Cr		5 000
Gain on sale of patent	Cr		60 000
(Acquisition of birdseed division from Dunedin Ltd)			
Acquisition costs payable	Dr	5 000	
Cash	Cr		5 000
(Payment of directly attributable costs)			
5 March			
Share capital	Dr	1 000	
Cash	Cr		1 000
(Costs of issuing shares)			
1 June			
Goodwill	Dr	2 000	
Plant and equipment	Cr		2 000
(Adjustment to the fair value of assets acquired from Dunedin Ltd)			
Accumulated depreciation	Dr	50	
Depreciation expense	Cr		50
(Being depreciation adjustment: 10% × $2000 for $\frac{1}{4}$ of a year, assuming depreciation is recorded elsewhere)			
31 July			
Provision for loss in value of shares	Dr	200	
Goodwill	Cr		200
(Contingency not having to be paid)			

FIGURE 12.15   Journal entries in the acquirer

LO 14   **12.6**   Disclosure — business combinations

Paragraphs 66–77 of IFRS 3 contain information on disclosures required in relation to business combinations. Paragraph 66 requires entities to disclose information about the nature and financial effect of business combinations occurring during the current reporting period as well as after the balance date but before the financial statements are authorised for issue. An example of the required disclosures is provided in figure 12.16 below.

NOTES continued			
26. Business combinations			**IFRS 3**
Acquisition of division from Dunedin Ltd			Para.
During the current reporting period, the company acquired the birdseed division of Dunedin Ltd. The acquisition date was 1 March 2006. The company has not had to dispose of any operations as a result of this combination.			*67(a)* *67(b)* *67(c)*
The cost of the combination was $248 382. The components of the cost were shares in the company, cash and a patent for packaging. The company also gave a guarantee relating to the maintenance of the company's share price. The company issued 100 000 shares, determining a fair value of $1.50 based on the current market price of the company at 1 March 2006 as reported by the stock exchange.			*67(d)* *67(d)(i)* *67(d)(ii)*
The assets and liabilities acquired from Dunedin Ltd were, as at 1 March 2006:			*67(f)*
	Carrying amount	Fair value	
Plant and equipment	$160 000	$167 000	
Land	70 000	75 000	
Motor vehicles	30 000	32 000	
Inventory	24 000	28 000	
Accounts receivable	18 000	16 000	
	302 000	318 000	
Accounts payable	35 000	35 000	
Bank overdraft	55 000	55 000	
	90 000	90 000	
Contingent liability acquired	8 000	8 000	
		98 000	
Net assets acquired		$220 000	
Goodwill of $33 382 was recognised in the acquisition, the extra consideration being paid due to the excellent reputation and customer following relating to the quality of the birdseed products.			*67(h)*
An adjustment of $2000 was made to the fair value of the plant and equipment and goodwill subsequent to the acquisition due to the provisional nature of the fair value of some of the specialised equipment determined at acquisition date.			*69* *73(b)*
Subsequent to the balance date, the provision in relation to the company's guarantee in relation to maintenance of the share price expired. No extra payment was required, as the share price had been maintained. Goodwill was reduced by $200.			*73(c)*

Acquisition of shares in Cages Ltd

On 1 August 2005, the company acquired 100% of the shares in Cages Ltd, a company primarily involved in manufacturing bird cages, for $65 000. The consideration paid was cash.

The assets and liabilities of Cages Ltd at acquisition date were:

	Carrying amount	Fair value
Plant and equipment	$ 82 000	$ 88 000
Vehicles	33 000	20 000
Cash	12 000	12 000
Accounts receivable	8 000	7 000
	124 000	127 000
Accounts payable	32 000	32 000
Net assets	$ 92 000	$ 95 000

Goodwill of $5000 was acquired, attributable to a quality, well-trained workforce.

The consolidated revenue for the consolidated group is $952 000. If the business combinations occurring during the year had occurred on 1 July 2005 instead of during the year, it is estimated that consolidated revenue would have been $985 000. The consolidated profit under the same assumption would have been $322 000 instead of $299 000.

Reference column (right side):
67(a), (b), (c)
67(d)
67(f)
67(f)

67(h)

70(a)

70(b)

27. Goodwill

Reference: 74

	2006	2005	
Gross amount at beginning of period	20 600	19 600	75(a)
Accumulated impairment losses	500	300	
	20 100	19 300	
Goodwill acquired	35 382	3 000	75(b)
	55 482	22 300	
Adjustments − tax assets recognised	−	2 000	75(c)
		20 300	
Impairment losses for current period	−	200	75(e)
Carrying amount at end of period	55 482	20 100	
Consisting of:			
Gross amount at end of period	55 982	20 600	75(h)
Accumulated impairment losses	500	500	
	55 482	20 100	

FIGURE 12.16 Disclosures required under IFRS 3

Figure 12.17 contains the disclosures provided by Danisco in its 2004–05 annual report concerning its acquisition of businesses. This information was provided in a note to the cash flow statement relating to the entity's cash flow from investing activities.

FIGURE 12.17 Disclosures of businesses acquired

NOTES TO THE CASH FLOW STATEMENT

GROUP

25   Purchase of undertakings and activities

Names of businesses acquired	Principal activity	Date of acquisition	Proportion of shares acquired	Purchase of undertakings and activities
Rhodia Food Ingredients	Production, sale and R&D	28/05/04	100%	2 265
Danisco Sweetener (Anyang) Co., Ltd.	Production and sale	15/03/05	54%	114
Genencor International Inc.	Production, sale and R&D	21/04/05	58%	3 529

	Rhodia Food Ingredients		Danisco Sweetener		Genencor		Total
DKK million	Book value prior to acquisition	Opening balance at fair value	Book value prior to acquisition	Opening balance at fair value	Book value prior to acquisition	Opening balance at fair value	2004/05
Intangible assets	14	185	–	–	–	–	185
Property, plant and equipment	358	370	47	71	696	696	1 137
Investments	40	40	–	–	101	97	137
Inventories	236	274	8	7	242	300	581
Receivables and prepayments	98	94	1	1	277	277	372
Cash and cash equivalents	2	2	–	–	551	551	553
Minority interests	–	–	(26)	(33)	(1)	(1)	(34)
Other provisions	–	(21)	–	–	(56)	(56)	(77)
Provisions for deferred tax	(15)	(6)	–	(7)	(17)	(39)	(52)
Financial liabilities	(6)	(6)	–	–	(106)	(106)	(112)
Non-interest-bearing debt	(149)	(145)	–	(1)	(136)	(214)	(360)
Corporation tax	–	–	–	–	(22)	(22)	(22)
Net assets	**578**	**787**	**30**	**38**	**1 529**	**1 483**	**2 308**
Goodwill on purchase of undertakings and activities		1 523		76		2 597	4 196
Adjustment of cash and cash equivalents		(2)		–		(551)	(553)
Cash purchase amount		2 308		114		3 529	5 951
Exchange adjustment		(43)		–		–	(43)
Purchase of undertakings and activities		2 265		114		3 529	5 908
Financial liabilities		6		–		106	112
Cost of acquisition total		2 271		114		3 635	6 020
Components of the cash purchase amount:							
Cash		2 253		110		2 982	5 345
Directly attributable acquisition costs		55		4		547	606
Cash purchase amount		2 308		114		3 529	5 951

Rhodia Food Ingredients:

On 28 May 2004 Danisco acquired 100% of the shares and net assets of Rhodia Food Ingredients (RFI). RFI is included in Danisco's results from that date. The Rhodia acquisition was partly an acquisition of net assets and partly of shares. The effect on Danisco's revenue and EBIT is estimated to DKK 1300 million and DKK 200 million respectively. Costs directly attributable to the acquisition include legal and audit fees, fees to investment bankers and other directly attributable external costs.

Danisco Sweetener (Anyang) Co. Ltd.:

Danisco acquired 54% of the shares in Danisco Sweeteners (Anyang) Co. Ltd. on 15 March 2005. The company is in the process of starting up production and has had no revenue or results in the financial year. Costs directly attributable to the acquisition include legal and audit fees and other directly attributable costs.

Genencor International Inc.:

At the beginning of the financial year, Danisco owned approximately 42% of the common stock and 50% of the preferred stock of Genencor International Inc. (Genencor). Genencor was included in Danisco's financial statements as an associate. On 27 January 2005, Danisco published an offer to acquire all of the outstanding shares of Genencor, and on 20 April 2005 Danisco announced the successful conclusion of the tender offer. Along with the purchase of common stock Danisco acquired the remaining part of preferred stock.

For accounting purposes the transaction by which Genencor became a group enterprise is seen as completed at 30 April 2005. Income from Genencor for the year 1 May 2004 to 30 April 2005 is accounted for as income from associates and Genencor's opening balance sheet at 30 April 2005 has been consolidated line by line into Danisco's balance sheet. Fair value adjustments are made on a preliminary basis due to the timing of the acquisition and an accurate allocation of the purchase price will take place in the next financial year. Costs directly attributable to the acquisition include payments related to termination of share option programmes in Genencor, realised and estimated fees to investment bankers, legal and audit fees and other directly attributable costs. Genencor's total revenues in 2004 were DKK 2356 million and EBITDA was DKK 402 million. Excluding the Health Care activities, EBITDA was DKK 534 million.

Source: Danisco (2005, p. 56).

LO 15

12.7 Business combinations (Phase II) considerations

In June 2005, the IASB issued the *Exposure Draft of Proposed Amendments to IFRS 3 Business Combinations.* This Amendments ED was a joint project developed between the IASB and the US Financial Accounting Standards Board (FASB) as part of their convergence project. The FASB issued the Amendments ED at the same time as the IASB. The initial expectation of the IASB was to have these amendments approved and applicable for annual reporting periods beginning on or after 1 January 2007. However, given the reactions in Europe and the United States to the Amendments ED, this timetable is unlikely to be met.

12.7.1 Proposed changes to IFRS 3

The major changes to IFRS 3 proposed in the Amendments ED are described below.

Scope of the Amendments ED

Whereas IFRS 3 excludes business combinations in which entities are brought together by contract alone and those involving mutual entities, these are included in the scope of the Amendments ED. Still excluded are business combinations where a joint venture is formed, and those involving entities under common control. Given the importance of the common-control scenario to many entities, it is disappointing that the Phase II considerations were not sufficiently theoretically advanced to be able to provide a solution to these situations.

Definitions

The definition of a 'business' is changed. In the Amendments ED, a business is defined as follows:

> A business is an integrated set of activities and assets that is capable of being conducted and managed for the purpose of providing either:
> (1) a return to investors, or
> (2) dividends, lower costs, or other economic benefits directly and proportionately to owners, members or participants.

There are two key changes in the definition. The first is the insertion of the word 'capable'. This emphasises that the integrated set of activities need not be conducted and managed; instead, they need only be capable of being conducted and managed. Where the activities are not at the point of being used for a specific purpose but a buyer might be willing to integrate them into an already existing business, then a business combination could occur. The second key change is that a business consists of inputs and processes but not necessarily outputs. For example, a mining operation that has not yet reached the production stage would still be classified as a business.

The definition of a 'business combination' has also changed. Paragraph 3 of the Amendments ED states:

> A business combination is a transaction or other event in which an acquirer obtains control of one or more businesses.

The IASB viewed the IFRS 3 definition as being too broad, and preferred to describe a business combination in terms of an economic event (Amendments ED, para. BC25). That economic event is one entity obtaining control over another. One effect of this is that combinations involving joint control are not business combinations, hence the exclusion of joint ventures from the Amendments ED.

Terminology

The term 'purchase method' has been replaced with 'acquisition method'. As the definition of a business combination is now defined in terms of an economic event, namely obtaining control of another entity, this may occur without any purchase occurring (for example, by contract). Hence, acquisition method would seem to be a broader descriptor than purchase method.

The term 'cost of the combination' is replaced with 'consideration paid'. As explained below in the discussion of the acquisition method, a key change in the Amendments ED is the move from a cost allocation approach to a fair value approach. Hence, the reference to cost is no longer applicable.

Acquisition method

A major change from IFRS 3 is the move from a cost allocation approach to a fair value measurement approach. According to paragraph 9 of the Amendments ED, the acquisition method has four steps:

(a) identifying the acquirer
(b) determining the acquisition date
(c) measuring the fair value of the acquiree
(d) measuring and recognising the assets acquired and the liabilities assumed.

Note that the steps in paragraph 16 of IFRS 3 relating to measuring the cost of the combination and the allocation of that cost are no longer used. The emphasis in the Amendments ED is not on the cost of the combination, but rather on the fair valuing of the acquiree. This eliminates the problem under IFRS 3 where there is a mixed model approach in that the purchase method is a cost allocation method that includes the fair valuing of the acquiree. The Amendments ED is a pure fair value model. In the Basis for Conclusions on the Amendments ED, paragraph BC17 contains the following key statements:

> Obtaining control over an acquired entity makes the acquirer accountable for all the acquiree's assets and liabilities — not just those that are identifiable and not just its proportionate share of those assets and liabilities. Therefore, the Board decided that the measurement objective in accounting for business combinations should be the fair value of the acquiree on the acquisition date rather than the costs incurred in a business combination.

As a result, the IASB decided that the following four fundamental principles should be applied in accounting for all business combinations (Basis for Conclusions on the Amendments ED, para. BC18):

(a) *The acquirer obtains control of the acquiree at the acquisition date and thereby becomes responsible and accountable for all the acquiree's assets, liabilities and activities, regardless of the percentage of its ownership in the acquiree.* The obtaining of control is a sufficiently significant event to warrant a remeasurement of the acquiree's assets and liabilities.

(b) *The total amount to be recognised for the acquiree should be the fair value of the acquiree as a whole.* Because the acquirer controls all the net assets of the acquiree, all these net assets should be remeasured regardless of the percentage ownership of the acquirer in the acquiree.

(c) *Business combinations are generally exchange transactions in which knowledgeable, unrelated willing parties are presumed to exchange equal values.* It is then expected in such a transaction that the fair value of the consideration paid by the acquirer equals the net fair value of the assets and liabilities acquired in the acquiree. In relation to measuring this transaction, measurement of either side of the transaction should give the same answer. However, there is a rebuttable presumption that the consideration paid by the acquirer is the best evidence of the fair value of the interest in the acquiree at the acquisition date.

(d) *The identifiable assets acquired and liabilities assumed in a business combination should be recognised at their fair values on the date control is obtained.*

Measurement of acquiree — including goodwill

All the assets and liabilities of the acquiree are to be measured at fair value. This includes goodwill. Goodwill is measured as the excess of the fair value of the acquiree as a whole over the net fair value of the recognised identifiable assets acquired and liabilities assumed (Amendments ED, para. BC49). Where an acquirer buys less than a 100% interest in an acquiree, under IFRS 3 only the goodwill attributable to the acquirer's interest in the acquiree is recognised. Under the Amendments ED, the full goodwill of the acquiree is recognised at acquisition date.

Under IFRS 3, the purchase method required the measurement of the identifiable assets, liabilities and contingent liabilities of the acquiree. In June 2005, the IASB issued the *Exposure Draft of Proposed Amendments to IAS 37 Provisions, Contingent Liabilities and Contingent Assets and IAS 19 Employee Benefits*. One of the proposals in this exposure draft was the removal of contingent liabilities. If approved, this proposal would affect the accounting for the liabilities of the acquiree, with no recognition of contingent liabilities as currently required in IFRS 3.

The Amendments ED also contains guidance on the recognition of some assets of the acquiree such as assets held for sale, operating leases and deferred taxes.

The Amendments ED proposes changes to the recognition criteria for assets and liabilities required by IFRS 3. It does not contain any *probability* recognition criterion. Resulting from the proposed changes to IAS 37, the IASB argues that where there is an unconditional right or obligation, it is certain that there will be an inflow of benefits or an outflow of resources. Hence, the probability criterion is always satisfied. This also applies to intangible assets. Similarly, there is no *reliability of measurement* recognition criterion. The IASB argues that sufficient information should always exist to reliably measure the fair value. In relation to intangible assets, where reliable measurement may be considered more difficult, relevance of information was considered of prime importance. Paragraph BC102 of the Amendments ED states:

> The Board concluded that an estimate of fair value and the separate recognition of intangible assets, rather than subsuming them in goodwill, provides better information to the users of financial statements, even though a significant degree of judgement could be involved in determining that fair value.

Consideration transferred

The fair value of the consideration transferred, according to paragraph 21 of the Amendments ED is the sum of:

(a) the acquisition-date fair value of the assets transferred, liabilities assumed and equity issued by the acquirer, and

(b) the acquisition-date fair value of any non-controlling equity interest in the acquiree at acquisition date.

Part (a) is not particularly different from the measurement used in IFRS 3 to measure the cost of the combination. If, however, at acquisition date the acquirer already holds an investment in the acquiree, part (b) provides a change from IFRS 3. Such an investment under IFRS 3 would continue to be measured at cost. Under the Amendments ED, at acquisition date the acquirer revalues the investment to fair value, taking the movement directly to profit and loss. If the investment prior to the acquisition date was revalued with movements going directly to equity, the amounts recognised directly in equity at acquisition date would be reclassified and taken to profit and loss as part of the gain or loss recognised at that date (Amendments ED, para. 56).

Two other changes in the measurement of the consideration transferred are contingent consideration and costs incurred in connection with the business combination. These are considered separately below.

Contingent consideration

Under IFRS 3, the principles for accounting for contingent consideration were carried forward from the old business combinations standard IAS 22 without review by the IASB. In general, IFRS 3 takes a cost accumulation approach, with subsequent changes to the measure of the contingent consideration affecting the cost of the combination and goodwill.

Under the Amendments ED, contingent consideration is measured at fair value at the acquisition date. Hence, if the acquirer agrees to transfer additional equity interests, cash or other assets to the former owners of the acquiree after the acquisition date dependent on specified future events occurring (such as sales or profit targets being met), the acquirer must measure the fair value of the contingency at acquisition date. Some of the contingent consideration may be difficult to measure but, as the IASB states in paragraph BC71 of the Amendments ED, not to measure the contingency at acquisition date fails to faithfully represent the economics of the business combination transaction. After acquisition date, any subsequent change in the fair value of the contingent consideration is treated as a post-acquisition event. If the contingent consideration consists of financial instruments, IAS 39 *Financial Instruments: Recognition and Measurement* is used to account for movements in the accounts. If the contingent payments are equity, they will not be remeasured after acquisition date.

Costs directly attributable to the business combination

Under IFRS 3, costs directly attributable to the combination are included in the cost of the combination and allocated to the identifiable assets and liabilities acquired. According to paragraph BC85 of the Amendments ED, these acquisition-related costs are not part of the fair value exchange between the buyer and the seller. Because the services received from the outlays have been consumed, the outlays do not give rise to assets. Hence, such costs must be expensed as incurred.

Goodwill and excess

As noted earlier, one of the main changes proposed in the Amendments ED is the recognition of the full goodwill of the acquiree. Where an excess arises — that is, where the fair value of the consideration transferred is less than the fair value of the acquirer's interest in the acquiree — the accounting is not significantly different from that in IFRS 3. Assessment of all aspects of measurement is required to ensure an excess really exists. If after this exercise an excess still exists, the acquirer accounts for it by reducing the goodwill recognised. If goodwill is reduced to zero, any remaining excess is recognised as a gain to the acquirer.

Step acquisitions

Under IFRS 3, each step acquisition prior to the obtaining of control is accounted for separately, with goodwill/excess being recognised at each step. Under the Amendments ED, the combined cost of past steps is revalued to fair value at acquisition date, with gains/losses taken to profit and loss.

12.7.2 Reaction to the Amendments ED

It was evident that the IASB and FASB were going to have problems getting agreement on the Amendments ED because there were five IASB members who expressed alternative views on various aspects of this exposure draft. All five disagreed with the use of the full goodwill method, arguing that goodwill is different from other assets and the process of measuring it is very difficult. They also disagreed conceptually with the approach taken by the IASB in its adoption of the economic entity approach.

The IASB has not published the comment letters to the Amendments ED. However, this was a joint project with the FASB, and the FASB has published comment letters on its website. Many of the letters to the FASB come from organisations outside the United States, including the responses from standard-setting bodies in the United Kingdom, Australia, Japan and South Africa, EFRAG (the European Financial Reporting Advisory Group), IOSCO (International Organization of Securities Commissions) and international companies such as Nestlé, Microsoft and the Ford Motor Company.

 WEBLINK

The comment letters can be found on the FASB website at
<www.fasb.org/ocl/fasb-getletters.php?project=1204-001> and
<www.fasb.org/ocl/fasb-getletters.php?project=1205-001>.

It is not the purpose of this section to report on all the responses to the standard-setting bodies, but to give some insight into the main areas of disagreement that respondents had to the Amendments ED. These are discussed below.

1. Conceptual approach adopted

A major source of disagreement was that respondents felt the IASB was introducing concepts into the accounting standards via the Business Combinations projects rather than having these concepts determined in other places such as the Conceptual Framework projects. There was a feeling that these concepts had not been fully discussed by the IASB and FASB prior to their being introduced into the Amendments ED. Some specific comments in this regard were:

> ... we do not support the proposals in the EDs. That is because we believe that the proposed approach does not produce more useful information than the current IFRS 3; indeed in many respects we believe that it will have the opposite effect. In addition, it will create major practical implementation issues. We also believe that it is inappropriate to introduce such radical and untested concepts through revision to specific standards at a time when the conceptual framework is under active review (EFRAG 2005, p.1).

> We are of the opinion that there are some of the changes which go beyond the short term convergence as they touch fundamental issues. These fundamental changes are:
> • Full fair value
> • Recognition of contingent assets and liabilities
> • Implementation of the full goodwill approach, derived from the entity view (Dansk Industries 2005, p. 2).

GASB [German Accounting Standards Board] noted that these proposed amendments are in line with the fair value approach as well as the entity theory the IASB pursues. But unfortunately these concepts have not been discussed on a more conceptual basis beforehand (GASB 2005, p. 3).

This led many to believe that the information provided by implementing the Amendments ED would not be useful to users:

However, intangible assets and especially goodwill are among the most difficult assets to measure and that's one of the particular tasks of financial analysts ... The figures provided for the goodwill will not be used by users in most cases to reach conclusion on valuation (French Society of Financial Analysts 2005, p. 2).

From our point of view it is not obvious that the proposed changes are in the interest of investors and investment analysts (GASB 2005, p. 3).

2. Use of the full goodwill method

There were mixed views on this question. At one end of the spectrum were respondents who favoured a cost accumulation method under which neither the net assets nor the goodwill of the acquiree are recognised at fair value in situations where the acquirer obtained less than 100% of the acquiree. A supporter of this approach was Microsoft:

We are opposed to the requirement to recognize 100 percent of the fair value of the acquiree at the acquisition date for step acquisitions or when the acquirer holds less than 100 percent of the equity interests of the acquiree ... However, we do not believe the Board's conclusion that recognizing the entire economic value of the acquiree, regardless of the ownership interest in the acquiree at the acquisition date, reflects the underlying economics ... In fact, we believe a method that involves accumulating and allocating costs provides relevant information over time in assessing an entity's returns from an acquisition relative to the costs incurred in acquiring another entity (Microsoft Corporation 2005, p. 1).

Other respondents to the Amendments ED agreed with the recognition of the acquiree's identifiable assets and liabilities at fair value but disagreed with recognising the goodwill at full fair value in a partial acquisition. This was the position taken by the majority of the respondents. Many of the US respondents argued that the FASB should converge to the existing requirements in IFRS 3. Major reasons for adopting this approach related to the nature of goodwill and the difficulties in measuring goodwill – views similar to those of the dissenting IASB members. These views included the following:

We expect constituents to face problems in estimating the full fair value of the acquiree in situations where the acquirer is acquiring less than a 100% stake. The presence of factors such as a control premium would make a simple extrapolation inappropriate. Any estimates would therefore require significant subjectivity and at best would only be directionally accurate (Citigroup 2005, p. 3).

The reasons why we disagree with the full goodwill method are as follows:
- The objective of accounting information is to provide information that helps users to estimate the corporate value, not to present the market's evaluation of the corporate value including internally generated goodwill.
- ... goodwill is different from other assets by its nature, because it is a component of the value of the business as a whole, after recognizing identifiable intangible assets, rather than having a separate existence.
- ... we believe that accounting for business combinations should [be] based on the actual transaction ...
- ... it is often impracticable to measure the fair value of the acquiree as a whole. In particular, it would be often impossible to distinguish between overpayments and control premiums (Accounting Standards Board of Japan 2005, pp. 4–5).

We are of the view that the recognition of 100 per cent of the acquiree, where an acquirer holds less than 100 per cent, requires a transaction to be recognised ... the minority is not a party to the transaction ...

Using the consideration transferred to estimate the fair value of the acquiree may not be appropriate because:
(i) it may fail to recognise any control premium included in the consideration transferred. The control premium may be difficult to measure with sufficient reliability; and
(ii) the consideration transferred is based on the acquirer's assessment of future returns it anticipates the investment will generate. These returns may include an assessment of future synergy benefits the acquirer anticipates it will achieve. Some of the synergy benefits may benefit the parent entity rather than the acquired entity and thereby have little or no relevance to the non-controlling interests in the acquired entity (Accounting Standards Board UK 2005, pp. 10, 12).

The reasons for our disagreement with the economic entity concept and with the full goodwill method [are] ...
• ... Goodwill, however is different from other assets, because it is a component of the value of the business as a whole, rather than having a separate existence.
• The process of measuring goodwill is extremely difficult ...
• The allocation of the goodwill between the parent and the subsidiary is also problematic ...
The proposals support 'what if' accounting, using a hypothetical valuation model to determine what price would be paid if 10% of the business were acquired when in fact less than 10% was acquired. ...

Furthermore, this accounting is contrary to the qualitative characteristic of substance over form, per the Framework ... The use of a hypothetical valuation model to derive a full fair value for goodwill is not substance over form, but fiction over form. (South African Institute of Chartered Accountants 2005, pp. 2, 6).

We are concerned with the requirement to record the full goodwill associated with a business combination in these situations for the following reasons:
a. Goodwill will be recorded based on a hypothetical or appraised value ...
b. ... As a residual, goodwill is distinctively different than any other asset recorded in a business combination whose value is easily understood and reliably measured ...
c. It is not clear what the full amount of goodwill represents and whether or how it will be viewed by investors ... (IOSCO 2005, p. 3).

There were, however, some respondents who agreed with the approach taken in the Amendments ED:

We agree with the conceptual thought behind recording the acquisition at its current fair value since we believe that a mixture of historical and current values co-existing in a single asset or liability makes financial statements less understandable and less useful, thus preventing the financial statements from faithfully representing the realities of the acquisition ...
We agree that recognizing 100 percent of the fair value of the acquiree is appropriate. We believe that this is crucial in erasing anomalies which were created when only the incremental ownership acquired was fair valued and the minority interest was reflected at its carryover basis (Ford Motor Company 2005, pp. 1, 3).

3. Accounting for costs directly associated with the acquisition

The Amendments ED proposed that these costs should be expensed. The majority of correspondents disagreed with this proposal, using two main arguments. First, they saw this as providing a departure from the accounting for such costs in other accounting standards such as IAS 16 *Property, Plant and Equipment*. Second, they viewed these costs as being an integral part of the acquisition price, with the outlays being incurred in order to generate future benefits. Some of their comments are reproduced overleaf.

We believe that the fees paid to external advisors that are directly attributable to the acquisition should be accounted for as part of the cost of the acquisition, considering consistency with IAS 2 "Inventories" and IAS 16 "Property, Plant and Equipment" (Accounting Standards Board of Japan 2005, p. 6).

We do not agree with the proposal to expense acquisition-related costs. In our view, such costs are an integral part of the purchase price ... The accounting proposed by the Board would effectively institute a separate model for transaction costs related to assets acquired as part of a business combination (expense) and those related to assets acquired outside a business combination, such as a direct acquisition of fixed assets (capitalized as part of asset). We are troubled by the notion that the form of a transaction would influence the accounting for a particular cost (Citigroup 2005, p. 4).

We do not concur with the conclusion in BC 87 that the intention of the buyer, including how acquisition-related costs are expected to be recovered, is distinct from fair value measurement of the acquiree. On the contrary we believe that it is the intention of how the buyer intends to recover the total cost of the investment (consideration and acquisition-related costs) combined with the seller's analysis of economic benefits from retaining ownership of the acquiree versus receiving a consideration minus divestment costs that forms a fair value of the acquiree (The Swedish Enterprise Accounting Group 2005, p. 2).

... such costs are an inherent and unavoidable part of the acquisition process — no acquisition could legally be completed without incurring such costs ... we cannot ignore the fact that there is a direct relationship between the incurrence of acquisition related transactions and the rights to the future benefits of the acquired entity that transfer to the acquirer as a result of those transactions. Therefore those costs cannot be disassociated with the acquisition (Texas Instruments 2005, p. 3).

4. Accounting for contingent consideration

The majority of correspondents disagreed with the proposal to recognise contingent consideration at fair value, although there was much support for this proposal. An interesting comment was provided by Citigroup, who stated:

Contingent consideration mechanisms are often negotiated to bridge differing views on the fair value of a business combination. As such, we find it curious to mandate fair value accounting for something that results directly from the inability of two parties to agree on fair value (Citigroup 2005, p. 4).

How the IASB and FASB react to the comments they have received is yet to be seen. Given the support by many Americans for the United States to converge by adopting IFRS 3, it may be that the IASB will choose to keep IFRS 3 for the time being and proceed with developing further the underlying concepts affecting accounting for business combinations.

12.8 Summary

IFRS 3 is the result of the IASB's deliberations on Phase I of the Business Combinations project. The project specifies accounting standards that have implications not only for the exchanges of assets between entities but also for the accounting for subsidiaries and associated entities. IFRS 3 specifies how the cost of the business combination is to be determined as well as how the assets and liabilities acquired are to be accounted for. The standard interacts with other standards such as IAS 38 *Intangible Assets* and IAS 37 *Provisions, Contingent Liabilities and Contingent Assets* because the acquirer has to recognise intangible assets and contingent liabilities acquired in a business combination. The nature and calculation of goodwill is also covered in this accounting standard, as is the treatment of an excess on acquisition.

The IASB has issued an exposure draft proposing changes to IFRS 3 under its Phase II project. These changes have not been received well by the respondents to the ED. Whether the IASB will continue with the current version of IFRS 3 or press ahead with its proposed changes is yet to be seen.

WEBLINK

Progress on Phase II of the Business Combinations project can be followed on the IASB website at <www.iasb.org> or the Deloitte website at <www.iasplus.com>.

1. Critically analyse the following comments made by the European Financial Reporting Advisory Group (EFRAG 2003) on page 5 of its response (dated 4 April 2003) to the IASB on ED 3 *Business Combinations*:

   The Exposure Draft proposes that the probability recognition criterion is always satisfied for separately acquired intangible assets (paragraph 22) and for intangible assets acquired in a business combination (paragraph 29). In addition it proposes that with the exception of an assembled workforce, sufficient information can reasonably be expected to exist to measure reliably the fair value of an intangible asset acquired in a business combination.

   We disagree with the Board's proposal because we believe that the general principle that an asset is recognised only (i) when future economic benefits will probably flow to the entity and (ii) the cost or value can be measured reliably, should be consistently applied in all situations, including business combinations. The current proposal results in an inconsistent treatment of internally generated goodwill and externally acquired intangible assets, because the probability criterion for recognition of an asset as defined in the Framework is now presumed to be satisfied in the case of a business combination or individual acquisition.

2. Critically analyse the following statement raised in the Basis for Conclusions on IFRS 3:

   Acquired goodwill is an asset that is consumed and replaced with internally generated goodwill. Amortisation therefore ensures that the acquired goodwill is written off and no internally generated goodwill is recognised in its place, consistently with the general prohibition in IAS 38 *Intangible Assets* on the recognition of internally generated goodwill.

3. Critically analyse the following statement raised in the Basis for Conclusions on IFRS 3:

   The useful life of acquired goodwill cannot be predicted with a satisfactory level of reliability, nor can the pattern in which that goodwill diminishes be known. However, systematic amortisation over an albeit arbitrary period of time provides an appropriate balance between conceptual soundness and operationality at an acceptable cost: i.e. it is the only practical solution to an intractable problem.

4. Outline what is meant by 'core goodwill'.

5. Some writers argue that goodwill is not an asset that should be recognised in the balance sheet. Discuss the nature of goodwill and whether it differs from other assets.

6. Under IFRS 3, the cost of the business combination is determined by calculating what is given up by the acquirer. Alternatively, the cost could be determined by analysing what the acquirer receives in exchange. Discuss the difference these approaches may have on the accounts of the acquirer, and the reasons why the IASB has taken its approach in IFRS 3.

7. Discuss the difference between the 'acquisition date' and the 'date of exchange'. Explain why it is necessary to distinguish between the two dates, and the effects on the acquirer's accounts.

8. In the IASB's Basis for Conclusions on IFRS 3, it noted the following case arising from its field visits:

   For example, one participant acquired water acquisition rights as part of a business combination. The rights are extremely valuable to many manufacturers operating in the same jurisdiction as the participant – the manufacturers cannot acquire water and, in many cases, cannot operate their plants without them. Local authorities grant the rights at little or no cost, but in limited numbers, for finite terms (normally 10 years), and renewal is certain at little or no cost. The rights cannot be sold other than as part of the sale of a business as a whole, therefore there exists no secondary market in the rights. If a manufacturer hands the rights back to the local authority, it is prohibited from reapplying.

   Discuss whether the participant should recognise an intangible asset as part of its accounting for the business combination.

9. White Ltd has been negotiating with Cloud Ltd for several months, and agreements have finally been reached for the two companies to combine. In considering the accounting for the combined entities, management realises that, in applying IFRS 3 *Business Combinations*, an acquirer must be identified. However, there is debate among the accounting staff as to which entity should be identified as the acquirer.

   (a) What factors/indicators should management consider in determining which entity is the acquirer?

   (b) Why is it necessary to identify an acquirer? In your answer, note the differences in accounting that would arise if White Ltd or Cloud Ltd were identified as the acquirer.

10. Should the costs incurred by the acquirer that are directly associated with the business combination be expensed rather than capitalised into the cost of the combination?

11. What is meant by a 'business combination'?

12. Is it possible in all business combinations to identify an acquirer?

13. Discuss the importance of identifying the acquisition date.

14. What is meant by 'contingent consideration' and how is it accounted for?

EXERCISE 12.1   ★

Accounting by the acquirer

On 1 July 2006, New Ltd acquired the following assets and liabilities from Zealand Ltd:

	Carrying amount	Fair value
Land	$300 000	$350 000
Plant (cost $400 000)	280 000	290 000
Inventory	80 000	85 000
Cash	15 000	15 000
Accounts payable	(20 000)	(20 000)
Loans	(80 000)	(80 000)

In exchange for these assets and liabilities, New Ltd issued 100 000 shares that had been issued for $1.20 per share but at 1 July 2006 had a fair value of $6.50 per share.

Required

1. Prepare the journal entries in the records of New Ltd to account for the acquisition of the assets and liabilities of Zealand Ltd.
2. Prepare the journal entries assuming that the fair value of New Ltd shares was $6 per share.

EXERCISE 12.2   ★

Accounting by an acquirer

Milford Ltd acquired all the assets and liabilities of Sound Ltd on 1 July 2007. At this date, the assets and liabilities of Sound Ltd consisted of:

	Carrying amount	Fair value
Current assets	$1 000 000	$ 980 000
Non-current assets	4 000 000	4 220 000
	5 000 000	5 200 000
Liabilities	500 000	500 000
	4 500 000	$4 700 000
Share capital — 100 000 shares	3 000 000	
Reserves	1 500 000	
	$4 500 000	

In exchange for these net assets, Milford Ltd agreed to:
- Issue 10 Milford Ltd shares for every Sound Ltd share. Milford Ltd shares were considered to have a fair value of $10 per share. Costs of share issue were $500.
- Transfer a patent to the former shareholders of Sound Ltd. The patent was carried in the records of Milford Ltd at $350 000 but was considered to have a fair value of $1 million
- Pay $5.20 per share in cash to each of the former shareholders of Sound Ltd.

Milford Ltd incurred $10 000 in costs associated with the acquisition of these net assets.

Required

1. Prepare an acquisition analysis in relation to this acquisition.
2. Prepare the journal entries in Milford Ltd to record the acquisition.

EXERCISE 12.3 ★   Acquisition of shares in acquiree

On 1 January 2006, Stewart Ltd acquired all the issued shares of Island Ltd. At this date the equity of Island Ltd consisted of:

Share capital — 100 000 shares issued at $5 per share	$500 000
General reserve	200 000
Asset revaluation surplus	100 000
Retained earnings	50 000

In exchange for these shares, Stewart Ltd agreed to pay the former shareholders of Island Ltd two shares in Stewart Ltd, these having a fair value of $4 per share, plus $1.50 cash for each share held in Island Ltd. The costs of issuing the shares were $800.

Required
Prepare the journal entries in the records of Stewart Ltd to record these events.

EXERCISE 12.4 ★   Accounting by an acquirer

Lower Ltd acquired the assets and liabilities of Hutt Ltd on 1 July 2006. These net assets measured at fair value consisted of:

Equipment	$ 50 000
Land	80 000
Trucks	40 000
Current assets	10 000
Current liabilities	(16 000)

Required
Prepare the journal entries in Lower Ltd to record this business combination assuming that, to acquire these net assets, Lower Ltd:
(a) issued 100 000 shares at $1.80 per share
(b) issued 100 000 shares at $1.60 per share.

EXERCISE 12.5 ★   Liquidation of the acquiree

Tokomaru Ltd acquired all the net assets of Bay Ltd, giving in exchange 100 000 shares, these having a fair value of $2.80 per share and $50 000 cash.

At the acquisition date, the balance sheet of Bay Ltd was as follows:

Cash	$ 10 000
Accounts receivable	20 000
Land	80 000
Plant	240 000
Vehicles	50 000
	400 000
Accounts payable	40 000
Loans	60 000
	100 000
Share capital	200 000
General reserve	40 000
Retained earnings	60 000
	$300 000

Costs of liquidation amounted to $1000.

Required
Prepare the journal entries to liquidate Bay Ltd.

EXERCISE 12.6 ★

Accounting for the acquisition of a business by the acquirer

On 1 December 2006, Greymouth Ltd acquired all the assets and liabilities of Opunake Ltd, with Greymouth Ltd issuing 100 000 shares to acquire these net assets. The fair values of Opunake Ltd's assets and liabilities at this date were:

Cash	$ 50 000
Furniture and fittings	20 000
Accounts receivable	5 000
Plant	125 000
Accounts payable	15 000
Current tax liability	8 000
Provision for annual leave	2 000

The financial year for Greymouth Ltd is January–December.

Required
1. Prepare the journal entries for Greymouth Ltd to record the business combination at 1 December 2006, assuming the fair value of each Greymouth Ltd share at acquisition date is $1.90. Prepare any note disclosures for Greymouth Ltd at 31 December 2006 in relation to the business combination.
2. Assume the fair value of each Greymouth Ltd share at acquisition date is $1.90. At acquisition date, the acquirer could only determine a provisional fair value for the plant. On 1 March 2007, Greymouth Ltd received the final value from the independent appraisal, the fair value at acquisition date being $131 000. Assuming the plant had a further five-year life from the acquisition date, explain how Greymouth Ltd will account for the business combination both at acquisition date and in the financial statements for 2007.
3. Prepare the journal entries for Greymouth Ltd to record the business combination at 1 December 2006, assuming the fair value of each Greymouth Ltd share at acquisition date is $1.70.

EXERCISE 12.7 ★

Determining the fair value of equity issued by the acquirer

The following are the balance sheets at 30 September 2006 of Gisborne Ltd and Oamaru Ltd.

Gisborne Ltd			
Share capital — 80 000 shares	$ 80 000	Non-current assets (at valuation	
Asset revaluation surplus	40 000	less depreciation)	$190 000
General reserve	60 000	Current assets	148 000
Retained earnings	30 000		
Creditors and provisions	28 000		
	$338 000		$338 000

Oamaru Ltd			
Share capital — 60 000 shares	$ 60 000	Non-current assets (at cost	
General reserve	20 000	less depreciation)	$ 50 000
Retained earnings	25 000	Current assets	65 000
Creditors and provisions	10 000		
	$ 115 000		$ 115 000

Additional information

(a) During September the shares of the companies have been selling on the stock exchange at or near the following prices:

Gisborne Ltd $5.80   Oamaru Ltd $1.80

(b) On 30 September the directors of Gisborne Ltd make an offer to the shareholders of Oamaru Ltd to acquire their shares on the basis of one fully paid share at $1 in Gisborne Ltd for every two fully paid shares at $1 in Oamaru Ltd.

The offer is open for one month and is contingent upon being accepted by the holders of at least 75% of Oamaru Ltd's capital.

(c) Immediately after the announcement, Gisborne Ltd's shares rise in price on the stock exchange to $6.20 and the shares of Oamaru Ltd rise to $3. The shares of both companies stay at or close to this price throughout October.

(d) By the end of October, holders of 90% of Oamaru Ltd shares accept the Gisborne Ltd offer and the latter company proceeds to acquire these shares on the agreed basis.

(e) By mid-November Gisborne Ltd shares drop in price on the stock exchange to $5.50.

(f) Costs of issuing and registering shares issued by Gisborne Ltd amounted to $2000.

Required

1. Give the journal entries necessary to record the transactions. (Show clearly to which company particular entries relate.)
2. State briefly why you selected the value adopted in recording the acquisition, and whether you consider there is any acceptable alternative recording value.
3. Show the balance sheet of Gisborne Ltd after the entries have been recorded.

EXERCISE 12.8 ★★   Liquidation of acquiree, accounting by acquirer

Westport Ltd, a supplier of snooker equipment, agreed to acquire the business of a rival firm, Manukau Ltd, taking over all assets and liabilities as at 1 June 2006.

The price agreed upon was $40 000, payable $20 000 in cash and the balance by the issue to the selling company of 16 000 fully paid shares in Westport Ltd, these shares having a fair value of $2.50 per share.

The trial balances of the two companies as at 1 June 2006 were as follows:

	Westport Ltd		Manukau Ltd	
	Dr	Cr	Dr	Cr
Share capital		$ 100 000		$ 90 000
Retained earnings		12 000	$ 24 000	
Accounts payable		2 000		20 000
Cash	$ 30 000		—	
Plant (net)	50 000		30 000	
Inventory	14 000		26 000	
Accounts receivable	8 000		20 000	
Government bonds	12 000		—	
Goodwill	—		10 000	
	$114 000	$ 114 000	$ 110 000	$ 110 000

All the identifiable net assets of Manukau Ltd were recorded by Manukau Ltd at fair value except for the inventory, which was considered to be worth $28 000. The plant had an expected remaining life of five years.

The business combination was completed and Manukau Ltd went into liquidation. Costs of liquidation amounted to $1000. Westport Ltd incurred incidental costs of $500 in relation to the acquisition. Costs of issuing shares in Westport Ltd were $400.

Required
1. Show the liquidation account and the shareholders' distribution account in the records of Manukau Ltd.
2. Prepare the journal entries in the records of Westport Ltd to record the business combination.
3. Show the balance sheet of Westport Ltd after completion of the business combination.
4. On 31 July 2006, Westport Ltd became aware that there had been an error in measuring the fair value of the plant at 1 June 2006. It in fact had a fair value at that date of $36 000. Explain how Westport Ltd is required to adjust for that error. Westport Ltd's balance date is 30 June.

EXERCISE 12.9 ★★

Cost of combination

On 1 September 2004, the directors of Ashburton Ltd approached the directors of Wanganui Ltd with the following proposal for the acquisition of the issued shares of Wanganui Ltd, conditional on acceptance by 90% of the shareholders of Wanganui Ltd by 30 November 2004.
- Two fully paid ordinary shares in Ashburton Ltd plus $3.10 cash for every preference share in Wanganui Ltd, payable at acquisition date.
- Three fully paid ordinary shares in Ashburton Ltd plus $1.20 cash for every ordinary share in Wanganui Ltd. Half of the cash is payable at acquisition, and the other half in one year's time.

By 30 November, 90% of the ordinary shareholders and all of the preference shareholders of Wanganui Ltd had accepted the offer. The directors of Ashburton Ltd decided *not* to acquire the remaining ordinary shares. Share transfer forms covering the transfer were dated 30 November 2004, and showed a price per Ashburton Ltd ordinary share of $4.20. Ashburton Ltd's incremental borrowing rate is 8% p.a.

The balance sheet of Wanganui Ltd at 30 November 2004 was as follows:

Wanganui Ltd Balance sheet as at 30 November 2004		
Current assets		$120 000
Non-current assets:		
Land and buildings	$203 000	
Plant and equipment	168 000	
Less: Accumulated depreciation	(45 000)	
Shares in other companies listed on stock exchange at cost		
(market $190 000)	30 000	
Government bonds, at cost	50 000	
Total non-current assets		406 000
Total assets		526 000
Current liabilities		30 000
Net assets		$496 000
Equity:		
Share capital		
80 000 ordinary shares fully paid	$160 000	
50 000 6% preference shares fully paid	100 000	$260 000
Retained earnings		236 000
Total equity		$496 000

Ashburton Ltd then appointed a new board of directors of Wanganui Ltd. This board took office on 1 December 2004 and immediately:

- revalued the asset 'Shares in Other Companies' to its market value (assume no tax effect)
- used the surplus so created to make a bonus issue of $32 000 to ordinary shareholders, each shareholder being allocated two ordinary shares for every ten ordinary shares held.

On 1 January 2005, directors of Wanganui Ltd declared interim dividends for the half-year ended 30 November 2004 of $9600 on ordinary shares and $3000 on the preference shares, both dividends to be paid from profits recognised before 30 November 2004.

The cash dividends were paid on 8 January 2005.

Required

Prepare all journal entries (in general form) to record the above transactions in the records of:

1. Ashburton Ltd
2. Wanganui Ltd.

EXERCISE 12.10 ★★★   Accounting for a business combination by both the acquirer and the acquiree

Blenheim Ltd was a company that was finding difficulty in raising finance for expansion. Napier Ltd was a company interested in achieving economies by marketing a wider range of products.

The following shows the financial positions of the companies at 30 June 2008.

	Blenheim Ltd	Napier Ltd
Share capital:		
40 000 shares	$ 40 000	
90 000 shares		$ 90 000
Retained earnings	12 000	30 000
	$ 52 000	$120 000
Liabilities:		
Debentures (secured by floating charge)	20 000	–
Accounts payable	42 000	12 000
	62 000	12 000
Total equity and liabilities	$114 000	$132 000
Assets:		
Cash	$ 12 000	$ 24 000
Accounts receivable	18 000	20 000
Inventory (at cost)	43 000	47 000
Land and buildings (at cost)	23 000	19 000
Plant and machinery (at cost)	52 000	41 000
Accumulated depreciation on plant and machinery	(34 000)	(19 000)
Total assets	$114 000	$132 000

It was agreed that it would be mutually advantageous for Blenheim Ltd to specialise in manufacturing, and for marketing, purchasing and promotion to be handled by Napier Ltd. Accordingly, Napier Ltd sold *part* of its assets to Blenheim Ltd on 1 July 2008, the identifiable assets acquired having the following fair values:

Inventory $22 000 (cost $15 000)
Land and buildings $34 000 (carrying amount $10 000)
Plant and machinery $27 000 (cost $38 000, accumulated depreciation $18 000)

The acquisition was satisfied by the issue of 40 000 'A' ordinary shares (fully paid) in Blenheim Ltd.

Required

1. Show the journal entries to record the above transactions in the records of Blenheim Ltd:
   (a) if the fair value of the 'A' ordinary shares of Blenheim Ltd was $2 per share
   (b) if the fair value of the 'A' ordinary shares of Blenheim Ltd was $2.20 per share. (Assume the assets acquired constitute a business entity.)
2. Show the journal entries in the records of Napier Ltd under (a) and (b) in part 1 above.
3. Show the balance sheet of Blenheim Ltd after the transactions, assuming the fair value of Blenheim's Ltd's 'A' ordinary shares was $2.20 per share. Provide the notes to the financial statements relating to the businss combinations.

PROBLEMS	

PROBLEM 12.1	★★	Liquidation of acquiree, accounting by acquirer

Hastings Ltd is seeking to expand its share of the widgets market and has negotiated to take over the operations of Timaru Ltd on 1 January 2006. The balance sheets of the two companies as at 31 December 2005 were as follows:

	Hastings Ltd	Timaru Ltd
Cash	$ 23 000	$ 12 000
Accounts receivable	25 000	34 700
Inventory	35 500	27 600
Freehold land	150 000	100 000
Buildings (net)	60 000	30 000
Plant and equipment (net)	65 000	46 000
Goodwill	25 000	2 000
	$383 500	$252 300
Accounts payable	$ 56 000	$ 43 500
Mortgage loan	50 000	40 000
Debentures	100 000	50 000
Share capital – 100 000 shares	100 000	–
– 60 000 shares	–	60 000
Other reserves	28 500	26 800
Retained earnings	49 000	32 000
	$383 500	$252 300

Hastings Ltd is to acquire all the assets, except cash, of Timaru Ltd. The assets of Timaru Ltd are all recorded at fair value except:

	Fair value
Inventory	$ 39 000
Freehold land	130 000
Buildings	40 000

In exchange, Hastings Ltd is to provide sufficient extra cash to allow Timaru Ltd to repay all of its outstanding debts and its liquidation costs of $2400, plus two fully paid shares in Hastings Ltd for every three shares held in Timaru Ltd. The fair value of a share in Hastings Ltd is $3.20. An investigation by the liquidator of Timaru Ltd reveals that at 31 December 2005 the following debts were outstanding but had not been recorded:

Accounts payable	$1 600
Mortgage interest	4 000

The debentures issued by Timaru Ltd are to be redeemed at a 5% premium. Costs of issuing the shares were $1200.

Required
1. Prepare the acquisition analysis and journal entries to record the business combination in the records of Hastings Ltd.
2. Prepare the liquidation, liquidators' cash, and shareholders' distribution accounts for Timaru Ltd.

PROBLEM 12.2 Accounting for business combination by acquirer, liquidation accounts of acquiree

On 1 July 2005, two companies — Plymouth Ltd and Whangarei Ltd — sign an agreement whereby the operations of Whangarei Ltd are to be taken over by Plymouth Ltd. Whangarei Ltd is to liquidate after the transfer is complete. The balance sheets of the two companies on that day were as follows:

	Plymouth Ltd	Whangarei Ltd
Cash	$ 50 000	$ 20 000
Accounts receivable	75 000	56 000
Inventory	56 000	29 000
Land	65 000	–
Plant and equipment	180 000	167 000
Accumulated depreciation – plant and equipment	(60 000)	(40 000)
Shares in Sefton Ltd	–	26 000
Debentures in Akaroa Ltd (face value)	10 000	–
	$376 000	$258 000
Accounts payable	$ 62 000	$ 31 000
Mortgage loan	75 000	21 500
10% Debentures (face value)	100 000	30 000
Contributed equity:		
Ordinary shares of $1, fully paid	100 000	–
'A' class shares of $2, fully paid	–	40 000
'B' class shares of $1, fully paid		60 000
Retained earnings	39 000	75 500
	$376 000	$258 000

Acquisition of Whangarei Ltd
Plymouth Ltd is to acquire all of the assets of Whangarei Ltd (except for cash). The assets of Whangarei Ltd are recorded at their fair values except for the items listed opposite.

	Carrying amount	Fair value
Inventory	$ 29 000	$ 39 200
Plant and equipment	127 000	140 000
Shares in Sefton Ltd	26 000	22 500

In exchange, the 'A' class shareholders of Whangarei Ltd are to receive one 7% debenture in Plymouth Ltd, redeemable on 1 July 2007, for every share held in Whangarei Ltd. The fair value of each debenture is $3.50. The 'B' class shareholders of Whangarei Ltd are to receive two shares in Plymouth Ltd for every three shares held in Whangarei Ltd. The fair value of each Plymouth Ltd share is $2.70. Costs to issue these shares will amount to $900.

Additionally, Plymouth Ltd is to provide Whangarei Ltd with sufficient cash, additional to that already held, to enable Whangarei Ltd to pay its liabilities. The outstanding debentures are to be redeemed at a 10% premium. Annual leave entitlements of $16 200 outstanding at 1 July 2005 and expected liquidation costs of $5000 have not been recognised by Whangarei Ltd. Costs to transport and install Whangarei Ltd's assets at Plymouth Ltd's premises will be $1600.

Required

1. Prepare the acquisition analysis and journal entries in the books of Plymouth Ltd to record the acquisition of Whangarei Ltd.
2. Prepare the liquidation, liquidator's cash and shareholders' distribution ledger accounts in the records of Whangarei Ltd.

PROBLEM 12.3 ★★   Accounting for business combination by acquirer, journal entries for liquidation of acquiree

Wanaka Ltd and Pongaroa Ltd are small family-owned companies engaged in vegetable growing and distribution. The Spencer family owns the shares in Pongaroa Ltd and the Rokocoko family own the shares in Wanaka Ltd. The head of the Spencer family wishes to retire but his two sons are not interested in carrying on the family business. Accordingly, on 1 July 2006, Wanaka Ltd is to take over the operations of Pongaroa Ltd, which will then liquidate. Wanaka Ltd is asset-rich but has limited overdraft facilities so that the following arrangement has been made.

Wanaka Ltd is to acquire all of the assets, except cash, delivery trucks and motor vehicles, of Pongaroa Ltd and will assume all of the liabilities except accounts payable. In return, Wanaka Ltd is to give the shareholders of Pongaroa Ltd a block of vacant land, two delivery vehicles and sufficient additional cash to enable the company to pay off the accounts payable and the liquidation costs of $1500. The land and vehicles had the following values at 30 June 2006:

	Carrying amount	Fair value
Freehold land	$ 50 000	$120 000
Delivery trucks	30 000	28 000

On the liquidation of Pongaroa Ltd, Mr Spencer is to receive the land and the motor vehicles and his two sons are to receive the delivery trucks.

The balance sheets of the two companies as at 30 June 2006 were as follows:

	Wanaka Ltd	Pongaroa Ltd
Cash	$ 3 500	$ 2 000
Accounts receivable	25 000	15 000
Freehold land	250 000	100 000
Buildings (net)	25 000	30 000
Cultivation equipment (net)	65 000	46 000
Irrigation equipment	16 000	22 000
Delivery trucks	45 000	36 000
Motor vehicles	25 000	32 000
	$454 500	$283 000
Accounts payable	26 000	23 500
Loan – Bank of NZ	150 000	80 000
Loan – Maori Bros	35 000	35 000
Loan – Long Cloud	70 000	52 500
Share capital – 100 000 shares	100 000	–
– 60 000 shares	–	60 000
Reserves	28 500	–
Retained earnings	45 000	32 000
	$454 500	$283 000

All the assets of Pongaroa Ltd are recorded at fair value, with the exception of:

	Fair value
Freehold land	$120 000
Buildings	40 000
Cultivation equipment	40 000
Motor vehicle	34 000

Required
1. Prepare the acquisition analysis and the journal entries to record the acquisition of Pongaroa Ltd's operations in the records of Wanaka Ltd.
2. Prepare the journal entries to record the liquidation of Pongaroa Ltd.
3. Prepare the balance sheet of Wanaka Ltd after the business combination, including any notes relating to the business combination.

PROBLEM 12.4   ★★   Accounting for business combination by acquirer

Rotorua Ltd and Waikato Ltd are two family-owned flax-producing companies in New Zealand. Rotorua Ltd is owned by the Wood family, while the Bradbury family owns Waikato Ltd. The Wood family has only one son, and he is engaged to be married to the daughter of the Bradbury family. Because the son is currently managing Waikato Ltd, it is proposed that he be allowed to manage both companies after the wedding. As a result, it is agreed by the two families that Rotorua Ltd should take over the net assets of Waikato Ltd.

The balance sheet of Waikato Ltd immediately prior to the takeover is as follows:

	Carrying amount	Fair value
Cash	$ 20 000	$ 20 000
Accounts receivable	140 000	125 000
Land	620 000	840 000
Buildings (net)	530 000	550 000
Farm equipment (net)	360 000	364 000
Irrigation equipment (net)	220 000	225 000
Vehicles (net)	160 000	172 000
	$2 050 000	
Accounts payable	80 000	80 000
Loan – Maori Bank	480 000	480 000
Share capital	670 000	
Retained earnings	820 000	
	$2 050 000	

The takeover agreement specified the following details:
- Rotorua Ltd is to acquire all the assets of Waikato Ltd except for cash, and one of the vehicles (having a carrying amount of $45 000 and a fair value of $48 000), and assume all the liabilities except for the loan from the Maori Bank. Waikato Ltd is then to go into liquidation.
- Rotorua Ltd is to supply sufficient cash to enable the debt to the Maori Bank to be paid off and to cover the liquidation costs of $5500. It will also give $150 000 to be distributed to Mr and Mrs Bradbury to assist in paying the wedding costs.
- Rotorua Ltd is also to give a piece of its own prime land to Waikato Ltd to be distributed to Mr and Mrs Bradbury, this eventually being available to be given to any offspring of the forthcoming marriage. The piece of land in question has a carrying amount of $80 000 and a fair value of $220 000.
- Rotorua Ltd is to issue 100 000 shares, these having a fair value of $14 per share, to be distributed via Waikato Ltd to the soon to-be-married-daughter of Mr and Mrs Bradbury, who is currently a shareholder in Waikato Ltd.

The takeover proceeded as per the agreement with Rotorua Ltd incurring incidental acquisition costs of $25 000, while there were $18 000 share issue costs.

Required
Prepare the acquisition analysis and the journal entries to record the acquisition of Waikato Ltd in the records of Rotorua Ltd.

PROBLEM 12.5 ★★★ Accounting for acquisitions of a business and shares in another entity

Foxton Ltd is seeking to expand its share of the pet care market and has negotiated to acquire the operations of Taupo Ltd and the shares of Picton Ltd.

The trial balances of the three companies at 1 July 2005 are shown overleaf.

	Foxton Ltd	Taupo Ltd	Picton Ltd
Cash	$145 000	$ 5 200	$ 84 000
Accounts receivable	34 000	21 300	12 000
Inventory	56 000	30 000	25 400
Shares in listed companies	16 000	22 000	7 000
Land and buildings (net)	70 000	40 000	36 000
Plant and equipment (net)	130 000	105 000	25 000
Goodwill (net)	6 000	5 000	5 600
	$457 000	$228 500	$195 000
Accounts payable	$ 65 000	$ 40 000	$ 29 000
Bank overdraft	0	0	1 500
Debentures	50 000	0	100 000
Mortgage loan	100 000	30 000	0
Contributed equity:			
Ordinary shares of $1, fully paid	200 000	150 000	60 000
Other reserves	15 000	6 500	2 500
Retained earnings (30/6/05)	27 000	2 000	2 000
	$457 000	$228 500	$195 000

Taupo Ltd

Foxton Ltd is to acquire all assets (except cash and shares in listed companies) of Taupo Ltd. Transfer and installation costs are expected to be $7600. The net assets of Taupo Ltd are recorded at fair value except for the following:

	Carrying amount	Fair value
Inventory	$ 30 000	$ 26 000
Land and buildings	40 000	80 000
Shares in listed companies	22 000	18 000
Accounts payable	(40 000)	(49 100)
Accrued leave	0	(29 700)

In exchange, the shareholders of Taupo Ltd are to receive, for every three Taupo Ltd shares held, one Foxton Ltd share worth $2.50 each. Costs to issue these shares will be $950. Additionally, Foxton Ltd will transfer to Taupo Ltd its 'Shares in listed companies' asset, which has a fair value of $15 000. These shares, together with those already owned by Taupo Ltd, will be sold and the proceeds distributed to the Taupo Ltd shareholders. Assume that the shares were sold for their fair values.

Foxton Ltd will also give Taupo Ltd sufficient additional cash to enable Taupo Ltd to pay all its creditors. Taupo Ltd will then liquidate. Liquidation costs are estimated to be $8700.

Picton Ltd

Foxton Ltd is to acquire all the issued shares of Picton Ltd. In exchange, the shareholders of Picton Ltd are to receive one Foxton Ltd share, worth $2.50, and $1.50 cash for every two Picton Ltd shares held.

Required

1. Prepare the acquisition analyses and journal entries to record the acquisitions in the records of Foxton Ltd.
2. Prepare the liquidation account and shareholders' distribution account for Taupo Ltd.

3. Explain in detail why, if Taupo Ltd has recorded a goodwill asset of $5000, Foxton Ltd calculates the goodwill acquired via an acquisition analysis. Why does Foxton Ltd not determine a fair value for the goodwill asset and record that figure as it has done for other assets acquired from Taupo Ltd?

4. If Foxton Ltd subsequently receives a dividend cheque for $1500 from Picton Ltd, paid from retained earnings earned prior to its acquisition of the shares in Picton Ltd, how should Foxton Ltd account for that cheque? Why?

5. Shortly after the business combination, the liquidator of Taupo Ltd receives a valid claim of $25 000 from a creditor. As Foxton Ltd has agreed to provide sufficient cash to pay all the liabilities of Taupo Ltd at acquisition date, the liquidator requests and receives a cheque for $25 000 from Foxton Ltd. How should Foxton Ltd record this payment? Why?

PROBLEM 12.6 ★★★   Acquisition of two businesses

Queenstown Ltd is a manufacturer of specialised industrial machinery seeking to diversify its operations. After protracted negotiations, the directors decided to purchase the assets and liabilities of Takapuna Ltd and the spare parts retail division of Nelson Ltd.

At 30 June 2006 the balance sheets of the three entities were as follows:

	Queenstown Ltd	Takapuna Ltd	Nelson Ltd
Land and buildings (net)	$ 60 000	$ 25 000	$ 40 000
Plant and machinery (net)	100 000	36 000	76 000
Office equipment (net)	16 000	4 000	6 000
Shares in listed companies	24 000	15 000	20 800
Debentures in listed companies	20 000	–	–
Accounts receivable	35 000	26 000	42 000
Inventory	150 000	54 000	30 200
Cash	59 000	11 000	9 000
Goodwill	–	7 000	–
	$464 000	$178 000	$224 000
Accounts payable	$ 26 000	$ 14 000	$ 27 000
Current tax liability	21 000	6 000	7 000
Provision for leave	36 000	10 000	17 500
Bank loan	83 000	16 000	43 500
Debentures	60 000	50 000	–
Share capital (issued at $1, fully paid)	200 000	60 000	90 000
Retained earnings	38 000	22 000	39 000
	$464 000	$178 000	$224 000

The acquisition agreement details are as follows:

Takapuna Ltd

Queenstown Ltd is to acquire all of the assets (other than cash) and liabilities (other than debentures, provisions and tax liabilities) of Takapuna Ltd for the following purchase consideration:

• Shareholders in Takapuna Ltd are to receive three shares in Queenstown Ltd, credited as fully paid, in exchange for every four shares held. The shares in Queenstown Ltd are to be issued at their fair value of $3.00 per share. Costs of share issue amounted to $2000.

• Queenstown Ltd is to provide sufficient cash which, when added to the cash already held, will enable Takapuna Ltd to pay out the current tax liability and provision for leave, to redeem the debentures at a premium of 5%, and to pay its liquidation expenses of $2500.

The fair values of the assets and liabilities of Takapuna Ltd are equal to their carrying amounts with the exception of the following:

	Fair value
Land and buildings	$60 000
Plant and machinery	50 000
Inventory	50 000

Incidental costs associated with the acquisition amount to $2500.

Nelson Ltd

Queenstown Ltd is to acquire the spare parts retail business of Nelson Ltd. The following information is available concerning that business, relative to the whole of Nelson Ltd:

	Total amount	Spare parts division	
	Carrying amount	Carrying amount	Fair value
Land and buildings (net)	$ 40 000	$ 20 000	$ 30 000
Plant and machinery (net)	76 000	32 000	34 500
Office equipment (net)	6 000	2 000	2 500
Accounts receivable	42 000	21 000	20 000
Inventory	30 200	12 000	12 000
Accounts payable	27 000	14 000	14 000
Provision for leave	17 500	7 000	7 000

The divisional net assets are to be acquired for $10 000 cash, plus 11 000 ordinary shares in Queenstown Ltd issued at their fair value of $3, as well as the land and buildings that have been purchased from Takapuna Ltd.

Incidental costs associated with the acquisition are $1000.

Required

1. Prepare the acquisition analyses for the acquisition transactions of Queenstown Ltd.
2. Prepare the liquidation account for Takapuna Ltd.
3. Prepare the journal entries for the acquisition transactions in the records of Queenstown Ltd and Nelson Ltd.

Visit these websites for additional information:

www.iasb.org   www.iasplus.com
www.asic.gov.au   www.ifac.org
www.aasb.com.au   www.nzica.com
www.accaglobal.com   www.capa.com.my

REFERENCES

Accounting Standards Board of Japan 2005, Letter of comment (no. 32) on *Exposure Draft of Proposed Amendments to IFRS 3 Business Combinations*, 28 October, viewed 29 June 2006, <www.fasb.org/ocl/fasb-getletters.php?project=1204-001>.

Accounting Standards Board UK 2005, Letter of comment (no. 130) on *Exposure Draft of Proposed Amendments to IFRS 3 Business Combinations*, 28 October, viewed 29 June 2006, <www.fasb.org/ocl/fasb-getletters.php?project=1204-001>.

Citigroup 2005, Letter of comment (no. 42) on *Exposure Draft of Proposed Amendments to IFRS 3 Business Combinations*, 28 October, viewed 29 June 2006, <www.fasb.org/ocl/fasb-getletters.php?project=1204-001>.

Danisco 2005, *Annual report 2004/05*, Danisco Corporation, Denmark, viewed March 2006, <www.danisco.com>.

Dansk Industries 2005, Letter of comment (no. 125) on *Exposure Draft of Proposed Amendments to IFRS 3 Business Combinations*, Confederation of Danish Industries, 2 November, viewed 29 June 2006, <www.fasb.org/ocl/fasb-getletters.php?project=1204-001>.

EFRAG 2005, Letter of comment (no. 268) on *Exposure Draft of Proposed Amendments to IFRS 3 Business Combinations*, European Financial Reporting Advisory Group, 28 November, viewed 29 June 2006, <www.fasb.org/ocl/fasb-getletters.php?project=1204-001>.

—2003, Letter of comment on ED 3, European Financial Reporting Advisory Group, 4 April.

French Society of Financial Analysts 2005, Letter of comment (no. 186) on *Exposure Draft of Proposed Amendments to IFRS 3 Business Combinations*, viewed 29 June 2006, <www.fasb.org/ocl/fasb-getletters.php?project=1204-001>.

GASB 2005, Letter of comment (no. 121) on *Exposure Draft of Proposed Amendments to IFRS 3 Business Combinations*, German Accounting Standards Board, 27 October, viewed 29 June 2006, <www.fasb.org/ocl/fasb-getletters.php?project=1204-001>.

IASB Amendments ED *see* IASB 2005b.

—Basis for Conclusions on IFRS 3.

— 2005a, Basis for Conclusions on *Exposure Draft of Proposed Amendments to IFRS 3 Business Combinations*, International Accounting Standards Committee Foundation, London.

— 2005b, *Exposure Draft of Proposed Amendments to IFRS 3 Business Combinations*, International Accounting Standards Committee Foundation, London.

—2004 Project Summary for Business Combinations (Phase II), International Accounting Standards Committee Foundation, London, January.

—2004, Project Update, 26 January, viewed 15 June 2004, <www.iasb.org>.

IOSCO 2005, Letter of comment (no. 260) on *Exposure Draft of Proposed Amendments to IFRS 3 Business Combinations*, International Organization of Securities Commissions, 29 November, <www.fasb.org/ocl/fasb getletters.php?project=1204 001>.

Johnson, LT & Petrone, KR 1998, 'Is goodwill an asset?', *Accounting Horizons*, vol. 12, no. 3, pp. 293–303.

Leo, KJ, Hoggett, JR & Radford, J 1995, *Accounting for identifiable intangibles and goodwill*, Australian Society of Certified Practising Accountants, Melbourne.

Microsoft Corporation 2005, Letter of comment (no. 21) on *Exposure Draft of Proposed Amendments to IFRS 3 Business Combinations*, 25 October, viewed 29 June 2006, <www.fasb.org/ocl/fasb-getletters.php?project=1204-001>.

Miller, M. & Islam, A 1988, *The definition and recognition of assets*, Accounting Theory Monograph No. 7, Australian Accounting Research Foundation, Melbourne.

Nokia 2005, *Nokia in 2005*, Nokia Corporation, Finland, viewed March 2006, <www.nokia.com>.

South African Institute of Chartered Accountants 2005, Letter of comment (no. 215) on *Exposure Draft of Proposed Amendments to IFRS 3 Business Combinations*, 28 October, viewed 29 June 2006, <www.fasb.org/ocl/fasb-getletters.php?project=1204-001>.

Swedish Enterprise Accounting Group 2005, Letter of comment (no. 185) on *Exposure Draft of Proposed Amendments to IFRS 3 Business Combinations*, International Organisation of Securities Commissions, 2 November, <www.fasb.org/ocl/fasb-getletters.php?project=1204-001>.

Texas Instruments 2005, Letter of comment (no. 91) on *Exposure Draft of Proposed Amendments to IFRS 3 Business Combinations*, International Organisation of Securities Commissions, 28 October, <www.fasb.org/ocl/fasb-getletters.php?project=1204-001>.

CHAPTER 13
Impairment of assets

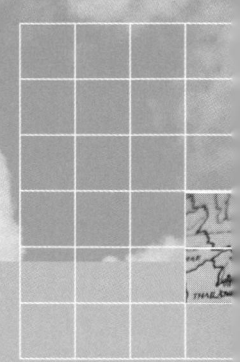

ACCOUNTING STANDARDS

International: IAS 36 *Impairment of Assets*
Australia: AASB 136 *Impairment of Assets*
New Zealand: NZ IAS 36 *Impairment of Assets*

CONCEPTS FOR REVIEW

Before studying this chapter, you should understand or, if necessary, revise:

- the IASB Framework
- the concept of depreciation adopted in IAS 16 *Property, Plant and Equipment*
- internally generated goodwill – its nature and accounting treatment under IAS 38 *Intangible Assets*
- acquired goodwill – its nature and accounting treatment under IFRS 3 *Business Combinations*.

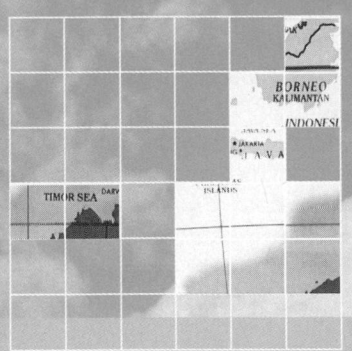

LEARNING OBJECTIVES

When you have studied this chapter, you should be able to:
1. understand the purpose of the impairment test for assets
2. understand when to undertake an impairment test
3. understand how to collect evidence to determine whether an impairment test is necessary
4. explain how to undertake an impairment test for an individual asset
5. explain how to calculate value in use
6. recognise and measure an impairment loss for an individual asset
7. understand what a cash-generating unit is, and how to identify one
8. account for an impairment loss for a cash-generating unit – not including goodwill
9. account for the impairment of goodwill
10. account for reversals of impairment losses
11. apply the disclosure requirements of IAS 36.

13.1 Introduction to IAS 36

Chapters 10 and 11 discuss the measurement and recognition criteria for property, plant and equipment, and intangibles. These assets are measured at cost or revalued amount and, for each asset, the cost or revalued amount is allocated over its useful life. The exception is where intangible assets have indefinite useful lives, in which case no amortisation is charged. In the balance sheet at the end of a reporting period, the assets are reported at cost or revalued amount less the accumulated depreciation/amortisation. As there are many judgements in the depreciation/amortisation process – estimates of useful life, residual values and the pattern of benefits – the question to be asked at balance date is whether the carrying amounts of the assets in the balance sheet overstate the worth of the assets. In other words, can an entity expect to recover in future periods the carrying amounts of an entity's assets? Recovery can be from future use of the asset and/or from the eventual disposal of the asset. If an entity does not expect to recover the carrying amount of an asset, the entity has an impairment loss in relation to that asset. Paragraph 6 of IAS 36 *Impairment of Assets* defines an impairment loss as follows: 'An impairment loss is the amount by which the carrying amount of an asset or a cash-generating unit exceeds its recoverable amount'.

The purpose of this chapter is to examine the impairment test for assets. The accounting standard covering impairment is IAS 36 *Impairment of Assets*. The standard was issued initially as IAS 36 in July 1998, amended on numerous occasions, exposed for further amendment in December 2002, and issued in its present form in 2004.

Under IAS 36, an entity is required to conduct impairment tests for its assets to see whether it has incurred any impairment losses. The purpose of the impairment test is to ensure that assets are not carried at amounts that exceed their recoverable amounts or, more simply, that assets are not overstated.

Key questions in relation to the impairment test are:
- How does the test work?
- Is the test the same for all assets?
- Should the test apply to individual assets or to groups of assets? If to groups, which groups?
- Is the accounting treatment the same for assets measured at cost and for those measured at revalued amount?
- When should the test be carried out? Should it be done annually? Every three years? Or some other time?
- Can the results of the impairment test be reversed; that is, if an asset is written down because it is impaired, can later events lead to the reversal of that write-down?

13.1.1 Scope of IAS 36

Paragraph 2 of IAS 36 notes that the standard does not apply to all assets; that is, not all assets are subject to impairment testing. Assets to which IAS 36 does not apply are:
- inventories – IAS 2 *Inventories*
- assets arising from construction contracts – IAS 11 *Construction Contracts*
- deferred tax assets – IAS 12 *Income Taxes*
- assets arising from employee benefits – IAS 19 *Employee Benefits*
- financial assets – IAS 39 *Financial Instruments: Recognition and Measurement*
- investment properties measured at fair value – IAS 40 *Investment Property*
- biological assets measured at fair value less estimated point-of-sale costs – IAS 41 *Agriculture*

- deferred acquisition costs and intangible assets relating to insurance contracts — IFRS 4 *Insurance Contracts*
- non-current assets or disposal groups classified as held for sale — IFRS 5 *Non-current Assets Held for Sale and Discontinued Operations.*

The accounting standards noted above contain the principles for recognition and measurement of the particular assets covered by those standards. Note that in some of these standards the assets are required to be recorded at fair value, or fair value less costs to sell. Where assets are recorded at fair value, there is no need to test for recoverability of the carrying amount of the asset. Under IAS 2, inventory is recorded at the lower of cost and net realisable value. As net realisable value is defined in terms of estimated selling price, IAS 2 has an inbuilt impairment test requiring inventory to be written down when the cost is effectively greater than the recoverable amount.

LO 2

13.2   When to undertake an impairment test

As noted earlier, the purpose of the impairment test is to ensure that disclosed assets do not have carrying amounts in excess of their recoverable amounts. However, under IAS 36 it is not necessary at each balance date to test each asset in order to determine if it is impaired. The only assets that need to be tested at balance date are those where there is any *indication* that an asset may be impaired (see paragraph 9 of IAS 36). An entity therefore must determine by looking at various sources of information whether there is sufficient evidence to suspect that an asset may be impaired. If there is no such evidence, then an entity can assume that impairment has not occurred.

For most assets, the need for an impairment test can be assessed by analysing sources of evidence. However, there are some assets for which an impairment test *must* be undertaken every year. Paragraph 10 identifies these assets:

- intangible assets with indefinite useful lives
- intangible assets not yet available for use
- goodwill acquired in a business combination.

The reason for singling out these assets for automatic impairment testing is that the carrying amounts of these assets are considered to be more uncertain than those of other assets. For intangible assets with indefinite useful lives, there is no annual amortisation charge, and hence no ongoing reduction in the carrying amounts of the assets. As the assets are not being reduced via amortisation, it is considered essential that the carrying amounts be tested against the recoverable amounts. Goodwill is calculated as a residual amount when a business combination occurs. (This is discussed in more detail later in this chapter.) Goodwill is also not subject to annual amortisation; instead, it is subject to an annual impairment test. However, impairment testing does not absolve management from being aware of events that may cause impairment to occur within an accounting period and accounting for such impairments as they occur.

Another important reason for remeasuring assets and testing for impairment relates to the concept of depreciation adopted by the IASB. As noted in chapter 10, depreciation is viewed as a process of allocation rather than as a valuation process, even when an asset is measured at a revalued amount. Hence, the carrying amount of an asset reflects the unallocated measure of the asset rather than the benefits to be derived from the asset in the future. The impairment test relates to the assessment of recoverability of the asset, which is not a feature of the depreciation allocation process.

LO 3

13.2.1   Collecting evidence of impairment

The purpose of the impairment test is to determine whether the carrying amount of an asset exceeds its recoverable amount. The evidence of impairment then relates to variables that may support the belief that the asset under investigation is not worth as much as it was previously. The indicators noted in IAS 36 are only the minimum that an entity's management should look at. Management should take into account the nature and use of a specific asset and determine the factors that may indicate deterioration in the asset's worth. The minimum indicators listed in IAS 36 are described in two groups: external sources of information, and internal sources of information.

External sources of information

Paragraph 12 of IAS 36 lists four sources of information relating to the external environment in which the entity operates:

1. *Market value.* Has the asset's market value declined more than would normally be expected during the period? This may occur for many reasons relating to changes in expectations concerning the operation of the entity. For example, there may have been a significant reduction in the entity's sales when new products or technologies, which the entity planned to introduce within a certain timeframe, are not introduced within that timeframe. Further, there may have been movements in key personnel that affect the productivity of the entity itself and provide increasing pressure from competitors who have employed these people.

2. *Entity's environment/market.* Have significant adverse changes occurred, or are they expected to occur, in the technological, market, economic or legal environment in which the entity operates, or in the market to which the asset is dedicated? For example, a competitor may have developed a product or technology that is likely to cause, or has caused, a significant and permanent reduction in the entity's market share.

3. *Interest rates.* Have market interest rates or market rates of return increased during the period, with potential changes in the interest rate used in assessing an entity's present value of future cash flows?

4. *Market capitalisation.* Is the carrying amount of the net assets of the entity greater than the market capitalisation of the entity?

Internal sources of information

Paragraph 12 of IAS 36 lists three sources of information based on events within the entity itself:

1. *Obsolescence or physical damage.* Does an analysis of the asset reveal physical damage, or obsolescence?

2. *Changed use within the entity.* Is the asset expected to be used differently within the entity? For example, the asset may become idle; there may be a restructure in the entity that changes the use of the asset; there may be plans to sell the asset; or the useful life of an intangible may be changed from indefinite to finite.

3. *Economic performance of the asset.* Do internal reports indicate that the economic performance of the asset is worse than expected? Evidence of this consists of:
   - actual cash flows for maintenance or operating the asset may be significantly higher than expected
   - actual cash inflows or profits may be lower than expected
   - expected cash flows for maintenance of operations may have increased, or expected profits may be lower.

In analysing the information from the above sources, paragraph 15 of IAS 36 notes that materiality must be taken into account. If, in previous analyses, the carrying amount of an asset was significantly lower than the asset's recoverable amount, minor movements in the factors listed above may cause the recoverable amount to be closer to the carrying amount but not large enough to expect the carrying amount to be greater than the recoverable amount. For example, if short-term interest rates changed, this may not be expected to affect long-term interest rates.

In its notes to the 2005 consolidated financial statements, Nokia provided details of the factors that trigger an impairment review for the entity. This is shown in figure 13.1.

Valuation of long-lived and intangible assets and goodwill

The Group assesses the carrying value of identifiable intangible assets, long-lived assets and goodwill annually, or more frequently if events or changes in circumstances indicate that such carrying value may not be recoverable. Factors that trigger an impairment review include underperformance relative to historical or projected future results, significant changes in the manner of the use of the acquired assets or the strategy for the overall business and significant negative industry or economic trends. The most significant variables in determining cash flows are discount rates, terminal values, the number of years on which to base the cash flow projections, as well as the assumptions and estimates used to determine the cash inflows and outflows. Amounts estimated could differ materially from what will actually occur in the future.

FIGURE 13.1 Indicators of impairment
Source: Nokia (2005, p. 25).

LO 4

13.3 Impairment test for an individual asset

The impairment test involves comparing the carrying amount of an asset with its recoverable amount. To understand the nature of this test, it is necessary to understand a number of definitions given in paragraph 6 of IAS 36:

> The **recoverable amount** of an asset or a cash-generating unit is the higher of its fair value less costs to sell and its value in use.

> **Fair value less costs to sell** is the amount obtainable from the sale of an asset or cash-generating unit in an arm's length transaction between knowledgeable, willing parties, less the costs of disposal.

> **Costs of disposal** are incremental costs directly attributable to the disposal of an asset or cash-generating unit, excluding finance costs and income tax expense.

> **Value in use** is the present value of the future cash flows expected to be derived from an asset or cash-generating unit.

Note the phrase 'an asset or cash-generating unit' in the above definitions. The discussion in this section focuses on an individual asset, and it is assumed that, for the asset being tested for impairment, there are specific cash flows that can be associated with the asset. Cash-generating units are discussed in section 13.4.

From the definition of recoverable amount, there are two possible amounts against which the carrying amount can be tested for impairment. These are fair value less costs to sell, and value in use. Although the definition of recoverable amount refers to the 'higher' of these two amounts, an impairment occurs if the carrying amount exceeds recoverable amount (para. 8). However, it is not always necessary to measure both amounts when testing for impairment. If either one of these amounts is greater than carrying amount, the asset is not impaired (para. 19). Where there are active markets, determining fair value less costs to sell is probably easier than calculating value in use. However, where the carrying amount exceeds the fair value less costs to sell, it is necessary to calculate the value in use. Figure 13.2 contains a diagrammatic representation of the impairment test based on a diagram provided by Picker and Johnson (1999).

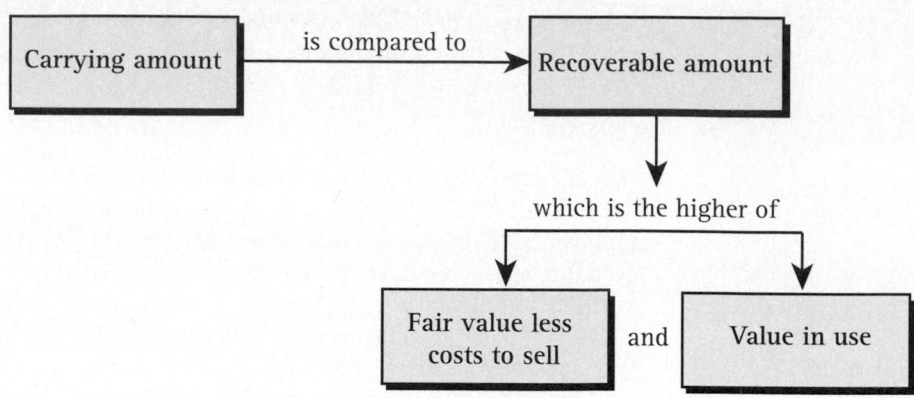

FIGURE 13.2 The impairment test
Source: Adapted from Picker & Johnson (1999, p. 7).

In calculating either fair value less costs to sell or value in use, paragraph 23 of IAS 36 notes that, in 'some cases, estimates, averages and computational shortcuts may provide reasonable approximations', rather than an entity having to perform in-depth calculations on an annual basis. It is also possible to use the most recent detailed calculation of recoverable amount made in a preceding year (para. 24) in the case of an intangible asset with an indefinite useful life. The latter is possible if *all* the following criteria are met:

• for the intangible asset, if tested as part of a cash-generating unit (see section 13.4 of this chapter), the other assets and liabilities in the unit have not changed significantly

• in the preceding year's calculation, the difference between the carrying amount and recoverable amount was substantial

• an analysis of all evidence relating to events affecting the asset suggests that the likelihood of the recoverable amount being less than carrying amount is remote.

13.3.1 Calculating fair value less costs to sell

There are two parts to the determination of fair value less costs to sell, namely *fair value* and *costs of disposal*. Where there is an active market, the fair value is the market price. If the market is not active, a fair value may be determined by observing evidence such as amounts paid in recent sales transactions. The fair value reflects what the entity could obtain from the sale of the asset to knowledgeable, willing buyers.

Paragraph 28 of IAS 36 provides the following examples of costs of disposal: legal costs, stamp duty and similar transaction taxes, costs of removing the asset, and direct incremental costs to bring the asset into condition for sale. The costs must be directly associated with either the sale of the asset or getting the asset ready for sale. Any costs arising subsequent to the sale of the asset, even if arising as a result of the sale, are not regarded as costs of disposal.

Paragraph 5 of IAS 36 provides guidance where an asset is measured under the alternative accounting treatment in IAS 16 – at a revalued amount (that is, fair value). Fair value as a measure does not include a consideration of disposal costs. Hence, if an asset's fair value is equal to its market value, the difference between fair value and fair value less costs to sell is the disposal costs of the asset. If the disposal costs are immaterial, then there is no significant difference between fair value and fair value less costs to sell. Therefore, where an asset is measured at fair value, revaluation decrements are not distinguishable from impairment losses. If the disposal costs are material, then fair value less costs to sell is less than the carrying amount (that is, fair value). The asset's value in use would then need to be calculated to determine whether it was less than fair value. If so, the asset is impaired and must be written down to recoverable amount, which is the higher of fair value less costs to sell and value in use.

LO 5

13.3.2 Calculating value in use

Value in use is the present value of future cash flows relating to the asset being measured. As paragraph 30 of IAS 36 notes, there are five elements to be reflected in the calculation of the value in use:

   (a) an estimate of the future cash flows the entity expects to derive from the asset;
   (b) expectations about possible variations in the amount or timing of those future cash flows;
   (c) the time value of money, represented by the current market risk-free rate of interest;
   (d) the price for bearing the uncertainty inherent in the asset;
   (e) other factors, such as illiquidity, that market participants would reflect in pricing the future cash flows the entity expects to derive from the asset.

The object is to measure the present value of the cash flows relating to the asset, in other words, to determine the cash flows and apply a discount rate. Some of the elements noted above − particularly (b), (d) and (e) − may affect either the measurement of the cash flows or the discount rate. Figure 13.3 contains an example of the calculation of value in use based on example 2 of the illustrative examples accompanying IAS 36.

Year	Long-term growth rates	Future cash flows	Present value factor at 15% discount rate	Discounted future cash flows
2002		230	0.869 57	200
2003		253	0.756 14	191
2004		273	0.657 52	180
2005		290	0.571 75	166
2006		304	0.497 18	151
2007	3%	313	0.432 33	135
2008	−2%	307	0.375 94	115
2009	−6%	289	0.326 90	94
2010	−15%	245	0.284 26	70
2011	−25%	184	0.247 19	45
2012	−67%	61	0.214 94	13
Value in use				1360

FIGURE 13.3 Calculation of value in use
Source: IAS 36, Illustrative Examples, Example 2.

As can be seen from figure 13.3, the calculation of value in use requires the estimation of future cash flows and a discount rate applied to these future cash flows.

Determining future cash flows

Paragraphs 33–54 of IAS 36 provide guidance in measuring future cash flows. Some important guidelines are:

- Cash flow projections should be based on *management's best estimate* of the range of economic conditions that will exist over the remaining useful life of the asset. These should be tempered by an analysis of past cash flows and management's success in the past in predicting future cash flows accurately. Where external evidence is available, this should be given greater weight than simple reliance on management's expectations.

- Cash flow projections should be based on the most recent *financial budgets and forecasts*. These projections should cover a maximum period of five years unless a longer period can be justified. For most entities, a detailed analysis of future operations rarely extends beyond five years.

- For years subsequent to the five-year budget projection, reliance should be placed on a steady or declining *growth rate*, unless there are specific reasons for predicting an increasing growth rate. In cases where an entity is doing particularly well, expectations of competitors entering the industry must be taken into consideration. The growth rate used should not exceed the long-term growth rate for the products, industries or country in which the entity operates. See figure 13.3 for an example of this.

- The cash inflows should include those from *continuing use* of the asset over its expected useful life as well as those expected to be received on *disposal* of the asset. Further, any cash *outflows* necessary to achieve the projected inflows must be taken into account. This may be particularly applicable at the time of the asset's disposal, where outlays are incurred to prepare the asset for disposal.

- Projected cash flows must be estimated for the asset in its *current* condition (paragraph 44). Where there is an expected restructuring of the entity in future periods, or where there are possibilities for improving or enhancing the performance of the asset by subsequent expenditure, projections of cash flows will not take these possible events into consideration. In the illustrative examples accompanying IAS 36, examples 5 and 6 demonstrate how cash flows are determined when restructuring and capital expenditure will be made to enhance performance. In both cases, if the value in use is being determined at 2006, and the restructuring/capital expenditure is not going to occur until 2007, the value in use at 2005 is determined by excluding the cash inflows/outflows relating to these future events. Once the entity is committed to the restructure, for example in 2006, the value in use calculated at that date could include the benefits from the restructure, such benefits being an increase in the expected cash flows. In the example of capital expenditure, using an aircraft as an example, management may include in its budget of 2005 capital expenditure for 2008 that is necessary to renew the operating capacity of the aircraft. However, the value in use at 2005 excludes expected renewal costs and subsequent benefits. When the capital expenditure is incurred in 2008, the increased benefits from the capital expenditure can be included in the calculation in order to determine the value in use at the end of that period. Day-to-day servicing costs are included in the outflows used to measure value in use, as are the costs of major inspections.

- Cash flows relating to *financing activities* or *income tax* are not included in the calculations of future cash flows. As the discount rate is based on a pre-tax basis, the future cash flows must also be on a pre-tax basis.

- In assessing cash flows from *disposal*, the expected disposal price will take into account specific future price increases/decreases. It will be based on an analysis of prices prevailing at the date of the estimate for similar assets in conditions similar to those expected for the asset under consideration at the end of its useful life.

- Appendix A to IAS 36, described as an 'integral part of the Standard', contains guidance on the use of present value techniques in measuring value in use. In paragraph

A2, two approaches to computing present value are noted. The first is the 'traditional' approach. It adjusts for expectations about possible variations in cash flow, the price for bearing uncertainty, and other factors used in pricing the asset by making the adjustments in the discount rate. The second is the 'expected cash flow' approach. It makes adjustments for these variables in arriving at risk-adjusted expected cash flows. The expected cash flows are based on consideration of all possible cash flows rather than just the most likely cash flow. Paragraph A7 provides the example of a situation where the possible cash flows and their related probabilities are as follows:

	Cash flow	Probability	Expected cash flow
Cash flow 1	$100	10%	$ 10
Cash flow 2	200	60%	120
Cash flow 3	300	30%	90
Expected cash flow			$220

It is also possible for the expected cash flow to take into account probabilities of being received in different years. As noted in paragraph A7, a cash flow of $1000 may be received in one year, two years or three years, with probabilities of 10%, 60% and 30% respectively:

	Present value	Probability	Expected cash flow
$1000 in 1 year at 5%	952.38	10%	$ 95.24
$1000 in 2 years at 5%	907.03	60%	544.22
$1000 in 3 years at 5%	863.84	30%	259.15
Expected present value			$898.61

A further refinement could be to apply different discount rates for different future periods where value in use is sensitive to a difference in risk for different periods or to the term structure of interest rates (para. A8):

	Present value	Probability	Expected cash flow
$1000 in 1 year at 5%	952.38	10%	$ 95.24
$1000 in 2 years at 5.25%	902.73	60%	541.64
$1000 in 3 years at 5.5%	851.61	30%	255.48
Expected present value			$892.36

Source: Adapted from IAS 36, appendix A, para. A8.

Undertaking this level of detail in measuring the expected cash flows must always be subject to a cost-benefit constraint (para. A12).

Paragraph A6 notes that there are further disadvantages with using the traditional approach because it relies on finding an interest rate that is commensurate with the risk. This requires isolating an asset existing in the market that has similar characteristics to the one being measured, and being able to observe the discount rate. The expected cash flow approach does not rely on finding such an asset but incorporates variations in risk and cash flows into the calculations of the expected cash flows. A range of possible outcomes is then built into the model, reducing the reliance on a single, most likely outcome.

Determining the discount rate

Paragraph 55 of IAS 36 notes that the discount rate should reflect:

(a) the time value of money; and

(b) the risks specific to the asset for which the future cash flow estimates have not been adjusted.

The rate may be determined by viewing rates used for similar assets in the market, or from the weighted average cost of capital of a listed entity that has a single asset, or portfolio of assets, similar to the asset under review (para. 56).

Paragraph A3 of appendix A notes that a general principle in choosing a discount rate is that the interest rate 'should reflect assumptions that are consistent with those inherent in the estimated cash flows'. Not to do so could lead to double counting. The example given in paragraph A3 (a) to illustrate this is as follows:

> For example, a discount rate of 12 per cent might be applied to contractual cash flows of a loan receivable. That rate reflects expectations about future defaults from loans with particular characteristics. That same 12 per cent rate should not be used to discount expected cash flows because those cash flows already reflect assumptions about future defaults.

Further advice contained in paragraphs A15–A21 of appendix A includes the following:

- As a starting point in choosing a discount rate, an entity may consider the current rates affecting the entity, such as the entity's weighted cost of capital, the entity's incremental borrowing rate and other market borrowing rates.
- The rate must reflect specific risks affecting the entity, with consideration being given to risks such as country risk, currency risk and price risk.
- The way in which the entity is financed as a whole, and the way in which the entity specifically financed the acquisition of the asset in question, should not affect the determination of the discount rate.

Figure 13.4 contains information provided in note 12 to the 2005 annual report of the Swatch Group Ltd. Note in particular the information provided about the calculation of the recoverable amount using value-in-use calculations.

Goodwill impairment testing

Goodwill is allocated to the Group's cash-generating units (CGUs), which correspond to the profit centers for the segment "watches and Jewelry" and the reportable segments for the business segments "Production" and "Electronic Systems". A segment-level summary of the goodwill allocation is presented below:

(CHF million)	31.12.2005	31.12.2004
Watches & jewelry	151	151
Production	22	22
Electronic systems	34	34
Total	207	207

The recoverable amount of a cash-generating unit is determined based on value-in-use calculations. These calculations use cash flow projections based on financial budgets approved by management covering a five-year period. Cash flows beyond the five-year period are extrapolated using conservatively estimated growth rates. The discount rates used (6.2%–7.5%) are derived from a capital asset pricing model using data from Swiss capital markets and reflect specific risks relating to the relevant segments. This is then adjusted to a pre-tax rate (8.25%–10.1%).

No impairment charge for goodwill had to be recorded in 2005. Management believes that any reasonably possible change in any of the key assumptions would not cause the carrying value of goodwill to exceed the recoverable amount.

FIGURE 13.4   Calculation of value in use

LO 6

13.3.3 ## Recognition and measurement of an impairment loss for an individual asset

Source: Swatch Group (2005, p. 149).

Paragraphs 58–64 of IAS 36 provide the principles for recognition and measurement of an impairment loss for an individual asset. If the recoverable amount of an asset is less than its carrying amount, an impairment loss occurs, and the asset must be written down from its carrying amount to the recoverable amount.

Where an asset is measured using the *cost model*, according to paragraph 60 of IAS 36, an impairment loss is recognised immediately in profit or loss. In relation to the other side of the accounting entry to the loss, reference should be made to paragraph 73(d) of IAS 16 *Property, Plant and Equipment*. According to this paragraph, for items of property, plant and equipment, 'the gross carrying amount and the accumulated depreciation (aggregated with accumulated impairment losses) at the beginning and end of the period' should be disclosed. When impairment occurs, there is no need to write off any existing accumulated depreciation or create a separate accumulated impairment account. The impairment write-down can be included in accumulated depreciation, preferably referred to as 'Accumulated depreciation and impairment losses'.

Hence, if an asset having a carrying amount of $100 (original cost $160) has a recoverable amount of $90, the appropriate journal entry to account for the impairment loss is:

Impairment loss	Dr	10	
Accumulated depreciation and			
impairment losses	Cr		10
(Impairment loss on asset)			

Where an asset is measured using the *revaluation model* (that is, at fair value) then, according to paragraph 60 of IAS 36, any impairment loss is treated as a revaluation decrement and accounted for as set out in IAS 16. If an asset at the end of an accounting period has a carrying amount of $100, being previously calculated as a fair value of $120 less accumulated depreciation of $20, and the asset's recoverable amount (and possibly its fair value) at the end of the period is determined to be $90, the accounting entry is:

Accumulated depreciation	Dr	20	
Revaluation write-down	Dr	10	
Asset	Cr		30
(Write-down of asset)			

If the revalued asset had a previous revaluation increment of $20, giving rise to a revaluation surplus of $14 and a deferred tax liability (using a tax rate of 30%) of $6, then the entry to write the asset down to a recoverable amount of $90 requires an adjustment directly against the revaluation surplus:

Accumulated depreciation	Dr	20	
Asset revaluation surplus	Dr	7	
Deferred tax liability	Dr	3	
Asset	Cr		30
(Write-down of asset to recoverable amount)			

Regardless of whether the cost model or the revaluation model is used, once the impairment loss is recognised, any subsequent depreciation/amortisation is based on the new recoverable amount. In accordance with paragraph 63 of IAS 36, the depreciation charge is that necessary to allocate the asset's revised carrying amount (the recoverable amount) less its residual value (if any) on a systematic basis over its remaining useful life. Consider the example of the asset recorded at cost of $160 less accumulated depreciation of $60 and having a recoverable amount of $90. The impairment loss of $10 is recognised, the remaining useful life of the asset is assessed (assume three years, with equal benefits per annum), and the residual value is determined (assume zero). Hence, in the year following recognition of the impairment loss, depreciation of $30 (being $\frac{1}{3} \times \$90$) is recognised.

It is possible that the recoverable amount is negative due to large expected future cash outflows relating to the asset, so the impairment loss could be greater than the carrying amount of the asset. According to paragraph 62 of IAS 16, a liability for the excess should be raised only if another standard requires it.

13.4   Cash-generating units — excluding goodwill

The discussion in section 13.3 focuses on individual assets and whether or not they have been impaired. The impairment test in such cases involves the determination of recoverable amount, and this requires the measurement of fair value less costs to sell and value in use of the asset being tested for impairment. However, for some assets, fair value less costs to sell may be determinable as the asset is separable and there exists a market for that asset, but it may be impossible to determine the value in use. Value in use requires determining the expected cash flows to be received from an asset. Some assets do not individually generate cash flows because the cash flows generated are the result of a combination of several assets. For example, a motor vehicle used by a manager does not by itself generate cash flows. Similarly, a machine in a factory works in conjunction with the rest of the assets in the factory to produce inventory which, when sold, creates cash inflows for an entity. For such assets, if the carrying amount exceeds the fair value less costs to sell, some other measure relating to value in use must be used. Figure 13.5 reproduces an example provided in IAS 36.

> **Example**
> A mining entity owns a private railway to support its mining activities. The private railway could be sold only for scrap value and it does not generate cash inflows that are largely independent of the cash inflows from the other assets of the mine.
>
> *It is not possible to estimate the recoverable amount of the private railway because its value cannot be determined and is probably different from scrap value. Therefore, the entity estimates the recoverable amount of the cash-generating unit to which the private railway belongs, i.e. the mine as a whole.*

FIGURE 13.5   Cash flows and individual assets
Source: IAS 36, para. 67.

The private railway described in figure 13.5 'could be sold only for scrap value', but this information is unimportant in determining the cash-generating unit. Even if the railway could be sold for a reasonable amount of money, the answer to what is the cash-generating unit is the same. The key question is whether the cash flows expected to be received by the entity as a whole can be allocated to the various parts of the entity. The railway by itself does not generate cash flows; the cash flows are generated by the combination of the mine and the railway. Hence, the railway is not a separate cash-generating unit. Because the railway is being used by the mining entity, there are no expected cash flows from disposal of the railway, so any consideration of the proceeds on sale of the railway is irrelevant.

Paragraph 66 of IAS 36 requires that, where there is any indication an asset may be impaired, if possible the recoverable amount should be estimated for the individual asset. However, if this is not possible, the entity should 'determine the recoverable amount of the cash-generating unit to which the asset belongs'. In other words, the impairment test is applied to a cash-generating unit rather than to an individual asset. Paragraph 6 contains the following definition of a cash-generating unit:

> A cash-generating unit is the smallest identifiable group of assets that generates cash inflows from continuing use that are largely independent of the cash inflows from other assets or groups of assets.

LO 7

13.4.1 Identifying a cash-generating unit

The identification of a cash-generating unit requires judgement. As is stated in the definition, the key is to determine the 'smallest identifiable group of assets', and this group must create 'independent' cash flows from continuing use. Guidelines given in paragraphs 67–73 of IAS 36 include the following:

- Consideration should be given to how management monitors the entity's operations; for example, by product lines, businesses, individual locations, districts or regional areas.
- Consideration should be given to how management makes decisions about continuing or disposing of the entity's assets and operations.
- If an active market exists for the output of a group of assets, this group constitutes a cash-generating unit.
- Even if some of the output of a group is used internally, if the output could be sold externally, then these prices can be used to measure the value in use of the group of assets.
- Cash-generating units should be identified consistently from period to period for the same group of assets.

Figure 13.6 contains examples adapted from those in the illustrative examples accompanying IAS 36 relating to the identification of cash-generating units.

One of the problems with using a cash-generating unit is that the identification of a particular unit within an entity is arbitrary. It requires judgement on the part of management, and the factors used in the determination will vary from entity to entity. There is no question of comparability between entities, because the cash-generating unit is used for internal accounting purposes and not external reporting disclosures. However, there is the issue of whether management will select cash-generating units with an eye to which assets may decrease in value, and ensure that such assets are included in units in which other assets increase in value.

One alternative to the cash-generating unit is the segment concept as in IAS 14 *Segment Reporting*. Although determination of segments is also arbitrary, an accounting standard covers the identification of segments, which should improve the comparability across entities, and the identified segments are reported to the public. Note, however, that IAS 36 allows a segment to be used as the cash-generating unit only if the segment equates to the smallest identifiable group of assets that generate independent cash flows. For example, in the notes to its 2005 annual report, Nokia stated that the entity:

> is organized on a worldwide basis into four primary business segments: Mobile Phones; Multimedia; Enterprise Solutions; and Networks. Nokia's reportable segments represent the strategic business units that offer different products and services for which monthly financial information is provided to the Board (Nokia 2005, p. 16).

Its impairment note in the 2005 report used these segments as the basis for reporting impairment losses, although the impairment losses seemed to relate to specific assets within those units. Figure 13.7 contains an extract from that note.

A: Retail store chain

Cool Surf City Store belongs to a retail store chain, Cool Surf Enterprises, which sells clothing under the Cool Surf brand. City Store makes all its retail purchases through Cool Surf Enterprises' purchasing centre. Pricing, marketing, advertising and human resource policies (except for hiring City Store's cashiers and salespersons) are set by Cool Surf Enterprises. Cool Surf Enterprises also owns five other stores in the same city as Cool Surf City Store (although in different neighbourhoods) and 20 other stores in other cities. All stores are managed in the same way. Is Cool Surf City Store a cash-generating unit?

Analysis

- *An entity should consider whether internal management reporting is organised to measure performance on a store-by-store basis, and whether the business is run on a store-by-store profit basis, or on a region/city basis.*
- *All City Surf Enterprises' stores are in different suburbs, and probably have different customer bases. So, although City Store is managed at a corporate level, it generates cash inflows that are largely independent of those of other Cool Surf stores. Therefore, it is likely that the City Store is a cash-generating unit.*

B: Magazine titles

A publisher owns 150 magazine titles, of which 70 were acquired and 80 were self-created. The price paid for a purchased magazine title is recognised as an intangible asset. The costs of creating magazine titles and maintaining existing titles are recognised as an expense as incurred. Cash inflows from direct sales and advertising are identifiable for each magazine title. Titles are managed by customer segments. The level of advertising income for a magazine title depends on the range of titles in the customer segment to which the magazine title relates. Management has a policy of abandoning old titles before the end of their economic lives and replacing them immediately with new titles for the same customer segment. Does an individual magazine title represent a separate cash-generating unit?

Analysis

- *It is likely that the recoverable amount of an individual magazine title can be assessed. Even though the level of advertising income for a title is influenced, to a certain extent, by the other titles in the customer segment, cash inflows from direct sales and advertising are identifiable for each title. In addition, although titles are managed by customer segments, decisions to abandon titles are made on an individual title basis.*
- *It is likely that individual magazine titles generate cash inflows that are largely independent of each other and that each magazine title is a separate cash-generating unit.*

C: Building half-rented to others and half-occupied for own use

Biscuits Ltd is a manufacturing company. It owns a headquarters building that used to be fully occupied for internal use. After downsizing, half of the building is now used internally and half is rented to third parties. The lease agreement with the tenant is for five years. Is the building a cash-generating unit?

Analysis

- *The primary purpose of the building is to serve as a corporate asset, supporting Biscuits Ltd's manufacturing activities. The building as a whole cannot be considered to generate cash inflows that are largely independent of the biscuit-making activities as a whole. It is likely that the cash-generating unit for the building is Biscuits Ltd as a whole.*
- *The building is not held as an investment. Therefore, it would not be appropriate to determine the value in use of the building based on projections of future market-related rents.*

FIGURE 13.6 Identifying cash-generating units
Source: Adapted from IAS 36, Illustrative Examples, Example 1.

Notes to the consolidated financial statements

9. Impairment

2005, EURm	Mobile Phones	Multimedia	Enterprise Solutions	Networks	Common Group Functions	Group
Impairment of available-for-sale investments	–	–	–	–	30	30
Total, net	–	–	–	–	30	30
2004, EURm						
Impairment of available-for-sale investments	–	–	–	–	11	11
Impairment of capitalized development costs	–	–	–	115	–	115
Total, net	–	–	–	115	11	126

During 2004, the Group recorded an impairment charge of EUR 65 million of capitalized development costs due to the abandonment of FlexiGateway and Horizontal Technology modules. In addition, an impairment charge of EUR 50 million was recorded on WCDMA radio access network program due to changes in market outlook. The impairment loss was determined as the difference between the carrying amount of the asset and its recoverable amount. The recoverable amount for WCDMA radio access network was derived from the discounted cash flow projections, which cover the estimated life of the WCDMA radio access network current technology, using a discount rate of 15%. The impaired technologies were part of Networks business group.

FIGURE 13.7 Segments and impairment
Source: Nokia (2005, p. 20).

LO 8

13.4.2 Impairment loss for a cash-generating unit — excluding goodwill

Impairment occurs when the carrying amount of the assets of a cash-generating unit exceed their recoverable amount.

Determining the impairment loss

In determining the carrying amount of the assets, all those assets that are directly attributable to the cash-generating unit and that contribute to generating the cash flows used in measuring recoverable amount must be included. There must be consistency between what is being measured for recoverable amount – namely cash flows relating to a group of assets – and the measurement of the carrying amount of those assets.

The principles for determining the recoverable amount of a cash-generating unit are the same as those described for an individual asset in section 13.3 of this chapter. However, note that paragraph 76(b) of IAS 36 requires that the carrying amount of a cash-generating unit does not include the carrying amount of any recognised liability. This is because, as stated in paragraph 43(b), the calculation of the future cash flows of the cash-generating unit does not include cash outflows that relate to obligations that have been recognised as liabilities, such as payables and provisions.

Accounting for an impairment loss in a cash-generating unit

If an impairment loss is recognised in a cash-generating unit that has not recorded any goodwill, paragraph 104 of IAS 36 states that the impairment loss shall be allocated to reduce the carrying amount of the assets of the unit by allocating the impairment loss on a pro-rata basis based on the carrying amount of each asset in the unit. The reduction in each carrying amount relates to each specific asset, and should be treated as an impairment of each asset, even though the impairment loss was based on an analysis of a cash-generating unit. The loss is accounted for in the same way as that for an individual asset as described in section 13.3, with losses relating to an asset measured at cost being recognised immediately in profit or loss.

Paragraph 105 of IAS 36 places some restrictions on an entity's ability to write down assets as a result of the allocation of the impairment loss across the carrying amounts of the assets of the cash-generating unit. For each asset, the carrying amount should not be reduced below the highest of the following:
- its fair value less costs to sell (if determinable)
- its value in use (if determinable)
- zero.

If there is an amount of impairment loss allocated to an asset, but a part of it would reduce the asset below, say, its fair value less costs to sell, then that part is allocated across the other assets in the cash-generating unit on a pro-rata basis (see illustrative example 13.1). However, as paragraph 106 notes, if the recoverable amount of each of the assets cannot be estimated without undue costs or effort, then an arbitrary allocation of the impairment loss between the assets of the unit will suffice because all the assets of a cash-generating unit work together.

ILLUSTRATIVE EXAMPLE 13.1

Impairment of a cash-generating unit

A cash-generating unit has been assessed for impairment and it has been determined that the unit has incurred an impairment loss of $12 000. The carrying amounts of the assets and the allocation of the impairment loss on a proportional basis are as follows:

	Carrying amount	Proportion	Allocation of impairment loss	Net carrying amount
Buildings	$ 500 000	5/12	$ 5 000	$495 000
Equipment	300 000	3/12	3 000	297 000
Land	250 000	2.5/12	2 500	247 500
Fittings	150 000	1.5/12	1 500	148 500
	$1 200 000		$12 000	

However, if the fair value less costs to sell of the buildings was $497 000, then this is the maximum to which these assets could be reduced. Hence, the balance of the allocated impairment loss to buildings of $2000 ($5000 − [$500 000 − $497 000]) has to be allocated across the other assets:

	Carrying amount	Proportion	Allocation of impairment loss	Net carrying amount
Buildings				$497 000
Equipment	$297 000	297/693	$ 857	296 143
Land	247 500	247.5/693	714	246 786
Fittings	148 500	148.5/693	429	148 071
	$693 000		$2 000	

The journal entry to reflect the recognition of the impairment loss is:

Impairment loss	Dr	12 000	
Accumulated depreciation and impairment losses – buildings	Cr		3 000
Accumulated depreciation and impairment losses – equipment	Cr		3 857
Land	Cr		3 214
Accumulated depreciation and impairment losses – fittings	Cr		1 929

Corporate assets

One problem that arises when dividing an entity into separate cash-generating units is dealing with corporate assets. Corporate assets, such as the headquarters building or the information technology support centre, are integral to all cash-generating units generating cash flows but do not by themselves independently generate cash flows. Paragraph 102 of IAS 36 sets out how corporate assets should be dealt with in determining impairment losses for an entity:

Step 1: If any corporate assets can be allocated on a reasonable and consistent basis to cash-generating units, then this should be done. Each unit is then, where appropriate, tested for an impairment loss. Where a loss occurs in a cash-generating unit, the loss is allocated on a pro-rata basis across the assets, including the portion of the corporate asset allocated to the unit.

Step 2: If some corporate assets cannot be allocated across the cash-generating units, the entity shall:
  (i) compare the carrying amount of each unit being tested, excluding the unallocated corporate asset, with its recoverable amount and recognise any impairment loss by allocating the loss across the assets of the unit;
  (ii) identify the smallest cash-generating unit that includes the unit under review and to which a portion of the unallocated corporate asset can be allocated on a reasonable and consistent basis; and
  (iii) compare the carrying amount of the larger cash-generating unit, including the portion of the corporate asset, with its allocated amount. Any impairment loss is then allocated across the assets of the larger cash-generating unit.

Figure 13.8 contains an example of an allocation of corporate assets based on example 8 of the illustrative examples accompanying IAS 36.

FIGURE 13.8 Allocation of corporate assets

An entity has three cash-generating units, A, B and C. As a result of adverse changes in the technological environment, impairment tests are conducted on each of the cash-generating units. At the end of 2004, the carrying amounts of A, B and C are $100, $150 and $200 respectively.

There are two corporate assets: the headquarters building carried at $150, and a research centre that has a carrying amount of $50. The relative carrying amounts of the cash-generating units are a reasonable indication of the proportion of the headquarters building devoted to each cash-generating unit. However, the carrying amount of the research centre cannot be allocated on a reasonable basis to the individual cash-generating units.

(continued)

The remaining estimated useful life of cash-generating unit A is 10 years, while the remaining useful lives of B and C and the headquarters are 20 years. The headquarters are depreciated on a straight-line basis.

The *first step* is to allocate that part of the corporate assets to the individual cash-generating units where it can be done in a reasonable manner. Here, this can be done for the headquarters building but not for the research centre. The allocation of the headquarters building has to be done on a weighted allocation basis because the useful lives of the units differ:

End of 2004	A	B	C	Total
Carrying amount	100	150	200	450
Useful life	10 years	20 years	20 years	
Weighting based on useful life	1	2	2	
Carrying amount after weighting	100	300	400	800
Pro-rata allocation of building	12% (100/800)	38% (300/800)	50% (400/800)	100%
Allocation of the carrying amount of building	19	56	75	150
Carrying amount after allocation of building	119	206	275	600

For each cash-generating unit, the carrying amount of the assets is compared with the recoverable amount. After calculating the present value of the expected cash flows for each unit as well as the entity as a whole, the recoverable amounts were determined to be:

	A	B	C	Entity
Recoverable amount	199	164	271	720

It is assumed that the entity as a whole has a recoverable amount greater than the sum of that for the individual units. Impairment losses can now be determined for each individual unit:

	A	B	C
Carrying amount	119	206	275
Recoverable amount	199	164	271
Impairment loss	0	42	4

The impairment losses are allocated across the assets of units B and C in proportion to their carrying amounts, including the allocated headquarters building:

	B		C	
To headquarters building	12	[42 × 56/206]	1	[4 × 75/275]
To other assets	30	[42 × 150/206]	3	[4 × 200/275]
	42		4	

The headquarters building is therefore to be written down from 150 to 137.

The *second step* is to deal with the research centre that could not be allocated in a reasonable manner across the units. This requires identifying the smallest cash-generating unit that includes the research centre. In this case, it is the entity as a whole. This unit is then tested for impairment (see opposite).

	A	B	^C	Building	Research centre	Entity
Carrying amount	100	150	200	150	50	650
Impairment loss		30	3	13		46
	100	120	197	137	50	604
Recoverable amount						720

The entity therefore has not incurred an impairment loss, because its recoverable amount is greater than its carrying amount. There is no need for a further write-down of the assets of the entity.

Source: Adapted from IAS 36, Illustrative Examples, Example 8.

13.5 Cash-generating units and goodwill

LO 9

In accounting for impairment losses for cash-generating units, one of the assets that may be recorded by an entity is goodwill. IAS 36 contains specific requirements for accounting for goodwill and how its existence affects the allocation of impairment losses across the assets of a cash-generating unit.

Goodwill is recognised only when it is acquired in a business combination. As discussed in chapter 11, IAS 38 *Intangible Assets* does not allow the recognition of internally generated goodwill, or the revaluation of any acquired goodwill. In accounting for a business combination, goodwill is calculated as a residual, being the difference between the cost of combination and the net fair value of the identifiable assets, liabilities and contingent liabilities acquired. (See chapter 12 for more information on business combinations.) Goodwill then consists of those assets that cannot be individually identified or separately recognised.

Goodwill is an accumulation of assets, and may include benefits arising from good labour relations and effective advertising campaigns, or from unrecognised intangibles that cannot be reliably measured. The assets that constitute goodwill increase the wealth of the entity and add to the expected future cash flows of the entity. However, for specific assets to be included in goodwill, either the cash flows associated with the specific assets cannot be reliably measured or the cash flows are earned in conjunction with other assets. Hence, it is not possible to determine a fair value less costs to sell for goodwill, or to identify a set of cash flows that relates specifically to goodwill. Any impairment of goodwill will not directly affect the cash flows of the entity, although the impairment will reduce the overall cash flows of the entity.

Accounting for goodwill acquired in a business combination is specified in IFRS 3 *Business Combinations*. Paragraph 52 requires the initial recognition of goodwill at an amount equal to the excess of the cost of the business combination over the acquirer's interest in the net fair value of the identifiable assets, liabilities and contingent liabilities. After initial recognition, as per paragraph 55 of IFRS 3, the acquirer measures goodwill acquired in a business combination at cost less any accumulated impairment losses. Goodwill is not subject to amortisation. Instead, the acquirer tests the carrying amount of goodwill annually in accordance with IAS 36.

When a business combination occurs, and goodwill is calculated as part of accounting for that combination, the goodwill acquired is allocated to one or more cash-generating units (IAS 36, para. 80). Even though goodwill was acquired in relation to the entity as a whole, the cash flow earning capacity of goodwill must be allocated across the cash-generating units. The aim is to allocate all assets, whether corporate assets or goodwill, to the cash-generating units so they can be associated with the cash flows received by those units.

When deciding which units should have goodwill allocated to them, consideration should be given to how internal management monitors the goodwill. According to paragraph 80, the goodwill should be allocated to the *lowest level* at which management monitors the goodwill. When the business combination occurred, the acquirer would have analysed the earning capacity of the entity it proposed to acquire, and would have equated aspects of goodwill to various cash-generating units. It is possible that the allocation of goodwill would be made to each of the segments identified by management under the application of IAS 14 *Segment Reporting.* Paragraph 80 of IAS 36 states that the units to which goodwill is allocated should not be larger than a segment based on either the entity's primary or secondary reporting format. This is due to the fact that IAS 14 requires the determination of business and geographical segments based on areas that are subject to different risks and return, and the internal financial reporting system within the entity is used as a basis for identifying these segments.

In its response to the Financial Accounting Standards Board (FASB) in the United States in relation to the board's deliberations on the impairment testing of goodwill, as reported in the FASB Summary of Comment Letters, Technology Network suggested that goodwill be tested at the enterprise level in all cases, or at least that option should be permitted:

> Many acquisitions are integrated into existing businesses for internal reporting purposes with many companies recording the goodwill at an operating or business unit level. However, over time, successful acquisitions frequently (and hopefully) create synergies with other internal reporting units and throughout an enterprise.
>
> The only way to ensure that this value is captured may be to perform impairment testing at the enterprise level. While we recognize that the Board has rejected such an approach, we believe that testing at the enterprise level would be appropriate in limited circumstances. For example, in the software industry, the acquired goodwill frequently becomes so integrated into the company's entire product line that it essentially becomes a new company platform. Thus, we do not believe there should be any firm rule prohibiting enterprise level testing. It should be allowed in appropriate circumstances (sourced from FASB Summary of Comment Letters).

The IASB (paragraph BC139 of the Basis for Conclusions on IAS 36) considered this argument and rejected impairment testing of goodwill at the level of the entity itself. It saw the important link as being the level at which goodwill is tested, with the level of internal reporting reflecting the management and reporting of goodwill that occurs within the entity itself.

As noted in paragraph BC139, the IASB was concerned that entities did not resort to testing the goodwill at the level of the entity itself. It stated that:

> there should be a link between the level at which goodwill is tested for impairment and the level of internal reporting that reflects the way an entity manages its operations and with which the goodwill naturally would be associated.

In that sense, the allocation of goodwill should not be an arbitrary process. As noted in paragraph 82 of IAS 36, the development of additional reporting systems should then not normally be necessary.

Under IFRS 3, there is an allowance for a provisional initial accounting for the business combination. Paragraph 84 of IAS 36 therefore provides, consistent with IFRS 3, that where the allocation of goodwill cannot be completed before the end of the annual period in which the business combination occurred, the initial allocation is to be completed before the end of the first annual period beginning after the acquisition date.

13.5.1 Impairment testing of goodwill

A cash-generating unit that has goodwill allocated to it must be tested for impairment *annually* or more frequently if there is an indication the unit may be impaired (IAS 36, para. 90). As with other impairment tests, this involves comparing the carrying amount of the unit's assets, including goodwill, with the recoverable amount of the unit's assets.

Recoverable amount exceeds carrying amount

If the recoverable amount exceeds the carrying amount, there is no impairment loss. In particular, there is no impairment of goodwill. The goodwill balance remains unadjusted; that is, it is not reduced due to impairment loss.

It should be noted that this test is not a robust test of the amount of goodwill recorded by the unit. Under this test, the goodwill is protected or 'cushioned' against impairment by:

1. *internally generated goodwill*. The benefits relating to the acquired goodwill may have been received by the entity, but unrecognised internally generated goodwill may exist in the entity. The internally generated goodwill may have arisen subsequent to the business combination, or could consist of that existing in the acquirer itself prior to the business combination.

2. *unrecognised identifiable net assets*. There may exist intangibles which do not meet the recognition criteria under IAS 38 *Intangible Assets*. These are not included in the measure of the carrying amount of the assets of the cash-generating unit, yet the cash flows generated by these assets increase the recoverable amount of the unit.

3. *excess value over carrying amount of recognised assets*. The impairment test uses the carrying amount of the unit's recognised assets. If the fair values of these assets are greater than their carrying amounts, the extra benefits relating to these assets increase the recoverable amount of the unit.

The IASB recognises that the above test provides a cushion against recognising impairment losses for goodwill. In paragraph BC135 of the Basis for Conclusions on IAS 36, it notes that the carrying amount of goodwill will always be shielded from impairment by internally generated goodwill. The impairment test for goodwill is at best ensuring that the carrying amount of goodwill is recoverable from cash flows generated by both acquired and internally generated goodwill. Such a cushion works, of course, only if the recoverable amount is being maintained; that is, if the value of the assets both identifiable and unidentifiable are being maintained by the entity. If the assets of the unit are being well managed then, in most cases, the goodwill of the unit is also being maintained. The test is then a screening mechanism. However, one advantage of the screening test is that it significantly reduces the cost of applying an impairment test, particularly in comparison to other tests that require a remeasurement of goodwill by measuring the net fair values of the identifiable assets and liabilities of the unit on an annual basis.

Figure 13.9 contains an extract from the 2005 annual report of Danisco (a Danish food-preparation company), explaining how the company conducted its impairment tests for goodwill that resulted in this case in not writing down goodwill.

Impairment test for goodwill:

As a result of the impairment tests there is no basis for writing down goodwill. Goodwill is allocated to the Group's two 'Cash Generating Units', Ingredients & Sweeteners and Sugar. Impairment tests are conducted annually in connection with the Board of Directors' and the Executive Board's strategy review. In the impairment test, the discounted values of future cash flows are for each unit compared against the carrying amounts. Future cash flows are based on the budget for 2005/06, strategy plans for the years 2006/07–2009/10 and projections for the following 10 years. Important parameters are sales, EBIT, working capital, tangible assets and growth assumptions subsequent to the indicated 15-year period. Budget and strategy plans build on specific commercial assessments of the business areas while projections that go beyond 2009/10 build on general parameters. For Ingredients & Sweeteners, the most important parameters in the projection for the period 2010/11 to 2019/20 are sales growth of 5% and corresponding EBIT growth. Working capital is assumed to be 30% of sales and maintenance of tangible assets is 15% of sales growth. The terminal value for the period after 2019/20 is set with the assumption of 2% growth. The rate of discount is 9.6% before tax, corresponding to a WACC of 7% after tax. The tax rate payable is assumed to be 27%.

For Sugar, the most important parameters in the projection for the period 2010/11 to 2019/20 are unchanged sales, a slightly declining EBIT and working capital of 35% of sales. Funds tied up in tangible assets are slightly declining. The terminal value for the period after 2019/20 is set with the assumption of 0% growth. The rate of discount is 8.6% before tax, corresponding to a WACC of 6.3% after tax. The tax rate payable is assumed to be 27%.

FIGURE 13.9 Impairment test for goodwill
Source: Danisco (2005, p. 48).

Carrying amount exceeds recoverable amount

If the carrying amount exceeds the recoverable amount, there is an impairment loss, and this loss is recognised in accordance with paragraph 104 of IAS 36. This paragraph states that the impairment loss must be allocated to reduce the carrying amount of the assets of the unit, or group of units, in the following order:

- first, to reduce the carrying amount of any goodwill allocated to the cash-generating unit
- then, to the other assets of the unit pro rata on the basis of the carrying amount of each asset in the unit.

These reductions in carrying amounts are treated as impairment losses on the individual assets of the unit and recognised as any other impairment losses on assets.

However, paragraph 105 of IAS 36 provides some restrictions on the write-downs to individual assets:

In allocating an impairment loss in accordance with paragraph 104, an entity shall not reduce the carrying amount of an asset below the highest of:
(a) its fair value less costs to sell (if determinable);
(b) its value in use (if determinable); and
(c) zero.
The amount of the impairment loss that would otherwise have been allocated to the asset shall be allocated pro rata to the other assets of the unit (group of units).

Figure 13.10 contains an example of accounting for an impairment loss for a cash-generating unit that contains goodwill. It is adapted from example 2 of the illustrative examples accompanying IAS 36.

FIGURE 13.10 Accounting for impairment loss in a cash-generating unit with allocated goodwill

At the end of 2005, entity T acquired entity M for $10 000. M has manufacturing plants in three countries. Each of these plants is considered to be a cash-generating unit. The goodwill recognised on the acquisition is allocated to these three units on a reasonable and consistent basis:

End of 2005	Allocation of purchase price	Fair value of identifiable assets	Goodwill
Activities in Country A	$ 3 000	$ 2 000	$ 1 000
Activities in Country B	2 000	1 500	500
Activities in Country C	5 000	3 500	1 500
Total	$ 10 000	$ 7 000	$ 3 000

Because goodwill has been allocated to each of the cash-generating units, each unit must be tested for impairment annually. For the years ending 2005 and 2006, the recoverable amount of each unit exceeded the carrying amount and hence the activities in each country as well as the goodwill allocated to these activities are regarded as not impaired.

At the beginning of 2007, a new government is elected in Country A and, as a result of government policies relating to export restrictions, there are concerns about the recoverability of the assets in Country A. The carrying amounts of assets in the Country A cash-generating unit at this point are:

Beginning of 2007	Goodwill	Identifiable assets	Total
Cost	$ 1 000	$ 2 000	$ 3 000
Accumulated depreciation (12-year life)	–	167	167
Carrying amount	$ 1 000	$ 1 833	$ 2 833

The recoverable amount of the Country A cash-generating unit is calculated as $1360, based on a value-in-use calculation. As the total carrying amount of the assets in this unit amount to $2833, there is an impairment loss of $1473 ($2833 − $1360).

The impairment loss is first allocated to the goodwill, writing it down to zero. The balance of the impairment loss ($473) is then allocated across the carrying amounts of the identifiable assets of the Country A cash-generating unit on a pro-rata basis:

Beginning of 2007	Goodwill	Identifiable assets	Total
Cost	$ 1 000	$ 2 000	$ 3 000
Accumulated depreciation (12-year life)	–	167	167
Carrying amount	1 000	1 833	2 833
Impairment loss	1 000	473	1 473
Carrying amount after impairment loss	$ 0	$ 1 360	$ 1 360

(*continued*)

The journal entries to record the allocation of the impairment loss are:

Impairment loss − goodwill	Dr	1 000	
Goodwill	Cr		1 000
(Impairment loss)			
Impairment loss	Dr	473	
Accumulated depreciation and			
impairment losses − plant			
and equipment	Cr		XXX
Land	Cr		XXX
(Allocation of impairment loss to assets on a			
pro-rata basis)			

Source: Adapted from IAS 36, Illustrative Examples, Example 2.

There has been much controversy over the goodwill impairment test. In fact, three IASB members dissented on the issue of IAS 36, primarily over aspects of this test. The advantage of the procedure used in IAS 36 is that it is not complex or costly, leading to a belief that the benefits outweigh the costs − see paragraph BC170 of the Basis for Conclusions on IAS 36. The criticism of the test is that it *does not measure whether good-will has been impaired.* Using the example in figure 13.10, although there is an impairment loss of $1473, there is no subsequent test to determine whether the goodwill has been impaired or whether some of the identifiable assets have been impaired. The method arbitrarily allocates the impairment loss first to goodwill − it assumes goodwill has been impaired. In the exposure draft to IAS 36, the impairment test suggested was a two-step approach as outlined in figure 13.11 (below and opposite).

Once an impairment loss is determined, the second step requires three actions:

Action 1: Calculate the implied value of goodwill.
The implied value of goodwill is calculated as follows:

Recoverable amount	*less*	net fair value of the identifiable assets, liabilities, and
of the cash-generating		contingent liabilities the entity would recognise if it
unit		acquired the cash-generating unit in a business combination
		on the date of the impairment test excluding any identifiable
		asset acquired in a business combination but not recognised
		separately from goodwill at the acquisition date.

Note that this measure of implied goodwill reduces the cushions. The assets and liabilities measured are not just those recorded by the entity, but those that would be recognised in an acquisition at the date the impairment test is made. Implied goodwill is then not protected by unrecognised identifiable assets because, under IFRS 3, these can be recognised in a business combination. Nor is it protected by excess values of the recognised assets because these assets are now measured at fair value rather than at carrying amount. If the object of the second step of the impairment test is to measure the current value of goodwill, then failing to exclude these other assets means the implied value of goodwill would consist of 'real' goodwill and identifiable assets.

The goodwill figure is still cushioned by internally generated goodwill, but it is not possible to distinguish between acquired goodwill and internally generated goodwill. There also does not seem any point in doing so because, if the purpose of the impairment test is to ensure that assets are not overstated, then whether the goodwill is 'old acquired' or 'new internally generated' does not matter. The question is whether at the time of the impairment test the unit has the carrying amount of goodwill as shown in the accounts.

Action 2: Compare the carrying amount of goodwill with the implied value of goodwill. If the carrying amount is *less than* the implied value, goodwill is not impaired, and no impairment loss needs to be recognised for goodwill. The impairment loss on the cash-generating unit then relates to the other assets of the unit. If the carrying amount is *greater than* the implied value, an impairment loss for goodwill has occurred and would be recognised immediately in profit or loss.

Action 3: Allocate the balance (if any) of the impairment loss to the other assets of the unit on a pro-rata basis according to the carrying amount of each asset in the unit. The accounting for the balance of the impairment loss is the same as for an impairment loss in a cash-generating unit where there is no goodwill.

Using the example in figure 13.10, having determined the impairment loss of $1473, the implied value of goodwill in Country A is then measured. The net fair value of the identifiable assets it would recognise if entity T acquired the Country A cash-generating unit at the date of the impairment test is calculated to be $1000. Hence, the implied value of goodwill is $360 ($1360 – $1000).

As the carrying amount of the goodwill of $1000 exceeds the implied value of $360, there is an impairment loss for goodwill of $640. The total impairment loss is $1473, so the balance of the impairment loss of $833 ($1473 – $640) is allocated across the carrying amounts of the identifiable assets of the Country A cash-generating unit:

Beginning of 2007	Goodwill	Identifiable assets	Total
Cost	$1 000	$2 000	$3 000
Accumulated depreciation (12-year life)	–	167	167
Carrying amount	1 000	1 833	2 833
Impairment loss	640	833	1 473
Carrying amount after impairment loss	$ 360	$1 000	$1 360

FIGURE 13.11 Accounting for impairment loss in a cash-generating unit with allocated goodwill — a two-step approach
Source: Adapted from IASB Exposure Draft to IAS 36.

Note in figure 13.11 that the process endeavours to measure the goodwill of the cash-generating unit, something IAS 36 does not do. The problem with the two-step process is that the calculation of the implied value for goodwill requires determining the fair values of the assets, liabilities and contingent liabilities of the cash-generating unit. This is seen by the IASB (para. BC166 of the Basis for Conclusions on IAS 36) as costly and impracticable. The field tests conducted by the IASB led it to change from the two-step method to the one-step method. An example of one company's opinion of the costliness of the approach is found in the comments of the Dow Chemical Company in its submission to the FASB on goodwill impairment, as reported in the Summary of Comment letters. The following Dow Chemical Company's comments were considered by the FASB to be representative of the majority of comments on this issue.

The mechanics of the impairment test will be cost prohibitive to undertake. The Board cannot seriously expect companies to regularly estimate the fair value of its assets and liabilities in attempting to calculate the implied fair value of goodwill. Our experience with obtaining such appraisals in the context of business acquisitions has led us to believe that any benefit from such precise impairment measurements is far outweighed by the prohibitive costs of retaining and regularly engaging outside valuation experts whose opinions can vary widely in their professional assessment. As a practical and cost-effective alternative, we strongly recommend the use of book values of reported assets for this purpose (sourced from FASB Summary of Comment Letters).

Timing of impairment tests

As noted earlier, goodwill has to be tested for impairment annually. However, the test does not have to occur at the end of the reporting period. As paragraph 96 of IAS 36 notes, the test may be performed at any time during the year, provided it is performed at the same time every year. According to paragraph BC171 of the Basis for Conclusions on IAS 36, this measure was allowed as a means of reducing the costs of applying the test. However, if a business combination has occurred in the current period, and an allocation has been made to one or more cash-generating units, all units to which goodwill has been allocated must be tested for impairment before the end of that year — see paragraph 96 of IAS 36 in this regard.

It is also not necessary for all cash-generating units to be tested for impairment at the same time. If there are two units being tested for impairment, one being a smaller cash-generating unit within a larger unit and the larger unit contains an allocation of goodwill, it is necessary to test the smaller unit for impairment first. This ensures that, if necessary, the assets of the smaller unit are adjusted prior to the testing of the larger unit. Similarly, if the assets of a cash-generating unit containing goodwill are being tested at the same time as the unit, then the assets must be tested first.

One of the reasons for requiring annual testing for both goodwill and intangibles with an indefinite life, apart from the uncertainty of measuring these assets, relates to the depreciation concept adopted by the IASB and discussed in chapter 10 of this book. Depreciation is seen as a 'process of allocation'. Hence, to have assets such as goodwill and indefinite life intangibles permanently on the records with no allocation to accounting periods seems to depart from the allocation process and to move to a valuation concept. As noted by the IASB (para. BC121 of the Basis for Conclusions on IAS 36), the board believes that 'non-amortisation of an intangible asset increases the reliance that must be placed on impairment reviews of that asset to ensure that its carrying amount does not exceed its recoverable amount'. However, in accordance with paragraph 10(a) for indefinite life intangibles and paragraph 96 for goodwill, both may be tested at any time during the year, provided it is performed at the same time every year. It must also be remembered that, as stated in paragraph BC122 of the Basis for Conclusions on IAS 36, annual testing is not a substitute for management being aware of events or changing circumstances that may indicate possible impairment and the need for additional testing.

Minority interest

A parent entity is one that controls the policies of another entity, called a subsidiary. In the majority of cases, the parent–subsidiary relationship is created when the parent acquires more than half of the issued shares of another entity. A minority interest (MI) consists of the ownership interest in the subsidiary not held by the parent. For example, A Ltd may own 60% of the shares of B Ltd. By virtue of its majority holding, A Ltd would control the management of B Ltd. The other 40% holding is the MI. These concepts are developed further in chapter 22.

Under IFRS 3, goodwill is calculated as the difference between the cost of the combination and the acquirer's or parent's share of the net fair value of the assets, liabilities and contingent liabilities of the acquiree. In other words, the goodwill calculated relates to the parent's share of the goodwill, not the total goodwill of the acquiree. In the A Ltd – B Ltd example above, the goodwill calculated would relate to the 60% acquisition of A Ltd in B Ltd. Goodwill attributable to the MI is not recognised.

Paragraphs 91–95 of IAS 36 cover impairment testing where a MI exists. In undertaking an impairment test relating to a subsidiary, the recoverable amount is calculated in relation to the subsidiary as a whole. This has to be compared to the sum of the carrying amounts of the subsidiary's net assets plus goodwill. However, as the goodwill relates only to the parent's share, it must be grossed up to calculate the goodwill of the subsidiary as a whole.

Example 7 of the illustrative examples accompanying IAS 36 deals with the impairment testing of cash-generating units with goodwill and MI. This example is used in figure 13.12, with part A showing the grossing up of the goodwill. Any impairment loss is firstly allocated to goodwill, and the balance allocated pro rata to the identifiable assets of the subsidiary. This is demonstrated in part B of figure 13.12.

FIGURE 13.12   Accounting for impairment testing with goodwill and MI

X Ltd acquires 80% of the shares of Y Ltd for $1600 on 1 January 2006. At this date, the identifiable net assets of Y Ltd have a fair value of $1500. Hence:

Net fair value of identifiable assets and liabilities of Y Ltd	= $1500
Net fair value acquired by X Ltd	= 80% × $1500
	= $1200
Cost of the combination	= $1600
Goodwill	= $400

Y Ltd is the smallest group of assets that generate cash inflows from continuing use that are largely independent of the cash flows from other assets. Y Ltd is a cash-generating unit.

At 31 December 2006, X Ltd determines that the recoverable amount of Y Ltd is $1000.

Part A: Testing Y Ltd for impairment
In order to test Y Ltd for impairment, the goodwill has to be grossed up. If goodwill of $400 relates to 80% of Y Ltd, then $500 (being $400/0.8) relates to 100 per cent of Y Ltd. In other words, the $400 goodwill is grossed up to $500.

Assuming $150 depreciation in relation to the identifiable assets of Y Ltd over the year, at 31 December 2006:

End of 2006	Goodwill	Identifiable assets	Total
Gross carrying amount	$400	$1 500	$1 900
Accumulated depreciation	–	(150)	(150)
Carrying amount	400	1 350	1 750
MI goodwill	100		100
Notionally adjusted carrying amount	$500	$1 350	$1 850

(*continued*)

As the recoverable amount is $1000 and the notionally adjusted carrying amount of Y Ltd is $1850, there is an impairment loss of $850.

Part B: Allocation of the impairment loss

The impairment loss of $500 is first allocated to goodwill, being $400 recorded and $100 not recorded. The remaining $350 impairment loss is allocated to the assets of Y Ltd:

End of 2006	Goodwill	Identifiable assets	Total
Gross carrying amount	$400	$1 500	$1 900
Accumulated depreciation	–	(150)	(150)
Carrying amount	400	1 350	1 750
Impairment loss	400	350	750
Carrying amount after impairment	$ 0	$1 000	$1 000

Source: Adapted from IAS 36, Illustrative Examples, Example 7.

Other impairment issues relating to goodwill

IAS 36 raises a number of other issues that need to be considered in accounting for the impairment of goodwill within a cash-generating unit:

- *Disposal of an operation within a cash-generating unit.* Where the cash-generating unit has a number of distinct operations and goodwill has been allocated to the unit, if one of the operations is disposed of, it is necessary to consider whether any of the goodwill relates to the operation disposed of. If there is any goodwill associated with the operation disposed of, the amount of goodwill is measured on the basis of the relative values of the operation disposed of and the portion of the cash-generating unit retained, unless the entity can demonstrate that some other method better reflects the goodwill associated with the operation disposed of. In calculating the gain or loss on disposal of the operation, the allocated portion of the goodwill is included in the carrying amount of the assets sold (para. 86).

  For example, if a part of a cash-generating unit was sold for $200, and the recoverable amount of the remaining part of the unit is $600, then it is assumed that 25% (200/[200 + 600]) of the goodwill has been sold and is included in the carrying amount of the operation disposed of.

- *Reorganisation of the entity.* Where an entity containing a number of cash-generating units restructures, changing the composition of the cash-generating units, and where goodwill has been allocated to the original units, paragraph 87 requires the reallocation of the goodwill to the new units. The allocation is done on a relative value basis similar to that used where a cash-generating unit is disposed of, again unless the entity can demonstrate that some other method better reflects the goodwill associated with the operation disposed of.

LO 10

13.6 Reversal of an impairment loss

An impairment loss is recognised after an entity analyses the future prospects of an individual asset or a cash-generating unit. Subsequent to an impairment loss occurring because of doubts about the performance of assets, it is possible for circumstances to change such that, when the recoverable amount of the assets increases, consideration can be given to a reversal of a past impairment loss. Paragraph 110 of IAS 36 requires that an entity assess *at each balance date* whether there are indications that an impairment loss recognised in previous periods may not exist or may have decreased. If such indications exist, the entity should estimate the recoverable amount of the asset or unit.

Similar to the assessment of whether there is an indication of an impairment loss, an entity needs to look at internal and external evidence to determine the existence of evidence for a reversal of the prior loss. Paragraph 111 of IAS 36 requires an entity to assess specific internal and external sources of information. These indicators are effectively the same as those for assessing the existence of a loss except that the indicators for a reversal relate to improvements in the entity's prospects. The indicators noted in paragraph 111 are (with italics added):

External sources of information

(a) the asset's market value has *increased* significantly during the period;

(b) significant changes with a *favourable effect* on the entity have taken place during the period, or will take place in the near future, in the technological, market, economic or legal environment in which the entity operates or in the market to which the asset is dedicated;

(c) market interest rates or other market rates of return on investments have *decreased* during the period, and those decreases are likely to affect the discount rate used in calculating the asset's value in use and increase the asset's recoverable amount materially;

Internal sources of information

(d) significant changes with a *favourable effect* on the entity have taken place during the period, or are expected to take place in the near future, in the extent to which, or manner in which, the asset is used or is expected to be used. These changes include capital expenditure incurred during the period to improve or enhance an asset in excess of its standard of performance assessed immediately before the expenditure is made or a commitment to discontinue or restructure the operation to which the asset belongs; and

(e) evidence is available from internal reporting that indicates that the economic performance of the asset is, or will be, *better* than expected.

It is possible, as envisaged by paragraph 113 of IAS 36, that a review of the evidence will not result in a reversal of a prior impairment loss, but instead may lead to changes in the depreciation/amortisation measure of an asset. The review may lead to changes in expectations about useful life, residual life, and the pattern of benefits to be received.

If the evidence is such that there is a change in the estimates in relation to an asset (and only if there has been a change in the estimates), a reversal of impairment loss can be recognised. The reversal process requires the recognition of an increase in the carrying amount of the asset to its recoverable amount.

The ability to recognise a reversal of an impairment loss and the accounting for that reversal are dependent on whether the reversal relates to an individual asset, a cash-generating unit or goodwill.

13.6.1 Reversal of an impairment loss — individual asset

Where the recoverable amount is greater than the carrying amount of an individual asset (other than goodwill), the reversal of a prior impairment loss requires adjusting the carrying amount of the asset to recoverable amount. In determining the amount by which the carrying amount is to be adjusted, one limitation, as outlined in paragraph 117 of IAS 36, is that the carrying amount cannot be increased to an amount in excess of the carrying amount that would have been determined had no impairment loss been recognised. Hence, for a depreciable asset, if there were changes made to the useful life, residual value or pattern of benefits as a result of the impairment loss in the prior period, then there needs to be a calculation of carrying amount using the depreciation variables applied prior to the impairment loss to determine what the carrying amount would have been if there had been no impairment loss. This latter amount is the maximum to which the actual carrying amount can be increased.

If the individual asset is recorded under the *cost model*, then the increase in the carrying amount is recognised immediately in profit or loss:

Accumulated depreciation/amortisation and impairment losses Income – impairment loss reversal (Reversal of impairment loss)	Dr Cr	XXX	XXX

If the individual asset is recorded under the *revaluation model*, namely at fair value, accounting for the reversal of the impairment loss depends on how the impairment loss was accounted for in a prior period. If the prior impairment loss was taken to profit or loss, then the reversal must also be taken to profit or loss, using the same entry as shown above for assets measured at cost. If the prior impairment loss was adjusted against revaluation surplus, then the reversal is treated as a revaluation increase:

Individual asset
    Deferred tax liability
    Asset revaluation surplus
(Reversal of impairment loss)
	Dr
	Cr
	Cr
		XXX	XXX
			XXX

After the reversal of the impairment loss and the adjustment of the asset to its new carrying amount, in accordance with paragraph 121 of IAS 36, the depreciation/amortisation charge must be adjusted so that the revised carrying amount, less any residual value, is allocated across the remaining useful life on a systematic basis.

13.6.2 Reversal of an impairment loss — cash-generating unit

If the reversal of the impairment loss relates to a cash-generating unit, in accordance with paragraph 122 of IAS 36, the reversal of the impairment loss is allocated to the assets of the unit, except for goodwill, pro rata with the carrying amounts of those assets. These reversals will then relate to the specific assets of the cash-generating unit and will be accounted for as detailed above for individual assets. In relation to those individual assets, the carrying amount of an asset cannot, as per paragraph 123 of IAS 36, be increased above the lower of:
- its recoverable amount (if determinable); and
- the carrying amount that would have been determined had no impairment loss been recognised for the asset in prior periods.

If the situation envisaged in paragraph 123 occurs, then the amount of impairment loss reversal that cannot be allocated to an individual asset is then allocated on a pro rata basis to the other assets of the cash-generating unit, except for goodwill.

13.6.3 Reversal of an impairment loss — goodwill

Paragraph 124 of IAS 36 states that an impairment loss recognised for goodwill shall *not* be reversed in a subsequent period. The reasons for this decision by the IASB are detailed in paragraphs BC187–C191 of the Basis for Conclusions on IAS 36.

The key principle driving the accounting for goodwill in a reversal of impairment loss situation is that established in IAS 38 *Intangibles*, namely that internally generated goodwill cannot be recognised. Where there is a reversal of an impairment loss, in order to be able to allocate some of the reversal amount to goodwill it would be necessary to establish that the old acquired goodwill still existed, rather than the increase in goodwill being recognition of internally generated goodwill. Because of the nature of goodwill, it is not possible to determine how much of any goodwill existing in an entity is remaining acquired goodwill or goodwill internally generated since the acquisition. To allow an impairment reversal to increase the carrying amount of goodwill is potentially allowing the recognition of internally generated goodwill — or, as described in paragraph BC190, 'backdoor' capitalisation of internally generated goodwill — hence the prohibition in IAS 36.

Some IASB members saw a potential inconsistency with disallowing the reinstatement of goodwill based on the grounds of non-recognition of internally generated goodwill and the allowance in IAS 36 of internally generated goodwill to act as a cushion to recognition of an impairment loss on goodwill. The IASB, however, concluded that to shield or cushion an impairment loss is not as bad as direct recognition of internally generated goodwill in a reversal situation. However, for those who argue that the IASB allows inconsistent accounting because the entity that has acquired goodwill is effectively allowed to recognise internally generated goodwill via the cushion effect in the impairment test, while at the same time those entities that have not acquired goodwill are not allowed to recognise internally generated goodwill, there is probably some truth in the accusation.

An example of a reversal of a prior period impairment loss within a cash-generating unit to which goodwill has been allocated is given in figure 13.13. This example is adapted from example 4 of the illustrative examples accompanying IAS 36.

FIGURE 13.13 Accounting for the reversal of an impairment loss

This example uses the situation in figure 13.10 in which the Country A cash-generating unit incurred an impairment loss and the assets and goodwill were written down by $473 and $1000 respectively.

In 2008, the business situation improves in Country A and government policies change. As a result, management re-estimates the recoverable amount of the Country A cash-generating unit, determining the recoverable amount to be $1910. This recoverable amount is compared with the carrying amount of the unit:

Beginning of 2007	Goodwill	Identifiable assets	Total
Historical cost	$1 000	$2 000	$3 000
Accumulated depreciation	–	(167)	(167)
Impairment loss	(1 000)	(473)	(1 473)
Carrying amount	$ 0	$1 360	$1 360
End of 2008			
Additional depreciation (2 years at new rate): $1360/11 × 2	–	(247)	(247)
Carrying amount	$ 0	$ 1 113	$ 1 113
Recoverable amount			1 910
Excess of recoverable amount over carrying amount			$ 797

As the excess of $797 cannot be allocated to goodwill, the question is whether the whole amount can be recognised as a reversal of impairment loss. The impairment reversal cannot exceed the carrying amount that would have been determined had

(*continued*)

no impairment loss been recognised. The carrying amount of the identifiable assets at 2008 if there had been no impairment loss is as follows (note that the depreciation rate prior to the impairment was straight-line over 12 years, whereas the rate has been adjusted subsequent to the impairment loss as a result of expected changes in the pattern of benefits of the assets):

End of 2008	Identifiable assets
Historical cost	$2 000
Accumulated depreciation (3/12 × $2000)	500
Depreciated historical cost	1 500
Actual carrying amount	1 113
Difference	$ 387

Hence, the maximum impairment loss reversal is $387. This amount is recognised immediately in profit or loss as income.

Source: Adapted from IAS 36, Illustrative Examples, Example 4.

LO 11

13.7 Disclosure

Paragraph 126 of IAS 36 requires the following disclosures for each class of assets:

(a) the amount of impairment losses recognised in profit or loss during the period and the line item(s) of the income statement in which those impairment losses are included.
(b) the amount of reversals of impairment losses recognised in profit or loss during the period and the line item(s) of the income statement in which those impairment losses are reversed.
(c) the amount of impairment losses on revalued assets recognised directly in equity during the period.
(d) the amount of reversals of impairment losses on revalued assets recognised directly in equity during the period.

As noted in chapter 10 of this book, paragraph 73(e) of IAS 16 *Property, Plant and Equipment* requires, in relation to the reconciliation of the carrying amount at the beginning and end of the period for each class of property, plant and equipment, disclosure of:
• increases or decreases during the period resulting from impairment losses recognised or reversed directly in equity
• impairment losses recognised in profit or loss during the period
• impairment losses reversed in profit or loss during the period.
Similar disclosures are required for intangibles under paragraph 118 of IAS 38 *Intangible Assets*, for each class of intangible asset.

As paragraph 128 of IAS 36 states, the disclosures required by paragraph 126 may be presented or included in a reconciliation of the carrying amount of assets at the beginning and end of the period. (Such disclosures were illustrated in section 10.8 of chapter 10.) For parts (a) and (b) of paragraph 126, disclosure is required of the relevant line item(s) used. If these were included in other expenses or other income then, in the note to the income statement relating to these line items in the income statement, information relating to impairment losses or reversals would be required. For example, the note to other expenses may be as shown in figure 13.14.

NOTE 5: Expenses			IAS 36 para.
Other operating expenses			
	2006	**2005**	
	$000	**$000**	
Amortisation of intangibles	521	435	
Impairment losses:			
Plant and equipment	100	–	*126(a)*
Land and buildings	–	–	
Trade receivables	52	21	
Patents	64	–	

FIGURE 13.14   Disclosures required by paragraph 126(a) of IAS 36

Paragraph 129 of IAS 36 details information to be disclosed for each reportable segment where an entity applies IAS 14 *Segment Reporting.*

Disclosures required by paragraph 130 of IAS 36 are illustrated in figure 13.15. If impairment losses related to items of property, plant and equipment, such a note could be included in the note detailing disclosures of property, plant and equipment. Disclosures concerning impairment losses for a cash-generating unit may be provided in a separate note or, if applicable, attached to the segment report. In figure 13.15, an impairment note is used because the information is given for both individual assets as well as a cash-generating unit.

Paragraph 133 of IAS 36 requires disclosures in relation to any goodwill that has not been allocated to a cash-generating unit at the balance date. In particular, an entity must disclose the amount of the unallocated goodwill and the reasons why that amount has not been allocated to the cash-generating units in the entity.

Because the calculation of recoverable amount requires assumptions and estimates relating to future cash flows, IAS 36 requires disclosures relating to the calculation of recoverable amount. Paragraph 132 encourages, but does not require, disclosure of *key assumptions* used to determine the recoverable amounts of assets or cash-generating units.

Paragraph 134 of IAS 36 requires disclosures about the *estimates* used to measure the recoverable amount of a cash-generating unit when goodwill or an intangible asset with an indefinite life is included in the carrying amount of the unit, and the carrying amount of goodwill or intangible assets with indefinite useful lives allocated to that unit is *significant* in comparison with the entity's total carrying amount of goodwill or intangible assets with indefinite useful lives. Where the carrying amount of goodwill or intangible assets is not significant for a unit, paragraph 135 requires that fact to be disclosed. If for a number of such units, the recoverable amounts are based on the same key assumptions and the aggregate carrying amount of goodwill or intangible assets with indefinite lives is significant in comparison to the total for the entity, paragraph 135 requires similar, but not as extensive, disclosures to that in paragraph 134.

Example 9 of the illustrative examples accompanying IAS 36 provides illustrative disclosures about such cash-generating units. This example is reproduced in figures 13.16 and 13.17, with references made to the appropriate part of paragraphs 134 and 135 of IAS 36 requiring that disclosure. Figure 13.16 contains the information about entity M for which the disclosures are made.

FIGURE 13.15 Disclosures required by paragraph 130 of IAS 36

14. IMPAIRMENT	IAS 36 Para. 130
The company incurred an impairment loss of $10 000 in relation to property held by the entity for future expansion, the item being written down to recoverable amount due to the pending closure of the plant. The value of the property was reduced due to there being environmental concerns over future development in that area.	*(b)* *(c)(i)* *(a)*
Impairment losses were also recognised in the current period in relation to the pet food division. This division is one of the company's cash-generating units as well as being a reportable segment of the company. The reason for the write-downs was the expected fall in future cash flows due to increased competition in the area, particularly given the lowering of government restrictions on imported products. The recoverable amount of the cash-generating unit is based on a value-in-use calculation. The discount rate used in the calculation of value in use was 10%, compared to the 11% rate used for a previous value-in-use calculation made in 2005. There has been no change in the aggregation of assets in the cash-generating unit since 2005. The impairment loss amounted to $2 600 000 and was allocated as follows:	*(d)(i)* *(a)* *(e)* *(g)* *(d)(iii)* *(b)* *(d)(ii)*

	$000
Land and buildings	500
Leasehood improvements	420
Plant and equipment	310
Leased plant and equipment	–
Patents and licences	480
Research and development	370
Goodwill	520
	$2 600

FIGURE 13.16 Background information for entity M

Entity M is a multinational manufacturing firm that uses geographical segments as its primary format for reporting segment information. M's three reportable segments based on that format are Europe, North America and Asia. Goodwill has been allocated for impairment testing purposes to three individual cash-generating units: two in Europe (units A and B) and one in North America (unit C), and to one group of cash-generating units (comprising operation XYZ in Asia).

  M acquired unit C, a manufacturing operation in North America, in December 2005. Unlike M's other North American operations, C operates in an industry with high margins and high-growth rates, and with the benefit of a ten-year patent on its primary product. The patent was granted to C just before M's acquisition of C. As part of accounting for the acquisition of C, M recognised, in addition to the patent, goodwill of $3000 and a brand name of $1000. M's management has determined that the brand name has an indefinite useful life. M has no other intangible assets with indefinite useful lives.

During the year ending 31 December 2006, M determines that there is no impairment of any of its cash-generating units containing goodwill or intangible assets with indefinite useful lives. The recoverable amounts of those units, including unit C, are determined on the basis of value-in-use calculations. XYZ has determined that the recoverable amount calculations are most sensitive to changes in the following assumptions:

European units containing goodwill	North American units containing goodwill (excluding unit C)	Unit C
Gross margin during the budget period (four years)	Five-year government bond rate during the budget period (five years)	Gross margin during the budget period (five years)
Market share during the budget period	Market share during the budget period	Market share during the budget period
Euro/US dollar exchange rate during the budget period	Raw material price inflation during the budget period	Raw material price inflation during the budget period
Growth rate used to extrapolate cash flows beyond the budget period	Growth rate used to extrapolate cash flows beyond the budget period	Growth rate used to extrapolate cash flows beyond the budget period

Source: Adapted from IAS 36, Illustrative Examples, Example 9.

Figure 13.17 contains the disclosures required for Entity M by paragraph 134 of IAS 36.

FIGURE 13.17 Disclosures required by paragraphs 134 and 135 of IAS 36

15. IMPAIRMENT: GOODWILL AND INTANGIBLE ASSETS	IAS 36
Goodwill has been allocated for impairment testing purposes to three individual cash-generating units — two in Europe (units A and B) and one in North America (unit C), and to one group of cash-generating units (comprising operation XYZ) in Asia. The carrying amount of goodwill allocated to unit C and operation XYZ is significant in comparison with the total carrying amount of goodwill, but the carrying amount of goodwill allocated to each of units A and B is not. Nevertheless, the recoverable amounts of units A and B are based on some of the same key assumptions, and the aggregate carrying amount of goodwill allocated to those units is significant. Unit C also has an intangible asset with an indefinite useful life for which the carrying amount is significant in comparison with the entity's total carrying amount of such assets.	Para. 135
Operation XYZ The carrying amount of goodwill allocated to this cash-generating unit is $1200. The recoverable amount of operation XYZ has been determined based on a value-in-use calculation. The recoverable amount calculations are most sensitive to changes in the following assumptions: • gross margin during the budget period (five years) • Japanese yen/US dollar exchange rate during the budget period • market share during the budget period • growth rate used to extrapolate cash flows beyond the budget period.	Para. 134 (a) (c) (d)(i)

(continued)

Management relies on past experience as well as reference to published market indicators and economists' forecasts to determine the values assigned to these key assumptions. *(d)(ii)*

The calculation of recoverable amount uses cash flow projections based on financial budgets approved by management covering a five-year period, and a discount rate of 8.4%. Cash flows beyond that five-year period have been extrapolated using a steady 6.3% growth rate. This growth rate does not exceed the long-term average growth rate for the market in which XYZ operates. Management believes that any reasonably possible change in the key assumptions on which XYZ's recoverable amount is based would not cause XYZ's carrying amount to exceed its recoverable amount. *(d)(iii)* *(d)(v)* *(d)(iv)* *(f)*

Unit C

The carrying amount of goodwill allocated to this unit is $1200. The unit has an intangible asset, being the brand name *Chanell*, which has a carrying amount of $1000. *(a)* *(b)*

The recoverable amount of unit C has been determined on a value-in-use calculation. That calculation is most sensitive to changes in the following assumptions: *(c)* *(d)(i)*

- five-year US government bond rate during the budget period (five years)
- raw materials price inflation during the budget period
- market share during the budget period
- growth rate use to extrapolate cash flows beyond the budget period.

Management relies on past experience as well as reference to published market indicators and economists' forecasts to determine the values assigned to these key assumptions. *(d)(ii)*

The calculation uses cash flow projections based on financial budgets approved by management covering a five-year period, and a discount rate of 8.4%. Cash flows beyond that five-year period have been extrapolated using a steady 6.3% growth rate. This growth rate does not exceed the long-term average growth rate for the market in which XYZ operates. Management believes that any reasonably possible change in the key assumptions on which XYZ's recoverable amount is based would *not* cause XYZ's carrying amount to exceed its recoverable amount. *(d)(iii)* *(d)(v)* *(d)(iv)*

Units A and B

Units A and B have an aggregate carrying amount of goodwill of $700 allocated to them. The recoverable amounts of units A and B have been determined on the basis of value-in-use calculations. Those units produce complementary products and their recoverable amounts are based on some of the same key assumptions. These assumptions are: *Para. 135* *(a)*

- gross margin during the budget period (four years)
- raw materials price inflation during the budget period
- market share during the budget period
- growth rate used to extrapolate cash flows beyond the budget period.

Management relies on past experience as well as reference to published market indicators and economists' forecasts to determine the values assigned to these key assumptions. *(c)* *(d)*

Management believes that reasonably possible change in any of these key assumptions would *not* cause the aggregate carrying amount of A and B to exceed the aggregate recoverable amount of those units. *(e)*

Source: Adapted from IAS 36, Illustrative Examples, Example 9.

In the example used in figures 13.16 and 13.17, the recoverable amount is based on value in use. Similar information is required to be disclosed if recoverable amount is based on fair value less costs to sell — see paragraph 134(e) of IAS 36 for details.

13.8 Summary

The balance sheet of an entity contains figures showing the amounts allocated to individual classes of assets as well as the total assets at the end of a reporting period. A concern for users and preparers of the financial statements is whether the assets have been overstated. The purpose of the impairment test is to ensure that management critically analyses the carrying amounts of these assets relative to the amounts expected to be recovered from them. Management must be aware of economic and market-based indications that one or more of an entity's assets may be impaired. The impairment testing may be undertaken for individual assets or for groups of assets constituting cash-generating units. A further purpose of the impairment testing process is to assess, on an ongoing basis, those assets that are not subject to amortisation, in particular, goodwill and intangible assets with indefinite lives. These assets are subject to annual impairment tests, and also require entities that carry them to provide extensive disclosures in relation to them.

1. La Grande Vache Ltd owns a large number of dairy farms in France. It has a number of factories that are used to produce milk products that are then sent to other factories to be converted into milk-based products such as yoghurt and custard. In applying IAS 36 *Impairment of Assets*, the accountant for La Grande Vache Ltd is concerned about correctly identifying the cash-generating units (CGUs) for the company, and has sought your advice on such questions as to whether the milk production section is a separate CGU even though the company does not sell milk directly to other parties, or whether it should be included in the milk-based products CGU.

   Write a report to the accountant of La Grande Vache Ltd, including the following:

   (a) Define a CGU.
   (b) Explain why impairment testing requires the use of CGUs, rather than being based on single assets.
   (c) Explain the factors that the accountant should consider in determining the CGUs for La Grande Vache Ltd.

2. In relation to IAS 36 *Impairment of Assets*, discuss how the accounting for internally generated goodwill affects both the impairment test and the accounting for reversals of impairment losses.

3. At 30 June 2006, France Ltd undertakes an impairment test. Having only recently adopted IFRSs, the management of B Ltd seeks your advice in relation to this test under IAS 36 *Impairment of Assets*. Write a report explaining

   (a) the purpose of the impairment test
   (b) how the existence of goodwill will affect the impairment test
   (c) the basic steps to be followed in applying the impairment test.

4. Eiffel Ltd has recently adopted IFRSs. In setting up its systems to apply IAS 36 *Impairment of Assets*, management wants to know how often the company needs to apply an impairment test on its assets, and what information it needs to generate to determine whether a test is needed. Prepare a response to management.

5. The Rennes City Council contracts out the bus routes in Rennes to various subcontractors based upon a tender arrangement. Some routes, such as the Express to City routes, are profitable, while others, such as those collecting schoolchildren from remote areas, are unprofitable. As a result, the city council requires tenderers to take a package of routes, some profitable, some less so. The Le Bon Bus Company has won the contract to operate its buses with a package of five separate routes, one of which operates at a significant loss. Specific buses are allocated by the Le Bon Bus Company to each route, and cash flows can be isolated to each route because drivers and takings are specific to each route.

   Discuss the determination of cash-generating units for the Le Bon Bus Company.

6. Evaluate the following comments (pages 4–5) made by the European Financial Reporting Advisory Group (EFRAG) in its response, dated 4 April 2003, to the IASB on the proposed amendments to IAS 36:

   Impairment Test

   The proposed impairment test does not distinguish between acquired goodwill and pre-existing goodwill of the acquirer nor between acquired goodwill and goodwill internally generated after the combination. This results in 'cushions', so avoiding recognition of real impairment losses of goodwill in certain situations when the impairment test is performed. We believe that this undermines the reliability of the information obtained.

   The Board claims that there seems to be no alternative design for the impairment test to avoid this. This may be true for the replacement of acquired goodwill by self-generated goodwill of the acquired business but we believe a stronger effort should be made to eliminate the cushion provided by the pre-acquisition self-generated goodwill of the acquirer. The current UK accounting standard FRS 11 *Impairment of Fixed Assets and Goodwill* attempts to make such a distinction.

   We urge the Board to delete the second step of the impairment test (paragraph 86). We believe that the second step, which measures the amount of goodwill impairment by comparing its carrying amount with its implied value, is costly and does not improve the quality of the information.

   In our view it suffices to allocate the identified impairment firstly to goodwill and then to intangible assets with indefinite useful lives that are part of the cash-generating unit and any remainder to other assets on a pro rata basis.

7. Evaluate the following comments (page 7) made by Deloitte Touche Tohmatsu in its comments, dated 4 April 2003, on the proposed amendments to IAS 36:

   We agree with the conclusion that goodwill acquired in a business combination should be recognised as an asset. With regard to the accounting for goodwill after initial recognition, we generally agree with the

Board's proposal. However, we note that there may be circumstances where goodwill has a finite life. For example, this may be the case when an entity has a specified life. In certain jurisdictions such as the People's Republic of China (the PRC), foreign investment is made by means of certain legal structures that expire after a specified number of years. At the end of the agreed period, the assets will revert to the PRC partner. In such circumstances, any goodwill will have an implied value of zero at the end of the entity's life.

Consequently, we believe that, in accounting for goodwill after initial recognition, there should be a rebuttable presumption that goodwill has an indefinite life and, therefore, accounted for at cost less any accumulated impairment losses. However, in those cases where that presumption is rebutted and sufficient persuasive evidence exists indicating that goodwill has a finite life, we believe that a method of systematic amortisation is preferable to 'impairment only' accounting. In such cases, we believe that goodwill, consistently with other intangible assets that have a finite life, should be amortised and tested for impairment when an indicator exists. The impairment test applied to goodwill with a definite life should be the same test as goodwill with an indefinite life.

8. Identify the cash-generating unit(s) in the following scenario:

Burger Queen is a chain of fast-food restaurants, with most reasonably sized towns in the country having a Burger Queen outlet. The key claim to fame of the Burger Queen restaurants is that their French fries are extra crunchy. Also, to ensure that there is a consistent standard of food and service across the country, the management of the chain of restaurants conducts spot checks on restaurants. Failure to provide the high standard expected by Burger Queen management can mean that the franchise to a particular location can be taken away from the franchisee. Burger Queen management is responsible for the television advertising across the country as well as the marketing program, including the special deals that may be available at any particular time.

Each restaurant is responsible for its own sales, cooking of food, training of staff, and general matters such as cleanliness of the store. However, all material used in the making of the burgers and other items sold are provided at a given cost from the central management, which can thereby control the quality and the price.

9. Identify the cash-generating unit(s) in the following scenario:

Louis Le Peu is in the business of making rubber tubing that comes in all sorts of sizes and shapes.

Louis has established three factories in the north, south and east parts of the city. Each factory has a large machine that can be adjusted to produce all the varieties of tubing that Louis sells. Each machine is capable of producing around 100 000 metres of tubing a week, depending on diameter and shape. Louis' current sales amount to about 250 000 metres a week. However, sales are sufficiently high that he cannot afford to shut one of the factories.

Each factory is never worked to full capacity. In order to satisfy customer demand as quickly as possible, all orders are directed to Louis, who allocates the jobs to the various factories depending on the current workload of each factory. This also ensures that efficient runs of particular types of tubing can be done at the same time. Each factory is managed individually in terms of maintenance of the machines, the hiring of labour and the packaging and delivery of the finished product.

10. (a) Identify the cash-generating unit(s) in the following scenario:

Fad Furniture Ltd has three separate operating divisions. The first, the timber division, is in charge of producing milled timber. This division manages a number of timber plantations and timber mills from which the finished timber is produced. The majority of the timber is sold, at an internal transfer price, to the second area of operations in Fad Furniture, the parts division. Any excess timber is sold to external parties. The parts division is responsible for turning the timber into parts for the making of timber furniture, both indoor and outdoor. These parts are suitable only for the manufacture of the furniture produced by Fad Furniture. The parts are then transferred at internal transfer prices to the third area of operations, the furniture division. This division assembles the furniture and delivers it to the various outlets that retail Fad Furniture's products.

(b) Would the determination of the cash-generating units be affected if the parts division was also responsible for kit furniture, where the parts are made available to customers for self-assembly?

11. Management is assessing the future cash flows in relation to an entity's assets, and considers that there are two possible scenarios for future cash flows. The first, for which there is a 70% probability of occurrence, would provide future cash flows of $5 million. The second, which has a probability of occurrence of 30%, would provide future cash flows of $8 million. Management believe that the calculation of value in use should be based on the most likely scenario,

namely the one that will produce $5 million cash flows. Discuss.

12. Eiffel Enterprises Ltd acquired a building in which to conduct its operations at a cost of $10 million. The building generates no cash flows on its own and is considered a part of the cash-generating unit, which is the firm as a whole. Since the building was acquired, the value of inner city properties has declined due to an overabundance of office space and the downturn in the economy. The firm would receive only $8 million dollars if it decided to sell the building now. However, the firm believes the building is serving its purpose and the profits of the firm are high, and there is no current intention to sell the building. Discuss whether the building should be written down to $8 million or not. Provide any journal entries necessary.

13. Versailles Ltd acquired a network facility for its administration section on 1 July 2004. The network facility cost $550 000 and was depreciated using a straight-line method over a five-year period, with a residual value of $50 000. On 30 June 2006, the company assessed the current market value of the facility given that there was an active market for such facilities as many companies used a similar network. The value was determined to be $300 000. Discuss whether the network facility asset is impaired and whether it should be written down to $300 000. Provide any journal entries necessary.

EXERCISES

EXERCISE 13.1   ★   Impairment loss

Paris Ltd has determined that its fine china division is a cash-generating unit. The carrying amounts of the assets at 30 June 2006 are as follows:

Factory	$210 000
Land	150 000
Equipment	120 000
Inventory	60 000

Paris Ltd calculated the value in use of the division to be $510 000.

Required
Provide the journal entry(ies) for the impairment loss, assuming that the fair value less costs to sell of the land are:
(a) $140 000
(b) $145 000.

EXERCISE 13.2   ★   Impairment loss, goodwill

On 1 January 2005, Orleans Ltd acquired all the assets and liabilities of Nantes Ltd. Nantes Ltd has a number of operating divisions, including one whose major industry is the manufacture of toy trains, particularly those having historical significance. The toy trains division is regarded as a cash-generating unit. In paying $2 million for the net assets of Nantes Ltd, Orleans calculated that it had acquired goodwill of $240 000. The goodwill was allocated to each of the divisions, and the assets and liabilities acquired measured at fair value at acquisition date.

At 31 December 2007, the carrying amounts of the assets of the toy train division were:

Factory	$250 000
Inventory	150 000
Brand — 'Froggy'	50 000
Goodwill	50 000

There is a declining interest in toy trains because of the aggressive marketing of computer-based toys, so the management of Orleans Ltd measured the value in use of the toy train division at 31 December 2007, determining it to be $423 000.

Required

Prepare the journal entries to account for the impairment loss at 31 December 2007.

EXERCISE 13.3   ★

Impairment loss, goodwill, partly owned subsidiary

Lyon Ltd acquired 60% of the issued shares of Toulouse Ltd on 1 January 2005 for $426 000. At this date, the net fair value of the identifiable assets and liabilities of Toulouse Ltd was $660 000.

At 31 December 2005, the tangible assets and liabilities of Toulouse Ltd as included in the consolidated financial statements of Lyon Ltd were as shown below.

Property, plant and equipment	$863 000
Accumulated depreciation	(120 000)
	743 000
Inventory	55 000
Cash	22 000
	820 000
Liabilities	(50 000)
	$770 000

Goodwill had not been written down over the year.

In conducting an impairment test on Toulouse Ltd as a cash-generating unit, Lyon Ltd assessed the recoverable amount of Toulouse Ltd to be $800 000.

Required

1. Explain how the impairment loss in relation to Toulouse Ltd should be allocated. Prepare journal entry(ies) in relation to the assets of Toulouse Ltd at 31 December 2005 as a result of the impairment test.
2. Explain the accounting for the impairment (if any) if the recoverable amount was $860 000.

PROBLEMS

PROBLEM 13.1   ★★

Impairment loss for a cash-generating unit, reversal of impairment loss

One of the cash-generating units of Marseille Ltd is that associated with the manufacture of wine barrels. At 30 June 2007, Marseille Ltd believed, based on an analysis of economic indicators, that the assets of the unit were impaired. The carrying amounts of the assets and liabilities of the unit at 30 June 2007 were:

Buildings	$420 000
Accumulated depreciation – buildings *	(180 000)
Factory machinery	220 000
Accumulated depreciation – machinery **	(40 000)
Goodwill	15 000
Inventory	80 000
Receivables	40 000
Allowance for doubtful debts	(5 000)
Cash	20 000
Accounts payable	30 000
Loans	20 000

*Depreciated at $60 000 per annum
** Depreciated at $45 000 per annum

Marseille Ltd determined the value in use of the unit to be $535 000. The receivables were considered to be collectible, except those considered doubtful. The company allocated the impairment loss in accordance with IAS 36.

During the 2007–08 period, Marseille Ltd increased the depreciation charge on buildings to $65 000 per annum, and to $50 000 per annum for factory machinery. The inventory on hand at 1 July 2007 was sold by the end of the year. At 30 June 2008, Marseille Ltd, due to a return in the market to the use of traditional barrels for wines and an increase in wine production, assessed the recoverable amount of the cash-generating unit to be $30 000 greater than the carrying amount of the unit. As a result, Marseille Ltd recognised a reversal of the impairment loss.

Required
1. Prepare the journal entries for Marseille Ltd at 30 June 2007 and 2008.
2. What differences would arise in relation to the answer in part 1 if the recoverable amount at 30 June 2008 was $20 000 greater than the carrying amount of the unit?
3. If the recoverable amount of the buildings at 30 June 2008 was $175 000, how would this change the answer to part 2?

PROBLEM 13.2   ★★   Allocation of corporate assets

Cognac Ltd has three cash-generating units: Avignon division, Brest division and Calais division. The company management has a headquarters office in the city, while the infrastructure for the divisions is located outside the city centre. Because of the potential for the company to have problems of an environmental nature or in relation to social justice, particularly with its mix of employees, Cognac Ltd has recently established a social responsibility centre (SRC), which interacts with the divisions generating information and statistics for the production of a triple-bottom-line social-responsibility report.

At 30 June 2006, the net assets relating to each of the divisions as well as the headquarters section and the SRC were as follows:

	Avignon division	Brest division	Calais division	Head office	SRC
Land	$120 000	$140 000	$ 80 000	$10 000	$ 5 000
Plant and equipment	420 000	310 000	270 000	40 000	15 000
Accumulated depreciation	(120 000)	(100 000)	(80 000)	(5 000)	(4 000)
Inventories	150 000	110 000	100 000	0	0
Accounts receivable	90 000	80 000	50 000	0	0
	660 000	540 000	420 000	45 000	16 000
Liabilities	60 000	50 000	50 000	0	0
Net assets	$600 000	$490 000	$ 370 000	$45 000	$16 000

Cognac Ltd believes that the corporation's headquarters supplies approximately equal service to the three divisions, and an immaterial amount to the SRC. Because the SRC has been established only recently, it is not possible at this stage to allocate the assets of the SRC to the three divisions. Economic indicators suggest that the company's assets may have been impaired, so management has determined the value in use of each of the divisions — the head office and the SRC do not generate cash inflows. The value in use of the three divisions were calculated to be:

	Avignon division	Brest division	Calais division
Value in use	$720 000	$500 000	$400 000

Required

Determine how Cognac Ltd should account for any impairment loss to the entity.

PROBLEM 13.3 ★★   Allocation of corporate assets and goodwill

Lourdes Ltd acquired all the assets and liabilities of Cherbourg Ltd on 1 January 2006. Cherbourg Ltd's activities were run through three separate businesses, namely the Chalais unit, the Tarbes unit and the Poitiers unit. These units comprise separate cash-generating units. Lourdes Ltd allowed unit managers to effectively operate each of the units, but certain central activities were run through the corporate office. Each unit was allocated a share of the goodwill acquired, as well as a share of the corporate office.

At 31 December 2006, the assets allocated to each unit were as follows:

	Chalais	Tarbes	Poitiers
Factory	$820	$750	$460
Accumulated depreciation	(420)	(380)	(340)
Land	200*	300**	150*
Equipment	300	410	560
Accumulated depreciation	(60)	(320)	(310)
Inventory	120	80	100*
Goodwill	40	50	30
Corporate property	200	150	120

* These assets have carrying amounts less than fair value less costs to sell.
** This asset has a fair value less costs to sell of $293.

Lourdes Ltd determined the value in use of each of the business units at 31 December 2006:

	Chalais	Tarbes	Poitiers
Value in use	$1 170	$900	$800

Required

Determine how Lourdes Ltd should allocate any impairment loss at 31 December 2006.

PROBLEM 13.4 ★★   Impairment, two cash-generating units

Le Mans Ltd has two divisions, Dieppe and Moulins. Each of these is regarded as a separate cash-generating unit.

At 31 December 2005, the carrying amounts of the assets of the two divisions were:

	Dieppe	Moulins
Plant	$1 500	$1 200
Accumulated depreciation	(650)	(375)
Patent	240	
Inventory	54	75
Receivables	75	82
Goodwill	25	20

The receivables were regarded as collectible, while the inventory's fair value less costs to sell was equal to its carrying amount. The patent had a fair value less costs to sell of $220. The plant at Dieppe was depreciated at $300 per annum, while that at Moulins was depreciated at $250 per annum.

Le Mans Ltd undertook impairment testing at 31 December 2005, and determined the value in use of the two divisions to be:

	Dieppe	Moulins
Value in use	$1 044	$990

As a result, management increased the depreciation of the Dieppe plant from $300 to $350 per annum.

By 31 December 2006, the performance in both divisions had improved, and the carrying amounts of the assets of both divisions and their recoverable amounts were as follows:

	Dieppe	Moulins
Carrying amount	$1 322	$1 433
Recoverable amount	$1 502	$1 520

Required

Determine how Le Mans Ltd should account for the results of the impairment tests at both 31 December 2005 and 31 December 2006.

PROBLEM 13.5 ★★　Impairment loss, allocation of goodwill

Bergerac Ltd is the parent of two subsidiaries. It owns all the issued shares of Reims Ltd, and 80% of the issued shares of Amiens Ltd.

At 31 July 2006, the carrying amounts of the assets of these entities within the group were as follows, including the goodwill allocated to these entities as a result of the consolidation process:

	Reims Ltd	Amiens Ltd
Land	$400 000	$150 000
Plant	300 000	520 000
Accumulated depreciation	(120 000)	(280 000)
Inventory	70 000	60 000
Cash	30 000	20 000
Goodwill	20 000	16 000

As a part of the impairment testing procedures undertaken by Bergerac Ltd, the recoverable amounts of the two cash-generating units were:

	Reims Ltd	Amiens Ltd
Recoverable amount	$650 000	$482 000

The fair value less costs to sell for inventory was greater than the carrying amount. In relation to land:

	Reims Ltd	Amiens Ltd
Fair value less costs to sell	$390 000	$155 000

Required

Determine the accounting adjustments required as a result of the impairment tests for each of the cash-generating units.

Visit these websites for additional information:

 **WEBLINK**

www.iasb.org　　　　　www.iasplus.com
www.asic.gov.au　　　　www.ifac.org
www.aasb.com.au　　　　www.nzica.com
www.accaglobal.com　　　www.capa.com.my

REFERENCES

Danisco 2005, *Annual report 2004/05*, Danisco Corporation, Denmark, viewed March 2006, <www.danisco.com>.

Deloitte Touche Tohmatsu 2003, Comments of Deloitte Touche Tohmatsu on Exposure Draft 3 *Business Combinations*, 4 April, p. 7, viewed 7 September 2004, <www.iasb.org/docs/ed03/ed3-cl44.pdf>.

European Financial Reporting Advisory Group 2003, Comments of EFRAG on Exposure Draft 3 *Business Combinations*, 4 April, p. 10, viewed 7 September 2004, <www.iasplus.com/efrag/0304ed3.pdf>.

FASB Summary of Comment Letters, Exposure Draft (Revised) *Business Combinations and Intangible Assets — Accounting for Goodwill*, <www.iasb.org>.

Nokia 2005, *Nokia in 2005*, Nokia Corporation, Finland, viewed March 2006 <www.nokia.com>.

Picker, R & Johnson, A-M 1999, 'Asset revaluations and impairment', *Accounting brief*, April, Ernst & Young.

Swatch Group 2005, *Annual report 2005*, The Swatch Group Ltd, Switzerland, viewed July 2006, <www.swatchgroup.com>.

CHAPTER 14
Leases

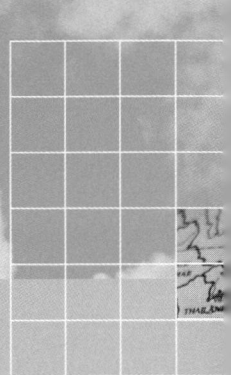

ACCOUNTING STANDARDS

International: IAS 17 *Leases*
Australia: AASB 117 *Leases*
New Zealand: NZ IAS 17 *Leases*

CONCEPTS FOR REVIEW

Before studying this chapter, you should understand or, if necessary, revise:
- the principles of accrual accounting
- the concept of an asset in the IASB Framework
- the concept of a liability in the Framework.

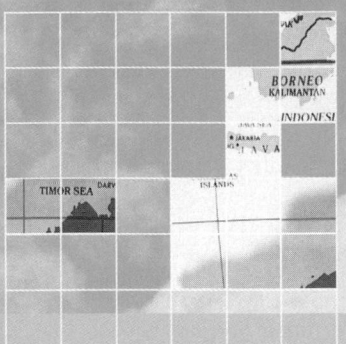

LEARNING OBJECTIVES

When you have studied this chapter, you should be able to:
1. discuss the characteristics of a lease
2. explain the difference between a finance lease and an operating lease
3. understand and apply the guidance necessary to classify leases
4. discuss the incentives to misclassify leases
5. account for finance leases from the perspective of a lessee
6. account for finance leases from the perspective of a lessor
7. account for operating leases from the perspective of both lessors and lessees
8. recognise and account for sale and leaseback transactions
9. discuss possible future changes to lease accounting.

14.1 Leases

The rapid growth of leasing as a means of gaining access to the economic benefits embodied in assets during the 1970s led to a concern among standard setters worldwide that the credibility of financial reports was compromised by extensive use of such 'off-balance-sheet' arrangements. Accordingly, the 1980s saw the issue of leasing standards by both international and national standard-setting bodies. These standards adopted similar accounting treatments based on the premise that, when a lease transfers substantially all of the risks and rewards incidental to ownership to the lessee, that lease is in substance equivalent to the acquisition of an asset on credit by the lessee, and to a sale or financing by the lessor. The mandatory recognition of the asset/liability related to the lease is justified by two arguments.

First, IAS 17, paragraph 21, states:

> Although the legal form of a lease agreement is that the lessee may acquire no legal title to the leased asset, in the case of finance leases the substance and financial reality are that the lessee acquires the economic benefits of the use of the leased asset for the major part of its economic life in return for entering into an obligation to pay for that right an amount approximating, at the inception of the lease, the fair value of the asset and the related finance charge.

Second, IAS 17, paragraph 22, states:

> If such lease transactions are not reflected in the lessee's balance sheet, the economic resources and the level of obligations of an entity are understated, thereby distorting financial ratios.

Interestingly, these justifications for the recognition of lease assets and liabilities make no reference to the Framework definitions and recognition criteria, but concentrate on the substance of the exchange of benefits and the reliability of financial information. This rationale seems to view the lease transaction as the quasi-purchase of an asset, in the sense that it records the acquisition of an asset even though no transfer of legal title takes place.

Apart from some minor amendments in the mid to late 1990s, these standards remained substantially unchanged until 1996. Concern that this accounting treatment was not compatible with the conceptual frameworks developed during the 1980s led to the publication in 1996 of a G4+1 special report authored by Warren McGregor and entitled *Accounting for leases: a new approach — recognition by lessees of assets and liabilities arising under lease contracts*. (G4 + 1 was a grouping of national accounting regulators. Initial membership consisted of standard setters from the United States, Canada, Australia and Great Britain, with the '+1' component being an IASB representative.) In preparing the 'stable platform' of accounting standards in 2004, the IASB made no major changes to IAS 17 *Leases*. A leasing project, led by the United Kingdom Accounting Standards Board, has been set up by the IASB.

WEBLINK ↗   Progress on this project can be followed by viewing the IASB website at <www.iasb.org>.

 LO 1

14.2 What is a lease?

Paragraph 4 of IAS 17 defines a lease as:

> an agreement whereby the lessor conveys to the lessee in return for a payment or series of payments the right to use an asset for an agreed period of time.

Thus, under a lease agreement the lessee acquires, not the asset itself, but the *right* to use the asset for a set time. Leased assets range from physical assets such as land, plant and vehicles, through to intangible assets such as patents, copyright and mineral rights.

Lease agreements may also result in the eventual transfer of ownership from lessor to lessee. For example, under a hire purchase agreement, the lessee will use the asset while paying for its acquisition. The agreed period of time may vary from a short period, such as the daily hire of a motor vehicle, to a longer period, such as the rental of office space by a company. The key feature of leases is the existence of an asset owned by one party (the lessor) but used, for some or all of its economic life, by another party (the lessee).

Service agreements relating to the provision of services, such as cleaning or maintenance, between two parties are not regarded as leases because the contract does not involve the use of an asset. These agreements are regarded as executory contracts; that is, both parties are still to perform to an equal degree the actions required by the contract. Thus, each party is regarded as having a right and obligation to participate in a future exchange or, alternatively, to compensate or be compensated for the consequences of not doing so. A cleaning contract entitles an entity to receive cleaning services on a regular basis and creates an obligation to pay for those services after they have been received. The key issue is the performance of the service. Until the cleaning services are delivered, the contract is merely an exchange of promises, not of future economic benefits. The existence of a non-cancellable service agreement or one that includes significant penalties for non-performance may, however, result in the service recipient acquiring control over future economic benefits (the right to receive cleaning services) that are likely to be delivered and can be reliably measured; in other words, an asset.

Accounting for leases is complicated by the fact that there are two parties involved — the lessor and the lessee.

14.2.1   Scope of application of IAS 17

Paragraph 2 of IAS 17 excludes the following types of leases from the scope of the accounting standard:
- lease agreements to explore for or use minerals, oil, natural gas and similar non-regenerative resources
- licensing agreements for such items as motion picture films, video recordings, plays, manuscripts, patents and copyrights.

No explanation is given for the exclusion of resource exploitation rights and licensing agreements, which means that the standard applies only to leases for assets with physical substance. Ironically, paragraph 3 states that 'this standard applies to agreements that transfer the right to use assets'. An agreement allowing a licensee to use a patented process provides future economic benefits to that licensee and meets the IASB Framework's definition of an asset in just the same way as a motor vehicle lease. The exclusion of these agreements from the scope of the standard is difficult to justify. Presumably, the expectation is that accounting standards on extractive industries, self-generating and renewable assets and intangibles will deal with leases of this type.

Additionally, paragraph 2 of IAS 17 mandates that the standard shall not be applied as the basis for measurement of leased investment properties or leased biological assets, as the measurement rules for such assets are contained in IAS 40 *Investment Property* and IAS 41 *Agriculture* respectively.

LO 2   14.3   Classification of leases

Paragraph 8 of IAS 17 requires both lessees and lessors to classify each lease arrangement as either an *operating lease* or a *finance lease* at the inception of the lease, which is defined in paragraph 4 as 'the earlier of the date of the lease agreement and the date of commitment by the parties to the principal provisions of the lease'. This classification process is vitally important because the accounting treatment and disclosures prescribed by the standard for each type of lease differ significantly.

IAS 17, paragraph 4, defines a finance lease as:

a lease that transfers substantially all the risks and rewards incidental to ownership of an asset. Title may or may not eventually be transferred.

An operating lease is simply defined as:

a lease other than a finance lease.

The key criterion of a finance lease is the transfer of substantially all of the risks and rewards without a transfer of ownership. The classification process therefore consists of three steps. First, the potential rewards and potential risks associated with the asset must be identified. Second, the lease agreement must be analysed to determine what rewards and risks are transferred from the lessor to the lessee. Third, an assessment must be made as to whether the risks and rewards associated with the asset have been substantially passed to the lessee.

The *risks* of ownership include:

• unsatisfactory performance, with the asset unable to provide benefits or service at the expected level or quality
• obsolescence, particularly with regard to the development of more technically advanced items
• idle capacity
• decline in residual value or losses on eventual sale of the asset
• uninsured damage and condemnation of the asset.

The *rewards* include:

• any benefits obtained from using the asset to provide benefit or service to the entity
• appreciation in residual value or gains on the eventual sale of the asset.

The risks and rewards relating to movements in realisable value are the most difficult to transfer without transferring the title. If the leased asset is to be returned to the lessor, then the risk of an adverse movement in realisable value has not been transferred unless the lessee guarantees some or all of the value of the asset at the end of the lease term.

IAS 17 does not define the term 'substantially' or prescribe classification criteria. This is left as a judgement call. By omitting quantitative examples, the IASB has placed the classification decision back in the hands of managers, who must decide what is 'substantial' for their entity and particular circumstances. The disadvantage of this approach is that similar or even identical lease agreements may be classified differently because of varying interpretations of what the terms 'major part' and 'substantially all' mean.

14.3.1 Classification guidance

To assist account preparers with this classification process, paragraphs 10 and 11 of IAS 17 provide the following series of situations that individually or in combination would normally lead to a lease transaction being classified as a finance lease:

• The lease transfers ownership of the asset by the end of the lease term.
• The lessee has the option to purchase the asset at a price that is expected to be sufficiently lower than the fair value at the date the option becomes exercisable for it to be reasonably certain that the option will be exercised.
• The lease term is for the major part of the economic life of the asset even if title is not transferred.

- At the inception of the lease, the present value of the minimum lease payments amounts to at least substantially all of the fair value of the leased asset.
- The leased assets are of such a specialised nature that only the lessee can use them without major modification.
- If the lessee can cancel the lease, the lessor's losses associated with the cancellation are borne by the lessee.
- Gains or losses from the fluctuation in the fair value of the residual accrue to the lessee.
- The lessee has the ability to continue the lease for a secondary period at a rental that is substantially less than market rent.

It should be noted that these pointers are guidelines in assessing whether substantially all the risks and rewards are transferred. Each pointer then relates to some measure of risk or reward.

For the purpose of analysis, the guidelines are classified into five categories, as represented in figure 14.1.

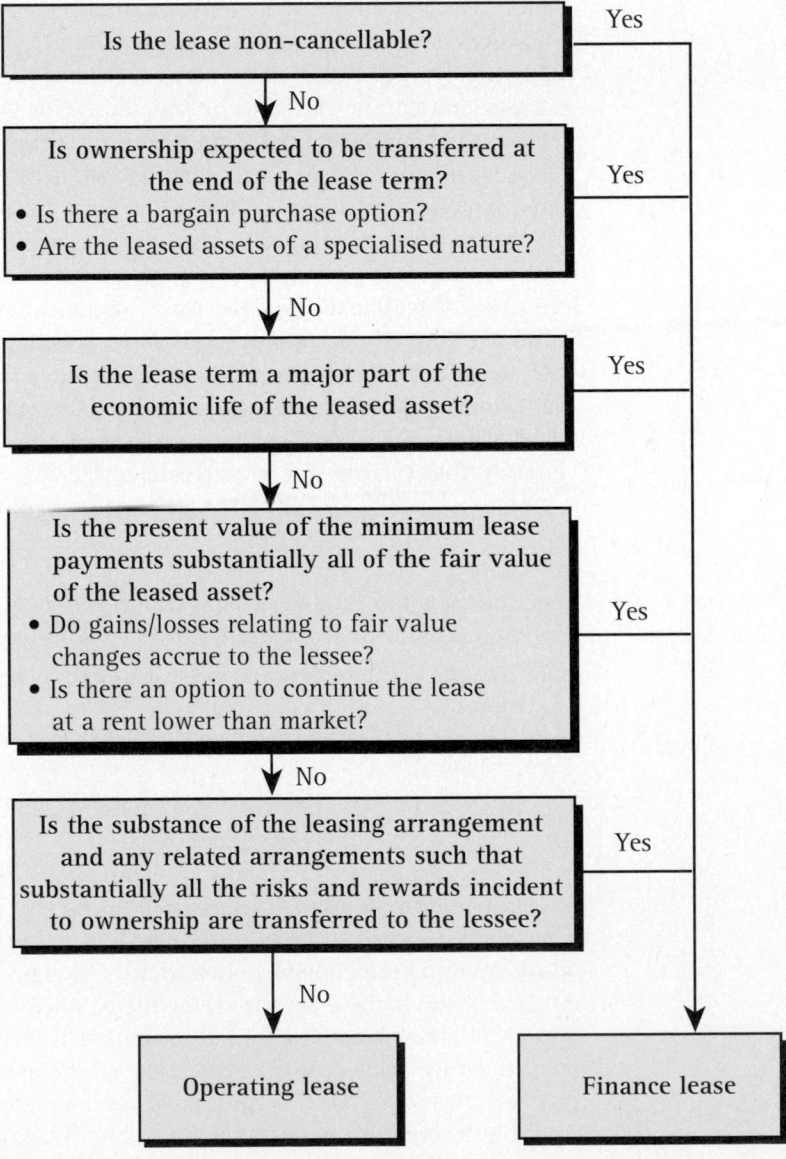

FIGURE 14.1 Guidelines for classifying a lease

LO 3

14.4   Applying the classification guidance

Therefore when classifying leases, managers will need to examine three main conditions of the lease agreement:
- cancellability of the lease
- extent of the asset's economic life transferred to the lessee
- present value of minimum lease payments.

14.4.1   Cancellability of the lease

A non-cancellable lease locks both parties into the agreement and ensures that the exchange of risks and rewards will occur. A lease from which both or either party could walk away at any time may result in only a limited transfer of risks and rewards. However, the application of this classification guidance is not a simple cancellable/non-cancellable choice. The definition of a non-cancellable lease provided in paragraph 4 of IAS 17 introduces shades of grey into the equation by deeming cancellable leases with the following characteristics to be 'non-cancellable':
- leases that can be cancelled only upon the occurrence of some remote contingency
- leases that can be cancelled only with the permission of the lessor
- leases where the lessee, upon cancellation, is committed to enter into a further lease for the same or equivalent asset with the same lessor
- leases that provide that the lessee, upon cancellation, incurs a penalty of such a magnitude that is expected to discourage cancellation in normal circumstances.

A careful examination of the lease agreement is necessary to ensure that cancellable leases are correctly designated.

It would appear that the standard setters have based the assessment of the probability that future risks and rewards have been transferred on whether or not a lease can be cancelled. That is, if a lease can be cancelled at any time without penalty, then there is no certainty that the transfer will be completed.

14.4.2   Extent of the asset's economic life transferred to the lessee

This classification guidance requires measurement of the lease term against the asset's economic useful life. Paragraph 4 of IAS 17 defines an asset's economic life as either:

(a) the period over which an asset is expected to be economically usable by one or more users; or

(b) the number of production or similar units expected to be obtained from the asset by one or more users.

The lease term is defined as the 'non-cancellable period for which the lessee has contracted to lease the asset' (para. 4).

This test represents an attempt to measure the extent of the transfer of rewards to the lessee. If title to the asset is transferred to the lessee at the end of the lease, or if there is a reasonable expectation at lease inception date that the lessee will purchase the asset (via a favourable purchase option clause) at the end of the lease term, then the lessee effectively holds the asset for all (or the balance remaining) of the asset's economic life. Where the asset is to be returned to the lessor at the end of the lease term, then judgement must be applied. What percentage of the asset's economic life represents a 'major' part — 60%? 70%? 80%? The lack of clear guidance in the accounting standard could result in differential classifications of similar lease arrangements. For example, a six-year lease of an asset with an economic life of eight years could be classified as a finance lease by entity A on the grounds that the lease term is 74% of the asset's economic life, but treated as an operating lease by entity B, which applies an 85% 'cut off'.

These classification criteria assume that the consumption pattern of economic benefits across the economic life of the asset will be straight-line (equal in each year). However, some assets, such as vehicles, may provide more of their benefits in the early years of their economic lives, so a time-based classification criterion may not be appropriate.

14.4.3 Present value of minimum lease payments

At lease inception date, the fair value of the asset measures the present value of the total benefits associated with the asset. The minimum lease payments (MLP) represent payments for benefits transferred to the lessee. This test therefore indicates the proportion of benefits being paid for by the lessee.

To apply this guidance, the following information must be gathered or determined at the inception of the lease:
- fair value of the leased asset
- minimum lease payments
- discount rate.

Fair value of the leased asset

Fair value is defined in IAS 17, paragraph 4, as:

> The amount for which an asset could be exchanged, or a liability settled, between knowledgeable, willing parties in an arm's length transaction.

The fair value is normally a market price. However, if the lease relates to specialised equipment constructed or obtained for the lease contract, a fair value may be difficult to obtain. The fair value is regarded as representing the future rewards available to the user of the asset, discounted by the market to allow for the risk that the rewards will not eventuate and for changes in the purchasing power of money over time.

Minimum lease payments

The definition of minimum lease payments, contained in paragraph 4 of the standard, can be expressed as follows:

Minimum lease payments =		(i) Payments over the lease term
	+	(ii) Guaranteed residual value
	+	(iii) Bargain purchase option
	−	(iv) Contingent rent
	−	(v) Reimbursement of costs paid by the lessor

(i) The *lease payments* are simply the total amounts payable under the lease agreement.

(ii) The *guaranteed residual value* is that part of the residual value of the leased asset guaranteed by the lessee or a third party related to the lessee (IAS 17, para. 4). The lessor will estimate the residual value of the leased asset at the end of the lease term based on market conditions at the inception of the lease, and the lessee will guarantee that, when the asset is returned to the lessor, it will realise at least that amount. The guarantee may range from 1% to 100% of the residual value and is a matter for negotiation between lessor and lessee. If the guarantee is provided by a party related to the lessor rather than the lessee, that part of the residual value is regarded, for the purposes of IAS 17, as unguaranteed. Where a lessee guarantees some or all of the residual value of the asset, the lessor has transferred risks associated with movements in the residual value to the lessee.

(iii) A *bargain purchase option* is a clause in the lease agreement allowing the lessee to purchase the asset at the end of the lease for a preset amount, significantly less than the expected residual value at the end of the lease term; hence, the 'bargain' description. In paragraph 4 of IAS 17, within the definition of minimum lease payments, the option price is described as one:

> that is expected to be sufficiently lower than fair value at the date the option becomes exercisable for it to be reasonably certain, at the inception of the lease, that the option will be exercised.

Together these amounts represent the maximum possible payment the lessee is legally obliged to make under the lease agreement, assuming that the guaranteed amount must be paid in full or the purchase option will be exercised.

(iv) Scheduled lease payments may be increased or decreased during the lease term by the occurrence of events specified in the lease agreement. Additional payments arising from such changes are called *contingent rent*. For example, an agreement to lease a photocopier may specify an additional charge where the number of copies made in a month exceed 100 000; or a motor vehicle lease charge may be decreased if the vehicle is driven only on sealed metropolitan roads. These charges/reductions relate to the use of the leased asset but, as the occurrence of the contingent event is uncertain at lease inception date, they are ignored when calculating the minimum lease payments.

(v) Lease payments may include two components; a charge for using the asset, and a charge to *reimburse the lessor for operating expenses* paid on behalf of the lessee. These operating amounts include insurance, maintenance, consumable supplies, replacement parts and rates. These costs are given the generic title 'executory costs' in this chapter. Amounts paid to reimburse such costs are excluded from minimum lease payments because they do not relate to the value of the asset transferred between lessor and lessee. Payments for such items give rise to equally unperformed contracts.

Discount rate

The minimum lease payments are discounted to present value by applying an appropriate discount rate. Discounting is not necessary if the lease contains a bargain purchase option or a 100% guaranteed residual value because, in both cases, the present value of the minimum lease payments will equal the fair value of the leased asset. Hence, a complete transfer of risks and rewards is deemed to have taken place.

To discount the minimum lease payments, the lessee/lessor will need to ascertain the interest rate implicit in the lease. This is defined in paragraph 4 of IAS 17 as:

> the discount rate that at the inception of the lease causes the aggregate present value of:
> (a) the minimum lease payments; and
> (b) the unguaranteed residual value
> to be equal to the sum of:
>   (i) the fair value of the leased asset, and
> (ii) any initial direct costs of the lessor.

Initial direct costs (IDC) are incremental costs that are directly attributable to negotiating and arranging a lease, except for such costs incurred by manufacturer or dealer lessors (IAS 17, para. 4). Examples include commission and legal fees and internal costs, but exclude general overheads such as those incurred by a sales and marketing team (para. 38). Initial direct costs incurred by a manufacturer/dealer lessor are excluded from the definition of initial direct costs (para. 38) because, according to paragraph 46, the costs of negotiating and arranging a finance lease are 'mainly related to earning the manufacturer's or dealer's selling profit'. How the IASB has reached this conclusion is hard to understand. Thus, for the purposes of determining the interest rate implicit in the lease, any initial direct costs incurred by a lessee or a manufacturer/dealer lessor are ignored.

The interest rate implicit in the lease is determined at the inception date of the lease, and this may differ from the commencement date of the lease term, which is a date set by the agreement. This may lead to the use of a distorted discount rate if the inception date of the lease differs from the commencement of the lease term, as this is the date from which the lessee is entitled to exercise its right to use the leased asset and presumably the date from which the lessee is entitled to receive the lease payments. As (a) and (b) from the paragraph 4 definition equal the future economic rewards obtainable from the asset, the interest rate is that used by the market to determine the fair value. From this comes the notion that the rate is implicit in the terms of the agreement.

If it is not possible to determine the fair value of the asset at the inception of the lease or the residual value at the end of the lease term, then the interest rate implicit in the lease cannot be calculated. In this situation, paragraph 20 of IAS 17 states that the lessee's (rather than the lessor's) incremental borrowing rate should be used to discount the minimum lease payments. The incremental borrowing rate is the rate of interest the lessee would have to pay on a similar lease or, if this is not determinable, the rate that (at the inception of the lease) the lessee would incur to borrow over a similar term, and with a similar security, the funds necessary to purchase the asset (para. 4).

Substantial transfer?

The present value of the minimum lease payments can be determined as a percentage of the fair value of the leased asset, and a judgement made as to whether this represents the transfer of 'substantially all' of the fair value of the asset from the lessor to the lessee. Again, a lack of quantitative guidelines may result in the inconsistent classification of similar lease arrangements.

ILLUSTRATIVE EXAMPLE 14.1

Classification of a lease agreement

For the purpose of illustrative examples within this chapter, the following percentages have been adopted to quantify the terms 'major part' and 'substantially all':
- Major part means that the lease term is 75% or more of the asset's economic life.
- Substantially all means that the present value of minimum lease payments (PV of MLP) is 90% or more of the fair value of the leased asset at inception of the lease.

On 30 June 2005, Edmonton Ltd leased a vehicle to Calgary Ltd. Edmonton Ltd had purchased the vehicle on that day for its fair value of $89 721. The lease agreement, which cost Edmonton Ltd $1457 to have drawn up, contained the following clauses:

Lease term	4 years
Annual payment, payable in advance on 30 June each year	$23 900
Economic life of vehicle	6 years
Estimated residual value at end of lease term	$15 000
Residual value guaranteed by lessee	$7 500

→

The lease is cancellable, but cancellation will incur a monetary penalty equivalent to two years' rental payments. Included in the annual payment is an amount of $1900 to cover reimbursement for the costs of insurance and maintenance paid by the lessor. The directors of Calgary Ltd have indicated that they intend to return the asset to Edmonton Ltd at the end of the lease term.

IAS 17 requires that the lease be classified as either a finance or an operating lease, based on the extent to which the risks and rewards associated with the vehicle have been effectively transferred between Edmonton Ltd and Calgary Ltd.

Is the lease non-cancellable?

The lease agreement is cancellable, but a significant monetary penalty equal to two years' rental payments will apply. This meets part (d) of the definition of non-cancellable in IAS 17, paragraph 4. Therefore, the lease is deemed to be non-cancellable.

Is ownership expected to be transferred at the end of the lease term?

The expectation is that the asset will be returned to the lessor.

Is the lease term a major part of the economic life of the leased asset?

The lease term is four years, which is only 60% of the asset's economic life of six years. Using 75% as the guideline, it would appear that the lease arrangement is not for the major part of the asset's life.

Is the present value of the minimum lease payments substantially all of the fair value of the leased asset?

Minimum lease payments
The minimum lease payments consist of:
- lease payments net of cost reimbursement — there is an immediate payment of $22 000 (being $23 900 – $1900) and four subsequent payments of $22 000
- contingent rental — which does not arise in this example
- guaranteed residual value — an amount of $7500 is guaranteed at the end of the fourth year.

The unguaranteed residual value is $7500.

Interest rate implicit in the lease
The discount rate is the rate that discounts the minimum lease payments and the unguaranteed residual value (UGRV) to the aggregate of the asset's fair value and any initial indirect costs of the lessor. In this example, the discount rate is the rate that discounts the lessee rental payments and the residual value to $91 178, which is the sum of the asset's fair value at 1 July 2005 of $89 721 and the initial direct costs of $1457 incurred by the lessor. This rate is found by trial and error using the present value tables (see appendix pages 645–6) or a financial calculator.

The implicit interest rate in this example is 7%, that is:

$$\text{Present value} = \$22\,000 + (\$22\,000 \times 2.6243 \, [T_2 \, 7\% \, 3y]) + (\$15\,000 \times 0.7629 \, [T_1 \, 7\% \, 4y])$$
$$= \$22\,000 + \$57\,735 + \$11\,443$$
$$= \$91\,178$$

where T = present value table
y = years

Note the following:
- As the first payment is made at the inception of the lease, it is not discounted.
- The discount factor used is an annuity factor based on three equal payments of $22 000 for the next three years at 7%.
- The discount factor used is based on a single payment of $15 000 (the residual value) at the end of the lease term in four years time at a rate of 7%. The $15 000 comprises $7500 guaranteed by the lessee plus the unguaranteed balance of $7500.

The present value is equal to the fair value plus initial direct costs, so the interest rate implicit in the lease is 7%.

Present value of minimum lease payments

PV of MLP = $22 000 + ($22 000 × 2.6243 [T_2 7% 3y]) + ($7500 × 0.7629 [$T_1$ 7% 4y])
= $22 000 + $57 735 + $5722
= $85 457

Fair value + IDC = $91 178

PV/(FV + IDC) = ($85 457/$91 178) × 100%
= 93.7%

Therefore, using 90% as the guideline, the present value of the minimum lease payments is substantially all of the fair value of the leased asset.

Classification of the lease

Application of the guidelines provides mixed signals. The key criterion in classifying leases is whether substantially all of the risks and rewards incident to ownership have been transferred. This requires an overall analysis of the situation, but insufficient information is given in the example to do this. The different signals coming from the lease term test and the present value test may be due to the fact that the majority of the rewards will be transferred in the early stages of the life of the asset, as with motor vehicles. This is reflected in the relatively low residual value at the end of the lease term. These mixed signals demonstrate that the guidelines must be used for guidance only and not treated as specific criteria that must be met.

Further, an analysis of the substance of the lease arrangement must be undertaken to ensure that it is not just the form of the lease agreement that is being accounted for (see section 14.5 of this chapter for more details).

Given no extra information, it is concluded that the lease agreement should be classified as a finance lease because substantially all the risks and rewards incident to ownership have been passed to the lessee.

LO 4

14.5 Substance over form: incentives to misclassify leases

The classification of lease arrangements as either finance leases or operating leases determines the accounting treatment of transactions associated with the lease. For finance leases, the lessee recognises an asset and liability at the inception of the lease. The leased asset is subsequently depreciated and the liability is reduced through rental payments. An annual interest charge is recognised in respect to the liability. For operating leases, the lessee treats rental payments as expenses.

These divergent accounting treatments provide an incentive to managers to classify lease arrangements as operating leases. Finance leases may have the following adverse impacts on a lessee entity's financial statements or on decisions made by users of those statements.

- The capitalisation of the leased asset increases the value of reported non-current assets and reduces return on asset ratios.
- Recognition of the present value of future lease payments as a liability will increase reported current and non-current liabilities. These will adversely affect debt-equity ratios and liquidity-solvency ratios, such as the current ratio (current assets/current liabilities). Reporting increased liabilities may result in entities breaching debt covenants, thereby causing debts to become due and payable immediately.
- Subsequent depreciation and interest expenses may exceed rental payments and result in lower profits being reported in the early years of the lease.
- Depreciation and interest expenses are not deductible for tax purposes, so additional liabilities may have to be recognised under IAS 12 *Income Taxes* when these expenses are less than the deduction for rental payments.
- More onerous disclosure requirements are required for finance leases.

The ability to manipulate gearing ratios and thereby possibly reduce the cost of capital or increase the availability of finance for an entity is the most significant reward of keeping financing arrangements off balance sheet by classifying them as operating leases. As a result, since the release of IAS 17, the leasing industry has been geared towards promoting lease structures or arrangements that meet the guidelines for classification as operating leases. As noted in paragraph 21 of IAS 17, classification and the subsequent accounting must be based on 'substance and financial reality and not merely with legal form'. Hence, after considering the guidelines, which concentrate on the form of the lease agreement, the process of classifying a lease must include an analysis of the substance of the lease arrangement.

Features of lease arrangements that can be manipulated include the lease term (in particular, using short terms with options to renew), residual values, economic life estimates and bargain price options.

McGregor (1996, appendix 2, pp. 33–4) gives the following examples of finance leases structured as operating leases:

- *Novated motor vehicle leases* – Under this arrangement, employees enter into finance lease arrangements with a lessor finance company to finance motor vehicles. The employer and employee then enter into a sub-lease. When the ultimate risk rests with the employee, the arrangement is an operating lease. However, if the employer assumes the risk by, for example, guaranteeing the lease payments, the lease may be in substance a finance lease.
- *Rolling stock sale and leaseback* – In Australia, public sector entities have entered into offshore sale and leaseback arrangements in respect of public transport. Typically, the leases are for periods of four to seven years with options for renewal, and are classified as operating leases. Assets involved include suburban trains, locomotives, light rail vehicles and buses. The unique rail gauges and other user-specific characteristics of this type of equipment make it unlikely that it would find a ready secondary market at the expiration of the lease term, and therefore underline the implausibility of any contention that the leases would not be renewed.
- *Private funding of public infrastructure* – Such funding arrangements often involve the establishment of a special purpose company by a financier to raise private sector finance by the issue of debt securities for the construction of buildings such as police

stations and courthouses. Apart from special purpose fitting out, the buildings are of a generic type for which alternative uses would therefore be readily available. The buildings are then leased to a government department or other public sector operator. The leases are invariably classified as operating leases by the government department or other public sector operator. An integral feature of most of these arrangements is that the government guarantees the debt securities, thereby ensuring that the bondholders are fully indemnified. Often the government also agrees to a pricing structure that ensures that capital as well as all other costs of the project will be recouped by the investor. Therefore, the risks and rewards of ownership are effectively transferred to the lessee (the government).

- *Separate arrangements for bargain purchase options or guaranteed residual values* — Some leases have been structured to include bargain purchase options or guaranteed residual values that are not specified directly as part of the lease agreements. For example, a bargain purchase option may be specified in an agreement completely separate from the lease agreement itself, and may be portrayed as unrelated to the lease agreement. Alternatively, a trust may be interposed between the lessor and lessee, with the lessee subscribing for units in the trust that are to be drawn against in the event of a shortfall in residual value. In these situations, the very existence of these arrangements may be difficult to detect and, even if detected, may be claimed to be unrelated to the lease and therefore not relevant to the lease classification process.

Shanahan (1989) described another scheme using an interposed entity. Under this arrangement, the lessor leases the asset to the interposed entity, which is owned 50/50 by the lessor and lessee, in the form of a finance lease. The interposed entity then subleases the asset to the ultimate lessee via a series of short-term operating leases, with options to renew. The lessor normally holds a 'put' option, whereby the lessor can force the lessee to buy its share of the interposed entity should the lessee fail to renew the operating lease. The lessee would then control the interposed entity and must consolidate its accounts (including the finance lease) with those of the lessee.

Tolling agreements (a non-lease) may also be used whereby the lessee has no right to use the leased equipment, but pays a toll to the lessor for provision of an asset *and* an operator for the asset. As the lessor's operator uses the asset, it is argued by those not wanting to recognise lease assets and liabilities that no lease as defined by IAS 17 exists.

The fact that managers can circumvent the requirements of the accounting standard and keep leases off balance sheet by using such contrivances means that the comparability and usefulness of financial reports is considerably diminished. As McGregor (1996, p. 3) points out:

> standards which do not require the recognition of assets and liabilities in respect of rights and obligations arising under certain financing arrangements have become a motivating factor in the selection of that type of financing arrangement over other forms of arrangement.

All of the arrangements described above are finance leases in substance, and a strict application of the IAS 17 definition of a finance lease should result in the classification of the arrangement as a finance lease. However, the notion of what is substantial is capable of a wide range of interpretations, and the lack of clear quantitative guidance in the accounting standard may allow unethical managers to manipulate the lease classification process.

14.5.1 SIC 27

In December 2001, the Standing Interpretations Committee (SIC) of the IASB issued SIC 27 *Evaluating the Substance of Transactions Involving the Legal Form of a Lease* in an attempt to provide authoritative guidance to assist in the classification decision. SIC 27 requires that a series of transactions that include a lease should be accounted for as a single transaction 'when the overall economic effect cannot be understood without reference to the series of transactions as a whole' (para. 3). This merely reiterates the 'substance over form' approach adopted by IAS 17. However, paragraph 5 of SIC 27 also provides the following indicators of arrangements that do not in substance involve a lease:

(a) an entity retains all the risks and rewards incident to ownership of an underlying asset and enjoys substantially the same rights to its use as before the arrangement;

(b) the primary reason for the arrangement is to achieve a particular tax result, and not to convey the right to use an asset; and

(c) an option is included on terms that make its exercise almost certain; (e.g. a put option that is exercisable at a price sufficiently higher than the expected fair value when it becomes exercisable).

Thus, the interpretation clearly details transactions that are *not* leases but does little to assist the classification of leases as either financing or operating, other than to state in paragraph 14:

When an entity does not control the assets that will be used to satisfy the lease payment obligations and is not obligated to pay the lease payments, it does not recognise the assets and lease payment obligations, because the definitions of an asset and a liability have not been met.

14.5.2 IFRIC 4

To further assist account preparers, the International Financial Reporting Interpretations Committee (IFRIC), which replaced the Standing Interpretations Committee, issued IFRIC 4 *Determining Whether an Arrangement Contains a Lease* in 2005. This interpretation was issued to assist account preparers in determining whether arrangements that are *not* in the legal form of a lease may in fact convey the right to use an item for an agreed period of time in return for a series of payments, and should therefore be treated as a lease for accounting purposes. Such arrangements may include:

- outsourcing arrangements
- arrangements in the telecommunications industry where suppliers of network capacity enter into contracts to provide purchases with rights to capacity
- take-or-pay contracts in which purchasers must make specified payments irrespective of whether they take delivery of services or products
- service concession arrangements where a supplier provides the use of an item of infrastructure to a purchaser.

The assessment of whether an arrangement contains a lease must be done at the inception of the arrangement using the information available at that time. If the provisions of the arrangement are subsequently changed, a reassessment will be made. Using the definition of a lease as an agreement whereby the lessor conveys to the lessee the right to use an asset for an agreed period of time in return for a payment or series of payments (IAS 17, paragraph 4), two criteria were developed to identify the lease component within an arrangement. These are stated in IFRIC 4, paragraph 6:

(a) fulfilment of the arrangement is dependent on the use of a specific asset or assets (the asset); and

(b) the arrangement conveys a right to use the asset.

IFRIC 4 uses an illustrative example of a purchaser who enters into a take-or-pay arrangement with an industrial gas supplier. If that supplier provides the gas from a plant that is built on the purchaser's premises and used solely to provide gas under the arrangement then, applying the above criteria, this lease is a 'de facto' lease of the gas plant.

If an arrangement does contain a lease component, then that part of the arrangement must be segregated and accounted for in accordance with IAS 17. This would require classification as an operating or financing lease at the inception of the arrangement. Payments made under the arrangement would need to be separated into lease payments and payments for other services on the basis of their relative fair values (IFRIC 4, para. 13).

LO 5

14.6 Accounting for finance leases by lessees

Once an arrangement has been classified as a finance lease, the asset and liability arising from it must be determined and recognised in the accounts.

14.6.1 Initial recognition

When a lease has been classified as a finance lease, paragraph 20 of IAS 17 requires the lessee to recognise, at the commencement of the lease term, an asset and a liability, each determined at the inception of the lease, equal in amount to the fair value of the leased property or, if lower, the present value of the minimum lease payments. The form of the entry is:

Lease asset	Dr	PV of MLP	
Lease liability	Cr		PV of MLP

The commencement of the lease term is the date from which the lessee is entitled to exercise its right to use the leased asset, and may be the same date as the inception of the lease or a later date. If not already determined as part of the classification process, the value of the asset or liability needs to be calculated at the inception of the lease by reference to the terms of the lease agreement. If the lessee incurs initial direct costs associated with the negotiation and securing of the lease arrangements then, according to paragraph 24 of IAS 17, these costs are added to the amount recognised as an asset. The journal entry is:

Lease asset	Dr	PV of MLP + IDC	
Lease liability	Cr		PV of MLP
Cash	Cr		IDC

14.6.2 Subsequent measurement

After initial recognition, IAS 17 prescribes differing accounting treatments for the lease asset and the lease liability.

Leased assets

Paragraph 27 of IAS 17 states that:

> the depreciation policy for depreciable leased assets shall be consistent with that for depreciable assets that are owned, and the depreciation recognised shall be calculated in accordance with IAS 16 *Property, Plant and Equipment* and IAS 38 *Intangible Assets*.

Depreciable assets are those whose future benefits are expected to expire over time or by use. The asset is depreciated over its useful life in a pattern reflecting the consumption or loss of the rewards embodied in the asset. The length of a leased asset's useful life depends on whether or not ownership of the asset will transfer at the end of the lease term. If the asset is to be returned to the lessor, then its useful life is the lease term. If ownership is reasonably certain to transfer to the lessee, then its useful life is its economic life or remainder thereof. Additionally, to determine whether a leased asset has become impaired, the lessee must apply IAS 36 *Impairment of Assets* (see chapter 13 of this book).

Lease liability

Because lease payments are made over the lease term, paragraph 25 of IAS 17 requires the payments to be divided into the following components:

- reduction of the lease liability
- interest expense incurred
- reimbursement of lessor costs
- payment of contingent rent.

The latter two are easily determined by reference to the lease agreement, but the first two need to be calculated. The lease liability recognised at the commencement of the lease term represents the present value of future lease payments relating to the use of the asset. This present value is determined by applying the interest rate implicit in the lease. Thus, the interest expense can be obtained by applying the same rate to the outstanding lease liability at the beginning of the payment period. A payments schedule can be used to determine the interest expense and the reduction in the liability over the lease period.

Accounting for the reimbursement of lessor costs and contingent rent

Paragraph 25 of IAS 17 requires contingent rent to be recognised as an expense of the year in which it is incurred. The accounting standard is silent about the component of lease payments that represents a reimbursement of costs incurred by the lessor. However, as the cost of such items is effectively borne by the lessee, the payment should be recognised as an expense. Consideration must be given to the pattern of consumption relating to those expenses and normal prepayment and accrual rules apply.

ILLUSTRATIVE EXAMPLE 14.2

Accounting for finance leases by lessees

Using the facts from illustrative example 14.1, the lease payments schedule prepared by Calgary Ltd, based on annual payments of $22 000 for the vehicle and an interest rate of 7%, would be:

Calgary Ltd Lease payments schedule				
	Minimum lease payments[1]	Interest expense[2]	Reduction in liability[3]	Balance of liability[4]
30 June 2005[6]				85 457[5]
30 June 2005	22 000	–	22 000	63 457
30 June 2006	22 000	4 442	17 558	45 899
30 June 2007	22 000	3 213	18 787	27 112
30 June 2008	22 000	1 898	20 102	7 010
30 June 2009	7 500	490	7 010	–
	95 500	10 043	85 457	–

Notes:

1. Four annual payments of $22 000 payable in advance on 30 June of each year, plus a guaranteed residual value of $7500 on the last day of the lease.
2. Interest expense = balance of liability each year multiplied by 7%. No interest expense is incurred in the first year because payment is made at the commencement of the lease.
3. Reduction in liability = minimum lease payments less interest expense. The total of this column must equal the initial liability, which may require rounding the final interest expense figure.
4. The balance is reduced each year by the amount in column 3.
5. Initial liability = present value of minimum lease payments. As the present value of minimum lease payments is less than the fair value of the asset, paragraph 20 of IAS 17 requires the lower amount to be recognised.
6. At lease inception.

The payment schedule is used to prepare lease journal entries and disclosure notes each year. The journal entries recorded by Calgary Ltd for the four years of the lease in accordance with IAS 17 are:

Calgary Ltd General journal			
Year ended 30 June 2005 30 June 2005 Leased vehicle Lease liability (Initial recording of lease asset/liability)	Dr Cr	85 457	85 457
Lease liability Prepaid executory costs Cash (First lease payment)	Dr Dr Cr	22 000 *1 900	23 900

*Executory costs have been capitalised because the insurance and maintenance benefits will not be received until the next reporting period.

Year ended 30 June 2006 1 July 2005 Executory costs Prepaid executory costs (Reversal of prepayment)	Dr Cr	1 900	1 900
30 June 2006 Lease liability Interest expense Prepaid executory costs Cash (Second lease payment)	Dr Dr Dr Cr	17 558 4 442 1 900	23 900
Depreciation expense Accumulated depreciation (Depreciation charge for the period [$85 457 – $7500]/4)*	Dr Cr	19 489	19 489

*Because the asset will be returned at the end of the lease term, the useful life is the lease term of four years and the depreciable amount is the cost less the guaranteed residual value.

Year ended 30 June 2007 1 July 2006 Executory costs Prepaid executory costs (Reversal of prepayment)	Dr Cr	1 900	1 900
30 June 2007 Lease liability Interest expense Prepaid executory costs Cash (Third lease payment)	Dr Dr Dr Cr	18 787 3 213 1 900	23 900
Depreciation expense Accumulated depreciation (Depreciation charge for the period [$85 457 – $7500]/4)	Dr Cr	19 489	19 489
Year ended 30 June 2008 1 July 2007 Executory costs Prepaid executory costs (Reversal of prepayment)	Dr Cr	1 900	1 900
30 June 2008 Lease liability Interest expense Prepaid executory costs Cash (Fourth lease payment)	Dr Dr Dr Cr	20 102 1 898 1 900	23 900
Depreciation expense Accumulated depreciation (Depreciation charge for the period [$85 457 – $7500]/4)	Dr Cr	19 489	19 489
Year ended 30 June 2009 1 July 2008 Executory costs Prepaid executory costs (Reversal of prepayment)	Dr Cr	1 900	1 900
30 June 2009 Lease liability Interest expense Leased vehicle* (Return of leased vehicle)	Dr Dr Cr	7 010 490	7 500
Depreciation expense Accumulated depreciation (Depreciation charge for the period [$85 457 – $7500]/4)*	Dr Cr	19 490	19 490
Accumulated depreciation Leased vehicle (Fully depreciated asset written off)	Dr Cr	77 957	77 957

*The final 'payment' is the return of the asset at its guaranteed residual value. If the asset is being purchased, this entry will record a cash payment. Another entry will then be required to reclassify the undepreciated balance of the asset from a 'leased' asset to an 'owned' asset.

14.6.3 Disclosures required

Paragraph 31 of IAS 17 requires that, in addition to meeting the requirements of IAS 32 *Financial Instruments: Disclosure and Presentation*, the following information must be disclosed by lessees:

- the carrying amount of each class of leased asset as at the balance date
- a reconciliation between the total future minimum lease payments at the balance sheet date and their present value
- the total of future minimum lease payments at the balance sheet date and their present value for each of the following periods:
  - not later than one year
  - later than one year and not later than five years
  - later than five years
- contingent rents recognised as an expense in the period
- the total of future minimum sublease payments expected to be received under non-cancellable subleases at the balance sheet date
- a general description of the lessee's material leasing arrangements.

(See chapter 6 of this book for more on IAS 32.)

Future minimum lease payments include all future amounts payable under the lease agreement less reimbursements of the lessor's costs and any known contingent rents. This reconciliation provides some information about future cash flows to financial statement users.

Figure 14.2 shows the leasing accounting policy disclosures and the lease commitments note to the financial statements of Telstra Corporation Ltd for the year ended 30 June 2005.

FIGURE 14.2 Note extracts from Telstra Corporation Ltd annual report 30 June 2005

NOTES TO THE FINANCIAL STATEMENTS (continued)

1: Summary of accounting policies (continued)

1.14 Leased plant and equipment (note 12)

We account for leases in accordance with AASB 1008: "Leases". We distinguish finance leases, which effectively transfer substantially all the risks and benefits incidental to ownership of the leased asset from the lessor to the lessee, from operating leases, under which the lessor effectively retains all such risks and benefits.

Where we acquire non current assets by using a finance lease, the present value of future minimum lease payments is disclosed as equipment under finance lease at the beginning of the lease term. Capitalised lease payments are amortised on a straight line basis over the shorter of the lease term or the expected useful life of the assets. A corresponding liability is also established and each lease payment is allocated between the liability and finance charges.

Operating lease payments are charged to the statement of financial performance in the periods in which they are incurred. Operating lease rental expense is disclosed in note 3.

Where we lease properties, costs of improvements to these properties are capitalised, and disclosed as leasehold improvements and amortised over the shorter of the useful life of the improvements or the term of the lease.

...

...

(continued)

NOTES TO THE FINANCIAL STATEMENTS (continued)

20. Expenditure commitments

	Telstra Group		Telstra Entity	
	As at 30 June		As at 30 June	
	2005 $m	2004 $m	2005 $m	2004 $m
...				
(b) Operating lease commitments				
Future lease payments for non-cancellable operating leases not recorded in the financial statements:				
Within 1 year	380	311	232	203
Within 1–2 years	260	245	154	156
Within 2–3 years	209	182	117	111
Within 3–4 years	149	153	64	86
Within 4–5 years	128	139	49	73
After 5 years	397	373	154	155
	1 523	1 403	770	784

In addition, in fiscal 2005 the Telstra Group has total future commitments under cancellable operating leases of $343 million (2004: $375 million). In fiscal 2005, the Telstra Entity has total future commitments under cancellable operating leases of $338 million (2004: $330 million).

Description of our operating leases
We have operating leases for the following major services:
- rental of land and buildings;
- rental of motor vehicles, caravan huts and trailers, and mechanical aids; and
- rental of personal computers, laptops, printers and other related equipment that are used in non communications plant activities.

The average lease term is:
- seven years for land and buildings;
- two years for motor vehicles, five years for light commercial vehicles and seven to twelve years for trucks and mechanical aids; and
- three years for personal computers and related equipment.

Contingent rental payments only exist for motor vehicles and are not significant compared with total rental payments made. These are based on unfair wear and tear, excess kilometres travelled, additional fittings and no financial loss to be suffered by the leasing company from changes to the original agreements. Our motor vehicles and related equipment must also remain in Australia.

We do not have any significant purchase options or non-cancellable sub-leases in our operating leases. Our property operating leases contain escalation clauses, which are fixed increases between 3% and 5%.

Operating leases related to our personal computers and associated equipment had average interest rates of 5.6% for fiscal 2005 (5.8% for fiscal 2004).

20. Expenditure commitments (continued)

	Note	Telstra Group		Telstra Entity	
		As at 30 June		As at 30 June	
		2005 $m	2004 $m	2005 $m	2004 $m
(c) Finance lease commitments					
Within 1 year		12	7	5	6
Within 1–2 years		10	6	5	6
Within 2–3 years		10	2	5	2
Within 3–4 years		8	2	5	2
Within 4–5 years		5	1	1	1
After 5 years		54	–	–	–
Total minimum lease payments		99	18	21	17
Future finance charges on finance leases		(47)	(1)	(4)	(1)
Present value of net future minimum lease payments		52	17	17	16
Recorded as current interest-bearing liabilities	16	5	7	4	6
Recorded as non current interest-bearing liabilities	16	47	10	13	10
Total finance lease liabilities	16	52	17	17	16

In addition to the above finance lease commitments, we previously entered into US finance leases for communications exchange equipment with various entities. We have prepaid all lease rentals due under the terms of these leases.

These entities lease the communications exchange equipment from the ultimate lessor and then sub-lease the equipment to us. We have guaranteed that the lease payments will be paid by these entities to the ultimate lessor as scheduled over the lease terms (refer to note 21 for further information).

The leases will expire in fiscal 2012. As part of the lease arrangements, we received guarantee fees, which have been recorded in revenue received in advance. The total revenue received in advance is insignificant and is being released to the statement of financial performance over the life of the leases.

Description of our finance leases
We have finance leases for the following major services:
- communications exchange equipment denominated in US dollars;
- property leases in our controlled entity; Telstra (PSINet) Limited;
- computer mainframes, computer processing equipment and other related equipment.

The average lease term is:
- eleven years for communications exchange equipment denominated in US dollars;
- eighteen years for property leases; and
- three years for computer mainframe and associated equipment.

Interest rates for our finance leases are:
- US dollar communication assets between 4.3% and 5.1%;
- property leases interest rate of 10.3%; and
- computer mainframe, computer processing equipment and associated equipment weighted average interest rate of 16.6%.

Refer to note 12 for further details on communication assets and equipment that are held under finance lease. We do not have any significant contingent rentals or non-cancellable sub-leases in our finance leases.

Source: Telstra Corporation Ltd (2005).

Figure 14.3 provides an illustration of the disclosures required by IAS 17.

	IAS 17 para. no.
Note 1: Summary of accounting policies (extract)	
Leasing Leases are classified as finance leases whenever the terms of the lease transfer substantially all the risks and rewards of ownership to the lessee. All other leases are classified as operating leases. *The entity as a lessee* Assets held under finance leases are recognised as assets of the entity at their fair value at the date of acquisition or, if lower, at the present value of the minimum lease payments. The corresponding liability to the lessor is included in the balance sheet as a finance lease liability. Lease payments are apportioned between finance charges and reduction of the lease liability to achieve a constant rate of interest on the remaining balance of the liability. Finance charges are charged directly against income unless they are directly attributable to qualifying assets, in which case they are capitalised in accordance with the entity's general policy on borrowing costs.	*31(e)*
Note 16: Property, plant and equipment (extract)	
The carrying amount of the entity's plant and equipment includes an amount of $46 479 (2006: $65 968) relating to leased assets.	

Note 36: Finance lease liabilities

	Minimum lease payments **2007**	PV of payments **2007**	Minimum lease payments 2006	PV of payments 2006	
Amounts payable under finance leases:					*31(b)*
Within one year	22 000	20 102	22 000	18 787	
After one year but not more than five years	7 500	7 010	29 500	27 112	
Total minimum lease payments	29 500	27 112	51 500	45 899	
Less Finance charges	(2 389)		(5 601)		
Present value of minimum lease payments	27 112		45 899		

In respect of finance leases, the following item has been recognised as an expense during the period:			*31(c)*
	2007	2006	
Contingent rent	1 200	0	

FIGURE 14.3   Illustrative disclosures required by IAS 17 for lessees of finance leases

LO 6

14.7 Accounting for finance leases by lessors

When a lease is classified as a finance lease, the lessor will need to 'derecognise' the leased asset and record a lease receivable.

14.7.1 Initial recognition

In theory, the classification process required by IAS 17 should result in identical classifications by both lessors and lessee. In reality, differing circumstances may result in the same lease being classified differently; for example, where the lessor benefits from a residual value guarantee provided by a party unrelated to the lessee (para. 9).

Paragraph 36 of IAS 17 requires the lessor to recognise assets held under a finance lease in its balance sheet and present them as a receivable at an amount equal to the net investment in the lease. The net investment in the lease is defined in paragraph 4 as the gross investment in the lease discounted at the interest rate implicit in the lease, with the gross investment being equal to:

(a) the minimum lease payments receivable by the lessor under a finance lease; and
(b) any unguaranteed residual value accruing to the lessor.

This value would normally equate to the fair value of the asset at the inception of the lease. Initial direct costs, except those incurred by manufacturer or dealer lessors, are included in the initial measurement of the finance lease receivable and reduce the amount of interest revenue recognised over the lease term. The definition of interest rate implicit in the lease automatically includes initial direct costs in the finance lease receivable, so there is no need to add them separately (para. 38). Lessees are required to recognise assets and liabilities associated with finance leases at the commencement of the lease term but no date for recognition is specified for lessors; presumably, it would be the same date.

The recognition of the fair value of the leased asset as a receivable raises an interesting issue in that the 'receivable', for those leases with no purchase option, has both a monetary component (the rent payments) and non-monetary component (the return of the asset). The problem with this 'combination asset' is that IAS 32 requires specific disclosures to be made for the rent part of the receivable, which is a financial asset as defined by that standard, but does not require disclosures with respect to the non-monetary component. Additionally, these components are subject to different risks, and recording both as an ostensible financial asset may mislead financial report users.

14.7.2   Subsequent measurement

As the lease payments are received from the lessee over the lease term, the receipts need to be analysed into the following components:

• reduction of the lease receivable
• interest revenue earned
• reimbursement of costs paid on behalf of the lessee
• receipt of contingent rent.

The latter two are easily determined by reference to the lease agreement, but the first two need to be calculated in a similar fashion to that used by the lessor. The lease receivable recognised at the commencement of the lease term represents the present value of future lease payments relating to the use of the asset. This present value is determined by applying the interest rate implicit in the lease. Thus, the interest revenue can be obtained by applying the same rate to the outstanding lease receivable at the beginning of the payment period. A receipts schedule can be used to determine the interest revenue and the reduction in the receivable over the lease period.

14.7.3   Accounting for executory costs and contingent rentals

IAS 17 is silent on the treatment of contingent rent and the reimbursements of costs incurred on behalf of the lessee. However, as these receipts meet the definition of income in the Framework, contingent rents should be recognised as revenue in the period they were earned, and reimbursements should be recorded as revenue in the same period in which the related expenses are incurred.

ILLUSTRATIVE EXAMPLE 14.3

Accounting for finance leases by lessors

On 30 June 2005, Edmonton Ltd leased a vehicle to Calgary Ltd. Edmonton Ltd had purchased the vehicle on that day for its fair value of $89 721. The lease agreement, which cost Edmonton Ltd $1457 to have drawn up, contained the following clauses:

Lease term	4 years
Annual payment, payable in advance on 30 June each year	$23 900
Economic life of vehicle	6 years
Estimated residual value at end of economic life	$2 000
Estimated residual value at end of lease term	$15 000
Residual value guaranteed by lessee	$7 500

The lease is cancellable, but cancellation will incur a monetary penalty equivalent to two years rental payments. Included in the annual payment is an amount of $1900 to cover reimbursement for the costs of insurance and maintenance paid by the lessor. The directors of Calgary Ltd have indicated that they will return the asset to Edmonton Ltd at the end of the lease term.

Classification of the lease by the lessor

Edmonton Ltd would apply IAS 17 guidelines and classify the lease as a finance lease. See illustrative example 14.1 for workings.

The lease receipts schedule based on annual payments of $22 000 for the vehicle and an interest rate implicit in the lease of 7% shows:

Edmonton Ltd Lease receipts schedule			
	Minimum lease receipts[1]	Interest revenue[2]	Reduction in receivable[3]	Balance of receivable[4]
---	---	---	---	---
30 June 2005				91 178[5]
30 June 2005	22 000	–	22 000	69 178
30 June 2006	22 000	4 842	17 158	52 020
30 June 2007	22 000	3 641	18 359	33 661
30 June 2008	22 000	2 356	19 644	14 017
30 June 2009	15 000	983	14 017	–
	103 000	11 822	91 178	–

Notes:
1. Four annual receipts of $22 000 payable in advance on 30 June of each year, plus a residual value of $15 000 (of which $7500 is guaranteed by the lessee) on the last day of the lease.
2. Interest revenue = balance of receivable each year multiplied by 7%. No interest revenue is earned in the first year because the payment is received at the inception of the lease.

3. Reduction in receivable = minimum lease receipts less interest revenue. The total of this column must equal the initial receivable, which may require rounding the final interest revenue figure.
4. The balance is reduced each year by the amount in column 3.
5. Initial receivable = fair value of $89 721 plus initial direct costs of $1457. This figure equals the present value of minimum lease payments receivable and the present value of the unguaranteed residual value.

The lease receipts schedule is used to prepare lease journal entries and disclosure notes each year, as shown below:

Edmonton Ltd General journal			
Year ended 30 June 2005 30 June 2005 Vehicle Cash (Purchase of motor vehicle)	Dr Cr	89 721	89 721
Lease receivable Vehicle (Lease of vehicle to Calgary Ltd)	Dr Cr	89 721	89 721
Lease receivable Cash (Payment of initial direct costs)	Dr Cr	1 457	1 457
Cash Lease receivable Reimbursement in advance (Receipt of first lease payment)	Dr Cr Cr	23 900	22 000 *1 900

*The reimbursement of executory cost has been carried forward to 2006, when Edmonton Ltd will pay the costs.

Year ended 30 June 2006 1 July 2005 Reimbursement in advance Reimbursement revenue (Reversal of accrual)	Dr Cr	1 900	1 900
30 June 2006 Insurance and maintenance Cash (Payment of costs on behalf of lessee)	Dr Cr	1 900	1 900
Cash Lease receivable Interest revenue Reimbursement in advance (Receipt of second lease payment)	Dr Cr Cr Cr	23 900	17 158 4 842 1 900

Year ended 30 June 2007			
1 July 2006			
Reimbursement in advance	Dr	1 900	
Reimbursement revenue	Cr		1 900
(Reversal of accrual)			
30 June 2007			
Insurance and maintenance	Dr	1 900	
Cash	Cr		1 900
(Payment of costs on behalf of lessee)			
Cash	Dr	23 900	
Lease receivable	Cr		18 359
Interest revenue	Cr		3 641
Reimbursement in advance	Cr		1 900
(Receipt of third lease payment)			
Year ended 30 June 2008			
1 July 2007			
Reimbursement in advance	Dr	1 900	
Reimbursement revenue	Cr		1 900
(Reversal of accrual)			
30 June 2008			
Insurance and maintenance	Dr	1 900	
Cash	Cr		1 900
(Payment of costs on behalf of lessee)			
Cash	Dr	23 900	
Lease receivable	Cr		19 644
Interest revenue	Cr		2 356
Reimbursement in advance	Cr		1 900
(Receipt of fourth lease payment)			
Year ended 30 June 2009			
1 July 2008			
Reimbursement in advance	Dr	1 900	
Reimbursement revenue	Cr		1 900
(Reversal of accrual)			
30 June 2009			
Insurance and maintenance	Dr	1 900	
Cash	Cr		1 900
(Payment of costs on behalf of lessee)			
Vehicle	Dr	15 000	
Interest revenue	Cr		983
Lease receivable	Cr		14 017
(Return of vehicle at end of lease)			

14.7.4 The initial direct costs anomaly

The inclusion (by the standard setters) of initial direct costs incurred by lessors in the definition of the interest rate implicit in the lease creates an interest rate differential between lessee and lessor where a lease agreement transfers all of the risks and rewards related to an asset.

To illustrate: consider the same situation as described in illustrative example 14.3 but increasing the guaranteed residual value to $15 000 (100% of the residual), which effectively transfers all of the benefits of the vehicle from Edmonton Ltd to Calgary Ltd. The present value of the minimum lease payments would then be:

$$\text{PV of MLP} = \$22\,000 + (\$22\,000 \times 2.6243\ [T_2\ 7\%\ 3y] + \$15\,000 \times 0.7629\ [T_1\ 7\%\ 4y])$$
$$= \$22\,000 + \$57\,735 + \$11\,443$$
$$= \$91\,178$$

This figure equals the fair value of the asset $89 721 plus the initial direct costs incurred by the lessor of $1457.

However, paragraph 20 of IAS 17 requires lessees to recognise, at the inception of the lease, an asset and a liability equal to the fair value of the leased asset or, if *lower*, the present value of the minimum lease payments. As the present value of the minimum lease payments using the 7% interest rate implicit in the lease is *higher* than the asset's fair value, it cannot be recognised by the lessee even though it would be recognised by the lessor. The lessee, Calgary Ltd, can only recognise a lease asset and liability of $89 721, and must recalculate the interest rate implicit in the lease in order to determine interest expense charges over the lease term.

The interest rate that discounts the lease payments to $89 721 is 8%, so Calgary Ltd will calculate its interest at 8% and Edmonton Ltd will calculate its interest revenue at 7%. The differential represents the recovery of the initial direct costs by Edmonton Ltd via the lease payments received.

14.7.5 Disclosures required

Paragraph 47 of IAS 17 requires that, in addition to disclosures required by IAS 32, the following information must be disclosed separately in the financial report in respect of finance leases:
- a reconciliation between the gross investment in the lease and the present value of the minimum lease payments at the balance sheet date
- the gross investment in the lease and the present value of minimum lease payments receivable at the balance sheet date, for each of the following periods:
  - not later than one year
  - later than one year and not later than five years
  - later than five years
- unearned finance income
- the unguaranteed residual values accruing to the benefit of the lessor
- the accumulated allowance for uncollectable minimum lease payments receivable
- contingent rents recognised as income in the period
- a general description of the lessor's material leasing arrangements.

Figure 14.4 provides an illustration of the disclosures required by IAS 17. The information used in this figure is derived from the Edmonton Ltd lease shown in illustrative example 14.3.

	IAS 17 para. no.
Note 1: Summary of accounting policies (extract)	

Leasing
Leases are classified as finance leases whenever the terms of the lease transfer substantially all the risks and rewards of ownership to the lessee. All other leases are classified as operating leases.   *47(f)*

The entity as a lessor
Amounts due from lessees under finance leases are recorded as a receivable at the amount of the entity's net investment in the leases. Finance lease income is allocated to accounting periods, so as to reflect a constant periodic rate of return on the entity's net investment outstanding in respect of the leases.

Note 36: Finance lease receivables

	Investment in lease **2007**	PV of receivables **2007**	Investment in lease 2006	PV of receivables 2006	
Amounts payable under finance leases:					*47(a)*
Within one year	22 000	19 644	22 000	18 359	
After one year but not more than five years	15 000	14 017	37 000	33 661	
Total minimum lease payments receivable	37 000	33 661	59 000	52 020	
Less Unearned finance income	(3 339)		(6 980)		*47(b)*
Present value of minimum lease payments	33 661		52 020		

Unguaranteed residual values of assets leased under finance leases at the balance sheet date are estimated at $7500 (2006: $7500)	*47(c)*
In respect of finance leases, contingent rents amounting to $1200 (2006: nil) were recognised as income during the period.	*47(e)*

FIGURE 14.4   Illustrative disclosures required by IAS 17 for lessors of finance leases

14.8 Accounting for finance leases by manufacturer or dealer lessors

When manufacturers or dealers offer customers the choice of either buying or leasing an asset, a lease arrangement gives rise to two types of income:
• profit or loss equivalent to the outright sale of the asset being leased, and
• finance income over the lease term.
Accounting for the lease is identical to that required by non-manufacturer/dealer lessors except for an initial entry to recognise profit or loss and the fact that initial direct costs are not included in the lease receivable amount.

IAS 17, paragraph 42, requires manufacturers and lessors to recognise selling profit or loss at the commencement of the lease, in accordance with the policy followed by the entity for outright sales. Where artificially low interest rates have been offered to entice the customer to enter the lease, the selling profit recorded must be restricted to that which would apply if a market rate of interest had been charged.

Hence, as well as recognising the lease receivable, the manufacturer or dealer records the profit or loss on sale (at market interest rates) at the commencement of the lease. The sales revenue recognised is equal to the fair value of the asset or, if lower, the minimum lease payments computed at a market rate of interest. The cost of sale expense is the cost or carrying amount of the leased property less the present value of any unguaranteed residual value. Sales revenue less cost of sales expense equals selling profit or loss. Additionally, paragraph 42 of IAS 17 requires the initial direct costs incurred by the manufacturer or dealer in negotiating and arranging the lease to be recognised as an expense when the profit is recognised. Such costs are regarded as part of earning the profit on sale rather than a cost of leasing (para. 46).

ILLUSTRATIVE EXAMPLE 14.4

Calculating and recognising profit on sale with initial direct costs

Saskatoon Ltd manufactures specialised moulding machinery for both sale and lease. On 1 July 2006, Saskatoon leased a machine to Grand Rapids Ltd, incurring $1500 in costs to negotiate, prepare and execute the lease document. The machine cost Saskatoon Ltd $195 000 to manufacture, and its fair value at the inception of the lease was $212 515. The interest rate implicit in the lease is 10%, which is in line with current market rates. Under the terms of the lease, Grand Rapids Ltd has guaranteed $25 000 of the asset's expected residual value of $37 000 at the end of the five-year lease term.

After classifying the lease as a finance lease, Saskatoon Ltd passes the following entries on 1 July 2006:

Lease receivable[1]	Dr	212 515	
Sales revenue[2]	Cr		205 063
Cost of sales[3]	Dr	187 548	
Inventory[4]	Cr		195 000
(Initial recognition of lease receivable and recording sale of machine)			
Lease costs	Dr	1 500	
Cash	Cr		1 500
(Payment of initial direct costs)			

Notes:
1. The lease receivable represents the net investment in the lease and is equal to the fair value of the leased machine.
2. Sales revenue represents the present value of the minimum lease payments, which in this situation is less than the fair value of the asset due to the existence of an unguaranteed residual value.
3. Cost of sales represents the cost of the leased machine ($195 000) less the present value of the unguaranteed residual value ($12 000 × 0.620 921 = $7452).
4. Inventory is reduced by the cost of the leased machine.

LO 7

14.9 Accounting for operating leases

Operating leases are those where substantially all the risks and rewards incident to ownership remain with the lessor. IAS 17 requires that such arrangements are treated as rental agreements, with all payments treated as income or expense by the respective parties.

14.9.1 Accounting treatment

Lessees

Paragraph 33 of IAS 17 requires the lessee to recognise lease payments as an expense on a straight-line basis over the lease term unless another systematic basis is more representative of the time pattern of the user's benefit.

Lessors

Lease receipts

Paragraph 50 of IAS 17 requires lessors to account for lease receipts from operating leases as income on a straight-line basis over the lease term unless another systematic basis is more representative of the time pattern in which the benefit derived from the leased asset is diminished.

Initial direct costs

Any initial direct costs incurred by lessors in negotiating operating leases are to be added to the carrying amount of the leased asset and recognised as an expense over the lease term on the same basis as the lease income (IAS 17, para. 52). The initial direct costs are then capitalised into a deferred costs account and disclosed as follows:

Asset	$XXX
Less Accumulated depreciation	XXX
	XXX
Plus Initial direct costs	XXX
	XXX

As the IAS 17 definition of initial direct costs excludes costs incurred by manufacturers and dealers in negotiating and executing a lease, paragraph 52 would apply only to costs incurred by non-dealer/manufacturer lessors.

Depreciation of leased assets

Paragraph 49 of IAS 17 requires the leased asset to be presented in the balance sheet according to the nature of the asset. According to paragraph 53, depreciation of assets provided under operating leases should be consistent with the lessor's normal depreciation policy for similar assets, and should be calculated in accordance with IAS 16 and IAS 38.

ILLUSTRATIVE EXAMPLE 14.5

Accounting for operating leases

On 1 July 2007, Medicine Hat Ltd leased a bobcat from Yellowknife Finance Ltd. The bobcat cost Yellowknife Finance Ltd $35 966 on that same day. The finance lease agreement, which cost Yellowknife Finance Ltd $381 to have drawn up, contained the following clauses.

→

Lease term	3 years
Estimated economic life of the bobcat	10 years
The lease is cancellable	
Annual rental payment, in arrears (commencing 30/6/07)	$3 900
Residual value at end of the lease term	$24 500
Residual guaranteed by Medicine Hat Ltd	$0
Interest rate implicit in lease	6%

IAS 17 requires that the lease be classified as either a finance or an operating lease based on the extent to which the risks and rewards associated with the vehicle have been effectively transferred between Medicine Hat Ltd and Yellowknife Finance Ltd.

Is the lease non-cancellable?

The lease agreement is cancellable; either party can walk away from the arrangement without penalty.

Is ownership expected to be transferred at the end of the lease term?

Medicine Hat Ltd expects to return the bobcat to Yellowknife Finance Ltd.

Is the lease term a major part of the economic life of the leased asset?

The lease term is three years, which is only 30% of the bobcat's economic life of 10 years. Therefore, it would appear that the lease arrangement is not for the major part of the asset's life.

Is the present value of the minimum lease payments substantially all of the fair value of the leased asset?

Minimum lease payments

The minimum lease payments consist of three payments, in arrears, of $3900. There are no contingent rentals, executory costs or guaranteed residual value.

Present value of minimum lease payments

$$
\begin{aligned}
\text{PV of MLP} &= \$3900 \times 2.6730 \ [3 \text{ years } T_2 \ 6\%] \\
&= \$10\,425 \\
\text{PV/FV} &= \$10\,425/\$35\,966 \\
&= 29\%
\end{aligned}
$$

Is the substance of the transaction such that substantially all of the risks and rewards incident to ownership have been transferred? The shortness of the lease term compared to the asset's economic life indicates that it is in substance an operating lease.

Classification of the lease

On the basis of the evidence available, there has not been an effective transfer of substantially all of the risks and rewards associated with the bobcat to the lessee. Hence, the lease should be classified and accounted for as an *operating lease*.

Journal entries

The following journal entries would be passed in the books of both the lessor and the lessee for the year ended 30 June 2008:

Medicine Hat Ltd General journal			
30 June 2008 Lease expense Cash (Payment of first year's rental)	Dr Cr	3 900	3 900

Yellowknife Finance Ltd General journal			
1 July 2007 Plant and equipment Cash (Purchase of bobcat)	Dr Cr	35 966	35 966
Deferred initial direct costs – Plant and equipment Cash (Initial direct costs incurred for lease)	Dr Cr	381	381
30 June 2008 Cash Lease income (Receipt of first year's rental)	Dr Cr	3 900	3 900

Lease expense
    Deferred initial direct costs
    – Plant and equipment
(Recognition of initial direct cost:
$381/3 years)
	Dr
	
	Cr
		127	127

Depreciation expense Accumulated depreciation (Depreciation charge for the period: $35 966/10)	Dr Cr	3 597	3 597

14.9.2 Disclosures required

Lessees

Paragraph 35 of IAS 17 requires lessees, in addition to meeting the requirements of IAS 32, to disclose the following information in respect of operating leases:

(a) the total of future minimum lease payments under non-cancellable operating leases for each of the following periods:
    (i) not later than one year;
    (ii) later than one year and not later than five years;
    (iii) later than five years.

(b) the total of future minimum sublease payments expected to be received under non-cancellable subleases at the balance sheet date.

(c) lease and sublease payments recognised as an expense in the period, with separate amounts for minimum lease payments, contingent rents, and sublease payments.

(d) a general description of the lessee's significant leasing arrangements ...

The key feature of these disclosures is the identification of future commitments with respect to those operating leases which are non-cancellable. This information allows users of financial statements to factor in lease expenses against expected future profits, and alerts potential creditors to the fact that some future cash flows are not available to service new liabilities.

Figure 14.5 provides an illustration of the disclosures required by IAS 17.

		IAS 17 para. no.
Note 1: Summary of accounting policies (extract)		
Leasing Leases are classified as finance leases whenever the terms of the lease transfer substantially all the risks and rewards of ownership to the lessee. All other leases are classified as operating leases.		*35(d)*
The entity as a lessee Rentals payable under operating leases are charged to income on a straight-line basis over the term of the relevant lease.		
Note 43: Operating lease arrangements		
Minimum lease payments recorded as expense amounted to $167 500 (2006: $152 100) for the period.		*35(c)*

Future minimum lease payments under non-cancellable operating leases are as follows:

	2007	2006	
Within one year	70 000	51 700	*35(a)*
After one year but not more than five years	115 500	100 000	
More than five years	76 200	64 800	
	261 700	216 500	

FIGURE 14.5   Illustrative disclosures required by IAS 17 for lessees of operating leases

Lessors

Paragraph 56 of IAS 17 requires lessors to make the following disclosures, in addition to those required by IAS 32, with respect to operating leases:

(a) the future minimum lease payments under non-cancellable operating leases in the aggregate and for each of the following periods:
  (i) not later than one year;
  (ii) later than one year and not later than five years;
  (iii) later than five years.

(b) total contingent rents recognised as income in the period.

(c) a general description of the lessee's leasing arrangements.

Figure 14.6 provides an illustration of the disclosures required by IAS 17.

	IAS 17 para. no.
Note 1: Summary of accounting policies (extract)	
Leasing Leases are classified as finance leases whenever the terms of the lease transfer substantially all the risks and rewards of ownership to the lessee. All other leases are classified as operating leases. *The entity as a lessor* Rental income from operating leases is recognised on a straight-line basis over the term of the relevant lease.	*56(c)*
Note 43: Operating lease arrangements	
Future minimum lease payments receivable under non-cancellable operating leases are as follows:	

	2007	2006	
Within one year	81 000	60 200	*56(a)*
After one year but not more than five years	317 900	324 000	
More than five years	153 900	228 800	
	552 800	613 000	

	IAS 17 para. no.
Contingent rent income amounting to $15 600 (2006: nil) was recognised during the period.	*56(b)*

FIGURE 14.6   Illustrative disclosures required by IAS 17 for lessors of operating leases

14.9.3   Accounting for lease incentives

In order to induce prospective lessees to enter into non-cancellable operating leases, lessors may offer lease incentives such as rent-free periods, upfront cash payments or contributions towards lessee expenses such as fit-out or removal costs. However attractive these incentives appear, it is unlikely that they are truly free because the lessor will structure the rental payments so as to recover the costs of the incentives over the lease term. Thus, rental payments will be higher than for leases that do not offer incentives.

IAS 17 is silent about incentives, and deals only with accounting for the rental payments made under the operating lease agreement. As a result, SIC 15 *Operating leases – Incentives* was issued in June 1998 to provide guidance on accounting for incentives by both lessors and lessees. Paragraph 3 of this interpretation requires that all incentives associated with an operating lease should be regarded as part of the net consideration agreed for the use of the leased asset, irrespective of the nature or form of the incentive or the timing of the lease payments.

- For lessors – the aggregate cost of the incentives is treated as a reduction in rental income over the lease term on a straight-line basis.
- For lessees – the aggregate benefit of incentives is treated as a reduction in rental expense over the lease term on a straight-line basis.

In both cases, another systematic basis can be used if it better represents the diminishment of the leased asset.

ILLUSTRATIVE EXAMPLE 14.6

Accounting for lease incentives

As an incentive to enter a four-year operating lease for a warehouse, Churchill Ltd receives an upfront cash payment of $600 upon signing an agreement to pay Orillia Ltd an annual rental of $11 150.

Churchill Ltd will make the following journal entries with respect to the lease incentive:

At inception of the lease			
Cash	Dr	600	
Incentive from lessor	Cr		600
(Recognition of liability to lessor)			
Payment entry (year 1)			
Lease expense	Dr	11 000	
Incentive from lessor*	Dr	150	
Cash	Cr		11 150
(Record payment of rent and reduction in liability)			

*Being 600/4.

Orillia Ltd will make the following journal entries with respect to the lease incentive:

At inception of the lease			
Incentive to lessee	Dr	600	
Cash	Cr		600
(Recognition of receivable)			
Receipt entry (year 1)			
Cash	Dr	11 150	
Incentive to lessee*	Cr		150
Rent income	Cr		11 000
(Record receipt of rent and reduction in receivable)			

*Being 600/4.

This broad-brush approach assumes that all incentives are the same, but a number of issues need to be addressed. In particular:

- the need to distinguish between 'capital' incentives such as property fit-outs, particularly in the retail industry, and 'cash' incentives such as rent-free periods
- the need to distinguish between property fit-outs that became part of the structure of a leased property and were owned by the lessor, and fit-outs that were owned by the lessee
- the difficulty of determining in practice whether market rentals were being paid by major tenants who had received incentives to lease space in a property
- the need to exclude incentives provided to achieve a desired tenancy mix aimed at improving rentals under future leases of the property.

To date, these matters have not been considered by the IASB.

14.10 Accounting for sale and leaseback transactions

A 'sale and leaseback' is a lease transaction that creates an accounting problem for lessees. Effectively, this type of arrangement involves the sale of an asset that is then leased back from the purchaser for all or part of its remaining economic life. Hence, the original owner becomes the lessee but the asset itself does not move. In substance, the lessee gives up legal ownership but still retains control over some or all of the asset's future economic benefits via the lease agreement. Generally, the asset is sold at a price equal to or greater than its fair value, and is leased back for lease payments sufficient to repay the purchaser for the cash invested plus a reasonable return. Therefore, the lease payment and the sale price are usually interdependent because they are negotiated as a package (IAS 17, para. 58).

Entities normally enter into sale and leaseback arrangements to generate immediate cash flows while still retaining the use of the asset. Such arrangements are particularly attractive where the fair value of an asset is considerably higher than its carrying amount, or where a large amount of capital is tied up in property and plant.

The major accounting issue revolves around the sale rather than the lease component of the transaction. The lease is classified and accounted for in exactly the same fashion as normal lease transactions, but accounting for the sale transaction differs according to whether the lease is classified as a finance lease or an operating lease.

14.10.1 Finance leases

According to IAS 17, paragraph 59:

> If a sale and leaseback transaction results in a finance lease, any excess of sales proceeds over the carrying amount shall not be immediately recognised as income by a seller-lessee. Instead, it shall be deferred and amortised over the lease term.

This accounting treatment is justified on the basis that the leaseback of the asset negates the sale transaction. In other words, there was a finance agreement between the lessor and the lessee – not a sale – with the asset used as security. Paragraph 60 of IAS 17 states that, for this reason 'it is not appropriate to regard an excess of sales proceeds over the carrying amount as income'. The accounting standard provides no guidance on how the deferred income is to be classified in the balance sheet. In this chapter, any deferred income is recognised separately and classified as 'other' liabilities on the balance sheet. Amortisation is on a straight-line basis over the lease term.

ILLUSTRATIVE EXAMPLE 14.7

Sale and leaseback

In an attempt to alleviate its liquidity problems, Banff Ltd entered into an agreement on 1 July 2007 to sell its processing plant to Lethbridge Ltd for $3.5 million (which is the fair value of the plant). At the date of sale, the plant had a carrying amount of $2.75 million. Lethbridge Ltd immediately leased the processing plant back to Banff Ltd. The terms of the lease agreement were:

Lease term	6 years
Economic life of plant	8 years
Annual rental payment, in arrears (commencing 30/6/08)	$700 000
Residual value of plant at end of lease term (fully guaranteed)	$500 000
Interest rate implicit in the lease	10%

The lease is non-cancellable. The annual rental payment includes $35 000 to reimburse the lessor for maintenance costs incurred on behalf of the lessee.

Accounting for the sale of the processing plant

Step 1 – Classify the leaseback

Banff Ltd must determine whether the leaseback has resulted in the company retaining substantially all of the risks and rewards associated with the processing plant, even though legal title has passed to Lethbridge Ltd, before classifying the lease as a finance lease in accordance with IAS 17 requirements.

Based on the following evidence, both lessor and lessee should conclude that the lease should be classified as a *finance lease*:

- the lease is non-cancellable
- ownership is not expected to be transferred at the end of the lease term
- the lease term is a major part of the economic life of the leased asset
- the present value of the minimum lease payments is substantially all of the fair value of the leased asset. It was calculated as follows:

$$
\begin{aligned}
\text{PV of MLP} &= \$665\,000 \times 4.3553 \quad + \quad \$500\,000 \times 0.5645 \\
&= \$2\,896\,275 \quad + \quad \$282\,250 \\
&= \$3\,178\,525 \\
\text{PV/FV} &= \$3\,178\,525/\$3\,500\,000 \\
&= 90.8\%
\end{aligned}
$$

Step 2 – Record the 'sale' transaction

This illustrative example will show only those journal entries relating to the sale of the processing plant to Lethbridge Ltd. The lease would be recorded as shown in illustrative example 14.2.

Banff Ltd General journal			

Year ended 30 June 2008
1 July 2007
Cash
    Deferred gain on sale
    Processing plant
(Sale of plant under sale and leaseback agreement)
	Dr
	Cr
	Cr
		3 500 000	750 000
			2 750 000

30 June 2008 Deferred gain on sale Gain on sale of leased plant (Amortisation of deferred gain: $750 000/6)	Dr Cr	125 000	125 000

The deferred gain is recognised as income on a straight-line basis over the lease term.

14.10.2   Operating leases

All operating leases are accounted for in the same way regardless of whether or not a sale and leaseback transaction is involved. The only accounting issue involves the initial recognition of the sale transaction.

The accounting treatment of the gain or loss on sale is determined by the relationship between the sale price of the asset and the asset's fair value on the date of sale. Essentially, a gain or loss on sale can be recognised immediately only when it equates to the gain or loss that would have been earned on a sale at fair value. Excess or reduced gains or losses are to be deferred and amortised over the lease term. Table 14.1 appears as an appendix to IAS 17, and sets out the alternative treatments as required by paragraphs 61–3 of the standard.

TABLE 14.1	Alternative treatments of gain or loss on sale		
Sale price at fair value (paragraph 61)	Carrying amount equal to fair value	Carrying amount less than fair value	Carrying amount above fair value
Profit	No profit	Recognise profit immediately	Not applicable
Loss	No loss	Not applicable	Recognise loss immediately
Sale price below fair value (paragraph 61)			
Profit	No profit	Recognise profit immediately	No profit (note 1)
Loss *not* compensated for by future lease payments at below market price	Recognise loss immediately	Recognise loss immediately	(note 1)
Loss compensated for by future lease payments at below market price	Defer and amortise loss	Defer and amortise loss	(note 1)
Sale price above fair value (paragraph 61)			
Profit	Defer and amortise profit	Defer and amortise excess of selling price over fair value. Recognise any excess of fair value over carrying amount immediately (note 3)	Defer and amortise profit (note 2)
Loss	No loss	No loss	(note 1)

Source: Adapted from IAS 17, appendix.

Notes:

1. These parts of the table represent circumstances dealt with in paragraph 63 of the standard. Paragraph 63 requires the carrying amount of an asset to be written down to fair value where it is subject to a sale and leaseback. This therefore results in a carrying amount equal to fair value.
2. Profit is the difference between the fair value and sale price because the carrying amount would have been written down to fair value in accordance with paragraph 63.
3. The excess profit (the excess of selling price over fair value) is deferred and amortised over the period for which the asset is expected to be used. Any excess of fair value over the carrying amount is recognised immediately.

14.10.3 Disclosures required

Sale and leaseback transactions are subject to the same disclosure requirements prescribed for lessees and lessors in relation to both operating and finance leases. Unique or unusual provisions of the agreement should be disclosed as part of the required description of material leasing arrangements. Additionally, sale and leaseback transactions may fall under the separate disclosure criteria in IAS 1 *Presentation of Financial Statements* with respect to gains or losses on the sale of assets.

14.10.4 Deferral and amortisation — some theoretical concerns

The accounting treatment mandated by IAS 17, paragraphs 59 and 61, relating to any gain or loss on the sale of an asset in a sale and leaseback transaction may result in the deferral of such gains or losses and their amortisation over the lease term. The Framework does not support this accounting treatment, because it results in reporting debit and credit balances in the balance sheet that do not meet the definitions of assets and liabilities. In illustrative example 12.7, Banff Ltd records a 'deferred gain' of $750 000 on 1 July 2007, but is this a liability? The Framework in paragraph 49 defines a liability as:

> a present obligation of the entity arising from past events, the settlement of which is expected to result in an outflow from the entity of resources embodying economic benefits.

The $750 000 credit balance recorded by the lessee certainly arises from a past transaction − the sale of the asset − but, as there is no future sacrifice in respect of this amount, it should not be classified and reported as a liability. Income is defined in paragraph 70 of the Framework as follows:

> Income is increases in economic benefits during the accounting period in the form of inflows or enhancements of assets or decreases of liabilities that result in increases in equity, other than those relating to contributions from equity participants.

The sale of its asset by Banff Ltd provides a cash inflow of $3.5 million and the loss of $2.75 million in future benefits, resulting in a net increase in equity of $750 000. This transaction clearly gives rise to income. The accounting treatment prescribed by IAS 17, paragraphs 59 and 61, results in entities incorrectly reporting income as liabilities, or expenses as assets. Accordingly, the profit reported in the income statement will be incorrect, as will the total asset and liability figures reported on the balance sheet. This 'error' situation will continue throughout the lease term as the 'deferred credit' or 'deferred debit' balances are amortised to profit and loss. Again, the rationale for this accounting treatment seems to be based on the notion that a lease is a quasi-sale transaction. There can be only one 'sale' recorded for a finance leaseback, and only a 'real' profit recorded for an operating leaseback. The reality, of course, is that the two transactions should be treated independently and recorded in accordance with the Framework.

LO 9   14.11 Likely future developments

The G4+1 1996 report *Accounting for leases: a new approach* identified the following unsatisfactory features of existing lease accounting standards (McGregor 1996, pp. 4–5):

- the standards do not require rights and obligations arising under operating leases to be recognised as assets and liabilities in the lessee's financial statements
- the standards have promoted the structuring of financial arrangements so as to meet the conditions for classification as operating leases, thus keeping these arrangements off balance sheet
- the accounting treatments detract from the comparability and usefulness of financial statements.

To this list could also be added:

- the creation of deferred debits and credits via accounting for sale and leaseback transactions, and initial direct costs of operating leases
- the exclusion of lease and licensing arrangements involving the exchange of intangible assets such as patents, copyright and mineral rights
- the recognition of residual interests in leased assets as receivables by lessors when such interests do not meet the definition of financial assets as per IAS 32.

Following on from the issue of the G4+1 paper, in 1999 the IASC issued *Leases: implementation of a new approach*, a discussion paper authored by the United Kingdom Accounting Standards Board on behalf of the international body. The discussion paper concluded that leases could be distinguished from executory contracts (contracts equally proportionately unperformed). The approach to lease accounting taken in the paper is based on the recognition that:

> leasing is different from and generally more flexible than other forms of asset financing – leases can be drawn up with terms that share asset risks and economic benefits between parties in any number of ways (sourced from Accounting Standards Board 1999, p. 28).

Hence, instead of applying artificial thresholds or classifications, the paper proposes that assets and liabilities arising under lease contracts be identified based on the fair values of the rights and obligations conveyed by the lease. Operating leases can give rise to such assets and liabilities. This approach should result in similar amounts being reported for similar leases.

The following accounting treatments are proposed in the discussion paper:

- Assets and liabilities should be recognised by a lessee in relation to the rights and obligations conveyed by a lease when the lessor has substantially performed its obligation to provide the lessee with access to the leased property for the lease term. Generally, this is when the leased property is delivered or otherwise made available to the lessee (3A, p. 60).
- The objective should be to record, at the beginning of the lease term, the fair value of the rights and obligations that are conveyed by the lease. Fair value is measured by the fair value of the consideration given, except where the fair value of the asset received is more clearly evident (3C, p. 60).
- The fair value of the rights obtained by the lessee cannot be less than the present value of the minimum lease payments required by the lease, assuming the lease is negotiated on an arm's-length basis (3D, p. 60).
- Two elements – a receivable in respect of payments required by the lease, and an interest in the residual value of the property – should be presented separately in the balance sheet by the lessors, reflecting the different property rights arising under the lease (8A, p. 153).
- The amounts receivable from the lessee should be recorded initially at the fair value of the consideration that the lessee has agreed to pay for the right to use the leased property (8B, p. 153).

These proposed changes would overcome the main criticisms of the current practice of accounting for leases. The classification decision would be replaced by a simple judgement relating to the lessor's performance under the lease agreement. These proposals should result in all lease assets and liabilities (subject to normal materiality considerations) being recognised and reported in the financial statements, irrespective of the nature or extent of the lease terms. Financial information should be more relevant when off-balance-sheet operating leases and leases of intangible assets are recognised and reported. Coincidentally, the changes will also remove incentives for management to structure leases so as to appear as operating leases. It may, of course, lead to a whole new industry devoted to making leases appear to be service contracts.

Since the release of this discussion paper, no further action has been taken. The United Kingdom Accounting Standards Board still leads the IASB's leasing project, but no timetable has been set for the project. An IASB project update issued in October 2005 indicated that the project was still continuing, and that the board has adopted a working assumption that 'assets and liabilities recognised in respect of leases should reflect the conveyance of the right of use and control of the associated future economic benefits for the period of the contract' (IASB 2005, p. 2). This approach is consistent with that proposed in the 1999 discussion paper. Thus, it would seem that the current standard will at some future time be completely overhauled and a new, more conceptually based approach taken to accounting for leases. A discussion paper is planned for publication in 2006.

14.12 Summary

This chapter analyses the content of IAS 17 *Leases* and provides guidance on its implementation. Accounting for leases requires management to exercise considerable judgement because the accounting standard adopts a principles-based approach that requires judgements concerning 'substance over form'. This means that judgement may initially be required to identify transactions that do not have the legal form of a lease but that, in substance, convey the right to use an asset in return for a series of payments and thus meet the IAS 17 definition of a lease. Each lease agreement is classified at the inception of the lease as either an operating lease or a finance lease. Accounting for finance leases requires the lessee to record a lease asset and a lease liability, both equal to the fair value of the leased asset or, if lower, the present value of the minimum lease payments at the inception of the lease. The lessor records its gross investment in the leased asset as a receivable. Accounting for operating leases requires lessees and lessors to record the lease payments as expense and income respectively in the period of payment. The accounting standard has been widely criticised for the classification requirement, which can result in similar leases being accounted for differently, and also for the fact that deferred debits and credits raised when accounting for certain sale and leaseback transactions under the standard do not meet the IASB Framework definitions of assets and liabilities. A review of the accounting standard is currently being undertaken by a project group of the international accounting body.

1. Leases are classified on the basis of 'substance over form'. What does this criterion mean and how does it relate to the capitalisation of finance leases?
2. What are 'minimum lease payments'?
3. What is meant by 'the interest rate implicit in a lease'?
4. If a lease agreement states that 'the lessee guarantees a residual value, at the end of the lease term, of $20 000', what does this mean?
5. Where a lessor incurs initial direct costs in establishing a lease agreement, how are these costs to be accounted for by the lessor?
6. If a lease has been capitalised as a finance lease, identify two circumstances in which the lease receivable raised by the lessor will differ from the lease asset raised by the lessee.
7. Explain how a profit made by a lessee on a sale and leaseback transaction is to be accounted for.
8. How, in accordance with IAS 17 requirements, are operating leases to be accounted for by lessors?
9. 'The accounting treatment required by IAS 17, paragraph 59, is not in accordance with the IASB Framework.' Discuss.
10. In the context of operating leases, what are lease incentives and how are they accounted for?

EXERCISES

EXERCISE 14.1 ★

Lease classification and determination of interest rates

This exercise contains four multiple choice questions. Select the correct answer and show any workings required.

1. Thunder Bay Ltd sells land that originally cost $150 000 to Victoria Ltd for $230 000 when the land's fair value is $215 000, and then enters into a cancellable lease agreement to use the land for two years at an annual rental of $2000. In the current year, how much profit would Thunder Bay Ltd record on the sale of the land?
   (a) $15 000
   (b) $80 000
   (c) $65 000
   (d) Nil

2. Using the information from part 1, how would Victoria Ltd record the annual cash received from Thunder Bay Ltd?
   (a) As rental revenue
   (b) As a reduction of the lease receivable
   (c) As rental expense
   (d) As interest revenue and a reduction of the lease receivable

3. On 1 July 2009, Sachs Harbour Ltd leases a machine with a fair value of $109 445 to Reliance Ltd for five years at an annual rental (in advance) of $25 000, and Reliance Ltd guarantees in full the estimated residual value of $15 000 on return of the asset. What would be the interest rate implicit in the lease?
   (a) 10%
   (b) 12%
   (c) 9%
   (d) 14%

4. Using the information from part 3, how would Reliance Ltd classify the lease?
   (a) As an operating lease
   (b) As a finance lease
   (c) As a sale and leaseback
   (d) As a lease incentive

EXERCISE 14.2   ★

Lease incentives

As an incentive to enter a non-cancellable operating lease for office premises for 10 years, the lessor has offered the lessee a rent-free period of two years. Rental payments under the lease commencing in year 3 are $5000 per annum.

Required
Prepare journal entries to account for the lease payment in year 3 of the lease in the books of both the lessor and the lessee.

EXERCISE 14.3   ★★

Finance lease — lessee

Trois Rivieres Ltd prepares the following lease payments schedule for the lease of a machine from Quebec Ltd. The machine has an economic life of six years. The lease agreement requires four annual payments of $33 000, and the machine will be returned to Quebec Ltd at the end of the lease term. The lease payments schedule is:

	MLP	Interest expense (10%)	Reduction in liability	Balance of liability
1 July 2009				98 512
1 July 2010	30 000	9 851	20 149	78 363
1 July 2011	30 000	7 836	22 164	56 199
1 July 2012	30 000	5 620	24 380	31 819
1 July 2013	35 000	3 181	31 819	–
	125 000	26 488	98 512	–

The following five multiple choice questions relate to the information provided above. Select the correct answer and show any workings required.

1. In its notes to the accounts at 30 June 2011, Trois Rivieres Ltd would disclose future lease payments of what amount?
   (a) $ 95 000
   (b) $ 65 000
   (c) $ 99 000
   (d) $104 000

2. For the year ended 30 June 2010, what would Trois Rivieres Ltd record in relation to the lease?
   (a) An interest payable of $26 488
   (b) An interest payable of $nil
   (c) An interest payable of $9851
   (d) An interest payable of $7836

3. How much annual depreciation expense would Trois Rivieres Ltd record?
   (a) $24 628
   (b) $16 419
   (c) $15 585
   (d) $23 378

4. If Quebec Ltd (the lessor) records a lease receivable of $102 327, the variance between this receivable and the liability of $98 512 recorded by Trois Rivieres Ltd could be due to what?
   (a) Initial direct costs paid by Quebec Ltd
   (b) An unguaranteed residual value
   (c) Both of the above
   (d) Neither of the above

5. Assume that the 1 July 2010 lease payment included an additional amount of $3000 for exceeding a limit for machine usage hours specified in the lease agreement. Trois Rivieres Ltd would account for this charge by recognising it as what?
   (a) An expense and disclosing the amount in the notes (if material)
   (b) Additional executory costs
   (c) Revenue
   (d) A reduction in the lease liability

EXERCISE 14.4 ★★   Lease identification

For the following arrangements, discuss whether they are 'in substance' lease transactions and thus fall under the ambit of IAS 17:

1. Entity A leases an asset to entity B, and obtains a non-recourse loan from a financial institution using the lease rentals and asset as collateral. Entity A sells the assets subject to the lease and the loan to a trustee, and leases the same asset back.
2. Entity A enters into an arrangement to buy petroleum products from entity B. The products are produced in a refinery built and operated by entity B on a site owned by entity A. While Entity B could provide the products from other refineries that it owns, it is not practical to do so. Entity B retains the right to sell products produced by the refinery to other customers, but there is only a remote possibility that it will do so. The arrangement requires entity A to make both fixed, unavoidable payments, and variable payments based on input costs at a target level of efficiency to entity B.
3. Entity A leases an asset to entity B for its entire economic life, and leases the same asset back under the same terms and conditions as the original lease. The two entities have a legally enforceable right to set off the amounts owing to one another, and an intention to settle these amounts on a net basis.
4. Entity A enters into a non-cancellable four-year lease with entity B for an asset with an expected economic life of ten years. Entity A has an option to renew the lease for a further four years at the end of the lease term. At the conclusion of the lease arrangement, the asset will revert back to entity B. In a separate agreement, entity B is granted a put option to sell the asset to entity A should its market value at the end of the lease be less than the residual value.

EXERCISE 14.5 ★★   Lease classification

Bower Ltd manufactures specialised moulding machinery for both sale and lease. On 1 July 2007, Bower Ltd leased a machine to Cuckoo Ltd. The machine being leased cost Bower Ltd $195 000 to make and its fair value at 1 July 2007 is considered to be $212 515. The terms of the lease are as follows:

The lease term is for five years, commencing on	1 July 2007
Annual lease payment, payable on 30 June each year	$57 500
Estimated useful life of machine (scrap value $2500)	8 years
Estimated residual value of machine at end of lease term	$37 000
Residual value guaranteed by Cuckoo Ltd	$25 000
Interest rate implicit in the lease	10%
The annual lease payment includes an amount of $7500 to cover annual maintenance and insurance costs.	
Cuckoo Ltd may cancel the lease but only with the permission of the lessor.	
Cuckoo Ltd intends to lease a new machine at the end of the lease term.	

Required
Classify the lease for both Bower Ltd and Cuckoo Ltd. Justify your answer.

EXERCISE 14.6   ★★★   Lease schedules and journal entries (year 1)

On 1 July 2007, Concrete Constructions Ltd leased a crane from Amazon Finance Ltd. The crane cost Amazon Finance Ltd $120 697, considered to be its fair value on that same day. The finance lease agreement contained the following clauses:

The lease term is for three years commencing on	1 July 2007
The lease is non-cancellable	
Annual lease payment, payable on 30 June each year	$39 000
Estimated useful life of crane	4 years
Estimated residual value of crane at end of lease term	$22 000
Residual value guaranteed by Concrete Constructions Ltd	$16 000
Interest rate implicit in the lease	7%
The lease was classified as a finance lease by both Concrete Constructions Ltd and Amazon Finance Ltd at 1 July 2007.	

Required

1. Prepare the lease schedules for both the lessee and the lessor.
2. Prepare the journal entries in the books of both the lessee and the lessor for the year ended 30 June 2008.

PROBLEMS

PROBLEM 14.1   ★   Finance lease — lessor

On 1 July 2005, Jane Smith decided she needed a new car. She went to the local car yard, Halifax Ltd, run by Fred Dealer. Jane discussed the price of a new Roadster Special with Fred, and they agreed on a price of $37 000. As Halifax Ltd had acquired the vehicle from the manufacturer for $30 000, Fred was pleased with the deal. On learning that Jane Smith wanted to lease the vehicle, Fred agreed to arrange for Moncton Ltd, a local finance company, to set up the lease agreement. Halifax Ltd then sold the car to Moncton Ltd for $37 000.

Moncton Ltd wrote a lease agreement, incurring initial direct costs of $1410 as a result. The lease agreement contained the following clauses:

Initial payment on 1 July 2005	$13 000
Payments on 1 July 2006 and 1 July 2007	$13 000
Guaranteed residual value at 30 June 2008	$10 000
Implicit interest rate in the lease	6%
The lease is non-cancellable.	

Moncton Ltd agreed to pay for the insurance and maintenance of the vehicle, the latter to be carried out by Halifax Ltd at regular intervals. The cost of these services is valued at $3000 per annum.

The vehicle had an expected useful life of four years. The expected residual value of the vehicle at 30 June 2008 was $12 000.

Costs of maintenance and insurance incurred by Moncton Ltd over the years ended 30 June 2006 to 30 June 2008 were $2810, $3020 and $2750 respectively. At 30 June 2008, Jane Smith returned the vehicle to Moncton Ltd, who sold the car for $9000 on 5 July 2008 and invoiced Jane Smith for the appropriate balance. Jane subsequently paid the debt on 13 July 2008.

Required
1. Assuming the lease is classified as a finance lease, prepare the journal entries in the books of Moncton Ltd in relation to the lease from 1 July 2005 to 31 July 2008.
2. In relation to finance leases, explain why the balance of the asset account raised by the lessee at the inception of the lease may differ from the balance of the receivable asset raised by the lessor.

PROBLEM 14.2 ★

Lease classification; accounting by lessee

On 1 July 2006, Moose Jaw Ltd leased a plastic moulding machine from Winnipeg Ltd. The machine cost Winnipeg $130 000 to manufacture and had a fair value of $154 109 on 1 July 2006. The lease agreement contained the following clauses:

Lease term	4 years
Annual rental payment, in advance on 1 July each year	$41 500
Residual value at end of the lease term	$15 000
Residual guaranteed by lessee	nil
Interest rate implicit in lease	8%
The lease is cancellable only with the permission of the lessor.	

The expected useful life of the machine is six years. Moose Jaw Ltd intends to return the machine to the lessor at the end of the lease term. Included in the annual rental payment is an amount of $1500 to cover the costs of maintenance and insurance paid for by the lessor.

Required
1. Classify the lease for both lessee and lessor based on the guidance provided in IAS 17. Justify your answer.
2. Prepare:
   (a) the lease schedules for the lessee (show all workings)
   (b) the journal entries in the books of the lessee for the year ended 30 June 2007.

PROBLEM 14.3 ★

Lease classification; accounting by lessor

Use the information contained in problem 14.2 for Moose Jaw Ltd to complete the following:
1. Classify the lease for both lessee and lessor based on the guidance provided in IAS 17. Justify your answer.
2. Prepare:
   (a) the lease schedules for the lessor (show all workings)
   (b) the journal entries in the books of the lessor for the year ended 30 June 2007.

PROBLEM 14.4 ★

Lease classification; accounting by lessor

On 1 July 2009, Haines Ltd leased a processing plant to Kitmat Ltd. The plant was purchased by Haines Ltd on 1 July 2009 for its fair value of $467 112. The lease agreement contained the clauses shown opposite.

Lease term	3 years
Economic life of plant	5 years
Annual rental payment, in arrears (commencing 30/06/2010)	$150 000
Residual value at end of the lease term	$90 000
Residual guaranteed by lessee	$60 000
Interest rate implicit in lease	7%
The lease is cancellable only with the permission of the lessor.	

Kitmat Ltd intends to return the processing plant to the lessor at the end of the lease term. The lease has been classified as a finance lease by both the lessee and the lessor.

Required
1. Prepare:
   (a) the lease payment schedule for the lessee (show all workings)
   (b) the journal entries in the books of the lessee for the year ended 30 June 2011.
2. Prepare:
   (a) the lease receipt schedule for the lessor (show all workings)
   (b) the journal entries in the books of the lessor for the year ended 30 June 2011.

PROBLEM 14.5 ★★ Lease classification; accounting for lessor and lessee

On 1 July 2008, Vancouver Ltd leased a photocopier from Kamloops Ltd, a company that manufactures, retails and leases copiers. The photocopier had cost Kamloops Ltd $30 000 to make but had a fair value on 1 July 2008 of $35 080. The lease agreement contained the following provisions:

Lease term	3 years
Annual payment, payable in advance on 1 July each year	$14 500
Economic life of the copier	4 years
Estimated residual value at the end of the lease term	
when the copier is returned to Kamloops Ltd	$3 000
Residual value guaranteed by Vancouver Ltd	$1 500
Interest rate implicit in the lease	10%
The lease is cancellable, provided another lease is immediately entered into.	

The annual payment included an amount of $2500 per annum to reimburse Kamloops Ltd for the cost of paper and toner supplied to Vancouver Ltd. Kamloops Ltd's solicitor prepared the lease agreement for a fee of $1365.

At the end of the lease term on 30 June 2011, Vancouver Ltd returned the copier to Kamloops Ltd, who sold the copier for $3000.

Required
1. Classify the lease for both the lessor and the lessee. Justify your answer.
2. Prepare the following:
   (a) For the lessee: the lease payment schedule and the journal entries for the year ended 30 June 2011 only.
   (b) For the lessor: the lease receipts schedule and the journal entries for the year ended 30 June 2009 only.

PROBLEM 14.6 ★★   Finance lease — lessee (including disclosures)

Ottawa Ltd decided to lease from Fredricton Ltd a motor vehicle that had a fair value at 30 June 2007 of $38 960. The lease agreement contained the following clauses:

Lease term (non-cancellable)	3 years
Annual rental payments (commencing 30/6/07)	$11 200
Guaranteed residual value (expected fair value at end of lease term)	$12 000
Extra rental per annum if the car is used outside the metropolitan area	$1 000

The expected useful life of the vehicle is five years. At the end of the three-year lease term, the car was returned to the lessor, who sold it for $10 000. The annual rental payments include an amount of $1200 to cover the cost of maintenance and insurance arranged and paid for by the lessor. The car was used outside the metropolitan area in the 2008–09 year. The lease is considered to be a finance lease.

Required
1. Prepare the journal entries for Ottawa Ltd from 30 June 2007 to 30 June 2010.
2. Prepare the relevant disclosures required under IAS 17 for the years ending 30 June 2008 and 30 June 2009.
3. How would your answer to part 1 change if the guaranteed residual value was only $10 000, and the expected fair value at the end of the lease term was $12 000?

PROBLEM 14.7 ★★★   Sale and leaseback

Montreal Ltd is asset rich but cash poor. In an attempt to alleviate its liquidity problems, it entered into an agreement on 1 July 2005 to sell its processing plant to Regina Ltd for $467 100. At the date of sale, the plant had a carrying amount of $400 000 and a future useful life of five years. Regina Ltd immediately leased the processing plant back to Montreal Ltd. The terms of the lease agreement were:

Lease term	3 years
Economic life of plant	5 years
Annual rental payment, in arrears (commencing 30/6/06)	$165 000
Residual value of plant at end of lease term	$90 000
Residual value guaranteed by Montreal Ltd	$60 000
Interest rate implicit in the lease	6%
The lease is cancellable, but only with the permission of the lessor.	

At the end of the lease term, the plant is to be returned to Regina Ltd. In setting up the lease agreement Regina Ltd incurred $9414 in legal fees and stamp duty costs. The annual rental payment includes $15 000 to reimburse the lessor for maintenance costs incurred on behalf of the lessee.

Required
1. Classify the lease for both lessor and lessee. Justify your answer.
2. Prepare a lease payments schedule and the journal entries in the books of Montreal Ltd for the year ending 30 June 2006. Show all workings.
3. Prepare a lease receipts schedule and the journal entries in the books of Regina Ltd for the year ending 30 June 2006. Show all workings.
4. Explain how and why your answer to parts 1 and 2 would change if the lease agreement could be cancelled at any time without penalty.
5. Explain how and why your answer to parts 1, 2 and 3 would change if the processing plant had been manufactured by Regina Ltd at a cost of $400 000.

PROBLEM 14.8 ★★★ Lease classification; accounting and disclosures

Toronto Ltd has entered into an agreement to lease a D9 bulldozer to Whitehorse Ltd. The lease agreement details are as follows:

Length of lease	5 years
Commencement date	1 July 2006
Annual lease payment, payable 30 June each year commencing 30 June 2007	$8 000
Fair value of the bulldozer at 1 July 2006	$34 797
Estimated economic life of the bulldozer	8 years
Estimated residual value of the plant at the end of its economic life	$2 000
Residual value at the end of the lease term, of which 50% is guaranteed by Whitehorse Ltd	$7 200
Interest rate implicit in the lease	9%

The lease is cancellable, but a penalty equal to 50% of the total lease payments is payable on cancellation. Whitehorse Ltd does not intend to buy the bulldozer at the end of the lease term. Toronto Ltd incurred $1000 to negotiate and execute the lease agreement. Toronto Ltd purchased the bulldozer for $34 797 just before the inception of the lease.

Required
1. State how both companies should classify the lease. Give reasons for your answer.
2. Prepare a schedule of lease payments for Whitehorse Ltd.
3. Prepare a schedule of lease receipts for Toronto Ltd.
4. Prepare journal entries to record the lease transactions for the year ended 30 June 2007 in the books of both companies.
5. Prepare an appropriate note to the financial statements of both companies as at 30 June 2007.

PROBLEM 14.9 ★★★ Finance lease with GRV and leaseback variations

On 1 July 2008, Valley Field Ltd acquired an item of plant for $31 864. On the same date, Valley Field Ltd entered into a lease agreement with Goja Haven Ltd in relation to the asset. According to the lease agreement, Goja Haven Ltd agreed to pay $12 000 immediately, with a further two payments of $12 000 on 1 July 2009 and 1 July 2010.

At 30 June 2011, the asset is to be returned to the lessor and its residual value is expected to be $6000. Goja Haven Ltd has agreed to guarantee the expected residual value at 30 June 2011. All insurance and maintenance costs are to be paid by Valley Field Ltd and are expected to amount to $2000 per annum. The costs of preparing the lease agreement amounted to $360. The interest rate implicit in the lease is 9%. The lease is classified as a finance lease. Plant is depreciable on a straight-line basis.

Required
1. Prepare a schedule of lease receipts for Valley Field Ltd and the journal entries for the year ended 30 June 2009.
2. Prepare a schedule of lease payments for Goja Haven Ltd and the journal entries for the year ended 30 June 2009.
3. Assume that Goja Haven Ltd guaranteed a residual value of only $4000. Prepare a lease schedule for both Valley Field Ltd and Goja Haven Ltd.
4. Instead of acquiring the plant for $31 864, assume that Valley Field Ltd manufactured the plant at a cost of $29 500 before entering into the lease agreement with Goja Haven Ltd. Prepare a schedule of lease receipts for Valley Field Ltd and the journal entries for the year ended 30 June 2009.

5. Assume that Goja Haven Ltd manufactured the plant itself at a cost of $29 500 and sold the plant to Valley Field Ltd for $31 864. Goja Haven Ltd then leased it back under the original terms of the finance lease, with Goja Haven Ltd guaranteeing a residual value of $4000. Prepare a lease schedule for both Valley Field Ltd and Goja Haven Ltd for the year ended 30 June 2009.

WEBLINK

Visit these websites for additional information:

www.iasb.org   www.iasplus.com
www.asic.gov.au   www.ifac.org
www.aasb.com.au   www.nzica.com
www.accaglobal.com   www.capa.com.my

REFERENCES

Accounting Standards Board UK 1999, *Leases: implementation of a new approach*, discussion paper prepared for the IASC, ASB Publications, Central Milton Keynes, UK.

G4+1 report — see McGregor 1996.

IASB 2005, *Project report*, International Accounting Standards Board UK, viewed 7 July 2006, <www.iasb.org>.

McGregor, W 1996, *Accounting for leases: a new approach — recognition by lessees of assets and liabilities arising under lease contracts*, FASB, July. Quoted material sourced from this publication.

Shanahan, J 1989, '$1 plus $1 equals a million-dollar lease', *Australian Business*, 14 June, pp. 79–80.

Telstra Corporation Ltd, 2005, *Annual report*, viewed 5 April 2006, <www.telstra.com.au>.

APPENDIX

APPENDIX A

Present value tables

TABLE A.1   Present value of $1: $PVIF = 1/(1 + k)^t$

Period	1%	2%	3%	4%	5%	6%	7%	8%	9%	10%	12%	14%	15%	16%	18%	20%	24%	28%	32%	36%
1	0.9901	0.9804	0.9709	0.9615	0.9524	0.9434	0.9346	0.9259	0.9174	0.9091	0.8929	0.8772	0.8696	0.8621	0.8475	0.8333	0.8065	0.7813	0.7576	0.7353
2	0.9803	0.9612	0.9426	0.9246	0.9070	0.8900	0.8734	0.8673	0.8417	0.8264	0.7972	0.7695	0.7561	0.7432	0.7182	0.6944	0.6504	0.6104	0.5739	0.5407
3	0.9706	0.9423	0.9151	0.8890	0.8638	0.8396	0.8163	0.7938	0.7722	0.7513	0.7118	0.6750	0.6575	0.6407	0.6086	0.5787	0.5245	0.4768	0.4348	0.3975
4	0.9610	0.9238	0.8885	0.8548	0.8227	0.7921	0.7629	0.7350	0.7084	0.6830	0.6355	0.5921	0.5718	0.5523	0.5158	0.4823	0.4230	0.3725	0.3294	0.2923
5	0.9515	0.9057	0.8626	0.8219	0.7835	0.7473	0.7130	0.6806	0.6499	0.6209	0.5674	0.5194	0.4972	0.4761	0.4371	0.4019	0.3411	0.2910	0.2495	0.2149
6	0.9420	0.8880	0.8375	0.7903	0.7462	0.7050	0.6663	0.6302	0.5963	0.5645	0.5066	0.4556	0.4323	0.4104	0.3704	0.3349	0.2751	0.2274	0.1890	0.1580
7	0.9327	0.8706	0.8131	0.7599	0.7107	0.6651	0.6227	0.5835	0.5470	0.5132	0.4523	0.3996	0.3759	0.3538	0.3139	0.2791	0.2218	0.1776	0.1432	0.1162
8	0.9235	0.8535	0.7894	0.7307	0.6768	0.6274	0.5820	0.5403	0.5019	0.4665	0.4039	0.3506	0.3269	0.3050	0.2660	0.2326	0.1789	0.1388	0.1085	0.0854
9	0.9143	0.8368	0.7664	0.7026	0.6446	0.5919	0.5439	0.5002	0.4604	0.4241	0.3606	0.3075	0.2843	0.2630	0.2255	0.1938	0.1443	0.1084	0.0822	0.0628
10	0.9053	0.8203	0.7441	0.6756	0.6139	0.5584	0.5083	0.4632	0.4224	0.3855	0.3220	0.2697	0.2472	0.2267	0.1911	0.1615	0.1164	0.0847	0.0623	0.0462
11	0.8963	0.8043	0.7224	0.6496	0.5847	0.5268	0.4751	0.4289	0.3875	0.3505	0.2875	0.2366	0.2149	0.1954	0.1619	0.1346	0.0938	0.0662	0.0472	0.0340
12	0.8874	0.7885	0.7014	0.6246	0.5568	0.4970	0.4440	0.3971	0.3555	0.3186	0.2567	0.2076	0.1869	0.1685	0.1372	0.1122	0.0757	0.0517	0.0357	0.0250
13	0.8787	0.7730	0.6810	0.6006	0.5303	0.4688	0.4150	0.3677	0.3262	0.2897	0.2292	0.1821	0.1625	0.1452	0.1163	0.0935	0.0610	0.0404	0.0271	0.0184
14	0.8700	0.7579	0.6611	0.5775	0.5051	0.4423	0.3878	0.3405	0.2992	0.2633	0.2046	0.1597	0.1413	0.1252	0.0985	0.0779	0.0492	0.0316	0.0205	0.0135
15	0.8613	0.7430	0.6419	0.5553	0.4810	0.4173	0.3624	0.3152	0.2745	0.2394	0.1827	0.1401	0.1229	0.1079	0.0835	0.0649	0.0397	0.0247	0.0155	0.0099
16	0.8528	0.7284	0.6232	0.5339	0.4581	0.3936	0.3387	0.2919	0.2519	0.2176	0.1631	0.1229	0.1069	0.0930	0.0708	0.0541	0.0320	0.0193	0.0118	0.0073
17	0.8444	0.7142	0.6050	0.5134	0.4363	0.3714	0.3166	0.2703	0.2311	0.1978	0.1456	0.1078	0.0929	0.0802	0.0600	0.0451	0.0258	0.0150	0.0089	0.0054
18	0.8630	0.7002	0.5874	0.4936	0.4155	0.3503	0.2959	0.2502	0.2120	0.1799	0.1300	0.0946	0.0808	0.0691	0.0508	0.0376	0.0208	0.0118	0.0068	0.0039
19	0.8277	0.6864	0.5703	0.4746	0.3957	0.3305	0.2765	0.2317	0.1945	0.1635	0.1161	0.0829	0.0703	0.0596	0.0431	0.0313	0.0168	0.0092	0.0051	0.0029
20	0.8195	0.6730	0.5537	0.4564	0.3769	0.3118	0.2584	0.2145	0.1784	0.1486	0.1037	0.0728	0.0611	0.0514	0.0365	0.0261	0.0135	0.0072	0.0039	0.0021
25	0.7798	0.6095	0.4776	0.3751	0.2953	0.2330	0.1842	0.1460	0.1160	0.0923	0.0588	0.0378	0.0304	0.0245	0.0160	0.0105	0.0046	0.0021	0.0010	0.0005
30	0.7419	0.5521	0.4120	0.3083	0.2314	0.1741	0.1314	0.0994	0.0754	0.0573	0.0334	0.0196	0.0151	0.0116	0.0070	0.0042	0.0016	0.0006	0.0002	0.0001
40	0.6717	0.4529	0.3066	0.2083	0.1420	0.0972	0.0668	0.0460	0.0318	0.0221	0.0107	0.0053	0.0037	0.0026	0.0013	0.0007	0.0002	0.0001	-	-
50	0.6080	0.3715	0.2281	0.1407	0.0872	0.0543	0.0339	0.0213	0.0134	0.0085	0.0035	0.0014	0.0009	0.0006	0.0003	0.0001	-	-	-	-
60	0.5504	0.3048	0.1697	0.0951	0.0535	0.0303	0.0173	0.0099	0.0057	0.0033	0.0011	0.0004	0.0002	0.0001	-	-	-	-	-	-

TABLE A.2 Present value of an annuity of \$1 per period for n periods:

$$PVIFA = \sum_{t-1}^{n} \frac{1}{(1+k)^t} = \frac{1 - \frac{1}{(1+k)^n}}{k}$$

Number of payments	1%	2%	3%	4%	5%	6%	7%	8%	9%	10%	12%	14%	15%	16%	18%	20%	24%	28%	32%
1	0.9901	0.9804	0.9709	0.9615	0.9524	0.9434	0.9346	0.9259	0.9174	0.9091	0.8929	0.8772	0.8696	0.8621	0.8475	0.8333	0.8065	0.7813	0.7576
2	1.9704	1.9416	1.9135	1.8861	1.8594	1.8334	1.8080	1.7833	1.7591	1.7355	1.6901	1.6467	1.6257	1.6052	1.5656	1.5278	1.4568	1.3916	1.3315
3	2.9410	2.8839	2.8286	2.7751	2.7232	2.6730	2.6243	2.5771	2.5313	2.4869	2.4018	2.3216	2.2832	2.2459	2.1743	2.1065	1.9813	1.8684	1.7663
4	3.9020	3.8077	3.7171	3.6299	3.5460	3.4651	3.3872	3.3121	3.2397	3.1699	3.0373	2.9137	2.8550	2.7982	2.6901	2.5887	2.4043	2.2410	2.0957
5	4.8534	4.7135	4.5797	4.4518	4.3295	4.2124	4.1002	3.9927	3.8897	3.7908	3.6048	3.4331	3.3522	3.2743	3.1272	2.9906	2.7454	2.5320	2.3452
6	5.7955	5.6014	5.4172	5.2421	5.0757	4.9173	4.7665	4.6229	4.4859	4.3553	4.1114	3.8887	3.7845	3.6847	3.4976	3.3255	3.0205	2.7594	2.5342
7	6.7282	6.4720	6.2303	6.0021	5.7864	5.5824	5.3893	5.2064	5.0330	4.8684	4.5638	4.2883	4.1604	4.0386	3.8115	3.6046	3.2423	2.9370	2.6775
8	7.6517	7.3255	7.0197	6.7327	6.4632	6.2098	5.9713	5.7466	5.5348	5.3349	4.9676	4.6389	4.4873	4.3436	4.0776	3.8372	3.4212	3.0758	2.7860
9	8.5660	8.1622	7.7861	7.4353	7.1078	6.8017	6.5152	6.2469	5.9952	5.7590	5.3282	4.9464	4.7716	4.6065	4.3030	4.0310	3.5655	3.1842	2.8681
10	9.4713	8.9826	8.5302	8.1109	7.7217	7.3601	7.0236	6.7101	6.4177	6.1446	5.6502	5.2161	5.0188	4.8332	4.4941	4.1925	3.6819	3.2689	2.9304
11	10.3876	9.7868	9.2526	8.7605	8.3064	7.8869	7.4987	7.1390	6.8052	6.4951	5.9377	5.4527	5.2337	5.0286	4.6560	4.3271	3.7757	3.3351	2.9776
12	11.2551	10.5753	9.9540	9.3851	8.8633	8.3838	7.9427	7.5361	7.1607	6.8137	6.1944	5.6603	5.4206	5.1971	4.7932	4.4392	3.8514	3.3868	3.0133
13	12.1337	11.3484	10.6350	9.9856	9.3936	8.8527	8.3577	7.9038	7.4869	7.1034	6.4235	5.8424	5.5831	5.3423	4.9095	4.5327	3.9124	3.4272	3.0404
14	13.0037	12.1062	11.2961	10.5631	9.8986	9.2950	8.7455	8.2442	7.7862	7.3667	6.6282	6.0021	5.7245	5.4675	5.0081	4.6106	3.9616	3.4587	3.0609
15	13.8651	12.8493	11.9379	11.1184	10.3797	9.7122	9.1079	8.5595	8.0607	7.6061	6.8109	6.1422	5.8474	5.5755	5.0916	4.6755	4.0013	3.4834	3.0764
16	14.7179	13.5777	12.5611	11.6523	10.8378	10.1059	9.4466	8.8514	8.3126	7.8237	6.9740	6.2651	5.9542	5.6685	5.1624	4.7296	4.0333	3.5026	3.0882
17	15.5623	14.2919	13.1661	12.1657	11.2741	10.4773	9.7632	9.1216	8.5436	8.0216	7.1196	6.3729	6.0472	5.7487	5.2223	4.7746	4.0591	3.5177	3.0971
18	16.3983	14.9920	13.7535	12.6593	11.6896	10.8276	10.0591	9.3719	8.7556	8.2014	7.2497	6.4674	6.1280	5.8178	5.2732	4.8122	4.0799	3.5294	3.1039
19	17.2260	15.6785	14.3238	13.1339	12.0853	11.1581	10.3356	9.6036	8.9501	8.3649	7.3658	6.5504	6.1982	5.8775	5.3162	4.8435	4.0967	3.5386	3.1090
20	18.0456	16.3514	14.8775	13.5903	12.4622	11.4699	10.5940	9.8181	9.1285	8.5136	7.4694	6.6231	6.2593	5.9288	5.3527	4.8696	4.1103	3.5458	3.1129
25	22.0232	19.5235	17.4131	15.6221	14.0939	12.7834	11.6536	10.6748	9.8226	9.0770	7.8431	6.8729	6.4641	6.0971	5.4669	4.9476	4.1474	3.5640	3.1220
30	25.8077	22.3965	19.6004	17.2920	15.3725	13.7648	12.4090	11.2578	10.2737	9.4269	8.0552	7.0027	6.5660	6.1772	5.5168	4.9789	4.1601	3.5693	3.1242
40	32.8347	27.3555	23.1148	19.7928	17.1591	15.0463	13.3317	11.9246	10.7574	9.7791	8.2438	7.1050	6.6418	6.2335	5.5482	4.9966	4.1659	3.5712	3.1250
50	39.1961	31.4236	25.7298	21.4822	18.2559	15.7619	13.8007	12.2335	10.9617	9.9148	8.3045	7.1327	6.6605	6.2463	5.5541	4.9995	4.1666	3.5714	3.1250
60	44.9550	34.7609	27.6756	22.6235	18.9293	16.1614	14.0392	12.3766	11.0480	9.9672	8.3240	7.1401	6.6651	6.2402	5.5553	4.9999	4.1667	3.5714	3.1250

PART 3
Disclosure

Part 3 examines the general disclosure standards established by the IASB to help ensure that IFRS-compliant financial statements attain the qualitative characteristics of financial statements discussed in chapter 2.

Chapter 15 addresses the general principles of disclosure, including fair presentation and the need for consistency of presentation and comparative information. It also discusses the general principles relating to accounting policies, changes in accounting estimates and errors, and the reporting of events after balance date.

Chapter 16 examines the objectives of a balance sheet, income statement and statement of changes in equity. It also outlines the information that must be presented on the face of these statements or in the notes. Chapter 17 deals with the objectives of a cash flow statement and the reporting of cash flows.

CHAPTER 15
Principles of disclosure – IAS 1, IAS 8 and IAS 10

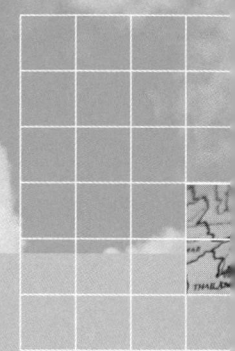

ACCOUNTING STANDARDS

International: IAS 1 *Presentation of Financial Statements*
IAS 8 *Accounting Policies, Changes in Accounting Estimates and Errors*
IAS 10 *Events After the Balance Sheet Date*

Australia: AASB 101 *Presentation of Financial Statements*
AASB 108 *Accounting Policies, Changes in Accounting Estimates and Errors*
AASB 110 *Events After the Balance Sheet Date*

New Zealand: NZ IAS 1 *Presentation of Financial Statements*
NZ IAS 8 *Accounting Policies, Changes in Accounting Estimates and Errors*
NZ IAS 10 *Events After the Balance Sheet Date*

CONCEPTS FOR REVIEW

Before studying this chapter, you should understand or, if necessary, revise:
• the IASB Framework, in particular the definitions of and recognition criteria for revenues and expenses.

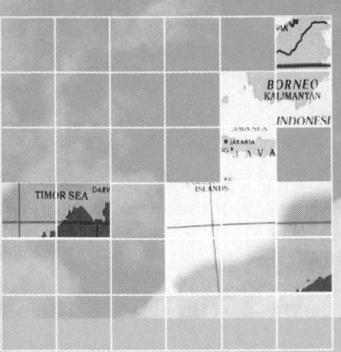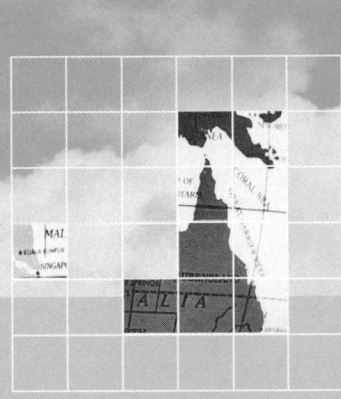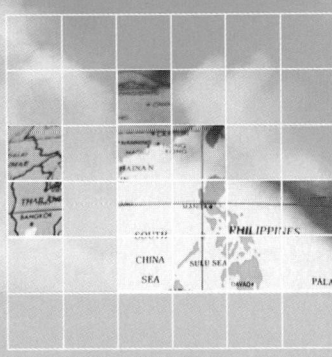

When you have studied this chapter, you should be able to:
1. explain the purpose of financial statements
2. describe the main components of financial statements
3. understand the overall considerations that are applied in the presentation of financial statements
4. understand the requirements of IAS 8 regarding the selection and application of accounting policies
5. distinguish between changes in accounting policies, changes in accounting estimates and errors
6. apply the requirements of IAS 8 in respect of changes in accounting policies, changes in accounting estimates and errors
7. apply the disclosure requirements of IAS 10
8. distinguish between adjusting and non-adjusting events after the balance sheet date.

15.1 Introduction to IAS 1, IAS 8 and IAS 10

IAS 1 *Presentation of Financial Statements*, IAS 8 *Accounting Policies, Changes in Accounting Estimates and Errors* and IAS 10 *Events After the Balance Sheet Date* are largely disclosure standards, although IAS 8 and IAS 10 also contain certain measurement requirements. These standards deal with fundamental disclosures and considerations that underpin financial statement presentation.

The overall principles and other considerations relating to the presentation of financial statements contained in IAS 1 are addressed in this chapter. Detailed matters relating to the presentation of a balance sheet, income statement, statement of changes in equity and notes are considered in chapter 16. The requirements for the presentation of a cash flow statement are outlined in chapter 17. IAS 8 and IAS 10 are addressed separately in this chapter.

LO 1

15.2 IAS 1 *Presentation of Financial Statements*

15.2.1 Purpose of financial statements

Financial statements are a structured presentation of the financial position and financial performance of an entity. The financial position of an entity is shown at a point in time — known as the reporting date or balance date — and is presented as a 'balance sheet' under IAS 1. The financial performance of an entity is shown for a specified period of time (usually one financial year) or an interim period such as a half-year. It is presented as an 'income statement' and 'cash flow statement' under IAS 1, showing the historic profit or loss and historic cash flows respectively for the period presented.

IAS 1 does not prescribe *who* must prepare financial statements. This is dealt with to some extent in the IASB Framework (refer to chapter 2 of this book) that sets out the objective of financial statements and defines general purpose financial statements. However, the requirement to *prepare* financial statements usually stems from a country's legislative environment and from individual entities' constitutions. For example, in Australia the Corporations Act requires most companies to prepare financial statements, with certain exceptions for small proprietary companies. In addition, non-corporate entities such as partnerships and trusts usually have a constitution or other enabling legislation that requires the preparation of financial statements. The relevant legislation or constitution will also specify *when* the entity must prepare its financial statements. This is usually for an annual reporting period or, for certain entities such as listed entities, an interim period as well. IAS 1, paragraph 49, states that financial statements shall be presented at least annually.

Whether or not those financial statements are *general purpose* financial statements depends on users' needs. Paragraph 3 of IAS 1 states that general purpose financial statements are those intended to meet the needs of users who are not in a position to demand reports that are tailored to their particular information needs. In Australia such an entity is called a 'reporting entity', but this term is not used in the IASB literature. Nevertheless, the concept is the same: if a user cannot command financial information tailored to his or her own needs, then the financial statements required of an entity must be *general purpose* financial statements. This means that entities (such as listed entities and many public companies) with large and varied groups of users (such as shareholders, creditors and employees) must prepare general purpose financial statements, and these general purpose financial statements must comply with the accounting standards of the IASB.

Paragraph 7 of IAS 1 states that the objective of general purpose financial statements is to provide information about the financial position, financial performance and cash flows of an entity that is useful to a wide range of users in making economic decisions.

Financial statements also show the results of management's stewardship of the resources entrusted to it. IAS 1 states that, to meet this objective, financial information should provide information about an entity's:
- assets
- liabilities
- equity
- income and expenses, including gains and losses
- other changes in equity
- cash flows.

LO 2

15.2.2   The components of financial statements

IAS 1 requires that a complete set of financial statements include the following:
- a balance sheet
- an income statement
- a statement of changes in equity
- a cash flow statement
- notes, comprising a summary of significant accounting policies and other explanatory notes.

Entities often present other information, such as certain financial ratios or a narrative review of operations by management or the directors. These reports are sometimes referred to as 'management discussion and analysis'. In some jurisdictions, entities are obliged under corporations legislation to prepare a 'directors' report' that covers, among other matters, commentary on the results of operations and financial position of the entity. In addition, some entities voluntarily prepare environmental and other reports. This other information is reported outside the financial statements and is not within the scope of International Financial Reporting Standards (IFRSs).

'Notes' are defined in paragraph 11 of IAS 1 as follows:

> Notes contain information in addition to that presented in the balance sheet, income statement, statement of changes in equity and cash flow statement. Notes provide narrative descriptions or disaggregations of items disclosed in those statements and information about items that do not qualify for recognition in those statements.

LO 3

15.2.3   Overall considerations in the presentation of financial statements

IAS 1 sets out seven overall considerations that need to be adhered to in the presentation of financial statements. These requirements are intended to ensure that the financial statements of an entity are a faithful presentation of its financial position, financial performance and cash flows.

1. Fair presentation and compliance with IFRSs

Paragraph 13 of IAS 1 states that financial statements shall present fairly the financial position, financial performance and cash flows of an entity. It goes on to define 'fair presentation' as follows:

> Fair presentation requires the faithful representation of the effects of transactions, other events and conditions in accordance with the definitions and recognition criteria for assets, liabilities, income and expenses set out in the *Framework*. The application of IFRSs, with additional disclosure when necessary, is presumed to result in financial statements that achieve a fair presentation.

Paragraph 14 of IAS 1 requires that an entity presenting financial statements that are compliant with IFRSs make an explicit and unreserved statement of such compliance in the notes to the financial statements. Such financial statements must comply with all the requirements of the IFRSs.

The last sentence of paragraph 13 is very significant. There is an assumption that full compliance with IFRSs will result in fair presentation. This also includes selecting and applying accounting policies in accordance with IAS 8; presenting information in a manner that provides relevant, reliable, comparable and understandable information (refer to chapter 2 of this book for the discussion of these qualitative characteristics of financial information); and providing additional disclosures to those specified by IFRSs, where necessary.

Paragraph 17 of IAS 1 says that, in extremely rare circumstances, management may depart from IFRSs. This is allowed only if two conditions are met:

- management concludes that compliance with a requirement in a standard or interpretation would be so misleading that it would conflict with the objective of financial statements set out in the Framework

- the relevant regulatory framework requires, or otherwise does not prohibit, such a departure. Note that IFRSs include IASB standards as well as interpretations of these standards issued by the International Financial Reporting Interpretations Committee (IFRIC).

Paragraph 22 of IAS 1 explains that an item of information would be in conflict with the objective of financial statements if it did not represent faithfully the transactions, other events and conditions that it either purports to represent or could reasonably be expected to represent. Consequently, it would be likely to influence economic decisions made by users of financial statements. The paragraph establishes a rebuttable presumption that an entity's compliance with a requirement of a standard or an interpretation would not be so misleading as to conflict with the objective of financial statements set out in the Framework; this is if other entities in similar circumstances comply with the requirement. Hence, when assessing whether non-compliance is supportable, management must assess whether the entity's circumstances differ from those of other entities that comply with the requirement.

Paragraphs 18–20 address the disclosure requirements when an entity makes such a departure. In such circumstances, the entity must disclose (paragraph 18):

(a) that management has concluded that the financial statements present fairly the entity's financial position, financial performance and cash flows;

(b) that it has complied with applicable Standards and Interpretations, except that it has departed from a particular requirement to achieve fair presentation;

(c) the title of the Standard or Interpretation from which the entity has departed, the nature of the departure, including the treatment that the Standard or Interpretation would require, the reason why that treatment would be so misleading in the circumstances that it would conflict with the objective of financial statements set out in the *Framework*, and the treatment adopted; and

(d) for each period presented, the financial impact of the departure on each item in the financial statements that would have been reported in complying with the requirement.

Paragraph 19 further requires that if a departure in a prior period affects the amounts recognised in the financial statements for the current period, the disclosures set out in (c) and (d) above are to be made.

Where the relevant regulatory framework prohibits the departure from the requirements of a standard or an interpretation, even in circumstances where compliance is considered to be so misleading that it would conflict with the objective of financial statements set out in the Framework, paragraph 21 of IAS 1 requires the following disclosures:

(a) the title of the Standard or Interpretation in question, the nature of the requirement, and the reason why management has concluded that complying with that requirement is so misleading in the circumstances that it conflicts with the objective of financial statements set out in the *Framework*; and

(b) for each period presented, the adjustments to each item in the financial statements that management has concluded would be necessary to achieve fair presentation.

The ability to depart from an accounting standard in the circumstances envisaged by paragraph 17 has commonly been termed the 'true and fair view override', and has been the subject of much debate in the accounting profession. In Australia, for example, the regulatory environment does not permit a company to depart from accounting standards, so a company incorporated in Australia and applying IAS 1 would not be able to avail itself of paragraph 17. However, Australian company legislation in the past did permit a true and fair view override. The override was removed in 1991 following concerns that companies were abusing the legislation, for example, to justify the use of a poor accounting policy that resulted in a higher profit figure than would have been attained by applying the relevant accounting standard correctly. This point illustrates the difficulty with paragraph 17 – it is open to abuse because it allows for a subjective determination of what 'presents fairly' means. If the presumption that compliance with IFRS results in fair presentation was applied, it would remove this area of subjectivity because all entities would then have to interpret the meaning of 'presents fairly' under the same framework.

Paragraph 17 also presents difficulties for auditors and users. Consider the examples shown in figure 15.1.

Example 1

Company A and company B have the same auditor, audit firm C. Company A and company B operate in the same industry (retail of consumer products) in Australia. Both companies routinely use leases as a means of obtaining their distribution and operating facilities. Company A applies IAS 17 *Leases* and capitalises all leases that meet the definition of a finance lease. Company B decides that, although its leases meet the definition of a finance lease under IAS 17, capitalisation of these leases would not result in fair presentation under paragraph 17 of IAS 1. Accordingly, company B departs from IAS 17.

Audit firm C must now decide whether it agrees with company A or with company B, since it is auditing both companies who have different interpretations of 'presents fairly' in exactly the same circumstances. If audit firm C agrees with company A, then it would have to qualify its audit opinion on the financial statements of company B on the basis that company B has departed from IAS 17 and IAS 1. If audit firm C agrees with company B, then it would have to qualify its audit opinion on the financial statements of company A on the basis that company A has, in complying with IAS 17, departed from IAS 1!

Example 2

Company A and company B have different auditors. Audit firm X audits company A and audit firm Z audits company B. Company A and company B operate in the same industry (retail of consumer products) in Australia. Both companies routinely use leases as a means of obtaining their distribution and operating facilities. Company A applies IAS 17 *Leases* and capitalises all leases that meet the definition of a finance lease. Company B decides that, although its leases meet the definition of a finance lease under IAS 17, capitalisation of these leases would not result in fair presentation under paragraph 17 of IAS 1. Accordingly, Company B departs from IAS 17.

Audit firm X agrees with company A's interpretation of IAS 17 and IAS 1, and signs an unqualified audit opinion on the financial statements of company A. Audit firm Z agrees with company B and signs an unqualified audit opinion on the financial statements of company B.

Ms Green is a shareholder of both companies. She reads the disclosures made by company B in accordance with IAS 1 and the audit opinion of audit firm Z, and understands that company B has departed from IAS 17 in order to provide a fair presentation of its financial statements, and that audit firm Z agrees with company B because the audit report is unqualified. Ms Green then reads the financial statements of company A and, because she cannot find any disclosure of a departure from IAS 17, correctly concludes that company A has fully complied with IAS 17. Ms Green is confused, however, because she knows that both companies are very similar. She rings her financial adviser, who is similarly confused. They ring a student of external financial reporting, who explains the objective of financial reporting. Ms Green and her financial adviser explain the situation with company A and company B to the student. All three are now confused, because the objective of financial reporting seems not to have been met – they are unable to confidently make economic decisions about either company.

FIGURE 15.1   Examples of the difficulties of the subjective test of 'presents fairly'

Although the examples given in figure 15.1 might be considered extreme, they illustrate the practical difficulties in applying paragraph 17 of IAS 1. It is true that the requirements of IFRSs are not faultless. Nonetheless, it can be argued that it is better for financial statement users to know that a consistent framework has been applied by companies, and to be able to rely on that consistency in making their economic decisions, instead of having to deal with the uncertainty and inconsistency caused by the 'true and fair view override'.

2. Going concern

Paragraph 23 of IAS 1 states that financial statements shall be prepared on a going concern basis unless management intends to either liquidate the entity or cease trading, or has no realistic alternative but to do so. The IASB Framework sets out a similar underlying assumption. When management is aware of any material uncertainties that cast doubt upon the entity's ability to continue as a going concern, those uncertainties must be disclosed. When financial statements are not prepared on a going concern basis, that fact must be disclosed, together with the basis on which the financial statements are prepared and the reason why the entity is not regarded as a going concern. An example of this is where an entity has been placed in receivership and it is anticipated that liquidation will follow. In such circumstances, the financial statements would be prepared on a 'liquidation' basis, which means that assets and liabilities are measured at the amounts expected to be received or settled on liquidation. In the case of assets, this will often be a 'fire-sale' value rather than a fair market value; in the case of liabilities, the creditors may forgive the company's debts. It is more common for a company (and its auditors) to disclose uncertainty regarding the going concern assumption than to prepare the financial statements on a liquidation basis.

3. Accrual basis of accounting

Financial statements, except for the cash flow statement, must be prepared using the accrual basis of accounting. This is discussed further in the IASB Framework (see chapter 2 of this book).

4. Consistency of presentation

Paragraph 27 of IAS 1 requires that the presentation and classification of items in the financial statements shall be retained from one period to the next unless:

  (a) following a significant change in the nature of the entity's operations or a review of its financial statements, it is apparent that another presentation or classification would be more appropriate having regard to the requirements of IAS 8; or
  (b) a Standard or Interpretation requires a change in presentation.

When such a change is made, the comparative information must also be reclassified. For example, an entity may present its assets and liabilities in current and non-current classifications, in accordance with paragraph 51 of IAS 1. However, paragraph 51 allows an entity to present its assets and liabilities in order of liquidity where this presentation is more reliable and relevant. Financial institutions, such as banks, frequently use the presentation in order of liquidity. If an entity begins to function like a financial institution after a change in the nature of its operations, it would be able to reclassify its assets and liabilities from the current/non-current presentation to the liquidity presentation, in accordance with paragraph 27.

5. Materiality and aggregation

Paragraph 11 of IAS 1 defines 'material' as follows:

Omissions or misstatements of items are material if they could, individually or collectively, influence the economic decisions of users taken on the basis of the financial statements. Materiality depends on the size and nature of the omission or misstatement judged in the surrounding circumstances. The size or nature of the item, or a combination of both, could be the determining factor.

Paragraph 29 states that each material class of similar items must be presented separately in the financial statements. Items of a dissimilar nature or function must be presented separately unless they are immaterial.

Financial statements result from processing large volumes of transactions that are then aggregated into classes according to their nature or function. These classes form the line items on the balance sheet, income statement, statement of changes in equity, and cash flow statement. IAS 1 specifies the minimum line items to be so presented; this is discussed in chapter 16.

6. Offsetting

IAS 1, paragraph 32, states that assets and liabilities, and income and expenses, shall not be offset unless required or permitted by a standard or interpretation. IAS 32 *Financial Instruments: Disclosure and Presentation* defines a right of set-off in respect of *financial* assets and liabilities (this is discussed further in chapter 6 of this book). Essentially, for items to be set off under IAS 32, there must be a *legal right* of set-off. This means that there must be a legal agreement documenting the right of the parties to set off amounts owed to/from each other. IAS 1 is not as prescriptive in relation to other *non-financial* items. Rather, it implies that offsetting is undesirable unless it reflects the substance of transactions or events (para. 33). Paragraphs 34 and 35 then go on to identify situations where offsetting would be appropriate. These include the following:

- gains and losses on the disposal of non-current assets should be reported net, instead of separately reporting the gross proceeds as income and the cost of the asset disposed of as an expense
- expenditure related to a provision recognised in accordance with IAS 37 (see chapter 5) may be offset against an amount reimbursed under a contractual arrangement with a third party
- gains and losses arising from a group of similar transactions, such as foreign exchange gains and losses arising on financial instruments held for trading, should be reported net unless they are material. This means that a net gain or loss may be reported, rather than separately reporting the gains and the losses. However, the gain or loss must be reported separately if it is material.

Because IAS 1 is not prescriptive about offsetting, this will be an area of judgement and subjectivity. Interestingly, in Australia prior to its adoption of IFRSs, gains and losses on the disposal of non-current assets were not permitted to be reported net, because Australia had a *gross* definition of revenue that did not permit revenue to be determined on a net basis. Thus, the revenue would include the proceeds on disposal, and expenses would include the cost of the asset disposed.

7. Comparative information

IAS 1, paragraph 36, requires the disclosure of comparative information in respect of the previous period for all amounts reported in the financial statements. This extends to narrative information where the comparative narrative information remains relevant. An example of this would be details of a contingent liability, where the development of the issue over time is relevant to users. In addition, IAS 1 requires that when the presentation or classification of items in the financial statements is amended, comparative amounts should be reclassified. This excludes changes in accounting policies or corrections of errors, which are dealt with in IAS 8 (and addressed later in this chapter).

15.2.4 Structure and content of financial statements: general requirements

The financial statements must be identified clearly and distinguished from other information in the same published document. For example, a company generally prepares an annual report that contains details of the company's operations during the year, a chairman's review and so on. This information is usually glossy and colourful, with the financial statements appended at the back in a less colourful style. As a result, it is usually quite clear where the financial statements are, but IAS 1 still requires them to be clearly identified as financial statements.

Other general requirements (IAS 1, paragraphs 46–50) are:

- each component of the financial statements must be identified clearly (balance sheet, income statement and so on)
- disclosure must be made of:
  - the name of the reporting entity and any change in that name from the preceding reporting date
  - whether the financial statements cover the individual entity or a group of entities
  - the balance sheet date or the period covered by the financial statements, whichever is appropriate to that component of the financial statements (the balance sheet date is appropriate to the balance sheet, and the period covered is appropriate to the income statement)
  - the presentation currency, as defined in IAS 21 *The Effects of Changes in Foreign Exchange Rates*
  - the level of rounding used in presenting amounts in the financial statements
- financial statements must be presented at least annually. If an entity's balance sheet date changes and financial statements are presented for a period longer or shorter than one year, the entity must disclose, in addition to the period covered by the financial statements:
  - the reason for using a longer or shorter period
  - the fact that comparative amounts for the income statement, statement of changes in equity, cash flow statement and related notes are not entirely comparable.

Paragraph 126 of IAS 1 requires an entity to disclose the following information in the notes (if it is not disclosed elsewhere in the financial statements):

(a) the domicile and legal form of the entity, its country of incorporation and the address of its registered office (or principal place of business, if different from the registered office);

(b) a description of the nature of the entity's operations and its principal activities; and

(c) the name of the parent and the ultimate parent of the group.

LO 4

15.3 IAS 8 Accounting Policies, Changes in Accounting Estimates and Errors

The objective of IAS 8 is to prescribe the criteria for selecting and changing accounting policies, together with associated disclosures. IAS 8 is especially relevant where there is no specific standard or interpretation dealing with a particular transaction or event, and the entity must therefore decide on its own how to account for such a transaction or event.

15.3.1 Selecting and applying accounting policies

IAS 8, paragraph 5, defines 'accounting policies' as:

the specific principles, bases, conventions, rules and practices applied by an entity in preparing and presenting financial statements.

IFRSs prescribe accounting policies for certain topics, transactions or events. IAS 8 deals with areas where there are no accounting standards, and sets out the principles that entities must apply in selecting appropriate accounting policies. The fundamental principle is set out in paragraph 10, shown opposite.

In the absence of a Standard or an Interpretation that specifically applies to a transaction, other event or condition, management shall use its judgement in developing and applying an accounting policy that results in information that is:

(a) relevant to the economic decision-making needs of users; and

(b) reliable, in that the financial statements:

    (i) represent faithfully the financial position, financial performance and cash flows of the entity;

    (ii) reflect the economic substance of transactions, other events and conditions, and not merely the legal form;

    (iii) are neutral, i.e. free from bias;

    (iv) are prudent; and

    (v) are complete in all material respects.

The concept of substance over form is particularly important. This is an area revealed as a weakness in the rule-based approach to standard setting used by the United States and implicated in some of the corporate collapses in that country in 2001 and 2002. Transactions that were, in substance, financing transactions were accounted for as sales, applying very literal interpretations of the US rules. Applying the principle of substance over form should result in transactions being accounted for appropriately. An example of where the substance over form principle is applied in IFRSs is in IAS 17 *Leases*, where certain lease transactions, which take the form of leases, in substance transfer the risks and rewards of ownership in the asset with an associated borrowing from lessor to lessee and are accounted for accordingly as finance leases.

Paragraphs 11 and 12 of IAS 8 go on to explain what is commonly termed the 'hierarchy' of relevant sources of information to be used by management in selecting and applying accounting policies:

11. In making the judgement described in paragraph 10, management shall refer to, and consider the applicability of, the following sources in descending order:

    (a) the requirements and guidance in Standards and Interpretations dealing with similar and related issues; and

    (b) the definitions, recognition criteria and measurement concepts for assets, liabilities, income and expenses in the *Framework*.

12. In making the judgement described in paragraph 10, management may also consider the most recent pronouncements of other standard-setting bodies that use a similar conceptual framework to develop accounting standards, other accounting literature and accepted industry practices, to the extent that these do not conflict with the sources in paragraph 11.

In the United States there are numerous detailed rules on how to account for specific transactions. In contrast, the IFRSs are generally principle-based standards and do not specify how to account for each and every type of transaction. An entity may find detailed guidance on how to account for a specific transaction in the rules of the US Emerging Issues Task Force (EITF), for example, but it may apply that EITF rule only if it is consistent with the IASB standards and the Framework.

Paragraph 13 of IAS 8 requires that an entity must apply accounting policies consistently for similar transactions, events or conditions unless otherwise required by an accounting standard or interpretation.

LO 5

15.3.2 Distinguishing between accounting policies, accounting estimates and errors

Accounting for a change in accounting policy is not a straightforward exercise. IAS 8 contains detailed measurement and disclosure requirements for changes in accounting policies as well as for changes in accounting estimates. It also specifies how errors must be accounted for. Before dealing with changes in these items, it is necessary to differentiate between them.

An accounting *policy* essentially comprises the principles or conventions applied in preparing the financial statements. By contrast, an accounting *estimate* is a judgement applied in determining the carrying amount of an item in the financial statements. The use of reasonable estimates is an essential part of the process of preparing financial statements because many elements of the financial statements — such as provisions for bad debts and inventory obsolescence, and assets' useful lives — cannot be calculated with exact precision. So, for example, an entity's accounting *policy* in respect of bad debts may be that it always makes a provision for expected bad debts based on past history and for all debtors that are more than 120 days overdue. The *calculation* of the amount of the bad debts provision is then an accounting *estimate* that applies this accounting policy.

An 'error' is an omission or misstatement in the financial statements. Errors may arise from mathematical mistakes, mistakes in applying accounting policies, oversights or misinterpretations of facts, and fraud (IAS 8, para. 5).

LO 6

15.3.3   Changes in accounting policies

IAS 8, paragraph 14, specifies only two circumstances in which an entity is permitted to change an accounting policy. These are:
- if the change is *required* by a standard or interpretation; or
- if the change, *made voluntarily*, results in the financial statements providing reliable and more relevant information about the effects of transactions, other events or conditions on the entity's financial position, financial performance or cash flows.

However, the initial application of a policy to revalue assets in accordance with IAS 16 *Property, Plant and Equipment* or IAS 38 *Intangible Assets* must be accounted for as a revaluation in accordance with those standards and not as a change in accounting policy under IAS 8. Note that this applies to the *initial* application of a revaluation policy only. IAS 8 would apply if an entity initially chooses the cost method under IAS 16 or IAS 38, and then changes to the revaluation method at a later date.

Where an entity changes an accounting policy because it is required to do so, it must account for that change as set out in the specific transitional provisions of the relevant accounting standard requiring the change. If the accounting standard does not specify how to account for the change, then the change must be applied *retrospectively*. Retrospective application is also required for all voluntary changes in accounting policy (IAS 8, para. 19). Retrospective application means applying a new accounting policy to transactions, other events and conditions as if that policy had always been applied (para. 5). When an entity applies the change retrospectively, the entity must adjust the *opening* balance of each affected component of equity for the earliest prior period presented, and the other comparative amounts disclosed for each prior period must be presented as if the new accounting policy had always been applied (para. 22).

Illustrative example 15.1 shows how to apply a change in accounting policy retrospectively.

ILLUSTRATIVE EXAMPLE 15.1

Applying a change in accounting policy retrospectively

During 2004, company A changed its accounting policy for training costs in order to comply with IAS 38. Previously, company A had capitalised certain training costs. Under IAS 38, it cannot capitalise training costs and, according to the transitional provisions of the standard, it must apply the change in accounting policy retrospectively.

→

During 2003, company A had capitalised training costs of $6000. In periods before 2003, it had capitalised training costs of $12 000. In 2004, it incurred training costs of $4500.

Company A's income statement for 2003 reported profit of $49 000 after income taxes of $21 000. Its income statement for 2004 reported profit of $56 000 after income taxes of $24 000. The training costs of $4500 were expensed in 2004.

Company A's retained earnings were $600 000 at the beginning of 2003 and $649 000 at the end of 2003. It had $100 000 in share capital throughout 2003 and 2004, representing 100 000 ordinary shares, and there were no other reserves.

Company A's tax rate was 30% for both periods. Its balance date is 30 June.

Applying the change in accounting policy retrospectively, Company A's income statement for 2004, with comparative figures, is as follows:

	2004 $	2003 (restated) $
Profit before income taxes	80 000	64 000[1]
Less Income taxes	24 000	19 200[2]
Profit	56 000	44 800

Company A's statement of changes in equity is as follows:

	Share capital $	Retained earnings $	Total $
Balance at 30 June 2002 as previously reported	100 000	600 000	700 000
Change in accounting policy for capitalisation of training costs		(8 400)[3]	(8 400)
Balance at 30 June 2002 as restated	100 000	591 600	691 600
Profit for the year ended 30 June 2003 (restated)		44 800	44 800
Balance at 30 June 2003	100 000	636 400	736 400
Profit for the year ended 30 June 2004		56 000	56 000
Balance at 30 June 2004	100 000	692 400	792 400

Notes:
1. Being $70 000 – 6000
2. Being $64 000 × 30%
3. Being $12 000 × 70%

Paragraphs 23–25 of IAS 8 deal with circumstances where retrospective application of a change in accounting policy is impracticable and thus cannot be applied. 'Impracticable' in the context of IAS 8 means that 'the entity cannot apply it after making every reasonable effort to do so' (para. 5). Hindsight is not used when applying a new accounting policy retrospectively. For example, an asset measured on the fair value basis retrospectively should be measured at the fair value as at the date of the retrospective adjustment and should not take into account subsequent events. When it is impracticable for an entity to apply a new accounting policy retrospectively because it cannot determine the cumulative effect of applying the policy to all prior periods, the entity should apply the new policy prospectively from the start of the earliest period practicable. This may be the current period.

Extensive disclosures are required when an entity changes its accounting policy. These are separated between mandatory changes and voluntary changes, as follows:

28. When initial application of a Standard or an Interpretation has an effect on the current period or any prior period, would have such an effect except that it is impracticable to determine the amount of the adjustment, or might have an effect on future periods, an entity shall disclose:
    (a) the title of the Standard or Interpretation;
    (b) when applicable, that the change in accounting policy is made in accordance with its transitional provisions;
    (c) the nature of the change in accounting policy;
    (d) when applicable, a description of the transitional provisions;
    (e) when applicable, the transitional provisions that might have an effect on future periods;
    (f) for the current period and each prior period presented, to the extent practicable, the amount of the adjustment:
        (i) for each financial statement line item affected; and
        (ii) if IAS 33 *Earnings per Share* applies to the entity, for basic and diluted earnings per share;
    (g) the amount of the adjustment relating to periods before those presented, to the extent practicable; and
    (h) if retrospective application required by paragraph 19(a) or (b) is impracticable for a particular prior period, or for periods before those presented, the circumstances that led to the existence of that condition and a description of how and from when the change in accounting policy has been applied.
    Financial statements of subsequent periods need not repeat these disclosures.
29. When a voluntary change in accounting policy has an effect on the current period or any prior period, would have an effect on that period except that it is impracticable to determine the amount of the adjustment, or might have an effect on future periods, an entity shall disclose:
    (a) the nature of the change in accounting policy;
    (b) the reasons why applying the new accounting policy provides reliable and more relevant information;
    (c) for the current period and each prior period presented, to the extent practicable, the amount of the adjustment:
        (i) for each financial statement line item affected; and
        (ii) if IAS 33 applies to the entity, for basic and diluted earnings per share;
    (d) the amount of the adjustment relating to periods before those presented, to the extent practicable; and
    (e) if retrospective application is impracticable for a particular prior period, or for periods before those presented, the circumstances that led to the existence of that condition and a description of how and from when the change in accounting policy has been applied.
    Financial statements of subsequent periods need not repeat these disclosures.

IAS 1, paragraph 96(d), also requires that the statement of changes in equity disclose the effects of changes in accounting policies and the correction of errors for each component of equity.

Following on from illustrative example 15.1, illustrative example 15.2 shows the additional disclosures required.

ILLUSTRATIVE EXAMPLE 15.2

Additional disclosures for the change in accounting policy shown in illustrative example 15.1

For the year ended 30 June 2004, company A applied IAS 38 *Intangible Assets* for the first time. As a result, certain training expenses that had been capitalised in the past were expensed. In accordance with the transitional provisions of IAS 38, the change in accounting policy was applied retrospectively. The comparative financial statements for 2003 have been restated. The effect of the change for each line item affected is tabulated below:

	Effect on 2003 $
(Decrease) in profit before tax	(6 000)
Decrease in income tax expense	1 800
(Decrease) in profit after tax	(4 200)
(Decrease) in intangible assets	(6 000)
Decrease in deferred tax liabilities	1 800
(Decrease) in retained earnings as at 30 June 2003	(12 600)[2]

	Effect on periods prior to 2003 $
(Decrease) in profit after tax	(8 400)[1]
(Decrease) in intangible assets	(12 000)
Decrease in deferred tax liabilities	3 600

Adjusted basic and diluted earnings per share for 2003 were 44.8 cents. Reported earnings per share for 2003 was 49 cents.

Notes:

1. This amount has been adjusted against opening retained earnings at 1 July 2002.
2. Per illustrative example 15.1, original closing retained earnings were $649 000 and adjusted closing retained earnings were $636 400. The difference is $12 600.

15.3.4 Changes in accounting estimates

As discussed in section 15.3.2, an accounting estimate is a judgement applied in determining the carrying amount of an item in the financial statements. An estimate may need revision if changes occur in the circumstances on which the estimate was based, or as a result of new information or more experience. Paragraph 36 of IAS 8 requires that a change in estimate be accounted for *prospectively*. Paragraph 5 explains that prospective application means:

- applying the new accounting estimate to transactions or events occurring after the date the estimate is changed; and
- recognising the effect of the change in the current and future periods affected by the change.

Paragraph 37 of IAS 8 goes on to state that if the change in estimate affects assets, liabilities or equity, then the carrying amounts of those items shall be adjusted in the period of the change. Paragraphs 39 and 40 contain the disclosure requirements for a change in an accounting estimate (shown overleaf).

39. An entity shall disclose the nature and amount of a change in an accounting estimate that has an effect in the current period or is expected to have an effect in future periods, except for the disclosure of the effect on future periods when it is impracticable to estimate that effect.

40. If the amount of the effect in future periods is not disclosed because estimating it is impracticable, an entity shall disclose that fact.

Illustrative example 15.3 demonstrates accounting for a change in accounting estimate, and the relevant disclosures.

ILLUSTRATIVE EXAMPLE 15.3

Accounting for a change in accounting estimate, and relevant disclosures

Company Z has historically depreciated its factory plant and equipment over 15 years. In 2004, company Z's directors determined that, due to technological developments in its industry, the factory plant and equipment should be depreciated over a shorter period: 10 years. Company Z's balance date is 30 June.

As at 1 July 2003, the balance of factory plant and equipment was as follows:

	$
Cost	150 000
Accumulated depreciation	(40 000)
Carrying amount	110 000

For the year ended 30 June 2004, company Z's depreciation expense will be $18 333. This is calculated as $110 000/6 (being the carrying amount of the asset at the date of the change in estimate, divided by the remaining useful life). Since the total useful life is reassessed to 10 years, and four years have already elapsed, the remaining useful life is six years.

Extract from company Z's financial statements for the year ended 30 June 2004:
Company Z has historically depreciated its factory plant and equipment over 15 years. As at 1 July 2003, the company's directors determined that, due to technological developments in its industry, the factory plant and equipment should be depreciated over a shorter period, being 10 years. The effect of the change in accounting estimate in the current period is an increase in depreciation expense and accumulated depreciation of $8333. In future periods, annual depreciation expense will be $18 333.

15.3.5 Correction of errors

As discussed in section 15.3.2, an 'error' is an omission or misstatement in the financial statements. Errors may arise from mathematical mistakes, mistakes in applying accounting policies, oversights or misinterpretations of facts, and fraud. (IAS 8, para. 5). If an error is discovered in a subsequent period, paragraph 42 states that the error must be corrected retrospectively by:

• restating the comparative amounts for the prior period/s presented in which the error occurred; or
• if the error occurred before the earliest prior period presented, restating the opening balances of assets, liabilities and equity for the earliest prior period presented.

As with changes in accounting policy, retrospective restatement is required unless it is impracticable to do so (paras 43–45). Similar disclosures are required for correction of errors as for changes in accounting policy (para. 49).

In practice, a change in accounting policy occurs more often than the correction of an error. Remember that the error must be material to the financial statements (IAS 8, paras 5 and 6), materiality being defined according to whether or not the omission or misstatement could influence the economic decisions of users. Materiality depends on the size and the nature of the item. If an error is material, the company and its auditors will usually suffer embarrassment, reputation damage or even litigation as a result of the restatement.

LO 7

15.4 IAS 10 *Events After the Balance Sheet Date*

The objective of IAS 10 is to prescribe when an entity should adjust its financial statements for events after the balance sheet date, and what disclosures the entity should make about events after the balance sheet date.

IAS 10, paragraph 3, defines two types of events after the balance sheet date:

Events after the balance sheet date are those events, favourable and unfavourable, that occur between the balance sheet date and the date when the financial statements are authorised for issue. Two types of events can be identified:

(a) those that provide evidence of conditions that existed at the balance sheet date (*adjusting events after the balance sheet date*); and

(b) those that are indicative of conditions that arose after the balance sheet date (*non-adjusting events after the balance sheet date*).

Usually the date at which financial statements are authorised for issue is the date on which the directors or other governing body formally approve the financial statements for issue to shareholders and/or other users. The fact that subsequent ratification by the shareholders at an annual meeting is required does not mean that the date of authorisation for issue is at that later ratification date.

LO 8

15.4.1 Adjusting events after the balance sheet date

Paragraph 8 of IAS 10 requires an entity to adjust the amounts recognised in its financial statements to reflect adjusting events after the balance sheet date. Examples of adjusting events after the balance sheet date include the following:

- The receipt of information after the balance sheet date indicates that an asset was impaired as at the balance sheet date. This may occur, for example, if a trade receivable recorded at the balance sheet date is shown to be irrecoverable because of the insolvency of the customer that occurs after the balance sheet date.

- The sale of inventories after the balance sheet date may give evidence of their net realisable value at the balance sheet date.

- The settlement after the balance sheet date of a court case confirms that the entity had a present obligation at the balance sheet date. The entity adjusts any previously recognised provision related to this court case in accordance with IAS 37 *Provisions, Contingent Liabilities and Contingent Assets* or recognises a new provision. (See chapter 5 of this book for further details.)

Illustrative example 15.4 shows how an adjusting event after the balance sheet date is accounted for.

ILLUSTRATIVE EXAMPLE 15.4

Accounting for an adjusting event after the balance sheet date

Company B is a retailer with a 30 June balance date. In its financial statements for the year ended 30 June 2004, company B included revenue and a receivable of $35 000 in respect of a large customer, company R. On 31 July 2004, before the financial statements were authorised for issue, company B was advised by the liquidator of company R that company R was insolvent and would be unable to repay the full amount owed to company B. The liquidator advised company B in writing that she would be paying all of company R's creditors 10 cents in the dollar for every dollar owed. The liquidator estimated that the amount would be paid in September 2004. Company B's financial statements were authorised for issue by the directors on 25 August 2004.

In accordance with IAS 8, the insolvency of company R is an adjusting event after the balance sheet date because it provides further evidence of the amount recognised as at 30 June 2004. Because the liquidator has confirmed in writing that $3500 will be paid in settlement, company B will adjust the receivable from $35 000 to $3500 as follows:

Expenses	Dr	31 500	
Receivables	Cr		31 500
(Impairment of receivable)			

Company B will need to reassess the carrying amount of this receivable at each reporting date. If, at the next reporting date, the liquidator has not settled the amount, company B will probably need to write off the receivable or, at a minimum, transfer it to non-current receivables, depending on the evidence available to support recoverability of the amount.

15.4.2 Non-adjusting events after the balance sheet date

Paragraph 10 of IAS 10 states that an entity shall not adjust the amounts recognised in its financial statements to reflect non-adjusting events after the balance sheet date. Examples of non-adjusting events include:
- a major business combination after the balance sheet date
- the destruction of property by fire after the balance sheet date
- the issuance of new share capital after the balance sheet date
- commencing major litigation arising solely out of events that occurred after the balance sheet date

Although these events are not adjusted for, paragraph 21 of IAS 10 requires the following disclosure:

> If non-adjusting events after the balance sheet date are material, non-disclosure could influence the economic decisions of users taken on the basis of the financial statements. Accordingly, an entity shall disclose the following for each material category of non-adjusting event after the balance sheet date:
> (a) the nature of the event; and
> (b) an estimate of its financial effect, or a statement that such an estimate cannot be made.

Paragraph 11 of IAS 10 refers to a controversial area of accounting for events after the balance sheet date. It states that a decline in the market value of investments between the balance sheet date and the date when the financial statements are authorised for issue is a non-adjusting event, because the decline in market value does not normally relate to the condition of the investments at the balance sheet date but instead reflects circumstances that have arisen subsequently. However, it could just as easily be argued that the same applies in the case of the receivables referred to in paragraph 9(b)(i) of IAS 10, regarding the insolvency of a debtor after the balance sheet date. IAS 10 paragraph 9(b)(i) states that this would constitute an adjusting event because the insolvency confirms that a loss existed at the balance sheet date. This is not necessarily true because the debtor may well have been solvent at the balance date.

The same applies to example 9(b)(ii) of IAS 10, regarding the sale of inventories after the balance sheet date. The issue is what are the *conditions* referred to in paragraph 3. Are they (1) subsequent events that provide further evidence about the *measurement* of items such as receivables, investments and inventories which existed at balance date, even if the evidence in relation to measurement occurred after the balance date; or (2) must the evidence in relation to measurement have existed at the balance date? It is submitted that (1) is the correct interpretation, which is applied in the examples in paragraph 9. Therefore, if an investment is recorded at cost in the balance sheet and there is a significant decline in market value after the balance date, this would be evidence that the investment is impaired and should be treated as an adjusting event. However, if the investment is being carried at fair value (in accordance with IAS 39 *Financial Instruments: Recognition and Measurement*), one could argue that fair value is determined as at the reporting date and, because of the mark-to-market accounting (fair value adjustments being made at each reporting date) being applied, the adjustment would be made only in the next reporting period.

15.4.3 Other disclosures

IAS 10 also requires other disclosures, namely:
* disclosure of the date the financial statements were authorised for issue (para. 17)
* updating disclosure about conditions at the balance sheet date (para. 19).

15.5 Summary

IAS 1 *Presentation of Financial Statements*, IAS 8 *Accounting Policies, Changes in Accounting Estimates and Errors* and IAS 10 *Events After the Balance Sheet Date* are largely disclosure standards, although IAS 8 and IAS 10 also contain certain measurement requirements. These standards deal with fundamental disclosures and considerations that underpin financial statement presentation.

IAS 1 prescribes the components of financial statements, overall considerations to be applied in the preparation of financial statements, and the structure and content of financial statements. IAS 8 distinguishes between accounting policies, accounting estimates and errors, and prescribes different requirements for each, particularly when there is a change. Any change in accounting policy must be applied retrospectively. Any change in an accounting estimate must be recognised prospectively. A correction of an error must be recognised, wherever possible, in the period when the error occurred.

IAS 10 distinguishes between two types of events after the balance sheet date – adjusting and non-adjusting. Adjusting events must be recognised in the financial statements, whereas non-adjusting events must be disclosed only.

DISCUSSION QUESTIONS

1. Discuss the seven overall considerations to be applied in the presentation of financial statements. Of these, which are the most subjective? Explain your answer.
2. Why is it important for entities to disclose the measurement bases used in preparing the financial statements?
3. Explain the difference between retrospective application of a change in accounting policy and prospective application of a change in accounting estimate. Why do you think the standard setters require prospective application of a change in accounting estimate?
4. Is it always clear whether an event occurring after the balance sheet date is adjusting or non-adjusting? Give examples to illustrate your answer.
5. What comprises a complete set of financial statements in accordance with IAS 1?
6. What is the difference between an accounting policy and an accounting estimate?

EXERCISES

EXERCISE 15.1 ★   Fair presentation

Under what circumstances can an entity depart from IFRSs? Are these circumstances expected to be common or rare? Explain your answer.

EXERCISE 15.2 ★   Fair presentation

Both company A and company B are manufacturers of plastic pipes. Company A complies with all IFRSs. Company B wishes to depart from IAS 39 in respect of hedge accounting, on the basis that compliance with the hedge accounting rules would result in company B's reported profit being misleading. Both company A and company B operate in a country whose regulatory framework permits departures from IFRSs. Must company B have regard to company A's accounting policies in making its decision to depart from IAS 39?

EXERCISE 15.3 ★   Consistency, materiality and aggregation

State whether each of the following statements is true or false:
(a) A material item is determined solely on the basis of its size.
(b) A class of assets or liabilities is determined by reference to items of a similar nature or function.
(c) Inventories and trade accounts receivable may be aggregated in the balance sheet.
(d) Cash and cash equivalents may be aggregated in the balance sheet.

EXERCISE 15.4 ★★   Materiality, offsetting

Company A is a retailer that imports about 30% of its goods. The following foreign exchange gains and losses were recognised during the year:

	Loss $m	Gain $m
Foreign currency borrowings with bank L	50	
Forward exchange contracts used as hedging instruments		1
Forward exchange contracts not used as hedges	3	
Foreign currency borrowings with bank S		10

Required

Identify which of the above gains and losses are permitted to be offset in company A's financial statements. Assume that materiality has been determined as $5 million for profit and loss purposes.

EXERCISE 15.5 ★★   Accounting policies, accounting estimates

State whether each of the following is an accounting policy or an accounting estimate for company A:

(a) The useful life of depreciable plant is determined as being six years.

(b) Company A's management determines that it will provide for all invoices in transit as at the balance date.

(c) Company A determines that it will calculate its warranty provision using past experience of defective products.

(d) The current year's warranty provision is calculated by providing for 1% of current year sales, based on last year's warranty claimed amounting to 1% of sales.

EXERCISE 15.6 ★★   Accounting policies, accounting estimates, errors

State whether the following changes should be accounted for retrospectively or prospectively:

(a) A change in accounting policy made voluntarily.

(b) A change in accounting policy required by an accounting standard or IFRIC interpretation.

(c) A change in an accounting estimate.

(d) An immaterial error discovered in the current year, relating to a transaction recorded two years ago.

(e) A material error discovered in the current year, relating to a transaction recorded two years ago. Management determines that retrospective application would cause undue cost and effort.

(f) A change in accounting policy required by an accounting standard. Retrospective application of that standard would require assumptions about what management's intent would have been in the relevant period(s).

EXERCISE 15.7 ★★★   Adjusting/non-adjusting post-balance date events

State whether each of the following would be an adjusting or non-adjusting event after the balance sheet date in the financial statements of company N. The financial statements of company N are authorised for issue on 12 August 2005, and the balance sheet date is 30 June 2005.

(a) At 30 June, company N had recorded $40 000 owed by company P, which is due 60 days after balance date. On 16 July, a receiver was appointed to company P. The receiver informed company N that the $40 000 would be paid in full by 30 September 2005.

(b) On 24 July, company N issued a corporate bond of $1 million, paying interest of 5% semi-annually in arrears.

(c) Company N measures its investments in listed shares as held-for-trading at fair value through profit and loss in accordance with IAS 39. As at 30 June, these investments were recorded at the market value at that date, which was $500 000. During the period leading up to 12 August 2005, there was a steady decline in the market values of all the shares in the portfolio, and at 12 August 2005 the fair value of the investments had fallen to $400 000.

(d) Company A had reported a contingent liability at 30 June 2005 in respect of a court case in which company A was the defendant. The case was not heard until the first week of August. On 11 August, the judge handed down her decision, against company A. The judge determined that company A was liable to pay damages and costs totalling $3 million.

(e) As in part (d), except that the damages and costs awarded against company A were $50 million, leading company A to place itself into voluntary liquidation.

PROBLEMS

PROBLEM 15.1 ★★

Change in accounting estimate

Company H has historically depreciated its administration buildings over 15 years. In 2005, company H's directors reviewed the depreciation rates for similar buildings used in its industry. Consequently, they decided that the buildings should be depreciated over a longer period, being 20 years. Company H's balance date is 30 June.

As at 1 July 2004, the balance of administration buildings was as follows:

	$
Cost	5 000 000
Accumulated depreciation	(1 666 667)
Carrying amount	3 333 333

Required

Prepare the note describing company H's change in accounting estimate for the year ended 30 June 2005, including comparative figures, in accordance with IAS 8. Show all workings.

PROBLEM 15.2 ★★★

Change in accounting policy — comprehensive problem

During 2005, company A changed its accounting policy for measuring property assets. Until 30 June 2005, company A had been applying the cost model under IAS 16 *Property, Plant and Equipment*. On 1 July 2005, the company's directors determined that the revaluation model would be more relevant and reliable, given that the fair value of the properties could be reliably measured. IAS 16 contains no rules about accounting for a change from the cost model to the revaluation model, so company A decided to apply IAS 8.

Company A had been depreciating the property over its useful life of 20 years. There was no change to the estimate of useful life when the change in accounting policy was made.

Relevant balances in company A's financial statements were as follows:

	30 June 2005 $	30 June 2004 $
Property assets – at cost	6 000 000	6 000 000
Accumulated depreciation	(1 500 000)	(1 200 000)
Carrying amount	4 500 000	4 800 000
Retained earnings	67 000 000	64 000 000
Share capital	40 000 000	40 000 000

Additional information
- Company A's income statement for 2005 reported a profit of $3 million after income taxes of $1 285 714.
- Company A's income statement for 2006 reported a profit of $3.5 million, after income taxes of $1.5 million and before the application of the change in accounting policy.

- The fair value of the property assets was determined by an independent valuer to be $7 800 000 as at 30 June 2005, and $6 800 000 as at 30 June 2004. No reliable measure could be determined for earlier periods. There was no change in fair value as at 30 June 2006.
- Company A's tax rate was 30% for both periods. Its balance date is 30 June, and it includes one year's comparative figures in its financial statements.

Required

Prepare the note disclosing the change in accounting policy for company A's financial statements for the year ended 30 June 2006. Include a full statement of changes in equity. Show comparative figures and all workings. Break down your workings as follows:

1. Calculate the age of the asset as at 30 June 2004.
2. Calculate the increase in the carrying amount of the asset (from depreciated cost to revalued amount) as at 30 June 2004.
3. Calculate the revised depreciation of the asset for the year ended 30 June 2005, based on the new carrying amount and the remaining life of the asset.
4. Calculate the revised carrying amount of the asset as at 30 June 2005 immediately prior to its revaluation (i.e. the revalued amount as at 30 June 2004 less that calculated in part 3).
5. Calculate the increase in the carrying amount of the asset as at 30 June 2005 (i.e. the revalued amount as at that date less that calculated in part 4).
6. Calculate the depreciation for the year ended 30 June 2006.
7. Prepare the note disclosure in accordance with IAS 8.

WEBLINK ↗

Visit these websites for additional information:

www.iasb.org	www.iasplus.com
www.asic.gov.au	www.ifac.org
www.aasb.com.au	www.nzica.com
www.accaglobal.com	www.capa.com.my

CHAPTER 16
Presentation of financial statements

ACCOUNTING STANDARDS

International: IAS 1 *Presentation of Financial Statements*
Australia: AASB 101 *Presentation of Financial Statements*
New Zealand: NZ IAS 1 *Presentation of Financial Statements*

CONCEPTS FOR REVIEW

Before studying this chapter, you should understand or, if necessary, revise:

- the IASB Framework, in particular the objectives and elements of financial statements
- the principles of disclosure relating to the presentation of financial statements
- the principles relating to the selection and changing of accounting policies
- the accounting treatment and disclosure of changes in accounting policies, accounting estimates and corrections of errors.

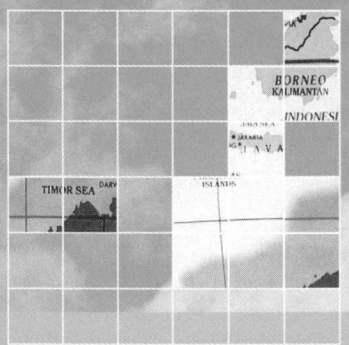

When you have studied this chapter, you should be able to:

1. understand the objective of a balance sheet and its limitations
2. understand and apply the requirements for the classification of balance sheet items
3. understand and apply the requirements for the presentation of information on the face of the balance sheet or in the notes
4. understand the objective of an income statement and its limitations
5. understand and apply the requirements for the presentation of information on the face of the income statement or in the notes
6. understand the objective of a statement of changes in equity
7. understand and apply the requirements for the presentation of information on the face of the statement in changes in equity or in the notes
8. understand and apply the requirements relating to the notes to financial statements.

16.1 Presentation of financial statements

The overall principles and other considerations relating to the presentation of financial statements as contained in IAS 1 *Presentation of Financial Statements* are addressed in chapter 15. This chapter deals with detailed matters relating to the presentation of a balance sheet, income statement, statement of changes in equity and notes. IAS 1 prescribes the structure and minimum content of these statements and notes. Other International Financial Reporting Standards (IFRSs) mandate disclosures relating to specific financial statement elements and transactions and events, as well as their recognition and measurement. Specific required disclosures relevant to the topics of the various chapters of this book are outlined in those chapters.

16.2 Scope

IAS 1 applies to all general purpose financial statements prepared and presented in accordance with IFRSs, except that its requirements relating to the structure and content of financial statements are not applicable to condensed interim financial statements. The structure and content requirements of condensed interim financial statements are contained in IAS 34 *Interim Financial Reporting*. The requirements of IAS 1 apply to the separate accounts of entities, as well as consolidated financial statements, which are required to be prepared under IAS 27 *Consolidated and Separate Financial Statements*.

Paragraph 5 of IAS 1 explains that the terminology used in IAS 1 is suitable for profit-oriented entities, including public sector business entities. However, if IAS 1 is applied to entities with not-for-profit activities in the private or public sectors there may be a need to amend the descriptions used for particular line items in the financial statements and for the financial statements themselves.

16.3 Balance sheet

LO 1

16.3.1 The objective of a balance sheet

One of the objectives of financial statements is to provide information about an entity's financial position. The balance sheet of an entity is the prime source for information about an entity's financial position because it summarises the elements directly related to the measurement of financial position: an entity's assets, liabilities and equity. It thus provides the basic information for evaluating an entity's capital structure and analysing its liquidity, solvency and financial flexibility. It also provides a basis for computing rates of return (e.g. return on total assets and equity and measures of solvency and liquidity).

However, the view of an entity's financial position presented by the balance sheet is by no means perfect and is often criticised by some commentators as being of limited value. These limitations primarily arise from:

- the optional measurement of certain assets at historical cost or depreciated historical cost rather than at a current value (refer to chapter 10 for further details)
- the mandatory omission of intangible self-generated assets from the balance sheet as a result of the recognition and measurement requirements of IAS 38 *Intangible Assets*. Significant examples include successful research expenditure and brand names, mastheads and similar assets (refer to chapter 11 for further details)
- financial engineering that frequently leads to off-balance-sheet rights and obligations. A significant example is the non-balance-sheet recognition of the rights and obligations pertaining to non-cancellable operating leases (refer to chapter 14 for further details).

Because of these limitations the balance sheet should be read in conjunction with the notes to the financial statements.

LO 2

16.3.2 Balance sheet classifications

The balance sheet presents a structured summary of the assets, liabilities and equity of an entity. Assets and liabilities are classified in a manner that facilitates the evaluation of an entity's financial structure and its liquidity, solvency and financial flexibility. Consequently, assets and liabilities are classified according to their function in the operations of the entity concerned and their liquidity and financial flexibility characteristics.

Paragraph 51 of IAS 1 requires an entity to classify assets and liabilities as current or non-current on the face of its balance sheet, except when a presentation based on liquidity is considered to provide more relevant and reliable information. When that exception arises, all assets and liabilities are required to be presented broadly in order of liquidity.

The current/non-current classification is ordinarily considered to be more relevant when an entity has a clearly identifiable operating cycle. This is because it distinguishes between those assets and liabilities that are expected to circulate within the entity's operating cycle and those used in the entity's long-term operations. The typical cycle operates from cash, purchase of inventory (in the case of a manufacturer, production) and then receivables through sales of inventory and finally back to cash through collection of the receivables. The average time of the operating cycle varies with the nature of the operations making up the cycle and may extend beyond 12 months. Industries where long operating cycles may exist include real estate development and construction, agriculture (such as plantation development) and property development.

Figure 16.1 shows the assets classified as current assets in the 31 December 2005 consolidated balance sheet of the Nokia Group, while figure 16.2 shows the liabilities classified as current.

Dec. 31	Notes	2005 EURm	2004 EURm
Current assets			
Inventories	19, 21	1 668	1 305
Accounts receivable, net of allowances for doubtful accounts (2005: EUR 281 million, 2004: EUR 361 million)	20, 21	5 346	4 382
Prepaid expenses and accrued income	20	1 938	1 429
Other financial assets		89	595
Available-for-sale investments	17	–	255
Available-for-sale investments, liquid assets	17	6 852	9 085
Available-for-sale investments, cash equivalents	17, 35	1 493	1 367
Bank and cash	35	1 565	1 090
		18 951	19 508

FIGURE 16.1 Current assets of the Nokia Group at 31 December 2005
Source: Nokia (2005, p. 7).

Dec. 31	Notes	2005 EURm	2004 EURm
Current liabilities			
Short-term borrowings	28	377	215
Accounts payable		3 494	2 669
Accrued expenses	29	3 320	2 604
Provisions	30	2 479	2 488
		9 670	7 976

FIGURE 16.2 Current liabilities of the Nokia Group at 31 December 2005
Source: Nokia (2005, p. 7).

Paragraph 54 of IAS 1 explains that for entities such as financial institutions a presentation based broadly on order of liquidity is usually considered to be more relevant than a current/non-current presentation. This is because such entities do not supply goods or services within a clearly identifiable operating cycle.

Figure 16.3 shows the balance sheet of the Dresdner Bank Group, in which the assets and liabilities of the group are presented in order of liquidity.

Balance sheet					
Assets	Note	31 Dec. 2005 € mn	31 Dec. 2004 € mn	Change € mn	%
Cash funds	(13)	4 295	2 266	2 029	89.5
Financial assets at fair value	(14)	165 806	192 570	−26 764	−13.9
Loans and advances to banks (net of loan loss allowance of €190m)	(15)	99 791	125 634	−25 843	−20.6
Loans and advances to customers (net of loan loss allowance of €1372m)	(16)	161 941	166 625	−4 684	−2.8
Investment securities	(19)	13 739	17 102	−3 363	−19.7
Investments in enterprises accounted for using the equity method	(19)	392	2 785	−2 393	−85.9
Property and equipment	(20)	2 432	4 451	−2 019	−45.4
Intangible assets	(21)	467	451	16	3.5
Assets held for sale	(22)	1 410	−	1 410	
Other assets	(23)	8 195	8 420	−225	−2.7
Deferred tax assets	(33)	2 904	3 566	−662	−18.6
Total assets		461 372	523 870	−62 498	−11.9
Liabilities and Equity	Note	31 Dec. 2005 € mn	31 Dec. 2004 € mn	Change € mn	%
Financial liabilities at fair value	(26)	81 322	99 799	−18 477	−18.5
Liabilities to banks	(27)	139 910	187 462	−47 552	−25.4
Liabilities to customers	(28)	155 785	154 513	1 272	0.8
Certificated liabilities	(29)	50 079	46 494	3 585	7.7
Provisions and other liabilities	(30)	11 976	13 462	−1 486	−11.0
Deferred tax liabilities	(33)	996	1 628	−632	−38.8
Subordinated liabilities	(34)	5 811	6 189	−378	−6.1
Profit-participation certificates	(35)	1 517	1 526	−9	−0.6
Equity	(36)	13 976	12 797	1 179	9.2
− Parent shareholders' equity		11 763	10 929	834	7.6
− Subscribed capital		1 503	1 503	0	0.0
− Additional paid-in capital		6 383	6 676	−293	−4.4
− Retained earnings		2 213	1 366	847	62.0
− Translation reserve		−380	−497	117	−23.5
− Cumulative remeasurement gains/losses on financial instruments		1 235	1 881	−646	−34.3
− Distributable profit		809	0	809	
− Minority interests		2 213	1 868	345	18.5
Total liabilities and equity		461 372	523 870	−62 498	−11.9

FIGURE 16.3   Balance sheet of the Dresdner Bank Group at 31 December 2005
Source: Dresdner Bank Corporation (2005, p. 117).

Where an entity has diverse operations, paragraph 55 of IAS 1 permits the use of both methods of presentation for the relevant assets and liabilities when this provides more relevant and reliable information.

Paragraphs 57 and 60 of IAS 1 mandate the classification of assets and liabilities as current or non-current as follows:

57. An asset shall be classified as current when it satisfies any of the following criteria:
    (a) it is expected to be realised in, or is intended for sale or consumption in, the entity's normal operating cycle;
    (b) it is held primarily for the purpose of being traded;
    (c) it is expected to be realised within twelve months after the balance sheet date; or
    (d) it is cash or a cash equivalent (as defined in IAS 7 *Cash Flow Statements*) unless it is restricted from being exchanged or used to settle a liability for at least twelve months after the balance date.
    All other assets shall be classified as non-current.
60. A liability shall be classified as current when it satisfies any of the following criteria:
    (a) it is expected to be settled in the entity's normal operating cycle;
    (b) it is held primarily for the purpose of being traded;
    (c) it is due to be settled within twelve months after the balance date; or
    (d) the entity does not have an unconditional right to defer settlement of the liability for at least twelve months after the balance date.
    All other liabilities shall be classified as non-current.

Figure 16.4 shows the assets classified as non-current assets in the 31 December 2005 consolidated balance sheet of the Nokia Group, while figure 16.5 shows the liabilities of the group classified as non-current.

Dec. 31	Notes	2005 EURm	2004 EURm
Non-current assets			
Capitalised development costs	14	260	278
Goodwill	14	90	90
Other intangible assets	14	211	209
Property, plant and equipment	15	1 585	1 534
Investments in associated companies	16	193	200
Available-for-sale investments	17	246	169
Deferred tax assets	27	692	623
Long-term loans receivable	18	63	–
Other non-current assets		7	58
		3 347	3 161

FIGURE 16.4 Non-current assets of the Nokia Group at 31 December 2005
Source: Nokia (2005, p. 7).

Dec. 31	Notes	2005 EURm	2004 EURm
Non-current liabilities	26		
Long-term interest-bearing liabilities		21	19
Deferred tax liabilities	27	151	179
Other long-term liabilities		96	96
		268	294

FIGURE 16.5 Non-current liabilities of the Nokia Group at 31 December 2005
Source: Nokia (2005, p. 7).

Under these classifications, current assets may include inventories and receivables that are expected to be sold, consumed or realised as part of the normal operating cycle beyond 12 months after balance sheet date. Similarly, current liabilities may include payables that are expected to be settled after more than 12 months after balance sheet date. Because of these possibilities paragraph 52 of IAS 1 requires that irrespective of whether assets and liabilities are classified on the current/non-current basis or in order of liquidity:

> ... for each asset and liability line item that combines amounts expected to be recovered or settled (a) no more than twelve months after the balance sheet date and (b) more than twelve months after the balance sheet date, an entity shall disclose the amount expected to be recovered or settled after more than twelve months.

Note 20 to the consolidated financial statements of the Nokia Group at 31 December 2005 reports that 'accounts receivable include EUR 166 million (EUR 118 million in 2004) due more than 12 months after the balance sheet date' (refer to figure 16.1 for total accounts receivable classified as a current asset).

The criteria for classifying liabilities as current or non-current are based solely on the conditions existing at the balance sheet date. Paragraph 61 of IAS 1 clarifies that financial liabilities that are due to be settled within 12 months after the balance sheet date are classified as current liabilities; this is even if an agreement to refinance or to reschedule payments on a long-term basis is completed after the balance sheet date and before the financial statements are authorised for issue. Consistent with this approach, paragraph 64 explains that if an entity expects and has the discretion to refinance or roll over an obligation for at least 12 months after the balance sheet date under an existing loan facility (i.e. one entered into before balance sheet date), the obligation is classified as non-current, even if it would otherwise be due within a shorter period. Similarly, paragraph 65 explains that if an entity breaches an undertaking under a long-term loan agreement on or before balance sheet date with the effect that the loan is repayable on demand, the loan is classified as current. This is unless the lender agrees by balance sheet date to waive the right to demand immediate repayment for at least 12 months after the balance sheet date. Such an agreement post-balance sheet date, but before the accounts are authorised for issue, does not change the required current classification.

The classification of liabilities as current or non-current is a particularly important issue for the purposes of assessing an entity's solvency. For example, an entity's current ratio (current assets to current liabilities) is often used as an indicator of solvency. Financiers, in setting the terms of borrowings, may also use it — some financiers will require that an entity not fall below a certain ratio of current assets to current liabilities. This is known as a 'negative pledge'. If the entity falls below that ratio then the financier has the right to demand repayment of the borrowing. These factors then affect the going concern assumption discussed in chapter 15.

LO 3

16.3.3 Information required to be presented on the face of the balance sheet

IAS 1 does not prescribe a standard balance sheet format that must be adopted. Rather, it prescribes a list of items that are considered to be sufficiently different in nature or function to warrant presentation on the face of the balance sheet as separate line items. These items are set forth in paragraph 68 and are:

(a) property, plant and equipment;
(b) investment property;
(c) intangible assets;
(d) financial assets (excluding amounts under (e), (h) and (i));
(e) investments accounted for using the equity method;
(f) biological assets;
(g) inventories;
(h) trade and other receivables;
(i) cash and cash equivalents;

(j) trade and other payables;

(k) provisions;⁻

(l) financial liabilities (excluding amounts shown under (j) and (k));

(m) liabilities and assets for current tax, as defined in IAS 12 *Income Taxes*;

(n) deferred tax liabilities and deferred tax assets, as defined in IAS 12;

(o) minority interest, presented within equity; and

(p) issued capital and reserves attributable to equity holders of the parent.

Paragraph 68A of IAS 1 requires disclosure of:

(a) the total of assets classified as held for sale and assets included in disposal groups classified as held for sale in accordance with IFRS 5 *Non-current Assets Held for Sale and Discontinued Operations*; and

(b) liabilities included in disposal groups classified as held for sale in accordance with IFRS 5.

Figure 16.6 shows the disclosures made in the Nokia Group's consolidated balance sheet at 31 December 2005 concerning the issued capital and reserves attributable to equity holders of the parent and minority interests.

Dec. 31	Notes	2005 EURm	2004 EURm
Capital and reserves attributable to equity holders of the parent			
Share capital	23	266	280
Share issue premium		2 458	2 366
Treasury shares, at cost		−3 616	−2 022
Translation differences		69	−126
Fair value and other reserves	22	−176	13
Retained earnings	25	13 154	13 720
		12 155	14 231
Minority interests		205	168
Total equity		12 360	14 399

FIGURE 16.6   Shareholders' equity attributable to the equity holders of Nokia Corporation and minority interests
Source: Nokia (2005, p. 7).

Paragraph 69 of IAS 1 requires additional line items, headings and subtotals to be presented on the face of the balance sheet when their inclusion is relevant to an understanding of the entity's financial position. Paragraph 72 explains that the judgement on whether additional items should be separately presented is based on an assessment of:

(a) the nature and liquidity of assets;

(b) the function of assets within the entity; and

(c) the amounts, nature and timing of liabilities.

16.3.4 Information required to be presented on the face of the balance sheet or in the notes

To enhance the understandability of the balance sheet line items, paragraph 74 of IAS 1 requires subclassifications of the line items to be presented either on the face of the balance sheet or in the notes in a manner appropriate to the entity's operations.

In some cases, the subclassifications are governed by a specific IFRS. For example, IAS 2 requires the total carrying amount of inventories to be broken down into classifications appropriate to the entity (refer to chapter 9). Such classifications may include merchandise, production supplies, materials, work in progress and finished goods. IAS 16 requires items of property, plant and equipment to be disaggregated into classes (refer to chapter 10). Entities typically separately report land and buildings from plant and equipment. Other examples are outlined in the other chapters included in part 2 of this book.

Figure 16.7 shows the subclassifications of inventories reported in note 19 to the 31 December 2005 consolidated financial statements of the Nokia Group.

19. Inventories	2005 EURm	2004 EURm
Raw materials, supplies and other	361	326
Work in progress	685	477
Finished goods	622	502
Total	1 668	1 305

FIGURE 16.7   Note 19 *Inventories* to the 31 December 2005 consolidated financial statements of the Nokia Group
Source: Nokia (2005, p. 23).

Paragraph 75 of IAS 1 explains that subclassifications of balance sheet line items are also dependent on the size, nature and function of the amounts involved and that judgement about the need for subclassifications should have regard to the same factors previously outlined when judging whether additional balance sheet line items should be presented (refer to section 16.3.3).

Other typical subclassifications include the disaggregation of:

(a) receivables between amounts receivable from trade customers, receivables from related parties and other amounts
(b) provisions into those for employee benefits, restructuring provisions, warranty provisions and other items
(c) equity into share capital, reserves and retained earnings.

Figure 16.8 shows the subclassifications of provisions reported in note 30 to the 31 December 2005 consolidated financial statements of the Nokia Group.

EURm	Warranty	IPR infringements	Tax	Other	Total
At Jan. 1, 2005, As revised	1 217	358	364	549	2 488
Exchange differences	22	–	–	–	22
Additional provisions	819	101	64	169	1 153
Change in fair value	–	–	–	3	3
Changes in estimates	–202	–41	–42	–39	–324
Charged to profit and loss account	617	60	22	133	832
Utilized during year	–675	–22	–	–166	–863
At Dec. 31, 2005	1 181	396	386	516	2 479

EURm	2005	2004
Analysis of total provisions at December 31:		
Non-current	788	726
Current	1 691	1 762

The IPR provision is based on estimated future settlements for asserted and unasserted past IPR infringements. Final resolution of IPR claims generally occurs over several periods. This results in varying usage of the provision year to year.

Other provisions include provisions for non-cancellable purchase commitments, provision for pension and other social costs on share-based awards and provision for losses on projects in progress.

FIGURE 16.8   Note 30 *Provisions* to the 31 December 2005 consolidated financial statements of the Nokia Group
Source: Nokia (2005, p. 30).

In addition, paragraph 76 of IAS 1 requires an entity to disclose the following, either on the face of the balance sheet or in the notes:

(a) for each class of share capital:
   (i) the number of shares authorised;
   (ii) the number of shares issued and fully paid, and issued but not fully paid;
   (iii) par value per share, or that the shares have no par value;
   (iv) a reconciliation of the number of shares outstanding at the beginning and at the end of the period;
   (v) the rights, preferences and restrictions attaching to that class including restrictions on the distribution of dividends and the repayment of capital;
   (vi) shares in the entity held by the entity or by its subsidiaries or associates; and
   (vii) shares reserved for issue under options and contracts for the sale of shares, including the terms and amounts; and
(b) a description of the nature and purpose of each reserve within equity.

16.3.5   Illustrative balance sheets

Part A of the guidance on implementing IAS 1 that accompanies, but is not part of, IAS 1 includes an illustrative balance sheet. The illustrative balance sheet is presented in figure 16.9, along with references to the relevant IAS 1 requirements. Figure 16.10 shows the group balance sheet of AngloGold Ashanti Ltd, a mining company incorporated in the Republic of South Africa, which is typical of a balance sheet prepared in accordance with IFRSs. Note 1 to AngloGold Ashanti's financial statements outlines its accounting policies and reports that the group's presentation currency is US dollars. The amounts have also been disclosed in SA Rand to help South African investors (refer to chapter 24 for a discussion of the issues relating to foreign currency translation).

FIGURE 16.9   Illustrative balance sheet

XYZ Group Balance sheet as at 31 December 20X2			
	In thousands of currency units		IAS 1, para. 46(a) 44, 46(c) 46(d), (e) 36
	20X2	20X1	
ASSETS			
Non-current assets			51
Property, plant and equipment	X	X	68(a)
Goodwill	X	X	68(c), 69
Other intangible assets	X	X	68(c), 69
Investments in associates	X	X	68(e)
Available-for-sale investments	X	X	68(d)
Total non-current assets	X	X	
Current assets			51
Inventories	X	X	68(g)
Trade receivables	X	X	68(h)
Other current assets	X	X	
Cash and cash equivalents	X	X	68(i)
Total current assets	X	X	
Total assets	X	X	

(continued)

EQUITY AND LIABILITIES			
Equity attributable to equity holders of the parent			
Share capital	X	X	75(e)
Other reserves	X	X	75(e)
Retained earnings	X	X	75(e)
	X	X	68(p)
Minority interest	X	X	68(o)
Total equity	X	X	
Non-current liabilities			51
Long-term liabilities	X	X	68(l), 70
Deferred tax	X	X	68(n)
Long-term provisions	X	X	68(k)
Total non-current liabilities	X	X	
Current liabilities			51
Trade and other payables	X	X	68(j)
Short-term borrowings	X	X	68(l)
Current portion of long-term borrowings	X	X	68(l)
Current tax payable	X	X	68(m)
Short-term provisions	X	X	68(k)
Total current liabilities	X	X	
Total liabilities	X	X	
Total equity and liabilities	X	X	

Source: IAS 1 Adapted from *Presentation of Financial Statements, Guidance on Implementing IAS 1.*

FIGURE 16.10 Group balance sheet of AngloGold Ashanti Limited

AngloGold Ashanti Group balance sheet as at 31 December 2005						
2004	2005	Figures in million	Notes	2005	2004
SA Rands				US Dollars	
		ASSETS			
		Non-current assets			
33 239	37 464	Tangible assets	17	5 905	5 888
2 458	2 533	Intangible assets	18	399	435
43	223	Investments in associates	19	35	8
608	645	Other investments	20	102	107
202	1 182	Inventories	22	186	35
1 055	243	Derivatives	40	38	187
55	124	Trade and other receivables	24	20	10
–	279	Deferred taxation	34	44	–
101	101	Other non-current assets	23	16	18
37 761	42 794			6 745	6 688

2004	2005	Figures in million	Notes	2005	2004
		AngloGold Ashanti **Group balance sheet (continued)**			
SA Rands				US Dollars	
		Current assets			
2 285	2 436	Inventories	22	384	406
1 700	1 589	Trade and other receivables	24	250	302
2 767	4 280	Derivatives	40	675	490
5	43	Current portion of other non-current assets	23	7	1
148	52	Cash restricted for use	25	8	26
1 630	1 328	Cash and cash equivalents	26	209	289
8 535	9 728			1 533	1 514
–	100	Non-current assets held for sale	27	16	–
8 535	9 828			1 549	1 514
46 296	52 622	Total assets		8 294	8 202
		EQUITY AND LIABILITIES			
18 987	19 047	Share capital and premium	28	3 002	3 364
(1 197)	(2 463)	Retained earnings and other reserves	29	(388)	(213)
17 790	16 584	Shareholders' equity		2 614	3 151
327	374	Minority interests	30	59	58
18 117	16 958	Total equity		2 673	3 209
		Non-current liabilities			
7 262	10 825	Borrowings	31	1 706	1 286
1 294	2 265	Environmental rehabilitation and other provisions	32	356	230
1 112	1 249	Provision for pension and post-retirement benefits	33	197	197
21	87	Trade, other payables and deferred income	35	14	4
3 033	2 460	Derivatives	40	388	537
7 653	7 353	Deferred taxation	34	1 159	1 356
20 375	24 239			3 820	3 610
		Current liabilities			
2 629	2 711	Trade, other payables and deferred income	35	427	466
1 800	1 190	Current portion of borrowings	31	188	319
3 007	6 814	Derivatives	40	1 074	533
368	710	Taxation		112	65
7 804	11 425			1 801	1 383
28 179	35 664	Total liabilities		5 621	4 993
46 296	52 622	Total equity and liabilities		8 294	8 202

Rounding of figures may result in computational discrepancies.
Source: AngloGold Ashanti (2005, p. 129).

16.4 Income statement

16.4.1 The objective of an income statement

LO 4

As explained in chapter 2, the income statement is the prime source for information about an entity's performance. Paragraph 78 of IAS 1 requires all items of income and expense recognised in a period to be included in profit or loss unless a standard or an interpretation requires otherwise. The income statement thus summarises the financial statement elements used to measure an entity's profit or loss, which is the most frequent measure of an entity's performance. Profit or loss is also used in the determination of other measures of an entity's performance, such as earnings per share or rates of return on total assets or return on equity.

The income statement can also be used to assist to predict an entity's future performance and future cash flows. This is particularly the case if there is appropriate disclosure of unusual items of income and expense that will assist a user in judging the quality of an entity's performance − in terms of the likely future sustainability of the reported profit or loss. The ability to identify likely non-recurring items of income or expense is of particular significance in making this judgement.

However, like the view of an entity's financial position presented by the balance sheet, the view of an entity's performance presented by the income statement is by no means perfect. The statement has its limitations that primarily arise from:

- the exclusion of some items of income and expense from profit or loss, including surpluses on the revaluation of property, plant and equipment (refer to chapter 10), certain gains or losses arising on translating the financial statements of a foreign operation (refer to chapter 24), and gains or losses on remeasuring available-for-sale financial assets and hedging instruments (refer to chapter 6)
- the mandatory expensing of expenditure relating to intangible self-generated assets as required by IAS 38 (refer to chapter 11)
- deliberate earnings management through the making of biased judgements relating to the measurement of items of income or expense, such as impairment and restructuring losses, with the objective of smoothing earnings or projecting an image of earnings growth.

LO 5

16.4.2 ## Information required to be presented on the face of the income statement

As for the balance sheet, IAS 1 does not prescribe a standard income statement format that must be adopted. Rather, it prescribes line items that are considered to be of sufficient importance to the reporting of the performance of an entity to warrant their presentation on the face of the income statement. These items are set forth in paragraph 81 of IAS 1 and are:

(a) revenue;
(b) finance costs;
(c) share of profit or loss of associates and joint ventures accounted for using the equity method;
(d) tax expense
(e) a single amount comprising the total of (i) the post-tax profit or loss of discontinued operations and (ii) the post-tax gain or loss recognised on the measurement to fair value less costs to sell or on the disposal of the assets or disposal group(s) constituting the discontinued operation; and
(f) profit or loss.

Paragraph 82 of IAS 1 requires disclosure of the following items as allocations of profit or loss for the period on the face of the income statement:

(a) profit or loss attributable to minority interest; and
(b) profit or loss attributable to equity holders of the parent.

In addition, paragraph 83 of IAS 1 requires additional line items, headings and subtotals to be presented on the face of the income statement when such presentation is relevant to an understanding of the entity's financial performance.

Paragraph 84 of IAS 1 explains that 'additional line items are included on the face of the income statement, and the descriptions used and the ordering of items are amended when this is necessary to explain the elements of financial performance.' Paragraph 84 further explains that the factors to be considered in making judgements concerning the inclusion of additional line items include the materiality and the nature and function of the components of income and expense.

However, paragraph 85 of IAS 1 specifically prohibits the presentation of any items of income and expense as 'extraordinary items' either on the face of the income statement or in the notes. This prohibition was inserted in IAS 1 following the IASB's decision to eliminate the concept of extraordinary items from IAS 8. IAS 8 previously defined 'extraordinary items' as 'income or expenses that arise from events or transactions that are clearly distinct from the ordinary activities of the enterprise and therefore are not expected to recur frequently or regularly'. In amending IAS 8 and prohibiting the presentation of 'extraordinary items' in the income statement or notes, the IASB concluded that items previously treated as extraordinary items resulted from the normal business risks faced by an entity and do not warrant presentation in a separate component of the income statement.

In the past, accounting standards have also classified items as 'abnormal' items depending on whether they were large or unusual. As with extraordinary items, this classification has been eliminated. The classification of items as abnormal or extraordinary allowed entities to report variations of their profit or loss for the period — for example, 'profit before abnormal items' or 'profit before extraordinary items'. Unfortunately the distinctions tended to be abused such that a profit figure was made to look better by reporting it before a large abnormal or extraordinary expense. Now that abnormal and extraordinary items have been eliminated, this practice should disappear. However, there is nothing in IAS 1 to prevent an entity from creating as many subtotals as it wishes. Thus, it could report a profit before and after any line item such as depreciation or impairment losses.

16.4.3 Information required to be presented on the face of the income statement or in the notes

To enhance the understandability of the income statement, paragraph 86 of IAS 1 requires the separate disclosure of the nature and amount of material items of income and expense. Paragraph 87 of IAS 1 explains that the circumstances that would give rise to the separate disclosure of items of income and expense include:

(a) write-downs of inventories to net realisable value or of property, plant and equipment to recoverable amounts, as well as reversals of such write-downs;
(b) restructurings of the activities of an entity and reversals of any provisions for the costs of restructurings;
(c) disposals of items of property, plant and equipment;
(d) disposals of investments;
(e) discontinued operations;
(f) litigation settlements; and
(g) other reversals of provisions.

Disclosure of these items is particularly important to a user of the income statement wishing to predict the likely future sustainability of the reported profit or loss.

Paragraph 88 of IAS 1 requires an entity to present an analysis of expenses classified either by their nature (for example, purchases of material, transport costs, employee benefits, depreciation and advertising costs) or their function within the entity (for example, costs of sales, costs of distribution and administrative activities), whichever provides the more relevant and reliable information. Paragraph 89 encourages, but does not require, the presentation of this expense analysis on the face of the income statement.

Figure 16.11 shows an example of a classification using the nature of expense method provided in paragraph 91 of IAS 1.

Revenue		X
Other income		X
Changes in inventories of finished goods and work in progress	X	
Raw materials and consumables used	X	
Employee benefit expense	X	
Depreciation and amortisation expense	X	
Other expenses	X	
	—	
Total expenses		(X)
		—
Profit		X
		=

FIGURE 16.11   Example of classification of expenses by nature
Source: IAS 1 *Presentation of Financial Statements,* paragraph 91.

Figure 16.12 shows an example of a classification using the function of expense method provided in IAS 1.

Revenue	X
Cost of sales	(X)
	—
Gross profit	X
Other income	X
Distribution costs	(X)
Administrative expenses	(X)
Other expenses	(X)
	—
Profit	X
	=

FIGURE 16.12   Example of classification of expenses by function
Source: IAS 1 *Presentation of Financial Statements,* paragraph 92.

If the classification of expenses by function method is used, additional information on the nature of expenses, including depreciation and amortisation expense and employee benefits expense, must be disclosed. Paragraph 94 of IAS 1 explains that this additional information is required because it is useful in predicting future cash flows.

Paragraph 95 of IAS 1 requires disclosure of, either on the face of the income statement or the statement of changes in equity or the notes, the amounts of dividends recognised as distributions to equity holders during the period, and the related amount per share.

16.4.4   Illustrative income statements

The guidance on implementing IAS 1 that accompanies, but is not part of, IAS 1 includes illustrative income statements. These illustrative income statements, along with references to IAS 1, are presented in figures 16.13 and 16.14. Figure 16.15 shows the consolidated profit and loss accounts (income statements) of the Nokia Group for the year ended 31 December 2005 together with comparatives for the preceding two years. Note that the comparatives are 'As revised'. The revisions made reflect the adoption of IFRS 2 *Share-based Payment* and revised IAS 39 *Financial Instruments: Recognition and Measurement* (refer to figure 16.18 on pages 690–2 for further information).

XYZ Group Income statement for the year ended 31 December 20X2			
	In thousands of currency units		IAS 1, para. 46(a) 44, 46(c) 46(d), (e)
	20X2	20X1	
Revenue	X	X	81(a)
Cost of sales	(X)	(X)	88, 92
Gross profit	X	X	
Other income	X	X	81(a)
Distribution costs	(X)	(X)	88, 92
Administrative expenses	(X)	(X)	88, 92
Other expenses	(X)	(X)	88, 92
Finance costs	(X)	(X)	81(b)
Share of profits of associates	X	X	81(c)
Profit before tax	X	X	
Income tax expense	(X)	(X)	81(d)
Profit for the period	X	X	81(f)
Attributable to:			
Equity holders of the parent	X	X	82(b)
Minority interest	X	X	82(a)
	X	X	

FIGURE 16.13 Illustrative income statement, illustrating the classification of expenses by function
Source: Adapted from IAS 1 *Presentation of Financial Statements, Guidance on Implementing IAS 1.*

XYZ Group Income statement for the year ended 31 December 20X2			
	In thousands of currency units		IAS 1, para. 46(a) 44, 46(c) 46(d), (e)
	20X2	20X1	
Revenue	X	X	81(a)
Other income	X	X	81(a)
Changes in inventories of finished goods and work in progress	(X)	(X)	88, 91
Work performed by the entity and capitalised	X	X	88, 91
Raw material and consumables used	(X)	(X)	88, 91
Employee benefits expense	(X)	(X)	88, 91
Depreciation and amortisation expense	(X)	(X)	88, 91
Impairment of property, plant and equipment	(X)	(X)	86, 88
Other expenses	(X)	(X)	88
Finance costs	(X)	(X)	81(b)
Share of profits of associates	X	X	81(c)
Profit before tax	X	X	
Income tax expense	(X)	(X)	81(d)
Profit for the period	X	X	81(f)
Attributable to:			
Equity holders of the parent	X	X	82(b)
Minority interest	X	X	82(a)
	X	X	

FIGURE 16.14 Illustrative income statement, illustrating the classification of expenses by nature
Source: Adapted from IAS 1 *Presentation of Financial Statements, Guidance on Implementing IAS 1.*

Nokia Group Consolidated profit and loss accounts, IFRS				
Financial year ended December 31	Notes	2005 EURm	2004 As revised EURm	2003 As revised EURm
Net sales		34 191	29 371	29 533
Cost of sales		−22 209	−18 179	−17 325
Gross profit		11 982	11 192	12 208
Research and development expenses		−3 825	−3 776	−3 788
Selling and marketing expenses	7	−2 961	−2 564	−2 657
Administrative and general expenses		−609	−611	−635
Other income	8	285	343	300
Other expenses	8, 9	−233	−162	−384
Customer finance impairment charges, net of reversals	9	–	–	226
Impairment of goodwill	9	–	–	−151
Amortization of goodwill	11	–	−96	−159
Operating profit	3, 4, 5, 6, 7, 8, 9, 10, 11	4 639	4 326	4 960
Share of results of associated companies	34	10	−26	−18
Financial income and expenses	12	322	405	352
Profit before tax		4 971	4 705	5 294
Tax	13	−1 281	−1 446	−1 697
Profit before minority interests		3 690	3 259	3 597
Minority interests		−74	−67	−54
Profit attributable to equity holders of the parent		3 616	3 192	3 543
Earnings per share (for profit attributable to the equity holders of the parent)	31	2005 EURm	2004 As revised EURm	2003 As revised EURm
Basic		0.83	0.69	0.74
Diluted		0.83	0.69	0.74
Average number of shares (000s shares)	31	2005	2004	2003
Basic		4 365 547	4 593 196	4 761 121
Diluted		4 371 239	4 600 337	4 761 160

FIGURE 16.15   Consolidated profit and loss accounts, IFRS of Nokia Group
Source: Nokia (2005, p. 6).

Note that in figure 16.15 the disclosure of earnings per share, and the average number of shares used to determine those per share amounts, are disclosed pursuant to the requirements of IAS 33 *Earnings per Share*.

16.5   Statement of changes in equity

LO 6

16.5.1   The objective of a statement of changes in equity

An assessment of the full performance of an entity requires consideration of not only the items of income and expense included in the determination of the profit or loss for the period, but also consideration of the gains and losses recognised directly in equity as required by a number of IFRSs (refer to section 16.4.1). To facilitate this consideration, the statement of changes in equity reports the profit or loss for the period and the other gains and losses recognised directly in equity. It may also report transactions with equity holders, such as new share issues and the payment of dividends.

An alternative approach to facilitating an assessment of the full performance of an entity would be to require the presentation of a comprehensive statement of financial performance that would include not only the content of the currently required income statement, but also the other gains and losses currently recognised directly in equity. One of the projects currently on the work program of the IASB concerns performance reporting. This project is being conducted jointly with the US Financial Accounting Standards Board. The IASB project summary reports that one of its tasks is to consider whether to require a single statement of comprehensive income that includes a subtotal similar to the concept of 'net income from continuing operations' (as required under US GAAP) or 'profit and loss'.

LO 7

16.5.2 Information required to be reported on the face of the statement of changes in equity

Paragraph 96 of IAS 1 requires the following information to be presented on the face of the statement of changes in equity:

(a) profit or loss for the period;

(b) each item of income and expense for the period that, as required by other Standards or by Interpretations, is recognised directly in equity, and the total of these items; and

(c) total income and expense for the period (calculated as the sum of (a) and (b)), showing separately the total amounts attributable to equity holders of the parent and to minority interest;

(d) for each component of equity, the effects of changes in accounting policies and corrections of errors recognised in accordance with IAS 8.

A statement of changes in equity that comprises only the above items is required to be called a 'statement of recognised income and expense'.

The requirements of IAS 8 are outlined in chapter 15.

16.5.3 Information to be presented on the face of the statement of changes in equity or in the notes

Paragraph 97 of IAS 1 requires an entity, to present, either on the face of the statement of changes in equity or in the notes:

(a) the amounts of transactions with equity holders acting in their capacity as equity holders, showing separately distributions to equity holders;

(b) the balance of retained earnings (ie accumulated profit or loss) at the beginning of the period and at the balance sheet date, and the changes during the period; and

(c) a reconciliation between the carrying amount of each class of contributed equity and each reserve at the beginning and the end of the period, separately disclosing each change.

16.5.4 Illustrative statements of changes in equity

The guidance on implementing IAS 1 that accompanies, but is not part of, IAS 1 includes two illustrative statements of changes in equity. The first example comprises a comprehensive reconciliation of the movements in each element of equity attributable to the equity holders of the parent and the minority interest and total equity for the current and the prior year. The second example illustrates an approach that presents only changes in equity representing income and expense in a separate component of the financial statements, titled 'Statement of Recognised Income and Expense'. Under this approach, the reconciliation of opening and closing balances of share capital, reserves and accumulated profit is presented in the notes, as permitted by paragraph 97 of IAS 1.

Figure 16.16 shows a sample comprehensive statement of changes in equity prepared in accordance with the requirements of IAS 1, with references to these requirements. This statement is based on the first illustration contained in the IAS 1 guidance.

Sunshine Ltd Group **Consolidated statement of changes in equity** **for the year ended 31 December 2007**								
	Attributable to equity holders of Sunshine Ltd							IAS 1, para. 46A, 44, 46(c), (d), (e)
$A millions	Share capital	Foreign currency	Other reserves	Retained earnings	Total	Minority interest	Total equity	
Balance at 31 December 2005	681	250	68	262	1 261	35	1 296	*97(c)*
Gain on property revaluation			20		20	5	25	*96(b)*
Available-for-sale investments								
Gains taken to equity			30		30		30	*96(b)*
Transferred to profit on sale			(15)		(15)		(15)	*96(b)*
Cash flow hedges								
Losses taken to equity			(25)		(25)	(3)	(28)	*96(b)*
Transferred to initial carrying								
amount of hedged items			10		10	(2)	8	*96(b)*
Transferred to profit for year			20		20	(8)	12	*96(b)*
Exchange differences on translating								
foreign operations		20			20	5	25	*96(b)*
Tax on items taken directly to or								
transferred from equity		(12)	(12)		(24)	1	(23)	*96(b)*
Net income recognised directly in equity		8	28		36	(2)	34	*96(b)*
Profit for year				135	135	8	143	*96(a)*
Total recognised income and expense **for the year**		8	28	135	171	6	177	*96(c)*
Dividends				(80)	(80)	(5)	(85)	*97(a)*
Share issue	90				90		90	*97(a)*
Balance at 31 December 2006	771	258	96	317	1 442	36	1 478	*97(c)*
Available-for-sale investments								
Gains taken to equity			10		10		10	*96(b)*
Transferred to profit on sale			(8)		(8)		(8)	*96(b)*
Cash flow hedges								
Profits taken to equity			20		20	3	23	*96(b)*
Transferred to initial carrying								
amount of hedged items			5		5	3	8	*96(b)*
Exchange differences on translating								
foreign operations		10			10	2	12	*96(b)*
Tax on items taken directly to or								
transferred from equity		(5)	(8)		(13)	(3)	(16)	*96(b)*
Net income recognised directly in equity		5	19		24	5	29	*96(b)*
Profit for year				129	129	6	135	*96(a)*
Total recognised income and expense **for the year**		5	19	129	153	11	164	*96(c)*
Dividends				(85)	(85)	(6)	(91)	*97(a)*
Balance at 31 December 2007	771	263	115	361	1 510	41	1 551	*97(c)*

FIGURE 16.16 Statement of changes in equity of Sunshine Ltd Group

Figure 16.17 presents the illustrative statement of recognised income and expense contained in the guidance on implementing IAS 1, along with references to IAS 1.

XYZ Group Statement of recognised income and expense for the year ended 31 December 20X2			
	In thousands of currency units		IAS 1, para. 46(a) 44, 46(c) 46(d), (e)
	20X2	20X1	
Gain/(loss) on revaluation of properties	(X)	X	96(b)
Available-for-sale investments:			
Valuation gains/(losses) taken to equity	(X)	(X)	96(b)
Transferred to profit or loss on sale	X	(X)	96(b)
Cash flow hedges:			
Gains/(losses) taken to equity	X	X	96(b)
Transferred to profit or loss for the period	(X)	X	96(b)
Transferred to the initial carrying amount of hedged items	(X)	(X)	96(b)
Exchange differences on translation of foreign operations	(X)	(X)	96(b)
Actuarial gains (losses) on defined benefit plans	X	(X)	96(b)
Tax on items taken directly to or transferred from equity	X	(X)	96(b)
Net income recognised directly in equity	(X)	X	96(b)
Profit for the period	X	X	96(a)
Total recognised income and expense for the period	X	X	96(c)
Attributable to:			
Equity holders of the parent	X	X	96(c)
Minority interest	X	X	96(c)
	X	X	
Effect of changes in accounting policy:			
Equity holders of the parent		(X)	96(c)(d)
Minority interest		(X)	96(c)(d)
		(X)	

FIGURE 16.17 Illustrative statement of recognised income and expense
Source: Adapted from IAS 1 *Presentation of Financial Statements, Guidance on Implementing IAS 1.*

16.6 Cash flow statement

IAS 7 *Cash Flow Statements* sets out the requirements for the presentation of cash flow statements and related disclosures. These requirements and disclosures are outlined in chapter 17.

LO 8

16.7 Notes

Notes are an integral part of the financial statements. Their objective is to enhance the understandability of the balance sheet, income statement, cash flow statement and statement of changes in equity. As far as practicable, each item on the face of these statements is cross-referenced to any related information in the notes (IAS 1, para. 104).

Paragraphs 103 to 124 of IAS 1 require that the notes disclose:

- a statement of compliance with IFRSs (para. 105(a); see also para. 14)
- the basis of the financial statements' preparation, including the measurement basis (or bases) (such as historical cost, net realisable value, fair value or recoverable amount) (paras 103(a) and 108(a))
- other accounting policies used that are relevant to an understanding of the financial statements (para. 108(b))
- information about the key assumptions concerning the future, and other key sources of estimation uncertainty at the balance sheet date, that have a significant risk of causing a material adjustment to the carrying amounts of assets and liabilities within the next financial year (e.g. assumptions used in performing significant asset impairment tests) (para. 116)
- other judgements management has made in the process of applying the entity's accounting policies that have the most significant effect on the amounts recognised in the financial statements (e.g. whether financial assets are held-to-maturity investments, whether a lease is a finance or operating lease and whether sales of goods are, in substance, financing arrangements) (para. 113)
- the information required by IFRSs that is not presented on the face of the balance sheet, income statement, statement of changes in equity or cash flow statement (para. 103(b))
- other additional information that is not presented on the face of the balance sheet, income statement, statement of changes in equity and cash flow statement, but is relevant to an understanding of one of them (para. 103(c)).

The summary of accounting policies is normally presented as the first note to the financial statements and ordinarily begins with the required statement of compliance with IFRSs. The disclosure of accounting policies is particularly relevant to an understanding of the financial statements where options exist in IFRSs. Examples include:

- the use of the equity method or proportionate consolidation for the recognition of an interest in a jointly controlled entity (refer to chapter 26)
- the expensing of all borrowing costs or the capitalisation of that portion of borrowing costs applicable to qualifying assets (under IAS 23 *Borrowing Costs*)
- the option to revalue property, plant and equipment as an alternative to using historical costs (refer to chapter 10)
- the option to classify certain investments as trading investments, held-to-maturity investments or available-for-sale investments (refer to chapter 6).

Figure 16.18 contains extracts from Note 1 to the 31 December 2005 consolidated financial statements of the Nokia Group which describes the accounting policies (referred to as accounting principles) of the group.

FIGURE 16.18 Extracts from Note 1 *Accounting principles* to the 31 December 2005 consolidated financial statements of the Nokia Group

Accounting principles
Basis of presentation
The consolidated financial statements of Nokia Corporation ("Nokia" or "the Group"), a Finnish limited liability company with domicile in Helsinki, are prepared in accordance with International Financial Reporting Standards (IFRS). The consolidated financial statements are presented in millions of euros (EURm), except as noted, and are prepared under the historical cost convention, except as disclosed in the accounting policies below. The notes to the consolidated financial statements also conform with Finnish Accounting legislation.

As of January 1, 2005 the Group adopted IFRS 2, Share-based Payment. The standard requires the recognition of share-based payment transactions in financial statements, including transactions with employees or other parties to be settled in cash, other assets, or equity instruments of the Company. Prior to the adoption of IFRS 2, the Group did not recognize the financial effect of share-based payments until such payments were settled. In accordance with the transitional provisions of IFRS 2, the Standard has been applied retrospectively to all grants of shares, share options or other equity instruments that were granted after November 7, 2002 and that were not yet vested at the effective date of the standard.

As of January 1, 2005 the Group adopted IAS 39(R), Financial Instruments: Recognition and Measurement, which supersedes IAS 39 (revised 2000). Under IAS 39(R), hedge accounting is no longer allowed under Treasury Center foreign exchange netting. This change is retrospective for the Group as an existing IFRS user.

The comparative figures for 2004 and 2003 have been revised to reflect the adoption of IFRS 2 and IAS 39(R) and the effects are summarized in the consolidated statement of changes in shareholders' equity, and further information is disclosed in the accounting policies and in Notes to the consolidated financial statements.

The Group adopted IFRS 3, Business Combinations together with IAS 36(R), Impairment of Assets, and IAS 38(R), Intangible Assets, as of January 1, 2005, resulting in a change in the accounting policy for goodwill. Until December 31, 2004, goodwill was amortized on a straight line basis over its expected useful life over a period ranging from two to five years and assessed for an indication of impairment, periodically. In accordance with the provisions of IFRS 3, the Group ceased amortization of goodwill from January 1, 2005 for all acquisitions made prior to March 31, 2004. Accumulated amortization as of December 31, 2004 has been eliminated with a corresponding decrease in the cost of goodwill. From January 1, 2005, goodwill is assessed for impairment annually, and whenever there are indications of impairment. Under the transitional provisions of IFRS 3, this change in accounting policy was effective immediately for acquisitions made after March 31, 2004.

Consequent upon the adoption of IAS 21(R), The Effects of Changes in Foreign Exchange Rates, the Group has changed its accounting policy for the translation differences of goodwill arising on acquisitions of foreign companies made after January 1, 2005. Goodwill on acquisitions of foreign companies made prior to that is translated to euros at historical rates. In accordance with IAS 21(R), goodwill on acquisitions of foreign companies made after January 1, 2005, is translated into euros at closing rates.

The impacts of IFRS 3 and IAS 21(R) are prospective from January 1, 2005. The adoption of IFRS 3, IAS 21(R), IAS 36(R) and IAS 38(R) did not have any impact to the Group's financial position, results of operations or cash flows.

Revenue recognition

Sales from the majority of the Group are recognized when persuasive evidence of an arrangement exists, delivery has occurred, the fee is fixed or determinable and collectibility is probable. An immaterial part of the revenue from products sold through distribution channels is recognized when the reseller or distributor sells the products to the end users. The Group records reductions to revenue for special pricing agreements, price protection and other volume based discounts.

In addition, sales and cost of sales from contracts involving solutions achieved through modification of complex telecommunications equipment are recognized on the percentage of completion method when the outcome of the contract can be estimated reliably. This occurs when total contract revenue and the costs to complete the contract can be estimated reliably, it is probable that the economic benefits

(continued)

associated with the contract will flow to the Group and the stage of contract completion can be measured. When the Group is not able to meet those conditions, the policy is to recognize revenues only equal to costs incurred to date, to the extent that such costs are expected to be recovered.

Completion is measured by reference to cost incurred to date as a percentage of estimated total project costs, the cost-to-cost method.

The percentage of completion method relies on estimates of total expected contract revenue and costs, as well as dependable measurement of the progress made towards completing a particular project. Recognized revenues and profits are subject to revisions during the project in the event that the assumptions regarding the overall project outcome are revised. The cumulative impact of a revision in estimates is recorded in the period such revisions become likely and estimable. Losses on projects in progress are recognized in the period they become likely and estimable.

The Group's customer contracts may include the provision of separately identifiable components of a single transaction, for example the construction of a network solution and subsequent network maintenance services. Accordingly, for these arrangements, revenue recognition requires proper identification of the components of the transaction and evaluation of their commercial effect in order to reflect the substance of the transaction. If the components are considered separable, revenue is allocated across the identifiable components based upon relative fair values.

All the Group's material revenue streams are recorded according to the above policies.

Accounts receivable

Accounts receivable are carried at the original invoice amount to customers less an estimate made for doubtful receivables based on a periodic review of all outstanding amounts, which includes an analysis of historical bad debt, customer concentrations, customer creditworthiness, current economic trends and changes in our customer payment terms. Bad debts are written off when identified.

Source: Nokia (2005, pp. 11, 12–13).

Other notes are then normally presented in the following order:
(a) supporting information for items presented on the face of the balance sheet, income statement, statement of changes in equity and cash flow statement, in the order in which each statement and each line is presented; and
(b) other disclosures that do not appear on the face of the balance sheet, income statement, cash flow statement and statement of changes in equity, including:
  • contingent liabilities (refer to chapter 5)
  • unrecognised contractual commitments, including commitments under operating leases (refer to chapter 14)
  • non-financial disclosures, such as an entity's risk management objectives and policies (refer to chapter 6).

Figure 16.19 shows the disclosure of commitments and contingencies made in note 32 to the 31 December 2005 consolidated financial statements of the Nokia Group.

FIGURE 16.19 Note 32 *Commitments and contingencies* to the Nokia Group's 31 December 2005 consolidated financial statements

32. Commitments and contingencies		
	2005 EURm	2004 EURm
Collateral for our own commitments		
Property under mortgages	18	18
Assets pledged	10	11
Contingent liabilities on behalf of Group companies		
Other guarantees	276	275
Contingent liabilities on behalf of other companies		
Guarantees for loans[1]	–	3
Other guarantees	2	2
Financing commitments		
Customer finance commitments[1]	13	56

1 See also Note 38 b.

The amounts above represent the maximum principal amount of commitments and contingencies.

Property under mortgages given as collateral for our own commitments include mortgages given to the Finnish National Board of Customs as a general indemnity of EUR 18 million in 2005 (EUR 18 million in 2004).

Assets pledged for the Group's own commitments include available-for-sale investments of EUR 10 million in 2005 (EUR 11 million of available-for-sale investments in 2004).

Other guarantees include guarantees of Nokia's performance of EUR 234 million in 2005 (EUR 223 million in 2004). However, EUR 182 million of these guarantees are provided to certain Networks' customers in the form of bank guarantees, standby letters of credit and other similar instruments. These instruments entitle the customer to claim payment as compensation for non-performance by Nokia of its obligations under network infrastructure supply agreements. Depending on the nature of the instrument, compensation is payable either immediately upon request, or subject to independent verification of non-performance by Nokia.

Guarantees for loans on behalf of other companies of EUR 0 million in 2005 (EUR 3 million in 2004) represent guarantees relating to payment by certain Networks' customers under specified loan facilities between such customers and their creditors. Nokia's obligations under such guarantees are released upon the earlier of expiration of the guarantee or early payment by the customer.

Financing commitments of EUR 13 million in 2005 (EUR 56 million in 2004) are available under loan facilities negotiated with customers of Networks. Availability of the amounts is dependent upon the borrower's continuing compliance with stated financial and operational covenants and compliance with other administrative terms of the facility. The loan facilities are primarily available to fund capital expenditure relating to purchases of network infrastructure equipment and services and to fund working capital.

The Group has been named as defendant along with certain of its senior executives in a class action complaint in the United States relating to certain public statements about its product portfolio and related financial projections in early 2004. The Group does not believe that the claim has merit and intends to vigorously defend itself.

(continued)

> The group is party to routine litigation incidental to the normal conduct of business. In the opinion of management the outcome of and liabilities in excess of what has been provided for related to these or other proceedings, in the aggregate, are not likely to be material to the financial conditions or results of operations.
>
> As of December 31, 2005, the Group had purchase commitments of EUR 1 919 million (EUR 1 236 million in 2004) relating to inventory purchase obligations, primarily for purchases in 2006.

Source: Nokia (2005, p. 31).

Paragraph 125 of IAS 1 requires the following note disclosures in regard to dividends of an entity:

(a) the amount of dividends proposed or declared before the financial statements were authorised for issue but not recognised as a distribution to equity holders during the period, and the related amount per share; and

(b) the amount of any cumulative preference dividends not recognised.

16.8 Summary

IAS 1 *Presentation of Financial Statements* is a disclosure standard that prescribes the structure and content of general-purpose financial statements, other than condensed interim financial statements. It prescribes various matters that are intended to ensure that the financial statements, which comprise a balance sheet, income statement, cash flow statement, statement of changes in equity and notes, faithfully present the financial position, financial performance and cash flows of an entity. These matters include various items that must be presented on the face of the balance sheet, income statement, cash flow statement and statement of changes in equity and other matters that may or must be presented in the notes. All such disclosures are designed to ensure the understandability of the financial statements by general users of the financial statements in their economic decision making.

DISCUSSION QUESTIONS

1. What is the objective of a balance sheet?
2. What are the major limitations of a balance sheet as a source of information for general users of financial statements?
3. Under what circumstances are assets and liabilities ordinarily classified broadly in order of liquidity rather than on a current/non-current classification?
4. Can an asset that is not realisable into cash within 12 months ever be classified as a current asset? If so, under what circumstances?
5. What is meant by classification of expenses by nature or function?
6. What is the objective of a statement of changes in equity?
7. The IASB is proposing to replace the income statement and statement of changes in equity with a comprehensive statement of financial performance. What are the reasons for this proposal?
8. Why is the required summary of accounting policies important to ensuring the understandability of financial statements to general users of the statements?
9. What are some of the more important judgements made that can lead to estimation uncertainty at a balance sheet date? What disclosures are required in the notes in regard to such matters?
10. What disclosures are required in the notes in regard to accounting policy judgements?

EXERCISES

EXERCISE 16.1   ★

Balance sheet classifications

The general ledger trial balance of Orange Limited includes the following balance sheet accounts:
(a) Trade receivables
(b) Work in progress
(c) Trade creditors
(d) Prepayments
(e) Property
(f) Goodwill
(g) Debentures outstanding
(h) Preference share capital
(i) Unearned revenue
(j) Accrued salaries
(k) Trading securities held
(l) Share capital
(m) Dividends payable

Required

Assume you are the accountant responsible for preparing a balance sheet of Orange Limited for consideration by the company's directors. In which balance sheet caption and classification would you include each of the above accounts? You should assume that assets and liabilities are classified into current and non-current categories and use the minimum line items permitted under IAS 1. If you need additional information to finalise your decision as to the appropriate classification or caption, indicate what information you require.

EXERCISE 16.2   Current asset and liability classifications

The general ledger trial balance of Banana Limited at 30 June 2007 includes the following balance sheet accounts:

		$
(a)	Dividends payable	25 000
(b)	Trade receivables	100 000
(c)	Accounts payable	85 000
(d)	Prepayments	12 000
(e)	Inventory of finished goods	120 000
(f)	Allowance for doubtful debts	5 000
(g)	Cash	10 000
(h)	Accrued liabilities	20 000
(i)	Inventory of raw materials	60 000
(j)	Loan repayable 31 October 2007	50 000
(k)	Bank overdraft	75 000
(l)	Current tax payable	30 000

Required

Assume you are the accountant of Banana Limited responsible for the preparation of the balance sheet of the company at 30 June 2007. Assume the company classifies assets and liabilities using a current/non-current basis. Prepare the current assets and current liabilities sections of the balance sheet, using the minimum line items permitted under IAS 1.

EXERCISE 16.3   ★   Income statement

The general ledger trial balance of Cowes Limited includes the following accounts at 30 June 2007:

(a)	Sales revenue	$1 200 000
(b)	Interest income	24 000
(c)	Proceeds on sale of fixed assets	50 000
(d)	Written-down value of assets sold	45 000
(e)	Valuation gain on trading investments	20 000
(f)	Dividends received	5 000
(g)	Cost of sales	840 000
(h)	Finance expenses	18 000
(i)	Selling and distribution expenses	76 000
(j)	Administrative expenses	35 000
(k)	Income tax expense	85 000

Required

Assume you are the accountant of Cowes Ltd, responsible for the preparation of the income statement of the company for the year ended 30 June 2007. The company classifies expenses by function. Prepare the income statement of Cowes Ltd, showing the analysis of expenses on the face of the income statement.

EXERCISE 16.4   Statement of changes in equity

The shareholders' equity section of the balance sheet of Newcastle Ltd at 30 June 2007 is shown opposite.

	2007	2006
Share capital	$200 000	$160 000
General reserve	50 000	40 000
Revaluation reserve	74 000	60 000
Retained earnings	170 000	160 000
	$494 000	$420 000

Additional information
- Newcastle Ltd issued 16 000 shares at $2.50 each on 31 May 2007 for cash.
- A transfer of $10 000 was made from retained earnings to the general reserve.
- Net profit for the year was $130 000.
- Dividends for the year comprised: interim dividend $50 000; final dividend provided $60 000.
- Land was revalued to current fair value, resulting in the recognition of a gross revaluation increment of $20 000 and a deferred tax liability of $6000.

Required
Prepare the statement of changes in equity of Newcastle Ltd for the year ended 30 June 2007 in accordance with IAS 1.

EXERCISE 16.5 ★

Current asset classifications

The general ledger trial balance of Apple Limited includes the following balance sheet accounts at 30 June 2007:

(a) Inventory	$100 000
(b) Trade receivables	120 000
(c) Prepaid insurance	8 000
(d) Listed investments held for trading purposes at fair value	20 000
(e) Available for sale investments	80 000
(f) Cash	30 000
(g) Deferred tax asset	15 000

Required
Assume you are the accountant of Apple Limited responsible for the preparation of the balance sheet of the company at 30 June 2007. Assume the company classifies assets and liabilities using a current/non-current basis. Prepare the current asset section of the balance sheet, using the minimum line items permitted under IAS 1.

EXERCISE 16.6 ★

Preparation of an income statement

The general ledger trial balance of Cucumber Ltd includes the following accounts at 30 June 2007:

(a) Sales revenue	$950 000
(b) Interest revenue	25 000
(c) Gain on sale of fixed assets	10 000
(d) Valuation gain on available for sale investments (no investments were disposed of during the year)	20 000
(e) Cost of goods sold	600 000
(f) Finance expenses	15 000
(g) Selling and distribution costs	50 000
(h) Administrative expenses	30 000
(i) Income tax expense	75 000

Required

Assume you are the accountant of Cucumber Ltd responsible for the preparation of the income statement of the company for the year ended 30 June 2007. Assume the company classifies expenses by function. Prepare the income statement of Cucumber Ltd, showing the analysis of expenses on the face of the income statement.

EXERCISE 16.7 ★★

Preparation of an income statement

The general ledger trial balance of Lemon Ltd includes the following accounts at 30 June 2007:

(a) Sales revenue	$975 000
(b) Interest income	20 000
(c) Share of profit of associates	15 000
(d) Other income	8 000
(e) Decrease in inventories of finished goods	25 000
(f) Raw materials and consumables used	350 000
(g) Employee benefit expenses	150 000
(h) Loss on translation of foreign operations (tax free)	30 000
(i) Depreciation of property, plant and equipment	45 000
(j) Impairment of property	80 000
(k) Finance costs	35 000
(l) Other expenses	45 000
(m) Income tax expense	75 000

Required

Assume you are the accountant of Lemon Ltd responsible for the preparation of the income statement of the company for the year ended 30 June 2007. Assume the company classifies expenses by nature. Prepare the income statement of Lemon Ltd, showing the analysis of expenses on the face of the income statement.

EXERCISE 16.8 ★★

Statement of changes in equity

The shareholders' section of the balance sheet of Hamilton Ltd at 30 June 2007 was as follows:

	2007	2006
Share capital	$300 000	$180 000
Available-for-sale investments revaluation reserve	60 000	40 000
Retained earnings	210 000	180 000
	$570 000	$400 000

Additional information
- Available-for-sale investments are regularly revalued to fair value. On the sale of an investment, any related revaluation increment is transferred to the income statement. Movements in the revaluation reserve during the year to 30 June 2007 comprised:
  - gross revaluation increments recognised $44 000 (related deferred income tax $14 000)
  - gross transfers on sale of investments $15 000 (related income tax $5000).
- Net profit for the year was $140 000.
- Dividends declared amounted to $110 000 (dividends subject to dividend reinvestment scheme $30 000).

Required

Prepare the statement of changes in equity of Hamilton Ltd for the year ended 30 June 2007 in accordance with IAS 1.

PROBLEM 16.1 ★   Preparation of a balance sheet

The general ledger summarised trial balance of Perth Ltd, a manufacturing company, includes the following accounts at 30 June 2007:

	Dr	Cr
Cash	$ 117 000	
Trade debtors	1 163 000	
Allowance for doubtful debts		$ 50 000
Sundry debtors	270 000	
Prepayments	94 000	
Sundry loans (current)	20 000	
Raw materials	493 000	
Finished goods	695 000	
Investments in unlisted companies (at cost)	30 000	
Land (at cost)	234 000	
Buildings (at cost)	687 000	
Accumulated depreciation – buildings		80 000
Plant and equipment (at cost)	6 329 000	
Accumulated depreciation – plant and equipment		3 036 000
Goodwill	2 425 000	
Brand names	40 000	
Patents	25 000	
Deferred income tax	189 000	
Trade creditors		1 078 000
Sundry creditors and accruals		568 000
Bank overdrafts		115 000
Bank loans		1 848 000
Other loans		646 000
Current tax payable		74 000
Provision for employee benefits		222 000
Dividends payable		100 000
Provision for warranty		20 000
Share capital		3 459 000
Retained earnings		1 515 000
	$12 811 000	$12 811 000

Additional information
- Bank loans include loans repayable within one year $620 000.
- Other loans outstanding are repayable within one year.
- Provision for employee benefits includes $143 000 payable within one year.
- Provision for warranty is in respect of a six-month warranty given over certain goods sold.

Required

Prepare the balance sheet of Perth Ltd at 30 June 2007 in accordance with IAS 1, using the balance sheet captions that a listed company is likely to use.

PROBLEM 16.2 ★   Preparation of a balance sheet

The general ledger summarised trial balance of Burnie Ltd, a manufacturing company, includes the following accounts at 30 June 2007:

	Dr	Cr
Cash	$ 175 000	
Deposits, at call	36 000	
Trade debtors	1 744 000	
Allowance for doubtful debts		$ 80 000
Sundry debtors	320 000	
Prepayments	141 000	
Raw materials	490 000	
Work in progress	151 000	
Finished goods	1 042 000	
Investments in listed companies (available for sale)	52 000	
Land, at valuation	250 000	
Buildings, at cost	1 030 000	
Accumulated depreciation – buildings		120 000
Plant and equipment	8 275 000	
Accumulated depreciation – plant and equipment		3 726 000
Leased assets	775 000	
Accumulated depreciation – leased assets		310 000
Goodwill	3 200 000	
Accumulated impairment – goodwill		670 000
Patents	110 000	
Trade creditors		1 617 000
Sundry creditors and accruals		715 000
Bank overdrafts		350 000
Bank loans		2 215 000
Debentures		675 000
Other loans		575 000
Lease liabilities		350 000
Current tax payable		152 000
Deferred tax		420 000
Provision for employment benefits		275 000
Provision for restructuring		412 000
Provision for warranty		42 000
Share capital		3 500 000
Investments revaluation reserve		25 000
Land revaluation reserve		81 000
Retained earnings		1 481 000
	$ 17 791 000	$ 17 791 000

Additional information
- Bank loans and other loans are all repayable beyond one year.
- $300 000 of the debentures is repayable within one year.
- Lease liabilities include $125 000 repayable within one year.

- Provision for employment benefits includes $192 000 payable within one year.
- The planned restructuring is intended to be completed within one year.
- Provision for warranty includes $20 000 estimated to be incurred beyond one year.

Required

Prepare the balance sheet of Burnie Ltd at 30 June 2007 in accordance with IAS 1, using the balance sheet captions that a listed entity is likely to use.

PROBLEM 16.3 ★   Preparation of a balance sheet

The summarised general ledger trial balance of Stawell Ltd, an investment company, includes the following accounts at 30 June 2007:

	Dr	Cr
Cash at bank	$ 7 000	
Deposits at call	112 869	
Dividends receivable	15 693	
Interest receivable	478	
Outstanding settlements receivable	4 900	
Trading securities	68 455	
Listed securities (available for sale)	1 880 472	
Deferred tax	655	
Outstanding settlements payable		$ 10 253
Interest payable		280
Other payables		83
Current tax payable		242
Provision for employee benefits		752
Deferred tax		56 414
Share capital		1 368 024
Revaluation reserve – investments		376 090
Retained earnings		278 384
	$2 090 522	$2 090 522

Additional information

Provision for employee benefits includes $525 payable within one year.

Required

Prepare the balance sheet of Stawell Ltd at 30 June 2007 in accordance with IAS 1, using the balance sheet captions that a listed company is likely to use.

PROBLEM 16.4 ★   Preparation of an income statement

The general ledger trial balance of Medco Ltd, a medical manufacturing and research company, includes the accounts at 30 June 2007 shown overleaf.

	Dr	Cr
Sales revenue		$1 300 000
Interest income		2 000
Proceeds from sale of plant		188 000
Rent		2 000
Royalties		10 000
Other revenue		1 000
Cost of sales	$820 000	
Interest on borrowings	33 000	
Sundry borrowing costs	1 000	
Research costs	51 000	
Advertising	25 000	
Sales staff	97 000	
Commission on sales	7 000	
Freight out	32 000	
Shipping supplies	16 000	
Depreciation on sales equipment	5 000	
Administrative salaries	72 000	
Legal and professional fees	13 000	
Office rent	30 000	
Insurance	14 000	
Depreciation of office equipment	16 000	
Stationery and supplies	5 000	
Miscellaneous expenses	2 000	
Cost of plant sold	162 000	
Income tax expense	31 000	

Required

Prepare the income statement of Medco Ltd for the year ended 30 June 2007, using a functional classification of expenses in accordance with IAS 1.

PROBLEM 16.5 ★ Preparation of an income statement

The general ledger trial balance of Investco Ltd, an investment company, includes the following revenue and expense items for the year ended 30 June 2007:

	Dr	Cr
Dividends from investments		$920 000
Distributions from trusts		70 000
Interest on deposits		70 000
Income from bank bills		10 000
Increment on revaluation of investments (available for sale)		45 000
Income from dealing in securities and derivatives (held for trading purposes)		40 000
Write-down of securities and derivatives (held for trading)	$60 000	
Other income		10 000
Interest	10 000	
Administrative staff costs	30 000	
Sundry administrative costs	40 000	
Income tax expense	30 000	

Required

Prepare the income statement of Investco Ltd for the year ended 30 June 2007, using a functional classification of expenses in accordance with IAS 1.

PROBLEM 16.6   ★★   Preparation of a balance sheet and income statement

The summarised general ledger trial balance of Westco Ltd, a distributor of goods, for the year ended 30 June 2007 is detailed below:

	Dr	Cr
Sales of goods		$ 7 360 000
Share of profits of associates		36 000
Rent received		9 000
Other income		6 000
Cost of goods sold	$ 4 978 000	
Distribution expenses	143 000	
Sales and marketing expenses	1 367 000	
Administration expenses	420 000	
Interest paid	74 000	
Other borrowing expenses	6 000	
Income tax expense	141 000	
Cash at bank	20 000	
Cash on deposits, at call	150 000	
Trade debtors	740 000	
Allowance for doubtful debts		24 000
Other debtors	154 000	
Employee share plan loans	260 000	
Raw materials	53 000	
Finished goods	1 190 000	
Investment in associates	375 000	
Land and buildings	426 000	
Accumulated depreciation – land and buildings		61 000
Plant and equipment	2 100 000	
Accumulated depreciation – plant and equipment		940 000
Trade names	60 000	
Accumulated impairment – trade names		15 000
Goodwill	1 450 000	
Bank loans		111 000
Other loans		810 000
Trade creditors		820 000
Employee benefit provisions		153 000
Provision for restructuring		62 000
Current tax payable		30 000
Provision for warranty		40 000
Deferred tax		100 000
Issued capital		2 920 000
Retained earnings, 30 June 2006		760 000
Dividends paid	150 000	
	$14 257 000	$14 257 000

Additional information
- Employee share plan loans include $50 000 due within one year.
- $25 000 of bank loans is repayable within one year.
- $400 000 of other loans is repayable within one year.
- Employee benefit provisions include $110 000 payable within one year.
- The planned restructuring is intended to be fully implemented within one year.
- Provision for warranty is in respect of a six-month warranty on certain goods sold.

Required

Prepare the balance sheet and income statement of Westco Ltd for the year ended 30 June 2007 in accordance with IAS 1, using statement captions that a listed company is likely to use.

PROBLEM 16.7   ★★★   Preparation of a balance sheet, income statement and statement of changes in equity

The summarised general trial balance of Beechworth Ltd, a manufacturing company, for the year ended 30 June 2007 is detailed below:

	Dr	Cr
Sales of goods		$4 469 000
Revaluation increment on available-for-sale investments		10 000
Tax on investment revaluation increment	$ 3 000	
Revaluation increment on land		50 000
Tax on land revaluation increment	15 000	
Interest		6 000
Cost of goods sold	2 987 000	
Distribution expenses	86 000	
Sales and marketing expenses	820 000	
Administration expenses	252 000	
Interest	44 000	
Other borrowing expenses	4 000	
Income tax expense	85 000	
Cash on hand	4 000	
Cash on deposit, at call	150 000	
Bank overdraft		50 000
Trade debtors	450 000	
Allowance for doubtful debts		14 000
Other debtors	93 000	
Raw materials	188 000	
Finished goods	714 000	
Listed investments (available for sale)	225 000	
Land and buildings	257 000	
Accumulated depreciation – land and buildings		36 000
Plant and equipment	1 260 000	
Accumulated depreciation – plant and equipment		564 000
Patents	45 000	
Goodwill	870 000	
Bank loans		66 000
Other loans		570 000
Trade creditors		510 000
Employee benefit provisions		93 000
Warranty provision		37 000
Current tax payable		25 000
Deferred tax		135 000
Retained earnings, 30 June 2006		326 000
Dividends	150 000	
Land revaluation reserve, 30 June 2006		15 000
Investments revaluation reserve, 30 June 2006		35 000
Share capital, 30 June 2006		1 541 000
Dividends reinvested		30 000
Share issue		120 000
	$8 702 000	$8 702 000

Additional information
• $30 000 of bank loans is repayable within one year.

- $110 000 of other loans is repayable within one year.
- Employee benefit provisions include $62 000 payable within one year.
- The warranty provision is in respect of a nine-month warranty given on certain goods sold.

Required

Prepare the balance sheet, income statement and statement of changes in equity of Beechworth Ltd for the year ended 30 June 2007 in accordance with the requirements of IAS 1, using statement captions that a listed company is likely to use.

PROBLEM 16.8 ★★★ Preparation of a balance sheet, income statement and statement of changes in equity

The summarised general ledger trial balance of Portland Ltd, a manufacturing company, for the year ended 30 June 2007 is detailed below:

	Dr	Cr
Sales of goods		$5 000 000
Interest income		22 000
Sundry income		25 000
Change in inventory of work in progress	$ 125 000	
Change in inventory of finished goods		60 000
Raw materials used	2 200 000	
Employee benefit expense	950 000	
Depreciation	226 000	
Impairment of patent	25 000	
Telecommunications costs	65 000	
Rental	70 000	
Advertising	142 000	
Insurance	45 000	
Freight out	133 000	
Doubtful debts	10 000	
Interest expense	30 000	
Other expenses	8 000	
Income tax expense	320 000	
Cash	4 000	
Cash on deposit, at call	120 000	
Bank overdraft		40 000
Trade debtors	495 000	
Allowance for doubtful debts		18 000
Other debtors	27 000	
Raw materials	320 000	
Finished goods	385 000	
Land	94 000	
Buildings	220 000	
Accumulated depreciation – land and buildings		52 000
Plant and equipment	1 380 000	
Accumulated depreciation – plant and equipment		320 000
Patents	90 000	
Goodwill	620 000	
Bank loans		92 000
Other loans		450 000
Trade creditors		452 000
Employee benefit provisions		120 000
Current tax payable		35 000
Deferred tax		140 000
Retained earnings, 30 June 2006		310 000
Dividends	210 000	
Share capital, 30 June 2006		1 007 000
Dividends reinvested		41 000
Share issue		130 000
	$8 314 000	$8 314 000

Additional information
- $20 000 of bank loans is repayable within one year.
- $90 000 other loans is repayable within one year.

Required
Prepare the balance sheet, income statement and statement of changes in equity of Portland Ltd for the year ended 30 June 2007 in accordance with the requirements of IAS 1, using statement captions that a listed company is likely to use.

WEBLINK

Visit these websites for additional information:

www.iasb.org   www.iasplus.com
www.asic.gov.au   www.ifac.org
www.aasb.com.au   www.nzica.com
www.accaglobal.com   www.capa.com.my

REFERENCES

AngloGold Ashanti 2008, *Annual report*, viewed 11 July 2006, <www.anglogold.com>.

Dresdner Bank Corporation 2005, *Annual report*, Frankfurt am Main viewed 23 February 2006, <www.dresdner-bank.com>.

IASB *Project Summary 2006 Performance reporting*, viewed 23 Feburary 2006, <www.iasb.org>.

Nokia 2005, *Nokia in 2005*, Nokia Corporation, Finland, viewed 10 July 2006, <www.nokia.com>.

CHAPTER 17
Cash flow statements

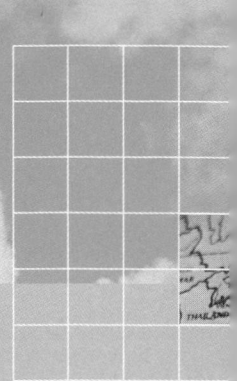

ACCOUNTING STANDARDS

International: IAS 7 *Cash Flow Statements*
Australia: AASB 107 *Cash Flow Statements*
New Zealand: NZ IAS 7 *Cash Flow Statements*

CONCEPTS FOR REVIEW

Before studying this chapter, you should understand or, if necessary, revise:
- the major items in an entity's income statement and statement of changes in equity
- the major items included in an entity's balance sheet.

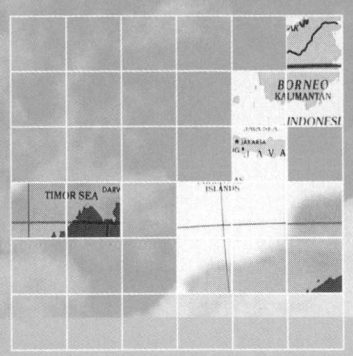

LEARNING OBJECTIVES

When you have studied this chapter, you should be able to:

1. explain the objectives of a cash flow statement and its usefulness
2. explain the definition of cash and cash equivalents
3. explain the classification of cash flow activities and classify cash inflows and outflows into operating, investing and financing activities
4. contrast the direct and indirect methods of presenting net cash flows from operating activities
5. prepare a cash flow statement
6. identify other disclosures required or encouraged by IAS 7
7. use a worksheet to prepare a statement of cash flows with more complex transactions.

17.1 Introduction to IAS 7

As explained in chapter 2, ultimately, all investors, creditors and other capital providers to an entity want to get cash out of their investment. Consequently, information about an entity's receipts and payments is of fundamental importance to such users of financial statements. The cash flow statement provides this information by reporting cash inflows and outflows classified into operating, investing and financing activities, and the net movement in cash and cash equivalents during the period.

17.2 Scope of IAS 7

IAS 7 *Cash Flow Statements* requires that a cash flow statement be prepared in accordance with the requirements of the standard, and be presented as an integral part of an entity's financial statements for each period for which financial statements are presented.

LO 1

17.3 Objectives of a cash flow statement

The overall objective of a cash flow statement is to present information about the historical changes in cash and cash equivalents of an entity during the period classified by operating, investing and financing activities. This information is particularly useful to investors, creditors and other users of financial statements to assist in:

- evaluating an entity's ability to generate cash and cash equivalents, and the timing and certainty of their generation
- evaluating an entity's financial structure (including liquidity and solvency) and its ability to meet its obligations and to pay dividends
- understanding the reasons for the difference between profit or loss for a period and the net cash flow from operating activities (the reasons for the differences are often helpful in evaluating the quality of earnings of an entity)
- comparing the operating performance of different entities, because net operating cash flows reported in cash flow statements are unaffected by different accounting choices and judgements under accrual accounting used in determining the profit or loss of an entity
- enabling its users to develop models to assess and compare the present value of the future cash flows of different entities.

LO 2

17.4 Defining cash and cash equivalents

Paragraph 6 of IAS 7 defines cash and cash equivalents as follows:

Cash comprises cash on hand and demand deposits.

Cash equivalents are short-term, highly liquid investments that are readily convertible to known amounts of cash and which are subject to an insignificant risk of changes in value.

Paragraph 7 of IAS 7 explains that cash equivalents are held for the purpose of meeting short-term cash commitments, and not for investment or other purposes. Since a cash-equivalent investment must by definition be readily convertible to cash and have an insignificant risk of changing in value, an investment will qualify as a cash equivalent only if it has a short maturity (usually three months or less). Equity investments will not qualify unless they are cash equivalents such as preferred shares acquired shortly before their specified maturity date.

Bank borrowings are ordinarily classified as a financing activity, except for bank overdrafts that are repayable on demand and which form an integral part of an entity's cash management. Such overdrafts may fluctuate from being overdrawn to being positive.

Cash flows reported in a cash flow statement exclude movements between items classified as cash or cash equivalents, such as the investment of excess cash in cash equivalents.

17.5 Classifying cash flow activities

As stated earlier, cash flow activities are reported in the cash flow statement classified into operating, investing and financing activities. Paragraph 6 of IAS 7 defines these activities as follows:

Operating activities are the principal revenue-producing activities of an entity and other activities that are not investing or financing activities.

Investing activities are the acquisition and disposal of long-term assets and other investments not included in cash equivalents.

Financing activities are activities that result in changes in size and composition of the equity capital and borrowings of the entity.

Figure 17.1 classifies the typical cash receipts and payments of an entity between operating, investing and financing activities.

Operating activities
Cash inflows from:
  Sale of goods
  Rendering of services
  Royalties, fees, commissions
  Interest received (may be investing)
  Dividends received (may be investing)
Cash outflows to:
  Suppliers for goods and services
  Employees
  Government for income and other taxes
  Lenders for interest (may be financing)
Investing activities
Cash inflows from:
  Sale of property, plant and equipment
  Sale of intangibles
  Sale of shares and debt instruments of other entities
  Repayment of loans to other parties

Cash outflows to:
  Acquire property, plant and equipment
  Acquire intangibles
  Acquire shares and debt instruments of other entities
  Lend money to other entities
Financing activities
Cash inflows from:
  Issuing shares and other equity instruments
  Issuing debentures, unsecured notes and other borrowings
Cash outflows to:
  Buy back shares
  Repay debentures, unsecured notes and other borrowings
  Pay dividends to shareholders (may be operating)

FIGURE 17.1 Typical cash receipts and payments classified by activity

17.5.1 Classifying interest and dividends received and paid

IAS 7 does not prescribe how interest and dividends received and paid should be classified. Rather, paragraph 31 of IAS 7 requires cash flows from interest and dividends received and paid to be disclosed separately and classified in a consistent manner from period to period as operating, investing or financing activities. Paragraph 33 of IAS 7 explains that interest paid and interest and dividends received are usually classified as operating cash flows for a financial institution, but there is no consensus on the classification of these cash flows for other entities. This is because interest paid and interest and dividends received may be classified as operating cash flows – they may be viewed as entering into the determination of profit or loss — or as financing cash flows (for interest paid) and investing cash flows (for interest and dividends received), being viewed as the costs of financing or the returns on investments respectively.

17.5.2 Classifying taxes on income

Paragraph 35 of IAS 7 requires that taxes on income be separately disclosed in the cash flow statement and classified as cash flows from operating activities, unless they can be specifically identified with financing and investing activities. Paragraph 36 of IAS 7 explains that, while the tax expense may be readily identifiable with investing or financing activities, the related tax flows are often impracticable to identify and may arise in a different period from the cash flows of the underlying transaction. For this reason, taxes paid are usually classified as cash flows from operating activities.

17.6 Format of cash flow statements

The general format of a cash flow statement follows the three cash flow activities. Cash flows from operating activities are presented first, followed by cash flows from investing activities and then those from financing activities. The resultant net increase or decrease in cash and cash equivalents during the period is then used to report the movement in cash and cash equivalents from the balance at the beginning of the period to the balance at the end of the period.

A typical format of a cash flow statement is presented in figure 17.2.

Cash flow statement For the year ended 31 December . . .		
Cash flows from operating activities		
Cash receipts from customers	$XXX	
Cash paid to suppliers and employees	(XXX)	
Cash generated from operations	XXX	
Interest received	XXX	
Interest paid	(XXX)	
Income taxes paid	(XXX)	
Net cash from operating activities		XXX
Cash flows from investing activities		
Acquisition of subsidiary, net of cash acquired	(XXX)	
Purchase of property and plant	(XXX)	
Proceeds from sale of plant	XXX	
Net cash used in investing activities		(XXX)
Cash flows from financing activities		
Proceeds from share issue	XXX	
Proceeds from borrowings	XXX	
Payment of borrowings	(XXX)	
Dividends paid	(XXX)	XXX
Net increase in cash and cash equivalents		XXX
Cash and cash equivalents at beginning of year		XXX
Cash and cash equivalents at end of year		XXX

FIGURE 17.2 Typical format of a cash flow statement using the direct method of reporting cash flows from operating activities

LO 4

17.6.1 Reporting cash flows from operating activities

Paragraph 18 of IAS 7 provides that cash flows from operating activities may be reported using one of two methods:

- the *direct method* — whereby classes of operating gross cash receipts and cash payments are disclosed, or
- the *indirect method* — whereby profit or loss is adjusted for the effect of transactions of a non-cash nature, any deferrals or accruals of past or future operating cash receipts or payments, and items of income or expense associated with investing or financing cash flows.

The direct method is encouraged.

The typical format of a cash flow statement set forth in figure 17.2 uses the direct method. Figure 17.3 illustrates the typical format of the indirect method of reporting cash flows from operating activities.

Cash flow statement For the year ended 31 December . . .	
Profit before tax	$XXX
Adjustments for:	
Depreciation	XXX
Foreign exchange loss	XXX
Loss on sale of equipment	XXX
Interest income	(XXX)
Interest expense	XXX
Increase in trade and other receivables	(XXX)
Decrease in inventories	XXX
Increase in accounts payable	XXX
Decrease in accrued liabilities	(XXX)
Cash generated from operations	XXX
Interest received	XXX
Interest paid	(XXX)
Income taxes paid	(XXX)
Net cash from operating activities	XXX

FIGURE 17.3 Typical format for the indirect method of reporting cash flows from operating activities

17.6.2 Reporting cash flows from investing and financing activities

Paragraph 21 of IAS 7 requires separate reporting of the major classes of gross cash receipts and gross cash payments arising from investing and financing activities, except for certain cash flows (outlined in the following section) that may be reported on a net basis.

17.6.3 Reporting cash flows on a net basis

Paragraph 22 of IAS 7 provides that cash flows arising from the following operating, investing or financing activities may be reported on a net basis:

(a) cash receipts and payments on behalf of customers when the cash flows reflect the activities of the customer rather than those of the entity; and

(b) cash receipts and payments for items in which the turnover is quick, the amounts are large, and the maturities are short.

Examples of cash receipts and payments covered by paragraph 22(a) are the acceptance and repayment of a bank's demand deposits, funds held for customers by an investment entity, and rents collected on behalf of and paid over to the owners of properties. Examples of cash receipts and payments referred to in paragraph 22(b) are principal amounts relating to credit card customers, and the purchase and sale of investments and other short-term borrowings (usually those that have a maturity period of three months or less).

Paragraph 24 of IAS 7 provides that cash flows from each of the following activities of a financial institution may be reported on a net basis:

(a) cash receipts and payments for the acceptance and repayment of deposits with a fixed maturity date;
(b) the placement of deposits with and withdrawal of deposits from other financial institutions; and
(c) cash advances and loans made to customers and the repayment of those advances and loans.

LO 5

17.7 Preparing a cash flow statement

Unlike the balance sheet and income statement, the cash flow statement is not prepared from an entity's general ledger trial balance. Preparation requires information to be compiled concerning the cash inflows and cash outflows of the relevant entity over the period covered by the statement. It is possible to compile the required information through a detailed analysis and summary of the cash records of the entity over the period. Ordinarily, though, a cash flow statement is prepared by using comparative balance sheets to determine the net amount of changes in assets, liabilities and equities over the period. The comparative balance sheets are supplemented by various income statement data and additional information extracted from the accounting records of the entity to enable certain cash receipts and payments to be fully identified. This method of preparation is demonstrated in simplified form using the information presented in figure 17.4 (below and opposite). The same method can be used to prepare a consolidated cash flow statement for a group of entities.

Beachwear Limited Income statement for the year ended 31 December 2007		
Revenue		
Sales revenue		$800 000
Interest		5 000
Gain on sale of plant		4 000
		809 000
Expenses		
Cost of goods sold	$480 000	
Wages and salaries expense	120 000	
Depreciation – plant and equipment	25 000	
Interest	4 000	
Other expenses	76 000	705 000
Profit before tax		104 000
Income tax expense		30 000
Profit for the year		$ 74 000

| | Beachwear Ltd Comparative balance sheets as at: | | |
	31 December 2006	31 December 2007	Increase (decrease)
Cash at bank	$ 60 000	$ 54 550	$(5 450)
Accounts receivable	70 000	79 000	9 000
Inventory	65 000	70 000	5 000
Prepayments	8 000	9 500	1 500
Interest receivable	150	100	(50)
A Plant	150 000	165 000	15 000
B Investments	12 000	14 000	2 000
B Intangibles	–	15 000	15 000
	$365 150	$407 150	
Accounts payable	42 000	45 000	3 000
Wages and salaries payable	4 000	5 000	1 000
Accrued interest	–	200	200
Other expenses payable	3 000	1 800	(1 200)
E Current tax payable	14 000	16 000	2 000
E Deferred tax	5 000	8 000	3 000
C Long-term borrowings	60 000	70 000	10 000
Share capital	200 000	200 000	–
D Retained earnings	37 150	61 150	24 000
	$365 150	$407 150	

Additional information extracted from the company's records:
A Plant that had a written-down value of $10 000 was sold for $14 000 cash.
   New equipment purchased for cash amounted to $50 000.
B Investments ($2000) and intangibles ($15 000) were acquired for cash.
C A borrowing of $10 000 was made during the year and received in cash.
D Dividends paid in cash were $50 000.
E Income tax expense for the year comprises:

Income tax currently payable	$27 000
Increase in deferred tax	3 000
	30 000

FIGURE 17.4 Financial statements and additional accounting information of Beachwear Ltd

17.7.1 Cash flows from operating activities

Ascertaining the net cash flows from operating activities is the first step in preparing a cash flow statement. The process used varies according to whether the direct or the indirect method of disclosure is used. The recommended direct method of preparation is demonstrated first.

Determining cash receipts from customers

The starting point for determining how much cash was received from customers is the sales revenue reported in the income statement. However, this figure reflects sales made by the entity during the period irrespective of whether the customers have paid for the sales. Credit sales are recorded by a debit to accounts receivable and a credit to sales revenue. On the other hand, cash received from customers includes sales made in the previous period that are not collected in cash until the current period, and excludes sales made in the current period that remain unpaid at the end of the period. Hence, cash received from customers (assuming there have been no bad debts written off or settlement discounts given) equals:

> Sales revenue + Beginning accounts receivable − Ending accounts receivable

Using the Beachwear Ltd information from figure 17.4, receipts from customers is determined as follows:

	Sales revenue	$800 000
+	Beginning accounts receivable	70 000
	Cash collectable from customers	870 000
−	Ending accounts receivable	(79 000)
	Receipts from customers	$791 000

If any bad debts had been written off during the period, cash collectable from customers would be further reduced by the amount of the write-offs in calculating the cash received from customers. A similar adjustment would be necessary if settlement discounts were given to customers for the payment of their accounts within prescribed credit terms. Such discounts reduce the cash received from customers, and necessitate the inclusion of a non-cash expense (discounts allowed) in the income statement.

The logic of this calculation is apparent from the following summarised accounts receivable account in the general ledger for the year:

Accounts receivable			
Opening balance	70 000	Bad debts	−
Sales	800 000	Discounts	−
		Cash receipts	791 000
		Closing balance	79 000
	870 0000		870 000

The above summarised general ledger account can be reconstructed from the balance sheet (the opening and closing balances) and income statement (bad debts, discount allowed and sales). The cash receipts amount is then determined by the difference in the accounts receivable account.

The above approach may be simplified by working with the change in receivables over the period. Under this approach, cash received from customers (assuming there are no bad debts written off or discounts allowed) equals:

> Sales revenue − Increase in accounts receivable
> or
> + Decrease in accounts receivable

Thus, cash received from customers for Beachwear Ltd can alternatively be determined as:

> $800 000 − $9000 = $791 000

Determining interest received

A similar approach is used to determine interest received, because interest received equals:

$$\text{Interest revenue} \quad - \quad \text{Increase in interest receivable}$$
$$\text{or}$$
$$+ \quad \text{Decrease in interest receivable}$$

Thus, Beachwear Ltd's interest received is:

$$\$5000 + \$50 = \$5050$$

Determining cash paid to suppliers and employees

Payments to suppliers may comprise purchases of inventory and payments for services. However, not all inventory purchased during the year is reflected in the income statement as cost of goods sold, because cost of goods sold includes beginning inventory and excludes ending inventory. Purchases of inventory made during the period equals:

$$\text{Cost of goods sold} - \text{Beginning inventory} + \text{Ending inventory}$$

Alternatively, this could be expressed as:

$$\text{Cost of goods sold} \quad + \quad \text{Increase in inventory}$$
$$\text{or}$$
$$- \quad \text{Decrease in inventory}$$

Using a similar approach to that outlined for cash receipts from customers, it is then necessary to adjust for accounts payable at the beginning and end of the period to arrive at cash paid to suppliers for purchases of inventory. Thus, cash paid to suppliers of inventories is calculated as:

$$\text{Purchases of inventories} + \text{Beginning accounts payable} - \text{Ending accounts payable}$$

Alternatively, this could be expressed as:

$$\text{Purchases of inventory} \quad + \quad \text{Decrease in accounts payable}$$
$$\text{or}$$
$$- \quad \text{Increase in accounts payable}$$

As shown in figure 17.4, Beachwear Ltd's comparative balance sheets report an increase in inventory of $5000 and in accounts payable of $3000. Hence, cash paid to suppliers for purchases is calculated as follows:

	Cost of goods sold	$480 000
+	Increase in inventory	5 000
	Purchases for year	485 000
−	Increase in accounts payable	(3 000)
	Payments to suppliers for purchases of inventory	$482 000

The logic of the previous calculations is apparent from the following summarised inventory and accounts payable (for inventory) accounts in the general ledger for the year:

Inventory				Accounts payable			
Opening balance	65 000	Cost of goods sold	480 000	Cash payments	482 000	Opening balance	42 000
Purchases	485 000	Closing balance	70 000	Closing balance	45 000	Purchases	485 000
	550 000		550 000		527 000		527 000

The above summarised general ledger accounts can be reconstructed from the information contained in the balance sheet (the opening and closing balances) and the income statement (cost of goods sold). The purchases amount is then determined by the difference in the inventory account and inserted in the accounts payable account. The amount of cash payments can then be determined by the difference in the accounts payable account.

A similar approach is taken to determine the amount of payments made to suppliers for services and to employees. Adjustments must be made to the relevant expenses recognised in the income statement for changes in the beginning and ending amounts of prepayments and relevant accounts payable and accrued liabilities. Thus, payments to suppliers for services is calculated as follows:

Expenses charged in income statement	−	Beginning prepayments
	+	Ending prepayments
	+	Beginning accounts payable/accruals
	−	Ending accounts payable/accruals

Alternatively, this could be expressed as:

Expenses charged in income statement	+	Increase in prepayments
		or
	−	Decrease in prepayments
	+	Decrease in accounts payable/accruals
		or
	−	Increase in accounts payable accounts

Beachwear Ltd's comparative balance sheet reports show:

Increase in prepayments	$1 500
Increase in wages and salaries payable	1 000
Decrease in other expenses payable	(1 200)

Thus cash paid to suppliers of services is calculated as follows:

Other expenses	$76 000
+ Increase in prepayments	1 500
+ Decrease in other expenses payable	1 200
Payments to suppliers of services	$78 700

Similarly, cash paid to employees is calculated as follows:

Wages and salaries expense	$120 000
− Increase in wages and salaries payable	1 000
Payments to employees	$119 000

Using the previous calculations, total payments to suppliers and employees to be reported in the cash flow statement comprises:

Payments to suppliers for purchases	$482 000
Payments to suppliers for services	78 700
Payments to employees	119 000
Total payments to suppliers and employees	$679 700

Determining interest paid

Using the same approach as for other expenses, Beachwear Ltd's interest paid is determined as follows:

Interest expense	$4 000
− Increase in accrued interest	200
Interest paid	$3 800

Determining income tax paid

The determination of income tax paid can be complicated by movements in the current and deferred tax accounts that are not reflected in the income tax expense recognised in the income statement. For example, as explained in chapter 8, deferred tax may arise from a revaluation of property, plant and equipment that causes a difference between the book and tax base of those assets, thereby resulting in a charge for income tax being made to the revaluation reserve account. Taxes may also be charged to other equity accounts such as a foreign currency translation reserve. As a result, it is often simplest to analyse the income tax currently payable liability account to determine the amount of tax paid during the year. To illustrate, the movement in Beachwear Ltd's current tax payable account may be summarised as follows:

Beginning balance	$14 000
+ Income tax expense	27 000
− Income tax paid	25 000
Ending balance	$16 000

For Beachwear Ltd, the amount of income tax paid consists of the final balance in respect of the previous year's current tax payable, and instalments (for example, quarterly) in respect of the current year. The income tax expense may include an adjustment for any under- or over-accrual for current tax payable at the beginning of the period.

The movement in the deferred income tax liability account for Beachwear Ltd may be summarised as follows:

Beginning balance	$5 000
+ Income tax expense	3 000
Ending balance	$8 000

In this example, total income tax expense recognised in the income statement comprises:

Income tax expense currently payable	$27 000
Increase in deferred income tax	3 000
Total income tax expense	$30 000

In this simplified situation, it is possible to derive the amount of income tax paid using the following approach:

Income tax expense – increase in current tax payable
– increase in deferred tax.

This is calculated as:

$$\$30\,000 - \$2000 - \$3000 = \$25\,000$$

Note that this approach has worked in this simplified example only because all charges for both current and deferred income tax are reflected in the income statement. In more complex situations involving the direct charging of tax to revaluation and other reserves, it will usually be simpler to identify actual payments of income tax by analysing the movements in the current tax payable account than to reconcile payments from the income tax expense charged in the income statement.

Summarising cash flows from operating activities

Using the direct method, the cash flows from the operating activities section of Beachwear Ltd's cash flow statement for the year are presented in figure 17.5.

Beachwear Ltd Cash flow statement (extract)	
Cash flows from operating activities	
Cash receipts from customers	$791 000
Cash paid to suppliers and employees	(679 700)
Cash generated from operations	111 300
Interest received	*5 050
Interest paid	**(3 800)
Income taxes paid	(25 000)
Net cash from operating activities	$ 87 550

* May be classified as investing
** May be classified as financing

FIGURE 17.5 Cash flows from operating activities (direct method)

The presentation of Beachwear Ltd's cash flows from operating activities under the indirect method is shown in figure 17.6.

Beachwear Ltd Cash flow statement (extract)	
Cash flows from operating activities	
Profit before tax	$104 000
Adjustment for:	
Depreciation	25 000
Interest income	(5 000)
Gain on sale of plant	(4 000)
Interest expense	4 000
Increase in accounts receivables	(9 000)
Increase in inventory	(5 000)
Increase in prepayments	(1 500)
Increase in accounts payable	3 000
Decrease in other payables	(200)
Cash generated from operations	111 300
Interest received	*5 050
Interest paid	**(3 800)
Income taxes paid	(25 000)
Net cash from operating activities	$ 87 550

* May be classified as investing
** May be classified as financing

FIGURE 17.6   Cash flows from operating activities (indirect method)

17.7.2   Cash flows from investing activities

Determining cash flows from investing activities requires identifying cash inflows and outflows relating to the acquisition and disposal of long-term assets and other investments not included in cash equivalents.

The comparative balance sheets of Beachwear Ltd in figure 17.4 show that plant has increased by $15 000 (A), investments by $2000 (B) and intangibles by $15 000 (B). To determine the cash flows relating to these increases, it is necessary to analyse the underlying transactions.

The net increase in plant reflects the recording of acquisitions, disposals and depreciation. Using the data provided, the analysis of the plant movement (which is net of accumulated depreciation) is as follows:

Beginning balance	$150 000
Acquisitions	50 000
Disposals	(10 000)
Depreciation for year	(25 000)
Ending balance	$165 000

The additional information provided in figure 17.4 states that the acquisitions were made for cash during the period, so no adjustment is necessary for year-end payables. Assuming that there were no outstanding payables for plant purchases at the beginning of the year, the cash flow for plant acquisitions for the year is $50 000 (A in figure 17.4). (If payables for plant purchases were outstanding at the beginning of the period, the amount would need to be included in plant purchases paid during the period.)

The proceeds on the sale of plant can be calculated as:

Net book value of plant disposed	+	Gain on disposal of plant
	or	
	−	Loss on disposal of plant

For Beachwear Ltd, the calculation is as follows:

$$\$10\,000 + 4000 = \$14\,000$$

However, the proceeds from the sale of plant equals the cash inflow for the year only if there are no receivables outstanding arising from the sale of plant at either the beginning or end of the year. If receivables exist, the cash inflow is determined using the approach that was previously outlined for sales revenue and interest receivable. For simplicity, it is assumed that Beachwear Ltd had no receivables outstanding, at the beginning or end of the year, arising from the sale of plant.

Issues similar to those outlined for the acquisition of plant arise in respect of investments and intangibles. The comparative balance sheets for Beachwear Ltd show that the movement in investments and intangibles equals the additional cash acquisitions made during the period, as detailed in the additional information presented in figure 17.4. Note, however, that the movement in these items equals the cash outflows for the year only if it is assumed that there were no outstanding accounts payable at the beginning of the year that were settled during the year. If payables exist, the cash outflow is determined using the approach that was previously outlined for cash paid to suppliers and employees.

Using the above information, Beachwear Ltd's cash flow statement showing the cash flows from investing activities for the current year is presented in figure 17.7.

Beachwear Ltd Cash flow statement (extract)	
Cash flows from investing activities	
Purchase of intangibles	$(15 000)
Purchase of investments	(2 000)
Purchase of plant	(50 000)
Proceeds from sale of plant	14 000
Net cash used in investing activities	$(53 000)

FIGURE 17.7 Cash flows from investing activities

17.7.3 Cash flows from financing activities

Determining cash flows from financing activities requires identifying cash flows that resulted in changes in the size and composition of equity capital and borrowings.

The additional information (C) in figure 17.4 confirms that the increase in borrowings of $10 000 derived from the comparative balance sheets of Beachwear Ltd arose from an additional borrowing. It would normally be necessary to analyse the net movement in borrowings in order to identify whether the movement reflects repayments and additional borrowings, and whether any new borrowings arose from non-cash transactions.

Share capital is unchanged at $200 000. The movement in retained earnings of $24 000 reflects:

Profit for the period	$74 000	
Dividends (paid in cash)	50 000	(D in figure 17.4)
Net movement	$24 000	

Using the previous information, Beachwear Ltd's cash flow statement showing the cash flows from financing activities for the current year is presented in figure 17.8.

Beachwear Ltd Cash flow statement (extract)	
Cash flows from financing activities	
Proceeds from borrowings	$10 000
Dividends paid	*(50 000)
Net cash used in financing activities	$(40 000)

*Dividends paid may be classified as an operating cash flow.

FIGURE 17.8   Cash flows from financing activities

All that remains to complete the statement of cash flows for Beachwear Ltd is the determination of the net increase or decrease for the period in cash held, and to use this total to reconcile cash at the beginning and end of the year.

The complete cash flow statement for Beachwear Ltd (using the direct method for reporting cash flows from operating activities) is shown in figure 17.9.

Beachwear Ltd Cash flow statement for the year ended 31 December 2007		
Cash flows from operating activities		
Cash receipts from customers	$ 791 000	
Cash paid to suppliers and employees	(679 700)	
Cash generated from operations	111 300	
Interest received	5 050	
Interest paid	(3 800)	
Income taxes paid	(25 000)	
Net cash from operating activities		$ 87 550
Cash flows from investing activities		
Purchase of intangibles	$ (15 000)	
Purchase of investments	(2 000)	
Purchase of plant	(50 000)	
Proceeds from sale of plant	14 000	
Net cash used in investing activities		(53 000)
Cash flows from financing activities		
Proceeds from borrowings	$ 10 000	
Dividends paid	(50 000)	
Net cash used in financing activities		(40 000)
Net decrease in cash and cash equivalents		(5 450)
Cash and cash equivalents at beginning of year		60 000
Cash and cash equivalents at end of year		$54 550

FIGURE 17.9   Complete cash flow statement of Beachwear Ltd

The balance of cash at year-end of $54 550 shown in figure 17.9 agrees with the cash at bank balance shown in the balance sheet at 31 December 2007 in figure 17.4. There are no cash equivalents such as short-term deposits or a bank overdraft. Where there are cash equivalents, paragraph 45 of IAS 7 requires that the cash and cash equivalents be disclosed, with the amounts reconciled in the cash flow statement and the equivalent items reported in the balance sheet. In addition, paragraph 48 requires an entity to disclose the amount of significant cash and cash-equivalent balances held that are not available for general use, for example, as a result of exchange controls that may affect the general availability of the cash held by a foreign subsidiary in the case of a consolidated cash flow statement.

LO 6

17.8 Other disclosures

Additional information is often necessary to obtain a complete picture of the change in an entity's financial position, because not all transactions are simple cash transactions. Significant changes can result from the acquisition or disposal of subsidiaries or other business units, or from transactions that do not involve current cash flows.

17.8.1 Acquisitions and disposals of subsidiaries and other business units

Chapters 19–24 of this book deal with the financial reporting of consolidated groups of entities. When a parent entity acquires an operating entity, or disposes of an existing subsidiary, a comparative consolidated balance sheet of the group before and after the acquisition or disposal will frequently disclose significant changes in the balance sheet amounts arising from the acquisition or disposal. Financial statement users need to be aware of such changes in order to understand the change in financial position of the consolidated group, so IAS 7 specifies additional reporting requirements relating to the acquisitions and disposals of subsidiaries and other business units. They are as follows:

39. The aggregate cash flows arising from acquisitions and from disposals of subsidiaries or other business units shall be presented separately and classified as investing activities.
40. An entity shall disclose, in aggregate, in respect of both acquisitions and disposals of subsidiaries or other business units during the period each of the following:
    (a) the total purchase or disposal consideration;
    (b) the portion of the purchase or disposal consideration discharged by means of cash and cash equivalents;
    (c) the amount of cash and cash equivalents in the subsidiary or business unit acquired or disposed of;
    (d) the amount of the assets and liabilities other than cash or cash equivalents in the subsidiary or business unit acquired or disposed of, summarised by each major category.

Separate presentation of the cash flow effects of acquisitions and disposals of subsidiaries and other business units is required. The cash flow effects of disposals are not deducted from those of acquisitions. Instead, the aggregate amount of the cash paid or received as purchase or sale consideration is reported in the cash flow statement net of cash equivalents acquired or disposed of.

17.8.2 Non-cash transactions

Not all investing or financing transactions involve current cash flows, although such transactions may significantly affect the financial structure of the entity. However, such transactions need to be understood in order to comprehend the change in financial position of an entity. Examples include:

• acquisition of assets by means of a finance lease or by assuming other liabilities
• acquisition of assets or an entity by means of an equity issue
• conversion of debt to equity and preference shares to ordinary shares
• refinancing of long-term debt
• payment of dividends through a share reinvestment scheme.

In regard to non-cash transactions, paragraph 43 of IAS 7 states:

Investing and financing transactions that do not require the use of cash or cash equivalents shall be excluded from a cash flow statement. Such transactions shall be disclosed elsewhere in the financial statements in a way that provides all the relevant information about these investing and financing activities.

17.8.3 Disclosures that are encouraged but not required

Paragraph 50 of IAS 7 encourages, but does not require, additional information that may be relevant to users in understanding the financial position and liquidity of an entity. They are as follows:

(a) the amount of undrawn borrowing facilities that may be available for future operating activities and to settle capital commitments, indicating any restrictions on the use of these facilities;
(b) the aggregate amounts of the cash flows from each of operating, investing and financing activities related to interests in joint ventures reported using proportionate consolidation;
(c) the aggregate amount of cash flows that represent increases in operating capacity separately from those cash flows that are required to maintain operating capacity; and
(d) the amount of the cash flows arising from the operating, investing and financing activities of each reported industry and geographical segment (see IAS 14 *Segment Reporting*).

Chapter 26 of this book provides an outline of proportionate consolidation of interests in joint ventures referred to in paragraph 50(b) of the standard. Chapter 18 deals with segment reporting referred to in paragraph 50(d).

LO 7

17.9 Comprehensive example

The example in this section demonstrates a more complex statement of cash flows prepared using a worksheet. Figure 17.10 presents the financial statements of Sports Action Ltd, and the worksheet is shown in figure 17.11. An explanation of the reconciling adjustments follows the worksheet. The indirect method is used to present cash flows from operating activities.

FIGURE 17.10   Financial statements of Sports Action Ltd

Sports Action Ltd Comparative balance sheets as at:			
	31 December 2006	31 December 2007	Increase (decrease)
Cash	$ 60 000	$ 69 800	$ 9 800
Short-term deposits	120 000	140 000	20 000
Accounts receivable, net	140 000	190 000	50 000
Inventory	130 000	155 000	25 000
Prepayments	16 000	19 000	3 000
Interest receivable	300	200	(100)
Investment in associate	40 000	45 000	5 000
Land	80 000	120 000	40 000
Plant	300 000	420 000	120 000
Accumulated depreciation	(50 000)	(65 000)	(15 000)
Intangibles	90 000	60 000	(30 000)
	$926 300	$1 154 000	$227 700
Accounts payable	84 000	90 000	6 000
Accrued liabilities	14 000	12 000	(2 000)
Current tax payable	28 000	32 000	4 000
Deferred tax	20 000	25 000	5 000
Borrowings	120 000	180 000	60 000
Share capital	600 000	680 000	80 000
Retained earnings	60 300	135 000	74 700
	$926 300	$1 154 000	$227 700

(continued)

Sports Action Ltd Income statement for the year ended 31 December 2007		
Revenue		
Sales revenue		$1 600 000
Interest		10 000
Share of profits of associate		10 000
Gain on sale of plant		8 000
		$1 628 000
Expenses		
Cost of goods sold	$960 000	
Wages and salaries	240 000	
Depreciation – plant	40 000	
Impairment – intangibles	30 000	
Interest	12 000	
Doubtful debts	8 000	
Other expenses	132 000	1 422 000
Profit before tax		206 000
Income tax expense		65 000
Profit for the year		$ 141 000

FIGURE 17.11 Cash flow statement worksheet

Other information used in worksheet:

(a) Changes in equity:

	Share capital	Accumulated profit
Balance at 31 December 2006	$600 000	$ 60 300
Profit for the year	–	141 000
Dividends – cash	–	(36 300)
– reinvested under dividend scheme	30 000	(30 000)
Cash share issue	50 000	–
Balance at 31 December 2007	$680 000	$135 000

(b) Investment in associate (equity method)

Balance at 31 December 2006	$ 40 000
Share of profit of associate	10 000
Dividend received	(5 000)
Balance at 31 December 2007	$ 45 000

(c) Land

Additional land acquired	$ 40 000
Finance provided by vendor	(35 000)
Cash paid	$ 5 000

(d) Plant
Acquisitions

Acquisitions	$180 000
Cash paid	171 000
Accounts payable outstanding at year-end	9 000
	$180 000
Disposals – cost	60 000
Accumulated depreciation	(25 000)
Proceeds received in cash	43 000

(e) Intangibles
There were no acquisitions or disposals.

Impairment write-down	$ 30 000

(f) Accounts payable
comprises:

	2006	2007
Purchase of inventory	$49 000	$ 56 000
Purchase of plant	15 000	9 000
Other purchases	20 000	25 000
	$84 000	$ 90 000

(g) Accrued liabilities comprises
accruals for:

	2006	2007
Interest	$ 1 200	$ 2 100
Wages and salaries	3 000	5 000
Other expenses	9 800	4 900
	$14 000	$ 12 000

(h) Borrowings of $60 000
Increase reflects:

Land vendor finance	$ 35 000
Additional cash borrowing	25 000
	$ 60 000

(i) Income tax expense comprises:

Currently payable	$ 60 000
Deferred tax	5 000
	$ 65 000

(j) Movement in current tax payable:

Balance at 31 December 2006	$ 28 000
Income tax expense	60 000
Payments made	(56 000)
Balance at 31 December 2007	$ 32 000

(continued)

	Balance 31.12.06	Reconciling items Debits	Reconciling items Credits	Balance 31.12.07
Sports Action Ltd **Cash flow statement worksheet** **for year ended 31 December 2007**				
Cash	$ 60 000	(26) $9 800		$ 69 800
Short-term deposits	120 000	(27) 20 000		140 000
Accounts receivable, net	140 000	(2) 50 000		190 000
Interest receivable	300		(13) 100	200
Inventory	130 000	(3) 25 000		155 000
Prepayments	16 000	(4) 3 000		19 000
Investment in associate	40 000	(7) 5 000		45 000
Land	80 000	(18) 5 000		
		(19) 35 000		120 000
Plant	300 000	(9) 8 000	(21) 43 000	
		(19) 180 000	(22) 25 000	420 000
Accumulated depreciation	(50 000)	(22) 25 000	(10) 40 000	(65 000)
Intangibles	90 000		(11) 30 000	60 000
	$926 300			$1 154 000
Accounts payable	84 000	(20) 6 000	(5) 12 000	90 000
Accrued liabilities	14 000	(6) 2 900	(14) 900	12 000
Current tax payable	28 000		(16) 4 000	32 000
Deferred tax	20 000		(17) 5 000	25 000
Borrowings	120 000		(19) 35 000	
			(22) 25 000	180 000
Share capital	600 000		(23) 50 000	
			(24) 30 000	680 000
Retained earnings	60 300	(15) 65 000	(1) 206 000	
		(24) 30 000		
		(25) 36 300		135 000
	$926 300			$1 154 000
Cash flow statement data **Operating activities**				
Profit before tax		(1) $206 000		$206 000
Increase in accounts receivable			(2) $ 50 000	(50 000)
Increase in inventory			(3) 25 000	(25 000)
Increase in prepayments			(4) 3 000	(3 000)
Increase in accounts payable		(5) 12 000		12 000
Decrease in accrued liabilities			(6) 2 900	(2 900)
Share of profits of associate			(7) 10 000	(10 000)
Interest income			(8) 10 000	(10 000)
Gain on sale of plant			(9) 8 000	(8 000)
Depreciation – plant		(10) 40 000		40 000
Impairment – intangibles		(11) 30 000		30 000
Interest expense		(12) 12 000		12 000
Cash generated from operations		300 000	108 900	191 100
Interest received		(8) 10 000		
		(13) 100		10 100
Dividend received from associate		(7) 5 000		5 000
Interest paid		(14) 900	(12) 12 000	(11 100)
Income tax paid		(16) 4 000		
		(17) 5 000	(15) 65 000	(56 000)
Net cash from operating activities		325 000	185 900	139 100

| | Balance 31.12.06 | Reconciling items | | Balance 31.12.07 |
		Debits	Credits	
Investing activities				
Purchase of land			(18) 5 000	(5 000)
Purchase of plant			(19) 180 000	
			(20) 6 000	(186 000)
Proceeds from sale of plant		(21) 43 000		43 000
Net cash used in investing activities		43 000	191 000	(148 000)
Financing activities				
Proceeds from borrowings		(22) 25 000		25 000
Proceeds from share issue		(23) 50 000		50 000
Payment of cash dividends			(25) 36 300	(36 300)
Net cash flows from financing activities		75 000	36 300	38 700
Net increase in cash and cash equivalents		443 000	413 200	$ 29 800
Increase in cash			(26) 9 800	
Increase in short-term deposits			(27) 20 000	
		$443 000	$443 000	

17.9.1   Explanation of reconciling adjustments in worksheet

Explanations of the reconciling adjustments made in compiling the cash flow statement data in figure 17.11 are set forth below.

A – Profit before tax

When using the indirect method of presenting cash flows from operating activities, the profit before tax of $206 000 is the starting point. An adjustment (1) is made to retained earnings to reflect the profit before tax for the year, and a separate adjustment (15) is made for income tax expense.

B – Increase in net accounts receivable

The net increase in accounts receivable of $50 000 is a movement that did not result in cash flows for the period. It must therefore be deducted from profit before tax (adjustment 2). Because the indirect method is being used, there is no need to include separate adjustments for bad debts written off, changes in any provision for doubtful debts or discounts allowed. Such adjustments are necessary to determine cash flows from customers only under the direct method.

C – Increase in inventory

The increase in inventory of $25 000 is an operating cash outflow subject to any increase funded through an increase in accounts payable (adjustment 3).

D – Prepayments

The increase in prepayments is an operating cash outflow during the period that is not reflected in profit before tax (adjustment 4).

E – Accounts payable

Accounts payable comprise:

	2006	2007	Increase (decrease)	
Amount arising from the:				
Purchase of inventory and services	$69 000	$81 000	$12 000	(Adjustment 5)
Purchase of plant	15 000	9 000	(6 000)	(Adjustment 20)
	$84 000	$90 000	$ 6 000	

The increase in accounts payable arising from the purchase of inventory and services does not involve an operating cash outflow for the period. In this example, it partly offsets the increase in inventory reflected in adjustment 3.

The reduction in accounts payable arising from the purchase of plant of $6000 increases the cash outflow for the purchase of plant (adjustment 20).

F – Accrued liabilities

Accrued liabilities comprise:

	2006	2007	Increase (decrease)
Amount arising from:			
Accrued interest	$ 1 200	$ 2 100	$ 900
Other	12 800	9 900	(2 900)
	$14 000	$12 000	($2 000)

The reduction in other accrued liabilities increases the operating cash outflows for the year and is reflected in adjustment 6. The increase in accrued interest payable does not involve a cash flow and is reflected in adjustment 14.

G – Equity earnings of associate

The investment in associate (accounted for under the equity method) increased by $5000, comprising the share of profits of the associate of $10 000, net of a dividend received of $5000. The $10 000 share of profits is excluded from cash generated from operations and the $5000 dividend received is included in net cash from operating activities. The $5000 net increase in the investment does not represent a cash flow and this is reflected in the $10 000 adjustment, net of the $5000 dividend (adjustment 7).

H – Interest income

Interest income is initially transferred out of profit before tax in order to arrive at cash generated from operations (adjustment 8), and is then increased by the reduction in interest receivable of $100 (adjustment 13) to arrive at the interest cash inflow. Alternatively, the interest cash inflow could be classified as an investing activity.

I – Gain on sale of plant

Gain on sale of plant of $8000 is not a cash inflow, so it is deducted from profit before tax in arriving at net cash from operating activities (adjustment 9). A separate adjustment is made for the proceeds from sale of plant of $43 000 as an investing cash flow. The cost of plant sold amount of $60 000 comprises the items shown opposite.

Proceeds	$43 000	(Adjustment 21)
− Gain on sale	(8 000)	(Adjustment 9)
+ Accumulated depreciation	25 000	(Adjustment 22)
Cost of plant sold	$60 000	

J — Depreciation of plant and impairment of intangibles

Both of these expenses in the income statement do not constitute cash flows in the current period, so they are added back in arriving at net cash from operating activities (depreciation adjustment 10 of $40 000 and impairment adjustment 11 of $30 000).

K — Interest expense

Interest expense is initially transferred out of profit before tax in order to arrive at cash generated from operations (adjustment 12). It is then reduced by the increase in accrued interest $900 (adjustment 14), to arrive at the interest cash outflow. Alternatively, the interest cash outflow could be classified as a financing activity.

L — Income tax paid

Income tax expense of $65 000 (adjustment 15) is reduced by the increase in current tax payable of $4000 (adjustment 16) and the increase in deferred income tax of $5000 (adjustment 17) to determine the income tax cash outflow of $56 000. In this example, there are no tax charges — such as on revaluation or translation reserve increments — made directly to equity accounts.

M — Purchase of land and plant

Additional land was acquired at a cost of $40 000, with $35 000 being financed by the vendor. Adjustment 18 records the cash outflow of $5000 and adjustment 19 records the non-cash component of $35 000. The other side of the adjustment is made to borrowings.

Plant acquisitions for the year are $180 000 (adjustment 19). This amount is increased by the reduction in plant accounts payable of $6000 (adjustment 20); this is discussed in part E above.

N — Proceeds from borrowings

The cash proceeds from borrowings of $25 000 comprise the gross increase in borrowings of $60 000 ($180 000 − $120 000) reduced by the $35 000 of land vendor finance (adjustment 19); this is discussed in part M above.

O — Proceeds from share issue and payment of cash dividends

To determine the proceeds from share issue (adjustment 23), the increase in share capital of $80 000 ($680 000 − $600 000) is reduced by the $30 000 of reinvested dividends (adjustment 24) because these dividends did not involve a cash inflow. Similarly, cash flows from financing activities include only the $36 300 of dividends paid in cash (adjustment 25).

P — Increase in cash and short-term deposits

Short-term deposits are considered to be cash equivalents. Therefore, the increase is included in the net increase in cash and cash equivalents for the period of $29 800 (adjustments 26 and 27).

Figure 17.12 contains Sports Action Ltd's cash flow statement for the year ended 31 December 2007 (without prior year comparatives).

Sports Action Ltd Cash flow statement for year ended 31 December 2007		
Cash flows from operating activities		
Profit before tax	$206 000	
Adjustments for:		
Depreciation	40 000	
Impairment of intangibles	30 000	
Gain on sale of plant	(8 000)	
Share of profits of associate	(10 000)	
Interest income	(10 000)	
Interest expense	12 000	
Increase in receivables	(50 000)	
Increase in inventory	(25 000)	
Increase in prepayments	(3 000)	
Increase in accounts payables	12 000	
Decrease in accrued liabilities	(2 900)	
Cash generated from operations	191 100	
Interest received	10 100	
Dividend received from associate	5 000	
Interest paid	(11 100)	
Income taxes paid	(56 000)	
Net cash from operating activities		$139 100
Cash flows from investing activities		
Purchase of land (Note A)	(5 000)	
Purchase of plant	(186 000)	
Proceeds from sale of plant	43 000	
Net cash used in investing activities		(148 000)
Cash flow from financing activities		
Proceeds from borrowings	25 000	
Proceeds from share issue (Note B)	50 000	
Dividends paid (Note B)	(36 300)	
Net cash from financing activities		38 700
Net increase in cash and cash equivalents		29 800
Cash and cash equivalents at beginning of year (Note C)		180 000
Cash and cash equivalents at end of year (Note C)		$209 800

Notes:

A Land

During the year, land at a cost of $40 000 was acquired by means of vendor finance of $35 000 and a cash payment of $5000.

B Dividends

During the year, shareholders elected to reinvest dividends amounting to $30 000 under the company's dividend share reinvestment scheme. (This information will be reported in the company's statement of changes in equity, so a cross-reference to that statement may be used instead of this note.)

C Cash and cash equivalents

Cash and cash equivalents included in the cash flow statement comprise the following balance sheet amounts:

	2007	2006
Cash	$ 69 800	$ 60 000
Short-term deposits	140 000	120 000
	$209 800	$180 000

FIGURE 17.12 Final cash flow statement of Sports Action Ltd

If the direct method of presenting operating cash flows is used, the cash receipts from customers and cash paid to suppliers and employees can be determined by reconstructing the relevant general ledger accounts or by using the equations previously given. For the purposes of this example, it is assumed that net accounts receivable comprises:

	2006	2007
Accounts receivable	$160 000	$215 000
Allowance for doubtful debts	20 000	25 000
	$140 000	$190 000

It is further assumed that bad debts of $3000 were deducted from the allowance for doubtful debts and the remaining allowance for doubtful debts was increased by a charge to the income statement of $8000 (refer to the income statement).

As demonstrated previously, the summarised general ledger accounts can be reconstructed from the balance sheet and supplementary information (opening and closing balances), and income statement and supplementary information (bad debts and sales). The cash receipts amount is then determined by the difference.

The reconstructed accounts receivable and allowance for doubtful debts general ledger accounts would appear as follows:

Accounts receivable			
Opening balance	160 000	Bad debts	3 000
Sales	1 600 000	Cash received	1 542 000
		Closing balance	215 000
	1 760 000		1 760 000

Allowance for doubtful debts			
Bad debts	3 000	Opening balance	20 000
Closing balance	25 000	Doubtful debts	8 000
	28 000		28 000

Cash paid to suppliers of inventory can be determined by reconstructing the relevant general ledger accounts. The purchases amount is determined as the difference between the opening and closing balances (obtained from the balance sheet) and cost of goods sold (obtained from the income statement). The determined amount of purchases is then recorded in the accounts payable (for inventory) account to calculate the cash payments to suppliers of inventory. This is shown as follows:

Inventory			
Opening balance	130 000	Cost of goods sold	960 000
Purchases	985 000	Closing balance	155 000
	1 115 000		1 115 000

Accounts payable — Inventory purchases			
Cash payments	978 000	Opening balance	49 000
Closing balance	56 000	Purchases	985 000
	1 034 000		1 034 000

Cash paid to other suppliers and employees can be similarly determined or found by using the equations previously given. Cash payments to other suppliers and employees comprise:

Other expenses	$132 000
Prepayments increase	3 000
Increase (decrease) in:	
accounts payable	(5 000)
Accruals liabilities	4 900
Total payments	$134 900
Wages and salaries	$240 000
Increase in accrued wages and salaries	(2 000)
Total payments	$238 000

Using the above calculations, total payments to suppliers and employees comprise:

Payments for:	
Inventory	$978 000
Other services	134 900
Employees	238 000
	$1 350 900

Using the above calculations, cash flows from operating activities presented under the direct method are shown in figure 17.13.

Cash flow from operating activities:	
Cash received from customers	$1 542 000
Cash payments to suppliers and employees	(1 350 900)
Cash generated from operations	191 100
Interest received	10 100
Dividend received from associate	5 000
Interest paid	(11 100)
Income taxes paid	(56 000)
Net cash from operating activities	$ 139 100

FIGURE 17.13 Cash flows from operating activities using the direct method

17.10 Extracts from financial reports

Figure 17.14 shows the information disclosed by the Nokia Group in its statement of cash flows and related notes for the year ended 31 December 2005, and figure 17.15 shows the disclosures as presented by the Danisco Group in its 30 April 2005 annual report.

FIGURE 17.14 Cash flow statements and related notes for Nokia, 2005

Consolidated cash flow statements, IFRS				
Financial year ended December 31	Notes	2005 EURm	2004 As revised EURm	2003 As revised EURm
Cash flow from operating activities				
Profit attributable to equity holders of the parent		3 616	3 192	3 543
Adjustments total	35	1 774	2 059	2 992
Profit attributable to equity holders of the parent before change in net working capital		5 390	5 251	6 535
Change in net working capital	35	−366	241	−184
Cash generated from operations		5 024	5 492	6 351
Interest received		353	204	256
Interest paid		−26	−26	−33
Other financial income and expenses, net received		47	41	118
Income taxes paid		−1 254	−1 368	−1 440
Net cash from operating activities		4 144	4 343	5 252
Cash flow from investing activities				
Acquisition of Group companies		−92	−	−7
Purchase of current available-for-sale investments, liquid assets		−7 277	−10 318	−11 695
Purchase of non-current available-for-sale investments		−89	−388	−282
Purchase of shares in associated companies		−16	−109	−61
Additions to capitalized development costs		−153	−101	−218
Long-term loans made to customers		−56	−	−97
Proceeds from repayment and sale of long-term loans receivable		−	368	315
Proceeds from (+)/payment of (−) other long-term receivables		14	2	−18
Proceeds from short-term loans receivable		182	66	63
Capital expenditures		−607	−548	−432
Proceeds from disposal of shares in Group companies, net of disposed cash		5	1	−
Proceeds from disposal of shares in associated companies		18	−	−
Proceeds from disposal of businesses		95	−	−
Proceeds from maturities and sale of current available-for-sale investments, liquid assets		9 402	9 737	8 793
Proceeds from sale of current available-for-sale investments		247	587	−
Proceeds from sale of non-current available-for-sale investments		3	346	381
Proceeds from sale of fixed assets		167	6	19
Dividends received		1	22	24
Net cash (used in) investing activities		1 844	−329	−3 215
Cash flow from financing activities				
Proceeds from stock option exercises		2	−	23
Purchase of treasury shares		−4 258	−2 648	−1 355
Proceeds from long-term borrowings		5	1	8
Repayment of long-term borrowings		−	−3	−56
Proceeds from (+)/repayment of (−) short-term borrowings		212	−255	−22
Dividends paid		−1 531	−1 413	−1 378
Net cash used in financing activities		−5 570	−4 318	−2 780
Foreign exchange adjustment		183	−23	−146
Net increase (+)/decrease(−) in cash and cash equivalents		601	−327	−889
Cash and cash equivalents at beginning of period		2 457	2 784	3 673

(*continued*)

Consolidated cash flow statements, IFRS				
Financial year ended December 31	Notes	2005 EURm	2004 As revised EURm	2003 As revised EURm
Cash and cash equivalents at end of period		3 058	2 457	2 784
Cash and cash equivalents comprised of:				
Bank and cash		1 565	1 090	1 145
Current available-for-sale investments, cash equivalents	1 738	1 493	1 367	1 639
		3 058	2 457	2 784

See Notes to consolidated financial statements.

The figures in the consolidated cash flow statement cannot be directly traced from the balance sheet without additional information as a result of acquisitions and disposals of subsidiaries and net foreign exchange differences arising on consolidation.

35. Notes to cash flow statement			
EURm	2005	2004 As revised	2003 As revised
Adjustments for:			
Depreciation and amortization (Note 11)	712	868	1 138
(Profit)/loss on sale of property, plant and equipment and available-for-sale investments	−131	26	170
Income taxes (Note 13)	1 281	1 446	1 697
Share of results of associated companies (Note 34)	−10	26	18
Minority interest	74	67	54
Financial income and expenses (Note 12)	−322	−405	−352
Impairment charges (Note 9)	66	129	453
Share-based compensation	104	62	41
Premium return	−	−160	−
Customer financing impairment charges and reversals	−	−	−226
Other	−	−	−1
Adjustments, total	1 774	2 059	2 992
Change in net working capital			
(Increase) Decrease in short-term receivables	−896	372	−205
Increase in inventories	−301	−193	−41
Increase in interest-free short-term borrowings	831	62	62
Change in net working capital	−366	241	−184
Non-cash investing activities			
Acquisition of:			
Current available-for-sale investments in settlement of customer loan	−	−	676
Company acquisitions	−	−	18
Total	−	−	694

Source: Nokia (2005, pp. 8–9, 34).

FIGURE 17.15   Cash flow statements and related notes for Danisco, 2005

	Cash flow statement 1 May 2004–30 April 2005	GROUP	
Note	DKK million	2003/04	2004/05
	Cash flow from operating activities		
	Profit for the year	1 009	1 242
26	Adjustments	1 978	1 457
	Change in inventories	(230)	(217)
	Change in receivables	(290)	(638)
	Change in trade payables etc.	26	409
	Change in working capital	(494)	(446)
	Results from other investments and securities	17	4
	Interest received	184	167
	Interest paid	(469)	(483)
22	Corporation tax paid	(558)	(563)
	Cash flow from operating activities	**1 667**	**1 378**
	Cash flow from investing activities		
25	Purchase of undertakings and activities	(42)	(5 908)
	Amount payable concerning purchase of activity	–	178
	Sale of undertakings and activities	–	65
	Purchase of property, plant and equipment	(868)	(757)
	Sale of property, plant and equipment	198	62
	Purchase of intangible assets	(153)	(119)
	Sale of intangible assets	47	–
	Change in financial assets, net	869	(3)
	Cash flow from investing activities	**51**	**(6 482)**
	Cash flow from financing activities		
27	Change in financial liabilities	(1 142)	5 751
	Buyback of own shares, net	(356)	(299)
	Dividends paid	(311)	(323)
	Change in minority interests	(2)	(39)
	Cash flow from financing activities	**(1 811)**	**5 090**
	Decrease/increase in cash and cash equivalents	**(93)**	**(14)**
	Cash and cash equivalents at 1 May	408	304
	Exchange adjustment of cash and cash equivalents	(11)	(8)
	Transferred from associates	–	447
	Cash and cash equivalents at 30 April	**304**	**729**
			(*continued*)

	Notes to the balance sheet		
		GROUP	
Note	DKK million	30 April 2004	30 April 2005
22	**Corporation tax**		
	Corporation tax payable at 1 May	325	201
	Additions due to new activities	–	22
	Transferred from associates	–	15
	Adjustment concerning previous years	–	35
	Tax on changes in equity	–	44
	Current tax on profit for the year	434	559
	Tax paid during the year	(558)	(563)
	Corporation tax payable at 30 April	201	313
	Corporation tax payable is stated in the balance sheet as follows:		
	Other receivables	70	65
	Corporation tax	271	378
	Corporation tax payable at 30 April	201	313

	Notes to the cash flow statement		
		GROUP	
Note	DKK million	2003/04	2004/05
25	**... purchase of undertakings and activities, continued**		
	Intangible assets	(3)	(185)
	Property, plant and equipment	(32)	(1 137)
	Investments	–	(137)
	Inventories	(3)	(581)
	Receivables and prepayments	–	(372)
	Cash and cash equivalents	–	(553)
	Minority interests	7	34
	Other provisions	–	77
	Provisions for deferred tax	–	52
	Financial liabilities	–	112
	Non-interest-bearing debt	6	360
	Corporation tax	–	22
	Net assets	(25)	(2 308)
	Goodwill on purchase of undertakings and activities	(17)	(4 196)
	Adjustment of cash and cash equivalents	–	553
	Cash purchase amount	(42)	(5 951)
	Exchange adjustment	–	43
	Purchase of undertakings and activities	(42)	(5 908)
	Financial liabilities	–	(112)
	Cost of acquisition total	(42)	(6 020)

Notes to the cash flow statement		
26 Adjustments		
Depreciation, writedowns and amortisation for the year	1 302	964
Gain from sale of investment in Amcor Flexible Europe A/S	(50)	.
Gain from sale of the oilseed rape business in Danisco Seed	–	(65)
Profit/loss on disposal of property, plant and equipment	(16)	(8)
Results of investments in associates	(53)	(54)
Results of investmens and securities	(17)	(4)
Financial income	(211)	(343)
Financial expenses	520	656
Other provisions	(20)	(123)
Expensed tax for the year	531	443
Non-financial prepayments and deferred income, etc.	(8)	(9)
Total	**1 978**	**1 457**
27 Change in financial liabilities		
Interest-bearing debt at 1 May	(9 828)	(8 591)
Exchange adjustment of opening value, etc.	13	2
Financial net liabilities assumed on purchase of undertakings and activities	–	(112)
Transferred from associates	–	(86)
Currency hedging of net investments in associates	188	146
Other movements	(36)	10
Interest-bearing debt at 30 April	8 591	14 382
Total	**(1 142)**	**5 751**

Source: Danisco (2005, pp. 44, 54, 57).

17.11 Summary

IAS 7 *Cash Flow Statements* is a disclosure standard requiring the presentation of a cash flow statement as an integral part of an entity's financial statements. The cash flow statement is particularly useful to investors, lenders and others when evaluating an entity's ability to generate cash and cash equivalents, and to meet its obligations and pay dividends. The statement is required to report cash flows classified into operating, investing and financing activities, as well as the net movement in cash and cash equivalents during the period. Net cash flows from operating activities may be presented using either the direct or the indirect method of presentation. IAS 7 requires additional information to be presented elsewhere in the financial reports concerning investing and financing activities that do not involve cash flows and are therefore excluded from a cash flow statement. The standard also requires additional disclosures relating to the acquisitions and disposals of subsidiaries and other business units.

DISCUSSION QUESTIONS

1. What is the objective of a cash flow statement?
2. How might a statement of cash flows be used?
3. What is the meaning of 'cash equivalent'?
4. Explain the required classifications of cash flows under IAS 7.
5. What sources of information are usually required to prepare a cash flow statement?
6. Explain the differences between the presentation of cash flows from operating activities under the direct method and their presentation under the indirect method. Do you consider one method to be more useful than the other? Why?
7. The cash flow statement is said to be of assistance in evaluating the financial strength of an entity, yet the statement can exclude significant non-cash transactions that can materially affect the financial strength of an entity. How does IAS 7 seek to overcome this issue?
8. An entity may report significant profits over a number of successive years and still experience negative cash flows from its operating activities. How can this happen?
9. An entity may report significant accounting losses over a number of successive years and still report net positive cash flows from operating activities over the same period. How can this happen?
10. What supplementary disclosures are required when a consolidated cash flow statement is being prepared for a group that has acquired or disposed of a subsidiary?

EXERCISES

EXERCISE 17.1   ★

Cash received from customers

At 30 June 2006, Swan Ltd had accounts receivable of $180 000. At 30 June 2007, accounts receivable were $220 000 and sales for the year amounted to $1 800 000.

Required

Calculate cash received from customers by Swan Ltd for the year ended 30 June 2007.

EXERCISE 17.2   ★

Cash payments to suppliers

Pigeon Ltd had the following balances:

	30 June 2006	30 June 2007
Inventory	$170 000	$210 000
Accounts payable for inventory purchases	51 000	65 000

Cost of goods sold was $1 700 000 for the year ended 30 June 2007.

Required

Calculate cash payments to suppliers for the year ended 30 June 2007.

EXERCISE 17.3   ★

Cash received from customers

At 30 June 2006, Pelican Ltd had accounts receivable of $200 000. At 30 June 2007, accounts receivable were $240 000 and sales for the year amounted to $2 100 000. Bad debts amounting to $50 000 had been written off during the year, and discounts of $17 000 had been allowed in respect of payments from customers made within prescribed credit terms.

Required

Calculate cash received from customers for the year ended 30 June 2007.

EXERCISE 17.4	★

Investing cash flows

The following information has been compiled from the accounting records of Lion Ltd for the year ended 30 June 2007:

Purchase of land, with the vendor financing $100 000 for two years	$350 000
Purchase of plant	250 000
Sale of plant:	
Book value	50 000
Cash proceeds	42 000

Required

Determine the amount of investing net cash outflows Lion Ltd would report in its cash flow statement for the year ended 30 June 2007.

EXERCISE 17.5	★

Financing cash flows

The following information has been compiled from the accounting records of Tiger Ltd for the year ended 30 June 2007:

Dividends — paid	$200 000
— share reinvestment scheme	120 000
Additional cash borrowing	300 000
Issue of shares — cash	340 000

Required

Determine the amount of net cash from financing activities Tiger Ltd would report in its cash flow statement for the year ended 30 June 2007.

EXERCISE 17.6	★★

Net investing cash flows

The accounting records of Giraffe Ltd at 30 June 2007 recorded the following non-current assets:

	30 June 2006	30 June 2007
Land, at independent valuation	$100 000	$120 000
Plant, at cost	70 000	85 000
Accumulated depreciation	(20 000)	(28 000)
Available-for-sale listed investments, at fair value	30 000	40 000
Goodwill	25 000	20 000
Additional information		
Land revaluation reserve	20 000	34 000
Investments revaluation reserve	5 000	11 000
Impairment of goodwill	—	5 000

- There were no acquisitions or disposals of land.
- There were no disposals of plant or investments.
- The land revaluation reserve increment is net of deferred tax of $6000.
- The investments revaluation reserve increment for the year is net of deferred tax of $2000.

Required

Determine the amount of net investing cash flows Giraffe Ltd would report in its cash flow statement for the year ended 30 June 2007, and prepare the investing section of the cash flow statement.

EXERCISE 17.7 ★★   Net financing cash flows

The following information has been extracted from the accounting records of Rabbit Ltd:

	30 June 2006	30 June 2007
Borrowings	$100 000	$200 000
Share capital	200 000	250 000
Property revaluation reserve	50 000	60 000
Retained earnings	75 000	95 000

Additional information

- Borrowings of $20 000 were repaid during the year to 30 June 2007. New borrowings include $80 000 vendor finance arising on the acquisition of a property.
- The increase in share capital includes $30 000 arising from the company's dividend reinvestment scheme.
- The movement in retained earnings comprises profit for the year $90 000, net of dividends $70 000.
- There were no dividends payable reported in the balance sheet at either 30 June 2006 or 30 June 2007.

Required

Determine the amount of financing cash flows Rabbit Ltd would report in its cash flow statement for the year ended 30 June 2007, and prepare the financing section of the cash flow statement.

EXERCISE 17.8 ★★★   Cash receipts from customers and cash paid to suppliers and employees

The accounting records of Sparrow Ltd recorded the following information:

	30 June 2006	30 June 2007
Accounts receivable	$40 000	$ 50 000
Inventories	32 000	34 000
Prepaid expenses	1 000	3 000
Accounts payable for inventory purchased	15 000	16 000
Employee liabilities	5 000	5 500
Other accruals (including accrued interest: 2006 − $700; 2007 − $850)	4 000	3 800
Sales revenue		600 000
Cost of goods sold		480 000
Expenses (including $5000 depreciation and $2000 interest)		75 000

Required

1. Calculate the amount of cash received from customers during the year ended 30 June 2007.
2. Calculate the amount of cash paid to suppliers and employees during the year ended 30 June 2007.

PROBLEMS

PROBLEM 17.1 ★

Preparation of a cash flow statement

A summarised comparative balance sheet of Leopard Ltd is presented below:

	30 June 2006	30 June 2007
Cash	$ 40 000	$ 55 000
Trade receivables	92 000	140 000
Investments, at cost	35 000	20 000
Plant	130 000	180 000
Accumulated depreciation	(45 000)	(60 000)
	$252 000	$335 000
Trade accounts payable	$ 75 000	$ 95 000
Share capital	100 000	150 000
Retained earnings	77 000	90 000
	$252 000	$335 000

Additional information
- An investment was sold for a profit of $15 000.
- There were no disposals of plant.
- The profit for the year was $60 000, after income tax expense of $30 000.
- A dividend of $47 000 was paid during the year.

Required
Using the indirect method of presenting cash flows from operating activities, prepare a cash flow statement in accordance with IAS 7 for the year ended 30 June 2007.

PROBLEM 17.2 ★

Preparation of a cash flow statement

A summarised comparative balance sheet of Blackall Ltd is presented below:

	30 June 2006	30 June 2007
Cash	$ 20 000	$ 91 000
Trade accounts receivable	65 000	90 000
Inventory	58 000	62 000
Prepayments	10 000	12 000
Land	80 000	90 000
Plant	280 000	320 000
Accumulated depreciation	(60 000)	(92 000)
	$453 000	$573 000
Accounts payable	$ 45 000	$ 48 000
Borrowings	160 000	200 000
Share capital	200 000	230 000
Retained earnings	48 000	95 000
	$453 000	$573 000

Additional information
- There were no disposals of land and plant during the year.
- A $30 000 borrowing was settled through the issue of ordinary shares. There were no other borrowing repayments.
- Profit for the year was $120 000, interest expense was $14 000, and income tax expense was $41 000.
- A $73 000 dividend was paid during the year.

Required

Using the indirect method of presenting cash flows from operating activities, prepare a cash flow statement in accordance with IAS 7 for the year ended 30 June 2007.

PROBLEM 17.3 ★ Presentation of a cash flow statement

A summarised comparative balance sheet of Cooran Ltd is presented below, together with the income statement for the year ended 30 June 2007:

	30 June 2006	30 June 2007
Cash	$ 30 000	$ 63 000
Trade receivables	46 000	70 000
Inventory	30 000	32 000
Investments	35 000	40 000
Plant	125 000	150 000
Accumulated depreciation	(23 000)	(35 000)
	$243 000	$320 000
Accounts payable	$ 39 000	$ 43 000
Accrued interest	3 000	5 000
Current tax payable	10 000	12 000
Borrowings	60 000	100 000
Share capital	100 000	100 000
Retained earnings	31 000	60 000
	$243 000	$320 000

Income statement for the year ended 30 June 2007	
Sales	$690 000
Cost of sales	483 000
Gross profit	207 000
Distribution costs	52 000
Administration costs	74 000
Interest	6 000
Profit before tax	75 000
Income tax expense	23 000
Profit for the year	$ 52 000

Additional information
- There were no disposals of investments or plant during the year.
- There are no deferred tax balances.
- A dividend of $23 000 was paid during the year.

Required

Using the direct method of presenting cash flows from operating activities, prepare a cash flow statement in accordance with IAS 7 for the year ended 30 June 2007.

Preparation of a cash flow statement

A summarised comparative balance sheet of Armadale Ltd is presented below:

	30 June 2006	30 June 2007
Cash	$ 96 000	$ 49 000
Accounts receivable	147 000	163 000
Prepayments	20 000	15 000
Inventory	60 000	104 000
Land	40 000	40 000
Plant	368 000	420 000
Accumulated depreciation	(45 000)	(70 000)
Deferred tax	20 000	24 000
	$706 000	$745 000
Accounts payable	$140 000	$152 000
Accrued liabilities	36 000	42 000
Current tax payable	24 000	31 000
Dividend payable	56 000	50 000
Borrowings	73 000	75 000
Share capital	335 000	345 000
Retained earnings	42 000	50 000
	$706 000	$745 000

Additional information
- Plant additions amounted to $72 000. Plant with a written-down value of $15 000 (cost $20 000, accumulated depreciation $5000) was sold for $22 000. The proceeds were outstanding at 30 June 2007.
- Accounts payable at 30 June 2006 include $34 000 arising from the acquisition of plant.
- Accrued liabilities include accrued interest of $3000 at 30 June 2006 and $4000 at 30 June 2007.
- The share capital increase of $10 000 arose from the reinvestment of dividends.
- The profit for the year was $92 000, after interest expense of $6000 and income tax expense of $46 000.
- Dividends declared out of profits for the year were: interim dividend $34 000, final dividend $50 000.

Required

Using the indirect method of presenting cash flows from operating activities, prepare a cash flow statement in accordance with IAS 7 for the year ended 30 June 2007.

Preparation of a cash flow statement

A summarised comparative balance sheet of Noosa Ltd is presented overleaf, together with an income statement for the year ended 30 June 2007.

	30 June 2006	30 June 2007
Cash	$ 45 000	$ 35 000
Trade receivables	69 000	105 000
Allowance for doubtful debts	(3 000)	(6 000)
Inventory	45 000	67 000
Available-for-sale investments	53 000	60 000
Plant	187 000	225 000
Accumulated depreciation	(35 000)	(53 000)
	$361 000	$433 000
Accounts payable	$ 65 000	$ 75 000
Accrued interest	5 000	7 000
Current tax payable	15 000	18 000
Deferred tax	30 000	37 000
Borrowings	80 000	100 000
Share capital	100 000	100 000
Investment revaluation reserve	2 000	7 000
Retained earnings	64 000	89 000
	$361 000	$433 000

Income statement for the year ended 30 June 2007	
Sales	$1 035 000
Cost of sales	774 000
Gross profit	261 000
Distribution costs	76 000
Administration costs	96 000
Interest	7 000
Profit before tax	82 000
Income tax expense	24 000
Profit for the year	$ 58 000

Additional information
- The movement in the allowance for doubtful debts for the year comprises:

Balance at 30 June 2006	$3 000
Charge for year	5 000
Bad debts written off	(2 000)
Balance at 30 June 2007	6 000

- Available-for-sale investments are valued at fair value, with increments/decrements being recognised in the investment revaluation reserve until investments are sold.
- The investments revaluation reserve increment for the year is net of deferred tax of $2000.
- There were no disposals of investments or plant during the year.
- A dividend of $33 000 was paid during the year.

Required
Using the direct method of presenting cash flows from operating activities, prepare a cash flow statement in accordance with IAS 7 for the year ended 30 June 2007.

| PROBLEM 17.6 | ★★ | Preparation of a cash flow statement |

A comparative balance sheet of Childers Ltd is presented below:

	30 June 2006	30 June 2007
Cash	$120 000	$ 218 000
Trade receivables	184 000	204 000
Inventory	100 000	160 000
Land (at valuation)	50 000	62 000
Plant	460 000	520 000
Accumulated depreciation	(90 000)	(120 000)
	$824 000	$1 044 000
Accounts payable	$150 000	$ 155 000
Accrued interest	12 000	16 000
Other accrued liabilities	45 000	43 000
Current tax payable	30 000	34 000
Provision for employee benefits	38 000	42 000
Dividend payable	–	60 000
Borrowings	95 000	105 000
Deferred tax	58 000	39 000
Share capital	350 000	380 000
Revaluation reserve	12 000	20 000
Retained earnings	34 000	150 000
	$824 000	$1 044 000

Income statement for the year ended 30 June 2007	
Sales	$3 580 000
Cost of sales	2 864 000
Gross profit	716 000
Gain on sale of plant	16 000
Dividends	4 000
Distribution costs	(185 000)
Administrative costs	(160 000)
Interest	(8 000)
Other costs	(40 000)
Profit before tax	343 000
Income tax expense	(103 000)
Profit for the year	$ 240 000

Additional information
- The land revaluation reserve increment for the year is net of deferred tax of $4000.
- Plant with a written-down value of $60 000 (cost $85 000, accumulated depreciation $25 000) was sold for $76 000.
- Accounts payable at 30 June 2007 include $22 000 in respect of plant acquisitions.
- There were borrowing repayments of $30 000 during the year.
- The increase in share capital of $30 000 arose from the company's dividend reinvestment scheme.
- Dividends declared out of profits for the year were: interim dividend $64 000, final dividend $60 000.

Required

Using the direct method of presenting cash flows from operating activities, prepare a cash flow statement in accordance with IAS 7 for the year ended 30 June 2007.

PROBLEM 17.7 ★★ Preparing cash flow statement information using the indirect method for operating cash flows

The comparative balance sheets and the income statement of Madrid Ltd are as follows:

Madrid Ltd Balance sheet as at 31 December		
	2006	2007
Current assets		
Deposits at call	$ 19 000	$ 30 000
Accounts receivable	340 000	320 000
Allowance for doubtful debts	(19 000)	(15 000)
Inventory	654 000	670 000
Prepayments	52 000	55 000
	$1 046 000	$1 060 000
Non-current assets		
Land	$ 400 000	$ 400 000
Buildings	1 175 000	1 850 000
Accumulated depreciation – buildings	(200 000)	(235 000)
Plant	850 000	940 000
Accumulated depreciation – plant	(375 000)	(452 000)
	1 850 000	2 503 000
Total assets	$2 896 000	$3 563 000
Current liabilities		
Bank overdraft	$ 140 000	$ 49 000
Accounts payable	553 000	570 000
Interest payable	25 000	30 000
Final dividend payable	205 000	230 000
Current tax payable	70 000	77 000
	993 000	956 000
Non-current liabilities		
Borrowings	900 000	1 300 000
Deferred tax	12 000	16 000
	912 000	1 316 000
Total liabilities	1 905 000	2 272 000
Equity		
Share capital	800 000	1 000 000
Retained earnings	191 000	291 000
	991 000	1 291 000
Total liabilities and equity	$2 896 000	$3 563 000

Madrid Ltd
Income statement
for the year ended 31 December 2007

Sales	$8 550 000
Less Cost of sales	4 517 000
Gross profit	4 033 000
Gain on sale of plant	18 000
	4 051 000
Distribution costs	1 635 000
Administration costs	1 566 000
Interest	70 000
Profit before tax	780 000
Income tax expense	250 000
Profit for the period	$ 530 000

The following additional information has been extracted from the accounting records of Madrid Ltd:

1. Movement in allowance for doubtful debts:

Balance 31 December 2006	$ 19 000
Charge for year	7 000
Bad debts written off	(11 000)
Balance 31 December 2007	$ 15 000

2. Building additions were completed at a cost of $675 000. There were no disposals.

3. The movement in plant and accumulated depreciation on plant comprised:

	Cost	Accumulated depreciation
Balance 31 December 2006	$ 850 000	$375 000
Additions – cash	160 000	
Disposals	(70 000)	(50 000)
Depreciation	–	127 000
Balance 31 December 2007	$ 940 000	$452 000
Cash proceeds from plant disposals	$ 38 000	

4. There was no outstanding interest payable at year-end.

5. Income tax expense comprised:

Income tax currently payable	$ 246 000
Deferred income tax	4 000
	$ 250 000

6. Additional cash borrowings $ 400 000

7. Movement in equity

	Share capital	Retained earnings
Balance 31 December 2006	$ 800 000	$191 000
Additional shares issued for cash	200 000	–
Profit for the period	–	530 000
Interim dividend – cash	–	(200 000)
Final dividend payable	–	(230 000)
Balance 31 December 2007	$1 000 000	$291 000

Required

1. Prepare a summary of cash flows from operating activities using the indirect method of presentation.
2. Prepare a summary of cash flows from investing activities.
3. Prepare a summary of cash flows from financing activities.

PROBLEM 17.8 ★★★ Preparing a cash flow statement with notes

The comparative balance sheets and the income statement of Adelaide Ltd were as follows:

Adelaide Ltd Balance sheet as at 31 December		
	2006	2007
Current assets		
Cash at bank	$ 46 000	$ 52 000
Cash deposits (30-day)	40 000	70 000
Accounts receivable	110 000	117 000
Allowance for doubtful debts	(12 000)	(16 000)
Interest receivable	2 000	3 000
Inventory	294 000	320 000
Prepayments	13 000	9 000
	493 000	555 000
Non-current assets		
Land	100 000	140 000
Plant	600 000	700 000
Accumulated depreciation	(140 000)	(180 000)
Plant, net	460 000	520 000
Investments in associate	80 000	92 000
Brand names	120 000	90 000
	760 000	842 000
Total assets	$1 253 000	$1 397 000
Current liabilities		
Accounts payable	$ 180 000	$ 196 000
Accrued liabilities	85 000	92 000
Current tax payable	40 000	43 000
Current portion of long-term borrowings	20 000	20 000
	325 000	351 000
Non-current liabilities		
Borrowings	98 000	138 000
Deferred tax	35 000	40 000
Employee benefits	40 000	43 000
	173 000	221 000
Total liabilities	498 000	572 000
Equity		
Share capital	500 000	530 000
Retained earnings	255 000	295 000
	755 000	825 000
Total liabilities and equity	$1 253 000	$1 397 000

Adelaide Ltd
Income statement
for the year ended 31 December 2007

Sales	$1 780 000
Cost of sales	1 030 000
Gross profit	750 000
Interest	2 000
Share of profits of associate	20 000
Gain on sale of plant	8 000
Total income	780 000
Expenses	
Salaries and wages	352 000
Depreciation	50 000
Discount allowed	8 000
Doubtful debts	6 000
Interest	21 000
Other (including impairment of brand names $30 000)	186 000
	623 000
Profit before tax	157 000
Income tax expense	(47 000)
Profit for the period	$ 110 000

The following additional information has been extracted from the accounting records of Adelaide Ltd:

1. 30-day cash deposits are used in the course of the daily cash management of the company.

2. Movement in allowance for doubtful debts:

Balance 31 December 2006	$ 12 000
Charge for year	6 000
Bad debts written off	(2 000)
Balance 31 December 2007	$ 16 000

3. Land

Additional cash purchase	$ 40 000

4. Plant

Purchases for year (including $50 000 purchase financed by vendor)	$150 000

5. Disposals

Proceeds (cash)	$ 48 000
Cost of disposals	50 000
Accumulated depreciation	(10 000)

6. Investments in associate

Share of profit	$ 20 000
Dividends received	8 000

(*continued*)

7.	Accounts payable Includes amounts owing in respect of plant purchases: 31 December 2006 31 December 2007		$ 12 000 18 000
8.	Accrued liabilities Includes accrued interest payable: 31 December 2006 31 December 2007		$ 4 000 5 000
9.	Income tax expense comprises: Current tax payable Deferred tax		$ 42 000 5 000
	Income tax expense		$ 47 000
10.	Dividends paid Under a dividend reinvestment share scheme, shareholders have the right to receive additional shares in lieu of cash dividends. Dividends paid comprised: Dividends paid in cash during the year Dividends reinvested		$ 40 000 30 000
	Total dividends		$ 70 000

Required

1. Using the direct method of presenting cash flows from operating activities, prepare a cash flow statement in accordance with IAS 7 for the year ended 31 December 2007.
2. Prepare a summary of cash flows from operating activities using the indirect method of presentation in accordance with IAS 7.
3. Prepare any notes to the cash flow statement that you consider are required under IAS 7.

WEBLINK

Visit these websites for additional information:

www.iasb.org   www.iasplus.com
www.asic.gov.au   www.ifac.org
www.aasb.com.au   www.nzica.com
www.accaglobal.com   www.capa.com.my

REFERENCES

Danisco 2005, *Annual report 2004/05*, Danisco A/S, Denmark, viewed 24 February 2006, <www.danisco.com>.
Nokia 2005, *Nokia in 2005*, Nokia Corporation, Finland, viewed 23 February 2006, <www.nokia.com>.

CHAPTER 18
Segment reporting – IAS 14

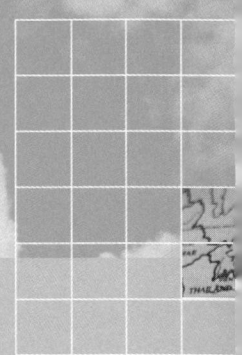

ACCOUNTING STANDARDS

International: IAS 14 *Segment Reporting*
Australia: AASB 114 *Segment Reporting*
New Zealand: NZ IAS 14 *Segment Reporting*

CONCEPTS FOR REVIEW

Before studying this chapter, you should understand or, if necessary, revise:

- the conceptual framework of the IASB, in particular the definitions of and recognition criteria for revenues and expenses
- the main disclosure standards of the IASB, in particular IAS 18 *Revenue* and IAS 1 *Presentation of Financial Statements*
- the basic requirements for accounting for goodwill and preparing consolidated financial statements.

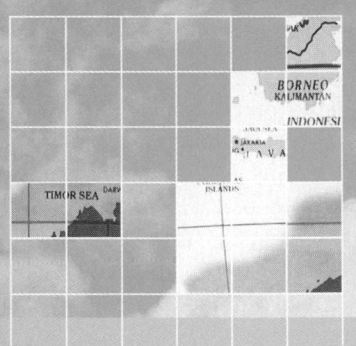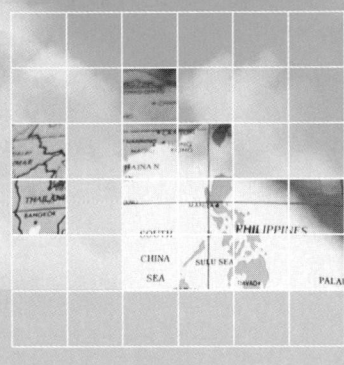

LEARNING OBJECTIVES

When you have studied this chapter, you should be able to:
1. understand the objectives of financial reporting by segments
2. distinguish between a business segment and a geographical segment
3. determine an entity's primary and secondary segment reporting formats
4. identify an entity's reportable segments
5. understand and apply the requirements for segment accounting policies, including the allocation of assets, liabilities, revenues and expenses to segments
6. understand and apply the disclosure requirements of IAS 14.

18.1   Introduction to IAS 14

IAS 14 *Segment Reporting* is primarily a disclosure standard and is particularly relevant for large organisations that operate in different geographic locations and/or in diverse businesses.

18.2   Scope

IAS 14 applies to entities whose equity or debt securities are publicly traded (i.e. entities listed on an authorised securities exchange such as the Australian Stock Exchange or the London Stock Exchange) and by entities that are in the process of listing.

If an entity voluntarily chooses to disclose segment information then it must fully comply with IAS 14. This may be the case, for example, where a large public company that is not listed, but has a large number of dependent users such as a number of minority shareholders, employees and creditors, elects to provide segment information. However, voluntary segment disclosures are not expected to be common, for reasons discussed in section 18.3.

Where the entity presents both consolidated financial statements and parent entity financial statements in a single financial report, then segment information need be presented only on the basis of the consolidated financial statements.

LO 1

18.3   Objectives of financial reporting by segments

Many entities operate in different geographical areas or provide products or services that are subject to differing rates of profitability, opportunities for growth, future prospects and risks. Information about an entity's geographical and business segments is relevant to assessing the risks and returns of a diversified or multinational entity where often that information cannot be determined from aggregated data. Therefore, segment information is regarded as necessary to help users of financial statements:
- better understand the entity's past performance
- better assess the entity's risks and returns
- make more informed judgements about the entity as a whole.

As we saw in 18.2, IAS 14 applies only to listed entities. Many securities analysts rely on the segment disclosures to help them assess not only an entity's past performance but also to help them predict future performance. Analysts use these assessments to determine an entity's share price. Segment disclosures are widely regarded as some of the most useful disclosures in financial reports because of the extent to which they disaggregate financial information into meaningful and often revealing groupings. For example, an entity may appear profitable on a consolidated basis, but segment disclosures may reveal that one part of the business is performing poorly while another part is performing well. The part that is performing poorly may be significant to the entity as a whole and over time continued poor performance by that part (or segment) may cause the entire entity's performance to suffer. This is the kind of information that impacts an entity's share price because analysts frequently look at predicted future cash flows in making their share price determinations.

On the other hand, preparers of financial reports may not wish to reveal too much information on a disaggregated basis to their competitors. Some may consider IAS 14's disclosure requirements to be too revealing. For example, a user can determine an entity's profit margin by segment when reading the segment disclosures. This is a key reason why it is unlikely that entities would volunteer to disclose segment information (see section 18.2). Another reason is that it is often a time-consuming exercise to prepare the segment disclosures.

LO 2

18.4 Business and geographical segments

18.4.1 Definitions

Paragraph 9 of IAS 14 defines business and geographical segments as follows:

> A *business segment* is a distinguishable component of an entity that is engaged in providing an individual product or service or a group of related products or services and that is subject to risks and returns that are different from those of other business segments. Factors that shall be considered in determining whether products and services are related include:
> (a) the nature of the products or services;
> (b) the nature of the production processes;
> (c) the type or class of customer for the products or services;
> (d) the methods used to distribute the products or provide the services; and
> (e) if applicable, the nature of the regulatory environment, for example, banking, insurance, or public utilities.
>   A *geographical segment* is a distinguishable component of an entity that is engaged in providing products or services within a particular economic environment and that is subject to risks and returns that are different from those of components operating in other economic environments. Factors that shall be considered in identifying geographical segments include:
> (a) similarity of economic and political conditions;
> (b) relationships between operations in different geographical areas;
> (c) proximity of operations;
> (d) special risks associated with operations in a particular area;
> (e) exchange control regulations; and
> (f) the underlying currency risks.

The predominant sources of risks affect how most entities are organised and managed. Therefore, IAS 14 (para. 27) states that an entity's organisational structure and internal financial reporting system should normally be the basis for identifying its segments. The risks and returns of an entity are influenced both by the geographical *location of its operations* (where its products are produced or where its service delivery activities are based) and also by the *location of its markets* (where its products are sold or services are rendered). The definition (para. 13) allows geographical segments to be based on either:

> (a) the location of an entity's production or service facilities and other assets; or
> (b) the location of its markets and customers.

Determining the composition of a business or geographical segment involves a certain amount of judgement. In making that judgement, entities should take into account the objective of reporting financial information by segment (as discussed in section 18.3) and the qualitative characteristics of financial statements as identified in the IASB Framework (see chapter 2). Those qualitative characteristics include:

- the relevance, reliability and comparability over time of financial information that is reported about an entity's different groups of products and services and about its operations in particular geographical areas; and
- the usefulness of that information for assessing the risks and returns of the entity as a whole.

Illustrative example 18.1 provides examples of business segments and geographical segments.

ILLUSTRATIVE EXAMPLE 18.1

Examples of business segments and geographical segments

Diversified manufacturing company A

Company A is a listed diversified manufacturing company. It produces most of its products in Australia and its markets are also mainly in Australia. It has three main product lines: wine, water heaters and olive oil. Each of these product lines has different production processes, markets and distribution processes. Company A is organised into three business units: wine, water heaters and olive oil. Each business unit reports separate financial and operational information to the chief executive officer (CEO) and chief financial officer (CFO). The results of all three business units are then aggregated to form the consolidated financial information. In preparing its financial statements in accordance with IAS 14, company A identifies three business segments: wine, water heaters and olive oil. It has only one geographical segment: Australia.

Manufacturing company B

Company B is a listed manufacturing company. It produces most of its products in Australia but it exports 70% of these products to Japan. It has only one main product line: grain-fed beef. Company B is organised into two business units: local and export. Each business unit reports separate financial and operational information to the chief executive officer (CEO) and chief financial officer (CFO). The results of the two business units are then aggregated to form the consolidated financial information. In preparing its financial statements in accordance with IAS 14, company B identifies two geographical segments: Australia and Japan. It has only one business segment: grain-fed beef.

LO 3

18.5 Primary and secondary segment reporting formats

18.5.1 Determining primary and secondary segment reporting formats

Illustrative example 18.1 provided some simple examples of business and geographical segments. Often, however, an entity will operate and/or have markets in different geographical locations as well as having different types of products and services. Therefore, an entity will often have both geographical segments and business segments. It is not always easy to delineate clearly business segments and geographical segments. However, IAS 14 requires an entity to determine which type of segment — business or geographical — will be its primary segment reporting format. The disclosures required for the primary segment format are extensive (IAS 14, paras 50–67) whereas the disclosures required for the secondary segment format are limited (IAS 14, paras 69–72).

Paragraph 26 of IAS 14 states:

> The dominant source and nature of an entity's risks and returns shall govern whether its primary segment reporting format will be business segments or geographical segments. If the entity's risks and rates of return are affected predominantly by differences in the products and services it produces, its primary format for reporting segment information shall be business segments, with secondary information reported geographically. Similarly, if the entity's risks and rates of return are affected predominantly by the fact that it operates in different countries or other geographical areas, its primary format for reporting segment information shall be geographical segments, with secondary information reported for groups of related products and services.

As noted earlier, IAS 14 requires that an entity's organisational structure and its internal financial reporting system should normally be the basis for identifying its segments (IAS 14, para 27). However, paragraph 27 goes on to say that:

(a) if an entity's risks and rates of return are strongly affected both by differences in the products and services it produces and by differences in the geographical areas in which it operates, as evidenced by a 'matrix approach' to managing the company and to reporting internally to the board of directors and the chief executive officer, then the entity shall use business segments as its primary segment reporting format and geographical segments as its secondary reporting format; and

(b) if an entity's internal organisational and management structure and its system of internal financial reporting to the board of directors and the chief executive officer are based neither on individual products or services or on groups of related products/services nor on geography, the directors and management of the entity shall determine whether the entity's risks and returns are related more to the products and services it produces or more to the geographical areas in which it operates and, as a consequence, shall choose either business segments or geographical segments as the entity's primary segment reporting format, with the other as its secondary reporting format.

For most entities, the predominant source of risks and returns determines how the entity is organised and managed. An entity's organisational and management structure and its internal financial reporting system normally provide the best evidence of the entity's predominant source of risks and returns for purposes of its segment reporting. Therefore, except in rare circumstances, an entity will report segment information in its financial statements on the same basis as it reports internally to top management. Its predominant source of risks and returns becomes its primary segment reporting format. Its secondary source of risks and returns becomes its secondary segment reporting format. Subparagraph 27(a) recognises, however, that some companies use a matrix approach for internal reporting. In such circumstances IAS 14 requires the company to select business segments as its primary format. This is aimed at enhancing comparability in financial reporting between different companies.

In some cases, an entity's internal reporting may have developed along lines unrelated either to differences in the types of products and services it produces or to the geographical areas in which it operates. For instance, internal reporting may be organised solely by legal entity, resulting in internal segments composed of groups of unrelated products and services. In those cases, the internally reported segment data will not meet the objective of IAS 14. Accordingly, paragraph 27(b) requires the directors and management of the entity to determine whether the entity's risks and returns are more product or service driven or geographically driven, and to choose either business segments or geographical segments as the entity's primary basis of segment reporting. Again, the objective is to achieve a reasonable degree of comparability with other entities, enhance comprehensibility of the resulting information and meet the needs of users for information about product or service-related and geographically related risks and returns. Paragraph 32 of IAS 14 explains how an entity should determine its segments in these circumstances, as follows:

(a) if one or more of the segments reported internally to the directors and management is a business segment or a geographical segment based on the factors in the definitions in paragraph 9 but others are not, subparagraph (b) below shall be applied only to those internal segments that do not meet the definitions in paragraph 9 (that is, an internally reported segment that meets the definition shall not be further segmented);

(b) for those segments reported internally to the directors and management that do not satisfy the definitions in paragraph 9, management of the entity shall look to the next lower level of internal segmentation that reports information along product and service lines or geographical lines, as appropriate under the definitions in paragraph 9; and

(c) if such an internally reported lower-level segment meets the definition of business segment or geographical segment based on the factors in paragraph 9, the criteria in paragraphs 34 and 35 for identifying reportable segments shall be applied to that segment.

Paragraphs 34 and 35 of IAS 14 deal with reportable segments, which are discussed in section 18.6.

Building on illustrative example 18.1, the following illustrative example shows how the companies would determine their primary and secondary segments:

ILLUSTRATIVE EXAMPLE 18.2

Primary and secondary segments

Diversified manufacturing company A

Company A is a listed diversified manufacturing company. It produces most of its products in Australia and its markets are also mainly in Australia. It has three main product lines: wine, water heaters and olive oil. Each of these product lines has different production processes, markets and distribution processes. Company A is organised into three business units: wine, water heaters and olive oil. Each business unit reports separate financial and operational information to the chief executive officer (CEO) and chief financial officer (CFO). The results of all three business units are then aggregated to form the consolidated financial information. In preparing its financial statements in accordance with IAS 14, company A identifies three business segments: wine, water heaters and olive oil. It has only one geographical segment: Australia. Because company A's risks and rates of return are affected predominantly by differences in the products and services it produces, its primary format for reporting segment information should be business segments, with secondary information reported geographically.

Manufacturing company B

Company B is a listed manufacturing company. It produces most of its products in Australia but it exports 70% of these products to Japan. It has only one main product line: grain-fed beef. Company B is organised into two business units: local and export. Each business unit reports separate financial and operational information to the chief executive officer (CEO) and chief financial officer (CFO). The results of the two business units are then aggregated to form the consolidated financial information. In preparing its financial statements in accordance with IAS 14, company B identifies two geographical segments: Australia and Japan. It has only one business segment: grain-fed beef. Because company B's risks and rates of return are affected predominantly by the fact that it operates in different countries, its primary format for reporting segment information should be geographical segments, with secondary information reported for its business segment.

In both of the above examples, the companies' predominant source of risks and returns determines their organisational and management structure and internal financial reporting. Therefore, their internal reporting structure is appropriate for segment reporting under IAS 14.

The following example illustrates the circumstances envisaged in IAS 14 paragraphs 27(b) and 32.

Diversified manufacturing company C

Company C is a listed diversified manufacturing company. It produces most of its products in Australia and its markets are also mainly in Australia. It has three main product lines: beer, picture frames and office workstation accessories. Each of these product

→

lines has different production processes, markets and distribution processes. Company C is organised into two business units: beer and other entities. The beer business unit reports separate financial and operational information to the chief executive officer (CEO) and chief financial officer (CFO). The other entities business unit is divided into six legal entities, each of which reports separate financial and operational information to the CEO and CFO. The reporting by the six legal entities does not reflect company C's predominant sources of risks and returns from the picture frames and office workstation accessories products. The results of the two business units are then aggregated to form the consolidated financial information. In preparing its financial statements in accordance with IAS 14, company C identifies three business segments: beer, picture frames and office workstation accessories. In doing so, it will need to determine the reported segment information for the picture frames and office workstation accessories business segments by further analysing and rearranging the information presented by the six legal entities. It has only one geographical segment: Australia. Because company C's risks and rates of return are affected predominantly by differences in the products and services it produces, its primary format for reporting segment information should be business segments, with secondary information reported geographically.

LO 4

18.6 Identifying an entity's reportable segments

18.6.1 Definition of a reportable segment

Paragraph 9 of IAS 14 defines a reportable segment as follows:

> A reportable segment is a business segment or a geographical segment identified based on the foregoing definitions for which segment information is required to be disclosed by this Standard.

This is not a very helpful definition. Paragraphs 34 through 43 go into detail about how an entity should determine its reportable segments. The requirements are complex and are best understood by reference to the decision tree included as appendix A to the standard and reproduced in figure 18.1 on page 763.

For ease of reference, the requirements of paragraphs 34 through 43 are reproduced below:

34. Two or more internally reported business segments or geographical segments that are substantially similar may be combined as a single business segment or geographical segment. Two or more business segments or geographical segments are substantially similar only if:
    (a) they exhibit similar long-term financial performance; and
    (b) they are similar in all of the factors in the appropriate definition in paragraph 9.
35. A business segment or geographical segment shall be identified as a reportable segment if a majority of its revenue is earned from sales to external customers and:
    (a) its revenue from sales to external customers and from transactions with other segments is 10 per cent or more of the total revenue, external and internal, of all segments; or
    (b) its segment result, whether profit or loss, is 10 per cent or more of the combined result of all segments in profit or the combined result of all segments in loss, whichever is the greater in absolute amount; or
    (c) its assets are 10 per cent or more of the total assets of all segments.

36. If an internally reported segment is below all of the thresholds of significance in paragraph 35:

(a) that segment may be designated as a reportable segment despite its size;

(b) if not designated as a reportable segment despite its size, that segment may be combined into a separately reportable segment with one or more other similar internally reported segment(s) that are also below all of the thresholds of significance in paragraph 35 (two or more business segments or geographical segments are similar if they share a majority of the factors in the appropriate definition in paragraph 9); and

(c) if that segment is not separately reported or combined, it shall be included as an unallocated reconciling item.

37. If total external revenue attributable to reportable segments constitutes less than 75 per cent of the total consolidated or entity revenue, additional segments shall be identified as reportable segments, even if they do not meet the 10 per cent thresholds in paragraph 35, until at least 75 per cent of total consolidated or entity revenue is included in reportable segments.

38. The 10 per cent thresholds in this Standard are not intended to be a guide for determining materiality for any aspect of financial reporting other than identifying reportable business and geographical segments.

39. By limiting reportable segments to those that earn a majority of their revenue from sales to external customers, this Standard does not require that the different stages of vertically integrated operations be identified as separate business segments. However, in some industries, current practice is to report certain vertically integrated activities as separate business segments even if they do not generate significant external sales revenue. For instance, many international oil companies report their upstream activities (exploration and production) and their downstream activities (refining and marketing) as separate business segments even if most or all of the upstream product (crude petroleum) is transferred internally to the entity's refining operation.

40. This Standard encourages, but does not require, the voluntary reporting of vertically integrated activities as separate segments, with appropriate description including disclosure of the basis of pricing inter-segment transfers as required by paragraph 75.

41. If an entity's internal reporting system treats vertically integrated activities as separate segments and the entity does not choose to report them externally as business segments, the selling segment shall be combined into the buying segment(s) in identifying externally reportable business segments unless there is no reasonable basis for doing so, in which case the selling segment would be included as an unallocated reconciling item.

42. A segment identified as a reportable segment in the immediately preceding period because it satisfied the relevant 10 per cent thresholds shall continue to be a reportable segment for the current period notwithstanding that its revenue, result, and assets all no longer exceed the 10 per cent thresholds, if the management of the entity judges the segment to be of continuing significance.

43. If a segment is identified as a reportable segment in the current period because it satisfies the relevant 10 per cent thresholds, prior period segment data that is presented for comparative purposes shall be restated to reflect the newly reportable segment as a separate segment, even if that segment did not satisfy the 10 per cent thresholds in the prior period, unless it is impracticable to do so.

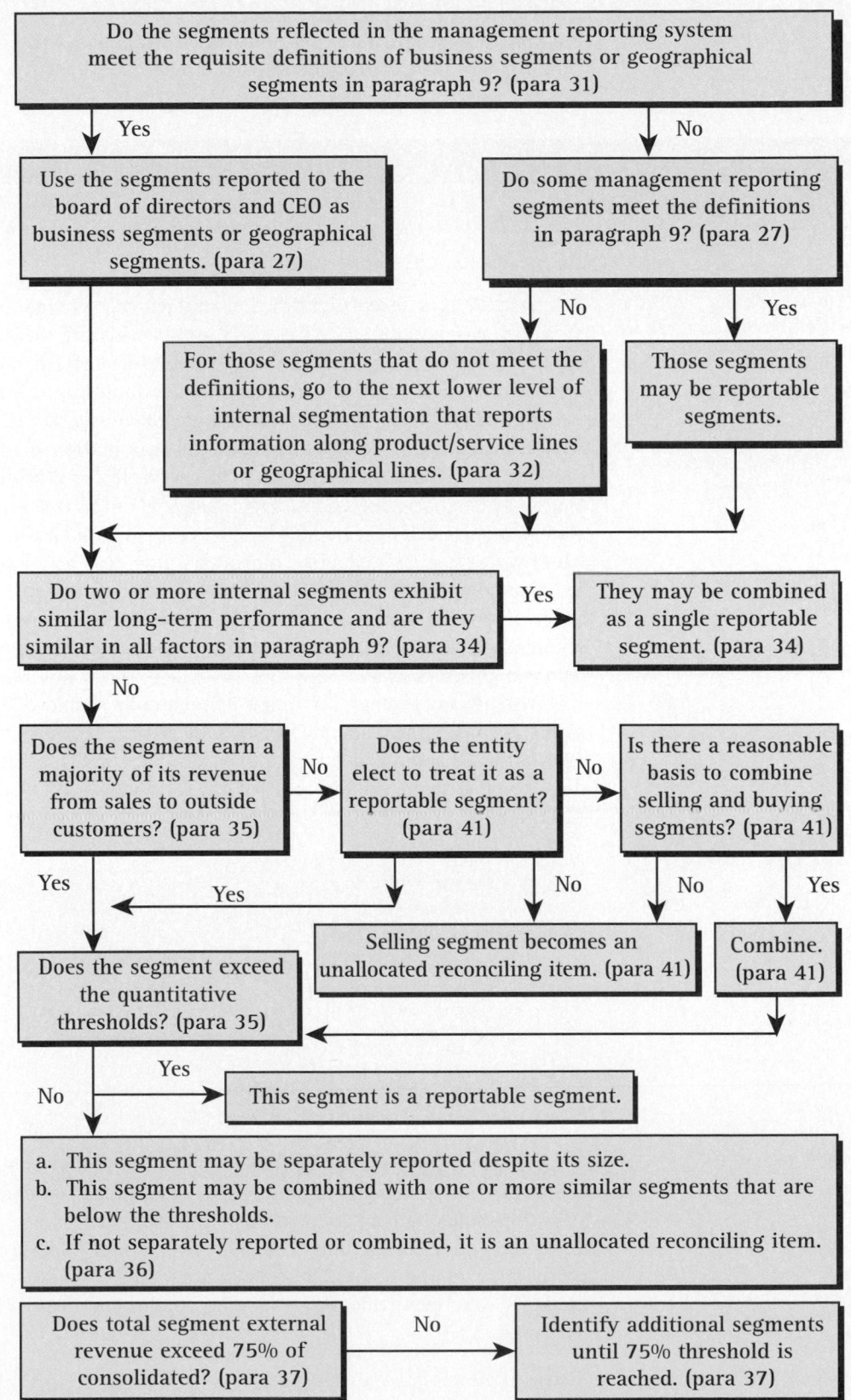

FIGURE 18.1 Reportable segments decision tree
Source: IAS 14 *Segment Reporting,* appendix A.

18.6.2   Applying the definition

Building on the previous two illustrative examples, the following illustrative example demonstrates how the companies would determine their reportable segments.

ILLUSTRATIVE EXAMPLE 18.3

Reportable segments

Diversified manufacturing company A

Company A is a listed diversified manufacturing company. It produces most of its products in Australia and its markets are also mainly in Australia. It has three main product lines: wine, water heaters and olive oil. Each of these product lines has different production processes, markets and distribution processes. Company A is organised into three business units: wine, water heaters and olive oil. Each business unit reports separate financial and operational information to the chief executive officer (CEO) and chief financial officer (CFO). The results of all three business units are then aggregated to form the consolidated financial information. In preparing its financial statements in accordance with IAS 14, company A identifies three business segments: wine, water heaters and olive oil. It has only one geographical segment: Australia. Because company A's risks and rates of return are affected predominantly by differences in the products and services it produces, its primary format for reporting segment information should be business segments, with secondary information reported geographically.

Now company A must determine its reportable segments. None of the business segments is substantially similar (per IAS 14, para. 34) and so they cannot be combined. The following additional information is provided: all three business units earn most of their revenue from external customers. Total consolidated revenue of company A is $253 million.

	Wine $	Water heaters $	Olive oil $	All segments $
Revenue	150m	90m	10m	250m
Segment result (profit)	14m	5m	1m	20m
Assets	500m	200m	100m	800m

All three segments are reportable segments because each earns a majority of its revenues from external customers and each equals or exceeds at least one of the 10% thresholds set out in paragraph 35. Wine and water heaters exceed all three and olive oil exceeds only the assets threshold. Because total external revenue attributable to the reportable segments exceeds 75% of total consolidated revenue, there is no requirement to identify additional segments in accordance with paragraph 37.

Manufacturing company B

Company B is a listed manufacturing company. It produces most of its products in Australia but it exports 70% of these products to Japan. It has only one main product line: grain-fed beef. Company B is organised into two business units: local and export. Each business unit reports separate financial and operational information to the chief executive officer (CEO) and chief financial officer (CFO). The results of the two business units are then aggregated to form the consolidated financial information. In preparing its financial statements in accordance with IAS 14, company B identifies two geographical segments: Australia and Japan. It has only one business segment: grain-fed beef. Because company B's risks and rates of return are affected predominantly by the fact that it operates in different countries, its primary format for reporting segment information should be geographical segments, with secondary information reported for its business segment.

Now company B must determine its reportable segments. Neither of the geographical segments is substantially similar (per IAS 14, para 34) and so they cannot be combined. The following additional information is provided: each business unit earns a majority of its revenues from external customers. Total consolidated revenue of company B is $750 million.

	Export $	Local $	All segments $
Revenue	490m	210m	700m
Segment result (profit)	80m	20m	100m
Assets	800m	200m	1 000m

Each geographical segment is a reportable segment because each earns a majority of its revenues from external customers and each equals or exceeds at least one of the 10% thresholds set out in paragraph 35. In fact, each exceeds all three of the thresholds. Because total external revenue attributable to the reportable segments exceeds 75% of total consolidated revenue, there is no requirement to identify additional segments in accordance with paragraph 37.

Diversified manufacturing company C

Company C is a listed diversified manufacturing company. It produces most of its products in Australia and its markets are also mainly in Australia. It has three main product lines: beer, picture frames and office workstation accessories. Each of these product lines has different production processes, markets and distribution processes. Company C is organised internally into two business units: beer and other entities. The beer business unit reports separate financial and operational information to the chief executive officer (CEO) and chief financial officer (CFO). The other entities business unit is divided into six legal entities, each of which reports separate financial and operational information to the CEO and CFO. The reporting by the six legal entities does not reflect company C's predominant sources of risks and returns from the picture frames and office workstation accessories products. The results of the two business units are then aggregated to form the consolidated financial information. In preparing its financial statements in accordance with IAS 14, company C identifies three business segments: beer, picture frames and office workstation accessories. In doing so, it needs to determine the reported segment information for the picture frames and office workstation accessories business segments by further analysing and rearranging the information presented by the six legal entities. It has only one geographical segment: Australia. Because company C's risks and rates of return are affected predominantly by differences in the products and services it produces, its primary format for reporting segment information should be business segments, with secondary information reported geographically.

Now company C must determine its reportable segments. None of the business segments is substantially similar (per IAS 14, para. 34) and so they cannot be combined. The following additional information is provided: all three business units earn a majority of their revenues from external customers. Total consolidated revenue of company C is $250 million.

	Beer $	Picture frames $	Office accessories $	All segments $
Revenue	150m	90m	10m	250m
Segment result (profit)	14m	5m	1m	20m
Assets	600m	150m	50m	800m

Only the beer and picture frames segments are reportable segments because each earns a majority of its revenues from external customers and each equals or exceeds at least one of the 10% thresholds set out in paragraph 35. In fact each exceeds all three of the thresholds. Office accessories is not a reportable segment because, although it earns a majority of its revenues from external customers, it does not equal or exceed any of the thresholds in paragraph 35. Company C may elect to designate office accessories as a reportable segment despite its size or include it as an unallocated reconciling item in the segment disclosures (IAS 14, para 36). Because total external revenue attributable to the reportable segments exceeds 75% of total consolidated revenue (it equals total consolidated revenue), there is no requirement to identify additional segments in accordance with paragraph 37.

LO 5

18.7 Segment accounting policies

18.7.1 Accounting policies and allocation of amounts to segments

Paragraph 44 of IAS 14 requires that segment information be prepared in conformity with the accounting policies adopted for preparing and presenting the financial statements of the consolidated group or entity.

This does not mean, however, that the consolidated or entity accounting policies are to be applied to reportable segments as if the segments were separate stand-alone reporting entities. A detailed calculation done in applying a particular accounting policy at the entity-wide level may be allocated to segments if there is a reasonable basis for doing so. Pension and other employee benefit calculations, for example, often are done for an entity as a whole, but the entity-wide figures may be allocated to segments based on salary and demographic data for the segments.

IAS 14 paragraph 47 states that assets that are jointly used by two or more segments should be allocated to segments if, and only if, their related revenues and expenses are also allocated to those segments.

At this point it is necessary to consider the definitions of segment assets, liabilities, revenues and expenses: They are defined in paragraph 16 of IAS 14 as follows:

Segment revenue is revenue reported in the entity's income statement that is directly attributable to a segment and the relevant portion of entity revenue that can be allocated on a reasonable basis to a segment, whether from sales to external customers or from transactions with other segments of the same entity. Segment revenue does not include:

(a) [deleted; this used to refer to 'extraordinary items', which are no longer permitted under IFRSs]

(b) interest or dividend income, including interest earned on advances or loans to other segments, unless the segment's operations are primarily of a financial nature; or

(c) gains on sales of investments or gains on extinguishment of debt unless the segment's operations are primarily of a financial nature.

Segment revenue includes an entity's share of profits or losses of associates, joint ventures, or other investments accounted for under the equity method only if those items are included in consolidated or total entity revenue.

Segment revenue includes a joint venturer's share of the revenue of a jointly controlled entity that is accounted for by proportionate consolidation in accordance with IAS 31, *Investments in Joint Ventures*.

Segment expense is expense resulting from the operating activities of a segment that is directly attributable to the segment and the relevant portion of an expense that can be allocated on a reasonable basis to the segment, including expenses relating to sales to external customers and expenses relating to transactions with other segments of the same entity. Segment expense does not include:

(a) [deleted]

(b) interest, including interest incurred on advances or loans from other segments, unless the segment's operations are primarily of a financial nature;

(c) losses on sales of investments or losses on extinguishment of debt unless the segment's operations are primarily of a financial nature;

(d) an entity's share of losses of associates, joint ventures, or other investments accounted for under the equity method;

(e) income tax expense; or

(f) general administrative expenses, head-office expenses, and other expenses that arise at the entity level and relate to the entity as a whole. However, costs are sometimes incurred at the entity level on behalf of a segment. Such costs are segment expenses if they relate to the segment's operating activities and they can be directly attributed or allocated to the segment on a reasonable basis.

Segment expense includes a joint venturer's share of the expenses of a jointly controlled entity that is accounted for by proportionate consolidation in accordance with IAS 31.

For a segment's operations that are primarily of a financial nature, interest income and interest expense may be reported as a single net amount for segment reporting purposes only if those items are netted in the consolidated or entity financial statements.

Segment result is segment revenue less segment expense. Segment result is determined before any adjustments for minority interest.

Segment assets are those operating assets that are employed by a segment in its operating activities and that either are directly attributable to the segment or can be allocated to the segment on a reasonable basis.

If a segment's segment result includes interest or dividend income, its segment assets include the related receivables, loans, investments, or other income-producing assets.

Segment assets do not include income tax assets.

Segment assets include investments accounted for under the equity method only if the profit or loss from such investments is included in segment revenue. Segment assets include a joint venturer's share of the operating assets of a jointly controlled entity that is accounted for by proportionate consolidation in accordance with IAS 31.

Segment assets are determined after deducting related allowances that are reported as direct offsets in the entity's balance sheet.

Segment liabilities are those operating liabilities that result from the operating activities of a segment and that either are directly attributable to the segment or can be allocated to the segment on a reasonable basis.

If a segment's segment result includes interest expense, its segment liabilities include the related interest-bearing liabilities.

Segment liabilities include a joint venturer's share of the liabilities of a jointly controlled entity that is accounted for by proportionate consolidation in accordance with IAS 31.

Segment liabilities do not include income tax liabilities.

Segment accounting policies are the accounting policies adopted for preparing and presenting the financial statements of the consolidated group or entity as well as those accounting policies that relate specifically to segment reporting.

The way in which asset, liability, revenue and expense items are allocated to segments depends on such factors as the nature of those items, the activities conducted by the segment and the relative autonomy of that segment. Paragraph 48 of IAS 14 states that it is not possible or appropriate to specify a single basis of allocation that should be adopted by all entities. Nor is it appropriate to force allocation of entity asset, liability, revenue and expense items that relate jointly to two or more segments if the only basis for making those allocations is arbitrary or difficult to understand.

At the same time, the definitions of segment revenue, expense, assets and liabilities are interrelated, and the resulting allocations should be consistent. Therefore, jointly used assets are allocated to segments if, and only if, their related revenues and expenses are also allocated to those segments. For example, an asset is included in segment assets if, and only if, the related depreciation or amortisation is deducted in measuring segment result. Segment assets do not include assets used for general entity or head-office purposes. These are disclosed as 'unallocated' head-office or corporate assets. Examples include income tax assets and buildings used for head-office administration only.

Similarly, the liabilities of segments whose operations are not primarily of a financial nature do not include borrowings and similar liabilities because segment result represents an operating, rather than a net-of-financing, profit or loss. Further, because debt is often issued at the head-office level on an entity-wide basis, it is often not possible to directly attribute, or reasonably allocate, the interest-bearing liability to the segment. Therefore these liabilities are disclosed as 'unallocated' head-office or corporate liabilities.

Measurements of segment assets and liabilities include adjustments to the prior carrying amounts of the identifiable segment assets and segment liabilities of a company acquired in a business combination, even if those adjustments are made only for the purpose of preparing consolidated financial statements and are not recorded in either the parent's or the subsidiary's separate financial statements. Similarly, if property, plant and equipment have been revalued subsequent to acquisition in accordance with the revaluation model in IAS 16, then measurements of segment assets reflect those revaluations (para. 21). Segment assets include goodwill that is directly attributable to a segment or that can be allocated to a segment on a reasonable basis, and segment expense includes any related impairment losses.

However, segment revenue, expense, assets and liabilities are determined before intragroup balances and intragroup transactions are eliminated as part of the consolidation process, except to the extent that such intragroup balances and transactions are between group entities within a single segment. Eliminations made on consolidation will be disclosed in a separate column as part of the reconciliation between the segment information and the consolidated information (see section 18.8 on disclosures).

While the accounting policies used in preparing and presenting the financial statements of the entity as a whole are also the fundamental segment accounting policies, segment accounting policies also include policies that relate specifically to segment reporting. These include identification of segments, method of pricing inter-segment transfers, and basis for allocating revenues and expenses to segments.

Note that, in relation to the determination of segment result, extraordinary items are no longer permitted under IAS 1 *Presentation of Financial Statements.*

Building on illustrative example 18.3, the following illustrative example shows how diversified manufacturing company A will determine its segment revenue, expense, assets and liabilities.

ILLUSTRATIVE EXAMPLE 18.4

Applying the requirements

Determining segment revenue, expense, assets and liabilities

The following financial information is provided for diversified manufacturing company A for the year ended 30 June 2005

	Wine $	Water heaters $	Olive oil $	All segments $
Segment revenue	150m	90m	10m	250m
Segment result (profit)	14m	5m	1m	20m
Segment assets	500m	200m	100m	800m

Total consolidated revenue of company A is $253 million. Total consolidated profit – after income tax expense of $5 million, interest income of $1 million and a gain on disposal of investments of $2 million – is $8 million. Total consolidated liabilities of company A are $200 million. These include borrowings of $150 million. Related interest expense is $10 million. $40 million of liabilities are trade creditors and other payables directly attributable to the wine segment. $10 million of liabilities are trade creditors and other payables directly attributable to the water heaters segment. All assets and related depreciation have been allocated to the business segments.

The allocation of segment revenue, expense, assets and liabilities is determined as follows:

	Wine $	Water heaters $	Olive oil $	Unallocated	Consolidated $
Revenue	150m	90m	10m	3m (interest income and gain on disposal of investments)	253m
Segment result (profit)	14m	5m	1m	3m revenue and 15m expenses (interest expense and income tax expense)	8m
Assets	500m	200m	100m	–	800m
Liabilities	40m	10m	–	150m (borrowings – not allocated because the segments' operations are not primarily of a financial nature)	200m

This example also shows that before an entity can determine its reportable segments (as demonstrated in illustrative example 18.3) it needs first to calculate correctly the segment allocations and unallocated amounts.

18.8 Disclosures

18.8.1 Outline of disclosure requirements

Paragraphs 50–67 of IAS 14 specify the disclosures required for reportable segments for an entity's *primary* segment reporting format. Paragraphs 68–72 identify the disclosures required for an entity's *secondary* reporting format. Paragraphs 74–83 address several other segment disclosure matters.

Appendix C to IAS 14 summarises the required disclosures and is quoted in figure 18.2 for ease of reference. You should refer to the detail in each relevant paragraph in IAS 14 when reviewing this table. Note also the 10% thresholds for secondary segment disclosures set out in paragraphs 69 through 71.

FIGURE 18.2 Appendix C to IAS 14: Summary of required disclosure

APPENDIX C Summary of required disclosure		
The appendix is illustrative only and does not form part of the standards. Its purpose is to summarise the disclosures required by paragraphs 49–83 for each of the three possible primary segment reporting formats. [¶xx] refers to paragraph xx in the Standard.		
Primary format is business segments	Primary format is geographical segments by location of assets	Primary format is geographical segments by location of customers
Required primary disclosures:	*Required primary disclosures:*	*Required primary disclosures:*
Revenue from external customers by business segment [¶51]	Revenue from external customers by location of assets [¶51]	Revenue from external customers by location of customers [¶51]
Revenue from transactions with other segments by business segment [¶51]	Revenue from transactions with other segments by location of assets [¶51]	Revenue from transactions with other segments by location of customers [¶51]
Segment result by business segment [¶52]	Segment result by location of assets [¶52]	Segment result by location of customers [¶52]
Carrying amount of segment assets by business segment [¶55]	Carrying amount of segment assets by location of assets [¶55]	Carrying amount of segment assets by location of customers [¶55]
Segment liabilities by business segment [¶56]	Segment liabilities by location of assets [¶56]	Segment liabilities by location of customers [¶56]
Cost to acquire property, plant, equipment and intangibles by business segment [¶57]	Cost to acquire property, plant, equipment and intangibles by location of assets [¶57]	Cost to acquire property, plant, equipment and intangibles by location of customers [¶57]
Depreciation and amortisation expense by business segment [¶58]	Depreciation and amortisation expense by location of assets [¶58]	Depreciation and amortisation expense by location of customers [¶58]
Non-cash expenses other than depreciation and amortisation by business segment [¶61]	Non-cash expenses other than depreciation and amortisation by location of assets [¶61]	Non-cash expenses other than depreciation and amortisation by location of customers [¶61]

Share of profit or loss of [¶64] and investment in [¶66] equity method associates or joint ventures by business segment (if substantially all within a single business segment)	Share of profit or loss of [¶64] and investment in [¶66] equity method associates or joint ventures by location of assets (if substantially all within a single business segment)	Share of profit or loss of [¶64] and investment in [¶66] equity method associates or joint ventures by location of customers (if substantially all within a single business segment)
Reconciliation of revenue, result, assets and liabilities by business segment [¶67]	Reconciliation of revenue, result, assets and liabilities [¶67]	Reconciliation of revenue, result, assets and liabilities [¶67]
Required secondary disclosures:	*Required secondary disclosures:*	*Required secondary disclosures:*
Revenue from external customers by location of customers [¶69]	Revenue from external customers by business segment [¶70]	Revenue from external customers by business segment [¶70]
Carrying amount of segment assets by location of assets [¶69]	Carrying amount of segment assets by business segment [¶70]	Carrying amount of segment assets by business segment [¶70]
Cost to acquire property, plant, equipment and intangibles by location of assets [¶69]	Cost to acquire property, plant, equipment and intangibles by business segment [¶70]	Cost to acquire property, plant, equipment and intangibles by business segment [¶70]
	Revenue from external customers by geographical customers if different from location of assets [¶71]	
		Carrying amount of segment assets by location of assets if different from location of customers [¶72]
		Cost to acquire property, plant, equipment and intangibles by location of assets if different from location of customers [¶72]
Other required disclosures:	*Other required disclosures:*	*Other required disclosures:*
Revenue for any business or geographical segment whose external revenue is more than 10% of entity revenue but that is not a reportable segment because a majority of its revenue is from internal transfers [¶74]	Revenue for any business or geographical segment whose external revenue is more than 10% of entity revenue but that is not a reportable segment because a majority of its revenue is from internal transfers [¶74]	Revenue for any business or geographical segment whose external revenue is more than 10% of entity revenue but that is not a reportable segment because a majority of its revenue is from internal transfers [¶74]
Basis of pricing inter-segment transfers and any change therein [¶75]	Basis of pricing inter-segment transfers and any change therein [¶75]	Basis of pricing inter-segment transfers and any change therein [¶75]
Changes in segment accounting policies [¶76]	Changes in segment accounting policies [¶76]	Changes in segment accounting policies [¶76]
Types of products and services in each business segment [¶81]	Types of products and services in each business segment [¶81]	Types of products and services in each business segment [¶81]
Composition of each geographical segment [¶81]	Composition of each geographical segment [¶81]	Composition of each geographical segment [¶81]

Source: IAS 14 *Segment Reporting*, Appendix C.

Appendix B to IAS 14 also provides a useful illustration of the required disclosures.

18.8.2 Additional disclosures that are encouraged but not required

IAS 14 contains a number of paragraphs encouraging, but not requiring, additional information. They are as follows:

> 53. If an entity can compute segment net profit or loss or some other measure of segment profitability other than segment result without arbitrary allocations, reporting of such amount(s) is encouraged in addition to segment result, appropriately described. If that measure is prepared on a basis other than the accounting policies adopted for the consolidated or entity financial statements, the entity will include in its financial statements a clear description of the basis of measurement.

IAS 14 states that an example of a measure of segment performance above segment result on the income statement is gross margin on sales. Examples of measures of segment performance below segment result on the income statement are profit or loss from ordinary activities (either before or after income taxes) and net profit or loss.

> 59. An entity is encouraged, but not required to disclose the nature and amount of any items of segment revenue and segment expense that are of such size, nature, or incidence that their disclosure is relevant to explain the performance of each reportable segment for the period.

IAS 1 states that when items of income or expense are material their nature and amount shall be disclosed separately. Paragraph 59 of IAS 14 is not intended to change the classification of any such items or to change the measurement of such items. The disclosure encouraged by that paragraph, however, does change the level at which the significance of such items is evaluated for disclosure purposes from the entity level to the segment level.

> 63. An entity that provides the segment cash flow disclosures that are encouraged by IAS 7 need not also disclose depreciation and amortisation expense pursuant to paragraph 58 or non-cash expenses pursuant to paragraph 61.

IAS 7 *Cash Flow Statements* notes that disclosing cash flow information for each reportable industry and geographical segment is relevant to understanding the entity's overall financial position, liquidity and cash flows. IAS 7 encourages the disclosure of such information. IAS 14 therefore also encourages the segment cash flow disclosures that are encouraged by IAS 7.

It is not common for entities to provide these 'encouraged' disclosures for a number of reasons, including competitive disadvantage (revealing too much information to competitors), cost of compiling the additional information and the arbitrary nature of more detailed segment allocations.

18.8.3 Comparative information

IAS 14, paragraph 76 states:

> Changes in accounting policies adopted for segment reporting that have a material effect on segment information shall be disclosed, and prior period segment information presented for comparative purposes shall be restated unless it is impracticable to do so. Such disclosure shall include a description of the nature of the change, the reasons for the change, the fact that comparative information has been restated or that it is impracticable to do so, and the financial effect of the change, if it is reasonably determinable. If an entity changes the identification of its segments and it does not restate prior period segment information on the new basis because it is impracticable to do so, then for the purpose of comparison the entity shall report segment data for both the old and the new bases of segmentation in the year in which it changes the identification of its segments.

Changes in accounting policies adopted at the entity level that affect segment information are dealt with in accordance with IAS 8 *Accounting Policies, Changes in Accounting Estimates and Errors*. Essentially, IAS 8 requires that a change in accounting policy should be applied retrospectively and that prior period information be restated unless it is impracticable to do. IAS 1 defines 'impracticable' as follows:

> Applying a requirement is impracticable when the entity cannot apply it after making every reasonable effort to do so.

Therefore, it is not sufficient for an entity to argue that it will take too much time or that it will incur too great a cost to restate comparative information. It is only if the entity cannot recalculate the information on a reasonable basis after making every effort to do so that it can say that it is impracticable. This requirement is particularly relevant for large organisations that frequently change their business segments; for example, as a result of internal changes in the way that the segments report to the CEO. Every time an internal reorganisation occurs, resulting in a change of business segments, restatement of comparative information using the new basis of segmentation is required.

18.8.4 Extracts from companies' financial reports

Some extracts from companies' recent financial reports are reproduced in figures 18.3–18.6. They are useful in understanding how companies in different industries produce segment information to meet users' needs.

FIGURE 18.3 Segment information from Queensland Cotton Holdings Ltd Annual Report 2005

Queensland Cotton Holdings Ltd
34. SEGMENT REPORTING

Inter-segment pricing is determined on an arm's length basis.

Segment results, assets and liabilities include items directly attributable to a segment as well as those that can be allocated on a reasonable basis. Unallocated items mainly comprise income-earning assets and revenue, interest-bearing loans, borrowings and expenses, and corporate assets and expenses.

Segment capital expenditure is the total cost incurred during the period to acquire segment assets that are expected to be used for more than one period.

Geographical segments
In presenting information on the basis of geographical segments, segment revenue, results, assets and liabilities is based on the geographical location of the assets. The consolidated entity's geographical segments reported are Australia, United States of America and Brazil.

Business segments
The consolidated entity comprises the following main business segments, based on the consolidated entity's management reporting system:

- Processing and sale of seed cotton and pulse crop
- Marketing of cotton
- Distribution and sale of chemicals, fertilisers and planting seed
- Provision of grower loans

Inter-segment pricing is determined on an arm's length basis.

(continued)

**Queensland Cotton Holdings Limited
and its controlled entities
Notes to the financial statements
for the year ended 28 February 2005**

Note 34. SEGMENT REPORTING (Continued)

Primary reporting
Geographical segments

	Australia 2005 $	Australia 2004 $	United States 2005 $	United States 2004 $	Brazil 2005 $	Brazil 2004 $	Consolidation 2005 $	Consolidation 2004 $
Revenue								
External segment revenue	417 838 423	301 311 914	226 483 939	244 663 076	38 783 264	–	683 105 626	545 974 990
Total segment revenue	417 838 423	301 311 914	226 483 939	244 663 076	38 783 264	–	683 105 626	545 974 990
Other unallocated revenue							455 963	956 180
Total revenue							683 561 589	546 931 170
Results								
Segment result	6 844 306	1 196 905	8 118 432	12 854 818	420 971	–	15 383 709	14 051 723
Unallocated corporate expenses							(6 190 890)	(7 424 333)
Profit from ordinary activities before income tax							9 192 819	6 627 390
Income tax (expense)/benefit							(2 901 341)	6 407 756
Net profit							6 291 478	13 035 146
Acquisition of property, plant and equipment including surplus assets held for sale	2 522 094	4 232 187	3 139 615	2 263 278	7 088	–	5 668 797	6 495 465
Depreciation and amortisation	(6 045 815)	(4 205 303)	(2 704 998)	(2 555 457)	–	–	(8 750 813)	(6 760 760)
Non-cash gains/(expenses other than depreciation)	3 302 683	1 956 431	(76 464)	443 209	–	–	3 226 219	2 399 640
Share of net profits of partnerships accounted for using the equity method included in segment results	–	–	145 008	9 978	–	–	145 008	9 978
Carrying value of equity accounted investments included in segment assets	–	–	1 789 658	2 915 303	–	–	1 789 658	2 915 303

Primary report (continued)

	2005 $	2004 $	2005 $	2004 $	2005 $	2004 $	Total 2005 $	Total 2004 $
Electricity rebates received	–	–	–	1 939 836	–	–	–	1 939 836
Assets								
Segment assets	214 218 039	255 319 294	141 168 044	116 084 487	5 839 260	–	361 225 343	371 403 781
Unallocated corporate assets							16 541 952	17 664 682
Consolidated total assets							377 767 295	389 068 463
Liabilities								
Segment liabilities	50 142 511	85 275 279	38 573 875	16 091 737	10 594 583	–	99 310 969	101 367 016
Unallocated corporate liabilities							136 942 583	151 023 665
Consolidated total liabilities							236 253 552	252 390 681

Secondary report
Business segments

	Segment revenues from external customers 2005 $	Segment revenues from external customers 2004 $	Carrying amount of segment assets 2005 $	Carrying amount of segment assets 2004 $	Acquisitions of property, plant & equipment 2005 $	Acquisitions of property, plant & equipment 2004 $
Processing and sale of seed cotton and pulse crop	143 957 904	92 047 526	135 166 989	127 610 567	4 865 011	5 817 071
Marketing of cotton	467 186 826	403 984 114	135 326 077	152 092 549	208 153	104 098
Distribution and sale of chemicals, fertilisers and planting seed	60 086 508	43 750 028	26 484 163	17 005 791	76 823	69 375
Provision of grower loans	3 355 707	3 771 470	38 281 056	50 261 228	–	–
Other	8 518 561	2 421 852	25 967 058	24 433 646	518 810	504 921
Total	683 105 626	545 974 990	361 225 343	371 403 781	5 668 797	6 495 465

External segment revenue by location of customer

	2005 $	2004 $
Australia	149 681 555	85 595 297
Indonesia	112 415 553	81 413 667
United States	104 853 997	81 181 983
Korea	67 728 610	63 776 245
Japan	60 477 917	45 991 721
China	58 895 474	54 531 930
Thailand	54 309 657	29 125 449
Pakistan	28 720 273	43 759 189
Italy	19 422 814	15 094 700
Other sales to external customers	26 599 776	45 504 809
Total segment revenue	683 105 626	545 974 990

Source: Queensland Cotton Holdings Ltd 2005, *Annual report*, pp. 59–61.

FIGURE 18.4   Segment information from ANZ Banking Group Financial Report 2005

ANZ BANKING GROUP
NOTES TO THE FINANCIAL STATEMENTS
40.   SEGMENT ANALYSIS

For management purposes the Group is organised into six major business segments including Personal, Institutional, New Zealand Business, Corporate, Esanda and UDC and Asia Pacific. An expanded description of the principal activities for each of the business segments is contained in the Glossary on pages 120 to 121.

A summarised description of each business segment is shown below:

Personal	Comprises the activities of Regional Commercial and Agribusiness Products, Banking Products, Consumer Finance, Wealth Management, Mortgages and other (including the branch network)
Institutional	Comprises businesses that provide a full range of financial services to the Group's largest corporate and institutional customers including Corporate and Structured Financing, Client Relationship Group, Markets and Trade and Transaction Services
New Zealand Business	Provides a full range of banking services for personal, small business and corporate customers in New Zealand and comprises ANZ Retail, NBNZ Retail, Corporate Banking, Rural Banking and Central Support
Corporate	Comprises Corporate Banking, Business Banking and Small Business banking in Australia
Esanda and UDC	Provides vehicle and equipment finance, rental services and fixed and at call investments. Operates in Australia as Esanda and Esanda FleetPartners and in New Zealand as UDC and Esanda FleetPartners
Asia Pacific	Provides retail banking services in the Pacific region and Asia, including ANZ's share of PT Panin Bank in Indonesia. This business excludes Institutional businesses in the Asia Pacific region that are included in the Institutional division.

As the composition of segments has changed over time, September 2004 comparatives have been adjusted to be consistent with the 2005 segment definitions. Comparatives for the year ended 30 September 2003 have not been provided because the data could not reasonably be disaggregated into the amended segments.

ANZ BANKING GROUP
NOTES TO THE FINANCIAL STATEMENTS
40. SEGMENT ANALYSIS (continued)

Business Segment Analysis[1,2]

Consolidated 30 September 2004	Personal $m	Institutional $m	New Zealand Business $m	Corporate $m	Esanda and UDC $m	Asia Pacific $m	Other[3] $m	Consolidated Total $m
External interest income	6 817	3 169	4 581	1 078	1 143	172	467	17 427
External interest expense	(1 585)	(2 581)	(2 932)	(623)	(695)	(163)	(3 050)	(11 629)
Net intersegment interest	(3 128)	174	(215)	242	(79)	154	2 852	–
Net interest income	2 104	762	1 434	697	369	163	269	5 798
Other external operating income	919	1 429	513	293	121	108	12	3 395
Share of net profit/loss of equity accounted investments	94	4	–	1	–	41	17	157
Net intersegment income	125	(30)	6	(94)	(9)	–	2	–
Operating income	3 242	2 165	1 953	897	481	312	300	9 350
Other external expenses	(1 363)	(623)	(950)	(232)	(162)	(172)	(1 013)	(4 515)
Net intersegment expenses	(276)	(143)	(5)	(62)	(26)	1	511	–
Operating expenses	(1 639)	(766)	(955)	(294)	(188)	(171)	(502)	(4 515)
Charge for doubtful debts	(198)	(139)	(92)	(66)	(62)	(23)	–	(580)
Income tax expense	(392)	(336)	(292)	(161)	(72)	(22)	41	(1 234)
Outside equity interests	–	(1)	–	–	–	(1)	(1)	(3)
Profit after income tax	1 013	923	614	376	159	95	(162)	3 018
Non-cash expenses								
Depreciation	(119)	(18)	(49)	(6)	(16)	(10)	(87)	(305)
Amortisation of goodwill	–	–	–	–	–	–	(179)	(179)
Financial position								
Total external assets	106 043	70 901	60 157	21 263	15 405	2 890	16 526	293 185
Associate investments	15	52	151	40	–	152	1 462	1 872
Total external liabilities	44 340	53 350	53 426	24 110	13 306	5 811	79 354	273 697

1 Results are equity standardised

2 Intersegment transfers are accounted for and determined on an arm's length or cost recovery basis

3 Includes Treasury, Operations, Technology & Shared Services, Corporate Centre, Risk Management, Group Financial Management and significant items

(continued)

ANZ BANKING GROUP
NOTES TO THE FINANCIAL STATEMENTS
40. SEGMENT ANALYSIS (continued)

The following analysis details financial information by business segment.

Business Segment Analysis[1,2]

Consolidated 30 September 2004	Personal $m	Institutional $m	New Zealand Business $m	Corporate $m	Esanda and UDC $m	Asia Pacific $m	Other[3] $m	Consolidated Total $m
External interest income	5 784	2 782	3 002	919	1 060	167	403	14 117
External interest expense	(1 334)	(2 647)	(1 623)	(529)	(593)	(123)	(2 014)	(8 863)
Net intersegment interest	(2 538)	573	(168)	250	(107)	109	1 881	–
Net interest income	1 912	708	1 211	640	360	153	270	5 254
Other external operating income	828	1 355	453	274	103	102	131	3 246
Share of net profit/loss of equity accounted investments	84	1	–	1	1	45	13	145
Net intersegment income	118	(23)	6	(86)	(8)	–	(7)	–
Operating income	2 942	2 041	1 670	829	456	300	407	8 645
Other external expenses	(1 263)	(576)	(801)	(214)	(159)	(145)	(868)	(4 026)
Net intersegment expenses	(270)	(144)	(17)	(66)	(27)	2	522	–
Operating expenses	(1 533)	(720)	(818)	(280)	(186)	(143)	(346)	(4 026)
Charge for doubtful debts	(183)	(160)	(97)	(61)	(67)	(23)	(41)	(632)
Income tax expense	(343)	(303)	(242)	(147)	(60)	(20)	(53)	(1 168)
Outside equity interests	–	(1)	–	–	–	(3)	–	(4)
Profit after income tax	883	857	513	341	143	111	(33)	2 815
Non-cash expenses								
Depreciation	(112)	(19)	(52)	(6)	(25)	(10)	(85)	(309)
Amortisation of goodwill	–	–	–	–	–	–	(146)	(146)
Financial position								
Total external assets	93 232	60 144	53 434	19 098	14 524	2 446	16 467	259 345
Associate investments	14	55	2	14	1	176	1 698	1 960
Acquisition of NBNZ assets including goodwill	–	11 225	28 521	–	–	–	3 265	43 011
Total external liabilities	40 454	48 747	47 247	21 836	12 261	5 298	65 577	241 420

1 Results are equity standardised
2 Intersegment transfers are accounted for and determined on an arm's length or cost recovery basis
3 Includes Treasury, Operations, Technology & Shared Services, Corporate Centre, Risk Management and Group Financial Management

The following analysis details financial information by geographic location.

Geographic Segment Analysis[4,5] Consolidated	2005		2004		2003	
	$m	%	$m	%	$m	%
Income						
Australia	13 496	64	11 767	67	9 508	73
New Zealand	6 211	30	4 632	27	2 149	17
Overseas markets	1 272	6	1 109	6	1 366	10
	20 979	100	17 508	100	13 023	100
Total assets						
Australia	195 500	67	170 455	66	151 538	77
New Zealand[6]	78 474	27	69 801	27	25 696	13
Overseas markets	19 211	6	19 089	7	18 357	10
	293 185	100	259 345	100	195 591	100
Net profit before tax[7]						
Australia	2 975	70	2 785	70	2 371	72
New Zealand	832	20	763	19	495	15
Overseas markets	448	10	439	11	411	13
	4 255	100	3 987	100	3 277	100

4 Intersegment transfers are accounted for and determined on an arm's length or cost recovery basis
5 The geographic segments represent the locations in which the transaction was booked
6 2004 amount includes NBNZ assets, including goodwill acquired of $3.1 billion
7 Includes outside equity interests

Source: ANZ Bank (2005, pp. 57–8).

FIGURE 18.5 Segment information from Colorado Group Ltd Financial Report 2005

Colorado Group Ltd
6. Segment reporting

Segment results, assets and liabilities include items directly attributable to a segment as well as those that can be allocated on a reasonable basis. Unallocated items mainly comprise income-earning assets and revenue, interest-bearing loans, borrowings and expenses, and corporate assets and expenses. Inter-segment pricing is on normal commercial items and conditions.

Business segments
The consolidated entity is principally engaged in the wholesale and retail distribution of footwear and apparel. The businesses are managed according to the nature of their operations and the products they provide. Each of the business segments represents a strategic business unit that offers products which are subject to risks and returns that are different from those of other business segments.

Geographical segments
The consolidated entity operates, and its customers are located, predominantly in Australia.

(continued)

Primary reporting business segments

	Retail 2005 $'000	Retail 2004 $'000	Wholesale 2005 $'000	Wholesale 2004 $'000	Eliminations 2005 $'000	Eliminations 2004 $'000	Consolidated 2005 $'000	Consolidated 2004 $'000
Revenue								
External segment revenue	416 522	391 880	50 008	48 874	–	–	466 530	440 754
Inter-segment revenue	–	–	13 833	10 668	(13 833)	(10 668)	–	–
Other revenue	483	366	2 725	2 211	–	–	3 208	2 577
Unallocated corporate revenue	–	–	–	–	–	–	1 439	589
Total segment revenue	**417 005**	**392 246**	**66 566**	**61 753**	**(13 833)**	**(10 668)**	**471 177**	**443 920**
Result								
Segment result	49 577	33 503	13 379	9 017	(656)	–	62 300	42 520
Unallocated corporate expenses	–	–	–	–	–	–	536	(1 057)
Profit from ordinary activities before income tax							62 836	41 463
Income tax expense							18 596	12 693
Profit from ordinary activities after income tax							**44 240**	**28 770**
Depreciation and amortisation	9 990	11 024	1 077	1 036	–	–	11 067	12 060
Assets								
Segment assets	92 091	72 265	44 554	42 357	(1 293)	(638)	135 352	113 984
Unallocated corporate assets							73 087	58 322
Consolidated total assets							**208 439**	**172 306**
Liabilities								
Segment liabilities	34 642	26 624	7 435	5 659	–	–	42 077	32 283
Unallocated corporate liabilities							21 385	27 214
Consolidated total liabilities							**63 462**	**59 497**
Acquisitions of non-current assets	15 139	11 485	1 460	468	–	–	16 599	11 953

Source: Colorado Group 2005, *Financial report*, p. 49.

FIGURE 18.6 Segment information from Wesfarmers Ltd Annual Report 2005

**Notes to and forming part of the accounts
for the year ended 30 June 2005 — Wesfarmers Limited and its controlled entities**

2 SEGMENT INFORMATION

The consolidated entity is comprised of the undermentioned business segments, operating predominantly in Australia. Revenue, expenses and results between segments are not considered material.

Hardware
- Retail building material and home and garden improvement products;
- Servicing project builders and the housing industry; and
- Bargain hardware and variety.

Energy
- Coal mining and development;
- Coal marketing to both domestic and export markets;
- National marketing and distribution of LPG;
- LPG extraction for domestic and export markets;
- Manufacture and marketing of industrial gases and equipment; and
- Electricity supply to mining operations and regional centres.

Insurance
Wesfarmers Federation Insurance is a supplier of specialist rural and small business regional insurance; and Lumley Insurance group was acquired on 14 October 2003 and provides general insurance in Australia and New Zealand. Information for the prior year includes results from the Lumley Insurance group for the eight and a half months since acquisition.

Industrial and safety distribution
Supplier and distributor of maintenance, repair and operating (MRO) products; and
Specialised supplier and distributor of industrial safety products and services.

Chemicals and fertilisers
Manufacture and marketing of chemicals for industry, mining and mineral processing;
Manufacture and marketing of broadacre and horticultural fertilisers; and
Soil and plant testing and agronomy advisory services.

Other
Rail transport
Fifty per cent ownership in Australian Railroad Group Pty Ltd which:
* has an interest in the South Australian and Western Australian rail freight businesses;
* provides rail services for bulk commodities and associated retail logistics operations; and
* owns track infrastructure under a 49 year lease.

Forest products
Manufacture of products to service the wholesale timber market in Australia; and
Forestry and timber operations ...

Property investment
Non-controlling interest in Bunnings Warehouse Property Trust, which acquires quality properties suitable as a Bunnings warehouse.

Gresham Partners Group Limited
Fifty per cent ownership in Gresham Partners Group Limited which:
* is an investment bank providing financial advisory and investment management services; and
* operates three separate units including Corporation Advisory, Private Equity and Specialist Funds.

Gresham Private Equity Funds
* Fifty per cent ownership in Gresham Private Equity Fund 1 which is a 10 year closed-end private equity fund targeting larger size private equity transactions in the areas of management buy-outs, expansion capital and corporate restructuring; and
* $150 million commitment to Gresham Private Equity Fund No. 2, which at 30 June 2005 had total direct and indirect commitments of $325 million. This represents approximately 67% of the units in Gresham Private Equity Fund No. 2 and some 46% of the overall funds committed through Gresham Private Equity Fund No. 2 and the Gresham Private Equity Co-Investment Fund, which two funds invest in parallel.

Rural services
Supplier of rural merchandise and fertilisers to cotton, cropping, viticulture, horticulture and grazing industries; and
Provider of:
* wool and livestock marketing services;
* real estate and rural property sales;
* seasonal finance, term loans and deposit facilities; and
* rural, domestic and commercial insurance.

Wesfarmers Landmark, the rural services business, was sold with effect from 29 August 2003. Information shown for the prior year covers only the period from 1 July to 29 August 2003.

(continued)

Notes to and forming part of the accounts
for the year ended 30 June 2005 — Wesfarmers Limited and its controlled entities

2 SEGMENT INFORMATION (continued)

	Hardware		Energy		Industrial and safety	
	2005 $000	2004 $000	2005 $000	2004 $000	2005 $000	2004 $000
Operating revenue	4 067 456	3 845 707	1 186 737	1 008 557	1 171 519	1 150 601
Earnings						
Earnings before interest, tax, depreciation, amortisation (EBITDA) and corporate overheads	464 680	436 116	395 240	319 039	125 055	124 397
Depreciation and amortisation of property, plant and equipment	(46 797)	(51 302)	(75 914)	(78 821)	(15 020)	(12 386)
Earnings before interest, tax, amortisation (EBITA) and corporate overheads	417 883	384 814	319 326	240 218	110 035	112 011
Amortisation of goodwill	(52 332)	(50 074)	(1 071)	(835)	(26 128)	(25 258)
Earnings before interest paid, tax (EBIT) and corporate overheads	365 551	334 740	318 255	239 383	83 907	86 753
Consolidation adjustment						
Borrowing expenses						
Corporate overheads						
Profit from ordinary activities before income tax expense						
Income tax expense						
Profit from ordinary activities after income tax expense						
Share of net profit or loss of associates included in earnings before interest paid, tax and corporate overheads	–	–	4 451	3 759	–	–
Non cash expenses other than depreciation and amortisation	35 128	67 033	30 999	21 826	13 299	15 882
Assets and liabilities						
Segment assets	2 225 318	2 248 446	1 363 040	1 024 553	924 385	934 019
Tax assets						
Consolidation adjustment						
Consolidated assets						
Segment liabilities	324 024	349 544	403 861	258 462	143 896	133 045
Tax liabilities						
Interest bearing liabilities						
Consolidated liabilities						
Investments accounted for using the equity method included in segment assets above	–	–	17 268	18 683	–	–
Acquisition of non-current assets	183 902	97 911	219 984	93 652	16 598	33 091

On 29 August 2003 the consolidated entity sold 100% of the capital of Wesfarmers Rural Holdings Limited, an Australian company owning the rural services segment of the group known as Landmark. Segment information for the prior year covers only the period from 1 July to 29 August 2003 and has been included in the 'Other' segment. Disposal proceeds and gains have also been included in the 'Other' segment.

On 14 October 2003 the consolidated entity acquired 100% of the capital of Edward Lumley Holdings Limited, a UK company with insurance businesses in Australia and New Zealand. Information for the prior year includes in the 'Insurance' segment the results from Lumley Insurance group for the eight and a half months since acquisition. Acquisition of non-current assets by the consolidated entity upon acquisition of the controlled entity have been included in acquisition of non-current assets above and are shown in note 25.

Notes to and forming part of the accounts
for the year ended 30 June 2005 — Wesfarmers Limited and its controlled entities

2 SEGMENT INFORMATION (continued)

Insurance		Chemicals and fertilisers		Other		Consolidated	
2005 $000	2004 $000	2005 $000	2004 $000	2005 $000	2004 $000	2005 $000	2004 $000
1 127 054	874 000	588 657	518 505	48 966	1 010 122	8 190 389	8 407 492
147 152	102 008	128 003	123 369	52 820	538 893	1 312 950	1 643 822
(8 374)	(6 211)	(38 660)	(37 720)	(2 338)	(7 408)	(187 103)	(193 848)
138 778	95 797	89 343	85 649	50 482	531 485	1 125 847	1 449 974
(10 636)	(7 541)	(263)	(262)	–	(1 566)	(90 430)	(85 536)
128 142	88 256	89 080	85 387	50 482	529 919	1 035 417	1 364 438
						(4 523)	(5 047)
						(102 837)	(80 296)
						(47 753)	(46 704)
						880 304	1 232 391
						(261 430)	(363 812)
						618 874	868 579
–	–	3 819	6 192	31 533	104 732	39 803	114 683
10 037	2 132	4 996	3 672	17 980	329 847	112 439	440 392
1 588 005	1 666 495	571 591	566 648	669 066	793 847	7 341 405	7 234 008
						57 867	65 118
						(84 924)	(27 726)
						7 314 348	7 271 400
1 173 048	1 162 159	100 329	110 484	91 021	83 513	2 236 179	2 097 207
						200 522	231 750
						1 796 628	1 611 918
						4 233 329	3 940 875
–	–	30 525	26 706	361 709	321 723	409 502	367 112
14 125	308 614	31 437	48 297	34 188	16 435	500 234	598 000

(continued)

Notes to and forming part of the accounts for the year ended 30 June 2005 — Wesfarmers Limited and its controlled entities					
2 SEGMENT INFORMATION (continued)					
		Consolidated		Wesfarmers Limited	
		2005 $000	2004 $000	2005 $000	2004 $000
Insurance segment disclosures					
Direct premium revenue[1]		1 069 033	825 218		
Reinsurance premiums expense		(335 596)	(287 662)		
Retained premiums		733 437	537 556		
Direct claims expense		(658 335)	(469 182)		
Claims settlement expense		(23 377)	(18 326)		
Reinsurance and other recoveries		246 265	173 493		
Net incurred claims		(435 447)	(314 015)		
Acquisition costs expense		(139 332)	(107 344)		
Earned exchange commissions		80 857	59 564		
General and administration expenses		(53 255)	(36 338)		
Other underwriting expenses[2]		(90 206)	(69 441)		
Net underwriting expenses		(201 936)	(153 559)		
Underwriting result		96 054	69 982		
Investment and other income		42 724	25 815		
Amortisation of goodwill		(10 636)	(7 541)		
Earnings before interest and tax		128 142	88 256		

1 Direct premium revenue includes $33 110 000 of fire services levy (2004: $29 418 000).
2 Other underwriting expenses includes $32 752 000 of fire services charges (2004: $24 411 000).

Source: Wesfarmers Ltd 2005, *Annual report,* pp. 63–66.

18.9   Expected future developments

In January 2006, the IASB issued ED 8 *Operating Segments*, which it proposed as a replacement to IAS 14. The ED is a significant step in the IASB's program for achieving convergence with standards issued by the US Financial Accounting Standards Board (FASB). ED 8 is essentially adopting the requirements of the FASB standard SFAS 131 *Disclosures about Segments of an Enterprise and Related Information*. The major change from IAS 14 is adoption of the management approach to identify segments as the *only* acceptable approach. The proposed operative date is annual reporting periods beginning on or after 1 January 2007.

18.10 Summary

IAS 14 *Segment Reporting* is primarily a disclosure standard and is particularly relevant for large organisations that operate in different geographical locations and/or in diverse businesses. Information about an entity's geographical and business segments is relevant to assessing the risks and returns of a diversified or multinational entity where often that information cannot be determined from aggregated data. IAS 14 requires that an entity should determine which type of segment — business or geographical — is its primary segment reporting format. The disclosures required for the primary segment format are extensive whereas the disclosures required for the secondary segment format are limited.

Determining the composition of a business or geographical segment involves a certain amount of judgement. In making that judgement, entities should take into account the objective of reporting financial information by segment and the qualitative characteristics of financial statements as identified in the IASB Framework. Similarly, allocating revenues, expenses, assets and liabilities to segments on a reasonable basis involves judgement. The allocations must be based on whether the items relate to the particular segment's operations, can be directly attributed to that segment or can be reasonably allocated to that segment.

1. Segment disclosures are widely regarded as some of the most useful disclosures in financial reports because of the extent to which they disaggregate financial information into meaningful and often revealing groupings. Discuss this assertion by reference to the objectives of financial reporting by segments.

2. IAS 14 contains a number of paragraphs encouraging, but not requiring, additional information to be disclosed. Do you think many reporting entities would voluntarily provide these disclosures? Explain your answer.

3. Discuss the meaning of 'impracticable' in the context of paragraph 76 of IAS 14. What reasons could a reporting entity validly give for not restating comparative segment information?

4. IAS 14 states that it is not possible or appropriate to specify a single basis of allocation of assets, liabilities, revenues and expenses to segments that should be adopted by all entities. Explain the main factors that an entity should consider in determining how to allocate amounts to segments.

5. The underlying rationale for the identification of segments espoused in IAS 14 is that business or geographical segments should reflect the entity's different groupings of risks and rewards, either by product or service or by location. Further, IAS 14 asserts that for most entities the predominant source of risks and returns determines how the entity is organised and managed. Discuss this rationale.

6. Discuss the extracts from companies' segment notes provided in section 18.8.4. What are the similarities and differences between the companies' disclosures? What do the disclosures indicate about the relative performance of segments within companies?

EXERCISES

EXERCISE 18.1 ★   Defining geographical segments

IAS 14 states that a geographical segment can be defined by reference either to location of assets or location of customers.

Required
Explain, by way of example, how an entity's location of assets could differ from its location of customers.

EXERCISE 18.2 ★   Identifying primary and secondary segments

Company B is a listed manufacturing company. It produces most of its products in Australia but exports 90% of these products to the United States, Canada and Germany. It has only one main product line: scientific equipment. Company B is organised internally into two main business units: local and export. The export business unit is in turn divided into two sub-units: North America and Germany (North America includes Canada). Each business unit reports separate financial and operational information to the chief executive officer (CEO) and chief financial officer (CFO). The results of the two business units are then aggregated to form the consolidated financial information. Details of the geographical groups are as follows:

	United States	Canada	Germany	Australia
Economic and political conditions	Stable	Stable. Closely related to US environment	Stable	Stable
Relationships between operations	Closely linked to Canadian operations	Closely linked to US operations	Self-sustaining	Self-sustaining

	United States	Canada	Germany	Australia
Proximity of operations	Closely linked to Canadian operations	Closely linked to US operations	Not close to other operations	Not close to other operations
Special risks	None	None	Stricter regulations	Small market
Exchange control regulations	None	None	None	None
Currency risks	Low	Low to medium	Low	Low to medium

Required

Identify company B's primary and secondary segment reporting formats.

EXERCISE 18.3 ★★   Identifying business and geographical segments

Using the information from exercise 18.2, identify company B's business and geographical segments.

EXERCISE 18.4 ★★   Identifying reportable segments

Company A is a listed diversified retail company. Its stores are located mainly in Australia. It has three main types of stores: general department stores, liquor stores and specialist toy stores. Each of these stores has different products, customer types and distribution processes. In accordance with IAS 14, company A has identified three business segments: general department stores, liquor stores and specialist toy stores.

All three business units earn most of their revenue from external customers. Total consolidated revenue of company A is $600 million.

	General department stores $	Liquor stores $	Toy stores $	All segments $
Revenue	400m	100m	50m	550m
Segment result (profit)	15m	7m	4m	26m
Assets	900m	200m	100m	1 200m

Required

Identify company A's reportable segments. Explain your answer.

EXERCISE 18.5 ★★   Analysing the information provided

Using the information provided about company A in exercise 18.4, analyse the relative profitability of the three business segments.

EXERCISE 18.6 ★★   Disclosures

Company X has three reportable segments A, B and C. It also has another segment, D, which is not classified as a reportable segment because it earns a majority of its revenue from sales to segments A and C. However, D's sales to external customers amount to 13% of company X's total sales to external customers.

Required

What, if anything, must company X disclose about segment D?

EXERCISE 18.7 ★★

Segment assets, liabilities, revenues and expenses

Company X, a listed manufacturing company, has two reportable segments, A and B. Both A and B are manufacturing segments.

Required

For each item listed, state whether or not it would be allocated to the reportable segments, identify the segments to which it would be allocated and explain why it would or would not be allocated.

1. Interest income
2. Dividend income
3. Share of profits from investments in equity-method associates attributable to segment A
4. Interest expense
5. Losses on sales of investments
6. Income tax expense
7. Payables and trade creditors attributable to segment B
8. Costs incurred at head-office level on behalf of segment A in relation to operating costs of segment A
9. Outside equity interest in company X's profit
10. Depreciation of equipment attributable to segment B

PROBLEMS

PROBLEM 18.1 ★★

Reportable segments, allocating amounts to segments

Company A is a listed diversified retail company. Its stores are located mainly in Australia. It has three main types of stores: general department stores, liquor stores and specialist toy stores. Each of these stores has different products, customer types and distribution processes. In accordance with IAS 14, company A has identified three business segments: general department stores, liquor stores and specialist toy stores.

For the year ended 30 June 2005 each business unit reported the following financial information to company A's CFO:

	General department stores $	Liquor stores $	Toy stores $	All segments $
Revenue	400m	100m	50m	550m
Segment result (profit)	15m	7m	4m	26m
Assets	900m	200m	100m	1 200m

All three business units earn a majority of their revenue from external customers. Total consolidated revenue of company A for the year ended 30 June 2005 is $800 million. Included in general department stores' revenue is $50 million of revenue from toy stores. As at balance date toy stores owed general department stores $45 million. This amount is included in general department stores' assets. Within the general department stores business unit there are five different legal entities including legal entities Y and Z. As at 30 June 2005 legal entity Z owed $23 million to legal entity Y. These amounts have not been eliminated in determining the assets of the general department stores segment.

Required

State whether the following statements are true or false. Give reasons for your answers.

1. Company A has three reportable segments.
2. The revenue figure that should be used by the general department stores segment for the purposes of determining whether or not it is a reportable segment is $350 million.
3. When company A discloses segment liabilities in accordance with IAS 14, the toy stores segment liabilities should include the $45 million owed to general department stores.
4. The assets figure that should be used by the general department stores segment for the purposes of determining whether or not it is a reportable segment is $900 million.
5. The assets figure that should be used by the general department stores segment for the purposes of determining whether or not it is a reportable segment is $855 million.
6. The assets figure that should be used by the general department stores segment for the purposes of determining whether or not it is a reportable segment is $832 million.
7. The assets figure that should be used by the general department stores segment for the purposes of determining whether or not it is a reportable segment is $877 million.

PROBLEM 18.2 ★★   Identifying business and geographical segments

Company A is a listed diversified manufacturing company. It produces most of its products in Australia and its markets are also mainly in Australia. It produces four types of products and services as follows:

	Home furniture	Office furniture	Interior design services	Soft furnishings
Nature of product/service	Timber tables, chairs, beds	Metal and plastic workstations and chairs	Advice on interior design	Curtains, cushions and bed linen
Production process	Mainly handmade, labour intensive, specialised machinery for timber products	Mainly machine-made, specialised machinery for metal and plastic products	None, labour intensive	Mainly handmade, labour intensive
Type of customer	Families, high income, aged 35–55 years	Corporate customers – company purchasing officers, no specific age group	Mainly females, high income, over age 35	Mainly females, high income, over age 35
Distribution process	Distributed through selected furniture stores and own home furniture outlets	Distributed through own specialised office furniture outlets	Distributed through own home furniture outlets	Distributed through own home furniture outlets
Regulatory environment	Not highly regulated	Specialised regulations	Not highly regulated	Not highly regulated

Company A is organised internally into three business units: manufacturing home furniture, manufacturing office furniture and stores. Stores include own home furniture outlets, own office furniture outlets and interior design. Manufacturing home furniture includes soft furnishings. Each business unit reports separate financial and operational information to the chief executive officer (CEO) and chief financial officer (CFO).

Required

Identify company A's business segments and geographical segments.

Comprehensive problem

Company A is a diversified financial institution. It provides three main types of services: banking, funds management and life insurance. Each of these services provides different products, serves different types of customer and has different distribution processes. Its operations are located mainly in Australia, although 12% of revenues from external customers are from bank branches in New Zealand. Company A is divided into three business units that report separately to top management. The business units are banking, funds management and life insurance. In accordance with IAS 14, company A has identified three business segments: banking, funds management and life insurance.

All three business units earn a majority of their revenues from external customers. The following financial information was reported to the company's CEO by each business unit for the year ended 30 June 2005:

	Banking $	Funds management $	Life insurance $	All segments $
Revenue – external sales	850m (all interest income)	90m (fees and commissions)	10m (premium income and other fees)	950m
Segment result (profit before amortisation, depreciation and income tax expense)	130m	16m	1m	147m
Segment assets	12 750m	630m	100m	13 480m

For the year ended 30 June 2005, the total consolidated revenue of company A is $984 million. Company A owns three properties with a total written-down value at 30 June 2005 of $300 million. One of the properties, with a written-down value of $220 million, is the corporate head office, where administration for the entire company is performed. The other two properties are large regional bank branches. Customers visiting those branches purchase mainly banking services but the company's full range of services may be provided at any bank branch office. The company's CFO has determined that these bank branch properties should be allocated to all three segments in proportion to the revenues generated by each business segment. Depreciation on the corporate head office property for the year was $4.4 million. Depreciation on the bank branch properties for the year was $1.6 million. During the year company A sold an investment property, realising a gain of $34 million. The investment property had not been allocated to any of the business segments in prior years.

The banking segment's assets are mainly loan receivables. A provision for doubtful debts of $630 million has been deducted in determining that segment's assets. During the year the provision was increased by $30 million. The banking segment's result also includes a share of profits from an associated entity of $2 million. The investment in the associated entity, carried at 30 June 2005 at $25 million, is included in the banking segment's assets because it is part of that segment's operations.

As at 30 June 2005, company A has $200 million of goodwill (written-down value) that it has not allocated to any of the business segments because there was no reasonable basis to do so. Goodwill amortisation for the year ended 30 June 2005 is $20 million.

For the year ended 30 June 2005, company A's total consolidated profit, after income tax expense of $36 million, is $85 million.

Total consolidated liabilities of company A at 30 June 2005 are $11 250 million. These include borrowings and deposits of $11 000 million that relate to the banking segment's operations and are directly attributable to that segment. Related interest expense for the year ended 30 June 2005 is $400 million. Creditors and policyholder liabilities that relate to the funds management and life insurance segments' operations and are directly attributable to those segments are $200 million and $50 million respectively. There is no related interest expense. A payable of $35 million from the life insurance segment to the wealth management segment was eliminated in calculating total consolidated liabilities of company A as at 30 June 2005. The related receivable is not included in the segment assets figure in the table shown on p. 790.

Other information

- Only 2% of company A's total assets are located in New Zealand.
- There were no inter-segment sales during the year.
- The products and services offered by each business segment are as follows:
  - banking: provides a full range of banking services for consumers and corporate customers
  - funds management: provides wealth creation, management and protection products and services to consumers
  - life insurance: provides life insurance policies and other protection products to consumers.
- There are no other internally reported segments.

Required

Prepare the segment disclosures note for company A for the year ended 30 June 2005 in accordance with IAS 14. Ignore comparative figures and show all workings. Perform your workings in the following order:

1. Identify the business segments and geographic segments.
2. Determine the primary segment reporting format.
3. Determine which segments are reportable segments.
4. Allocate relevant assets, liabilities, revenues and expenses to the reportable segments. In doing so, specifically consider:
   (a) the corporate head office and related depreciation
   (b) the regional bank branch properties and related depreciation
   (c) the gain on sale of investment properties
   (d) the investment in the associated entity and related share of profits
   (e) goodwill and related amortisation
   (f) interest income and interest expense.
5. Identify which segment assets, liabilities, revenues and expenses require separate disclosure, including amounts to be disclosed or eliminated on consolidation.
6. Calculate consolidated profit after tax.
7. Prepare the required segment disclosures.

WEBLINK

Visit these websites for additional information:

www.iasb.org
www.asic.gov.au
www.aasb.com.au
www.accaglobal.com

www.iasplus.com
www.ifac.org
www.nzica.com
www.capa.com.my

REFERENCES

ANZ Bank 2005, *2005 ANZ Financial report*, Australia and New Zealand Banking Group Limited, viewed 10 March 2006, <www.anz.com.au>.

Colorado Group Ltd 2005, *Financial report*.

Queensland Cotton Holdings Ltd 2003, *Annual report*.

Wesfarmers Ltd 2005, *Annual report*, viewed 16 March 2006, <www.wesfarmers.com.au>.

PART 4
Economic entities

Part 4 examines the application of accounting standards to situations where the accounting entity consists of more than one legal entity.

Chapters 19–23 are concerned with the preparation of consolidated financial statements that show the financial performance and position of the group. Chapter 19 contains an analysis of the criteria for determining a parent–subsidiary relationship. Chapters 20–23 are concerned with the preparation of the consolidated financial statements, and chapter 24 analyses the translation of the financial statements of foreign subsidiaries into a currency suitable for consolidation with the parent. Chapters 25 and 26 discuss the accounting for associates and joint ventures.

CHAPTER 19
Controlled entities — the consolidation method

ACCOUNTING STANDARDS

International: IAS 27 *Consolidated and Separate Financial Statements*

IFRS 3 *Business Combinations*

Australia: AASB 127 *Consolidated and Separate Financial Statements*

AASB 3 *Business Combinations*

New Zealand: NZ IAS 27 *Consolidated and Separate Financial Statements*

NZ IFRS 3 *Business Combinations*

CONCEPTS FOR REVIEW

Before studying this chapter, you should understand or, if necessary, revise:

• the IASB Framework

• accounting for business combinations (see chapter 12 of this book).

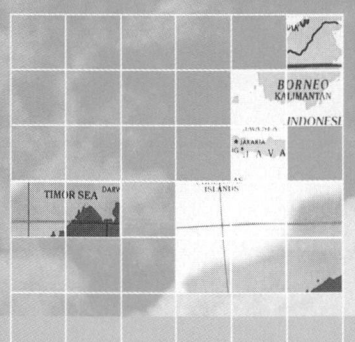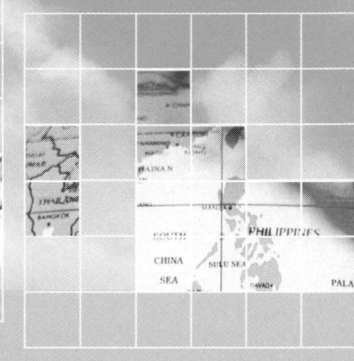

LEARNING OBJECTIVES

When you have studied this chapter, you should be able to:
1. understand the nature and various forms of controlled entities
2. explain how the consolidation method is applied
3. define the term 'control' as used in determining a parent–subsidiary relationship
4. explain the factors to consider in determining whether an entity has the power to govern the policies of another entity
5. explain the benefits that can arise from a controlled relationship
6. discuss the importance of ownership in determining parent–subsidiary relationships
7. discuss the reasons for consolidating the financial statements of entities
8. explain the reporting entity concept
9. discuss which entities should prepare consolidated financial statements
10. explain the interrelationship between a parent and an acquirer in a business combination
11. understand the alternative concepts of consolidation
12. explain the differences in report format between single entities and consolidated entities.

19.1 Introduction

The purpose of this chapter is to discuss the preparation of a single set of financial statements, referred to as the consolidated financial statements, for a number of entities that are managed as a single economic entity and, in particular, a group of entities that are under the control of one of those entities. The preparation of the consolidated financial statements involves the combining of the financial statements of the individual entities so that they show the financial position and performance of the group of entities, presented as if they were a single economic entity.

As well as analysing the form the consolidated financial statements might take, this chapter also considers the concept of control as the criterion for consolidation; that is, as the key characteristic that determines the existence of which entities' financial statements should be combined. In section 19.2 a number of combinations of entities for which consolidated financial statements could be prepared are considered. However, the concentration of the chapter, and the following four chapters in this book, is on the particular situation where one entity, the parent, controls another entity, the subsidiary, and the preparation of the consolidated financial statements for such a group of entities. However, it needs to be appreciated that consolidation is not a process that is used exclusively for parent–subsidiary relationships. The concept of control is applicable to combinations of entities other than parents and their subsidiaries, and the process of consolidation is the same for all these combinations.

The two accounting standards that are primarily used in this chapter are IFRS 3 *Business Combinations* and IAS 27 *Consolidated and Separate Financial Statements*. The latter standard deals only with the preparation of consolidated financial statements for parent–subsidiary situations.

LO 1

19.2 Forms of controlled entities

Appendix A of IFRS 3 contains the following definition of a business combination:

> The bringing together of separate entities or businesses into one reporting entity.

A business combination thus involves the formation of an entity that consists of a number of separate entities that together form a combined entity, with users of financial information requiring information about that entity as a whole. Some examples of such business combinations are given below.

19.2.1 Acquisition of shares in another entity

Entity A may acquire all or part of the issued shares of another entity. For example, as shown in figure 19.1, Entity A may acquire 80% of the issued shares of Entity B. Entity A will record an investment in Entity B, and the giving up of some form of consideration such as cash, or shares, in Entity A itself. As the transaction is between Entity A and the shareholders in Entity B, there are no accounting entries in Entity B in relation to this transaction.

Depending on the percentage of shares held in Entity B, as well as other factors, Entity A may have the ability to control the decision making in relation to Entity B. The two entities may then operate as a combined entity, with the wealth of the shareholders in Entity A being dependent on the capacity of both entities to generate profits. The shareholders in Entity A are then interested in the combined financial performance and financial position of the two entities.

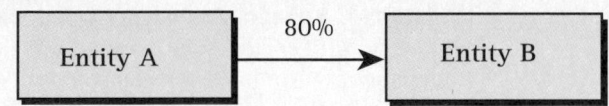

FIGURE 19.1   Acquisition of shares in another entity

As is discussed in more detail later in this chapter, where Entity A controls the operations of Entity B, the business combination results in the formation of a parent–subsidiary relationship; that is, Entity A is regarded as the parent, with Entity B as its subsidiary. The application of IFRS 3 and IAS 27 will require the preparation of a special set of financial statements – the consolidated financial statements – to report the economic performance and position of the two entities as a combined entity.

19.2.2 Formation of a new entity to acquire the shares of two other entities

A variation on the first example is where, instead of Entity A acquiring the shares of Entity B, after negotiations between Entity A and Entity B, the two entities agree to the formation of a new entity, Entity C. Entity C acquires all the shares of the other two entities, as in figure 19.2.

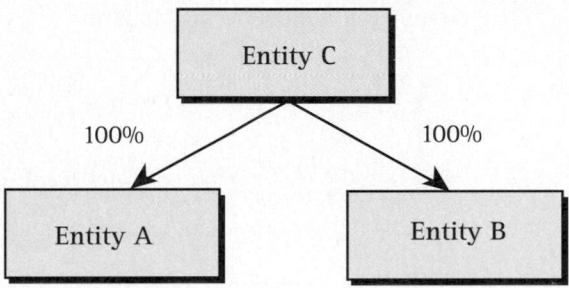

FIGURE 19.2   Formation of new entity

The shareholders in Entity A and Entity B receive shares in Entity C in exchange for their shares in the other entities. The business combination has resulted in the three entities being brought together into one entity as Entity C now controls the operations of both Entity A and Entity B. The shareholders in Entity C are then interested in the combined entity, which consists of all three entities. Their information needs are better met by the production of a set of consolidated financial statements showing the financial position and performance of the combined entities as a single entity.

19.2.3 Stapled securities

Some legal entities listed on a stock exchange may issue equity securities that are combined with, or stapled to, the securities issued by another legal entity. The stapled securities cannot be traded separately, and are quoted on the stock exchange at a single price. The result of the stapling is that the investors in one of the legal entities are also investors in the other legal entity. The reason for the stapling is because, given particular legislative, taxation or operating factors, this is the most cost-effective structure for the two entities to act as a joint operation.

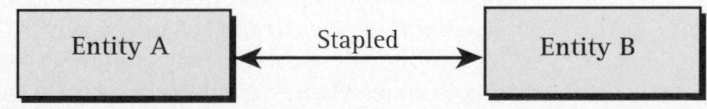

FIGURE 19.3   Stapled securities

In figure 19.3, Entity A does not acquire any of the shares or net assets of Entity B, nor does Entity B make any such acquisitions in relation to Entity A. The structure is formed by agreement or contract between the two entities. For the shareholders in both Entity A and Entity B, the worth of their investment is dependent on the performance of both entities. The price of the quoted security is dependent on the performance of the two entities as a group. The stapling is a form of business combination because the two entities have been brought together into one reporting entity.

19.2.4 Dual-listed entities

A 'dual-listed' structure involves the formation of a contractual arrangement between two entities under which the activities of both entities are brought together, managed and operated on a unified basis as if they were a single entity, while retaining their separate legal entities, tax residencies and stock exchange listings. An example of such a structure is that between the Australian company, BHP Ltd, and the UK company, Billiton Plc.

WEBLINK Visit <www.bhpbilliton.com> for more information on these two companies.

Figure 19.4 diagrammatically illustrates dual-listed entities. For example, Entity A may be a listed entity in Australia while Entity B may be a listed entity in Hong Kong. Assume the following information:

Entity A:	Number of issued shares	100
	Value per share	$1
Entity B	Number of issued shares	100
	Value per share	$3

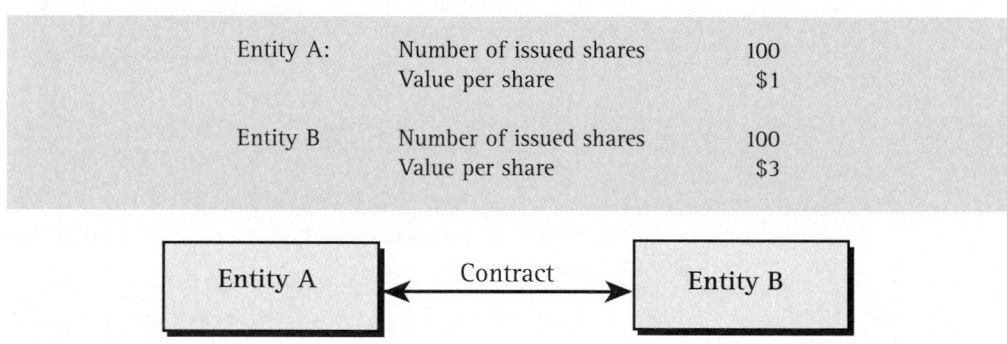

FIGURE 19.4 Dual-listed entities

The two entities could agree to an arrangement whereby each entity retains its own listing, and the shareholders in each entity retain their ownership in their respective entities, but there is a sharing of rights between the shareholder groups such that the shareholders have an economic interest in the combined assets of both entities. In this example, Entity B could issue 200 bonus shares so that the number of shares issued increases to 300 to reflect the fact that Entity B is three times as valuable as Entity A. The rights of both shares in Entity A and shares in Entity B are changed so that they are entitled to a 1/400 interest per share in the combined wealth of both entities. The two entities are managed on a unified basis, with shareholders of both companies being able to vote on substantial issues affecting their combined interests, such as the appointment of directors. The shareholders in both entities are interested in the preparation of a set of financial statements about the combined entities rather than just the individual entities themselves.

The common feature of these business combinations is the interest of users of financial statements in the financial performance and position of the combined entities rather than the individual entities. These financial statements are the consolidated financial statements because they are prepared by adding together the financial statements of the individual entities within the business combination. A key question to be addressed later in this chapter is which entities should be required to prepare consolidated financial statements? In other words, what is the concept or criterion that provides the basis for consolidation?

19.3 Applying the consolidation method

Although, as shown in section 19.2, there are a number of situations where business combinations may usefully apply the consolidation process to prepare a set of consolidated financial statements for the combined entities, the only IASB accounting standard that currently requires the application of the consolidation method is IAS 27. IAS 27 applies to situations as depicted in figures 19.1 and 19.2, specifically, where parent and subsidiary entities exist. Paragraph 4 of IAS 27 contains the following definitions:

> *Consolidated financial statements* are the financial statements of a group presented as those of a single economic entity.
>
> A *group* is a parent and all its subsidiaries.
>
> A *parent* is an entity that has one or more subsidiaries.
>
> A *subsidiary* is an entity, including an unincorporated entity such as a partnership, that is controlled by another entity (known as the parent).

In figure 19.1, Entity A is the parent and Entity B is the subsidiary — if we assume that, because of its 80% holding in Entity B, Entity A is able to control Entity B (the meaning of 'control' is discussed in section 19.4). Entity A and Entity B as a combined unit, or economic entity, are referred to as a group. The consolidated financial statements are then the financial statements of the group, and the process of preparing the consolidated financial statements is referred to as consolidation.

Paragraph 22 of IAS 27 states that in preparing the consolidated financial statements, 'the financial statements of the parent and its subsidiaries [are combined] line-by-line by adding together like items of assets, liabilities, equity, income and expenses'. For example, assuming that at a specified balance date, Entity A and Entity B both report cash balances in the financial statements for their individual legal entities, the cash for the group, as reported in the consolidated financial statements, is determined by adding the cash balances of the parent and the subsidiary:

	Entity A	+	Entity B	=	Group [Consolidated Financial Statements]
Cash	$50 000	+	$20 000	=	$70 000

This aggregation process is subject to a number of adjustments, which are covered in detail in the following chapters. These adjustments are necessary because of intragroup shareholdings and transactions between entities within the group. However, at this stage the process of consolidation should be seen as being simply a process of aggregation of the financial statements of all the entities in the group. Note that the consolidation process does not involve making adjustments to the individual financial statements or the accounts of the entities in the group. The consolidated financial statements are an additional set of financial statements and, as demonstrated in chapter 20, are prepared using a worksheet or spreadsheet to facilitate the addition and adjustment process.

The consolidated financial statements consist of a consolidated balance sheet, consolidated income statement, consolidated statement of changes in equity, and a consolidated cash flow statement. The format of these statements is as presented in chapters 15–17.

It is important to understand that the preparation of the consolidated financial statements does not necessarily overcome the need or requirement to prepare financial statements for the individual entities within the group. The consolidated financial statements are required in addition to the individual financial statements. The need for the individual financial statements is dependent on legal requirements within a specific jurisdiction, and application of the reporting entity concept (see section 19.4.6).

LO 3

19.4 Control as the criterion for consolidation

In paragraph 4 of IAS 27, a subsidiary is defined as an entity that is *controlled* by another entity, the parent. The criterion for identifying a parent–subsidiary relationship, and hence the basis for consolidation, is control. The determination of whether one entity controls another is then crucial to the determination of which entities should prepare consolidated financial statements.

Although IAS 27 contains a definition of control, and provides some discussion on the meaning of the term, there still exists much disagreement on what constitutes control. The IASB is currently debating the definition of control, but as of 2006 had not yet agreed on any change to the definition in IAS 27. To assist in providing an understanding of the debate, as well as providing an insight into the application of IAS 27, extensive references will be made in this chapter to the debate within the Financial Accounting Standards Board (FASB) in the United States, as this reflects many aspects of the debate happening within the IASB.

Paragraph 4 of IAS 27 contains the following definition of control:

> Control is the power to govern the financial and operating policies of an entity so as to obtain benefits from its activities.

Note that there are two parts to this definition of control:
- the ability to direct the financial and operating policies of another entity (*the power criterion*)
- the ability to obtain benefits from the other entity (*the benefit criterion*).

In February 1999, the FASB issued an *Exposure Draft on Consolidated Financial Statements: Purpose and Policy* (hereafter referred to as the FASB ED). The FASB ED was very controversial and, as reported in the 28 February 2001 edition of the FASB *Status Report*, 'at this time, there is not sufficient Board member support to proceed with either a final statement on consolidation policy, or an exposure draft on entities with specific limits on their powers (SPEs)'. However, the concepts in the FASB ED are not dissimilar from those in IAS 27, and give insight into the meaning of terms used in IAS 27. In the FASB ED, control is defined as follows:

> The ability of an entity to direct the policies and management that guide the ongoing activities of another entity so as to increase its benefits and limit its losses from that other entity's activities. For purposes of consolidated statements, control involves decision-making ability that is not shared with others.

This definition also relies on the power criterion and the benefit criterion used in the IAS 27 definition. However, it also emphasises an interlinking between these two criteria – the ability to control another entity should be such as to allow the controller to use that power to increase its benefits and limit its losses from the subsidiary's activities. This dimension effectively requires that the benefits relate to the use of the power, rather than being independent of the power. In the use of the words 'so as' in the definition of control in IAS 27, this same dimension is inherent in that definition.

LO 4

19.4.1 Power to govern the financial and operating policies of an entity

The IASB uses the term 'power to govern' while the FASB uses 'ability to direct'. There is no difference between the two terms, both referring to an entity's *capacity* to control. One of the key elements of the debate on the meaning of control is the distinction between the notion of 'capacity to control' and that of 'actual control'. Capacity to control does not require the holder to actually exercise control. Similarly, an entity that is actually controlling another may not have the capacity to control.

Some factors to consider in determining the existence of capacity to control are as follows:

Passive versus active control

The entity having the power to govern, or the capacity to control, may not be actively involved in the management of the controlled entity; the controller may play a passive role. However, in situations where another party is actively formulating the policies of a subsidiary, in order for another entity to be the controlling entity, it must have the ability to change or modify those policy decisions if the need for change is seen to exist. The existence of actual control, (i.e. determining the actual policies of the subsidiary) often signals the existence of capacity to control, but the two are not necessarily coexistent.

Non-shared control

Regardless of whether the control is passive or active, there can be only one controlling entity; there cannot be two or more entities that share the control. It is possible that one entity may delegate control to another entity, but the first entity has the capacity to control even if it is the delegated party that actually controls the subsidiary.

In the FASB ED, the FASB argued (para. 11) that the parent's ability to control a subsidiary is an exclusionary power. The decision-making ability cannot be shared and the parent must be able to:

- direct the use of and access to another entity's assets, generally by having the power to set the policies that guide how those assets are used in ongoing activities, and
- hold the management of that other entity accountable for the conduct of its ongoing activities, including the use of that entity's assets, generally by having the power to select, terminate, and determine the compensation of the management responsible for carrying out the directives of the parent.

However, as the FASB ED noted (para. 12), this does not mean that the parent must be able to make any decision it likes in relation to another entity, as the parent will be constrained by 'laws, regulations, corporate charters, shareholder and partnership agreements, debt covenants, and other agreements that impose limits to protect the interests of noncontrolling investors, creditors, and others'. These are protective rights and do not affect the ability of one entity to control another.

Level of share ownership

Paragraph 13 of IAS 27 states that control is presumed to exist when the parent owns, directly or indirectly through subsidiaries, more than half of the voting power of an entity. Hence, where the parent owns more than 50% of the shares of another entity, it is expected that the latter is a subsidiary of the former.

Ownership of shares normally provides voting rights that enable the holder of the majority of shares to dominate the appointment of directors or an entity's governing board. As paragraph 13 of IAS 27 states, control exists (when the parent owns half or less of the voting power of an entity) where there is:

(c) power to appoint or remove the majority of the members of the board of directors or equivalent governing body and control of the entity is by that board or body; or

(d) power to cast the majority of votes at meetings of the board of directors or equivalent governing body and control of the entity is by that board or body.

There is no debate about the existence of control where the parent has a majority shareholding in the subsidiary. However, where the ownership interest is less than 50% or is based on possible future actions, there is less consensus about whether control exists. As the FASB noted in its 2001 Status Report:

> Several FASB Board members are concerned about the appropriateness of determining that nonshared decision-making ability can exist based on the anticipated nonaction by other holders of voting rights.

Control under IAS 27 is *non-shared* control. A distinction needs to be made between non-shared control and what can be described as 'unilateral control'. Unilateral control means that the controlling party is not dependent on the support of others to exercise control, which is the case where the parent owns more than 50% of the shares of the subsidiary. Where the holding is less than 50%, the parent has a non-shared or dominant control. This is not control in a legal sense as with unilateral control, but is control that is achieved both because of its own actions and because of the actions (or inactions) of other parties. This form of control is referred to by the FASB (see figure 19.5 for an example) as 'effective control', and appears to be the form adopted by IAS 27.

In determining the existence of effective control it is necessary to examine the actions of other parties. In particular, factors to assess include:

- *the existence of contracts.* Paragraph 13 of IAS 27 identifies two circumstances where control exists because of the existence of contracts:

   (a) power over more than half of the voting rights by virtue of an agreement with other investors;
   (b) power to govern the financial and operating policies of the entity under a statute or an agreement.

   The contract or agreement may take many forms; however, a contract may cover a limited time period. Control will then exist only while the contract is current.
- *size of the voting interest.* Although all shareholders may attend general meetings and vote in matters relating to governance of an entity, it is rare for this to occur. If, therefore, only 60% of the eligible votes are cast at a general meeting and an entity has more than a 30% interest in that entity, it can cast the majority of votes at that meeting. It then has effective control of the entity.
- *dispersion of other shareholders.* Shareholders can be dispersed geographically as well as in numbers of shares held. The annual general meeting may be held in Sydney, Australia, but the majority of shareholders may live in South-East Asia. The probability of these shareholders attending the general meeting is then lessened by location.

   Further, even if all the shareholders lived in Sydney, if all shareholders held small parcels of shares, then the probability of attendance at general meetings is reduced. For example, if the number of shares issued by the subsidiary was 1000, the shareholders would be more dispersed if there were 1000 shareholders with one share each than if there were four shareholders with 250 shares each. However, assuming the prospective parent has a 40% interest, it is not clear where the cut-off point is between lack of control, where there are two other shareholders with 30% each, and having control, where there are 60 other shareholders with 1% each.
- *level of disorganisation or apathy of the remaining shareholders.* This factor is affected by the dispersion of the shareholders, and reflected in their attendance at general meetings. Holders of small parcels of shares are often not organised into forming voting blocks. Shareholders with environmental or ethical concerns may be less apathetic about the actions of the entity and its management policies, and may form voting blocks.

Figure 19.5 is an abbreviated version of an example given in paragraphs 87–94 of the FASB ED to illustrate the application of the concept of control where the parent has less than 50% of the shareholding in a subsidiary. In the example, the ownership by Company A of shares in Company B reduces over time from 100%, to 60%, to 45%, and finally, to 35%. The question is whether Company A retains control of Company B as its shareholding decreases. The FASB argues in this example that control is maintained even at the 35% level, applying factors such as those discussed earlier.

However, it is the assessment of the non-action of others in determining the existence of control that caused some FASB board members to be concerned, particularly because of the subjectivity of assessing the reasons for the shareholders' actions. Do the non-voting shareholders not vote because they are happy with the management ability of Company A as opposed to their being apathetic? Would they be willing to combine to outvote Company A if the latter's decisions were considered untenable? The success of Company B's operations under the control of Company A is a further measure of the potential for generally passive shareholders to be sufficiently concerned to cast a vote at the next general meeting. While shareholders see positive results, they are less likely to react against Company A. When the company is performing poorly, the interest of shareholders increases as well as their willingness to become involved. Poor performance with resultant lowering of share price may also result in a current or new shareholder acquiring a large block of shares and changing the voting mix at general meetings.

Company A, a cement manufacturer, acquired all of the voting shares of Company B, a rug manufacturer, as part of a diversification program.

Several years later, Company A decided as part of its corporate strategy to commit capital resources only to its primary line of business, and was unwilling to support the projected growth of Company B. Company A caused Company B to issue additional shares in an initial public offering, resulting in a reduction in Company A's ownership interest in Company B from 100% to 60%.

Shortly after the offering, the newly issued shares are widely held, no other party having more than 3% of Company B's outstanding shares. Both before and after the initial public offering, Company A's shareholding represents a majority interest in Company B, which leads to a presumption of control in the absence of evidence to the contrary (FASB ED, para. 18(a)). Moreover, there is no evidence that demonstrates that Company A, through its 60% interest, no longer has the ability to dominate the nomination and selection of the members of the board of Company B.

Five years later, to raise additional capital needed to finance the growth of Company B, Company A causes Company B to issue additional shares, which reduces Company A's ownership of outstanding shares to 45%. At this time, Company A's 45% holding is the largest block of shares held by any single party, and the remaining shares outstanding continue to be widely held – no other party holds more than 3% of the outstanding shares. Ten days after the public offering, Company A is able, through the board of directors of Company B, to cause the renomination of all of its choices for the 11 board members of Company B.

During the preceding five years, about 80% of the eligible rights to vote in an election of the board of directors of Company B were cast at any given annual meeting of Company B. The percentage of votes cast in each of the past five years are as follows (the last being the most recent): 76, 81, 82, 79, and 82. Company A voted all of its shares each year, but only about half of the other eligible votes were cast in each of those years.

In this case, Company A no longer has legal control of Company B but, based on the facts, effective control has not been lost. Company A still has the ability to dominate the process of nominating and electing the members of the board of Company B, which is based primarily on 2 factors: Company A's large minority holding and the wide dispersion of the remaining shares.

About two years later, another issuance of Company B's shares reduces Company A's holdings to 35%, and the voting patterns and all other facts remain constant. Company A's 35% holding is now less than half of the 80% of votes typically cast in past elections and may still be nearly half of the votes cast in future elections.

In this case, Company A's ability to maintain control becomes questionable. However, assurance of an entity's ability to maintain its control is not a condition for consolidation. Rather, the assessment is based on whether an entity has a current ability to control another entity. In this case, based on the facts and the weight of evidence, the 35% voting interest, the strong ties to the directors of Company B and the continuing success of Company B's operations under its control, collectively give Company A the ability to dominate the nomination and election of Company B's board of directors. In this case, there is no evidence that demonstrates that control of Company B has been lost.

FIGURE 19.5 Controlling partially owned entities

A number of problems arise in applying the concept of effective control. First, there is the question of temporary control. Where the parent holds more than 50% of the shares of the subsidiary, there is no danger of a change in the identity of the parent. However, if the identification of the parent is based on factors that may change over time, the process becomes difficult. For example, the percentage of votes cast at general meetings may historically be 70%, but in a particular year it may be 50%. A shareholder with 30% of the voting power has control in the latter circumstance but not in the former. This control may, however, last for only a year until the next general meeting.

Second, the ability of an entity to control another may be affected by relationships with other parties. For example, a holder of 40% of the voting power may be 'friendly' with the holder of another 11% of the votes. This friendly relationship could include a financial institution that has invested in the holder of the 40% votes and plans to vote with that party to increase its potential for repayment of loans. However, business relationships and loyalties are not always permanent.

Third, a minority holder that did not have control may, due to changing circumstances, find itself with the capacity to control. For example, a holder of a 30% block of shares may not have had control because the remaining shares were tightly held by a small number of parties. However, if one or more of these parties sold their shares in small lots, the minority holder could have the controlling parcel of shares. Regardless of whether this shareholder wanted to exercise that control or not, he or she has the capacity to control and is the parent.

The theoretical question is whether in these circumstances an entity really controls in its own right or in fact has control that is shared with the other shareholders, as control is affected by their actions. The practical question relates to how to determine control in changing circumstances. Is it sufficient to rely on *usual circumstances*, such as the average attendance at general meetings, or the *probability* of how other shareholders will act?

19.4.2 Potential voting rights

Paragraphs 14–15 of IAS 27 discuss the issue of potential voting rights. For example, an entity may have share call options or convertible instruments which, if exercised or converted, give the entity voting power over the financial and operating policies of another entity. There are two types of convertible voting rights that need to be considered:
- potential voting rights that are currently exercisable or convertible
- potential voting rights that cannot be exercised or converted until a future date or until the occurrence of a future event.

The second circumstance does not influence the current assessment of capacity to control and hence such potential voting rights are not considered in assessment of control. In relation to a situation, where at balance date the holder of an instrument has the capacity to exercise the instrument and obtain the power to govern the financial and operating policies of another entity, then that entity is a parent of the other entity.

It may be argued that control should be based on the actual situation at balance date and, as the holder of the convertible instrument has not exercised the instrument, the actual situation is that the holder is not yet in control. In other words, it would require an action on the part of the holder to have a current capacity to control. However, as expressed previously in this chapter, control exists even when the holder is passive. A holder of 51% of the shares of another entity is the parent of that entity even if it does not attend general meetings or participate in determination of the directors of the entity.

The implementation guidance to IAS 27 provides a number of illustrative examples to assist in determining when potential voting rights should be taken into consideration in the assessment of the existence of control.

LO 5

19.4.3   Ability to obtain benefits from the other entity's activities

The second part of the IAS 27 definition of control is concerned with a parent's ability to use that power to increase the benefits it derives and limit the losses it suffers from the activities of its subsidiary.

This characteristic of control acts to exclude such parties as trustees and those with fiduciary relationships with the subsidiary. These parties may be able to direct certain activities of the subsidiary but, apart from fees for service, the activities do not lead to increased or decreased benefits to these parties.

Apart from the obvious benefits in terms of dividends relating to the holding of an ownership interest, there are other benefits that can accrue to the controlling entity. Paragraph 38 of the FASB ED lists some of these:

- benefits from structuring transactions with a subsidiary to obtain necessary and scarce raw materials on a priority basis, at strategic locations, or at reduced costs of delivery
- benefits from gaining access to the subsidiary's distribution network, patents, or proprietary production techniques
- benefits from combining certain functions of the parent and subsidiary to create economies of scale in, for example, costs of management, employee benefits, or insurance
- benefits from denying or regulating access to a subsidiary's assets by its non-controlling investors, creditors, competitors and others.

The FASB argued (para. 217) that 'because of the stewardship responsibilities and risks associated with being in control of an entity, the Board believes that an entity rarely acquires control of another entity without obtaining significant opportunities to benefit from that control'. No entity wants to control another entity for purely altruistic reasons.

In March 2002, the Accounting Standards Board (ASB) in the United Kingdom in a draft paper on consolidation policy provided some principles to be used in applying a control-based consolidation policy, particularly in relation to linking controlling policies with benefits to be accrued from their application:

- *The commercial outcomes for each party should be assessed.* Arrangements between entities should be assessed from a perspective that makes commercial sense for each of the entities involved. This perspective requires that, at the outset at least, no entity should expect benefit without exposure to commensurate risk and no entity should be exposed to risks without expecting commensurate benefit.
- *Control requires both the ability to direct and to benefit.* Control has two aspects: the ability to direct the operating and financial policies and the ability to benefit or suffer from that direction.
- *The ability to benefit and the exposure to risk assume particular importance where policies of direction are pre-determined.* Where through pre-determination or otherwise, there is no real present choice of financial and operating policies, the ability to direct becomes irrelevant in deciding issues of control. Decisions on consolidation then depend on the nature of the ability to benefit of the different entities involved and their exposure to the risks inherent in those benefits.

The philosophy being expressed in these principles is that there is an association between benefits and risk, and one of the risks relates to taking control of another entity. Identification of the controlling entity should therefore be assisted by an analysis of which entities are bearing the risks in relation to another entity, and which entities are likely to benefit from their association with that entity. Importantly, the ability to be able to vary the amount of benefits or to affect the generation of benefits is also important in identifying who is in control.

The third principle noted by the UK ASB relates to the situation where a parent may set up a special purpose entity in which it has a small shareholding and the majority shareholding might be held by the party which finances the activities of the special purpose entity. However, the entity is set up such that the operating and financial policies are virtually fixed (see figure 19.6 for a case example). In this case, as the ASB noted, the determination of the parent then focuses on the ability to benefit and the exposure to risk rather than the ability to determine policies of the special purpose entity. Corporation J does not control the Board of Directors of Corporation X. However, there are not many decisions left for Corporation X to make as the product and dealers are all predetermined. In terms of benefits, the investor group receives a return on the entity as the inventory is sold. However, Corporation J receives a greater range of benefits as Corporation X is acting as a sales agent for its boats. Corporation X still runs all the risks in relation to production of the boats and disposing of any unsold boats, and receives the major benefits from the sale of the boats via the fee for services. Corporation J is then the parent of Corporation X.

Corporation J, a public company, is a boat manufacturer specialising in sailboats for private use. Corporation J, with the assistance of an investment banker and in conjunction with an independent investor group, created Corporation X.

The business purpose of Corporation X is to purchase all of Corporation J's luxury line sailboats upon completion of production. The investor group contributed $600 000 and Corporation J contributed $400 000 to capitalise Corporation X. The investor group will own 60% of the voting interest in Corporation X, with Corporation J having the remaining 40% voting interest. Corporation X is governed by a board of directors and consists of ten directors: six appointed by the investor group and four appointed by Corporation J. All significant business decisions must be approved by 60% of the board, except for decisions relating to liquidation, issuance of additional debt or equity capital and changes to the size of board of directors, these decisions requiring approval by 80% of the board.

Corporation X's operations consist of acquiring 100% of Corporation J's luxury line sailboats at cost of production. Corporation X may, at its option, return any unsold inventory to Corporation J after one year at cost. Corporation X is allowed to enter into other transactions with unrelated parties, but the investor group and Corporation J have agreed that Corporation X will not enter into such transactions. Corporation J has an agreement with Corporation X to maintain relationships with its dealer network. Corporation J will provide all necessary post-production storage facilities, arrange for shipment to dealers, provide incentive plans to dealers and provide manufacturer's warranties. Apart from inventory, Corporation X will not have any substantive assets.

Corporation J receives a fee for services provided to Corporation X equal to the revenue from sales after deducting the cost of sales, financing fees and a facilitation fee paid to the investor group.

FIGURE 19.6 Special purpose entity
Source: Adapted from a case written by the FASB as part of its testing of the FASB ED.

LO 6

19.4.4   ## Alternatives to control

In the Discussion Memorandum issued in 1991, written by Paul Pacter, and issued by the FASB prior to determining the exposure draft on consolidation policy and procedures, the FASB requested comments on three possible conditions for consolidation:

- a parent's level of ownership in another entity, even if not controlled by the parent
- control of an entity by a parent without a specified level of ownership or
- control and a level of ownership as two separate and necessary conditions.

As reported in paragraph 203 of the FASB ED, nearly all respondents agreed that control is a necessary condition, rejecting ownership without control. However, a majority of respondents supported the third possibility listed above − namely, that both control and a significant level of ownership should be required for determining the existence of a parent–subsidiary relationship. Most of the respondents suggested an ownership level of 50% or more.

The FASB rejected the advice of the respondents, giving a number of reasons (paras. 215–218):

- *There is no link between ownership and control.* The level of ownership does not affect whether a parent controls a subsidiary. An entity can direct the use of the assets of another entity regardless of the level of its direct ownership interest. An analogy can be drawn with the definition of an asset in the IASB Framework. There is no requirement in the definition of an asset for an entity to have ownership in order to have an asset; the requirement is that an entity control the benefits expected to flow from the resource.
- *Stewardship responsibilities.* If an entity is in control of another entity it has a responsibility to be accountable for management of all assets and liabilities under its command.
- *Reporting of risks and benefits.* There are risks associated with controlling an entity, and an entity rarely acquires control of another entity without obtaining significant opportunities to benefit from that control.
- *Not to require consolidation for entities where there is less than 50% ownership would be a significant step backward in the evolution of consolidated financial statements.* The historical development of consolidation has been to move from a legalistic greater than 50% ownership to a more conceptual position of control. To revert back to reliance on ownership percentages is to move backwards in terms of conceptual accounting.

LO 7

19.4.5 Reasons for consolidation

Given the amount of debate on the criterion of consolidation, is there any potential solution to the problem? It seems that there has to be a compromise between those who want unilateral control, which equates to control with greater than 50% ownership, and proponents of effective control. The choice of the criterion for consolidation must be based on the reasons for requiring consolidation; that is, the reasons for requiring the preparation of consolidated financial statements.

A key purpose for all financial reporting is the discharge of accountability. Entities that are responsible or accountable for managing a pool of resources, being the recipients of economic benefits and responsible for paying economic benefits, are generally required to report on their activities, and are held accountable for their management of those activities. Those who are in control of resources are accountable for their use. The definition of control should reflect this aspect of accountability.

The FASB, in its arguments against the use of a joint ownership-control criterion, placed emphasis on the need to consider the qualitative characteristics of accounting information. The requirement to prepare consolidated financial statements must then be associated with the need for that information:

- In paragraph 179 of the FASB ED, it is argued that the consolidated financial statements must *represent as faithfully* as possible the financial position, financial performance and cash flows of a parent and its subsidiaries. These statements must then show all the elements under the control of the parent.
- The consolidated financial statements must provide the information that is *relevant* to the users of those statements. Which entities should be combined with the parent to provide the information needed by users to make their economic decisions?
- The information must be *understandable* to the users, providing information exceeding that provided in the separate financial statements of the entities in the group.
- The information must increase the ability of the users to *compare* the position and performance of the group with other entities that are organised differently such as by the use of divisions and branches.

This emphasis on user needs leads to a consideration of the role of a reporting entity, as the key feature of a reporting entity is the existence of users who are dependent on a set of financial statements to make their economic decisions.

LO 8

19.4.6   The reporting entity concept

What is a reporting entity? Appendix A to IFRS 3 contains the following definition of a reporting entity:

> An entity for which there are users who rely on the entity's general purpose financial statements for information that will be useful to them for making decisions about the allocation of resources. A reporting entity can be a single entity or a group comprising a parent and all of its subsidiaries.

Paragraph 8 of the Framework states that it applies to 'reporting entities', a reporting entity being 'an entity for which there are users who rely on the financial statements as their major source of financial information about the entity'.

The key feature of a reporting entity is therefore the existence of dependent users; that is, when a group is formed as a result of a business combination, it is a reporting entity if there exist users who require information about the group. Consider the situation in figure 19.7 where Entity A acquires all the shares of Entity B, the combined entities forming a group:

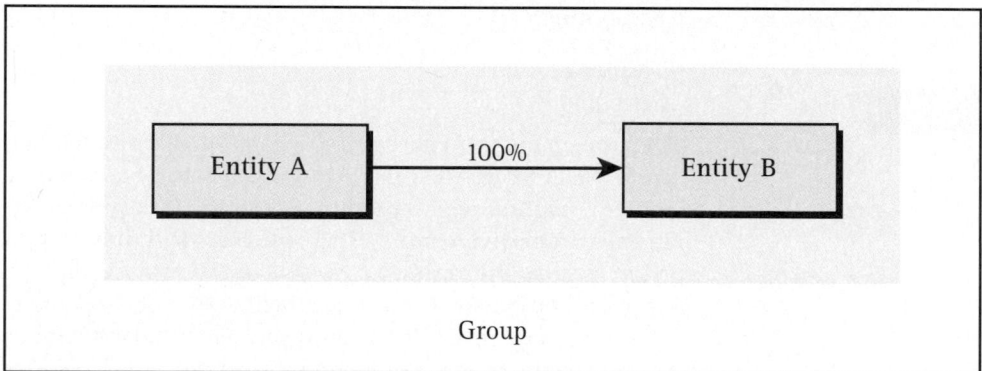

FIGURE 19.7   Combined entities

The law may require each of the individual entities to prepare financial reports about each separate entity, but there may be users of financial information who want information about the group (i.e. the combination of the two legal entities). For example, as Entity A owns all the shares of Entity B, the wealth of the shareholders of Entity A is dependent on the combined performance of both A and B. The combined businesses then become a reporting entity as there are users of financial information who want a financial report on the combined entities A and B.

Who are the users?

Paragraph 9 of the IASB Framework identifies seven user groups that are important in determining the existence of a reporting entity:
- investors
- employees
- lenders
- suppliers and other trade creditors
- customers
- governments and their agencies
- the public.

These users could be classified into the following three groups:
- resource providers: shareholders, employees, suppliers and lenders
- recipients of goods and services: customers
- parties having a review or oversight function: governments, regulatory agencies, unions and the media.

The problem with this listing is that there is no potential user group excluded. All people or entities, regardless of the strength of their link with an entity, can effectively fit within the 'users' category. The difficulty of having such a broad category of users is twofold. First, for an entity's management to attempt to isolate the existence of dependent users, to have to analyse the position with respect to such a broad grouping is very time consuming and costly. Second, the breadth of the grouping introduces many parties that have tenuous relationships with an entity, such as environmental groups.

It should be noted that the users have to be 'dependent users'. There are user groups who, because of their relationship with an entity, are not dependent on the issue of general-purpose financial statements to obtain information about an entity. For example, lenders such as banks often have the capacity to require entities to supply required information, and the entities are willing to do so in order to obtain loans at lower interest rates than if the information were not supplied. The banks are then not dependent users. In Statement of Accounting Concepts 1 (SAC 1) *Definition of the Reporting Entity*, issued by the Australian Accounting Research Foundation in Australia in 1990, a number of factors were given in paragraphs 19–22 to assist in the identification of dependent users:
- *Separation of management from economic interest.* The further the owners are removed from the management of the entity, the more likely it is that the owners will be dependent on the supply of information about the entity.
- *Economic or political importance/influence.* An entity could be economically and politically important for many reasons (e.g. it is involved in a strategic industry such as defence, or in oil and gas production; it is a major employer in a particular part of the country; it is involved in environmentally sensitive areas; it enjoys monopoly privileges or tariff protection). Entities that have dominant positions or privileges will always attract interested parties and potentially dependent users.
- *Financial characteristics.* Characteristics to consider include the amount of debt, number of employees, size of profit, value of sales and value of assets. Users will be attracted to particular characteristics based on their interest in the entity. Investors will be interested in investment, employees in long-term employment and the survival of the entity, suppliers in long-term markets and solvency, and customers in solvency and profitability affecting worth of warranties and after-sales service.

To illustrate the application of the reporting entity concept, consider the economic entity structure in figure 19.8.

Assume A Ltd owns 80% of the issued shares of B Ltd, while B Ltd owns all the issued shares of C Ltd. It should be noted that the ownership interest in B Ltd consists of two parties: the parent interest, A Ltd, of 80% and the minority interest (MI) of 20%. The minority interest shareholders in an entity are the shareholders other than the parent. The question is how many reporting entities are there in figure 19.8?
- It is possible that each of the individual entities A Ltd, B Ltd and C Ltd are each reporting entities. Resource providers, such as employees and creditors, and recipients of goods and

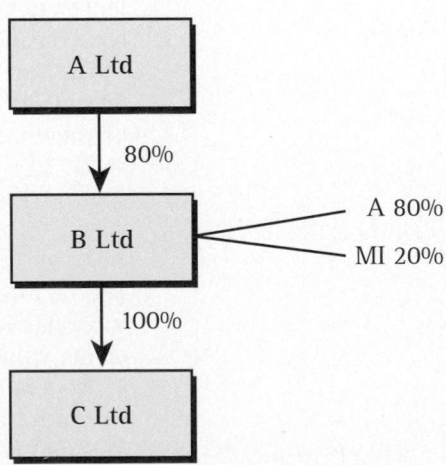

FIGURE 19.8 Reporting entity concept (1)

services, such as customers, would be interested in the financial performance and position of each of the entities as a separate unit. From a shareholder perspective, it is possible that A Ltd is not a reporting entity as the shareholders in A Ltd are more concerned with a report about the combination of entities A Ltd, B Ltd and C Ltd than about the individual performance of A Ltd.

- The combined group of A Ltd, B Ltd and C Ltd is also probably a reporting entity. The wealth and earning capacity of the equity holders in A Ltd is dependent not only on the performance of A Ltd, but also of B Ltd and C Ltd, given the investment that A Ltd has in these entities.

- It is also possible that the group of B Ltd and C Ltd is also a reporting entity. As A Ltd owns only 80% of the shares of B Ltd, there is a minority interest holding in B Ltd of 20%. The minority interest in B Ltd has no financial interest in A Ltd and would be concerned only with the financial performance of the combined grouping of B Ltd and C Ltd.

There are therefore five possible reporting entities in figure 19.8.

If figure 19.8 were changed to that in figure 19.9 such that A Ltd owned all the issued shares of B Ltd, would there be any change in the number of reporting entities? The possible change is whether the group of B Ltd and C Ltd would still be a reporting entity. This is, as per the definition of a reporting entity, determined by identifying the dependent users in relation to that group. Considering shareholders as a possible user group, there are no shareholders who are interested in the group of B Ltd and C Ltd. The shareholders in A Ltd are still interested in the combination of A Ltd, B Ltd and C Ltd. For the group of B Ltd and C Ltd to be a reporting entity, interested parties other than shareholders would need to be identified. As far as lenders are concerned, lenders are often able to demand

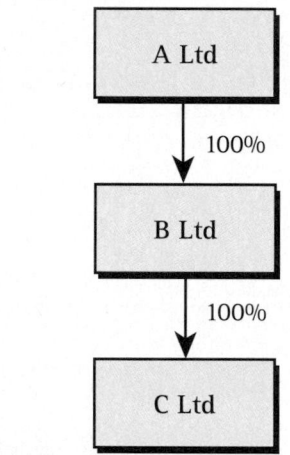

FIGURE 19.9 Reporting entity concept (2)

specific purpose reports and do not qualify as users interested in general-purpose financial reports. Further, lenders are often associated with individual entities rather than economic entities because of the nature of the lending contract. One possible scenario where lenders would be interested in the group of B Ltd and C Ltd would be where a lender to C Ltd has its loan guaranteed by B Ltd. The probability of the lender having the loan repaid is then dependent on the combined resources of B Ltd and C Ltd.

The key question in determining the existence of a reporting entity is whether dependent users can be identified. This will require the exercise of judgement on the part of those charged with preparation and verification of the financial reports of the entity under analysis.

19.4.7 Control and reporting entities

The reporting entity concept can be used to help determine the definition of control for consolidation purposes — the appropriate definition should lead to the financial statements required by the dependent users. Consider the following two situations:

1. Assume A Ltd owns 45% of B Ltd, but adopts a passive position making no effort to control B Ltd. Control is held by another entity, C Ltd, that holds 40% of B Ltd. Hence, A Ltd has the capacity to control but C Ltd actually controls B Ltd on a day-to-day basis. Who should prepare consolidated financial statements: A Ltd or C Ltd? Who is

responsible or accountable for the use of the resources of B Ltd: A Ltd or C Ltd? The answer lies in applying the reporting entity concept. Do the users want consolidated financial statements about A Ltd + B Ltd and/or C Ltd + B Ltd?

2. If A Ltd owns 40% of B Ltd and there are two other shareholders in B Ltd, each holding 30%, it is generally argued that A Ltd does not have the capacity to control B Ltd. Consider the case where A Ltd actually controls B Ltd because the other two investors are passive investors, or have high regard for A Ltd's managerial expertise. A Ltd is then actually controlling the policies of both A Ltd and B Ltd, but does not have the capacity to control. Should A Ltd prepare consolidated financial statements for A Ltd + B Ltd? Application of the reporting entity concept should assist in determining whether there is a need for such a set of financial statements.

As the IASB is currently debating the definition of control for consolidation purposes, it is possible that changes will be made to IAS 27 in the near future.

LO 9

19.5 Presentation of consolidated financial statements

Paragraph 9 of IAS 27 requires all parents – other than those described in paragraph 10 – to present consolidated financial statements.

The exclusion under paragraph 10 of IAS 27 is as follows:

A parent need not present consolidated financial statements if and only if:

(a) the parent itself is a wholly-owned subsidiary or is a partially-owned subsidiary of another entity and its other owners, including those not otherwise entitled to vote, have been informed about, and do not object to, the parent not presenting consolidated financial statements;

(b) the parent's debt or equity securities are not traded in a public market (a domestic or foreign stock exchange or an over-the-counter market, including local and regional markets);

(c) the parent did not file, nor is it in the process of filing, its financial statements with a securities commission or other regulatory organisation for the purpose of issuing any class of securities in a public market; and

(d) the ultimate or any intermediate parent of the parent publishes consolidated financial statements that comply with International Financial Reporting Standards.

The situation envisaged in part (a) of this paragraph is as shown in figure 19.10.

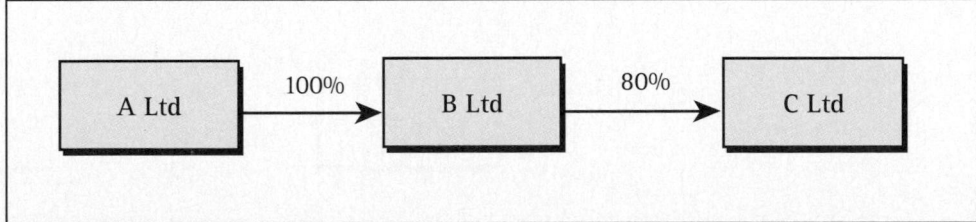

FIGURE 19.10   Wholly-owned subsidiary

The exemption given is in line with the concept of the reporting entity. As discussed in section 19.4.6, the reporting entity concept requires presentation of financial statements only where there are dependent users. In relation to the group of B Ltd and C Ltd, there are no shareholders who require a set of consolidated financial statements for this group. As noted in paragraph 10 of IAS 27, if A Ltd owned, say, 90% of the shares of B Ltd, and B Ltd could obtain the unanimous consent of the 10% minority shareholders then B Ltd again would not have dependent users who would require the preparation of a set of consolidated financial statements for the group of B Ltd and C Ltd.

IAS 27 does not allow a parent to exclude any subsidiary from being included in the consolidated financial statements. Paragraph 12 of IAS 27 requires that the consolidated financial reports include *all* subsidiaries of the parent.

IAS 27 specifically notes some areas where exclusions of subsidiaries from consolidation are *not* permitted, namely, where:
- the business activities of a subsidiary are different from those for other subsidiaries (see IAS 27, para. 20); and
- the investor is not a company, such as a trust, a partnership, a mutual fund or a venture capital organisation.

Similarly, exclusions from consolidation do not exist where:
- there is a large minority interest; or
- there are severe long-term restrictions that impair the ability to transfer funds to the parent.

LO 10   19.6   Parent entities and identification of an acquirer — reverse acquisitions

As noted in chapter 12, accounting for a business combination under the purchase method requires the identification of an acquirer. Paragraph 17 of IFRS 3 states that the 'acquirer is the combining entity that obtains control of the other combining entities or businesses'. Hence, as the criterion for identification of a parent–subsidiary relationship is control, it is expected that when a business combination is formed by the creation of a parent–subsidiary relationship, the parent would be identified as the acquirer. However, paragraphs 21–22 of IFRS 3 refer to situations where the parent is not identified as the acquirer.

Consider the situation in figure 19.11 in which A Ltd and B Ltd combine by the formation of a new entity, C Ltd, which acquires all the shares of both of these entities with the issue of shares in C Ltd. C Ltd controls both A Ltd and B Ltd.

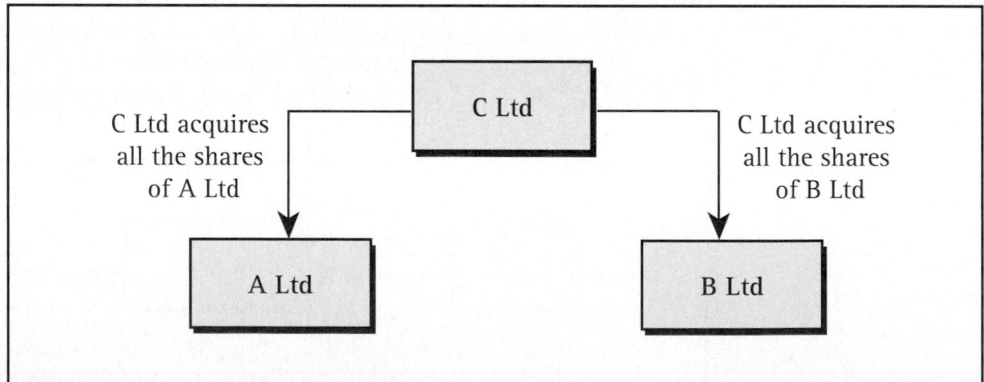

FIGURE 19.11   Identification of an acquirer where new entity formed

Paragraph 22 of IFRS 3 states that when 'a new entity is formed to issue equity instruments to effect a business combination, one of the combining entities that existed before the combination shall be adjudged the acquirer on the evidence available'. In other words, even though C Ltd is acquiring the shares of both A Ltd and B Ltd, it is not to be considered the acquirer; either A Ltd or B Ltd must be considered to be the acquirer. Deciding which entity is the acquirer involves a consideration of such factors as which of the combining entities initiated the combination, and whether the assets and revenues of one of the combining entities significantly exceed those of the others (IFRS 3, para. 23). The reasons for this decision by the IASB are given in paragraphs BC62–BC66 of the Basis of Conclusions on IFRS 3.

The key reason for the IASB's decision is in paragraph BC45. The argument is that the new entity, C Ltd, may have no economic substance, and the accounting result for the combination of the three entities should be the same if A Ltd simply combined with B Ltd without the formation of C Ltd. Paragraph BC65 argues that if this is not the case, 'both comparability and reliability (which rests on the notions of accounting for the substance of transactions and representational faithfulness, i.e. that similar transactions are accounted for in the same way) are diminished'.

However, the problem that then arises in the figure 19.11 scenario is that a choice has to be made: is A Ltd or B Ltd the acquirer? As paragraph BC64 notes, this decision is an arbitrary one, and even the IASB thought the usefulness of the resultant information was questionable. In deciding on which entity is the acquirer, paragraph 20 of IFRS 3 provides some indicators to consider in situations where it may be difficult to identify an acquirer. The entity likely to be the acquirer is the one:

- that has a significantly greater fair value
- that gives up the cash or other assets, in the case where equity instruments are exchanged for cash or other assets, or
- whose management is able to dominate subsequent to the business combination.

The problem with these criteria is that they are arbitrary. Consider, for example, the second of the above criteria involving the exchange of cash or other assets for equity instruments. Why is one form of consideration more important than another in determining an acquirer? They are both simply forms of consideration, selected in the exchange as the form necessary to make the deal as the consideration appeals to the other party involved in the deal.

A further situation considered in paragraph 21 of IFRS 3 is the 'reverse acquisition' form of business combination. Consider the situation in figure 19.12.

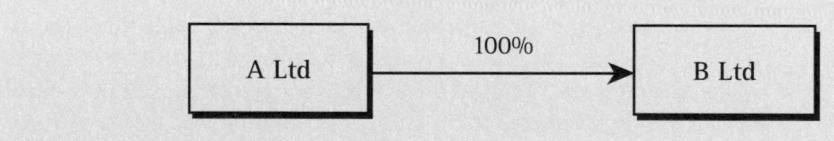

Prior to business combination
Share capital – 100 shares   Share capital – 60 shares
Fair value per share – $12   Fair value per share – $40

Terms of combination
A Ltd issues 2.5 shares in exchange for each B Ltd share.
Hence, A Ltd issues 150 shares to the former shareholders of B Ltd.

Subsequent to combination
A Ltd holds all the shares in B Ltd.
The holders of shares in A Ltd consist of the holders of the 100 shares existing prior to the business combination, and the former shareholders of B Ltd who now hold 150 shares in A Ltd.

FIGURE 19.12 Reverse acquisition

A Ltd acquired all the shares in B Ltd, and B Ltd can therefore legally control the financial and operating policies of B Ltd. However, an analysis of the shareholding in A Ltd shows that the former shareholders of B hold 60% (i.e. 150/250) of the shares of

A Ltd. Some argue that the substance of the business combination is that B Ltd has really taken over A Ltd because the former shareholders of B Ltd are in control. Paragraph 21 of IFRS 3 provides a further example of a reverse acquisition:

> In some business combinations, commonly referred to as reverse acquisitions, the acquirer is the entity whose equity interests have been acquired and the issuing entity is the acquiree. This might be the case when, for example, a private entity arranges to have itself 'acquired' by a smaller public entity as a means of obtaining a stock exchange listing. Although legally the issuing public entity is regarded as the parent and the private entity is regarded as the subsidiary, the legal subsidiary is the acquirer if it has the power to govern the financial and operating policies of the legal parent so as to obtain benefits from its activities.

The problem with the reverse acquisitions argument is that it relies on an analysis of which *shareholders* control the decision making; that is, the acquiring entity is the one whose *owners* control the combined entity and who have the power to govern the financial and operating policies of the entity so as to obtain benefits from its activities.

The accounting for reverse acquisitions is covered in chapter 20.

LO 11

19.7 Concepts of consolidation

Having decided on the criterion for consolidation, and hence the definitions of 'parent' and 'subsidiary', a further decision made by standard setters is the choice of a concept of consolidation. The accounting literature makes reference to many concepts of consolidation; the most common are the proprietary concept, the parent entity concept and the entity concept.

Differences in consolidation arise under these concepts only if the parent does not own all the equity in a subsidiary; in other words if a minority interest exists. The term 'minority interest' is defined in IAS 27 paragraph 4 as follows:

> Minority interest is that portion of the profit or loss and net assets of a subsidiary attributable to equity interests that are not owned, directly or indirectly through subsidiaries, by the parent.

In figure 19.13, it can be seen that in B Ltd the parent has an ownership interest of 60% and there is a minority interest (MI) of 40%. Similarly in Y Ltd there is a parent interest of 35% and a MI of 65%. Even though it is termed a 'minority' interest, the percentage interest could be greater than that of the parent because the criterion for consolidation is control and not ownership interest. The meaning and measurement of the MI are discussed in more detail in chapters 22–23.

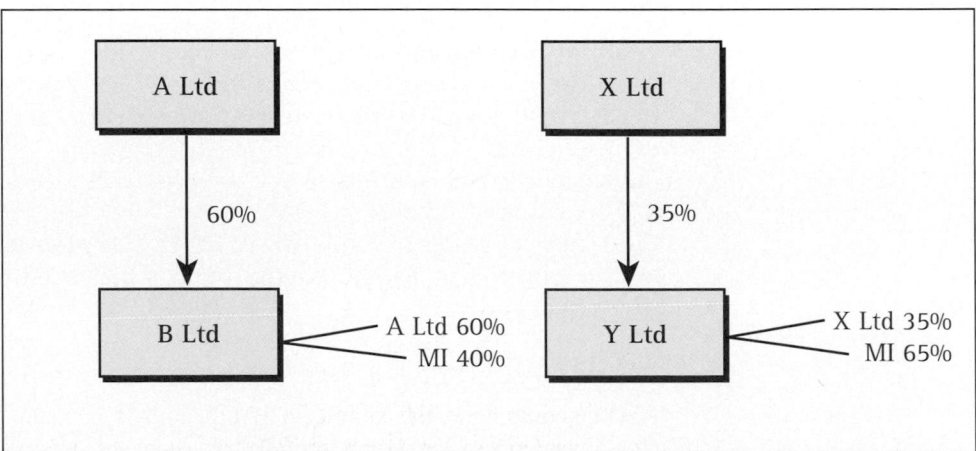

FIGURE 19.13   Minority interest

The main areas affected in the preparation of consolidated financial statements by the choice of concept of consolidation are:

- *the assets and liabilities of a subsidiary included in the consolidated financial statements*. This relates to whether all the net assets of a subsidiary are included in the consolidated group or just those attributable to the parent interest.
- *the classification of the MI as equity or liability, and the measurement of the MI*. The consolidated assets consist of the sum of the assets of the parent and those of the subsidiaries. The choice of concept affects the amount shown as total consolidated liabilities and equity, since the choice of concept affects the category into which the MI is placed as well as the calculation of the amount of the MI.
- *the adjustments for the effects of transactions within the group*. The consolidated financial statements show the performance and financial position of the group in its dealings with parties external to the group. Where, for example, profits are made by one part of the group, such as a subsidiary, in selling inventory to another part of the group, such as the parent, the effects of these transactions must be eliminated with adjustments being made to the profits recorded by the subsidiary. The choice of concept affects whether all the profit on such transactions is adjusted for or whether only part of the profit is eliminated.

No specific concept of consolidation is explicitly recognised in IAS 27. However, the accounting treatments adopted in IAS 27 are consistent with the adoption of the entity concept of consolidation. In this chapter, only a brief outline of the alternative concepts of consolidation is given. A more detailed analysis can be found in Leo (1987) and Pacter (1991).

19.7.1 Entity concept of consolidation

Under this concept:

- the group consists of the assets and liabilities of the parent as well as all the assets and liabilities of the subsidiaries
- the MI is classified as an equity holder or contributor of capital to the group in the same capacity as the equity holders of the parent.

Diagrammatically, the group under the entity concept is as shown in figure 19.14.

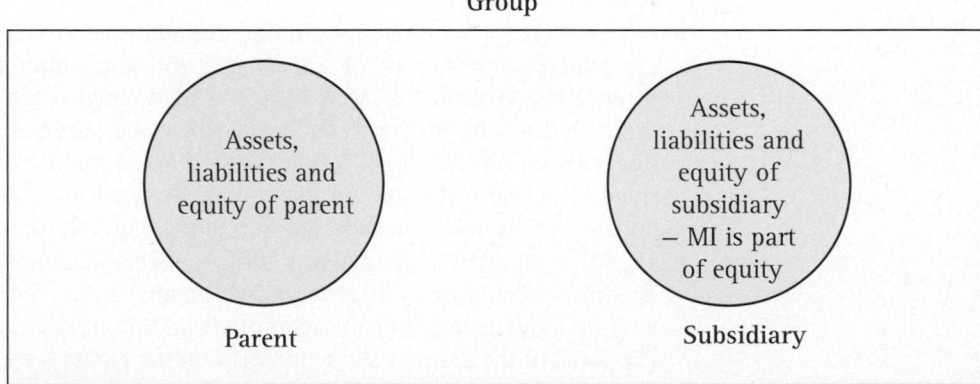

FIGURE 19.14   Group under the entity concept

The implications of adopting the entity concept of consolidation to the preparation of the consolidated financial statements are as follows:

- Where there are transactions between members of the group, the effects of these transactions are adjusted in full, as required by paragraph 17 of IAS 27 (see chapter 21 for a detailed discussion). This accords with the view that the consolidated financial statements should show the results of transactions between the group and parties external to the group. The adjustments are then unaffected by the extent of the parent's ownership interest in the subsidiary.

- As the MI is classified as a contributor of equity to the group, it is disclosed in the equity section of the consolidated financial statements, as per paragraphs 68 and 82 of IAS 1 *Presentation of Financial Statements* and paragraph 33 of IAS 27.
- Because of the classification of the MI as equity, its measurement is based on a share of consolidated equity and not on a share of the recorded equity of the subsidiary in which the MI ownership interest is held (discussed in more detail in chapter 19).

19.7.2 Parent entity concept of consolidation

Under the parent entity concept:
- The consolidated group consists of the assets and liabilities of the parent and all the assets and liabilities of the subsidiaries.
- The MI is classified as a liability.

Diagrammatically, the group under the parent entity concept is as shown in figure 19.15.

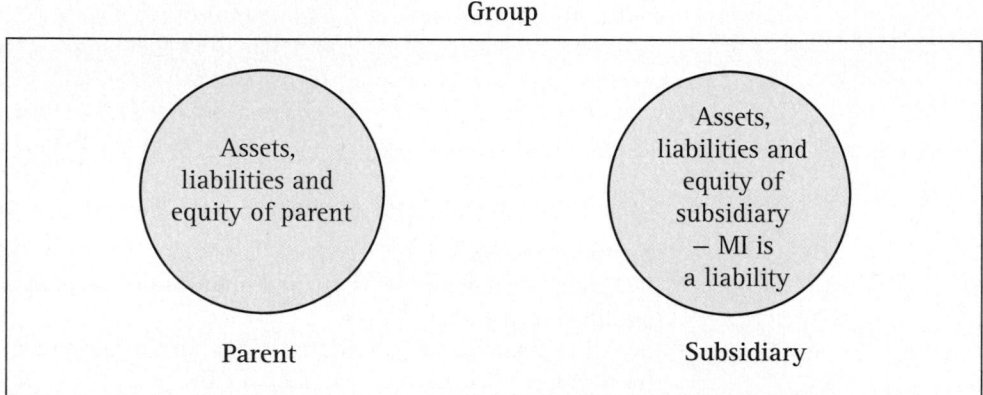

FIGURE 19.15   Group under the parent entity concept

Under this concept:
- Adjustments for transactions within the group involve both partial (i.e. to the extent of the parent's interest in the subsidiary) and total elimination procedures. Only the parent's share of the intragroup profit is eliminated where the subsidiary is the selling entity, but all the profit is eliminated where the parent is the seller. The rationale for this is based on the classification of the MI as a liability, and the need to increase the share of the MI when the subsidiary makes a profit on transacting with the parent. The justification is based on the need to report accurately the liability to the MI.
- The MI is reported in the liability section of the balance sheet.
- The MI is calculated as its proportionate share of the recorded equity of the subsidiary, with no adjustments for transactions within the group.

The focus of the parent entity concept is on the parent's equity holders as the prime user group. All controlled assets and liabilities are included in the consolidated financial statements, but the claim by the parent's equity holders is net of the liability claim of the MI.

19.7.3 Proprietary concept of consolidation

This concept is sometimes referred to as proportional consolidation or pro-rata consolidation. Under the proprietary concept:
- The group consists of the assets and liabilities of the parent and the parent's proportional share of the assets and liabilities of the subsidiary. Hence, the consolidated financial statements do not include all the net assets of a subsidiary, only the parent's share.

- As the MI is outside the group, the MI share of subsidiary equity is not disclosed, and neither is the MI share of the net assets of the subsidiary.

Diagrammatically, the group under the proprietary concept is as shown in figure 19.16.

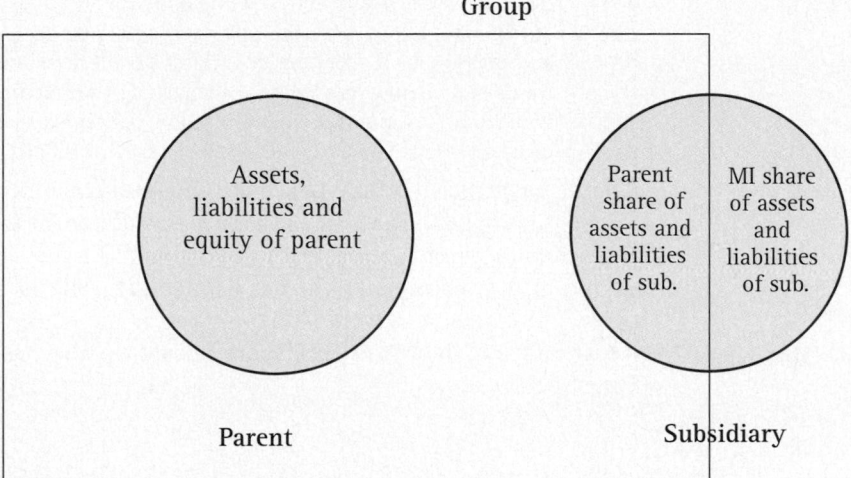

FIGURE 19.16   Group under the proprietary concept

Under this concept:

- Transactions between the parent and the subsidiary are adjusted proportionally (i.e. to the extent of the parent's ownership interest in the subsidiary).
- MI is not disclosed.

19.7.4 Choice of concept

As noted earlier in this section, the IASB has effectively chosen the entity concept of consolidation. The main reasons for this would probably be (it is not possible to be definitive about the reasons, as the IASB has not stated any reasons) that under the entity concept:

- The consolidated financial statements include all the assets and liabilities of the group. Given the choice of control as the criterion for consolidation, it seems appropriate that all the consolidated financial statements include all the assets under the control of the parent.
- The MI does not fit into the definition of a liability under the IASB Framework. The group has no obligation to outlay resources to the MI. The MI has the same claim on the net assets of a subsidiary, as does the parent. The MI does not have a priority claim, which is normally the case with liability claims. In the Basis for Conclusions to IAS 27, the IASB made the following comments in relation to the MI:

BC24.   The Board decided to amend this requirement and to require minority interests to be presented in the consolidated balance sheet within equity, separately from the parent shareholders' equity. The Board noted that a minority interest is not a liability of a group because it does not meet the definition of a liability in the *Framework for the Preparation and Presentation of Financial Statements*.

BC25.   Paragraph 49(b) of the *Framework* states that a liability is a present obligation of the entity arising from past events, the settlement of which is expected to result in an outflow from the entity of resources embodying economic benefits. Paragraph 60 of the *Framework* further indicates that an essential characteristic of a liability is that the entity has a present obligation and that an obligation is a duty or responsibility to act or perform in a particular way. The Board noted that the existence of a minority interest in the net assets of a subsidiary does not give rise to a present obligation of the group, the settlement of which is expected to result in an outflow of economic benefits from the group.

BC26. Rather, the Board noted that a minority interest represents the residual interest in the net assets of those subsidiaries held by some of the shareholders of the subsidiaries within the group, and therefore meets the *Framework's* definition of equity. Paragraph 49(c) of the *Framework* states that equity is the residual interest in the assets of the entity after deducting all its liabilities.

BC27. The Board acknowledged that this decision gives rise to questions about the recognition and measurement of minority interest but it concluded that as further deliberations would not change its conclusion regarding their appropriate classification, there was no need to postpone its implementation. It decided that the recognition and measurement questions should be addressed as part of its project on business combinations.

One of the members of the IASB, Tatsumi Yamada, dissented on the issue of IAS 27. In his dissenting opinion, Mr Yamada argued that the IASB is taking the entity view without giving enough consideration to the fundamental issues of what information should be provided in the consolidated financial statements, and to whom the information is being provided. This requires an in-depth analysis of the objectives of consolidation. Since the issue of IAS 27, there has been more debate on the choice of concept. This debate is outlined below.

19.8 Exposure drafts on consolidation

In June 2005, the IASB issued *Exposure Draft on Proposed Amendments to IAS 27 Consolidated and Separate Financial Statements*. At the same time, the FASB issued its *Exposure Draft on Consolidated Financial Statements, Including Accounting and Reporting of Noncontrolling Interests in Subsidiaries*. Although the FASB ED covered similar material to that of the IASB, and both EDs were issued as part of the joint convergence project between the IASB and the FASB on business combinations, the FASB ED was not drafted jointly with the IASB.

Unfortunately, the comment letters to the IASB ED are not available to the public. However, the FASB received 49 responses to its ED, and these are available on its website. In general, the respondents did not support the changes proposed by the FASB, preferring the current practice to the changes proposed. Two key issues arising from the ED were the classification and disclosure of the minority interest (MI) and the adoption of the entity versus the parent entity concept of consolidation. It is these two issues that are commented on in this section.

 WEBLINK

The comment letters can be found on the FASB website at
<www.fasb.org/ocl/fasb-getletters.php?project=1204-001> and
<www.fasb.org/ocl/fasb-getletters.php?project=1205-001>.

19.8.1 Classification of the MI

A majority of the respondents to the FASB's ED disagreed with the proposal that the non-controlling equity interest in the subsidiaries, the MI, should be classified as equity in the consolidated group. There were a number of differing reasons given by respondents for reaching this conclusion:

- Although the MI does not meet the definition of a liability, it is still not equity to the group. Proponents of this approach included Microsoft and ACLI (the American Council of Life Insurers):

  ... we disagree with the Board's conclusion that shares of a consolidated subsidiary that represent the noncontrolling interests should be accounted for and reported as equity of the consolidated entity.

> While we agree with the Board that noncontrolling interests do not meet the current definition of liabilities ... we believe it is compelling that a substantial majority of respondents to the consolidations ED and the liabilites and equity ED asserted that noncontrolling interests are not equity interests in consolidated financial statements (Microsoft 2005, p. 1).

> We concur with the FASB's suggestion that the liability does not represent a liability as defined in FASB Concept Statement No. 6. We also believe, though, that noncontrolling interests do not fit within the definition of equity. We do not agree with the Board's conclusion that noncontrolling interests own a residual interest in a component of consolidated equity (ACLI 2005, p. 1).

- The MI is not equity, primarily because the MI does not comprise residual equity holders and, although the MI holders have an equity interest in a specific subsidiary, they do not have an interest in the consolidated group. Representatives of this view were Wells Fargo and Royal Dutch Shell plc:

> We believe that noncontrolling interests do not meet the definition of equity because they do not have an ownership interest in the consolidated equity of the company. Equity reflected in consolidated financial statements should include only equity owned by the shareholders of the parent company. Holders of noncontrolling interests are not shareholders of the company and their interests should not be classified as equity (Wells Fargo 2005, p. 1).

> We do not believe that the noncontrolling interest is or should be considered simply as part of equity. Preparers and users of financial statements focus on the parent's interest and therefore balances and transactions with the minority interest should continue to be seen as in effect with a third party (Royal Dutch Shell 2005, p. 2).

- The MI is neither equity nor a liability, but should be disclosed between liabilities and equity, the so-called mezzanine treatment, which is probably the most common form of disclosure used in the United States. Supporters of this view were Dennis Beresford (former chair of the FASB) and Citigroup:

> First, the Board states that there is diversity in practice for the accounting for minority interests in subsidiaries. However, as the Board notes, most companies report minority interests in between liabilities and equity in balance sheets, to reflect the fact that these amounts don't mesh nicely with the notions of liabilities or of equity of the shareholders of the reporting company. Companies reporting these amounts as liabilities probably do so only because the amounts are so small that a separate caption isn't warranted. Thus, I'm not sure that practice is all that diverse for minority interests. It is understandable that the Board does not wish to explicitly endorse the long-standing, so-called mezzanine treatment for minority interests, but simply leaving this matter alone would be better than the changes proposed (Beresford 2005, p. 2).

> We disagree with the classification of noncontrolling interests as equity of the consolidated entity. The proposed classification would imply that noncontrolling interest holders have an interest in the consolidated group – a conclusion we disagree with under a parent company view ... We recommend that the FASB mandate the classification of noncontrolling interest as a 'mezzanine item' between liabilities and equity (Citigroup 2005, p. 3).

- Some supported the mezzanine view, suggesting to the FASB that it complete its conceptual framework projects prior to reaching a definite conclusion to this debate. This view was presented by Deloitte:

> We agree with the FASB's conclusion that a noncontrolling interest in a consolidated subsidiary does not represent a liability. However, we do not believe that until the FASB completes its analysis of noncontrolling interests under its conceptual framework project it is appropriate to conclude that a noncontrolling interest represents an ownership interest in the consolidated entity. We note that these interests do not represent residual equity in the consolidated equity. Therefore, we question the conclusion that noncontrolling interests

must be equity because they are not liabilities. As such, we believe that the current practice of presenting such amounts between liabilities and equity provides useful information to financial statement users, and, therefore, should be retained for the present time (Deloitte 2005, p. 3).

- Support for completion of the Conceptual Framework projects was given by PricewaterhouseCoopers, with the suggestion that this may result in the MI being classified as a different type of equity interest:

  > We agree with the Boards' view that a non-controlling interest in a subsidiary is an equity interest and that most non-controlling interests do not meet the definition of a liability in the conceptual frameworks. Nonetheless, we believe that the consolidated financial statements should only include parent company equity in the equity section of the balance sheet. Non-controlling interests are a different type of equity interest, separate and distinct from the equity interests of the parent entity shareholders. We therefore believe the conceptual framework should be enhanced to include another category of equity to be presented separately from consolidated equity (PricewaterhouseCoopers 2005, appendix A, p. 2).

- Many commentators to the ED believed that disclosure of the MI as equity would lead to the provision of less relevant information to users of the consolidated financial statements. This was the view expressed by Wells Fargo and ACLI:

  > We are very concerned that classification of noncontrolling interests as equity in consolidated financial statements will significantly reduce the transparency and relevance of financial information provided to financial statement users ... We are concerned with the impact that including noncontrolling interests in consolidated equity and reporting net income for the entire economic entity, including the noncontrolling interests, will have on key financial ratios for a financial services company. These ratios include regulatory capital ratios, leverage ratios and profitability ratios calculated using consolidated equity balances (Wells Fargo 2005, p. 2).

  > We believe that this view of equity is a departure from the view of users of financial statements including regulatory agencies and stockholders. We further believe that this disconnect has a high likelihood of misleading users of financial statements (ACLI 2005, p. 1)

- Other respondents were willing to accept that the MI should be classified as equity. However, acceptance of this view was then not to be seen as support for adoption of the economic entity view and the resultant accounting for changes in movements in shareholdings by parties within the group. KPMG and Ernst & Young made comments along these lines:

  > We do not object to the proposal and current requirement in IAS 27 that noncontrolling interests be included in consolidated equity (which represents a change from current practice in the US of presenting noncontrolling interests outside of equity) if presented separately from the parent company's equity. However, classification of noncontrolling interests in equity should only relate to presentation and not be regarded as an argument for an economic entity approach which in our view is not an appropriate basis for preparing the consolidated financial statements of the parent company (KPMG 2005, p. 4).

  > While we agree with the Boards that noncontrolling interests do not meet the definition of a liability in the IASB Framework/FASB Concepts Statements, we are not convinced that this should necessarily lead to the rejection of the parent company extension concept in favour of the economic entity concept (Ernst & Young 2005, pp. 2–3).

It would seem then the FASB will have a hard job in the short term, particularly prior to the completion of its Conceptual Framework projects, to convince its constituents that the MI should be accounted for as equity of the consolidated group.

Although the comment letters to the IASB are not made public, it would appear that the IASB received a similar message from its constituents. In their responses to the *Exposure Draft of Proposed Amendments to IFRS 3 Business Combinations* (the Amendments ED; see chapter 12), European commentators replied to the FASB as well as to the

IASB because this was a joint project between the IASB and the FASB, with the FASB publishing the responses on its website. Some of the responses to the classification of the MI as equity from European constituents were as follows:

> Whilst we agree with the Board that non-controlling interests do not meet the definition of a liability as per the IASB Framework/FASB Concepts Statements, we are not convinced that this fact alone should lead to the rejection of the parent company approach in favour of the economic entity approach (South African Institute of Chartered Accountants 2005, p. 2)

> - Owners of the parent entity control the entire group, whereas minority shareholders have only interests in a particular subsidiary ...
> - We agree that non-controlling interests should be presented as equity because they do not meet the definition of a liability. However, we do not believe that controlling interests and non-controlling interests should be treated equivalently in determining net income (Accounting Standards Board of Japan 2005, p. 2).

> We agree that non-controlling interests do not meet the definition of a liability. However, we do not accept that ... it follows that an economic entity view has to be applied. In our view the economic entity view issue is of much broader dimension and we disagree with the proposal mainly for the reason that it moves away from the fundamental objective of financial statements, which is primarily providing information to the shareholders of the parent entity (European Financial Reporting Advisory Group (EFRAG) 2005, p. 4).

19.8.2 Economic entity versus parent entity concepts

Just as the comment letters expressed disapproval for the proposed changes in relation to MI, the letters were equally loud in their lack of support for the economic entity concept. Reasons given for this view were:

- Lack of decision-usefulness of the economic concept

> The economic unit concept introduced in the ED further obfuscates the understandability and therefore the usefulness of financial statements. Investors use financial statements to predict the rate of return on their investments in the parent company. To reflect more than is economically owned by the parent company in the financial statements results in confusion, at a minimum. We are not aware of any investor need for such a dramatic change to current practice (PepsiCo 2005, p. 1).

> However, nearly a quarter century of research and deliberations on these matters has not resulted in final decisions in this area. And the consolidation practices that would result from this ED and the related one on Business Combinations would be much more complicated than at present while producing arguably less useful financial information ... the economic unit theory for consolidation has never received much support vs the much more widely accepted view of consolidation based on the parent company theory. In particular, I believe there is an extensive record that users of financial statements such as equity analysts and credit officers in lending institutions are far more interested in financial information from the parent company's perspective than they are in economic unit financial information ... The bottom line seems to be that the Board is more concerned with what it views as conceptual purity than useful information (Beresford 2005, pp. 1, 3).

- Lack of sufficient research demonstrating any conceptual superiority for the entity concept

> In that regard, we believe that the Boards need to explain in greater detail the accounting theory and conceptual support for each approach and the reasons why the economic entity view of consolidated financial statements is believed by the Boards to be superior to the parent company view ... In summary, we do not believe that the Boards have either carried out sufficient due process or made a sufficiently compelling case for the adoption of the 'economic entity' approach rather than the 'parent company' approach (Ernst & Young 2005, pp. 3, 4).

We are not aware that financial statement users have expressed significant concern about the parent company approach used to account for business combinations and to prepare consolidated financial statements. Additionally, we are not aware of a body of research that supports the decision-usefulness of the economic entity approach and the resulting use of full fair value in accounting for business combinations ...

However, we believe that the parent–company approach as defined in that same document provides more relevant information to users of the consolidated financial statements because it allows users of consolidated financial statements to understand the investment of the parent in the acquired entity (KPMG 2005, p. 2).

Various proposals on consolidation policy and procedures have been issued over the years and all have invariably relied upon the 'economic unit' theory. In our experience, most constituents, including analysts and other financial statement users, favour a parent company approach to financial reporting ... only after accepting that the 'economic unit' view is conceptually superior to the 'parent company' view can one accept many of the conclusions reached in this Proposal. We strongly favour the 'parent company' view as being the most relevant to both current and future investors, though we acknowledge that no consensus has yet been reached despite decades of debate (Citigroup 2005, p. 1).

Again, it was not only US constituents who favoured the parent entity approach. This was evident also in many of the responses by non-American commentators to the Amendments ED:

The proposed standard is predicated on the economic entity concept of consolidated financial statements. Whether this concept is the preferable one seems to us to be a precursor question to determining the accounting for the establishment of a parent–subsidiary relationship, such as occurs in a business combination ... If the Board is going to move forward with the economic entity concept, then we believe it needs to make the case for this approach, and in doing so to consider the direction(s) of its other projects, such as Performance Reporting (International Organization of Securities Commissions (IOSCO 2005, p. 2).

In particular, the case must be made why the entity view of the reporting entity, on which the proposed model is based, provides superior information for investors and creditors of the parent company (Canadian Accounting Standards Board 2005, p. 2).

We support the parent entity view from the viewpoint of usefulness of the information provided to investors. In our view, the purpose of consolidated financial statements is to report net income, that is, changes in equity attributable to owners of the parent entity other than changes arising from direct transactions with shareholders (Accounting Standards Board of Japan 2005, p. 1).

The ASB continues to believe that the 'parent entity approach' provides a better focus for financial reporting than the entity approach ... the primary objective of consolidated financial statements is to provide information about the financial performance of an entity to the investors in the parent entity (Accounting Standards Board UK, p. 2).

GASB noted that these proposed amendments are in line with the fair value approach as well as the entity theory the IASB pursues. But unfortunately these concepts have not been discussed on a more conceptual basis beforehand. From our point of view it is not obvious that the proposed changes are in the interest of investors and investment analysts (German Accounting Standards Board 2005, p. 3).

As noted in particular in the comments by Dennis R Beresford, there has been much debate over many years on the nature of the consolidated group and the interrelationships between the various interests in that group. It is not going to be an easy task for either the IASB or the FASB to convince constituents that there is an obvious answer to the issues. To try and introduce solutions via the Phase II Business Combinations project was probably not the best approach. Conceptual solutions with open debate would be a better approach.

19.9 Format of consolidated financial statements

The format of the consolidated financial statements is the same as that for single entities, as per IAS 1 *Presentation of Financial Statements* (discussed in chapter 16). The only additional requirements are in relationship to the disclosure of the MI.

Paragraph 33 of IAS 27 states:

Minority interests shall be presented in the consolidated balance sheet within equity, separately from the parent shareholders' equity. Minority interests in the profit or loss of the group shall also be separately disclosed.

These disclosures link with that in IAS 1. According to paragraph 82 of IAS 1:

The following items shall be disclosed on the face of the income statement as allocations of profit or loss for the period:
(a) profit or loss attributable to minority interest; and
(b) profit or loss attributable to equity holders of the parent.

Figure 19.17 demonstrates this form of disclosure.

Consolidated income statement (extract) for the year ended 30 June 2006	2006 $000	2005 $000
Profit before tax	X	X
Income tax expense	X	X
Profit for the period	X	X
Attributable to:		
Equity holders of the parent	X	X
Minority interest	X	X
	X	X

FIGURE 19.17 Illustrative disclosures of MI in the consolidated income statement

In the consolidated statement of changes in equity, IAS 1 paragraph 96 requires the disclosure of:

(c) total income and expense for the period ... showing separately the total amounts attributable to equity holders of the parent and to minority interest.

There are various formats for the statement of changes in equity. However, the format illustrated in the Guidance on Implementing IAS 1 is shown in figure 19.18.

Consolidated statement of changes in equity (extract) for the year ended 30 June 2006		Attributable to equity holders of the parent				Minority interest	Total equity
	Share capital	Other reserves	Translation reserve	Accumulated profits	Total		
Balance at 1 July 2005	X	X	X	X	X	X	X
Profit for the period				X	X	X	X

FIGURE 19.18 Illustrative disclosures of MI in the consolidated statement of changes in equity

Note that the information required by paragraph 96(c) could be provided as shown in figure 19.19 overleaf.

Consolidated statement of changes in equity (extract) for the year ended 30 June 2006	Consolidated	Parent
Net income recognised directly in equity	X	X
Profit for the period	X	X
Total recognised income and expense for the period	X	X
Attributable to:		
Members of the parent	X	X
Minority interest	X	X
	X	X

FIGURE 19.19   Illustrative disclosures of MI in the consolidated statement of changes in equity

In relation to the information required by paragraph 97 concerning movements in the equity accounts, only the consolidated figures are required. However, it is expected that most entities will disclose both a consolidated and a parent column as in figure 19.19.

Paragraph 68 of IAS 1 states:

As a minimum, the face of the balance sheet shall include line items that present the following amounts:

...

(o) minority interest, presented within equity; and

(p) issued capital and reserves attributable to equity holders of the parent.

Figure 19.20 illustrates this disclosure in the consolidated balance sheet.

Consolidated balance sheet (extract) as at 30 June 2006	2006 $000	2005 $000
EQUITY AND LIABILITIES		
Equity attributable to equity holders of the parent		
Share capital	X	X
Other reserves	X	X
Retained earnings	X	X
	X	X
Minority interest	X	X
Total equity	X	X

FIGURE 19.20   Illustrative disclosures of MI in the consolidated balance sheet

19.9.1 Other disclosures required by IAS 27

Paragraph 40 of IAS 27 requires the following disclosures in the consolidated financial statements:

(c) the nature of the relationship between the parent and a subsidiary of which the parent does not own, directly or indirectly through subsidiaries, more than half of the voting power;

(d) the reasons why the ownership, directly or indirectly through subsidiaries, of more than half of the voting or potential voting power of an investee does not constitute control;

(e) the reporting date of the financial statements of a subsidiary when such financial statements are used to prepare consolidated financial statements and are as of a reporting date or for a period that is different from that of the parent, and the reason for using a different reporting date or different period; and

(f) the nature and extent of any significant restrictions (e.g. resulting from borrowing arrangements or regulatory requirements) on the ability of subsidiaries to transfer funds to the parent in the form of cash dividends or to repay loans or advances.

Where, in accordance with paragraph 10 of IAS 27, an entity elects not to prepare consolidated financial statements, paragraph 41 requires the following disclosures in the separate financial statements of the parent:

(a) the fact that the financial statements are separate financial statements; that the exemption from consolidation has been used; the name and country of incorporation or residence of the entity whose consolidated financial statements that comply with International Financial Reporting Standards have been produced for public use; and the address where those consolidated financial statements are obtainable;

(b) a list of significant investments in subsidiaries, jointly controlled entities and associates, including the name, country of incorporation or residence, proportion of ownership interest and, if different, proportion of voting power held; and

(c) a description of the method used to account for the investments listed under (b).

Other than those parent entities applying paragraph 10, in the separate financial statements of a parent, the following disclosures are required by paragraph 42:

(a) the fact that the statements are separate financial statements and the reasons why those statements are prepared if not required by law;

(b) a list of significant investments in subsidiaries, jointly controlled entities and associates, including the name, country of incorporation or residence, proportion of ownership interest and, if different, proportion of voting power held; and

(c) a description of the method used to account for the investments listed under (b);

and shall identify the financial statements prepared in accordance with paragraph 9 of this Standard, IAS 28 and IAS 31 to which they relate.

19.10   Summary

The effect of many business combinations is that there are situations where there are a number of entities under the control of a single management. Users of financial information about those entities are provided with more relevant information when the financial statements of those entities are consolidated into one set of financial statements: the consolidated financial statements. Although there is still debate within the financial community concerning the criteria for consolidation, the predominant view is that control, being the power to govern the financial and operating policies, is the key determinant. Under the accounting standards, consolidated financial statements are required where parent–subsidiary organisational structures exist. Assessment of whether one entity, the parent, controls another entity, the subsidiary, is a subjective decision and requires an in-depth understanding of the concept of control. IAS 27 provides definitions and disclosures in relation to the preparation of consolidated financial statements. As the IASB is currently debating the definition of control, IAS 27 could be subject to change in the near future.

1. What is a subsidiary?

2. What is meant by the term 'control'?

3. Why should control be the key criterion for consolidation?

4. For what purposes are the consolidated financial statements prepared?

5. What factors could be considered in determining when one entity controls another?

6. Should potential voting rights be considered when deciding if one entity controls another?

7. How does the reporting entity concept affect the determination of whether an entity should prepare consolidated financial statements?

8. Should the minority interest be classified as a liability or as equity?

9. What is meant by the entity concept? How does the choice of this concept affect the preparation of consolidated financial statements?

10. What is meant by the parent entity concept? How does the choice of this concept affect the preparation of consolidated financial statements?

11. Should the IASB choose the parent entity or the entity concept of consolidation?

12. Where should the minority interest be disclosed in the consolidated balance sheet?

13. Which users of financial statements would be interested in consolidated financial statements rather than just the financial statements of the entities within a group?

14. Should only those entities in which another entity owns more than 50% of the issued shares be classified as subsidiaries?

15. What benefits could be sought by an entity that obtains control over another entity?

16. Koriyama Ltd establishes Tokyo Ltd for the sole purpose of developing a new product to be manufactured and marketed by Koriyama Ltd. Koriyama Ltd engages Mr Smith to lead the team to develop the new product. Mr Smith is named Managing Director of Tokyo Ltd at an annual salary of $100 000, $10 000 of which is advanced to Mr Smith by Tokyo Ltd at the time Tokyo Ltd is established. Mr Smith invests $10 000 in the project and receives all of Tokyo Ltd's initial issue of ten shares of voting ordinary shares.

Koriyama Ltd transfers $500 000 to Tokyo Ltd in exchange for 7%, ten-year debentures convertible at any time into 500 shares of Tokyo Ltd voting ordinary shares. Tokyo Ltd has enough shares authorised to fulfil its obligation if Koriyama Ltd converts its debentures into voting ordinary shares.

The constitution of Tokyo Ltd provides certain powers for the holders of voting common shares and the holders of securities convertible into voting ordinary shares that require a majority of each class voting separately. These include:

(a) The power to amend the corporate purpose of Tokyo Ltd, and

(b) The power to authorise and issue voting shares of securities convertible into voting shares.

At the time Tokyo Ltd is established, there are no known economic legal impediments to Koriyama Ltd converting the debt.

Required

Discuss whether Tokyo Ltd is a subsidiary of Koriyama Ltd.

Source: Adapted from Case V issued by the FASB as a part of its Consolidations project.

17. Nagoya Ltd is a production company that produces movies and television shows. It also owns cable television systems that broadcast its movies and television shows. Nagoya Ltd transferred its cable assets and the shares in its previously owned and recently acquired cable television systems, which broadcast Nagoya Ltd's movies, to Kyoto Ltd. Kyoto Ltd assumed approximately $200 million in debt related to certain of the companies it acquired in the transaction. After the transfer date, Kyoto Ltd acquired additional cable television systems, incurring approximately $2 billion of debt, none of which was guaranteed by Nagoya Ltd.

Kyoto Ltd was initially established as a wholly-owned subsidiary of Nagoya Ltd. Several months after the transfer, Kyoto Ltd issued ordinary shares in an initial public offering, raising nearly $1 billion in cash and reducing Nagoya Ltd's interest in Kyoto Ltd to 41%. The remaining 59% of Kyoto Ltd's voting interest is widely held.

The president of Kyoto Ltd was formerly vice-president of broadcast operations for Nagoya Ltd. Half the directors of Kyoto Ltd are or were executive officers of Nagoya Ltd.

Kyoto Ltd and its subsidiaries have entered individually into broadcast contracts with Nagoya Ltd, pursuant to which Kyoto Ltd and its cable system subsidiaries must purchase 90% of their television shows from Nagoya Ltd at payment terms, and other terms and conditions of supply as determined from time to time by Nagoya Ltd. That agreement gives Kyoto Ltd and its cable television system subsidiaries the exclusive right to broadcast Nagoya Ltd's movies and television shows in specific geographic areas containing approximately 45% of the country's population. Kyoto Ltd and its cable television subsidiaries determine the advertising rates charged to their broadcast advertisers.

Under its agreement with Nagoya Ltd, Kyoto Ltd has limited rights to engage in businesses other than the sale of Nagoya Ltd's movies and television shows. In its most recent fiscal year, approximately 90% of Kyoto Ltd's sales were Nagoya Ltd movies and television shows. Nagoya Ltd provides promotional and marketing services and consultation to the cable television systems that broadcast its movies and television shows. Kyoto Ltd rents office space from Nagoya Ltd in its headquarters facility through a renewable lease agreement, which will expire in five years.

Required
(a) Should Nagoya Ltd consolidate Kyoto Ltd? Why?
(b) If Nagoya Ltd had not established Kyoto Ltd but had instead purchased 41% of Kyoto Ltd's voting shares on the open market, does this change your answer to part (a)? Why?

Source: Adapted from Case III issued by the FASB as a part of its Consolidations project.

18. Hiroshima Ltd and Nagasaki Ltd own 80% and 20% respectively of the ordinary shares that carry voting rights at a general meeting of shareholders of Osaka Ltd. Hiroshima Ltd sells one half of its interest to Kobe Ltd and buys call options from Kobe Ltd that are exercisable at any time at a premium to the market price when issued, and if exercised would give Hiroshima Ltd its original 80% ownership interest and voting rights. At 30 June 2006, the options are out of the money.

Required
Discuss whether Hiroshima Ltd is the parent of Osaka Ltd.

Source: Adapted from the Implementation Guidance to IAS 27.

19. Kurashiki Ltd, Sasebo Ltd and Kanzawa Ltd each own one third of the ordinary shares that carry voting rights at a general meeting of shareholders of Saga Ltd. Kurashiki Ltd, Sasebo Ltd and Kanzawa Ltd each

have the right to appoint two directors to the board of Saga Ltd. Kurashiki Ltd also owns call options that are exercisable at a fixed price at any time and, if exercised, would give it all the voting rights in Saga Ltd. The management of Kurashiki Ltd does not intend to exercise the call options, even if Sasebo Ltd and Kanzawa Ltd do not vote in the same manner as Kurashiki Ltd.

Required
Discuss whether Saga Ltd is a subsidiary of any of the other entities.

Source: Adapted from the Implementation Guidance to IAS 27.

20. Nagano Ltd and Matsue Ltd own 55% and 45% respectively of the ordinary shares that carry voting rights at a general meeting of shareholders of Toyota Ltd. Matsue Ltd also holds debt instruments that are convertible into ordinary shares of Toyota Ltd. The debt can be converted at a substantial price, in comparison with Matsue Ltd's net assets, at any time and if converted would require Matsue Ltd to borrow additional funds to make the payment. If the debt were to be converted, Matsue Ltd would hold 70% of the voting rights and Nagano Ltd's interest would reduce to 30%. Given the effect of increasing its debt on its debt-equity ratio, Matsue Ltd does not believe that it has the financial ability to enter into conversion of the debt.

Required
Discuss whether Matsue Ltd is a parent of Toyota Ltd.

Source: Adapted from the Implementation Guidance to IAS 27.

21. Okuchi Ltd has acquired, during the current year, the following investments in the shares issued by other companies:

Tottori Ltd	$120 000 (40% of issued capital)
Susaki Ltd	$117 000 (35% of issued capital)

Okuchi Ltd is unsure how to account for these investments and has asked you, as the auditor, for some professional advice.

Specifically, Okuchi Ltd is concerned that it may need to prepare consolidated financial statements under IAS 27. To help you, the company has provided the following information about the two investee companies:

Tottori Ltd
- The remaining shares in Tottori Ltd are owned by a diverse group of investors who each hold a small parcel of shares.

- Historically, only a small number of the share-holders attend the general meetings or question the actions of the directors.
- Okuchi Ltd has nominated three new directors and expects that they will be appointed at the next annual general meeting. The current board of directors has five members.

Susaki Ltd

- The remaining shares in Susaki Ltd are owned by a small group of investors who each own approximately 15% of the issued shares. One of these shareholders is Tottori Ltd, which owns 17%.
- The shareholders take a keen interest in the running of the company and attend all meetings.
- Two of the shareholders, including Tottori Ltd, already have representatives on the board of directors who have indicated their intention of nominating for re-election.

Required

1. Advise Okuchi Ltd as to whether, under IAS 27, it controls Tottori Ltd and/or Susaki Ltd. Support your conclusion.
2. Would your conclusion be different if the remaining shares in Tottori Ltd were owned by three institutional investors each holding 20%? If so, why?

22. **Part A**

Morioka Ltd owns 40% of the shares of Hirosaki Ltd, and holds the only substantial block of shares in that entity, no other party owning more than 3% of the shares. The annual general meeting of Hirosaki Ltd is to be held in a month's time. Two situations that may arise are:

- Morioka Ltd will be able to elect a majority of Hirosaki Ltd's board of directors as a result of exercising its votes as the largest holder of shares. As only 75% of shareholders voted in the previous year's annual meeting, Morioka Ltd may have the majority of the votes that are cast at the meeting.
- By obtaining the proxies of other shareholders and, after meeting with other shareholders who normally attend general meetings of Hirosaki Ltd, by convincing these shareholders to vote with it, Morioka Ltd may obtain the necessary votes to have its nominees elected as directors of the board of Hirosaki Ltd, regardless of the attendance at the general meeting.

Required

Discuss the potential for Hirosaki Ltd being classified as a subsidiary of Morioka Ltd.

Part B

Assume that, at the annual general meeting of Hirosaki Ltd, Morioka Ltd's nominees are elected as the board members of Hirosaki Ltd.

Required

Discuss whether Hirosaki Ltd is a subsidiary of Morioka Ltd given that the annual general meeting was attended by shareholders who held (a) 75% of the voting shares, (b) 90% of the voting shares.

23. On 1 March 2005, Yonago Ltd acquired 40% of the voting shares of Onada Ltd. Under the company's constitution, each share is entitled to one vote per share. On the basis of past experience, only 65% of the eligible votes are typically cast at the annual general meetings of Onada Ltd. No other shareholder holds a major block of shares in Onada Ltd.

The financial year of Onada Ltd ends on 30 June each year. The directors of Yonago Ltd argue that they are not required under IAS 27 to include Onada Ltd as a subsidiary in Yonago Ltd's consolidated financial statements at 30 June 2005 as there is no conclusive evidence that Yonago Ltd can control the financial and operating policies of Onada Ltd. The auditors of Yonago Ltd disagree, referring specifically to past years' voting figures.

Provide a report to Yonago Ltd on whether it should regard Onada Ltd as a subsidiary in its preparation of consolidated financial statements at 30 June 2005.

24. Critically analyse the following article, in particular whether IAS 27 overcomes the problems noted. Note that AASB 1024 on consolidation is not significantly different from IAS 127.

Consolidation standard – in practice

Those who drafted the new consolidation standard AASB 1024 insist that it contains hard and fast rules for identifying which 'subsidiaries' accounts are to be consolidated with a 'parent entity'.

Others (your correspondent included) have criticised the standard for incorporating subjective rather than objective tests.

Under AASB 1024, consolidation is required for all entities over which a parent has 'capacity to control'. Identification of the existence of capacity to 'control' is a matter of 'professional judgment'; whether an entity has control is to be 'decided in the light of the prevailing circumstances'.

More fundamental, perhaps, is the question of whether determining the ambit of consolidation in terms of tests of 'control' – rather than, say, levels of beneficial ownership – produces accounting data that is relevant to the judgments viewed by major users of financial statements.

Even more basic are concerns that AASB 1024 may fail to prevent companies from selectively deconsolidating subsidiaries with the aim of hiding losses or placing debt 'off-balance sheet'.

Whatever one's views about these questions, AASB 1024 is now in operation. The standard affects companies with financial years ending on or after December 31, 1991.

One of the first companies to report under this new regime was BTR Nylex. Before reviewing BTR Nylex's accounts, it is emphasised that the following commentary is not intended in any way to suggest that BTR Nylex is involved in 'creative accounting', or has taken any steps to evade the rules established within the Companies Act and Codes, the Corporations Law, AAS 24 or AASB 1024 regarding the ambit of consolidation.

But the fact remains that BTR Nylex's investment relationships provide an interesting case study of how AASB 1024 is being interpreted. For that matter, BTR Nylex's past reports are also interesting illustrations of consolidation practices.

A starting point is BTR Nylex's 1988 accounts. At that time, BTR Nylex held 100 per cent of a finance company called Bridge Wholesale Acceptance Corporation (Australia) Limited – formerly known as Borg-Warner Acceptance Corporation (Australia) Limited.

Instead of consolidating Bridge Wholesale Acceptance Corporation (BWAC), BTR Nylex chose to present BWAC's accounts separately, and to record BWAC's results on an 'equity accounting' basis.

Then in 1990, BTR Nylex sold off 50 per cent of BWAC. Since BWAC was deemed not to be a subsidiary, BTR was able to record a group profit on disposal of $24.64 million.

With only a 50 per cent holding, BWAC accounts were not consolidated in BTR Nylex's 1990 accounts. It is noteworthy that non-consolidation meant that BTR Nylex's consolidated balance sheet was not affected by the high gearing of the BWAC business: total liabilities of $365.7 million, as opposed to total share capital and reserves of $17.4 million.

The 50 per cent interest in BWAC was sold by BTR Nylex to Austrim Limited. Austrim was incorporated in Tasmania on September 1, 1987, and subsequently listed on the Perth second-board. What makes the consolidation practices even more interesting is that the sale of 50 per cent of the BWAC shares was partly on credit – and, it would seem, on interest-free terms. By June 30, 1991 only $22,500,000 of the $45 million price had been paid to the vendor.

It is at this point that the BTR–Austrim–BWAC relationships raise some questions about the way AASB 1024 delineates parent–subsidiary relationships, and the way the tests of 'capacity to control' in AASB 1024 are being interpreted.

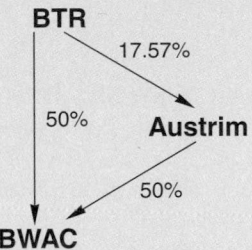

As shown in the diagram above, BTR Nylex held shares in Austrim, so that BTR Nylex's beneficial interest in BWAC exceeded 50 per cent. Still, that situation did not trigger the tests for consolidation contained in the old Companies Code.

The accounting period of BTR Nylex ends December 31; for Austrim it ends June 30. At June 30, 1991 BTR held 7,260,000 shares in Austrim – or 17.57 per cent of Austrim's issued share capital. In February 1992 Austrim issued a prospectus to raise additional capital so as to pay off its debt to BTR Nylex for the purchase of BWAC. That prospectus showed BTR's stake in Austrim was still 17.57 per cent.

So, at BTR Nylex's balance date of December 31, 1991, BTR's beneficial interest in BWAC amounted to around 58.8 per cent.

AASB 1024 suggests that a factor which may indicate the existence of control is ownership interest. The holding of an ownership interest usually entitles the investor to an equivalent percentage interest in the voting rights of the investee. 'Consequently, a majority ownership interest would normally, though not necessarily, be accompanied by the existence of control.' In this case, BTR has not regarded a 58 per cent beneficial interest as giving rise to control over BWAC.

Another factor which AASB 1024 says might indicate the existence of control by one entity over another entity is the capacity to dominate the composition of the board of directors of another entity. In this case, the board of Austrim included BTR Nylex chairman Mr Alan R Jackson, and BTR Nylex director Mr Kenneth H Parker. Between them they also held a direct and indirect interest in some 1,479,001 Austrim shares.

The standard suggests that evidence of the existence of a 'capacity to control' might be revealed by an entity being able to obtain financial information from the other entity

(continued)

on request. Of course, the presence of common directors makes that test meaningless.

It would appear that BTR Nylex directors took the view that they did not control Austrim; perhaps control vested with another director, Perth entrepreneur Kerry Stokes. The test is linked with capacity to dominate decision-making.

An interesting feature of the BTR Nylex–BWAC relationship is the fact that, as part of the original deal whereby BTR sold 50 per cent of BWAC's shares to Austrim, the latter company and its subsidiary Pitman Pty Ltd agreed to reinvest 40 per cent (or 'such other percentage as may be agreed') of any dividend received from BWAC.

However, AASB 1024 refers to the capacity to dominate decision-making so as to enable another entity to operate with it achieving the former's objectives. This contractual arrangement, on its own, may not meet the test established in the standard.

Nor would the fact that BTR Nylex's major loan to BWAC may have placed it in the position to demand repayment or refinancing of the loan.

So, to return to AASB 1024. The existence of 'control' is to be decided in the 'light of the prevailing circumstances'. In this case, the circumstances involved the existence of a 58.8 per cent beneficial interest, common directors, and the presence of a major loan.

Non-consolidation of BWAC may well be the natural outcome of using a test of 'control' in the standard. But to this writer, there is an urgent need to rewrite AASB 1024 so that it includes an additional test of consolidation: majority beneficial ownership.

Source: Walker (1992).

25. IAS 27 implicitly adopts the entity concept of consolidation. In his dissenting opinion to the issue of IAS 27 in 2004, Mr Yamada argued that the IASB was taking the entity concept without giving enough consideration to the objectives of consolidated financial statements.

Required
Discuss the following:
(a) What are the main objectives of preparing consolidated financial statements?
(b) How would the choice of objectives affect the adoption of particular concepts of consolidation?

26. Okinawa Ltd has 37% of the voting interest in Naha Ltd. An investment bank with which it has business relationships holds a 15% voting interest. Because of the closeness of the business relationship with the bank, Okinawa Ltd believes it can rely on the bank's support to ensure it cannot be outvoted at general meetings of Naha Ltd.

Required
Given that there is no guarantee that the bank will always support Okinawa Ltd, particularly if there is a potential for economic loss, discuss whether Okinawa Ltd is a parent of Naha Ltd.

27. Some have argued that the criteria for consolidation should be control plus significant risks and rewards or ownership or economic benefits. These parties argue that the consolidated financial statements are not meaningful if they include subsidiaries in which the parent's level of benefits is less than 50% or is not significant.

Required
Discuss:
(a) the place of a benefits criterion in the definition of control
(b) possible benefits that could occur as a result of obtaining control of another entity
(c) the need to place a specified level of benefits in the definition of control.

WEBLINK

Visit these websites for additional information:
www.iasb.org
www.asic.gov.au
www.aasb.com.au
www.accaglobal.com

www.iasplus.com
www.ifac.org
www.nzica.com
www.capa.com.my

REFERENCES

Accounting Standards Board of Japan 2005, Letter of comment (no. 32) on *Exposure Draft of Proposed Amendments to IFRS 3 Business Combinations*, 28 October, viewed July 2006, <www.fasb.org/ocl/fasb-getletters.php?project=1204-001>.

Accounting Standards Board UK 2005, Letter of comment (no. 130) on *Exposure Draft of Proposed Amendments to IFRS 3 Business Combinations*, 28 October, viewed July 2006, <www.fasb.org/ocl/fasb-getletters.php?project=1204-001>.

ACLI 2005, Letter of comment (no. 30) on *Exposure Draft on Consolidated Financial Statements, Including Accounting and Reporting of Noncontrolling Interests in Subsidiaries*, American Council of Life Insurers, 28 October, viewed July 2006, <www.fasb.org/ocl/fasb-getletters.php?project=1205-001>.

Beresford, DR 2005, Letter of comment (no. 2) on *Exposure Draft on Consolidated Financial Statements, Including Accounting and Reporting of Noncontrolling Interests in Subsidiaries*, 16 September, viewed July 2006, <www.fasb.org/ocl/fasb-getletters.php?project=1205-001>.

Canadian Accounting Standards Board 2005, Letter of comment (no. 248) on *Exposure Draft of Proposed Amendments to IFRS 3 Business Combinations*, 25 October, viewed July 2006, <www.fasb.org/ocl/fasb-getletters.php?project=1204-001>.

Citigroup 2005, Letter of comment (no. 14) on *Exposure Draft on Consolidated Financial Statements, Including Accounting and Reporting of Noncontrolling Interests in Subsidiaries*, 28 October, viewed July 2006, <www.fasb.org/ocl/fasb-getletters.php?project=1205-001>.

Deloitte 2005, Letter of comment (no. 7) on *Exposure Draft on Consolidated Financial Statements, Including Accounting and Reporting of Noncontrolling Interests in Subsidiaries*, 26 October, viewed July 2006, <www.fasb.org/ocl/fasb-getletters.php?project=1205-001>.

EFRAG 2005, Letter of comment (no. 268) on *Exposure Draft of Proposed Amendments to IFRS 3 Business Combinations*, European Financial Reporting Advisory Group, 28 November, viewed July 2006, <www.fasb.org/ocl/fasb-getletters.php?project=1204-001>.

Ernst & Young 2005, Letter of comment (no. 46) on *Exposure Draft on Consolidated Financial Statements, Including Accounting and Reporting of Noncontrolling Interests in Subsidiaries*, 2 November, viewed July 2006, <www.fasb.org/ocl/fasb-getletters.php?project=1205-001>.

German Accounting Standards Board 2005, Letter of comment (no. 121) on *Exposure Draft of Proposed Amendments to IFRS 3 Business Combinations*, 27 October, viewed July 2006, <www.fasb.org/ocl/fasb-getletters.php?project=1204-001>.

IOSCO 2005, Letter of comment (no. 260) on *Exposure Draft of Proposed Amendments to IFRS 3 Business Combinations*, International Organization of Securities Commissions, 29 November, viewed July 2006, <www.fasb.org/ocl/fasb-getletters.php?project=1204-001>.

KPMG 2005, Letter of comment (no. 33) on *Exposure Draft on Consolidated Financial Statements, Including Accounting and Reporting of Noncontrolling Interests in Subsidiaries*, 28 October, viewed July 2006, <www.fasb.org/ocl/fasb-getletters.php?project=1205-001>.

Leo, KJ 1987, *Consolidated financial statements*, Discussion Paper No. 11, Australian Accounting Research Foundation, Melbourne.

Microsoft 2005, Letter of comment (no. 16) on *Exposure Draft on Consolidated Financial Statements, Including Accounting and Reporting of Noncontrolling Interests in Subsidiaries*, 28 October, viewed July 2006, <www.fasb.org/ocl/fasb-getletters.php?project=1205-001>.

Pacter, P 1991, *Consolidation policy and procedures*, Discussion Memorandum, Financial Accounting Standards Board, Norwalk (Connecticut), USA.

PepsiCo 2005, Letter of comment (no. 282) on *Exposure Draft of Proposed Amendments to IFRS 3 Business Combinations*, viewed July 2006, <www.fasb.org/ocl/fasb-getletters.php?project=1204-001>.

Pricewaterhouse Coopers 2005, Letter of comment (no. 12) on *Exposure Draft on Consolidated Financial Statements, Including Accounting and Reporting of Noncontrolling Interests in Subsidiaries*, 28 October, viewed July 2006, <www.fasb.org/ocl/fasb-getletters.php?project=1205-001>.

Royal Dutch Shell 2005, Letter of comment (no. 35) on *Exposure Draft on Consolidated Financial Statements, Including Accounting and Reporting of Noncontrolling Interests in Subsidiaries*, viewed July 2006, <www.fasb.org/ocl/fasb-getletters.php?project=1205-001>.

South African Institute of Chartered Accountants 2005, Letter of comment (no. 215) on *Exposure Draft of Proposed Amendments to IFRS 3 Business Combinations*, 28 October, viewed July 2006, <www.fasb.org/ocl/fasb-getletters.php?project=1204-001>.

Walker, B 1992, 'Consolidation standard – in practice', *New Accountant*, 28 May, p. 24.

Wells Fargo 2005, Letter of comment (no. 19) on *Exposure Draft on Consolidated Financial Statements, Including Accounting and Reporting of Noncontrolling Interests in Subsidiaries*, 28 October, viewed July 2006, <www.fasb.org/ocl/fasb-getletters.php?project=1205-001>.

CHAPTER 20
Consolidated financial statements: wholly owned subsidiaries

ACCOUNTING STANDARDS

International: IAS 27 *Consolidated and Separate Financial Statements*

IFRS 3 *Business Combinations*

Australia: AASB 127 *Consolidated and Separate Financial Statements*

AASB 3 *Business Combinations*

New Zealand: NZ IAS 27 *Consolidated and Separate Financial Statements*

NZ IFRS 3 *Business Combinations*

CONCEPTS FOR REVIEW

Before studying this chapter, you should understand or, if necessary, revise:
- the IASB Framework (see chapter 2 of this book)
- accounting for business combinations (see chapter 12 of this book).

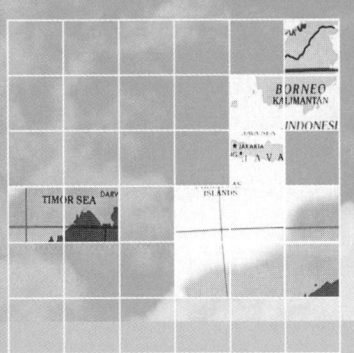

When you have studied this chapter, you should be able to:

1. understand the nature of the group covered in this chapter, and the initial adjustments required to subsidiary statements
2. explain how a consolidation worksheet is used
3. prepare an acquisition analysis for the parent's acquisition in a subsidiary
4. explain why business combination valuation entries are required and how to prepare them at acquisition date
5. explain the purpose of the pre-acquisition entries, and be able to prepare them at acquisition date
6. complete a consolidation worksheet
7. adjust the acquisition analysis where the subsidiary has recorded goodwill at acquisition date
8. adjust the acquisition analysis where the subsidiary has a dividend payable at acquisition date
9. account for an excess on acquisition
10. prepare the business combination valuation entries in periods subsequent to the acquisition date
11. adjust pre-acquisition entries for changes in business combination valuation entries
12. adjust pre-acquisition entries for dividends paid or payable from pre-acquisition equity
13. adjust pre-acquisition entries for movements in reserves
14. prepare the disclosures required by IFRS 3 and IAS 27.

20.1 The consolidation process

The purpose of this chapter is to discuss the preparation of consolidated financial statements. As stated in paragraph 12 of IAS 27 *Consolidated and Separate Financial Statements*, consolidated statements are the result of combining the financial statements of a parent and all its subsidiaries. (The determination of whether an entity is a parent or a subsidiary is discussed in chapter 19 of this book.) The two accounting standards that are primarily used in this chapter are IAS 27 and IFRS 3 *Business Combinations*. Chapter 12 of this book contains the accounting principles relevant for business combinations. An in-depth understanding of that chapter is essential to the preparation of consolidated financial statements because the parent's acquisition of shares in a subsidiary is simply one form of a business combination.

IFRS 3 distinguishes 'date of exchange' from 'acquisition date':

Acquisition date   The date on which the acquirer effectively obtains control of the acquiree.

Date of exchange   When a business combination is achieved through a single exchange transaction, the date of exchange is the acquisition date. When a business combination involves more than one exchange transaction, for example when it is achieved in stages by successive shares purchases, the date of exchange is the date that each individual investment is recognised in the financial statements of the acquirer.

As discussed in chapter 12 of this book, the cost of the combination is calculated at the date of exchange, whereas the fair values of the identifiable assets, liabilities and contingent liabilities of the subsidiary are measured at the acquisition date. In this chapter, the only combinations considered are those where the parent acquires its controlling interest in a subsidiary in a single transaction – not where control is achieved after a number of purchases of shares by the parent. Further, it is assumed in this chapter that the acquisition of the shares gives the parent control of the subsidiary. Hence, in all cases in this chapter, the acquisition date is the same as the date of exchange.

Note, however, as discussed in chapter 19 of this book, control of a subsidiary does not necessarily involve the parent acquiring shares in a subsidiary. The consolidated financial statements of a parent and its subsidiaries include information about a subsidiary from the date the parent obtains control of the subsidiary; that is, from the acquisition date. A subsidiary continues to be included in the parent's consolidated financial statements until the parent no longer controls that entity; that is, until the date of disposal of the subsidiary (IAS 27, para. 30).

Before undertaking the consolidation process, it may be necessary to make adjustments in relation to the content of the financial statements of the subsidiary:
- If a subsidiary's balance date does not coincide with the parent's balance date, adjustments must be made for the effects of significant transactions and events that occur between those dates, with additional financial statements being prepared where it is practicable to do so (IAS 27, para. 26). In most cases, where there are different dates, the subsidiary will prepare adjusted financial statements as at the parent's reporting date, so that adjustments are not necessary on consolidation. Where the preparation of adjusted financial statements is unduly costly, the financial statements of the subsidiary prepared at a different reporting date from the parent may be used, subject to adjustments for significant transactions. However, as paragraph 27 states, for this to be a viable option, the difference between the reporting dates can be no longer than three months. Further, the length of the reporting periods, as well as any difference between the reporting dates, must be the same from period to period.

- The consolidated financial statements are to be prepared using uniform accounting policies for like transactions and other events in similar circumstances (IAS 27, para. 28). Where different policies are used, adjustments are made so that like transactions are accounted for under a uniform policy in the consolidated financial statements.

Journal entry adjustments

The preparation of the consolidated financial statements involves adding together the financial statements of the parent and its subsidiaries. As a part of this summation process, a number of adjustments are made, these being expressed in the form of journal entries:

- As required by IFRS 3, at the acquisition date, the acquirer must recognise the identifiable assets and liabilities and contingent liabilities of the subsidiary at fair value. Adjusting the carrying amounts of the subsidiary's assets and liabilities to fair value and recognising any identifiable assets, liabilities and contingent liabilities acquired as a part of the business combination, but not recorded by the subsidiary, is a part of the consolidation process. The entries used to make these adjustments are referred to in this chapter as the *business combination valuation entries*. As noted in section 20.2 of this chapter, these adjusting entries are generally not made in the records of the subsidiary itself but in a consolidation worksheet.
- Where the parent has an ownership interest (it owns shares) in a subsidiary, adjusting entries are made, referred to in this chapter as the *pre-acquisition entries*. As noted in paragraph 22(a) of IAS 27, this involves eliminating the carrying amount of the parent's investment in each subsidiary, and the parent's portion of pre-acquisition equity in each subsidiary. The name of these entries is derived from the fact that the equity of the subsidiary at the acquisition date is referred to as pre-acquisition equity, and it is this equity that is being eliminated. As explained in section 20.4.1 of this book, any recognition of goodwill on consolidation is made in the pre-acquisition entries. These entries are also made in the consolidation worksheet and not in the records of the subsidiary.
- The third set of adjustments to be made is for transactions between the entities within the group subsequent to the acquisition date, including events such as sales of inventory or non-current assets. These intragroup transactions are referred to in IAS 27 paragraph 24, and adjustments for these transactions are discussed in detail in chapter 21 of this book.

Group under discussion

In this chapter, the group under discussion is one where:

- There are only two entities within the group: one parent and one subsidiary. The group is then as shown in figure 20.1.

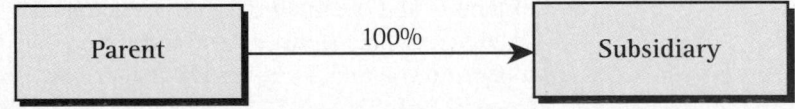

FIGURE 20.1   A wholly owned group

- Both entities have share capital.
- The parent owns all the issued shares of the subsidiary (the subsidiary is wholly owned). Partially owned subsidiaries, where it is necessary to account for the minority interest, are covered in chapter 22 of this book.
- The parent entity acquired its ownership interest in the subsidiary as a result of a single transaction, with control being achieved as a result of this acquisition.
- There are no intragroup transactions between the parent and its subsidiary subsequent to the acquisition date.

LO 2   20.2 Consolidation worksheets

The consolidated financial statements are prepared by adding together the financial statements of the parent and the subsidiary. It is the *financial statements* of the parent and the subsidiary, rather than the underlying accounts, which are added together. There are no consolidated ledger accounts. The financial statements that are added together are the balance sheets, income statements and statements of changes in equity prepared by the management of the parent and the subsidiary. Consolidated cash flow statements must also be prepared, but these are not covered in this book.

To facilitate the addition process, particularly where there are a number of subsidiaries, as well as to make the necessary valuation and pre-acquisition entry adjustments, a worksheet or computer spreadsheet is often used. From the worksheet, the external reports are prepared: the consolidated balance sheet, income statement and statement of changes in equity.

The format for the worksheet is presented in figure 20.2, which contains the information used for the consolidation of the parent, P Ltd, and the subsidiary, S Ltd.

Financial statements	Parent P Ltd	Subsidiary S Ltd	Adjustments				Consolidation
				Dr	Cr		
	$	$		$	$		$
Retained earnings	25 000	12 000	*1*	5 000			32 000
Share capital	30 000	15 000	*1*	15 000			30 000
	55 000	27 000					62 000
Shares in S Ltd	20 000	–			20 000	*1*	–
Other assets	35 000	27 000					62 000
	55 000	27 000		20 000	20 000		62 000

FIGURE 20.2 Consolidation worksheet — basic format

Note the following points about the worksheet:
- Column 1 contains the names of the accounts, as the financial statements are combined on a line-by-line basis.
- Columns 2 and 3 contain the internal financial statements of the parent, P Ltd, and its subsidiary, S Ltd. These statements are obtained from the separate legal entities. The number of columns is expanded if there are more subsidiaries within the group (see chapter 23 of this book).
- The next four columns, headed 'Adjustments', are used to make the adjustments required in the consolidation process. These include adjustments for valuations at acquisition date, pre-acquisition equity, and intragroup transactions such as sales of inventory between the parent and subsidiary. The adjustments, written in the form of journal entries, are recorded on the worksheet. Where there are many adjustments, each journal entry should be numbered so that it is clear which items are being affected by a particular adjustment entry. In figure 20.2 there is only one worksheet entry, hence the number 1 is entered against each adjustment item. The worksheet adjustment entry is shown opposite.

1. Retained earnings	Dr	5 000	
Share capital	Dr	15 000	
Shares in S Ltd	Cr		20 000

- As noted earlier, the process of consolidation is one of adding the financial statements of the members of the group and making various adjustments. Hence, figures for each line item in the right-hand column, headed 'Consolidation', arise through addition and subtraction as you proceed horizontally across the worksheet. For example, for share capital:

$$\$30\,000 + \$15\,000 - \$15\,000 = \$30\,000$$

The figures in the right-hand column provide the information for the preparation of the consolidated financial statements of P Ltd and S Ltd.

- In the 'Consolidation' column, the totals and subtotals are a product of the preceding items in that column rather than being added across the rows. For example, the total consolidated equity of $62 000 is determined by adding the retained earnings balance of $32 000 and the share capital balance of $30 000, both the latter balances appearing in the 'Consolidation' column. It is from this column that the information for preparing the consolidated income statement, statement of changes in equity and balance sheet are prepared. These statements will not include all the line items in the consolidation worksheet. However, information for the notes to these statements is also obtained from line items in the worksheet.

In preparing the consolidated financial statements, *no* adjustments are made in the accounting records of the individual entities that constitute the group. The adjustment entries recorded in the columns of the worksheet do not affect the accounts of the individual entities. They are recorded in a separate consolidation journal, not in the journals of any of the member entities, and are then recorded on the consolidation worksheet. Hence, where consolidated financial statements are prepared over a number of years, a particular entry (such as a pre-acquisition entry) needs to be made every time a consolidation worksheet is prepared because the entry never affects the actual financial statements of the individual entities.

LO 3

20.3 The acquisition analysis

As noted in chapter 12 of this book, the parent records its investment in the subsidiary at the cost of the business combination, which is the fair value of the consideration paid. Where the cost of the business combination is greater than the acquirer's interest in the net fair value of the identifiable assets, liabilities and contingent liabilities of the acquiree, goodwill is recognised. Where the reverse occurs, the excess is recognised as a gain. An acquisition analysis is conducted at acquisition date because it is necessary to recognise the identifiable assets and liabilities of the subsidiary at fair value, and to determine if there has been an acquisition of goodwill or an excess. As noted in chapter 10, this may give rise to the recognition of assets, liabilities and contingent liabilities that are not recognised in the records of the subsidiary. For example, the business combination may give rise to intangibles that were not capable of being recognised in the subsidiary's records.

The first step in the consolidation process is to undertake the above acquisition analysis in order to obtain the information necessary for making both the business combination valuation and pre-acquisition entry adjustments for the consolidation worksheet. Consider the example in figure 20.3.

On 1 July 2006, Parent Ltd acquired all the issued share capital of Sub Ltd, giving in exchange 100 000 shares in Parent Ltd, these having a fair value of $5 per share. At acquisition date, the balance sheets of Parent Ltd and Sub Ltd, and the fair values of Sub Ltd's assets and liabilities, were as follows:

| | Parent Ltd | Sub Ltd | |
	Carrying amount	Carrying amount	Fair value
EQUITY AND LIABILITIES			
Equity			
Share capital	$550 000	$300 000	
Retained earnings	350 000	140 000	
Total equity	900 000	440 000	
Liabilities			
Provisions	30 000	60 000	$ 60 000
Payables	27 000	34 000	34 000
Tax liabilities	10 000	6 000	6 000
Total liabilities	67 000	100 000	
Total equity and liabilities	$967 000	$540 000	
ASSETS			
Land	$120 000	$150 000	$170 000
Equipment	620 000	480 000	330 000
Accumulated depreciation	(380 000)	(170 000)	
Shares in Sub Ltd	500 000		
Inventory	92 000	75 000	80 000
Cash	15 000	5 000	5 000
Total assets	$967 000	$540 000	

At acquisition date, Sub Ltd has an unrecorded patent with a fair value of $20 000, and a contingent liability with a fair value of $15 000.

The tax rate is 30%.

FIGURE 20.3 Information at acquisition date

The analysis at acquisition date then consists of comparing the fair value of the consideration paid and the net fair value of the identifiable assets, liabilities and contingent liabilities acquired. The net fair value of the subsidiary could be calculated by revaluing the assets and liabilities of the subsidiary from the carrying amounts to fair value, remembering that under IAS 12 *Income Taxes* revaluation of assets requires a recognition of the tax effect of the revaluation because there is a difference between the carrying amount and the tax base caused by the revaluation. However, in calculating the net fair value acquired, because particular information is required to prepare the valuation and pre-acquisition entries, the calculation is done by adding the recorded equity of the subsidiary (which represents the recorded net assets of the subsidiary) and the differences between the carrying amounts of the assets and liabilities and their fair values, adjusted for tax. The book equity of the subsidiary in figure 20.3 consists of:

$300 000 capital + $140 000 retained earnings

The equity relating to the differences in fair value and carrying amounts for assets and liabilities recorded by Sub Ltd – as well as for assets, liabilities and contingent liabilities not recognised by the subsidiary but recognised as being acquired as part of the business combination – is referred to in this chapter as the *business combination valuation reserve* (BCVR). This reserve is not an account recognised in the subsidiary's records, but it is recognised in the consolidation process as part of the business combination. For example, for land there is a $20 000 difference between fair value and carrying amount. On revaluation of the land to fair value, a business combination valuation reserve of $14 000 [being $20 000 (1 – 30%)] is raised.

The acquisition analysis, including the determination of the goodwill of the subsidiary is as shown in figure 20.4.

At 1 July 2006:
 Net fair value of identifiable assets,
 liabilities and contingent
 liabilities of Sub Ltd   = $300 000 + $140 000 (recorded equity)
                 + ($170 000 – $150 000) (1 – 30%) (BCVR – land)
                 + ($330 000 – $310 000) (1 – 30%) (BCVR – equipment)
                 + ($80 000 – $75 000) (1 – 30%) (BCVR – inventory)
                 + $20 000 (1 – 30%) (BCVR – patent)
                 – $15 000 (1 – 30%) (BCVR – contingent liability)
                 = $475 000
 Cost of the combination = 100 000 × $5
                 = $500 000
 Goodwill   = $500 000 – $475 000
                 = $25 000

FIGURE 20.4 Acquisition analysis

Having completed the acquisition analysis, the information from this analysis is used to prepare the adjustment entries for the consolidation worksheet. These entries are the business combination valuation entries and the pre-acquisition entries.

In this book, it is assumed that the tax base of the subsidiary's assets and liabilities is not changed by the parent's acquisition of the subsidiary. In some jurisdictions, where the group becomes the taxable entity, there is a change in the tax base to the fair value amounts. In this case, no tax effect would be recognised in relation to the assets and liabilities acquired.

20.4 Worksheet entries at the acquisition date

As noted earlier, the consolidation process does not result in any entries being made in the actual records of either the parent or the subsidiary. The adjustment entries are made in the consolidation worksheet. Hence, adjustment entries need to be passed in each worksheet prepared, and these entries change over time. In the rest of this section, the adjustment entries that would be passed in a consolidation worksheet prepared *immediately after the acquisition date* are analysed.

20.4.1 Business combination valuation entries

LO 4

In figure 20.3, there are three identifiable assets recognised by the subsidiary whose fair values differ from their carrying amounts at acquisition date, as well as an intangible asset and a contingent liability recognised as part of the business combination. The entries for the business combination valuations are done in the consolidation worksheet rather than in the records of the subsidiary. (See section 20.7 for a discussion in relation to making these adjustments in the records of the subsidiary itself.) The assets and liabilities that require adjustment to fair value can be easily identified by reference to the acquisition analysis in figure 20.4; namely land, equipment, inventory, patent and the contingent liability. In relation to the goodwill to be recognised on consolidation, under IFRS 3 only the goodwill acquired by the parent is recognised on consolidation. This has no effect where the parent acquires all the shares in the subsidiary. However, where the parent acquires less than all the shares in a subsidiary, the goodwill attributable to the minority interest is not recognised on consolidation (see chapter 22 of this book). It is for this reason that goodwill is recognised in the pre-acquisition entries rather than in the business combination valuation entries. The latter recognise the full fair value of the identifiable assets, liabilities and contingent liabilities of the subsidiary regardless of the percentage ownership of the parent in the subsidiary.

Consolidation worksheet adjustment entries for each of these assets and the contingent liability are given in figure 20.5. Note that the total balance of the business combination valuation reserve is $35 000. The adjustments to assets, liabilities and contingent liabilities at acquisition date could be achieved by one adjustment entry, giving a net balance to the business combination valuation reserve. However, in order to keep track of movements in that reserve as assets are depreciated or sold and liabilities paid, it is practical to prepare a valuation entry for each component of the valuation process. The valuation entries are passed in the adjustment columns of the worksheet, which is illustrated in section 20.4.3 of this book.

Business combination valuation entries			
1. Land	Dr	20 000	
Deferred tax liability	Cr		6 000
Business combination valuation reserve	Cr		14 000
2. Accumulated depreciation – equipment	Dr	170 000	
Equipment	Cr		150 000
Deferred tax liability	Cr		6 000
Business combination valuation reserve	Cr		14 000
3. Inventory	Dr	5 000	
Deferred tax liability	Cr		1 500
Business combination valuation reserve	Cr		3 500
4. Patent	Dr	20 000	
Deferred tax liability	Cr		6 000
Business combination valuation reserve	Cr		14 000
5. Business combination valuation reserve	Dr	10 500	
Deferred tax asset	Dr	4 500	
Contingent liability	Cr		15 000

FIGURE 20.5 Business combination valuation entries at acquisition date

LO 5

20.4.2 Pre-acquisition entries

As noted in paragraph 22(a) of IAS 27, the pre-acquisition entries are required to eliminate the carrying amount of the parent's investment in the subsidiary and the parent's portion of pre-acquisition equity. The pre-acquisition entries then involve three areas:

• The investment account, shares in subsidiary, as shown in the financial statements of the parent.

- The equity of the subsidiary at the acquisition date (the pre-acquisition equity). The pre-acquisition equity is not just the equity recorded by the subsidiary but includes the business combination valuation reserve recognised on consolidation via the valuation entries. Because the accounts containing pre-acquisition equity may change over time as a result of dividends and reserve transfers, more than one pre-acquisition entry may be required in a particular year.
- Recognition of goodwill. Note that, as stated in paragraph 21 of IAS 12 *Income Taxes*, there is no recognition of a deferred tax liability in relation to goodwill because goodwill is a residual, and the recognition of a deferred tax liability would increase its carrying amount.

Using the example in figure 20.3, and reading the information from the acquisition analysis in figure 20.4, including goodwill and the business combination valuation reserve for the revalued assets and the contingent liability, the pre-acquisition entry at acquisition date is as shown in figure 20.6. The pre-acquisition entry in this figure is numbered 6 because there were five previous valuation entries.

Pre-acquisition entry			
6. Retained earnings (1/7/06)	Dr	140 000	
Share capital	Dr	300 000	
Business combination valuation reserve	Dr	35 000	
Goodwill	Dr	25 000	
Shares in Sub Ltd	Cr		500 000

FIGURE 20.6 Pre-acquisition entry at acquisition date

The pre-acquisition entry is necessary to avoid overstating the equity and net assets of the group. To illustrate, consider the information in figure 20.3 relating to Parent Ltd's acquisition of the shares of Sub Ltd. Having acquired the shares in Sub Ltd, Parent Ltd records the asset 'Shares in Sub Ltd' at $500 000. This asset represents the actual net assets of Sub Ltd; that is, the ownership of the shares gives Parent Ltd the right to the net assets of Sub Ltd. To include both the asset 'Shares in Sub Ltd' and the net assets of Sub Ltd in the consolidated balance sheet would double-count the assets of the group, because the investment account is simply the right to the other assets. On consolidation, the investment account is therefore eliminated and, in its place, the net assets of the subsidiary are included in the consolidated balance sheet.

Similarly, to include both the equity of the parent and the equity of the subsidiary in the consolidated balance sheet would double-count the equity of the group. In the example, Parent Ltd has equity of $900 000, which is represented by its net assets including the investment in the subsidiary. Because the investment in the subsidiary is the same as the net assets of the subsidiary, the equity of the parent effectively relates to the net assets of the subsidiary. To include in the consolidated balance sheet the equity of the subsidiary at acquisition date as well as the equity of the parent would double-count equity in relation to the net assets of the subsidiary.

LO 6

20.4.3 ## Consolidation worksheet

Figure 20.7 contains the consolidation worksheet prepared at acquisition date, with adjustments being made for business combination valuation and pre-acquisition entries. The right-hand column reflects the consolidated balance sheet, showing the position of the group. Note in relation to the figures in this column:
- In relation to the three equity accounts — share capital, business combination valuation reserve and retained earnings — only the parent's balances are carried into the consolidated balance sheet. At acquisition date, all the equity of the subsidiary is pre-acquisition and is eliminated.

- With the business combination valuation reserve, the valuation entries establish the reserve, while the pre-acquisition entry eliminates it because it is by nature pre-acquisition equity.
- The assets of the subsidiary are carried forward into the consolidated balance sheet at fair value.
- The subsidiary's goodwill is recognised on consolidation.
- The debit and credit adjustment columns each total $730 000. This means that the adjusting journal entries have equal debits and credits, which is essential if the balance sheet is to balance.

Financial statements	Parent Ltd	Sub Ltd	Adjustments				Consolidation
				Dr	Cr		
	$	$		$	$		$
Retained earnings	350 000	140 000	6	140 000			350 000
Share capital	550 000	300 000	6	300 000			550 000
Business combination valuation reserve			5	10 500	14 000	1	–
			6	35 000	14 000	2	
					3 500	3	
					14 000	4	
	900 000	440 000					900 000
Provisions	30 000	60 000					90 000
Payables	27 000	34 000					61 000
Tax liabilities (net of tax assets)	10 000	6 000	5	4 500	6 000	1	31 000
					6 000	2	
					1 500	3	
					6 000	4	
Contingent liability	–	–			15 000	5	15 000
	67 000	100 000					197 000
Total equity and liabilities	967 000	540 000					1 097 000
Cash	15 000	5 000					20 000
Land	120 000	150 000	1	20 000			290 000
Equipment	620 000	480 000			150 000	2	950 000
Accumulated depreciation	(380 000)	(170 000)	2	170 000			(380 000)
Shares in Sub Ltd	500 000	–			500 000	6	–
Inventory	92 000	75 000	3	5 000			172 000
Patent	–	–	4	20 000			20 000
Goodwill	–	–	6	25 000			25 000
Total assets	967 000	540 000		730 000	730 000		1 097 000

FIGURE 20.7 Consolidation worksheet at acquisition date

20.4.4   ## Subsidiary has recorded goodwill at acquisition date

In the example used in section 20.4.3, at acquisition date the subsidiary did not have any recorded goodwill. Consider the situation where the assets recorded by the subsidiary at acquisition date are the same as in figure 20.3 except that now there is recorded goodwill, as follows:

	Sub Ltd	
	Carrying amount	Fair value
Cash	$ 5 000	$ 5 000
Land	150 000	170 000
Equipment	480 000	330 000
Accumulated depreciation	(170 000)	
Goodwill	10 000	
Inventory	75 000	80 000
	$550 000	

Assume that the retained earnings balance is now $150 000 rather than $140 000. The acquisition analysis is then as follows:

Net fair value of identifiable assets, liabilities and contingent liabilities of Sub Ltd	= $300 000 + $150 000 (equity)
	+ ($170 000 − $150 000) (1 − 30%) (BCVR − land)
	+ ($330 000 − $310 000) (1 − 30%) (BCVR − equipment)
	+ ($80 000 − $75 000) (1 − 30%) (BCVR − inventory)
	+ $20 000 (1 − 30%) (BCVR − patent)
	− $15 000 (1 − 30%) (BCVR − contingent liability)
	− $10 000 (goodwill)
	= $475 000
Cost of the combination	= 100 000 × $5
	= $500 000
Goodwill	= $500 000 − $475 000
	= $25 000
Recorded goodwill	= $10 000
Unrecorded goodwill	= $15 000

Note that, as the first calculation of the acquisition analysis relates to the fair value of the *identifiable* net assets, the goodwill of the subsidiary (unidentifiable assets) must be subtracted. Further, it is necessary to calculate the additional goodwill not recorded by the subsidiary, this being the amount recognised on consolidation. The amount of goodwill recognised in the pre-acquisition entry is $15 000, and the pre-acquisition entry is:

Retained earnings	Dr	150 000	
Share capital	Dr	300 000	
Business combination valuation reserve	Dr	35 000	
Goodwill	Dr	15 000	
Shares in Sub Ltd	Cr		500 000

The line item for goodwill in the consolidation worksheet would show:

Financial statements	Parent Ltd	Sub Ltd		Adjustments			Consolidation
				Dr	Cr		
Goodwill	–	10 000	6	15 000			25 000

The consolidated balance sheet thus shows the total acquired goodwill of the subsidiary.

20.4.5   ## Subsidiary has recorded dividends at acquisition date

Using the information in figure 20.3, assume that one of the payables at acquisition date is a dividend payable of $10 000. The parent can acquire the shares in the subsidiary on a cum div. or an ex div. basis.

If the shares are acquired on a cum div. basis, then the parent acquires the right to the dividend declared at acquisition date. In this case, if Parent Ltd pays $500 000 for the shares in Sub Ltd, then the entry it passes to record the business combination is:

Shares in Sub Ltd	Dr	490 000	
Dividend receivable	Dr	10 000	
Share capital	Cr		500 000

In other words, the parent acquires two assets: the investment in the subsidiary, and the dividend receivable. In calculating the goodwill in the subsidiary, using the information in figure 20.3, the acquisition analysis is:

Net fair value of identifiable assets,
   liabilities and contingent
   liabilities of Sub Ltd = $300 000 + $140 000 (equity)
      + ($170 000 − $150 000) (1 − 30%) (BCVR − land)
      + ($330 000 − $310 000) (1 − 30%) (BCVR − equipment)
      + ($80 000 − $75 000) (1 − 30%) (BCVR − inventory)
      + $20 000 (1 − 30%) (BCVR − patent)
      − $15 000 (1 − 30%) (BCVR − contingent liability)
   = $475 000
Cost of the combination = (100 000 × $5) − $10 000 dividend receivable
   = $490 000
Goodwill = $490 000 − $475 000
   = $15 000

In other words, the fair value of the consideration paid must be that for the investment in the subsidiary, excluding the amount paid for the dividend receivable. The pre-acquisition entry is then:

Retained earnings	Dr	140 000	
Share capital	Dr	300 000	
Business combination valuation reserve	Dr	35 000	
Goodwill	Dr	15 000	
Shares in Sub Ltd	Cr		490 000

A further consolidation worksheet entry is also required:

| Dividend payable | Dr | 10 000 | |
| Dividend receivable | Cr | | 10 000 |

This entry is necessary in order for the consolidated balance sheet to show only the assets and liabilities of the group; that is, only those benefits receivable from and obligations payable to parties external to the group. In relation to the dividend receivable recorded by Parent Ltd, this is not an asset of the group, because that entity does not expect to receive dividends from a party external to it. Similarly, the dividend payable recorded by the subsidiary is not a liability of the group. This dividend will be paid within the group, not to parties outside the group.

LO 9

20.4.6   ## Excess

In the example in figure 20.3, Parent Ltd paid $500 000 for the shares in Sub Ltd. Consider the situation where Parent Ltd paid $470 000 for these shares. The acquisition analysis is as shown in figure 20.8.

Net fair value of identifiable assets,
    liabilities and contingent
    liabilities of Sub Ltd   = $300 000 + $140 000 (equity)
                + ($170 000 − $150 000) (1 − 30%) (BCVR − land)
                + ($330 000 − $310 000) (1 − 30%) (BCVR − equipment)
                + ($80 000 − $75 000) (1 − 30%) (BCVR − inventory)
                + $20 000 (1 − 30%) (BCVR − patent)
                − $15 000 (1 − 30%) (BCVR − contingent liability)
            = $475 000
Cost of the combination = $470 000
Excess   = $475 000 − $470 000
            = $5000

FIGURE 20.8   Excess

As the net fair value of the identifiable assets, liabilities and contingent liabilities of the subsidiary is greater than the cost of the combination, in accordance with paragraph 56 of IFRS 3, the acquirer must firstly reassess the identification and measurement of the subsidiary's identifiable assets, liabilities and contingent liabilities as well as the measurement of the cost of the combination. The expectation under IFRS 3 is that an excess is usually the result of measurement errors rather than being a real gain to the acquirer. However, having confirmed the identification and measurement of both amounts paid and net assets acquired, if an excess still exists, under paragraph 56(b) the excess is recognised immediately in profit and loss.

Existence of an excess has no effect on the business combination valuation entries. The pre-acquisition entry is as shown in figure 20.9. (Note that the entry does not include that relating to goodwill as recognised previously.)

Pre-acquisition entry			
6. Retained earnings (1/7/06)	Dr	140 000	
Share capital	Dr	300 000	
Business combination valuation reserve	Dr	35 000	
Excess	Cr		5 000
Shares in Sub Ltd	Cr		470 000

FIGURE 20.9   Pre-acquisition entry at acquisition date — excess

LO 10

20.5 Worksheet entries subsequent to the acquisition date

At acquisition date, the business combination valuation entries result in the economic entity recognising assets and liabilities not recorded by the subsidiaries. Subsequently, changes in these assets and liabilities occur as assets are depreciated or sold and liabilities paid. Movements in pre-acquisition equity also occur as dividends are paid or declared, and transfers made within equity.

20.5.1 Business combination valuation entries

In the example used in figure 20.3, there were five items for which valuation entries were made: land, equipment, inventory, patent and contingent liabilities. In this section, a three-year time period subsequent to the acquisition date, 1 July 2006, is analysed with the following events occurring:

- the land is sold in the 2008–09 period
- the equipment is depreciated on a straight-line basis over a five-year period
- the inventory on hand at 1 July 2006 is all sold by 30 June 2007, the end of the first year
- the patent has an indefinite life, and is tested for impairment annually, with an impairment loss of $5000 recognised in the 2007–08 period
- the contingent liability results in a payment of $10 000 in June 2007, with no further liability existing.

Each of the assets will now be analysed separately with the consolidation worksheet subsequently shown for the 2008–09 period.

Land

At acquisition date, 1 July 2006, the business combination valuation entry is:

Land	Dr	20 000
Deferred tax liability	Cr	6 000
Business combination valuation reserve	Cr	14 000

At *30 June 2007*, because the land is still on hand, the same valuation entry is made in the consolidation worksheet used to prepare the consolidated financial statements at that date. It is assumed in this period that the asset is not held for sale and is recorded at cost.

Assume in the *2007–08 financial period* that the land is classified as held for sale and is accounted for under IFRS 5 *Non-current Assets Held for Sale and Discontinued Operations*. The land is then recorded at the lower of its carrying amount and fair value less costs to sell. Assuming the carrying amount is the lower value, the business combination valuation entry in the consolidation worksheet prepared at 30 June 2008 is the same as that for 30 June 2007.

Assume in the *2008–09 financial period* that the land is sold for $200 000, with $1000 costs to sell being incurred. Sub Ltd will record a gain on sale of $49 000 (being $200 000 − $150 000 − $1000). From the group's perspective, the gain on sale is only $29 000 (being $200 000 − $170 000 − $1000). On consolidation, an adjustment to reduce the recorded gain by $20 000 is required. The carrying amount of the land sold causes the difference in gain on sale. The cost of the land is greater to the group than to the subsidiary. As the asset has been sold, the deferred tax liability is reversed, with an adjustment being made to income tax expense. If the subsidiary records both proceeds on sale and carrying amount of land sold, the valuation entry at 30 June 2008 is as shown opposite.

Carrying amount of land sold	Dr	20 000	
Income tax expense	Cr		6 000
Business combination valuation reserve	Cr		14 000

Alternatively, if the subsidiary's financial statements show a gain on sale:

Gain on sale of land	Dr	20 000	
Income tax expense	Cr		6 000
Business combination valuation reserve	Cr		14 000

In subsequent periods, the valuation entry is:

| Retained earnings (opening balance) | Dr | 14 000 | |
| Business combination valuation reserve | Cr | | 14 000 |

This entry has no effect on total equity. It reflects the fact that, whereas the subsidiary recognised the increase in worth of the land in retained earnings, the group recognised the increased value in the business combination valuation reserve. Where revalued assets are derecognised, as noted in paragraph 41 of IAS 16 *Property, Plant and Equipment*, it is usual business practice to transfer the revaluation reserve to retained earnings. If this principle is applied on consolidation, then the business combination valuation entries in the year of sale of the land are:

Carrying amount of land sold/gain on sale	Dr	20 000	
Income tax expense	Cr		6 000
Business combination valuation reserve	Cr		14 000

Business combination valuation reserve	Dr	14 000	
Transfer from business combination			
valuation reserve (retained earnings)	Cr		14 000

These two entries can be simplified into one entry:

Carrying amount of land sold/gain on sale	Dr	20 000	
Income tax expense	Cr		6 000
Transfer from business combination			
valuation reserve	Cr		14 000

Because this entry has no effect on retained earnings, no consolidation worksheet entries are required in subsequent periods.

Equipment
The business combination valuation entry at 1 July 2006 is:

Accumulated depreciation – equipment	Dr	170 000	
Equipment	Cr		150 000
Deferred tax liability	Cr		6 000
Business combination valuation reserve	Cr		14 000

The asset is depreciated on a straight-line basis evenly over a five-year period (at 20% per annum). Because the asset is recognised on consolidation at an amount that is $20 000 greater than that recognised in the records of the subsidiary, the depreciation expense to the group must also be greater. The difference in depreciation reflects the extra amount paid for the equipment by the group. The adjustment for depreciation results in changes to the carrying amount of the asset. Differences between the tax base and the carrying amount are reflected in the deferred tax liability. As the asset is recovered by use, the deferred tax liability recognised at acquisition date is progressively reversed, with the movement being in proportion to depreciation charges — in this case 20% per annum. The adjustments for depreciation and the related tax effects are recognised in the consolidation worksheet valuation entries in the periods subsequent to acquisition date.

The business combination valuation entries for equipment at 30 June 2007 are:

Accumulated depreciation – equipment	Dr	170 000	
Equipment	Cr		150 000
Deferred tax liability	Cr		6 000
Business combination valuation reserve	Cr		14 000
Depreciation expense	Dr	4 000	
Accumulated depreciation	Cr		4 000
(20% × $20 000 p.a.)			
Deferred tax liability	Dr	1 200	
Income tax expense	Cr		1 200
(20% × $6000, or 30% × $4000 p.a.)			

Note that the first entry is the same as that made at acquisition date, with the other two entries reflecting subsequent depreciation and tax-effect changes.

The valuation entries at 30 June 2009 reflect the need to adjust for three years' depreciation (for two prior periods and a current period):

Accumulated depreciation – equipment	Dr	170 000	
Equipment	Cr		150 000
Deferred tax liability	Cr		6 000
Business combination valuation reserve	Cr		14 000
Depreciation expense	Dr	4 000	
Retained earnings (1/7/08)	Dr	8 000	
Accumulated depreciation	Cr		12 000
(20% × $20 000 p.a.)			
Deferred tax liability	Dr	3 600	
Income tax expense	Cr		1 200
Retained earnings (1/7/08)	Cr		2 400
(20% × $6000, or 30% × $4000 p.a.)			

The equipment is fully depreciated by 30 June 2011. In that year, the valuation entries for equipment are:

Accumulated depreciation – equipment	Dr	170 000	
Equipment	Cr		150 000
Deferred tax liability	Cr		6 000
Business combination valuation reserve	Cr		14 000
Depreciation expense	Dr	4 000	
Retained earnings (1/7/10)	Dr	16 000	
Accumulated depreciation	Cr		20 000
(20% × $20 000 p.a.)			

Deferred tax liability	Dr	6 000	
Income tax expense	Cr		1 200
Retained earnings (1/7/10)	Cr		4 800
(20% × $6000, or 30% × $4000 p.a.)			

Since the equipment is fully consumed and then derecognised, a further entry is required:

| Equipment | Dr | 150 000 | |
| Accumulated depreciation – equipment | Cr | | 150 000 |

These entries could be combined as follows:

Depreciation expense	Dr	4 000	
Income tax expense	Cr		1 200
Retained earnings (1/7/10)	Dr	11 200	
Business combination valuation reserve	Cr		14 000

As with the land example, and because the asset is derecognised at 30 June 2011, the credit could be made to 'Transfer from business combination valuation reserve' instead of to 'Business combination valuation reserve'. Consequently, there would be no need for any valuation adjustment entries for equipment in subsequent periods.

Inventory

The valuation entry for inventory at acquisition date, 1 July 2006, is:

Inventory	Dr	5 000	
Deferred tax liability	Cr		1 500
Business combination valuation reserve	Cr		3 500

The key event affecting the subsequent accounting for inventory is the sale of the inventory by the subsidiary. Assume the inventory is sold in the 2006–07 period for $90 000. The subsidiary records cost of sales at the carrying amount of $75 000, whereas the cost to the group is $80 000. In the consolidation worksheet, instead of the $5000 adjustment to inventory, a $5000 adjustment to cost of sales is required. As the inventory is sold, the deferred tax liability is reversed. As with land and equipment, the business combination valuation reserve is transferred to retained earnings because the asset is derecognised.

The valuation entry at 30 June 2007 is then:

Cost of sales	Dr	5 000	
Income tax expense	Cr		1 500
Transfer from business combination valuation reserve	Cr		3 500

Because this entry has a zero effect on closing retained earnings, no consolidation worksheet entry is required in subsequent years.

In relation to the sale of inventory, a comparison of what is recorded by Sub Ltd and what is shown in the consolidated financial statements at 30 June 2007 is as follows:

	Sub Ltd	Consolidation	
Sales	$90 000	$90 000	
Cost of sales	75 000	80 000	(75 000 + 5000)
Profit before income tax	15 000	10 000	
Income tax expense	4 500	3 000	(4500 − 1500)
Profit	$10 500	$ 7 000	

If at 30 June 2007 only 80% of the inventory had been sold, then the valuation entry must reflect adjustments both to cost of sales and ending inventory. The consolidation worksheet valuation entries, reflecting the 80% sold and the 20% still on hand, are:

Cost of sales	Dr	4 000	
Income tax expense	Cr		1 200
Transfer from business combination			
valuation reserve	Cr		2 800

This entry has no effect on subsequent periods' consolidation worksheets.

Inventory	Dr	1 000	
Deferred tax liability	Cr		300
Business combination valuation reserve	Cr		700

Assuming the inventory is all sold by 30 June 2008, the valuation entry in the consolidation worksheet prepared at that date is:

Cost of sales	Dr	1 000	
Income tax expense	Cr		300
Transfer from business combination			
valuation reserve	Cr		700

Patent

The business combination valuation entry at acquisition date, 1 July 2006, is:

Patent	Dr	20 000	
Deferred tax liability	Cr		6 000
Business combination valuation reserve	Cr		14 000

This entry is used in each year that the patent continues to have an indefinite life. A change occurs only if there is an impairment loss. In this example, an impairment loss of $5000 occurs in the 2007–08 period. The business combination valuation entries at 30 June 2008 are then:

Patent	Dr	20 000	
Deferred tax liability	Cr		6 000
Business combination valuation reserve	Cr		14 000
Impairment loss	Dr	5 000	
Accumulated impairment losses	Cr		5 000
Deferred tax liability	Dr	1 500	
Income tax expense	Cr		1 500

The entries at 30 June 2009 are:

Patent	Dr	20 000	
Deferred tax liability	Cr		6 000
Business combination valuation reserve	Cr		14 000
Retained earnings (1/7/08)	Dr	3 500	
Deferred tax liability	Dr	1 500	
Accumulated impairment losses	Cr		5 000

Contingent liabilities

The business combination valuation entry at 1 July 2006 is:

Business combination valuation reserve	Dr	10 500	
Deferred tax asset	Dr	4 500	
Contingent liability	Cr		15 000

If the contingent liability is paid or derecognised, then the above entry changes. In this example, a payment of $10 000 is made during the first year in relation to the liability. The subsidiary records an expense of $10 000. As there is no expense to the group, it must be eliminated on consolidation. Instead, a gain of $5000 is recognised by the group as the contingent liability of $15 000 is settled for $10 000. The business combination valuation entry at 30 June 2007 is:

Transfer from business combination valuation reserve	Dr	10 500	
Income tax expense	Dr	4 500	
Expense	Cr		10 000
Gain on write-down of liability	Cr		5 000

No entry is required in 30 June 2009.

Business combination valuation entries at 30 June 2009

The valuation entries for all assets at 30 June 2009 are as shown in figure 20.10.

1. Carrying amount of land sold/gain	Dr	20 000	
Income tax expense	Cr		6 000
Transfer from business combination valuation reserve	Cr		14 000
2. Accumulated depreciation – equipment	Dr	170 000	
Equipment	Cr		150 000
Deferred tax liability	Cr		6 000
Business combination valuation reserve	Cr		14 000
Depreciation expense	Dr	4 000	
Retained earnings (1/7/08)	Dr	8 000	
Accumulated depreciation	Cr		12 000
(20% × $20 000 p.a.)			
Deferred tax liability	Dr	3 600	
Income tax expense	Cr		1 200
Retained earnings (1/7/08)	Cr		2 400
(20% × $6000, or 30% × $4000 p.a.)			
3. Patent	Dr	20 000	
Deferred tax liability	Cr		6 000
Business combination valuation reserve	Cr		14 000
Retained earnings (1/7/08)	Dr	5 000	
Accumulated impairment losses	Cr		5 000

FIGURE 20.10   Business combination valuation entries at 30 June 2009

20.5.2 Pre-acquisition entries

The pre-acquisition entry at acquisition date, relating to the example in figure 20.3, is:

Retained earnings (1/7/06)	Dr	140 000	
Share capital	Dr	300 000	
Business combination valuation reserve	Dr	35 000	
Goodwill	Dr	25 000	
Shares in Sub Ltd	Cr		500 000

There are four events that can cause a change in this entry subsequent to acquisition date:
- impairment of goodwill
- transfers from business combination valuation reserve, as undertaken in the consolidation worksheet valuation entries
- dividends paid and payable from pre-acquisition equity
- transfers to and from pre-acquisition retained earnings and other reserves.

In any particular year, some of these events will have occurred in prior periods, and some will occur in the current period. The pre-acquisition entries for the current period consist of the combined pre-acquisition entry at the beginning of the current period (the pre-acquisition entry at the acquisition date adjusted for the effects of all pre-acquisition equity changes up to the beginning of the current period) and entries relating to changes in pre-acquisition equity in the current period.

Impairment of goodwill

The impairment of goodwill affects the pre-acquisition entry. Impairment tests for goodwill are undertaken annually. Assume that goodwill is written down by $5000 in the 2007–08 period as a result of an impairment test. In the consolidation worksheet prepared at 30 June 2008, the pre-acquisition entry will recognise the $25 000 goodwill acquired. However, a further entry is required to recognise the impairment of the goodwill:

Impairment expense	Dr	5 000	
Accumulated impairment losses	Cr		5 000

At 30 June 2009, assuming no further impairment, the pre-acquisition entry incorporating the impairment of the goodwill is:

Retained earnings (1/7/08)*	Dr	145 000	
Share capital	Dr	300 000	
Business combination valuation reserve	Dr	35 000	
Goodwill	Dr	25 000	
Accumulated impairment losses	Cr		5 000
Shares in Sub Ltd	Cr		500 000

* $140 000 + $5000

Changes in business combination valuation entries

LO 11

For the items affected by business combination valuation adjustments, four changes since acquisition date have affected the pre-acquisition entry. Two of these occurred in the year ending 30 June 2007:
- the sale of inventory on hand at acquisition date
- the payment and write-off of the contingent liability.

In both cases, the adjustment was made to 'Transfer from business combination valuation reserve' in the business combination valuation entries at 30 June 2007.

This transfer affects the pre-acquisition entry because the valuation reserves are created in the valuation entries and, being part of pre-acquisition equity, are eliminated in the pre-acquisition entry (see for example the worksheet in figure 20.7). If the valuation entry gives rise to a transfer from the business combination valuation reserve, instead of a business combination valuation reserve, then the adjustment in the pre-acquisition entry must also be made to the transfer account. This is done by adding an additional entry to the pre-acquisition entry in the year of transfer (see below). The need to make an extra adjustment in the pre-acquisition entry should be obvious from viewing the valuation entries. It is only if there is, or has been in prior periods, a transfer in the valuation entries that this flows through to the pre-acquisition entry.

The pre-acquisition entries at 30 June 2007 affected by the sale of inventory and the payment of the contingent liability are then:

Retained earnings (1/7/06)	Dr	140 000	
Share capital	Dr	300 000	
Business combination valuation reserve	Dr	35 000	
Goodwill	Dr	25 000	
Shares in Sub Ltd	Cr		500 000
Business combination valuation reserve	Dr	7 000	
Transfer from business combination			
valuation reserve	Cr		7 000
($3500 inventory and $10 500 contingent liability)			

In the consolidation worksheet at 30 June 2008, assuming no other transfers or events, the pre-acquisition entries are the combination of the two entries from the previous period's worksheet plus the adjustment for goodwill impairment:

Retained earnings (1/7/07)	Dr	133 000	
Share capital	Dr	300 000	
Business combination valuation reserve	Dr	42 000	
Goodwill	Dr	25 000	
Shares in Sub Ltd	Cr		500 000
Impairment expense	Dr	5 000	
Accumulated impairment losses	Cr		5 000

In the 2008–09 period (the current period), pre-acquisition balances are affected by the sale of the land. As can be seen from the valuation entry for land in section 20.5.1, in the current period there is a transfer from the business combination valuation reserve to retained earnings of $14 000. This then requires the following entry to be included in the pre-acquisition entries for the current period:

Transfer from business combination valuation reserve	Dr	14 000	
Business combination valuation reserve	Cr		14 000

In summary, the pre-acquisition entries to be passed in the consolidation worksheet at 30 June 2009 are as shown in figure 20.11. These are affected by the sale of inventory and payment of the contingent liability in 2006–07, the impairment of goodwill in 2007–08 and the sale of land in 2008–09.

4. Retained earnings (1/7/08)*		Dr	138 000	
Share capital		Dr	300 000	
Business combination valuation reserve		Dr	42 000	
Goodwill		Dr	25 000	
Accumulated impairment losses		Cr		5 000
Shares in Sub Ltd		Cr		500 000
5. Transfer from business combination valuation reserve		Dr	14 000	
Business combination valuation reserve		Cr		14 000

*$138 000 = $140 000 + $3500 (inventory) + $5000 (goodwill impairment) − $10 500 (contingent liability paid)

FIGURE 20.11 Pre-acquisition entries at 30 June 2009

Figure 20.12 (below and opposite) shows the consolidation worksheet at 30 June 2009, with the worksheet containing the adjustment entries from figures 20.10 and 20.11.

Financial statements	Parent Ltd	Sub Ltd	Adjustments Dr			Adjustments Cr		Consolidation
	$	$		$		$		$
Revenues	120 000	95 000						215 000
Expenses	85 000	72 000	2	4 000				161 000
	35 000	23 000						54 000
Gain on sale of non-current assets	15 000	31 000	1	20 000				26 000
Profit before tax	50 000	54 000						80 000
Income tax expense	15 000	21 000				6 000	1	
						1 200	2	28 800
Profit for the period	35 000	33 000						51 200
Retained earnings (1/7/08)	420 000	220 000	2	8 000		2 400	2	
			3	5 000				
			4	138 000				491 400
Transfer from business combination valuation reserve	–	–	5	14 000		14 000	1	–
Retained earnings (30/6/09)	455 000	253 000						537 100
Share capital	550 000	300 000	4	300 000				550 000
Business combination valuation reserve	–		4	42 000		14 000	2	–
						14 000	3	
						14 000	5	
	1 005 000	553 000						1 092 600
Provisions	40 000	40 000						80 000
Payables	32 000	24 000						56 000

Financial statements	Parent Ltd	Sub Ltd		Adjustments			Consolidation
				Dr	Cr		
	$	$		$	$		$
Tax liabilities	12 000	16 000	2	3 600	6 000	2	
					6 000	3	36 400
	84 000	80 000					172 400
Total equity and liabilities	1 089 000	633 000					1 265 000
Cash	65 000	95 000					160 000
Land	170 000	50 000					220 000
Equipment	750 000	683 000			150 000	2	1 283 000
Accumulated depreciation	(448 000)	(270 000)	2	170 000	12 000	2	(560 000)
Shares in Sub Ltd	500 000	–			500 000	4	–
Inventory	52 000	75 000					127 000
Patent	–	–	3	20 000			20 000
Accumulated impairment losses	–	–			5 000	3	(5 000)
Goodwill	–	–	4	25 000			25 000
Accumulated impairment losses					5 000	3	(5 000)
Total assets	1 089 000	633 000		749 600	749 600		1 265 000

FIGURE 20.12   Consolidation worksheet at 30 June 2009

LO 12

Dividends from pre-acquisition equity

Dividends are commonly declared and paid by the subsidiary after the acquisition date. The examples in this chapter assume that the parent owns all the shares in the subsidiary, so all subsidiary dividends are paid to the parent. These dividends may be paid from pre-acquisition equity or post-acquisition equity. Dividends from post-acquisition equity are discussed in chapter 21 of this book.

This chapter assumes that the subsidiary will pass the following entries for dividends paid and declared in its own records:

Dividend paid		Dr	XXX
Cash		Cr	XXX
(Dividend paid in the current period)			
Dividend declared		Dr	XXX
Dividend payable		Cr	XXX
(Dividend declared in the current period)			

Because the dividends are paid or declared from pre-acquisition equity, the parent will recognise the dividend as a reduction in the investment in the subsidiary rather than as revenue. It represents a return of equity acquired at acquisition date rather than a return on the investment. Therefore, the format of the entries in the parent's records is:

Cash	Dr	XXX	
Shares in subsidiary	Cr		XXX
(Dividend paid by subsidiary)			
Dividend receivable	Dr	XXX	
Shares in subsidiary	Cr		XXX
(Dividend declared by subsidiary)			

Because the dividends are paid or declared from pre-acquisition equity, the consolidation worksheet adjustment entry that is affected is the pre-acquisition entry. Assume for all the cases illustrated below that the pre-acquisition entry for the year ending 30 June 2007, apart from the effect of dividends, is as follows:

Retained earnings (1/7/06)	Dr	140 000	
Share capital	Dr	300 000	
Business combination valuation reserve	Dr	60 000	
Shares in subsidiary	Cr		500 000

Case 1: Dividend paid in the current period

Assume that in the 2006–07 period the subsidiary pays a dividend of $5000. The entries passed in the parent and the subsidiary as a result of the dividend are:

Parent			
Cash	Dr	5 000	
Shares in subsidiary	Cr		5 000

Subsidiary			
Dividend paid	Dr	5 000	
Cash	Cr		5 000

Note that the parent now records the investment in the subsidiary at $495 000. The pre-acquisition entries for the 2006–07 period are shown in figure 20.13.

Retained earnings (1/7/06)	Dr	140 000	
Share capital	Dr	300 000	
Business combination valuation reserve	Dr	60 000	
Shares in subsidiary	Cr		500 000
Shares in subsidiary	Dr	5 000	
Dividend paid	Cr		5 000

FIGURE 20.13 Dividend paid in the current period

The dividend paid of $5000 is eliminated because the group has not paid any dividends to parties external to the group. Therefore, the dividend paid and reported by the subsidiary in its financial statements cannot be carried forward into the consolidated financial statements.

In subsequent periods, the pre-acquisition entry becomes:

Retained earnings (opening balance)*	Dr	135 000	
Share capital	Dr	300 000	
Business combination valuation reserve	Dr	60 000	
Shares in subsidiary	Cr		495 000

* $140 000 – $5000

Case 2: Dividend declared in the current period

Assume that in the 2006–07 period the subsidiary declares but does not pay a dividend of $6000. The entries passed in the parent and the subsidiary as a result of the dividend are:

Parent				Subsidiary			
Dividend receivable	Dr	6 000		Dividend declared	Dr	6 000	
Shares in subsidiary	Cr		6 000	Dividend payable	Cr		6 000

Note that the parent now records the investment in the subsidiary at $494 000. The pre-acquisition entries for the 2006–07 period are shown in figure 20.14.

Retained earnings (1/7/06)	Dr	140 000	
Share capital	Dr	300 000	
Business combination valuation reserve	Dr	60 000	
Shares in subsidiary	Cr		500 000
Shares in subsidiary	Dr	6 000	
Dividend receivable	Cr		6 000
Dividend payable	Dr	6 000	
Dividend declared	Cr		6 000

FIGURE 20.14   Dividend declared in the current period

The group has neither an obligation to pay dividends to external parties nor an expectation of receiving dividends from external parties. Hence, the dividend payable and the dividend receivable must be eliminated on consolidation.

If the dividend is paid in the 2007–08 period, the pre-acquisition entry in the consolidation worksheet prepared at 30 June 2008 is:

Retained earnings (1/7/07)*	Dr	134 000	
Share capital	Dr	300 000	
Business combination valuation reserve	Dr	60 000	
Shares in subsidiary	Cr		494 000

* $140 000 – $6000

The dividend receivable raised by the parent and the dividend payable raised by the subsidiary are closed in the records of the parent and the subsidiary on payment of the dividend. They are therefore no longer present in these entities' financial statements at 30 June 2008.

Case 3: Bonus share dividend

Assume that in the 2006–07 period the subsidiary pays a dividend of $3000 by the issue of bonus shares. The entries passed in the parent and the subsidiary as a result of the dividend are:

Parent				Subsidiary			
No entry required				Bonus dividend paid	Dr	3 000	
				Share capital	Cr		3 000

No entry is required in the parent because its share of wealth in the subsidiary is unchanged by the bonus share issue. The pre-acquisition entries for the 2006–07 period are shown in figure 20.15.

Retained earnings (1/7/06)	Dr	140 000	
Share capital	Dr	300 000	
Business combination valuation reserve	Dr	60 000	
Shares in subsidiary	Cr		500 000
Share capital	Dr	3 000	
Bonus dividend paid	Cr		3 000

FIGURE 20.15 Dividend provided for in the current period

The effect of the bonus dividend is to increase the share capital of the subsidiary by $3000 and to reduce the retained earnings by the same amount. There is no overall change in the pre-acquisition equity of the subsidiary, just a transfer from one equity account to another. Accordingly, there is no change in the balance of the investment account in the records of the parent.

The pre-acquisition entry in subsequent periods is:

Retained earnings (opening balance)*	Dr	137 000	
Share capital	Dr	303 000	
Business combination valuation reserve	Dr	60 000	
Shares in subsidiary	Cr		500 000

* $140 000 – $3000

LO 13

Pre-acquisition reserve transfers

From time to time the subsidiary may transfer retained earnings to reserves, or make transfers from reserves to retained earnings. These do not cause any change in the total pre-acquisition equity but simply change the composition of that equity. Therefore, there is no change in the investment account recorded by the parent entity. In fact, the parent is unaffected by these transfers.

Assume for the cases illustrated below that the pre-acquisition entry for the year ending 30 June 2007, apart from the effect of reserve transfers, is as follows:

Retained earnings (1/7/06)	Dr	140 000	
Share capital	Dr	300 000	
Business combination valuation reserve	Dr	60 000	
Shares in subsidiary	Cr		500 000

Case 1: Transfer from retained earnings to other reserves

Assume that in the 2006–07 period the subsidiary transfers $4000 to general reserve from retained earnings. The entry passed in the subsidiary as a result of the transfer is:

| Transfer to general reserve | Dr | 4 000 | |
| General reserve | Cr | | 4 000 |

The pre-acquisition entries for the 2006–07 period are shown in figure 20.16.

Retained earnings (1/7/06)	Dr	140 000	
Share capital	Dr	300 000	
Business combination valuation reserve	Dr	60 000	
Shares in subsidiary	Cr		500 000
General reserve	Dr	4 000	
Transfer to general reserve	Cr		4 000

FIGURE 20.16 Transfer to general reserve in the current period

As both the transfer to general reserve account and the general reserve account are pre-acquisition in nature, they are eliminated as part of the pre-acquisition entry. The pre-acquisition entry in subsequent periods is:

Retained earnings (opening balance)*	Dr	136 000	
Share capital	Dr	300 000	
Business combination valuation reserve	Dr	60 000	
General reserve	Dr	4 000	
Shares in subsidiary	Cr		500 000

* $140 000 – $4000

In this case, as well as the following cases, the only equity account in which movements (transfers to and from) are specifically identified is retained earnings. Movements within the general reserve account are not specifically noted. This is because, as illustrated in figure 20.12, the retained earnings account and changes therein are used to connect the income statement accounts and the balance sheet accounts. In preparing the consolidated statement of changes in equity, where movements in all equity accounts are disclosed, adjustments for pre-acquisition transfers must be taken into account. Whether such adjustments are necessary can be seen from viewing the consolidation worksheet and the adjustments made to individual equity accounts. A similar issue arises in preparing other notes to the consolidated financial statements (such as property, plant and equipment) where movements such as additions and disposals must be disclosed.

Case 2: Transfers to retained earnings from reserves

This case uses the information in case 1, in which a $4000 general reserve was created. Assume that in the 2007–08 period the subsidiary transfers $1000 to retained earnings from general reserve. The entry passed in the subsidiary as a result of the transfer is:

General reserve	Dr	1 000	
Transfer from general reserve	Cr		1 000

The pre-acquisition entries for the 2007–08 period are shown in figure 20.17.

Retained earnings (1/7/07)	Dr	136 000	
Share capital	Dr	300 000	
Business combination valuation reserve	Dr	60 000	
General reserve	Dr	4 000	
Shares in subsidiary	Cr		500 000
Transfer from general reserve	Dr	1 000	
General reserve	Cr		1 000

FIGURE 20.17   Transfer from general reserve in the current period

As both the transfer from general reserve account and general reserve account are pre-acquisition in nature, they are eliminated as part of the pre-acquisition entry. The pre-acquisition entry in subsequent periods is:

Retained earnings (opening balance)*	Dr	137 000	
Share capital	Dr	300 000	
Business combination valuation reserve	Dr	60 000	
General reserve	Dr	3 000	
Shares in subsidiary	Cr		500 000

* $140 000 – $4000 + $1000

20.6 Comprehensive example

On 1 July 2005, Oslo Ltd acquired 100% of the issued shares of Helsinki Ltd on a cum div. basis. The fair value of the consideration paid was measured at $335 000. At this date, the records of Helsinki Ltd included the following information:

Share capital	$200 000
General reserve	5 000
Retained earnings	100 000
Dividend payable	20 000
Goodwill	5 000

The dividend liability at 1 July 2005 was paid in August 2005. At 1 July 2005, all the identifiable assets and liabilities of Helsinki Ltd were recorded in the subsidiary's books at fair value except for the following assets:

	Carrying amount	Fair value
Inventory	$ 40 000	$ 43 000
Plant (cost $240 000)	$180 000	$185 000

The inventory was all sold by 30 June 2006. The plant has a further five-year life and is depreciated on a straight-line basis. Goodwill was not impaired in any period. When assets are sold or fully consumed, any relating business combination valuation reserve is transferred to retained earnings. The tax rate is 30%.

The summarised financial statements of the entities within the group at 30 June 2007 were as shown in figure 20.18. Both the dividend paid in the 2006–07 period and the transfer to general reserve were from profits earned prior to acquisition date. In the 2005–06 period, a $5000 dividend was paid from pre-acquisition profits.

Problem

Prepare the consolidated income statement, statement of changes in equity, and balance sheet for Oslo Ltd at 30 June 2007.

Solution: Acquisition analysis

At 1 July 2005	
Net fair value of identifiable assets, liabilities and contingent liabilities of Helsinki Ltd	= $200 000 + $5000 + $100 000 (equity)
	− $5000 goodwill recorded
	+ ($5000) (1 − 30%) (BCVR − plant)
	+ ($3000) (1 − 30%) (BCVR − inventory)
	= $305 600
Cost of combination	= $335 000 − $20 000 (dividend receivable)
	= $315 000
Goodwill	= $315 000 − $305 600
	= $9400
Unrecorded goodwill	= $9400 − $5000
	= $4400

Consolidation worksheet adjustment entries at 30 June 2007

Business combination valuation entries at 30 June 2007

1. Accumulated depreciation – plant	Dr	60 000	
Plant	Cr		55 000
Deferred tax liability	Cr		1 500
Business combination valuation reserve	Cr		3 500
Depreciation expense	Dr	1 000	
Retained earnings (1/7/06)	Dr	1 000	
Accumulated depreciation	Cr		2 000
(20% × $5000 p.a. for two years)			
Deferred tax liability	Dr	600	
Income tax expense	Cr		300
Retained earnings (1/7/06)	Cr		300

Pre-acquisition entries at 30 June 2007

The pre-acquisition entry at acquisition date is:

Retained earnings (1/7/06)	Dr	100 000	
Share capital	Dr	200 000	
General reserve	Dr	5 000	
Business combination valuation reserve	Dr	5 600	
Goodwill	Dr	4 400	
Shares in Helsinki Ltd	Cr		315 000

Between the acquisition date and the beginning of the current period:
• the inventory on hand at acquisition date has been sold
• the business combination valuation reserve of $2100 created at acquisition date has been transferred to retained earnings
• a $5000 dividend from pre-acquisition profits was paid in the 2005–06 period, thereby reducing both the retained earnings and the balance of the investment account as recorded by the parent entity.

The pre-acquisition entry at the beginning of the 2006–07 period is then:

2. Retained earnings (1/7/06)*	Dr	97 100	
Share capital	Dr	200 000	
General reserve	Dr	5 000	
Business combination valuation reserve**	Dr	3 500	
Goodwill	Dr	4 400	
Shares in Helsinki Ltd***	Cr		310 000

* $100 000 + $2100 (inventory) – $5000 (dividend)
** $5600 – $2100 (inventory)
*** $315 000 – $5000 (dividend)

Two further events in the current period affect the balances of pre-acquisition equity:
• a $10 000 dividend from pre-acquisition profits was paid in the current period
• a transfer to general reserve of $15 000 was made in the current period.

Two extra entries are then required:

3. Shares in Helsinki Ltd	Dr	10 000	
Dividend paid	Cr		10 000
4. General reserve	Dr	15 000	
Transfer to general reserve	Cr		15 000

Both the business combination valuation entries and the pre-acquisition entries are then passed through the consolidation worksheet as shown in figure 20.18.

Financial statements	Oslo Ltd	Helsinki Ltd	Adjustments				Consolidation
				Dr	Cr		
	$	$		$	$		$
Revenues	125 000	90 000					215 000
Expenses	85 000	65 000	1	1 000			151 000
Profit before tax	40 000	25 000					64 000
Income tax expense	15 500	10 200			300	1	25 400
Profit for the period	24 500	14 800					38 600
Retained earnings (1/7/08)	150 000	85 000	1	1 000	300	1	
			2	97 100			137 200
	174 500	99 800					175 800
Transfer to general reserve	20 000	15 000			15 000	4	20 000
Dividend paid	15 000	10 000			10 000	3	15 000
	35 000	25 000					35 000
Retained earnings (30/6/09)	139 500	74 800					140 800
Share capital	500 000	200 000	2	200 000			500 000
Business combination valuation reserve	–	–	2	3 500	3 500	1	–
General reserve	50 000	20 000	2	5 000			
			4	15 000			50 000
	689 500	294 800					690 800
Tax liabilities	11 000	16 000	1	600	1 500	1	27 900
Other liabilities	50 000	20 000					70 000
	61 000	36 000					97 900
Total equity and liabilities	750 500	330 800					788 700
Cash	25 000	5 000					30 000
Inventory	60 000	75 000					135 000
Plant	500 000	300 000			55 000	1	745 000
Accumulated depreciation	(160 000)	(80 000)	1	60 000	2 000	1	(182 000)
Shares in Helsinki Ltd	300 000	–	2	10 000	310 000	2	–
Fixtures and fittings	40 000	38 000					78 000
Accumulated depreciation	(14 500)	(12 200)					(26 700)
Goodwill	–	5 000	2	4 400			9 400
Total assets	750 500	330 800		397 600	397 600		788 700

FIGURE 20.18 Consolidation worksheet

The consolidated financial statements of Oslo Ltd at 30 June 2007 are as shown in figure 20.19.

FIGURE 20.19 Consolidated income statement, statement of changes in equity and balance sheet

Oslo Ltd Consolidated income statement for the year ended 30 June 2007	
Revenues	$ 150 000
Expenses	151 000
Profit before tax	64 000
Income tax expense	25 400
Profit for the period	$ 38 600

Oslo Ltd Consolidated statement of changes in equity for the year ended 30 June 2007	
Profit for the period	$ 38 600
Amount recognised directly in equity	–
Total recognised income and expense for the period	$ 38 600
Retained earnings balance at 1 July 2006	$ 137 200
Profit for the period	38 600
Dividend paid	(15 000)
Transfer to general reserve	(20 000)
Retained earnings balance at 30 June 2007	$ 140 800
General reserve balance at 1 July 2006	$ 30 000
Transfer from retained earnings	20 000
General reserve balance at 30 June 2007	$ 50 000
Share capital balance at 1 July 2006	$ 500 000
Share capital balance at 30 June 2007	$ 500 000

Oslo Ltd Consolidated balance sheet as at 30 June 2007		
EQUITY AND LIABILITIES		
Equity		
Share capital		$ 500 000
Other reserves – general reserve		50 000
Retained earnings		140 800
Total equity		690 800
Non-current liabilities		
Tax liabilities		27 900
Other		70 000
Total non-current liabilities		97 900
Total equity and liabilities		$ 788 700
ASSETS		
Non-current assets		
Plant	$ 745 000	
Accumulated depreciation	(182 000)	$ 563 000
		(*continued*)

Fixtures and fittings	78 000	
Accumulated depreciation	(26 700)	51 300
Goodwill		9 400
		623 700
Current assets		
Cash		30 000
Inventory		135 000
		165 000
Total assets		$ 788 700

20.7 Revaluations in the records of the subsidiary at acquisition date

IFRS 3 does not discuss whether the valuation of the assets of the subsidiary at acquisition date should be done in the consolidation worksheet or in the records of the subsidiary. It is expected that most entities will make their adjustments in the consolidation worksheet, for two reasons:

• Adjustments for assets such as goodwill and inventory would not be allowed in the actual records of the subsidiary. Goodwill is not allowed to be revalued because it would amount to the recognition of internally generated goodwill, while inventory cannot be written to an amount greater than cost.

• The revaluation of non-current assets in the records of the subsidiary means that the subsidiary has effectively adopted the revaluation model of accounting for those assets. As discussed in chapter 10 of this book, IAS 16 *Property, Plant and Equipment* then requires that the assets be kept at amounts not materially different from fair value. For entities wanting to measure assets using the cost model, the revaluation of subsidiary assets would then be undertaken in the consolidation worksheet.

Note that the business combination valuation entries applied in the consolidation worksheet for property, plant and equipment assets in this chapter are of the same form as those applied for property, plant and equipment in chapter 10. Hence, the consolidated financial statements at acquisition date would be the same regardless of whether revaluation occurs on consolidation or in the records of the subsidiary. In future periods, differences would arise because there is no requirement for valuations done in the consolidation worksheet to be updated for subsequent changes in the fair values of the assets.

LO 14

20.8 Disclosure

Paragraphs 66–77 of IFRS 3 cover the disclosure of information about business combinations. These paragraphs require an acquirer to disclose information that enables users of its financial statements to evaluate the nature and financial effect of business combinations that occurred during the reporting period, as well as those that occurred between the balance date and when the financial statements are authorised for issue. Examples of disclosures required by these paragraphs are given in figure 20.20.

FIGURE 20.20 Disclosure of business combinations

Note 4 Business combinations	IFRS 3 Para.
On 20 October 2005, Stockholm Ltd acquired 100% of the voting shares of Uppsala Ltd, a listed Swedish company specialising in the manufacture of electronic parts for sound equipment. To acquire this ownership interest, Stockholm Ltd issued 600 000 ordinary shares, valued at $2.50 per share, which rank equally for dividends after the acquisition date. The fair value is based on the published market price at acquisition date.	67(a)(b)(c) 67(d)(i)(ii)

No operations were disposed of as part of the combination.   *67(e)*

The total cost of the business combination was $1 800 000 and   *67(d)*
consisted of:

	$000
Shares issued, at fair value	1 500
Cash paid	240
Cash payable in two years time	60
Total cost of combination	1 800

The fair values and the carrying amounts of the assets acquired and liabilities assumed in Uppsala Ltd as at 20 October 2005 were:

	Fair value $000	Carrying amount $000	
Property, plant and equipment	1 240	1 020	*67(f)*
Receivables	340	340	
Inventory	160	130	
Intangibles	302	22	
Goodwill	54	0	
	2 096	1 512	
Payables	152	152	
Provisions	103	103	
Tax liabilities	41	41	
	296	296	
Fair value of net assets of Uppsala Ltd	1 800		

Goodwill in Uppsala Ltd can be attributed to the synergies existing   *67(h)*
within the company, and relate to the high level of training given to
the staff as well as the professional expertise of the employees.
Further, there exist in-process research activities in Uppsala Ltd for
which it was impossible to determine reliable fair values for the
separate recognition of intangible assets.

Uppsala Ltd earned a profit for the period from 20 October 2005 to   *67(i)*
30 June 2006 of $520 000. This has been included in the
consolidated profit for the year ended 30 June 2006.

None of the above information has been prepared on a provisional   *69*
basis.

(continued)

The consolidated profit is shown in the income statement at $5 652 000, which includes the $520 000 contributed by Uppsala Ltd from 20 October 2005 to the end of the period. If Uppsala Ltd had been acquired at 1 July 2005, it is estimated that the consolidated entity would have reported:	70

	$000
Consolidated revenue	36 654
Consolidated profit	6 341

In relation to the business combination in the 2004 period, when Stockholm Ltd acquired all the shares in Turku Ltd, an adjustment was made in the current period due to an error in measurement of property held by Turku Ltd. A loss of $250 000 was recognised in the current reporting period due to the write-down of this property.	72
In the current period profit are included gains on the sale of land acquired as a part of the business combination with Uppsala Ltd. The gain amounted to $100 000 and arose due to an upsurge in demand for inner-city properties.	73(a)

Goodwill *75, 76*

	$000	
Gross amount at 1 July 2005	120	76(a)
Accumulated impairment losses	15	
Carrying amount at 1 July 2005	105	
Goodwill recognised in current period	54	76(b)
Carrying amount at 30 June 2006	159	
Gross amount at 30 June 2006	174	76(h)
Accumulated impairment losses	15	
Carrying amount at 30 June 2006	159	

IAS 27 also requires disclosures in relation to a parent's interest in its subsidiaries. Figure 20.21 illustrates some of these disclosures.

FIGURE 20.21 Disclosures concerning subsidiaries

Note 5 Subsidiaries	IAS 27 Para.
Bergen Ltd has a 40% interest in Vaasa Ltd. Although it has less than half the voting power, Bergen Ltd believes it has control of the financial and operating policies of XYZ Ltd. Bergen Ltd is able to exercise this control because the remaining ownership in Vaasa Ltd is diverse and widely spread, with the next single largest ownership block being 11%.	40(c)
Bergen Ltd has invested in a special purpose entity established by Tampere Ltd. Tampere Ltd established Eura Ltd as a vehicle for distributing the sailing boats that it makes. Bergen Ltd currently owns 60% of the shares issued by Eura Ltd. Because of the limited decisions that the board of Eura Ltd can make due to the constitution of that entity, Bergen Ltd believes that it does not have any real power over the operations of Eura Ltd, so it sees its role in Eura Ltd as that of an investor.	40(d)

Bergen Ltd has a wholly owned subsidiary, Rauma Ltd, which operates within the electricity generating industry. Its balance date is 31 May. Rauma Ltd continues to use this balance date because the government regulating authority requires all entities within the industry to provide financial information to it based on financial position at that date.	*40(e)*
Bergen Ltd has a wholly owned subsidiary, Trelleborg Ltd, in the country of Mambo. Because of constraints on assets leaving the country recently imposed by the new military government, there are major restrictions on the subsidiary being able to transfer funds to Bergen Ltd.	*40(f)*

Paragraph 10 of IAS 27 provides certain parent entities relief from having to prepare consolidated financial statements:

A parent need not present consolidated financial statements if and only if:

(a) the parent is itself a wholly-owned subsidiary, or is a partially-owned subsidiary of another entity and its other owners, including those not otherwise entitled to vote, have been informed about, and do not object to, the parent not presenting consolidated financial statements;

(b) the parent's debt or equity instruments are not traded in a public market (a domestic or foreign stock exchange or an over-the-counter market, including local and regional markets);

(c) the parent did not file, nor is it in the process of filing, its financial statements with a securities commission or other regulatory organisation for the purpose of issuing any class of instruments in a public market; and

(d) the ultimate or any intermediate parent of the parent produces consolidated financial statements available for public use that comply with International Financial Reporting Standards.

Paragraph 41 details disclosures required by such parent entities, these disclosures being made in their separate financial statements:

(a) the fact that the financial statements are separate financial statements; that the exemption from consolidation has been used; the name and country of incorporation or residence of the entity whose consolidated financial statements that comply with International Financial Reporting Standards have been produced for public use; and the address where those consolidated financial statements are obtainable;

(b) a list of significant investments in subsidiaries, jointly controlled entities and associates, including the name, country of incorporation or residence, proportion of ownership interest and, if different, proportion of voting power held; and

(c) a description of the method used to account for the investments listed under (b).

Paragraph 42 requires similar disclosures by parent entities that prepare separate financial statements as well as consolidated financial statements. These disclosures are made in the separate financial statements:

(a) the fact that the statements are separate financial statements and the reasons why those statements are prepared if not required by law;

(b) a list of significant investments in subsidiaries, jointly controlled entities and associates, including the name, country of incorporation or residence, proportion of ownership interest and, if different, proportion of voting power held; and

(c) a description of the method used to account for the investments listed under (b);

and shall identify the financial statements prepared in accordance with paragraph 9 of this Standard, IAS 28 and IAS 31 to which they relate.

20.9 Reverse acquisitions

According to IFRS 3, where a business combination is effected through an acquisition of equity interests, the acquirer is the combining entity that has the power to govern the financial and operating policies of the other entity so as to obtain benefits from its activities. A reverse acquisition occurs when the legal subsidiary has this form of control over the legal parent. The usual circumstance creating a reverse acquisition is where an entity (the legal parent) obtains ownership of the equity of another entity (the legal subsidiary) but, as part of the exchange transaction, it issues enough voting equity as consideration for control of the combined entity to pass to the owners of the legal subsidiary.

To illustrate, consider the following example, which is taken from example 5 in the illustrative examples to IFRS 3. Assume Entity A and Entity B agree to merge. The capital structure of each entity is:

> Entity A – 100 ordinary shares
> Entity B – 60 ordinary shares

Entity A issues $2\frac{1}{2}$ shares in exchange for each ordinary share of Entity B. All of Entity B's shareholders exchange their shares for Entity A shares. Entity A therefore issues 150 shares ($60 \times 2\frac{1}{2}$) for the 60 shares in Entity B. The position subsequent to the share exchange is:

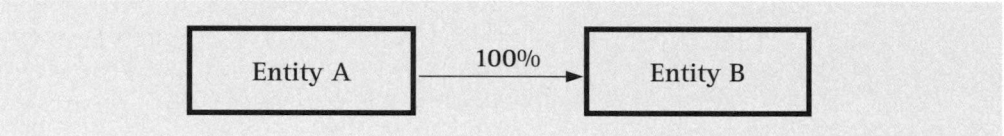

Entity A is now the legal parent of the subsidiary Entity B. However, analysing the shareholding in Entity A shows that it consists of the 100 shares existing prior to the merger and 150 new shares held by the former shareholders in B. In essence, the former shareholders of Entity B now control both Entities A and B. The former Entity B shareholders have a 60% interest in Entity A (150/(100 + 150). The IASB argues that there has been a reverse acquisition, and that Entity B is effectively the acquirer of Entity A.

The key accounting effect of deciding that Entity B is the acquirer is that the assets and liabilities of Entity A are to be valued at fair value. This is contrary to normal acquisition accounting, based on Entity A being the legal parent of entity B, which would require the assets and liabilities of Entity B to be valued at fair value.

Illustrative example 20.1 demonstrates the accounting where a reverse acquisition occurs.

ILLUSTRATIVE EXAMPLE 20.1

Reverse acquisitions

This example is adapted from the illustrative example developed by the IASB and appended to the exposure draft, and uses the Entity A–Entity B scenario described above.

The balance sheets of A Ltd and B Ltd at 30 June 2005 were as shown opposite.

→

	A Ltd	B Ltd
Current assets	$ 500	$ 700
Non-current assets	1 300	3 000
Total assets	$1 800	$ 3 700
Share capital		
100 shares	$ 300	
60 shares		$ 600
Retained earnings	800	1 400
	1 100	2 000
Current liabilities	300	600
Non-current liabilities	400	1 100
	700	1 700
Total equity and liabilities	$1 800	$ 3 700

On 1 July 2005, A Ltd acquired all the issued shares of B Ltd, giving in exchange $2\frac{1}{2}$ A Ltd shares for each ordinary share of B Ltd. A Ltd thus issued 150 shares to acquire the 60 shares issued by B Ltd.

The fair value of each ordinary share of B Ltd at 1 July 2005 is $40, while the quoted market price of A Ltd's ordinary shares is $16. The fair values of A Ltd's identifiable assets and liabilities at acquisition date are the same as their carrying amounts except for the non-current assets whose fair value was $1500. The tax rate is 30%.

In acquiring the shares in B Ltd, A Ltd issued 150 shares at $16 each. Therefore, A Ltd would have raised an investment in B Ltd at $2400. However, under reverse acquisition accounting, the cost of the combination is based on what it would have cost for B Ltd to acquire all the shares in A Ltd, and for the former B Ltd shareholders to have a 60% interest in the combined entities. Because B Ltd has, prior to the acquisition date, a share capital of 60, B Ltd needs to issue 40 shares to the shareholders of A Ltd in exchange for their shares in order for the former B Ltd shareholders to have a 60% interest in B Ltd. If B Ltd issued these 40 shares, it would record a cost of the combination of $1600 (being 40 × $40).

The acquisition analysis then relates the imputed cost of combination of $1600 to the fair value of A Ltd:

Net fair value of A Ltd	= $300 + $800 (equity) +
	$200 (1 − 30%) (BCVR − non-current assets)
	= $1240
Cost of combination	= $1600
Goodwill	= $360

The consolidation worksheet entries are:

1. Change in cost of combination

The purpose of these entries is to eliminate the investment account actually raised by A Ltd and substitute for it the entry that B Ltd would have made if it had actually acquired the shares in A Ltd:

Share capital − A Ltd	Dr	2 400	
Shares in B Ltd	Cr		2 400
Shares in A Ltd	Dr	1 600	
Share capital − B Ltd	Cr		1 600

2. Business combination valuation entries

These entries revalue the assets of A Ltd:

Non-current assets	Dr	200	
Deferred tax liability	Cr		60
Business combination			
valuation reserve	Cr		140

3. Pre-acquisition entry

This entry eliminates the newly created investment in A Ltd from entry 1 above against the equity of A Ltd that existed prior to the merger, but including any valuation reserve raised on consolidation:

Share capital – A Ltd	Dr	300	
Retained earnings	Dr	800	
Business combination valuation			
reserve	Dr	140	
Goodwill	Dr	360	
Shares in A Ltd	Cr		1 600

The consolidation worksheet at acquisition date is shown in figure 20.22. Note:
- the equity of A Ltd on hand at acquisition date is eliminated
- the capital that B Ltd would have issued if it had acquired the shares in A Ltd is carried forward into the balance sheet
- it is A Ltd's assets that are revalued.

Financial statements	A Ltd	B Ltd		Adjustments			Consolidation
				Dr	Cr		
Retained earnings	800	1 400	3	800			1 400
Share capital	2 700	600	1	2 400	1 600	1	
			3	300			2 200
Business combination valuation reserve	–	–	3	140	140	2	–
Current liabilities	300	600					900
Deferred tax liability					60	2	60
Non-current liabilities	400	1 100					1 500
	4 200	3 700					6 060
Current assets	500	700					1 200
Shares in B Ltd	2 400	–			2 400	1	–
Shares in A Ltd			1	1 600	1 600	3	–
Non-current assets	1 300	3 000	2	200			4 500
Goodwill			2	360			360
	4 200	3 700		5 800	5 800		6 060

FIGURE 20.22 Consolidation worksheet — reverse acquisition accounting

20.10 Summary

This chapter is concerned with the preparation of the consolidated financial statements for a group consisting of a parent and a wholly owned subsidiary. Because of the requirements of IFRS 3 to recognise the identifiable net assets of an acquired entity at fair value, an initial adjustment to be made on consolidation is to adjust any assets or liabilities for which there are differences between fair value and carrying amount at the acquisition date. Further, although the identifiable intangible assets and contingent liabilities of the subsidiary may not have been recognised in the subsidiary's records, they are recognised as part of the business combination. These adjustments are made on consolidation in the consolidation worksheet via business combination valuation entries. Where the parent has an investment in the shares of a subsidiary, adjustments via the pre-acquisition entries are necessary to avoid double-counting the group's assets and equities. As a part of the analysis at acquisition date, the existence of goodwill or excess is determined. Adjustments for these amounts are processed via the pre-acquisition entries. Using a consolidation worksheet, the financial statements of the individual entities in the group are added together, the adjustments noted above are made, and the consolidated financial report produced.

1. What is the purpose of the pre-acquisition entries in the preparation of consolidated financial statements?
2. When there is a dividend payable by the subsidiary at acquisition date, under what conditions should the existence of this dividend be taken into consideration in preparing the pre-acquisition entries?
3. Why is it necessary to distinguish pre-acquisition dividends from post-acquisition dividends?
4. If the subsidiary has recorded goodwill in its records at acquisition date, how does this affect the preparation of the pre-acquisition entries?
5. How does the existence of an excess affect the pre-acquisition entries, both in the year of acquisition and in subsequent years?
6. If, at the date the parent acquires a controlling interest in a subsidiary, the carrying amounts of the subsidiary's assets are not equal to fair value, explain why adjustments to these assets are required in the preparation of the consolidated financial statements.
7. How does IFRS 3 *Business Combinations* affect the acquisition analysis?
8. What is the purpose of the business combination valuation entries?
9. Using an example, explain how the business combination entries affect the pre-acquisition entries.
10. Why are some adjustment entries in the previous period's consolidation worksheet also made in the current period's worksheet?

EXERCISES

EXERCISE 20.1   ★

Consolidation worksheet entries one year after acquisition date

At 1 July 2005, Uppsala Ltd acquired all the shares of Malmo Ltd for $283 000. At this date, the equity of Malmo Ltd consisted of:

Share capital — 100 000 shares	$100 000
General reserve	50 000
Retained earnings	20 000

All the identifiable assets and liabilities of Malmo Ltd were recorded at amounts equal to fair value except for the following assets:

	Carrying amount	Fair value
Inventory	$ 60 000	$ 65 000
Plant (cost $280 000)	200 000	210 000

The inventory was all sold by 30 June 2006. The plant has a further five-year life, and depreciation is calculated on a straight-line basis. When revalued assets are sold or fully consumed, any related revaluation surplus is transferred to retained earnings.

The tax rate is 30%.

Required

Prepare the consolidation worksheet entries at 30 June 2006 for the preparation of the consolidated financial statements of Uppsala Ltd.

EXERCISE 20.2   ★

Acquisition analysis, worksheet entries at acquisition date

At 1 July 2005, Arvika Ltd acquired all the shares of Brunnsberg Ltd for $255 000 on a cum div. basis. At this date, the equity of Brunnsberg Ltd consisted of:

Share capital	$160 000
Retained earnings	40 000

At this date, the identifiable assets and liabilities of Brunnsberg Ltd were recorded at fair value except for:

	Carrying amount	Fair value
Inventory	$ 40 000	$ 44 000
Plant (cost $120 000)	100 000	105 000

At 1 July 2005, Brunnsberg Ltd's assets and liabilities included a dividend payable of $5000 and goodwill of $6000 (net of $4000 accumulated impairment losses). An analysis of the unrecorded intangibles of Brunnsberg Ltd revealed that the company had unrecorded internally generated brands, considered to have a fair value of $50 000. Further, Brunnsberg Ltd had expensed research outlays of $80 000 that were considered to have a fair value of $20 000. In its financial statements at 30 June 2005, Brunnsberg Ltd had reported a contingent liability relating to a potential claim by customers for unsatisfactory products, the fair value of the claim being $10 000.

The tax rate is 30%.

Required

Prepare the acquisition analysis at 1 July 2005, and the consolidation worksheet entries for preparation of consolidated financial statements of Arvika Ltd at that date.

EXERCISE 20.3   ★

Business combination valuation and pre-acquisition entries

On 1 July 2005, Kimito Ltd acquired all the share capital of Rauma Ltd for $218 500. At this date, Rauma Ltd's equity comprised:

Share capital — 100 000 shares	$100 000
General reserve	50 000
Retained earnings	36 000

All the identifiable assets and liabilities of Rauma Ltd were recorded at fair value as at 1 July 2005 except for the following:

	Carrying amount	Fair value
Inventory	$27 000	$35 000
Land	75 000	90 000
Equipment (cost $100 000)	50 000	60 000

The equipment is expected to have a further 10-year life. All the inventory was sold by June 2006.

The tax rate is 30%.

On 1 January 2006, Rauma Ltd paid an interim dividend of $10 000 from retained earnings held at 1 July 2005. On 30 June 2006, the directors of Rauma Ltd decided to transfer $25 000 from the general reserve to retained earnings.

Required

Prepare the consolidation worksheet entries for the preparation of consolidated financial statements for Kimito Ltd and its subsidiary Rauma Ltd as at:

1. 1 July 2005
2. 30 June 2006.

EXERCISE 20.4   ★

Pre-acquisition entries, recorded goodwill

On 1 July 2006, Frondheim Ltd acquired the issued shares (cum div.) of Alesund Ltd for $120 000. At that date, the financial statements of Alesund Ltd included the following items:

Share capital	$52 500
General reserve	45 000
Retained earnings	9 000
Dividend payable	7 500

At 1 July 2006, Alesund Ltd had recorded goodwill of $2000, and all of its identifiable assets and liabilities were recorded at fair value. Share capital represents 75 000 shares paid to 70 cents per share. $22 500 of uncalled capital was called up on 1 October 2006. The dividend was paid on 20 October 2006. The tax rate is 30%.

Required
Prepare the pre-acquisition entries for the preparation of consolidated financial statements at:
1. 1 July 2006, immediately after combination
2. 31 December 2006.

EXERCISE 20.5   ★★

Consolidation worksheet

Kristianstad Ltd acquired all the share capital of Angelholm Ltd for $102 000 on 1 July 2003 when the equity of Angelholm Ltd consisted of:

Share capital — 50 000 shares	$50 000
Retained earnings	30 000

All identifiable assets and liabilities of Angelholm Ltd were recorded at amounts equal to fair value, except as follows:

	Carrying amount	Fair value
Inventory	$20 000	$25 000
Plant (cost $80 000)	60 000	70 000

The plant is expected to have a further useful life of five years. All the inventory on hand at 1 July 2003 was sold by 31 December 2003.

On 30 June 2005, the directors of Angelholm Ltd declared a dividend of $5000 payable out of profits earned before 1 July 2003. The income tax rate is 30%.

At 30 June 2005, the following information was obtained from both entities:

	Kristianstad Ltd	Angelholm Ltd
Profit before tax	$ 50 000	$ 40 000
Income tax expense	20 000	15 000
Profit	30 000	25 000
Retained earnings (1/7/04)	50 000	35 000
	80 000	60 000
Dividend declared	20 000	5 000
Retained earnings (30/6/05)	$ 60 000	$ 55 000
Share capital	$150 000	$ 50 000
General reserve	35 000	—
Retained earnings	60 000	55 000
Total equity	245 000	105 000

Provisions	65 000	15 000
Dividend payable	20 000	5 000
Total liabilities	85 000	20 000
Total equity and liabilities	$330 000	$125 000
Cash	$ 13 000	$ 14 000
Accounts receivable	30 000	25 000
Dividend receivable	5 000	–
Inventory	70 000	50 000
Shares in Angelholm Ltd	97 000	–
Plant	200 000	80 000
Accumulated depreciation	(85 000)	(44 000)
Total assets	$330 000	$125 000

Required

1. Prepare the consolidation worksheet entries for the preparation of consolidated financial statements for Kristianstad Ltd and its subsidiary, Angelholm Ltd, as at 1 July 2003.
2. Prepare the consolidation worksheet entries and the consolidation worksheet for the preparation of consolidated financial statements for Kristianstad Ltd and its subsidiary, Angelholm Ltd, as at 30 June 2005.

EXERCISE 20.6   Recorded goodwill, dividends, unrecorded intangible

On 1 July 2005, Kurikka Ltd acquired all the share capital (cum div.) of Vaasa Ltd, giving in exchange 50 000 shares in Kurikka Ltd, these having a fair value at acquisition date of $5 per share. Costs incurred in undertaking the acquisition amounted to $10 000. The dividend payable at the acquisition date was paid in September 2005. At 30 June 2005, the balance sheet of Vaasa Ltd was as follows:

Balance sheet as at 30 June 2005			
Plant and equipment	$218 000	Share capital (150 000 shares)	$150 000
Goodwill	6 000	Retained earnings	84 000
Current assets	44 000	Dividend payable	10 000
		Other liabilities	24 000
	$268 000		$268 000

The recorded amounts of the identifiable assets and liabilities of Vaasa Ltd at the acquisition date were equal to their fair values. Vaasa Ltd had not recorded an internally developed trademark. Kurikka Ltd valued this at $20 000. It was assumed to have a four-year life. The tax rate is 30%. Since 1 July 2005, the following events have occurred:

- On 1 September 2005, Vaasa Ltd paid a $12 000 dividend from profits earned before 1 July 2005.
- On 31 December 2007, Vaasa Ltd paid a bonus share dividend from pre-acquisition profits, the dividend being one share for every three held.
- On 21 September 2008, Vaasa Ltd paid a $5000 dividend from profits earned before 1 July 2005. The dividend had been declared in June 2008.

Required

Prepare the consolidation worksheet entries for the preparation of consolidated financial statements at 30 June 2009.

EXERCISE 20.7   ★★   Excess, consolidation worksheet

As part of a corporate expansion plan, Stavanger Ltd acquired all the share capital (cum div.) of Askoy Ltd on 1 July 2006 for $138 000 cash. The balance sheets of both companies at 30 June 2006 were as follows:

	Stavanger Ltd	Askoy Ltd
Share capital	$180 000	$ 80 000
Retained earnings	82 000	45 000
Total equity	$262 000	$125 000
Provisions	88 000	27 000
Dividend payable	20 000	10 000
Total liabilities	108 000	37 000
Total equity and liabilities	$370 000	$162 000
Cash	$150 000	$ 10 000
Receivables	40 000	25 000
Inventory	55 000	42 000
Plant	190 000	100 000
Accumulated depreciation	(65 000)	(15 000)
Total assets	$370 000	$162 000

All identifiable assets and liabilities of Askoy Ltd were recorded at fair value as at 1 July 2006 except for the following:

	Carrying amount	Fair value
Inventory	$42 000	$45 000
Plant (cost $100 000)	85 000	90 000

The plant is expected to have a further useful life of five years. Inventory held at 1 July 2006 was all sold by 30 June 2007. The dividend payable at 1 July 2006 was paid in October 2006. A dividend of $15 000 was declared on 30 June 2007 out of profits earned before 1 July 2006. The company tax rate is 30%.

Required
1. Prepare the consolidation worksheet entries, the consolidation worksheet and the consolidated balance sheet for Stavanger Ltd and its subsidiary, Askoy Ltd, as at 1 July 2006.
2. Prepare the consolidation worksheet entries for the preparation of consolidated financial statements for Stavanger Ltd and its subsidiary, Askoy Ltd, as at 30 June 2007.

EXERCISE 20.8 ★★

Goodwill, excess, adjustments to goodwill by the subsidiary

The balance sheet of Halmstad Ltd at 30 June 2006 was as follows:

Halmstad Ltd Balance sheet as at 30 June 2006		
Share capital (150 000 shares)		$150 000
Retained earnings		98 000
Total equity		248 000
Dividend payable		10 000
Other liabilities		24 000
Total liabilities		34 000
Total equity and liabilities		$282 000
Inventory		$ 44 000
Non-current assets: Plant and equipment	$390 000	
Accumulated depreciation	(158 000)	
	232 000	
Goodwill	6 000	238 000
Total assets		$282 000

The recorded amounts of the identifiable assets and liabilities of Halmstad Ltd at this date were equal to their fair values except for inventory and plant and equipment, whose fair values were $50 000 and $236 000 respectively. The plant and equipment has a further five-year life. All the inventory was sold by Halmstad Ltd by December 2006. The tax rate is 30%.

On 1 July 2006, Kalkenberg Ltd acquired all the shares (cum div.) in Halmstad Ltd, giving in exchange 50 000 shares in Kalkenberg Ltd, these having a fair value at acquisition date of $5 per share. Costs incurred by Kalkenberg Ltd in undertaking the acquisition amounted to $10 000. The dividend payable was paid in August 2006.

Required

1. Prepare the consolidation worksheet adjustment entries for the preparation of consolidated financial statements at 30 June 2010.
2. Discuss the effects on these entries at 1 July 2006 if the costs incurred in the acquisition were only $5000.
3. Discuss the effects on the adjustment entries at 1 July 2006 if the subsidiary adjusted the goodwill in its records based upon an analysis of Kalkenberg Ltd's acquiring its shares in Halmstad Ltd. (Assume the incidental acquisition costs are $10 000.)

PROBLEMS

PROBLEM 20.1 ★

Worksheet entries after the acquisition date

This problem is based on the information in exercise 20.2.
In relation to the assets and liabilities recognised at acquisition date:
- The inventory was all sold by 30 June 2006.
- The plant had an expected useful life of five years, with depreciation being on a straight-line basis.
- Brunnsberg Ltd recorded an impairment loss of $1500 in relation to goodwill during the year ending 30 June 2006.

- In January 2007, $8000 of capitalised research outlays recognised on consolidation was written off.
- Brands were considered to have an indefinite life.
- The contingent liability was settled in February 2007, with Brunnsberg Ltd paying $12 000 to the dissatisfied customers.
- When assets are sold, written off or fully consumed or liabilities settled, any revaluation reserves are transferred to retained earnings.

Required
Prepare the consolidation worksheet entries for the preparation of consolidated financial statements at 30 June 2007.

PROBLEM 20.2   ★★   Excess, consolidation worksheet

Lahti Ltd gained control of Jokela Ltd by acquiring its share capital on 1 January 2002. The balance sheet of Jokela Ltd at that date showed:

Share capital	$ 60 000	Land	$ 20 000
Retained earnings	60 000	Plant and machinery	120 000
Liabilities	15 000	Accumulated depreciation	(20 000)
		Inventory	15 000
	$135 000		$135 000

At 1 January 2002, the recorded amounts of Jokela Ltd's assets and liabilities were equal to their fair values except as follows:

	Carrying amount	Fair value
Plant and machinery	$100 000	$102 000
Inventory	15 000	18 000

All this inventory was sold by Jokela Ltd in the following three months. The depreciable assets have a further five-year life, benefits being received evenly over this period. Any business combination valuation adjustments are made on consolidation. Immediately after acquisition, Jokela Ltd declared and paid a $4000 dividend. The tax rate is 30%.

At 31 December 2002, the following information was obtained from both entities:

	Lahti Ltd	Jokela Ltd
Profit before tax	$100 000	$ 15 000
Income tax expense	20 000	5 000
Profit	80 000	10 000
Retained earnings (1/1/02)	133 000	60 000
	213 000	70 000
Dividend paid	10 000	4 000
Retained earnings (31/12/02)	$203 000	$ 66 000
Share capital	$445 000	$ 60 000
Retained earnings	203 000	66 000
Liabilities	52 000	12 000
	$700 000	$138 000

Land	–	$ 20 000
Plant and machinery	$595 000	120 000
Accumulated depreciation	(20 000)	(25 000)
Inventory	15 000	23 000
Shares in Jokela Ltd	110 000	–
	$700 000	$138 000

Required

1. Prepare the consolidated financial statements for Lahti Ltd at 31 December 2002.
2. Prepare the valuation and pre-acquisition entries at 31 December 2006, assuming that, on consolidation, business combination valuation reserves are transferred to retained earnings when the related asset is sold or fully consumed.

PROBLEM 20.3   ★★   Revaluation in subsidiary's records, dividends

On 1 July 2004, Sandefjord Ltd acquired all the shares of Arendal Ltd (totalling $40 000) for a cash outlay of $100 000. At that date the other reserves and retained earnings of Arendal Ltd were as follows:

General reserve	$30 000
Retained earnings	20 000

All identifiable assets and liabilities of Arendal Ltd were recorded at fair value at 1 July 2004 except as follows:

	Carrying amount	Fair value
Land	$30 000	$34 000
Plant (cost $28 000)	20 000	22 000
Inventory	40 000	44 000

The plant has a further five-year life. Of the inventory on hand at 1 July 2004, 90% was sold by 30 June 2005. Neither company had any recorded goodwill. The tax rate is 30%.

Required

1. Prepare the consolidation worksheet entries at 30 June 2005, assuming:
   (a) Arendal Ltd revalued the land and plant to their fair values in its records at 1 July 2004.
   (b) all business combination valuations are made in the consolidation worksheet.
2. If, during December 2005, Arendal Ltd declared and paid a $15 000 dividend from profits earned before 1 July 2004, and the balance of inventory was sold, what would be the business combination valuation and pre-acquisition entries at 30 June 2006, assuming 1(b) above?
3. If, during June 2006, Arendal Ltd declared (but did not pay) a further dividend of $5000 from retained earnings recognised before 1 July 2004, what would be the pre-acquisition entry at 30 June 2006?
4. If, during June 2006, Arendal Ltd also transferred $6000 from general reserve (pre-acquisition) to retained earnings (earned before 1 July 2004), what would be the pre-acquisition entry at 30 June 2006?

Excess, consolidation worksheet

The account balances of Norrkoping Ltd and Vastervick Ltd at 1 July 2005 were as follows:

	Norrkoping Ltd	Vastervick Ltd
	$000	$000
Share capital — 600 000 shares	600	–
— 200 000 shares	–	200
General reserve	200	50
Asset revaluation surplus	150	40
Retained earnings	200	160
Dividend payable	10	15
Other liabilities	320	15
	1 480	480
Land	400	200
Machinery	500	250
Accumulated depreciation	(100)	(50)
Inventory	480	75
Cash	200	5
	1 480	480

The fair values of Vastervick Ltd's assets at 1 July 2005 were:

	$000
Land	240
Machinery	220
Inventory	95

The two companies decided to combine on 1 July 2005 with Norrkoping Ltd issuing one share (fair value $2) and 50c cash for each share in Vastervick Ltd. Vastervick Ltd's shares were acquired cum div.

The tax rate is 30%.

Required
1. Prepare the consolidated balance sheet immediately after Norrkoping Ltd's acquisition of shares in Vastervick Ltd.
2. Prepare the consolidation worksheet entries required for the consolidation worksheet at 30 June 2006, assuming both dividends were paid during September 2005. Assume all inventory on hand at 1 July 2005 was sold in the following three months, and that the machinery has a further four-year life.

PROBLEM 20.5   ★★   Consolidation worksheet, dividends and reserve transfer

Financial statements	Ruovesi Ltd	Savonlinna Ltd	Adjustments			Consolidation
			Dr	Cr		
Profit	6 000	4 000				
Retained earnings (1/7/05)	22 000	18 000				
	28 000	22 000				
Transfer from general reserve	5 000	3 000				
	33 000	25 000				
Dividend paid	6 000	5 000				
Retained earnings (30/6/06)	27 000	20 000				

An extract from the consolidation worksheet of Ruovesi Ltd and its subsidiary, Savonlinna Ltd, as at 30 June 2006, is shown above. Ruovesi Ltd acquired all the share capital (cum div.) of Savonlinna Ltd on 1 July 2002 for $127 000 when the equity of Savonlinna Ltd consisted of:

Share capital	$85 000
General reserve	18 000
Retained earnings	12 000

All the identifiable assets and liabilities of Savonlinna Ltd at 1 July 2002 were recorded at fair value except for:

	Carrying amount	Fair value
Plant (cost $100 000)	$80 000	$82 000
Inventory	6 000	7 000

The plant had a further five-year life. All the inventory was sold by Savonlinna Ltd by 22 September 2002. The tax rate is 30%. The liabilities of Savonlinna Ltd included a dividend payable of $6000. Savonlinna Ltd had not recorded any goodwill. At 1 July 2002, Savonlinna Ltd had incurred research and development outlays of $5000, which it had expensed. Ruovesi Ltd placed a fair value of $2000 on this item. The project was still in progress at 30 June 2006, with Savonlinna Ltd capitalising $3000 in the 2005–06 period. Valuation adjustments are made on consolidation.

All other dividends paid by Savonlinna Ltd have been from post-acquisition profits except an interim dividend of $2000 paid in January 2004 and the dividend of $5000 paid during the current period. The transfer from general reserve during the current period ending 30 June 2006 is also from pre-acquisition reserves, and is the only such transfer since the acquisition date.

Required
1. Prepare the consolidation worksheet entries at 30 June 2006.
2. Complete the worksheet extract above.

PROBLEM 20.6 ★★★   Contingent liabilities and reserve transfers

On 1 July 2006, Vetlanda Ltd acquired all the share capital of Jonkoping Ltd when the equity of Jonkoping Ltd consisted of:

100 000 ordinary shares issued at $1, paid to 75c each	$75 000
General reserve	15 000
Retained earnings	12 000

All identifiable assets and liabilities of both companies were recorded at fair value except as follows:

	Carrying amount	Fair value
Inventory	$20 000	$25 000
Machinery (net)	80 000	95 000

The machinery has a further five-year life. Of the inventory on hand at 1 July 2006, 90% was sold by 31 December 2006. At 1 July 2006, Jonkoping Ltd was involved in a court case with an entity that was claiming damages from it. Jonkoping Ltd had not raised a liability in relation to any expected damages. Vetlanda Ltd measured the fair value of the contingent liability at $5000. By 31 December 2006, the expectation of winning the court case had improved, so the fair value was considered to be $1000. The tax rate is 30%. Valuation adjustments are made on consolidation.

On 1 November 2006, Jonkoping Ltd paid an interim dividend of $3750 out of retained earnings in existence at 1 July 2006. Also, $6500 of these retained earnings were transferred to the general reserve account.

On 1 December 2006, Jonkoping Ltd made a call of 25c per share, all call money being received by 20 December 2006.

At 31 December 2006, the balance sheet of Vetlanda Ltd showed shares in Jonkoping Ltd at $143 500.

Required

Prepare the consolidation worksheet entries for the preparation of the consolidated financial statements for Vetlanda and its subsidiary, Jonkoping Ltd, as at 31 December 2006.

PROBLEM 20.7 ★★★   Excess, consolidation worksheet

The financial statements of Lapua Ltd and its subsidiary, Kouvola Ltd, at 30 June 2005 contained the following information:

	Lapua Ltd	Kouvola Ltd
Profit before tax	$ 3 200	$ 1 800
Income tax expense	1 300	240
Profit	1 900	1 560
Retained earnings at 1/7/04	1 500	2 100
	3 400	3 600
Dividend paid	500	200
Retained earnings at 30/6/05	2 900	3 460
Share capital	25 000	10 000
General reserve	8 000	3 000
Liabilities	6 000	2 000
	$41 900	$18 460

Land	$ 8 600	$ 5 100
Plant	20 000	10 000
Accumulated depreciation	(5 000)	(1 000)
Inventory	3 000	4 000
Cash	500	360
Shares in Kouvola Ltd	14 800	–
	$41 900	$18 460

Lapua Ltd had acquired all the share capital of Kouvola Ltd on 1 July 2003 for $15 000 when the equity of Kouvola Ltd consisted of:

Share capital – 10 000 shares	$10 000
General reserve	2 000
Retained earnings	1 500

At the acquisition date by Lapua Ltd, Kouvola Ltd's non-monetary assets consisted of:

	Carrying amount	Fair value
Land	$4 000	$6 000
Plant (cost $6000)	5 500	6 500
Inventory	3 000	4 000

The plant had a further five-year life. All the inventory was sold by 30 June 2004. All valuation adjustments to non-current assets are made on consolidation. The land was sold in January 2005 for $6000. The relevant business combination valuation reserves are transferred, on consolidation, to retained earnings. The tax rate is 30%.

Since acquisition date, all dividends have been from post-acquisition profits except the dividend of $200 paid by Kouvola Ltd in February 2005. Also, in September 2003, Kouvola Ltd transferred $500 from its general reserve, earned before 1 July 2003, to retained earnings.

Required
Prepare the consolidated financial statements for the year ended 30 June 2005.

PROBLEM 20.8 ★★★ Unrecognised intangible, contingent liability, dividends

On 30 September 2006, Lillehammer Ltd acquired all the shares of Honefoss Ltd for $3 per share in cash. The equity of Honefoss Ltd at that date was:

Share capital – 10 000 shares	$10 000
General reserve	3 000
Retained earnings	12 000

At this date, all the identifiable assets and liabilities of Honefoss Ltd were recorded at fair value except for machinery and inventory whose carrying amounts were each $2000 less than their fair values. All this inventory was sold by Honefoss Ltd before December 2006. The machinery had a further five-year life. The tax rate is 30%.

In a previous period, Honefoss Ltd had purchased some goodwill that had been written down to a carrying amount of $2000 as at 30 September 2006. Honefoss Ltd had developed a business magazine containing economic indicators for the coal industry. The magazine was widely sought after. Lillehammer Ltd placed a value of $1500 on the masthead. The intangible asset, not recognised by Honefoss Ltd at 30 September 2006, was considered to have an indefinite life.

At 30 September 2006, Finn Ltd had sued Honefoss Ltd for alleged damaging statements made in the magazine, and a court case was in progress. Honefoss Ltd had not recognised any liability for damages. Lillehammer Ltd assessed potential damages at a fair value of $2000. In January 2008, the court handed down its decision, and Honefoss Ltd was required to pay damages of $2500.

Between 30 September 2006 and 30 June 2007 (balance date for both companies), the following movements occurred in the books of Honefoss Ltd:

- Honefoss Ltd transferred $3000 from pre-acquisition retained earnings to the general reserve.
- Honefoss Ltd had declared and paid a bonus share issue of one share for every two shares held at 1 October 2006 out of the general reserve ($3000) and partly out of the retained earnings.
- A 10% final dividend was declared on the revised capital amounts to be paid from retained earnings earned before 30 September 2006. This was paid in October 2007.

Required

1. Prepare the consolidation worksheet adjustment entries for consolidation of the financial statements of Lillehammer Ltd and Honefoss Ltd on:
   (a) 30 September 2006
   (b) 30 June 2007.
2. Given no further movements in pre-acquisition equity of Honefoss Ltd, prepare the worksheet entries at 30 June 2008.

PROBLEM 20.9 ★★★   Consolidation worksheet, unrecognised intangibles and liabilities

Kotka Ltd gained control of Grimstad Ltd by acquiring all its shares on 1 July 2003. The equity at that date was:

Share capital	$100 000
Retained earnings	35 000

At 1 July 2003, all the identifiable assets and liabilities of Grimstad Ltd were recorded at fair value except for:

	Carrying amount	Fair value
Inventory	$ 18 000	$ 22 000
Land	120 000	130 000
Plant (cost $120 000)	95 000	98 000

The inventory was all sold by 30 June 2004. The plant had a further five-year life but was sold on 1 January 2006 for $50 000. The land was sold in March 2004 for $150 000.

Where revalued assets are sold or fully consumed, any associated amounts in the business combination valuation reserve are transferred to retained earnings. At 1 July 2003, Grimstad Ltd had guaranteed a loan taken out by Swede Ltd. Grimstad Ltd had not raised a liability in relation to the guarantee but, as Swede Ltd was not performing well, Kotka Ltd valued the contingent liability at $5000. In January 2006, Swede Ltd repaid the loan. Grimstad Ltd had also invented a special tool and patented the process. No asset was raised by Grimstad Ltd, but Kotka Ltd valued the patent at $6000, with an expected useful life of six years. The tax rate is 30%.

Financial information for these companies for the year ended 30 June 2006 is as follows:

	Kotka Ltd	Grimstad Ltd
Profit before tax	$ 50 000	$ 15 000
Income tax expense	20 000	6 000
Profit	30 000	9 000
Retained earnings as at 1 July 2005	37 000	45 000
	67 000	54 000
Dividend paid	20 000	10 000
Transfer to general reserve	–	20 000
	20 000	30 000
Retained earnings at 30 June 2006	$ 47 000	$ 24 000
Share capital	$150 000	$100 000
General reserve	42 000	20 000
Retained earnings	47 000	24 000
Total equity	239 000	144 000
Payables	19 000	12 000
Loan	25 000	–
	44 000	12 000
Total equity and liabilities	$283 000	$156 000
Cash	$ 15 000	$ 9 000
Inventory	30 000	21 000
Plant and equipment	150 000	163 000
Accumulated depreciation	(62 000)	(37 000)
Shares in Grimstad Ltd	150 000	–
Total assets	$283 000	$156 000

The dividend paid and the transfer to general reserve during the year ended 30 June 2006 were from profits earned before 1 July 2003.

Required

Prepare the consolidated financial statements for Kotka Ltd as at 30 June 2006. Your answer should include all consolidation adjustment journal entries and a consolidation worksheet.

Visit these websites for additional information:

www.iasb.org	www.iasplus.com
www.asic.gov.au	www.ifac.org
www.aasb.com.au	www.nzica.com
www.accaglobal.com	www.capa.com.my

CHAPTER 21
Consolidated financial statements: intragroup transactions

ACCOUNTING STANDARDS

International: IAS 27 *Consolidated and Separate Financial Statements*

Australia: AASB 127 *Consolidated and Separate Financial Statements*

New Zealand: NZ IAS 27 *Consolidated and Separate Financial Statements*

CONCEPTS FOR REVIEW

Before studying this chapter, you should understand or, if necessary, revise:

- the nature of the consolidated group and the purpose of preparing consolidated financial statements
- the preparation of pre-acquisition entries and business combination valuation entries
- the use and format of the consolidation worksheet.

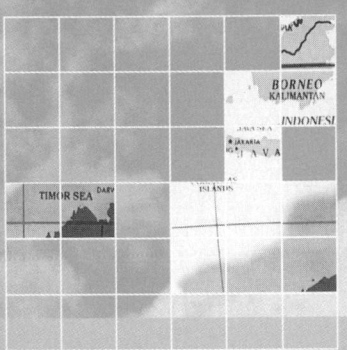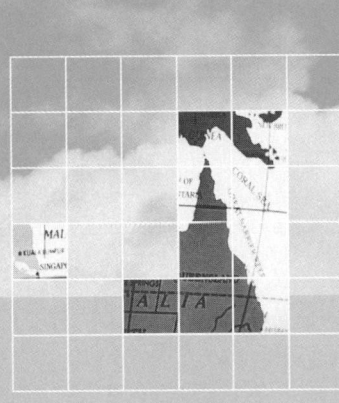

LEARNING OBJECTIVES

When you have studied this chapter, you should be able to:

1. explain the need for making adjustments for intragroup transactions
2. prepare worksheet entries for intragroup transactions involving profits and losses in beginning and ending inventory
3. prepare worksheet entries for intragroup transactions involving profits and losses on the transfer of non-current assets in both the current and previous periods
4. prepare worksheet entries for intragroup transactions involving transfers from inventory to non-current assets and from non-current assets to inventory
5. prepare worksheet entries for intragroup services such as management fees
6. prepare worksheet entries for intragroup dividends from post-acquisition equity
7. prepare worksheet entries for intragroup borrowings.

21.1 Introduction

In this chapter, the group under discussion is restricted to one where:
- there are only two entities within the group (i.e. one parent and one subsidiary)
- the parent owns all the shares of the subsidiary.
    Diagrammatically, then, the group is as shown in figure 21.1.

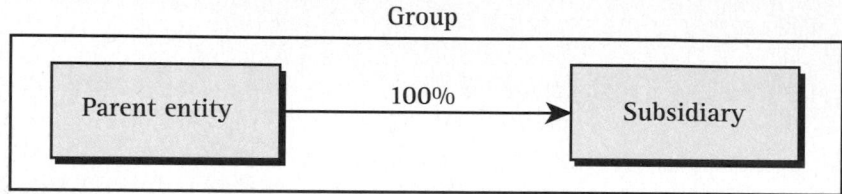

FIGURE 21.1   Group

In chapter 19, it was explained that the process of consolidation involves adding together the financial statements of a parent and its subsidiaries to reflect an overall view of the financial affairs of the group of entities as a single economic entity. It is also pointed out that two major adjustments are necessary to effect the process of consolidation:
(a) adjustments involving equity at the acquisition date, namely the business combination valuation entry (if any) and the pre-acquisition entry, eliminating the investment account in the parent's financial statements against the pre-acquisition equity of the subsidiary (see chapter 20)
(b) elimination of intragroup balances and the effects of transactions whereby profits or losses are made by different members of the group through trading with each other.
    This chapter focuses on (b), adjustments for intragroup balances and transactions. The chapter analyses transactions involving inventory, depreciable assets, services, dividends and borrowings.

21.2 Rationale for adjusting for intragroup transactions

LO 1

Whenever related entities trade with each other, or borrow and lend money to each other, the separate legal entities disclose the effects of these transactions in the assets and liabilities recorded and the profits and losses reported. For example, if a subsidiary sells inventory to its parent, the subsidiary records a sale of inventory, including the profit on sale and reduction in inventory assets, and the parent records the purchase of inventory at the amount paid to the subsidiary. If, then, in preparing the consolidated financial statements, the separate financial statements of the legal entities are simply added together without any adjustments for the effects of the intragroup transactions, the consolidated financial statements include not only the results of the group transacting with external parties (i.e. parties outside the group) but also the results of transactions within the group. This conflicts with the purpose of the consolidated financial statements to provide information about the financial performance and financial position of the group as a result of its dealings with external parties. Hence, the effects of transactions within the group must be adjusted for in the preparation of the consolidated financial statements.
    The requirement for the full adjustment for the effects of intragroup transactions is stated in paragraph 24 of IAS 27 *Consolidated and Separate Financial Statements*:

Intragroup balances, transactions, income and expenses shall be eliminated in full.

The requirement to adjust for the full effects of the transactions is consistent with the entity concept of consolidation, as the whole of the parent and the subsidiary are within the group.

Besides adjusting for the effects of transactions occurring in the current period, it is also necessary to adjust the current period's consolidated financial statements for the ongoing effects of transactions in previous periods. Because the consolidation adjustment entries are applied in a worksheet only, and not in the accounts of either the parent or the subsidiary, any continuing effects of previous periods' transactions must be considered. This affects transactions such as loans between, say, a parent and a subsidiary where a balance owing at the end of a number of periods is reduced over time as repayments are made. Similarly, where assets such as inventory are transferred at the end of one period and then are still on hand at the beginning of the next period, consolidation adjustments are required to be made in both periods.

Some intragroup transactions do not affect the carrying amounts of assets and liabilities (e.g. where there is a management fee paid by one entity to another within the group). In that case, the items affected are fee revenue and fee expense. However, in other circumstances, there are assets and liabilities recognised by the group at amounts different from the amounts recognised by the individual legal entities. For example, consider the situation where a subsidiary sold an item of inventory to the parent for $1000, and the inventory had cost the subsidiary $800. The parent recognises the inventory at cost of $1000, while the cost of the inventory to the group is only $800. As is explained in more detail later in this chapter, consolidation adjustment entries are necessary to adjust for both the profit on the intragroup transaction and the carrying amount of the inventory.

Under IAS 12 *Income Taxes*, deferred tax accounts must be raised where there are temporary differences between the carrying amount of an asset or liability and its tax base. Any difference between the carrying amount of an asset or a liability and its tax base in a legal entity within the group is accounted for by the legal entity. However, on consolidation, in relation to intragroup transactions, adjustments may be made to the carrying amounts of assets and liabilities. Hence, in adjusting for intragroup transactions wherever there are changes to the carrying amounts of assets and liabilities, any associated tax effect must be considered. Paragraph 25 of IAS 27 recognises the need to apply tax-effect accounting for temporary differences arising from the elimination of profits and losses from intragroup transactions.

For example, assume an asset is recorded by a subsidiary at a carrying amount of $1000, and that the tax base is $800. In the records of the subsidiary, the application of tax-effect accounting will account for the temporary difference of $200, raising a deferred tax liability of $60, assuming a tax rate of 30%. If, on consolidation, an adjustment is made to reduce the carrying amount of the asset, say to $950, the consolidation adjustment entries must include an adjustment for the tax effect of the change in the carrying amount of the asset, namely a reduction in the deferred tax liability of $15 (i.e. 30% × $50). The consolidated financial statements then show a deferred tax liability of $45 (i.e. $60 − $15). The combination of the tax-effect entries in the subsidiaries and the tax-effect adjustments on consolidation will account for the temporary difference caused by the group showing the asset at $950 and the tax base being $800, namely a deferred tax liability of $45 (i.e. 30% × ($950 − $800)).

As can be seen in this example, in preparing the consolidation adjustments it is unnecessary to consider the tax-effect entries made in the individual entities in the group. If the appropriate tax-effect adjustments are made for the changes in the carrying amounts of the assets, then the combination of those adjustments and the tax-effect entries made in the entities themselves will produce the correct answer.

In this book, it is assumed that each subsidiary is a tax paying entity. Under the tax consolidation system in some countries, groups comprising a parent and its wholly owned subsidiaries can elect to consolidate and be treated as a single entity for tax purposes. Such entities prepare a consolidated tax return, and the effects of intragroup transactions are eliminated. Under such a scheme, the tax-effect adjustments demonstrated in this chapter would not apply.

Just as the pre-acquisition entry is used in a consolidation worksheet to eliminate the investment and to adjust for pre-acquisition equity, adjustment journal entries are prepared for intragroup transactions and are recorded in the consolidation worksheet. The same two adjustment columns are used to effect these adjustments. For example, if it were necessary to adjust downwards by $10 000 the sales revenue recorded by the legal entities, the consolidation worksheet would show the following line:

	Parent	Subsidiary		Adjustments			Group
				Dr	Cr		
Sales revenue	100 000	80 000	4	10 000			170 000

In the following sections of this chapter, three types of intragroup transactions are discussed — transfers of inventory, transfers of non-current assets and intragroup services. In each of the specific sections covering these transactions, the process of determining when profits are realised for the different types of transactions is discussed.

LO 2

21.3 Transfers of inventory

In the following examples, assume that Beijing Ltd owns all the share capital of Shanghai Ltd, and that the consolidation process is being carried out on 30 June 2006, for the year ending on that date. Assume also a tax rate of 30%. All entries shown as being for the individual entities assume the use of a perpetual inventory system, and adjustments will be made, where necessary, to the cost of sales account.

21.3.1 Sales of inventory

Example

On 1 January 2006, Beijing Ltd acquired $10 000 worth of inventory for cash from Shanghai Ltd. The inventory had previously cost Shanghai Ltd $8000.

In Shanghai Ltd, the following journal entries are made on 1 January 2006:

Cash	Dr	10 000	
Sales revenue	Cr		10 000
Cost of sales	Dr	8 000	
Inventory	Cr		8 000

In Beijing Ltd, the journal entry is:

Inventory	Dr	10 000	
Cash	Cr		10 000

From the viewpoint of the group in relation to this transaction, no sales of inventory were made to any party outside the group, nor has the group acquired any inventory from external parties. Hence, if the financial statements of Beijing Ltd and Shanghai Ltd are simply added together for consolidation purposes, 'sales', 'cost of sales' and 'inventory' would need to be adjusted on consolidation as the consolidated financial statements must show only the results of transactions with parties external to the group.

21.3.2 Realisation of profits or losses

Paragraph 25 of IAS 127 states that the profits and losses resulting from intragroup transactions that require consolidation adjustments to be made are those 'recognised in assets'. These profits can be described as 'unrealised profits'. The test for realisation is the involvement of an external party in relation to the item involved in the intragroup transaction. If an item of inventory is transferred from a subsidiary to the parent entity (or vice versa), no external party is involved in that transaction. The profit made by the subsidiary is unrealised to the group. If the parent then sells that inventory item to a party external to the group, the intragroup profit becomes realised to the group. For example, assume a subsidiary, Shanghai Ltd, sells inventory to its parent, Beijing Ltd, for $100, and that inventory cost Shanghai Ltd $90. The profit on this transaction is unrealised. If Beijing Ltd sells the inventory to an external party for $100, the intragroup profit is realised. The group sold inventory to an external party for $100 that cost the group $90. The group has made $10 profit. Hence, the consolidation adjustments for profits on intragroup transfers of inventory depend on whether the acquiring entity has sold the inventory to parties outside the group. In other words, the adjustments depend on whether the acquiring entity still carries some or all of the transferred inventory as ending inventory at the end of the financial period.

21.3.3 Profits in ending inventory

The following example uses the information in the example in section 21.3.1 and provides information about whether the inventory transferred is still on hand at the end of the financial period.

> **Example: Transferred inventory still on hand**
> On 30 June 2006, all the inventory sold by Shanghai Ltd to Beijing Ltd is still on hand.

The adjustment entries in the consolidation worksheet at 30 June 2006 are:

Sales revenue	Dr	10 000	
Cost of sales	Cr		8 000
Inventory	Cr		2 000

The sales adjustment is necessary to eliminate the effects of the original sale in the current period. Shanghai Ltd recorded sales of $10 000. From the group's viewpoint, as no external party was involved in the transaction, no sales should be shown in the consolidated financial statements. To adjust sales revenue downwards, a debit adjustment is necessary. The effect of this adjustment on the consolidation process is seen in figure 21.2. Hence, an adjustment is necessary to eliminate the sales recorded by Shanghai Ltd.

Using similar reasoning as with the adjustment for sales revenue, the subsidiary has recorded cost of sales of $8000, but the group has made no sales to parties external to the group. Hence, the consolidation worksheet needs to have a reduction in cost of sales of $8000 in order to show a zero amount in the consolidation column. Note also that adjusting sales by $10 000 and cost of sales by $8000 effectively reduces consolidated profit by $2000. In other words, the $2000 profit recorded by Shanghai Ltd on selling inventory to Beijing Ltd is eliminated and there is a zero profit shown on consolidation. As no external party was involved in the transfer of inventory, the whole of the profit on the intragroup transaction is unrealised. This is illustrated in figure 21.2.

	Parent	Subsidiary		Adjustments Dr		Adjustments Cr		Group
Sales revenue	0	10 000	*1*	10 000				0
Cost of sales	0	8 000			8 000		*1*	0
		2 000						
Tax expense	0	600			600		*2*	0
Profit		1 400						0
Inventory	10 000	0			2 000		*1*	8 000
Deferred tax asset	0	0	*2*	600				600

FIGURE 21.2 Extract from consolidation worksheet — profit in closing inventory

The previous explanation dealing with the effect on profit covers only the income statement part of the adjustment. Under an historical cost system, assets in the consolidated balance sheet must be shown at cost to the group. Inventory is recorded in Beijing Ltd at $10 000, the cost to Beijing Ltd. The cost to the group is, however, $8000, the amount that was paid for the inventory by Shanghai Ltd to parties external to the group. Hence, if inventory is to be reported at $8000 in the consolidated financial statements, and it is recorded in Beijing Ltd's records at $10 000, a credit adjustment of $2000 is needed to reduce the inventory to $8000, the cost to the group. This effect is seen in figure 21.2.

Beijing Ltd has recorded the inventory in its records at $10 000. This amount is probably also its tax base. However, as explained in section 21.2, any difference between the tax base and the carrying amount in Beijing Ltd is accounted for in the tax-effect entries in Beijing Ltd. On consolidation, a tax-effect entry is necessary where an adjustment entry causes a difference between the carrying amount of an asset or a liability in the records of the legal entity and the carrying amount shown in the consolidated financial statements. In the adjustment entry relating to profit in ending inventory in the above example, the carrying amount of inventory is reduced downwards by $2000. The carrying amount and tax base of the inventory in Beijing Ltd is $10 000, but the carrying amount in the group is $8000. This $2000 difference is a deductible temporary difference giving rise to a deferred tax asset of $600 (i.e. 30% × $2000), as well as a corresponding decrease in income tax expense. The appropriate consolidation worksheet adjustment entry is:

Deferred tax asset	Dr	600	
Income tax expense	Cr		600

The effects of this entry are shown in figure 21.2.

The deferred tax asset recognises that the group is expected to earn profits in the future that will not require the payment of tax to the Taxation Office. When the inventory is sold by Beijing Ltd in a future period, this temporary difference is reversed. To illustrate this effect, assume that in the following period Beijing Ltd sells this inventory to an external entity for $11 000. Beijing Ltd will record a before-tax profit of $1000 (i.e. $11 000 − $10 000) and an associated tax expense of $300. From the consolidated group position, the profit on sale is $3000 (i.e. $11 000 − $8000). The group will show current tax payable of $300, will reverse the $600 deferred tax asset, and recognise an income tax expense of $900. These effects are further illustrated below.

Example: Transferred inventories partly sold

On 1 January 2006, Beijing Ltd acquired $10 000 worth of inventory for cash from Shanghai Ltd. The inventory had previously cost Shanghai Ltd $8000. By the end of the year, 30 June 2006, Beijing Ltd had sold $7500 of the transferred inventory for $14 000 to external parties. Thus, $2500 of the inventory is on hand in Beijing Ltd at 30 June 2006.

The adjustment entry for the preparation of consolidated financial statements at 30 June 2006 is:

Sales	Dr	10 000	
Cost of sales	Cr		9 500
Inventory	Cr		500

The total sales recorded by the *legal entities* are $24 000 (i.e. $10 000 by Shanghai Ltd and $14 000 by Beijing Ltd). The sales by the group, being those sold to entities external to the group, are $14 000. The consolidation adjustment to sales revenue is then $10 000, being the amount necessary to eliminate the sales within the group.

The total cost of sales recorded by the legal entities is $15 500 (i.e. $8000 by Shanghai Ltd and $7500 by Beijing Ltd (i.e. 75% × $10 000)). The cost of sales to the group, being those to parties external to the group, is $6000 (i.e. 75% × $8000). Hence, the consolidation adjustment is $9500 (i.e. $15 500 (sum of recorded sales) less $6000 (group)). The adjustment is that necessary to adjust the sum of the amounts recorded by the legal entities to that to be recognised by the group.

Note that the combined adjustments to sales and cost of sales result in a $500 reduction in before-tax profit. Of the $2000 intragroup profit on the transfer of inventory from Shanghai Ltd to Beijing Ltd, as three-quarters of the inventory has been sold by Beijing Ltd to an external party, $1500 of the profit is realised to the group and only $500, the profit remaining in ending inventory, is unrealised. It is the unrealised profit that is adjusted for in the worksheet entry.

The group profit is then $500 less than that recorded by the legal entities. The sum of profits recorded by the legal entities is $8500, consisting of $2000 recorded by Shanghai Ltd and $6500 (being sales of $14 000 less cost of sales of $7500) recorded by Beijing Ltd. From the group's viewpoint, profit on sale of inventory to external parties is only $8000, consisting of sales of $14 000 less cost of sales of $6000 (being 75% of original cost of $8000). Hence, an adjustment of $500 is necessary to reduce recorded profit of $8500 to group profit of $8000.

The $500 adjustment to inventory reflects that proportion of the total profit on sale of the transferred inventory that remains in the inventory on hand at the end of the period. Since 25% of the transferred inventory is still on hand at the end of the period, then 25%

of the total profit on transfer of inventory (i.e. 25% × $2000) needs to be adjusted at the end of the period. The adjustment entry reduces the inventory on hand at 30 June 2006 from the recorded cost to Beijing Ltd of $2500 to the group cost of $2000 (being 25% of the original cost of $8000).

Consider the *tax effect* of this adjustment. The carrying amount of the inventory is reduced by $500, reflecting the fact that the carrying amount to the group is $500 less than the carrying amount in Beijing Ltd. This gives rise to a deductible temporary difference of $500. Hence, a deferred tax asset of $150 (i.e. 30% × $500) must be raised on consolidation with a corresponding effect on income tax expense. The expectation of the group is that, in some future period, it will recognise the remaining $500 profit in transferred inventory when it sells the inventory to an external party, but will not have to pay tax on the $500 as Shanghai Ltd has already paid the relevant tax. This expected tax saving to the group will be shown in the consolidated financial statements by a debit adjustment of $150 to the deferred tax asset account.

The tax-effect adjustment entry is then:

Deferred tax asset	Dr	150	
Income tax expense	Cr		150

Example: Transferred inventory completely sold

On 1 January 2006, Beijing Ltd acquired $10 000 worth of inventory for cash from Shanghai Ltd. The inventory had previously cost Shanghai Ltd $8000. By the end of the year, 30 June 2006, Beijing Ltd had sold all the transferred inventory to an external party for $18 000.

Shanghai Ltd records a profit of	$ 2 000	(i.e. $10 000 less $8000)
Beijing Ltd records a profit of	$ 8 000	(i.e. $18 000 less $10 000)
Total recorded profit is	$10 000	

Profit to the group = Selling price to external parties less cost to the group
                      = $18 000 − $8000
                      = $10 000

Since the recorded profit equals the profit to the group, there is no need for a profit adjustment on consolidation. Further, as there is no transferred inventory still on hand, there is no need for an adjustment to inventory. As all the inventory has been sold to an external party, the whole of the intragroup profit is realised to the group. Note, however, that an adjustment for the sales and cost of sales is still necessary. As noted previously, the sales within the group amount to $18 000 while the sales recorded by the legal entities total $28 000 (i.e. $10 000 + $18 000). Hence, sales must be reduced by $10 000. The total recorded cost of sales is $18 000, being $8000 by Shanghai Ltd and $10 000 by Beijing Ltd. The group's cost of sales is the original cost of the transferred inventory, $8000. Hence, cost of sales is reduced by $10 000 on consolidation. The adjustment entry is then:

Sales	Dr	10 000	
Cost of sales	Cr		10 000

Since there is no adjustment to the carrying amounts of assets or liabilities, there is no need for any *tax-effect* adjustment.

Where inventory is transferred in the current period and some or all of that inventory is still on hand at the end of the period, the general form of the worksheet entries is:

Sales revenue	Dr	X	
Cost of sales	Cr		X
Inventory	Cr		X
(The adjustment to inventory is based on the profit remaining in inventory on hand at the end of the period)			
Deferred tax asset	Dr	X	
Income tax expense	Cr		X
(Being the tax rate times the adjustment to ending inventory)			

21.3.4 Profits in opening inventory

Any transferred inventory remaining unsold at the end of one period is still on hand at the beginning of the next period. Because the consolidation adjustments are made only in a worksheet and not in the records of any of the legal entities, any differences in balances between the legal entities and the consolidated group at the end of one period must still exist at the beginning of the next period.

Example: Transferred inventory on hand at the beginning of the period

On 1 July 2005, the first day of the current period, Shanghai Ltd has on hand inventory worth $7000, transferred from Beijing Ltd in June 2005. The inventory had previously cost Beijing Ltd $4500. The tax rate is 30%.

In this example, in the preparation of the consolidated financial statements at 30 June 2005 the following adjustment entries for the $2500 profit in ending inventory would have been made in the consolidation worksheet:

Sales	Dr	7 000	
Cost of sales	Cr		4 500
Inventory	Cr		2 500
Deferred tax asset	Dr	750	
Income tax expense	Cr		750
(30% × $2500)			

Since the ending inventory at 30 June 2005 becomes the beginning inventory for the next year, an adjustment is necessary in the consolidated financial statements prepared at 30 June 2006. The required adjustment is:

Retained earnings (1/7/05)	Dr	2 500	
Cost of sales	Cr		2 500

In making this consolidation worksheet adjustment, it is assumed that the inventory is sold to external parties in the current period. If this is not the case, then the adjustment to inventory as made at 30 June 2005 would need to be made again in preparing the consolidated financial statements at 30 June 2006.

In making a *credit adjustment* of $2500, cost of sales is reduced. The cost of sales recorded by Shanghai Ltd in the 2005–06 period is $2500 greater than that which the group wants to show, because the cost of sales recorded by Beijing Ltd is $7000, whereas the cost of sales to the group is only $4500. A reduction in cost of sales means an increase in profit. Hence, in the 2005–06 period, the group's profit is greater than the sum of the legal entities' profit.

The *debit adjustment* to the opening balance of retained earnings reduces that balance, that is, the group made less profit in previous years than the sum of the retained earnings recorded by the legal entities. This is because, in June 2005, Beijing Ltd recorded a $2500 profit on the sale of inventory to Shanghai Ltd, this profit not being recognised by the group until the 2005–06 period.

Consider the *tax effect* of these entries. If the previous period's tax-effect adjustment were carried forward into this year's worksheet it would be:

Deferred tax asset	Dr	750	
Retained earnings (1/7/05)	Cr		750

On sale of the inventory in the 2005–06 period, the deferred tax asset is reversed, with a resultant effect on income tax expense:

Income tax expense	Dr	750	
Deferred tax asset	Cr		750

On combining these two entries, the worksheet entry required is:

Income tax expense	Dr	750	
Retained earnings (1/7/05)	Cr		750

The adjustment to cost of sales, retained earnings and income tax expense can be combined into one entry as follows:

Income tax expense	Dr	750	
Retained earnings (1/7/05)	Dr	1 750	
Cost of sales	Cr		2 500

Note that this entry has no effect on the closing balance of retained earnings at 30 June 2006. As the inventory has been sold outside the group, the whole of the profit on the intragroup transaction is realised to the group. There is no unrealised profit to be adjusted for at the end of the period.

Where inventory was transferred in a previous period and some or all of that inventory is still on hand at the beginning of the current period, the general form of the entries is:

Retained earnings (opening balance)	Dr	X	
Cost of sales	Cr		X
Income tax expense	Dr	X	
Retained earnings (opening balance)	Cr		X

It can be seen that the consolidation worksheet entries for inventory transferred within the current period are different from those where the inventory was transferred in a previous period. *Before preparing the adjustment entries, it is essential to determine the timing of the transaction.*

LO 3

21.4 Transfers of non-current assets

Besides transferring inventory, it is possible for non-current assets to be transferred within the group. The worksheet adjustment entries are shown in two parts: (1) the entries to adjust for any profit or loss on sale of the assets, and (2) the entries relating to any depreciation of the assets after sale. As realisation of the profit or loss on sale is related to the depreciation of the transferred asset, the depreciation entries are covered in section 21.4.2 in conjunction with the discussion on realisation. If a non-depreciable asset is transferred, only the first of these entries is required, and realisation of the profit or loss occurs, as with inventory, on sale of the asset to an external party.

21.4.1 Sales of non-current assets

Example: Transfer in current year

Beijing Ltd sold Shanghai Ltd plant for $18 500 cash at 1 July 2005. It had cost Beijing Ltd $20 000 when acquired one year previously. Depreciation charged on plant by Beijing Ltd is 10% p.a. on cost, and Shanghai Ltd applies a rate of 6% p.a. on cost. The income tax rate is 30%.

The journal entries in the records of Beijing Ltd and Shanghai Ltd at the date of sale, 1 July 2005, are:

Beijing Ltd

Cash	Dr	18 500	
Proceeds from sale of plant	Cr		18 500
Carrying amount of plant sold	Dr	18 000	
Accumulated depreciation	Dr	2 000	
Plant	Cr		20 000

Shanghai Ltd

Plant	Dr	18 500	
Cash	Cr		18 500

The consolidation adjustment entry is:

Proceeds from sale of plant	Dr	18 500	
Carrying amount of plant sold	Cr		18 000
Plant	Cr		500

From the group's viewpoint, there is no sale of plant to parties external to the group. Since the legal entity Beijing Ltd recorded such a sale, the consolidation adjustment involves eliminating the effects of the sale. The adjustment entry includes a debit to revenue and a credit to the expense account, carrying amount of plant sold, to eliminate the effect of these accounts raised by Beijing Ltd. As a result of the sale, the plant is recorded by Shanghai Ltd at cost of $18 500. From the group's perspective, the cost of the asset at the time of transfer within the group is the carrying amount in the records of the selling company, Beijing Ltd (i.e. $18 000). So that the asset is reported in the consolidated financial statements at cost to the group, an adjustment entry reducing the asset from a recorded amount of $18 500 to the group's cost of $18 000 is necessary. Hence, a credit to the asset of $500 is required.

Under International Financial Reporting Standards, there is no requirement to disclose separately the income on sale of non-current assets, nor the carrying amounts of assets sold. Some entities may disclose on a net basis a gain or loss on sale of non-current assets. In the above example, there is a gain on sale to Beijing Ltd of $500. If Beijing Ltd had recorded a gain on sale of non-current assets, the consolidation adjustment entry would be:

Gain on sale of non-current asset	Dr	500	
Plant	Cr		500

In the consolidated income statement, it is the gain or loss on sale of the non-current asset that is reported.

The consolidation adjustment reduces plant by $500. As with inventory, any adjustment on consolidation to the carrying amount of an asset provides a difference between the carrying amount and the tax base of the asset. Hence, there is a deductible temporary difference in relation to the plant. It is then necessary to recognise a deferred tax asset and an adjustment to income tax expense equal to the tax rate times the temporary difference, namely 30% × $500 equal to $150. The consolidation worksheet adjustment entry is:

Deferred tax asset	Dr	150	
Income tax expense	Cr		150
(30% × $500)			

A deferred tax asset is recognised because there is a reduction in the carrying amount of the asset. This may in fact be a reduction in a deferred tax liability raised by the legal entity if for some reason the carrying amount of the asset in the legal entity were greater than the asset's tax base. As deferred tax assets and liabilities are netted off for disclosure purposes, a problem as to whether the adjustment is reducing a deferred tax liability or increasing a deferred tax asset is not important.

As long as the depreciable asset remains within the group, an adjustment entry is necessary to reduce Beijing Ltd's recorded prior-period profits and to reduce the cost of the asset as recorded by Shanghai Ltd. The adjustment entry in years after the year of sale of the asset is:

Retained earnings (opening balance)	Dr	500	
Plant	Cr		500

In periods after the year of sale, as long as the asset remains on hand, the tax-effect entry is:

Deferred tax asset	Dr	150	
Retained earnings (opening balance)	Cr		150

In summary, in the *year of transfer*, the general form of the consolidation worksheet entries is:

Proceeds on sale	Dr	X	
Carrying amount of asset sold	Cr		X
Non-current asset	Cr		X
Deferred tax asset	Dr	X	
Income tax expense	Cr		X

In *years after the transfer*, the entries become:

Retained earnings (opening balance)	Dr	X	
Non-current asset	Cr		X
Deferred tax asset	Dr	X	
Retained earnings (opening balance)	Cr		X

If a loss is made on transfer of a non-current asset, consolidation adjustments are needed to eliminate the loss and bring the non-current asset back to cost to the group. The tax-effect worksheet entry then recognises a deferred tax liability. The pro forma consolidation entries are:

Non-current asset	Dr	X	
Proceeds on sale	Dr	X	
Carrying amount of asset sold	Cr		X
Income tax expense	Dr	X	
Deferred tax liability	Cr		X

In years after the transfer, the entries become:

Non-current asset	Dr	X	
Retained earnings (opening balance)	Cr		X
Retained earnings (opening balance)	Dr	X	
Deferred tax liability	Cr		X

Paragraph 25 of IAS 27 notes that intragroup losses may indicate an impairment. In that case, an impairment loss and related accumulated impairment loss would be recognised in the consolidation worksheet.

21.4.2 Depreciation and realisation of profits or losses

Realisation of profits or losses on depreciable asset transfers

For intragroup transactions such as inventory transfers or sale of land, the determination of whether the profit on the intragroup sale is realised is simple. The profit is realised when the buying entity, say the parent, sells the transferred inventory or land to an external party. However, where transactions occur involving depreciable assets, no external party ever becomes *directly* involved in these transactions, as the transferred item remains within the group. Hence, either the profits or losses on transfer of these items are to be regarded as never being realised, or some assumption is made about the point of realisation. The former course of action is impractical because adjustments for the profit would have to be made for every year in the life of the group after the transaction occurred. In practice, the second course of action is followed.

The realisation of the profit or loss on a depreciable asset transferred within the group is *assumed* to occur when the future benefits embodied in the asset are consumed by the group. In other words, the depreciable asset transferred within the group will never be sold to an external party, but will be used up within the group to generate benefits for the group. As the asset is used up within the group, the benefits are received by the group. A useful measure of the pattern of benefits received by the group can be obtained by reference to the depreciation charged on the asset, since the depreciation allocation is related to the pattern of benefits from the use of the assets. Hence, for depreciable assets, the involvement of external parties in the transaction occurs on an indirect basis with the assumption being made that realisation occurs in a pattern consistent with the allocation of the depreciation of the non-current asset.

Assume a subsidiary sells a depreciable asset to the parent at a profit of $100, and the parent depreciates the asset on a straight-line basis of 10% p.a. On the date of sale, the unrealised profit is $100. In the first year after the sale, $10 (i.e. 10% × $100) of that profit is realised, leaving $90 unrealised profit at the end of the year. In that year the group shows $90 less profit than the sum of the profits of the parent and the subsidiary. In the second year, the group realises a further $10 profit, and shows $10 more profit than the sum of the net profits of the parent and the subsidiary. The process of realisation occurs via the adjustments for the depreciation of the asset subsequent to the point of sale, and is explained in the following section on depreciation.

Depreciation

In the previous example, plant was transferred from Beijing Ltd to Shanghai Ltd for $18 500 at a before-tax gain of $500. Since the asset is transferred at the beginning of the current period, Shanghai Ltd uses the asset and charges depreciation at 6% p.a. on a straight-line basis. The adjustment for depreciation at the end of the first year after the sale is determined by comparing the depreciation charge on the cost to the legal entity with the depreciation charge on the cost to the group:

Shanghai Ltd:	Cost of asset	= $18 500
	Depreciation expense	= 6% × $18 500
		= $1110
Group:	Cost of asset	= $18 000
	Depreciation expense	= 6% × $18 000
		= $1080
	Adjustment	= $1110 − $1080
		= $30

On consolidation, depreciation is reduced by $30. The worksheet entry is:

Accumulated depreciation	Dr	30	
Depreciation expense	Cr		30

This adjustment increases the group's profit by $30, that is, the group has realised $30 of the $500 profit on sale of the plant. The adjustment for the gain on sale reduces the group's profit by $500, and the adjustment for depreciation results in recognising some of that profit being realised as the asset is used up. The amount of profit realised is in proportion to the depreciation charged, namely 6% p.a.

In determining whether the depreciation rate used should be Beijing Ltd's or Shanghai Ltd's, remember that Beijing Ltd sold the asset to Shanghai Ltd. The purpose of making the consolidation adjustments is not to show the financial statements as they would have been if the transaction had not occurred, but to eliminate the effects of the intragroup transactions. Within the group, the plant has been transferred from one place of use, namely from Beijing Ltd. As a result, the plant is subject to the wear and tear, life expectations and so on associated with Shanghai Ltd's assets rather than Beijing Ltd's assets. Hence, the appropriate depreciation rate for consolidation purposes is that of the entity in which the asset is used.

The difference between the carrying amount in the legal entity and that in the group at date of sale was $500 (i.e. $18 500 − $18 000). At the end of the first year after sale, the difference is $470 (i.e. by adjusting for 6% depreciation, 94% × $18 500 less

94% × $18 000). The reduction in the carrying amount difference is $30, giving rise to a reversal of the initial temporary difference of $9 (i.e. 30% × $30). The worksheet adjustment entry for the tax effect of the depreciation adjustment is:

Income tax expense	Dr	9	
Deferred tax asset	Cr		9

The tax-effect adjustment is calculated as the tax rate times the adjustment to depreciation (i.e. 30% × $30). This depreciation adjustment causes the carrying amount to change each period, thus reducing the temporary difference created on the initial transfer of the asset. The net effect of the depreciation and the tax-effect adjustment on the net profit of the group is an increase of $21 (i.e. $30 − $9). The $350 after-tax profit on the sale of the plant is being realised at $21 (i.e. 6% × $350) p.a.

While the asset remains on hand, depreciation will be charged. Hence, when preparing the consolidated financial statements for the period 2006–07, the adjustment for depreciation must reflect the effects of the differences in depreciation for both the current year and the previous year. The adjustment relating to the previous period's depreciation is made against retained earnings (opening balance). The adjustment at 30 June 2007 is:

Accumulated depreciation	Dr	60	
Depreciation expense	Cr		30
Retained earnings (1/7/06)	Cr		30

In this worksheet entry, both the current period's and the previous period's accounting profit is increased by the reduction in depreciation expense. From a tax-effect accounting perspective, there must be an increase in income tax expense both for the current period and for the previous period. Reversal of the deferred tax asset raised in relation to the gain on sale occurs throughout the life of the asset as it is depreciated, causing its carrying amount to fall. The consolidation adjustment entry at 30 June 2007 for the tax effect of the depreciation adjustment entry is:

Retained earnings (1/7/06)	Dr	9	
Income tax expense	Dr	9	
Deferred tax asset	Cr		18

It can be seen that over the expected life of the asset, as it is depreciated, the deferred tax asset raised on the intragroup sale of the asset is progressively being reversed.

In relation to the realisation of the profit on sale, the unrealised after-tax profit on the sale of the vehicle is $350 (i.e. $500 × (1 − 0.3)). The profit is being realised at $21 ($30 − $9) p.a. At the end of the second year after the sale, a total of $42 is realised, $21 in the previous year and $21 in the current year. When the asset is fully depreciated, the whole of the profit on sale is realised.

In the *year of transfer*, the general form of consolidation entries for depreciation of a transferred asset is:

Accumulated depreciation	Dr	X	
Depreciation expense	Cr		X

Income tax expense	Dr	X	
Deferred tax asset	Cr		X

In the *years after the transfer*, the entries are:

Accumulated depreciation	Dr	X	
Depreciation expense	Cr		X
Retained earnings (opening balance)	Cr		X
Income tax expense	Dr	X	
Retained earnings (opening balance)	Dr	X	
Deferred tax asset	Cr		X

Note that, if a loss were made on the transfer, these entries would be reversed and the tax-effect entry would reduce the deferred tax liability created as a result of the loss on transfer. Again, intragroup losses may indicate an impairment loss that requires recognition on consolidation.

LO 4

21.4.3 Transfers from inventory to non-current assets

It is possible that an item which is regarded by one entity within the group as inventory is classified as a non-current asset by another entity. The key to determining the appropriate adjustment entries in these cases is to prepare the journal entries for the intragroup transaction in the records of the entities involved. In this section, the situation analysed is where the selling entity regards the transferred item as inventory and the acquiring entity classifies it as a depreciable asset.

> **Example: Inventory transferred to non-current asset**
> Shanghai Ltd sells to Beijing Ltd an item of inventory on 1 January 2006, that is, halfway through the current accounting period, for $6000 cash. The item cost Shanghai Ltd $3000 earlier in the current year. Beijing Ltd intends to use the item as a depreciable asset with a useful life of 10 years, and no estimated salvage value. A straight-line depreciation rate of 10% p.a. is applicable. The tax rate is 30%.

This transfer is examined in two stages, that is, sale and depreciation.

Sale

The entries in the accounts of the two entities are:

Shanghai Ltd

Cash	Dr	6 000	
Sales	Cr		6 000
Cost of sales	Dr	3 000	
Inventory	Cr		3 000

Beijing Ltd

Non-current asset	Dr	6 000	
Cash	Cr		6 000

Hence, from the legal entities' perspectives, there has been a sale of inventory and the acquisition of a non-current asset.

From the viewpoint of the group, there has been no sale of inventory and no acquisition of a non-current asset. Instead, the asset previously classified as inventory is now classified as a non-current asset which cost the group $3000. The three elements determining the consolidation adjustment are the profit on the sale of inventory by Shanghai Ltd, the revenue and expense items raised by Shanghai Ltd in relation to inventory, and the reporting of the non-current asset at cost to the group.

The worksheet entry for the year ended 30 June 2006 is:

Sales	Dr	6 000	
Cost of sales	Cr		3 000
Non-current asset	Cr		3 000

The debit and credit to sales and cost of sales respectively remove the $3000 profit recorded by Shanghai Ltd. Note that, in comparison with the inventory-to-inventory transfers (section 21.3.1), the sales and cost of sales in the above entry are both adjustments to Shanghai Ltd's income statement.

The consolidation worksheet adjustment reduces the carrying amount of the non-current asset by $3000. This gives rise to a deductible temporary difference, with the recognition of a deferred tax asset and an adjustment to income tax expense. The adjustment is equal to $900 (i.e. 30% × $3000). The consolidation worksheet adjustment entry is:

Deferred tax asset	Dr	900	
Income tax expense	Cr		900

If the acquisition by Beijing Ltd had taken place in the previous period, the sales and cost of sales of Shanghai Ltd for the current period would not be affected. Further, the profit of $3000 would be reflected in Shanghai Ltd's opening balance of retained earnings, causing the consolidation adjustment entries for the year ended 30 June 2007 to be:

Retained earnings (1/7/06)	Dr	3 000	
Non-current asset	Cr		3 000
Deferred tax asset	Dr	900	
Retained earnings (1/7/06)	Cr		900

Depreciation

Beijing Ltd has recorded the asset at $6000 and charges depreciation at the rate of 10% p.a. on cost. The depreciation expense per year is, then, $600. For the half-year ended 30 June 2006, the depreciation charge is $300. From the group's viewpoint, the depreciation is based on the cost of $3000, giving depreciation for the half-year of $150. To convert the legal entity figure of $300 to the $150 required for the group, the required consolidation adjustment entry for the year ended 30 June 2006 is:

Accumulated depreciation	Dr	150	
Depreciation expense	Cr		150

The tax-effect entry for consolidation purposes is:

Income tax expense	Dr	45	
Deferred tax asset	Cr		45

The adjustment to depreciation expense results in a decrease in the difference between the carrying amounts of the asset to the legal entity and to the group. Income tax expense must then be increased by $45 (i.e. 30% × $150) as the credit to deferred tax asset reflects the reversal of the temporary difference.

For the year ended 30 June 2007, the consolidation adjustment entries for depreciation are:

Accumulated depreciation	Dr	450	
Depreciation expense	Cr		300
Retained earnings (1/7/06)	Cr		150
Income tax expense	Dr	90	
Retained earnings (1/7/06)	Dr	45	
Deferred tax asset	Cr		135

21.4.4　Transfers from non-current assets to inventory

Assume Shanghai Ltd sold a non-current asset to Beijing Ltd, which classified it as inventory. On sale of the asset, Shanghai Ltd would pass journal entries relevant to the sale of a non-current asset while Beijing Ltd would record the purchase of inventory. Further, as Beijing Ltd regards the item as inventory, no depreciation would be charged. From the group's perspective, there has been a change in the asset classification from a non-current asset to inventory.

Assuming the inventory is not still on hand at the end of the year, the form of the consolidation entries in the year of the transfer is:

Proceeds from sale of non-current asset*	Dr	X	
Carrying amount of asset sold*	Cr		X
Cost of sales	Cr		X

* Instead of these two lines, a debit adjustment to the 'Gain on sale of non-current asset' account could be used.

21.5　Comprehensive example: intragroup transfers of assets

ILLUSTRATIVE EXAMPLE 21.1

Determination of cost

The following example illustrates procedures for the preparation of a consolidated income statement, statement of changes in equity and a consolidated balance sheet where the subsidiary is 100% owned. The pre-acquisition entry and pre-acquisition dividends as discussed in chapter 20 are also featured, as well as a number of intragroup inventory and non-current asset transfers.

Details
On 1 July 2002, Rongjiang Ltd acquired all the share capital of Weifang Ltd for $472 000. Weifang Ltd's equity at that date is shown opposite.

→

Share capital	$300 000
General reserve	96 000
Retained earnings	56 000

At 1 July 2002, all the identifiable assets and liabilities of Weifang Ltd were recorded at fair value.

Financial information for Rongjiang Ltd and Weifang Ltd for the year ended 30 June 2006 is presented in the left-hand columns of the worksheet illustrated in figure 21.3 (pp. 907–8). It is assumed that both companies use the perpetual inventory system.

Additional information

(a) During the year, Weifang Ltd paid a dividend of $30 000 from profits earned before 30 June 2002.

(b) On 1 January 2006, Weifang Ltd sold merchandise costing $30 000 to Rongjiang Ltd for $50 000. Half of this merchandise was still on hand at 30 June 2006.

(c) On 1 January 2005, Weifang Ltd sold an item of inventory costing $2000 to Rongjiang Ltd for $4000. Rongjiang Ltd treated this item as part of its equipment and depreciated it at 5% p.a. on a straight-line basis.

(d) On 31 March 2006, Rongjiang Ltd sold plant to Weifang Ltd for $6000 which was $1000 below its carrying amount to Rongjiang Ltd at that date. Weifang Ltd charged depreciation at the rate of 10% p.a. on this item.

(e) In the 2003–04 period, Rongjiang Ltd sold a block of land to Weifang Ltd at $20 000 above cost. The land is still held by Weifang Ltd.

(f) There was a profit in the beginning inventory of Rongjiang Ltd of $6000 on goods acquired from Weifang Ltd in the previous period.

(g) The tax rate is 30%.

Required

Prepare the consolidated financial statements for the year ended 30 June 2006.

Solution

Consolidation worksheet entries

1. *Pre-acquisition entry*

   At 1 July 2002:

Net fair value of the identifiable assets, liabilities and contingent liabilities of Weifang Ltd	= $300 000 + $96 000 + $56 000
	= $452 000
Cost of the combination	= $472 000
Goodwill	= $20 000

The pre-acquisition entry at 30 June 2006, taking into effect the dividend of $30 000 paid in the current year from pre-acquisition equity, is:

Retained earnings (1/7/05)	Dr	56 000	
Share capital	Dr	300 000	
General reserve	Dr	96 000	
Goodwill	Dr	20 000	
Shares in Weifang Ltd	Cr		472 000
Shares in Weifang Ltd	Dr	30 000	
Dividend paid	Cr		30 000

2. *Profit in ending inventory*

Sales	Dr	50 000	
Cost of sales	Cr		40 000
Inventory	Cr		10 000
($10 000 = $\frac{1}{2}$ × [$50 000 − $30 000])			
Deferred tax asset	Dr	3 000	
Income tax expense	Cr		3 000
(30% × $10 000)			

3. *Sale of inventory, classified as equipment*
   Note: The transfer occurred in a previous period.

Retained earnings (1/7/05)	Dr	2 000	
Plant and equipment	Cr		2 000
Deferred tax asset	Dr	600	
Retained earnings (1/7/05)	Cr		600
(30% × $2000)			

4. *Depreciation*

Recorded depreciation		Group depreciation	
Previous period			
5% × $4000 × $\frac{1}{2}$ year = $ 100		5% × $2000 × $\frac{1}{2}$ year = $ 50	
Current period			
5% × $4000 = 200		5% × $2000 = 100	
$300		$150	

The accumulated depreciation adjustment is $300 − $150 = $150.

Accumulated depreciation	Dr	150	
Depreciation expense	Cr		100
Retained earnings (1/7/05)	Cr		50
Income tax expense	Dr	30	
Retained earnings (1/7/05)	Dr	15	
Deferred tax asset	Cr		45
($30 = 30% × $100; $15 = 30% × $50)			

5. *Loss on sale of plant*

Plant and equipment	Dr	1 000	
Proceeds from sale of plant	Dr	6 000	
Carrying amount of plant sold	Cr		7 000
Income tax expense	Dr	300	
Deferred tax liability	Cr		300
(30% × $1000)			

→

6. *Depreciation on plant*

Recorded depreciation			Group depreciation		
$10\% \times \$6000 \times \frac{1}{4}$ year	$=$	$\$150$	$10\% \times \$7000 \times \frac{1}{4}$ year	$=$	$\$175$

Depreciation expense	Dr	25	
Accumulated depreciation	Cr		25
Deferred tax liability	Dr	8	
Income tax expense	Cr		8
$(30\% \times \$25 = 7.5,$ round to $\$8)$			

7. *Profit on sale of land in previous period*

Retained earnings (1/7/05)	Dr	20 000	
Land	Cr		20 000
Deferred tax asset	Dr	6 000	
Retained earnings (1/7/05)	Cr		6 000
$(30\% \times \$20\ 000)$			

8. *Profit in beginning inventory*

Retained earnings (1/7/05)	Dr	6 000	
Cost of sales	Cr		6 000
Income tax expense	Dr	1 800	
Retained earnings (1/7/05)	Cr		1 800
$(30\% \times \$6000)$			

Figure 21.3 shows the completed worksheet for preparation of the consolidated financial statements of Rongjiang Ltd and its subsidiary Weifang Ltd at 30 June 2006. Once the effects of all adjustments are added or subtracted horizontally in the worksheet to calculate figures in the right-hand 'consolidation' column, the consolidated financial statements can be prepared, as shown in figure 21.4 (p. 909).

FIGURE 21.3 Consolidation worksheet — intragroup transfers of assets

Financial statements	Rongjiang Ltd	Weifang Ltd		Dr	Cr		Consolidation
				Adjustments			
Sales revenue	1 196 000	928 000	2	50 000			2 074 000
Cost of sales	888 000	670 000			40 000 6 000	2 9	1 512 000
Wages and salaries	57 500	32 000					89 500
Depreciation	5 200	4 800	6	25	100	4	9 925
Other expenses	4 000	—					4 000
Total expenses	954 700	706 800					1 615 425
	241 300	221 200					458 575

(continued)

Financial statements	Ronjiang Ltd	Weifang Ltd		Adjustments Dr	Cr		Consolidation
Proceeds from sale of plant	6 000	–	5	6 000			–
Carrying amount of plant sold	7 000	–			7 000	5	–
Gain (loss)	(1 000)	–					–
Profit before income tax	240 300	221 200					458 575
Income tax expense	96 120	88 480	4	30	3 000	2	183 722
			5	300	8	6	
			8	1 800			
Profit	144 180	132 720					274 853
Retained earnings (1/7/05)	100 820	70 280	1	56 000	600	3	95 535
			3	2 000	50	4	
			4	15	6 000	7	
			7	20 000	1 800	8	
			8	6 000			
	245 000	203 000					370 388
Dividend paid	80 000	30 000			30 000	1	80 000
Retained earnings (30/6/06)	165 000	173 000					290 388
Share capital	500 000	300 000	1	300 000			500 000
General reserve	140 000	96 000	1	96 000			140 000
Deferred tax liability	52 000	43 000	2	3 000	45	4	85 737
			3	600	300	5	
			6	8			
			7	6 000			
	857 000	612 000					1 016 125
Shares in Weifang Ltd	442 000	–			442 000	1	–
Cash	80 000	73 000					153 000
Inventory	168 000	36 000			10 000	2	194 000
Other current assets	25 000	368 000					393 000
Land	100 000	120 000			20 000	7	200 000
Plant and equipment	52 000	28 000	5	1 000	2 000	3	79 000
Accumulated depreciation	(10 000)	(13 000)	4	150	25	6	(22 875)
Goodwill	–	–	1	20 000			20 000
	857 000	612 000		568 928	568 928		1 016 125

Rongjiang Ltd
Consolidated income statement
for the year ended 30 June 2006

Revenues	$2 074 000
Expenses	1 615 425
Profit before income tax	458 575
Income tax expense	183 722
Profit for the period	$ 274 853

Rongjiang Ltd
Consolidated statement of changes in equity
for the year ended 30 June 2006

Profit for the period	$274 853
Amounts recognised directly in equity	–
Total recognised income and expense for the period	$274 853
Retained earnings at 1 July 2005	$ 95 535
Profit for the period	274 853
Dividend paid	(80 000)
Retained earnings at 30 June 2006	$290 388
General reserve at 1 July 2005	$140 000
General reserve at 30 June 2006	$140 000
Share capital at 1 July 2005	$500 000
Share capital at 30 June 2006	$500 000

Rongjiang Ltd
Consolidated balance sheet
as at 30 June 2006

Current assets			
Cash assets			$ 153 000
Inventories			194 000
Other			393 000
Total current assets			740 000
Non-current assets			
Property, plant and equipment:			
Plant and equipment	$79 000		
Accumulated depreciation	(22 875)	$ 56 125	
Land		200 000	256 125
Goodwill			20 000
Total non-current assets			276 125
Total assets			1 016 125
Non-current liabilities			
Deferred tax liabilities			85 737
Net assets			$ 930 388
Equity			
Share capital			$ 500 000
Other reserves:			
General reserve			140 000
Retained earnings			290 388
Total equity			$ 930 388

FIGURE 21.4   Consolidated financial statements

21.6 Intragroup services

Many different examples of services between related entities exist. For instance:

- Beijing Ltd may lend to Shanghai Ltd some specialist personnel for a limited period of time for the performance of a particular task by Shanghai Ltd. For this service, Beijing Ltd may charge Shanghai Ltd a certain fee, or expect Shanghai Ltd to perform other services in return.
- One entity may lease or rent an item of plant or a warehouse from the other.
- A subsidiary may exist solely for the purpose of carrying out some specific task; for example, research activities for the parent, a fee for such research being duly charged. In this situation, all service revenue earned by the subsidiary is paid for by the parent, and must be adjusted in the consolidation process.

Example: Intragroup services

During 2005–06, Beijing Ltd offered the services of a specialist employee to Shanghai Ltd for two months in return for which Shanghai Ltd paid $30 000 to Beijing Ltd. The employee's annual salary is $155 000, paid for by Beijing Ltd.

The journal entries in the records of Beijing Ltd and Shanghai Ltd in relation to this transaction are:

Beijing Ltd

Cash	Dr	30 000	
Service revenue	Cr		30 000

Shanghai Ltd

Service expense	Dr	30 000	
Cash	Cr		30 000

From the group's perspective there has been no service revenue received or service expense made to parties external to the group. Hence, to adjust from what has been recorded by the legal entities to the group's perspective, the consolidation adjustment entry is:

Service revenue	Dr	30 000	
Service expense	Cr		30 000

No adjustment is made in relation to the employee's salary since, from the group's view, the salary paid to the employee is a payment to an external party.

Since there is no effect on the carrying amounts of assets or liabilities, there is no temporary difference and no need for any income tax adjustment.

Example: Intragroup rent

Beijing Ltd rents office space from Shanghai Ltd for $150 000 p.a.

In accounting for this transaction, Beijing Ltd records rent expense of $150 000 and Shanghai Ltd records rent revenue of $150 000. From the group's view, the intragroup rental scheme is purely an internal arrangement, and no revenue or expense is incurred.

The recorded revenue and expense therefore need to be eliminated. The appropriate consolidation adjustment entry is:

| Rent revenue | Dr | 150 000 | |
| Rent expense | Cr | | 150 000 |

There is no tax-effect entry necessary as assets and liabilities are unaffected by the adjustment entry.

21.6.1 Realisation of profits or losses

With the transfer of services within the group, the consolidation adjustments do not affect the profit of the group. In a transaction involving a payment by a parent to a subsidiary for services rendered, the parent shows an expense and the subsidiary shows revenue. The net effect on the group's profit is zero. Hence, from the group's view, with intragroup services there are no realisation difficulties.

LO 6

21.7 Intragroup dividends from post-acquisition equity

In this section, consideration is given to dividends declared and paid from profits earned after Beijing Ltd's acquisition of Shanghai Ltd. These are commonly referred to as post-acquisition dividends. In contrast to pre-acquisition dividends, which are accounted for as a reduction in the investment, post-acquisition dividends are accounted for as revenue in the records of Beijing Ltd.

Three situations are considered in this section:
* dividends declared in the current period but not paid
* dividends declared and paid in the current period
* bonus share dividends.

It is assumed that the company expecting to receive the dividend recognises revenue when the dividend is declared.

21.7.1 Dividends declared in the current period but not paid

Assume that, on 25 June 2006, Shanghai Ltd declares a dividend of $4000 from profits earned since the acquisition date. At the end of the period, the dividend is unpaid.

The entries passed by the legal entities are:

Shanghai Ltd

| Dividend declared (in retained earnings) | Dr | 4 000 | |
| Dividend payable | Cr | | 4 000 |

Beijing Ltd

| Dividend receivable | Dr | 4 000 | |
| Dividend revenue | Cr | | 4 000 |

The entry made by Shanghai Ltd both reduces retained earnings and raises a liability account. From the group's perspective, there is no reduction in equity and the group has no obligation to pay dividends outside the group. Similarly, the group expects no dividends to be received from parties outside the group. Hence, the appropriate consolidation adjustment entries are shown on the next page.

Dividend payable	Dr	4 000	
Dividend declared	Cr		4 000
(To adjust for the effects of the entry made by Shanghai Ltd)			
Dividend revenue	Dr	4 000	
Dividend receivable	Cr		4 000
(To adjust for the effects of the entry made by Beijing Ltd)			

In the following period when the dividend is paid, no adjustments are required in the consolidation worksheet. As there are no dividend revenue, dividend declared, or receivable items left open at the end of the period, then the position of the group is the same as the sum of the legal entities' financial statements.

21.7.2 Dividends declared and paid in the current period

Assume Shanghai Ltd declares and pays an interim dividend of $4000 in the current period.

Entries by the *legal entities* are:

Beijing Ltd

| Cash | Dr | 4 000 | |
| Dividend revenue | Cr | | 4 000 |

Shanghai Ltd

| Interim dividend paid (in retained earnings) | Dr | 4 000 | |
| Cash | Cr | | 4 000 |

From the outlook of the group, no dividends have been paid and no dividend revenue has been received. Hence, the adjustment necessary for the consolidated financial statements to show the affairs of the group is:

| Dividend revenue | Dr | 4 000 | |
| Interim dividend paid | Cr | | 4 000 |

21.7.3 Bonus share dividends

A subsidiary may occasionally pay a dividend to its parent in the form of shares rather than cash.

For example, assume a bonus share dividend of $5000 is paid by Shanghai Ltd out of post-acquisition profits.

The journal entry made by Shanghai Ltd is:

| Bonus share dividend paid (in retained earnings) | Dr | 5 000 | |
| Share capital | Cr | | 5 000 |

Since the bonus share dividend is paid by the subsidiary out of post-acquisition profits, these profits which, for consolidation purposes, are normally available for dividends have been capitalised as share capital.

In the records of Beijing Ltd, no entry is required as the bonus share dividend does not give Beijing Ltd an increased share of Shanghai Ltd, that is, Beijing Ltd receives nothing that it did not previously own. Furthermore, if the investment is to be recorded strictly at the historical purchase price for the pre-acquisition equity of Shanghai Ltd, the investment is unaffected by the bonus dividend out of post-acquisition equity.

For consolidation purposes, two alternative adjustments are possible:

(a) Eliminate the bonus dividend paid against the share capital of Shanghai Ltd, that is, reverse the entry made by the subsidiary to record the dividend:

Share capital	Dr	5 000	
Bonus share dividend paid	Cr		5 000

If this entry is used, the fact that Shanghai Ltd has provided for a bonus dividend does not appear in the consolidated financial statements unless disclosed by way of a note. The capitalisation of Shanghai Ltd's retained earnings does not affect consolidated retained earnings, but does result in the inclusion in the consolidated retained earnings balance of those profits which have been capitalised and are not available for the payment of dividends.

(b) Do not eliminate the bonus dividend paid but set up a new capitalised profits reserve in the consolidation worksheet. The entry is:

Share capital	Dr	5 000	
Capitalised profits reserve	Cr		5 000

The purpose of creating the reserve is to disclose the fact that part of the retained earnings of the group has been capitalised by the subsidiary and is therefore no longer available for payment of cash dividends to the parent.

Alternative (b) is recommended as the preferred treatment of bonus share dividends as it raises the capitalised profits reserve in the consolidated financial statements as a non-distributable reserve. From the group's viewpoint, distribution of this capitalised profits reserve to shareholders in the group is impossible and therefore is correctly treated as non-distributable.

Tax effect of dividends

Generally, dividends are tax-free. There are then no tax-effect adjustment entries required in relation to dividend-related consolidation adjustment entries.

ILLUSTRATIVE EXAMPLE 21.2

Post-acquisition dividends

On 1 July 2008, Fuzhow Ltd acquired all the share capital of Wuhan Ltd and Jinan Ltd for $187 500 and $150 000 respectively. At that date, equity of the three companies was:

	Fuzhow Ltd	Wuhan Ltd	Jinan Ltd
Share capital	$150 000	$100 000	$100 000
General reserve	90 000	60 000	40 000
Retained earnings	20 000	17 500	10 000

At 1 July 2008, the identifiable net assets of all companies were recorded at fair values.

For the year ended 30 June 2009, the summarised financial statements of the three companies show the following details:

	Fuzhow Ltd	Wuhan Ltd	Jinan Ltd
Sales revenue	$398 500	$200 000	$150 000
Dividend revenue	9 000	–	–
Total revenues	407 500	200 000	150 000
Total expenses	360 000	176 000	138 000
Profit before income tax	47 500	24 000	12 000
Income tax expense	15 000	10 000	5 000
Profit	32 500	14 000	7 000
Retained earnings (1/7/08)	20 000	17 500	10 000
Total available for appropriation	52 500	31 500	17 000
Interim dividend paid	7 500	2 500	–
Bonus share dividend paid	–	–	4 000
Final dividend declared	15 000	5 000	1 500
Transfer to general reserve	2 000	5 000	–
	24 500	12 500	5 500
Retained earnings (30/6/09)	28 000	19 000	11 500
Shares in Wuhan Ltd	$187 500	–	–
Shares in Jinan Ltd	150 000	–	–
Dividend receivable	6 500	–	–
Property, plant and equipment	23 500	$205 000	$167 000
Total assets	367 500	205 000	167 000
Final dividend payable	15 000	5 000	1 500
Non-current liabilities	82 500	16 000	10 000
Total liabilities	97 500	21 000	11 500
Net assets	$270 000	$184 000	$155 500
Share capital	$150 000	$100 000	$104 000
General reserve	92 000	65 000	40 000
Retained earnings	28 000	19 000	11 500
Total equity	$270 000	$184 000	$155 500

Required

Prepare the consolidated financial statements as at 30 June 2009 for Fuzhow Ltd and its two subsidiaries, Wuhan Ltd and Jinan Ltd. Assume all dividends and reserve transfers are from post-acquisition profits.

Solution

From an examination of the financial statements of the three companies, the following facts are discernible:

(a) The relationship between the parent and subsidiaries may be expressed as shown in figure 21.5.

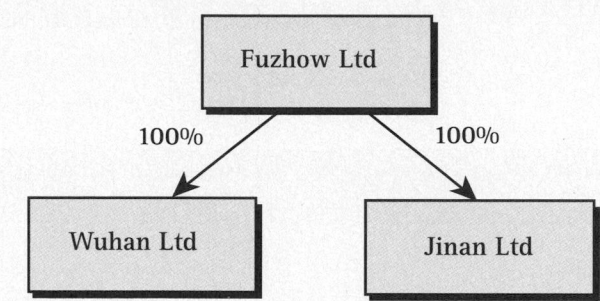

FIGURE 21.5 Relationship between parent and subsidiaries

(b) Fuzhow Ltd has recognised both the interim and final dividends from Wuhan Ltd and Jinan Ltd as revenue. Note the dividend receivable of $6500 in the balance sheet.

(c) Fuzhow Ltd has made no entry with respect to the bonus share dividend paid by Jinan Ltd. It is assumed in the following solution that treatment (b) as discussed in section 21.7.3 on page 913 is adopted.

Figure 21.6 overleaf illustrates the consolidation worksheet necessary to consolidate the financial statements of Fuzhow Ltd and its two subsidiaries. Detailed discussion of each adjustment is provided below.

Consolidation worksheet adjustment entries

1. *Pre-acquisition entry: Fuzhow Ltd and Wuhan Ltd*

   At 1 July 2008:

Net fair value of identifiable assets, liabilities and contingent liabilities of Wuhan Ltd	= $100 000 + $60 000 + $17 500
	= $177 500
Cost of the combination	= $187 500
Goodwill	= $10 000

The pre-acquisition entry at 30 June 2009 is then:

Retained earnings (1/7/08)	Dr	17 500	
Share capital	Dr	100 000	
General reserve	Dr	60 000	
Goodwill	Dr	10 000	
Shares in Wuhan Ltd	Cr		187 500

2. *Pre-acquisition entry: Fuzhow Ltd and Jinan Ltd*

   At 1 July 2008:

Net fair value of identifiable assets, liabilities and contingent liabilities of Jinan Ltd	= $100 000 + $40 000 + $10 000
	= $150 000
Cost of the combination	= $150 000
Goodwill	= zero

3. *Interim dividend: Wuhan Ltd*

Dividend revenue	Dr	2 500	
Dividend paid	Cr		2 500

4. Bonus share dividend: Jinan Ltd

	Dr	4 000	
Share capital			
Capitalised profits reserve	Cr		4 000

Financial statements	Fuzhow Ltd	Wuhan Ltd	Jinan Ltd		Adjustments Dr	Cr		Consolidation
Sales revenue	398 500	200 000	150 000					748 500
Dividend revenue	9 000	—	—	3	2 500			—
				5	5 000			
				6	1 500			
	407 500	200 000	150 000					748 500
Expenses	360 000	176 000	138 000					674 000
Profit before income tax	47 500	24 000	12 000					74 500
Income tax expense	15 000	10 000	5 000					30 000
Profit	32 500	14 000	7 000					44 500
Retained earnings (1/7/08)	20 000	17 500	10 000	1	17 500			20 000
				2	10 000			
	52 500	31 500	17 000					64 500
Interim dividend paid	7 500	2 500	—			2 500	3	7 500
Bonus dividend paid	—	—	4 000					4 000
Final dividend declared	15 000	5 000	1 500			5 000	5	15 000
						1 500	6	
Transfer to general reserve	2 000	5 000	—					7 000
	24 500	12 500	5 500					33 500
Retained earnings (30/6/09)	28 000	19 000	11 500					31 000
Share capital	150 000	100 000	104 000	1	100 000			150 000
				2	100 000			
				4	4 000			
General reserve	92 000	65 000	40 000	1	60 000			97 000
				2	40 000			
Capitalised profits reserve						4 000	4	4 000
Final dividend payable	15 000	5 000	1 500	5	5 000			15 000
				6	1 500			
Non-current liabilities	82 500	16 000	10 000					108 500
	367 500	205 000	167 000					405 500
Shares in Wuhan Ltd	187 500	—	—			187 500	1	—
Shares in Jinan Ltd	150 000	—	—			150 000	2	—
Dividend receivable	6 500	—	—			5 000	5	—
						1 500	6	
Property, plant and equipment	23 500	205 000	167 000					395 500
Goodwill	—	—	—	1	10 000			10 000
	367 500	205 000	167 000		357 000	357 000		405 500

FIGURE 21.6 Consolidation worksheet — post-acquisition dividends

→

5. *Final dividend declared: Wuhan Ltd*

Final dividend payable	Dr	5 000	
Final dividend declared	Cr		5 000
Dividend revenue	Dr	5 000	
Dividend receivable	Cr		5 000

6. *Final dividend declared: Jinan Ltd*

Final dividend payable	Dr	1 500	
Final dividend declared	Cr		1 500
Dividend revenue	Dr	1 500	
Dividend receivable	Cr		1 500

Notes
1. No adjustment entries are made for transfers to and from reserves if post-acquisition equity only is affected.
2. The dividends paid and declared by the parent to its shareholders are not adjusted for in the consolidated financial statements as these dividends are dividends paid by the group to external parties.

From figure 21.6, after all adjustments have been entered in the worksheet and amounts totalled across to the consolidation column, the consolidated financial statements can be prepared in suitable format as shown in figure 21.7.

FIGURE 21.7 Consolidated financial statements — adjustments for dividends

Fuzhow Ltd
Consolidated income statement
for the year ended 30 June 2009

Revenues	$ 718 500
Expenses	674 000
Profit before income tax	74 500
Income tax expense	30 000
Profit for the period	$ 44 500

Fuzhow Ltd
Consolidated statement of changes in equity
for the year ended 30 June 2009

Profit for the period	$ 44 500
Amounts recognised directly in equity	–
Total recognised income and expense for the period	$ 44 500
Retained earnings at 1 July 2008	$ 20 000
Profit for the period	44 500
Interim dividend paid	(7 500)
Bonus dividend paid	(4 000)
Final dividend declared	(15 000)
Transfer of general reserve	(7 000)
Retained earnings at 30 June 2009	$ 31 000
	(*continued*)

General reserve at 1 July 2008	$ 90 000
Transfer from retained earnings	7 000
General reserve at 30 June 2009	$ 97 000
Capitalised profits reserve at 1 July 2008	$ 0
Increase due to bonus dividend paid	4 000
Capitalised profits reserve at 30 June 2009	$ 4 000
Share capital as at 1 July 2008	$ 150 000
Share capital at 30 June 2009	$ 150 000

Fuzhow Ltd
Consolidated balance sheet
as at 30 June 2009

Non-current assets		
Property, plant and equipment		$ 395 500
Goodwill		10 000
Total non-current assets		405 500
Total assets		405 500
Current liabilities		
Final dividend payable		15 000
Non-current liabilities		108 500
Total liabilities		123 500
Net assets		$ 282 000
Equity		
Share capital		$ 150 000
Other reserves:		
General reserve	$97 000	
Capitalised profits reserve (Note 1)	4 000	101 000
Retained earnings		31 000
Total equity		$ 282 000

Note 1: The capitalised profits reserve represents the non-distributable profit created by the capitalisation of profits in a subsidiary by means of a bonus share dividend.

LO 7

21.8 Intragroup borrowings

Members of a group often borrow and lend money among themselves, and charge interest on the money borrowed. In some cases, an entity may be set up within the group solely for the purpose of handling group finances and for borrowing money on international money markets. Consolidation adjustments are necessary in relation to these intragroup borrowings and interest thereon because, from the stance of the group, these transactions create assets and liabilities and revenues and expenses that do not exist in terms of the group's relationship with external parties.

Example: Advances

Beijing Ltd lends $100 000 to Shanghai Ltd, the latter paying $15 000 interest to Beijing Ltd.

The relevant journal entries in each of the legal entities are:

Beijing Ltd

Advance to Shanghai Ltd	Dr	100 000	
Cash	Cr		100 000
Cash	Dr	15 000	
Interest revenue	Cr		15 000

Shanghai Ltd

Cash	Dr	100 000	
Advance from Beijing Ltd	Cr		100 000
Interest expense	Dr	15 000	
Cash	Cr		15 000

The consolidation adjustments involve eliminating the monetary asset created by Beijing Ltd, the monetary liability raised by Shanghai Ltd, the interest revenue recorded by Beijing Ltd and the interest expense paid by Shanghai Ltd:

Advance from Beijing Ltd	Dr	100 000	
Advance to Shanghai Ltd	Cr		100 000
Interest revenue	Dr	15 000	
Interest expense	Cr		15 000

The adjustment to the asset and liability is necessary as long as the intragroup loan exists. In relation to any past period's payments and receipt of interest, no ongoing adjustment to accumulated profits (opening balance) is necessary as the net effect of the consolidation adjustment is zero on that item.

As the effect on net assets of the consolidation adjustment is zero, no tax-effect entry is necessary.

> ### Example: Debentures acquired at date of issue
> On 1 January 2006, Beijing Ltd issues 1000 $100 debentures having an interest rate of 15% p.a. payable on 1 January of each year. Shanghai Ltd, a wholly owned subsidiary of Beijing Ltd, acquires half the debentures issued.

The journal entries made by Beijing Ltd and Shanghai Ltd for the year ended 30 June 2006 are:

Beijing Ltd

01–Jan–06	Cash	Dr	100 000	
	Debentures	Cr		100 000
	(Issue of debentures)			
30–Jun–06	Interest expense	Dr	7 500	
	Interest payable	Cr		7 500
	(Accrued interest payable of 15%			
	for 6 months)			

Shanghai Ltd

01-Jan-06	Debentures in Beijing Ltd	Dr	50 000	
	Cash	Cr		50 000
	(Debentures acquired)			
30-Jun-06	Interest receivable	Dr	3 750	
	Interest revenue	Cr		3 750
	(Accrued interest revenue)			

The consolidation entries to adjust for the entries recorded in the legal entities are:

Debentures	Dr	50 000	
Debentures in Beijing Ltd	Cr		50 000
Interest payable	Dr	3 750	
Interest receivable	Cr		3 750
Interest revenue	Dr	3 750	
Interest expense	Cr		3 750

Example: Debentures acquired on the open market

Beijing Ltd issued, on 1 July 2005, 1000 $100 15% debentures at nominal value. Interest is payable half-yearly on 31 December and 30 June. Debentures are to be redeemed after ten years. Assume that Shanghai Ltd acquired 300 of these debentures cum div. on the open market for $95 on 31 March 2006.

Journal entries made by Beijing Ltd and Shanghai Ltd for the year ended 30 June 2006 are:

Beijing Ltd

01-Jul-05	Cash	Dr	100 000	
	Debentures	Cr		100 000
	(Issue of debentures)			
31-Dec-05	Interest expense	Dr	7 500	
	Cash	Cr		7 500
	(Interest paid on 31/12/05)			
30-Jun-06	Interest expense	Dr	7 500	
	Cash	Cr		7 500
	(Interest paid on 30/6/06)			

Shanghai Ltd

31-Mar-06	Debentures in Beijing Ltd	Dr	28 500	
	Cash	Cr		28 500
	(300 debentures acquired on the open market)			
30-Jun-06	Cash	Dr	2 250	
	Debentures in Beijing Ltd	Cr		1 125
	Interest revenue	Cr		1 125
	(Interest before 31/3/06 was included in the purchase price)			

From the group's perspective, the purchase by Shanghai Ltd on the open market effectively redeemed 300 of the debentures issued by Beijing Ltd. Since the debentures were acquired cum div., the interest expense for the period 1 January to 31 March 2006 has been paid for by the group when the debentures were acquired by Shanghai Ltd. The group has redeemed 300 of the debentures at a price less than nominal value and is entitled to recognise income in the consolidation worksheet to the extent of the discount received on purchase or redemption. The consolidation adjustment entries necessary at 30 June 2006 are:

Debentures	Dr	30 000	
Debentures in Beijing Ltd	Cr		27 375*
Income on redemption of debentures	Cr		2 625
* $27 375 = $28 500 − $1125			
Interest revenue	Dr	1 125	
Interest expense	Cr		1 125

In future periods, while the debentures are still outstanding in the records of Beijing Ltd, the consolidation adjustment entries for debentures and interest must continue to be made. However, the income on redemption of debentures is considered to have occurred on 31 March 2006. Hence, in future periods, a credit entry is made to retained earnings (opening balance). To illustrate, the consolidation entries necessary at 30 June 2007 are as follows:

Debentures	Dr	30 000	
Debentures in Beijing Ltd	Cr		27 375
Retained earnings (1/7/06)	Cr		2 625
Interest revenue	Dr	4 500	
Interest expense	Cr		4 500
(Being a full year's interest on 300 debentures)			

There is no tax effect in the group because the assets and liabilities are reduced equally.

Example: Redemption of debtors

Assume the debentures issued in the previous example are redeemed on 30 June 2015.

For the year ended 30 June 2015 the journal entries made by the legal entities are as follows:

Beijing Ltd

31-Dec-14	Interest expense	Dr	7 500	
	Cash	Cr		7 500
	(Interest paid)			
30-Jun-15	Interest expense	Dr	7 500	
	Cash	Cr		7 500
	(Interest paid)			
	Debentures	Dr	100 000	
	Cash	Cr		100 000
	(Redemption of debentures)			

Shanghai Ltd

31-Dec-14	Cash	Dr	2 250	
	Interest revenue	Cr		2 250
30-Jun-15	Cash	Dr	2 250	
	Interest revenue	Cr		2 250
	Cash	Dr	30 000	
	Debentures in Beijing Ltd	Cr		27 375
	Income on redemption			
	of debentures	Cr		2 625

On consolidation, besides the elimination of the interest paid during the period, an adjustment is necessary to eliminate the income on redemption recorded by Shanghai Ltd. This income is not income to the group in the year ended 30 June 2015. From the group's viewpoint, the debentures were effectively redeemed when Shanghai Ltd acquired the debentures on the open market in 2006. The consolidated financial statements in that year reflected the income on redemption. The consolidation adjustment entries for the year ended 30 June 2015 are:

Interest revenue	Dr	4 500	
Interest expense	Cr		4 500
Income on redemption of debentures	Dr	2 625	
Retained earnings (1/7/14)	Cr		2 625

21.9 Summary

This chapter introduces the problems of intragroup transfers of inventory, non-current assets, services, dividends and debentures and their adjustment in the consolidation process. Associated with these transfers is a need to consider the implications of applying tax-effect accounting in the consolidation process.

The basic approach adopted to determine the consolidation adjustment entries for intragroup transfers is:

(a) Analyse the events within the records of the legal entities involved in the intragroup transfer. Determine whether the transaction is a prior period or current period event.

(b) Analyse the position from the group's viewpoint.

(c) Create adjusting entries to change from the legal entities' position to that of the group.

(d) Consider the tax effect of the adjusting entries.

Note again that there are no actual adjusting entries made in the records of the individual legal entities which constitute the group. However, if required, a special journal could be set up by the parent entity to keep a record of the adjustments made in the process of preparing the consolidated financial statements. Alternatively, the consolidation process may be performed by the use of special consolidation worksheets.

DISCUSSION QUESTIONS

1. Why is it necessary to make adjustments for intragroup transactions?

2. In making adjustments for intragroup transactions, entries are sometimes made for the tax effect of the adjustments. Given that the consolidated group, being a non-legal entity, pays no income tax, why are the tax-effect entries made? Also, in what circumstances are they made?

3. If Beijing Ltd sold an item of inventory to its wholly owned subsidiary, Shanghai Ltd, for $15 000, the item previously costing Beijing Ltd $12 000, the adjusting entries at the end of the period – assuming Shanghai Ltd subsequently sold half of the items to external parties, and the tax rate is 30% – are:

Sales	Dr	15 000	
Cost of sales	Cr		13 500
Inventory	Cr		1 500
Deferred tax asset	Dr	450	
Income tax expense	Cr		450

Explain why the above entries are made, noting the adjustment to each item separately.

4. Using the information in question 3, determine the consolidation worksheet entries in the following year, and explain the adjustments to each item separately.

5. At the beginning of the current period, Beijing Ltd sold a used depreciable asset to its wholly owned subsidiary, Shanghai Ltd, for $80 000. Beijing Ltd had originally paid $200 000 for this asset, and at time of sale to Shanghai Ltd had charged depreciation of $150 000.

In calculating the depreciation expense for the consolidated group (as opposed to that recorded by Shanghai Ltd), should it be based on:
(a) $200 000
(b) $50 000
(c) $80 000?
Explain your choice.

6. If the parent entity purchases on the open market, for an amount less than nominal value, some debentures previously issued by the subsidiary, the adjustment in the worksheet includes the raising of 'income on redemption'. What does this represent? Does an adjustment to income, or subsequently to retained earnings, have to be made for the rest of the life of the group? If not, what event causes the discontinuation of this adjustment entry?

7. If a subsidiary sells inventory to its parent entity at the same amount it would sell that inventory to non-related entities, why should profits on these transactions be adjusted on consolidation?

8. How should the parent treat the receipt of a bonus dividend paid from the subsidiary's post-acquisition profits? What effect does this treatment have on the consolidation adjustments in the worksheet?

EXERCISES

Note: In all exercises, at acquisition date, the identifiable assets and liabilities of the subsidiary are recorded at fair value.

EXERCISE 21.1 ★

Intragroup transactions

Maoming Ltd owns all the share capital of Wugang Ltd. In relation to the following intragroup transactions, prepare adjusting journal entries for the consolidation worksheet at 30 June 2006. Assume an income tax rate of 30% and that all income on sale of assets is taxable and expenses are deductible.

(a) During the year ending 30 June 2006, Wugang Ltd sold $50 000 worth of inventory to Maoming Ltd. Wugang Ltd recorded a $10 000 profit before tax on these transactions. At 30 June 2006, Maoming Ltd has one-quarter of these goods still on hand.

(b) Wugang Ltd sold a warehouse to Maoming Ltd for $100 000. This had originally cost Wugang Ltd $82 000. The transaction took place on 1 January 2005. Maoming Ltd charges depreciation at 5% p.a. on a straight-line basis.

(c) During the 2005–06 period, Maoming Ltd sold inventory costing $12 000 to Wugang Ltd for $18 000. One-third of this was sold to Hong Ltd for $9500 and one-third to Kong Ltd for $9000.

(d) On 1 January 2005, Wugang Ltd sold inventory costing $6000 to Maoming Ltd at a transfer price of $8000. On 1 September 2005, Maoming Ltd sold half of these goods back to Wugang Ltd, receiving $3000 from Wugang Ltd. Of the remainder kept by Maoming Ltd, half was sold in January 2006 to China Ltd at a loss of $200.

(e) On 25 June 2006, Maoming Ltd declared a dividend of $10 000. On the same day, Wugang Ltd declared a $5000 dividend.

(f) On 1 October 2005, Maoming Ltd issued 1000 15% debentures of $100 at nominal value. Wugang Ltd acquired 400 of these. Interest is payable half-yearly on 31 March and 30 September. Accruals have been recognised in the legal entities' accounts.

(g) During the 2004–05 period, Maoming Ltd sold inventory to Wugang Ltd for $10 000, recording a before-tax profit of $2000. Half this inventory was unsold by Wugang Ltd at 30 June 2005.

EXERCISE 21.2 ★ Intragroup transactions

Wudu Ltd owns all of the share capital of Shashi Ltd. In relation to the following intragroup transactions, all parts of which are independent unless specified, prepare the consolidation worksheet adjusting entries for preparation of the consolidated financial statements as at 30 June 2008. Assume an income tax rate of 30% and that all income on sale of assets is taxable and expenses are deductible.

(a) In January 2008, Wudu Ltd sells inventory to Shashi Ltd for $15 000. This inventory had previously cost Wudu Ltd $10 000, and it remains unsold by Shashi Ltd at the end of the period.

(b) All the inventory in (a) above is sold to Hong Ltd, an external party, for $20 000 on 2 February 2008.

(c) Half the inventory in (a) above is sold to Kong Ltd, an external party, for $9000 on 22 February 2008. The remainder is still unsold at the end of the period.

(d) Wudu Ltd, in March 2008, sold inventory for $10 000 that was transferred from Shashi Ltd three years ago. It had originally cost Shashi Ltd $6000, and was sold to Wudu Ltd for $12 000.

(e) Shashi Ltd sold some land to Wudu Ltd in December 2007. The land had originally cost Shashi Ltd $25 000, but was sold to Wudu Ltd for only $20 000. To help Wudu Ltd pay for the land, Shashi Ltd gave Wudu Ltd an interest-free loan of $12 000, the balance being paid in cash. Wudu Ltd has as yet made no repayments on the loan.

(f) On 1 July 2007, Wudu Ltd sold a depreciable asset costing $10 000 to Shashi Ltd for $12 000. Wudu Ltd had not charged any depreciation on the asset before the sale. Both entities depreciate assets at 10% p.a. on cost.

(g) On 1 July 2007, Wudu Ltd sold an item of machinery to Shashi Ltd for $6000. This item had cost Wudu Ltd $4000. Wudu Ltd regarded this item as inventory whereas Shashi Ltd intended to use it as a non-current asset. Shashi Ltd charges depreciation at the rate of 10% p.a. on cost.

EXERCISE 21.3 ★ Intragroup transactions

Kaifeng Ltd owns all the share capital of Yinchuan Ltd. The following transactions relate to the period ended 30 June 2008. Assuming an income tax rate of 30%, provide adjustment entries to be included in the consolidation worksheet as at 30 June 2008.

(a) On 1 July 2007, Kaifeng Ltd sold a motor vehicle to Yinchuan Ltd for $15 000. This had a carrying amount to Kaifeng Ltd of $12 000. Both entities depreciate motor vehicles at a rate of 10% p.a. on cost.

(b) Yinchuan Ltd manufactures items of machinery which are used as non-current assets by other companies, including Kaifeng Ltd. On 1 January 2008, Yinchuan Ltd sold such an item to Kaifeng Ltd for $62 000, its cost to Yinchuan Ltd being only $55 000 to manufacture. Kaifeng Ltd charges depreciation on these machines at 20% p.a. on the diminishing value.

(c) Kaifeng Ltd manufactures certain items which it then markets through Yinchuan Ltd. During the current period, Kaifeng Ltd sold for $12 000 items to Yinchuan Ltd at cost plus 20%. Yinchuan Ltd has sold 75% of these transferred items at 30 June 2008.

(d) Yinchuan Ltd also sells second-hand machinery. Kaifeng Ltd sold one of its depreci-able assets (original cost $40 000, accumulated depreciation $32 000) to Yinchuan Ltd for $5000 on 1 January 2008. Yinchuan Ltd had not resold the item by 30 June 2008.

(e) Yinchuan Ltd sold a depreciable asset (carrying amount of $22 000) to Kaifeng Ltd on 1 January 2007 for $25 000. Both entities charge depreciation at a rate of 10% p.a. on cost in relation to these items. On 31 December 2007, Kaifeng Ltd sold this asset to China Ltd for $20 000.

EXERCISE 21.4 ★

Intragroup transactions

For each of the following intragroup transactions, assume that the consolidation process is being undertaken at 30 June 2007, and that an income tax rate of 30% applies. Prepare the consolidation worksheet adjustment entries for these transactions. All parts are inde-pendent unless specified. Yuanling Ltd owns all the share capital of Gaoping Ltd.

(a) On 1 January 2007, Yuanling Ltd sold an item of plant to Gaoping Ltd for $1000. Immediately before the sale, Yuanling Ltd had the item of plant on its accounts for $1500. Yuanling Ltd depreciated items at 5% p.a. on the reducing balance and Gaoping Ltd used the straight-line method over 10 years.

(b) A non-current asset with a carrying amount of $1000 was sold by Yuanling Ltd to Gaoping Ltd for $800 on 1 January 2007. Gaoping Ltd intended to use this item as inventory, being a seller of second-hand goods. Both entities charged depreciation at the rate of 10% p.a. on the reducing balance. The item was still on hand at 30 June 2007.

(c) On 1 May 2007, Gaoping Ltd sold inventory costing $200 to Yuanling Ltd for $400 on credit. On 30 June 2007, only half of these goods had been sold by Yuanling Ltd, but Yuanling Ltd had paid $300 back to Gaoping Ltd.

(d) During March 2007, Gaoping Ltd declared a $3000 dividend. The dividend was paid in August 2008.

(e) In December 2006, Gaoping Ltd paid a $1500 interim dividend.

(f) In February 2006, Yuanling Ltd sold inventory to Gaoping Ltd for $6000, at a mark-up of 20% on cost. One-quarter of this inventory was unsold by Gaoping Ltd at 30 June 2006.

(g) On 1 January 2005, Gaoping Ltd sold a new tractor to Yuanling Ltd for $20 000. This had cost Gaoping Ltd $16 000 on that day. Both entities charged depreciation at the rate of 10% p.a. on the reducing balance.

(h) Gaoping Ltd rented a spare warehouse to Yuanling Ltd and also to China Ltd during 2006–07. The total charge for the rental was $300, and Yuanling Ltd and China Ltd both agreed to pay half of this amount to Gaoping Ltd.

EXERCISE 21.5 ★★

Pre-acquisition entry and intragroup transactions

On 1 January 2003, Shengrao Ltd acquired all the share capital of Kunming Ltd for $300 000. The equity of Kunming Ltd at 1 January 2003 was:

Share capital	$200 000
Retained earnings	50 000
General reserve	20 000
	$270 000

At this date, all identifiable assets and liabilities of Kunming Ltd were recorded at fair value. Goodwill is tested annually for impairment. By 31 December 2006, no impairment has occurred. At 1 January 2003, no goodwill had been recorded by Kunming Ltd.

On 1 May 2006, Kunming Ltd transferred $15 000 from the general reserve (pre-acquisition) to retained earnings. All dividends have been paid from post-acquisition profits except a dividend of $4000 that was declared and paid in December 2003 out of the general reserve. The current tax rate is 30%. Assuming consolidated financial statements are required for the period 1 January 2006 to 31 December 2006, provide journal entries (including the pre-acquisition entry) to show the adjustments that would be made in the consolidation worksheets. Use the following information:

(a) At 31 December 2006, Kunming Ltd holds $100 000 of 7% debentures issued by Shengrao Ltd on 1 January 2005. All necessary interest payments have been made.
(b) At balance date, Kunming Ltd owes Shengrao Ltd $1000 for items sold on credit.
(c) Kunming Ltd undertook an advertising campaign for Shengrao Ltd during the year. Shengrao Ltd paid $8000 to Kunming Ltd for this service.
(d) The beginning and ending inventories of Shengrao Ltd and Kunming Ltd in relation to the current period included the following unsold intragroup inventory:

	Shengrao Ltd	Kunming Ltd
Beginning inventory:		
Transfer price	$2 000	$1 200
Original cost	1 400	800
Ending inventory:		
Transfer price	500	900
Original cost	300	700

Shengrao Ltd sold inventory to Kunming Ltd during the current period for $3000. This was $500 above the cost of the inventory to Shengrao Ltd. Kunming Ltd sold inventory to Shengrao Ltd in the current period for $2500, recording a pre-tax profit of $800.

(e) Shengrao Ltd sold an item of inventory to Kunming Ltd on 1 July 2006 for use as part of plant and machinery. The item cost Shengrao Ltd $4000 and was sold to Kunming for $6000. Kunming Ltd depreciated the item at 10% p.a. straight-line.
(f) Shengrao Ltd received dividends totalling $63 000 during the current period from Kunming Ltd. All of this related to dividends declared in the current period.

EXERCISE 21.6 ★★   Intragroup transactions, explanation of rationale

Changchun Ltd owns 100% of the shares of Shenyang Ltd. During the 2006–07 period, the following events occurred:

(a) Changchun Ltd sold inventory for $10 000 which had been sold to it by Shenyang Ltd in June 2006. The inventory originally cost Shenyang Ltd $6000 and was sold to Changchun Ltd for $9000.
(b) Changchun Ltd recorded depreciation of $10 000 on machinery sold to it by Shenyang Ltd on 1 January 2006. The machinery had a carrying amount in Shenyang Ltd at the date of sale of $80 000. Both entities apply a depreciation rate of 10% p.a. on a straight-line basis for this type of machinery.

Required
1. For each of the above transactions, prepare the adjustments required in the consolidation worksheet at 30 June 2007, assuming an income tax rate of 30%.
2. Explain the rationale behind each of the entries you have prepared.

PROBLEM 21.1 ★★

Consolidation worksheet, intragroup transactions

On 1 July 2005, Anshan Ltd acquired cum div. all the shares of Yingkow Ltd, at which date the equity and liability sections of Yingkow Ltd's balance sheet showed the following balances:

Share capital (300 000 shares)	$300 000
Other reserves	60 000
Retained earnings	10 000
Dividend payable	20 000

The dividend payable was subsequently paid in August 2005. In June 2008, Yingkow Ltd declared a $4000 dividend from profits earned before July 2005, to be paid in August 2008. A bonus dividend, on the basis of one ordinary share for every ten ordinary shares held, was paid in January 2008 out of other reserves existing at acquisition date.

On 1 July 2005, all the identifiable assets and liabilities of Yingkow Ltd were recorded at fair value except for:

	Carrying amount	Fair value
Inventory	$120 000	$130 000
Machinery (cost $200 000)	160 000	165 000

The inventory was all sold by 30 November 2005. The machinery had a further five-year life but was sold on 1 January 2008. At the acquisition date, Yingkow Ltd had a contingent liability of $20 000 that Anshan Ltd considered to have a fair value of $12 000. This liability was settled in June 2006. At 1 July 2005, Yingkow Ltd had not recorded any goodwill.

On 30 June 2008, the trial balances of Anshan Ltd and Yingkow Ltd were as follows:

Trial balances as at 30 June 2008		
	Anshan Ltd	Yingkow Ltd
Shares in Yingkow Ltd	$ 396 000	$ —
Inventory	180 000	160 000
Other current assets	29 000	15 000
Bank	25 000	10 000
Plant and machinery	572 500	412 000
Land	154 200	65 000
Income tax expense	35 000	40 000
Dividend declared	10 000	4 000
	$1 401 700	$ 706 000
Share capital	$ 800 000	$ 330 000
Other reserves	150 000	60 000
Retained earnings at 1 July 2007	15 000	12 000
Profit before income tax	80 000	90 000
Debentures	100 000	40 000
Other current liabilities	34 700	60 000
Dividend payable	10 000	4 000
Accumulated depreciation — plant and machinery	212 000	110 000
	$1 401 700	$ 706 000

Additional information

(a) On 1 July 2006, Anshan Ltd sold an item of plant to Yingkow Ltd at a profit before tax of $4000. Anshan Ltd depreciates this particular item of plant at a rate of 20% p.a. on cost and Yingkow Ltd applies a rate of 10% p.a. on cost.

(b) At 30 June 2008, Anshan Ltd has on hand some items of inventory purchased from Yingkow Ltd in June 2007 at a profit of $500.

(c) The tax rate is 30%.

Required

1. Prepare the adjusting journal entries for the consolidation worksheet at 30 June 2008.
2. Prepare the consolidated income statement, consolidated statement of changes in equity and the consolidated balance sheet at 30 June 2008.
3. In relation to parts (a) and (b) above, explain why you made the consolidation adjustment worksheet entries used in preparing the consolidated financial statements at 30 June 2008.

PROBLEM 21.2 ★★

Goodwill, consolidation worksheet, intragroup transactions

Pingnan Ltd owns all the shares of Ganzhow Ltd. The shares were acquired on 1 July 2006 by Pingnan Ltd at a cost of $60 000. At acquisition date, the capital of Ganzhow Ltd consisted of 44 000 ordinary shares each fully paid at $1. There were retained earnings of $4000. All the identifiable assets and liabilities of Ganzhow Ltd were recorded at amounts equal to fair value, except for:

	Carrying amount	Fair value
Inventory	$12 000	$15 000
Land	60 000	70 000
Machinery (cost $100 000)	80 000	82 000

The land was sold on 1 June 2007 for $94 000. The machinery had a further five-year life. The inventory was all sold by 31 December 2006. Ganzhow Ltd has not recorded any goodwill at 1 July 2006. Goodwill has not been impaired.

The trial balances of the two entities at 30 June 2008 are shown below.

Trial balances as at 30 June 2008				
	Pingnan Ltd		Ganzhow Ltd	
	Dr	Cr	Dr	Cr
Share capital		$ 64 000		$ 44 000
Retained earnings (1/7/07)		32 000		21 000
Current liabilities		21 400		17 000
Machinery	$ 38 000		$ 71 500	
Shares in Ganzhow Ltd	60 000		–	
Inventory	19 000		16 400	
Receivables	5 500		8 300	
Sales revenue		43 000		52 000
Cost of sales	20 600		30 900	
Selling expenses	3 200		6 000	
Administrative expenses	5 300		2 700	
Depreciation/amortisation expenses	1 200		2 600	
Income tax expense	7 400		4 700	
Accumulated depreciation – machinery		12 200		22 300
Deferred tax assets	5 400		6 300	
Plant (net of depreciation)	8 000		7 400	
Proceeds from sale of machinery		6 000		10 000
Carrying amount of machinery sold	5 000		9 500	
	$178 600	$178 600	$166 300	$166 300

Additional information

(a) Intragroup sales of inventory for the year ended 30 June 2008 from Pingnan Ltd to Ganzhow Ltd, $14 000; and from Ganzhow Ltd to Pingnan Ltd, $3000.

(b) Intragroup inventory on hand:
   (i) at 1 July 2007: held by Ganzhow Ltd, purchased from Pingnan Ltd at a profit of $400.
   (ii) at 30 June 2008: held by Pingnan Ltd, purchased from Ganzhow Ltd at a profit of $200.

(c) Intragroup machinery on hand at 30 June 2008:
   (i) Pingnan Ltd: purchased from Ganzhow Ltd on 1 July 2007 for $10 000 at a profit to Ganzhow Ltd of $500. Depreciation rate is 10% p.a. on cost.
   (ii) Ganzhow Ltd: purchased from Pingnan Ltd on 1 January 2007 for $12 000, at a loss to Pingnan Ltd of $500. Depreciation rate is 10% p.a. on cost.

(d) Ganzhow Ltd had purchased from Pingnan Ltd an item of inventory which Pingnan Ltd had treated as plant. Carrying amount in Pingnan Ltd's records at time of sale (1 January 2008) was $5000 and it was sold at a profit of $1000. The item is still on hand in Ganzhow Ltd's inventory at 30 June 2008.

(e) The income tax rate is 30%.

Required

Prepare a worksheet for consolidating the financial statements of Pingnan Ltd and Ganzhow Ltd as at 30 June 2008.

PROBLEM 21.3 ★★   Consolidation worksheet, consolidated financial statements

On 1 July 2007, Tianshui Ltd acquired all the shares of Lanzhou Ltd for $160 000. The financial statements of the two entities at 30 June 2008 contained the following information:

	Tianshui Ltd	Lanzhou Ltd
Sales revenue	$239 800	$200 000
Dividend revenue	12 000	–
Other income	6 600	–
	258 400	200 000
Cost of sales	123 000	120 000
Other expenses	34 600	20 000
	157 600	140 000
Profit before income tax	100 800	60 000
Income tax expense	32 000	20 000
Profit for the period	68 800	40 000
Retained earnings (1/7/07)	24 000	12 000
Total available for appropriation	92 800	52 000
Dividend paid from 2006–07 profit	18 800	5 000
Interim dividend paid from 2007–08 profit	16 000	4 800
Dividend declared from 2007–08 profit	16 000	7 200
Transfer to general reserve	8 000	–
	58 000	17 000
Retained earnings (30/6/08)	$ 34 800	$ 35 000

(continued)

Current assets		
Cash	$ 1 000	$ 40
Receivables	27 000	12 100
Allowance for doubtful debts	(500)	(300)
Inventory	68 000	57 000
Total current assets	95 500	68 840
Non-current assets		
Plant and machinery	100 000	72 000
Accumulated depreciation	(40 000)	(26 000)
Land	107 300	190 000
Debentures in Lanzhou Ltd	57 000	–
Shares in Lanzhou Ltd	155 000	
Total non-current assets	379 300	236 000
Total assets	474 800	304 840
Current liabilities		
Dividend payable	16 000	7 200
Provisions	12 000	8 800
Bank overdraft	–	14 840
Current tax liabilities	11 000	10 000
Total current liabilities	39 000	40 840
Non-current liabilities		
12% mortgage debentures	–	80 000
Deferred tax liabilities	13 000	5 000
Total non-current liabilities	13 000	85 000
Total liabilities	52 000	125 840
Net assets	$422 800	$179 000
Equity		
Share capital	$320 000	$120 000
General reserve	68 000	24 000
Retained earnings	34 800	35 000
Total equity	$422 800	$179 000

Additional information

(a) At 1 July 2007, all identifiable assets and liabilities of Lanzhou Ltd were recorded at fair values except for inventory, for which the fair value was $1000 greater than the carrying amount. This inventory was all sold by 30 June 2008. At 1 July 2007, Lanzhou Ltd had research and development outlays that it had expensed as incurred. Tianshui Ltd measured the fair value of the in-process research and development at $8000. By 30 June 2008, it was assessed that $2000 of this was not recoverable. At 1 July 2007, Lanzhou Ltd had reported a contingent liability relating to a guarantee that was considered to have a fair value of $7000. This liability still existed at 30 June 2008. At 1 July 2007, Lanzhou Ltd had not recorded any goodwill.

(b) The debentures were issued by Lanzhou Ltd at nominal value on 1 July 2006, and are redeemable on 30 June 2012. Tianshui Ltd acquired its holding ($60 000) of these debentures on the open market on 1 January 2008, immediately after the half-yearly interest payment had been made. All interest has been paid and brought to account in the records of both entities.

(c) During the 2007–08 period, Tianshui Ltd sold inventory to Lanzhou Ltd for $40 000, at a mark-up of cost plus 25%. At 30 June 2008, $10 000 worth of inventory is still held by Lanzhou Ltd.

(d) On 1 January 2008, Lanzhou Ltd sold an item of inventory to Tianshui Ltd which planned to use it as a non-current asset, depreciable at 10% p.a. on cost. Tianshui Ltd paid $30 000 for this item, with Lanzhou Ltd having manufactured it at a cost of $24 000.

(e) The income tax rate is 30%.

Required

Prepare the consolidated income statement, consolidated statement of changes in equity and the consolidated balance sheet for Tianshui Ltd and its subsidiary as required for the year ended 30 June 2008.

| PROBLEM 21.4 | ★★ | Consolidation worksheet, impairment of goodwill |

The following financial information for Chengdu Ltd and its 100% owned subsidiary, Nanchong Ltd, for the year ended 31 December 2007 has been provided.

	Chengdu Ltd	Nanchong Ltd
Sales revenue	$25 000	$23 600
Dividend revenue	500	–
Other income	1 500	2 000
Proceeds from sale of non-current assets	5 000	22 000
Total	32 000	47 600
Cost of sales	21 000	18 000
Other expenses	3 000	1 000
Carrying amount of non-current assets sold	4 000	20 000
Total expenses	28 000	39 000
Profit before income tax	4 000	8 600
Income tax expense	1 350	1 950
Profit for the period	2 650	6 650
Retained earnings (1/1/07)	6 000	3 000
	8 650	9 650
Interim dividend paid	2 500	1 000
Retained earnings (31/12/07)	$ 6 150	$ 8 650

Chengdu Ltd acquired its shares in Nanchong Ltd at 1 January 2007, buying the 10 000 shares in Nanchong Ltd for $20 000. The shares were bought on a cum div. basis as Nanchong Ltd had declared a dividend of $3000 that was not paid until March 2007. The interim dividend paid in the current period was derived equally from pre- and post-acquisition profits.

At 1 January 2007, all identifiable assets and liabilities of Nanchong Ltd were recorded at fair value except for inventory, for which the carrying amount of $2000 was $400 less than fair value. Some of this inventory has been a little slow to sell, and 10% of it is still on hand at 31 December 2007. Inventory on hand in Nanchong Ltd at 31 December 2007 also includes some items acquired from Chengdu Ltd during the year. These were sold by Chengdu Ltd for $5000, at a profit before tax of $1000. Half of the goodwill was written off as the result of an impairment test on 31 December 2007.

During March 2007, Chengdu Ltd provided some management services to Nanchong Ltd at a fee of $500.

On 1 July 2007, Nanchong Ltd sold machinery to Chengdu Ltd at a gain of $2000. This machinery had a carrying amount to Nanchong Ltd of $20 000, and was considered by Chengdu Ltd to have a five-year life.

The tax rate is 30%.

Required

1. What is the balance of the shares in Nanchong Ltd in the records of Chengdu Ltd at 31 December 2007?
2. Prepare the consolidated income statement for Chengdu Ltd and its subsidiary, Nanchong Ltd, at 31 December 2007.
3. Discuss the concept of 'realisation' using the intragroup transactions in this problem to illustrate the concept.

PROBLEM 21.5 ★★ Consolidation worksheet, consolidated income statement

The following financial information for Wuwei Ltd and Lingling Ltd for the year ended 30 June 2007 has been provided:

	Wuwei Ltd	Lingling Ltd
Sales revenue	$80 000	$ 40 000
Proceeds from sale of office furniture	–	3 000
Dividend revenue	2 400	1 600
Total income	82 400	44 600
Cost of sales	60 000	30 000
Other expenses	10 800	7 500
Total expenses	70 800	37 500
Profit before income tax	11 600	7 100
Income tax expense	3 000	2 200
Profit for the period	8 600	4 900
Retained earnings (1/7/06)	14 500	2 800
	23 100	7 700
Interim dividend paid	4 000	2 000
Final dividend provided	8 000	2 400
	12 000	4 400
Retained earnings (30/6/07)	$ 11 100	$ 3 300

Additional information

(a) On 1 July 2005, Wuwei Ltd purchased 100% of the shares of Lingling Ltd for $50 000. At that date the equity of the two entities was as follows:

	Wuwei Ltd	Lingling Ltd
General reserve	$25 000	$ 4 000
Retained earnings	14 500	2 800
Share capital	50 000	40 000

At 1 July 2005, all the identifiable assets and liabilities of Lingling Ltd were recorded at fair value except for the following:

	Carrying amount	Fair value
Plant and equipment (cost $80 000)	$60 000	$61 000
Inventory	3 000	3 500

All of this inventory was sold by December 2005. The plant and equipment had a further five-year life. Any valuation adjustments are made on consolidation.

(b) The interim dividend paid by Lingling Ltd in the current year was out of the pre-acquisition profit.

(c) The final dividend declared by both entities is being paid out of current profits.

(d) Wuwei Ltd records dividends receivable as revenue when dividends are declared.

(e) The opening inventory of Lingling Ltd included goods which cost Lingling Ltd $2000. Lingling Ltd purchased this inventory from Wuwei Ltd at cost plus $33\frac{1}{3}\%$.

(f) Intragroup sales totalled $10 000 for the year. Sales from Wuwei Ltd to Lingling Ltd, at cost plus 10%, amounted to $5600. The closing inventory of Wuwei Ltd included goods which cost Wuwei Ltd $4400. Wuwei Ltd purchased this inventory from Lingling Ltd at cost plus 10%.

(g) On 31 December 2006, Lingling Ltd sold Wuwei Ltd office furniture for $3000. This furniture originally cost Lingling Ltd $3000 and was written down to $2500 when sold. Wuwei Ltd depreciates furniture at the rate of 10% p.a. on cost.

(h) The tax rate is 30%.

Required

Prepare the consolidated income statement for the year ended 30 June 2007.

PROBLEM 21.6 ★★★   Consolidated worksheet, consolidated income statement

On 1 April 2006, Hancheng Ltd acquired all the issued ordinary shares (cum div.) of Nanyang Ltd for $100 000. At that date, relevant balances in the records of Nanyang Ltd were:

Share capital	$80 000
General reserve	5 000
Retained earnings	5 000
Dividend payable	4 000

All the identifiable assets and liabilities of Nanyang Ltd were recorded at fair values except for the following:

	Carrying amount	Fair value
Inventory	$10 000	$12 000
Plant (cost $80 000)	50 000	53 000

Immediately after the acquisition of its shares by Hancheng Ltd, Nanyang Ltd revalued its plant to fair value. The plant was expected to have a further five-year life. All the inventory on hand at 1 April 2006 was sold by the end of the financial year.

At 1 April 2006, Nanyang Ltd had recorded goodwill of $2000. As the result of an impairment test on 31 March 2007, Nanyang Ltd wrote goodwill down by $1500.

The dividend payable was subsequently paid in June 2006. During 2006, Nanyang Ltd paid an interim dividend of $4000 from profits earned before 1 April 2006.

During the period ending 31 March 2007, intragroup sales consisted of $40 000 from Hancheng Ltd to Nanyang Ltd at a profit to Hancheng Ltd of $10 000. These were all sold to external parties by Nanyang Ltd for $42 000 before 31 March 2007. Nanyang Ltd also sold some inventory to Hancheng Ltd for $10 000. This had cost Nanyang Ltd $6000. Hancheng Ltd since has sold all the items to external parties for $8000, except one batch on which Nanyang Ltd recorded a $500 profit before tax (original cost to Nanyang Ltd was $1000).

On 1 October 2006, Hancheng Ltd sold an item, regarded by Hancheng Ltd as a non-current asset, to Nanyang Ltd which regarded it as inventory. At time of sale, the carrying amount of the item to Hancheng Ltd was $28 000, and was sold to Nanyang Ltd for $30 000. Hancheng Ltd was using a 10% p.a. depreciation rate applied to cost. The item remains unsold by Nanyang Ltd at 31 March 2007.

The following information was obtained from the companies for the year ended 31 March 2007:

	Hancheng Ltd	Nanyang Ltd
Sales	$ 150 000	$ 120 000
Proceeds on sale of non-current asset	30 000	–
	180 000	120 000
Cost of sales	88 000	68 000
Other expenses	44 000	19 000
	132 000	87 000
Profit before income tax	48 000	33 000
Income tax expense	12 000	14 000
Net profit	36 000	19 000
Retained earnings (1/4/06)	10 000	5 000
Total available for appropriation	46 000	24 000
Dividend paid	8 000	4 000
Retained earnings (31/3/07)	$ 38 000	$ 20 000

Required

1. Prepare the consolidated income statement as at 31 March 2007. Assume a tax rate of 30%.
2. Explain the consolidation worksheet adjustment for the sale of the non-current asset to Nanyang Ltd at 1 October 2006 by Hancheng Ltd.

PROBLEM 21.7   Consolidation worksheet, consolidated financial statements

On 31 December 2000, Shantou Ltd acquired all the issued shares of Chifeng Ltd. On this date, the share capital of Chifeng Ltd consisted of 200 000 shares paid to 50c per share. Other reserves and retained earnings at this date consisted of:

General reserve	$25 000
Retained earnings	20 000

At 31 December 2000, all the identifiable assets and liabilities of Chifeng Ltd were recorded at fair value except for some plant and machinery. This plant and machinery, which cost $100 000, had a carrying amount of $85 000 and a fair value of $90 000. The estimated remaining useful life was 10 years. Adjustments for fair values are made on consolidation.

Immediately after acquisition, a dividend of $10 000 was declared and paid out of retained earnings. Also, one year after acquisition, Chifeng Ltd used $20 000 from the general reserve to partly pay the balance unpaid on the issued shares.

The trial balances of Shantou Ltd and Chifeng Ltd at 31 December 2005 were as shown opposite.

Trial balances as at 31 December 2005		
	Shantou Ltd	Chifeng Ltd
Credits		
Share capital	$500 000	$120 000
General reserve	25 000	5 000
Retained earnings (1 January 2005)	40 000	65 000
Current tax liabilities	22 000	18 000
Deferred tax liabilities	6 240	5 200
Payables	22 000	14 000
Sales revenue	250 000	120 000
Other income	20 000	5 000
Proceeds from sale of non-current assets	14 000	50 000
	$899 240	$402 200
Debits		
Income tax expense	$ 20 000	$ 10 000
Dividend declared	10 000	8 000
Plant and machinery	460 000	361 000
Accumulated depreciation	(300 000)	(261 000)
Motor vehicles	284 200	152 600
Accumulated depreciation	(160 000)	(100 000)
Receivables	25 000	7 310
Inventory	106 440	72 000
Bank	46 900	5 990
Deferred tax assets	12 700	6 300
Shares in Chifeng Ltd	160 000	–
Cost of sales	188 000	80 000
Other expenses	28 000	5 000
Carrying amount of non-current assets sold	18 000	55 000
	$899 240	$402 200

Additional information

(a) During the current period, Shantou Ltd sold inventory to Chifeng Ltd for $20 000. This had originally cost Shantou Ltd $18 200. Chifeng Ltd has, by 31 December 2005, sold half of this inventory for $12 310.

(b) Some of the items manufactured by Chifeng Ltd are used as plant by Shantou Ltd. One of the plant items held by Shantou Ltd at 31 December 2005 was purchased from Chifeng Ltd on 1 July 2002 for $25 000. It had cost Chifeng Ltd $17 500 to manufacture this item. Shantou Ltd depreciates such items at 10% p.a. on cost.

(c) At 1 January 2005, Chifeng Ltd sold a machine to Shantou Ltd for $50 000. This item had a carrying amount at time of sale to Chifeng Ltd of $55 000. Both entities use a 5% p.a. on cost depreciation rate for this item.

(d) The tax rate is 30%.

Required

Prepare the consolidated income statement, the consolidated statement of changes in equity and the consolidated balance sheet as at 31 December 2005.

PROBLEM 21.8   ★★★   Consolidation worksheet

On 1 July 2005, Minhe Ltd acquired all the shares of Luoyang Ltd for $142 200. At acquisition date, the equity of Luoyang Ltd was as shown overleaf.

Share capital	$80 000
General reserve	16 000
Retained earnings	21 000

On this date, all the identifiable assets and liabilities of Luoyang Ltd were recorded at fair value except for the following assets:

	Carrying amount	Fair value
Inventory	$50 000	$56 000
Motor vehicles (cost $18 000)	15 000	16 000
Furniture and fittings (cost $30 000)	24 000	32 000
Land	18 480	24 480

The inventory and land on hand in Luoyang Ltd at 1 July 2005 were sold during the following 12 months. The motor vehicles, which at acquisition date were estimated to have a four-year life, were sold on 1 January 2007. Except for land, valuation adjustments are made on consolidation and, on realisation of a business combination valuation reserve, a transfer is made to retained earnings on consolidation. The furniture and fittings were estimated to have a further eight-year life. At 1 July 2005, Luoyang Ltd had not recorded any goodwill.

The following trial balances were prepared for the companies at 30 June 2007:

Credits	Minhe Ltd	Luoyang Ltd
Share capital	$ 170 000	$ 80 000
General reserve	41 000	22 000
Retained earnings (1/7/06)	16 000	29 500
Debentures	120 000	–
Final dividend payable	10 000	3 000
Current tax liabilities	8 000	2 500
Other payables	34 800	10 100
Advance from Minhe Ltd	–	10 000
Sales revenue	85 000	65 000
Other income	23 000	22 000
Accumulated depreciation		
– Motor vehicles	4 000	2 000
– Furniture and fittings	2 000	6 000
	$ 513 800	$ 252 100
Debits		
Cost of sales	$ 65 000	$ 53 500
Other expenses	22 000	27 000
Shares in Luoyang Ltd	137 200	–
Land	–	24 480
Motor vehicles	28 000	22 000
Furniture and fittings	34 000	37 300
Inventory	171 580	70 320
Other assets	8 620	3 100
Income tax expense	7 200	2 000
Interim dividend paid	4 000	2 000
Final dividend declared	10 000	3 000
Deferred tax assets	16 200	7 400
Advance to Luoyang Ltd	10 000	–
	$ 513 800	$ 252 100

Additional information

(a) All dividends have been from post-acquisition profits except for part of the dividend declared by Luoyang Ltd in June 2006. The dividend of $10 000 included $5000 from profits earned before 1 July 2005. The dividend was paid in September 2006.

(b) Intragroup transfers of inventory consisted of:

1/7/05 to 30/6/06:	
Sales from Minhe Ltd to Luoyang Ltd	$12 000
Profit in inventory on hand 30/6/06	200
1/7/06 to 30/6/07:	
Sales from Minhe Ltd to Luoyang Ltd	15 000
Profit in inventory on hand 30/6/07	
(incl. $50 from previous period sales)	1 000

(c) On 1 January 2006, Luoyang Ltd sold furniture and fittings to Minhe Ltd for $8000. This had originally cost Luoyang Ltd $12 000 and had a carrying amount at time of sale of $7000. Both entities charge depreciation at the rate of 10% p.a.

(d) The tax rate is 30%.

Required

Prepare the consolidation worksheet for the preparation of the consolidated financial statements for the period ended 30 June 2007.

Visit these websites for additional information:

WEBLINK

www.iasb.org   www.iasplus.com
www.asic.gov.au   www.ifac.org
www.aasb.com.au   www.nzica.com
www.accaglobal.com   www.capa.com.my

CHAPTER 22
Consolidated financial statements: minority interest

ACCOUNTING STANDARDS

International: IAS 27 *Consolidated and Separate Financial Statements*

Australia: AASB 127 *Consolidated and Separate Financial Statements*

New Zealand: NZ IAS 27 *Consolidated and Separate Financial Statements*

CONCEPTS FOR REVIEW

Before studying this chapter, you should understand or, if necessary, revise:

- the nature of the group
- the entity concept of consolidation
- the rationale for business combination valuation and pre-acquisition entries for wholly owned subsidiaries
- the consolidation worksheet adjustments used for valuation and pre-acquisition adjustments
- adjustment entries for intragroup transactions
- the concept of realisation in relation to intragroup transactions.

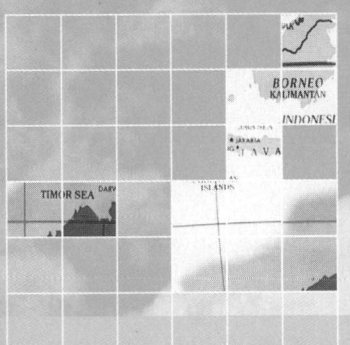

When you have studied this chapter, you should be able to:
1. discuss the nature of the minority interest (MI)
2. explain the effects of the MI on the consolidation process
3. explain how to calculate the MI share of equity
4. calculate the MI share of equity at acquisition date
5. calculate the MI share of equity for periods subsequent to acquisition date
6. explain how the calculation of the MI is affected by the existence of intragroup transactions
7. prepare a set of consolidated financial statements for a parent and a partly owned subsidiary
8. explain how the MI is affected by the existence of an excess.

22.1 Introduction

In chapters 20 and 21, the group under consideration consisted of two entities where the parent owned *all* the share capital of the subsidiary. In this chapter, the group under discussion consists of a parent that has only a *partial* interest in the subsidiary; that is, the subsidiary is less than wholly owned by the parent.

22.1.1 Nature of the minority interest (MI)

Ownership interests in a subsidiary other than the parent are referred to as the minority interest, or MI. Paragraph 4 of IAS 27 *Consolidated and Separate Financial Statements* contains the following definition of MI:

> Minority interest is that portion of the profit or loss and net assets of a subsidiary attributable to equity interests that are not owned, directly or indirectly through subsidiaries, by the parent.

Note that the term 'minority' interest is not a good one in that a parent may control another entity with less than a 50% ownership. In such cases, a minority interest may in fact have a majority shareholding in the subsidiary.

In figure 22.1, the group shown is illustrative of those discussed in this chapter. In this case, the parent entity owns 75% of the shares of a subsidiary. Under the entity concept of consolidation (see chapter 19 of this book), the group consists of the combined assets and liabilities of the parent and the subsidiary. There are two equity holders in this group — the parent shareholders and the MI. The MI is a contributor of equity to the group.

Group

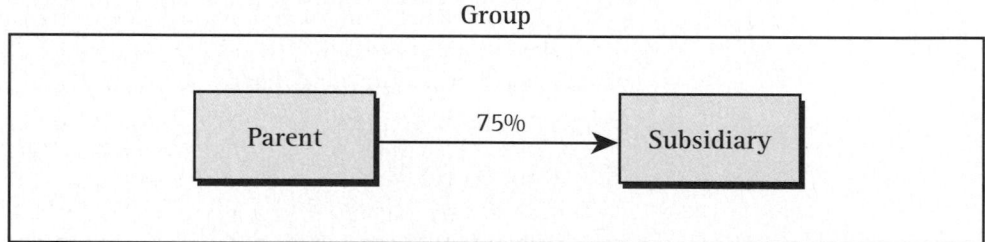

FIGURE 22.1   The group

According to paragraph 33 of IAS 27, the MI is to be identified and presented within equity, separately from the parent shareholders' equity; that is, it is regarded as an equity contributor to the group, rather than a liability of the group. This is because the MI does not meet the definition of a liability as contained in the Framework, because the group has no present obligation to provide economic outflows to the MI. The MI receives a share of consolidated equity, and is therefore a participant in the residual equity of the group. IAS 27, although not explicitly recognising the fact, adopts the entity concept of consolidation as it adjusts for the effects of intragroup transactions in full (paragraph 24) and categorises the MI as equity. (See chapter 19 for a full discussion of the concepts of consolidation and the classification of MI as equity or liability.)

Classification of the MI as equity affects both the calculation of the MI as well as how it is disclosed in the consolidated financial statements.

22.1.2 Calculation of the MI share of equity

The MI is entitled to a share of *consolidated equity*, as it is a contributor of equity to the consolidated group. Because consolidated equity is affected by profits and losses made in relation to transactions within the group, the calculation of the MI is affected by the existence of intragroup transactions. In other words, the MI is entitled to a share of the equity of the subsidiary adjusted for the effects of profits and losses made on intragroup transactions. This is discussed in more detail in section 22.6 of this chapter.

22.1.3 Disclosure of the MI

According to paragraph 33 of IAS 27:

> Minority interests shall be presented in the consolidated balance sheet within equity, separately from the parent shareholders' equity. Minority interests in the profit or loss of the group shall be separately presented.

IAS 1 *Presentation of Financial Statements* confirms these disclosures. Paragraph 82 of IAS 1 requires the profit or loss to be disclosed on the face of the income statement, showing separately that attributable to minority interest, and that attributable to equity holders of the parent.

Figure 22.2 shows how the income statement may be shown. Note that in terms of the various line items in the income statement, such as revenues and expenses, it is the total consolidated balance that is disclosed. It is only the consolidated profit that is divided into parent share and MI share.

Moscow Ltd Consolidated income statement for the year ended 30 June 2006		
	2006 $000	2005 $000
Revenue	(XXX)	XXX
Expenses	XXX	(XXX)
Gross profit	XXX	XXX
Finance costs	(XXX)	(XXX)
	XXX	XXX
Share of after-tax profit of associates	XXX	XXX
Profit before tax	XXX	XXX
Income tax expense	(XXX)	(XXX)
Profit for the period	XXX	XXX
Attributable to:		
Equity holders of the parent	XXX	XXX
Minority interest	XXX	XXX
	XXX	XXX

FIGURE 22.2   Disclosure of MI in the income statement

According to paragraph 96(c) of IAS 1, the total income and expense for the period must be disclosed in the statement of changes in equity, showing separately the total amounts attributable to equity holders of the parent and to minority interest. Figures 22.3 and 22.4 provide examples of disclosures in the statement of changes in equity. In relation to the figure 22.4 disclosure, a further note is required, as per paragraph 97 of IAS 1. Note that the only line item for which the MI must be shown is the total income and expense for the period. There is no requirement to show the MI share of each equity account.

Moscow Ltd Consolidated statement of changes in equity (extract) for the year ended 30 June 2006							
	Attributable to equity holders of the parent					Minority interest	Total equity
	Share capital	Other reserves	Translation reserve	Retained earnings	Total		
Balance at 1 July 2005	XXX	XXX	XXX	XXX	XXX	XXX	XXX
Changes in equity for 2006							
Gain on property valuation		XXX			XXX	XXX	XXX
Profit for the period				XXX	XXX	XXX	XXX
Total recognised income and expense for the period		XXX		XXX	XXX	XXX	XXX
Dividends				(XXX)	(XXX)	(XXX)	(XXX)
Issue of share capital	XXX				XXX	XXX	XXX
Balance at 30 June 2006	XXX	XXX	XXX	XXX	XXX	XXX	XXX

FIGURE 22.3   Disclosure of MI in the statement of changes in equity — see Guidance on Implementing IAS 1

Moscow Ltd Statement of changes in equity for the year ended 30 June 2006					
	Note	Consolidated		Attributable to equity holders of the parent	
		2006	2005	2006	2005
		$m	$m	$m	$m
Gain/loss on revaluation of properties		XXX	XXX	XXX	XXX

Available-for-sale investments:
    Valuation gains/(losses) taken to equity
    Transferred to profit or loss on sale
		
		XXX
		XXX
			
			XXX
			XXX
				
				XXX
				XXX
					
					XXX
					XXX

Exchange differences on translation of foreign operations		XXX	XXX	XXX	XXX
Gains (losses) on cash flow hedges		XXX	XXX	XXX	XXX
Net income recognised directly in equity		XXX	XXX	XXX	XXX
Profit for the period		XXX	XXX	XXX	XXX
Total recognised income and expense for the period		XXX	XXX	XXX	XXX

Attributable to:
    Equity holders of the parent
    Minority interest
		
		XXX
		XXX
			
			XXX
			XXX
				
				XXX
				–
					
					XXX
					–

		XXX	XXX	XXX	XXX

Effect of changes in accounting policy:
    Equity holders of the parent
    Minority interest
			
			XXX
			XXX
					
					XXX
					–

			XXX		XXX

FIGURE 22.4   Statement of changes in equity

Similarly, in paragraph 68(o) of IAS 1, the total MI share of equity is required to be disclosed on the face of the balance sheet. The equity section of the balance sheet could then appear as in figure 22.5. On the face of the balance sheet, only the total MI share of equity is disclosed, rather than the MI share of the different categories of equity. The MI share of the various categories of equity and the changes in those balances can be seen in the statement of changes in equity. Note that the consolidated assets and liabilities are those for the whole of the group; it is only equity that is divided into parent and MI shares.

Moscow Ltd Balance sheet (extract) as at 30 June 2006		
	2006	2005
EQUITY		
Equity attributable to equity holders of the parent		
Share capital	XXX	XXX
Other reserves	XXX	XXX
Retained earnings	XXX	XXX
	XXX	XXX
Minority interest	XXX	XXX
Total equity	XXX	XXX

FIGURE 22.5 Disclosure of MI in the balance sheet

22.2 Effects of an MI on the consolidation process

LO 2

The existence of an MI in the subsidiary causes a number of changes to the consolidation process discussed in chapter 20.

22.2.1 Business combination valuation entries

The existence of an MI has no effect on the valuation entries for differences between carrying amounts and fair values at acquisition date. All identifiable assets, liabilities and contingent liabilities of the subsidiary are revalued to fair value. The fact that the parent acquired only a portion of the equity of the subsidiary does not affect the requirement to show all the assets and liabilities of the subsidiary at fair value at acquisition date.

22.2.2 Acquisition analysis and pre-acquisition entry

Where the parent acquires less than all the shares of a subsidiary, it acquires only a portion of the total equity or total net assets of the subsidiary. The cost of combination paid by the parent represents the cost of acquiring only a proportion of the net assets or equity of the subsidiary.

To illustrate, assume that P Ltd paid $169 600 for 80% of the shares of S Ltd on 1 July 2006. All identifiable assets and liabilities of the subsidiary were recorded at fair value, except for land for which the fair value was $10 000 greater than cost. The tax rate is 30%. At acquisition date, the equity of S Ltd consisted of:

Share capital	$100 000
General reserve	60 000
Retained earnings	40 000

The acquisition analysis is as follows:

Net fair value of identifiable assets,
   liabilities and contingent liabilities of S Ltd = $100 000 + $60 000 + $40 000
                                                      + $10 000 (1 − 30%) (BCVR − land)
                                                  = $207 000
Net fair value acquired   = 80% × $207 000
                                                  = $165 600
Cost of combination   = $169 600
Goodwill acquired   = $169 600 − $165 600
                                                  = $4000

Note the following:
- BCVR refers to the business combination valuation reserve.
- Goodwill is calculated by comparing the fair value of the consideration paid with a proportionate share of the net fair value of the identifiable assets, liabilities and contingent liabilities of the subsidiary. This is then the parent's share of the goodwill of the subsidiary.
- The total goodwill of the subsidiary may be inferred from the acquisition transaction. In this case, the goodwill of $4000 relates to an acquisition of 80% of the shares of the subsidiary. Hence, the total goodwill of the subsidiary could be inferred to be $5000 (being $4000/0.8). However, under IFRS 3 *Business Combinations*, only the goodwill acquired by the parent is recognised.

In relation to the equity on hand at acquisition date, only 80% is attributable to the parent, and 20% is attributable to the MI. The pre-acquisition entry relates to the investment by the parent in the subsidiary, and thus relates to 80% of the amounts shown in the acquisition analysis. The adjustments to equity in the pre-acquisition entry are then determined by taking 80% of the recorded equity of the subsidiary, plus 80% of the business combination valuation reserves recognised as a result of differences between fair value and carrying amounts of the subsidiary's identifiable net assets at acquisition date. The appropriate consolidation worksheet entries for the above example at acquisition date are:

Business combination valuation entry

Land	Dr	10 000	
Deferred tax liability	Cr		3 000
Business combination valuation reserve	Cr		7 000

Pre-acquisition entry

Share capital (80% × $100 000)	Dr	80 000	
General reserve (80% × $60 000)	Dr	48 000	
Business combination valuation reserve (80% × $7000)	Dr	5 600	
Retained earnings (80% × $40 000)	Dr	32 000	
Goodwill	Dr	4 000	
Shares in S Ltd	Cr		169 600

22.2.3 Intragroup transactions

As noted in chapter 21, because IAS 27 adopts the entity concept of consolidation, the full effects of transactions within the group are adjusted on consolidation. In essence, the worksheet adjustment entries used in chapter 21 are the same regardless of whether the subsidiary is wholly or partly owned by its parent. The only exception to the entries used in chapter 21 is for dividends.

Where an MI exists, any dividends declared or paid by a subsidiary are paid proportionately (to the extent of the ownership interest in the subsidiary) to the parent and proportionately to the MI. In adjusting for dividends paid by a subsidiary, only the dividend paid or payable to the parent is eliminated on consolidation. In other words, there is a proportional adjustment of the dividend paid or declared. As with other intragroup transactions, the adjustment relates to the flow within the group. A payment or a declaration of dividends by a subsidiary reduces the MI share of subsidiary equity because the equity of the subsidiary is reduced by the payment or declaration of dividends. In calculating the MI share of subsidiary equity, the existence of dividends must be taken into consideration (see section 22.4.2 of this chapter). Where a dividend is declared, the MI share of equity is reduced, and a liability to pay dividends to the MI is shown in the consolidated balance sheet.

To illustrate, assume a parent owns 80% of the share capital of a subsidiary. In the current period, the subsidiary pays a $1000 dividend and declares a further $1500 dividend. The adjustment entries in the consolidation worksheet in the current period are:

Dividend revenue	Dr	800	
Dividend paid	Cr		800
(80% × $1000)			
Dividend payable	Dr	1 200	
Dividend declared	Cr		1 200
(80% × $1500)			
Dividend revenue	Dr	1 200	
Dividend receivable	Cr		1 200
(80% × $1500)			

22.2.4 Consolidation worksheet

Because the disclosure requirements for the MI require the extraction of the MI share of various equity items, the consolidation worksheet is changed to enable this information to be produced. Figure 22.6 contains an example of the changed worksheet. In particular, note that two new columns are added, a *debit column* and a *credit column* for the calculation of the MI share of equity. These two columns are not adjustment or elimination columns. Instead, they are used to divide consolidated equity into MI share and parent entity share. The worksheet shown in figure 22.6 also contains a column showing the figures for the consolidated group. This column is shown between the adjustment columns and the MI columns, and it is the summation of the financial statements of the group members and the consolidation adjustments. The parent figures are then determined by subtracting the MI share of equity from the total consolidated equity of the group.

In figure 22.6, the amounts in the debit MI column record the MI share of the relevant equity item. This amount is subtracted in the consolidation process so that the consolidation column contains the parent's share of consolidated equity.

The first line in figure 22.6 is the consolidated profit/(loss) for the period. This amount is then attributed to the parent and the MI. In all subsequent equity lines, the MI share is recorded in the debit MI column, and the parent's share of each equity account is calculated. The total MI share of equity is then added to the parent column to give total consolidated equity.

The MI share of retained earnings is increased by subsidiary profits and transfers from reserves, and decreased by transfers to reserves and payments and declarations of dividends. The total MI share of equity is then the sum of the MI share of capital, other reserves and retained earnings. The assets and liabilities of the group are shown in total and not allocated to the equity interests in the group (see the liabilities section in figure 22.6).

Financial statements	P Ltd	S Ltd	Adjustments			Group		Minority interest			Parent
			Dr	Cr				Dr	Cr		
Profit/(loss)	XXX	XXX				XXX		XXX			XXX
Retained earnings (opening balance)	XXX	XXX				XXX		XXX			XXX
Transfer from reserves	XXX	XXX				XXX		XXX			XXX
Total available for appropriation	XXX	XXX				XXX					XXX
Interim dividend paid	XXX	XXX				XXX			XXX		XXX
Final dividend declared	XXX	XXX				XXX			XXX		XXX
Transfer to reserves	XXX	XXX				XXX			XXX		XXX
	XXX	XXX				XXX					XXX
Retained earnings (closing balance)	XXX	XXX				XXX					XXX
Share capital	XXX	XXX				XXX		XXX			XXX
Other reserves	XXX	XXX				XXX		XXX			XXX
Total equity: parent											XXX
Total equity: MI									XXX		XXX
Total equity	XXX	XXX				XXX		XXX	XXX		XXX
Current liabilities	XXX	XXX				XXX					
Non-current liabilities	XXX	XXX				XXX					
Total liabilities	XXX	XXX				XXX					
Total equity and liabilities	XXX	XXX				XXX					

FIGURE 22.6   Consolidation worksheet containing MI columns

LO 3

22.3   Calculating the MI share of equity

According to paragraph 22(c) of IAS 27, minority interests in the net assets consist of:

(i) the amount of those minority interests at the date of the original combination calculated in accordance with IFRS 3; and

(ii) the minority's share of changes in equity since the date of the combination.

In relation to part (ii), changes in equity since the acquisition date must be taken into account. Note that these changes are not only in the recorded equity of the subsidiary, but they also relate to other changes in consolidated equity. As noted earlier in this chapter, the MI is entitled to a share of consolidated equity under the entity concept of consolidation. This requires taking into account adjustments for profits and losses made as a result of intragroup transactions because these profits and losses are not recognised by the group.

The calculation of the MI is therefore done in two stages: (1) the MI share of recorded equity is determined (see section 22.4 of this book), and (2) this share is adjusted for the effects of intragroup transactions (see section 22.5).

22.4 MI share of recorded equity of the subsidiary

The equity of the subsidiary consists of the equity contained in the actual records of the subsidiary as well as any business combination valuation reserves created on consolidation at the acquisition date, where the identifiable assets and liabilities of the subsidiary are recorded at amounts different from their fair values. The MI is entitled to a share of subsidiary equity at balance date, which consists of the equity on hand at acquisition date plus any changes in that equity between acquisition date and reporting date. The calculation of the MI share of equity at a point in time is done in three steps:

1. Determine the MI share of equity of the subsidiary at acquisition date.
2. Determine the MI share of the change in subsidiary equity between the acquisition date and the beginning of the current period for which the consolidated financial statements are being prepared.
3. Determine the MI share of the changes in subsidiary equity in the current period.

The calculation could be represented diagrammatically, as shown in figure 22.7.

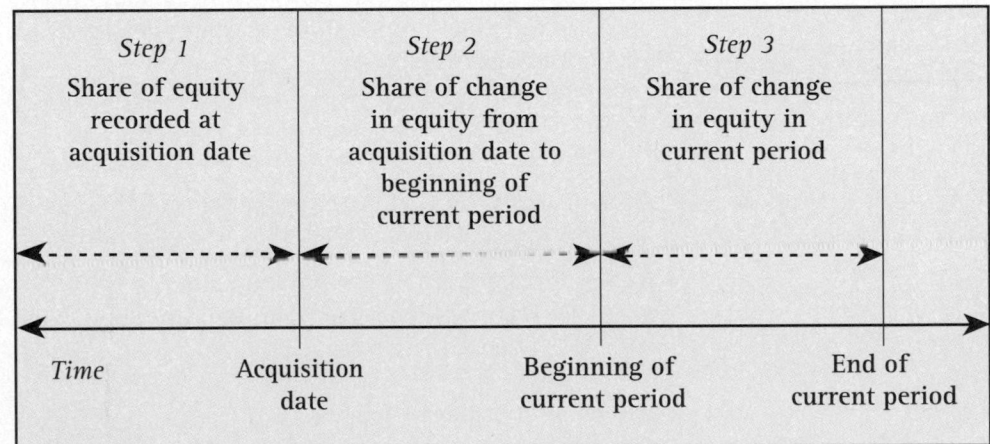

FIGURE 22.7 Calculating the MI share of equity
Source: Based on a diagram by Peter Gerhardy, School of Commerce, Flinders University.

Note that, in calculating the MI share of equity at the end of the current period, the information relating to the MI share of equity from steps 1 and 2 should be available from the previous period's consolidation worksheet.

To illustrate the above procedure, consider the calculation of the MI share of retained earnings over a five-year period. Assume the following information in relation to Tartu Ltd:

Retained earnings as at 1 July 2000	$10 000
Retained earnings as at 30 June 2004	50 000
Profit for the 2004–05 period	15 000
Retained earnings as at 30 June 2005	65 000

Assume that Vilnius Ltd had acquired 80% of the share capital of Tartu Ltd at 1 July 2000, and the consolidated financial statements were being prepared at 30 June 2005. The 20% MI in Tartu Ltd is therefore entitled to a share of the retained earnings balance of $65 000, a share equal to $13 000. This share is calculated in three steps:

1. A share of the balance at 1 July 2000 (20% × $10 000) = $ 2 000
2. A share of the change in retained earnings from the acquisition date to the beginning of the current period (20% × [$50 000 − $10 000]) = $ 8 000
3. A share of the current period increase in retained earnings (20% × $15 000) = $ 3 000

$13 000

The increase in retained earnings is broken into these three steps because accounting is based on time periods. The MI is entitled to a share of the profits of past periods as well as a share of the profits of the current period. Note that, in calculating the MI share of retained earnings for Tartu Ltd at 30 June 2006 (one year after the above calculation), the total of steps 1 and 2 for the 2006 calculation would be $13 000, as calculated above. The only additional calculation would be the share of changes in equity in the 2005–06 period.

These separate calculations are not based on a division of equity into pre-acquisition and post-acquisition equity. The division of equity is based on *time* — changes in equity are calculated on a period-by-period basis for accounting purposes.

The MI columns in the consolidation worksheet contain the amounts relating to the three steps noted above. The journal entries used in the MI columns of the consolidation worksheet to reflect the MI share of equity are based on the three-step approach. The form of these entries is:

Step 1: MI at acquisition date

Share capital	Dr	XXX	
Business combination valuation reserve	Dr	XXX	
Retained earnings (opening balance)	Dr	XXX	
MI	Cr		XXX

Step 2: MI share of changes in equity between acquisition date and beginning of the current period

Retained earnings (opening balance)	Dr	XXX	
MI	Cr		XXX

Step 3: MI share of changes in equity in the current period

MI share of profit/(loss)	Dr	XXX	
MI	Cr		XXX
MI	Dr	XXX	
Dividend paid	Cr		XXX
MI	Dr	XXX	
Dividend declared	Cr		XXX

The effects of these journal entries can be seen in the consolidation worksheet in figure 22.6. The above entries are illustrative only, and there may be others where there are transfers to or from reserves that affect the balances of equity in the subsidiary. The effects of these transactions are illustrated in the next section.

LO 4

22.4.1 ## Accounting at acquisition date

This section illustrates the effects that the existence of an MI has on the valuation entries, the acquisition analysis and the pre-acquisition entry, as well as the step 1 calculation of the MI share of equity at acquisition date.

ILLUSTRATIVE EXAMPLE 22.1

Consolidation worksheet entries at acquisition date

On 1 July 2005, Gorki Ltd acquired 60% of the shares (cum div.) of Minsk Ltd for $45 600 when the equity of Minsk Ltd consisted of:

Share capital	$40 000
General reserve	2 000
Retained earnings	2 000

At acquisition date, the liabilities of Minsk Ltd included a dividend payable of $1000. All the identifiable assets and liabilities of Minsk Ltd were recorded at fair value except for equipment and inventory:

	Carrying amount	Fair value
Equipment (cost $250 000)	$180 000	$200 000
Inventory	40 000	50 000

The tax rate is 30%.

Acquisition analysis

Net fair value of identifiable assets, liabilities and contingent liabilities of Minsk Ltd	= $40 000 (capital) + $2000 (general reserve) + $2000 (retained earnings) + $20 000 (1 − 30%) (BCVR − equipment) + $10 000 (1 − 30%) (BCVR − inventory)
	= $65 000
Net fair value acquired by Gorki Ltd	= 60% × $65 000
	= $39 000
Cost of combination	= $45 600 − (60% × $1000) (dividend receivable)
	= $45 000
Goodwill acquired by Gorki Ltd	= $6000

Where an MI exists, because the parent acquires only a part of the ownership interest of the subsidiary, the parent acquires only a proportionate share of each of the equity amounts in the subsidiary.

1. Business combination valuation entries

The valuation entries are unaffected by the existence of an MI. The purpose of these entries, in accordance with IFRS 3, is to show the assets and liabilities of the subsidiary at fair value at acquisition date. These entries for a consolidation worksheet (see figure 22.8, p. 951) prepared at acquisition date are shown overleaf.

Accumulated depreciation – equipment	Dr	70 000	
Equipment	Cr		50 000
Deferred tax liability	Cr		6 000
Business combination valuation reserve	Cr		14 000
Inventory	Dr	10 000	
Deferred tax liability	Cr		3 000
Business combination valuation reserve	Cr		7 000

The business combination valuation reserve is pre-acquisition equity because it is recognised on consolidation at acquisition date. The MI is entitled to a proportionate share of this reserve. As the reserve is recognised by the group, but not in the records of the subsidiary, this affects later calculations for the MI share of equity.

2. Pre-acquisition entries

The first pre-acquisition entry is read from the pre-acquisition analysis. The parent's proportionate share of the various recorded equity accounts of the subsidiary, as well as the parent's share of the business combination valuation reserves, are eliminated against the investment account in the pre-acquisition entry. In this illustrative example, the pre-acquisition entry is:

Retained earnings (1/7/05)	Dr	1 200	
(60% × $2000)			
Share capital	Dr	24 000	
(60% × $40 000)			
Business combination valuation reserve	Dr	12 600	
(60% × [$14 000 + $7000])			
General reserve	Dr	1 200	
(60% × $2000)			
Goodwill	Dr	6 000	
Shares in Minsk Ltd	Cr		45 000

At acquisition date, the subsidiary has recorded a dividend payable and the parent entity a dividend receivable. An adjustment entry is required because these are not dividends receivable or payable to parties external to the group. The adjustment is a proportionate one as it relates only to the amount payable within the group:

Dividend payable	Dr	600	
Dividend receivable	Cr		600
(60% × $1000)			

No further adjustment is required once the dividend has been paid.

3. MI share of equity at acquisition date

The MI at acquisition date (the step 1 calculation) is determined as the proportionate share of the equity recorded by the subsidiary at that date and the valuation reserves recorded on consolidation (see opposite).

→

Share capital	40% × $40 000	= $16 000
General reserve	40% × $2000	= 800
Business combination valuation reserve	40% × ($14 000 + $7000)	= 8 400
Retained earnings	40% × $2000	= 800
		$26 000

The following entry is then passed in the MI columns of the consolidation worksheet:

Retained earnings (1/7/05)	Dr	800	
Share capital	Dr	16 000	
Business combination valuation reserve	Dr	8 400	
General reserve	Dr	800	
MI	Cr		26 000

This entry is passed as the step 1 MI entry in *all* subsequent consolidation worksheets. It is never changed. Any subsequent changes in pre-acquisition equity are dealt with in the step 2 MI calculation. Figure 22.8 shows an extract from a consolidation worksheet for Gorki Ltd and its subsidiary, Minsk Ltd, at acquisition date. Only the equity section of the worksheet is shown. The worksheet entries are (1) the business combination valuation entries, (2) the pre-acquisition entries (the dividend adjustment is not shown in figure 22.8 because only an extract from the worksheet is reproduced), and (3) the MI step 1 entry.

Financial statements	Gorki Ltd	Minsk Ltd	Adjustments	Dr	Cr		Group		Minority interest Dr	Cr		Parent
Retained earnings	50 000	2 000	2	1 200			50 800	3	800			50 000
Share capital	100 000	40 000	2	24 000			116 000	3	16 000			100 000
General reserve	20 000	2 000	2	1 200			20 800	3	800			20 000
Business combination valuation reserve			2	12 600	14 000 7 000	1 1	8 400	3	8 400			0
Total equity: parent												170 000
Total equity: MI										26 000	3	26 000
Total equity	170 000	44 000					196 000		26 000	26 000		196 000

FIGURE 22.8 Consolidation worksheet (extract) at acquisition date

In figure 22.8, the adjustment columns eliminate the parent's share of the pre-acquisition equity accounts and the MI columns extract the MI share of total equity. The parent column contains only the parent's share of post-acquisition equity, which in this case, being at acquisition date, is zero.

22.4.2 Accounting subsequent to acquisition date

Using illustrative example 22.1, the consolidation worksheet entries at the end of the period three years after the acquisition date will now be considered. Assume that:

- all inventory on hand at 1 July 2005 is sold by 30 June 2006
- the dividend payable at acquisition date is paid in August 2005
- the equipment has an expected useful life of five years
- goodwill has not been impaired
- in the three years after the acquisition date, Minsk Ltd recorded the changes in equity shown in figure 22.9.

	2005–06	2006–07	2007–08
Profit for the period	$ 8 000	$12 000	$15 000
Retained earnings (opening balance)	2 000	7 800	16 000
	10 000	19 800	31 000
Transfer from general reserve	–	–	500
	10 000	19 800	31 500
Transfer to general reserve	–	1 000	–
Dividend paid*	1 000	1 200	1 500
Dividend declared	1 200	1 600	2 000
	2 200	3 800	3 500
Retained earnings (closing balance)	7 800	16 000	28 000
Share capital	40 000	40 000	40 000
General reserve	2 000	3 000	2 500

* In the 2007–08 period, $1000 of the dividend paid is from pre-acquisition profits.

FIGURE 22.9   Changes in equity over a three-year period

In preparing the consolidated financial statements at 30 June 2008, the consolidation worksheet contains the valuation entries, the pre-acquisition entries, the MI entries and the adjustments for the dividend transactions.

1. Business combination valuation entries

The valuation entries for the 2007–08 period differ from those prepared at acquisition date in that the equipment is depreciated, and the inventory has been sold. The entries at 30 June 2008 are:

Accumulated depreciation – equipment	Dr	70 000	
Equipment	Cr		50 000
Deferred tax liability	Cr		6 000
Business combination valuation reserve	Cr		14 000
Depreciation expense	Dr	4 000	
Retained earnings (1/7/07)	Dr	8 000	
Accumulated depreciation	Cr		12 000
(20% × $20 000 p.a.)			
Deferred tax liability	Dr	3 600	
Income tax expense	Cr		1 200
Retained earnings (1/7/07)	Cr		2 400
(30% × $4000 p.a.)			

2. Pre-acquisition entries

The pre-acquisition entries have to take into consideration the following events occurring since acquisition date:

- The dividend of $1000 on hand at acquisition date has been paid.
- A $1000 pre-acquisition dividend has been paid in the current period.
- The inventory on hand at acquisition date has been sold.

The entry at 30 June 2008 is:

Retained earnings (1/7/07)*	Dr	5 400	
Dividend paid	Cr		600
Share capital	Dr	24 000	
Business combination valuation reserve**	Dr	8 400	
General reserve	Dr	1 200	
Goodwill	Dr	6 000	
Shares in Minsk Ltd ***	Cr		44 400

* $1200 + (60% × $7000) (BCVR transfer — inventory)
** 60% × $14 000
*** $45 000 − $600 current dividend

3. MI share of equity at acquisition date (step 1)

The MI share of equity at acquisition date is as calculated previously. This entry is never changed from the amount calculated at that date.

Retained earnings (1/7/05)	Dr	800	
Share capital	Dr	16 000	
Business combination valuation reserve	Dr	8 400	
General reserve	Dr	800	
MI	Cr		26 000

4. MI share of changes in equity between acquisition date and beginning of the current period (step 2)

To calculate this entry, it is necessary to note any changes in subsidiary equity between the two dates (from 1 July 2005 to 30 June 2007). The changes will generally relate to movements in retained earnings and reserves, but changes could occur in share capital, such as when a bonus dividend is paid. In this example, there are three changes in subsidiary equity, as shown in figure 22.9:

- Retained earnings increased from $2000 to $16 000. This will increase the MI share of retained earnings.
- In the 2006–07 period, $1000 was transferred to the general reserve. Because the transfer has reduced retained earnings, the MI share of retained earnings as calculated above has been reduced by this transfer, and an increase in the MI share of general reserve needs to be recognised as well as an increase in MI in total.
- The sale of inventory in the 2005–06 period resulted in a transfer of $7000 from the business combination valuation reserve to retained earnings. Because the profits from the sale of inventory are recorded in the profits of the subsidiary, the MI receives a share of the increased wealth relating to inventory. The MI share of the business combination valuation reserve as recognised in step 1 must be reduced, with a reduction in MI in total.

Before noting the effects of these events in journal entry format, the equipment on hand at acquisition date needs adjustment. In the business combination valuation entry, the equipment on hand at acquisition date was revalued to fair value and the increase taken to the valuation reserve. By recognising the asset at fair value at acquisition date, the group recognises the extra benefits over and above the asset's carrying amount to be earned by the subsidiary. As expressed in the depreciation of the equipment (see the valuation entries above), the group expects the subsidiary to realise extra after-tax benefits of $2800 (being $4000 depreciation expense less the credit of $1200 to income tax expense) in each of the five years after acquisition. Whereas the group recognises these extra benefits at acquisition date via the valuation reserve, the subsidiary recognises these benefits as profit in its records only as the equipment is used. Hence, the profit after tax recorded by the subsidiary in each of the five years after acquisition date will contain $2800 benefits from the equipment that the group recognised in the valuation reserve at acquisition date.

In calculating the MI share of equity from acquisition date to the beginning of the current period, the MI will double-count the benefits from the equipment if there is no adjustment for the depreciation of the equipment. This occurs because the share of the MI in equity calculated at acquisition date includes a share of the business combination valuation reserve created at that date in the consolidation worksheet. Therefore, giving the MI a full share of the recorded profits of the subsidiary in the five years after the acquisition date would double-count the benefits relating to the equipment. The MI has already received a share of the valuation reserve in the step 1 calculation. Hence, in calculating the MI share of changes in equity between acquisition date and the beginning of the current period (the step 2 calculation), there needs to be an adjustment for the extra depreciation of the equipment in relation to each of the years since acquisition date.

The adjustment for depreciation can be read directly from the valuation entry that records the depreciation on the equipment since acquisition date. In the valuation entry required for the 2007–08 consolidated financial statements, there is a net debit adjustment to retained earnings (1/7/07) of $5600 (being the $8000 adjustment for prior periods' depreciation less the $2400 adjustment for prior periods' tax effect) in relation to the after-tax effects of depreciating the equipment. This reflects the extra benefits received by the subsidiary as a result of using the equipment and recorded by the subsidiary in its retained earnings account.

In this example, the only adjustment to retained earnings in the business combination valuation entry is that relating to the equipment. In other examples, there may be a number of adjustments to retained earnings according to the number of assets being revalued. All such adjustments must be taken into account in order not to double-count the MI share of equity. In other words, to determine the required adjustments needed to avoid double-counting, all adjustments to retained earnings in the valuation entries must be taken into consideration.

In illustrative example 22.1, the MI share of changes in retained earnings is determined by calculating the change in retained earnings over the period, less the adjustment against retained earnings in the valuation entry relating to depreciation of the equipment. The amount is calculated as follows:

$$40\% \times (\$16\,000 - \$2000 - [\$8000 - \$2400]) = \$3360$$

The MI is also entitled to a share of the change in *general reserve* between acquisition date and the beginning of the current period, the change being the transfer to general reserve in the 2006–07 period. As the general reserve is increased, the MI share of that account is also increased. The calculation is:

$$40\% \times \$1000 = \$400$$

The MI is also affected by the transfer on consolidation from the business combination valuation reserve to retained earnings as a result of the sale of inventory. The MI share of the valuation reserve is decreased, with a reduction in MI in total. The calculation is:

$$40\% \times \$7000 = \$2800$$

The consolidation worksheet entries in the MI columns for the step 2 MI calculation are:

Retained earnings (1/7/07)	Dr	3 360	
MI	Cr		3 360
(40% × [$16 000 − $2000 − ($8000 − $2400)])			
General reserve	Dr	400	
MI	Cr		400
(40% × $1000)			
MI	Dr	2 800	
Business combination valuation reserve	Cr		2 800
(40% × $7000)			

These entries may be combined as:

Retained earnings (1/7/07)	Dr	3 360	
General reserve	Dr	400	
Business combination valuation reserve	Cr		2 800
MI	Cr		960

5. MI share of current period changes in equity (step 3)

From figure 22.9 on page 952, it can be seen that there are three changes in equity in the 2007–08 period:

- Minsk Ltd has reported a profit of $15 000.
- There has been a transfer from general reserve of $500.
- The subsidiary has paid a dividend of $1500 and declared a dividend of $2000.

In relation to both dividends and transfer to/from reserves, from an MI perspective it is irrelevant whether the amounts are from pre- or post-acquisition equity. The MI receives a share of all equity accounts regardless of whether it existed prior to acquisition date or was created after that date.

The MI share of *current period profit* is based on a 40% share of the recorded profit of $15 000. However, just as in step 2, there must be an adjustment made to avoid the double-counting caused by the subsidiary recognising profits from the use of the equipment, these benefits having been recognised on consolidation in the business combination valuation reserve. Again, reference needs to be made to the valuation entries and, in particular to the amounts in these entries affecting current period profit. In the valuation entries, there is a debit adjustment to depreciation expense of $4000 and a credit adjustment to income tax expense of $1200. In other words, in the current period, Minsk Ltd recognised in its profit an amount of $2800 from the use of the equipment that was recognised by the group in the business combination valuation reserve. Since the MI has been given a share of the valuation reserve in step 1, giving the MI a share of the recorded profit without adjusting for the current period's depreciation would double-count the MI share of equity. The MI share of current period profit is therefore 40% of the net of recorded profit of $15 000 less the after-tax depreciation adjustment of $2800.

The consolidation worksheet entry in the MI columns is:

MI share of profit/(loss) 　　MI (40% × [$15 000 − ($4000 − $1200)])	Dr Cr	4 880	4 880

In the current period, a change in equity is caused by the $500 *transfer from general reserve* to retained earnings. This transaction does not change the amount of equity in total because it is a transfer between equity accounts, so there is no change to the MI in total. However, the MI share of general reserve has decreased and the MI share of retained earnings has increased. For the latter account, the appropriate line item is 'Transfer from general reserve'. The consolidation worksheet entry in the MI columns is:

Transfer from general reserve 　　General reserve (40% × $500)	Dr Cr	200	200

The third change in equity in the current period relates to *dividends paid and declared*. Dividends are a reduction in retained earnings. The MI share of equity is reduced as a result of the payment or declaration of dividends. Where dividends are paid, the MI receives a cash distribution as compensation for the reduction in equity interest. Where dividends are declared, the group recognises a liability to make a future cash payment to the MI as compensation for the reduction in equity. The consolidation worksheet entries in the MI column are:

MI 　　Dividend paid (40% × $1500)	Dr Cr	600	600
MI 　　Dividend declared (40% × $2000)	Dr Cr	800	800

6. Adjustments for intragroup transactions: dividends

The following entries in the adjustment columns of the worksheet are necessary to adjust for the dividend transactions in the current period. The amounts are based on the proportion of dividends paid within the group:

Dividend revenue 　　Dividend paid (60% × $500)	Dr Cr	300	300

Note that the above adjustment entry relates only to post-acquisition dividends, as the adjustment for pre-acquisition dividends is made in the pre-acquisition entry.

Dividend payable 　　Dividend declared (60% × $2000)	Dr Cr	1 200	1 200
Dividend revenue 　　Dividend receivable (60% × $2000)	Dr Cr	1 200	1 200

Using the figures for the subsidiary as given in figure 22.8, and assuming information for the parent, a consolidation worksheet showing the effects of the entries developed in illustrative example 22.1 is given in figure 22.10.

Financial statements	Gorki Ltd	Minsk Ltd		Adjustments			Group		Minority interest			Parent
				Dr	Cr				Dr	Cr		
Profit (loss) for the period	20 000	15 000	1 6 6	4 000 300 1 200	1 200	1	30 700	5	4 880			25 820
Retained earnings (1/7/07)	25 000	16 000	1 2	8 000 5 400	2 400	1	30 000	3 4	800 3 360			25 840
Transfer from general reserve	–	500					500	5	200			300
	45 000	31 500					61 200					51 960
Dividend paid	10 000	1 500			600 300	2 6	10 600			600	5	10 000
Dividend declared	5 000	2 000			1 200	6	5 800			800	5	5 000
	15 000	3 500					16 400					15 000
Retained earnings (30/6/08)	30 000	28 000					44 800					36 960
Share capital	100 000	40 000	2	24 000			116 000	3	16 000			100 000
General reserve	20 000	2 500	2	1 200			21 300	3 4	800 400	200	5	20 300
Business combination valuation reserve	–	–	2	8 400	14 000	1	5 600	3	8 400	2 800	1	
Total equity: parent												157 260
Total equity: MI								5 5	600 800	26 000 960 4 880	3 4 5	30 440
Total equity	150 000	70 500					187 700		36 240	36 240		187 700

FIGURE 22.10   Consolidation worksheet with MI columns

22.5 Adjusting for the effects of intragroup transactions

The justification for considering adjustments for intragroup transactions in the calculation of the MI share of equity is that, under the entity concept of consolidation, the MI is classified as a contributor of capital to the group. Thus, the calculation of the MI is based on a share of *consolidated equity* and not equity as recorded by the subsidiary. Consolidated equity is determined as the sum of the equity of the parent and the subsidiaries after making adjustments for the effects of intragroup transactions. The MI share of that equity must therefore be based on subsidiary equity after adjusting for the effects of intragroup transactions that affect the subsidiary's equity.

To illustrate, assume that during the current period, a subsidiary in which there exists an MI of 20% has recorded a profit of $20 000. This includes a before-tax profit of $2000 on the sale of $18 000 inventory to the parent. The inventory is still on hand at the end of the current period. In the adjustment columns of the consolidation worksheet, the adjustment entries for the sale of inventory (assuming a tax rate of 30%) are:

Sales	Dr	18 000	
Cost of sales	Cr		16 000
Inventory	Cr		2 000
Deferred tax asset	Dr	600	
Income tax expense	Cr		600

The group does not regard the after-tax profit of $1400 as being a part of consolidated profit. Hence, in calculating the MI share of consolidated profit, the MI is entitled to $3720 (being 20% of the recorded profit of $20 000 less intragroup profit of $1400).

The MI share of equity is therefore adjusted for the effects of intragroup transactions. Note that the MI share of consolidated equity is essentially based on a share of *subsidiary* equity. Therefore, only intragroup transactions that affect the subsidiary's equity need to be taken into consideration. Profits made on inventory sold by the parent to the subsidiary do not affect the calculation of the MI because the profit is recorded by the parent, not the subsidiary; the subsidiary equity is unaffected by the transaction.

In section 22.4 of this book, it is explained that the MI share of the equity recorded by the subsidiary is calculated in three steps, namely:

- share of equity at acquisition date
- share of changes in equity between acquisition date and the beginning of the current period
- share of changes in equity in the current period.

These calculations are based on the *recorded* subsidiary equity; that is, equity that will include the effects of the intragroup transactions. Having calculated the MI as a result of the three-step process, further adjustments must be made by the subsidiary for the effects of intragroup transactions. Instead of adjusting for these transactions in the MI entries relating to the three-step process, the adjustments to the MI are determined when the adjustments are made for the effects of the specific intragroup transactions.

Consider the case above where a subsidiary, in which the MI is 20%, records a profit of $20 000. This includes a $2000 before-tax profit on the sale of inventory to the parent (cost $4000, selling price $6000). In the step 3 MI calculation, the worksheet entry passed in the MI columns is:

MI share of profit/(loss)	Dr	4 000	
MI	Cr		4 000
(20% × $20 000 recorded profit)			

In making the adjustment for the effects of intragroup transactions to be passed in the adjustment columns of the worksheet, the following entries are made:

Profit in closing inventory: subsidiary to parent

Sales	Dr	6 000	
Cost of sales	Cr		4 000
Inventory	Cr		2 000
Deferred tax asset	Dr	600	
Income tax expense	Cr		600
(30% × $2000)			

As this adjustment affects the profit of the subsidiary by an amount of $1400 after tax (being $2000 − $600), this triggers the need to make an adjustment to the MI. The following entry is passed in the MI columns of the worksheet:

MI		Dr	280	
MI share of profit/(loss)		Cr		280
(20% × $1400)				

This entry is explained in more detail in illustrative example 22.2 later in this chapter. The combined effect of the step 3 MI entry and this last entry is that the MI totals $3720 (being $4000 less $280). Thus, the MI is given a share of recorded profit adjusted for the effects of intragroup transactions.

22.5.1 The concept of 'realisation' of profits and losses

Not all transactions require an adjustment entry for the MI. For a transaction to require an adjustment to the calculation of the MI share of equity, it must have the following characteristics:

- The transaction must result in the subsidiary recording a profit or a loss.
- After the transaction, the other party to the transaction (this is the parent for two-company structures) must have on hand an asset, such as inventory, on which the unrealised profit is accrued.
- The initial consolidation adjustment for the transaction should affect both the balance sheet and the income statement (including appropriations), unlike payments of debenture interest, which affect only the income statement.

In determining the transactions requiring an adjusting entry for the MI, it is important to determine which transactions involve unrealised profit. The concept of 'realisation' is discussed in chapter 21. The test for realisation is the involvement of a party external to the group, and it is based on the concept that the consolidated financial statements report the affairs of the group in terms of its dealings with parties external to the group. Consolidated profits are therefore realised profits because they result from dealing with parties external to the group. Profits made by transacting within the group are unrealised because no external party is involved. Once the profits/losses on an intragroup transaction become realised, the MI share of equity no longer needs to be adjusted for the effects of an intragroup transaction as the profits/losses recorded by the subsidiary are all realised profits.

In this section, the key point to note is when (for different types of transactions) unrealised profits on intragroup transactions become realised.

Inventory

With inventory, realisation occurs when the acquiring entity sells the inventory to an entity outside the group. Consolidation adjustments for inventory are based on the profit/loss remaining in inventory on hand at the end of a financial period. If inventory is sold in the current period by the subsidiary to the parent at a profit, giving the MI a share of the recorded profit will overstate the MI share of consolidated equity because the group does not recognise the profit until the inventory is sold outside the group. Hence, whenever consolidated adjustments are made for profit remaining in inventory on hand at the end of the period, an MI adjustment is necessary to reduce the MI share of current period profit and the MI total. Following the consolidation adjustment for the unrealised profit in inventory, an MI adjustment entry is made in the MI columns of the worksheet. The general form of the entry is:

| MI | | Dr | XXX | |
| MI share of profit/(loss) | | Cr | | XXX |

If there is inventory on hand at *the beginning of the current period*, the MI share of the previous period's profit must be reduced because the subsidiary's previous year's recorded profit contains unrealised profit. As the group realises the profit in the current period when the inventory is sold to external parties, the MI share of current period's profit must be increased. Following the worksheet adjustment for the profit remaining in beginning inventory, an MI adjustment entry is made in the MI columns of the worksheet. The general form of the MI entry is:

| MI share of profit/(loss) | Dr | XXX | |
| Retained earnings (opening balance) | Cr | | XXX |

Depreciable non-current assets

With depreciable non-current assets, profit is realised as the asset is used up within the group. Realisation of the profit occurs as the future benefits embodied in the asset are consumed by the group, and occurs in proportion to the depreciation of the asset. If the subsidiary sells a non-current asset in the current period to the parent, an adjustment is made for the profit on sale because the profit is unrealised to the group. The MI share of current period profit must then be reduced. Following the worksheet adjustment for the profit on sale, an MI adjustment is made in the MI columns of the worksheet. The general form of the adjustment entry is:

| MI | Dr | XXX | |
| MI share of profit/(loss) | Cr | | XXX |

As the asset is depreciated, some of the profit becomes realised, increasing the MI share of profit. Following the worksheet adjustment entry for depreciation, an MI entry is made in the MI columns of the worksheet. The general form of the MI reflecting the increased share of profit is:

| MI share of profit/(loss) | Dr | XXX | |
| MI | Cr | | XXX |

It can be seen that the MI adjustment for the profit on sale reduces the MI share of equity, and the MI adjustment relating to depreciation increases the MI share of equity. This reflects the fact that the profit becomes realised as the asset is used up.

Intragroup transfers for services and interest

For transactions involving services and interest, the group's profit is unaffected because the general consolidation adjustment reduces expense and revenue equally. However, from the MI's perspective, there has been a change in the equity of the subsidiary; for example, the subsidiary may have recorded interest revenue as a result of a payment to the parent entity relating to an intragroup loan. The revenue is unrealised in that no external entity has been involved in the transaction. Theoretically, the MI should be adjusted for such transactions. However, as noted in paragraph 25 of IAS 27, it is profits and losses 'recognised in assets' that are of concern. In other words, where there are transfers between entities that do not result in the retention within the group of assets on which the profit has been accrued, it is *assumed* that the profit is realised by the group immediately on payment within the group. For transactions such as payments for intragroup services, interest and dividends, there are no assets recorded with accrued profits attached, since the transactions are cash transactions. Hence, the profit is assumed to be immediately realised. The reason for the assumption of immediate realisation of profits on these types of transactions is a pragmatic one based on the cost–benefit of determining a point of realisation.

An example of the process of calculating MI when intragroup transactions exist is given in illustrative example 22.2.

ILLUSTRATIVE EXAMPLE 22.2

MI and intragroup transactions

LO 7

Ivanova Ltd acquired 80% of the shares of Murmansk Ltd in 1 July 2003 for $520 000, when the equity of Murmansk Ltd consisted of:

Share capital	$500 000
General reserve	100 000
Retained earnings	50 000

All identifiable assets and liabilities of Murmansk Ltd are recorded at fair value at this date. Financial information for both companies at 30 June 2007 is as follows:

	Ivanova Ltd	Murmansk Ltd
Sales revenue	$720 000	$530 000
Other revenue	240 000	120 000
	960 000	650 000
Cost of sales	610 000	410 000
Other expenses	230 000	160 000
	840 000	570 000
Profit before tax	120 000	80 000
Tax expense	40 000	25 000
Profit for the period	80 000	55 000
Retained earnings at 1/7/06	200 000	112 000
	280 000	167 000
Dividend paid	20 000	10 000
Dividend declared	25 000	15 000
	45 000	25 000
Retained earnings at 30/6/07	235 000	142 000
Share capital	600 000	500 000
General reserve	100 000	150 000
Total equity	935 000	792 000
Dividend payable	25 000	15 000
Other liabilities	25 000	25 000
Total liabilities	50 000	40 000
Total equity and liabilities	$985 000	$832 000
Receivables	$ 80 000	$ 30 000
Inventory	100 000	170 000
Plant and equipment	300 000	580 000
Accumulated depreciation	(115 000)	(88 000)
Shares in Murmansk Ltd	516 800	–
Deferred tax assets	53 200	40 000
Other assets	50 000	100 000
Total assets	$985 000	$832 000

→

The following transactions took place between Ivanova Ltd and Murmansk Ltd:

(a) During the 2006–07 period, Murmansk Ltd sold inventory to Ivanova Ltd for $23 000, recording a profit before tax of $3000. Ivanova Ltd has since resold half of these items.

(b) During the 2006–07 period, Ivanova Ltd sold inventory to Murmansk Ltd for $18 000, recording a profit before tax of $2000. Murmansk Ltd has not resold any of these items.

(c) On 1 June 2007, Murmansk Ltd paid $1000 to Ivanova Ltd for services rendered.

(d) During the 2005–06 period, Murmansk Ltd sold inventory to Ivanova Ltd of which, at 30 June 2006, there was still on hand inventory on which Murmansk Ltd had recorded a before-tax profit of $4000.

(e) On 1 July 2005, Murmansk Ltd sold plant to Ivanova Ltd for $150 000, recording a profit of $20 000 before tax. Ivanova Ltd applies a 10% p.a. straight-line method of depreciation in relation to these assets.

(f) In relation to the dividend paid in the current period, $4000 is from profits earned before 1 July 2003.

Required

Given an income tax rate of 30%, prepare the consolidated financial statements for Ivanova Ltd for the year ended 30 June 2007.

Solution
Acquisition analysis

Net fair value of Murmansk Ltd	= $500 000 + $100 000 + $50 000
	= $650 000
Net fair value acquired by Ivanova Ltd	= 80% × $650 000
	= $520 000
Cost of combination	= $520 000
Goodwill	= 0

Consolidation worksheet entries at 30 June 2007

There are no business combination valuation entries because all the assets and liabilities of the subsidiary are recorded at fair value.

1. Pre-acquisition entry

Retained earnings (1/7/06)	Dr	40 000	
Dividend paid	Cr		3 200
Share capital	Dr	400 000	
General reserve	Dr	80 000	
Shares in Murmansk Ltd	Cr		516 800

The only event affecting the pre-acquisition entry since acquisition is the payment of the $4000 pre-acquisition dividend in the current period.

Minority interest

2. MI share of equity at acquisition date, 1 July 2003 (step 1)

Recorded equity of Murmansk Ltd		20%
Retained earnings	$ 50 000	$ 10 000
Share capital	500 000	100 000
General reserve	100 000	20 000
		$ 130 000

The worksheet entry in the MI columns is:

Retained earnings (1/7/06)	Dr	10 000	
Share capital	Dr	100 000	
General reserve	Dr	20 000	
MI	Cr		130 000

3. MI share of equity from 1 July 2003 to 30 June 2006 (step 2)

	Change in equity	20%
General reserve ($150 000 − $100 000)	$50 000	$10 000
Retained earnings ($112 000 − $50 000)	62 000	12 400

The worksheet entry in the MI columns is:

Retained earnings (1/7/06)	Dr	12 400	
General reserve	Dr	10 000	
MI	Cr		22 400

4. MI in equity from 1 July 2006 to 30 June 2007 (step 3)

Profit	
Current period's profit	$55 000
MI share − 20%	11 000

The worksheet entry in the MI columns is:

MI share of profit/(loss)	Dr	11 000	
MI	Cr		11 000

Dividend paid

The dividend paid by the subsidiary reduces the equity of the subsidiary. Pre-acquisition dividends reduce subsidiary equity in the same way as post-acquisition dividends. Hence, the adjustment to the MI share of equity as a result of the dividend paid must take into consideration the full dividend paid (both pre- and post-acquisition dividend) with the effect of reducing the MI share of total equity. The entry in the MI columns of the worksheet is:

MI	Dr	2 000	
Dividend paid	Cr		2 000
(20% × $10 000)			

Dividend declared

As with the dividend paid, the MI has been given a full share of equity before the declaration of dividends. As the dividend declared reduces the equity of the subsidiary, the MI share of equity is also reduced. The entry in the MI columns of the worksheet is:

MI	Dr	3 000	
Dividend declared	Cr		3 000
(20% × $15 000)			

→

Intragroup transactions
5. Dividend paid

Of the current period dividend paid, $6000 is from post-acquisition equity and $4000 is from pre-acquisition equity. The pre-acquisition dividend is dealt with in the pre-acquisition entry. The entry to adjust for the post-acquisition dividend in the adjustment columns is:

Dividend revenue	Dr	4 800	
Dividend paid	Cr		4 800
(80% × $6000)			

6. Dividend declared

The subsidiary declared a dividend of $15 000, of which $12 000 is paid within the group. The entries in the adjustment columns of the worksheet are:

Dividend payable	Dr	12 000	
Dividend declared	Cr		12 000
Dividend revenue	Dr	12 000	
Dividend receivable	Cr		12 000

7. Sale of inventory: Murmansk Ltd to Ivanova Ltd

The worksheet entries in the adjustment columns are:

Sales	Dr	23 000	
Cost of sales	Cr		21 500
Inventory	Cr		1 500
(Unrealised profit on sale of inventory, being 50% × $3000)			
Deferred tax asset	Dr	450	
Income tax expense	Cr		450
(Tax effect, being 30% × $1500)			

8. Adjustment to MI: unrealised profit in ending inventory

The profit on sale was made by the subsidiary. The MI is therefore affected. The total after-tax profit on the intragroup sale of inventory was $2100 (being $3000 − $900 tax). However, as half of the inventory is sold to an external entity, this portion is realised. The adjustment to the MI relates only to the unrealised profits remaining in the inventory still on hand (half of $2100, or $1050). This is the same after-tax figure used to adjust profits in entry 7 above.

The transaction occurs in the current period. Therefore, it is the MI share of current period profit that is affected. In adjustment entry 4, the MI is given a share of the total recorded subsidiary profit for the current period. As the realised profit is less than the recorded profit, the MI share of equity must be reduced, specifically the MI share of current period profit.

The worksheet entry in the MI columns of the worksheet is:

MI	Dr	210	
MI share of profit/(loss)	Cr		210
(20% × $1050)			

The debit adjustment shows a reduction in total equity attributable to the MI, and the credit adjustment shows a reduction in the MI share of current period's profits.

9. Sale of inventory: Ivanova Ltd to Murmansk Ltd
The entries in the adjustment columns of the worksheet are:

Sales	Dr	18 000	
Cost of sales	Cr		16 000
Inventory	Cr		2 000
Deferred tax asset	Dr	600	
Income tax expense	Cr		600

As the profit on the transaction is made by the parent entity and does not affect the equity of the subsidiary, there is no need to make any adjustment to the MI.

10. Payment for services: Murmansk Ltd to Ivanova Ltd
The entry in the adjustment columns of the worksheet is:

Other revenues	Dr	1 000	
Other expenses	Cr		1 000

The profit of the subsidiary is affected by the transaction even though the payment may in effect be from the parent to the subsidiary. However, if it is assumed that realisation occurs on payment for the services for this type of transaction, then no unrealised profit/loss exists in the subsidiary. Hence, there is no need to make any adjustment to the MI share of equity.

11. Sale of inventory in previous period: Murmansk Ltd to Ivanova Ltd
The entries in the adjustment columns of the worksheet are:

Retained earnings (1/7/06)	Dr	2 800	
Income tax expense	Dr	1 200	
Cost of sales	Cr		4 000

12. Adjustment to MI: unrealised profit in beginning inventory
The profit on this transaction was made by the subsidiary, so an adjustment to the MI share of equity is required. There are two effects on the MI because the transaction affects both last year's and the current period's figures.

First, the profit made by the subsidiary in the previous period was unrealised last year. Hence, the subsidiary's retained earnings (1/7/06) account contains $2800 unrealised profit. An adjustment is necessary to reduce the MI share of the previous period's profit. The adjustment is:

MI	Dr	560	
Retained earnings (1/7/06)	Cr		560
(20% × $2800)			

Second, in relation to the current period, as the inventory transferred last period is sold in the current period to an external entity, the profit previously recorded by the subsidiary becomes realised in the current period. Since the profit is realised to the MI in the current period but was recorded by the subsidiary last period, the MI share of current period profit needs to be increased. The adjustment is shown overleaf.

→

MI share of profit/(loss)	Dr	560	
MI	Cr		560
(20% × $2800)			

These two entries can be combined and passed in the MI columns of the worksheet:

| MI share of profit/(loss) | Dr | 560 | |
| Retained earnings (1/7/06) | Cr | | 560 |

This entry has no effect on the total MI share of equity. It simply reduces the MI share of equity recorded last period and increases the MI share of current period profit. This reflects the fact that the subsidiary recorded the profit in the previous period whereas the group recognised the profit in the current period.

13. Sale of depreciable asset in previous period: Murmansk Ltd to Ivanova Ltd
The sale occurred at the beginning of the previous period. The entries in the adjustment columns of the worksheet are:

Retained earnings (1/7/06)	Dr	14 000	
Deferred tax asset	Dr	6 000	
Plant and equipment	Cr		20 000

14. Adjustment to MI: unrealised profit in depreciable asset in previous period
Because the subsidiary recorded the profit on the transaction, the MI is affected. As the transaction occurred in the previous period, the subsidiary's recorded retained earnings (1/7/06) balance contains an after-tax unrealised profit of $14 000. The MI share of last year's profits must then be reduced by $2800 (being 20% × $14 000).
The worksheet entry in the MI columns is:

| MI | Dr | 2 800 | |
| Retained earnings (1/7/06) | Cr | | 2 800 |

Worksheet entries relating to the sale of the asset and the associated MI adjustment are made in each year of the asset's life. Realisation of this profit is dealt with in relation to the depreciation adjustment entry.

15. Depreciation on non-current asset sold
The entries in the adjustment columns of the worksheet reflect the depreciation of the transferred asset over a two-year period on a straight-line basis, given an overall asset life of 10 years (see opposite).

Accumulated depreciation	Dr	4 000	
Depreciation expense	Cr		2 000
Retained earnings (1/7/06)	Cr		2 000
(Depreciation of 10% × $20 000 p.a. for two years)			
Retained earnings (1/7/06)	Dr	600	
Income tax expense	Dr	600	
Deferred tax asset	Cr		1 200

16. Adjustment to MI: realisation of profit via depreciation

The assumption made in relation to the $14 000 unrealised profit is that realisation will occur over the life of the asset as the benefits of the depreciable asset are consumed by the group. The profit is then realised in proportion to the depreciation charged on the asset. As can be seen from adjustment entry 15, the after-tax adjustment to depreciation expense is $1400 (being $2000 – $600). In other words, the $14 000 profit recognised last period by the subsidiary will be recognised as realised to the extent of $1400 p.a. over the next 10 years. Hence, $1400 is realised in the 2005–06 period, and a further $1400 is realised in the 2006–07 period. The MI share of last year's profits is therefore increased, as is the MI share of the current period's profits.

The worksheet entry in the MI columns is:

MI share of profit/(loss)	Dr	280	
Retained earnings (1/7/06)	Dr	280	
MI	Cr		560
(20% × $1400 p.a.)			

In each of the 10 years following the transfer of the asset, the group realises an extra $1400 profit. This increases the MI share of profit by $280 per year, and effectively reverses the reduction in the MI share of profit relating to the gain on sale shown in entry 14. As the profit becomes realised over time, the MI share of equity increases. Combining the effects of entries 14 and 16, the effect on MI share of retained earnings (opening balance) over time is as follows:

MI share of retained earnings (1/7/06)	$2800 less $280
MI share of retained earnings (1/7/07)	$2800 less (2 × $280)
MI share of retained earnings (1/7/08)	$2800 less (3 × $280)
MI share of retained earnings (1/7/14)	$2800 less (9 × $280)

In the period ended 30 June 2014, the profit becomes fully realised as the asset becomes fully depreciated. In the 2014–15 period, no adjustments are necessary in relation to the transfer of the depreciable asset.

The consolidation worksheet for Ivanova Ltd at 30 June 2007 is shown in figure 22.11.

FIGURE 22.11　Consolidation worksheet showing MI and the effects of intragroup transactions

Financial statements	Ivanova Ltd	Murmansk Ltd		Adjustments Dr	Adjustments Cr		Group		Minority interest Dr	Minority interest Cr		Parent
Sales revenue	720 000	530 000	7 9	23 000 18 000			1 209 000					
Other revenues	240 000	120 000	5 6 10	4 800 12 000 1 000			342 200					
	960 000	650 000					1 551 200					
Cost of sales	610 000	410 000			21 500 16 000 4 000	7 9 11	978 500					
Other expenses	230 000	160 000			1 000 2 000	10 15	387 000					
	840 000	570 000					1 365 500					
Profit before tax	120 000	80 000					185 700					
Tax expense	40 000	25 000	11 15	1 200 600	600 450	9 7	65 750					
Profit	80 000	55 000					119 950	4 12 16	11 000 560 280	210	8	108 320
Retained earnings (1/7/06)	200 000	112 000	1 11 13 15	40 000 2 800 14 000 600	2 000	15	256 600	2 3 16	10 000 12 400 280	560 2 800	12 14	237 280
	280 000	167 000					376 550					345 600
Dividend paid	20 000	10 000			3 200 4 800	1 5	22 000			2 000	4	20 000
Dividend declared	25 000	15 000			12 000	6	28 000			3 000	4	25 000
	45 000	25 000					50 000					45 000
Retained earnings (30/6/07)	235 000	142 000					326 550					300 600
Share capital	600 000	500 000	1	400 000			700 000	2	100 000			600 000
General reserve	100 000	150 000	1	80 000			170 000	2 3	20 000 10 000			140 000
Total equity: parent												1 040 600
Total equity: MI								4 4 8 14	2 000 3 000 210 2 800	130 000 22 400 11 000 560	2 3 4 16	155 950
Total equity	935 000	792 000					1 196 550		172 530	172 530		1 196 550
Dividend payable	25 000	15 000	6	12 000			28 000					
Other liabilities	25 000	25 000					50 000					
Total liabilities	50 000	40 000					78 000					

Financial statements	Ivanova Ltd	Murmansk Ltd	Adjustments			Group	Minority interest			Parent
			Dr	Cr			Dr	Cr		
Total equity and liabilities	985 000	832 000				1 274 550				
Receivables	80 000	30 000		12 000	6	98 000				
Inventory	100 000	170 000		1 500	7	266 500				
				2 000	9					
Plant and equipment	300 000	580 000		20 000	13	860 000				
Accumulated depreciation	115 000	(88 000)	15	4 000			(199 000)			
Shares in Murmansk Ltd	516 800			516 800	1	–				
Deferred tax asset	53 200	40 000	7	450	1 200	15	99 050			
			9	600						
			13	6 000						
Other assets	50 000	100 000				150 000				
Total assets	985 000	832 000	621 050	621 050		1 274 550				

The consolidated financial statements for Ivanova Ltd and its subsidiary, Murmansk Ltd, for the year ended 30 June 2007 are as shown in figure 22.12.

FIGURE 22.12 Consolidated financial statements

Ivanova Ltd Consolidated income statement for the year ended 30 June 2007	
Revenue:	
Sales	$1 209 000
Other	342 200
Total revenue	1 551 200
Expenses:	
Cost of sales	978 500
Other	387 000
Total expenses	1 365 500
Profit before tax	185 700
Income tax expense	65 750
Profit for the period	$ 119 950
Attributable to:	
Equity holders of the parent	108 320
Minority interest	11 630
	$ 119 950

(continued)

Ivanova Ltd
Consolidated statement of changes in equity
for the year ended 30 June 2007

	Consolidated	Parent
Profit for the period	$ 119 950	$ 108 320
Net income recognised directly in equity	–	–
Total recognised income and expense for the period	$ 119 950	$ 108 320
Attributable to:		
Equity holders of the parent	$ 108 320	
Minority interest	11 630	
	$ 119 950	
Retained earnings at 1 July 2006	$256 600	$237 280
Profit for the period	119 950	108 320
Dividend paid	(22 000)	(20 000)
Dividend declared	(28 000)	(25 000)
Retained earnings at 30 June 2007	$326 550	$300 600
General reserve at 1 July 2006	$ 170 000	$ 140 000
General reserve at 30 June 2007	$ 170 000	$ 140 000
Share capital at 1 July 2006	$ 700 000	$ 600 000
Share capital at 30 June 2007	$ 700 000	$ 600 000

Ivanova Ltd
Consolidated balance sheet
as at 30 June 2007

EQUITY AND LIABILITIES

Equity attributable to equity holders of the parent

Share capital	$ 600 000
Other reserves – general reserve	140 000
Retained earnings	300 600
	1 040 600
Minority interest	155 950
Total equity	1 196 550
Liabilities	
Current liabilities – dividend payable	28 000
Non-current liabilities	50 000
Total liabilities	78 000
Total equity and liabilities	$1 274 550

ASSETS

Non-current assets

Plant and equipment	$ 860 000
Accumulated depreciation	(199 000)
Deferred tax asset	99 050
Other	150 000
	910 050
Current assets	
Receivables	$ 98 000
Inventory	266 500
	364 500
Total assets	$1 274 550

LO 8

22.6 Excess on acquisition

This chapter has used examples of business combinations in which goodwill has been acquired. In the rare case that an excess on acquisition arises, such an excess has no effect on the calculation of the MI share of equity. Further, whereas the goodwill of the subsidiary may be determined by calculating the goodwill acquired by the parent entity and then grossing this up to determine the goodwill for the subsidiary, this process is not applicable for the excess on acquisition. The excess is a gain made by the parent paying less than the net fair value of the acquirer's share of the identifiable assets, liabilities and contingent liabilities of the subsidiary. The MI receives a share of the fair value of the subsidiary, and has no involvement with the excess on acquisition.

To illustrate, assume a subsidiary has the following balance sheet:

Equity	$80 000
Identifiable net assets	$80 000

Assume all identifiable assets and liabilities of the subsidiary are recorded at amounts equal to fair value. If a parent acquires 80% of the shares of the subsidiary for $63 000, then the acquisition analysis is:

Net fair value of subsidiary	= $80 000
Net fair value acquired by parent	= 80% × $80 000
	= $64 000
Cost of combination	= $63 000
Excess	= $64 000 − $63 000
	= $1000

Assuming all fair values have been measured accurately, the consolidation worksheet entries at acquisition date are as shown below:

Business combination valuation entry
No entry is required in this simple example.

Pre-acquisition entry

Equity	Dr	64 000	
Excess – gain on acquisition	Cr		1 000
Shares in subsidiary	Cr		63 000

Minority interest (step 1)

Equity	Dr	16 000	
MI	Cr		16 000
(20% × $80 000)			

Note that the MI does not receive any share relating to the excess.

22.7 Summary

This chapter has concentrated on the effect the existence of an MI has on the preparation of the consolidated financial statements. In relation to the preparation of the entries in the consolidation worksheet, the existence of an MI has no effect on the business combination valuation entries, but it does affect the pre-acquisition entries because they reflect only the parent's acquisition in the subsidiary. The calculation of the MI share of equity is affected by the existence of intragroup transactions as the MI is entitled to a share of consolidated equity, being a contributor of equity to the group. In preparing the consolidated financial statements, the MI share of equity must be disclosed, together with the parent's share of equity.

DISCUSSION QUESTIONS

1. The consolidated financial statements are designed to show the financial performance and financial position of a group as a single economic entity. Discuss the relationship of the parent shareholders and the MI in this entity.

2. The MI is calculated in three steps, taking into consideration three time periods. What are these steps and why is this approach used in calculating the MI share of equity?

3. Although a parent does not own all the share capital of a subsidiary, it is required on consolidation to value the identifiable assets, liabilities and contingent liabilities at fair value at the acquisition date. If the cost of the combination relates only to the portion acquired by the parent, why is it necessary to fully value these assets?

4. How is the calculation of the MI affected by whether the MI is classified as a liability or as equity?

5. The consolidation worksheet contains adjustments for the effects of intragroup transactions. Why are these adjustments taken into consideration in the calculation of the MI share of equity?

6. In calculating the MI share of subsidiary equity, adjustments are made for unrealised profit on intragroup transactions. What is meant by 'unrealised profit'? When does profit become realised? Use examples to illustrate your answer.

7. When a subsidiary records interest revenue from a payment by the parent, this revenue affects the equity of the subsidiary but does not result from involvement with a party external to the group. Should this transaction affect the calculation of the MI share of equity?

8. In calculating the MI share of equity from the acquisition date to the beginning of the current period, what changes could occur between those two dates? How would they affect the calculation of the MI share of equity?

EXERCISES

EXERCISE 22.1   ★

Consolidation worksheet, consolidated financial statements

Novgorod Ltd purchased 75% of the capital of Gomel Ltd for $250 000 on 1 July 2000. At this date the equity of Gomel Ltd was:

Share capital	$100 000
General reserve	60 000
Retained earnings	40 000

At this date, Gomel Ltd had not recorded any goodwill, and all identifiable assets and liabilities were recorded at fair value except for the following assets:

	Carrying amount	Fair value
Inventory	$ 70 000	$100 000
Plant (cost $170 000)	150 000	190 000
Land	50 000	100 000

The plant has a remaining useful life of 10 years. As a result of an impairment test, all goodwill was written off in 2003. All the inventory on hand at 1 July 2000 was sold by 30 June 2001. Differences beween carrying amounts and fair values are recognised on consolidation. The tax rate is 30%.

The trial balances of Novgorod Ltd and Gomel Ltd at 30 June 2006 are:

	Novgorod Ltd	Gomel Ltd
Shares in Gomel Ltd	$ 250 000	−
Plant	425 500	$ 190 000
Land	110 000	50 000
Current assets	162 000	84 000
Cost of sales	225 000	35 000
Other expenses	65 000	7 000
Income tax expense	50 000	5 000
	$ 1 287 500	$ 371 000
Share capital	$ 400 000	$ 100 000
General reserve	60 000	80 000
Retained earnings (1/7/05)	120 000	75 000
Sales revenue	510 600	80 000
Payables	72 900	12 000
Accumulated depreciation (plant)	124 000	24 000
	$ 1 287 500	$ 371 000

Required

1. Prepare the consolidation worksheet entries immediately after acquisition date.
2. Prepare the consolidation worksheet entries for Novgorod Ltd at 30 June 2001. Assume a profit for Gomel Ltd for the 2000–01 period of $40 000.
3. Prepare the consolidated financial statements as at 30 June 2006.

EXERCISE 22.2   ★

Consolidation worksheet entries including MI

On 1 July 2000, Norilsk Ltd acquired 90% of the capital of Rudny Ltd for $290 160. The equity of Rudny Ltd at this date consisted of:

Share capital	$200 000
Retained earnings	80 000

The carrying amounts and fair values of the assets and liabilities recorded by Rudny Ltd at 1 July 2000 were as follows:

	Carrying amount	Fair value
Fittings	$ 20 000	$ 20 000
Land	90 000	100 000
Inventory	10 000	12 000
Machinery (net)	200 000	220 000
Liabilities	40 000	40 000

The machinery and fittings have a further 10-year life, benefits to be received evenly over this period. Differences between carrying amounts and fair values are recognised on consolidation.

The tax rate is 30%. All inventory on hand at 1 July 2000 is sold by 30 June 2001.

Required

1. What are the entries for the consolidation worksheet if prepared immediately after 1 July 2000?
2. What are the entries for the consolidation worksheet if prepared at 30 June 2001? Assume a profit for Rudny Ltd for the 2000–01 period of $20 000.

Consolidation worksheet entries, excess, recorded goodwill

On 1 July 2003, Odessa Ltd acquired 75% of the shares of Riga Ltd for $123 525. At this date, the balance sheet of Riga Ltd consisted of:

Share capital – 100 000 shares	$ 100 000	Cash	$ 5 000
General reserve	20 000	Inventories	20 000
Retained earnings	40 000	Plant (cost $100 000)	80 000
Liabilities	60 000	Fittings (cost $80 000)	50 000
		Receivables	5 000
		Land	60 000
	$220 000		$220 000

In relation to the assets of Riga Ltd, the fair values at 1 July 2003 were:

Cash	$ 5 000
Inventories	25 000
Plant	86 000
Fittings	51 000
Receivables	4 000
Land	80 000

The inventories were all sold and the receivables all collected by 30 June 2004. The plant and fittings each have an expected useful life of five years. The plant was sold on 1 January 2006. The tax rate is 30%.

Additional information
(a) At 1 July 2005, the retained earnings of Riga Ltd were $80 000, and the general reserve was $30 000.
(b) During the 2005–06 period, Riga Ltd recorded a profit of $15 000.
(c) In June 2005, a dividend of $8000 was declared by Riga Ltd, and was paid in August 2005. An interim dividend of $5000 was paid in January 2006, and a final dividend of $4000 declared in June 2006.

Required
Prepare the worksheet entries for the preparation of the consolidated financial statements of Odessa Ltd and its subsidiary, Riga Ltd, at 30 June 2006.

Consolidation worksheet entries, dividends, equity transfers

On 1 July 2004, Kisinev Ltd acquired 80% of the shares (cum div.) of Tula Ltd for $202 000. At this date, the equity of Tula Ltd consisted of:

Share capital – 100 000 shares	$100 000
General reserve	40 000
Retained earnings	50 000

The carrying amounts and fair values of the assets of Tula Ltd were as shown overleaf.

	Carrying amount	Fair value
Land	$70 000	$90 000
Plant (cost $100 000)	80 000	85 000
Fittings (cost $40 000)	20 000	20 000
Goodwill	5 000	10 000

Any adjustment for the differences in carrying amounts and fair values is recognised on consolidation. Both plant and fittings were expected to have a further five-year life, with benefits being received evenly over those periods. The plant was sold on 1 January 2007. In the year of the sale of plant, on consolidation the valuation reserve relating to the plant was transferred to retained earnings. At 1 July 2004, Tula Ltd had not recorded an internally generated trademark that Kisinev Ltd considered to have a fair value of $50 000. This intangible asset was considered to have an indefinite useful life.

Additional information
(a) The following profits were recorded by Tula Ltd:

For the 2004–05 period	$20 000
For the 2005–06 period	25 000
For the 2006–07 period	30 000

(b) In June 2006, Tula Ltd transferred $5000 to general reserve, and in June 2007, a further $6000 was transferred.
(c) In August 2004, the dividend payable of $5000 on hand at 1 July 2004 was paid by Tula Ltd.
(d) Other dividends declared or paid since 1 July 2004 are:
  • $8000 dividend declared in June 2005, paid in August 2005; half of this dividend was from profits earned before 1 July 2004
  • $6000 dividend declared in June 2006, paid in August 2006
  • $5000 dividend paid in December 2006
  • $8000 dividend declared in June 2007, expected to be paid in August 2007.

Required
Prepare the worksheet entries for the preparation of the consolidated financial statements of Kisinev Ltd and its subsidiary, Tula Ltd, at 30 June 2007.

EXERCISE 22.5 ★★

Consolidation worksheet entries, multiple years

On 1 July 2004, Orenburg Ltd acquired 75% of the issued shares of Kusva Ltd for $125 750. At this date, the accounts of Kusva Ltd included the following balances:

Share capital	$80 000
General reserve	20 000
Retained earnings	40 000

All the identifiable assets and liabilities of Kusva Ltd were recorded at fair value except for the following:

	Carrying amount	Fair value
Plant (cost $50 000)	$35 000	$41 000
Land	50 000	70 000
Goodwill	20 000	24 000

Adjustments for the differences between carrying amounts and fair values are to be made on consolidation. The plant has a further three-year life. All the inventory was sold by 30 June 2005.

During the four years since acquisition, Kusva Ltd has recorded the following annual results:

Year ended	Profit (loss)
30 June 2005	$10 000
30 June 2006	23 000
30 June 2007	(6 000)
30 June 2008	22 000

There have been no transfers to or from the general reserve or any dividends paid or declared by Kusva Ltd since the acquisition date.

The land owned by Kusva Ltd on 1 July 2004 was sold on 1 March 2006 for $75 000. The group transfers the valuation reserves to retained earnings when an asset is sold or fully consumed. The tax rate is 30%.

Required
1. Prepare the consolidation worksheet entries as at 1 July 2004.
2. Prepare the consolidation worksheet entries for the year ended 30 June 2005.
3. Prepare the consolidation worksheet entries for the year ended 30 June 2006.
4. Prepare the consolidation worksheet entries for the year ended 30 June 2007.
5. Prepare the consolidation worksheet entries for the year ended 30 June 2008.

EXERCISE 22.6 ★★

Consolidation worksheet entries, multiple years

On 1 July 2006, Kalinin Ltd acquired 60% of the shares of Bratsk Ltd for $111 700. At this date, the equity of Bratsk Ltd consisted of:

Share capital	$120 000
General reserve	10 000
Retained earnings	30 000

At this date, the identifiable assets and liabilities of Bratsk Ltd were recorded at fair value except for the following assets:

	Carrying amount	Fair value
Equipment (cost $80 000)	$65 000	$75 000
Land	80 000	90 000
Inventory	45 000	50 000

Adjustments for the differences between carrying amounts and fair values are to be made on consolidation. The equipment has a further five-year life. Half the inventory on hand at the acquisition date was sold by 30 June 2007, with the remainder being sold in the 2007–08 financial year. At 30 June 2009, the goodwill was written down by $3000 as the result of an impairment test.

During the three years since acquisition, Bratsk Ltd has recorded the annual results shown overleaf.

Year ended	Profit
30 June 2007	$15 000
30 June 2008	27 000
30 June 2009	12 000

There have been no transfers to or from the general reserve or any dividend paid or declared by Bratsk Ltd since the acquisition date.

The equipment owned by Bratsk Ltd on 1 July 2006 was sold on 1 January 2008 for $70 000. On consolidation, the group transfers the valuation reserve to retained earnings when an asset is sold or fully consumed. The tax rate is 30%.

Required
1. Prepare the consolidation worksheet entries as at 1 July 2006.
2. Prepare the consolidation worksheet entries for the year ended 30 June 2007.
3. Prepare the consolidation worksheet entries for the year ended 30 June 2008.
4. Prepare the consolidation worksheet entries for the year ended 30 June 2009.

EXERCISE 22.7 ★★   Consolidation worksheet, unrecorded intangible, dividends

On 1 July 2003, Kiev Ltd acquired 70% of the shares (cum div.) of Harkov Ltd for $138 950. At this date, the equity of Harkov Ltd consisted of:

Share capital	$100 000
General reserve	40 000
Retained earnings	25 000

Harkov Ltd's records showed a dividend payable at 1 July 2003 of $10 000. The dividend was paid on 1 November 2003.

A comparison of the carrying amounts and fair values of the assets of Harkov Ltd at 1 July 2003 revealed the following:

	Carrying amount	Fair value
Plant (cost $75 000)	$45 000	$60 000
Vehicles (cost $40 000)	23 000	23 000
Goodwill	10 000	

Adjustments for the differences in carrying amounts and fair values are recognised on consolidation. Both plant and vehicles were expected to have a further five-year life, with benefits being received evenly over those periods. Harkov Ltd had not recorded an internally generated brand name for an item that was considered by Kiev Ltd to have a fair value of $20 000. The brand name is regarded as having an indefinite useful life. At 30 June 2004, goodwill was considered to be impaired by $1000, and a further impairment loss of $2000 was recognised in 2005.

Additional information
(a) The dividends paid and declared since 1 July 2003 are:
  • $10 000 dividend declared in June 2004, paid in October 2004; this dividend was appropriated from profits earned before 1 July 2003
  • $5000 dividend declared in June 2005, paid in September 2005; half of this dividend was appropriated from profits earned before 1 July 2003
  • $8000 dividend paid in April 2006 from post-acquisition profits.
(b) In June 2005, Harkov Ltd transferred an amount of $20 000 from the general reserve to retained earnings.

(c) The plant on hand at 1 July 2003 was sold on 30 June 2006. On consolidation, the group decided to transfer the valuation reserve relating to the plant to retained earnings.
(d) On 30 June 2006, the financial data of both companies were:

	Kiev Ltd	Harkov Ltd
Revenues	$280 000	$190 000
Expenses	220 000	140 000
Profit before tax	60 000	50 000
Income tax expense	26 000	14 000
Profit for the period	34 000	36 000
Retained earnings (1/7/05)	76 000	65 000
Total available for appropriation	110 000	101 000
Dividend paid	20 000	8 000
Retained earnings (30/6/06)	90 000	93 000
Share capital	100 000	100 000
General reserve	50 000	20 000
Payables	20 000	12 000
	$260 000	$225 000
Current assets	$ 33 800	$ 43 000
Vehicles	35 000	50 000
Accumulated depreciation	(12 000)	(30 000)
Plant and equipment	100 000	150 000
Accumulated depreciation	(50 000)	(75 000)
Land	30 000	—
Goodwill	—	10 000
Accumulated impairment	—	(3 000)
Trademarks	—	80 000
Shares in Harkov Ltd	123 200	—
	$260 000	$225 000

Required
Prepare the consoldiated financial statements of Kiev Ltd as at 30 June 2006.

PROBLEMS

PROBLEM 22.1   ★

Consolidation worksheet, consolidated financial statements

In June 2006, Penza Ltd made an offer to the shareholders of Tambov Ltd to acquire a controlling interest in the company. Penza Ltd was prepared to pay $1.50 cash per share, provided that 70% of the shares could be acquired (enough shares to gain control).

The directors of Tambov Ltd recommended that the offer be accepted. By 1 July 2006, when the offer expired, 75% of the shares had changed hands and were now in the possession of Penza Ltd. The balance sheet of Tambov Ltd on that date is shown overleaf.

Tambov Ltd Balance sheet as at 1 July 2006	
Current assets	$368 000
Non-current assets	244 000
	$612 000
Share capital — 400 000 shares	$400 000
General reserve	120 000
Retained earnings	40 000
Current liabilities	52 000
	$612 000

At 1 July 2006, all the identifiable assets and liabilities of Tambov Ltd were recorded at fair value.

The draft financial statements of the two companies on 30 June 2007 revealed the following details:

	Penza Ltd	Tambov Ltd
Sales revenue	$ 878 900	$388 900
Cost of sales	374 400	112 400
Gross profit	504 500	276 500
Other income	302 100	112 500
	806 600	389 000
Other expenses	216 200	115 800
Profit before tax	590 400	273 200
Income tax expense	112 400	50 000
Profit	478 000	223 200
Retained earnings as at 1 July 2006	112 000	40 000
	590 000	263 200
Dividend paid	40 000	30 000
Dividend declared	50 000	10 000
	90 000	40 000
Retained earnings as at 30 June 2007	500 000	223 200
Share capital	1 200 000	400 000
General reserve	124 000	150 000
Current liabilities	177 000	124 400
	$2 001 000	$897 600
Receivables	$ 320 000	$175 000
Inventory	287 500	210 600
Investments — Shares in Tambov Ltd	435 000	—
Other investments	62 000	—
Equipment	650 000	460 000
Accumulated depreciation	(250 000)	(160 000)
Other non-current assets	496 500	212 000
	$2 001 000	$897 600

Additional information

(a) Penza Ltd had made an advance of $80 000 to Tambov Ltd. This advance was repayable in June 2008.

(b) Tambov Ltd paid an interim dividend of $30 000 during the year; $20 000 of this dividend had come from profits earned in the year ended 30 June 2006.

(c) The directors of Penza Ltd and Tambov Ltd had declared final dividends of $50 000 and $10 000 respectively, from current period's profits.

(d) Tambov Ltd holds at balance date inventory purchased from Penza Ltd during the year for $55 000. Penza Ltd invoices goods to its subsidiary at cost plus 10%.

(e) On 1 July 2006, Tambov Ltd sold to Penza Ltd some display equipment for $60 000. At that date, the carrying amount of the equipment was $52 000 and the equipment was estimated to have a useful life of 10 years if used constantly over that period.

(f) Assume a tax rate of 30%.

Required

Prepare the consolidated financial statements for Penza Ltd and its subsidiary as at 30 June 2007.

PROBLEM 22.2 ★★   Consolidation worksheet, consolidated financial statements

On 1 July 2001, Kartaly Ltd acquired 75% of the share capital of Voronez Ltd at a cost of $27 600. At this date, the capital of Voronez Ltd consisted of 30 000 ordinary shares each fully paid, and retained earnings were $6000.

At 1 July 2001, Voronez Ltd had not recorded any goodwill, and all the identifiable net assets of Voronez Ltd were recorded at fair value.

The trial balances of the two companies as at 30 June 2006 are as shown below.

Trial balances as at 30 June 2006				
	Kartaly Ltd		Voronez Ltd	
	Dr	Cr	Dr	Cr
Share capital		$ 40 000		$ 30 000
Retained earnings (1 July 2005)		19 000		14 500
General reserve				5 000
Current tax liability		8 500		2 900
Plant	$ 30 000		$ 70 000	
Accumulated depreciation – plant		17 000		30 500
Shares in Voronez Ltd	27 600			
10% debentures in Voronez Ltd	2 500			
Inventory	12 000		15 500	
Other current assets	14 050		1 500	
Deferred tax asset	2 000		5 000	
Sales revenue		50 000		80 000
Cost of sales	34 000		58 500	
Selling expenses	4 000		6 000	
Other expenses	1 500		1 500	
Financial expenses	1 500		2 000	
Income tax expense	5 000		5 500	
Interest received from debentures		250		
Dividend revenue		1 800		
Dividend paid			2 400	
10% debentures	2 400			5 000
	$136 550	$136 550	$167 900	$167 900

Additional information

(a) Intragroup sales for the year ended 30 June 2006 from Voronez Ltd to Kartaly Ltd: $19 000.

(b) Unrealised profits on inventory held at 1 July 2005: inventory held by Kartaly Ltd purchased from Voronez Ltd at a profit before tax of $800.

(c) Unrealised profits on inventory held at 30 June 2006: inventory held by Kartaly Ltd purchased from Voronez Ltd at a profit before tax of $1200.

(d) The tax rate applicable is 30c in the dollar.

Required

Prepare the consolidated financial statements for the year ended 30 June 2006.

PROBLEM 22.3 ★★   Consolidated worksheet, consolidated financial statements

On 1 July 2005, Kurgan Ltd acquired 80% of the share capital of Abakan Ltd for $264 800. This was sufficient for Kurgan Ltd to gain control over Abakan Ltd. On that date, the balance sheet of Abakan Ltd consisted of:

Share capital	$250 000
General reserve	10 000
Retained earnings	10 000
Liabilities	180 000
	$450 000
Cash	$ 35 000
Inventories	70 000
Land	50 000
Plant and equipment	300 000
Accumulated depreciation	(130 000)
Trademark	100 000
Goodwill	25 000
	$450 000

All the identifiable assets and liabilities of Abakan Ltd were recorded at fair value except for:

	Carrying amount	Fair value
Inventories	$ 70 000	$ 80 000
Land	50 000	70 000
Plant and equipment (cost $300 000)	170 000	190 000
Trademark	100 000	110 000

The plant and equipment had a further five-year life and was expected to be used evenly over that time. The trademark was considered to have an indefinite life. Any adjustments for differences between carrying amounts at acquisition date and fair values are made on consolidation.

During the year ended 30 June 2006, all inventories on hand at the beginning of the year were sold, and the land was sold on 28 February 2006 to Werst Ltd for $80 000. Any valuation reserve created in relation to the land was transferred on consolidation to retained earnings.

The income tax rate is assumed to be 30%.

The summarised income information of Kurgan Ltd and Abakan Ltd for the year ended 30 June 2006 is as shown below:

	Kurgan Ltd	Abakan Ltd
Sales revenue	$200 000	$172 000
Other income	85 000	35 000
	285 000	207 000
Cost of sales	162 000	128 000
Other expenses	53 000	31 000
	215 000	159 000
Profit before tax	70 000	48 000
Income tax expense	20 000	18 000
Profit	50 000	30 000
Retained earnings (1/7/05)	30 000	10 000
Transfer from general reserve	–	8 000
	80 000	48 000
Interim dividend paid	12 000	10 000
Final dividend declared	6 000	4 000
	18 000	14 000
Retained earnings (30/6/06)	$ 62 000	$ 34 000

Of the interim dividend paid by Abakan Ltd in the current year, $5000 was from profits earned before acquisition date. All other dividends were from the current year's profits.

During the current year, Abakan Ltd sold a quantity of inventory to Kurgan Ltd for $8000. The original cost of these items to Abakan Ltd was $5000. One-third of this inventory was still on hand at the end of the year.

On 31 March 2006, Abakan Ltd transferred an item of plant with a carrying amount of $10 000 to Kurgan Ltd for $15 000. Kurgan Ltd treated this item as inventory. The item was still on hand at the end of the year. Abakan Ltd applied a 20% depreciation rate to this type of plant.

Required

1. Prepare the consolidation worksheet entries necessary for preparation of the consolidated financial statements for Abakan Ltd and its subsidiary for the year ended 30 June 2006.
2. Prepare the consolidated income statement and statement of changes in equity for Kurgan Ltd and its subsidiary at 30 June 2006.

PROBLEM 22.4 ★★★   Consolidation worksheet entries

On 1 July 2002, Kursk Ltd acquired 75% of the shares of Belgorod Ltd for $40 000. The following balances appeared in the records of Belgorod Ltd at this date:

Share capital	$20 000
General reserve	2 000
Retained earnings	10 000

At 1 July 2002, all the identifiable assets and liabilities of Belgorod Ltd were recorded at fair value except for the following:

	Carrying amount	Fair value
Machinery (cost $36 000)	$30 000	$40 000
Inventory	16 000	20 000
Receivables	20 000	18 000

The machinery, which had a remaining useful life of five years, was adjusted to fair value after the acquisition date in the consolidation worksheet. The machinery was sold by Belgorod Ltd on 1 January 2007 for $4000, with the related valuation reserve being transferred on consolidation to retained earnings. By 30 June 2003, receivables had all been collected and inventory sold.

For the year ended 30 June 2007, the following information is available:

(a) Intragroup sales were: Belgorod Ltd to Kursk Ltd — $40 000. The mark-up on cost of all sales was 25%.

(b) At 30 June 2007, inventory of Kursk Ltd included $2000 of items acquired from Belgorod Ltd.

(c) At 30 June 2006, inventory of Kursk Ltd included goods of $1000 resulting from a sale on 1 March 2006 of non-current assets by Belgorod Ltd at a before-tax profit of $200. These items were sold by Kursk Ltd on 1 September 2006. This class of non-current assets is depreciated using a 10% depreciation rate on a straight-line basis.

(d) On 1 January 2007, Belgorod Ltd sold an item of plant to Kursk Ltd for $2000 at a before-tax profit of $800. For plant assets, Belgorod Ltd applies a 10% p.a. straight-line depreciation rate, and Kursk Ltd uses a 2.5% p.a. straight-line method.

(e) The current tax rate is 30%.

(f) All dividends declared in the current year are from post-acquisition profits except for a $4000 interim dividend declared and paid by Belgorod Ltd from pre-acquisition profits.

(g) Financial information for the year ended 30 June 2007 includes the following:

	Kursk Ltd	Belgorod Ltd
Sales revenue	$ 92 000	$52 000
Other revenue	8 000	8 000
Total revenue	100 000	60 000
Cost of sales	58 000	26 000
Other expenses:		
Selling and administrative (including depreciation)	4 000	2 000
Financial	2 000	1 000
Carrying amount of non-current assets sold	6 000	5 000
	70 000	34 000
Gross profit	30 000	26 000
Dividend revenue	3 000	–
Profit before tax	33 000	26 000
Income tax expense	13 200	10 400
Profit	19 800	15 600
Retained earnings at 1 July 2006	40 000	20 000
	59 800	35 600
Transfer to general reserve	3 800	1 000
Interim dividend paid	4 000	8 000
Final dividend declared	4 000	4 000
	11 800	13 000
Retained earnings at 30 June 2007	$ 48 000	$22 600

Required

1. Prepare the consolidation worksheet entries for the preparation of the consolidated financial statements of Kursk Ltd at 30 June 2007.
2. (a) In relation to the transaction in additional information (c), prepare the adjustment entry for the consolidation worksheet for the period ending 30 June 2006.
   (b) Explain, in relation to the transaction in additional information (c), the rationale for the related MI entry for the period ending 30 June 2007.

PROBLEM 22.5 ★★★   Consolidation worksheet entries, recorded goodwill, leases

At 1 July 2005, Smolensk Ltd acquired 80% of the share capital of Toropec Ltd for $290 000. At this date the balance sheet of Toropec Ltd, including comparative information on fair values for assets, was as shown below.

		Carrying amount	Fair value
Current assets			
Inventory		$ 60 000	$ 65 000
Receivables	$ 40 000		
Allowance for doubtful debts	5 000	35 000	35 000
Total current assets		95 000	
Non-current assets			
Plant and machinery (at cost)	200 000		
Accumulated depreciation	125 000	75 000	90 000
Vehicles (at cost)	80 000		
Accumulated depreciation	10 000	70 000	75 000
Buildings (at cost)	120 000		
Accumulated depreciation	5 000	115 000	115 000
Trademark (at valuation)		100 000	100 000
Other assets		40 000	40 000
Goodwill		20 000	
Total non-current assets		420 000	
Total assets		$515 000	
Equity			
Share capital		$200 000	
Asset revaluation surplus		50 000	
Retained earnings		50 000	
Total equity		300 000	
Current liabilities			
Accounts payable		40 000	
Dividend payable		20 000	
Total current liabilities		60 000	
Non-current liabilities			
Debentures		155 000	
Total liabilities		215 000	
Total equity and liabilities		$515 000	

At 1 July 2005, it was expected that the depreciable assets had the following remaining useful lives:

Plant and machinery	5 years
Vehicles	10 years
Trademark	100 years
Buildings	10 years

All the inventory on hand at 1 July 2005 was sold by Toropec Ltd by 30 June 2006. Adjustments for differences between fair values and carrying amounts at acquisition date are made on consolidation. The tax rate is 30%.

Additional information
(a) The dividend payable in the records of Toropec Ltd at 1 July 2005 was paid in September 2005.
(b) On 1 January 2008, one of the machines that was on hand in Toropec Ltd at 1 July 2005 was sold for $6000. At 1 July 2005, the machine was recorded at cost of $50 000 with accumulated depreciation of $30 000, and had a fair value of $23 000. Any related revaluation reserve was transferred on consolidation to retained earnings.
(c) During the 2007–08 period, Toropec Ltd transferred $10 000 from the asset revaluation surplus (on hand at 1 July 2005) to retained earnings, and transferred $20 000 to general reserve from retained earnings.
(d) Information on dividends paid and declared is as follows:
   2005–06 period:
   • paid a $5000 dividend from equity earned before 1 July 2005
   2006–07 period:
   • paid a $4000 interim dividend
   • declared, in June 2007, a $6000 dividend
   2007–08 period:
   • paid the $6000 dividend declared in the previous period
   • paid a $5000 interim dividend
   • declared, in June 2008, an $8000 dividend.
(e) Information on inventory sold by Toropec Ltd to Smolensk Ltd at cost plus 25%:
   • At 1 July 2007, Smolensk Ltd had $10 000 of inventory on hand.
   • During the 2007–08 period, $50 000 worth of inventory was sold, with 10% still on hand in Smolensk Ltd at 30 June 2008.
(f) On 1 July 2007, Smolensk Ltd leased a machine from Toropec Ltd under a direct financing lease arrangement. The fair vaue of the asset leased was $25 000, and the lease agreement had an implicit interest rate of 10%. The lease term was for the whole of the machine's useful life, being five years. The residual value at the end of the lease term was expected to be zero. At 30 June 2008, Smolensk Ltd made a lease payment to Toropec Ltd of $7500, which included an amount of $1500 to cover the costs of insurance and maintenance, both supplied by Toropec Ltd.
(g) The retained earnings balance at 30 June 2007 in Toropec Ltd was $60 000. The profit for the year ended 30 June 2008 was $25 000.

Required
Prepare consolidated worksheet journal entries for preparing the consolidated financial statements of Smolensk Ltd at 30 June 2008.

Consolidation worksheet entries

On 1 July 2003, Kaunas Ltd acquired (cum div.) a 70% interest in Rovno Ltd. The following balances appeared in the records of Rovno Ltd at this date:

Share capital – 100 000 shares	$100 000
General reserve	20 000
Retained earnings	52 000
Dividend payable	5 000

At 1 July 2003, a comparison of the carrying amounts and fair values of Rovno Ltd's identifiable assets and liabilities revealed the following:

	Carrying amount	Fair value
Cash	$ 10 000	$ 10 000
Accounts receivable	28 000	26 000
Inventory	51 000	55 000
Vehicles (cost $25 000)	17 000	18 000
Plant (cost $100 000)	66 000	70 000
Furniture and fittings (cost $60 000)	34 500	34 500
	206 500	213 500
Dividend payable	5 000	5 000
Provisions	33 000	33 000
	38 000	38 000
Identifiable assets and liabilities	$168 500	$175 500

Any differences between carrying amounts at acquisition and fair values are adjusted on consolidation. The non-current assets were deemed to have the following remaining useful lives:

Vehicles	5 years
Plant	8 years
Furniture and fittings	7 years

In addition, Rovno Ltd had recorded goodwill of $3500 at 1 July 2003. The following events occurred between the acquisition date and 30 June 2006.
(a) By 30 June 2004, 80% of the inventory on hand at 1 July 2003 had been sold, and all accounts receivable deemed to be collectable at 1 July 2003 had been received.
(b) On 15 September 2003, the dividend declared as at 1 July 2003 was paid.
(c) On 15 March 2004, Rovno Ltd paid a $12 000 dividend from profits earned before 1 July 2003.
(d) On 30 June 2005, Rovno Ltd transferred $15 000 from pre-acquisition retained earnings to the general reserve.
(e) On 1 January 2006, Rovno Ltd paid a bonus share dividend from the general reserve, the dividend being one share for each ten held.
(f) On 20 June 2006, Rovno Ltd declared a dividend of $5000 from pre-acquisition profits. The dividend was paid on 10 October 2006.
For the year ended 30 June 2007, the following information is available:
(a) The dividend declared during the year was 50% from pre-acquisition and 50% from post-acquisition profits.

(b) Kaunas Ltd recognises dividend revenue when the dividends are declared by Rovno Ltd.
(c) The transfer was from pre-acquisition reserves.
(d) The balance of the 'Shares in Rovno Ltd' account was $101 880 at 30 June 2007.
(e) On 30 June 2007, vehicles on hand at the acquisition date were sold for $6500. Any related valuation reserve was transferred on consolidation to retained earnings.
(f) The company tax rate is 30%.
(g) Financial information for the year ended 30 June 2007 included the following:

	Kaunas Ltd	Rovno Ltd
Profit before tax	$42 000	$36 000
Income tax expense	16 800	14 400
Profit	25 200	21 600
Retained earnings (1/7/06)	55 600	66 800
Transfer from general reserve	–	10 000
Total available for appropriation	80 800	98 400
Dividend paid	15 000	8 000
Dividend declared	10 000	16 000
	25 000	24 000
Retained earnings (30/6/07)	$55 800	$74 400

Required
Prepare the consolidation worksheet entries for the preparation of the consolidated financial statements of Kaunas Ltd at 30 June 2007.

PROBLEM 22.7   Consolidation worksheet, revaluation in subsidiary's records

On 1 July 2004, Vinnica Ltd acquired 80% of the share capital of Baranovici Ltd for $198 000. At this date, the equity of Baranovici Ltd consisted of:

Share capital	$150 000
General reserve	30 000
Retained earnings	20 000

At 1 July 2004, all the identifiable assets and liabilities of Baranovici Ltd were recorded at fair value except for the following assets:

	Carrying amount	Fair value
Plant (cost $120 000)	$90 000	$100 000
Land	80 000	120 000

The plant had a further five-year life, with benefits expected to be received evenly over that period. The land was sold by Baranovici Ltd in January 2006 for $150 000. Baranovici Ltd had revalued both these assets in its records at 1 July 2004.

Financial information for these two companies at 30 June 2006 included:

	Vinnica Ltd	Baranovici Ltd
Sales revenue	$920 000	$780 000
Other income	65 000	82 000
	985 000	862 000
Cost of sales	622 000	580 000
Other expenses	223 000	162 000
	845 000	742 000
Profit before tax	140 000	120 000
Income tax expense	30 000	40 000
Profit	110 000	80 000
Retained earnings (1/7/05)	80 000	60 000
Transfer from asset revaluation surplus		28 000
	190 000	168 000
Transfer to general reserve		15 000
Dividend paid	20 000	15 000
Dividend declared	25 000	20 000
	45 000	50 000
Retained earnings (30/6/06)	$145 000	$118 000

Additional information
(a) All dividends paid or provided for by Baranovici Ltd are from post-acquisition profits except for half of the $10 000 dividend declared in June 2005 and paid in August 2005.
(b) In the 2004–05 period, Baranovici Ltd transferred $10 000 from the general reserve to retained earnings. No other transfers to or from reserves took place in that period. In the 2005–06 period, the transfer from asset revaluation surplus is as a result of Baranovici Ltd's selling of the land on hand at 1 July 2004. The transfer to general reserve is from post-acquisition profits. The balance of Baranovici Ltd's asset revaluation surplus at 1 July 2005 was $50 000, with an increase of $5000 recognised at 30 June 2006.
(c) During the 2004–05 period, Baranovici Ltd sold some inventory to Vinnica Ltd for $8000. This had originally cost Baranovici Ltd $6000. At 30 June 2005, 10% of these goods remained unsold by Vinnica Ltd.
(d) The ending inventory of Vinnica Ltd included inventory sold to it by Baranovici Ltd at a profit of $3000 before tax. This had cost Baranovici Ltd $32 000.
(e) On 1 January 2005, Baranovici Ltd sold an item of inventory to Vinnica Ltd for $50 000. This had originally cost Baranovici Ltd $40 000. Vinnica Ltd uses the item as a non-current asset (plant) and depreciates it on a straight-line basis over a five-year period.
(f) The tax rate is 30%.

Required
1. Prepare the consolidation worksheet entries for the preparation of the consolidated financial statements of Vinnica Ltd at 30 June 2006.
2. Prepare the consolidated income statement and statement of changes in equity at 30 June 2006.

PROBLEM 22.8   ★★★   Consolidation worksheet, consolidated financial statements

Financial information at 30 June 2008 of Kazan Ltd and its subsidiary company, Sevastopol Ltd included that shown below.

	Kazan Ltd	Sevastopol Ltd
Sales revenue	$316 000	$220 000
Other revenue:		
Debenture interest	5 000	–
Management and consulting fees	5 000	–
Dividend from Sevastopol Ltd	12 000	–
Total revenues	338 000	220 000
Cost of sales	130 000	85 000
Manufacturing expenses	90 000	60 000
Depreciation on plant	15 000	15 000
Administrative	15 000	8 000
Financial	11 000	5 000
Other expenses	14 000	12 000
Total expenses	275 000	185 000
Profit before tax	63 000	35 000
Income tax expense	25 000	17 000
Profit	38 000	18 000
Retained earnings (1/7/07)	50 000	45 000
	88 000	63 000
Transfer to general reserve	3 000	–
Interim dividend paid	10 000	10 000
Final dividend declared	10 000	5 000
	23 000	15 000
Retained earnings (30/6/08)	65 000	48 000
General reserve	63 000	20 000
Share capital	300 000	100 000
Debentures	200 000	100 000
Current tax liability	25 000	17 000
Dividend payable	10 000	5 000
Deferred tax liability	–	7 000
Other liabilities	90 000	12 000
	$753 000	$309 000
Debentures in Sevastopol Ltd	$ 100 000	–
Shares in Sevastopol Ltd	130 000	–
Plant (cost)	120 000	$ 102 000
Accumulated depreciation – plant	(65 000)	(55 000)
Other depreciable assets	126 000	115 000
Accumulated depreciation	(40 000)	(25 000)
Inventory	90 000	85 000
Deferred tax asset	87 000	30 000
Land	201 000	57 000
Dividend receivable	4 000	–
	$753 000	$309 000

At 1 July 2005, the date Kazan Ltd acquired its 80% shareholding in Sevastopol Ltd, all the identifiable assets and liabilities of Sevastopol Ltd were at fair value except for the following assets:

	Carrying amount	Fair value
Plant (cost $75 000)	$50 000	$55 000
Land	30 000	38 000

The plant has an expected life of 10 years, with benefits being received evenly over that period. Differences between carrying amounts and fair values are adjusted on consolidation. The land on hand at 1 July 2005 was sold on 1 February 2006 for $40 000. Any valuation reserve in relation to the land is transferred on consolidation to retained earnings.

Additional information
(a) At the acquisition date of 80% of its issued shares by Kazan Ltd, the equity of Sevastopol Ltd was:

Share capital (100 000 shares)	$100 000
General reserve	3 000
Retained earnings	37 000

The balance of pre-acquisition profit was drawn upon in June 2007 when the directors of Sevastopol Ltd paid a 2% dividend from it.
(b) Inventory on hand of Sevastopol Ltd at 1 July 2007 included a quantity priced at $10 000 that had been sold to Sevastopol Ltd by its parent. This inventory had cost Kazan Ltd $7500. It was all sold by Sevastopol Ltd during the year.
(c) In Kazan Ltd's inventory at 30 June 2008 were various items sold to it by Sevastopol Ltd at $5000 above cost.
(d) During the year, intragroup sales by Sevastopol Ltd to Kazan Ltd were $60 000.
(e) It was also learned that Sevastopol Ltd had sold to Kazan Ltd an item from its inventory for $20 000 on 1 January 2007. Kazan Ltd had treated this item as an addition to its plant and machinery. The item was put into service as soon as received by Kazan Ltd and depreciation charged at 20% p.a. The item had been fully imported by Sevastopol Ltd at a landed cost of $15 000.
(f) Management and consulting fees derived by Kazan Ltd were all from Sevastopol Ltd and represented charges made for administration $2200 and technical services $2800. The latter were charged by Sevastopol Ltd to manufacturing expenses.
(g) All debentures issued by Sevastopol Ltd are held by Kazan Ltd.
(h) The tax rate is 30%.

Required
Prepare the consolidated financial statements for Kazan Ltd and its subsidiary, Sevastopol Ltd, for the year ended 30 June 2008.

Visit these websites for additional information:
WEBLINK

www.iasb.org   www.iasplus.com
www.asic.gov.au   www.ifac.org
www.aasb.com.au   www.nzica.com
www.accaglobal.com   www.capa.com.my

CHAPTER 23
Consolidated financial statements: indirect ownership interests

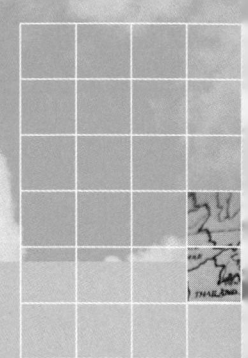

ACCOUNTING STANDARDS	International: IAS 27 *Consolidated and Separate Financial Statements*
	Australia: AASB 127 *Consolidated and Separate Financial Statements*
	New Zealand: NZ IAS 27 *Consolidated and Separate Financial Statements*

CONCEPTS FOR REVIEW

Before studying this chapter, you should understand or, if necessary, revise:

- the consolidation process for a group containing a parent and a single subsidiary
- the nature and calculation of the minority interest (MI) share of equity.

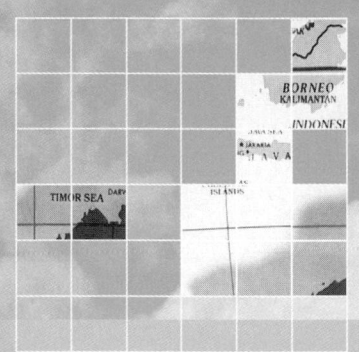

LEARNING OBJECTIVES

When you have studied this chapter, you should be able to:

1. explain the difference between direct minority interest (DMI) and indirect minority interest (IMI)
2. understand the difference between sequential and non-sequential acquisitions
3. explain why and how the calculation of the DMI and IMI is different
4. calculate the MI share of equity in a sequential acquisition situation
5. adjust for the effects of intragroup transactions within a group containing multiple subsidiaries
6. adjust for the effects of dividends paid and declared within a group containing multiple subsidiaries
7. prepare a set of consolidated financial statements for a parent with multiple subsidiaries
8. explain the effects on the consolidation process where the acquisition is non-sequential
9. explain the nature of reciprocal ownership between subsidiaries
10. calculate the MI share of equity for a group containing reciprocal ownership interests.

23.1 Introduction

In chapter 22, the group under discussion consisted of two companies in which the parent had a partial interest in the subsidiary. Hence, in the subsidiary, there were two ownership interests: the parent and the minority interest (MI). In this chapter there are two different forms of group discussed. First, the parent may have an interest in a subsidiary that has an interest in a subsidiary of its own. Some examples of this are given in figure 23.1.

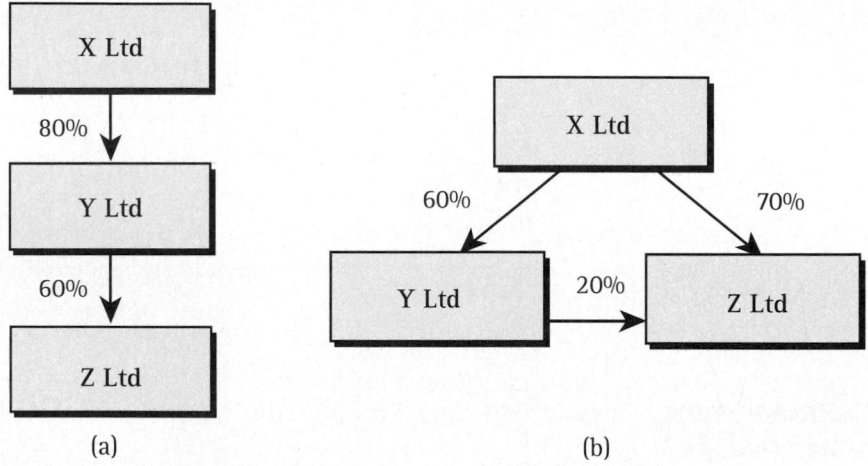

FIGURE 23.1   Indirect ownership interests

Note in both the structures illustrated in figure 23.1 that the parent, X Ltd, has an interest in Z Ltd indirectly through Y Ltd. In (a), X Ltd has a 48% indirect interest in Z Ltd (i.e. 80% × 60%). In (b) X Ltd has an 82% interest in Z Ltd: a 70% direct interest and a 12% (i.e. 60% × 20%) indirect interest via Y Ltd. This form of structure gives rise to two types of MI: a direct minority interest (DMI) and an indirect minority interest (IMI); these are explained in more detail later in this chapter.

The second structure discussed in this chapter is where a parent and a subsidiary have ownership interests in each other, or where subsidiaries have ownership interests in each other. These are referred to as reciprocal ownerships. Examples of such structures are shown in figure 23.2.

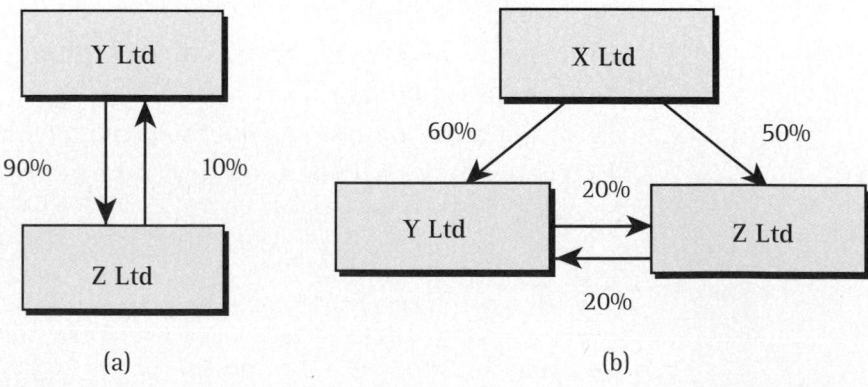

FIGURE 23.2   Reciprocal holdings

In both diagrams in figure 23.1, Y Ltd and Z Ltd hold shares in each other.

23.2 Direct and indirect minority interest (MI)

One feature of multiple subsidiary structures where a parent has an interest in a subsidiary that is itself a parent of another subsidiary is the need to classify the MI ownership in the subsidiaries into direct MI (DMI) and indirect MI (IMI). Consider the group in figure 23.3.

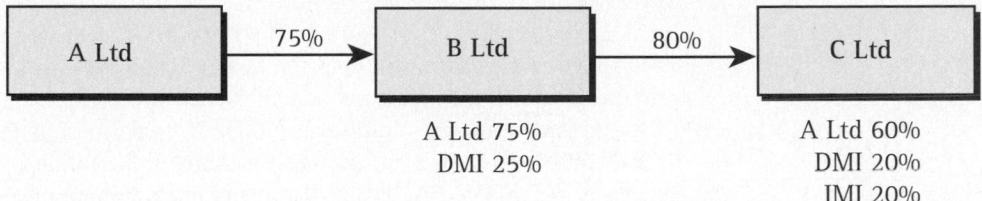

FIGURE 23.3 Group with both IMI and DMI

In relation to B Ltd, the MI has a direct ownership in this entity. Hence, the MI of 25% is classified as a DMI. In relation to C Ltd, as B Ltd owns 80% of C Ltd, there is a DMI of 20% (i.e. an MI that holds shares directly in C Ltd). B Ltd owns 80% of C Ltd, but B Ltd has two owners: A Ltd (75%) and the DMI (25%). Hence, A Ltd owns 60% of C Ltd, being 75% × 80%, while the DMI in B Ltd owns 20%, being 25% × 80%, of C Ltd. The DMI in B Ltd's ownership in C Ltd is referred to as an IMI in C Ltd as the DMI in B Ltd does not directly own shares in C Ltd; its ownership in C Ltd is indirectly through B Ltd. It is important to note that the IMI in C Ltd is the same party as the DMI in B Ltd.

Figure 23.4 provides another example of the existence of an IMI.

Note in figure 23.4 that if A Ltd's ownership in B Ltd was changed to 100% there would be no IMI in C Ltd. For an IMI to exist there has to be a DMI in the immediate parent of that entity.

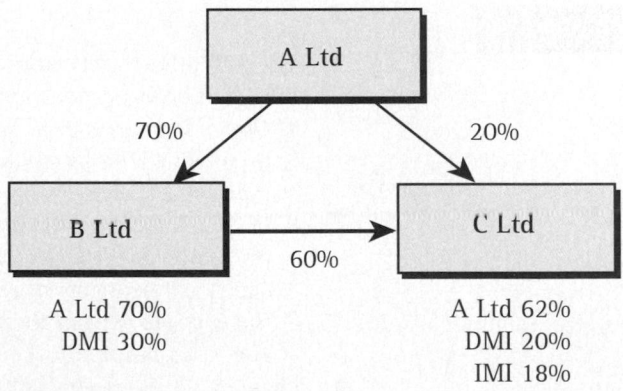

FIGURE 23.4 Indirect and direct MI

23.3 Sequential acquisitions

In accounting for multiple subsidiary structures, such as in figure 23.3 where A Ltd holds shares in B Ltd which holds shares in C Ltd, the accounting treatment depends on the sequence in which the acquisitions occurred. In this chapter, a *sequential acquisition* is one where A Ltd acquires its shares in B Ltd before B Ltd acquires its shares in C Ltd, or both acquisitions occur on the same date. A *non-sequential acquisition* is one where B Ltd acquires its shares in C Ltd prior to A Ltd acquiring its shares in B Ltd. As is discussed in more detail in section 23.4, the problem with a non-sequential acquisition is that when A Ltd acquires its shares in B Ltd, one of the assets of B Ltd is 'shares in C Ltd'; that is, the fair value of B Ltd is affected by the fair value of C Ltd.

In dealing with sequential acquisitions, what differences arise in preparing consolidated financial statements for a multiple acquisition subsidiary structure such as in figure 23.5?

FIGURE 23.5 Group with both IMI and DMI

The steps involved in preparing the consolidation worksheet are essentially the same as outlined in previous chapters; the main difference is that there are two business combinations rather than one. The combining of P Ltd and A Ltd and the combining of A Ltd and B Ltd are analysed in exactly the same fashion as for any two-entity combination because the combination involves the two companies in the transaction. It does not matter which of the two combinations is analysed first. Hence:

- the acquisition analysis, business combination valuation entries and pre-acquisition entries for P Ltd's acquisition of A Ltd are unchanged from that demonstrated in previous chapters.
- the acquisition analysis, business combination valuation entries and pre-acquisition entries for A Ltd's acquisition of B Ltd are unchanged from that demonstrated in previous chapters.

The accounting for intragroup transactions does not change from that discussed in chapter 21. If the transactions are within the group, the effects of these transactions must be adjusted for in full. This is regardless of whether B Ltd sells to P Ltd, or A Ltd sells to B Ltd or any other combination of entities is involved. The only area where a difference occurs is with dividends, and this is discussed in section 23.3.3.

The major area of difference when multiple subsidiaries are involved is the calculation of the MI share of equity.

LO 3

23.3.1 Calculation of MI share of equity

The difference in accounting for the MI arises because of the existence of both a DMI and an IMI. The basic rules are as follows:

- *Direct MI* receives a proportionate share of all equity recorded by the subsidiary — these equity balances include both *pre-acquisition* and *post-acquisition* amounts.
- *Indirect MI* receives a proportionate share of a subsidiary's *post-acquisition* equity only.
- In calculating the MI share of equity, it is consolidated equity rather than recorded equity on which the MI is calculated. Hence, in calculating both the DMI and IMI share of equity, adjustments must be made to eliminate any unrealised profits/losses arising from transactions within the group.

The calculation of the DMI share of equity is therefore the same as illustrated in chapter 22. The extra adjustments have to be made for the IMI as it receives a share of post-acquisition equity only. First, however, why is the IMI limited to a share of post-acquisition equity only? Consider the group of P Ltd in figure 23.6.

In analysing why the IMI receives a share of only post-acquisition equity, it is important to remember that an IMI arises only when a partly owned subsidiary holds shares in another subsidiary. In figure 23.6, the IMI arises in B Ltd only because there exists a DMI in A Ltd. The DMI in A Ltd is the same group of shareholders as the IMI in B Ltd.

The DMI in A Ltd is entitled to a share of the net assets of A Ltd. This share is calculated as a 30% share of the equity of A Ltd. However, one of the assets of A Ltd is the investment Shares in B Ltd, which reflects the right of A Ltd to 60% of the net assets of B Ltd. As the IMI in B Ltd is the same party as the DMI in A Ltd, it would be double counting to give the IMI a share of the equity of B Ltd relating to the pre-acquisition assets of B Ltd. The double counting issue arises because the investment, Shares in B Ltd, reflects the pre-acquisition equity and assets of B Ltd. When B Ltd earns post-acquisition equity, represented by post-acquisition assets, this equity is not reflected in A Ltd because the investment account, shares in B Ltd, is recorded at cost. Hence, the double counting issue does not arise in relation to B Ltd's post-acquisition equity, and the IMI is then given a share of the post-acquisition equity of B Ltd.

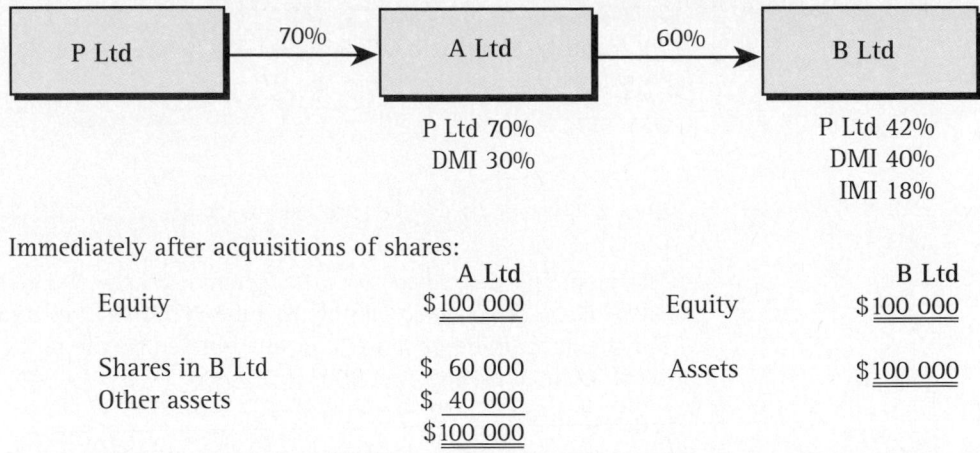

Immediately after acquisitions of shares:

	A Ltd			B Ltd
Equity	$100 000		Equity	$100 000
Shares in B Ltd	$ 60 000		Assets	$100 000
Other assets	$ 40 000			
	$100 000			

FIGURE 23.6 Group with both IMI and DMI

In relation to the pre-acquisition equity of B Ltd, it can be seen that 60% is eliminated in the pre-acquisition entry for A Ltd's acquisition of B Ltd and the DMI in B Ltd is given a 40% direct share. This effectively allocates all the pre-acquisition equity of B Ltd — there is none left for the IMI. This is not a problem because, as explained above, the IMI is entitled to a share of post-acquisition equity only.

As explained in previous chapters, where assets are recorded at amounts that differ from fair value, these affect *pre-acquisition* equity. In other words, as goodwill is impaired, inventory sold or non-current assets depreciated, there is an adjustment made to the balance of pre-acquisition amounts via the business combination valuation entries. As the IMI receives a share of post-acquisition equity only, the adjustment to pre-acquisition equity reflected through the pre-acquisition entry must be considered when calculating the IMI share of equity.

As explained in chapter 22, the calculation of the MI share of equity takes place in three steps:
• share of equity at acquisition date
• share of changes in equity from acquisition date to the beginning of the current period
• share of changes in equity in the current period.

There are only *two steps* in calculating the IMI share of equity. Since, by definition, all the equity on hand at acquisition date is *pre-acquisition*, the IMI does not receive a share of equity at that date.

ILLUSTRATIVE EXAMPLE 23.1

Calculation of the MI share of equity

LO 4

Using the P Ltd – A Ltd – B Ltd example in figure 23.6, assume A Ltd pays $55 200 for its 60% interest in B Ltd when the equity of B Ltd at 1 July 2003 is:

Share capital	$40 000
General reserve	30 000
Retained earnings	15 000

All identifiable assets and liabilities of B Ltd are recorded at fair value except for the following:

	Carrying amount	Fair value
Plant	$50 000	$55 000
Inventory	20 000	25 000

The plant is expected to last a further five years. Of the inventory, 90% is sold by 30 June 2004 and it is all sold by 30 June 2005. The tax rate is 30%.

For the accounting period ending 30 June 2005, the profit is $10 000, and the balance of retained earnings (1/7/04) is $24 000.

Required

Prepare the consolidation worksheet entries relating to A Ltd's acquisition of B Ltd, including the MI entries relating to B Ltd, required for the preparation of the consolidated financial statements at 30 June 2005.

Solution

Acquisition analysis

At 1 July 2003:
Net fair value of the identifiable assets,
   liabilities and contingent liabilities of B Ltd = $40 000 (capital) + $30 000 (reserve)
                                    + $15 000 (retained earnings)
                                    + $5000 (1 − 0.3) (BCVR − plant)
                                    + $5000 (1 − 0.3) (BCVR − inventory)
                                  = $92 000
Net fair value acquired by A Ltd   = 60% × $92 000
                                    = $55 200
Cost of combination   = $55 200
Goodwill/excess   = zero

The consolidation worksheet entries at 30 June 2005 are:

1. Business combination valuation entries

Plant	Dr	5 000	
Deferred tax liability	Cr		1 500
Business combination valuation reserve	Cr		3 500
Depreciation expense	Dr	1 000	
Retained earnings (1/7/04)	Dr	1 000	
Accumulated depreciation	Cr		2 000
(20% × $5000 p.a.)			
Deferred tax liability	Dr	600	
Income tax expense	Cr		300
Retained earnings (1/7/04)	Cr		300
Cost of sales	Dr	500	
Income tax expense	Cr		150
Transfer from business combination			
valuation reserve	Cr		350

2. Pre-acquisition entries

At 1 July 2003:			
Retained earnings (1/7/03)	Dr	9 000	
Share capital	Dr	24 000	
General reserve	Dr	18 000	
Business combination valuation reserve	Dr	4 200	
Shares in B Ltd	Cr		55 200
(60% of equity balances)			

At 30 June 2005, the inventory has been all sold, resulting in a transfer of valuation reserve to retained earnings.

Retained earnings (1/7/04)*	Dr	10 890	
Share capital	Dr	24 000	
General reserve	Dr	18 000	
Business combination valuation reserve	Dr	2 310	
Shares in B Ltd	Cr		55 200

* $10 890 = 60% [$15 000 + 90%($5000 − $1500) (inventory sold in prior period)]

Transfer from business combination			
valuation reserve	Dr	210	
Business combination valuation reserve	Cr		210

3. MI share of equity at acquisition date, 1 July 2003 (step 1)

The DMI receives a share of the equity on hand at acquisition date. As this equity is pre-acquisition, the IMI does not receive a share. The entry in the MI columns is:

Retained earnings (1/7/04)	Dr	6 000	
Share capital	Dr	16 000	
General reserve	Dr	12 000	
Business combination valuation reserve*	Dr	2 800	
MI	Cr		36 800
(40% of balances)			

* $2800 = 40% of BCVR of $7000 at acquisition date

4. MI share of changes in equity from 1 July 2003 to 30 June 2004 (step 2)

DMI share

The DMI of 40% in B Ltd is entitled to a share of the change in equity from 1 July 2003 to 30 June 2004. The *retained earnings* balance has changed from $15 000 at acquisition date to $24 000 at 30 June 2004. To avoid double counting the MI share of equity, an adjustment must be made for the depreciation of plant as evidenced in the valuation entry. The entry in the MI columns of the worksheet is:

Retained earnings (1/7/04)	Dr	3 320	
MI	Cr		3 320
(40% × [$24 000 − $15 000 − ($1000 − $300)])			

The DMI is also affected by the transfer on consolidation of $3150 from the business combination valuation reserve on sale of 90% of the inventory. The entry is:

MI	Dr	1 260	
Business combination valuation reserve	Cr		1 260
(40% × 90% × $3500)			

IMI share

The IMI of 18% in B Ltd is entitled to a share of post-acquisition changes in equity over this period. The retained earnings balance of $24 000 at 30 June 2004 contains three items relating to pre-acquisition equity:

- the $15 000 balance on hand at acquisition date
- there has been a $3150 transfer from the business combination valuation reserve relating to the 90% of inventory sold
- there has been a $700 after-tax depreciation charge in relation to the plant.

In relation to the first two of these items, the effect can be read from an analysis of the pre-acquisition entry at 30 June 2005. In this entry, there is a debit adjustment to retained earnings (1/7/04) of $10 890. This amount reflects 60% (the parent's share) of the pre-acquisition subsidiary balance at 1 July 2004. The total balance of B Ltd's pre-acquisition retained earnings is then $10 890/0.6, which is $18 150.

The post-acquisition equity in the retained earnings (1/7/04) balance is then:

$$\$24\,000 - \$10\,890/0.6 - (\$1000 - \$300) = \$5150$$

The IMI share of this is $927, being 18% × $5150. The worksheet entry at 30 June 2005 in the MI columns is:

Retained earnings (1/7/04)	Dr	927	
MI	Cr		927

There is no need for any entry relating to the business combination valuation reserve. First, this is pre-acquisition equity, and second, the effects of the transfer have been taken into consideration in the grossing-up process with retained earnings.

5. MI share of equity from 1 July 2004 to 30 June 2005 (step 3)
During this period, B Ltd records a profit of $10 000.

DMI share

The DMI share of profit is adjusted for the effects of the depreciation on plant and the sale of the rest of the inventory, as evidenced in the valuation entry. The entry in the MI columns of the worksheet is:

MI share of profit	Dr	3 580	
MI	Cr		3 580
(40% × [$10 000 − ($1000 − $300) − ($500 − $150)])			

Besides the increase in equity caused by the earning of profit, the equity of B Ltd in the current period is affected by the transfer from business combination valuation reserve to retained earnings of $350 as a result of the sale of inventory that was on hand at acquisition date. This equity change is a movement within pre-acquisition equity and therefore affects only the DMI, not the IMI. The entry in the MI columns of the worksheet is:

Transfer from business combination valuation reserve	Dr	140	
Business combination valuation reserve	Cr		140
(40% × $350)			

IMI share

In the pre-acquisition entry at 30 June 2005, there are no adjustments to current period profit, indicating that there are no items affecting pre-acquisition equity that require an adjustment in the calculation of the IMI share of current period profit. However, as with the DMI calculation, an adjustment must be made for the depreciation on the plant and the sale of the remaining inventory. The entry in the MI columns is:

MI share of profit	Dr	1 611	
MI	Cr		1 611
(18% × [$10 000 − ($1000 − $300) − ($500 − $350)])			

23.3.2 The effects of intragroup transactions on the calculation of MI

As noted earlier, the adjustments for the effects of transactions within the group in structures, such as in figure 23.7, are the same as those for the two-company structure illustrated in chapter 22. The effects of the transactions must be adjusted in full regardless of the amount of MI existing in any entity.

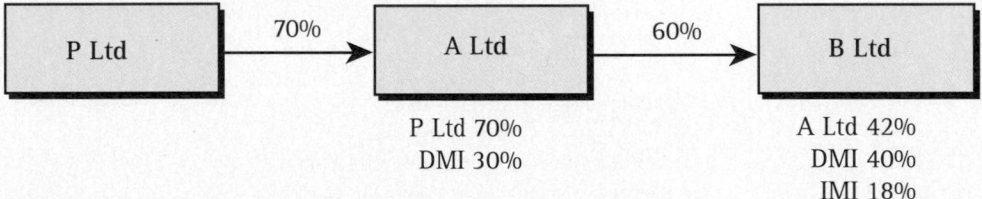

FIGURE 23.7   Group with both IMI and DMI

What must be considered is the effect on the MI of such adjustments. The key to this is determining which entity recorded the profit on the transaction. Using the structure in figure 23.7:

- if A Ltd earned the profit/loss — whether by selling to P Ltd or B Ltd — the MI adjustment is based on the 30% DMI in A Ltd.
- if B Ltd made the profit/loss — whether by selling to P Ltd or A Ltd — the MI adjustment is based on the total MI in B Ltd of 58%, which is the sum of the 40% DMI and 18% IMI.

Assume that, during the current period, B Ltd sold $25 000 of inventory to P Ltd at a profit before tax of $5000. The inventory is on hand at the end of the year.

The consolidation worksheet entries are:

Sale of inventory: B Ltd to P Ltd

Sales	Dr	25 000	
Cost of sales	Cr		20 000
Inventory	Cr		5 000
Deferred tax asset	Dr	1 500	
Income tax expense	Cr		1 500

Adjustment to MI in B Ltd

MI	Dr	2 030	
MI share of profit	Cr		2 030
([40% + 18%] × [$5000 − $1500])			

Where items of property, plant and equipment are transferred within the group, the effects of the existence of an IMI must be taken into account. For example, assume B Ltd at the beginning of the previous year sold plant to A Ltd for $800 000 at a profit before tax of $20 000, with the asset having an expected life of five years.

The consolidation worksheet entries are:

Transfer of plant: B Ltd to A Ltd

Retained earnings (opening balance)	Dr	14 000	
Deferred tax asset	Dr	6 000	
Plant	Cr		20 000

Adjustment to MI

MI	Dr	8 120	
Retained earnings (opening balance)	Cr		8 120
([40% + 18%] × $14 000)			

Depreciation of plant

Accumulated depreciation	Dr	8 000	
Depreciation expense	Cr		4 000
Retained earnings (opening balance)	Cr		4 000
(Depreciation of 20% × $20 000 p.a.)			
Income tax expense	Dr	1 200	
Retained earnings (opening balance)	Dr	1 200	
Deferred tax asset	Cr		2 400

Adjustment to MI in B Ltd

Retained earnings (opening balance)	Dr	1 624	
MI share of profit	Dr	1 624	
MI	Cr		3 248
([40% + 18%] × $2800 = $1624			

LO 6

23.3.3 Dividends

As explained in chapter 22, in calculating the DMI share of retained earnings, the DMI is given a share of current period's profits and opening balance of retained earnings adjusted by a share of dividends paid and declared, and transfers to and from reserves. The IMI is allocated a share of the current period's post-acquisition profits, opening balance of post-acquisition retained earnings, and transfers to and from post-acquisition reserves. The IMI share of these balances is not reduced through allocation of dividend paid or declared. In this regard, consider the following consolidation worksheet in relation to dividends paid by B Ltd (using the figure 23.7 structure). An extract from the worksheet shows that the adjustment for the intragroup transaction and the allocation to the 40% DMI in B Ltd eliminates the total balance of the dividend paid:

Financial statements	P Ltd	A Ltd	B Ltd	Adjustments		Minority interest		Consol.
				Dr	Cr	Dr	Cr	
Dividend paid	–	–	2 000		1 200		800	–

No dividend is paid directly to the IMI. The IMI in B Ltd receives its share through the DMI in A Ltd receiving a share of the profit of A Ltd, which includes dividend revenue from B Ltd. By the DMI in A Ltd receiving a share of profit of A Ltd, it receives a share of the profit of B Ltd because the dividend paid by B Ltd is a distribution of B Ltd's profit. This raises a problem of double counting because the IMI of B Ltd, which receives a share of the profit of B Ltd, is the same party as the DMI in A Ltd, which receives a share of the profit of B Ltd through the dividend revenue from B Ltd being included in the profit of A Ltd. This problem does not arise in a two-entity situation as any dividend paid by the subsidiary is paid to the parent of the group. With multiple subsidiaries, the problem arises when a dividend paid or declared by one subsidiary is recognised as revenue by another subsidiary, both of which contain a MI.

The group in figure 23.7 is used to discuss the effects on the MI of dividends paid or declared by a subsidiary whose ownership includes an IMI.

The simplified income statements for the period ended 30 June 2005 are:

	P Ltd	A Ltd	B Ltd
Profit for the period	$ 40 000	$28 000	$10 000
Retained earnings (opening balance)	90 000	25 000	24 000
	130 000	53 000	34 000
Dividend paid	10 000	3 000	2 000
Dividend declared	10 000	5 000	3 000
Transfer to reserves	10 000	5 000	6 000
	30 000	13 000	11 000
Retained earnings (closing balance)	$100 000	$40 000	$23 000

The DMI of 30% in A Ltd and the DMI of 40% in B Ltd receive their share of all equity accounts within their respective entities (see overleaf).

	DMI — A Ltd 30%	DMI — B Ltd 40%
Profit for the period	$ 8 400	$ 4 000
Retained earnings (opening balance)	7 500	9 600
	15 900	13 600
Dividend paid	900	800
Dividend declared	1 500	1 200
Transfer to reserves	1 500	2 400
	3 900	4 400
Retained earnings (closing balance)	$12 000	$ 9 200

Dividend paid in the current period

In the group illustrated in figure 23.7, the profit of A Ltd includes $1200 dividend revenue (60% × $2000); that is, A Ltd's share of the dividend paid by B Ltd from its current profit. The issue here is that, if the IMI in B Ltd is allocated a share of the profit of B Ltd and the DMI in A Ltd is allocated a share of the profit of A Ltd, which includes the dividend revenue from B Ltd, then, because the DMI and the IMI are the same party, the calculation of the MI share of equity involves double counting. As noted earlier, in calculating the IMI share of B Ltd's equity, the IMI is not given a share of the dividend paid, which means there is no reduction in the IMI share of B Ltd's equity.

In calculating the MI share of equity it is necessary to make an adjustment to eliminate the double counting. This could be done by adjusting the IMI of B Ltd's equity or the DMI share of A Ltd's equity, since the problem is caused by the fact that A Ltd has recognised some of B Ltd's profit through dividend revenue. In this case the adjustment is made by affecting the DMI share of A Ltd's equity. Hence, when making the adjustment for the $2000 dividend paid from B Ltd to A Ltd, the following consolidation worksheet entries are made:

Dividend paid by B Ltd

Dividend revenue	Dr	1 200	
Dividend paid	Cr		1 200
(60% × $2000)			

Step 3: MI calculation for A Ltd

Dividend revenue	Dr	800	
Dividend paid	Cr		800
(40% × $2000)			

MI	Dr	360	
MI share of profit	Cr		360
(Being the reduction of the DMI share of profit in A Ltd as the latter includes the dividend from B Ltd: 30% × $1200)			

Dividend declared

B Ltd has declared a $3000 dividend but not paid it by the end of the period. A Ltd will still recognise 60% of this, $1800, as dividend revenue. Hence, the same double counting problem that arose with dividend paid also arises with dividend declared. An extra entry to overcome the double counting is again required. The consolidation worksheet entries are shown opposite.

Dividend declared by B Ltd

Dividend payable	Dr	1 800	
Dividend declared	Cr		1 800
(60% × $3000)			

Dividend revenue	Dr	1 800	
Dividend receivable	Cr		1 800

Step 3: MI calculation for A Ltd

MI	Dr	1 200	
Dividend paid	Cr		1 200
(40% × $3000)			

MI	Dr	540	
MI share of profit	Cr		540
(30% × $1800)			

ILLUSTRATIVE EXAMPLE 23.2

Effects of intragroup transactions on the calculation of MI

LO 7

On 1 July 2004, Oak Ltd acquired 60% of the shares of Ash Ltd for $163 980. On the same day, Ash Ltd acquired 75% of the shares of Beech Ltd for $129 050. At this date, an extract from the balance sheets of Ash Ltd and Beech Ltd disclosed the following:

	Ash Ltd	Beech Ltd
Share capital	$240 000	$164 000
General reserve	8 000	–
Retained earnings	1 600	2 400
Dividend payable	14 400	–

The dividend payable by Ash Ltd was subsequently paid. No other dividends have been paid from pre-acquisition equity.

On 1 July 2004, all the identifiable assets and liabilities of Beech Ltd were recorded at fair value except for the non-monetary assets. A comparison of the non-monetary assets' carrying amounts and fair values revealed the following information:

	Beech Ltd	
	Carrying amount	Fair value
Inventory	$ 5 000	$ 6 000
Plant (cost $160 000)	128 000	133 000
Land	56 000	60 000

The plant was expected to provide further benefits evenly over the next five years. All inventory was sold by 30 June 2005.

On 1 July 2004, all the identifiable assets and liabilities of Ash Ltd were recorded at fair value except for the following:

	Ash Ltd	
	Carrying amount	Fair value
Inventory	$ 6 000	$ 8 000
Plant (cost $147 000)	126 000	130 000

The balance of goodwill recorded at 1 July 2004 by Ash Ltd was $6000. The financial data as at 30 June 2006 of the three companies are as follows:

	Oak Ltd	Ash Ltd	Beech Ltd
Sales revenue	$675 360	$444 800	$290 000
Dividend revenue	18 720	13 200	–
Debenture interest	–	3 200	3 840
Total revenue	694 080	461 200	293 840
Cost of sales	490 400	333 600	232 000
Other expenses	44 080	42 800	20 000
Total expenses	534 480	376 400	252 000
Profit before tax	159 600	84 800	41 840
Income tax expense	64 000	32 000	16 000
Profit for the period	95 600	52 800	25 840
Retained earnings (1/7/05)	4 000	10 400	8 800
	99 600	63 200	34 640
Dividend paid	20 000	14 400	8 000
Dividend declared	30 000	16 800	9 600
	50 000	31 200	17 600
Retained earnings (30/6/06)	49 600	32 000	17 040
Share capital	420 000	240 000	164 000
General reserve	12 000	16 000	8 000
Total equity	481 600	288 000	189 040
Debentures	160 000	–	–
Provisions	20 000	29 600	16 000
Dividend payable	30 000	16 800	9 600
Current tax liability	64 400	32 000	16 000
Total liabilities	274 400	78 400	41 600
Total equity and liabilities	$756 000	$366 400	$230 640
Inventory	$ 5 600	$ 4 400	$ 5 120
Receivables	21 860	15 550	1 520
Cash	28 000	10 600	21 600
Debentures in Oak Ltd	–	40 000	48 000
Shares in Ash Ltd	155 340	–	–
Shares in Beech Ltd	–	129 050	–
Plant	500 000	147 000	160 000
Accumulated depreciation	(204 000)	(63 000)	(64 000)
Land	200 000	70 000	56 000
Deferred tax asset	32 000	6 800	2 400
Goodwill	17 200	6 000	–
Total assets	$756 000	$366 400	$230 640

Additional information

(a) Sales and purchases included the following transactions:
  - sales by Ash Ltd to Oak Ltd invoiced at cost plus $33\frac{1}{3}$% were $120 000
  - sales by Beech Ltd to Oak Ltd invoiced at cost plus 25% were $36 000.

(b) Inventory on hand of Oak Ltd at 30 June 2006 included $1600 acquired from Ash Ltd and $1200 acquired from Beech Ltd.

(c) Inventory of Ash Ltd at 1 July 2005 included $160 profit on goods received from Beech Ltd.

(d) Receivables and payables included $3600 owed by Oak Ltd to Ash Ltd.

(e) The tax rate is 30%.

Required

Based on the above information, prepare the consolidated financial statements for Oak Ltd and its subsidiaries as at 30 June 2006.

Solution

The first step in the consolidation process is to establish the structure of the group and percentage ownership of the MI (see figure 23.8).

The next step is to choose one of the acquisitions, prepare the acquisition analysis, the business combination valuation and pre-acquisition entries and the MI entries.

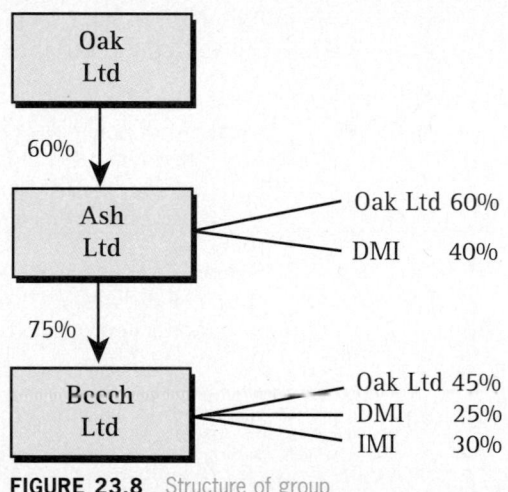

FIGURE 23.8 Structure of group

Acquisition analysis: Ash Ltd and Beech Ltd

At 1 July 2004:
Net fair value of identifiable assets,
  liabilities and contingent liabilities of Beech Ltd = $164 000 (capital) + $2400 (retained earnings)
  + $1000 (1 − 0.3) (BCVR − inventory)
  + $5000 (1 − 0.3) (BCVR − plant)
  + $4000 (1 − 0.3) (BCVR − land)
  = $173 400
Net fair value acquired by Ash Ltd = 75% × $173 400
  = $130 050
Cost of combination = $129 050
Excess = $1000

1. Business combination valuation entries: Ash Ltd and Beech Ltd
At 1 July 2004:

Inventory	Dr	1 000	
Deferred tax liability	Cr		300
Business combination valuation reserve	Cr		700
Accumulated depreciation – plant	Dr	32 000	
Plant	Cr		27 000
Deferred tax liability	Cr		1 500
Business combination valuation reserve	Cr		3 500
Land	Dr	4 000	
Deferred tax liability	Cr		1 200
Business combination valuation reserve	Cr		2 800

At 30 June 2006, the valuation entries for plant require adjustment to reflect depreciation of $1000 p.a., being $\frac{1}{5}$ of $5000. The inventory was all sold in the 2004–05 period. The valuation entries at 30 June 2006 are:

Accumulated depreciation – plant	Dr	32 000	
Plant	Cr		27 000
Deferred tax liability	Cr		1 500
Business combination valuation reserve	Cr		3 500
Depreciation expense	Dr	1 000	
Retained earnings (1/7/05)	Dr	1 000	
Accumulated depreciation	Cr		2 000
($\frac{1}{5} \times$ $5000)			
Deferred tax liability	Dr	600	
Income tax expense	Cr		300
Retained earnings (1/7/05)	Cr		300
Land	Dr	4 000	
Deferred tax liability	Cr		1 200
Business combination valuation reserve	Cr		2 800

2. Pre-acquisition entry: Ash Ltd and Beech Ltd
The pre-acquisition entry at 1 July 2004 is:

Retained earnings (1/7/04)	Dr	1 800	
Share capital	Dr	123 000	
Business combination valuation reserve	Dr	5 250	
Excess – other income	Cr		1 000
Shares in Beech Ltd	Cr		129 050

The inventory is all sold in the 2004–05 period, and the related valuation reserve (75% × $700) transferred to retained earnings.

At 30 June 2006, the entry is:

Retained earnings (1/7/05)*	Dr	1 325	
Share capital	Dr	123 000	
Business combination valuation reserve	Dr	4 725	
Shares in Beech Ltd	Cr		129 050

*$1325 = $1800 − $1000 excess + (75% × $700) inventory

3. MI share of equity in Beech Ltd at 1 July 2004

Retained earnings (1/7/05)	Dr	600	
Share capital	Dr	41 000	
Business combination valuation reserve	Dr	1 750	
MI	Cr		43 350

4. MI share of changes in equity from 1 July 2004 to 30 June 2005

Retained earnings of Beech Ltd at 30 June 2005 have increased by $6400 (i.e. from $2400 to $8800) but adjustments must be made for the after-tax depreciation on plant, as shown in the business combination valuation entries:

DMI (25%)

Retained earnings (1/7/05)	Dr	1 425	
MI	Cr		1 425
(25% × [$6400 − ($1000 − $300)])			

IMI (30%)

The IMI receives a share of post-acquisition equity only. As the pre-acquisition entry at 30 June 2006 has a debit adjustment of $1325, the pre-acquisition retained earnings of Beech Ltd are $1767 (i.e. $1325/0.75) plus the adjustments for the depreciation of plant ($1000 − $300), a total of $2467. The IMI share of post-acquisition retained earnings is then:

$$30\% \times [\$8800 - \$1325/0.75 - (\$1000 - \$300)] = \$1900$$

The worksheet entry is:

Retained earnings (1/7/05)	Dr	1 900	
MI	Cr		1 900

The *business combination valuation reserve* in relation to inventory has been transferred to retained earnings. This affects the DMI only as it relates to pre-acquisition profits.

DMI (25%)

MI	Dr	175	
Business combination valuation reserve	Cr		175
(25% × $700)			

The *general reserve* has increased from a zero balance at acquisition date to $8000, an increase of $8000. As this has resulted from a transfer from post-acquisition retained earnings, both the DMI and IMI are affected.

DMI (25%) and IMI (30%)

General reserve	Dr	4 400	
MI	Cr		4 400
([25% + 30%] × $8000)			

5. MI share of equity in Beech Ltd from 1 July 2005 to 30 June 2006
As there is no adjustment to the current period profit in the pre-acquisition entry, both the DMI and IMI receive a share of the recorded profit of $25 840 adjusted for the depreciation of plant:

MI share of profit	Dr	13 827	
MI	Cr		13 827
([25% + 30%] × [$25 840 − ($1000 − $300)])			

Beech Ltd has *paid a dividend* of $8000. This affects the DMI only.

MI	Dr	2 000	
Dividend paid	Cr		2 000
(25% × $8000)			

Beech Ltd has *declared a dividend* of $9600. Only the DMI is affected.

MI	Dr	2 400	
Dividend declared	Cr		2 400
(25% × $9600)			

The next step is to deal with the other acquisition: Oak Ltd's acquisition of Ash Ltd.

Acquisition analysis: Oak Ltd and Ash Ltd

Net fair value of identifiable assets, liabilities and contingent liabilities of Ash Ltd	= $240 000 (capital) + $8000 (general reserve)
	+ $1600 (retained earnings)
	+ $2000 (1 − 0.3) (BCVR − inventory)
	+ $4000 (1 − 0.3) (BCVR − plant)
	− $6000 goodwill
	= $247 800
Net fair value acquired by Oak Ltd	= 60% × $247 800
	= $148 680
Cost of combination	= $163 980 − (60% × $14 400) (dividend)
	= $155 340
Goodwill acquired by Oak Ltd	= $6660
Non-recorded goodwill	= $6660 − (60% × $6000)
	= $3060

6. Business combination valuation entries: Oak Ltd and Ash Ltd
At 1 July 2004:

Inventory	Dr	2 000	
Deferred tax liability	Cr		600
Business combination valuation reserve	Cr		1 400
Accumulated depreciation	Dr	21 000	
Plant	Cr		17 000
Deferred tax liability	Cr		1 200
Business combination valuation reserve	Cr		2 800

The entries at 30 June 2006 take into account that the inventory is sold in 2005, and the plant is depreciated at $1000 p.a., being $\frac{1}{4}$ of $4000.

The entries at 30 June 2006 are:

Accumulated depreciation	Dr	21 000	
Plant	Cr		17 000
Deferred tax liability	Cr		1 200
Business combination valuation reserve	Cr		2 800
Depreciation expense	Dr	1 000	
Retained earnings (1/7/05)	Dr	1 000	
Accumulated depreciation	Cr		2 000
Deferred tax liability	Dr	600	
Income tax expense	Cr		300
Retained earnings (1/7/05)	Cr		300

7. Pre-acquisition entries
At 1 July 2004:

Retained earnings (1/7/04)	Dr	960	
Share capital	Dr	144 000	
General reserve	Dr	4 800	
Business combination valuation reserve	Dr	2 520	
Goodwill	Dr	3 060	
Shares in Ash Ltd	Cr		155 340
Dividend payable	Dr	8 640	
Dividend receivable	Cr		8 640

By 30 June 2006, the dividend has been paid and the inventory sold with the relevant valuation reserve transferred to retained earnings. The entry is:

Retained earnings (1/7/05)	Dr	1 800	
Share capital	Dr	144 000	
General reserve	Dr	4 800	
Business combination valuation reserve*	Dr	1 680	
Goodwill	Dr	3 060	
Shares in Ash Ltd	Cr		155 340

* $2520 − (60% × $1400)

8. MI in equity of Ash Ltd at 1 July 2004

Retained earnings (1/7/05)	Dr	640	
Share capital	Dr	96 000	
General reserve	Dr	3 200	
Business combination valuation reserve	Dr	1 680	
MI	Cr		101 520
(40% of balances at acquisition)			

9. MI share of equity in Ash Ltd from 1 July 2004 to 30 June 2005
The *retained earnings* for Ash Ltd have increased from $1600 to $10 400, an increase of $8800. This has to be adjusted for the after-tax depreciation on plant, $1000 – $300.

Retained earnings (1/7/05)	Dr	3 240	
MI	Cr		3 240
(40% × $8800 – [$1000 – $300])			

The *business combination valuation reserve* relating to inventory has been transferred to retained earnings:

MI	Dr	560	
Business combination valuation reserve	Cr		560
(40% × $1400)			

The *general reserve* has increased from $8000 to $16 000:

General reserve	Dr	3 200	
MI	Cr		3 200
(40% × $8000)			

10. MI share of equity of Ash Ltd from 1 July 2005 to 30 June 2006
Current period profit: This is $52 800, and is adjusted for the after-tax depreciation on plant.

MI share of profit	Dr	20 840	
MI	Cr		20 840
(40% × [$52 800 – ($1000 – $300)])			

Dividend paid of $14 400:

MI	Dr	5 760	
Dividend paid	Cr		5 760
(40% × $14 400)			

Dividend declared of $16 800:

MI	Dr	6 720	
Dividend declared	Cr		6 720

Dividend revenue from Beech Ltd of $13 200: Beech Ltd paid a dividend of $8000 and declared a dividend of $9600. Ash Ltd therefore recorded dividend revenue of $13 200 (i.e. 75% × ($8000 + $9600)). As the IMI has received a share of the profit of Beech Ltd, to avoid double counting, the DMI in Ash Ltd must be adjusted in relation to the dividend revenue from Beech Ltd:

MI	Dr	5 280	
MI share of profit	Cr		5 280
(40% × $13 200)			

Intragroup transactions
11. Dividend paid – Beech Ltd

Dividend revenue	Dr	6 000	
Interim dividend paid	Cr		6 000
(75% × $8000)			

12. Dividend paid – Ash Ltd

Dividend revenue	Dr	8 640	
Interim dividend paid	Cr		8 640
(60% × $14 400)			

13. Dividend declared – Ash Ltd

Dividend payable	Dr	10 080	
Dividend declared	Cr		10 080
(60% × $16 800)			
Dividend revenue	Dr	10 080	
Dividend receivable	Cr		10 080

14. Dividend declared – Beech Ltd

Dividend payable	Dr	7 200	
Dividend declared	Cr		7 200
(75% × $9600)			
Dividend revenue	Dr	7 200	
Dividend receivable	Cr		7 200

15. Profit in ending inventory: Sales by Ash Ltd to Oak Ltd

Sales revenue	Dr	120 000	
Cost of sales	Cr		119 600
Inventory	Cr		400
Deferred tax asset	Dr	120	
Income tax expense	Cr		120

16. Adjustment to MI in Ash Ltd

MI	Dr	112	
MI share of profit	Cr		112
(40% × [$400 – $120])			

17. Profit in ending inventory: Sales by Beech Ltd to Oak Ltd

Sales revenue	Dr	36 000	
Cost of sales	Cr		35 760
Inventory	Cr		240
Deferred tax asset	Dr	72	
Income tax expense	Cr		72

18. Adjustment to MI in Beech Ltd

MI	Dr	92	
MI share of profit	Cr		92
([25% + 30%] × [$240 – $72])			

19. Profit in opening inventory: Sales by Beech Ltd to Ash Ltd

Retained earnings (1/7/05)	Dr	112	
Income tax expense	Dr	48	
Cost of sales	Cr		160

20. Adjustment to MI in Beech Ltd

MI share of profit	Dr	62	
Retained earnings (1/7/05)	Cr		62
([25% + 30%] × [$160 – $48])			

21. Intragroup balances
Amount owing by Oak Ltd to Ash Ltd is $3600.

Payables	Dr	3 600	
Receivables	Cr		3 600

22. Intragroup debentures
Intragroup debentures held amount to $88 000.

8% Debentures	Dr	88 000	
Debentures in Oak Ltd	Cr		88 000

23. Debenture interest
Interest paid by Oak Ltd is 8% of the sum of $40 000 and $48 000.

Debenture interest revenue	Dr	7 040	
Debenture interest expense	Cr		7 040

The consolidation worksheet is shown in figure 23.9.

FIGURE 23.9 Consolidation worksheet — indirect ownership interests

Financial statements	Oak Ltd	Ash Ltd	Beech Ltd	Adjustments Dr (ref)	Adjustments Dr	Adjustments Cr	Adjustments Cr (ref)	Group	Minority interest Dr (ref)	Minority interest Dr	Minority interest Cr	Minority interest Cr (ref)	Parent
Sales revenue	675 360	444 800	290 000	15 / 17	120 000 / 36 000			1 254 160					
Dividend revenue	18 720	13 200	–	11 / 12 / 13 / 14	6 000 / 8 640 / 10 080 / 7 200			–					
Debenture interest	–	3 200	3 840	23	7 040			–					
Total revenue	694 080	461 200	293 840					1 254 160					
Cost of sales	490 400	333 600	232 000			119 600 / 35 760 / 160	15 / 17 / 19	900 480					
Other expenses	44 080	42 800	20 000	1 / 6	1 000 / 1 000	7 040	23	101 840					
Total expenses	534 480	376 400	252 000					1 002 320					
Profit before tax	159 600	84 800	41 840					251 840					
Tax expense	64 000	32 000	16 000	19	48	300 / 300 / 120 / 72	1 / 6 / 15 / 17	111 256					
Profit for the period	95 600	52 800	25 840					140 584	5 / 10 / 20	13 827 / 20 840 / 62	5 280 / 112 / 92	10 / 16 / 18	111 339
Retained earnings (1/7/05)	4 000	10 400	8 800	1 / 2 / 5 / 7 / 19	1 000 / 1 325 / 1 000 / 1 800 / 112	300 / 300	1 / 6	18 563	3 / 4 / 4 / 8 / 9	600 / 1 425 / 1 900 / 640 / 3 240	62	20	10 820
	99 600	63 200	34 640					159 147					122 159

(continued)

Financial statements	Oak Ltd	Ash Ltd	Beech Ltd	Adjustments Dr	Adjustments Cr	Group	MI Dr	MI Cr	Parent
Dividend paid	20 000	14 400	8 000		6 000 (11); 8 640 (12)	27 760		2 000 (5); 5 760 (10)	20 000
Dividend declared	30 000	16 800	9 600		10 080 (13); 7 200 (14)	39 120		2 400 (5); 6 720 (10)	30 000
	50 000	31 200	17 600			66 880			50 000
Retained profits (30/6/06)	49 600	32 000	17 040			92 267			72 159
Share capital	420 000	240 000	164 000	123 000 (2); 144 000 (7)		557 000	41 000 (3); 96 000 (8)		420 000
General reserve	12 000	16 000	8 000	4 800 (7)		31 200	4 400 (4); 3 200 (8); 3 200 (9)		20 400
Business combination valuation reserve	–	–	–	4 725 (2); 1 680 (7)	3 500 (1); 2 800 (1); 2 800 (6)	2 695	1 750 (3); 1 680 (8)	175 (4); 560 (9)	–
Total equity: Parent									512 559
Total equity: MI							175 (4); 2 000 (5); 2 400 (5); 500 (9); 5 760 (10); 6 720 (10); 5 280 (10); 112 (16); 92 (18)	43 350 (3); 1 425 (4); 1 900 (4); 4 400 (4); 13 827 (5); 101 520 (8); 3 240 (9); 3 200 (9); 20 840 (10)	170 603
Total equity	481 600	288 000	189 040			683 162	216 863	216 863	683 162

Financial statements	Oak Ltd	Ash Ltd	Beech Ltd	Ref	Adjustments Dr	Adjustments Cr	Ref	Group	Minority interest Dr	Minority interest Cr	Parent
Debentures	160 000	–	–	22	88 000			72 000			
Provisions	20 000	29 600	16 000	21	3 600			62 000			
Dividend payable	30 000	16 800	9 600	13 14	10 080 7 200			39 120			
Current tax liability	64 400	32 000	16 000					112 400			
Deferred tax liability	–	–	–	1 6	600 600	1 500 1 200 1 200	1 1 6	2 700			
Total liabilities	274 400	78 400	41 600					288 220			
Total equity and liabilities	756 000	366 400	230 640					971 382			
Inventory	5 600	4 400	5 120			400 240	15 17	14 480			
Receivables	21 860	15 550	1 520			3 600 10 080 7 200	21 13 14	18 050			
Cash	28 000	10 600	21 600					60 200			
Debentures in Oak Ltd	–	40 000	48 000			88 000	22	–			
Shares in Ash Ltd	155 340	–	–			155 340	7	–			
Shares in Beech Ltd	–	129 050	–			129 050	2	–			
Plant	500 000	147 000	160 000			27 000 17 000	1 6	763 000			
Accumulated depreciation	(204 000)	(63 000)	(64 000)	1 6	32 000 21 000	2 000 2 000	1 6	(282 000)			
Land	200 000	70 000	56 000	1	4 000			330 000			
Deferred tax asset	32 000	6 800	2 400	15 17	120 72			41 392			
Goodwill	17 200	6 000	–	7	3 060			26 260			
Total assets	756 000	366 400	230 640		650 782	650 782		971 382			

The consolidated financial statements for Oak Ltd at 30 June 2006 are shown in figure 23.10 (below and opposite).

Oak Ltd Consolidated income statement for the year ended 30 June 2006	
Revenue: sales	$1 254 160
Expenses:	
Cost of sales	900 480
Other	101 840
Total expenses	1 002 320
Profit before income tax	251 840
Income tax expense	111 256
Profit for the period	$ 140 584
Attributable to:	
Equity holders of the parent	$ 111 339
Minority interest	29 245
	$ 140 584

Oak Ltd Consolidated balance sheet as at 30 June 2006	
EQUITY AND LIABILITIES	
Equity attributable to equity holders of the parent	
Share capital	$420 000
Other reserves: general	20 400
Retained earnings	72 159
	512 559
Minority interest	170 603
Total equity	683 162
Non-current liabilities	
Debentures	72 000
Deferred tax liabilities	2 700
Total non-current liabilities	74 700
Current liabilities	
Provisions	62 000
Dividend payable	39 120
Current tax liabilities	112 400
Total current liabilities	213 520
Total liabilities	288 220
Total equity and liabilities	$971 382

ASSETS

Non-current assets

Plant and equipment	$763 000
Accumulated depreciation	(282 000)
Land	330 000
Deferred tax assets	41 392
Goodwill	26 260
Total non-current assets	878 652

Current assets

Inventories	$ 14 480
Receivables	18 050
Cash	60 200
Total current assets	92 730
Total assets	$971 382

Oak Ltd
Consolidated statement of changes in equity
for year ended 30 June 2006

Profit for the period	$140 584
Net income recognised directly in equity	0
Total recognised income and expense for the period	$140 584
Attributable to:	
Equity holders of the parent	$ 111 339
Minority interest	$ 29 245

	Consolidated	Parent
Share capital		
Balance at beginning of year	$557 000	$420 000
Balance at end of year	557 000	420 000
General reserve		
Balance at beginning of year	$ 31 200	$ 20 400
Balance at end of year	31 200	20 400
Retained earnings		
Balance at beginning of year	$ 18 563	$ 10 820
Profit for the period	140 584	111 339
Dividends paid and declared	(66 880)	(50 000)
Balance at end of year	92 267	72 159

FIGURE 23.10 Consolidated financial statements

LO 8 **23.4** Non-sequential acquisitions

Consider the following group in which Y Ltd is a subsidiary of X Ltd and Z Ltd is a subsidiary of Y Ltd:

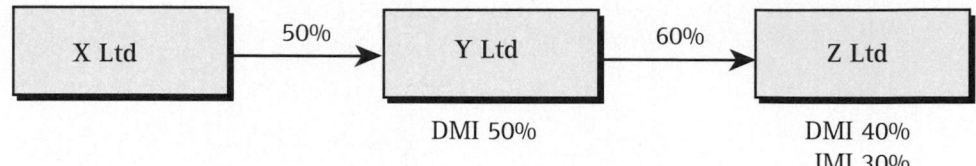

DMI 50%   DMI 40%
                           IMI 30%

The sequence in which the two acquisitions occurred was:

> 1 July 2004: Y Ltd acquired its interest in Z Ltd
> 1 July 2005: X Ltd acquired its interest in Y Ltd

The problem that the non-sequential acquisition causes is that, in relation to X Ltd's acquisition of Y Ltd, one of the assets of Y Ltd is 'shares in Z Ltd'. At the date of X Ltd's acquisition in Y Ltd, the fair value of the investment 'shares in Z Ltd' will have increased due to the increased worth of Z Ltd. In other words, when X Ltd considers the fair value of the consideration to pay for shares in Y Ltd, it considers not only the value of Y Ltd but also the value of Z Ltd. The fair value of Y Ltd's investment in Z Ltd related to the increased wealth of Z Ltd between 1 July 2004 and 1 July 2005.

Assume Y Ltd acquired its 60% interest in Z Ltd on 1 July 2004 for $420 when the financial position of Z Ltd was:

	Carrying amount	Fair value
Share capital	$300	
Retained earnings	230	
	$530	
Land	$200	$300
Other assets	330	330
	$530	

The acquisition analysis of Y Ltd's acquisition of Z Ltd is then:

Net fair value of Z Ltd	=	$300 + $230 + $100 (1 − 30%) (BCVR − land)
	=	$600
Net fair value acquired	=	60% × $600
	=	$360
Cost of combination	=	$420
Goodwill acquired	=	$60

The worksheet entries at acquisition date, 1 July 2004, for this acquisition are:

Business combination valuation entry − Z Ltd

Land	Dr	100	
Deferred tax liability	Cr		30
Business combination valuation reserve	Cr		70

Pre-acquisition entry

Share capital [60% × $300]	Dr	180	
Retained earnings [60% × $230]	Dr	138	
Business combination valuation reserve [60% × $70]	Dr	42	
Goodwill	Dr	60	
Shares in Z Ltd	Cr		420

MI at acquisition date

Share capital	Dr	120	
Retained earnings	Dr	92	
Business combination valuation reserve	Dr	28	
MI	Cr		240
(40% of balances)			

On 1 July 2005, X Ltd acquires 50% of the shareholding in Y Ltd for $650 when the financial positions of Y Ltd and Z Ltd are:

	Y Ltd Carrying amount	Y Ltd Fair value			Z Ltd Carrying amount	Z Ltd Fair value
Share capital	$500			Share capital	$300	
Retained earnings	600			Retained earnings	300	
Business combination valuation reserve*		$120		Business combination valuation reserve*		$140
				Liabilities*		60
Shares in Z Ltd	$420	$540		Land	$200	400
Other assets	680	680		Other assets	400	400

* These relate to the valuation of the assets, with the valuation of the land being tax-effected.

Hence, in relation to Z Ltd at 1 July 2005:
* Retained earnings has increased by $70 (i.e. from $230 to $300)
* Land has increased its fair value by $100 (i.e. from $300 to $400)

Worksheet entries at 1 July 2005:
Because X Ltd acquires the group of Y Ltd–Z Ltd, the assets of both Y Ltd and Z Ltd are revalued at 1 July 2005.

1. Business combination valuation entries – Z Ltd

Land	Dr	100	
Deferred tax liability	Cr		30
Business combination valuation reserve	Cr		70
Land	Dr	100	
Deferred tax liability	Cr		30
Business combination valuation reserve	Cr		70

It is useful to raise the increases in valuation separately as the MI has to be increased by these amounts. In subsequent periods, the entries may be combined.

2. Pre-acquisition entry at 1 July 2005: Y Ltd–Z Ltd

There is no change from the entry at 1 July 2004:

Share capital [60% × $300]	Dr	180	
Retained earnings [60% × $230]	Dr	138	
Business combination valuation reserve [60% × $70]	Dr	42	
Goodwill	Dr	60	
Shares in Z Ltd	Cr		420

3. 40% DMI at acquisition date

There is no change from the entry at 1 July 2004:

Share capital	Dr	120	
Retained earnings	Dr	92	
Business combination valuation reserve	Dr	28	
MI	Cr		240
(40% of balances)			

4. 40% DMI share of equity from 1 July 2004 to 1 July 2005

Retained earnings	Dr	28	
MI	Cr		28
(40% × $70)			

Business combination valuation reserve	Dr	28	
MI	Cr		28
(40% × $70 land)			

The IMI of 30% receives no amount at this stage because there are no post-acquisition profits in Z Ltd. The MI in Y Ltd (which is the same party as the IMI in Z Ltd) receives a share of the business combination valuation reserves in Y Ltd at 1 July 2005, which reflects any increase in Z Ltd's wealth between 1 July 2004 and 1 July 2005. Hence, post-acquisition equity, to which the IMI in Z Ltd is entitled to a share, occurs only after 1 July 2005.

5. Business combination valuation entries – Y Ltd at 1 July 2005

Shares in Z Ltd	Dr	120	
Business combination valuation reserve	Cr		120
($540 – $420)			

Note that only $420 is eliminated in the pre-acquisition entry for Y Ltd to Z Ltd. This is based on the following acquisition analysis for X Ltd–Y Ltd:

Net fair value of Y Ltd	=	$500 + $600 + $120 (BCVR – Shares in Z)
	=	$1220
Net fair value acquired by X Ltd	=	50% × $1220
	=	$610
Cost of combination	=	$650
Goodwill acquired	=	$40

6. Pre-acquisition entry: X Ltd–Y Ltd

Share capital	Dr	250	
Retained earnings	Dr	300	
Business combination valuation reserve	Dr	60	
Goodwill	Dr	40	
Shares in Y Ltd	Cr		650

Retained earnings [60% × $70]	Dr	42
Business combination valuation reserve [60% × $70]	Dr	42
Goodwill*	Dr	36
Shares in Z Ltd	Cr	120

* This reflects Y Ltd's share of the extra goodwill in Z Ltd between 1 July 2004 and 1 July 2005. The goodwill of Z Ltd is not revalued at 1 July 2005; hence, there is no share of equity recognised as occurs with assets such as land.

The last entry eliminates the extra worth in Z Ltd, which is reflected in the revaluation of 'shares in Z Ltd' in the accounts of Y Ltd. The whole of the fair value of this account is now eliminated on consolidation. In future worksheets this entry should be included in the valuation entries for Z Ltd because any changes in land (sale or impairment) may affect the nature of the equity accounts associated with Z Ltd.

7. 50% DMI in Y Ltd

Share capital	Dr	250
Retained earnings	Dr	300
Business combination valuation reserve [50% × $120]	Dr	60
MI	Cr	610

Financial statements	X Ltd	Y Ltd	Z Ltd		Adjustments Dr		Adjustments Cr		Minority interest Dr		Minority interest Cr	Consol.
Retained earnings	800	600	300	2 6 6	138 300 42			3 4 7	92 28 300			800
Share capital	900	500	300	2 6	180 250			3 7	120 250			900
Business combination valuation reserve	–	–	–	2 6 6	42 60 42	1 1 5	70 70 120	3 4 7	28 28 60			–
Liabilities	–	–	–			1 1	30 30					60
MI										3 4 4 7	240 28 28 610	906
	1700	1100	600									2666
Shares in Y Ltd	650	–	–	5		6	650					–
Shares in Z Ltd	–	420	–	5	120	2 6	420 120					–
Land	–	–	200	1 1	100 100							400
Other assets	1050	680	400									2130
Goodwill	–	–	–	2 6 6	60 40 36							136
	1700	1100	600		1510		1510		906		906	2666

FIGURE 23.11   Consolidation worksheet: non-sequential acquisition

The consolidation worksheet at 1 July 2005 is shown in figure 23.11. For retained earnings, share capital and the business combination valuation reserve, the consolidation amounts are those for X Ltd (i.e. there are no post-acquisition subsidiary amounts in these accounts attributable to the parent).

23.5 Reciprocal ownership

LO 9

Reciprocal shareholdings, otherwise known as mutual holdings or crossholdings, exist when a parent and a subsidiary own shares in each other. They also exist when a parent has more than one subsidiary and two or more of the subsidiaries own shares in each other. Some illustrative structures are as shown in figures 23.12 and 23.13.

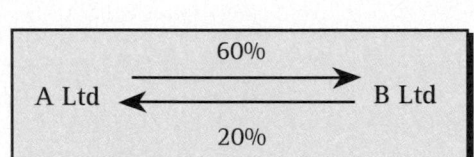

FIGURE 23.12 Reciprocal holdings

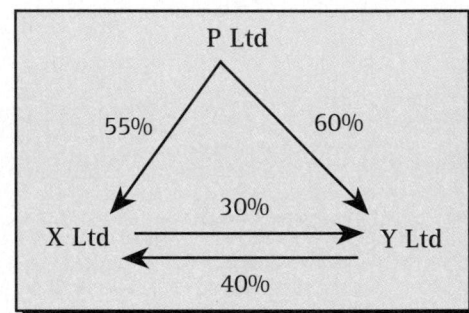

FIGURE 23.13 Reciprocal holdings

In some jurisdictions, such as Australia, subsidiaries are not allowed to hold shares in the parent entity. Hence, structures such as in figure 23.12 are not allowed to exist. However, structures such as in figure 23.13, where the crossholding is between the subsidiaries, are allowed.

23.5.1 Pre-acquisition and valuation entries

Using the structure in figure 23.13, business combination valuation entries are necessary for both X Ltd and Y Ltd, while there are four pre-acquisition entries:
- P Ltd's acquisition of X Ltd
- P Ltd's acquisition of Y Ltd
- X Ltd's acquisition of Y Ltd
- Y Ltd's acquisition of X Ltd.

Timing of these acquisitions will affect the valuations made, and the form of the pre-acquisition entries, particularly in relation to the crossholding between X Ltd and Y Ltd. If X Ltd acquires shares in Y Ltd prior to Y Ltd acquiring its shares in X Ltd, then in preparing the pre-acquisition/valuation entries for the latter acquisition, one of the assets of X Ltd is its investment in Y Ltd. In other words, where non-sequential acquisitions occur, particular adjustments must be taken into account, as demonstrated in section 23.4 of this chapter.

23.5.2 Minority interest

Consider the following structure:

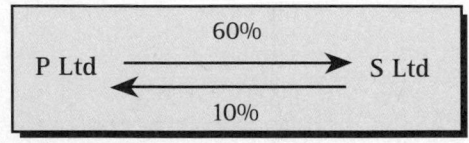

What are the ownership interests in each entity?

In relation to *S Ltd*, there is a DMI of 40%. However, it is a little more difficult to determine P Ltd's interest in S Ltd because of the reciprocal holding. Similarly, in relation to P Ltd, there is an MI in P Ltd, but its exact percentage interest is not immediately obvious.

A further factor complicating the calculation of the MI share of equity is the timing of the various acquisitions; that is, whether P Ltd acquired its share in S Ltd before S Ltd acquired its shares in P Ltd or vice versa. The profits recorded by the two entities can be broken into three parts:

- those on hand at the first acquisition (e.g. P Ltd's acquisition of S Ltd)
- those on hand at the second acquisition (S Ltd's acquisition of P Ltd); this is the date the reciprocal ownership arises
- those earned subsequent to the point of the mutual ownership occurring. These are referred to here as *post-acquisition profits*; that is, after the point that the reciprocal holding was raised.

Allocation of pre-acquisition equity to the MI

A series of small examples containing variations in the timing of acquisitions will be examined to demonstrate the approach to be taken in calculating the shares of pre-acquisition equity attributable to the parent and the MI. The P Ltd–S Ltd group is used in these examples. *It is assumed for these examples that no business combination valuation entries are required (i.e. all assets are at fair value and no goodwill arises on acquisition).* Because the calculations are concerned with the allocation of *pre-acquisition* equity only the DMI is of concern.

Example 1: Shares acquired on the same date

On 1 July 2004, P Ltd acquired 60% of the shares of S Ltd and S Ltd acquired 10% of the shares of P Ltd. The only DMI is the 40% in S Ltd. It is entitled to a share of all equity of S Ltd at acquisition date, 1 July 2004.

Example 2: P Ltd acquires shares in S Ltd before S Ltd acquires shares in P Ltd

Information concerning the acquisitions is as follows:

	P Ltd	S Ltd	
	1/7/05	1/7/04	1/7/05
Share capital	$40 000	$25 000	$25 000
Retained earnings	30 000	10 000	15 000
Shares in S Ltd	21 000		
Shares in P Ltd			7 300
Other assets	49 000	35 000	32 700

P Ltd acquired 60% of the shares of S Ltd for $21 000 at 1 July 2004 when the retained earnings of S Ltd were $10 000. On 1 July 2005, S Ltd acquired 10% of the shares in P Ltd for $7300. At this date, the retained earnings of S Ltd had increased by $5000 and the fair value of the shares in S Ltd account in P Ltd increased to $24 000 (a $3000 increase, which is 60% × $5000).

The consolidation worksheet entries at 1 July 2005 are:

P Ltd's acquisition of S Ltd
Pre-acquisition entry

Share capital [60% × $25 000]	Dr	15 000	
Retained earnings [60% × $10 000]	Dr	6 000	
Shares in S Ltd	Cr		21 000

MI in S Ltd at acquisition date

Share capital	Dr	10 000	
Retained earnings	Dr	4 000	
MI	Cr		14 000
(40% of balances)			

MI share of equity from 1/7/04 to 30/6/05

Retained earnings	Dr	2 000	
MI	Cr		2 000
(40% × [$15 000 − $10 000])			

S Ltd's acquisition of P Ltd
Valuation of P Ltd's assets

Shares in S Ltd	Dr	3 000	
Business combination valuation reserve	Cr		3 000

Pre-acquisition entries

Share capital [10% × $40 000]	Dr	4 000	
Retained earnings [10% × $30 000]	Dr	3 000	
Business combination valuation reserve [10% × $3000]	Dr	300	
Shares in P Ltd	Cr		7 300
Retained earnings	Dr	3 000	
Shares in S Ltd	Cr		3 000
(60% × [$15 000 − $10 000])			

This latter entry results in the total $15 000 of S Ltd's retained earnings now either being eliminated or allocated to the MI. The parent's share is recognised in the business combination valuation reserve.

Example 3: S Ltd acquires shares in P Ltd before P Ltd acquires shares in S Ltd
Information concerning the acquisitions is as follows:

	S Ltd	P Ltd	
	1/7/05	1/7/04	1/7/05
Share capital	$25 000	$40 000	$40 000
Retained earnings	10 000	30 000	40 000
Shares in S Ltd			21 600
Shares in P Ltd	7 000		
Other assets	28 000	70 000	58 400

On 1 July 2004, S Ltd acquired a 10% interest in P Ltd for $7000.

On 1 July 2005, P Ltd acquired a 60% controlling interest in S Ltd for $21 600. S Ltd's asset 'shares in P Ltd' had a fair value at this date of $8000, reflecting the increase in equity of P Ltd of $10 000.

Consolidation worksheet entries at 1 July 2005 are:

S Ltd's acquisition of P Ltd
Pre-acquisition entry

Share capital [10% × $40 000]	Dr	4 000	
Retained earnings [10% × $30 000]	Dr	3 000	
Shares in P Ltd	Cr		7 000

P Ltd's acquisition of S Ltd
Valuation of S Ltd's assets

Shares in P Ltd	Dr	1 000	
Business combination valuation reserve	Cr		1 000
($8000 – $7000)			

Pre-acquisition entries

Share capital [60% × $25 000]	Dr	15 000	
Retained earnings [60% × $10 000]	Dr	6 000	
Business combination valuation reserve [60% × $1000]	Dr	600	
Shares in S Ltd	Cr		21 600

Retained earnings [10% ($40 000 – $30 000)]	Dr	1 000	
Shares in P Ltd	Cr		1 000

MI share at 1/7/04 (note the MI has an interest in S Ltd at this date)

Share capital [40% × $25 000]	Dr	10 000	
Retained earnings [40% × $10 000]	Dr	4 000	
MI	Cr		14 000

MI share of equity from 1/7/04 to 1/7/05

Business combination valuation reserve [40% × $1000]	Dr	400	
MI	Cr		400

(Note that this reflects the increased worth of P Ltd between these two dates. The 40% DMI in S Ltd actually has an IMI share of the equity of P Ltd between the two acquisition dates of (40% × 10%) ($40 000 – $30 000) = $400.)

Allocation of post-acquisition equity

In the above section, the MI has been given a share of equity of both entities up to the date of the formation of the reciprocal holding. The purpose of this section is to demonstrate the allocation of the changes in equity subsequent to the formation of the reciprocal ownership.

The difficulty in this process is that there is no easy way of determining the relative ownership interests in the entities within the group because the entities are inter-dependent. Consider again the following structure:

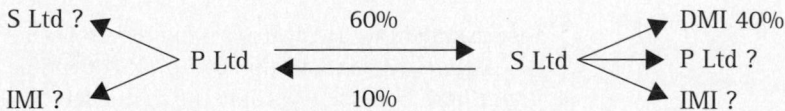

The only percentage easily calculable is the DMI in S Ltd. There are various methods that are used to overcome the problem of interdependency. For two companies simultaneous equations may be used. Using the group of P Ltd and S Ltd:

Let P = recorded profit of P Ltd
S = recorded profit of S Ltd
p = 'real' or 'true' profits of P Ltd
s = 'real' or 'true' profits of S Ltd.

(The 'real' profits of P Ltd consist of the recorded profits of P Ltd plus the profits of S Ltd that can be claimed by P Ltd because of its ownership interest in S Ltd.)

$$p = P + 0.6s \text{ (1)}$$
$$s = S + 0.1p \text{ (2)}$$

Substituting for p in equation (2):

$$s = S + 0.1(P + 0.6s)$$
$$= S + 0.1P + 0.06s$$
$$0.94s = S + 0.1P$$
$$s = 1/0.94S + 0.1P/0.94$$

As both P and S are known, being the recorded profits, the post-acquisition profits of P Ltd and S Ltd are calculable. The MI share of post-acquisition profits is based on the DMI in S Ltd of 40% receiving a share of s (i.e. a 40% share of the real post-acquisition profits of S Ltd). There is no need to calculate any IMI share of equity as, by calculating the real profits of S Ltd, the DMI gets the appropriate share, including that from the crossholdings.

ILLUSTRATIVE EXAMPLE 23.3

Calculation of the MI share of equity

LO 10

The following example is used to illustrate the calculation of the MI where reciprocal holdings exist between subsidiaries. The structure of the group is shown in figure 23.14:

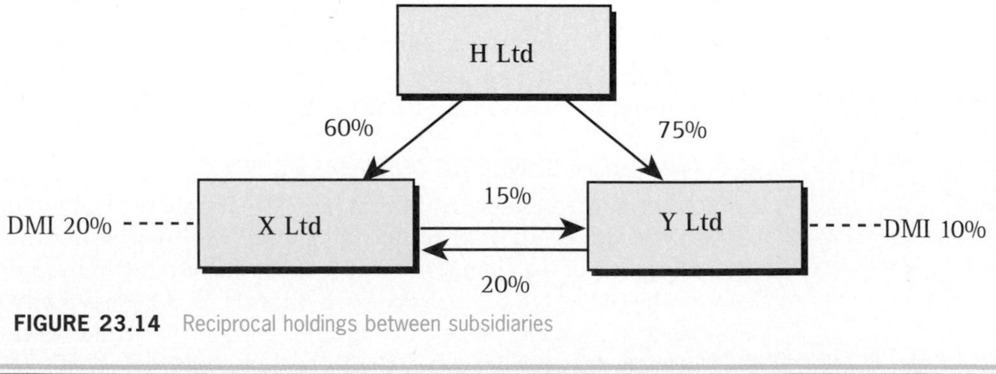

FIGURE 23.14 Reciprocal holdings between subsidiaries

It is assumed that H Ltd has an interest in both X Ltd and Y Ltd prior to the occurrence of the reciprocal relationship. The pre-acquisition entries for these acquisitions will not be given here because they have no influence on the calculation of the MI.

Assume X Ltd and Y Ltd acquired their shareholdings in each other on 1 July 2004:

- X Ltd paid $15 720 for 15% of Y Ltd's issued shares when the retained earnings of Y Ltd were $20 000. All the identifiable net assets of Y Ltd were recorded at fair value except for plant, for which the fair value was $4000 greater than carrying amount. The plant has a remaining useful life of four years.
- Y Ltd paid $30 000 for 20% of X Ltd's issued shares when the retained earnings of X Ltd were $40 000. All of the identifiable net assets of X Ltd were recorded at fair value except for inventory, for which the fair value was $5000 greater than fair value. The inventory was all sold within the following year.
- The tax rate is 30% and when revalued assets are sold or consumed, any related valuation reserve relating to those assets is transferred to retained earnings.

At 30 June 2006, the financial statements of X Ltd and Y Ltd contained the following information:

	X Ltd	Y Ltd
Dividend revenue	$ 750	$ 1 000
Other income	20 000	10 000
Profit before income tax	20 750	11 000
Income tax expense	8 000	5 000
Profit for the period	12 750	6 000
Retained earnings (1/7/05)	65 000	45 000
	77 750	51 000
Dividend paid	5 000	5 000
Retained earnings (30/6/06)	72 750	46 000
Share capital	100 000	80 000
	$172 750	$126 000
Shares in X Ltd	–	$ 30 000
Shares in Y Ltd	$ 15 720	–
Other assets	157 030	96 000
	$172 750	$126 000

Acquisition analysis: X Ltd–Y Ltd

Net fair value of Y Ltd	=	$80 000 + $20 000
		+ $4000 (1 – 30%) (BCVR – plant)
	=	$102 800
Net fair value acquired by X Ltd	=	15% × $102 800
	=	$15 420
Cost of combination	=	$15 720
Goodwill	=	$300

Acquisition analysis: Y Ltd–X Ltd

Net fair value of X Ltd	=	$100 000 + $40 000
		+ $5000 (1 – 30%) (BCVR – inventory)
	=	$143 500
Net fair value acquired by Y Ltd	=	20% × $143 500
	=	$28 700
Cost of combination	=	$30 000
Goodwill	=	$1300

The consolidation worksheet entries at 30 June 2006 are:

Business combination valuation entries: X Ltd–Y Ltd

Plant	Dr	4 000	
Deferred tax liability	Cr		1 200
Business combination valuation reserve	Cr		2 800
Depreciation expense	Dr	1 000	
Retained earnings (1/7/05)	Dr	1 000	
Accumulated depreciation	Cr		2 000
($\frac{1}{4}$ × $4000 p.a.)			
Deferred tax liability	Dr	600	
Income tax expense	Cr		300
Retained earnings (1/7/05)	Cr		300

Pre-acquisition entry: X Ltd–Y Ltd

Share capital	Dr	12 000	
Retained earnings (1/7/05)	Dr	3 000	
Business combination valuation reserve	Dr	420	
Goodwill	Dr	300	
Shares in Y Ltd	Cr		15 720

DMI in Y Ltd at acquisition date (10%)

Share capital	Dr	8 000	
Retained earnings (1/7/05)	Dr	2 000	
Business combination valuation reserve	Dr	280	
MI	Cr		10 280

Business combination valuation entries: Y Ltd–X Ltd
There are none as the inventory has been sold.

Pre-acquisition entry: Y Ltd–X Ltd

Share capital	Dr	20 000	
Retained earnings (1/7/05)*	Dr	8 700	
Goodwill	Dr	1 300	
Shares in Y Ltd	Cr		30 000

* 20% × $40 000 + 20% × $3500 inventory sold

DMI in X Ltd at acquisition date (20%)

Share capital	Dr	20 000	
Retained earnings (1/7/05)	Dr	8 000	
Business combination valuation reserve	Dr	700	
MI	Cr		28 700

MI share of changes in equity in Y Ltd and X Ltd from 1/7/04 to 30/6/05
In calculating the MI share of changes in equity for both X Ltd and Y Ltd, simultaneous equations are used. Assume:

$$X = \text{recorded profits of X Ltd}$$
$$Y = \text{recorded profits of Y Ltd}$$
$$x = \text{real profits of X Ltd}$$
$$y = \text{real profits of Y Ltd}$$

$$x = X + 0.15y$$
$$y = Y + 0.2x$$
$$x = X + 0.15(Y + 0.2x)$$
$$= X + 0.15Y + 0.03x$$
$$0.97x = X + 0.15Y$$
$$x = 1/0.97X + 0.15/0.97Y$$

This change in equity is after the date of formation of the reciprocal relationship. However, an adjustment needs to be made to the change in retained earnings in Y Ltd between these two dates to reflect the profits recognised by the subsidiary due to the use of the revalued plant and for the sale of inventory in relation to the retained earnings of X Ltd.

$$x = 1/0.97(\$65\,000 - \$8700/0.2 \text{ pre-acq.})$$
$$+ 0.15/0.97(\$45\,000 - \$3000/0.15 \text{ pre-acq.} - (\$1000 - \$300) \text{ plant})$$
$$= \$25\,923$$
$$y = Y + 0.2x$$
$$= (\$45\,000 - \$3000/0.15 \text{ pre-acq.} - (\$1000 - \$300) \text{ plant}) + 0.2 \times \$25\,923$$
$$= \$29\,485$$

$$MI = 20\%x + 10\%y$$
$$= (20\% \times \$25\,923) + (10\% \times \$29\,485)$$
$$= \$8133$$

The MI entry is:

Retained earnings (1/7/05)	Dr	8 133	
MI	Cr		8 133

There also needs to be recognition of the fact that in X Ltd, on sale of the inventory, the business combination valuation reserve was transferred to retained earnings. The MI entry is:

Retained earnings (1/7/05)	Dr	700	
Business combination valuation reserve	Cr		700
(20% × $3500)			

MI share of changes in equity in X Ltd and Y Ltd from 1/7/05 to 30/6/06
The same equations as above are used for the *current period's* changes in equity:

$$x = 1/0.97X + 0.15/0.97Y$$
$$y = Y + 0.2x$$

Adjustments must be made in relation to Y Ltd for the continued depreciation of the plant. Further adjustments must be made in both X Ltd and Y Ltd for any dividend revenue recognised by either company based on dividends paid and declared by the other company to ensure no double counting of equity.

$$
\begin{aligned}
x &= 1/0.97(\$12\,750 - \$750 \text{ dividend revenue from Y Ltd}) \\
&\quad + 0.15/0.97(\$6000 - \$1000 \text{ dividend revenue from X Ltd} \\
&\quad - (\$1000 - \$300) \text{ plant depreciation}) \\
&= \$13\,036 \\
y &= Y + 0.2x \\
&= (\$6000 - \$1000 \text{ dividend revenue} - (\$1000 - \$300) \text{ plant depreciation}) \\
&\quad + (0.2 \times \$13\,036) \\
&= \$6907
\end{aligned}
$$

$$
\begin{aligned}
MI &= 20\%x + 10\%y \\
&= (20\% \times \$13\,036) + (10\% \times \$6907) \\
&= \$3298
\end{aligned}
$$

The MI entry is:

MI share of profit	Dr	3 298
MI	Cr	3 298

23.6 Summary

This chapter has been concerned with the preparation of consolidated financial statements for groups of entities where the minority interest in an entity is not directly in the entity itself, but arises because of the ownership of another partly owned entity in that entity. It is necessary then to distinguish between direct and indirect minority interests. This is important in calculating the indirect minority interest share of equity because it receives a share of only post-acquisition equity. The chapter also considers complications arising from the timing of the acquisitions where a number of entities are involved; that is, where the acquisitions can be sequential or non-sequential. The principles relating to the measurement of indirect minority interests and the timing of acquisitions are employed in accounting for reciprocal ownerships, where entities have ownership interests in each other. These areas provide much difficulty in determining the parent's and minority interest's share of equity. Reference back to basic principles is consistently required in order to achieve the right answers to difficult problems.

DISCUSSION QUESTIONS

1. What is the difference between direct and indirect minority interests?
2. Why does the indirect minority interest receive a share of *post-acquisition* equity only?
3. Whenever there is an indirect minority interest and dividends have been paid by the third company out of post-acquisition profits, an adjustment must be made to the direct outside equity interest's share of profits in the second company in certain circumstances. Describe those circumstances and explain why the adjustment is necessary.
4. In the pre-acquisition entry, why are only partial eliminations of equity made when a minority interest exists?
5. P Ltd owns 60% of A Ltd and A Ltd owns 70% of B Ltd. Determine all minority interests assuming the existence of a group.
6. P Ltd owns 60% of A Ltd and 20% of B Ltd. A Ltd also owns 70% of B Ltd. Determine all minority interests in the group.
7. What are the effects on the consolidation process when the acquisition is non-sequential?
8. What are reciprocal ownership interests, and how are they accounted for on consolidation?

Why is no adjustment made for an indirect minority interest when preparing consolidated financial statements immediately after acquisition?

EXERCISES

Note: In all exercises, at the acquisition date, the identifiable assets and liabilities of the subsidiary are recorded at amounts equal to fair values.

EXERCISE 23.1   ★   Consolidation worksheet entries, three companies

On 1 July 2005, Jakarta Ltd acquired 80% of the shares of Bandung Ltd and Bandung Ltd acquired 75% of the shares of Surabaya Ltd. All shares were acquired cum div.

Equity of the companies at 1 July 2005 was as follows:

	Bandung Ltd	Surabaya Ltd
Share capital	$80 000	$60 000
Asset revaluation surplus	5 000	–
Retained earnings	1 000	4 000
Dividend payable	8 000	5 000

At 1 July 2005, all identifiable assets and liabilities of Bandung Ltd and Surabaya Ltd were recorded at fair value. No goodwill or excess arose in any of the share acquisitions.

The financial statements of the three companies at 30 June 2007 contained the following information:

	Jakarta Ltd	Bandung Ltd	Surabaya Ltd
Share capital	$130 000	$80 000	$60 000
Asset revaluation surplus	–	5 000	–
Retained earnings (1/7/06)	10 000	10 500	13 000
Dividend payable	13 000	8 000	6 000
Profit	4 000	2 000	1 500

The final dividends were declared out of profits for the year ended 30 June 2007.

Since 1 July 2005, the following intragroup transactions have occurred:

(a) Bandung Ltd sold to Surabaya Ltd an item of machinery for $12 000 on 31 December 2005. The machinery had originally cost Bandung Ltd $14 000 and at the time of sale had been depreciated to $11 200. The group charges depreciation at 10% straight-line.

(b) During the year ended 30 June 2007, inventory was transferred by Surabaya Ltd to Bandung Ltd at 25% on cost to Surabaya Ltd. $4000 of this inventory is included in the inventory of Bandung Ltd as at 30 June 2007. The tax rate is 30%.

Required
Prepare the consolidation worksheet entries for the year ended 30 June 2007.

EXERCISE 23.2   ★   Calculation of minority interest

On 1 July 2006, Surakarta Ltd acquired 75% of the shares of Malang Ltd at a cost of $280 000 and Malang Ltd acquired 80% of the shares of Lumajang Ltd at a cost of $135 000. At acquisition date, the equity of Malang Ltd and Lumajang Ltd was as follows and represented the fair values of identifiable assets and liabilities at that date:

	Malang Ltd	Lumajang Ltd
Share capital	$150 000	$140 000
General reserve	20 000	–
Retained earnings	50 000	20 000

On 30 June 2008, Malang Ltd transferred the general reserve back to retained earnings and declared a dividend of $20 000 which was paid on 1 November 2008.

On 30 June 2010, the companies provided the following information.

	Malang Ltd	Lumajang Ltd
Profit before income tax	$ 48 000	$32 000
Income tax expense	20 000	15 000
Profit	28 000	17 000
Retained earnings (1/7/09)	75 000	42 000
	103 000	59 000
Transfer to general reserve	–	20 000
Dividend paid	10 000	–
Dividend declared	15 000	10 000
	25 000	30 000
Retained earnings (30/6/10)	$ 78 000	$29 000

Required
Calculate the minority interest share of retained earnings (30/6/10) for Malang Ltd and Lumajang Ltd.

EXERCISE 23.3   ★   Consolidation worksheet entries, multiple subsidiaries

On 1 July 2004, Medan Ltd acquired 70% of the shares of Tarutung Ltd for $100 000 and Tarutung Ltd acquired 60% of Pakanbaru Ltd for $70 000. The equity of the companies at 1 July 2004 was:

	Tarutung Ltd	Pakanbaru Ltd
Share capital	$100 000	$80 000
Retained earnings	40 000	30 000

At 1 July 2004, all the identifiable assets and liabilities of both Tarutung Ltd and Pakanbaru Ltd were recorded at fair value.

At 30 June 2007, the financial data of the three companies were as follows:

	Medan Ltd	Tarutung Ltd	Pakanbaru Ltd
Sales revenue	$120 000	$102 000	$ 84 000
Other revenue	60 000	44 000	36 000
Total revenues	180 000	146 000	120 000
Cost of sales	90 000	80 000	72 000
Other expenses	60 000	41 000	26 000
Total expenses	150 000	121 000	98 000
Profit before income tax	30 000	25 000	22 000
Income tax expense	8 000	8 000	5 000
Profit for the period	22 000	17 000	17 000
Retained earnings (1/7/06)	55 000	46 000	25 000
Total available for appropriation	77 000	63 000	42 000
Dividend paid	15 000	10 000	5 000
Retained earnings (30/6/07)	62 000	53 000	37 000
Share capital	148 000	100 000	80 000
Net assets	$210 000	$153 000	$117 000

All dividends paid in the year ended 30 June 2007 are from post-acquisition profits except for that paid by Medan Ltd. In the year ended 30 June 2006, Pakanbaru Ltd paid a dividend of $15 000 from profits earned before 1 July 2004.

Since 1 July 2004, the following transactions have occurred between the three companies:

• During the current year, Tarutung Ltd sold inventory valued at $20 000 to Medan Ltd, this having cost Tarutung Ltd $15 000. Half of this inventory is still on hand at 30 June 2007.

• On 1 July 2006, Pakanbaru Ltd sold a motor vehicle to Tarutung Ltd for $25 000. The carrying amount of the vehicle at the date of sale was $23 000. Vehicles are depreciated at 30% p.a. on a straight-line basis.

The company tax rate is 30%.

Required

Prepare the consolidation worksheet journal entries for the year ended 30 June 2007.

EXERCISE 23.4	★

Calculation of minority interest share of retained earnings

On 1 July 2005, Padang Ltd acquired 60% of the shares of Jambi Ltd for $300 000, and Jambi Ltd acquired 80% of the shares of Bangko Ltd for $190 000. It was considered that Padang Ltd exercised control over Jambi Ltd and Bangko Ltd. At acquisition date, the equity for Jambi Ltd and Bangko Ltd was as follows, and represented the fair values of identifiable assets and liabilities at that date:

	Jambi Ltd	Bangko Ltd
Share capital	$200 000	$140 000
General reserve	130 000	70 000
Retained earnings	80 000	20 000

Three years later, the companies provided the following information:

	Jambi Ltd	Bangko Ltd
Profit before income tax	$ 24 000	$18 000
Income tax expense	10 000	7 500
Profit	14 000	10 500
Retained earnings (1/7/07)	88 000	27 500
	102 000	38 000
Dividend declared	10 000	8 000
Retained earnings (30/6/08)	$ 92 000	$30 000

There was a transfer to reserves of $4000 from pre-acquisition profits in the period ended 30 June 2007 by Bangko Ltd.

Required
Calculate the minority interest's share of retained earnings (30/6/08) of Jambi Ltd and Bangko Ltd.

EXERCISE 23.5 ★★   Consolidation worksheet, consolidated income statement

Bogor Ltd acquired 75% of the shares of Tegal Ltd on 1 July 2002 for $1 900 000. The identifiable assets and liabilities of Tegal Ltd at fair value on the acquisition date were represented by:

Share capital	$ 500 000
General reserve	800 000
Retained earnings	1 200 000
	$2 500 000

On the same date, Tegal Ltd acquired 60% of Semarang Ltd for $1 100 000. The identifiable assets and liabilities of Semarang Ltd at the acquisition date at fair value were represented by:

Share capital	$ 660 000
General reserve	500 000
Retained earnings	500 000
	$1 660 000

The financial information provided by the three companies for the year ended 30 June 2007 is shown opposite.

	Bogor Ltd	Tegal Ltd	Semarang Ltd
Sales revenue	$2 850 000	$1 100 000	$ 880 000
Other revenue	420 000	200 000	60 000
Total revenues	3 270 000	1 300 000	940 000
Cost of sales	1 410 000	520 000	380 000
Other expenses	200 000	80 000	110 000
Total expenses	1 610 000	600 000	490 000
Profit before income tax	1 660 000	700 000	450 000
Income tax expense	580 000	160 000	140 000
Profit	1 080 000	540 000	310 000
Retained earnings (1/7/06)	4 070 000	2 300 000	1 120 000
Total available for appropriation	5 150 000	2 840 000	1 430 000
Dividend paid	400 000	160 000	80 000
Dividend declared	400 000	200 000	90 000
Transfer to general reserve	100 000	50 000	40 000
	900 000	410 000	210 000
Retained earnings (30/6/07)	$4 250 000	$2 430 000	$1 220 000

The following additional information was obtained:
(a) Dividends paid by Semarang Ltd ($80 000) were considered to be paid from profits earned before 1 July 2002. All other dividends paid or declared were from profits earned in the current year.
(b) All transfers to general reserve were from post-acquisition profits.
(c) Included in the plant and machinery of Semarang Ltd was a machine sold by Tegal Ltd on 30 June 2004 for $75 000. The asset had originally cost $130 000 and it had been written down to $60 000. Semarang Ltd had depreciated the machine on a straight-line basis over five years, with no residual value.
(d) Semarang Ltd had transferred one of its motor vehicles (carrying amount of $15 000) to Bogor Ltd on 31 March 2006 for $12 000. Bogor Ltd regarded this vehicle as part of its inventory. The vehicle was sold by Bogor Ltd on 31 July 2006 for $17 000.
(e) The tax rate is 30%.

Required
Prepare the consolidated income statement and statement of changes in equity (not including movements in the general reserve and share capital) for the group for the year ended 30 June 2007.

EXERCISE 23.6   ★★★   Consolidated financial statements

On 1 July 2003, the following balances appeared in the ledgers of the following three companies:

	Pemalang Ltd	Bekasi Ltd	Memboro Ltd
Retained earnings	$20 000	$10 000	$ 5 000
General reserve	8 000	2 000	1 000
Dividend payable	4 000	2 000	–
Share capital	80 000	60 000	20 000

The dividend payable on 1 July 2003 was paid in October 2003.

For the year ended 30 June 2008, the following information is available:
- Inter-company sales were:
  Bekasi Ltd to Pemalang Ltd $20 000
  Memboro Ltd to Pemalang Ltd $15 000
  The mark-up on cost on all sales was 25%.
- At 30 June 2008, inventory of Pemalang Ltd included:
  $1000 of goods purchased from Bekasi Ltd
  $1800 of goods purchased from Memboro Ltd.
- The current income tax rate is 30%.
- All dividends paid or declared in the current year are from post-acquisition profits except for a $2000 dividend paid by Memboro Ltd out of pre-acquisition profits.
- Pemalang Ltd paid $67 200 for 80% of the shares of Bekasi Ltd at 1 July 2003 when all identifiable assets and liabilities of Bekasi Ltd were recorded at fair value.
- Bekasi Ltd paid $18 750 for 75% of the shares of Memboro Ltd at 1 July 2003 when all identifiable assets and liabilities of Memboro Ltd were recorded at fair value as below.

Receivables	$ 9 000
Inventory	10 000
Plant	20 000
Total assets	39 000
Liabilities	13 000
Net assets	$26 000

- The plant has an expected remaining useful life of five years. By 30 June 2004, all receivables had been collected and inventory sold.

The financial information for the year ended 30 June 2008 for all three companies was as follows:

	Pemalang Ltd	Bekasi Ltd	Memboro Ltd
Sales revenue	$ 98 400	$ 50 000	$30 000
Cost of sales	61 000	29 000	13 000
Gross profit	37 400	21 000	17 000
Expenses:			
Selling and administrative (inc. depn)	10 000	5 000	3 000
Financial	3 000	1 000	1 000
	13 000	6 000	4 000
	24 400	15 000	13 000
Dividend revenue	3 200	3 000	–
Profit before income tax	27 600	18 000	13 000
Income tax expense	12 000	8 100	5 200
Profit	15 600	9 900	7 800
Retained earnings (1/7/07)	40 000	20 000	10 000
Total available for appropriation	55 600	29 900	17 800
Transfer to general reserve	4 000	1 900	–
Dividend paid	5 000	2 000	4 000
Dividend declared	5 000	2 000	2 000
	14 000	5 900	6 000

Retained earnings (30/6/08)	41 600	24 000	11 800
General reserve	12 000	3 900	1 000
Share capital	80 000	60 000	20 000
Equity	$133 600	$ 87 900	$32 800
Receivables	$ 18 000	$ 25 000	$11 000
Inventory	25 000	26 400	13 800
Shares in Bekasi Ltd	65 600	–	–
Shares in Memboro Ltd	–	17 250	–
Plant	50 000	41 250	20 000
Total assets	158 600	109 900	44 800
Provisions	20 000	20 000	10 000
Dividend payable	5 000	2 000	2 000
Total liabilities	25 000	22 000	13 000
Net assets	$133 600	$ 87 900	$31 800

Required

Prepare the consolidated financial statements of Pemalang Ltd at 30 June 2008.

PROBLEMS

Note: In all problems, at the acquisition date, the identifiable assets and liabilities of the subsidiary are recorded at amounts different from fair values.

PROBLEM 23.1 ★★

Consolidation worksheet entries

The balance sheets of Melaka Ltd, Anson Ltd and Ipoh Ltd for the year ended 30 June 2006 are shown below.

	Melaka Ltd	Anson Ltd	Ipoh Ltd
Share capital	$150 000	$50 000	$21 000
Retained earnings	60 000	18 000	4 000
Dividend payable	30 000	10 000	6 000
	$240 000	$78 000	$31 000
Non-current assets	$120 000	$20 000	$10 000
Shares in Anson Ltd	55 800	–	–
Shares in Ipoh Ltd	–	21 000	–
Inventory	10 000	25 000	20 000
Receivables	54 200	12 000	1 000
	$240 000	$78 000	$31 000

For the year ended 30 June 2006, Anson Ltd and Ipoh Ltd recorded a profit of $2000 and $1000 respectively.

Anson Ltd acquired 90% of the ordinary shares of Ipoh Ltd for a total consideration of $20 730. At the acquisition date, 1 July 2003, Ipoh Ltd's equity comprised:

Share capital (21 000 shares)	$21 000
Retained earnings	1 000

At this date, all identifiable assets and liabilities of Ipoh Ltd were recorded at fair value except for some plant for which the fair value of $8000 was $1000 greater than the carrying amount of $7000 (i.e. original cost of $8500 less accumulated depreciation of $1500). The plant is expected to last a further five years.

On the same day, the directors of Melaka Ltd made a successful offer for 45 000 of Anson Ltd's fully paid shares. The consideration was $54 990 and, at the acquisition date, Anson Ltd's equity comprised:

Share capital (50 000 shares)	$50 000
Retained earnings	4 000

At this date, all identifiable assets and liabilities of Melaka Ltd were recorded at fair value except for some machinery whose fair value was $3000 greater than its recorded amount of $6000, the latter being $10 000 cost less accumulated depreciation of $4000. The machinery is expected to have a further useful life of three years. When assets are sold or fully consumed, any related valuation reserves are transferred to retained earnings.

Required
Prepare the consolidation worksheet entries for the preparation of the consolidated financial statements of Melaka Ltd at 30 June 2006.

PROBLEM 23.2 ★★ Consolidation worksheet, consolidated income statement and statement of changes in equity

On 1 July 2007, Pattani Ltd acquired 80% of the shares in Bentong Ltd (cum div.) for $44 760. At this date, Bentong Ltd had not recorded any goodwill and all its identifiable net assets were recorded at fair value except for the following.

	Carrying amount	Fair value
Land	$ 8 000	$10 000
Inventory	12 000	15 000

Half of this inventory still remained on hand at 30 June 2008. Immediately after the acquisition date, Bentong Ltd revalued the land to fair value. The land was still on hand at 30 June 2008.

At 1 July 2007, Bentong Ltd acquired 75% of the shares in Sungai Ltd for $15 300. Sungai Ltd had not recorded any goodwill and all its identifiable assets and liabilities were recorded at fair value except for the following:

	Carrying amount	Fair value
Inventory	$10 000	$14 000

All the inventory was sold by 30 June 2008. When assets are sold or fully consumed, any related valuation reserves are transferred to retained earnings.

At the acquisition date, the financial statements of the three companies showed the following:

	Pattani Ltd	Bentong Ltd	Sungai Ltd	
Share capital	$80 000	$32 000	$20 000	
General reserve	20 000	3 200	–	
Asset revaluation surplus	16 000	6 400	–	
Retained earnings	6 400	4 800	3 200	(Dr)
Dividend payable	12 000	3 200	–	

The following information was provided for the year ended 30 June 2008:

	Pattani Ltd	Bentong Ltd	Sungai Ltd
Sales revenue	$108 000	$72 000	$54 000
Cost of sales	72 000	61 200	40 500
Gross profit	36 000	10 800	13 500
Less: Distribution and administrative			
expenses	9 000	2 700	2 880
	27 000	8 100	10 620
Plus: Interim dividend revenue	1 280	1 500	–
Profit before income tax	28 280	9 600	10 620
Income tax expense	8 480	1 920	2 400
Profit	19 800	7 680	8 220
Retained earnings (1/7/07)	6 400	4 800	(3 200)
	26 200	12 480	5 020
Less: Dividend paid	4 000	–	1 000
Dividend declared	4 000	1 600	1 000
	8 000	1 600	2 000
Retained earnings (30/6/08)	$ 18 200	$10 880	$ 3 020

Additional information
(a) Dividends declared for the year ended 30 June 2007 were duly paid.
(b) Intragroup purchases (at cost plus $33\frac{1}{3}$%) were:
  • Pattani Ltd from Bentong Ltd – $43 200
  • Bentong Ltd from Sungai Ltd – $37 800.
(c) Intragroup purchases valued at cost to the purchasing company were included in inventory at 30 June 2008, as follows:
  • Pattani Ltd – $5400
  • Bentong Ltd – $4500.
(d) The tax rate is 30%.

Required
1. Prepare the consolidation worksheet entries for the preparation of the consolidated financial statements of Pattani Ltd at 30 June 2008.
2. Prepare the consolidated income statement and statement of changes in equity (not including movements in share capital and other reserves) at 30 June 2008.

PROBLEM 23.3 ★★   Consolidation worksheet entries

On 1 July 2005, Sungai Ltd acquired (ex div.) 80% of the shares of Kampar Ltd for $146 400. At this date, the equity of Kampar Ltd consisted of:

Share capital	$100 000
General reserve	50 000
Retained earnings	20 000

In the accounts at this date, Kampar Ltd had recorded a dividend payable of $5000, goodwill of $13 000, and furniture at cost of $80 000 less accumulated depreciation of $10 000. All the identifiable assets and liabilities of Kampar Ltd were recorded at fair value except for the following.

	Carrying amount	Fair value
Plant (cost $120 000)	$90 000	$100 000
Inventory	40 000	45 000

The plant has a further five-year life, and is depreciated using the straight-line method. On the inventory, 90% was sold by 30 June 2006, the remaining 10% being sold by 30 June 2007.

During the 2005–06 period, Kampar Ltd recorded a profit of $40 000. There were no changes in reserves. During the 2006–07 period, Kampar Ltd recorded a profit of $36 000, and recorded a transfer to general reserve of $6000.

On 1 January 2006, Kampar Ltd acquired a 50% interest in Yala Ltd for $57 000, giving it a capacity to control that entity. At this date, the equity of Yala Ltd consisted of:

Share capital	$80 000
General reserve	40 000
Retained earnings	(10 000)

The identifiable assets and liabilities of Yala Ltd consisted of:

	Carrying amount	Fair value
Land	$50 000	$56 000
Plant (cost $110 000)	80 000	82 000
Inventory	10 000	12 000

All the inventory on hand at 1 January 2006 was sold by 30 June 2006. The plant had a further 10-year life, and was depreciated using the straight-line method. The land was sold by Yala Ltd in the 2006–07 period.

The profit of Yala Ltd for the period from 1 January 2006 to 30 June 2006 was $8000. There were no movements in the general reserve during this period. During the 2006–07 period, Yala Ltd earned a $20 000 profit. Yala Ltd also transferred $20 000 from general reserve to retained earnings during the 2006–07 period.

Assume an income tax rate of 30%. When assets are sold or fully consumed, any related valuation reserves are transferred to retained earnings.

Required

Prepare, in general journal entry format, the consolidation worksheet entries for the preparation of the consolidated financial statements of Sungai Ltd at 30 June 2007.

PROBLEM 23.4 ★★   Consolidation worksheet entries

On 1 July 2004, Mersing Ltd acquired 75% of the issued shares of Kulai Ltd for $320 000. At this date the balance sheet of Kulai Ltd was as follows:

Current assets	$ 20 000
Non-current assets	500 000
	520 000
Liabilities	120 000
Net assets	$400 000
Share capital	$100 000
General reserve	100 000
Retained earnings	200 000
Total equity	$400 000

All the identifiable assets and liabilities of Kulai Ltd were recorded at fair value except for some land for which the fair value was $10 000 greater than the carrying amount and some depreciable assets with a further five-year life for which the fair value was $12 000 greater than the carrying amount. The tax rate is 30%.

On 1 July 2006, Pekan Ltd acquired 60% of the issued shares of Mersing Ltd for $350 000. At this date, the balance sheet of Mersing Ltd was as follows:

Current assets		$120 000
Non-current assets		
Investment in Kulai Ltd	$320 000	
Other	280 000	600 000
		720 000
Liabilities		220 000
Net assets		$500 000
Share capital		$200 000
Retained earnings		300 000
		$500 000

All the identifiable assets and liabilities of Mersing Ltd were recorded at fair value except for the investment in Kulai Ltd which had a fair value of $400 000. The balance sheet of Kulai Ltd at 1 July 2006 was as follows:

Current assets	$ 30 000
Non-current assets	600 000
	630 000
Liabilities	130 000
	$500 000
Share capital	$100 000
General reserve	120 000
Retained earnings	280 000
	$500 000

All the identifiable assets and liabilities of Kulai Ltd at this date were recorded at fair value except for the land held at 1 July 2004 which, at 1 July 2006, had a fair value of $20 000 greater than carrying amount, and the depreciable assets which have a further three-year life have a fair value of $8000 greater than carrying amount.

Financial information about Pekan Ltd, Mersing Ltd and Kulai Ltd at 30 June 2007 is shown overleaf.

	Pekan Ltd	Mersing Ltd	Kulai Ltd
Current assets	$ 200 000	$150 000	$ 35 000
Non-current assets			
Investment in Mersing Ltd	350 000	–	–
Investment in Kulai Ltd	–	320 000	–
Land	100 000	50 000	40 000
Depreciable assets	500 000	400 000	620 000
Accumulated depreciation	(80 000)	(80 000)	(40 000)
	1 070 000	840 000	655 000
Liabilities	250 000	260 000	120 000
Net assets	$ 820 000	$580 000	$535 000
Share capital	$ 300 000	$200 000	$100 000
General reserve	200 000	–	120 000
Retailed earnings (1/7/06)	150 000	300 000	280 000
Profit for the period	170 000	80 000	35 000
	$ 820 000	$580 000	$535 000

Required

Prepare the worksheet entries for the consolidated financial statements at 30 June 2007.

PROBLEM 23.5 ★★★   Consolidation worksheet entries, analysis of minority interest

A client of yours is the chief accountant of Ranong Ltd which, at 30 June 2006, has two subsidiaries, Phuket Ltd and Trang Ltd. He is unsure how to prepare the consolidated financial statements and has asked for your help. He has provided you with the information below concerning the group, and has determined a series of questions for which he wants clear, well-written answers. Provide the answers to these questions. Assume an income tax rate of 30%.

Part A

Ranong Ltd acquired 40% of the capital of Phuket Ltd on 1 July 2003 for $79 400, consisting of $9400 cash and 14 000 Ranong Ltd shares having an estimated fair value of $5 per share. The equity of Phuket Ltd at this date is shown below.

Share capital	$100 000
General reserve	50 000
Retained earnings	40 000

All the identifiable assets and liabilities of Phuket Ltd were recorded at fair value except for plant (carrying amount $60 000, net of $10 000 depreciation) for which the fair value was $65 000. The plant has a further five-year life.

During January 2004, Phuket Ltd paid a dividend of $5000, of which half was from profits earned before 1 July 2003. Further, in January 2004, a transfer to retained earnings of $4000 was made from the general reserve established before 1 July 2003.

Required

1. Prepare the business combination valuation and pre-acquisition entries in relation to Ranong Ltd's acquisition of Phuket Ltd at 30 June 2004, assuming Phuket Ltd is a subsidiary of Ranong Ltd at this date.

2. Explain how the calculations used in requirement A meet the requirements of IFRS 3 *Business Combinations*.
3. If Ranong Ltd acquired its shares in Phuket Ltd at 1 July 2003, but did not achieve control until 1 July 2004 when the retained earnings of Phuket Ltd were $60 000 and the fair value of plant was $30 000 greater than the carrying amount, should the fair values be measured at 1 July 2003, or at 1 July 2004 when Ranong Ltd obtained control of Phuket Ltd? Explain your answer, referring to requirements of appropriate accounting standards to justify your answer.
4. If Phuket Ltd earned a $10 000 profit between 1 July 2003 and 30 June 2004, determine the minority interest share of Phuket Ltd's equity at 30 June 2004.
5. Explain your calculation of the minority interest share of profit in requirement 4.

Part B

Phuket Ltd acquired 75% of the issued shares of Trang Ltd at 1 January 2004 for $137 000 when the equity of Trang Ltd consisted of $100 000 capital and $62 000 retained earnings which included profit of $12 000, earned from 1 July 2003. At acquisition date, all the identifiable assets and liabilities of Trang Ltd were recorded at fair value except for the following assets:

	Carrying amount	Fair value
Land	$80 000	$90 000
Plant (net of accumulated depreciation of $15 000)	60 000	65 000
Inventory	20 000	25 000

Of the inventory, 90% was sold by 30 June 2004 and the remainder by 30 June 2005. The land was sold in January 2006 for $120 000. The plant has a further five-year life. When assets are sold or fully consumed, any related valuation reserves are transferred to retained earnings.

Required
Prepare the business combination valuation and pre-acquisition entries at 30 June 2004 and 30 June 2006.

Part C

The following transactions affect the preparation of consolidated financial statements at 30 June 2006:
(a) Sale of inventory in June 2005 from Trang Ltd to Ranong Ltd — the inventory cost Trang Ltd $2000, and was sold to Ranong Ltd for $3000. At 30 June 2006, the inventory was all sold by Ranong Ltd.
(b) Sale of plant on 1 January 2005 from Trang Ltd to Ranong Ltd — the plant had a carrying amount in Trang Ltd of $12 000 at time of sale, and was sold for $15 000. The plant had a further five-year life.
(c) Dividend of $10 000 declared in June 2006 by Trang Ltd to be paid in August 2006.
(d) Payment of a $4500 management fee from Trang Ltd to Ranong Ltd in February 2006.

Required
In relation to the preparation of the consolidated financial statements *at 30 June 2006*:
1. Provide consolidation worksheet journal entries for the above transactions, including related minority interest adjustments.
2. If the retained earnings (1/7/05) of Trang Ltd was $80 000 and the profit for the 2005–06 period was $10 000, calculate the minority interests share of Trang Ltd's equity at 30 June 2006, assuming no changes in reserves.

3. The calculation of minority interest is based on the concept of sharing only those profits that are realised to the group. Explain this concept, showing how it is implemented using transactions (a), (b) and (d) in part C.
4. Explain the minority interest adjustment entry in relation to transaction (c).
5. Explain the adjustment entry for transaction (a).

PROBLEM 23.6 ★★★   Consolidated financial statements

On 1 July 2006, Pattani Ltd acquired 60% of the shares of Kantang Ltd for $108 000. On the same day, Kantang Ltd acquired 80% of the shares (cum div.) of Phenom Ltd for $71 600. At the acquisition date, Kantang Ltd's and Phenom Ltd's financial statements showed the following balances:

	Kantang Ltd	Phenom Ltd
Share capital	$100 000	$60 000
General reserve	30 000	20 000
Retained earnings	15 000	8 000
Dividend payable	–	5 000

The dividend of Phenom Ltd was paid later in 2006.

On 1 July 2006, all identifiable assets and liabilities of Kantang Ltd and Phenom Ltd were recorded at fair values except for the following.

	Kantang Ltd		Phenom Ltd	
	Carrying amount	Fair value	Carrying amount	Fair value
Plant and machinery (cost $80 000)	$60 000	$80 000	–	–
Inventory	40 000	50 000	$30 000	$40 000
Vehicles (cost $80 000)	–	–	50 000	55 000

The vehicles have an expected useful life of four years and the plant is expected to last a further 10 years. Benefits are expected to be received evenly over these periods. All inventory on hand at 1 July 2006 was sold by 30 June 2007. When assets are sold or fully consumed, any related valuation reserves are transferred to retained earnings.

The financial statements of the three companies at 30 June 2007 are shown opposite.

	Pattani Ltd	Kantang Ltd	Phenom Ltd
Sales revenue	$520 000	$365 000	$115 000
Other revenue	160 000	105 000	58 000
	680 000	470 000	173 000
Cost of sales	410 000	190 000	86 000
Other expenses	146 000	180 000	42 000
	556 000	370 000	128 000
Profit before income tax	124 000	100 000	45 000
Income tax expense	51 000	40 000	20 000
Profit	73 000	60 000	25 000
Retained earnings (1/7/06)	24 000	15 000	8 000
	97 000	75 000	33 000
Dividend from profits earned before 1/7/06	–	5 000	–
Interim dividend paid	10 000	10 000	3 000
Final dividend declared	16 000	8 000	4 000
Transfer to general reserve	25 000	6 000	4 000
	51 000	29 000	11 000
Retained earnings (30/6/07)	46 000	46 000	22 000
Share capital	250 000	100 000	60 000
General reserve	145 000	36 000	24 000
Bank overdraft	21 000	6 000	20 000
Provisions	41 000	30 000	20 000
Current tax liability	55 000	42 000	26 000
Deferred tax liability	25 000	12 000	8 000
Dividend payable	16 000	8 000	4 000
	$599 000	$280 000	$184 000
Bank	$ 52 000	$ 25 000	$ 32 000
Receivables	61 200	17 000	16 000
Inventory	103 000	41 800	68 000
Dividend receivable	4 800	3 200	–
Shares in Kantang Ltd	105 000	–	–
Shares in Phenom Ltd	–	67 600	–
Deferred tax asset	21 000	15 400	8 000
Plant	200 000	180 000	–
Accumulated depreciation	(48 000)	(70 000)	–
Vehicles	130 000	–	100 000
Accumulated depreciation	(30 000)	–	(40 000)
	$599 000	$280 000	$184 000

Additional information

(a) Included in the ending inventory of Kantang Ltd was inventory purchased from Phenom Ltd for $10 000. This had originally cost Phenom Ltd $8000.

(b) Pattani Ltd had sold inventory to Phenom Ltd during the period for $25 000. This had cost Pattani Ltd $20 000. Half of this has been sold to external parties by Phenom Ltd during the year for $15 000.

(c) The tax rate is 30%.

Required

Prepare the consolidated financial statements for Pattani Ltd and its subsidiaries, Kantang Ltd and Phenom Ltd, for the period ending 30 June 2007.

PROBLEM 23.7 ★★★   Consolidated financial statements

On 1 July 2005, Kuala Ltd acquired 60% of the shares of Lumpur Ltd for $150 500. On the same day, Lumpur Ltd acquired 80% of the shares of Muar Ltd for $103 400. Equities of the subsidiaries at acquisition date were:

	Lumpur Ltd	Muar Ltd
Share capital	$140 000	$110 000
General reserve	60 000	10 000
Retained earnings	15 000	2 000

On 1 July 2005, Lumpur Ltd had recorded all its identifiable assets and liabilities at fair value except for the following assets:

	Carrying amount	Fair value
Plant (cost $120 000)	$100 000	$110 000
Inventory	15 000	20 000

By 30 June 2006, 90% of this inventory had been sold to parties outside the group. The other 10% was all sold by 30 June 2007.

The plant was expected to have a further useful life of five years, benefits being received evenly over this period.

On 1 July 2005, Muar Ltd's liabilities were all recorded at fair value. A comparison of the carrying amounts and fair values of its identifiable assets showed:

	Carrying amount	Fair value
Plant (cost $95 000)	$80 000	$80 000
Furniture (cost $60 000)	40 000	48 000
Inventory	16 000	20 000
Receivables	20 000	20 000
Cash	8 000	8 000

By 30 June 2006, all of this inventory had been sold to parties external to the group. The plant had a further expected life of five years and the furniture 10 years. When assets are sold or fully consumed, any related valuation reserves are transferred to retained earnings.

Additional information
(a) All dividends have been from post-acquisition profits.
(b) In June 2006, Lumpur Ltd declared a dividend of $10 000 and Muar Ltd declared a dividend of $5000. These were paid in September 2006.
(c) Included in the ending inventory of Lumpur Ltd is inventory of $5000 purchased from Kuala Ltd at cost plus 25%.
(d) On 1 January 2006, Lumpur Ltd sold some plant to Kuala Ltd for $22 000. This had a carrying amount at time of sale by Lumpur Ltd of $18 000. Both companies depreciate plant at 10% p.a. straight-line on cost.
(e) The tax rate is 30%.

Required
Using the financial information opposite for the companies at 30 June 2007, prepare the consolidated financial statements of Kuala Ltd.

	Kuala Ltd	Lumpur Ltd	Muar Ltd
Sales revenue	$250 000	$180 000	$112 000
Other revenue	20 000	16 000	23 000
Other income	30 000	14 000	20 000
	300 000	210 000	155 000
Cost of sales	190 000	102 000	85 000
Other expenses	48 000	70 000	45 000
	238 000	172 000	130 000
Profit before income tax	62 000	38 000	25 000
Income tax expense	20 000	16 000	11 200
Profit	42 000	22 000	13 800
Retained earnings (1/7/06)	18 000	47 000	13 500
	60 000	69 000	27 300
Dividend paid	10 000	7 500	5 000
Dividend declared	15 000	10 000	7 500
Transfer to general reserve	5 000	3 000	2 000
	30 000	20 500	14 500
Retained earnings (30/6/07)	$ 30 000	$ 48 500	$ 12 800

	Kuala Ltd	Lumpur Ltd	Muar Ltd
Credits			
Share capital	$200 000	$140 000	$110 000
General reserve	70 000	65 000	15 000
Retained earnings	30 000	48 500	12 800
Debentures		–	100 000
Dividend payable	15 000	10 000	7 500
Provisions	40 000	31 250	10 250
Advance from Lumpur Ltd	6 000	–	–
Other non-current liabilities	102 000	16 000	2 000
	$463 000	$310 750	$257 550
Debits			
Shares in Lumpur Ltd	$150 500	–	–
Shares in Muar Ltd	–	$103 400	–
Debentures in Muar Ltd	30 000	–	–
Inventory	42 500	19 600	$ 19 200
Receivables	87 100	43 600	25 400
Advance to Kuala Ltd	–	6 000	
Deferred tax asset	20 300	5 150	20 450
Plant	120 000	173 000	150 000
Accumulated depreciation	(37 400)	(40 000)	(27 500)
Furniture	80 000	–	100 000
Accumulated depreciation	(30 000)	–	(30 000)
	$463 000	$310 750	$257 550

Consolidated financial statements

On 1 July 2003, Sedao Ltd acquired 10% of the issued capital of Kulim Ltd for $60 000. At this date the equity of Kulim Ltd consisted of:

Share capital	$100 000
Retained earnings	450 000

All the identifiable assets and liabilities of Kulim Ltd were recorded at fair value except for some machinery for which the fair value was $20 000 greater than carrying amount. The machinery had a further five-year life, with benefits expected to be received evenly over this period.

On 1 January 2006, Kulim Ltd acquired 60% of the issued capital of Sedao Ltd for $132 000, obtaining control over the financial and operating policies of Sedao Ltd. At this date the equity of Sedao Ltd consisted of:

Share capital	$100 000
Retained earnings (1/7/05)	50 000
Profit to 1/1/06	50 000

All the identifiable assets and liabilities of Sedao Ltd were recorded at fair value except for plant and machinery (expected life of five years) whose fair value was $5000 greater than carrying amount, and the investment account 'Shares in Kulim Ltd' which had a fair value of $70 000. The financial statements of Kulim Ltd at 1 January 2006 contained the following information:

	Carrying amount	Fair value
Current assets	$120 000	$120 000
Non-current assets		
Plant and machinery	470 000	490 000
Other	200 000	200 000
	790 000	810 000
Liabilities	160 000	160 000
Net assets	$630 000	$650 000
Share capital	$100 000	
Retained earnings (1/7/05)	500 000	
Profit to 1/1/06	30 000	
Equity	$630 000	

The plant and machinery of Kulim Ltd whose fair value was greater than carrying amount had a further four-year life.

At 30 June 2006 Sedao Ltd had not disposed of its shares in Kulim Ltd.

At 30 June 2006, the financial statements of Kulim Ltd and its subsidiary Sedao Ltd included the information shown opposite.

	Kulim Ltd	Sedao Ltd
Profit before income tax	$ 50 000	$ 80 000
Income tax expense	10 000	20 000
Profit	40 000	60 000
Retained earnings at 1/7/05	500 000	50 000
	540 000	110 000
Dividends paid at 28/6/06	20 000	10 000
Retained earnings at 30/6/06	$520 000	$100 000
Current assets	$ 80 000	$ 30 000
Non-current assets		
Shares in Sedao Ltd	132 000	–
Shares in Kulim Ltd	–	60 000
Plant and machinery	600 000	140 000
Accumulated depreciation	(72 000)	(20 000)
Other	80 000	50 000
Total assets	820 000	260 000
Liabilities	200 000	60 000
Net assets	$620 000	$200 000
Equity		
Share capital	100 000	100 000
Retained earnings	520 000	100 000
Total equity	$620 000	$200 000

Required

Prepare the consolidated financial statements at 30 June 2006. Where necessary, make calculations to the nearest dollar.

Visit these websites for additional information:

www.iasb.org   www.iasplus.com
www.asic.gov.au   www.ifac.org
www.aasb.com.au   www.nzica.com
www.accaglobal.com   www.capa.com.my

CHAPTER 24
Consolidated financial statements: foreign subsidiaries

ACCOUNTING STANDARDS

International: IAS 21 *The Effects of Changes in Foreign Exchange Rates*

Australia: AASB 121 *The Effects of Changes in Foreign Exchange Rates*

New Zealand: NZ IAS 21 *The Effects of Changes in Foreign Exchange Rates*

CONCEPTS FOR REVIEW

Before studying this chapter, you should understand or, if necessary, revise:

- the preparation of consolidated financial statements
- the nature of the minority interest and the calculation of its share of equity
- the rationale underlying the adjustments on consolidation for intragroup transactions.

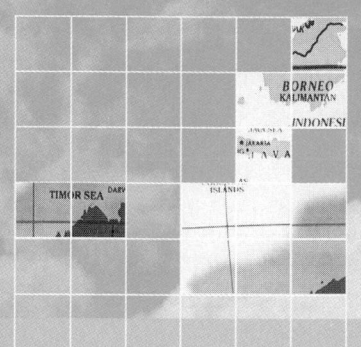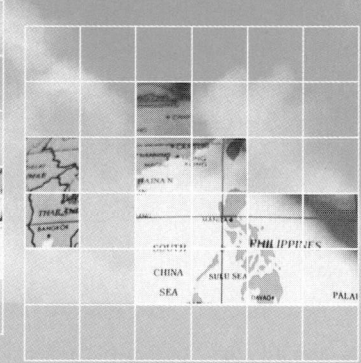

When you have studied this chapter, you should be able to:
1. explain the difference between functional and presentation currencies
2. understand the rationale underlying the choice of a functional currency
3. apply the indicators in choosing a functional currency
4. translate a set of financial statements from local currency into the functional currency
5. account for changes in the functional currency
6. translate financial statements into the presentation currency
7. prepare consolidated financial statements including foreign subsidiaries
8. explain what constitutes the net investment in a foreign operation
9. prepare the disclosures required by IAS 21.

24.1 Translation of foreign subsidiary's statements

A parent entity may have subsidiaries that are domiciled in a foreign country. In most cases, the financial statements of the foreign subsidiary are prepared in the currency of the foreign country. In order for the financial statements of the foreign operation to be included in the consolidated financial statements of the parent, it is necessary to translate the foreign operation's financial statements to the currency used by the parent entity for reporting purposes. The purpose of this chapter is to discuss the process for translating and presenting the consolidated financial statements of a parent entity where at least one of its subsidiaries is a foreign subsidiary.

The accounting standard that deals with this process is IAS 21 *The Effects of Changes in Foreign Exchange Rates*. IAS 21 was first issued by the International Accounting Standards Committee (IASC) in July 1983, revised in 1993, and further revised as a part of the Improvements project in 2003. This latter revision provided convergence with Generally Accepted Accounting Principles (GAAP) in the United States, in particular Statement of Financial Accounting Standards No. 52 (SFAS 52) *Foreign Currency Translation*.

LO 1

24.2 Functional and presentation currencies

Paragraph 3 of IAS 21 notes that its two areas of application are:
- translating the results and financial position of foreign operations that are included in the financial statements of the entity by consolidation or the equity method; and
- translating an entity's results and financial position into a presentation currency.

Note that there are two different translation processes here. In order to understand this, it is necessary to distinguish between three different types of currency: local currency, functional currency and presentation currency. Not all foreign subsidiaries experience all three currencies.
- *Local currency*. This is the currency in which the foreign operation measures and records its transactions.
- *Functional currency*. This is defined in paragraph 8 of IAS 21 as 'the currency of the primary economic environment in which the entity operates'. As is explained in more detail later, it is this currency that affects the economic wealth of the entity.
- *Presentation currency*. Paragraph 8 defines this as 'the currency in which the financial statements are presented'.

To illustrate, Foreign Ltd is a subsidiary of Parent Ltd. Parent Ltd is an Australian company and Foreign Ltd operates in Singapore. The operations in Singapore are to sell goods manufactured in France. In this case, Foreign Ltd would most likely maintain its accounts in Singaporean dollars, the local currency, while the functional currency could be the euro, reflecting the major economic operations in France. However, for presentation in the consolidated financial statements of Parent Ltd, the presentation currency could be the Australian dollar. As the accounts are maintained in Singaporean dollars, they may firstly have to be translated into the functional currency, the euro, and then translated again into the Australian dollar for presentation purposes. It is these two translation processes that are referred to in paragraph 3 of IAS 21.

LO 2

24.3 The rationale underlying the functional currency choice

This section relies heavily on the discussion in the seminal paper by Lawrence Revsine, published in 1983, in which he emphasised the need to understand the rationale underlying the choice of an exchange rate as an entity's functional currency.

As noted by Revsine (1984, p. 514):

> A much more real danger is that firms, their auditors, and outside analysts may not understand the subtle philosophy that underlies the functional currency choice. As a consequence, innocent but incorrect choices and assessments may be made, and compatibility may not be achieved.

According to paragraphs 4(a) and 4(b) of SFAS 52, the objectives of the translation process are:

1. to provide information that is generally compatible with the expected economic effects of an exchange rate change on an entity's cash flows and equity
2. to reflect in consolidated statements the financial results and relationships of the individual consolidated entities as measured in their functional currencies in conformity with US generally accepted accounting principles.

Note in particular the first objective. As the foreign subsidiary operates in another country, it is important that the financial effects on the parent entity of a change in the exchange rate are apparent from the translation process. The parent entity has an investment in a foreign operation and so has assets that are exposed to a change in the exchange rate. Capturing the extent of this exposure should be reflected in the choice of translation method. The economic relationship between the parent and the subsidiary affects the extent to which a change in exchange rate affects the parent entity. This can be seen by noting the differences in the following three cases adapted from Revsine (1984).

24.3.1   Case 1

Wildcat Ltd is an Australian company that wants to sell its product in Hong Kong. On 1 January 2004, when the exchange rate is A$1 = HK$5, Wildcat Ltd acquires a building in Hong Kong to be used to distribute the Australian product. The building cost HK$1 million, equal to A$200 000. It also deposited A$55 000 (equal to HK$275 000) in a Hong Kong bank. By 31 January 2004, the company had made credit sales in Hong Kong of HK$550 000. The exchange rate at this time was still A$1 = HK$5. The goods sold had cost A$90 000 to manufacture. The receivables were collected in February 2004 when the exchange rate was A$1 = HK$5.5. This cash receipt is transferred back to Australia immediately.

Note, in this case the company has no subsidiary but acquired an overseas asset, deposited money in an overseas bank and sold goods overseas. The company would record these transactions as follows, in Australian dollars:

Building	Dr	200 000	
Cash	Cr		200 000
Cash – HK Bank	Dr	50 000	
Cash	Cr		50 000
Receivables	Dr	110 000	
Sales	Cr		110 000
Cost of sales	Dr	90 000	
Inventory	Cr		90 000
Foreign exchange loss	Dr	10 000	
Receivables	Cr		10 000
(Loss on receivables when exchange rate changed from 1:5 to 1:5.5)			

(*continued*)

Cash	Dr	100 000	
Receivables	Cr		100 000
Foreign exchange loss	Dr	5 000	
Cash in HK Bank	Cr		5 000
(Loss on holding HK$55 000 when exchange rate changed from 1:5.0 to 1:5.5)			

Note two effects of this accounting procedure:
- Foreign currency transactions, whether completed (the sale) or uncompleted (the deposit), have an immediate or potentially immediate effect on the future cash flows of the parent. As a result, foreign currency gains/losses are recorded as they occur and immediately affect income.
- Non-monetary assets held in the foreign country are recorded at historical cost and are unaffected by exchange rate changes.

24.3.2 Case 2

Assume that, instead of transacting directly with customers in Hong Kong, Wildcat Ltd formed a subsidiary, Dragon Ltd, to handle the Hong Kong operation. As with case 1, all goods are transferred from the Australian parent to the Hong Kong subsidiary, which sells them in Hong Kong and remits profits back to the Australian parent.

Hence, Dragon Ltd is established with a capital structure of HK$1 250 000 (equal to A$250 000), an amount necessary to acquire the Hong Kong building and establish the bank account. On selling the inventory to Dragon Ltd, Wildcat Ltd passes the following entries:

Receivable – Dragon Ltd	Dr	110 000	
Sales revenue	Cr		110 000
Cost of sales	Dr	90 000	
Inventory	Cr		90 000

Assuming that the parent bills the subsidiary in Hong Kong dollars, namely HK$110 000, on receipt of the cash, the parent would pass the entry:

Foreign exchange loss	Dr	10 000	
Cash	Dr	100 000	
Receivable	Cr		110 000

The subsidiary will show:

Sales	HK$ 110 000
Cost of sales	110 000
Profit	–
Equity	HK$1 250 000
Building	HK$1 000 000
Cash	250 000
	HK$1 250 000

Note that the underlying transactions are the same in case 1 and case 2. The organisational form does not change the underlying economic effects of the transactions. The translation of the HK subsidiary must therefore show the position as if the parent had undertaken the transactions itself. This is the purpose behind the choice of the functional currency approach.

Where the subsidiary is simply a conduit for transforming foreign currency transactions into dollar cash flows, the consolidation approach treats the foreign currency statements of the subsidiary as artefacts that must be translated into the currency of the parent.

In case 2, the translation of the subsidiary's statements must show:

- the assets of the subsidiary at cost to the parent; that is, what the parent would have paid in its currency at acquisition date
- the revenues and expenses of the subsidiary at what it would have cost the parent in its currency at the date those transactions occurred
- monetary gains and losses being recognised immediately in income as they affect the parent directly.

Note, in case 2, that the functional currency of the subsidiary is the Australian dollar. It is the currency of the primary economic environment in which the entity operates. The inventories are sourced in Australian dollars, the dollars financing the subsidiary are Australian dollars, and the cash flows that influence the actions of the parent in continuing to operate in Hong Kong are Australian dollars.

The key to determining the functional currency in case 2 is the recognition of the subsidiary as an *intermediary for the parent's activities*. The alternative is for the subsidiary to act as a *free-standing unit*. Consider case 3 in this regard.

24.3.3 Case 3

Assume that Wildcat Ltd establishes a subsidiary in Hong Kong for HK$1 250 000, the money again being used to acquire a building and set up a bank account. However, in this case the Hong Kong operation is established to manufacture products in Hong Kong for sale in Hong Kong.

Chinese labour is used in the manufacturing process and profits are used to reinvest in the business for expansion purposes. Remittances of cash to the parent are in the form of dividends.

The economics of case 3 are different from those in case 2. The subsidiary is not just acting as a conduit for the parent. Apart from the initial investment, the cash flows, both inflows and outflows, for the subsidiary are dependent on the economic environment of Hong Kong rather than Australia. The effect of a change in the exchange rate between Australia and Hong Kong has no immediate effect on the operations of the Hong Kong subsidiary. It certainly affects the worth of the parent's investment in the subsidiary, but it has no immediate cash flow effect on the parent. In this circumstance, the functional currency is the Hong Kong dollar rather than the Australian dollar.

In analysing the success of the overseas subsidiary, the interrelationships between variables such as sales, profits, assets and equity should be the same whether they are expressed in Hong Kong or Australian dollars. In other words, the translation process should adjust all items by the same exchange rate to retain these interrelationships.

The key point of Revsine's article is that the choice of translation method should be such as to reflect the underlying economics of the situation. In particular, it is necessary to select the appropriate functional currency to reflect these underlying economic events.

LO 3

24.4 Identifying the functional currency

Paragraphs 9–12 of IAS 21 provide information on determining the functional currency:

- Para 9: normally the one in which it primarily *generates and expends cash*
  Consider the currency:
  - in which *sales prices* are denominated or which influences sales prices
  - of the country whose competitive forces and regulations influence *sales prices*
  - in which *input costs* – labour, materials – are denominated and settled, or which influences such costs
- Para 10: consider two factors:
  - the currency in which funds from *financing activities* are generated
  - the currency in which *receipts from operating activities* are retained.
- Para 11: consider:
  - whether the activities of the foreign operation are carried out as an *extension* of the reporting entity
  - whether *transactions with the reporting entity* are a high or low proportion of the foreign operation's activities
  - whether *cash flows* from the activities of the foreign operation *directly affect* the cash flows of the reporting entity and are readily available for remittance to it
  - whether *cash flows* from the foreign operation are sufficient to *service existing and expected debt* obligations without funds being made available by the reporting entity
- Para 12: management should use judgement to determine which currency most faithfully reflects the economic effects of the underlying transactions and events.

These factors are not significantly different from those stated in paragraph 42 of the FASB's SFAS 52. Jeter and Chaney (2003, p. 618) provided the basis for the information provided in figure 24.1, which illustrates the functional currency indicators as set down by the FASB.

Economic indicators	Indicators pointing to local overseas currency as functional currency	Indicators pointing to parent entity's currency as functional currency
Cash flows	Primarily in the local currency and do not affect the parent's cash flows.	Directly affect the parent's cash flows on a current basis and are readily available for remittance to the parent.
Sales prices	Are not primarily responsive in the short term to exchange rate changes. They are determined primarily by local conditions.	Are primarily responsive to exchange rate changes in the short term and are determined primarily by worldwide competition.
Sales market	Active local market, although there may be significant amounts of exports.	Sales are mostly in the country of the parent entity, or denominated in the parent entity's currency.
Expenses	Production costs and operating expenses are determined primarily by local conditions.	Production costs and operating expenses are obtained primarily from parent entity sources.
Financing	Primarily denominated in the local currency, and the foreign entity's cash flow from operations is sufficient to service existing and normally expected obligations.	Primarily from parent or other parent country-denominated obligations, or the parent entity is expected to service the debt.
Intragroup transactions	Low volume of intragroup transactions and there is not an extensive interrelationship between the operations of the foreign entity and those of the parent. However, the foreign entity may rely on the parent's or affiliates' competitive advantages, such as patents and trademarks.	High volume of intragroup transactions; there is an extensive interrelationship between the operations of the parent and those of the foreign entity or the foreign entity is an investment or financing device for the parent.

FIGURE 24.1 Functional currency indicators — FASB *Source:* Jeter and Chaney (2003, p. 618).

In applying the criteria shown in figure 24.1 for a parent and a single subsidiary, such as an Australian parent and a subsidiary in Hong Kong, there are three scenarios:
1. the functional currency of the subsidiary is the Australian dollar
2. the functional currency is the Hong Kong dollar
3. the functional currency is another currency, say, the Malaysian ringgit.

In relation to the choice between the first two alternatives, the extreme situations are those alluded to in the analysis of the Revsine cases. For the *Australian dollar* to be the functional currency, the expectation is that the subsidiary is a conduit for the parent entity. In the easy case, the product being sold is made in Australia, and the selling price is determined by worldwide competition. Further, because the entire product sold by the subsidiary emanates from the parent, there is significant traffic between the two entities, including cash being transferred from the subsidiary to the parent. For the *Hong Kong dollar* to be the functional currency, it is expected that the Hong Kong operation is independent of the parent entity. The products are sourced in Hong Kong and the sales prices depend on the local currency. The only regular transactions between the two entities are the annual dividends.

However, between these two scenarios there are many others where the determination of the functional currency is blurred. For example, the product being sold may require some Australian raw materials but be assembled in Hong Kong using some local raw materials. There are then material transactions between the two entities, but the subsidiary may be self-sufficient in terms of finance. In these cases, cash is generated in Hong Kong but expended in both Australia and Hong Kong. In determining the functional currency, management will need to apply judgement. The key to making a correct decision is, in accordance with Revsine, understanding what the translation process is trying to achieve in terms of reporting the underlying economic substance of the events and transactions.

In relation to the situation where another currency, such as the Malaysian ringgit, is the functional currency, this could occur where the Australian parent establishes a subsidiary in Hong Kong that imports raw materials from Malaysia and elsewhere, assembles them in Hong Kong and sells the finished product in Malaysia.

It is possible therefore for a parent entity that has a large number of foreign subsidiaries to have a number of functional currencies, particularly if the foreign subsidiaries are all relatively independent. An example of this is the US company 3M, which in 2002 was a US$16 billion diversified technology company that had operations in more than 60 countries, sold products in nearly 200 countries and had 29 international subsidiaries. The subsidiaries ran manufacturing operations ranging from small converting operations to full-scale manufacturing of multiple product lines. In the notes to its 31 December 2002 annual report, 3M's policy statement on foreign currency translation stated:

> Local currencies generally are considered the functional currencies outside the United States. Assets and liabilities for operations in local-currency environments are translated at year-end exchange rates. Income and expense items are translated at average rates of exchange prevailing during the year. Cumulative translation adjustments are recorded as a component of accumulated other comprehensive income in stockholders' equity.

As the functional currencies for the offshore operations were the local currencies, 3M had to deal with the accounting for a number of functional currencies.

LO 4

24.5 Translation into the functional currency

In the situation where it is determined that the Hong Kong dollar is the functional currency for the Hong Kong subsidiary, the financial statements of the subsidiary prepared in Hong Kong dollars are automatically in the functional currency. Where the Hong Kong subsidiary uses the Australian dollar as its functional currency, it is necessary to translate the Hong Kong accounts from Hong Kong dollars into Australian dollars.

The process of translating one currency into another is given in paragraphs 21 and 23 of IAS 21. Paragraph 21 deals with items reflected in the income statement that concern transactions occurring in the current period:

> A foreign currency transaction shall be recorded, on initial recognition in the functional currency, by applying to the foreign currency amount the spot exchange rate between the functional currency and the foreign currency at the date of the transaction.

Hence, in translating the revenues and expenses in the income statement, theoretically each item of revenue and expense should be translated at the spot exchange rate between the functional currency and the foreign currency on the date that the transaction occurred. However, given the large number of transactions being reported on in the income statement, paragraph 22 of IAS 21 provides for an averaging system to be used. A rate that approximates the actual rate at the date of the transaction can be used; for example, an average rate for a week or month might be used for all transactions within those periods. The extent to which averaging can be used depends on the extent to which there is a fluctuation in the exchange rate over a period and the evenness with which transactions occur throughout the period. For example, where the transactions are made evenly throughout a financial year — no seasonal effect, for example — and there is an even movement of the exchange rate over that year, a yearly average exchange rate could be used.

In relation to balance sheet accounts, paragraph 23 of IAS 21 states:

> At each balance sheet date:
> (a) foreign currency monetary items shall be translated using the closing rate;
> (b) non-monetary items that are measured in terms of historical cost in a foreign currency shall be translated using the exchange rate at the date of the transaction; and
> (c) non-monetary items that are measured at fair value in a foreign currency shall be translated using the exchange rates at the date when the value was determined.

Monetary items are defined in paragraph 8 as 'units of currency held and assets and liabilities to be received or paid in a fixed or determinable number of units of currency'. As noted in paragraph 16, examples of monetary liabilities include pensions and other employee benefits to be paid in cash and provisions to be settled in cash, including cash dividends that are recognised as a liability. Examples of monetary assets include cash and accounts receivable. All of these items are translated using the spot exchange rate at balance sheet date — the closing rate. As noted in case 1 previously, this reflects the amounts available in the functional currency.

For non-monetary items such as plant and equipment, IAS 16 *Property, Plant and Equipment* (see chapter 10) allows the use of the cost basis or the revaluation model of measurement. Where the cost basis is used, the appropriate translation rate is the spot rate at the date the asset was initially recorded by the subsidiary. Where the revaluation model is used, the appropriate rate is the spot rate at the date of the valuation to fair value. Paragraph 25 of IAS 21 notes that certain non-monetary assets such as inventory are to be reported at the lower of cost and net realisable value in accordance with IAS 2 *Inventory*. In such a case, it is necessary to calculate the cost, translated using the spot rate at acquisition date, and the net realisable value translated at the spot rate at the date of valuation. The lower amount is then used — this may require a write-down in the functional currency statements that would not occur in the local currency statements.

The basic principles of the translation method follow.

24.5.1   Balance sheet items

- *Assets.* Assets should first be classified as monetary or non-monetary. Monetary assets are translated at the current rate existing at balance date. With a non-monetary asset, the exchange rate used is that current at the date at which the recorded amount for the asset has been entered into the accounts. Hence, for non-monetary assets recorded at historical cost, the rates used are those existing when the historical cost was recorded. For non-monetary assets that have been revalued, whether upwards or downwards, the exchange rates used will relate to the dates of revaluation.

- *Liabilities.* The principles enunciated for assets apply also for liabilities. The liabilities are classified as monetary and non-monetary and, for the latter, it is the date of valuation that is important.
- *Equity.* In selecting the appropriate exchange rate two factors are important. First, equity existing at the date of acquisition or investment is distinguished from post-acquisition equity. Second, movements in other reserves and retained earnings constituting transfers within or internal to equity are treated differently from other reserves.
- *Share capital.* If on hand at acquisition or created by investment, the capital is translated at the rate existing at acquisition or investment. If the capital arises as the result of a transfer from another equity account, such as a bonus dividend, the rate is that current at the date the amounts transferred were originally recognised in equity.
- *Other reserves.* If on hand at acquisition, the reserves are translated at the rate existing at acquisition. If the reserves are post-acquisition and result from internal transfers, the rate used is that at the date the amounts transferred were originally recognised in equity. If the reserves are post-acquisition and not created from internal transfers, the rate used is that current at the date the reserves are first recognised in the accounts.
- *Retained earnings.* If on hand at acquisition, the retained earnings are translated at the rate of exchange current at the acquisition date. Any dividends paid from pre-acquisition profits are also translated at this rate. Post-acquisition profits are carried forward balances from translation of previous periods' income statements.

24.5.2   Income statement items

- *Income and expenses.* In general, these are translated at the rates current at the dates the applicable transactions occur. For items that relate to non-monetary items, such as depreciation and amortisation, the rates used are those used to translate the related non-monetary items.
- *Dividends paid.* These are translated at the rate current at the date of payment.
- *Dividends declared.* These are translated at the rate current at the date of declaration.
- *Transfers to/from reserves.* As noted earlier, if internal transfers are made, the rates applicable are those existing when the amounts transferred were originally recognised in equity.

The application of these rules will result in exchange differences. Exchange differences arise mainly from translating the foreign operation's monetary items at current rates in the same way as for the foreign currency monetary items of the entity. Because the non-monetary items are translated using a historical rate that is the same for year to year, no exchange differences arise in relation to the non-monetary items. Further, items in the income statement such as sales, purchases and expenses give rise to monetary items such as cash, receivables and payables. Hence, the exchange difference over the period can be explained by examining the movements in the monetary items over the period. The accounting for the exchange difference is explained in paragraph 28 of IAS 21:

> Exchange differences arising on the settlement of monetary items or on translating monetary items at rates different from those at which they were translated on initial recognition during the period, or in previous financial statements, shall be recognised in profit or loss in the period in which they arise, except as described in paragraph 32.

The exchange differences are then taken to the current period's income statement in the same way as movements in the exchange rates on an entity's own foreign currency monetary items. See section 24.10 of this chapter for a discussion of the paragraph 32 exception.

As stated in paragraph 34 of IAS 21, the application of the basic principles of the translation method means that when an entity keeps its records in a currency other than its functional currency all amounts are remeasured in the functional currency. This produces the same amounts in that currency as would have occurred had the items been recorded initially in the functional currency.

ILLUSTRATIVE EXAMPLE 24.1

Translation from local currency into functional currency

Golden Lion Ltd, a company operating in Singapore, is a wholly owned subsidiary of Kiwi Ltd, a company listed in New Zealand. Kiwi Ltd formed Golden Lion Ltd on 1 July 2004 with an investment of NZ$310 000. Golden Lion Ltd's records and financial statements are prepared in Singaporean dollars (S$). Golden Lion Ltd has prepared the financial information at 30 June 2005, as shown in figure 24.2.

Golden Lion Ltd Balance sheet as at 30 June 2005	
	2005 S$
Current assets:	
Inventory	210 000
Monetary assets	190 000
Total current assets	400 000
Non-current assets:	
Land – acquired 1/7/04	100 000
Buildings – acquired 1/10/04	120 000
Plant and equipment – acquired 1/11/04	110 000
Accumulated depreciation	(10 000)
Deferred tax asset	10 000
Total non-current assets	330 000
Total assets	730 000
Current liabilities:	
Current tax liability	70 000
Borrowings	50 000
Payables	100 000
Total current liabilities	220 000
Non-current liabilities:	
Borrowings	150 000
Total liabilities	370 000
Net assets	360 000
Equity:	
Share capital	310 000
Retained earnings	50 000
Total equity	360 000

→

Golden Lion Ltd Income statement for the year ended 30 June 2005		
	2005	
	S$	S$
Sales revenue		1 200 000
Cost of sales:		
Purchases	1 020 000	
Ending inventory	210 000	810 000
Gross profit		390 000
Expenses:		
Selling	120 000	
Depreciation	10 000	
Interest	20 000	
Other	90 000	240 000
Profit before income tax		150 000
Income tax expense		60 000
Profit for the period		90 000

The only movement in equity, other than in profit, was a dividend paid during the period of S$40 000.

Additional information

(a) Exchange rates over the period 1 July 2004 to 30 June 2005 were:

	S$1.00 = NZ$
1 July 2004	1.00
1 October 2004	0.95
1 November 2004	0.90
1 January 2005	0.85
1 April 2005	0.75
30 June 2005	0.75
Average rate for year	0.85
Average rate for final quarter	0.77

(b) Proceeds of long-term borrowings were received on 1 July 2004 and are payable in four annual instalments commencing 1 July 2005. Interest expense relates to this loan.

(c) The inventory on hand at balance date represents approximately the final three months' purchases.

(d) Revenues and expenses are spread evenly throughout the year.

(e) Deferred tax asset relates to depreciation of the plant and equipment.

(f) The dividends were paid on 1 April 2005.

Required

The functional currency is determined to be the New Zealand dollar. Translate the financial statements of Golden Lion Ltd into the functional currency.

Solution

The translation process is as shown in figure 24.2.

	S$	Rate	NZ$
Sales	1 200 000	0.85	1 020 000
Cost of sales:			
Purchases	1 020 000	0.85	867 000
Ending inventory	210 000	0.77	161 700
	810 000		705 300
Gross profit	390 000		314 700
Expenses:			
Selling	120 000	0.85	102 000
Depreciation	10 000	0.90	9 000
Interest	20 000	0.85	17 000
Other	90 000	0.85	76 500
	240 000		204 500
			110 200
Foreign exchange translation loss	0		1 000
Profit before tax	150 000		109 200
Income tax expense	60 000	0.85	51 000
Profit for the period	90 000		58 200
Retained earnings at 1/7/04	0		0
	90 000		58 200
Dividends paid	40 000	0.75	30 000
Retained earnings at 30/6/05	50 000		28 200
Share capital	310 000	1.00	310 000
Non-current borrowings	150 000	0.75	112 500
Current tax liability	70 000	0.75	52 500
Current borrowings	50 000	0.75	37 500
Payables	100 000	0.75	75 000
	730 000		615 700
Inventory	210 000	0.77	161 700
Monetary assets	190 000	0.75	142 500
Land	100 000	1.00	100 000
Buildings	120 000	0.95	114 000
Plant and equipment	110 000	0.90	99 000
Accumulated depreciation	(10 000)	0.90	(9 000)
Deferred tax asset	10 000	0.75	7 500
	730 000		615 700

FIGURE 24.2   Translation into functional currency

Exchange differences arise mainly from translating the foreign operation's monetary items at current rates in the same way as for the foreign currency monetary items of the entity. Because the non-monetary items are translated using a historical rate that is the same from year to year, exchange differences in relation to non-monetary items arise only in the periods in which they are acquired or sold. Items in the income statement such as sales, purchases and expenses give rise to monetary items such as cash, receivables and payables. Hence, exchange differences are going to arise by examining the movements in the monetary items over the period.

From figure 24.2, the net monetary assets of Golden Lion Ltd at 30 June 2005 consist of:

	S$
Monetary assets	190 000
Deferred tax asset	10 000
Borrowings: non-current	(150 000)
Borrowings: current	(50 000)
Current tax liability	(70 000)
Payables	(100 000)
Net monetary assets at 1/7/04	(170 000)

The changes in the net monetary assets are determined from the income statement. The exchange differences are calculated by comparing the difference between the exchange rate used in the translation process and the current rate at the reporting date:

	S$	Current rate less rate applied	NZ$ gain (loss)
Net monetary assets at 1 July 2004	310 000	(0.75–1.00)	(77 500)
Increases in monetary assets:			
Sales	1 200 000	(0.75–0.85)	(120 000)
	1 510 000		(197 500)
Decreases in monetary assets:			
Land	100 000	(0.75–1.00)	25 000
Buildings	120 000	(0.75–0.95)	24 000
Plant	110 000	(0.75–0.90)	16 500
Purchases	1 020 000	(0.75–0.85)	102 000
Selling expenses	120 000	(0.75–0.85)	12 000
Interest	20 000	(0.75–0.85)	2 000
Other expenses	90 000	(0.75–0.85)	9 000
Dividend paid	40 000	(0.75–0.75)	–
Income tax expense*	60 000	(0.75–0.85)	6 000
	1 680 000		196 500
Net monetary assets at 30 June 2005	(170 000)		(1 000)

* The entry for the period is:		S$	S$
Income tax expense	Dr	60 000	
Deferred tax asset	Dr	10 000	
Current tax liability	Cr		70 000

In preparing the translated financial statements for the following period, it should be noted that the balance of retained earnings at 30 June 2005, as translated in figure 24.2, is carried forward into the next period. In other words, there is no direct translation of the retained earnings (opening balance) within the translation process.

LO 5

24.6 Changing the functional currency

In the example used in the previous section, the foreign operation in Singapore used the New Zealand dollar as its functional currency. Because of changes in the foreign operation's circumstances, such as the source of raw materials or the variables that determine the selling price of the entity's products, it may be that the functional currency changes into, for example, Japanese yen. According to paragraph 33 of IAS 21, where there is a change in the functional currency the translation procedures apply from the date of the change. Further, paragraph 35 notes that the effect of a change is accounted for prospectively.

Assume, therefore that the Singaporean operation used New Zealand dollars as the functional currency until 1 June 2007, and then decided that the Japanese yen was the appropriate functional currency. The financial statements of the Singaporean entity at the date of change, 1 June 2007, would then be translated at the rate of exchange between the Japanese yen and the Singaporean dollar. This rate would be the historical rate for all non-monetary assets held at the date of change. Any exchange differences recognised in the statements translated into New Zealand dollars would not be recognised in the new translation. These gains/losses would resurface until the parent disposed of the foreign operation, and all exchange gains/losses would be taken into account at that point.

LO 6

24.7 Translation into the presentation currency

Consider an Australian entity that has two subsidiaries, one in Malaysia and one in Hong Kong, and the functional currency for each of these subsidiaries is the Hong Kong dollar. The Australian parent will have to prepare a set of consolidated financial statements for the group. In which currency should the consolidated financial statements be prepared?

Theoretically, any currency could be the presentation currency. It may be the Australian dollar if management perceives it as the currency in which users prefer to read the financial statements. In that case, the two subsidiaries' financial statements would be prepared in Hong Kong dollars, which is the functional currency for them both. These would then be translated into Australian dollars and consolidated with the parent entity's statements.

It is possible that the presentation currency could be the Hong Kong dollar, for example if the majority of shareholders in the parent entity were Hong Kong residents. In that case, the parent entity's statements would be translated from the Australian dollar into the Hong Kong dollar and consolidated with those of the subsidiaries as presented in their functional currency.

Hence, having prepared the parent's and the subsidiaries' financial statements in the relevant functional currencies, a presentation currency is chosen and all statements not already in that currency are translated into the presentation currency. Obviously, a number of presentation currencies could be chosen, and multiple translations undertaken.

Paragraph 39 of IAS 21 states the principles for translating from the functional currency into the presentation currency:

> The results and financial position of an entity whose functional currency is not the currency of a hyperinflationary economy shall be translated into a different presentation currency using the following procedures:
> (a) assets and liabilities for each balance sheet presented (i.e. including comparatives) shall be translated at the closing rate at the date of that balance date;
> (b) income and expenses for each income statement (i.e. including comparatives) shall be translated at exchange rates at the dates of the transactions; and
> (c) all resulting exchange differences shall be recognised as a separate component of equity.

Paragraph 40 notes that average rates over a period for income statement items may be used unless exchange rates fluctuate significantly over the period.

An elaboration of these procedures for a foreign subsidiary is as follows.

24.7.1 Balance sheet items

- *Assets*. All assets, whether current or non-current, monetary or non-monetary, are translated at the exchange rate current at the reporting date. This includes all contra-asset accounts such as accumulated depreciation and allowance for doubtful debts.
- *Liabilities*. All liabilities are translated at the same rate as assets, namely the exchange rate current at the reporting date.
- *Equity*. In selecting the appropriate rate, two factors need to be kept in mind. First, equity existing at the acquisition date or investment is distinguished from post-acquisition equity. Second, movements in other reserves and retained earnings constituting transfers within or internal to shareholders' equity are treated differently from other reserves.
- *Share capital*. If on hand at acquisition date or created by investment, this is translated at the rate current at acquisition date or investment. If created by transfer from a reserve, such as general reserve via a bonus issue, this is translated at the rate current at the date the amounts transferred were originally recognised in equity.
- *Other reserves*. If on hand at acquisition date, these are translated at the current exchange rate existing at acquisition date. If reserves are post-acquisition and created by an internal transfer within equity, they are translated at the rate existing at the date the reserve from which the transfer was made was originally recognised in the accounts. If post-acquisition and not the result of an internal transfer (e.g. an asset revaluation surplus), the rate used is that current at the date the reserve is recognised in the accounts.
- *Retained earnings*. If on hand at acquisition date, they are translated at the current exchange rate existing at acquisition. Any dividends from pre-acquisition profits are also translated at this rate. Post-acquisition profits are carried forward balances from translation of previous periods' income statements.

24.7.2 Income statement items

- *Income and expenses*. These are translated at the rates current at the applicable transaction dates. For items, such as purchases of inventory and sales, that occur regularly throughout the period, for practical reasons average or standard rates that approximate the relevant rates may be employed. This will involve considerations of materiality. In relation to items such as depreciation, which are allocations for a period, even though they may be recognised in the accounts only at year-end (because they reflect events occurring throughout the period) an average-for-the-period exchange rate may be used.
- *Dividends paid*. These are translated at the rates current when the dividends were paid.
- *Dividends declared*. These are translated at the rates current when the dividends are declared, generally at end-of-year rates.
- *Transfers to/from reserves*. As noted earlier, if these are transfers internal to equity, the rate used for the transfer and the reserve created is that existing when the amounts transferred were originally recognised in equity.

Using the example in figure 24.2 and, assuming that the functional currency of Golden Lion Ltd is Singaporean dollars, the translation into New Zealand dollars as a presentation currency is shown in figure 24.3.

	S$	Rate	NZ$
Sales	1 200 000	0.85	1 020 000
Cost of sales:			
Purchases	1 020 000	0.85	867 000
Ending inventory	210 000	0.77	161 700
	810 000		705 300
Gross profit	390 000		314 700
Expenses:			
Selling	120 000	0.85	102 000
Depreciation	10 000	0.85	8 500
Interest	20 000	0.85	17 000
Other	90 000	0.85	76 500
	240 000		204 000
Profit before tax			110 700
Income tax expense	60 000	0.85	51 000
Profit for the period	90 000		59 700
Retained earnings at 1/7/04	0		0
	90 000		59 700
Dividends paid	40 000	0.75	30 000
Retained earnings at 30/6/05	50 000		29 700
Share capital	310 000	1.00	310 000
Non-current borrowings	150 000	0.75	112 500
Current tax liability	70 000	0.75	52 500
Current borrowings	50 000	0.75	37 500
Payables	100 000	0.75	75 000
Foreign currency translation reserve			(69 700)
	730 000		547 500
Inventory	210 000	0.75	157 500
Monetary assets	190 000	0.75	142 500
Land	100 000	0.75	75 000
Buildings	120 000	0.75	90 000
Plant and equipment	110 000	0.75	82 500
Accumulated depreciation	(10 000)	0.75	(7 500)
Deferred tax asset	10 000	0.75	7 500
	730 000		547 500

FIGURE 24.3 Translation into presentation currency

The exchange difference arising as a result of the translation is NZ$(86 500) — there has been an exchange loss over the period. This loss arises for two reasons, as explained in paragraph 41 of IAS 21:

• *The income and expense items are translated at dates of the transactions and not the closing rate:*

The profit represents the net movements in income and expenses:

Profit	=	S$90 000
Profit as translated	=	NZ$59 700
Profit × closing rate	=	S$90 000 × 0.75
	=	NZ$67 500
Translation gain	=	NZ$(7800)

- *In the case of a net investment in a foreign operation, translating the opening net assets at an exchange rate different from the closing rate:*

Net investment at 1 July 2004	=	S$310 000
Net investment × opening rate	=	S$310 000 × 1.00
	=	NZ$310 000
Net investment × closing rate	=	S$310 000 × 0.75
	=	NZ$232 500
Translation loss	=	NZ$(77 500)

- The total translation loss is NZ$(69 700) equal to (NZ$7800 + NZ$(77 500)).

Note the following in relation to the translation into presentation currency:

- The exchange differences are not taken into current period income or expense. As explained in paragraph 41 of IAS 21, these exchange differences have little or no direct effect on the present and future cash flows from operations. The translation is for presentation only. It is the functional currency statements that recognise exchange differences in current period income and expense.
- In the Basis for Conclusions to the 2004 revisions, in paragraphs BC10–BC14, the IASB discussed whether the standard should (a) be permitted to present its financial statements in a currency other than the functional currency, (b) be allowed a limited choice of presentation currencies or (c) be permitted to present their financial statements in any currency. The IASB concluded that entities should be permitted to present in any currency or currencies. The IASB noted that some jurisdictions require the use of a specific presentation which will put constraints on some entities anyway. Further, many large groups have a large number of functional currencies and it is not clear which currency should be the presentation currency. In fact, in such circumstances management may prefer to use a number of presentation currencies.

When the AASB in Australia issued an exposure draft requesting responses to whether or not Australian accounting standards should require the use of the Australian dollar as the presentation currency, the following response was given by the Rinker Group Ltd (sourced from AASB 2003, p. 7):

> It is our view that mandated presentation currency is not now appropriate to the circumstances of Rinker and that adoption of an Australian converged standard which is identical to the proposals outlined in the improvement to IAS 21 would serve the users of our financial reports far better.
>
> While Rinker is domiciled in Australia, is listed on the Australian Stock Exchange and currently has a shareholder base which is approximately 80% Australian, it is overwhelmingly a US economic entity. Over 80% of its revenue, profit, and assets are in the US. Ninety-nine percent of its debt is in the US. The clearly stated strategy of the company is to grow in the US. One of the characteristics of the industry in which Rinker participates (heavy building materials) is that revenues and costs are totally denominated in the local currency (US revenue and costs are completely in US dollars; Australian revenue and costs are completely in Australian dollars). As a result, variances in US dollar/Australian dollar exchange rates represent purely translation variances with no economic impact on the intrinsic value of the entity ...
>
> ... mandated reporting in Australian dollars may provide misleading information to the users of financial reports, particularly in periods when there are significant movements in the US dollar/Australian dollar exchange rates ...

In the AASB papers summarising these responses, the example shown in figure 24.4 was provided to illustrate the point being made by Rinker.

	2001	2002	2003
Debtors – $US	10	13	16
Actual growth	–	30%	23%
Exchange rate: A$1 = US$	0.5	0.56	0.67
Translate to presentation currency – A$			
Debtors – A$	20	23	24
Growth reported	–	15%	4%
Difference between growth rates	–	15%	19%

FIGURE 24.4   Illustration of the argument for non-monetary presentation currency
Source: From AASB (2003), p. 4.

The financial statements in the functional currency show the financial performance and position of the entity in the currency that primarily affects the operations of that entity. The translation process should not result in a different performance/position being shown. Note the effect on the comparative analysis of the change in exchange rates. The only way that the problem is overcome is if, in comparing the 2003 results with the 2002 results, the 2002 results are translated at the 2003 exchange rate rather than the 2002 rate. In other words, comparative figures must be continuously updated for exchange rate changes. This is a similar process to that used in accounting for inflation where both the current year's and prior year's accounts must be presented in current year dollars as the buying power of the dollar changes due to inflation.

- Paragraphs BC15–BC23 of the Basis for Conclusions on IAS 21 discuss the translation method for translating from the functional currency to a different presentation currency. In paragraph BC16, the IASB emphasises that the translation process 'should not change the way in which the underlying items are measured'. Rather, the translation method should merely *express* the underlying amounts, as measured in the functional currency, in a different currency. In this regard, refer to figure 24.4. Note the following ratios:

	S$	NZ$
Current ratio	400 000/730 000 = 0.548	300 000/547 500 = 0.548
Debt to equity	370 000/360 000 = 1.03	277 500/270 000 = 1.03
Profit to sales	90 000/1 200 000 = 0.075	76 500/1 020 000 = 0.075
However, note:		
Profit to equity	90 000/360 000 = 0.25	76 500/270 000 = 0.28

The ratios are only ever going to be fully retained if all items in both the income statement and the balance sheet are translated at the closing rate. Using the exchange rates at the date of transaction means that retaining the ratios will not be possible. Paragraph BC17 notes that the IASB considered the method of translating all amounts at the most recent closing rate, noting that the method is simple, does not generate exchange differences and does not change ratios such as return on assets. However, the IASB prefers the method adopted in IAS 21, arguing that this method gives the same result if you translate the foreign entity's statements first into a functional currency and then into a different presentation currency or translate them directly into the presentation currency. For example, consider a Singaporean entity that has a functional currency of Hong Kong dollars but a presentation currency of Australian dollars. In relation to, say, a S$100 sales revenue transaction on 1 January 2005, whether you translate (a) using the spot rate for Singaporean dollars to Hong Kong dollars, and then translate this amount to Australian dollars using the spot rate on 1 January 2005 for Hong Kong dollars to Australian dollars; or (b) using the spot rate on 1 January 2005 for Singaporean dollars to Australian dollars the answer is the same. This occurs because both the translation to functional currency and the translation to presentation currencies for income statement items use the spot rate at the date of the transaction. In contrast, if the presentation translation used the closing rate for all accounts, a different answer would be obtained. However, the translation directly into the presentation currency does not isolate the exchange differences affecting income/expense that arise under a functional currency translation; rather it includes these exchange differences and those arising on a presentation translation into one amount affecting equity rather than income/expense.

LO 7

24.8 Consolidating foreign subsidiaries — where local currency is the functional currency

Paragraphs 44–47 of IAS 21 deal with matters relating to the consolidation of foreign subsidiaries. As noted in paragraph 45, normal consolidation procedures as set down in IAS 27 apply to foreign subsidiaries. Where a parent establishes or sets up a subsidiary in a foreign country, the determination of what exists at acquisition date is relatively simple. This is because generally the investment recorded by the parent is equal to the initial share capital of the subsidiary. Where a parent entity obtains an overseas subsidiary by acquiring an already existing operation, the date of control determines the point of time at which historical rates for translation are determined.

For example, assume on 1 July 2006 Austco Ltd acquires all the shares of Ishikawa Ltd, a Japanese entity that has been in existence for many years. The group commences on the date of control, namely 1 July 2006. Ishikawa Ltd may have some land that it acquired in 2000 for 1000 yen. The historical cost in the records of the company is 1000 yen. In other words, even though the overseas entity has held the land prior to the date that Austco Ltd obtained control over the foreign entity, the date for measurement of the historical rate is the date of control. This is because, under IFRS 3 *Business Combinations*, all assets and liabilities of the subsidiary are measured at fair value at acquisition date.

24.8.1 Acquisition analysis

Assume that Austco Ltd acquired all the shares of Ishikawa Ltd at 1 July 2006 for A$30 000, when the exchange rate between the Australian dollar and the Japanese yen was 1:5. At acquisition date, the equity of that company consisted of:

	¥	A$
Share capital	100 000	20 000
Retained earnings	40 000	8 000

All the identifiable assets and liabilities of Ishikawa Ltd were recorded at fair value except for plant, for which the fair value was ¥5000 (equal to A$1000) greater than the carrying amount. The plant has a further five-year life. The Japanese tax rate is 20%. The Australian tax rate is 30%. At 30 June 2007, the exchange rate is A$1 = ¥6. The average rate for the year is A$1 = ¥5.5.

At acquisition date:	
Net fair value of identifiable assets and liabilities of Ishikawa Ltd	= A$20 000 + $8000 + A$1000(1 − 20%) (BCVR − plant)
	= A$28 800
Cost of the combination	= A$30 000
Goodwill	= A$1200
	= ¥(1200 × 5)
	= ¥6000

As noted in paragraph 47 of IAS 21, the goodwill is regarded as an asset of the subsidiary.

24.8.2   Business combination valuation entries

Goodwill

At acquisition date, the entry in Japanese yen is:

		¥	¥
Goodwill	Dr	6 000	
Business combination valuation reserve	Cr		6 000

The valuation reserve continues to be translated at the rate at acquisition date as it is pre-acquisition equity. Assuming the functional currency is the yen, the financial statements of Ishikawa Ltd would be translated into Australian dollars for presentation purposes. The goodwill is translated at the closing rate of 1:5, giving rise to a foreign currency translation loss, recognised in equity. Hence, on consolidation, the worksheet entry at 30/6/07 is:

		A$	A$
Goodwill	Dr	1 000	
Foreign currency translation reserve	Dr	200	
Business combination valuation reserve	Cr		1 200

Plant

Similarly to goodwill, as noted in paragraph 47 of IAS 21, any fair value adjustments to the carrying amounts of assets and liabilities at acquisition date are treated as assets and liabilities of the foreign operation.

At acquisition date, the valuation entry is:

		A$	A$
Plant (¥5000/5)	Dr	1 000	
Deferred tax liability	Dr		200
Business combination valuation reserve	Cr		800

At 30 June 2007, the valuation reserve is translated at the exchange rate at acquisition date and, as with goodwill, a foreign exchange loss is recognised — in this case on both the plant and the deferred tax liability:

		A$	A$
Plant (¥5000/6)	Dr	833	
Foreign currency translation reserve	Dr	134	
Deferred tax liability (20% × 833)	Cr		167
Business combination valuation reserve	Cr		800

The plant is depreciated at 20% per annum. This is based on the ¥5000 adjustment, giving a depreciation of ¥1000 per annum. The plant is translated at closing rates while the depreciation is translated at average rates.

Depreciation expense [¥1000/5.5]	Dr	182	
Accumulated depreciation [¥1000/6.0]	Cr		167
Foreign currency translation reserve	Cr		15
Deferred tax liability [¥200/6.0 or 20% × 167]	Dr	33	
Income tax expense [¥200/5.5]	Cr		36
Foreign currency translation reserve	Dr	3	

24.8.3 Pre-acquisition entry

The entry at acquisition date and at 30 June 2007 is:

Retained earnings (1/7/06)	Dr	8 000	
Share capital	Dr	20 000	
Business combination valuation reserve [800 + 1200]	Dr	2 000	
Shares in Ishikawa Ltd	Cr		30 000

24.8.4 Minority interest

The MI receives a share of the recorded equity of the subsidiary as well as the valuation reserves raised on consolidation. The MI also receives a share of the foreign currency translation reserve raised on the translation into the presentation currency. This share will need to be adjusted for any movements in that reserve as a result of movements raised via the revaluation process.

24.8.5 Intragroup transactions

As with any transactions within the group, the effects of transactions between a parent and its foreign subsidiaries, or between foreign subsidiaries, must be eliminated in full. Neither IAS 21 nor IAS 27 provide specific guidance in relation to transactions with foreign entities. A key matter of concern is whether the adjustment should be affected by changes in the exchange rate. In this regard, note paragraphs 136 and 137 of the Basis for Conclusions relating to the US Statement of Financial Accounting Standards (SFAS) No. 52 *Foreign Currency Translation*:

> 136. An intercompany sale or transfer of inventory, machinery, etc., frequently produces an intercompany profit for the selling entity and, likewise, the acquiring entity's cost of the inventory, machinery, etc., includes a component of intercompany profit. The Board considered whether computation of the amount of intercompany profit to be eliminated should be based on exchange rates in effect on the date of the intercompany sale or transfer, or whether that computation should be based on exchange rates as of the date the asset (inventory, machinery, etc.) or the related expense (cost of sales, depreciation, etc.) is translated.

137. The Board decided that any intercompany profit occurs on the date of sale or transfer and that exchange rates in effect on that date or reasonable approximations thereof should be used to compute the amount of any intercompany profit to be eliminated. The effect of subsequent changes in exchange rates on the transferred asset or the related expense is viewed as being the result of changes in exchange rates rather than being attributable to intercompany profit.

It needs to be emphasised that the process of making the consolidation adjustments is to eliminate the *effects* of intragroup transactions. The exchange rate change is not an effect of the transaction but an economic effect on the group resulting from having assets in foreign entities.

Example 1: Parent sells inventory to foreign subsidiary

Assume Aust Ltd, an Australian company, owns 100% of the shares of a foreign operation, F Ltd. During the current period, when the exchange rate is F1 = $2, Aust Ltd sells $10 000 worth of inventory to F Ltd, at a before-tax profit of $2000. At the end of the period, F Ltd still has all inventory on hand. At the year-end balance date, the exchange rate is F1 = $2.50. The Australian tax rate is 30%, while the tax rate in the foreign country is 20%.

Assuming the financial statements of F Ltd have been translated from the functional currency (F) to the presentation currency (Australian dollars), the consolidation worksheet adjustment entries for the intragroup transaction are:

Sales	Dr	10 000	
Cost of sales	Cr		8 000
Inventory	Cr		2 000
Deferred tax asset	Dr	400	
Income tax expense	Cr		400
(20% × 2000)			

The above entries eliminate the sales and cost of sales as recorded by the parent. The inventory would have been recorded by F Ltd at F5000. The translation process at balance date would mean the F5000 of inventory would be translated using the closing rate of F1 = $2.50, giving a translated figure for inventory of $12 500. After passing the consolidation adjustment entry, inventory in the consolidated balance sheet would be reported at $10 500 (i.e. $12 500 – $2000). This figure is greater than the original cost of $8000 due to the exchange rate change between the transaction date and the balance date. The US FASB would argue that no further entry is necessary as the effect of changes in the exchange rates on the transferred asset is viewed as the result of changes in exchange rates rather than intragroup profit.

Note that the tax rate used is that of the country holding the asset — in this case, the foreign country. This is because the adjustment for the tax effect is required because of the adjustment to the carrying amount of the inventory in the first journal entry. As the inventory is held by the foreign entity, it is the foreign country's tax rate that is applicable.

Example 2: Foreign subsidiary sells inventory to parent

Assume F Ltd, the foreign subsidiary, sells an item of inventory to Aust Ltd, the Australian parent, during the current period. The inventory had cost F Ltd F5000 and was sold to Aust Ltd for F7500. At the date of sale, the exchange rate was F1 = $2. The tax rate in Australia is 30%. All inventory was still on hand at the end of the period when the closing exchange rate was F1 = $2.50.

The consolidation worksheet entry is:

Sales	Dr	15 000	
Cost of sales	Cr		10 000
Inventory	Cr		5 000
Deferred tax asset	Dr	1 500	
Income tax expense	Cr		1 500

Both sales and cost of sales as recorded by F Ltd are translated at the exchange rate existing at the date of the transaction, namely F1 = $2. The inventory sold to the parent is recorded by that entity at $15 000. The profit on sale is adjusted against inventory at the exchange rate existing at date of sale, giving an adjustment of $5000. Hence, in the consolidated balance sheet at the end of the period, the inventory is reported at $10 000, equal to the original cost to F Ltd.

ILLUSTRATIVE EXAMPLE 24.2

Consolidation — functional currency is the subsidiary's local currency

On 1 January 2004, Kangaroo Ltd, an Australian company, acquired 80% of the shares of Kiwi Ltd, a New Zealand company, for A$2 498 000. The 2004 trial balance of Kiwi Ltd prepared in New Zealand dollars, which is also the functional currency, showed the following information:

	1 January 2004 NZ$000	31 December 2004 NZ$000
Revenue		6 450
Cost of sales		4 400
Gross profit		2 050
Expenses:		
Depreciation		280
Other		960
		1 240
Profit before income tax		810
Income tax expense		120
Profit		690
Retained earnings at beginning of year		1 440
		2 130
Dividend paid		100
Dividend declared		100
		200
Retained earnings at end of year		1 930

(continued)

	1 January 2004 NZ$000	31 December 2004 NZ$000
Cash and receivables	1 000	1 760
Inventories	1 200	1 000
Land	800	800
Buildings	2 200	2 200
Accumulated depreciation	(900)	(990)
Equipment	1 130	1 330
Accumulated depreciation	(200)	(390)
Total assets	5 230	5 710
Current liabilities	590	420
Non-current liabilities	1 200	1 360
Total liabilities	1 790	1 780
Net assets	3 440	3 930
Share capital	2 000	2 000
Retained earnings	1 440	1 930
Total equity	3 440	3 930

Additional information

1. Direct exchange rates for the New Zealand dollar are as follows:

1 January 2004	1.20
1 July 2004	1.25
1 November 2004	1.35
31 December 2004	1.40
Average for the year	1.30

2. At 1 January 2004, all the assets and liabilities of Kiwi Ltd were recorded at fair value except for the land, for which the fair value was NZ$1 000 000, and the equipment, for which the fair value was $1 010 000. The undervalued equipment had a further four-year life. The tax rate in New Zealand is 25%.

3. Additional equipment was acquired on 1 July 2004 for NZ$200 000 by issuing a note for NZ$160 000 and paying the balance in cash.

4. Sales and expenses were incurred evenly throughout the year.

5. Dividends of NZ$100 000 were paid on 1 July 2004.

6. On 1 November 2004, Kiwi Ltd sold inventory to Kangaroo Ltd for NZ$25 000. The inventory had cost Kiwi Ltd $20 000. Half of the inventory is still on hand at 31 December 2004. The Australian tax rate is 30%.

Required

1. Translate the New Zealand financial statements into the Australian dollar, which is the presentation currency.

2. Prepare the consolidation worksheet entries for consolidating the New Zealand subsidiary into the consolidated financial statements of Kangaroo Ltd.

Solution
1. Translation into presentation currency

	NZ$	Rate	A$
Revenue	6 450	1/1.30	4 962
Cost of sales	4 400	1/1.30	3 385
Gross profit	2 050		1 577
Depreciation	280	1/1.30	215
Other	960	1/1.30	739
	1 240		954
Profit before tax	810		623
Income tax expense	120	1/1.30	92
Profit	690		531
Retained earnings as at 1/1/04	1 440	1/1.20	1 200
	2 130		1 731
Dividend paid	100	1/1.25	80
Dividend declared	100	1/1.40	71
	200		151
Retained earnings as at 31/12/04	1 930		1 580
Share capital	2 000	1/1.20	1 667
Non-current liabilities	1 360	1/1.40	971
Current liabilities	420	1/1.40	300
Foreign currency translation reserve			(439)
	5 710		4 079
Cash and receivables	1 760	1/1.40	1 257
Inventories	1 000	1/1.40	714
Land	800	1/1.40	572
Buildings	2 200	1/1.40	1 572
Accumulated depreciation	(990)	1/1.40	(707)
Equipment	1 330	1/1.40	950
Accumulated depreciation	(390)	1/1.40	(279)
	5 710		4 079

In relation to the foreign currency translation reserve:
- *The income and expense items are translated at dates of the transactions and not the closing rate:*
  The profit represents the net movements in income and expenses:

Profit	=	NZ$690 000
Profit as translated	=	A$530 800
Profit × closing rate	=	NZ$690 000 × 1/1.40
	=	A$492 857
Translation loss	=	A$(37 943)
Dividend paid as translated	=	A$80 000
Dividend paid at closing rate	=	NZ$100 000 × 1/1.40
	=	A$71 429
Translation gain	=	A$8571

→

- *In the case of a net investment in a foreign operation, translating the opening net assets at an exchange rate different from the closing rate:*

Net investment at 1 July 2004	=	NZ\$3 440 000
Net investment × opening rate	=	NZ\$3 440 000 × 1/1.20
	=	A\$2 866 667
Net investment × closing rate	=	NZ\$3 440 000 × 1/1.40
	=	A\$2 457 143
Translation loss	=	A\$(409 524)

- Total translation loss is A\$(438 896) = (A\$(37 943) + A\$(409 524)) + \$8571

2. **Consolidation worksheet entries:**
   (in \$000)

Net fair value of identifiable assets and liabilities of Kiwi Ltd	=	A\$[2000 + 1440 + 200(1 − 25%) (land) + 80(1 − 25%) (equipment)] 1/1.20
	=	A\$[1667 + 1200 + 125 + 50]
Net fair value acquired	=	80% × A\$[1667 + 1200 + 125 + 50]
	=	A\$[1334 + 960 + 100 + 40]
	=	A\$2434
Cost of combination	=	A\$2498
Goodwill acquired	=	A\$64
	=	NZ\$77 (i.e. 64 × 1.20)

(i) Business combination valuation entries

Land (200/1.40)	Dr	143	
Foreign currency translation reserve	Dr	18	
Business combination valuation reserve (150/1.20)	Cr		125
Deferred tax liability (50/1.40)	Cr		36
Accumulated depreciation (200/1.40)	Dr	143	
Equipment (120/1.40)	Cr		86
Foreign currency translation reserve	Dr	7	
Deferred tax liability (25% × (80/1.40))	Cr		14
Business combination valuation reserve (60/1.20)	Cr		50
Depreciation expense ([1/4 × 80]/1.30)	Dr	15	
Accumulated depreciation ([1/4 × 80]/1.40)	Cr		14
Foreign currency translation reserve	Cr		1
Deferred tax liability ([25% × 20]/1.30)	Dr	3.5	
Income tax expense ([25% × 20]/1.30)	Cr		3.8
Foreign currency translation reserve	Dr	0.3	

(At acquisition the deferred tax liability was NZ\$20 = 25% × NZ\$80)

(ii) Pre-acquisition entry

Retained earnings (1/1/04)	Dr	960	
Share capital	Dr	1 334	
Business combination valuation reserve	Dr	140	
Goodwill	Dr	64	
Shares in Kiwi Ltd	Cr		2 498
Foreign currency translation reserve	Dr	9	
Goodwill (77/1.40 − 64)	Cr		9

(iii) Minority interest
Share at acquisition date

Retained earnings (1/1/04) (20% × 1200)	Dr	240	
Share capital (20% × 1667)	Dr	333	
Business combination valuation reserve (20% [125 + 50])	Dr	35	
MI	Cr		608

Share from 1/1/04–31/12/04
(i) Current period profit – the share is based on the translated profit of the subsidiary

MI share of profit	Dr	104	
MI	Cr		104
(20% × A$[531 − (15 − 3.8)])			

(ii) The share of the foreign currency translation reserve is based on the amount of the reserve calculated as a result of the translation process adjusted by any changes in that reserve recognised in the valuation entries

MI	Dr	93	
Foreign currency translation reserve	Cr		93
(20% [439 + 18 + 7 + 1 + 0.3])			

(iii) Dividend paid

MI	Dr	16	
Dividend paid	Cr		16
(20% × A$80)			

(iv) Dividend declared

MI	Dr	14	
Dividend declared	Cr		14
(20% × A$71)			

Intragroup transactions:

(i) Dividends

Dividend revenue	Dr	64	
Dividend paid	Cr		64
(80% × 100/1.25)			

Dividend revenue	Dr	57	
Dividend receivable	Cr		57
(80% × 100/1.40)			

Dividend payable	Dr	57	
Dividend declared	Cr		57

(ii) Sale of inventory: subsidiary to parent

Sales revenue (25/1.35)	Dr	19	
Cost of sales	Cr		17
Inventory (1/2 × 5 × 1/1.35)	Cr		2

Deferred tax asset (30% × 2)	Dr	0.6	
Income tax expense	Cr		0.6

(iii) Adjustment to MI

MI	Dr	0.28	
MI share of profit	Cr		0.28
(20% × (2 − 0.6))			

24.9 Consolidating foreign subsidiaries — where functional currency is that of the parent entity

In this circumstance, the subsidiary's financial statements are prepared in the local currency, and, as the parent's currency is the functional currency, they are translated into the parent's currency. The main difference in preparing the consolidated financial statements in this case is in the valuation entries. This is because the translation of non-monetary assets differs when the translation is for presentation purposes rather than for functional currency purposes.

Under the method described in paragraph 23 of IAS 21, the non-monetary assets of the subsidiary are translated using exchange rates at the date of the transaction (i.e. historical rates). In contrast, in illustrative example 24.2, where the translation is based on paragraph 39 of IAS 21, the non-monetary assets are translated at the closing rate.

Using the information in illustrative example 24.2:

- at acquisition date, 1 January 2004, goodwill of the subsidiary was measured to be NZ$96
- the land had a fair value-carrying amount difference of NZ$200
- the equipment had a fair value-carrying amount difference of NZ$80, with an expected remaining useful life of 25%
- the NZ tax rate is 25%
- the direct exchange rates for the NZ dollar are shown opposite.

1 January 2004	1.20
1 July 2004	1.25
1 November 2004	1.35
31 December, 2004	1.40
Average for the year	1.30

The business combination valuation entries are then:

The goodwill balance is translated at the historical rate:

Goodwill (96/1.20)	Dr	80	
Business combination valuation reserve (96/1.20)	Cr		80

The land is translated at the historical rate, but the deferred tax liability is translated at the closing rate. As the net monetary assets held at the beginning of the period are affected by changes in the exchange rate, an exchange gain is recognised.

Land (200/1.20)	Dr	167	
Foreign exchange gain	Cr		6
Business combination valuation reserve (150/1.20)	Cr		125
Deferred tax liability (50/1.40)	Cr		36

The equipment and related accumulated depreciation are translated at the historical rate, while the deferred tax liability is translated at the closing rate, giving rise to a foreign exchange gain.

Subsequent depreciation is based on the historical rate.

Accumulated depreciation (200/1.20)	Dr	167	
Equipment (120/1.20)	Cr		100
Foreign exchange gain	Cr		3
Deferred tax liability ((25% × 80)1.40))	Cr		14
Business combination valuation reserve (60/1.20)	Cr		50
Depreciation expense ([1/4 × 80]/1.20)	Dr	17	
Accumulated depreciation ([1/4 × 80]/1.20)	Cr		17
Deferred tax liability ([25% × 20]/1.40)	Dr	3.5	
Income tax expense ([25% × 20]/1.30)	Cr		3.8
Foreign currency exchange loss	Dr	0.3	

(At acquisition the deferred tax liability was NZ$20 = 25% × NZ$80)

LO 8

24.10 Net investment in a foreign operation

Paragraph 15 of IAS 21 notes that the investment in a foreign operation may consist of more than just the ownership of shares in that operation. An entity may have a monetary item that is receivable or payable to the foreign subsidiary. According to paragraph 15, where there is an item for which settlement is neither planned nor likely to occur in the foreseeable future, it is in substance a part of the entity's net investment in that foreign operation. These items include long-term receivables and payables but not trade receivables or payables.

Consider the situation where an Australian parent entity has made a long-term loan of 100 000 yen to a Japanese subsidiary when the exchange rate is $2 = ¥1. The parent entity records a receivable of $200 000, while the subsidiary records a payable of ¥100 000. If during the following financial period the exchange rate changes to $3 = ¥1, in accordance with paragraph 28 of IAS 21 the Australian parent passes the following entry in its own records:

| Loan receivable | Dr | 100 000 | |
| Exchange gain | Cr | | 100 000 |

This results in the receivable being recorded at $300 000. The subsidiary does not pass any entry because it still owes ¥100 000. On translation of the subsidiary into the presentation currency (the Australian dollar), the payable is translated into $300 000. On consolidation of the subsidiary, both the payable and the receivable are eliminated. However, because the receivable is regarded as part of the parent's net investment in the subsidiary, the accounting for the exchange gain is in accord with paragraph 32 of IAS 21:

> Exchange differences arising on a monetary item that forms part of a reporting entity's net investment in a foreign operation (see paragraph 15) shall be recognised in profit or loss in the separate financial statements of the reporting entity or the individual financial statements of the foreign operation, as appropriate. In the financial statements that include the foreign operation and the reporting entity (e.g. consolidated financial statements where the foreign operation is a subsidiary), such exchange differences shall be recognised initially in a separate component of equity and recognised in profit or loss on disposal of the net investment in accordance with paragraph 48.

Hence, the exchange gain of $100 000 recognised as income by the parent must, on consolidation, be reclassified to the foreign currency translation reserve raised as part of the translation process. Hence, in the consolidation worksheet the adjustment entry is:

| Exchange gain | Dr | 100 000 | |
| Foreign currency translation reserve | Cr | | 100 000 |

LO 9

24.11 Disclosure

Paragraphs 51–57 contain the disclosure requirements under IAS 21. In particular, an entity must disclose:
- the amount of exchange differences included in profit or loss for the period
- net exchange differences classified in a separate component of equity, and a reconciliation of the amount of such exchange differences at the beginning and end of the period
- when the presentation currency of the parent entity is different from the functional currency:
  - the fact that they are different
  - the functional currency
  - the reason for using a different presentation currency
- when there is a change in the functional currency, the fact that such a change has occurred.

Some examples of accounting policies notes in relation to currency translation are given in figure 24.5.

Example 1: Nokia Corporation, a Finnish limited liability company domiciled in Helsinki

Transactions in foreign currencies

Transactions in foreign currencies are recorded at the rates of exchange prevailing at the dates of the individual transactions. For practical reasons, a rate that approximates the actual rate at the date of the transaction is often used. At the end of the accounting period, the unsettled balances on foreign currency receivables and liabilities are valued at the rates of exchange prevailing at the year-end. Foreign exchange gains and losses arising from balance sheet items, as well as fair value changes in the related hedging instruments, are reported in Financial Income and Expenses.

Foreign Group companies

In the consolidated accounts all items in the profit and loss accounts of foreign subsidiaries are translated into euro at the average foreign exchange rates for the accounting period. The balance sheets of foreign Group companies are translated into euro at the year-end foreign exchange rates with the exception of goodwill arising on the acquisition of a foreign company prior to the adoption of IAS 21 (revised 2004) as of January 1, 2005, which is translated to euro at historical rates. Differences resulting from the translation of profit and loss account items at the average rate and the balance sheet items at the closing rate are treated as an adjustment affecting consolidated shareholders' equity. On the disposal of all or part of a foreign Group company by sale, liquidation, repayment of share capital or abandonment, the cumulative amount or proportionate share of the translation difference is recognized as income or as expense in the same period in which the gain or loss on disposal is recognized.

Source: Nokia (2005, p. 11).

Example 2: Bayer Group, which has headquarters in Germany and activities in Europe, North America and Asia

Foreign currency translation

In the financial statements of the individual consolidated companies, foreign currency receivables and payables are translated at closing rates, irrespective of whether they are exchange-hedged. Forward contracts that, from an economic point of view, serve as a hedge against fluctuations in exchange rates are stated at fair value.

The majority of consolidated companies outside the euro zone are to be regarded as foreign entities since they are financially, economically and organizationally autonomous. Their functional currencies according to IAS 21 (The Effects of Changes in Foreign Exchange Rates) are thus the respective local currencies. The assets and liabilities of these companies are therefore translated at closing rates, while income and expense items are translated at average rates for the year.

Where the operations of a company outside the euro zone are integral to those of Bayer AG, the functional currency is the euro. Property, plant and equipment, intangible assets, investments in affiliated companies and other securities included in investments are translated at the historical exchange rates on the dates of addition, along with any relevant amortization, depreciation and write-downs. All other balance sheet items are translated at closing rates. Income and expense items (except amortization, depreciation and write-downs) are translated at average rates for the year.

Exchange differences arising from the translation of foreign companies' balance sheets are shown in a separate stockholders' equity item.

In case of divestiture, the respective exchange differences are reversed and recognized in income.

The exchange rates for major currencies against the euro varied as follows:

€1		Closing rate		Average rate	
		2004	2005	2004	2005
Argentina	ARS	4.05	3.57	3.66	3.64
Brazil	BRL	3.62	2.76	3.64	3.04
UK	GBP	0.71	0.69	0.68	0.68
Japan	JPY	139.65	138.90	134.40	136.86
Canada	CAD	1.64	1.37	1.62	1.51
Mexico	MXN	15.23	12.59	14.04	13.58
Switzerland	CHF	1.54	1.56	1.54	1.55
USA	USD	1.36	1.18	1.24	1.24

Source: Bayer (2006, p. 93).

FIGURE 24.5   Accounting policies on foreign currency translation

Notice in figure 24.5, that the Bayer Group provides information about the functional currencies of the entities within the group, which relates to the disclosures required by paragraph 53 of IAS 21.

Illustrative disclosures relating to paragraph 52 of IAS 21 are given in figure 24.6.

NOTE			IAS 21 Para.
Movements in reserves			
Foreign Currency Translation Reserve	**2005**	**2004**	*52(b)*
Balance at beginning of period	(2 420)	(3 020)	
Exchange differences arising on translation of overseas operations	(540)	600	
Balance at end of period	(2 960)	(2 420)	
Profit from operations			
	2005	**2004**	
Profit from operations has been arrived at after charging:			
Amortisation	x	x	
Research and development costs	x	x	
Net foreign exchange losses/(gains)	765	(346)	*52(a)*

FIGURE 24.6 Disclosures required by paragraph 50 of IAS 21

24.12 Summary

A parent entity may have investments in subsidiaries that are incorporated in countries other than that of the parent. The foreign operation will record its transactions generally in the local currency. However, the local currency may not be that of the economy that determines the pricing of those transactions. To this end, IAS 21 requires the financial statements of a foreign operation to be translated into its functional currency, being the currency of the primary economic environment in which the entity operates. Determination of the functional currency is a matter of judgement, and the choice of the appropriate currency requires an analysis of the underlying economics of the foreign operation. A further problem addressed by IAS 21 is where the financial statements of the foreign operation need to be presented in a currency different from the functional currency. IAS 21 then provides principles relating to the translation of a set of financial statements into the presentation currency. Whenever a translation process is undertaken, foreign exchange translation adjustments arise. It is necessary to determine whether these adjustments are taken to current income or to a separate component of equity.

Where the foreign operation is a subsidiary, having translated the financial statements of the foreign operation into the currency in which the consolidated financial statements are to be presented, consolidation worksheet adjustments are required as a part of the normal consolidation process. In assessing the assets and liabilities held by the subsidiary at acquisition date, as well as any goodwill or excess arising as a result of the acquisition, the effects of movements in exchange rates on these assets and liabilities must be taken into consideration. The consolidation adjustments are affected by the process of translation used to translate the foreign entity's financial statements from the local currency into either the functional currency or the presentation currency.

DISCUSSION QUESTIONS[1]

1. What is the purpose of translating financial statements from one currency to another?
2. What is meant by 'functional currency'?
3. What is the rationale behind the choice of an exchange rate as an entity's functional currency?
4. What guidelines are used to determine the functional currency of an entity?
5. How are income statement items translated from the local currency into the functional currency?
6. How are balance sheet items translated from the local currency into the functional currency?
7. How are foreign exchange gains and losses calculated when translating from local currency to functional currency?
8. What is meant by 'presentation currency'?
9. How are income statement items translated from functional currency to presentation currency?
10. How are balance sheet items translated from functional currency to presentation currency?
11. What causes a foreign currency translation reserve to arise?
12. Why are gains/losses on translation taken to a foreign currency translation reserve rather than to profit and loss for the period?
13. In relation to the following case situations, discuss the choice of a functional currency.

Case 1
A Malaysian operation manufactures a product using Malaysian materials and labour. Specialised equipment and senior operations staff are supplied by its Australian parent. Reimbursement invoices for these services are denominated in the Malaysian ringgit. The product is sold in the Malaysian market at a price, denominated in Malaysian ringgit, which is determined by competition with similar locally produced products. The foreign operation retains sufficient cash to meet wages and day-to-day operating costs with the remainder being remitted to the Australian parent. The receipt of dividends from the foreign operation is important to the parent's cash management function. Long-term financing is arranged and serviced by the parent.

Case 2
A Korean operation is a wholly owned subsidiary of an Australian company which regards the operation as a long-term investment, and thus takes no part in the day-to-day decision making of the operation. The operation purchases parts from various non-related Australian manufacturers for assembly by Korean labour. The finished product is exported to a number of countries but Australia is the major market. Consequently, sales prices are determined by competition within Australia.

14. In relation to the following case situations, discuss whether you regard the reporting entity as exposed to foreign exchange gains and losses in relation to the foreign entity.

Case 1
A foreign operation extracts mineral ores that are shipped to Australia for processing at the parent entity's smelters. All senior personnel at the foreign operation are parent entity employees. Monthly invoices for ore supplied to the parent are denominated in US dollars. The parent entity pays these invoices with US dollars obtained by selling its finished product to US customers, thus taking advantage of a natural hedge. Payments to the foreign operation cover all running costs but long-term financing is provided by the parent entity.

Case 2
A foreign operation extracts a mineral product that it exports worldwide. The sales price is subject to daily fluctuations. The Australian parent regards the operation as an investment only but the extreme volatility of the foreign operation's sales prices impacts on the price of the parent's shares on the Australian stock exchange because the investment in the foreign operation is one of the parent's significant assets.

15. In relation to the following case situations, discuss which currency is the functional currency of the foreign entity.

Case 1
An Indonesian operation manufactures a product using Indonesian materials and labour. Patented processes and senior operations staff are supplied by its Australian parent. Reimbursement invoices for these services are denominated in Indonesian rupiah. The product is sold in the Indonesian market at a price, denominated in rupiah, that is determined by

---

1. (*Note:* The cases in discussion questions 13–15 were used in the project by Radford (1996) to test the implementation of AASB 1012 by Australian companies.)

competition with similar locally produced products. The Indonesian operation remits all revenue to the Australian parent, retaining only sufficient cash to meet wages and day-to-day operating costs. The receipt of cash from the Indonesian operation is important to the parent's cash management function. Long-term financing is arranged and serviced by the parent.

Case 2

A New Zealand operation is a wholly owned subsidiary of an Australian company. The parent regards the operation as a long-term investment and all financial and operational decisions are made by New Zealand management. The New Zealand operation purchases parts from various non-related Australian manufacturers for assembly in New Zealand. The finished product is exported to a number of countries with Australia as the major market. Consequently, sales prices are determined by competition within Australia.

16. Foreign Ltd is a Queensland software developer that specialises in software that controls the operations of open cut mining. To exploit opportunities in the US market, the firm has established a fully owned subsidiary operating in Atlanta, Georgia. The operations of the subsidiary (Opencut Inc.) essentially involve the marketing of software initially developed in Australia but which is further developed by the US subsidiary to suit the special requirements of particular US customers. Foreign Ltd does not charge Opencut Inc. for the software successfully amended and marketed in the United States. At this stage no dividends have been paid by Opencut Inc; however, it is expected that dividends will commence within 12 months. With respect to working capital, Opencut Inc. has a 'revolving credit' agreement (overdraft facility) with the Bank of Georgia, which has been guaranteed by the Australian parent.

    Discuss the process of translating the financial statements of Opencut Inc. for consolidation with Foreign Ltd.

17. The accounts listed below are for a wholly owned foreign subsidiary. In the space provided indicate the exchange rate that would be used to translate the accounts into Australian dollars. Use the following letters to indicate the appropriate exchange rate:

    H — historical exchange rate

C — current exchange rate at the end of the current period
A — average exchange rate for the current period.

	Australian dollar is the functional currency	Foreign currency is the functional currency
Cash		
Prepaid expenses		
Equipment		
Goodwill		
Accounts payable		
Inventory — at cost		
Inventory — at net realisable value		
Capital		
Sales		
Depreciation expense		

18. Victory Ltd is an Australian company with two overseas subsidiaries, one in Indonesia and the other in South Korea. The Indonesian subsidiary has as its major activity the distribution in Indonesia of Victory Ltd's products. It has been agreed that the subsidiary will, for a period of time, retain all profits in order to expand its distribution network in Indonesia. In the past it has remitted most of its profits to the Australian parent company.

    The South Korean subsidiary has been established to manufacture a range of products for the South-East Asian market. There is also an expectation that it could in the future become the major manufacturing plant for Victory Ltd and provide a supply of products for the Australian market.

    Based on the above, determine the functional currency of the foreign subsidiaries. Explain your choice.

19. Discuss the differences in the translation process when translating from a local currency to a functional currency compared with translating from a functional currency to a presentation currency.

20. Discuss the use of a foreign currency translation reserve to account for movements in exchange rates compared with taking gains/losses as a result of movements in exchange rates directly to the income statement.

21. Explain what is meant by the 'net investment in a foreign operation'. Provide an example and explain the accounting implications.

EXERCISES

EXERCISE 24.1 ★

Translation into functional currency

Cloud Ltd is a manufacturer of sheepskin products in New Zealand. It is a fully owned subsidiary of a Hong Kong company, Asian Ltd. The following assets are held by Cloud Ltd at 30 June 2006:

Plant:	Cost NZ$	Useful life (years)	Acquisition date	Exchange rate on acquisition date (NZ$1 = HK$)
Tanner	40 000	5	10/8/02	5.4
Benches	20 000	8	8/3/04	5.8
Presses	70 000	7	6/10/05	6.2

Plant is depreciated on a straight-line basis, with zero residual values. All assets acquired in the first half of a month are allocated a full month's depreciation.

Inventory:
- At 1 July 2005, the inventory on hand of $25 000 was acquired during the last month of the 2004–05 period.
- Inventory acquired during the 2005–06 period was acquired evenly throughout the period. Total purchases of $420 000 was acquired during that period.
- The inventory of $30 000 on hand at 30 June 2006 was acquired during June 2006.

Relevant exchange rates (quoted as NZ$1 = HK$) are as follows:

Average for June 2005	7.2
1 July 2005	7.0
Average for 2005–06	7.5
Average for June 2006	7.7
30 June 2006	7.8

Required
1. Assuming the functional currency for Cloud Ltd is the NZ$, calculate:
   (a) the balances for the plant items and inventory in HK$ at 30 June 2006
   (b) the depreciation and cost of sales amounts in the income statement for 2005–06.
2. Assuming the functional currency is the HK$, calculate:
   (a) the balances for the plant items and inventory in HK$ at 30 June 2006
   (b) the depreciation and cost of sales amounts in the income statement for 2005–06.
3. Discuss the differences in the results achieved in parts 1 and 2 above, and why the choice of the functional currency gives a different set of accounting numbers.

EXERCISE 24.2 ★★

Translation into presentation currency

Bruce Ltd, an Australian company, acquired all the issued shares of Yukon Ltd, a US company, on 1 January 2005. At this date, the net assets of Yukon Ltd are shown overleaf.

	US$
Property, plant and equipment	155 000
Accumulated depreciation	(30 000)
	125 000
Cash	10 000
Inventory	20 000
Accounts receivable	10 000
Total assets	165 000
Accounts payable	15 000
Net assets	150 000

The trial balance of Yukon Ltd at 31 December 2005 was:

	US$ Dr	US$ Cr
Share capital		100 000
Retained earnings		50 000
Accounts payable		42 000
Sales		90 000
Accumulated depreciation – plant and equipment		45 000
Property, plant and equipment	155 000	
Accounts receivable	40 000	
Inventory	45 000	
Cash	12 000	
Cost of sales	30 000	
Depreciation	15 000	
Other expenses	30 000	
	327 000	327 000

Additional information
1. No property, plant and equipment were acquired in the 2005 period.
2. All sales and expenses were acquired evenly throughout the period. The inventory on hand at the end of the year was acquired during December 2005.
3. Exchange rates were (A$1 = US$):

1 January 2005	0.52
31 December 2005	0.60
Average for December 2005	0.58
Average for 2005	0.56

4. The functional currency for Yukon Ltd is the US dollar.

Required
1. Prepare the financial statements of Yukon Ltd at 31 December 2005 in the presentation currency of Australian dollars.
2. Verify the translation adjustment.
3. Discuss the differences that would occur if the functional currency of Yukon Ltd were the Australian dollar.
4. If the functional currency were the Australian dollar, calculate the translation adjustment.

EXERCISE 24.3 ★★   Translation of financial statements into functional currency

Orchard Ltd, a company incorporated in Singapore, acquired all the issued shares of Nathan Ltd, a Hong Kong company, on 1 July 2005. The trial balance of Nathan Ltd at 30 June 2006 was:

	HK$ Dr	HK$ Cr
Share capital		800 000
Retained earnings (1/7/05)		240 000
General reserve		100 000
Payables		160 000
Deferred tax liability		120 000
Current tax liability		20 000
Provisions		80 000
Sales		610 000
Proceeds on sale of land		250 000
Accumulated depreciation – plant		340 000
Plant	920 000	
Land	400 000	
Cash	240 000	
Accounts receivable	300 000	
Inventory at 1 July 2005	60 000	
Purchases	260 000	
Depreciation – plant	156 000	
Carrying amount of land sold	200 000	
Income tax expense	50 000	
Other expenses	134 000	
	2 720 000	2 720 000

Additional information

1. Exchange rates based on equivalence to HK$1 were:

	S$
1 July 2005	0.20
8 October 2005	0.25
1 December 2005	0.28
1 January 2006	0.30
2 April 2006	0.27
30 June 2006	0.22
Average during last quarter 2005–06	0.24
Average 2005–06	0.26

2. Inventory was acquired evenly throughout the year. The closing inventory of HK$60 000 was acquired during the last quarter of the year.
3. Sales and other expenses occurred evenly throughout the year.
4. The Hong Kong tax rate is 20%.
5. The land on hand at the beginning of the year was sold on 8 October 2005. The land on hand at the end of the year was acquired on 1 December 2005.

6. Movements in plant over 2005–06 were:

Plant at 1 July 2005	HK$600 000
Acquisitions – 8 October 2005	200 000
– 2 April 2006	120 000
Plant at 30 June 2006	920 000

Depreciation on plant is measured at 20% per annum on cost. Where assets are acquired during a month, a full month's depreciation is charged.

7. The functional currency of the Hong Kong operation is the Singaporean dollar.

Required
1. Prepare the financial statements of Nathan Ltd in Singaporean dollars at 30 June 2006.
2. Verify the translation adjustment.

EXERCISE 24.4 ★★ Consolidation worksheet entries for foreign subsidiary

Using the information in exercise 21.3, assume that Orchard Ltd acquired the shares in Nathan Ltd for HK$1 250 000. All the identifiable assets and liabilities of Nathan Ltd at acquisition date were recorded at amounts equal to fair value except for the following assets:

	HK$ Carrying amount	HK$ Fair value
Inventory	60 000	70 000
Land	200 000	250 000
Plant (cost HK$800 000)	600 000	640 000

The plant is expected to have a further four-year life. The inventory is all sold by 30 June 2006. The tax rate in Hong Kong is 20%.

Required
Prepare the consolidation worksheet entries for the preparation of the consolidated financial statements of Orchard Ltd at 30 June 2006.

EXERCISE 24.5 ★★ Different functional currencies, consolidation adjustments

On 1 July 2005, an Australian company, Bruce Ltd, acquired all the issued capital of a Swedish company, Mikael Ltd, for $997 400. At the date of acquisition, the equity of Mikael Ltd consisted of:

	Krona (K)
Share capital	800 000
General reserve	200 000
Retained earnings	635 000

All the identifiable assets and liabilities of Mikael Ltd were recorded at fair value except for plant for which the fair value was K100 000 greater than carrying amount. The plant has a further five-year life.

The internal financial statements of Mikael Ltd at 30 June 2006 are shown opposite.

Income statement		
	K	K
Revenues		2 585 000
Cost of sales:		
Opening stock	600 000	
Purchases	1 800 000	
	2 400 000	
Closing stock 580 000	1 820 000	
Gross profit		765 000
Expenses:		
Depreciation	125 000	
Other	270 000	395 000
Profit before income tax		370 000
Income tax expense		200 000
Profit for the period		170 000
Retained earnings as at 1 July 2005		635 000
		805 000
Dividend paid		100 000
Retained earnings as at 30 June 2006		705 000

Balance sheet		
1/7/05 K		30/6/06 K
	Current assets	
500 000	Cash and receivables	500 000
600 000	Inventory	580 000
1 100 000	Total current assets	1 080 000
	Non-current assets	
300 000	Land	300 000
700 000	Buildings	700 000
(100 000)	Accumulated depreciation	(130 000)
800 000	Plant	900 000
(235 000)	Accumulated depreciation	(330 000)
1 465 000	Total non-current assets	1 440 000
2 565 000	Total assets	2 520 000
350 000	Current liabilities	235 000
	Non-current liabilities	
580 000	Notes – issued September 2005	580 000
930 000	Total liabilities	815 000
1 635 000	Net assets	1 705 000
	Equity	
800 000	Share capital	800 000
200 000	General reserve	200 000
635 000	Retained earnings	705 000
1 635 000	Total equity	1 705 000

Additional information

1. Exchange rates for the Swedish krona were as follows:

	1 krona = $A
1 July 2005	0.54
Average 2005–06	0.52
January 2006	0.52
30 June 2006	0.50
Average for the last four months of the 2005–06 period	0.51

2. Mikael Ltd acquired additional plant for K100 000 on 1 January 2006 by issuing a note for K80 000 and paying the balance in cash.
3. Sales, purchases and other expenses were incurred evenly through the year.
4. Depreciation for the period in krona was as follows:

Buildings	30 000
Plant	
– acquired before 1 July 2005	85 000
– acquired 1 January 2006	10 000

5. The inventory is valued on a FIFO basis. The opening stock was acquired when the exchange rate was 0.55, and the closing stock was acquired during the last four months of the 2005–06 period.
6. Dividends of K50 000 were paid on 2 July 2005 and 1 January 2006. The former were from profits earned prior to 1 July 2005.
7. The tax rate for Mikael Ltd is 25%.

Required

1. Translate the accounts of the foreign subsidiary, Mikael Ltd, into Australian dollars at 30 June 2006, assuming:
   (a) the functional currency is the Swedish krona, and the presentation currency is the Australian dollar
   (b) the functional currency is the Australian dollar, as is the presentation currency.
2. Verify the translation adjustments in 1.
3. Prepare for each of (a) and (b) above the business combination valuation and pre-acquisition entries for the preparation of the consolidated financial statements at 30 June 2006.

PROBLEMS	
PROBLEM 24.1 ★★	Consolidation of foreign currency translation reserve

On 1 July 2004, Koala Ltd, an Australian company, acquired shares in Wai Chen Ltd, a company based in Hong Kong. At this date, the equity of Wai Chen Ltd was:

	HK$
Share capital	200 000
General reserve	100 000
Retained earnings	300 000

At 30 June 2005 and 2006 respectively, the retained earnings balances of Wai Chen Ltd were HK$400 000 and HK$450 000 respectively. All transactions occurred evenly

throughout these years. The internal financial statements of the two companies at 30 June 2007 were as follows:

Income statements		
	Koala Ltd A$	Wai Chen Ltd HK$
Sales	700 000	595 000
Cost of sales	300 000	400 000
	400 000	195 000
Expenses	210 200	100 000
	189 800	95 000
Dividend revenue	12 000	–
Profit before income tax	201 800	95 000
Tax expense	51 800	20 000
Profit	150 000	75 000
Retained earnings as at 1/7/06	750 000	450 000
	900 000	525 000
Dividend paid	100 000	25 000
Retained earnings as at 30/6/07	800 000	500 000

Balance sheets		
	Koala Ltd A$	Wai Chen Ltd HK$
Current assets	311 520	250 000
Shares in Wai Chen Ltd	288 480	–
Property, plant and equipment (net)	700 000	500 000
Patents and trademarks	100 000	150 000
Total assets	1 400 000	900 000
Liabilities	100 000	100 000
Net assets	1 300 000	800 000
Equity:		
Share capital	500 000	200 000
General reserve	–	100 000
Retained earnings	800 000	500 000
Total equity	1 300 000	800 000

Additional information
1. The dividend paid by Wai Chen Ltd was paid on 1 May 2007.
2. Some relevant exchange rates are:

1 July 2004	HK$1 = $A0.80
Average 2004–05	0.82
1 July 2005	0.85
Average 2005–06	0.88
1 July 2006	0.90
Average 2006–07	0.85
1 May 2007	0.80
30 June 2007	0.78

Required

Translate the financial statements of Wai Chen Ltd as at 30 June 2007 into the presentation currency of Australian dollars, assuming that the functional currency is the Hong Kong dollar.

Translation into presentation currency, consolidation adjustments

Dragon Boat Ltd is an international company resident in Singapore. It acquired 80% of the issued shares of an Australian company, Black Swan Ltd, on 1 July 2005 for A$560 000. All the identifiable assets and liabilities of Black Swan Ltd were recorded at fair value except for the following:

	Carrying amount A$	Fair value A$
Plant (net)	180 000	240 000
Inventory	68 000	90 000
Brand names	0	140 000

The plant is considered to have a remaining life of five years, with depreciation being calculated on a straight-line basis. All inventory on hand at acquisition date was sold within the following 12-month period. The brand names are considered to have an indefinite life, and are adjusted only if impaired.

At 30 June 2006, the following information was available about the two companies:

	Dragon Boat Ltd S$	Black Swan Ltd A$
Share capital	560 000	350 000
Retained earnings as at 1/7/05	330 000	170 000
Provisions	45 000	30 000
Payables	14 000	40 000
Sales	620 000	310 000
Dividend revenue	6 400	0
Accumulated depreciation – plant	210 000	160 000
	1 785 400	1 060 000
Cash	92 100	30 000
Accounts receivable	145 300	115 000
Inventory	110 000	80 000
Shares in Black Swan Ltd	336 000	0
Buildings (net)	84 000	220 000
Plant	420 000	400 000
Cost of sales	390 000	120 000
Depreciation – plant	85 000	40 000
Tax expense	23 000	15 000
Other expenses	50 000	10 000
Dividend paid	20 000	10 000
Dividend provided	30 000	20 000
	1 785 400	1 060 000

Additional information

1. Sales, purchases and other expenses were incurred evenly throughout the 2005–06 period. The dividend was paid by Black Swan Ltd on 1 January 2006, while the dividend was declared on 30 June 2006.
2. The tax rate in Australia is 30% and the tax rate in Singapore is 20%.
3. Black Swan Ltd acquired A$100 000 additional new plant on 1 January 2006. Of the depreciation charged in the 2005–06 period, A$8000 related to the new plant.
4. The rates of exchange between the Australian dollar and the Singapore dollar were (expressed as A$1 = S$0.6):

1 July 2005	0.60
1 December 2005	0.64
1 January 2006	0.68
30 June 2006	0.70
Average for the 2005–06 period	0.65

5. The functional currency of the Australian subsidiary is the Australian dollar.
6. On 1 January 2006, Black Swan Ltd sold some inventory to Dragon Boat Ltd for A$20 000. The inventory had cost the subsidiary $18 000. Only 10% of this inventory remained unsold by the parent entity at 30 June 2006.

Required

1. Translate the financial statements of Black Swan Ltd into Singapore dollars for inclusion in the consolidated financial statements of Dragon Boat Ltd.
2. Verify the translation adjustment.
3. Prepare the consolidation worksheet entries necessary for the preparation of the consolidated financial statements at 30 June 2006.

PROBLEM 24.3 ★★★   Translation into functional currency, intragroup transactions

On 1 January 2003, Aussie Ltd formed a company, Dundee Ltd, in the United States to sell Australian products such as boomerangs and cuddly koalas and kangaroos. The initial capital was US$500 000. On 1 February 2004, a lease was signed on a shop for US$20 000, payable on the first day of each month. On 15 February, store furnishings were acquired for $448 000; these were expected to have a useful life of four years. On 10 June 2003, more fittings were acquired at a cost of $124 000, again with an expected life of four years. The financial statements of Dundee Ltd at 31 December 2003 were:

Additional information

1. Where non-current assets are acquired during a month, a full month's depreciation is applied.
2. The tax rate in the United States is 20%, while the tax rate in Australia is 30%.
3. The functional currency for Dundee Ltd is the Australian dollar.
4. Exchange rates for the financial year were (A$1 = US$):

1 January 2003	0.60
1 February	0.63
15 February	0.64
10 June	0.66
30 June	0.65
Average for first half year	0.63
30 September	0.66
1 December	0.69
Average for second half year	0.65
31 December 2003	0.70

5. Sales in the first half of the year amounted to $210 000.

6. Expenses, other than depreciation, leases costs and purchases, in the first half of the year amounted to $60 000.

7. Aussie Ltd sold inventory to Dundee Ltd at cost plus 20%. Inventory transferred to Dundee Ltd during the year consisted of:

1 February	US$50 000
30 June	US$60 000
30 September	US$40 000
1 December	US$80 000

All the inventory was sold by Dundee Ltd except for $20 000 of the stock transferred on 1 December 2003.

8. Financial information relating to Dundee Ltd for the year ending 31 December 2003 is:

	US$
Sales revenue	680 000
Closing inventory	20 000
Accumulated depreciation – furniture and fittings	120 750
Accounts payable	40 000
Share capital	500 000
	1 360 750
Lease expenses	220 000
Purchases	230 000
Inventory	20 000
Other expenses	150 000
Depreciation – furniture and fittings	120 750
Furniture and fittings	572 000
Cash	14 600
Accounts receivable	33 400
	1 360 750

Required

1. Translate the financial statements of Dundee Ltd into Australian dollars for inclusion in the consolidated financial statements of Aussie Ltd at 31 December 2003.

2. Prepare the consolidation worksheet entries for adjusting for the effects of the inventory sales from the parent to the subsidiary.

PROBLEM 24.4 ★★★ Translation into presentation currency, consolidation entries

On 1 July 2006, Koala Ltd, an Australian company, acquired 80% of the issued shares of Grizzly Ltd, a company incorporated in the United States for US$789 600 (= A$1 579 200). The draft income statement and balance sheet of Grizzly Ltd at 30 June 2007 are shown opposite.

	US$	US$
Sales revenues		1 600 000
Cost of sales:		
Opening inventory	140 000	
Purchases	840 000	
	980 000	
Closing inventory	280 000	700 000
Gross profit		900 000
Expenses:		
Depreciation	90 000	
Other	270 000	360 000
Profit before income tax		540 000
Income tax expense		200 000
Profit		340 000
Retained earnings as at 1 July 2006		200 000
		540 000
Dividend paid	120 000	
Dividend declared	200 000	320 000
Retained earnings as at 30 June 2007		220 000

	2007 US$	2006 US$
Current assets:		
Inventory	280 000	140 000
Accounts receivable	20 000	130 000
Cash	20 000	570 000
Total current assets	320 000	840 000
Non-current assets:		
Patent	80 000	80 000
Plant	720 000	600 000
Accumulated depreciation	(130 000)	(80 000)
Land	500 000	300 000
Buildings	920 000	820 000
Accumulated depreciation	(120 000)	(80 000)
Total non-current assets	1 970 000	1 640 000
Total assets	2 290 000	2 480 000
Current liabilities:		
Provisions	500 000	620 000
Accounts payable	320 000	940 000
Total current liabilities	820 000	1 560 000
Non-current liabilities:		
Loan from Koala Ltd	530 000	–
Total liabilities	1 350 000	1 560 000
Net assets	940 000	920 000
Equity:		
Share capital	720 000	720 000
Retained earnings	220 000	200 000
Total equity	940 000	920 000

Additional information

1. At acquisition date, all the assets and liabilities of Grizzly Ltd were recorded at fair value except for:

	Fair value US$
Plant	540 000
Land	324 000
Inventory	182 000

   The plant was expected to have a further five-year life. The inventory was all sold by July 2007. The US tax rate is 25%.

2. On 1 January 2007, Grizzly Ltd acquired new plant for US$120 000. This plant is depreciated over a five-year period.

3. On 1 April 2007, Grizzly Ltd acquired US$200 000 worth of land.

4. On 1 October 2006, Grizzly Ltd acquired US$100 000 worth of new buildings. These buildings are depreciated evenly over a 10-year period.

5. The interim dividend was paid on 1 January 2007, half of which was from profits earned prior to 1 July 2006, while the dividend payable was declared on 30 June 2007.

6. Sales, purchases and expenses occurred evenly throughout the period. The inventory on hand at 30 June 2007 was acquired during June 2007.

7. The loan of US$530 000 from Koala Ltd was granted on 1 July 2006. The interest rate is 8% per annum. Interest is paid on 30 June and 1 January each year.

8. Koala Ltd sold raw materials to Grizzly Ltd at 20% mark-up on cost. During the 2006–07 period there were three shipments of raw materials, costing Grizzly Ltd:

1 October 2006	US$120 000
1 January	US$96 000
1 April 2007	US$132 000

   At 30 June 2007, 20% of the shipment in April remains on hand in Grizzly Ltd. The Australian tax rate is 30%.

9. The exchange rates for the financial year were as follows:

	US$1 = A$
1 July 2006	2.00
1 October 2006	1.80
1 January 2007	1.70
1 April 2007	1.60
30 June 2007	1.50
Average June 2007	1.52
Average for 2006–07	1.75

Required

1. If the functional currency for Grizzly Ltd is the US dollar, prepare the financial statements of Grizzly Ltd at 30 June 2007 in the presentation currency of the Australian dollar.

2. Verify the foreign currency translation adjustment.

3. Prepare the consolidation worksheet entries to consolidate the translated financial statements of Grizzly Ltd with its parent entity at 30 June 2007.

PROBLEM 24.5   Translation into foreign currency, consolidation effects

Use the information in problem 24.4.

Required

1. If the functional currency for Grizzly Ltd is the Australian dollar, prepare the financial statements of Grizzly Ltd at 30 June 2007 in the functional currency.
2. Verify the foreign currency translation adjustment.
3. Prepare the consolidation worksheet entries to consolidate the translated financial statements of Grizzly Ltd with its parent entity at 30 June 2007.
4. Assume on 1 January 2007, Grizzly Ltd sold the patent to Koala Ltd for US$100 000 and that Koala Ltd depreciates this asset evenly over a 20-year period. Prepare the consolidation worksheet adjustment entries at 30 June 2007.

WEBLINK

Visit these websites for additional information:

www.iasb.org   www.iasplus.com

www.asic.gov.au   www.ifac.org

www.aasb.com.au   www.nzica.com

www.accaglobal.com   www.capa.com.my

REFERENCES

AASB 2003, *Presentation Currency of Australia Financial Reports* (Agenda paper 12.2), collation of submissions on the invitation to comment meeting of the AASB, 15–16 October, Glenelg, South Australia.

Bayer 2006, *Bayer Annual Report 2005*, Bayer AG, Germany, viewed 20 April 2006, <www.bayer.com>.

FASB 1981, *Foreign currency translation: Statement of Financial Accounting Standards No. 52*, Norwalk, Connecticut.

Jeter, DC & Chaney, PK 2003, *Advanced accounting*, 2nd edn, John Wiley, US.

Nokia 2005, *Nokia in 2005*, Nokia Corporation, Finland, viewed 20 April 2006, <www.nokia.com>.

Radford, J 1996, *Foreign currency translation: clarity or confusion?*, project written as part of a Masters of Commerce degree, Curtin University of Technology, Perth, Western Australia.

Revsine, L 1984, 'The rationale underlying the functional currency choice', *The Accounting Review*, vol. 59 no. 3, pp. 505–14.

CHAPTER 25
Accounting for investments in associates

ACCOUNTING STANDARDS

International: IAS 28 *Investments in Associates*
Australia: AASB 128 *Investments in Associates*
New Zealand: NZ IAS 28 *Investments in Associates*

CONCEPTS FOR REVIEW

Before studying this chapter, you should understand or, if necessary, revise:

- the criteria for consolidation
- the criteria for identifying parent entities and subsidiaries
- the adjustments at acquisition date when preparing consolidated financial statements
- accounting for the effects on consolidation of intragroup transactions.

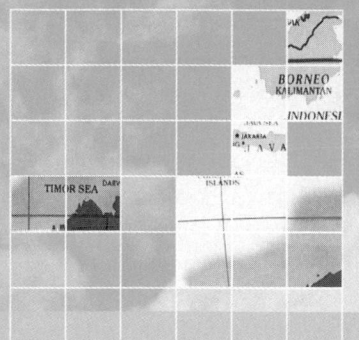

LEARNING OBJECTIVES

When you have studied this chapter, you should be able to:

1. apply the criteria for identifying associates
2. explain in which entities the equity method is applied
3. explain the basic principles of the equity method
4. adjust for goodwill and fair value differences at acquisition date
5. adjust for movements in equity from dividends and reserves, and the effects of different accounting policies
6. adjust for the effects of inter-entity transactions
7. account for losses recorded by the associate
8. prepare the disclosures required by IAS 28
9. prepare a set of financial statements applying the equity method to associates.

25.1 Accounting for equity investments in other entities

It is a common feature of global business that entities hold investments in other entities. Accounting standards provide different methods for accounting for those investments, depending on the nature of the investments and the relationship between the investor and the investee. Traditionally, investments in other entities have been recorded using the cost model, under which the investment has been recorded at its cost of acquisition. Changes to the recorded amount of the investment occur only if the asset is impaired, while increases in the worth of the investment are not recognised. The investor recognises revenue in relation to the investment only when the investee declares or pays a dividend from post-acquisition equity.

As detailed in chapter 6 of this book, IAS 39 *Financial Instruments: Recognition and Measurement* provides standards on the accounting for equity investments in other entities. When a financial asset is recognised initially, it is measured at cost, which is the *fair value* of the consideration given. For the purpose of measuring a financial asset subsequent to initial recognition, IAS 39 classifies financial assets into four categories. Where financial assets are held for trading, gains and losses from changes in fair value are recognised in profit or loss for the period; while for financial assets classified as available-for-sale, the changes in fair value are recognised directly in equity (except for impairment losses) until the asset is derecognised.

However, as stated in paragraph 1 of IAS 39, that standard does not apply to 'investments in subsidiaries, associates and joint ventures', except under certain conditions. Hence, investments in financial assets are accounted for under IAS 39 until they meet the criteria for classification as subsidiaries, associates or joint ventures. They are then accounted for under the relevant standard for that classification. In this book, chapters 19–24 are concerned with the accounting for subsidiaries. Because of the particular relationship that exists between a parent and a subsidiary (which is based on the control of the parent over the subsidiary), the standard setters believe that a special form of accounting other than the cost method or the fair value method is applicable, so that users of the financial statements can obtain a more informed picture of the financial position and performance of the combined economic entity or group. Hence, IAS 27 *Consolidated and Separate Financial Statements* requires the use of the *consolidation method* to account for parents and subsidiaries. The consolidation method results in the financial statements of the parent and each of its subsidiaries being combined to form the consolidated financial statements. These consolidated statements report all the assets, liabilities, revenues and expenses of these entities. The information about the entities is presented on a detailed, line-by-line basis in both the income statement and the balance sheet. The accounts of the investor are not affected by the application of the consolidation method.

Just as a subsidiary is seen as having a special relationship with its parent so that a particular form of accounting is required to provide the necessary information about those companies, the relationship between an investor and its associated entities is seen as being of special significance so that a specific accounting method – the equity method of accounting – is required to provide information about the investor and its associates. As with subsidiaries, the nature of the investor–associate relationship is clearly defined, in this case in IAS 28 *Investments in Associates*, and the principles of the equity method specifically established. The accounting for investments in associates is the focus of this chapter. The accounting for joint ventures is covered in chapter 26.

25.2 Identifying associates

An associate is defined in paragraph 2 of IAS 28 as follows:

> An associate is an entity, including an unincorporated entity such as a partnership, over which the investor has significant influence and that is neither a subsidiary nor an interest in a joint venture.

Significant influence

The key characteristic determining the existence of an associate is that of significant influence. This term is defined in paragraph 2 of IAS 28 as follows:

> Significant influence is the power to participate in the financial and operating policy decisions of the investee but is not control or joint control over those policies.

Note the following features of this definition:

- The definition requires the investor to have the power, or the capacity, to affect the investee. As with the definition of control identifying a parent–subsidiary relationship (see chapter 19), the definition does not require the investor to actually exercise that power. Instead, the focus is on the existence of the power or capacity.
- The specific power is that of being able to participate in the financial and operating decisions of the investee. Whereas the parent–subsidiary relationship was defined in terms of the power or capacity to *dominate* the financial and operating decisions of the subsidiary, the investor–associate relationship relates to the power to *participate* in those same decisions. Hence, the investor–associate relationship is of the same nature as that existing between a parent and subsidiary, the difference being the level of control that can be exercised.
- The definition recognises three types or levels of control that one entity can exercise over another: control or dominance (relating to subsidiaries), significant influence (relating to associates), and joint control. The latter relates to joint ventures, and is discussed in chapter 26 of this book.
- In the definitions of an associate and significant influence, there is no requirement for the investor to hold any shares, or have a beneficial interest, in the associate. However, as is discussed in more detail in section 25.3 of this chapter, the application of the equity method of accounting is based on the investor owning shares in the associate. In other words, if significant influence is exercised by one entity over another by virtue of an association or contract other than from the holding of shares, then the equity method cannot be applied in relation to the associate. Even in such cases, however, some of the disclosures required by IAS 28 in relation to associates may still be required.

The assessment of the existence of significant influence requires judgement on the part of accountants. To assist in this determination, IAS 28 provides further guidance in paragraphs 6–10:

- Paragraph 6 provides that where an investor holds, directly or indirectly (for example, through subsidiaries) 20% or more of the voting power of the investee, it is presumed that the investor has significant influence over the investee. This is a rebuttable presumption because if the investor can demonstrate that such influence does not exist, then the investee is not classified as an associate. Further, where the investor owns less than 20% of another entity, there is a presumption that the investee is *not* an associate. It is therefore possible for more than one entity to have significant influence over another entity, but there can be only one parent entity in relation to a subsidiary.
- Paragraph 7 provides a list of factors that may evidence the existence of significant influence:
  (a) representation on the board of directors or equivalent governing body of the investee
  (b) participation in policy-making processes, including participation in decisions about dividends or other distributions

(c) material transactions between the investor and the investee

(d) interchange of managerial personnel

(e) provision of essential technical information.

In all the above examples, the evidence relates to actual participation. In general, the most common form of participation is that of representation on the board of directors. In other words, because of the significance of the ownership interest of the investor in the associate, the investor is able to obtain representation on the board of directors and hence influence the decision making in the investee.

- Paragraph 8 raises the issue of whether ownership of securities such as options or convertible notes should be used in assessing the existence of significant influence. This paragraph requires the potential effect of the exercise of such securities to be considered in cases where the holder currently has the ability to exercise or convert those rights. Where the rights are not exercisable because they are subject to a time constraint, they should not be taken into consideration. Note that there must be a current ability to exercise power, not a future ability to do so.

Exclusions

As noted above, where the level of influence is such that the investor has control or joint control, the investee is not regarded as an associate. Further, some entities that would meet the definition of associates are also excluded from the requirements of IAS 28. Paragraph 1 states that IAS 28 does not apply to investments in associates held by:

- venture capital organisations, or
- mutual funds, unit trusts and similar entities including investment-linked insurance funds

that are classified as held for trading and accounted for at fair value in accordance with IAS 39. Such entities must recognise changes in the fair values of those investments in the current period profit or loss. According to the Basis for Conclusions on IAS 28, paragraphs BC5 and BC6, these exclusions were made because of the lack of relevance of equity-accounted information to those entities, as well as the frequent changes in the level of ownership in these investments by such entities.

Paragraph 13 of IAS 28 also provides exclusions from the application of the equity method to associates. In particular:

- Where the investment in the associate is acquired and held exclusively with a view to its disposal within 12 months of acquisition, and the management is actively seeking a buyer, the equity method does not have to be applied to that associate. Appendix B of IFRS 5 *Non-current Assets Held for Sale and Discontinued Operations* establishes criteria for classifying assets as 'held for sale'. Such assets are required to be measured at the lower of their carrying amounts and fair values less costs to sell. According to paragraph 15 of IAS 28, if the associate is not disposed of within the requisite 12 months, the financial statements must be restated and the investment accounted for in accordance with the equity method.

  Where all these conditions apply, the entity shall account for the associate as a held-for-trading investment and accounted for at fair value, with changes in fair value affecting current period profit or loss.

- Where all the following apply, an investor need not apply the equity method of accounting:
  - the investor is a wholly-owned subsidiary, or is a partially-owned subsidiary of another entity and its owners have been informed about and do not object to the investor not applying the equity method
  - the investor's debt or equity securities are not traded in a public market such as a domestic or foreign stock exchange

– the investor did not file, nor is in the process of filing, its financial statements with a securities commission or other regulatory organisation, for the purpose of issuing any class of securities in a public market
– the ultimate or any intermediate parent of the investor publishes consolidated financial statements that comply with International Financial Reporting Standards.

25.3 Application — consolidated or separate financial statements

LO 2

Paragraph 1 of IAS 28 requires that investments in associates be accounted for by the equity method, as detailed in this standard.

Where the investor prepares consolidated financial statements, investments in associates held by the parent and its subsidiaries are accounted for in the consolidated financial statements by the equity method. Therefore, the accounting entries applying the equity method to the investment in the associate are made in the *consolidation worksheet*. The adjustment entries must then be made on a year-to-year basis, because no permanent entries for the equity accounting are made in the records of the investor.

Where the investor has no subsidiaries and therefore does not prepare consolidated financial statements, the investor must apply the equity method to its associates in the *accounting records of the investor*. The accounts of the investor are therefore affected by the application of the equity method, in contrast to the situation where the equity method entries are made in the consolidation worksheet.

Paragraph 4 of IAS 28 makes reference to 'separate financial statements'. These statements are in addition to those mentioned in the previous paragraph. For example, where the investor prepares consolidated financial statements, the financial statements of the investor itself are separate financial statements. In such a situation, according to paragraph 35 of IAS 28, an investment in an associate is accounted for in the financial records of the investor in accordance with paragraphs 37–39 of IAS 27 *Consolidated and Separate Financial Statements*; namely, at cost or in accordance with IAS 39 *Financial Instruments: Recognition and Measurement*.

25.4 Application of the equity method of accounting

Applying the equity method requires an analysis of the acquisition similar to that undertaken when accounting for subsidiaries. Whether there is any goodwill or an excess to be accounted for is determined by this analysis.

25.4.1 Rationale for the method

As can be seen from the discussion in relation to the identification of associates in section 25.2 above, the criterion of control used for identifying subsidiaries has similarities with the definition of significant influence used for associates. Paragraph 20 of IAS 28 states:

> Many of the procedures appropriate for the application of the equity method are similar to the consolidation procedures described in IAS 27. Furthermore, the concepts underlying the procedures used in accounting for the acquisition of a subsidiary are also adopted in accounting for the acquisition of an investment of an associate.

Because of the similarity with the principles and procedures used in applying the consolidation method to subsidiaries, the equity method of accounting has sometimes been described as 'one-line consolidation'. However, IAS 28 does not consistently use the consolidation principles in its application of the equity method.

IAS 28 does not justify the information, or the need for the information, provided by the application of the equity method. In paragraph 17 of IAS 28, it is argued that the cost method may be unsatisfactory for associates because the recognition of dividends may not be an adequate measure of the income earned by the investor. Further, it is argued that applying the equity method 'provides more informative reporting of the net assets and profit or loss of the investor'. However, the standard does not explain why the equity method is superior to the fair value method or other measurement methods. Similarly, where there is a departure from consolidation principles, IAS 28 does not supply a justification for the departure. This makes it difficult to evaluate the equity method on the basis of its being a one-line consolidation method or simply another measurement method competing with fair value.

Similarities and differences between the consolidation method and the equity method are noted in section 25.4.3 of this chapter, where the latter method is described in detail.

25.4.2 Acquisition date and date of exchange

IFRS 3 *Business Combinations* contains the following definitions:

> **Acquisition date:** The date on which the acquirer effectively obtains control of the acquiree.

> **Date of exchange:** When a business combination is achieved through a single exchange transaction, the date of exchange is the acquisition date. When a business combination involves more than one exchange transaction, for example, when it is achieved in stages by successive share purchases, the date of exchange is the date that each individual investment is recognised in the financial statements of the acquirer.

In applying the standards in IFRS 3 to the preparation of consolidated financial statements, the cost of the combination is calculated at the date of exchange, while the fair values of the subsidiary's assets, liabilities and contingent liabilities are measured at acquisition date.

Similar concepts would apply in relation to the investor–associate relationship. The term 'acquisition date' is not really applicable to equity accounting because the definition relates to one entity having *control* over another, whereas equity accounting applies where one entity has *significant influence* over another. Therefore, in this chapter the term 'date of acquisition' or 'acquisition date', as used in IAS 28 but not defined in that standard, is defined as 'the date on which the investor effectively obtains significant influence over the investee'. As with consolidation, the cost of acquiring the shares in the associate is determined at the date of exchange, while the measurement of the fair values of the assets and liabilities of the associate occurs at the acquisition date.

Theoretically, the acquisition date and the date of exchange could be different. For example, assume Lausanne Ltd acquired a 20% ownership interest in Bern Ltd on 1 July 2004 but, because of the particular distribution of the balance of voting power, Lausanne Ltd did not significantly influence the decisions of Bern Ltd. However, on 1 January 2005, as a result of sales of certain large shareholdings in Bern Ltd, Lausanne Ltd was able to significantly influence Bern Ltd's decisions. Hence, 1 July 2004 is the date of exchange (the date the shares were acquired), while 1 January 2005 is the date of acquisition (the date significant influence is achieved). The accounting for the situation where an investee becomes an associate subsequent to initial acquisition of an ownership is illustrated in section 25.4.4 of this chapter.

The recognition of the existence of significant influence – the date of acquisition – is the key to determining when the standards in IAS 28 are to apply. As paragraph 23 states, 'An investment in an associate is accounted for using the equity method from the date on which it becomes an associate'.

25.4.3   Applying the equity method

Paragraph 11 of IAS 28 provides a description of the basics of the equity method. The key steps are:

1. Recognise the initial investment in the associate at cost.
2. Increase or decrease the carrying amount of the investment by the investor's share of the profit or loss of the investee after the date of acquisition (post-acquisition profit or loss).
3. Reduce the carrying amount of the investment by distributions (such as dividends) received from the associate.
4. Increase or decrease the carrying amount of the investment for changes in the investor's share of the reserves of the associate. This applies only to reserves where changes in the associate's equity have not already been included in profit or loss. Hence, changes in asset revaluation and foreign currency translation reserves (or surpluses) are recognised; but movements in general reserve, which are an appropriation from retained earnings, are not recognised.

Although potential voting rights may be used in the assessment of the existence of significant influence, they are not used in any of the above calculations (para. 12, IAS 28).

ILLUSTRATIVE EXAMPLE 25.1

Basic application of the equity method

1. Investor does not prepare consolidated financial statements

On 1 July 2005, Zurich Ltd acquired 25% of the shares of Geneva Ltd for $42 500. At this date, all the identifiable assets and liabilities of Geneva Ltd were recorded at amounts equal to fair value, and the equity of Geneva Ltd consisted of:

Share capital	$100 000
General reserve	30 000
Asset revaluation surplus	20 000
Retained earnings	20 000

During the 2005–06 year, Geneva Ltd reported a profit of $25 000. The asset revaluation surplus increased by $5000. Geneva Ltd paid a $4000 dividend and transferred $3000 to general reserve.

At 1 July 2005, Zurich Ltd recorded the investment in Geneva Ltd at $42 500. At 30 June 2005, the journal entries to apply the equity method, as passed in the records of the investor, are:

(a) Recognition of share of profit or loss of associate

Investment in associate	Dr	6 250	
Share of profit or loss of associate	Cr		6 250
(Share of associate's profit: 25% × $25 000)			

(b) Recognition of increase in asset revaluation surplus

Shares in associate	Dr	1 250	
Asset revaluation surplus	Cr		1 250
(Share of surplus: 25% × $5000)			

Note that there is no recognition of the increase in the general reserve because the share of the reserve has been recognised in the share of profit for the period.

(c) Adjustment for dividend paid by associate

Cash	Dr	1 000	
Investment in associate	Cr		1 000
(Adjustment for dividend paid by associate: 25% × $4000)			

Because the investor has recognised its share of the equity of the associate, the dividend is simply a receipt of equity already recognised in the investment account.

At 30 June 2005, the investment in the associate is measured at $49 000 (being $42 500 + $6250 + $1250 − $1000). The equity of Geneva Ltd consists of:

Share capital	$100 000
Asset revaluation surplus ($20 000 + $5000)	25 000
General reserve ($30 000 + $3000)	33 000
Retained earnings ($20 000 + $25 000 − $4000 − $3000)	38 000
	$196 000

The investor's share of the equity of the associate is 25% of $196 000, being $49 000, which is the same as the recorded amount of the investment in the associate. In other words, the equity method, in this case, is designed to show the investment in the associate at an amount equal to the investor's share of the reported equity of the associate. As explained later in this chapter, this relationship is not always achieved due to the effects of pre-acquisition equity, the existence of goodwill, and adjustments made for the effects of inter-entity transactions.

2. Investor prepares consolidated financial statements

In this circumstance, the entries are not made in the accounting records of the entities themselves but in the consolidation worksheet instead. The first two entries are the same as shown in part 1 of this example. The entry that differs is that for the dividend. The consolidation worksheet entry is:

(c) Adjustment for dividend paid by associate

Dividend revenue	Dr	1 000	
Investment in associate	Cr		1 000
(Adjustment for dividend paid by associate: 25% × $4000)			

When Geneva Ltd paid the $4000 dividend, Zurich Ltd recorded the receipt of cash and recognised dividend revenue. The effect of the above entry on the application of the equity method is to eliminate the dividend revenue previously recognised by the investor. Because the investor recognises a share of the whole of the profit of the associate, the dividend revenue cannot also be recognised as income by the investor. However, the payment of the dividend reduces the investment in the associate.

Goodwill and fair value adjustments

The description of the equity method in paragraph 11 of IAS 28 refers to the recognition of *post-acquisition* equity. Further, paragraph 20 of this standard notes that many of the procedures appropriate to the application of the equity method are similar to the consolidation procedures described in IAS 27. To this end, any differences between fair values and carrying amounts of identifiable assets and liabilities acquired, as well as any goodwill or excess on acquisition, must be taken into account. Paragraph 23 of IAS 28 states:

> An investment in an associate is accounted for using the equity method from the date on which it becomes an associate. On acquisition of the investment any difference between the cost of the investment and the investor's share of the net fair value of the associate's identifiable assets, liabilities and contingent liabilities is accounted for in accordance with IFRS 3 *Business Combinations*. Therefore:
>
> (a) goodwill relating to an associate is included in the carrying amount of the investment. However, amortisation of that goodwill is not permitted and is therefore not included in the determination of the investor's share of the associate's profits or losses.
>
> (b) any excess of the investor's share of the net fair value of the associate's identifiable assets, liabilities and contingent liabilities over the cost of the investment is excluded from the carrying amount of the investment and is instead included as income in the determination of the investor's share of the associate's profit or loss in the period in which the investment is acquired.
>
> Appropriate adjustments to the investor's share of the associate's profits or losses after acquisition are also made to account, for example, for depreciation of the depreciable assets, based on their fair values at the acquisition date. Similarly, appropriate adjustments to the investor's share of the associate's profits or losses after acquisition are made for impairment losses recognised by the associate, such as for goodwill or property, plant and equipment.

As with consolidated financial statements, at the acquisition date the cost of acquisition is compared with the net fair value of the identifiable assets, liabilities and contingent liabilities of the associate acquired by the investor in order to determine whether any goodwill is acquired or whether there is an excess.

The purpose of this acquisition analysis is to determine the real post-acquisition equity of the associate. Because the cost of acquisition is the amount paid for the net fair value of the identifiable assets and liabilities acquired and the goodwill (if any), then the recorded profits of the associate after the acquisition date are not all post-acquisition equity. They will include profits recognised and paid for by the acquiring entity at acquisition date. Hence, in determining the investor's share of post-acquisition profits of the associate, adjustments will have to be made for differences between carrying amounts and fair values at the acquisition date, as well as for any goodwill impairment or excess.

These adjustments are only notional adjustments; they are not made in the records of the associate, but are made in calculating the incremental adjustment to the share of profit of the associate. Because the adjustment is made to a share of profit or loss, the adjustment is calculated on an after-tax basis. Therefore, adjustments relating to the depreciation of non-current assets or the cost of inventory sold must be calculated on an after-tax basis.

ILLUSTRATIVE EXAMPLE 25.2

Goodwill and fair value adjustments

On 1 July 2004, Zermatt Ltd acquired 25% of the shares of Grenchen Ltd for $49 375. At this date, the equity of Grenchen Ltd consisted of:

Share capital	$100 000
General reserve	50 000
Retained earnings	20 000

At the acquisition date, all the identifiable assets and liabilities of Grenchen Ltd were recorded at fair value, except for plant for which the fair value was $10 000 greater than its carrying amount and inventory whose fair value was $5000 greater than its cost. The tax rate is 30%. The plant has a further five-year life. The inventory was all sold by 30 June 2005.

In the reporting period ending 30 June 2005, Grenchen Ltd reported a profit of $15 000. The acquisition analysis at 1 July 2004 is as follows:

Net fair value of the identifiable assets, liabilities and contingent liabilities of Grenchen Ltd	= ($100 000 + $50 000 + $20 000) (equity) + $10 000 (1 – 30%) (plant) + $5000 (1 – 30%) (inventory) = $180 500
Net fair value acquired by Zermatt Ltd	= 25% × $180 500 = $45 125
Cost of acquisition	= $49 375
Goodwill	= $4250
Depreciation (net of tax) of plant p.a.	= 20% × (25% × [$10 000 (1 – 30%)]) = $350
Effect of sale of inventory (net of tax)	= 25% × $5000 (1 – 30%) = $875

The amount of the adjustment needed in applying equity accounting to the investment in the associate at 30 June 2005 is determined as follows:

Share of profit recorded by associate (25% × $15 000)		$3 750
Pre-acquisition adjustments:		
Depreciation of plant	(350)	
Sale of inventory	(875)	(1 225)
Share of post-acquisition profit of associate		$2 525

The journal entry to reflect the application of the equity method to the investment in the associate is:

Investment in Grenchen Ltd	Dr	2 525	
Share of profit or loss of associate	Cr		2 525
(Recognition of share of post-acquisition profit of associate)			

This entry is the same regardless of whether the investor prepares consolidated financial statements.

ILLUSTRATIVE EXAMPLE 25.3

Excess

IFRS 3 *Business Combinations* requires any excess to be taken to profit and loss, subject to an analysis of the fair values calculated for the identifiable assets and liabilities of the acquiree.

Assume in illustrative example 22.2 that the cost of acquisition was $45 000. The acquisition analysis would then show:

Net fair value acquired by Zermatt Ltd	= 25% × $180 500
	= $45 125
Cost of acquisition	= $45 000
Excess	= $125
Depreciation (net of tax) of plant p.a.	= 20% × (25% × [$10 000 (1 – 30%)])
	= $350
Effect of sale of inventory (net of tax)	= 25% × $5000 (1 – 30%)
	= $875

The amount of the adjustment needed in applying equity accounting to the investment in the associate at 30 June 2005 is then as follows:

Share of profit recorded by associate (25% × $15 000)		$3 750
Pre-acquisition adjustments:		
Excess	$125	
Depreciation of plant	(350)	
Sale of inventory	(875)	(1 100)
Share of post-acquisition profit of associate		$2 650

The journal entry to reflect the application of the equity method to the investment in the associate is:

Investment in Grenchen Ltd	Dr	2 650	
Share of profit or loss of associate	Cr		2 650
(Recognition of share of post-acquisition profit of associate)			

LO 5

Dividends, reserves and accounting policies

The accounting for dividends, reserves and differing accounting policies is discussed below, and then demonstrated in illustrative example 22.4.

1. Pre-acquisition dividends

Where dividends are paid by the associate from pre-acquisition equity, the investor records the following:

Cash	Dr	XXX	
Investment in associate	Cr		XXX

In applying the equity method to the associate, there is no need to make any adjustments where the dividends are paid or declared from pre-acquisition equity. The adjustment to the investment account is already made in the records of the investor.

2. Post-acquisition dividends

When the associate pays or declares a dividend from post-acquisition equity, the investor records dividend revenue. As noted earlier in this chapter, because the investment account has been adjusted for the investor's share of all post-acquisition equity, applying the equity method requires the investment account to be adjusted for dividends paid or declared.

Where no consolidated financial statements are prepared, the entry in the investor's records is:

Cash	Dr	XXX	
Investment in associate	Cr		XXX

Where consolidated financial statements are prepared, the consolidation worksheet entry is:

Dividend revenue	Dr	XXX	
Investment in associate	Cr		XXX

3. Preference shares

Paragraph 28 of IAS 28 states:

> If an associate has outstanding cumulative preference shares that are held by parties other than the investor and classified as equity, the investor computes its share of profits or losses after adjusting for the dividends on such shares, whether or not the dividends have been declared.

This discussion relates only to dividends that are classified as equity because, for those preference shares classified as debt, the payments to the holders are treated as interest and deducted before calculating profit for the period. For preference shares treated as equity, the payments to holders are classified as dividends and appropriated subsequent to the calculation of profit.

The equity attributable to the ordinary shareholders in the associate is net of dividends to the preference shareholders. Hence, in calculating the share of the current period equity attributable to the investor, adjustments need to be made for:
- preference dividends paid or declared in the current period, and
- preference dividends that are cumulative in the current period, but have not been paid or declared.

This applies to preference dividends relating to preference shares regardless of whether the investor owns the preference shares in the associate or whether other parties own the shares. The calculation is then (assuming the dollar amounts):

Profit of associate	$100
Less Preference dividends paid/declared	20
	80
Investor's share: 20% of $80	$ 16

4. Reserves

The equity of the investee may also increase/decrease via changes in reserve balances in the associate. There are three situations to consider:

- *Where post-acquisition reserves are created directly in the associate*

  An example of this is where the associate recognises an increase in the asset revaluation surplus – the increase in equity does not go to the income statement but directly to the surplus. The investor's share of the asset revaluation surplus is recognised on application of the equity method via the following entry:

Investment in associate	Dr	XXX	
Asset revaluation surplus	Cr		XXX

  This entry is the same regardless of whether it is made in the investor's records or in the consolidation worksheet.

- *Where reserves are created by the associate but reflect pre-acquisition equity*

  Reserves on hand at acquisition date may be transferred to other equity accounts subsequent to that date. As these amounts are recognised in the investor's cost of acquisition, and thus the carrying amount of the investment in the associate, no further adjustment is necessary on application of the equity method for movements in pre-acquisition equity.

- *Where the associate creates reserves by transferring amounts from retained earnings*

  For example, the investor may transfer an amount from retained earnings to general reserve. As the investor's share of the equity in the retained earnings account has already been recognised by the investor, there is no need to adjust for the increase in the general reserve.

5. Dissimilar accounting policies

Paragraphs 26 and 27 of IAS 28 state:

> 26. The investor's financial statements shall be prepared using uniform accounting policies for like transactions and events in similar circumstances.

> 27. If an associate uses accounting policies other than those of the investor for like transactions and events in similar circumstances, adjustments shall be made to conform the associate's accounting policies to those of the investor when the associate's financial statements are used by the investor in applying the equity method.

In the calculation of the investor's share of the profit of the associate, adjustments must then be made to the recorded profit of the associate where that figure has been measured based on policies that are different from those applied by the investor.

6. Different reporting dates

Paragraph 25 of IAS 28 requires that, unless it is impracticable to do so, the associate should prepare financial statements as of the same date as the financial statements of the investor so that the equity method can be applied by the investor. Where the financial statements of the associate are prepared as of a different date, in applying the equity method, adjustments should be made for significant transactions or events that have occurred between the dates of the statements of the two entities. Paragraph 25 of IAS 28 sets a maximum difference between the reporting dates of the investor and the associate as no more than three months.

Dividends, reserves and dissimilar accounting policies

On 1 July 2005, St Moritz Ltd acquired 40% of the shares of Thun Ltd for $122 400. The equity of Thun Ltd at acquisition date consisted of:

Ordinary share capital	$200 000
10% preference share capital	100 000
Retained earnings	80 000

At 1 July 2005, all the identifiable assets and liabilities of Thun Ltd were recorded at fair value except for the following:

	Carrying amount	Fair value
Machinery	$140 000	$160 000
Inventory	60 000	70 000

By 30 June 2006, the inventory on hand at 1 July 2005 had been sold by Thun Ltd. The machinery was expected to provide future benefits evenly over the next two years. The tax rate is 30%.

In relation to the preference shares, there were no arrears of dividend outstanding at 1 July 2005. However, no dividends were paid in the 2006–07 period, and the shares are cumulative. The dividends paid in the 2007–08 period included the previous period's arrears.

All the ordinary dividends are from post-acquisition equity. Dividends declared at 30 June are paid within the following three months, with liabilities being raised at the date of declaration.

In January 2008, Thun Ltd revalued furniture upwards by $6000, affecting the asset revaluation surplus.

Both companies have interests in exploring mining leases. Whereas St Moritz Ltd has adopted a policy of capitalising its exploration expenditure, Thun Ltd has adopted a policy of expensing exploration outlays. This has resulted in Thun Ltd expensing $4500 and $6500 in the periods 2006–07 and 2007–08 respectively.

The income statements and statements of changes in equity of Thun Ltd over three periods contained the following information:

	30 June 2006	30 June 2007	30 June 2008
Profit	$ 40 000	$ 60 000	$ 70 000
Retained earnings (opening balance)	80 000	88 000	113 000
	120 000	148 000	183 000
Ordinary dividend paid	5 000	10 000	15 000
Ordinary dividend declared	7 000	15 000	20 000
Preference dividend paid	10 000	–	20 000
Transfer to general reserve	10 000	10 000	–
	32 000	35 000	55 000
Retained earnings (closing balance)	88 000	113 000	128 000

Required

Prepare the entries in the consolidation worksheet of St Moritz Ltd to apply the equity method to its investment in Thun Ltd for each of the three years ending 30 June 2006, 2007 and 2008.

Solution

Acquisition analysis

Net fair value of identifiable assets, liabilities and contingent liabilities of Thun Ltd	= ($200 000 + $80 000) (equity)
	+ $20 000 (1 – 30%) (machinery)
	+ $10 000 (1 – 30%) (inventory)
	= $301 000
Net fair value acquired by St Moritz Ltd	= 40% × $301 000
	= $120 400
Cost of acquisition	= $122 400
Goodwill	= $2000
Depreciation of machinery p.a. after tax	= 50% × (40% × $20 000 (1 – 30%))
	= $2800
Pre-acquisition after-tax inventory effect	= 40% × $10 000 (1 – 30%)
	= $2800

Year ended 30 June 2006: workings

Recorded profit		$40 000
Adjustments:		
Preference dividend paid	$(10 000)	(10 000)
		30 000
Investor's share — 40%		12 000
Pre-acquisition adjustments:		
Sale of inventory	(2 800)	
Depreciation of machinery	(2 800)	(5 600)
		$ 6 400

The journal entries in the consolidation worksheet of St Moritz at 30 June 2006 are:

Investment in Thun Ltd	Dr	6 400	
Share of profit or loss of associate	Cr		6 400
(Recognition of equity-accounted profit of associate)			
Dividend revenue	Dr	4 800	
Investment in Thun Ltd	Cr		4 800
(Adjustment for ordinary dividends from associate: 40% × [$5000 + $7000])			

Note that the net increase in equity and the investment account for the year is $1600 (being $6400 – $4800).

Year ended 30 June 2007: workings

Recorded profit		$60 000
Adjustments:		
Expensing of exploration outlays		
net of tax effect (4500 × [1 − 30%])	$ 3 150	
Preference dividend in arrears	(10 000)	(6 850)
		53 150
Investor's share — 40%		21 260
Pre-acquisition adjustments:		
Depreciation of machinery	(2 800)	(2 800)
		$18 460

The journal entries in the consolidation worksheet of St Moritz at 30 June 2007 are:

Investment in Thun Ltd	Dr	1 600	
Retained earnings (1/7/06)	Cr		1 600
(Share of prior period profits of associate)			

Note that the above entry is necessary because the equity accounting entries are made in the consolidation worksheet and not in the actual records of the investor.

Investment in Thun Ltd	Dr	18 460	
Share of profit or loss of associate	Cr		18 460
(Recognition of equity-accounted profit of associate)			
Dividend revenue	Dr	10 000	
Investment in Thun Ltd	Cr		10 000
(Adjustment for ordinary dividends from associate: 40% × [$10 000 + $15 000])			

Note that the net increase in equity and in the investment account as a result of applying the equity method is $10 060 (being $1600 + $18 460 − $10 000).

Year ended 30 June 2008: workings

Recorded profit		$70 000
Adjustments:		
Expensing of exploration outlays		
($6500 [1 − 30%])	$ 4 550	
Preference dividend paid in relation to		
current year	(10 000)	(5 450)
		64 550
Investor's share — 40%		$25 820

The journal entries in the consolidation worksheet of St Moritz at 30 June 2008 are:

Investment in Thun Ltd	Dr	10 060	
Retained earnings (1/7/07)	Cr		10 060
(Share of prior period profits of associate)			
Shares in Thun Ltd	Dr	25 820	
Share of profit or loss of associate	Cr		25 820
(Recognition of equity-accounted profit of associate)			
Dividend revenue	Dr	14 000	
Investment in Thun Ltd	Cr		14 000
(Adjustment for ordinary dividends from associate: 40% × [$15 000 + $20 000])			
Investment in Thun Ltd	Dr	1 680	
Asset revaluation surplus	Cr		1 680
(Share of associate's surplus: 40% × ($6000[1 – 30%]))			

25.4.4   Becoming an associate after acquiring an ownership interest

An investor may acquire an ownership interest in an investee on a certain date, but the investee may not be classified as an associate until a later date. This may occur when, for example, the investor acquires more shares in the investee.

The initial accounting for this investment is governed by IAS 39. The investor initially recognises its investment in the investee at its cost of acquisition, based on the fair value of what was given up to acquire the investment. Applying IAS 39, the investor classifies the investment (for example, as a held-for-trading financial instrument), and accounts for it accordingly. If the asset is classified as held for trading, it will be measured at fair value and changes in fair value will be recognised in profit or loss for the period. If the investor obtains significant influence over the investee, the latter becomes an associate and the accounting for the investment by the investor is governed by IAS 28.

The equity method is applied at the acquisition date, which is the date the investor obtains significant influence over the investee. At this date, the investor completes the following:

Step 1   Derecognises any fair value adjustments to the carrying amount of the investment between the date of exchange and the date of acquisition.

Step 2   Measures the fair values of the identifiable assets, liabilities and contingent liabilities of the investee.

Step 3   Measures any goodwill or excess as the difference between the cost of the investment and the investor's share of the fair value of the identifiable assets, liabilities and contingent liabilities acquired.

ILLUSTRATIVE EXAMPLE 25.5

Obtaining significant influence after acquiring ownership interest

Assume Neuchatel Ltd acquired 20% of the shares of Morez Ltd on 1 January 2005 for $28 000. At this date, the equity of Morez Ltd consisted of $100 000 capital and $20 000 retained earnings. At 1 July 2005, Neuchatel Ltd obtained significant influence over Morez Ltd. The investment in Morez Ltd had been classified as held for trading and was measured at 1 July 2005 at its fair value of $28 500. At this date, the investor measured the fair values of the identifiable assets and liabilities of Morez Ltd at $138 000.

At 1 July 2005, the acquisition date, Neuchatel Ltd would undertake an acquisition analysis:

Net fair value of identifiable assets, liabilities and contingent liabilities of Morez Ltd	= $138 000
Net fair value acquired by Neuchatel Ltd	= 20% × $138 000
	= $27 600
Cost of investment	= $28 000
Goodwill	= $28 000 − $27 600
	= $400

Neuchatel Ltd would apply the equity method to the investment from 1 July 2005. Assuming that Morez Ltd reported a $10 000 profit for the six months to 31 December 2005, and that at the acquisition date there were no differences in the fair value carrying amounts in relation to the assets and liabilities of the investee, the journal entries in the records of Neuchatel Ltd to apply the equity method are:

2005 **1 July** Gains/losses on investments (profit or loss) Investment in associate (Re-measurement of investment on adoption of equity method: $28 500 − $28 000)	Dr Cr	500	500
31 December Investment in associate Share of profit or loss of associate (Share of profit of associate: 20% × $10 000)	Dr Cr	2 000	2 000

25.4.5 Investing in an associate in stages

Besides there being a time difference between the initial investment and the acquisition date, a further complication arises where the investor's investment in the associate is achieved in stages before obtaining a sufficient investment in the investee to wield significant influence. The accounting for this is not covered in IAS 28. The principles for business combinations involving stages, as outlined in paragraphs 58–60 of IFRS 3, must be applied. In essence, each exchange transaction is treated separately for the purpose of calculating differences in fair value/carrying amounts in relation to the investee's net assets, and any goodwill or excess is calculated at each step.

ILLUSTRATIVE EXAMPLE 25.6

Step acquisitions

Assume Neuchatel Ltd acquired 10% of the shares of Morez Ltd on 1 January 2005 for $13 000. At this date, the equity of Morez Ltd consisted of $100 000 capital and $20 000 retained earnings, and all the identifiable assets and liabilities of Morez Ltd were recorded at fair value except for inventory, whose fair value was $10 000 greater than carrying amount. The inventory was all sold by 31 December 2006. The tax rate is 30%. At 31 December 2006, the fair value of the investment was $16 200. The investment was designated as held for sale.

On 1 July 2006, Neuchatel Ltd acquired a further 10% of the share capital of Morez Ltd for $17 200 (this also being the fair value of the initial investment in Morez Ltd at this date), when the equity of Morez Ltd consisted of:

Share capital	$100 000
Asset revaluation surplus	12 000
Retained earnings (1/1/06)	38 000
Profit (1/1/06–30/6/06)	8 000

The identifiable assets and liabilities of Morez Ltd were recorded at fair value at this date except for inventory, whose fair value was $15 000 greater than carrying amount. This acquisition gives Neuchatel Ltd significant influence over Morez Ltd.

At each of the dates of exchange, the investor would have to undertake an acquisition analysis:

At step 1:   1 January 2005

Net fair value of identifiable assets, liabilities and contingent liabilities of investee	= $100 000 + $20 000 + $10 000 (1 − 30%)
	= $127 000
Net fair value acquired	= 10% × $127 000
	= $12 700
Cost of investment	= $13 000
Goodwill	= $300

At step 2:   1 July 2006

Net fair value of identifiable assets, liabilities and contingent liabilities of investee	= $100 000 + $12 000 + $38 000 + $8000
	+ $15 000 (1 − 30%)
	= $168 500
Net fair value acquired	= 10% × $168 500
	= $16 850
Cost of investment	= $17 200
Goodwill	= $350

At 1 January 2005, Neuchatel Ltd would record the investment in Morez Ltd at $13 000. At 1 July 2006, the investment would be recorded at $17 200, being the fair value at that date. Neuchatel Ltd would have recognised the change in fair value, being $3200 in the 2005 profit and $800 in the 2006 profit for the first half-year.

As Morez Ltd became an associate at 1 July 2006, the application of the equity method requires the following journal entries:

Derecognition of the IAS 39 fair value adjustments

Gains/losses on investments (profit or loss)	Dr	4 200	
Investment in associate	Cr		4 200
(Re-measurement of investment on classification as associate: $17 200 – $13 000)			

Re-measurement to equity-accounted amount at date investor becomes an associate
At 1 July 2006, the investor will recognise an increment of $3100 as a result of applying the equity method to the first step acquisition. This amount is calculated as follows:

- Its share of the profit or loss of the investee recorded between the two dates, adjusted for the effects of the pre-acquisition equity relating to the inventory.
- Retained earnings: 10% × ($38 000 – $20 000 – $10 000[1 – 30%]) = $1100
- Profit for half-year: 10% × $8000 = $800
- Asset revaluation surplus: 10% × $12 000 = $1200

The required entry is:

Investment in associate	Dr	3 100	
Gains/losses on investments	Cr		1 900
Asset revaluation surplus	Cr		1 200
(Adjustment of carrying amount of associate to the equity-accounted amount)			

The carrying amount of the investment at 1 July 2006 is then $33 300, being:

Investment at 1 January 2005	$13 000
Re-measurement to fair value at 31/12/05 under IAS 39	3 200
Re-measurement to fair value at 1/7/06 under IAS 39	1 000
Investment at 1 July 2006	17 200
Derecognition of fair value re-measurements	(4 200)
Adjustment to equity-accounted carrying amount	3 100
Cost of step 2 investment	17 200
Equity-accounted investment at 1 July 2006	$33 300

If Morez Ltd then recorded a profit of $22 000 for the second half of the 2006 year, Neuchatel Ltd would recognise its 20% share of that amount, adjusted for the after-tax profit on the sale of inventory on hand at 1 July 2006:

Investment in associate	Dr	2 300	
Share of profit or loss of associate	Cr		2 300
(Recognition of share of post-acquisition profits of associate: 20% × [$22 000 – $15 000 (1 – 30%)])			

The above entries are the same regardless of whether the equity accounting is being applied in the consolidation worksheet or in the actual accounts of the investor.

LO 6

25.4.6   Inter-entity transactions

Paragraph 22 of IAS 28 states:

> Profits and losses resulting from 'upstream' and 'downstream' transactions between an investor (including its consolidated subsidiaries) and an associate are recognised in the investor's financial statements only to the extent of unrelated investors' interests in the associate. 'Upstream' transactions are, for example, sales of assets from an associate to the investor. 'Downstream' transactions are, for example, sales of assets from the investor to an associate. The investor's share in the associate's profits and losses resulting from these transactions is eliminated.

As detailed in chapter 21 of this book, in the preparation of consolidated financial statements, adjustments are made to eliminate the effects of transactions between the parent and its subsidiaries, and between the subsidiaries themselves. This procedure requires the full effect of the transactions to be eliminated, and the adjustments are made against the particular accounts affected by the transactions. Under IAS 28, the adjustments for the effects of inter-entity transactions are not consistent with those used on consolidation. The principles for adjusting for the effects of inter-entity transactions under IAS 28 are as follows:

- Adjustments must be made for transactions between the associate and the investor that give rise to unrealised profits or losses. Realisation of such profits or losses occurs when the asset on which the profit or loss accrued is sold to an external party or as the future benefits embodied in the asset are consumed. Unlike consolidation, there is no need to adjust for all transactions between the investor and the associate; only the transactions where profit is affected require adjustment. Therefore, transactions such as the holding of debentures by one entity in another entity, and the payment of interest on those debentures, do not require an adjustment under equity accounting.
- Unlike adjustments for unrealised profits and losses within a consolidated group, adjustments for transactions between an investor and an associate are done on a proportionate basis, determined in accordance with the investor's ownership interest in the associate. This is reasonable given that, under the equity method, only the investor's share of the equity of the associate is recognised and not the full equity of the associate.
- IAS 28 does not detail which accounts should be adjusted in this process. For example, if the associate sells an item of inventory to the investor at a profit, it is necessary to adjust the investor's share of the recorded profits of the associate. However, should the other side of the adjustment be to the inventory of the investor, because it is this asset that is affected by the inter-entity transaction? In this chapter, the adjustments are made on an after-tax basis to the accounts 'Investment in associate' and 'Share of profit or loss of associate'. In other words, there are no adjustments to specific asset accounts such as property, plant and equipment or inventory.

The effect of this is that the adjustments are the same for upstream and downstream transactions, because the only accounts affected by the adjustments are the carrying amount of the investment and the investor's share of profit or loss. Hence, the direction of the transaction is irrelevant in determining the accounts affected by the application of the equity method.

There are no good arguments for this method apart from simplicity. If the adjustments were consistent with those used under the consolidation method, then:

- where the investor transferred inventory to the associate, adjustments would be made to sales and cost of sales of the investor and the carrying amount of the investment in the associate, as the latter reflects the assets of the associate
- where the associate transferred inventory to the investor, the adjustments would be made to the share of profit of the associate and the inventory account of the investor.

Failing to adjust the individual accounts where appropriate departs from the approach of applying the equity method as a one-line consolidation method, and makes it more equivalent to a measurement method or valuation technique.

Another effect of the approach to adjust only the two accounts for all inter-entity transactions relating to downstream transactions is seen where the investor records a profit on the sale of inventory to an associate. Under equity accounting, an adjustment is made to the account 'Share of profit or loss of associate'. This account is affected even though the profit is made by the investor and the profits of the associate are unaffected by the transaction. The incremental change in the investment account does not therefore reflect only changes in the equity of the associate, but includes unrealised profits made by the investor.

Examples of inter-entity transactions

In the following examples, assume that the reporting period is for the year ending 30 June 2007, and that the investor, Laufen Ltd, owns 25% of Matterhorn Ltd. Laufen Ltd acquired its ownership interest in Matterhorn Ltd on 1 July 2005, when the retained earnings balance of Matterhorn Ltd was $100 000. At this date, all the identifiable assets and liabilities of Matterhorn Ltd were recorded at fair value. At 30 June 2006, the retained earnings balance in Matterhorn Ltd is $140 000, and the profit recorded for the 2006–07 period is $30 000. The tax rate is 30%.

The adjustment entries may differ according to whether they are made in the consolidation worksheet or in the accounting records of the investor. Differences in particular arise where the effects of a transaction occur across two or more years.

Example 1:   Sale of inventory from associate to investor in the current period

During the 2006–07 period, Matterhorn Ltd sold $5000 worth of inventory to Laufen Ltd. These items had previously cost Matterhorn Ltd $3000. All the items remain unsold by the investor at 30 June 2007.

The calculations for applying the equity method are as follows:

2005–06 period

Change in retained earnings since acquisition date:	
$140 000 – $100 000	$40 000
Investor's share — 25%	$10 000

2006–07 period

Current period's profit	$30 000
Adjustments for inter-entity transactions:	
Unrealised after-tax profit in ending inventory	
$2000 (1 – 30%)	(1 400)
	28 600
Investor's share — 25%	$ 7 150

If the investor prepares consolidated financial statements, the entries in the consolidation worksheet to apply the equity method to its associate are:

Investment in associate	Dr	10 000	
Retained profits (1/7/06)	Cr		10 000
Investment in associate	Dr	7 150	
Share of profit or loss of associate	Cr		7 150

If the investor does not prepare consolidated financial statements, the first of the two entries is recorded by the investor at 30 June 2006 (except that the credit is made to 'Share of profit or loss of associate'), and the second entry is recorded at 30 June 2007.

Example 2:   Sale of inventory from investor to associate in the current period

Details are the same as in example 1, except that Laufen Ltd sells the inventory to Matterhorn Ltd.

The calculations and journal entries are exactly the same as in example 1. The flow of the transaction, whether upstream or downstream, does not affect the accounting for the transaction.

Example 3:   Sale of inventory in the current period, part remaining unsold

During the 2006–07 period, Matterhorn Ltd sold $5000 worth of inventory to Laufen Ltd. These items had previously cost Matterhorn Ltd $3000. Half of the items remain unsold by Laufen Ltd at 30 June 2007.

The increment to the investment account is calculated in a similar fashion to example 1, but the adjustment is based only on the profit remaining in inventory on hand at the end of the period because it is this inventory that contains the unrealised profit. The calculations are as follows:

2005–06 period
As for example 1:

Increment	$10 000

2006–07 period

Current period's recorded profit	$30 000
Adjustment for inter-entity transactions:	
Unrealised after-tax profit in ending inventory	
$1000 (1 – 30%)	(700)
	29 300
Investor's share – 25%	$ 7 325

If the investor prepares consolidated financial statements at 30 June 2007, the entries in the consolidation worksheet to apply the equity method to its associate are:

Investment in associate	Dr	10 000	
Retained earnings (1/7/06)	Cr		10 000
Investment in associate	Dr	7 325	
Share of profit or loss of associate	Cr		7 325

If the investor does not prepare consolidated financial statements, in the 2006–07 period only the second of the above two entries is required.

Example 4:   Sale of inventory in the previous period

During the 2005–06 period, Laufen Ltd sold $5000 worth of inventory to Matterhorn Ltd. These items had previously cost Laufen Ltd $3000. All the items remain unsold by Matterhorn Ltd at 30 June 2006. These were eventually sold in the following period.

The calculations for applying the equity method are as follows:

2005–06 period

Change in retained earnings since acquisition date:	
$140 000 – $100 000	$40 000
Adjustment for inter-entity transactions:	
Unrealised after-tax profit in ending inventory	
$2000 (1 – 30%)	(1 400)
	38 600
Investor's share – 25%	$ 9 650

2006–07 period

Current period's profit	$30 000
Adjustment for inter-entity transactions:	
Realised after-tax profit in opening inventory	
$2000 (1 – 30%)	1 400
	31 400
Investor's share – 25%	$ 7 850

In the 2006-07 period, the profit that was unrealised in the previous period becomes realised. Hence, the amount is added back in the calculation of the 2006-07 share of equity. The addition of the 2005-06 and the 2006-07 increments results in the inter-entity transaction having a zero effect since, by 30 June 2007, the profit on the sale is realised.

If the investor prepares consolidated financial statements at 30 June 2007, the entries in the consolidation worksheet to apply the equity method to its associate are:

Investment in associate	Dr	9 650	
Retained earnings (1/7/06)	Cr		9 650
Investment in associate	Dr	7 850	
Share of profit or loss of associate	Cr		7 850

If the investor does not prepare consolidated statements, the first of the above entries is recorded in the accounts of the investor at 30 June 2006 (except that the credit is made to 'Share of profit or loss of associate'), and the second entry at 30 June 2007.

Example 5:   Sale of depreciable non-current asset

On 1 July 2005, Matterhorn Ltd sold an item of plant to Laufen Ltd for $8000. The carrying amount of the asset on this date in Matterhorn Ltd's records was $3000. The plant had a remaining useful life of five years.

The calculations for applying the equity method are as follows:

2005–06 period

Change in retained earnings since acquisition date	$40 000
Adjustments for inter-entity transactions:	
Unrealised after-tax profit on sale of plant	
$5000 (1 – 30%)	(3 500)
Realised profit on sale of plant: $\frac{1}{5} \times \$3500$	700
	37 200
Investor's share – 25%	$ 9 300

Note that the profit on the sale of the plant is unrealised because the plant was not sold to external parties. It is expected to be realised as the asset is consumed. The consumption of benefits is measured by the depreciation of the asset. Hence, as the plant is depreciated on a straight-line basis over a five-year period, one-fifth of the profit is realised in each year after the inter-entity transfer.

2006–07 period

Current period's recorded profit	$30 000
Adjustment for inter-entity transactions:	
Realised after-tax profit on sale of plant	
$\frac{1}{5} \times \$3500$	700
	30 700
Investor's share – 25%	$ 7 675

A further fifth of the unrealised profit is realised in the 2006–07 period as the benefits from the asset are further consumed. After a five-year period, the whole of the profit is realised.

If the investor prepares consolidated financial statements at 30 June 2007, the entries in the consolidation worksheet to apply the equity method to its associate are:

Investment in associate	Dr	9 300	
Retained earnings (1/7/06)	Cr		9 300
Investment in associate	Dr	7 675	
Share of profit or loss of associate	Cr		7 675

If the investor does not prepare consolidated statements, the first of the above entries is recorded in the accounts of the investor at 30 June 2006 (except that the credit is made to 'Share of profit or loss of associate'), and the second entry at 30 June 2007.

Example 6:   Payment of interest
On 1 July 2005, Laufen Ltd lent $10 000 to Matterhorn Ltd. Interest of $1000 p.a. was paid by Matterhorn Ltd.

Although the profit of Matterhorn Ltd includes the interest expense from this transaction, no adjustment is required because the revenue/expense on the transaction is assumed to be realised. Profits are considered to be unrealised only when there remains an asset in the investor/associate transferred at a profit or loss from the associate/investor.

25.4.7   Transactions between associates
Assume that Laufen Ltd owned 25% of the shares of Matterhorn Ltd as well as 40% of the shares of Adelbaden Ltd. Where transactions occur between two associates, the proportional adjustment is 10% (being 40% × 25%, which is the product of the ownership interests in the associate).

Example 7:   Sale of inventory between associates
In the current period, Matterhorn Ltd sold inventory to Adelbaden Ltd at an after-tax profit of $100. The inventory remains unsold at the end of the period.

The unrealised profit on the transaction is $100. The adjustment affects 'Share of profit or loss of associate' and the carrying amount of the investment. However, is it the investment in Matterhorn Ltd or the investment in Adelbaden Ltd? Where transactions are between associates, the flow of the transaction is of concern. In this example, the unrealised profit relates to Matterhorn Ltd because it was Matterhorn Ltd who sold the inventory to Adelbaden Ltd. Therefore, if Matterhorn Ltd recorded a $1000 profit:

Recorded profit	$1 000.0
Adjustment for inter-entity transactions:	
Unrealised profit in inventory	
$(25\% \times 40\%) \times \$100$	10.0
	990.0
Investor's share – 25%	$ 247.5

The equity accounting entry is:

Investment in associate – Matterhorn Ltd	Dr	247.5	
Share of profit or loss of associate			
– Matterhorn Ltd	Dr		247.5
(Share of profit of associate)			

LO 7

25.4.8   Share of losses of the associate

Paragraph 29 of IAS 28 discusses the accounting for losses made by an associate. In this situation, the investor recognises losses only to the point where the carrying amount of the investment reaches zero. As paragraph 29 states, the investor discontinues the use of the equity method when the share of losses equals or exceeds the carrying amount of the investment.

A further point made in paragraph 29 is that the carrying amount of the investment is not just the balance of the investment account 'Investment in associate'. The investor's interest in the associate also includes other long-term interests in the associate, such as preference shares or long-term receivables or loans. The base against which the losses are offset is then the investor's net investment in the associate. Where the associate incurs losses, the carrying amount of the account 'Investment in associate' is first reduced to zero. If losses exceed this carrying amount, they are then applied against the other components of the investor's interest in the associate in the reverse order of their seniority, or priority in liquidation. The logic is that, if the associate is making losses, then the probability of the other investments in the associate being realised is lessened.

Paragraph 30 of IAS 28 states that: 'If the associate subsequently reports profits, the investor resumes recognising its share of those profits only after its share of the profits equals the share of losses not recognised'. In other words, once the equity-accounted balance of the investment returns to a positive amount, equity accounting resumes.

ILLUSTRATIVE EXAMPLE 25.7

Share of losses of the associate

On 1 July 2004, Leuk Ltd acquired 25% of the shares of Jungfrau Ltd for $100 000. At that date, the equity of Jungfrau Ltd was $400 000, with all identifiable assets and liabilities being measured at amounts equal to fair value. Table 25.1 shows the profits and losses made by the associate over the first five years of operations after 1 July 2004, with their effects on the carrying amount of the investment.

		TABLE 25.1			Profits and losses made by associate over first five years of operations		

Year	Profit/(loss)	Share of profit/loss	Cumulative share	Equity-accounted balance of investment
2004–05	$20 000	$5 000	$5 000	$105 000
2005–06	(200 000)	(50 000)	(45 000)	55 000
2006–07	(250 000)	(62 500)	(107 500)	0
2007–08	16 000	4 000	(103 500)	0
2008–09	20 000	5 000	(98 500)	1 500

The table shows that the investment account is initially recorded by Leuk Ltd at $100 000, and is progressively adjusted for Leuk Ltd's share of the profits and losses of Jungfrau Ltd. In the 2006–07 year, when the cumulative share of the losses of the associate exceed the cost of the investment, the investor discontinues recognising its share of future losses. Even though profits are recorded by the associate in the 2007–08 year, the balance of the investment stays at zero because the profits are not sufficient to offset losses not recognised.

The journal entries in the consolidation worksheets of Leuk Ltd over these periods are:

30 June 2005

Investment in associate	Dr	5 000	
Share of profit or loss of associate	Cr		5 000

30 June 2006

Share of profit or loss of associate	Dr	50 000	
Retained earnings (1/7/05)	Cr		5 000
Investment in associate	Cr		45 000

30 June 2007

Share of profit or loss of associate	Dr	55 000	
Retained earnings (1/7/05)	Dr	45 000	
Investment in associate	Cr		100 000

30 June 2008

Retained earnings (1/7/07)	Dr	100 000	
Investment in associate	Cr		100 000

30 June 2009

Retained earnings (1/7/08)	Dr	100 000	
Investment in associate	Cr		98 500
Share of profit or loss of associate	Cr		1 500

25.4.9 Impairment losses

In situations where the associate records losses, as illustrated in section 22.4.8 of this chapter, if there are indications that the investment may be impaired, the investor should apply IAS 36 *Impairment of Assets*. Paragraph 33 of IAS 28 states that, in determining the value in use of the investment, an investor estimates:

(a) its share of the present value of the estimated future cash flows expected to be generated by the associate, including the cash flows from the operations of the associate and the proceeds on the ultimate disposal of the investment; or

(b) the present value of the estimated future cash flows expected to arise from dividends to be received from the investment and from its ultimate disposal.

Under appropriate assumptions, both methods give the same result.

LO 8

25.5 Disclosure

Paragraphs 37–40 of IAS 28 contain the disclosures required in relation to associates.

In relation to the investment account 'Shares in associate', paragraph 38 requires investments in associates accounted for using the equity method to be classified as non-current assets and disclosed as a separate item in the balance sheet. Similarly, the account 'Share of profit or loss of associate' must be disclosed as a separate item in the income statement. The investor's share of any discontinuing operations of such associates must also be separately disclosed. Paragraph 39 also requires separate disclosure in the statement of changes in equity of the investor's share of changes recognised directly in the associate's equity.

Note the following disclosure requirements:

- *Paragraph 37(c):* Where an investor holds less than 20% of the voting or potential voting power of the investee, but has applied the equity method because it believes it has significant influence, the investor must disclose the reasons why the presumption that it does not have such influence is overcome.
- *Paragraph 37(d):* Where an investor holds more than 20% of the voting or potential voting power of the investee, but has not applied the equity method because it believes it does not have significant influence, the investor must disclose the reasons why the presumption that it does have such influence is overcome.
- *Paragraph 37(g):* Where an investor has discontinued the application of the equity method because the associate has incurred losses, the investor must disclose the unrecognised share of losses of an associate, both for the period and cumulatively.
- *Paragraphs 37(h) and (i):* Paragraph 13 of IAS 28 provides a number of exemptions to the application of the equity method in accounting for associates. Paragraph 37(h) requires the disclosure of the fact that an associate is not accounted for under the equity method in accordance with paragraph 13. Paragraph 37(i) requires the disclosure of summarised financial information – including the amounts of total assets, total liabilities, revenues and profit or loss – either individually or in groups, of associates that are not accounted for under the equity method.

Other disclosures required in relation to associates are illustrated in figure 25.1.

Note 22: Investments in associates	IAS 28
The entity has a 35% interest in Swiss Ltd. The fair value of the investment at balance date is $650 000.	*Para. 37(a)*
The following information is obtained from the balance sheet and income statement of Swiss Ltd at 31 December 2006:	*37(b)*

	$000
Assets	2 400
Liabilities	900
Revenues	10 630
Profit	320

The reporting dates of the company and its associate are different in that Swiss Ltd, because of legislative requirements relating to the nature of the industry it is primarily involved in, has a reporting date of 28 February. Any significant transactions and events occurring between the two dates have been adjusted for when applying the equity method to the investment.	*37(e)*
Because of the nature of the industry that Swiss Ltd operates in, government regulations require that Swiss Ltd notify and obtain approval from the regulatory authority before paying dividends.	*37(f)*
Swiss Ltd has recorded a contingent liability of $10 000 relating to a guarantee it has offered. The company's share of the liability incurred jointly with other investors in Swiss Ltd is $3500.	*40*

FIGURE 25.1 Disclosures concerning investments in associates

LO 9

25.6 Comprehensive example

On 1 July 2006, Montreaux Ltd paid $2 696 000 for 40% of the shares of Fribourg Ltd, a company involved in the manufacture of garden equipment. At that date, the equity of Fribourg Ltd consisted of:

	$000
Share capital – 3 000 000 shares	3 000
Retained earnings	3 000

At 1 July 2006, all the identifiable assets and liabilities of Fribourg Ltd were recorded at fair value except for the following:

	Carrying amount	Fair value
	$000	$000
Inventory	1 000	1 200
Plant (cost $3 200 000)	2 500	3 000

The inventory was all sold by 30 June 2007. The plant had a further expected useful life of five years.

Additional information
(a) On 1 July 2007, Montreaux Ltd held inventory sold to it by Fribourg Ltd at a profit before income tax of $200 000.
(b) In February 2008, Fribourg Ltd sold inventory to Montreaux Ltd at a profit before income tax of $600 000. Half of this was still held by Montreaux Ltd at 30 June 2008.

(c) On 30 June 2008, Fribourg Ltd held inventory sold to it by Montreaux at a profit before income tax of $200 000. This had been sold to Fribourg Ltd for $2 million.

(d) On 2 July 2006, Fribourg Ltd sold some equipment to Montreaux Ltd for $1.5 million, with Fribourg Ltd recording a profit before income tax of $400 000. The equipment had a further four-year life, with the benefits being expected to occur evenly in these years.

(e) All dividends have come from profits earned after 1 July 2006, except for a $500 000 dividend paid in December 2006. In June 2007, Fribourg Ltd provided for a dividend of $1 million. This dividend was paid in August 2007. Dividend revenue is recognised when the dividend is provided for.

(f) The balances in the general reserve have resulted from transfers from retained earnings.

(g) The tax rate is 30%.

(h) Each share in Fribourg Ltd has a fair value at 30 June 2008 of $4.

(i) The consolidated financial statements of Montreaux Ltd and the financial statements of Fribourg Ltd at 30 June 2008, not including the equity-accounted figures, are as follows:

Income statements for the year ended 30 June 2008		
	Montreaux Ltd	Fribourg Ltd
	$000	$000
Revenue	25 000	18 600
Expenses	19 200	13 600
Profit before tax	5 800	5 000
Income tax expense	2 200	1 100
Profit for the period	3 600	3 900

Statements of changes in equity for the year ended 30 June 2008		
	Montreaux Ltd	Fribourg Ltd
	$000	$000
Profit for the period	3 600	3 900
Amounts recognised directly in equity	–	–
Total recognised income and expense for the period	3 600	3 900
Retained earnings as at 1/7/07	4 000	4 000
Profit	3 600	3 900
	7 600	7 900
Transfer to general reserve	–	1 000
Dividend paid	3 000	1 500
Dividend declared	1 500	1 000
	4 500	3 500
Retained earnings as at 30/6/08	3 100	4 400
Asset revaluation surplus as at 1/7/07	–	200
Increase in 2007–08		400
Asset revaluation surplus as at 30/6/08		600
General reserve as at 1/7/07	1 000	1 500
Increase in 2007–08	–	1 000
General reserve at 30/6/08	1 000	2 500

Balance sheets as at 30 June 2008		
	Montreaux Ltd	Fribourg Ltd
	$000	$000
EQUITY AND LIABILITIES		
Equity		
Share capital	8 000	3 000
Asset revaluation surplus	–	600
General reserve	1 000	2 500
Retained earnings	3 100	4 400
Total equity	12 100	10 500
Total liabilities	1 500	1 400
Total equity and liabilities	13 600	11 900
ASSETS		
Non-current assets		
Property, plant and equipment	6 104	9 000
Investment in Fribourg Ltd	2 496	–
	8 600	9 000
Current assets		
Inventory	4 000	2 000
Receivables	1 000	900
	5 000	2 900
Total assets	13 600	11 900

Required

1. Prepare the consolidated financial statements of Montreaux Ltd at 30 June 2008, applying the equity method of accounting to the investment in Fribourg Ltd.
2. Prepare the notes to the consolidated financial statements relating to the investment in the associate, Fribourg Ltd.

Solution

Acquisition analysis
At 1 July 2006:

Net fair value of identifiable assets, liabilities and contingent liabilities of Fribourg Ltd	= ($3 000 000 + $3 000 000) (equity) + $200 000 (1 – 30%) (inventory) + $500 000 (1 – 30%) (plant) = $6 490 000
Net fair value acquired by Fribourg Ltd	= 40% × $6 490 000 = $2 596 000
Cost of acquisition	= $2 696 000
Goodwill	= $100 000
Depreciation of plant p.a.	= 20%(40% × $500 000 (1 – 30%)) = $28 000
Pre-acquisition inventory effect	= 40% × $200 000 (1 – 30%) = $56 000

Consolidation worksheet entries at 30 June 2008

(i) *Share of changes in equity in previous periods* $000 $000

Post-acquisition retained earnings from acquisition
date to beginning of the current period:

$4 000 000 − ($3 000 000 − $500 000 pre-acquisition dividend)		1 500
Change in general reserve in prior periods		1 500
Adjustments for inter-entity transactions:		
Inventory on hand at 30/6/08: $200 000 (1 − 30%)	(140)	
Unrealised profit on sale of equipment:		
Original profit $400 000 (1 − 30%) less depreciation		
p.a. of $\frac{1}{4} \times $280 000$	(210)	(350)
		2 650
Investor's share − 40%		1 060
Pre-acquisition adjustments:		
Depreciation of plant	(28)	
Sale of inventory	(56)	(84)
Investor's share of retained earnings at 1/7/07		976
Share of asset revaluation surplus in prior periods:		
40% × $200 000		80
Total increase in equity-accounted carrying amount		
in previous periods		1 056

The consolidation worksheet entry in relation to previous period's equity is:

Investment in associate − Fribourg Ltd	Dr	1 056 000	
Retained earnings (1/7/07)	Cr		976 000
Asset revaluation surplus	Cr		80 000

(ii) *Share of profit in current period* $000 $000

Recorded profit		3 900
Adjustments for inter-entity transactions:		
Realised profit in opening inventory	140	
Realised profit on plant: $\frac{1}{4} \times $280 000$	70	
Unrealised profit in Montreaux Ltd's ending inventory:		
$\frac{1}{2} \times $600 000 (1 − 30%)$	(210)	
Unrealised profit in Fribourg Ltd's ending inventory:		
$200 000 (1 − 30%)	(140)	(140)
		3 760
Investor's share − 40%		1 504
Pre-acquisition adjustments:		
Depreciation of plant		(28)
Investor's share of profit of associate		1 476
Share of increment in asset revaluation surplus: 40% × $400 000		160
Total increase in equity-accounted carrying amount in current period		$1 636

The consolidation worksheet entry is:

Investment in associate − Fribourg Ltd	Dr	1 636 000	
Share of profit or loss of associate	Cr		1 476 000
Asset revaluation surplus	Cr		160 000

(iii) Dividends paid and declared by associate

During the current period, Fribourg Ltd paid a $1.5 million dividend and declared a $1 million dividend. The consolidation worksheet adjustment is:

Dividend revenue	Dr	1 000 000	
Investment in associate – Fribourg Ltd			
(40% of [$1 500 000 + $1 000 000])	Cr		1 000 000

On the basis of the above worksheet entries, the carrying amount of the investment in the associate, Fribourg Ltd, is $4 188 000, being $2 496 000 + $1 056 000 + $1 636 000 – $1 000 000.

1. Consolidated financial statements at 30 June 2008

The consolidated financial statements of Montreaux Ltd at 30 June 2008, including the investment in the associate being accounted for under IAS 28, are as follows:

Montreaux Ltd Consolidated income statement for year ended 30 June 2008	
	$000
Revenue ($25 000 000 – $1 000 000)	24 000
Expenses	19 200
	4 800
Share of profit or loss of associate accounted for using the equity method	1 476
Profit before tax	6 276
Income tax expense	2 200
Profit for the period	4 076

Montreaux Ltd Consolidated statement of changes in equity for financial year ended 30 June 2008	
	$000
Profit for the period	4 076
Amounts recognised directly in equity	160
Total recognised income and expense for the period	4 236
Retained earnings at 1/7/07 ($4 000 000 + $976 000)	4 976
Profit	4 076
	9 052
Dividend paid	(3 000)
Dividend declared	(1 500)
Retained earnings at 30/6/08	4 552
Asset revaluation surplus at 1/7/07	80
Increment from associate	160
Asset revaluation surplus at 30/6/08	240
General reserve at 1/7/07	$1 000
General reserve at 30/6/08	$1 000

Montreaux Ltd Consolidated balance sheet as at 30 June 2008	
EQUITY AND LIABILITIES	$000
Equity	
Share capital	8 000
Other reserves – Asset revaluation surplus	240
– General reserve	1 000
Retained earnings	4 552
Total equity	13 792
Total liabilities	1 500
Total equity and liabilities	15 292
ASSETS	
Non-current assets	
Property, plant and equipment	6 104
Investment in associates (Note 1)	4 118
	10 292
Current assets	
Inventories	4 000
Receivables	1 000
	5 000
Total assets	15 292

2. Notes to the consolidated financial statements

Note 1: Investment in associate

Montreaux Ltd has a 40% investment in Fribourg Ltd, which is classified as an associated company of Montreaux Ltd. The fair value of the investment at balance date is $4 800 000.

Information about Fribourg Ltd extracted from its financial statements at 30 June 2008 is as follows:

	$000
Assets	11 900
Liabilities	1 400
Revenues	18 600
Profit	3 900

25.7   Summary

When an entity has equity investments in other entities, accounting standards require the investments to be classified according to the nature of the investments and the relationship between the investor and the investee. The relationship between parent entities and their subsidiaries is based on the capacity of the parent to control or dominate the decisions made by the subsidiaries. In this chapter, another type of investment is analysed – one in which the investee also has a special relationship with the investor. With such an investee, called an associate, the investor has significant influence over the financial and operating decisions made by the associate. Because of this relationship, the accounting standards require specific information to be provided so that users can properly assess their investments.

The accounting method applied to associates is called the equity method of accounting, sometimes referred to as one-line consolidation. The method involves recognising the investor's share of the post-acquisition equity of the associate – the share of movements in the current period's post-acquisition equity being disclosed in a single line in the income statement – and measuring the carrying amount of the investment in the balance sheet as the sum of the original cost of the investment plus this share of associate's equity. Some traditional consolidation techniques, such as adjusting for the effects of intragroup transactions and for fair value/carrying amount differences in assets held at the date of acquisition, are used in applying the equity method. However, the method adopted in IAS 28 is not totally consistent with a true one-line consolidation approach. The IASB, in its future analysis of IAS 28, needs to consider the place of the equity method in the light of its Framework, in particular whether equity accounting is one-line consolidation or just another measurement method.

1. How is an associate defined in IAS 28? Why should associates be distinguished from other investments held by the investor?
2. What are the similarities and differences between the criteria used to identify subsidiaries and those used to identify associates?
3. Discuss the relative merits of accounting for investments by the cost method, the fair value method and the equity method.
4. Outline the accounting adjustments required in relation to transactions between the investor and an associate. What is the rationale for these adjustments?
5. Compare the accounting for the effects of inter-entity transactions for transactions between parent entities and subsidiaries and between investors and associates.
6. Should the equity method be viewed as a form of consolidation or a valuation technique?
7. Why is equity accounting sometimes referred to as 'one-line consolidation'?
8. Explain the differences in application of the equity method of accounting where the method is applied in the records of the investor compared with the application in the consolidation worksheet of the investor.
9. Explain the treatment of dividends from the associate under the equity method of accounting.
10. What is the difference between 'significant influence' and 'control'?
11. What factors should be considered in determining whether one entity has significant control over another entity?
12. How does an investee account for post-acquisition movements in the reserves (other than retained earnings) of an associate?
13. If an associate pays a dividend in the current period, explain the difference in application of the equity method if the dividend is classified as a pre-acquisition dividend rather than a post-acquisition dividend.
14. If, at acquisition date, an associate has inventory for which the fair value is greater than the carrying amount, how does this affect the application of the equity method in accounting for the associate?
15. In its submission to the Australian Accounting Standards Board on Exposure Draft (ED) 71 on the use of the equity method in Australia, Ernst & Young provided the following example.

	Investor	Associate
Cash	$20 000	
Investment	5 000	
Asset A		$20 000
	$25 000	$20 000
Capital	5 000	10 000
Profits	20 000	–
Liabilities		10 000
	$25 000	$20 000

Example 1 – Unrealised profit of the investee
The investor has a 50% associate whose $10 000 capital is in the form of cash. The investor sells asset A (which has nil book value) to the associate for $20 000. The associate has not traded and hence has no profit or loss.

Adjust the investor's profit?
The profit is in the investor and ED 71 does *not* appear to require adjustment against the investor's profit (which would, in any case, be inconsistent with a view that equity accounting is a technique for measuring the investment and not a consolidation technique).

Adjust the associate's profit?
If 50% of the unrealised profit does need to be eliminated then – to avoid making a consolidation adjustment against the investor's profit – the entries must be between the share of associate's profit and the investment. This would show, in the first instance, a loss of $10 000 from the associate despite it having not traded! As this would have the effect of reducing the investment to less than zero the loss would be restricted to $5000 and the investment would be carried at zero. It seems appropriate to reduce the value of the investment to nil in this way when the associate has not had any adverse result and the intrinsic value of the investment is still $5000.

Required
Comment on the example used by Ernst & Young, and discuss which accounts should be affected in adjusting for the effects of inter-entity transactions between investors and associates.

EXERCISES

EXERCISE 25.1 ★

Adjustments where investor prepares and does not prepare consolidated financial statements

Moutier Ltd acquired a 30% interest in Romont Ltd for $50 000 on 1 July 2006. The equity of Romont Ltd at the acquisition date was:

Share capital	$ 30 000
Retained earnings	120 000
	$150 000

All the identifiable assets and liabilities of Romont Ltd were recorded at fair value. Profits and dividends for the years ended 30 June 2007 to 2009 were as follows:

	Profit before tax	Income tax expense	Dividends paid
2007	$80 000	$30 000	$80 000*
2008	70 000	25 000	15 000
2009	60 000	20 000	10 000

* Includes $60 000 relating to profits earned before 1 July 2006.

Required

1. Prepare journal entries in the records of Moutier Ltd for each of the years ended 30 June 2007 to 2009 in relation to its investment in the associate, Romont Ltd. (Assume Moutier Ltd does not prepare consolidated financial statements.)
2. Prepare the consolidation worksheet entries to account for Moutier Ltd's interest in the associate, Romont Ltd. (Assume Moutier Ltd does prepare consolidated financial statements.)

EXERCISE 25.2 ★

Accounting for an associate by an investor

Chur Ltd acquired a 40% interest in Flims Ltd for $170 000 on 1 July 2004. The share capital, reserves and retained earnings of Flims Ltd at the acquisition date and at 30 June 2005 were as follows:

	1 July 2004	30 June 2005
Share capital	$300 000	$300 000
Asset revaluation surplus	–	100 000
General reserve	–	15 000
Retained earnings	100 000	109 000
	$400 000	$524 000

At 1 July 2004, all the identifiable assets and liabilities of Flims Ltd were recorded at fair value.

The following is applicable to Flims Ltd for the year to 30 June 2005:

(a) Profit (after income tax expense of $11 000): $39 000
(b) Increase in reserves
   • General (transferred from retained earnings): $15 000
   • Asset revaluation (revaluation of freehold land and buildings at 30 June 2005): $100 000
(c) Dividends paid to shareholders: $15 000.

Additionally, depreciation is provided by Flims Ltd on the diminishing balance method, whereas Chur Ltd uses the straight-line method. Had Flims Ltd used the straight-line method, the accumulated depreciation on non-current assets would be increased by $20 000 (2004 − $10 000). The tax rate is 30%.

Chur Ltd does not prepare consolidated financial statements.

Required
Prepare the journal entries in the records of Chur Ltd for the year ended 30 June 2005 in relation to its investment in the associate, Flims Ltd.

EXERCISE 25.3   ★   Inter-entity transactions where investor has no subsidiaries

Baden Ltd acquired 20% of the ordinary shares of Kloten Ltd on 1 July 2004. At this date, all the identifiable assets and liabilities of Baden Ltd were recorded at fair value. An analysis of the acquisition showed that $2000 of goodwill was acquired.

Baden Ltd has no subsidiaries, and records its investment in the associate, Kloten Ltd, in accordance with IAS 28. In the 2005–06 period, Kloten Ltd recorded a profit of $100 000, paid an interim dividend of $10 000 and, in June 2006, declared a further dividend of $15 000. In June 2005, Kloten Ltd had declared a $20 000 dividend, which was paid in August 2005, at which date it was recognised by Baden Ltd.

The following transactions have occurred between the two entities (all transactions are independent unless specified).
(a) In January 2006, Kloten Ltd sold inventory to Baden Ltd for $15 000. This inventory had previously cost Kloten Ltd $10 000, and remains unsold by Baden Ltd at the end of the period.
(b) In February 2006, Baden Ltd sold inventory to Kloten Ltd at a before-tax profit of $5000. Half of this was sold by Kloten Ltd before 30 June 2006.
(c) In June 2005, Kloten Ltd sold inventory to Baden Ltd for $18 000. This inventory had cost Kloten Ltd $12 000. At 30 June 2005, this inventory remained unsold by Baden Ltd. However, it was all sold by Baden Ltd before 30 June 2006.
The tax rate is 30%.

Required
Prepare the journal entries in the records of Baden Ltd in relation to its investment in Kloten Ltd for the year ended 30 June 2006.

EXERCISE 25.4   ★   Inter-entity transactions where investor does not prepare consolidated financial statements

Glarus Ltd owns 25% of the shares of its associate, Althorp Ltd. At the acquisition date, there were no differences between the fair values and the carrying amounts of the identifiable assets and liabilities of Althorp Ltd.

For 2004–05, Althorp Ltd recorded a profit of $100 000. During this period, Althorp Ltd paid a $10 000 dividend, declared in June 2004, and an interim dividend of $8000. The tax rate is 30%.

The following transactions have occurred between Glarus Ltd and Althorp Ltd:
(a) On 1 July 2003, Althorp Ltd sold a non-current asset costing $10 000 to Glarus Ltd for $12 000. Glarus Ltd applies a 10% p.a. on cost straight-line method of depreciation.
(b) On 1 January 2005, Althorp Ltd sold an item of plant to Glarus Ltd for $15 000. The carrying amount of the asset to Althorp Ltd at time of sale was $12 000. Glarus Ltd applies a 15% p.a. straight-line method of depreciation.
(c) A non-current asset with a carrying amount of $20 000 was sold by Althorp Ltd to Glarus Ltd for $28 000 on 1 June 2005. Glarus Ltd regarded the item as inventory and still had the item on hand at 30 June 2004.

(d) On 1 July 2003, Glarus Ltd sold an item of machinery to Althorp Ltd for $6000. This item had cost Glarus Ltd $4000. Glarus Ltd regarded this item as inventory whereas Althorp Ltd intended to use the item as a non-current asset. Althorp Ltd applied a 10% p.a. on cost straight-line depreciation method.

Required

Glarus Ltd applies IAS 28 in accounting for its investment in Althorp Ltd. Assuming Glarus Ltd does not prepare consolidated financial statements, prepare the journal entries in the records of Glarus Ltd for the year ended 30 June 2005 in relation to its investment in Althorp Ltd.

EXERCISE 25.5 ★★

Investor prepares consolidated financial statements, multiple periods

On 1 July 2004, Zug Ltd purchased 30% of the shares of Horgen Ltd for $60 050. At this date, the ledger balances of Horgen Ltd were:

Capital	$150 000	Assets	$225 000
Other reserves	30 000	*Less:* Liabilities	30 000
Retained earnings	15 000		
	$195 000		$195 000

At 1 July 2004, all the identifiable assets and liabilities of Horgen Ltd were recorded at fair value except for plant whose fair value was $5000 greater than carrying amount. This plant has an expected future life of five years, the benefits being received evenly over this period. Dividend revenue is recognised when dividends are declared. The tax rate is 30%.

The results of Horgen Ltd for the next three years were:

	30 June 2005	30 June 2006	30 June 2007
Profit/(loss) before income tax	$50 000	$40 000	$(5 000)
Income tax expense	20 000	20 000	–
Profit/(loss)	30 000	20 000	(5 000)
Dividend paid	15 000	5 000	2 000
Dividend declared	10 000	5 000	1 000

Required

Prepare, in journal entry format, for the years ending 30 June 2005, 2006 and 2007, the consolidation worksheet adjustments to include the equity-accounted results for the associate, Horgen Ltd, in the consolidated financial statements of Zug Ltd.

EXERCISE 25.6 ★★

Consolidated worksheet entries to include investment in associate

On 1 July 2005, Sursee Ltd acquired 30% of the shares of Burgdorf Ltd for $60 000. At this date, the equity of Burgdorf Ltd consisted of:

Share capital (100 000 shares)	$100 000
Asset revaluation surplus	50 000
Retained earnings	20 000

At this date, all the identifiable assets and liabilities of Burgdorf Ltd were recorded at fair value except for the assets overleaf.

	Carrying amount	Fair value
Machinery	$20 000	$25 000
Inventory	10 000	12 000

The machinery was expected to have a further five-year life, benefits being received evenly over this period. The inventory was all sold by 30 June 2006.

On 1 July 2005, the ownership interest of 30%, together with board representation and a diverse spread of remaining shareholders, was sufficient for the investor to demonstrate significant influence, and accordingly to begin accounting for the investment as an associate. At this date, the equity of Burgdorf Ltd consisted of:

Share capital (100 000 shares)	$100 000
Asset revaluation surplus	60 000
General reserve	10 000
Retained earnings	40 000

Dividends paid by Burgdorf Ltd in the 2005–06 period were $10 000, and $12 000 was paid in the 2006–07 period. In June 2007, Burgdorf Ltd declared a dividend of $10 000. Dividend revenue is recognised when dividends are declared.

During the period ending 30 June 2008, the following events occurred:

(a) Burgdorf Ltd sold to Sursee Ltd some inventory, which had previously cost Burgdorf Ltd $8000, for $10 000. Sursee Ltd still had one-quarter of these items on hand at 30 June 2008.

(b) On 1 January 2008, Sursee Ltd sold a non-current asset to Burgdorf Ltd for $50 000, giving a profit before tax of $10 000 to Sursee Ltd. Burgdorf Ltd applied a 12% p.a. on cost straight-line depreciation method to this asset.

(c) On 31 December 2007, Burgdorf Ltd paid an interim dividend of $5000.

(d) At 30 June 2008, Burgdorf Ltd calculated that it had earned a profit of $32 000, after an income tax expense of $8000. Burgdorf Ltd then declared a $5000 dividend, to be paid in September 2008, and transferred $3000 to the general reserve.

(e) The tax rate is 30%.

Required

Prepare the journal entries for the consolidation worksheet of Sursee Ltd at 30 June 2008 for the inclusion of the equity-accounted results of Burgdorf Ltd.

PROBLEMS

PROBLEM 25.1   ★★

Adjustments where investor does and does not prepare consolidated financial statements

On 1 July 2005, Interlaken Ltd acquired a 30% interest in one of its suppliers, Grindelwald Ltd, at a cost of $13 650. The directors of Interlaken Ltd believe they exert 'significant influence' over Grindelwald Ltd.

The equity of Grindelwald Ltd at acquisition date was:

Share capital (20 000 shares)	$20 000
Retained earnings	10 000
	$30 000

All the identifiable assets and liabilities of Grindelwald Ltd at 1 July 2005 were recorded at fair values except for some depreciable non-current assets with a fair value of $15 000 greater than carrying amount. These depreciable assets are expected to have a further five-year life.

Additional information
(a) At 30 June 2007, Interlaken Ltd had inventory costing $100 000 (2006 – $60 000) on hand which had been purchased from Grindelwald Ltd. A profit before tax of $30 000 (2006 – $10 000) had been made on the sale.
(b) All companies adopt the recommendations of IAS 12 regarding tax-effect accounting. Assume a tax rate of 30% applies.
(c) Information about income and changes in equity of Grindelwald Ltd as at 30 June 2007 is:

Profit before tax		$360 000
Income tax expense		180 000
Profit		180 000
Retained earnings at 1/7/06		50 000
		230 000
Dividend paid	$50 000	
Dividend declared	50 000	100 000
Retained earnings at 30/6/07		$130 000

(d) All dividends may be assumed to be out of the profit for the current year. Dividend revenue is recognised when declared by directors.
(e) The equity of Grindelwald Ltd at 30 June 2007 was:

Share capital	$ 20 000
Asset revaluation surplus	30 000
General reserve	5 000
Retained earnings	130 000
	$185 000

The asset revaluation surplus arose from a revaluation of freehold land made at 30 June 2007. The general reserve arose from a transfer from retained earnings in June 2006.

Required
1. Assume Interlaken Ltd does not prepare consolidated financial statements. Prepare the journal entries in the records of Grindelwald Ltd for the year ended 30 June 2007 in relation to the investment in Grindelwald Ltd.
2. Assume Interlaken Ltd does prepare consolidated financial statements. Prepare the consolidated worksheet entries for the year ended 30 June 2007 for inclusion of the equity-accounted results of Grindelwald Ltd.

Accounting for an associate within — and where there are no — consolidated financial statements

On 1 July 2004, Gstaad Ltd purchased 40% of the shares of Aigle Ltd for $63 200. At that date, equity of Aigle Ltd consisted of:

Share capital	$125 000
Retained earnings	11 000

At 1 July 2004, the identifiable assets and liabilities of Aigle Ltd were recorded at fair value.

During the year ended 30 June 2005, Aigle Ltd paid a dividend of $7500 from profits earned before 1 July 2004. Information about income and changes in equity for both companies for the year ended 30 June 2007 was as follows:

	Gstaad Ltd	Aigle Ltd
Profit before tax	$26 000	$23 500
Income tax expense	10 600	5 400
Profit	15 400	18 100
Retained earnings (1/7/06)	18 000	16 000
	33 400	34 100
Dividend paid	5 000	4 000
Dividend declared	10 000	5 000
	15 000	9 000
Retained earnings (30/6/07)	$18 400	$25 100

Additional information
(a) Gstaad Ltd recognised the final dividend revenue from Aigle Ltd before receipt of cash. Aigle Ltd declared a $6000 dividend in June 2006, this being paid in August 2006.
(b) On 31 December 2005, Aigle Ltd sold Gstaad Ltd a motor vehicle for $12 000. The vehicle had originally cost Aigle Ltd $18 000 and was written down to $9000 for both tax and accounting purposes at time of sale to Gstaad Ltd. Both companies depreciated motor vehicles at the rate of 20% p.a. on cost.
(c) The beginning inventory of Aigle Ltd included goods at $4000 bought from Gstaad Ltd; their cost to Gstaad Ltd was $3200.
(d) The ending inventory of Gstaad Ltd included goods purchased from Aigle Ltd at a profit before tax of $1600.
(e) The tax rate is 30%.

Required
1. Prepare the journal entries in the records of Gstaad Ltd to account for the investment in Aigle Ltd in accordance with IAS 28 for the year ended 30 June 2007 assuming Gstaad Ltd does not prepare consolidated financial statements.
2. Prepare the consolidated worksheet entries in relation to the investment in Aigle Ltd, assuming Gstaad Ltd does prepare consolidated financial statements at 30 June 2007.

Consolidated financial statements including investments in associates

Morges Ltd acquired 90% of the ordinary shares of Andermatt Ltd on 1 July 2005 at a cost of $150 750. At that date the equity of Andermatt Ltd was:

Share capital (100 000 shares)	$100 000
Reserve	8 000
Retained earnings	12 000

At 1 July 2005, all the identifiable assets and liabilities of Andermatt Ltd were at fair value except for the following assets:

	Carrying amount	Fair value
Inventory	$10 000	$15 000
Depreciable assets	25 000	35 000

The inventory was all sold by 30 June 2006. Depreciable assets have an expected further five-year life, with depreciation being calculated on a straight-line basis. Valuation adjustments are made on consolidation.

In the year following acquisition, a dividend of $2000 was paid from pre-acquisition retained earnings. All other dividends have been from post-acquisition profits.

On 1 July 2008, Morges Ltd acquired 25% of the capital of Davos Ltd for $3500. All the identifiable assets and liabilities of Davos Ltd were recorded at fair value except for the following:

	Carrying amount	Fair value
Inventory	$1 000	$1 500
Depreciable assets	6 000	7 000

All this inventory was sold in the 12 months after 1 July 2008. The depreciable assets were considered to have a further five-year life.

Information on Davos Ltd's equity position is as follows:

	1 July 2008	30 June 2009
Share capital	$10 000	$10 000
General reserve	–	2 000
Retained earnings	2 150	4 000

For the year ended 30 June 2010, Davos Ltd recorded a profit before tax of $2600 and an income tax expense of $600. Davos Ltd paid a dividend of $200 in January 2010. Morges Ltd regards Davos Ltd as an associated company.

During the year ended 30 June 2010, Davos Ltd sold inventory to Andermatt Ltd for $6000. The cost of this inventory to Davos Ltd was $4000. Andermatt Ltd has resold only 20% of these items. However, Andermatt Ltd made a profit before tax of $500 on the resale of these items.

On 1 January 2009, Morges Ltd sold Davos Ltd a motor vehicle for $4000, at a profit before tax of $800 to Morges Ltd. Both companies treat motor vehicles as non-current assets. Both companies charge depreciation at 20% p.a. on the reducing balance. Assume a tax rate of 30%.

Information about income and changes in equity for Morges Ltd and its subsidiary, Andermatt Ltd, for the year ended 30 June 2010 is as follows:

	Morges Ltd	Andermatt Ltd
Sales revenue	$200 000	$60 000
Less: Cost of sales	110 000	30 000
Gross profit	90 000	30 000
Less: Depreciation	16 000	4 000
Other expenses	22 000	3 000
	38 000	7 000
	52 000	23 000
Plus: Other revenue	30 000	5 000
Profit before income tax	82 000	28 000
Less: Income tax expense	20 000	10 000
Profit	62 000	18 000
Plus: Retained earnings (1/7/09)	120 000	80 000
	182 000	98 000
Less: Dividend paid	20 000	4 000
Retained earnings (30/6/10)	$162 000	$94 000

Required
1. Prepare the consolidated income statement and statement of changes in equity of Morges Ltd and its subsidiary Andermatt Ltd as at 30 June 2010.
2. In the consolidated balance sheet, what would be the balance of the investment shares in Davos Ltd?

PROBLEM 25.4

Consolidation worksheet entries including investments in associates

You are given the following details for the year ended 30 June 2008:

	Jungfrau Ltd	Neuchatel Ltd	Biel Ltd
Profit before tax	$100 000	$30 000	$25 000
Income tax expense	31 000	10 000	6 000
Profit	69 000	20 000	19 000
Retained earnings at 1 July 2007	20 000	12 000	11 000
	89 000	32 000	30 000
Dividend paid	14 000	6 000	2 000
Dividend declared	15 000	4 000	8 000
Transfer to general reserve (from current period's profit)	10 000	5 000	6 000
	39 000	15 000	16 000
Retained earnings at 30 June 2008	$50 000	$17 000	$14 000

Additional information
(a) Jungfrau Ltd owns 80% of the participating shares in Neuchatel Ltd and 20% of the shares in Biel Ltd (enough to cause Jungfrau Ltd to have significant influence over Biel Ltd).
(b) On 1 July 2006, all identifiable assets and liabilities of Neuchatel Ltd were recorded at fair value. Jungfrau Ltd purchased 80% of Neuchatel Ltd's shares on 1 July 2006, and paid $5000 for goodwill, none of which had been recorded on Neuchatel Ltd's records.

(c) At the date Jungfrau Ltd acquired its shares in Biel Ltd, Biel Ltd's equity was recorded as:

Share capital	$100 000
General reserve	15 000
Retained earnings	5 000

All the identifiable assets and liabilities of Biel Ltd were recorded at fair value.

Jungfrau Ltd paid $25 000 for its shares in Biel Ltd on 1 July 2006. There was $3000 transferred to general reserve by Biel Ltd in the year ended 30 June 2007, out of equity earned since 1 July 2006.

(d) Included in the beginning inventory of Jungfrau Ltd were profits before tax made by Neuchatel Ltd: $5000; Biel Ltd: $3000.

(e) Included in the ending inventory of Neuchatel Ltd were profits before tax made by Biel Ltd: $4000.

(f) Biel Ltd had recorded a profit (net of $500 tax) of $2000 in selling certain non-current assets to Jungfrau Ltd on 1 January 2008. Jungfrau Ltd treats the items as non-current assets and charges depreciation at the rate of 25% p.a. straight-line from that date.

(g) Jungfrau Ltd purchased for $10 000 an item of plant from Neuchatel Ltd on 1 September 2006. The carrying amount of the asset at that date was $7000. The asset was depreciated at the rate of 20% p.a. straight-line from 1 September 2006.

(h) During the year ended 30 June 2008, Biel Ltd has revalued upwards one of its non-current assets by $8000. There had been no previous downward revaluations.

(i) Dividend revenue is recognised when dividends are declared.

(j) The tax rate is 30%.

Required

Prepare the consolidation worksheet entries (in general journal form) needed for the consolidated statements for the year ended 30 June 2008 for Jungfrau Ltd and its subsidiary Neuchatel Ltd. Include the equity-accounted results of Biel Ltd.

 PROBLEM 25.5 ★★★ Consolidated financial statements including investments in associates

On 1 July 2006, Adelboden Ltd acquired 60% of the shares of Uster Ltd for $200 000. On the same day, Adelboden Ltd acquired 40% of the shares of Monthey Ltd for $64 000. Included in the balances of Uster Ltd and Monthey Ltd at that date were the following items:

	Uster Ltd	Monthey Ltd
Share capital (all shares issued for $1)	$200 000	$100 000
General reserve	80 000	20 000
Retained earnings	20 000	12 000
Dividend payable	10 000	10 000

The dividends of both companies were subsequently confirmed on 15 September 2006 and paid to the holders of shares on the register at that date.

At 1 July 2006, when Adelboden Ltd acquired its shares in Uster Ltd, all the identifiable assets and liabilities of Uster Ltd were recorded at fair value except for some plant with a written-down carrying amount of $100 000 (net of accumulated depreciation of $20 000) and a fair value of $110 000. This plant was expected to last a further five years.

At 1 July 2006, Adelboden Ltd acquired sufficient shares to be able to control Uster Ltd. Any valuation adjustments at this date are done in the consolidation worksheet.

At 1 July 2006, when Adelboden Ltd acquired its shares in Monthey Ltd, all the identifiable assets and liabilities of Monthey Ltd were recorded at fair value except for some machinery which had a written-down carrying amount of $50 000 (net of accumulated depreciation of $10 000) and a fair value of $60 000. The machinery was expected to last a further five years. At 1 July 2006, Adelboden Ltd did not exercise significant influence over Monthey Ltd. However, by 30 June 2007, Adelboden Ltd was able to exercise significant influence over Monthey Ltd due to a change of members on the board of directors.

Financial information for the three companies for the year ended 30 June 2009 is shown below and opposite.

	Adelboden Ltd	Uster Ltd	Monthey Ltd
Revenues	$700 000	$560 000	$180 000
Expenses	500 000	430 000	120 000
Profit before tax	200 000	130 000	60 000
Income tax expense	50 000	30 000	28 000
Profit	150 000	100 000	32 000
Retained earnings (1/7/08)	70 000	40 000	20 000
	220 000	140 000	52 000
Dividend paid			
(from profits earned to 30/6/06)	–	10 000	–
Interim dividend paid	20 000	20 000	5 000
Final dividend declared	30 000	20 000	10 000
Transfer to general reserve	60 000	20 000	6 000
	110 000	70 000	21 000
Retained earnings (30/6/09)	$110 000	$ 70 000	$ 31 000
Non-current assets			
Plant and equipment	$ 650 000	$224 000	$161 000
Accumulated depreciation	(69 000)	(102 000)	(30 000)
Investment in Uster Ltd	188 000	–	–
Investment in Monthey Ltd	60 000	–	–
Deferred tax asset	40 000	24 000	60 000
Property	127 000	204 000	30 000
Current assets			
Cash	92 000	102 000	42 000
Receivables	104 000	72 000	44 000
Inventory	96 000	80 000	42 000
Total assets	1 288 000	604 000	347 000
Non-current liabilities			
Debentures	246 000	61 000	97 000
Current liabilities			
Payables	60 000	68 000	34 000
Current tax liability	58 000	37 000	23 000
Dividend payable	30 000	20 000	10 000
Total liabilities	394 000	186 000	164 000
Net assets	$ 894 000	$418 000	$183 000

	Adelboden Ltd	Uster Ltd	Monthey Ltd
Equity			
Share capital	$ 400 000	$200 000	$100 000
Reserves:			
Asset revaluation surplus	64 000	48 000	16 000
Dividend equalisation reserve	50 000	–	–
General reserve	270 000	100 000	36 000
Retained earnings	110 000	70 000	31 000
Total equity	$ 894 000	$418 000	$183 000

Additional information
(a) All dividend revenue is recognised before receipt of cash.
(b) Apart from the general reserve, the only movements in reserve accounts in the period ended 30 June 2009 were caused by increases in the asset revaluation surplus of Uster Ltd of $8000 and Monthey Ltd of $5000.
(c) Included in the ending inventory of Uster Ltd was inventory purchased from Uster Ltd for $16 000. Original cost to Uster Ltd was $12 000.
(d) Included in the ending inventory of Adelboden Ltd was inventory purchased from Monthey Ltd for $12 000. This had originally cost Monthey Ltd $10 000.
(e) Included in the beginning inventory of Adelboden Ltd was inventory purchased from Monthey Ltd for $10 000. This had originally cost Monthey Ltd $7000.
(f) Included in the receivables of Adelboden Ltd are amounts of $6000 and $4000 owing by Uster Ltd and Monthey Ltd respectively.
(g) The tax rate is 30%.

Required
Prepare the consolidation income statement, statement of changes in equity, and balance sheet for Adelboden Ltd and its subsidiary Uster Ltd, as at 30 June 2009. Include the equity-accounted results for Monthey Ltd.

PROBLEM 25.6 ★★★   Multiple associates, consolidated financial statements

Winterthur Ltd has one subsidiary, Lech Ltd, and two associated companies, Arosa Ltd and Dornbirn Ltd, and Lech Ltd has one associated company, Thusis Ltd.

	Lech Ltd	Thusis Ltd	Arosa Ltd	Dornbirn Ltd
Share capital				
Ordinary:				
Held by group	$1 200	$ 250	$200	$ 250
Held by other interests	800	750	600	750
	$2 000	$1 000	$800	$1 000

Information about the companies for the year ended 30 June 2008 is as follows:

	Winterthur Ltd	Lech Ltd	Thusis Ltd	Arosa Ltd	Dornbirn Ltd
Trading profit (loss)	$ 200	$1 000	$600	$2 400	$1 200
Dividend revenue	600	400	100	–	–
Profit before tax	800	1 400	700	2 400	1 200
Income tax expense	100	500	300	1 200	600
Profit	700	900	400	1 200	600
Dividend paid	500	500	200	1 000	200
	200	400	200	200	400
Retained earnings (1/7/07)	6 800	3 600	230	2 000	1 210
Retained earnings (30/6/08)	$7 000	$4 000	$430	$2 200	$1 610

	Winterthur Ltd	Lech Ltd	Thusis Ltd	Arosa Ltd	Dornbirn Ltd
Investments	$ 4 008	$3 000	$ 800	–	–
Other non-current assets (net)	6 000	3 000	400	2 000	2 400
Current assets	1 992	2 000	800	1 600	$1 000
Total assets	$12 000	$8 000	$2 000	$3 600	$3 400
Share capital	$ 1 000	$2 000	$1 000	$800	$1 000
Asset revaluation surplus	1 000	–	200	–	–
Retained earnings	7 000	4 000	430	2 200	1 610
Total equity	9 000	6 000	1 630	3 000	2 610
Liabilities	3 000	2 000	370	600	790
Total equity and liabilities	$12 000	$8 000	$2 000	$3 600	$ 3 00

Additional information
(a) *Lech Ltd:* Winterthur Ltd acquired a 60% interest on 30 June 2000 for $3000. Shareholders' equity at 30 June 2000 was:

Share capital	$2 000
Retained earnings	2 000
	$4 000

At the acquisition date, Lech Ltd had not recorded any goodwill. All the identifiable assets and liabilities of Lech Ltd were recorded at fair value except the following:

	Carrying amount	Fair value
Inventory	$ 500	$ 600
Non-current assets (net)	1 200	1 500

By 30 June 2000, all the inventory had been sold by Lech Ltd. The non-current assets had a further expected life of ten years, with benefits from use being received evenly over these years.

(b) *Thusis Ltd:* Lech Ltd acquired, on 1 July 2007, 25% of the share capital for $400. Equity at 30 June 2007 was:

Share capital	$1 000
Retained earnings	230

At 30 June 2007, Thusis Ltd had not recorded any goodwill. All the identifiable assets and liabilities were recorded at fair value except for the following:

	Carrying amount	Fair value
Inventory	$500	$600
Non-current assets (net)	200	400

By 30 June 2008, half the inventory had been sold to external parties. The non-current assets were revalued in the records of Thusis Ltd on 1 July 2007.

(c) *Winterthur Ltd:* Included in current assets of Winterthur Ltd at 30 June 2008 is inventory that was purchased from Lech Ltd for $900. Lech Ltd sells its goods at cost plus 50% mark-up.

(d) *Winterthur Ltd:* Included in current assets of Winterthur Ltd at 30 June 2007 was inventory that was purchased from Lech Ltd for $600.

(e) *Lech Ltd:* Included in the non-current assets of Lech Ltd at 30 June 2008 is an item of plant that was sold to Lech Ltd by Thusis Ltd on 1 July 2007 for $1200. At the date of sale, this asset had a carrying amount to Thusis Ltd of $1000. It had an expected future useful life of five years, with benefits being received evenly over these years.

(f) *Arosa Ltd:* Winterthur Ltd acquired a 25% interest on 30 June 2005 for $400. Equity at 30 June 2005 was:

Share capital	$800
Retained earnings	600

At this date, Arosa Ltd had not recorded any goodwill. All the identifiable assets and liabilities of Arosa Ltd were recorded at fair value except for the following assets:

	Carrying amount	Fair value
Inventory	$100	$120
Non-current assets (net)	500	600

The inventory was all sold by 30 June 2006. The non-current assets had a further useful life of four years.

(g) *Dornbirn Ltd:* Winterthur Ltd acquired a 25% interest on 1 July 2007 for $600. A comparison of carrying amounts and fair values at 30 June 2007 is shown overleaf.

	Carrying amount	Fair value
Share capital	$1 000	
Retained earnings	1 210	
Liabilities	790	$ 790
	$3 000	
Inventory	$ 800	1 000
Non-current assets:		
Plant	1 000	1 200
Equipment	1 200	1 500
	$3 000	

The plant had a further five-year life and the equipment had a further six-year life. By 30 June 2008, all the undervalued inventory had been sold.

(h) *Arosa Ltd:* On 1 July 2006, Arosa Ltd sold a non-current asset to Winterthur Ltd for $500. At the time of sale, this asset had a carrying amount of $450. Winterthur Ltd depreciated this asset evenly over a five-year period.

(i) *Dornbirn Ltd:* At 30 June 2008, Winterthur Ltd held inventory that was sold to it by Dornbirn Ltd at a profit before tax of $200 during the previous period.

(j) *Winterthur Ltd:* On 30 June 2008, Winterthur Ltd held inventory that had been sold to it during the previous six months by Arosa Ltd for $1000. Arosa Ltd made $400 profit before tax on the sale.

(k) The tax rate is 30%.

Required

Prepare the consolidated income statement, statement of changes in equity, and balance sheet of Winterthur Ltd for the year ended 30 June 2008. Include all the associates accounted for under the equity method.

 WEBLINK

Visit these websites for additional information:

www.iasb.org   www.iasplus.com
www.asic.gov.au   www.ifac.org
www.aasb.com.au   www.nzica.com
www.accaglobal.com   www.capa.com.my

CHAPTER 26
Interests in joint ventures

ACCOUNTING STANDARDS

International: IAS 31 *Interests in Joint Ventures*
Australia: AASB 131 *Interests in Joint Ventures*
New Zealand: NZ IAS 31 *Interests in Joint Ventures*

CONCEPTS FOR REVIEW

Before studying this chapter, you should understand or, if necessary, revise:
- the criteria for identification of parent entities and subsidiaries
- the criteria for identification of associates
- the application of the equity method of accounting
- the IASB Framework, particularly the definition of an asset.

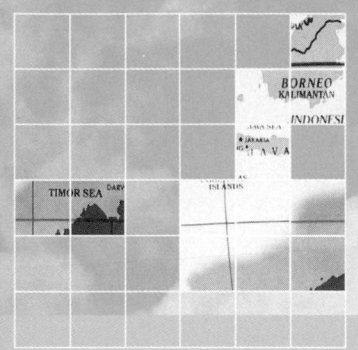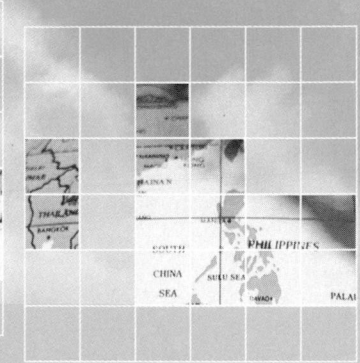

LEARNING OBJECTIVES

When you have studied this chapter, you should be able to:

1. discuss the defining characteristics of a joint venture
2. explain the different forms of a joint venture
3. account for jointly controlled operations
4. account for jointly controlled assets
5. account for an unincorporated joint venture that is sharing output
6. adjust for the effects of contributions of non-monetary assets by a joint venturer
7. account for a joint venture entity sharing profit
8. debate the advantages and disadvantages of using the proportionate consolidation method or the equity method
9. prepare the disclosures required by IAS 31.

26.1 Investments in other entities

In earlier chapters of this book two types of investments are analysed. First, there is the investment in a *subsidiary*, where a parent entity has the capacity to control the financial and operating policies of another entity. Where this control relationship exists, the consolidation method is used for the preparation of consolidated financial statements to report the financial performance and position of the group of entities. The consolidated financial statements provide detailed line-by-line information about the entities in the group. Second, there is the investment in an *associate*, where the investor has the capacity to significantly influence the financial and operating decisions of another entity, the associate. The accounting method used to provide information about this form of investment is the equity method, a form of one-line consolidation method where the carrying amount of the investment in the associate is adjusted for the investor's share of movements in the post-acquisition equity of the associate. Information on investments in associates as provided by applying the equity method is considerably less than that for subsidiaries resulting from applying the consolidation method.

In this chapter, another form of investment is analysed: the investment in a joint venture. As is explained in detail in the following section, the level of control that the investor has in the investee is again used to determine the existence of a joint venture. Further, both the consolidation and equity methods are used to develop a method of providing information about investments in joint ventures.

LO 1

26.2 The nature of a joint venture

26.2.1 Defining a joint venture

Paragraph 3 of IAS 31 *Interests in Joint Ventures* contains the following definitions:

> A *joint venture* is a contractual arrangement whereby two or more parties undertake an economic activity that is subject to joint control.

> A *venturer* is a party to a joint venture and has joint control over that joint venture.

> An *investor in a joint venture* is a party to a joint venture and does not have joint control over that joint venture.

Note first that in the definition of a joint venture reference is made to an 'economic activity'. As is explained in detail in section 26.2.2, the form of economic activity does not require the formation of another entity, and may relate to a single asset.

There are two major characteristics of a joint venture:

1. *Contractual arrangement*
   As noted in paragraph 9 of IAS 31, it is the existence of a contractual arrangement that distinguishes certain investments in associates (see chapter 25) from investments in joint ventures. The venturers are bound by the contractual arrangement that details the operation and management of the joint venture. Paragraph 10 of IAS 31 notes that the contractual arrangement may exist in a number of forms, such as a specific contract, or may be detailed in the articles or other by-laws of the joint venture. This paragraph also notes that the contractual arrangement is usually in writing and deals with such matters as:

   (a) the activity, duration and reporting obligations of the joint venture;
   (b) the appointment of the board of directors or equivalent governing body of the joint venture and the voting rights of the venturers;
   (c) capital contributions by the venturers; and
   (d) the sharing by the venturers of the output, income, expenses or results of the joint venture.

2. *Joint control*

As noted earlier in this chapter, a parent–subsidiary relationship is evidenced by the existence of a capacity to control or dominate, while an investor–associate relationship is evidenced by the existence of significant influence. The characteristic of joint control also relies on the control relationship between the joint venturers. A single joint venturer cannot control the joint venture; otherwise that venturer would be a parent entity. It must also be a different relationship than just significantly influencing the decisions made in the joint venture.

Joint control is defined in IAS 31, paragraph 3, as:

> the contractually agreed sharing of control over an economic activity.

The IASB (see *IASB Update*, November 2003) expressed concern that this definition was not sufficiently explicit about the nature of the sharing of control; for example, the parties could contractually agree that all the essential strategic operating, investing and financing decisions require the consent of most of the owners. The IASB preferred the concept that all parties had to agree (i.e. unanimously consent to the decisions) to be built into the definition. As a result, there was a preference for the definition of joint control proposed in the 1999 G4+1[1] Discussion Paper ('G4-DP'), 'Reporting Interests in Joint Ventures and Similar Arrangements', principally written by Canadians J Alex Milburn and Peter D Chant (1999).

> Joint control over an enterprise exists when no one party alone has the power to control its strategic operating, investing, and financing decisions, but two or more parties can do so, and each of the parties sharing control (joint venturers) must consent.

As at March 2006, however, no change had been made to the definition of joint control in IAS 31.

Paragraphs 11 and 12 of IAS 31 provide the following guidance in determining the existence of joint control:

- no single venturer is in a position to control the activity unilaterally
- the decisions in areas essential to the goals of the joint venture require the consent of the venturers
- one venturer may be appointed as the manager or operator of the joint venture; however, this party acts within the financial and operating policies detailed in the contractual arrangement and consented to by the venturers.

The ownership of a majority ownership interest may often be used to indicate the existence of control because voting power is generally associated with ownership interest. However, it may be possible for joint control to exist even where there are varying ownership interests. For example, if holdings are in the proportions of 50:30:20, joint control still exists so long as the unanimous agreement of each party is necessary for strategic decisions to be made. The key factor is that no single party can unilaterally control the financial and operating decisions of the venture. Joint control might exist by each venturer being given a veto power over the strategic decisions. Note that IAS 31 distinguishes between a 'venturer' and an 'investor'. For example, where there are three parties in the venture sharing output on a 50:30:20 basis, it may be that the first party is only an investor while the other two parties are the venturers. The difference is that only the parties that have joint control are venturers – in this case, the first party would not have a veto power.

---

1. The G4+1 organisation consisted of the accounting standards boards in Australia, Canada, New Zealand, the United Kingdom and the United States, as well as the International Accounting Standards Committee. G4+1 was disbanded when the International Accounting Standards Board was established.

26.2.2   Forms of joint ventures

IAS 31 identifies three forms of joint venture:

- *Jointly controlled operations* (paragraphs 13–17). As stated in paragraph 13, with a jointly controlled operation, there is no corporation, partnership or financial structure established separate from the venturers themselves. Each joint venturer uses its own assets and incurs its own expenses to create a joint product. An example is the manufacture of an aeroplane. One joint venturer makes the body, another manufactures and installs the engines while another fits out the aircraft. Each venturer is involved in its own part of the overall activity. The venturers then share the revenue on sale of the product according to the contractual arrangement.
- *Jointly controlled assets* (paragraphs 18–23). The joint venture may relate to the shared use of a single asset such as an oil or gas pipeline, a communications network or a property such as farm land. The contractual arrangement provides for each venturer to use the asset at particular periods of time or for a particular number of hours. As with the jointly owned operation, there is no specific structure created for the joint venture; the venturers simply share an asset.

  In some cases the joint venture may require the use of a number of shared assets. For example, if the joint venture is established to operate a mine, each venturer may provide an initial contribution for the establishment of the mining operation, possibly including the property, plant and equipment necessary to run the mine. The venturers then share in the output of the mine, with each party being responsible for the ultimate sale or internal use of the output. As paragraph 19 states, each venturer has control over its share of future economic benefits through its share of the jointly controlled asset.
- *Jointly controlled entities* (paragraphs 24–29). Paragraph 24 states that a jointly controlled entity is a joint venture that 'involves the establishment of a corporation, partnership or other entity in which each venturer has an interest'. Each venturer then has an interest in the entity rather than an interest in the individual assets of the joint venture. Further, as noted in paragraph 25, rather than sharing the output of the joint venture, as the joint venture earns income, the venturers share the profits of the joint venture. However, paragraph 25 notes that even in the case of a jointly controlled entity, there could be a sharing of the output.

The key difference between the first two categories (jointly controlled operations and assets) and the third category (jointly controlled entities) is that in the first two categories the venturers have an undivided interest in the assets of the joint venture. Hence, if venturers X and Y entered into a joint arrangement to extract uranium from a mine, then each venturer would hold an undivided interest in the property, plant and equipment and other assets used in the mining venture, as well as joint and several responsibility for any liabilities. With a jointly controlled entity, a separate entity is created to carry on the activity of the joint venture. The entity controls the resources contributed by the venturers, rather than the resources being controlled by the venturers, and the liabilities would be obligations of the entity itself.

Recognition that entities may have undivided interests in assets is recognised in the Statement of Financial Accounting Concepts No. 6, paragraph 185, issued by the US Financial Accounting Standards Board:

> The definition of assets focuses primarily on the future economic benefit to which an entity has access and only secondarily on the physical things and other agents that provide future economic benefits. Many physical things and other agents are in effect bundles of future economic benefits that can be unbundled in various ways, and two or more entities may have different future economic benefits from the same agent at the same time or the same

continuing future economic benefit at different times. For example, two or more entities may have undivided interests in a parcel of land. Each has a right to future economic benefit that may qualify as an asset under the definition in paragraph 25, even though the right of each is subject at least to some extent to the rights of the other(s) (FASB 1985, pp. 57–8).

With jointly controlled operations, each venturer may not have any assets in which there are undivided interests because each venturer simply contributes to the overall project. With individual assets, the undivided interests could be based on time (e.g. each venturer can use the asset for a specified day of the week) or the capacity of the resource (e.g. each venturer has a proportionate share of the capacity of a pipeline).

In both the 1994 Discussion Paper 'Associates and Joint Ventures' ('UK-DP') issued by the Accounting Standards Board in the United Kingdom and the G4-DP, the question of whether joint ventures should be restricted to jointly controlled entities is raised.

In the UK-DP (paragraph 3.16), it is argued that a joint venture should be viewed as a strategic alliance in which the investor acts as a partner in the investee's business. Joint venture activities would then be limited to situations where the joint activities constituted a 'business'. Jointly controlled operations and jointly controlled assets would not be seen as giving rise to a business, and hence should not be described as joint ventures. Paragraph 3.17 of UK-DP states:

> Many joint activities stand alone as businesses in their own right. However, some joint activities amount only to a sharing of facilities. A joint activity is a shared facility rather than a business if the joint venturers derive their benefit from product or services taken in kind rather than receiving a share in the profits of trading.

The G4-DP contained similar arguments. Paragraph 2.15 states:

> ... a joint venture must be an enterprise, that is, it must be a separate entity that carries on activities with its own assets and liabilities. The essence of the definition is that unless the joint venture is a separate entity carrying on its own activities with its own resources to achieve its own distinct purposes, it does not have a separate decision-making identity so as to be capable of independent control by external joint venturers. It may be incorporated or it may not be ... As an example, several hospitals may set up a joint venture to provide a laundry service that is a separate entity with its own resources and decision-making identity.

The emphasis in the G4-DP is on the criterion of joint control as opposed to a shared facility. A joint venture must be an activity in which the venturers together control it, consenting to all the essential decisions. Where two parties simply share a pipeline, or similar asset, there are no strategic decisions to be made because there is no ongoing business activity. Similarly, where there are joint operations, such as the making of an aeroplane, each party manages their own contribution within a planned framework. The parties do not become involved in jointly managing a business activity.

Paragraph 2.27 of the G4-DP illustrates the nature of a joint venture:

> For example, suppose that enterprises A and B together acquire a mine and agree to share the output between them on a specified basis, to sell any surplus production, and to share costs and revenues. This activity may be set up in several different ways:
>
> (a) In some jurisdictions, A and B may hold an undivided interest in each of the assets of the mine (the mining property, buildings, equipment, working capital, etc.) and assume joint and several responsibility for any liabilities. Management is appointed to manage the mine on behalf of A and B, with costs and revenues being allocated to them for net cash settlement. (Either A or B may act as manager.) In this case, A and B will each reflect their undivided interest in the assets and share of the liabilities and will record their share of revenues and costs as an extension of its business operations. A and B would be expected to disclose the undivided interest nature of these assets and liabilities and any contingent liabilities.

(b) …

(c) A different economic arrangement could be established under which the mine is set up as a *joint venture*, that is, as a separate enterprise, as described in paragraph 2.15. In this case, rather than share costs and revenues, the joint venture would commit to acquire amounts of the output of the mine (perhaps at fixed or variable prices under a take-or-pay contract). A and B would then have a joint interest in the venture and would be entitled to share in the net profits or losses of the enterprise in accordance with their respective joint venture interests, regardless of the amount of profits or losses that resulted from each venture's transactions with the joint venture.

An alternative way of categorising the different forms of joint ventures is to make a distinction between jointly controlled assets and jointly controlled businesses. If it is agreed that a joint venture should involve a business, potentially the definition of business used in IFRS 3 *Business Combinations* could be used:

An integrated set of activities and assets conducted and managed for the purpose of providing:
(a) a return to investors; or
(b) lower costs or other economic benefits directly and proportionately to policyholders or participants.
A business generally consists of inputs, processes applied to those inputs, and resulting outputs that are, or will be, used to generate revenues. If goodwill is present in a transferred set of activities and assets, the transferred set shall be presumed to be a business.

If this is the case, then some jointly controlled assets, such as a mining operation sharing output, would be better classified as a jointly controlled entity. The term entity is normally defined to include organisational structures other than corporations and partnerships. For example, an entity is defined in the Australian concepts document SAC 1 'Definition of the Reporting Entity' as 'any legal, administrative, or fiduciary arrangement, organisational structure or other party (including a person) having the capacity to deploy scarce resources in order to achieve objectives'.

The UK FRS 9 *Associates and Joint Ventures* (1997) drew a similar conclusion, arguing that an arrangement should not be defined as a joint venture unless it constituted an entity. Paragraph 8 of FRS 9 states:

For a joint entity arrangement to amount to an entity, it must carry on a trade or business, meaning a trade or business of its own and not just part of its participants' trades or businesses. In its activities the joint arrangement must therefore have some independence (within the objectives set by the agreement governing the joint arrangement) to pursue its own commercial strategy in its buying and selling; it must either have access to the market in its own right for its main inputs and outputs or, at least, be able to obtain them from the participants or sell them to the participants on generally the same terms as are available in the market. The following indicate that the joint activities undertaken in a joint arrangement do not amount to its carrying on a trade or business of its own — and therefore that the joint arrangement is not an entity:
(a) the participants derive their benefit from product or services taken in kind rather than by receiving a share in the results of trading, or
(b) each participant's share of the output or result of the joint activity is determined by its supply of key inputs to the process producing that output or result.

This definition of an entity is more narrow than the IASB definition of an entity as a 'business'. FRS 9 effectively requires a joint venture to trade and hence produce a profit or loss. It is doubtful that an entity that has inputs, processes and outputs, with the latter being distributed to the investors, is any less an entity than a trading entity.

In determining the appropriate accounting method to be used it is essential that the nature of a joint venture be clearly identified. In IAS 31, as detailed later in this chapter, jointly controlled entities are accounted for differently from jointly controlled assets and operations. However, in section 26.8, after an analysis of these methods, it is argued that joint ventures should be limited to jointly controlled businesses, while shared facilities (jointly controlled operations and assets) should be accounted for in the same way as other assets; as such they should be excluded from an accounting standard on joint ventures.

LO 3

26.3 Jointly controlled operations

Paragraph 15 of IAS 31 states:

> In respect of its interests in jointly controlled operations, a venturer shall recognise in its financial statements:
> (a) the assets that it controls and the liabilities that it incurs; and
> (b) the expenses that it incurs and its share of the income that it earns from the sale of goods or services by the joint venture.

As each venturer uses its own property, plant and equipment the venturer automatically includes these assets in its own records. As the venturer incurs costs in relation to a particular project, such as assisting in the manufacture of an aeroplane, the venturer accumulates those costs in a work in progress account:

| Work in progress – joint venture | Dr | X | |
| Cash | Cr | | X |

If the venturer has to contribute towards some joint costs of the venture, these are also capitalised into work in progress.

When the aircraft is sold, the venturer receives a share of the proceeds:

| Cash | Dr | X | |
| Revenue from joint venture | Cr | | X |

and the work in progress is recognised as cost of product sold:

| Cost of product – joint venture | Dr | X | |
| Work in progress | Cr | | X |

LO 4

26.4 Jointly controlled assets

Paragraph 21 of IAS 31 details the accounting for interests in jointly controlled assets:

> In respect of its interest in jointly controlled assets, a venturer shall recognise in its financial statements:
> (a) its share of the jointly controlled assets, classified according to the nature of the assets;
> (b) any liabilities that it has incurred;
> (c) its share of any liabilities incurred jointly with the other venturers in relation to the joint venture;
> (d) any income from the sale or use of its share of the output of the joint venture, together with its share of any expenses incurred by the joint venture; and
> (e) any expenses that it has incurred in respect of its interest in the joint venture.

Assume that a venturer has a half-share of a jointly controlled gas pipeline that cost $100 000 to construct. Each venturer will pass the following journal entry:

Pipeline – Property, plant and equipment	Dr	50 000	
Cash	Cr		50 000

As the pipeline is the subject of a joint control agreement, there is some debate as to whether or not each venturer should recognise its share of the pipeline as an asset. Paragraph 2.21 of G4-DP states:

> Some may argue that joint ownership of an asset (for example, a 50 percent joint interest in a mine) does not technically meet the definition of an asset, which is a resource controlled by the entity, not jointly controlled. But the distinction must be made between the mining property per se and the reporting enterprise's rights in it. The reporting enterprise's asset is its contractual joint ownership rights. The enterprise controls these rights and the benefits that flow from them. It can determine how to use them, and it may decide to sell them, hold them, or pledge them as collateral.

However, if the real asset is the rights to the pipeline, then the asset is an intangible asset, and not one of property, plant and equipment. The question of asset recognition is discussed further in section 26.8.

26.5 Jointly controlled assets where output is shared — accounting by the joint venture

Where the joint venture is undertaken outside a formal structure, such as a corporation or partnership, separate accounting records do not need to be kept for the joint venture. However, for accountability reasons it is expected that the joint venture agreement would require these records.

IAS 31 does not provide standards on accounting for the joint venture operation itself. If the joint venture does not sell the output produced, but rather distributes it to the venturers, there is no profit or loss account raised by the venture. In preparing accounts for the joint venture, the main purpose is to accumulate costs as incurred. These are capitalised into a work in progress account, which is transferred to the venturers as inventory. Further, the joint venture accounts provide information about the assets and liabilities relating to the joint venture as well as the contributions from the venturers. Hence, a balance sheet is the joint venture's main financial statement.

Illustrative example 26.1 illustrates the accounting system within the joint venture operation. The journal entries represent the establishment of the joint venture operation and its activities throughout the year. Transactions that occur regularly throughout the year, such as payment of wages, are accumulated into one entry.

ILLUSTRATIVE EXAMPLE 26.1

Accounting by an unincorporated joint venture

On 1 July 2006, X Ltd and Y Ltd signed an agreement to form a joint venture to manufacture a product called Plasboard. This product is used in the packaging industry and has the advantages of the strength and protection qualities of cardboard as well as the flexibility and durability of plastic.

To commence the venture, both venturers contributed $1 500 000 in cash. In the example it is assumed that not all the raw materials are used during the period, and not all finished goods have been transferred to the venturers.

- *Contributions of cash by the venturers*

Cash	Dr	3 000 000	
X Ltd − contribution	Cr		1 500 000
Y Ltd − contribution	Cr		1 500 000
(Contributions by venturers)			

- *Use of cash and loan to buy equipment and raw materials*

Equipment	Dr	800 000	
Cash	Cr		500 000
Loan − equipment	Cr		300 000
(Acquisition of equipment)			

Raw materials	Dr	650 000	
Trade creditors	Cr		650 000
(Acquisition of materials)			

- *Payment of wages*

Wages − management	Dr	200 000	
Wages − other	Dr	520 000	
Cash	Cr		700 000
Accrued wages	Cr		20 000
(Annual wages)			

- *Borrowing from the bank*

Cash	Dr	500 000	
Bank loan	Cr		500 000
(Amount borrowed)			

- *Repayment of loan and other expenses*

Loan − equipment	Dr	100 000	
Cash	Cr		100 000
(Part-payment for loan on equipment)			

Trade creditors	Dr	420 000	
Cash	Cr		420 000
(Payment of trade creditors)			

Overhead expenses	Dr	1 300 000	
Cash	Cr		1 300 000
(Payment of manufacturing expenses such as electricity)			

→

- *Depreciation of equipment*

Depreciation expense	Dr	80 000	
Accumulated depreciation	Cr		80 000
(Depreciation of equipment)			

- *Transfer of expenses to work in progress*

Work in progress	Dr	2 580 000	
Wages	Cr		720 000
Raw materials	Cr		480 000
Overhead expenses	Cr		1 300 000
Depreciation expense	Cr		80 000
(Allocating of costs to work in progress)			

- *Transfer from work in progress to inventory*

Inventory	Dr	1 800 000	
Work in progress	Cr		1 800 000
(Allocation to finished goods)			

- *Transfer of inventory to venturers throughout the year*

X Ltd	Dr	800 000	
Y Ltd	Dr	800 000	
Inventory	Cr		1 600 000
(Delivery of output to venturers)			

The major ledger accounts of interest in relation to the joint venture are as follows:

Cash

	$		$
Contribution – X Ltd	1 500 000	Equipment	500 000
Contribution – Y Ltd	1 500 000	Wages	700 000
Bank loan	500 000	Loan – equipment	100 000
		Trade creditors	420 000
		Overhead expenses	1 300 000
		Balance c/f	480 000
	3 500 000		3 500 000
Balance b/f	480 000		

Work in progress

	$		$
Wages	720 000	Inventory	1 800 000
Raw materials	480 000		
Overhead	1 300 000		
Depreciation	80 000	Balance c/f	780 000
	2 580 000		2 580 000
Balance b/f	780 000		

→

The balance sheet of the joint venture at 30 June 2007 would be:

Balance sheet as at 30 June 2007		
Current assets		
Raw materials	$ 170 000	
Inventory	200 000	
Work in progress	780 000	
Cash	480 000	
Total current assets		$1 630 000
Non-current assets		
Equipment	800 000	
Accumulated depreciation	(80 000)	720 000
Total assets		2 350 000
Current liabilities		
Trade creditors	230 000	
Accrued wages	20 000	
Total current liabilities		250 000
Non-current liabilities		
Bank loan	500 000	
Loan – equipment	200 000	
Total non-current liabilities		700 000
Total liabilities		950 000
Net assets		$1 400 000
Venturers' equity		
X Ltd: Contributions – at 1/7/06	$1 500 000	
Cost of inventory distributed	(800 000)	$700 000
Y Ltd: Contributions – at 1/7/06	1 500 000	
Cost of inventory distributed	(800 000)	700 000
Total venturers' equity		$1 400 000

From this example, we can see that the costs of producing the output are accumulated in the joint venture operation, and the inventory, at cost, distributed to the joint venturers. In this example, all costs are capitalised into inventory. In some cases, the costs may be transferred to the venturers' accounts as expenses and matched in the records of the venturers with the revenue from sale of the output. For example, if the joint venture operation involved exploring for minerals, it may be desirable to expense the costs of exploration and evaluation rather than capitalise them for allocation to future inventory. Similarly, where depreciation is charged on non-current assets, the depreciation expense may not, as in this example, be charged in the accounts of the joint venture itself. Instead, in the records of the venturers themselves, a charge for depreciation may be made.

LO 5

26.6 Jointly controlled assets where output is shared — accounting by a venturer

Theoretically, there are two methods that the venturer can use in accounting for its interest:
- *The one-line method.* Under this method, the venturer records its investment in the joint venture, adjusting only for any contributions it makes to the joint venture and any distributions or allocations made by the joint venture to the venturer. The joint venturer may provide note disclosure on the assets and liabilities underlying that investment.
- *The line-by-line method.* Under this method, the records of the venturer include, on a line-by-line basis, its share of the assets and liabilities in the joint venture.

The merits of these methods are discussed in section 26.8, with a preference being expressed for the one-line method. Because IAS 31 classifies this form of joint venture as jointly controlled assets, it requires the line-by-line method set out in paragraph 21 to be used. In illustrative examples 26.2 and 26.3, both methods are illustrated. Because paragraph 56 of IAS 31 requires disclosures of assets, liabilities, income and expenses in relation to a joint venture, in the following examples a distinction is made between joint venture elements and those belonging to the venturer. This is similar to the need to distinguish between leased assets and acquired assets.

The venturer's accounting records are affected by the nature of its contributions. The contributions can be in the form of cash, non-current assets or provision of services. In the following sections, examples of venturers' accounting records for different forms of contributions are provided.

26.6.1 Cash contributions

ILLUSTRATIVE EXAMPLE 26.2

Contribution of cash by a joint venturer

On 1 July 2005, X Ltd and Y Ltd establish a joint venture operation to manufacture a product. Each company has a 50% interest in the venture and shares output equally. To commence the venture, both companies contribute cash of $1 500 000 on 1 July 2005. Each venturer depreciates equipment at 10% p.a. on cost.

The following information was extracted from the accounts and financial statements of the joint venture operation as at 30 June 2006:

Balance sheet (extract) as at 30 June 2006	
Assets	
Cash	$ 420 000
Raw materials	100 000
Work in progress	650 000
Inventory	200 000
Equipment	1 500 000
Total assets	2 870 000
Liabilities	
Accounts payable (raw materials)	120 000
Accrued expenses (wages)	150 000
Bank loan	1 000 000
Total liabilities	1 270 000
Net assets	$1 600 000

Cash receipts and payments for the year ended 30 June 2006		
	Payments	Receipts
Contributions		$3 000 000
Bank loan		1 000 000
Equipment (purchased 3/7/05)	$1 500 000	
Wages	500 000	
Accounts payable (raw materials)	380 000	
Overhead expenses	1 200 000	
	$3 580 000	$4 000 000

Costs incurred for the year ended 30 June 2006	
Wages	$ 650 000
Raw materials	400 000
Overhead expenses	1 200 000
	2 250 000
Less: Cost of inventory	1 600 000
Work in progress at 30/6/06	$ 650 000

Required

Prepare the journal entries in the records of X Ltd and Y Ltd for the year ended 30 June 2006.

Solution

1. Line-by-line method

Records of X Ltd

At 1 July 2005, X Ltd records its interest in the joint venture, the asset cash being distinguished as an asset in a joint venture:

Cash in joint venture (JV)	Dr	1 500 000	
Cash	Cr		1 500 000

At 30 June 2006, the joint venture has used the cash to acquire various assets, undertake loans, incur expenses and manufacture inventory. As a contributor of 50% of the cash into the joint venture, X Ltd is entitled to 50% of all the assets, liabilities, expenses and output of the joint venture. From the balance sheet of the joint venture, it should be noted that the net assets of the joint venture amount to $1 600 000 (i.e. $2 870 000 – $1 270 000). The inventory in the balance sheet is $200 000. From the costs incurred information, it can be seen that the joint venture has produced $1 600 000 worth of inventory. If only $200 000 is still on hand in the joint venture, then $1 400 000 worth of inventory must have been transferred to the joint venturers: $700 000 each. The contributions section of the balance sheet is shown overleaf.

X Ltd:	Initial contribution	$1 500 000		
	Inventory transferred	(700 000)		$ 800 000
Y Ltd:	Initial contribution	1 500 000		
	Inventory transferred	(700 000)		800 000
				$1 600 000

At 30 June 2006, X Ltd makes the following entry in its records to replace 'Cash in JV' with a 50% share of each of the accounts in the balance sheet of the joint venture at 30 June 2006. The entry also recognises the inventory of $700 000 transferred to X Ltd from the joint venture.

Raw material in JV	Dr	50 000		[100 000/2]
Work in progress in JV	Dr	325 000		[650 000/2]
Inventory in JV	Dr	100 000		[200 000/2]
Equipment in JV	Dr	750 000		[1 500 000/2]
Inventory	Dr	700 000		[1 400 000/2]
Accounts payable in JV	Cr		60 000	[120 000/2]
Accrued expenses in JV	Cr		75 000	[150 000/2]
Bank loan in JV	Cr		500 000	[1 000 000/2]
Cash in JV	Cr		1 290 000	[1 500 000 − (420 000/2)]

Note that X Ltd's share of cash in the joint venture is calculated by finding the difference between the share at the beginning of the period and the share at the end of the period.

X Ltd depreciates the equipment in its own records. Therefore, having recognised an asset at $750 000, X Ltd would also pass the following entry at 30 June 2006:

Depreciation expense	Dr	75 000		[10% × 750 000]
Accumulated depreciation	Cr		75 000	
(Depreciation on equipment in the joint venture)				

Records of Y Ltd

As Y Ltd contributed the same asset (cash of $1 500 000) to the joint venture as X Ltd, the journal entries in the records of Y Ltd would be the same as that in X Ltd.

2. One-line method

As in the line-by-line method, each venturer records the initial contribution; however, this time as an investment in the joint venture:

Investment in joint venture	Dr	1 500 000	
Cash	Cr		1 500 000

On receipt of the inventory of $700 000 from the joint venture, the venturer reduces its investment in the joint venture:

Inventory	Dr	700 000	
Investment in joint venture	Cr		700 000

The depreciation is capitalised into the cost of the inventory:

Inventory	Dr	75 000	
Investment in joint venture	Cr		75 000

As the investment is recognised on a one-line basis, to provide more information about the assets and liabilities underlying the investment, the joint venturer could disclose this information in the notes to the accounts:

The investment of $725 000 in the joint venture relates to the following assets and liabilities jointly controlled within the joint venture entity:

Raw material	$ 50 000
Work in progress	325 000
Inventory	100 000
Equipment	750 000
Accumulated depreciation	(75 000)
Cash	210 000
Total assets	1 360 000
Accounts payable	60 000
Accrued expenses	75 000
Bank loan	500 000
Total liabilities	635 000
Net assets	$ 725 000

LO 6

26.6.2 Contributions of non-monetary assets

Where a venturer contributes a non-current asset to the joint venture, the value of the contribution is effectively the fair value of that non-current asset. Hence, if one venturer contributed $100 000 cash and the other venturer a non-current asset, then for both parties to agree to join there would have to be agreement that the non-current asset being contributed had a fair value of $100 000. If all venturers contributed non-current assets, then some form of valuation of the contributions would need to be made by the parties involved.

Paragraph 48 of IAS 31 provides guidance on accounting for contributions of non-monetary assets provided by a venturer. It states:

> When a venturer contributes or sells assets to a joint venture, recognition of any portion of a gain or loss from the transaction shall reflect the substance of the transaction. While the assets are retained by the joint venture, and provided the venturer has transferred the significant risks and rewards of ownership, the venturer shall recognise only that portion of the gain or loss that is attributable to the interests of the other venturers. The venturer shall recognise the full amount of any loss when the contribution or sale provides evidence of a reduction in the net realisable value of current assets or an impairment loss.

Assume venturer A carries a non-current asset at fair value in its accounts; for example, an item of plant for $100 000. If this asset is contributed to a joint venture where the other venturer, B, contributes cash of $100 000, the journal entry to record the contribution in the records of venturer A under the *line-by-line method* is shown overleaf.

Cash in JV	Dr	50 000		[100 000/2]
Plant in JV	Dr	50 000		[100 000/2]
Plant	Cr		100 000	

In the records of venturer B, the entry is:

Cash in JV	Dr	50 000		[100 000/2]
Plant in JV	Dr	50 000		[100 000/2]
Cash	Cr		100 000	

Note that in the records of both venturers the plant in the joint venture is recorded at the same amount − $50 000.

Under the *one-line method*, both venturers would record an investment of $100 000, one giving up cash and the other giving up plant.

The accounting records of a venturer that contributes a non-current asset become more complicated when the venturer carries the contributed asset in its records at an amount less than fair value.

In contributing an asset to the joint venture, the venturer is effectively selling a proportion of that asset to the other joint venturers, and retaining a proportion for itself. Where the carrying amount of the asset is lower than the fair value, the venturer makes a profit on selling the proportion of the asset to the other venturers. The profit is the difference between the fair value and carrying amount of the proportion of the asset sold. Assume venturer A contributed a non-current asset with a fair value of $100 000, and a carrying amount of $80 000, while venturer B contributed cash of $100 000. Venturer A can then recognise a profit on sale of half the non-current asset of $10 000 (being $\frac{1}{2}$ ($100 000 − $80 000)). The entry in the records of venturer A under the line-by-line method is:

Cash in JV	Dr	50 000		[100 000/2]
Plant in JV	Dr	40 000		[80 000/2]
Carrying amount of plant sold	Dr	40 000		[80 000/2]
Proceeds on sale of plant	Cr		50 000	[100 000/2]
Plant	Cr		80 000	

The whole of the plant at carrying amount is given up by the venturer, with half being sold to the other venturer at a profit and the other half being the asset held in the joint venture. Note that venturer A has the plant in the joint venture recorded at half of the carrying amount and not at half of the fair value.

For venturer B, under the line-by-line method, the entry in its records is:

Cash in JV	Dr	50 000		[100 000/2]
Plant in JV	Dr	50 000		[100 000/2]
Cash	Cr		100 000	

Note that venturer B has the non-current asset recorded in its records at half of fair value. Hence, venturer A and venturer B have their equal share of the plant recorded in their records at different amounts.

The fact that the venturers have the non-current asset recorded at different amounts in their records affects the calculation of the cost of the inventory distributed to the venturers from the joint venture. If the asset is depreciated, and the depreciation included in the cost of inventory, then, as the venturers have the asset recorded at different amounts, the depreciation expense for each of the venturers differs and so does the cost of inventory transferred.

Where the asset is depreciated in the joint venture's records, this depreciation is based on the fair value of the asset. For venturer B, the depreciation charge is then the appropriate one and no adjustment is necessary. However, for venturer A, an adjustment is necessary, as the depreciation charged by the joint venture is too great. As the depreciation is capitalised into inventory and work in progress in the records of the joint venture, in the accounts of venturer A, when A recognises its share of the assets of the joint venture, a further entry is necessary to reduce the balances of the inventory-related accounts. This extra entry in venturer A's records is demonstrated in illustrative example 26.3.

Under the *one-line method*, venturer A records its investment at $90 000, with the giving up of the $80 000 asset and the recognition of a $10 000 gain on sale. Venturer B's investment is recorded at $100 000 with the giving up of cash for the same amount.

ILLUSTRATIVE EXAMPLE 26.3

Contribution of a non-current asset by a venturer

On 1 July 2005, X Ltd and Y Ltd established a joint venture to manufacture a product. Each company has a 50% interest in the venture and shares output equally. To commence the venture, on 1 July 2005, X Ltd contributed cash of $1 500 000 and Y Ltd contributed equipment which had a carrying amount of $1 000 000, and a fair value of $1 500 000. The equipment is depreciated in the joint venture's accounts at 10% p.a. on cost.

The following information was extracted from the joint venture's financial statements as at 30 June 2006:

Balance sheet (extract) as at 30 June 2006	
Assets	
Cash	$ 420 000
Raw materials	100 000
Work in progress	800 000
Inventory	200 000
Equipment	1 500 000
Accumulated depreciation – equipment	(150 000)
Total assets	2 870 000
Liabilities	
Accounts payable	120 000
Accrued expenses (wages)	150 000
Bank loan	1 000 000
Total liabilities	1 270 000
Net assets	$1 600 000

Cash receipts and payments for the year ended 30 June 2006		
	Payments	Receipts
Contributions		$1 500 000
Bank loan		1 000 000
Wages	$ 500 000	
Accounts payable (raw materials)	380 000	
Overhead expenses	1 200 000	
	$2 080 000	$2 500 000

Costs incurred for the year ended 30 June 2006	
Wages	$ 650 000
Raw materials	400 000
Depreciation	150 000
Overhead expenses	1 200 000
	2 400 000
Less: Cost of inventory	1 600 000
Work in progress at 30 June 2006	$ 800 000

Required

Prepare the journal entries in the records of each of the venturers for the year ended 30 June 2006.

Solution

1. Line-by-line method

Records of X Ltd

In this example, X Ltd contributes cash to the joint venture, and Y Ltd contributes equipment. At 1 July 2005, X Ltd gives up the cash contribution and recognises a share of the cash and the equipment in the joint venture. X Ltd will recognise a share of the *fair value* of the asset. The entry is:

Cash in JV	Dr	750 000		[1 500 000/2]
Equipment in JV	Dr	750 000		[1 500 000/2]
Cash	Cr		1 500 000	

At 30 June 2006, X Ltd recognises a share of the assets and liabilities in the balance sheet of the joint venture. Note that the joint venture has produced inventory of $1 600 000, of which $1 400 000 has been transferred to the venturers. Further, the joint venture has depreciated the equipment, the depreciation being based on the fair value of the equipment. The entry at 30 June 2006 in X Ltd's accounts is shown opposite.

→

Raw material in JV	Dr	50 000		[100 000/2]
Work in progress in JV	Dr	400 000		[800 000/2]
Inventory in JV	Dr	100 000		[200 000/2]
Inventory	Dr	700 000		[1 400 000/2]
Accumulated depreciation — equipment in JV	Cr		75 000	[150 000/2]
Accounts payable in JV	Cr		60 000	[120 000/2]
Accrued expenses in JV	Cr		75 000	[150 000/2]
Bank loan in JV	Cr		500 000	[1 000 000/2]
Cash in JV	Cr		540 000	[750 000 – (420 000/2)]

As depreciation has been based on fair value in the joint venture, and X Ltd has its share of the equipment in the joint venture recorded at fair value, the correct amount of depreciation has been capitalised into the cost of inventory. No adjusting entry is necessary.

Records of Y Ltd

At 1 July 2005, Y Ltd contributes equipment to the joint venture, this having a carrying amount in Y Ltd different from the fair value of the asset. In recording its contribution to the joint venture, Y Ltd therefore recognises a gain on selling half of the equipment to X Ltd. X Ltd's share of the equipment in the joint venture is then based on the original carrying amount of the asset. The entry is:

Cash in JV	Dr	750 000		[1 500 000/2]
Equipment in JV	Dr	500 000		[1 000 000/2]
Carrying amount of equipment sold	Dr	500 000		[1 000 000/2]
Equipment	Cr		1 000 000	
Proceeds from sale of equipment	Cr		750 000	[1 500 000/2]

At 30 June 2006, Y Ltd recognises its share of the accounts in the balance sheet of the joint venture as well as its share of the inventory transferred from the joint venture. The entry is:

Raw material in JV	Dr	50 000		[100 000/2]
Work in progress in JV	Dr	400 000		[800 000/2]
Inventory in JV	Dr	100 000		[200 000/2]
Inventory	Dr	700 000		[1 400 000/2]
Accumulated depreciation — equipment in JV	Cr		75 000	[150 000/2]
Accounts payable in JV	Cr		60 000	[120 000/2]
Accrued expenses in JV	Cr		75 000	[150 000/2]
Bank loan in JV	Cr		500 000	[1 000 000/2]
Cash in JV	Cr		540 000	[750 000 – (420 000/2)]

Note that this entry is the same as that for X Ltd.

The depreciation recognised by X Ltd is $75 000, which is based on the fair value of the asset. However, the equipment in the joint venture has been recognised by Y Ltd at only $500 000, which is half of the original carrying amount. Y Ltd would want to recognise only $50 000 depreciation, which is 10% of $500 000. Hence, whereas the work in progress and inventory recognised by Y Ltd includes depreciation of $75 000, the real cost of these assets to Y Ltd is less, to the amount of $25 000. A further entry is necessary to reduce the accumulated depreciation recognised by Y Ltd and to reduce the cost of the work in progress and inventory relating to the joint venture. This means that the cost of these assets to Y Ltd is different from that recognised by X Ltd. This is because the cost of the equipment in the joint venture is less for Y Ltd than for X Ltd.

As the depreciation is capitalised into work in progress and inventory (both that amount still on hand in the joint venture as well as that transferred to Y Ltd), the adjustment to depreciation is proportionately allocated across these accounts:

Share of $25 000			
Work in progress	$ 400 000	1/3	$ 8 333
Inventory in JV	100 000	1/12	2 083
Inventory	700 000	7/12	14 584
	$1 200 000		$25 000

The entry in the records of Y Ltd to adjust the accumulated depreciation and the cost of the inventory-related accounts is then:

Accumulated depreciation – equipment in JV	Dr	25 000		[10% × (750 000 – 500 000)]
Work in progress in JV	Cr		8 333	
Inventory in JV	Cr		2 083	
Inventory	Cr		14 584	

2. One-line method
Records of X Ltd
At 1 July 2005, X Ltd records its initial investment in the joint venture:

Investment in joint venture	Dr	1 500 000	
Cash	Cr		1 500 000

At 30 June 2006, X Ltd reduces the investment on receipt of the inventory from the joint venture:

Inventory	Dr	700 000	
Investment in joint venture	Cr		700 000

The investment now has a carrying amount of $800 000. Note disclosure about the underlying assets and liabilities could be as shown opposite.

The investment of $800 000 in the joint venture relates to the following assets and liabilities jointly controlled within the joint venture entity:

Cash	$ 210 000
Raw materials	50 000
Work in progress	400 000
Inventory	100 000
Equipment	750 000
Accumulated depreciation	(75 000)
	1 435 000
Accounts payable	60 000
Accrued expenses	75 000
Bank loan	500 000
	635 000
Net assets	$ 800 000

Records of Y Ltd

At 1 July 2005, Y Ltd records its investment in the joint venture. This is at a lower amount than that recognised by X Ltd because of the contribution of the asset:

Investment in joint venture	Dr	1 250 000	
Equipment	Cr		1 000 000
Gain on sale	Cr		250 000

At 30 June 2006, Y Ltd reduces the investment on receipt of the inventory:

Inventory	Dr	700 000	
Investment in joint venture	Cr		700 000

As shown in the line-by-line method, an adjustment is required to inventory because of the difference in equipment recognised by Y Ltd:

Investment in joint venture	Dr	14 584	
Inventory	Cr		14 584

The investment now has a carrying amount of $564 584. Note disclosure about the underlying assets and liabilities could be:

The investment of $564 584 in the joint venture relates to the following assets and liabilities jointly controlled within the joint venture entity:

Cash	$ 210 000
Raw materials	50 000
Work in progress [400 000 − 8333]	391 667
Inventory [100 000 − 2083]	97 917
Equipment [750 000 − 250 000]	500 000
Accumulated depreciation [75 000 − 25 000]	(50 000)
	1 199 584
Accounts payable	60 000
Accrued expenses	75 000
Bank loan	500 000
	635 000
Net assets	$ 564 584

26.6.3   Contributions of services

Contributions of cash and non-current assets result in the immediate provision of assets to the joint venture. With the provision of services, the venturer supplying the services raises a liability, which is the obligation to supply the services when required by the joint venture, while the joint venture recognises an asset, which is the services receivable from the venturer.

The principles established in accounting for the contributions of non-current assets where the fair value differs from the carrying amount apply to the accounting for services provided. Where a venturer has the expertise to provide services, normally the venturer supplies those services at fair value. This means that the cost of the services provided by the venturer differs from the fair value of the services. Hence:

- in providing services to the other venturers, a venturer records a profit on the supply of the services. However, the services provided to itself (i.e. its share of the joint venture) must be supplied at cost, no profit being earned.
- the joint venture will record the services receivable at fair value and capitalise the cost of the services when supplied into the cost of the work in progress and inventory. For the venturer supplying the services, an adjustment is necessary to reduce the cost of the work in progress and inventory as recorded by the joint venture back to the lower cost to the venturer.

ILLUSTRATIVE EXAMPLE 26.4

Contribution of services by a venturer

On 1 July 2005, X Ltd and Y Ltd established a joint venture to manufacture a product. Each company has a 50% interest in the venture and shares output equally. To commence the venture, on 1 July 2005, X Ltd contributed cash of $1 000 000 and Y Ltd undertook to contribute two years' worth of administration and production services ($1 000 000 fair value). Y Ltd estimated the cost of providing the services over the next two years at $750 000 (i.e. Y Ltd earning a profit on the provision of services). Each venturer depreciated equipment at 10% p.a. on cost.

The following information was extracted from the accounts and financial statements of the joint venture operation as at 30 June 2006:

Balance sheet (extract) as at 30 June 2006	
Assets	
Cash	$ 20 000
Services receivable	500 000
Raw materials	100 000
Work in progress	650 000
Inventory	200 000
Equipment	800 000
Total assets	2 270 000
Liabilities	
Accounts payable (raw materials)	120 000
Accrued expenses (wages)	50 000
Bank loan	1 500 000
Total liabilities	1 670 000
Net assets	$ 600 000

$\longrightarrow$

Cash receipts and payments for the year ended 30 June 2006		
	Payments	Receipts
Contributions		$1 000 000
Bank loan		1 500 000
Equipment (purchased 3/7/05)	$ 800 000	
Wages	100 000	
Accounts payable (raw materials)	380 000	
Overhead expenses	1 200 000	
	$2 480 000	$2 500 000

Costs incurred for the year ended 30 June 2006	
Wages	$ 150 000
Raw materials	400 000
Services received	500 000
Overhead expenses	1 200 000
	2 250 000
Less: Cost of inventory	1 600 000
Work in progress at 30 June 2006	$ 650 000

Required

Prepare the journal entries in the records of both venturers for the year ended 30 June 2006.

Solution — Line-by-line method

Records of X Ltd

At 1 July 2006, X Ltd supplies cash to the joint venture and Y Ltd promises to provide services. The entry in X Ltd is:

Cash in JV	Dr	500 000		[1 000 000/2]
Services receivable in JV	Dr	500 000		[1 000 000/2]
Cash	Cr		1 000 000	

The joint venture would raise an asset, Services Receivable, at $1 000 000. When the first year's services are supplied by Y Ltd, the joint venture reduces the receivable account by $500 000 and capitalises $500 000 into the work in progress account, leaving a balance of $500 000 in services receivable. This can be seen in the balance sheet and costs incurred statement of the joint venture at 30 June 2006.

At 30 June 2006, X Ltd recognises its half share in the assets and liabilities of the joint venture and the inventory transferred from the joint venture. The entry by X Ltd is shown overleaf.

Raw material in JV	Dr	50 000		[100 000/2]
Work in progress in JV	Dr	325 000		[650 000/2]
Inventory in JV	Dr	100 000		[200 000/2]
Equipment in JV	Dr	400 000		[800 000/2]
Inventory	Dr	700 000		[1 400 000/2]
Accounts payable in JV	Cr		60 000	[120 000/2]
Accrued expenses in JV	Cr		25 000	[50 000/2]
Bank loan in JV	Cr		750 000	[150 000/2]
Cash in JV	Cr		490 000	[500 000 – (20 000/2)]
Services receivable in JV	Cr		250 000	[500 000 – (500 000/2)]

As the venturers depreciate the equipment in their own records, a further entry is necessary by X Ltd:

Depreciation expense – equipment in JV	Dr	40 000		[10% × 400 000)]
Accumulated depreciation	Cr		40 000	

Records of Y Ltd

At 1 July 2006, Y Ltd recognises a profit on selling services to X Ltd and raises an obligation to supply services to X Ltd. It does not raise any obligation, nor recognise a profit, in relation to the supply of services to itself. Y Ltd does not, therefore, recognise a share of the services receivable account raised by the joint venture, as it cannot hold an asset in itself. The entry by X Ltd is:

Cash in JV	Dr	500 000		[1 000 000/2]
Obligation to supply services to JV	Cr		375 000	[750 000/2]
Gain – supply of services	Cr		125 000	[(1 000 000 – 750 000)/2]

During the 2005–06 period, Y Ltd supplies services to the joint venture. The cost of supplying the services to the joint venture is $375 000. Y Ltd recognises a reduction in the liability to supply services to X Ltd as well as the cost of supplying services to itself. The entry in the records of Y Ltd when the services are provided is:

Services provided to JV	Dr	187 500		[375 000/2]
Obligation to supply services	Dr	187 500		[375 000/2]
Cash	Cr		375 000	[750 000/2]

At 30 June 2006, Y Ltd recognises its share of the balance sheet accounts of the joint venture as well as the inventory transferred from the joint venture to Y Ltd. As Y Ltd did not recognise a share of the services receivable account raised by the joint venture, in recognising a share of the joint venture's accounts at 30 June 2006, it is

necessary to make an adjustment for the services recognised by the joint venture. This adjustment is in two parts:

- In the accounts of the joint venture, the services provided based on their fair value have been capitalised into the cost of the work in progress and inventory. Hence, the expense account 'Services Provided to JV' raised by Y Ltd during 2005–06 needs to be eliminated – Y Ltd cannot have the cost of the services capitalised into inventory as well as recognising a period operating expense. A credit adjustment of $187 500 is then made to the 'Services provided to JV' account.

- As the amount that the joint venture has capitalised into work in progress and inventory is based on fair value, an adjustment is necessary in relation to the profit element on the provision of the services. The cost of the inventory to Y Ltd is less than that to X Ltd as Y Ltd recognises the services at cost while X Ltd pays fair value for them. The profit element on providing services must then be proportionately adjusted against the work in progress and inventory accounts recognised by the joint venture. The profit on supplying services for one year for one venturer is $62 500 (being $\frac{1}{2} \times \frac{1}{2} \times \$250\,000$). The allocation across the inventory-related accounts is as follows:

Share of $62 500			
Inventory in JV	$ 100 000	100/1125	$ 5 555
Inventory	700 000	700/1125	38 890
Work in progress in JV	325 000	325/1125	18 055
	$1 125 000		$62 500

These amounts are then credited to the appropriate accounts to eliminate the profit element on the provision of services, and hence reduce their cost to Y Ltd.

The entry at 30 June 2006 for Y Ltd is then:

Raw material in IV	Dr	50 000		[100 000/2]
Work in progress in JV	Dr	325 000		[650 000/2]
Inventory in JV	Dr	100 000		[200 000/2]
Equipment in JV	Dr	400 000		[800 000/2]
Inventory	Dr	700 000		[1 400 000/2]
Accounts payable in JV	Cr		60 000	[120 000/2]
Accrued expenses in JV	Cr		25 000	[50 000/2]
Bank loan in JV	Cr		750 000	[1 500 000/2]
Cash in JV	Cr		490 000	[500 000 –
				20 000/2]
Services provided to JV	Cr		187 500	
Inventory in JV	Cr		5 555	
Inventory	Cr		38 890	
Work in progress in JV	Cr		18 055	

As the venturers depreciate the equipment in their own records, a further entry is necessary in Y Ltd:

Depreciation expense – equipment in JV	Dr	40 000		[10% × 400 000]
Accumulated depreciation	Cr		40 000	

26.6.4 Contributions of assets with ownership retained

In section 26.6.2, the situation analysed is where a venturer contributed a non-current asset to the joint venture, potentially to be used by the joint venture. In this section, the situation under consideration is where the non-current asset contributed to the venture is used for the life of the joint venture and then returned to the venturer. In essence, the venturer supplying the asset retains ownership of the asset and contributes some part of the benefits of the asset to the joint venture. For example, a venturer could allow the joint venture to use some land owned by a venturer, or a venturer may have a patent that the joint venture is allowed to use for a period of time.

In accounting for the contribution of such an asset, it needs to be recognised that what the venturer is contributing to the joint venture is the fair value of the benefits given up by the venturer. Assume a venturer owns an asset with a fair value of $100 000 and this is supplied to the joint venture for the next two years, at the end of which the fair value of the asset is $80 000. The venturer is then supplying an asset to the joint venture that has a value of $20 000. The venturer then has two assets: an asset of $80 000 and a proportionate share of the $20 000 asset in the joint venture.

ILLUSTRATIVE EXAMPLE 26.5

Contribution of a non-current asset by a venturer, with ownership retained

On 1 July 2005, X Ltd and Y Ltd established a joint venture to manufacture a product. Each company has a 50% interest in the venture and shares output equally. To commence the venture, on 1 July 2005, X Ltd contributed cash of $100 000 and Y Ltd undertook to contribute the use of equipment owned by it. At 1 July 2005, the equipment is recorded by Y Ltd at $150 000, being the fair value of the asset; the asset has a remaining 15-year life. Depreciation on the equipment is charged using a straight-line depreciation method. The asset has a fair value of $50 000 at the end of ten years – this being the life of the joint venture.

The following information was extracted from the accounts and financial statements of the joint venture operation as at 30 June 2006:

Balance sheet (extract) as at 30 June 2006	
Assets	
Cash	$ 52 000
Raw materials	1 000
Work in progress	24 000
Inventory	10 000
Equipment	100 000
Accumulated depreciation – equipment	(10 000)
Total assets	177 000
Liabilities	
Accounts payable	2 000
Accrued expenses (wages)	5 000
Total liabilities	7 000
Net assets	$170 000

Cash receipts and payments for the year ended 30 June 2006		
	Payments	Receipts
Contributions		$100 000
Wages	$35 000	
Accounts payable (raw materials)	3 000	
Overhead expenses	10 000	
	$48 000	$100 000

Costs incurred for the year ended 30 June 2006	
Wages	$40 000
Raw materials	4 000
Equipment used	10 000
Overhead expenses	10 000
	64 000
Less: Inventory	40 000
Work in progress at 30 June 2006	$24 000

Required

Prepare the journal entries in the records of X Ltd and Y Ltd for the year ending 30 June 2006.

Solution — Line-by-line method

Records of X Ltd

As the asset has a fair value of $150 000 at 1 July 2005 and a fair value at the end of the life of the joint venture of $50 000, Y Ltd contributes an asset worth $100 000 to the joint venture. At 1 July 2005, X Ltd passes the following entry:

Equipment in JV	Dr	50 000		[100 000/2]
Cash in JV	Dr	50 000		[100 000/2]
Cash	Cr		100 000	

The joint venture recognises the equipment at $100 000 and depreciates this over the ten years at $10 000 per annum. At 30 June 2006, X Ltd recognises its share of the assets and liabilities of the joint venture and the inventory transferred to it from the joint venture. In relation to the latter, the joint venture has produced $40 000 worth of inventory, of which $30 000 has been transferred to the venturers and $10 000 remains in the joint venture. The entry at 30 June 2006 is:

Raw material in JV	Dr	500		[1 000/2]
Work in progress in JV	Dr	12 000		[24 000/2]
Inventory in JV	Dr	5 000		[10 000/2]
Inventory	Dr	15 000		[30 000/2]
Accounts payable in JV	Cr		1 000	[2 000/2]
Accrued expenses in JV	Cr		2 500	[5 000/2]
Accumulated depreciation — equipment in JV	Cr		5 000	[10 000/2]
Cash in JV	Cr		24 000	[50 000 – 52 000/2]

Records of Y Ltd

The accounting records of Y Ltd are very similar to those shown in illustrative example 26.3 because Y Ltd sells half of the asset to X Ltd, potentially earning a profit on the sale. The asset being sold in this example has a carrying amount of $100 000 and a fair value of $100 000, so no profit is recorded. The entry in Y Ltd at 1 July 2005 is:

Equipment in JV	Dr	50 000		[100 000/2]
Cash in JV	Dr	50 000		[100 000/2]
Carrying amount of equipment				
sold to JV	Dr	50 000		[100 000/2]
Equipment	Cr		100 000	
Proceeds on sale of				
equipment to JV	Cr		50 000	[100 000/2]

In the records of Y Ltd there are now two assets: equipment at $50 000 and equipment in the joint venture at $50 000.

At 30 June 2006, Y Ltd recognises its share of the assets and liabilities of the joint venture as well as the inventory transferred from the joint venture. As the carrying amount of the equipment at 1 July 2005 equalled the fair value, no adjustment is necessary in relation to the carrying amount of the equipment or the cost of the work in progress and inventory. The entry is:

Raw material in JV	Dr	500		[1 000/2]
Work in progress in JV	Dr	12 000		[24 000/2]
Inventory in JV	Dr	5 000		[10 000/2]
Inventory	Dr	15 000		[30 000/2]
Accounts payable in JV	Cr		1 000	[2 000/2]
Accrued expenses in JV	Cr		2 500	[5 000/2]
Accumulated depreciation –				
equipment in JV	Cr		5 000	[10 000/2]
Cash in JV	Cr		24 000	[50 000 – 52 000/2]

This entry is the same as for X Ltd.

ILLUSTRATIVE EXAMPLE 26.6

Contribution of a non-current asset by a venturer, where the fair value is greater than the carrying amount

Assume the same information as in illustrative example 26.5, except that the equipment supplied by Y Ltd had a carrying amount of $140 000 at 1 July 2005. Hence, the equipment being supplied has, at 1 July 2005, a carrying amount of $140 000 and a fair value of $150 000, with the residual value after 10 years being $50 000.

→

The journal entries for X Ltd as given in the solution in illustrative example 26.5 are not affected by the carrying amount being different from the fair value at 1 July 2005. However, Y Ltd will record a gain on selling half the equipment to X Ltd and record the asset in the joint venture at half of the carrying amount. The entry in the records of Y Ltd at 1 July 2005 is:

Equipment in JV	Dr	45 000		[90 000/2]
Cash in JV	Dr	50 000		[100 000/2]
Carrying amount of equipment				
sold to JV	Dr	45 000		[90 000/2]
Equipment	Cr		90 000	
Proceeds on sale of				
equipment to JV	Cr		50 000	[100 000/2]

Y Ltd then has two assets: equipment at $50 000 and equipment in the joint venture at $45 000. In relation to the latter, the joint venture depreciates an asset that cost $100 000. The annual charge is $10 000, this being included in the cost of the work in progress and inventory accounts. For Y Ltd, the cost of these assets is less than for X Ltd as the equipment cost Y Ltd less than X Ltd. Hence, as demonstrated in illustrative example 26.3, an adjustment entry of the following form would need to be passed in the records of Y Ltd at 30 June 2006:

Accumulated depreciation —				[10% × (50 000 −
equipment in JV	Dr	500		45 000)]
Work in progress in JV	Cr		X	
Inventory in JV	Cr		X	
Inventory	Cr		X	

26.6.5 Management fees paid to a venturer

In section 26.6.3, the situation where a venturer supplied services as its contribution to the joint venture was discussed. In this section, the analysis is concerned with the case where a venturer supplies a service in the normal course of business to the joint venture. This includes payment to a joint venturer to act in a management capacity to the joint venture.

In accounting for these payments, the joint venture pays cash to a joint venturer, with the cost of the service being capitalised into work in progress and inventory produced by the joint venture. For a venturer that does not supply the service there are no accounting adjustments necessary because of the transaction. For the venturer that does supply the service, normally it would incur a cost to supply the service and earn a profit on the supply of that service. In accounting for its interest in the joint venture, the venturer supplying the service has to consider the following:

- As with supplying services as part of the initial contribution, a venturer cannot earn a profit on supplying services to itself.
- As the joint venture capitalises the amount paid to the venturer into the cost of work in progress and inventory, an adjustment is necessary to inventory related accounts because the cost of these items to the venturer supplying the services is less than that to the other venturer(s).

ILLUSTRATIVE EXAMPLE 26.7

Management fees paid to a venturer

X Ltd and Y Ltd have formed a joint venture and share equally in the output of the joint venture. During the current period ending 30 June 2006, the joint venture pays a management fee of $400 000 to X Ltd. The cost to X Ltd of supplying management services to the joint venture is $320 000. At the end of the current period, X Ltd's share of the inventory-related assets from the joint venture as recorded for X Ltd is:

Work in progress in JV	$300 000
Inventory in JV	200 000
Inventory	500 000

The joint venture has capitalised the management services fee of $400 000 into the cost of these assets. In the records of X Ltd at 30 June 2006, the following entries are required:

To record revenue on payment of the service fee by the joint venture

Cash	Dr	400 000
Fee revenue	Cr	400 000

To record the cost of supplying the services

Cost of supplying services	Dr	320 000
Cash	Cr	320 000

To adjust for the profit on X Ltd supplying services to itself

The total profit to X Ltd on supplying the management service is $80 000. Half this profit is made on supplying services to Y Ltd and the other $40 000 on supplying services to itself. An adjustment is necessary to eliminate the revenue and the expense on supplying services to itself. The following entry eliminates from the fee revenue only the amount of the expense − the profit element in the revenue is eliminated in the next entry:

Fee revenue	Dr	160 000	[320 000/2]
Cost of supplying services	Cr	160 000	

To adjust the cost of the inventory-related assets from the joint venture

The profit element on supplying services to itself, $40 000, is proportionately adjusted across the inventory-related assets as follows:

			Share of $40 000
Inventory in JV	$ 200 000	20%	$ 8 000
Inventory	500 000	50%	20 000
Work in progress in JV	300 000	30%	12 000
	$1 000 000		$40 000

→

The entry is:

Fee revenue	Dr	40 000	
Inventory in JV	Cr		8 000
Inventory	Cr		20 000
Work in progress in JV	Cr		12 000

Note that the combination of this entry and the immediately preceding one results in adjusting fee revenue for a total of $200 000, which is half the revenue paid by the joint venture to X Ltd.

If X Ltd had provided the services but the joint venture had not yet paid the fee by the end of the period, the liabilities of the joint venture need to be adjusted. Further, the fee receivable account of $400 000 raised by X Ltd needs to be adjusted. The entry is:

Accruals in JV	Dr	200 000	
Fee receivable	Cr		200 000

LO 7

26.7 Accounting by a venturer in a jointly controlled entity that is sharing profit

A joint venture entity that is established to generate profits to be shared between the venturers can be organised within a number of organisational structures, including corporations and partnerships. As noted in paragraph 20 of IAS 31, a jointly controlled entity maintains its own accounting records and prepares and presents financial statements in the same way as other entities in conformity with International Financial Reporting Standards.

On commencement of the joint venture, each venturer contributes cash or other assets and passes a journal entry of the following order:

Investment in joint venture	Dr	X	
Cash/other asset	Cr		X
(Initial contribution to joint venture entity)			

IAS 31 then provides two methods of accounting for jointly controlled entities.

Proportionate consolidation

Paragraph 33 of IAS 31 provides details on this method. The basic principles are:
- in its own balance sheet, the venturer includes its share of the assets that it controls jointly and its share of the liabilities for which it is jointly responsible
- in its own income statement, the venturer includes its share of the income and expenses of the jointly controlled entity.

The method thus involves a line-by-line recognition of the venturer's share of the accounts of the joint venture. By taking a line-by-line approach, the method is similar to the consolidation method as applied to subsidiaries under IAS 27, but dissimilar to that method because only the venturer's share of the other entity is recognised.

Paragraph 34 of IAS 31 provides for the use of alternative reporting formats under the proportionate consolidation method. The venturer may:

- combine the share of the joint venture's activities within each line of its own financial statements, for example, the venturer's share of property, plant and equipment is included with the venturer's property, plant and equipment; or
- include separate line items for each major classification of assets, liabilities, income and expenses — this format enables the users of the venturer's financial statements to separate out the activities of the venturer from that of the joint venture. An illustration of various formats is given in figure 26.3.

Equity method

The equity method of accounting is discussed in detail in chapter 25. The basic principles of the method, as stated in the definition in paragraph 3 of IAS 31, are as follows:

- In the balance sheet, initially record the investment in the joint venture at cost and adjust thereafter for the post-acquisition change in the venturer's share of net assets of the jointly controlled entity; the increase in net assets will equate to the profit/loss recorded by the joint venture and any increases in reserves created directly in equity.
- In the income statement, recognise the venturer's share of the profit or loss of the jointly controlled entity.

The equity method, as described in IAS 28, is also a consolidation technique, often being described as a one-line consolidation method.

The major difference between the two methods is that the equity method recognises the investment in the joint venture as the asset held by the venturer, whereas the proportionate consolidation method recognises the undivided interest in the individual assets and liabilities of the joint venture. The arguments for and against the two methods are discussed in section 26.8.

26.7.1 Applying the two methods of accounting for a jointly controlled entity

On 1 January 2005, Dublin Ltd signed a joint venture agreement with another venturer for the production of bottled water. One venturer had access to mineral springs and the other technical experience in manufacturing. A corporation, Cork Ltd was established for that purpose. It was agreed that both joint venturers would initially contribute $500 000 each, receive 100 000 $5 shares in the new company and share profits equally.

At the end of the first year, 31 December 2005, the financial statements of the joint venture showed:

Revenues	$ 200 000
Expenses	140 000
Profit before tax	60 000
Income tax expense	14 000
Profit for the period	46 000
Share capital	1 000 000
Payables	140 000
Provisions	150 000
	$1 336 000
Property, plant and equipment	$ 940 000
Accumulated depreciation	(50 000)
Inventory	250 000
Cash	36 000
Receivables	160 000
	$1 336 000

On establishment of the joint venture and the contribution for the shares in Cork Ltd, Dublin Ltd passed the following entry in its records:

Investment in Cork Ltd	Dr	500 000	
Cash	Cr		500 000
(Being investment in joint venture)			

Under the proportionate consolidation method, at 31 December 2005, Dublin Ltd recognises 50% of all the accounts of Cork Ltd. As per the consolidation method, this process requires an adjustment to eliminate the investment account in the joint venture as recorded by Dublin Ltd and the pre-acquisition equity of the joint venture. This process is shown in figure 26.1.

Financial statements	Dublin Ltd	Share of Cork Ltd	Adjustments Dr		Adjustments Cr	Proportionate consolidation
Revenues	5 400 000	100 000				5 500 000
Expenses	4 400 000	70 000				4 470 000
Profit before tax	1 000 000	30 000				1 030 000
Tax expense	240 000	7 000				247 000
Profit	760 000	23 000				783 000
Share capital	1 500 000	500 000	*1*	500 000		1 500 000
Retained earnings	460 000					460 000
Payables	250 000	70 000				320 000
Provisions	170 000	75 000				245 000
	3 140 000	668 000				3 308 000
Property, plant and equipment	1 950 000	470 000				2 420 000
Accumulated depreciation	(350 000)	(25 000)				(375 000)
Inventory	420 000	125 000				545 000
Cash	380 000	18 000				398 000
Receivables	240 000	80 000				320 000
Investment in Cork Ltd	500 000			*1*	500 000	
	3 140 000	668 000	500 000		500 000	3 308 000

FIGURE 26.1 Proportionate consolidation method

If the equity method is applied in the same situation, the joint venturer recognises as an increase to the carrying amount of the investment, its share of the post-acquisition profit/loss of the joint venture, in this case a 50% share of the $46 000 profit: $23 000. The adjusting journal entry passed in the worksheet is then:

Investment in Cork Ltd	Dr	23 000	
Share of profit of joint venture	Cr		23 000

The worksheet under the equity method is shown in figure 26.2.

Financial statements	Dublin Ltd		Adjustments				Equity-accounted statements
				Dr		Cr	
Revenues	5 400 000						5 400 000
Expenses	4 400 000						4 400 000
Profit before tax	1 000 000						1 000 000
Tax expense	240 000						240 000
Trading profit	760 000						760 000
Share of profit of joint venture					1	23 000	23 000
Profit for the period							783 000
Share capital	1 500 000						1 500 000
Retained earnings	460 000						460 000
Payables	250 000						250 000
Provisions	170 000						170 000
	3 140 000						3 163 000
Property, plant and equipment	1 950 000						1 950 000
Accumulated depreciation	(350 000)						(350 000)
Inventory	420 000						420 000
Cash	380 000						380 000
Receivables	240 000						240 000
Investment in Cork Ltd	500 000		1	23 000			523 000
	3 140 000			23 000		23 000	3 163 000

FIGURE 26.2 Equity method

LO 8

26.8 Equity method versus proportionate consolidation

In this section, the form of joint venture being analysed is the jointly controlled entity or business, and not the shared facility or jointly controlled asset. This entity may be incorporated or be an unincorporated association established by the venturers. Further, the venturers may agree to share profit or output of the venture. Where the distribution is in the form of output, the traditional equity method based upon recognition of a share of the profits of the investee is not appropriate because the joint venture does not generate a profit. In these cases, a one-line asset recognised by the joint venturer is the equivalent of the equity method for a profit-making entity. The choice being debated is effectively whether a one-line method or a proportionate multi-line method is appropriate.

Arguments for and against the two methods are given in chapter 3 of G4-DP and in chapter 4 of UK-DP. There are two main areas of debate: what assets are controllable by a joint venturer, and the need for disclosure about the assets and liabilities of the joint venture.

The control debate

The key argument here is that the proportionate consolidation method is at odds with the definition of an asset in the IASB Framework. The definition of an asset in the Framework is:

> An asset is a resource controlled by the entity as a result of past events and from which future economic benefits are expected to flow to the entity.

There is no definition of control given in the Framework. In G4-DP, in paragraphs 2.8 and 2.9, definitions of control as given in accounting standards, such as IAS 31 on consolidated financial statements, are quoted. However, these definitions relate to criteria for consolidation rather than asset definition and are therefore not necessarily applicable. It is therefore questionable how much of those concepts of control can be used in determining the existence of assets.

In IAS 38 *Intangible Assets*, paragraphs 13–16 contain a discussion of control in relation to recognition of intangible assets. In paragraph 15, the following statements are made in relation to recognition of skilled staff as assets:

> The entity may also expect that the staff will continue to make their skills available to the entity. However, an entity usually has insufficient control over the expected future economic benefits arising from a team of skilled staff and from training for these items to meet the definition of an intangible asset.

It is important to note the distinction here between the ability and the right of the entity to deny access of others to the benefits of the staff skills and the ability of the entity to be able to govern or manage the extent of those benefits. While the skilled staff remain, the benefits will flow to the entity and not to other parties. However, whether the staff remain is beyond the control of the entity. In relation to an unincorporated joint venture, each venturer is entitled to a share of output. The venturer can deny or regulate the access of the other venturers to that output. However, a venturer cannot determine or regulate the extent of the production from the joint venture. It requires the consent of all venturers to make decisions on the use of the joint venture assets.

It is this element of being able to determine the policies in relation to the deployment of resources that could commonly exist between the definitions of control for consolidation purposes and for asset definition purposes. Control for asset definition purposes therefore would require the entity to be able to affect the amount of benefits to be received rather than simply having a right to the ultimate benefits.

Note the following comments in relation to leases from the G4+1 Discussion Paper (2000) entitled 'Leases: Implementation of a New Approach':

> A central feature of the definitions of assets is that past transactions or events have resulted in control over the capacity to obtain future economic benefits. [Para. 2.8]

> The nature of assets that arise under leases is different from those that are obtained by ownership. An owner of property is typically free to use it in any way he wishes and may sell, pledge or dispose of it. In contrast, a lessee can use the leased property only in the ways permitted by the lease contract, and usually has no rights to pledge or dispose of it. Nonetheless, the right granted by the lease to use the property is a source of economic benefits controlled by the lessee and, as such, is an asset. [Para.1.13]

The entity does not have to have an unfettered ability to do what it likes with a resource in order to have control. With leased properties, the ability of lessees to control the benefits is limited. But lessees have the capacity to make the benefits larger or smaller by their actions and by implementation of the policies they adopt for managing the leased property. If such an ability does not exist the asset is simply an investment.

Consider the notion of control in relation to the pipeline example given by Dieter and Wyatt (1978, p. 89) in their argument against proportionate consolidation:

> For example, assume a manufacturing company has a 20 percent interest in a pipeline project joint venture, organized to supply natural gas to it as a power source. Four other coventurers also have a 20 percent equity interest. The debt of the project is guaranteed, via a throughput agreement with each of the venturers, in the same proportion as their equity interests. Under these circumstances, no one venturer has direct control over the pipeline or even a portion thereof (i.e., a pipeline per se is not divisible). By combining 20 percent of the cost of the pipeline directly with the property, plant and equipment of the manufacturing operations of the investor, a reader of the investor's financial statements could be left with an erroneous impression of the amount of assets the investor's management directly controls and supervises.

These arguments are not correct. The sharing of the pipeline is no different from a number of parties leasing a taxi; one drives it in the mornings, one in the evenings and one on weekends. However, as each party has control over the manner of use and hence the extent of benefits to be received, each party has an asset. Therefore, for jointly controlled assets, or shared facilities, it is appropriate for each party to recognise its share of the resource as an asset.

If these arguments are applied to the use of proportionate consolidation for joint venture entities, then the method conflicts with the definition of an asset. This was the conclusion reached in the G4-DP, paragraph 3.12:

> There is general recognition and acceptance among the conceptual frameworks of G4+1 members that an essential condition of an asset is that it be a *resource controlled by the reporting enterprise*. Proportionate consolidation is fundamentally inconsistent with this basic economic concept because a venturer cannot control (that is, use or direct the use of) its pro rata share of individual assets in a joint venture.

Hence, to be consistent with the Framework, the IASB should not permit the use of proportionate consolidation or line-by-line accounting for joint venture entities. To assist in reaching the right conclusion in this area, it is necessary for the IASB to expand the Framework to clarify the meaning of the term 'control'. This seems to be an urgent need given the conclusions reached by Willett (1995) in his discussion of the debate on accounting for joint ventures in Canada, and by Schuetze (1993):

> The board concluded that the term 'control', as used in Section 1000, could be interpreted as dealing with the level of assurance that future economic benefits can be obtained or yielded in the future from the assets and liabilities held. The sense of the term 'control' is different from the way in which it is used in consolidations, which has more to do with 'managerial' control' (sourced from Willett 1995, p. 60).

> [the asset definition] is so complex, so abstract, so open-ended, so all-inclusive, and so vague that we cannot use it to solve problems (sourced from Scheutze 1993, p. 67).

The disclosure debate

Those who argue in favour of the proportionate consolidation method argue that 'the one-line method simply is uninformative in conveying the economic effects of the investment in and commitment to the joint venture by the investor in many of these joint ventures' (Dieter & Wyatt 1978, p. 90). More succinctly, the G4-DP in paragraph 3.18 stated:

> At the heart of the case of those arguing for proportionate consolidation is their strongly held belief that it is more useful accounting. They argue that portraying the venturer's share of the activities of the joint venture as part of the venturer's operations provides a broader and more comprehensive representation of the extent of venturer operations and assets and liabilities. Further, they claim that proportionate consolidation provides a better representation of the performance of enterprise management, and an improved basis for predicting the ability of the venturer to generate cash and cash equivalents in the future, particularly where a significant portion of business is conducted using joint ventures.

Some specific comments were made in the UK-DP (paragraph 4.10) concerning the disadvantages of the disclosures required by application of the equity method:

(a) By bringing in only the net amounts for the results and assets of associates and joint ventures the equity method distorts financial ratios such as gearing and profit margin. Associates and joint venture extend the economic activities of the investor and the net amounts do not give much information on the operations of such entities and, therefore, the effect on the investor of its interests in them.

(b) The net amounts shown under the equity method do not reveal the level of liabilities held by the associates and joint ventures or the structure of their financing. In general, the potential benefits and risks related to the investor's interests in strategic alliances are obscured by the presentation of net amounts.

If the one-line method is preferred, the deficiencies in relation to information disclosed in the financial statements can be overcome by providing additional disclosure. There have been a number of solutions advanced by various authors in this regard:

- **Gross equity method** (UK Financial Reporting Standard 9 'Associates and Joint Ventures' 1997)

  Under this method, the basic equity method is applied, but additional disclosure is required:
  - in the consolidated income statement, the investor's share of the joint venture's turnover is separately disclosed
  - in the consolidated balance sheet, the investor's share of the gross assets and liabilities is disclosed.

  The main criticism of this method is that it has the same shortcomings as the proportionate consolidation method because it portrays the assets and liabilities of the joint venture as being assets and liabilities of the investor.

- **The expanded equity method** (Dieter & Wyatt 1978)

  Under this method, the investor discloses its proportionate share of the assets and liabilities of the joint venture in its financial statements, but with separate disclosure and without combining the numbers with those of the investor. Dieter and Wyatt (1978) provide a number of formats. In figure 26.3, Exhibit 1 from their article is reproduced showing a comparison of the disclosures under the equity method, proportionate consolidation and two variants of the expanded equity method.

  These authors argued that the expanded equity method overcomes the objections directed at proportionate consolidation of including both controlled and jointly controlled items in the one financial statement. This is because under the expanded equity method the two types of assets and liabilities are kept separate. They argued that the expanded equity method has the advantages of:

  (1) distinguishing those assets and liabilities directly owned and controlled by the investor from those represented by its interest in the joint venture's assets and liabilities and
  (2) highlighting the extent of the investor's involvement in joint venture activities.

- **Summarised note disclosure** (G4-DP)

  The authors of G4-DP argued that the expanded equity method is a compromise proposal between the equity method and the proportionate consolidation method. As they noted (paragraph 3.26), the use of the expanded equity method has the same conceptual shortcomings of the proportionate consolidation method because the assets and liabilities of the joint venture are not those of the investor. If the use of the expanded equity method in the financial statements presents the joint venture's assets and liabilities as belonging to the investor, then this is conceptually incorrect. To overcome this conceptual problem, in G4-DP it was recommended (paragraph 4.4) that note disclosure be used, and the summarised financial statements of the joint venture operation be disclosed in the notes, including at least the investor's share of the following amounts:
  - current assets and long-term assets
  - current liabilities and long-term liabilities (with a maturity profile of material amounts of long-term debt)
  - revenues and expenses by major components, and net income before and after taxes
  - cash flow from operating, investing and financing activities.

Which method should be used? There seems to be general agreement that there is a need for more disclosure than required under the basic equity method. Conceptually, that information cannot be provided on the face of the financial statements. Standard setters could move to innovative disclosure formats such as the use of different colours, as suggested by Wallman (1996), so that joint venture information was provided on the face of the financial statements but separated from the investor's own information by the use of colour. Until such innovations occur, provision of the additional disclosures in the notes would appear to be the best solution.

FIGURE 26.3 Expanded equity method

ABC JOINT VENTURE
Balance sheet as at 31 December 1977

Assets		Liabilities and capital		
Current assets:		**Current liabilities:**		
Cash	$100 000	Current maturities of long-term debt		$200 000
Receivables	100 000	Accounts payable		100 000
Supplies	200 000	Accrued expenses		100 000
Total current assets	400 000	Total current liabilities		400 000
		Long-term debt, less current maturities:		
		Mortgage loans		$4 000 000
		Term loan		700 000
		Total long-term debt		$4 700 000
Fixed assets, at cost:			Capital	Earnings
Steam-generating facility	$6 000 000	**Capital:**		
Less: Accumulated		XYZ Corp. (30%)	$60 000	$30 000
depreciation	1 000 000	A Corp. (35%)	70 000	35 000
		B Corp. (35%)	70 000	35 000
Total fixed assets	$5 000 000		$200 000	$100 000
		Total capital		300 000
	$5 400 000			$5 400 000

XYZ CORPORATION
Balance sheet as at 31 December 1977

	Traditional one-line equity method presentation (APB Opinion No.18)	Proportionate consolidation proposed by Reklau (1997)	Expanded equity method presentation	
			Alternative 1	Alternative 2
Current assets:				
Cash	$ 500 000	$ 530 000	$ 500 000	$ 500 000
Receivables	1 000 000	1 030 000	1 000 000	1 000 000
Inventories	3 000 000	3 060 000	3 000 000	3 000 000
Company share of current assets of joint venture	N/A	N/A	N/A	120 000
Total current assets	$4 500 000	$4 620 000	$4 500 000	$4 620 000
Fixed assets:				
Land	$100 000	$100 000	$100 000	$100 000
Plant	4 000 000	5 800 000	4 000 000	4 000 000
Machinery and equipment	2 000 000	2 000 000	2 000 000	2 000 000
	$6 100 000	$7 900 000	$6 100 000	$6 100 000
Less: Accumulated depreciation	2 100 000	2 400 000	2 100 000	2 100 000
	4 000 000	5 500 000	4 000 000	4 000 000
Company share of steam-generating plant, net, of joint venture	N/A	N/A	N/A	1 500 000
	$4 000 000	$5 500 000	$4 000 000	$5 500 000

XYZ CORPORATION Balance sheet as at 31 December 1977			
Investment in equity of 30% owned joint venture	$ 90 000	–	–	–

Company share of investment in joint venture:				
Current assets	N/A	N/A	$ 120 000	N/A
Fixed assets, net			1 500 000	
			1 620 000	
Total assets	$8 590 000	$10 120 000	$10 120 000	$10 120 000
Liabilities and stockholders' equity				
Current liabilities:				
Current maturities of long-term debt	$1 000 000	$ 1 060 000	$ 1 000 000	$ 1 000 000
Accounts payable and accrued expenses	2 000 000	2 060 000	2 000 000	2 000 000
Company share of current liabilities of joint venture	N/A	N/A	N/A	120 000
	$3 000 000	$3 120 000	$ 3 000 000	$ 3 120 000
Long-term debt, less current maturities:				
Mortgage loan	$3 000 000	$ 4 200 000	$ 3 000 000	$ 3 000 000
Term loan	N/A	210 000	N/A	N/A
Company share of long-term debt of joint venture	N/A	N/A	N/A	1 410 000
	$3 000 000	$ 4 410 000	$ 3 000 000	$ 4 410 000
Company share of liabilities of joint venture:				
Current liabilities			$ 120 000	
Long-term debt, less current liabilities	N/A	N/A	1 410 000	N/A
			$ 1 530 000	
Stockholders' equity:				
Common stock	$1 800 000	$ 1 800 000	$ 1 800 000	$ 1 800 000
Retained earnings	790 000	790 000	790 000	790 000
	$2 590 000	$ 2 590 000	$ 2 590 000	$ 2 590 000
Total liabilities and stockholders' equity	$8 590 000	$10 120 000	$10 120 000	$10 120 000

Source: Dieter & Wyatt (1978, pp. 92–93).

In the *IASB Update* of December 2005, the following paragraphs were included:

The Board discussed addressing the accounting for interests in joint ventures in the context of a short-term convergence project. The Board decided that the existing option of proportionate consolidation in IAS 31 *Interests in Joint Ventures* should be removed.

However, the Board decided that the definition of a joint venture in IAS 31 does not address adequately the difference between a joint venture entity and an undivided interest in the assets and liabilities of a joint arrangement. The Board decided that the scope of the project should be expanded to consider the definition of a joint venture (IASB 2005, p. 4).

Hence, the expectation is that the proportionate consolidation method will be removed. However, at June 2006, there has been no change to IAS 31. The IASB currently has projects relating to the definition of an asset (as part of its Conceptual Framework project) and measurement. Whether the equity method itself will survive the Measurement project is unknown.

During 2005–06, technical staff of the Australian Accounting Standards Board worked on a long-term research project on joint ventures for the IASB. In the March 2006 *IASB Update*, the following was reported:

> The research team proposed defining a joint venture as a jointly controlled 'integrated resource arrangement'. The Board decided not to adopt this definition.
>
> The Board decided that the driver for accounting by participants in joint arrangements should be their contractual rights and obligations that are created by the joint arrangement agreement, rather than whether the arrangement is of a particular type or form. Accordingly, participants should account separately for contractual rights to share the net results of the arrangement's operations and any contractual rights they control unilaterally (such as rights of use). Participants in a jointly controlled business (as defined in the Exposure Draft of Amendments to IFRS 3 *Business Combinations*) would have contractual rights to share the net results of the arrangement's operations, but might also have contractual rights that they control unilaterally.
>
> The Board thanked the research team for its work. The Board decided that, in view of the potential effects of developments in current Board projects (such as the consolidations and conceptual framework projects and, in particular, the short-term convergence project) on accounting for joint ventures, work on the long-term research project should be suspended, pending the outcome of those developments (IASB 2006, p. 3).

So, at March 2006, IAS 31 remains unchanged. Future developments will be driven by the short-term convergence project with the FASB. What compromises will emerge from this project remain to be seen.

LO 9   26.9 Disclosures required by IAS 31

IAS 31 requires three types of disclosure:
- *Paragraph 54.* A venturer is required to disclose the aggregate amount of various contingent liabilities, unless the probability of loss is remote, separately from the amount of other contingent liabilities.
- *Paragraph 55.* A venturer is required to disclose the aggregate amount of various capital commitments.
- *Paragraph 56.* A venturer shall disclose a listing and description of interests in significant joint ventures and the proportion of ownership interest held in jointly controlled entities.
- *Paragraph 56.* For jointly controlled entities disclosure is required of the aggregate amounts of each of current assets, long-term assets, current liabilities, long-term liabilities, income and expenses relating to interests in joint ventures.
- *Paragraph 57.* A venturer shall disclose the method it uses to recognise its interest in jointly controlled entities.

Illustrative disclosures required by IAS 31 are provided in figure 26.4.

	IAS 31 Para.
Note 1: Summary of significant accounting policies Interests in jointly controlled entities are accounted for by proportionate consolidation which involves recognising a proportionate share, on a line-by-line basis, of each joint venture's assets, liabilities, income and expenses in the consolidated financial statements.	*57*

Note: Interest in joint ventures *56*

The Group has interests in the following joint venture entities:

Joint venture	Description	% interest
Mineral Valley	Oil and gas	50
North Sea	Oil and gas	33

The Group's share of current assets, long-term assets, current liabilities, long-term liabilities, income and expenses of the joint venture entities which are included in the consolidated financial statements at 31 December are as follows:

In €000	2006	2005
Current assets	220	200
Non-current assets	750	620
Current liabilities	140	120
Non-current liabilities	224	215
Income	50	38
Expenses	35	27

Note: Commitments and contingencies *55*

Capital expenditure commitments *(b)*

In relation to the joint venture, North Sea, in which the Group has a 33% interest, that entity has purchase commitments for property, plant and equipment totalling €340 000 (2005 €180 000)

Contingent liabilities *54* *(a)*

In relation to the joint venture Mineral Valley, in which the Group has a 50% interest, the parent company has guaranteed the performance of a contract for that entity for €40 000. Management does not expect a liability to arise from this guarantee.

The Group is not contingently liable for the liabilities of the other joint venturers in the joint ventures in which the Group has investments. *(c)*

FIGURE 26.4 Illustrative disclosure — IAS 31

To illustrate how companies have disclosed their investments in joint ventures, figure 26.5 reproduces the note disclosure provided in the 2005 annual report published in March 2006 by the German-based company Bayer AG.

Five joint ventures – the same number as in the previous year – are included by proportionate consolidation in compliance with IAS 31 (Financial Reporting of Interests in Joint Ventures) . . .

The effect of joint ventures on the Group balance sheet and income statement is as follows:

€ million	2005	€ million	2005
Current assets	15	Income	50
Noncurrent assets	62	Expenses	(47)
Current liabilities	(23)		
Noncurrent liabilities	(10)		
Net assets	44	Income after taxes	3

FIGURE 26.5   Illustrative disclosure from Bayer
Source: Bayer (2006, pp. 112–13).

26.10   Summary

One of the difficult tasks faced by accounting standard setters is the determination of how to classify and account for the various investments held by one entity in another entity. Some investments are classified as subsidiaries, others as associates and others as joint ventures. In all cases, the investor has some form of special relationship with the investee relating to the involvement by the investor in the formation of the strategic policies and decisions of the investee. With joint ventures, the specific relationship between the joint venturer and the joint venture is that of joint control, requiring the joint venturer to interact with the other venturers in order for the strategic decisions about the joint venture to be made.

There is still much debate within the international community about accounting for joint ventures. The classification and definition of joint ventures is still under debate, with different opinions about the inclusion of arrangements other than entities being included in the classification of joint ventures. Debate also occurs in relation to the appropriate accounting method to be applied, particularly between those who favour proportionate consolidation and those who prefer the equity accounting method. Mixed with this is debate about the effect of the conceptual framework definitions on the choice of these methods.

IAS 31 has not significantly altered in recent years. However, it is expected that significant change will occur as answers are sought to the questions raised in this chapter. Will both the proportionate consolidation method and the equity method survive that process? The Australian Accounting Standards Board deleted the option to use the proportionate consolidation method from its accounting standards, which are equivalent to international accounting standards, in the belief that this method would not survive future revisions to IAS 31. Whether their decision was correct is yet to be determined.

DISCUSSION QUESTIONS

1. Assume Entity A owns 50% of the voting shares of Entity X, and that Entities B and C each control 25%. Discuss whether Entity A should be treated as a joint venturer in accounting for its interest in Entity X.

2. Where a venturer has joint control over another entity, it also has significant influence over that entity. It is questionable then whether the same accounting methods should be applied to associates and joint ventures. In the UK-DP, the equity accounting method was recommended for both associates and joint ventures, with additional information being provided in the notes to the accounts. Discuss whether the accounting required for joint ventures should differ from that required for associates.

3. Discuss the key difference(s) between a joint venture operation and a joint venture entity. How do these differences affect the accounting for these joint ventures?

4. Distinguish between a subsidiary, an associate, a joint venture and a partnership. Why are different accounting methods required when accounting for each of these entities?

5. IAS 31 *Interests in Joint Ventures* uses joint control as a characteristic of a joint venture. Discuss what is meant by the term joint control.

6. The FASB's definition [of an asset] is so complex, so abstract, so open-ended, so all-inclusive, and so vague that we cannot use it to solve problems ... Defining an asset as a probable future economic benefit is to use a high-order abstraction. Under such an approach, if an enterprise owns a truck, the truck *per se* is not the asset. The asset is the present value of the cash flows that will come from using the truck ... (Schuetze 1993, pp. 67–8)

   Discuss whether, under the IASB Framework definition of an asset, proportions of items such as cash, accounts receivable or plant held by a joint venture are assets to a joint venturer.

7. Discuss the differences in disclosures for joint venture entities under IAS 31 and the expanded entity methods raised by Reklau and Dieter and Wyatt.

8. In accounting for jointly controlled entities under IAS 31, preparers have a choice between the use of proportionate consolidation and the equity method. Explain the differences between the two methods, and the arguments for and against the use of each of the methods.

EXERCISES

EXERCISE 26.1 ★   Determination of a joint venture

Emerald Ltd and Isle Ltd decide to jointly undertake the manufacture of an electric car. They form Eire Ltd, which undertakes the manufacture of the car. Emerald Ltd and Isle Ltd provide the various parts for the manufacture of the car, which is assembled by Eire Ltd.

Emerald Ltd and Isle Ltd each hold 50% of the voting rights in Eire Ltd and receive 50% of the output or profits from Eire Ltd. The constitution of Eire Ltd requires that the operations of the company must be in accordance with a business plan prepared annually, and to which both Emerald Ltd and Isle Ltd both agree. Eire Ltd has six directors, with three being appointed by Emerald Ltd and three by Isle Ltd.

Required

Evaluate whether this situation should be accounted for under IAS 31.

EXERCISE 26.2 ★   Accounting for an asset used by a number of companies

Omagh Ltd and Dungannon Ltd are companies that have newly discovered oilwells in a Middle-Eastern country. There is some distance to the nearest port and, rather than build separate pipelines, they have agreed to jointly build a pipeline to the port and share the use of the pipeline for transporting oil. Sperrin Ltd also has oilwells in the area and has agreed to use any excess capacity of the pipeline.

Required

Discuss how you would account for the pipeline.

EXERCISE 26.3 ★

Accounting for a jointly used asset

In an area famous for its wine, it has become popular for people to retire here, establish a vineyard and grow their own grapes. Because these people have only small vineyards, they do not have the equipment to press their own grapes to extract the juice. A number of these people agreed to acquire a wine press that could be used jointly by the group. Each person in the group would have a right to use the machine for a specified number of days of the year. For those days, each person could use the machine as they saw fit, including leasing it to a third party. However, no party can sell or modify the machine. Eventual disposal or replacement of the machine is a joint decision of the group.

Required
Discuss the accounting for the wine press.

EXERCISE 26.4 ★

Accounting for different joint arrangements

Discuss how you would account for each of the following three situations:
1. Kil Ltd and Kenny Ltd enter into a joint arrangement to mine iron ore. Each party contributes equally to the acquisition of the necessary equipment and working capital. They assume joint and several responsibility for any liabilities that arise. A manager is appointed to run the operation. The output of the mine is distributed equally to the two companies for disposal.
2. Kil Ltd and Kenny Ltd enter into an agreement to mine iron ore. They establish a company in which they hold an equal number of shares. Both shareholders contribute an equal amount of capital to establish the company, and a manager is appointed to run the mining company. When the iron ore is extracted, it is distributed to each of the shareholders in equal proportions.
3. Kil Ltd and Kenny Ltd enter into an agreement to mine iron ore. They establish a company in which they hold an equal number of shares. Both shareholders contribute an equal amount of capital to establish the company, and a manager is appointed to run the mining company. The mining company signs contracts with the two shareholders whereby each of the shareholders agrees to acquire the output of the mine at a fixed price. The shareholders share equally in any profits or losses of the mining company.

EXERCISE 26.5 ★

Joint venturers share output

On 1 July 2005, Belfast Ltd entered into a joint venture agreement with Londonderry Ltd to form an unincorporated entity to produce a new type of widget. It was agreed that each party to the agreement would share the output equally. Belfast Ltd's initial contribution consisted of $2 000 000 cash and Londonderry Ltd contributed machinery that was recorded in the records of Londonderry Ltd at $1 900 000. During the first year of operation both parties contributed a further $3 000 000 each.

On 30 June 2006, the venture manager provided the following statements (in $000):

Costs incurred for the year ended 30 June 2006	
Wages	$1 840
Supplies	2 800
Overheads	2 200
	6 840
Cost of inventory	4 840
Work in progress at 30 June 2006	$2 000

Receipts and payments for year ended 30 June 2006		
Receipts:		
Original contributions		$2 000
Additional contributions		6 000
		8 000
Payments:		
Machinery (2/7/05)	$ 800	
Wages	1 800	
Supplies	3 000	
Overheads	2 100	
Operating expenses	200	7 900
Closing cash balance		$ 100

Assets and liabilities at 30 June 2006	
Assets	
Cash	$ 100
Machinery	2 800
Supplies	400
Work in progress	2 000
Total assets	5 300
Liabilities	
Accrued wages	40
Creditors	300
Total liabilities	340
Net assets	$4 960

Each venturer depreciates machinery at 20% per annum on cost.

Required

1. Prepare the journal entries in the records of Belfast Ltd and Londonderry Ltd in relation to the joint venture, assuming the line-by-line method of accounting is used.
2. Prepare the journal entries in the records of Londonderry Ltd assuming that the joint venture, not the venturers, had depreciated the machinery and included that expense in the cost of inventory transferred.

EXERCISE 26.6	★

Unincorporated joint venture, line-by-line method

On 1 July 2004, Donegal Ltd entered into a joint venture agreement with Bangor Ltd to establish an unincorporated joint venture to manufacture timber-felling equipment. It was agreed that the output of the venture would be shared: Donegal Ltd 60% and Bangor Ltd 40%.

To commence the venture, contributions were as follows:

- Donegal Ltd: cash of $1 100 000 and equipment having a carrying amount of $300 000 and a fair value of $400 000
- Bangor Ltd: cash of $600 000 and plant having a carrying amount of $450 000 and a fair value of $400 000.

Bangor Ltd revalued the plant it contributed to the joint venture to fair value prior to its transfer to the joint venture. Plant and equipment was depreciated (to the nearest month) in the joint venture's books at 20% p.a. on cost. During December 2004, an additional $1 000 000 cash was contributed by the venturers in the same proportion as their initial contributions.

The following information, in relation to the joint venture's operations for the year ended 30 June 2005, was provided by the venture manager:

(a) *Costs incurred for the year ended 30 June 2005*

Wages	$ 400 000
Raw materials	1 200 000
Overheads	650 000
Depreciation	205 000
	2 455 000
Less: Cost of inventory	2 005 000
Work in progress at 30 June 2005	$ 450 000

(b) *Receipts and payments for year ended 30 June 2005*

	Payments	Receipts
Contributions		$2 700 000
Plant (3 January 2005)	$ 450 000	
Wages	350 000	
Accounts payable	980 000	
Overhead costs	610 000	
Operating expenses	40 000	
	$2 430 000	$2 700 000

(c) *Assets and liabilities at 30 June 2005*

	Dr	Cr
Cash	$ 270 000	
Raw materials	100 000	
Work in progress	450 000	
Inventory	255 000	
Plant and equipment	1 250 000	
Accumulated depreciation – plant and equipment		$205 000
Accounts payable		320 000
Accrued expenses – wages and overheads		90 000

Required

Prepare the journal entries in the records of Donegal Ltd in relation to the joint venture for the year ended 30 June 2005, assuming the use of the line-by-line method. (Round all amounts to the nearest dollar and show all relevant workings.)

EXERCISE 26.7   ★★   Equity method, proportionate consolidation

On 1 January 2006, Dingle Ltd entered into an arrangement to establish an incorporated joint venture with Arklow Ltd. Both entities had had previous experience in the extractives industry, and they hoped their joint skills would enable them to find an economically viable ore deposit. Under the contractual arrangement, the two parties were to share equally in the profits/losses of any viable mining venture. On 1 January 2006, they both contributed $750 000 in cash, receiving shares in the new company Skibbereen Ltd.

One year later they had undertaken an extensive exploration program. Although no major find had been discovered, there was sufficient promise in the evaluation of their current workings to continue prospecting. All outlays for exploration had been capitalised.

At 31 December 2006, the balance sheet of Skibbereen Ltd showed:

Cash	$ 365 000
Land	520 000
Capitalised exploration costs	430 000
Equipment	220 000
Provisions	(35 000)
Share capital	$1 500 000

The balance sheet of Dingle Ltd at 31 December 2006 was as follows:

Current assets	
Cash	$ 100 000
Inventory	400 000
Receivables	200 000
Total current assets	700 000
Non-current assets	
Investment in joint venture	750 000
Land	600 000
Plant and equipment	1 200 000
Accumulated depreciation	(440 000)
Deferred exploration costs	840 000
Intangibles	220 000
Total non-current assets	3 170 000
Total assets	3 870 000
Current liabilities	
Payables	120 000
Provisions	320 000
Total current liabilities	440 000
Non-current liabilities	1 400 000
Total liabilities	1 840 000
Net assets	$2 030 000
Equity	
Share capital	1 200 000
Retained earnings	830 000
Total equity	$2 030 000

Required
1. Prepare the balance sheet of Dingle Ltd assuming:
   (a) the use of the equity method in accounting for the interest in the joint venture
   (b) the use of the proportionate consolidation method.
2. Explain the differences in accounting if the venturers had formed an unincorporated joint venture to undertake their activities, agreeing to share the output of the mine.

| EXERCISE 26.8 | ★★ | Venturers share output |

Abbeyfeale Ltd enters into an arrangement with another venturer, Foxford Ltd, to establish an unincorporated joint venture to produce a drug that assists both hay fever sufferers and those with sinus problems. To produce the drug requires a combination of the technical and pharmaceutical knowledge of both companies. Each company will receive an equal share of the output of the drug, which they will retail through their own preferred outlets, potentially under different names. Abbeyfeale Ltd agrees to manage the project for a fee of $100 000 per annum. Abbeyfeale Ltd estimates that it will cost $80 000 to provide the service. The management fee is capitalised into the cost of inventory produced.

The venture commences on 1 January 2006, with each venturer providing $1 million cash. At the end of the first year, the balance sheet of the joint venture showed:

Assets:	
Vehicles	$ 200 000
Accumulated depreciation	(50 000)
Equipment	820 000
Accumulated depreciation	(60 000)
Inventory	80 000
Work in progress	320 000
Materials	210 000
Total assets	1 520 000
Liabilities:	
Provisions	80 000
Payables	40 000
	120 000
Net assets	$1 400 000
Venturers' equity	
Initial contributions	2 000 000
Inventory delivered	(400 000)
General administration costs	(200 000)
Total equity	$1 400 000

Required

1. Prepare the journal entries in the records of Abbeyfeale Ltd during 2006 assuming:
    (a) the use of the line-by-line method to account for the joint venture
    (b) the use of the one-line method.
2. What differences would occur if the management fee paid to Abbeyfeale Ltd were treated as general administration costs?

| PROBLEMS | |

| PROBLEM 26.1 | ★★ | Use of line-by-line method |

During 2005, a group of academics were undertaking a bonding exercise in the Portadown hills. While tracking through the hills, they came across a spring of pure sweet water. They formed a company called Galway Ltd and decided to establish the extent of their find. In the process they expended funds, obtained from teaching overseas students, on equipment and employing geologists and mining experts. The general conclusion was that the find was significant and a commercially profitable business selling mineral water was feasible. As they were academics, and had no practical experience in the real world of big business, they decided to establish a joint venture with Kilrush Ltd who would establish a factory to produce bottled water. The joint venture agreement was signed on 1 January 2006, with Galway Ltd and Kilrush Ltd having a 50% share in the unincorporated joint venture.

The initial contributions by the two venturers were as follows:

Galway Ltd:	
Capitalised expenses	$ 800 000
Equipment	800 000
Cash	2 400 000
Kilrush Ltd:	
Cash	$4 000 000

The capitalised expenses were recorded in the books of Galway Ltd at $320 000, while the equipment was recorded at a carrying amount of $640 000. In order to supply the cash, Galway Ltd borrowed $800 000 of its required contribution. It is expected that the reserves of water will be depleted within 10 years, and the equipment is expected to have a similar useful life.

On 1 June 2006, the joint venture was ready to start producing bottles of water. The joint venture's accounts at 30 June 2007 contained the following information:

Balance sheet (extract)	2006	2007
Work in progress		$ 200 000
Capitalised costs	$ 800 000	800 000
Plant and equipment	8 360 000	7 760 000
Cash	80 000	240 000
Accounts payable – plant	(240 000)	(800 000)
Accrued expenses – wages etc.	(160 000)	(200 000)

Cash receipts and payments (extract)	2007	
	Payments	Receipts
Materials and supplies	$480 000	
Administration	160 000	
Wages	560 000	
Accounts payable – plant	960 000	
Contributions from joint venturers		$2 000 000

The output of the first year's operations was distributed equally to the joint venturers. Production in the first year was estimated to be 15% of the reserves. At 30 June 2007, Galway Ltd held 10% of its share of output in inventory, having sold the rest to its customers for $2 000 000. Expenses of the joint venture incurred up to 30 June 2007 were allocated to the venturers.

At 30 June 2007, the joint venture had ordered new plant and equipment of $300 000 which had not yet arrived. Because of some damage to the environment caused by the establishment of the pumping station to extract the water, there is a potential restoration cost to be incurred at closure of the joint venture. Whether this will be required will depend on the result of current legal inquiries.

Required
1. Prepare the journal entries in the records of Galway Ltd for the periods ending 30 June 2006 and 2007, assuming the use of the line-by-line method.
2. Prepare any notes that must be attached to the accounts of Galway Ltd for the year ending 30 June 2007 in relation to the joint venture, as required by IAS 31.

PROBLEM 26.2	★★

Venturers share output, line-by-line method

On 1 July 2006, Wicklow Ltd entered into a joint venture agreement with Waterford Ltd to manufacture stevedoring equipment. It was agreed that each party to the agreement would share the output equally.

To commence the venture, contributions were as follows:
- Wicklow Ltd: cash of $2 000 000 and equipment having a $400 000 carrying amount and a fair value of $600 000
- Waterford Ltd: cash of $1 800 000 and plant having a carrying amount of $900 000 and a fair value of $800 000.

Waterford Ltd revalued the plant it contributed to the joint venture prior to its transfer to the joint venture.

Plant and equipment is depreciated (to the nearest month) in the joint venture's books at 20% per annum on cost.

During December 2006, both parties contributed an additional $1 500 000 cash.

The following information, in relation to the joint venture's operations for the year ended 30 June 2007, was provided by the venture manager.

(a) *Costs incurred for the year ended 30 June 2007*

Wages	$1 200 000
Raw materials	2 150 000
Overheads	1 860 000
Depreciation	470 000
	5 680 000
Less: Cost of inventory	2 580 000
Work in progress at 30 June 2007	$3 100 000

(b) *Receipts and payments for the year ended 30 June 2007*

	Payments	Receipts
Contributions		$6 800 000
Plant (10 July 2006)	$ 950 000	
Wages	1 150 000	
Accounts payable	1 980 000	
Overhead costs	1 810 000	
Operating expenses	440 000	
	$6 330 000	$6 800 000

(c) *Assets and liabilities as at 30 June 2007*

	Dr	Cr
Cash	$ 470 000	
Raw materials	360 000	
Work in progress	3 100 000	
Inventory	580 000	
Plant and equipment	2 350 000	
Accumulated depreciation – plant and equipment		$470 000
Accounts payable		530 000
Accrued expenses		100 000

Required

Prepare the journal entries in the records of Wicklow Ltd and Waterford Ltd in relation to the joint venture for the year ended 30 June 2002, assuming the use of the line-by-line method.

PROBLEM 26.3 ★★★   Unincorporated joint venture managed by one of the venturers

During 2004, discussions took place between Boyle Ltd, a company concerned with the design of specialised tools and machines, and two companies, Roscommon Ltd and Wexford Ltd, which could potentially assist in the manufacture of a new tool. The new tool is called SmartTool and is to be used in the making of high grade mining instruments. On 1 June 2005, the three companies agreed to form an unincorporated joint venture to achieve this purpose. It was agreed that the relative interests in the joint venture would be:

Boyle Ltd	50%
Roscommon Ltd	25%
Wexford Ltd	25%

It was further agreed that Wexford Ltd would undertake a management role in relation to the new venture, being responsible for operating decisions and for record keeping. Wexford Ltd would be paid a management fee by the joint venture of $20 000. In establishing the joint venture, the various parties agreed to provide the following assets as their initial contribution:

• Boyle Ltd was to provide the patent to SmartTool, which was being recorded by Boyle Ltd at a capitalised development cost of $1 400 000. The venturers agreed that this asset had a fair value of $2 000 000, with an expected useful life of ten years.

• Roscommon Ltd was to provide cash of $1 000 000.

• Wexford Ltd was to provide the basic plant and equipment to manufacture the new tool. The plant and equipment was recorded in the books of Wexford Ltd at $600 000, but the venturers agreed that it had a fair value of $1 000 000. The plant and equipment was estimated to have a further useful life of five years.

During the first period of the joint venture's operation, the output of the joint venture was distributed to each of the venturers in proportion to their agreed interests. By 30 June 2006, Wexford Ltd had sold 80% of the output received from the joint venture for $300 000. The joint venture had not paid the management fee to Wexford Ltd by 30 June 2006.

Information from the financial statements of the joint venture as at 30 June 2006 is shown overleaf.

Assets	
Cash	$ 40 000
Plant and equipment	1 080 000
Accumulated depreciation	(208 000)
Patent	2 000 000
Accumulated depreciation	(200 000)
Office equipment	88 000
Accumulated depreciation	(8 800)
Work in progress	40 000
Liabilities	
Creditors – for materials	$ 136 000
Accruals – salaries etc, including the management fee	112 000
Cash payments	
Salaries	$ 220 000
Materials	488 000
Operating expenses	84 000

Required

1. Prepare the journal entries in the records of Boyle Ltd and Roscommon Ltd at the commencement of the joint venture, assuming the use of the line-by-line method.
2. Prepare the journal entries in the records of Wexford Ltd for the financial year ending 30 June 2006.

PROBLEM 26.4 ★★★ Venturers share output, contributions include tangible assets and the provision of services

Ballycastle Ltd, a development corporation associated with Belfast University, has developed and patented a new process to produce synthetic anti-ageing hormones. Due to a lack of resources, Ballycastle Ltd entered into a five-year joint venture with Edenderry Ltd and Kenmare Ltd to produce the hormone. The venturers are to share the output equally and will contribute to the unincorporated joint venture as follows:

Ballycastle Ltd

Cash $400 000 and Patent $360 000. The patent is currently recorded in the records of Ballycastle Ltd at $240 000.

Edenderry Ltd

Cash $460 000 and Services of Scientific Staff $300 000. Edenderry Ltd estimates that the cost of providing the services to the joint venture will be $225 000. Additional support staff will be employed and paid by the venture.

Kenmare Ltd

Cash $160 000 and a Laboratory Facility which has a fair value of $1 900 000 (carrying amount $1 800 000). The laboratory facility is to be returned by the joint venture at the end of the project when its expected carrying value will be $1 300 000. In addition, Kenmare Ltd is to provide the joint venture with autoclaving services as a part of the normal course of business. These services are charged out at cost plus 20%.

The joint venture commenced on 1 July 2006. The joint venture's accounts at 30 June 2007 were as follows:

Cash receipts and payments		
	Payments	Receipts
Contributions received		$1 020 000
Materials	$280 000	
Equipment**	360 000	
Administrative expenses	84 000	
Support staff wages	120 000	
Autoclaving services	36 000	

** Depreciation is to be charged by the venture at 20% p.a.; the equipment has on average been in use for six months during the year ended 30 June 2007.

Balance sheet (extract)		
Assets		
Cash		$ 140 000
Equipment	$360 000	
Accumulated depreciation	(36 000)	324 000
Patent	360 000	
Accumulated amortisation	(72 000)	288 000
Laboratory facility	600 000	
Accumulated depreciation	(120 000)	480 000
Materials inventory		30 000
Work in progress		37 000
Services receivable		240 000
		1 539 000
Liabilities		
Accounts payable (materials)		66 000
Account payable (autoclaving)		60 000
Accrued wages		30 000
		156 000
Net assets		$1 383 000

Required

1. Prepare the journal entries in the records of all venturers at the commencement of the joint venture, assuming the use of the line-by-line method.
2. Prepare the journal entries in the records of Edenderry Ltd for the year ended 30 June 2007.
3. Prepare the journal entries in the records of Kenmare Ltd for the year ended 30 June 2007.

PROBLEM 26.5 ★★★ Joint venturers, contributions include non-current assets and services

Tullamore Ltd has discovered a new way of providing the extra fizz to soft drinks that is necessary to capture the next generation of soft-drink consumers. To exploit this new invention, it enters into a joint agreement with two other soft-drink manufacturers, Jamieson Ltd and Annalee Ltd. The joint venture agreement was signed on 1 July 2006. The agreement contains the following specifications:

- Tullamore Ltd is to have a 50% interest in the joint venture, with Tullamore Ltd supplying the patent for the secret extra fizz to the joint venture for the next ten years, at which point the patent will be returned to Tullamore Ltd. At 1 July 2006, the fair value of the patent is considered to be at $15 million. Tullamore Ltd has capitalised outlays during the development of the new formula for fizz and has capitalised costs of $12 million at 1 July 2006. At the end of the ten years, it is estimated that the fair value of the patent will be $5 million. The patent is depreciated in the books of each of the venturers, and not included in the cost of inventory.
- Jamieson Ltd is to have a 25% interest in the joint venture, supplying $4 million cash as well as management services to the joint venture. The services are worth $1 million and will be supplied evenly over the first five years of the joint venture. Jamieson Ltd believes that supplying the services will cost it $750 000.
- Annalee Ltd is to have a 25% interest in the joint venture. Annalee Ltd is to supply plant and equipment to the joint venture at a fair value of $5 million. The plant and equipment is currently recorded in the books of Annalee Ltd at a carrying amount of $4 million (related accumulated depreciation is $1 million). The plant and equipment

has an expected remaining useful life of five years. Annalee Ltd is to play a major role in the management of the joint venture, and will be paid a management fee of $200 000 per annum. The expected cost to Annalee Ltd of supplying these services is $170 000. The fee was paid on 25 June 2007.

Information in relation to the operations of the joint venture at the end of the first year, 30 June 2007, is as follows (in $000):

Balance sheet			
Cash	$ 200	Venturers' equity	$14 600
Work in progress	200	Trade creditors	600
Plant and equipment	6 000	Accrued expenses	800
Accumulated depreciation	(1 200)		
Services receivable	800		
Patent	10 000		
	$16 000		$16 000

Statement of cash flows		
Cash balance at 1/7/06		$4 000
Less: Wages and salaries	$ 860	
Supplies and materials	1 520	
Plant and equipment	1 000	
Administration expenses	420	3 800
Cash balance at 30/6/07		$ 200

Cost of production	
Wages and salaries	$1 560
Supplies and materials	2 120
Administration expenses	520
Services	200
Depreciation – plant and equipment	1 200
	5 600
Work in progress at 30 June 2007	200
Cost of inventory produced	$5 400

Required

Prepare the journal entries in the records of each of the venturers for the year ending 30 June 2007, assuming the use of the line-by-line method.

PROBLEM 26.6 ★★★   Proportionate consolidation, equity method, expanded equity method

Tramore Ltd and Limerick Ltd both operate in the pharmaceutical business. Both companies have been privately working on a cure for the Ross River virus, a disease carried by mosquitoes. Because of a lack of success, and after discussions between the scientists involved, the two companies agreed to establish a joint venture company, Greystones Ltd, for the purpose of conducting joint research.

The company was established on 1 January 2006 with share capital of $800 000, with both parties contributing equally to the joint venture entity. As part of its $400 000 contribution, Tramore Ltd supplied a research laboratory to the joint venture. This laboratory was recorded by Tramore Ltd at $200 000, but was considered to have a fair value of $250 000. The laboratory was considered to have a ten-year life, and depreciated on a straight-line basis. The joint venture was to generate cash inflows by the sale of by-product drugs produced during the research process.

At 31 December 2006, the project was proceeding well. The venturers had agreed in November 2006 that Greystones Ltd should order $400 000 worth of new computerised equipment to be delivered early in 2007. It was also agreed that the joint venture should borrow a further $500 000 in March 2007, as the laboratory facilities needed some renovations. As with the current long-term loan, both venturers agreed to act as guarantors for that loan. At 31 December 2006, the consolidated financial statements of Tramore Ltd – excluding any adjustments for the joint venture – and the financial statements of Greystones Ltd showed the following information (in $000):

	Tramore Ltd (Group)	Greystones Ltd
Revenues:		
Sales of products	$2 600	$ 860
Dividends	30	
	2 630	
Expenses:		
Wages	840	440
Depreciation – laboratories	65	25
Depreciation – equipment	95	60
Supplies	620	240
Other	120	15
	1 740	780
Profit before tax	890	80
Income tax expense	210	20
Profit	680	60
Retained earnings at 1 January 2006	1 450	
	2 130	
Dividend paid	80	20
Retained earnings at 31 December 2006	$2 050	$ 40
Current assets		
Supplies	$ 550	$40
Cash	80	50
Receivables	320	60
Total current assets	950	150
Non-current assets		
Laboratories	3 850	250
Accumulated depreciation	(860)	(25)
Equipment	1 370	420
Accumulated depreciation	(770)	(60)
Capitalised development	2 400	455
Investment in joint venture – Greystones Ltd	400	–
Total non-current assets	5 390	1 030
Total assets	6 340	1 180

(continued)

Current liabilities		
Payables	120	60
Provisions	170	80
Total current liabilities	290	140
Non-current liabilities		
Loan	1 000	200
Total liabilities	1 290	340
Net assets	$5 050	$ 840
Equity		
Share capital	$3 000	$800
Retained earnings	2 050	40
Total equity	$5 050	$ 840

Required

1. Prepare the consolidated financial statements of Tramore Ltd using:
   (a) the proportionate consolidation method
   (b) the equity method
   (c) the expanded equity method.
2. Prepare the note disclosures provided by IAS 31 in relation to the joint venture entity.

PROBLEM 26.7 ★★★   Venturers share output, line-by-line method

After prospecting unsuccessfully for a number of years for gold, in November 2006 Armagh Ltd finally found an economically viable deposit. Realising that it did not have sufficient expertise to operate a gold mine successfully, Armagh Ltd formed an unincorporated joint venture with Dungannon Ltd, agreeing to share the output of the mine equally. It was agreed that the two venturers would initially contribute the following assets:

Armagh Ltd:	
Capitalised exploration costs, including permits licences, and mining rights, currently recorded by Armagh Ltd at $200 000	$800 000
Cash	700 000
Dungannon Ltd:	
Cash	1 500 000

The joint venture commenced on 1 January 2007. By 31 December 2007, the mine had been operating successfully. It was reliably estimated at the commencement of the project that the mine had expected reserves of 100 000 tons.

In the first year following commencement, 5000 tons of gold were extracted, while in 2008, 10 000 tons were extracted. This output was distributed to the venturers equally.

All costs except general administration costs were capitalised into the cost of the output, with depreciation of equipment and capitalised exploration costs being written off in proportion to the depletion of the reserves. General administration expenses were allocated to the venturers equally.

The financial report of the joint venture over the first two years of operation showed the following information:

Cash receipts and payments		
	2007	2008
Balance at 1 January	–	$ 300 000
Contributions from venturers	$2 200 000	1 200 000
	2 200 000	1 500 000
Plant and equipment	800 000	190 000
Wages	600 000	660 000
Materials	200 000	240 000
General administration	300 000	300 000
	1 900 000	1 390 000
Balance at 31 December	$ 300 000	$ 110 000

Balance sheet		
	2007	2008
Capitalised exploration costs	$ 760 000	$ 680 000
Plant and equipment	800 000	990 000
Accumulated depreciation	(40 000)	(140 000)
Cash	300 000	110 000
Materials	50 000	40 000
	1 870 000	1 680 000
Accrued wages	10 000	20 000
Accounts payable (materials)	20 000	30 000
	30 000	50 000
Net assets	$1 840 000	$1 630 000
Venturers' equity:		
Contributions as at 1 January	3 000 000	1 840 000
Additional contributions		1 200 000
	3 000 000	3 040 000
Less: Output distributed	860 000	1 110 000
Allocation: general administration	300 000	300 000
	1 160 000	1 410 000
Balance at 31 December	$1 840 000	$1 630 000

Required

Prepare the journal entries in the records of Armagh Ltd using the line-by-line method to record its interest in the joint venture for the years ending 31 December 2007 and 2008.

Visit these websites for additional information:

www.iasb.org   www.iasplus.com
www.asic.gov.au   www.ifac.org
www.aasb.com.au   www.nzica.com
www.accaglobal.com   www.capa.com.my

REFERENCES

Accounting Standards Board 1994, 'Associates and joint ventures', Discussion paper, Accounting Standards Board, London.

Bayer 2005, *Bayer Annual Report 2005*, Bayer AG, Germany, viewed 19 May 2006, <www.bayer.com>.

Dieter, R & Wyatt, AR 1978, 'The expanded equity method – an alternative in accounting for investments in joint ventures', *Journal of Accountancy* June, pp. 89–94.

FASB 1985, *Statement of Financial Accounting Concepts No. 6*, Financial Accounting Standards Board, December, Norwalk (Connecticut), USA, viewed 14 July 2006, <www.fasb.org>.

G4+1, 2000, 'Leases: Implementation of a new approach', G4+1 Position Paper, published separately by the Accounting Standards Board in Australia, Canada, New Zealand, United Kingdom, United States and by the International Accounting Standards Committee.

IASB 2006, *IASB Update*, International Accounting Standards Committee Foundation, March, London, viewed 14 July 2006, <www.iasb.org>.

–2005, *IASB Update*, December.

–2003, *IASB Update*, November.

Milburn, JA & Chant, PD 1999, 'Reporting interests in joint ventures and similar arrangements', published separately by the Accounting Standards Board in Australia, Canada, New Zealand, United Kingdom, United States and by the International Accounting Standards Committee.

Reklau, DL 1997, 'Accounting for investments in joint ventures – a re-examination', *Journal of Accountancy*, September, pp. 96–103.

Scheutze, WP 1993, 'What is an asset?', *Accounting Horizons*, September, pp. 66–70.

Wallman, SMH 1996, 'The future of accounting and financial reporting, Part II: the colorized approach', *Accounting Horizons*, June, pp. 138–48.

Willett, P 1995, 'Joint enterprise', *CA Magazine*, June/July, pp. 59–62.

*us*eful terms

Accounting estimates Measurement judgements applied in preparing the financial statements.

Accounting policies The specific principles, bases, conventions, rules and practices applied by an entity in preparing and presenting financial statements.

Accounting profit Profit for a period (determined in accordance with accounting standards and statements of accounting concepts) before deducting tax expense.

Accrual basis Recognising the effects of transactions and other events when they occur, rather than when cash or its equivalent is received or paid.

Acquisition date The date on which the acquirer effectively obtains control of the acquiree.

Active market A market in which all the following conditions exist: (a) the items traded in the market are homogeneous; (b) willing buyers and sellers can normally be found at any time; and (c) prices are available to the public.

Adjusting event after the balance sheet date An event that provides evidence of conditions that existed at the balance sheet date

Agreement date The date that a substantive agreement between the combining parties is reached

Allotment The process whereby directors of the company allocate shares to applicants. Alternatively, an account recording an amount of money receivable from successful applicants once shares are allotted.

Amortisation The systematic allocation of the depreciable amount of an intangible asset over its useful life. *See* depreciation

Amortised cost The amount at which the financial asset or financial liability is measured at initial recognition minus principal repayments, plus or minus the cumulative amortisation using the effective interest method of any difference between that initial amount and the maturity amount, and minus any reduction (directly or through the use of an allowance account) for impairment or uncollectability.

Application The process whereby prospective shareholders apply to the company for an allotment of shares. Alternatively, an account used to record the amount of money receivable by the company from applicants for shares.

Asset A resource controlled by an entity as a result of past events and from which future economic benefits are expected to flow to the entity.

Associate An entity over which the investor has significant influence and that is neither a subsidiary nor an interest in a joint venture.

Available-for-sale financial assets Those non-derivative financial assets that are designated as available for sale or that are not classified as (a) loans and receivables, (b) held-to-maturity investments or (c) financial assets at fair value through profit or loss.

Balance sheet A financial statement that presents assets, liabilities and equity of an entity at a given point in time.

Bargain purchase option A clause in the lease agreement allowing the lessee to purchase the asset at the end of the lease for a preset amount, significantly less than the expected residual value at the end of the lease term.

Bonus issue or bonus shares An issue of shares to existing owners as a substitute for the payment of cash, particularly as a substitute for a cash dividend.

Business An integrated set of activities and assets conducted and managed for the purpose of providing (a) a return to investors, or (b) lower costs or other economic benefits directly and proportionately to policyholders or participants.

Business combination The bringing together of separate entities or businesses into one reporting entity.

Business segment A distinguishable component of an entity that is engaged in providing an individual product or service or a group of related products or services and that is subject to risks and returns that are different from those of other business segments.

Call An account used to record amounts of money receivable on shares that have been allotted by shareholders whose shares were forfeited.

Carrying amount The amount at which an asset is recognised in the balance sheet after deducting any accumulated amortisation and accumulated impairment losses thereon.

Cash Includes cash on hand, currency, cheques, money orders or electronic transfer that a bank will accept as a deposit.

Cash basis Recognising the effects of transactions and other events when cash or its equivalent is received or paid, rather than when the transactions or other events occur.

Cash equivalents Short-term, highly liquid investments that are readily convertible to known amounts of cash and which are subject to an insignificant risk of changes in value.

Cash flow statement Provides information about the cash payments and cash receipts of an entity during a period.

Cash-generating unit The smallest identifiable group of assets that generates cash inflows that are largely independent of the cash inflows from other assets or groups of assets.

Cash or settlement discount An incentive for early payment of amounts owing on credit transactions, normally quoted as a percentage.

Cash-settled share-based payment transaction A share-based payment transaction in which the entity acquires goods or services by incurring a liability to transfer cash or other assets to the supplier of those goods or services for amounts that are based on the price (or value) of the entity's shares or other equity instruments of the entity.

Class of assets A category of assets having a similar nature or function in the operations of an entity, and which, for the purposes of disclosure, is shown as a single item without supplementary disclosure.

Closing rate The spot exchange rate at the reporting date.

Comparability The quality of accounting information that results from similar accounting recognition, measurement, disclosure, and presentation standards being used by all entities.

Component of an entity Operations and cash flows that can be clearly distinguished, operationally and for financial reporting purposes, from the rest of the entity.

Consolidated financial statements The financial statements of a group of entities, prepared by combining the financial statements of the parent and each of its subsidiaries, subject to necessary adjustments, and presenting them as those of a single economic entity.

Constructive obligation An obligation that derives from an entity's actions where: (a) by an established pattern of past practice, published policies or a sufficiently specific current statement, the entity has indicated to other parties that it will accept certain responsibilities; and (b) as a result, the entity has created a valid expectation on the part of those other parties that it will discharge those responsibilities.

Contingency A condition arising from past events that exists at reporting date and gives rise to either a possible asset or a possible liability, the outcome of which will be confirmed only on the occurrence of one or more uncertain future events that are outside the control of the entity.

Contingent asset A possible asset that arises from past events and whose existence will be confirmed only by the occurrence or non-occurrence of one or more uncertain future events not wholly within the control of the entity.

Contingent liability (a) A possible obligation that arises from past events and whose existence will be confirmed only by the occurrence or non-occurrence of one or more uncertain future events not wholly within the control of the entity, or (b) a present obligation that arises from past events but is not recognised because (i) it is not probable that an outflow of resources embodying economic events will be required to settle the obligation, or (ii) the amount of the obligation cannot be measured with sufficient reliability.

Contingent rent That portion of the lease payments that is not fixed in amount but is based on the future amount of a factor that changes other than with the passage of time.

Control The power to govern the financial and operating policies of an entity so as to obtain benefits from its activities.

Corporate assets Assets other than goodwill that contribute to the future cash flows of both the cash-generating unit under review and other cash-generating units.

Corporate governance The system by which companies are directed and managed. It influences how the objectives of the company are set and achieved, how risk is monitored and assessed, and how performance is optimised. Good corporate governance structures encourage companies to create value (through entrepreneurism, innovation, development and exploration) and provide accountability and control systems commensurate with the risks involved.

Cost The amount of cash or cash equivalent paid or the fair value of the other consideration given to acquire an asset at the time of its acquisition or construction.

Costs of conversion Costs directly related to the units of production plus a systematic allocation of fixed and variable overheads that are incurred in converting materials into finished goods.

Costs of disposal Incremental costs directly attributable to the disposal of an asset or cash-generating unit, excluding finance costs and income tax expense.

Costs of purchase Costs such as purchase price, import duties and other taxes (other than those subsequently recoverable by the entity from the taxing authorities), transport, handling and other costs directly attributable to the acquisition of finished goods, materials and services.

Costs to sell The incremental costs directly attributable to the disposal of an asset (or disposal group), excluding finance costs and income tax expense.

Cumulative In relation to preference shares, shares on which undeclared dividends in one year accumulate to the following year/s until paid.

Current liability A liability that (a) is expected to be settled in the normal course of the entity's operating cycle, or (b) is at call or due or expected to be settled within 12 months of the reporting date.

Current tax The amount of income taxes payable in respect of the taxable profit for a period.

Date of exchange The date when each individual investment is recognised in the financial report of the acquirer.

Deductible temporary differences Temporary differences that will result in amounts that are deductible in determining taxable profit of future periods when the carrying amount of the asset or liability is recovered or settled.

Deferred tax asset Amounts of income taxes recoverable in future periods in respect of deferred temporary differences; the carry forward of unused tax losses and the carry forward of unused tax credits.

Deferred tax liability Amounts of income taxes payable in future periods in respect of taxable temporary differences.

Depreciable amount The cost of an asset, or other amount substituted for cost, less its residual value.

Depreciation (amortisation) The systematic allocation of the depreciable amount of an asset over its useful life.

Derivatives A financial instrument that derives its value from another underlying item, such as a share price or an interest rate. The definition requires all of the following three characteristics to be met: (a) its value must change in response to a change in an underlying variable such as a specified interest rate, price, or foreign exchange rate; (b) it must require no initial net investment or an initial net investment that is smaller than would be required for other types of contracts with similar responses to changes in market factors; (c) it is settled at a future date.

Development The application of research findings or other knowledge to a plan or design for the production of new or substantially improved materials, devices, products, processes, systems or services before the start of commercial production or use.

Direct minority interest (DMI) The MI held directly in an entity, and not indirectly through another entity.

Discontinued operation A component of an entity that either has been disposed of or is classified as held for sale and (a) represents a separate major line of business or geographical area of operations; (b) is part of a single coordinated plan to dispose of a separate major line of business or geographical area of operations; or (c) is a subsidiary acquired exclusively with a view to resale.

Disposal group A group of assets to be disposed of, by sale or otherwise, together as a group in a single transaction, and liabilities directly associated with those assets that will be transferred in the transaction.

Dividends A distribution of profit to the equity holders of a company.

Economic life For an asset, is either (a) the period over which an asset is expected to be economically useable by one or more users; or (b) the number of production or similar units expected to be obtained from the asset by one or more users.

Effective interest method A method of calculating the amortised cost of a financial asset or a financial liability, and of allocating the interest income or interest expense over the relevant period.

Effective interest rate The rate that exactly discounts estimated future cash payments or receipts through the expected life of the financial instrument (or, when appropriate, a shorter period) to the net carrying amount of the financial asset or financial liability.

Embedded derivative A component of a combined (or 'hybrid') instrument that also includes a non-derivative host contract, with the effect that some of the cash flows of the combined instrument vary in a way similar to a stand-alone instrument.

Employees and others providing similar services Individuals who render personal services to the entity and either (a) the individuals are regarded as employees for legal or tax purposes, (b) the individuals work for the entity under its direction in the same way as individuals who are regarded as employees for legal or tax purposes, or (c) the services rendered are similar to those rendered by employees. For example, the term encompasses all management personnel, that is, those persons having authority and responsibility for planning, directing and controlling the activities of the entity, including non-executive directors.

Entity concept of consolidation The group consists of all the assets and liabilities of the parent and its subsidiaries, and the minority interest is classified as a contributor of equity to the group.

Equity The residual interest in the assets of the entity after deducting all its liabilities.

Equity instrument Any contract that evidences a residual interest in the assets of an entity after deducting all of its liabilities.

Equity instrument granted The right (conditional or unconditional) to an equity instrument of the entity conferred by the entity on another party, under a share-based payment arrangement.

Equity-settled share-based payment transaction A share-based payment transaction in which the entity receives goods or services as consideration for equity instruments of the entity (including shares or share options).

Equity method The method of accounting whereby the investment is initially recognised at cost and subsequently adjusted for the post-acquisition change in the investor's share of net assets of the associate. The profit or loss of the investor includes the investor's share of the profit or loss of the investee.

Errors Omissions from or misstatements in the financial statements.

Exchange difference The difference resulting from translating a given number of units of one currency into another currency at different exchange rates.

Exchange rate The ratio of exchange for two currencies.

Executory contracts Contracts under which neither party has performed any of its obligations or both parties have partially performed their obligations to an equal extent.

Executory costs Operating amounts (including insurance, maintenance, consumable supplies, replacement parts and rates) that are paid by the lessor on behalf of the lessee.

Expenses Decreases in economic benefits during the accounting period in the form of outflows or depletions of assets or incurrences of liabilities that result in decreases in equity, other than those relating to distributions to equity participants.

Fair value The amount for which an asset could be exchanged, or a liability settled, between knowledgeable, willing parties in an arm's-length transaction.

Fair value less costs to sell The amount obtainable from the sale of an asset or cash-generating unit in an arm's-length transaction between knowledgeable, willing parties, less the costs of disposal.

Finance lease A lease that transfers substantially all of the risks and rewards incidental to ownership of an asset. Title may or may not eventually be transferred.

Financial asset Any asset that is: (a) cash (b) an equity instrument of another entity (c) a contractual right: (i) to receive cash or another financial asset from another entity; or (ii) to exchange financial assets or financial liabilities with another entity under conditions that are potentially favourable to the entity; or (d) a contract that will or may be settled in the entity's own equity instruments that is: (i) a non-derivative for which the entity is or may be obliged to receive a variable number of the entity's own equity instruments; or (ii) a derivative that will or may be settled other than by the exchange of a fixed amount of cash or another financial asset for a fixed number of the entity's own equity instruments. For this purpose the entity's own equity instruments do not include instruments that are themselves contracts for the future receipt or delivery of the entity's own equity instruments.

Financial assets at fair value through profit or loss Financial assets held for trading and measured at fair value with any gain or loss from a change in fair value recognised in profit or loss, or financial assets that upon initial recognition are designated by the entity as at fair value through profit or loss.

Financial instrument Any contract that gives rise to a financial asset of one entity and a financial liability or equity instrument of another.

Financial liability Any liability that is: (a) a contractual obligation: (i) to deliver cash or another financial asset to another entity; or (ii) to exchange financial assets or financial liabilities with another entity under conditions that are potentially unfavourable to the entity; or (b) a contract that will or may be settled in the entity's own equity instruments and is: (i) a non-derivative for which the entity is or may be obliged to deliver a variable number of the entity's own equity instruments; or (ii) a derivative that will or may be settled other than by the exchange of a fixed amount of cash or another financial asset for a fixed number of the entity's own equity instruments. For this purpose the entity's own equity instruments do not include instruments that are themselves contracts for the future receipt or delivery of the entity's own equity instruments.

Financial position The assets, liabilities, and residual equity interest of an entity at a given point in time.

Financing activities Those activities that result in changes in the size and composition of the equity capital and borrowings of the entity.

Firm commitment A binding agreement for the exchange of a specified quantity of resources at a specified price on a specified future date or dates.

First-in, first-out (FIFO) A method of allocating cost to inventory items that assumes that the items first purchased will be the items first sold.

FOB destination A condition of sale under which the seller pays all freight costs (FOB means 'free on board').

FOB shipping A condition of sale under which freight costs incurred from the point of shipment are paid by the buyer (FOB means 'free on board').

Forecast transaction An uncommitted but anticipated future transaction.

Foreign currency A currency other than the functional currency of the entity.

Foreign operation An entity that is a subsidiary, associate, joint venture or branch of a reporting entity, the activities of which are based or conducted in a country or currency other than those of the reporting entity.

Forfeited shares account An account initially recording the amount of funds supplied by shareholders whose shares were forfeited.

Framework for the Preparation and Presentation of Financial Statements The pronouncement of the International Accounting Standards Board that sets out the concepts underlying the preparation and presentation of financial statements for external users.

Functional currency The currency of the primary economic environment in which the entity operates.

General purpose financial statements The financial statements that a business entity prepares and presents at least annually to meet the common information needs of a wide range of users external to the entity.

Geographical segment A distinguishable component of an entity that is engaged in providing products or services within a particular economic environment and that is subject to risks and returns that are different from those of components operating in other economic environments.

Going concern An entity that is expected to continue in operation for the foreseeable future.

Goodwill Future economic benefits arising from assets that are not capable of being individually identified and separately recognised.

Grant date The date at which the entity and another party (including an employee) agree to a share-based payment arrangement, being when the entity and the counterparty have a shared understanding of the terms and conditions of the arrangement. At grant date the entity confers on the counterparty the right to cash, other assets, or equity instruments of the entity, provided the specified vesting conditions, if any, are met. If that agreement is subject to an approval process (for example, by shareholders), grant date is the date when that approval is obtained.

Gross investment For the lessor, the aggregate of the minimum lease payments receivable by the lessor under a finance lease, and any unguaranteed residual value accruing to the lessor.

Group A parent and its subsidiaries.

Guaranteed residual value That part of the residual value of the leased asset guaranteed by the lessee or a third party related to the lessee.

Hedge effectiveness The degree to which changes in the fair value or cash flows of the hedged item that are attributable to a hedged risk are offset by changes in the fair value or cash flows of the hedging instrument.

Hedged item An asset, liability, firm commitment, highly probable forecast transaction or net investment in a foreign operation that (a) exposes the entity to risk of changes in fair value or future cash flows and (b) is designated as being hedged.

Hedging instrument A designated derivative or (for a hedge of the risk of changes in foreign currency exchange rates only) a designated non-derivative financial asset or non-derivative financial liability whose fair value or cash flows are expected to offset changes in the fair value or cash flows of a designated hedged item.

Held-to-maturity investments Investments that the entity has the positive intention and ability to hold to maturity (e.g. debt instruments, such as debentures held in another entity or redeemable preference shares) other than: (a) those that the entity upon initial recognition designates as at fair value through profit or loss; (b) those that the entity designates as available for sale; and (c) those that meet the definition of loans and receivables.

Highly probable Significantly more likely than probable.

Impairment loss The amount by which the carrying amount of an asset exceeds its recoverable amount.

Inception of the lease The earlier of the date of the lease agreement and the date of commitment by the parties to the principal provisions of the lease.

Income Increases in economic benefits during the accounting period in the form of inflows or enhancements of assets or decreases of liabilities that result in increases in equity, other than those relating to contributions from equity participants.

Income statement The statement reports on the entity's revenues and expenses for the reporting period.

Incremental borrowing rate The rate of interest the lessee would have to pay on a similar lease or, if that is not determinable, the rate that (at the inception of the lease) the lessee would incur to borrow over a similar term, and with a similar security, the funds necessary to purchase the asset.

Indirect minority interest (IMI) The MI in an entity held indirectly through another entity, caused by there being a DMI in the latter entry.

Initial direct costs Incremental costs that are directly attributable to negotiating and arranging a lease, except for such costs incurred by the manufacturer or dealer lessors.

Intangible asset An identifiable non-monetary asset without physical substance.

Interest rate implicit in the lease rate The rate that, at the inception of the lease, causes the aggregate present value of the minimum lease payments and the unguaranteed residual value to be equal to the sum of the fair value of the leased asset and any initial direct costs of the lessor.

Intrinsic value The difference between the fair value of the shares to which the counterparty has the (conditional or unconditional) right to subscribe or which it has the right to receive, and the price (if any) the counterparty is (or will be) required to pay for those shares. For example, a share option with an exercise price of CU15 (currency units) on a share with a fair value of CU20, has an intrinsic value of CU5.

Inventories Assets held for sale in the ordinary course of business, in the process of production for such sale, or in the form of materials or supplies to be consumed in the production process or in the rendering of services.

Investing activities Those activities which relate to the acquisition and disposal of long-term assets and other investments not included in cash equivalents.

Investment property Property (land or a building, or part of a building, or both) held to earn rentals or for capital appreciation or both, rather than for (a) use in the production or supply of goods or services or for administrative purposes, or (b) sale in the ordinary course of business.

Joint control The contractually agreed sharing of control over an economic activity that exists only when the strategic financial and operating decisions relating to the activity require the unanimous consent of the parties sharing the control (the venturers).

Joint venture A contractual arrangement whereby two or more parties undertake an economic activity that is subject to joint control.

Lease An agreement whereby the lessor conveys to the lessee in return for a payment or series of payments the right to use an asset for an agreed period of time.

Lease term The non-cancellable period for which the lessee has contracted to lease the asset, together with any further terms for which the lessee has the option to continue to lease the asset, with or without further payment, when at the inception of the lease it is reasonably certain that the lessee will exercise the option.

Liability A present obligation of the entity arising from past events, the settlement of which is expected to result in an outflow from the entity of resources embodying economic benefits.

Loans and receivables Non-derivative financial assets with fixed or determinable payments that are not quoted in an active market and which the entity has no intention of trading, e.g. loan to a subsidiary.

Market condition A condition upon which the exercise price, vesting or exercisability of an equity instrument depends that is related to the market price of the entity's equity instruments, such as attaining a specified share price or a specified amount of intrinsic value of a share option, or achieving a specified target that is based on the market price of the entity's equity instruments relative to an index of market prices of equity instruments of other entities.

Materiality The notion of materiality guides the margin of error acceptable, the degree of precision required and the extent of the disclosure required when preparing general purpose financial reports.

Measurement The process of determining the monetary amount at which an asset, liability, income or expense is reported in the financial statements.

Measurement date The date at which the fair value of the equity instruments granted is measured for the purposes of this IFRS. For transactions with employees and others providing similar services, the measurement date is grant date. For transactions with parties other than employees (and those providing similar services), the measurement date is the date the entity obtains the goods or the counterparty renders service.

Minimum lease payments The payments over the lease term that the lessee is or can be required to make, excluding contingent rent, costs for services and taxes to be paid by and reimbursed to the lessor, together with (a) for a lessee, any amounts guaranteed by the lessee or by a party related to the lessee; or (b) for a lessor, any residual value guaranteed to the lessor.

Minority interest (MI) The part of the profit or loss and net assets of a subsidiary attributable to equity interest that are not owned, directly or indirectly through subsidiaries, by the parent.

Monetary assets Money held and assets to be received in fixed or determinable amounts of money.

Monetary items Units of currency held and assets and liabilities to be received or paid in a fixed or determinable number of units of currency.

Net assets Total assets minus liabilities.

Net investment in a foreign operation The amount of the reporting entity's interest in the net assets of that operation.

Net realisable value The estimated selling price in the ordinary course of business less the estimated costs of completion and the estimated costs necessary to make the sale.

Non-adjusting event after the balance sheet date An event that is indicative of conditions that arose after the balance sheet date.

Non-cancellable lease A lease that is cancellable only (a) upon the occurrence of some remote contingency; (b) with the permission of the lessor; (c) if the lessee enters into a new lease for the same or an equivalent asset with the same lessor; or (d) upon payment by the lessee of such an additional amount that, at inception of the lease, makes the continuation of the lease reasonably certain.

Notes Notes are prepared in accordance with IAS 1 and form part of a set of general purpose financial statements. They contain information in addition to that presented in the balance sheet, income statement, statement of changes in equity and cash flow statement. They provide narrative descriptions of the basis of preparation of the financial statements and accounting policies adopted, as well as disaggregations of items disclosed in the financial statements and information about items that do not qualify for recognition in those statements.

Obligating event An event that creates a legal or constructive obligation that results in an entity having no realistic alternative to settling that obligation.

Onerous contract A contract in which the unavoidable costs of meeting the obligations under the contract exceed the economic benefits expected to be received under it.

Operating activities Those activities which relate to the main revenue-producing activities of the entity and other activities that are not investing or financing activities.

Operating lease A lease other than a finance lease.

Parent An entity that has one or more subsidiaries.

Participating In relation to preference shares, shares that receive extra dividends above a fixed rate once a certain level of dividends has been paid on ordinary shares.

Performance The ability of an entity to earn a profit on the resources that have been invested in it.

Periodic method A system of recording inventory whereby the value of inventory is determined and recorded on a periodic basis (normally annually).

Perpetual method A system of recording inventory whereby inventory records are updated each time a transaction involving inventory takes place.

Pre-acquisition equity The equity of the subsidiary at acquisition date. It is not just the equity recorded by the subsidiary, but is determined by reference to the cost of the business combination.

Presentation currency The currency in which the financial report is presented.

Private placement An issue of shares usually to a large institutional investor such as a finance company, superannuation fund or life insurance company.

Probable More likely than not.

Property, plant and equipment Tangible assets held by an entity for use in the production or supply of goods or services, for rental to others, or for administrative purposes, and which are expected to be used during more than one period.

Prospective application Means applying the change to transactions, events or other conditions occurring after the date of the change and recognising the effect in the current and future periods.

Provision A liability of uncertain timing or amount.

Public company A company entitled to raise funds from the public by lodging a disclosure document with ASIC and have its shares or other ownership documents traded on the stock exchange. It may be a limited company, unlimited company or no-liability company.

Reciprocal shareholdings Where two entities hold shares in each other.

Recognition The process of incorporating in the financial statements an item that meets the definition of an asset, liability, income or expense.

Recoverable amount For an asset or a cash-generating unit, the higher of its fair value less costs to sell and its value in use.

Relevance That quality of information that exists when the information influences economic decisions made by users.

Reliability Information has the quality of reliability when it is free from material error and bias and can be depended on by users to represent faithfully that which it either purports to represent or could reasonably be expected to represent.

Reload feature A feature that provides for an automatic grant of additional share options whenever the option holder exercises previously granted options using the entity's shares, rather than cash, to satisfy the exercise price.

Reload option A new share option granted when a share is used to satisfy the exercise price of a previous share option.

Reportable segment A business segment or a geographical segment identified based on the definitions for either a business segment or geographical segment.

Reporting entity An entity in respect of which it is reasonable to expect the existence of users who rely on the entity's general purpose financial report for information that will be useful to them for making and evaluating decisions about the allocation of scarce resources. A reporting entity can be a single entity or a group comprising a parent and all of its subsidiaries.

Research Original and planned investigation undertaken with the prospect of gaining new scientific or technical knowledge and understanding.

Reserve A category of equity that is not contributed capital.

Revenue The gross inflow of economic benefits during the period arising in the course of the ordinary activities of an entity when those inflows result in increases in equity, other than increases relating to contributions from equity participants.

Residual value The estimated amount that an entity would currently obtain from disposal of the asset, after deducting the estimated costs of disposal, if the asset were already of the age and in the condition expected at the end of its useful life.

Retrospective application Means applying a new accounting policy to transactions, other events and conditions as if that policy had always been applied.

Revaluation decrement (increment) The amount by which the revalued carrying amount of a non-current asset as at the revaluation date is less than (exceeds) its previous carrying amount.

Rights issue An issue of new shares giving existing shareholders the right to an additional number of shares in proportion to their current shareholdings.

Segment accounting policies Accounting policies adopted for preparing and presenting the financial statements of the consolidated group or entity as well as those accounting policies that relate specifically to a segment.

Segment assets Operating assets that are employed by a segment in its operating activities and that either are directly attributable to the segment or can be allocated to the segment on a reasonable basis.

Segment expense Expense resulting from the operating activities of a segment that is directly attributable to the segment and the relevant portion of an expense that can be allocated on a reasonable basis to the segment, including expenses relating to sales to external customers and expenses relating to transactions with other segments of the same entity.

Segment liabilities Operating liabilities that result from the operating activities of a segment and that either are directly attributable to the segment or can be allocated to the segment on a reasonable basis.

Segment result Segment revenue less segment expense. Segment result is determined before any adjustments for minority interest.

Segment revenue Revenue reported in the entity's income statement that is directly attributable to a segment and the relevant portion of entity revenue that can be allocated on a reasonable basis to a segment, whether from sales to external customers or from transactions with other segments of the same entity.

Separate financial statements The financial statements prepared by a parent in which its investments are accounted for on the basis of the direct equity interest rather than on the basis of the reported results and net assets of the investees.

Share-based payment arrangement An agreement between the entity and another party (including an employee) to enter into a share-based payment transaction, which thereby entitles the other party to receive cash or other assets of the entity for amounts that are based on the price of the entity's shares or other equity instruments of the entity, or to receive equity instruments of the entity, provided the specified vesting conditions, if any, are met.

Share-based payment transaction A transaction in which the entity receives goods or services as consideration for equity instruments of the entity (including shares or share options), or acquires goods or services by incurring liabilities to the supplier of those goods or services for amounts that are based on the price of the entity's shares or other equity instruments of the entity.

Share buy-back The repurchase of a company's shares by the company from its shareholders.

Share issue costs Costs incurred on the issue of equity instruments. These include underwriting costs, stamp duties and taxes, professional advisers' fees and brokerage.

Share option A contract that gives the holder the right, but not the obligation, to subscribe to the entity's shares at a fixed or determinable price for a specified period of time.

Significant influence The power to participate in the financial and operating policies of the investee without having control or joint control over those policies.

Specific identification A method of allocating cost to inventory based on identifying and aggregating all costs directly related to each individual inventory item.

Spot exchange rate The exchange rate for immediate delivery.

Statement of changes in equity A financial statement prepared in accordance with IAS 1 for inclusion in general purpose financial reports. The statement reports on the changes in the entity's equity for the reporting period. Changes in equity disclosed may include movements in retained earnings for the period, items of income and expense recognised directly in equity, and movements in each class of share and each reserve.

Subsidiary An entity, including an unincorporated entity such as a partnership, that is controlled by another entity (known as the parent).

Substance over form The accounts will reflect the underlying economic reality of transactions and not their legal form.

Tax base Of an asset or liability, is the amount attributed to that asset or liability for tax purposes.

Tax expense The aggregate amount included in the determination of profit or loss for the period in respect of current tax and deferred tax.

Taxable profit The profit for a period, determined in accordance with the rules established by the taxation authorities, upon which income taxes are payable.

Taxable temporary differences Temporary differences that will result in taxable amounts in determining taxable profit of future periods when the carrying amount of the asset and liability is recovered or settled.

Temporary difference The difference between the carrying amount of an asset or liability and the tax base of that asset or liability.

Trade discount A reduction in selling prices granted to customers.

Understandability The ability of financial information to be comprehended by financial statement users who have a reasonable knowledge of business and economic activities and accounting, and a willingness to study the information with reasonable diligence.

Underwriter An entity which, for a fee, undertakes to subscribe for any shares not allotted to applicants as a result of an undersubscription.

Unguaranteed residual value That portion of the residual value of the leased asset, the realisation of which is not assured by the lessor or is guaranteed solely by a party related to the lessor.

Useful life The period over which an asset is expected to be available for use by an entity, or the number of production or similar units expected to be obtained from the asset by an entity.

Value in use The present value of future cash flows expected to arise from the continuing use of an asset and from its disposal at the end of its useful life.

Venturer A party to a joint venture that has joint control over that joint venture.

Vest To become an entitlement. Under a share-based payment arrangement, a counterparty's right to receive cash, other assets, or equity instruments of the entity vests upon satisfaction of any specified vesting conditions.

Vesting conditions The conditions that must be satisfied for the counterparty to become entitled to receive cash, other assets or equity instruments of the entity, under a share-based payment arrangement. Vesting conditions include service conditions, which require the other party to complete a specified period of service, and performance conditions, which require specified performance targets to be met (such as a specified increase in the entity's profit over a specified period of time).

Vesting period The period during which all the specified vesting conditions of a share-based payment arrangement are to be satisfied.

Weighted average A method of allocating cost to inventory items based on the weighted average of the cost of similar items at the beginning of a period and the cost of similar items purchased or produced during the period.

index